Gar Alperovitz

THE DECISION TO USE THE ATOMIC BOMB

Gar Alperovitz, a historian and political economist, is president of the National Center for Economic Alternatives. He is also Senior Research Scientist in the Department of Government and Politics at the University of Maryland, and a Fellow of the Institute for Policy Studies. Formerly a Fellow of King's College, Cambridge, and of the Institute of Politics at Harvard, he has served as Legislative Assistant in the U.S. House of Representatives, Legislative Director in the U.S. Senate, and Special Assistant in the Department of State. His books include *Atomic Diplomacy: Hiroshima and Potsdam*, and he has written numerous articles for *The New York Times*, the *Wall Street Journal*, the *Washington Post*, the *Los Angeles Times*, *The Nation*, *Foreign Policy*, *The Atlantic Monthly*, and many other academic and popular publications.

ALSO BY GAR ALPEROVITZ

Rebuilding America: A Blueprint for the New Economy (with Jeff Faux) (1984)

American Economic Policy (edited with Roger Skurski) (1984)

Strategy and Program (with Staughton Lynd) (1973)

Cold War Essays (1970)

Atomic Diplomacy: Hiroshima and Potsdam (1965)

THE DECISION TO USE
THE ATOMIC BOMB

THE
DECISION
TO USE THE
ATOMIC BOMB

Gar Alperovitz

with the assistance of
Sanho Tree, Edward Rouse Winstead,
Kathryn C. Morris, David J. Williams, Leo C. Maley III,
Thad Williamson, and Miranda Grieder

Vintage Books
A Division of Random House, Inc.
New York

FIRST VINTAGE BOOKS EDITION, AUGUST 1996

The Library of Congress has cataloged the Knopf edition as follows:
Alperovitz, Gar.
The decision to use the atomic bomb, and the architecture of an
American myth / by Gar Alperovitz.
p.   cm.
Includes bibliographical references and index.
ISBN 0-679-44331-2
1. World War, 1939–1945—United States.   2. World War,
1939–1945—Japan.   3. Strategy.   4. World War, 1939–1945—
Campaigns—Japan.   5. Hiroshima-shi (Japan)—History—
Bombardment, 1945.   6. United States—Foreign relations—
1945–1953.   7. United States—Foreign relations—Soviet Union.
8. Soviet Union—Foreign relations—United States. I. Title.
D769.2.A5 1995   95-8778
940.54′25—dc20   CIP
Vintage ISBN: 0-679-76285-X

Random House Web address: http://www.randomhouse.com/

Printed in the United States of America
10 9 8 7 6 5 4 3 2 1

FOR SHARON

Like traumatized people, we have been cut off from the knowledge of our past. Like traumatized people, we need to understand the past in order to reclaim the present and the future.

—Judith Lewis Herman,
Trauma and Recovery

Contents

Preface

The traditional story of the decision to use the atomic bomb has been told countless times in the last five decades, and there is no longer serious dispute about many of its basic elements. It is well understood, for instance, that Japan was in dire straits long before the war ended—and that Russia (which from 1941 on had maintained a neutral stance towards Japan) was scheduled to enter the fray sometime in early August 1945.

Similarly, it is known that a debate occurred within the U.S. government over whether to allow Japan to keep its Emperor—and that long before the atomic bomb was used, many officials believed a clearly expressed decision to do so would be likely to produce a surrender. There is also no dispute that in May 1945 a high-level group of presidential advisers—the Interim Committee—made recommendations as to how and when the atomic bomb should be dropped. Finally, there is no real disagreement that the final decision to go forward occurred in July 1945 while President Harry Truman was in Potsdam, Germany, meeting with Prime Minister Winston Churchill and Soviet Premier Joseph Stalin.

Although the following account recapitulates the essential history covering these basic elements of the tale, it does not attempt to reproduce many well-known but non-essential details. Instead, it focuses primary attention on the major issues most historians recognize to be fundamental, and it probes these in depth as it attempts to reach the heart of the historic controversy.

The most important issue, of course, is whether it was understood before the atomic bomb was used that the war with Japan could be ended by other means without significant loss of life. In turn, a serious exploration of this question requires that we consider what is now known about the two most obvious alternatives defined for President Truman during the months before he made his decision:

First, to what degree was the president advised—and to what degree did he understand—that a clarification of the officially stated demand for "unconditional surrender" specifying that Japan could keep its Emperor would be likely to end the war?

Second, to what degree was he advised—and to what degree did he understand—that the force of a Russian declaration of war might itself bring about an early end to the fighting?

In the pages which follow, the atomic bomb decision is brought into sharp relief by exploring just what is and what is not known about decision-making concerning each of the two major options—step by step, throughout the period which led up to the final events at Potsdam.

Inevitably an investigation of this kind also illuminates a host of other, subordinate issues—including: precisely what counsel the president was given by his military advisers; the degree to which diplomatic considerations related to the Soviet Union influenced the president; the extent to which various factions within the Japanese government, particularly the hard-line army groups, were judged to be amenable to surrender; why a city, rather than a strictly military target, was selected for bombing; whether an August delay to explore surrender issues might have been possible before the first landing on the island of Kyushu (scheduled for planning purposes in November), or before the full invasion (scheduled for much later, in the spring of 1946); and whether it was necessary to use two atomic bombs.

The challenge for both the historian and the reader is to abandon the safe posture of disinterested observer: Judgments must be made at each step of the way concerning what is known (and still not known) about the decisions that were made during the summer of 1945—and about the information we now have concerning what the men who made them believed to be the choices available to them at the time.

THE DECISION TO USE
THE ATOMIC BOMB

Introduction

A PERSONAL NOTE

Among the many remaining puzzles surrounding the decision to use the atomic bomb, perhaps the most intriguing concern two of the nation's highest World War II military leaders. A few years after Hiroshima and Nagasaki were destroyed, Admiral William D. Leahy went public with the following statement:

> It is my opinion that the use of this barbarous weapon at Hiroshima and Nagasaki was of no material assistance in our war against Japan. The Japanese were already defeated and ready to surrender. . . .
>
> My own feeling was that in being the first to use it, we had adopted an ethical standard common to the barbarians of the Dark Ages. I was not taught to make war in that fashion, and wars cannot be won by destroying women and children. . . .[1]

Leahy was not what one might call a typical critic of American policy. Not only had the five-star admiral presided over the U.S. Joint Chiefs of Staff (and the Combined American-British Chiefs of Staff), but he had simultaneously been chief of staff to the commander-in-chief of the army and navy, serving Roosevelt in that capacity from 1942 to 1945 and Truman from 1945 to 1949.[2] Moreover, he was a good friend of Truman's and the two men respected and liked each other; his public criticism of the Hiroshima decision was hardly personal.

We can imagine what it would mean today if General Colin Powell were to go public with a similar critique, say, of the massive bombings he presided over as chairman of the Joint Chiefs of Staff during the 1991 Persian Gulf War—and on decisions made by his friend President George Bush.

A similar puzzle concerns Dwight D. Eisenhower, the triumphant Supreme Commander of the Allied Expeditionary Force who directed British and American operations against Hitler—and also, subsequently, of course, president of the United States. In the midst of the Cold War—shortly after his famous Farewell Address criticizing the "military-industrial complex"—Eisenhower also went public with a statement about the Hiroshima decision.

Recalling the 1945 moment when Secretary of War Henry L. Stimson informed him the atomic bomb would be used against Japanese cities, Eisenhower stated:

> During his recitation of the relevant facts, I had been conscious of a feeling of depression and so I voiced to him my grave misgivings, first on the basis of my belief that Japan was already defeated and that dropping the bomb was completely unnecessary, and secondly because I thought that our country should avoid shocking world opinion by the use of a weapon whose employment was, I thought, no longer mandatory as a measure to save American lives. It was my belief that Japan was, at that very moment, seeking some way to surrender with a minimum loss of "face." . . .[3]

Something clearly had caused Leahy and Eisenhower to break the unwritten rule that requires high officials to maintain a discreet silence in connection with controversial matters about which they have special knowledge. But as we shall see, Leahy and Eisenhower were not the only military figures who broke the rule. Moreover, less than a year after the bombings an extensive official study by the U.S. Strategic Bombing Survey published its conclusion that Japan would likely have surrendered in 1945 without atomic bombing, without a Soviet declaration of war, and without an American invasion.

Again, it is not only the substance of the conclusion reached by this official body, but the fact that it was made public and received wide publicity, which forces itself into awareness, now, nearly fifty years after the fact.

I have had the privilege of participating in the policy process at high levels of the U.S. Department of State and of directing legislative work in both the U.S. Senate and the U.S. House of Representatives. Statements made by important military figures and by official bodies, even those designated as independent or semi-independent, which run directly contrary to major government decisions rarely see the light of day.

On the fortieth anniversary of the launching of the nuclear era, historian Paul Boyer introduced a thoughtful reflection on the meaning of the atomic bombings in this fashion: " 'Hiroshima.' 'Nagasaki.' The very words, familiar to the point of banality but restlessly alive, remind us that we have yet to assimilate fully what they represent into our political, cultural, or moral history."[4]

In part, this book had its origins in a recurring feeling that we have, in fact, overlooked something profoundly important by not probing the Hiroshima story deeply—by not, for instance, asking serious questions about statements like those made by Leahy, Eisenhower, and the Strategic Bombing Survey.

The issue goes far beyond the validity of military judgments, important as they are. Most of us—unlike Leahy and Eisenhower—have not as yet allowed our response to Hiroshima to move to what Boyer called "a deeper plane of moral complexity." Exceptions to the "denial of the enormity of the event" are few and far between.[5] In connection with the more difficult issues silence mostly reigns—and denial.

The gnawing sense that it is simply wrong to continue to pass over the troubling underlying questions as the fiftieth anniversary of Hiroshima approached was one of the things which prompted me to undertake this study. Another was personal:

Many years ago, as a young graduate student at Britain's Cambridge University, I happened upon the then recently opened diaries of Henry Stimson. These clearly showed that before the atomic bomb had been tested, American leaders had begun to calculate that the new force might greatly strengthen their hand against their wartime ally, the Soviet Union. In May 1945, for instance, Stimson judged that

> [I]t may be necessary to have it out with Russia on her relations to Manchuria and Port Arthur and various other parts of North China, and also the relations of China to us. Over any such tangled wave of problems, S-1 [i.e., the atomic bomb] secret would be dominant. . . .[6]

Stimson's diary shows him to have urged that until the new weapon was tested,

> . . . the time now and the method now to deal with Russia was to keep our mouths shut and let our actions speak for words. . . . It is a case where we have got to regain the lead and perhaps do it in a pretty rough and realistic way. . . . this was a place where we really held all the cards. . . . They can't get along without our help and industries and we have coming into action a weapon which will be unique. . . . Now the thing is not to get into unnecessary quarrels by talking too much and not to indicate any weakness by talking too much; let our actions speak for themselves.[7]

When the Cambridge Ph.D. thesis I wrote using such documents was published under the title *Atomic Diplomacy: Hiroshima and Potsdam*, it became the center of a controversy over why the atomic bomb had been used. This question had not, in fact, been my primary focus. I had been interested in how the bomb influenced diplomacy, not why it was used. In a few concluding remarks, however, I had observed that the then available evidence "strongly suggested" that the view James F. Byrnes had reportedly urged to three atomic scientists (also in May 1945) was an accurate statement of policy:

Mr. Byrnes did not argue that it was necessary to use the bomb against the cities of Japan in order to win the war. . . . Mr. Byrnes's . . . view [was] that our possessing and demonstrating the bomb would make Russia more manageable in Europe. . . .[8]

Since Byrnes was Truman's personal representative on crucial atomic bomb issues and the man he subsequently chose to be his secretary of state, I thought his views significant. I had also written that I did not believe questions concerning the influence of diplomatic considerations on the decision could be fully answered "on the basis of the presently available evidence"; that "no final conclusion can be reached on this question"; and that "more research and more information are needed to reach a conclusive understanding of why the atomic bomb was used."[9]

Atomic Diplomacy was researched and written in the late 1950s and very early 1960s. However, in the atmosphere of heated debate over the escalating Vietnam War after its 1965 publication—as Professor Gaddis Smith has observed—fine distinctions and careful caveats were not much in vogue.[10] Oversimplified versions of my argument (together with some obvious graduate-student errors) were pounced upon by critics who could not abide criticism of the Hiroshima decision.[11] In part, I suppose the following text is thus also a much-delayed response to my own call for "more research and more information" on these matters. Although the once-controversial idea that diplomatic considerations related to the Soviet Union played a significant part in the Hiroshima decision is now commonplace among serious scholars, I should stress that this book is not primarily—or even significantly—an attempt to resolve remaining questions of the precise impact diplomatic considerations had on the Hiroshima decision.*

I am largely concerned with other, perhaps even more difficult matters as we enter the fifty-first year since the events reported in these pages occurred.

In a very real sense this book is the result of my own extended confrontation with the psychological resistance I, too, share to penetrating to "a deeper plane of moral complexity" concerning the bombings. What pushed me over the edge (in 1990) was an encounter with the following statement:

Careful scholarly treatment of the records and manuscripts opened over the past few years has greatly enhanced our understanding of why the Truman administration used atomic weapons against Japan. Experts continue to disagree on some issues, but critical questions have been answered. The consensus among scholars is that the bomb was not needed to avoid an invasion of Japan and to end the war within a relatively

---

*See the Afterword for a discussion of the continuing debate on this issue.

short time. It is clear that alternatives to the bomb existed and that Truman and his advisers knew it.[12]

The writer was J. Samuel Walker, chief historian of the U.S. Nuclear Regulatory Commission—the institutional locus of conservative, often pronuclear thinking. Nor was Walker stating a personal opinion; he was offering a summary of the most recent expert research on the Hiroshima decision in the respected scholarly journal *Diplomatic History*. (The conclusion of a similar review in another journal was that the most recent documentary discoveries were "devastating" to the traditional explanation of the decision.[13])

What struck me initially was the simple honesty of the challenging assessment of the literature which Walker had provided. If after surveying the modern expert research, a government scholar could come to this conclusion, it occurred to me that just possibly others might be able to confront the Hiroshima story in a new way. Some scholars, of course, still disagree with the general "consensus" in the most recent research Walker described; and the implications of the expert literature have not yet reached many general historians who are not specialists in this particular area.* And, of course, in the following pages each significant remaining objection must be examined and confronted head-on. Walker, however, was unequivocal about a central point: "It is certain that the hoary claim that the bomb prevented one-half million American combat deaths is unsupportable."[14]

A rather obvious question now fairly jumped off the page—one which, of course, had been there all along, at least since the time of the Leahy, Eisenhower, and Strategic Bombing Survey statements:

How could it be that what leading military figures believed—and now many historians had concluded—was so radically different from what the majority of Americans still believed?

Throughout the half century that has passed since Hiroshima, poll after poll has shown that most Americans think that the bombings were totally justified—and, moreover, that they had saved a very significant number of lives which might otherwise have been lost in an invasion.[15]

Either Leahy, Eisenhower, the Strategic Bombing Survey, and now many modern researchers were totally wrong about the facts—or the American people had been allowed to believe something that was false. That was the question which now would not go away. Even leaving aside continuing expert differences and the remaining areas of uncertainty, the possibility of some measure of deception—or at least extraordinary exaggeration—could not be excluded.

---

*See below, pp. 520–21, 643, for instance, for a discussion of the handling of one important issue in David McCullough's recent, widely read *Truman*.

Initially, I thought I might do a short article on the problem. As I dug into the modern documents with the help of a group of young researchers, however, I found important new evidence about how the decision to use the atomic bomb was really made. And as I probed the question of why the views of most Americans came to be what they were, I discovered, not surprisingly, that this was no accident. Some leading officials (and their associates) had *wanted* the American people to believe what they came to believe—and they had worked hard to make sure that they achieved their objective.

An article, clearly, could not do justice to such issues, and (after timely nudges and encouragement from my friends Bernd Greiner and Ronald Goldfarb) I decided to undertake a full-blown study. In what follows, Book I attempts straightforwardly to assemble and report what is now known (and still not known) about the decision to use the atomic bomb. Book II explores why, precisely, what most Americans still believe is different.

In an Afterword to the main text, I examine certain additional points and several "theories" concerning the Hiroshima bombing which have been offered by various authors. The word "theories" may surprise some readers—but this is in fact the only appropriate term when there are significant gaps in the record. Historians like to substitute the softer word "interpretation" for "theory," and some seem to write from atop Mount Olympus, as if they had all the facts and therefore were simply telling the unquestioned story of what happened. However, very few knowledgeable scholars, if pressed, would claim they could offer definitive answers to some of the most important questions.

As the reader will soon see, much of the information contained in the following pages is not presented in the usual narrative mode of most history writing (including my own previous work). Instead, I have chosen to reproduce substantial passages from White House and other documents at numerous points of the argument. Often the reader is spared the details of the living documents of the time. In my experience—and especially in connection with some of the truly critical issues—the documents themselves are far more compelling than any interpretation offered by after-the-fact writers.

Another reason for inviting the reader into the documentary discovery process has to do with the question of why what we now know is so different from what most Americans have been taught to believe. Practically speaking, the way "history" is constructed is that documents are discovered; then new facts are put together with old facts; then a new "story" emerges from the resulting new mosaic. When we look back over five decades, it is extraordinary how the available documents, known facts, and resulting "story" have changed over time. Especially during the last decade and a half there have been important documentary "finds."

A firsthand feel for the actual documents is necessary to grasp how our understanding of events actually emerged over time—how (sometimes very erratically) some of the most important facts were discovered, and how new insights were agonizingly developed. Book I is thus not only an attempt to assemble "what we now know," but also a cautionary illustration (and warning) about the way "official" versions of reality get promoted, and how later—often far too much later—they are commonly contradicted by previously suppressed or otherwise unavailable evidence.

Some of the issues connected with the decision to use the atomic bomb are still so controversial that nothing can be gained by taking shortcuts. The only way to answer the hardest questions is to lay out the evidence. Furthermore, on some crucial matters there are still huge gaps in the record (and in some cases evidence of the destruction of important documents). The most straightforward approach in situations where direct evidence on an important issue is simply not available is to assemble all the information that can be found, and then attempt to narrow the field of possibilities. Although some additional detail must be presented, this, too, allows the reader to join in the process of investigation so he or she can judge the import of the available evidence. (Whenever feasible I have for this reason also cited accessible published sources in addition to difficult-to-check archival files.)

Although I think the scholarly detective aspects of the tale have a certain fascination of their own, I have also tried to limit the scope of the reporting in certain areas—in part simply to hold down the length of this book. As we shall see, the real decisions connected with the use of the atomic bomb were made by a tiny group of officials. I have accordingly focused in Book I on what men at the very top of the U.S. government did during the summer of 1945, and I have referred readers to other studies for additional detail. Many excellent accounts are now available of how the atomic bomb was developed; of lower-level bureaucratic and other infighting; of, say, how some atomic scientists maneuvered at the last minute to attempt to head off the weapon's use by urging a "demonstration" rather than the destruction of a city.[16]

Book II proceeds in a slightly different manner in its exploration of the question of how the American people came to believe what most still believe about the bombing of Hiroshima.

Ask nine out of ten people why the United States used the atomic bomb at the end of World War II and the answer almost always is: "To save perhaps a million lives by making an invasion unnecessary." In a special 1985 *Nightline* broadcast on the fortieth anniversary of the bombings, ABC's Ted Koppel put it this way:

What happened over Japan . . . was a human tragedy. . . . But what was planned to take place in the war between Japan and the United States would almost certainly have been an even greater tragedy. . . .[17]

Where, precisely, did this idea come from? How did it become so wide-spread? If, in fact, the bomb was not needed to prevent an invasion—and especially, of course, if this was known at the time—the notion that it was the only way to save large numbers of lives is clearly a myth. And clearly, too, in a very general sense the public has been misled.

We have been very poorly served by the print and electronic media in connection with the Hiroshima story. Over the past fifty years most journalists have reported what government officials have said about the decision as if it were fact—evidence to the contrary notwithstanding. An impressive thread of challenging reporting does exist—a reminder that there have always been people willing to speak out, to penetrate the silence. (As we shall see, some of the most forthright reporting was done not only by critics but by highly respected military journalists and well-known business magazines.)

At another level, there is the matter of routine government classification of major documents for a substantial period (usually thirty years in the case of significant diplomatic and military issues). For decades—especially during the early postwar period when the public's views about Hiroshima were being consolidated—thousands of documents were off-limits to researchers. Classification practices—and especially the all-too-easy manner in which claims of "national security" are used to suppress information—clearly need to be questioned.

We also lack knowledge of many private discussions between James F. Byrnes and President Truman during April, May, and June 1945, when Byrnes served as the president's personal representative on the Interim Committee. And we know almost nothing about the critical planning sessions the two men held during the eight-day Atlantic crossing before the Potsdam conference and, on the return, just before the bombing itself.

That the documents one would need to fully resolve many of the most difficult issues related to the Hiroshima decision have not been made available is understood by the nation's best scholars. The author of one important study, Martin Sherwin, asked in 1973: "Was an implicit warning to Moscow, then, the principal reason for deciding to use the atomic bomb against Japan? In light of the ambiguity of the available evidence the question defies an unequivocal answer."[18] Three decades after Hiroshima, Barton Bernstein similarly observed that several key questions "cannot be definitively answered on the basis of presently available evidence. . . ."[19]

An obvious question arises: Why is this so? If the decision to use the atomic bomb was simply a matter of obvious military necessity—as had repeatedly been stated—why hadn't everything long since been made public? What was there to hide?

In impressive displays of scholarly reflection and integrity over time, a number of historians—including Sherwin and Bernstein—have revised various aspects of their interpretations of the decision, and of their judgments. Bernstein stated to a 1990 gathering: "The task I have is to try as a historian, as an individual, to make some sense on a problem that I've labored on for many years. I've had various formulations . . . I'm sure that each would change and will change over time." He continued:

> Evidence almost never on interesting matters entails answers. It only provides leverage for answers. [On other matters] . . . evidence is useful, the leverage is more contingent, and well-intentioned, ardently researching people looking at the same material can plausibly come to different conclusions.[20]

Still another well-known scholar, Stephen Ambrose, sent me a personal note on the subject in early 1993 which stated: "For my part I've gone back and forth on the A-bomb decision so many times I can't have much confidence in hard conclusions."[21]

As I began to probe the more puzzling aspects of the record, it also appeared that something besides the usual government classification procedures had been at work. The documentary trail is, in fact, punctuated by numerous quite obvious gaps—in some cases because apparently no records of important discussions were kept; in others, for reasons that are unexplained. Also, some documents appear to have been hidden or destroyed.

Specialized work being done on certain specific elements of the story by other scholars also pointed to a common problem: Many important documents had evidently been actively suppressed—and others appeared to have been manipulated in odd ways or even in certain cases systematically rewritten to "improve" the historical record.

It seemed plain that the oddities also turning up in other research (for instance, concerning the suppression of information related to human radiation experimentation) were no accident—that there was a general problem which needed to be investigated.

The modern term for a process characterized by practices of the kind we are discussing is "cover-up." However, the term is far too blatant and conspiratorial for our purposes. Perhaps the plural form, "cover-ups," might be more appropriate. Moreover, although some of the men involved were indeed blatant and conspiratorial, others appear to have been caught up in events and seem themselves to have been somewhat blinded to what was happening.

What they did, even if it resulted in the suppression of information, was not the same as a blatant cover-up.

Several of the people involved, it seems clear, also may ultimately have come to believe the things they later said which are now contradicted by the available documents. Nonetheless, some form of misrepresentation was—and is—certain; and as we shall see, misstatements of fact, manipulation of the documentary record, the withholding of information for many decades, and in some instances, clear evidence of outright lying, define a process which would easily warrant more dramatic labeling in our own era.

Put another way, it would be very surprising indeed if the widespread and continued belief in the mistaken notion that the atomic bomb had been needed to prevent massive loss of life had simply occurred without official encouragement and the denial of access to contrary information.

How were the ideas most people were taught propagated and sustained?

Any effort to find out is handicapped from the outset: The process is inherently covert. Moreover, some of the parties involved were diligent in covering their tracks. Still, it is possible to sketch the main outlines of what happened by assembling bits and pieces of information from a wide range of sources—and, also, by comparing the public statements of key officials with the evidence which, after fifty years, is now in hand.

The various officials are all rather different. Each in his own way is complex; there are no cardboard characters in this drama. President Truman, to take the most notable example, is a far more interesting figure than many commonly understand. He is not simply the straight-shooting, lovable, cracker-barrel "man of the people" of recent mythology.[22] Truman was, after all, the handpicked senatorial candidate of the notorious Kansas City Pendergast machine—and a shrewd poker player to boot. There is indisputable evidence that on several occasions the president misrepresented important aspects of the Hiroshima story—both to the American people and to his own Cabinet. Moreover, as we shall see, his writings on the subject systematically eliminate information on many crucial aspects of the tale which, we can now document, run counter to the official version of events.

On the other hand, Truman was a newcomer to office and for a long time was clearly in over his head. There is also ample evidence that at the outset of his Administration he was manipulated by the shrewd politician he made his personal representative for atomic bomb matters—the man he privately called his "conniving" secretary of state, James F. Byrnes. Often the record shows the president's personal instincts to have been quite different from Byrnes' policy. Through a rather complex process, it appears that ultimately Truman himself came to believe what he said on many occasions—namely that the bomb had to be used to prevent an invasion. (It does not seem to be the case, however, that the question never troubled him.*)

The other major figures involved range from the ailing and aging secretary of war, Henry L. Stimson, to the tough-minded, aggressive general in charge of the Manhattan Project, Leslie R. Groves; and they include a host of lesser military and other officials. During his last years Stimson was rolled forward once again onto the stage of history to set out the official line (with the help of a young man who later became famous in his own right, McGeorge Bundy). Characteristically, Stimson—a man of great personal integrity—was to change his mind on what he initially said with Bundy's help, and he subsequently retreated on some crucial issues. Groves was always clear about what had to be done; he did not hesitate to suppress documents and propagandize to make sure his version of events was broadcast far and wide.

Then, of course, there is Byrnes, who, in the end, was perhaps most responsible for advice on the decision and for convincing the president to reject available alternatives. We shall learn a great deal about this man—including his nimble capacity to stay out of the line of fire for decades after the fact in connection with the Hiroshima decision.

We should also reflect on an obvious psychological reality concerning why the Hiroshima myth has been sustained for so long. How many people, in truth, could find the strength to publicly repudiate what had been done and what been said? It is understandable in human terms that many of the men involved probably came themselves to accept as fact things which documents now available show they did not believe at the time.

In our own time, most Americans have come to take for granted the fact that government officials regularly lie to the people and then attempt to cover their tracks. Many people are cynical in a way they were not fifty years ago. We are also sentimental: We don't like to think that the men of earlier days might possibly have acted as men do today.

The Hiroshima story reminds us that government deceit (even by good men) is hardly a recent invention.

I wish to stress that term: "good men." None of the officials involved in this tale had evil intentions. What can be said of them, I believe, is that some became so taken by the power the atomic bomb seemed to give them to do good (as they defined it) that they seem to have gotten carried away. Stimson put his finger on a key point when he observed privately to his colleague Joseph Grew that they were "very fine men"—but also that they "should have known better. . . ."[23]

*See below, pp. 562–70.

This returns us to the question of why certain individuals like Leahy and Eisenhower not only reached the conclusions they did about the Hiroshima decision, but why they chose not to continue to affirm the public myth by their personal silence. Both, it seems clear, felt that the use of force could not be allowed to transcend all ethical limits—even the use of force for what was judged to be good: ". . . so I voiced to him my grave misgivings. . . ." "I was not taught to make war in that fashion. . . ."[24]

The manipulation of the public by elites, the seductive belief that overwhelming force confers unlimited power to determine good and evil, and the fragile nature of the limits we seem willing to accept on our own prerogatives are all ongoing issues—as, finally, is the terrible question of what it means for a democracy to delegate to one person such extraordinary discretionary power in an era when the next Hiroshima could be the globe.

As Maya Angelou urged in the poem she read on Inaugural Day, January 20, 1993:

> History, despite its wrenching pain,
> Cannot be unlived, but if faced
> With courage, need not to be lived again.[25]

Hiroshima and Nagasaki—now—I think, have very little to do with the past.

How we choose to deal with them, I believe, may have everything to do with the future.

We are all fine Americans who should have known better about our own silent refusal to confront the enormity of nuclear weapons.

Book One

THE DECISION

[I]t wasn't necessary to hit them with that awful thing. . . .
—President Dwight D. Eisenhower

Chapter 1

THE TRAJECTORY OF
JAPAN'S DECLINE

We believe that a considerable portion of the Japanese population now consider absolute military defeat to be probable. The increasing effects of sea blockade and the cumulative devastation wrought by strategic bombing, which has already rendered millions homeless and has destroyed from 25% to 50% of the builtup [sic] area of Japan's most important cities, should make this realization increasingly general.
—Combined U.S.–British Intelligence Committee, July 8, 1945

Among historians of World War II it is now a commonplace that Japanese power disintegrated rapidly in the spring and summer of 1945—that from the early months of that year, their defeat was certain. Robert J. C. Butow describes the dire situation as of the end of 1944:

> . . . the scales of war had been tipped so steeply against the Japanese that no counterweights at their disposal could possibly have balanced them. Germany, which for the Japanese had been a seemingly invincible first line of defense, was facing inevitable destruction; the defense perimeter that the Japanese had created far out beyond their island base had been cracked and deeply penetrated; worst of all, Japan's military potential was dropping rapidly with her industrial capacity, as American submarines and planes cut the last of her economic lifelines to the outside world and great aerial armadas began the methodical destruction of her cities.[1]

The Pacific War had initially moved relatively slowly as President Roosevelt gave priority to the European struggle against Hitler. The famous Pacific battles—Midway: June 1942; Guadalcanal: August–November 1942; New

Guinea: September 1942–April 1944; Marianas: June–August 1944—along with the U.S. Navy slowly tightening its stranglehold on Japanese shipping—were dramatic, but far different from what was about to come. In the late summer of 1944, Japan's plight became severe. The fall of Saipan in early July and of Tinian and Guam one month later provided bases which brought the home islands into much better B-29 bombing range. In September, Lieutenant General George C. Kenney, Commander of Air Forces in the Southwest Pacific, was able to tell General "Hap" Arnold, Commander of the Army Air Forces:

> The situation is developing rapidly and there are trends which indicate that the Jap is not going to last much longer.
>
> His sea power is so badly depleted that it is no match for any one of several task forces we could put into action.
>
> His air power is in a bad way. He has a lot of airplanes—probably more than he had a year ago—but he has lost his element, flight, squadron and group leaders and his hastily trained replacements haven't the skill or ability or combat knowledge to compete with us. . . .
>
> Without the support of his sea power and air power his land forces cannot do anything except hold out in isolated, beleaguered spots all over the map until bombs, bullets, disease and starvation kill them off. . . .[2]

The end-products of America's enormous industrial capacity—the battleships and carriers of the U.S. Navy and the heavy bombers of the Army Air Forces—now began to pummel Japan mercilessly. On November 24, the war was brought home to millions of Japanese when the Nakajima Aircraft works in the suburbs of Tokyo were struck. A few months later the firebombing of Tokyo (March 9–10, 1945) produced a military and human catastrophe. Some sixteen square miles of one of the world's most densely packed residential districts was completely burnt out, and at least 84,000 people were killed in the firestorm; total losses may have numbered upwards of 120,000. With the collapse of Iwo Jima in the last week of March, U.S. fighter planes could provide cover for heavy bombing missions to Japan—which now went forward on a massive scale. As another historian, Herbert Feis, has succinctly put it: "The structure of Japanese life and production was being smashed and burned."[3]

On April 1, 1945, the U.S. Tenth Army—consisting of three Marine Corps divisions and four Army divisions—landed on Okinawa, the gateway to the home islands. At this time, too, the Russians signaled the likely end of their neutrality. The Koiso government, only nine months old, collapsed. An aging admiral known for his moderation, Baron Kantaro Suzuki, took over amidst growing chaos.[4]

* * *

What was known within the U.S. government at the time—and, specifically, how much did top officials understand the meaning both of particular developments and, equally important, of the trajectory and developing trend of events?

Although most of the American public and servicemen in the field were led to envisage a long and fierce battle—and the high probability of an invasion—now, a half century later, we know a great deal more both about what was actually happening and about what was known by Washington. Clearly, Japan was defeated and preparing to surrender before the atomic bomb was used. Though the question of timing was in dispute, it is also certain that this was generally understood in the U.S. government at the time.

Shortly after the Suzuki government took over, a confidential internal U.S. government assessment by the Office of Strategic Services (OSS) concluded:

> Admiral Suzuki stands a world apart from the Kwantung Army faction which has exercised a paramount influence in Japanese politics since the February 26th military revolt in 1936. . . . Suzuki's appointment has all the appearance of a desperate stop-gap arrangement, an effort to by-pass these extremists and yet provide a new political alignment which can lay the basis for peace negotiations if possible.[5]

At the same time, the Joint Intelligence Committee (JIC) of the Joint Chiefs of Staff put forward a devastating report on Japan's situation. "With respect to essential raw materials for her war industries," it observed, "Japan is even more dependent than Great Britain upon imports from overseas. . . ."

> Due to the shortage of ocean shipping, Japan's main rail lines are already overburdened, while motor transport is totally inadequate. . . . The continued heavy destruction of machinery and equipment will make it impossible for Japan to replace losses with her existing or potential machine tool and heavy equipment industry. . . .
>
> Under these circumstances the Japanese "will" to continue the war may be expected to weaken progressively. Entirely apart from the physical results obtained by air-sea blockade combined with strategic bombing, the psychological effects upon the Japanese people as a whole will be most detrimental and will progressively undermine their confidence in victory or even confidence in the hope of avoiding complete and inevitable defeat.[6]

Major international developments added to the crisis. In early April the Soviet Union gave notice that it would not renew its existing Neutrality Pact with Japan. If Stalin was no longer prepared to maintain neutrality once his vast armies had completed their work against Hitler, it would be disastrous:

The third Great Power would join a victorious Britain and United States in an all-out assault on an already devastated Japan.[7]

U.S. intelligence experts had long since broken Japanese codes and were regularly reading top-secret high-level cable and radio traffic.[8] An intercepted March 1 cable from Japan's ambassador to Moscow Naotake Sato predicted that abrogation of the Neutrality Pact would plunge the Japanese people into a state of "unprecedented despair and despondency."[9] When word of the Soviet Union's decision actually reached Tokyo, Japanese officials scrambled to attempt somehow to insure that the Neutrality Pact would last out the year. On April 24 Foreign Minister Shigenori Togo cabled Sato instructing him to seek an immediate meeting with Soviet Foreign Minister Vyacheslav M. Molotov. "Since Japan is facing a grave situation which permits no delay, it is urgently necessary that we should sound out Russia's real intentions [toward Japan] and exhaust all possibilities of bringing about a new turn in the situation. . . ."[10]

U.S. officials, of course, were fully aware of the importance of the Soviet announcement. The OSS report on the replacement of Koiso by Suzuki pointed out that the "loss of Iwo Jima and the present invasion of Okinawa have seriously intensified the domestic political situation. . . ." However, it noted, "it seems highly probable that Russia's abrogation of the Neutrality Pact was the actual spark which touched off these accumulated explosives."[11] By April 11 the Joint Intelligence Staff (JIS) of the Joint Chiefs of Staff was reporting its judgment that: "If at any time the U.S.S.R. should enter the war, all Japanese will realize that absolute defeat is inevitable."[12]

Other extraordinary international events also rocked Japanese politics. Hitler's suicide on April 30 and Germany's surrender on May 8 were political and psychological body blows to those within Japan who argued for a continuation of the war. Italy had already disintegrated, and with the collapse of Germany, the three Axis powers were no more: Japan was alone. A May 12 intercepted message revealed Sato cabling: ". . . once the enemy's European air forces are transferred to the Pacific, our damages will exceed anything we can imagine, so that we may be facing the same situation that led to the downfall of Hitler Germany."[13] On May 15, an internal memorandum from Major General Clayton Bissell, assistant chief of staff for Intelligence to Lieutenant General John E. Hull, assistant chief of staff for the War Department's Operations Division (OPD), put it bluntly:

> The Japanese have been brought to a cold realization of their isolated position by the surrender of Germany, and evidence indicates that they are appalled by the destruction wrought on German cities.[14]

Officials at various levels of the government were beginning to draw quite specific conclusions. In his May 15 memorandum, for instance, Bissell recommended an immediate surrender ultimatum. The Military Intelligence Division believed that with Germany's collapse and Japan's new fears of a Soviet onslaught, "the present moment will be an excellent one for an unconditional surrender demand upon Japan when she can be assured that surrender would be made to the Anglo-Americans only."[15]

On June 1, the Office of War Information's (OWI's) Foreign Morale Analysis Division stressed that assuming that "the military pressure is sustained, the psychological and social tensions now handicapping the Japanese will continue to mount in severity until they actively cripple the Japanese war effort."[16]

On June 21 the United States announced successful completion of the bloody Okinawa campaign—a loss which had a profound effect on Japanese military leaders. As the end approached, Japanese Army leaders called a full-dress meeting of the Supreme Council for the Direction of the War. An appraisal before them stated:

> The people are losing confidence in their leaders, and the gloomy omen of deterioration of public morale is present. The spirit of public sacrifice is lacking and among leading intellectuals there are some who advocate peace negotiations as a way out. . . .
>
> There is also a strong possibility that a considerable portion of Japan's various industrial areas will soon have to suspend operations for want of coal. From mid-year on, there will be a shortage of basic industrial salts, making it difficult for us to produce light metals, synthetic oil, and explosives. Henceforth, prices will rise sharply—bringing on inflation. This, in turn, will seriously undermine our wartime economy.[17]

Within the United States, Secretary of War Stimson provided this overview to President Truman in a top-secret memorandum written on July 2, less than two weeks after Okinawa's collapse:

> We have the following enormously favorable factors on our side—factors much weightier than those we had against Germany:
>
> Japan has no allies.
>
> Her navy is nearly destroyed and she is vulnerable to a surface and underwater blockade which can deprive her of sufficient food and supplies for her population.
>
> She is terribly vulnerable to our concentrated air attack upon her crowded cities, industrial and food resources.
>
> She has against her not only the Anglo-American forces but the rising forces of China and the ominous threat of Russia.
>
> We have inexhaustible and untouched industrial resources to bring to bear against her diminishing potential.

We have great moral superiority through being the victim of her first sneak attack.[18]

In a similar vein, the Combined U.S.-British Intelligence Committee submitted a report to the Combined Chiefs of Staff in the first week of July which stated:

The Japanese ruling groups are aware of the desperate military situation. . . .

We believe that a considerable portion of the Japanese population now consider absolute military defeat to be probable. The increasing effects of sea blockade and the cumulative devastation wrought by strategic bombing, which has already rendered millions homeless and has destroyed from 25% to 50% of the builtup [sic] area of Japan's most important cities, should make this realization increasingly general.[19]

As if to underscore these assessments, in the first week of July the Japanese government publicly announced a 10 percent cut in staple rations, together with new plans to manufacture starch from potato vine and other plants.[20] The Board of Technology stated that it would begin processing 150 million acorns as a substitute for rice. Radio Tokyo went "all out" in praise of acorns—and declared that a campaign to popularize the idea of eating acorns would follow.[21]

At this time Radio Tokyo also noted that pine-root oil was now being worked on as an experimental airplane fuel and that a "wooden aircraft production department" had been established in the Japanese Munitions Ministry.[22]

Chapter 2

GENERAL EFFORTS
TO END THE WAR

His Majesty the Emperor, mindful of the fact that the present war daily brings greater evil and sacrifice upon the peoples of all belligerent powers, desires from his heart that it may be quickly terminated.

— Intercepted message from Foreign Minister Togo
to Ambassador Sato in Moscow, July 12, 1945

As Japan's situation deteriorated, the frequency and intensity of secret diplomatic moves and so-called "peace feelers" mounted. At the same time American cryptographers intercepted increasingly revealing cable traffic as Japanese officials began maneuvering to end the war. Again the general trajectory is no longer in doubt.

Preliminary indications of Japanese diplomatic movement appeared as early as July and August 1944, after the loss of Saipan and the fall of the Tojo government. On August 11, under the heading "Japanese consider peace possibilities," War Department MAGIC reports of intercepted messages (designated "Eyes Only" for the president and his closest advisers) pointed out:

Foreign Minister Shigemitsu has instructed Ambassador Sato [in Moscow] to find out whether Russia is willing to assist in bringing about a negotiated peace. Shigemitsu's instructions, although cautiously worded, clearly imply that he has in mind a move by Russia to initiate peace discussions between Japan and the Anglo-Americans. . . . [I]t seems hardly likely that he would have taken such a step without having consulted at least some of the more important members of the new Japanese Cabinet.

The summary also noted:

This is the first time that the Japanese have been willing to suggest to Russia directly that they are ready for peace.[1]

Appended to this report was the text of Shigemitsu's August 7 message, which included an internal Japanese assessment:

> In the Pacific, the American offensive is becoming violent. The enemy has already broken into our territorial waters and by means of absolute superiority on the sea and in the air is steadily drawing nearer to our homeland itself with the intention of severing our sea communications and destroying our shore installations. This situation will become increasingly serious as Germany's military strength diminishes. . . .[2]

On September 26, the British ambassador to the United States gave Secretary of State Cordell Hull a paraphrase of a telegram sent from Sweden's minister in Tokyo:

> I learn from a very reliable source that in important civilian circles in Japan the peace problem is being discussed with increasing anxiety. A speedy German collapse is expected and it is not believed that Japan can then continue the war. It is therefore considered necessary to get peace as soon as possible before the country and towns are destroyed. . . . If any willingness appeared to exist in London the Japanese would be ready for preliminary discussions through Swedish channels.
> Behind the man who gave me this message stands one of the best known statesmen in Japan and there is no doubt that this attempt must be considered as a serious one.[3]

The British government decided not to respond to this indirect approach.[4] In his reply on September 29, however, Hull agreed to Halifax's suggestion that Moscow should be told of the "peace feeler" (his term).[5] On October 10, a summary of the episode was also sent to Admiral Leahy.[6]

Two weeks later, on October 25—under the heading "Japanese peace moves in China"—MAGIC analysts reported:

> On 30 August Foreign Minister Shigemitsu informed Ambassador Tani in Nanking that the Supreme Council for the Conduct of the War had decided that "political activities" designed to effect peace with Chungking should be undertaken through the Nanking Government.[7]

This summary included an October 14 cable from Ambassador Tani to Foreign Minister Shigemitsu which stated: "The situation in Europe is regarded as disadvantageous to the Axis, and the progress America is making in the Pacific indicates the defeat of Japan."[8]

An unexpected resurgence of Nazi resistance—the German Army's surprise Ardennes counteroffensive which began on December 16—delayed Germany's surrender. This in turn, it appears, may have slowed the pace of Japanese peace maneuvers. Nevertheless, on January 30, 1945, the State Department received from the OSS

> . . . a series of reports in regard to Japanese negotiations, beginning in early January, 1945, with the Vatican looking toward mediation by the Pope in the war of the Pacific. . . . [I]t appears that the Japanese Government is involved, as negotiations are now being conducted at the Vatican by the Japanese Minister (Ken Harada) and his assistants.[9]

As the Yalta Conference approached, there was an unmistakable burst of anxiety in the intercepted cable traffic. At Yalta the United States and Britain would be talking directly to the Soviet Union, and the consequences could be disastrous. On February 9, U.S. military intelligence intercepted the following urgent cable from Shigemitsu to Sato:

> I believe that the Three Power Conference will soon be over, and I want you to seek an interview with Molotov and then to inform me as to what you learn from him concerning the details of the Conference and of Russia's attitude toward Japan. I should like you to make a regular practice of ascertaining Russia's policy toward Japan from now on, and also on some appropriate occasion to sound out her feeling about the continuance of the Neutrality Pact.[10]

By April 6 the following report by Sweden's minister in Tokyo was sent to the State Department through the U.S. minister in Stockholm:

> . . . it seems probable that very far-reaching conditions would be accepted by the Japanese by way of negotiation. . . . Exchange of the Japanese constitution must also be considered as excluded. The Emperor must not be touched. However, the Imperial power could be somewhat democratized as is that of the English King.[11]

Though the U.S. minister expressed some wariness as to the source of this information, the following day he assured Hull that it "represented views expressed to Swedish Minister Bagge in Tokyo by 'Jap officials of very high rank.' "

> It is Foreign Office opinion although Bagge did not say so that these views were intentionally given to Bagge in expectation they would come to attention of United States and British Governments. Bagge's report was received 2 days before Russian denunciation of the neutrality pact with Japan.[12]

As the Soviet denunciation of the pact, the installation of the new Suzuki government, and the impending German surrender came together, peace feelers and diplomatic maneuvering began to multiply. On May 5 the following message to Berlin from the German naval attaché in Tokyo was intercepted:

An influential member of the Admiralty Staff has given me to understand that, since the situation is clearly recognized to be hopeless, large sections of the Japanese armed forces would not regard with disfavor an American request for capitulation even if the terms were hard, provided they were halfway honorable.[13]

On May 12—four days after Germany's surrender—William Donovan, director of the OSS, reported to Truman:

[A] source, on 11 May, talked with Shunichi Kase, the Japanese Minister to Switzerland. He reports that Kase expressed a wish to help arrange for a cessation of hostilities between the Japanese and the Allies. Kase reportedly considers direct talks with the Americans and the British preferable to negotiations through the USSR, because the latter eventuality would increase Soviet prestige so much that the whole Far East would become Communist.[14]

On June 2, a similar report was submitted directly to Truman, this time of peace feeler activity in Portugal:

On May 7, 1945 the OSS representative reported that . . . [a] source stated that he had been asked by Masutaro Inoue, Counsellor of the Japanese Legation in Portugal, to contact United States representatives. Source quoted Inoue as saying that the Japanese are ready to cease hostilities, provided they are allowed to retain possession of their home islands. . . .

On 19 May, the OSS representative reported Inoue again had repeated to source his desire to talk with an American representative. On this occasion Inoue declared that actual peace terms were unimportant so long as the term "unconditional surrender" was not employed.[15]

Still another report was received from Switzerland a few days later, on June 4:

Source is in touch with Fujimura, who is understood to be one of the principal Japanese Naval representatives in Europe . . . Fujimura indicated to source that the Navy circles who now control [?] the Japanese Government would be willing to surrender but wish, if possible, to save some face from the present wreckage. These Navy circles, he declares, particularly stress the necessity of preserving the Emperor in order to avoid Communism and chaos. Fujimura emphasizes that Japan cannot supply itself with basically essential foodstuffs.[16]

On July 7 an account of peace feeler activity in Sweden was sent to the Secretary of State:

Major General Onodera, Jap Mil Attaché, stated that Japs know war has been lost. . . . Onodera referred to Emperor and pointed out that by reason of Emperor's position contact will have to be made by Swed [sic] King. He further stated that Emperor must be maintained in his position after the capitulation. No other conditions of surrender were specified.[17]

And on July 13, just before Truman's Potsdam meeting with Churchill and Stalin, OSS representative Allen Dulles reported from Wiesbaden, Germany:

Per Jacobsson, a Swedish national and economic adviser to the Bank for International Settlements, has been approached by Kojiro Kitamura, a director of the Bank, a representative of the Yokohama Specie Bank and former financial attaché in Berlin. Kitamura indicated to Jacobsson that he was anxious to establish immediate contact with American representatives and implied that the only condition on which Japan would insist with respect to surrender would be some consideration for the Japanese Imperial family.[18]

On July 16, Donovan sent the president Dulles' follow-up report of Jacobsson's activities:

Throughout discussions with Jacobsson, the Japanese officials stressed only two points: (a) the preservation of the Emperor, and (b) the possibility of returning to the constitution promulgated in 1889.[19]

None of these approaches, of course, carried formal, official authorization, and, accordingly, they were treated with considerable caution: There was obviously an enormous difference between a general mid-level (or even high-level) probe and a true Japanese initiative. Moreover, experts in Washington differed as to the appropriate weight to attach to various moves at various points in time as the summer progressed.

Nevertheless, the increasing pace of contacts involving important Japanese representatives was an obvious indication of Japan's deteriorating internal situation—and, too, of the clear trajectory of change. In particular, as General Charles H. Bonesteel III, chief of the Policy Section in the War Department's Operations Division (OPD), was later to recall: "the poor damn Japanese were putting feelers out by the ton so to speak through Russia. . . ."[20] A major turning point—and by far the most important development of the summer—occurred on July 13, when U.S. intelligence experts intercepted explicit and dramatic evidence of Japan's desire to end the war: The Emperor had decided to intervene personally to attempt to end the fighting. The MAGIC summary of July 13 revealed Foreign Minister Togo instructing his ambassador (on July 12) in Moscow "to inform the Russians of the Imperial will concerning the ending of the war. . . ."

> His Majesty the Emperor, mindful of the fact that the present war daily brings greater evil and sacrifice upon the peoples of all belligerent powers, desires from his heart that it may be quickly terminated. . . .
>
> It is the Emperor's private intention to send Prince Konoye to Moscow as a Special Envoy with a letter from him containing the statements given above. Please inform Molotov of this and get the Russians' consent to having the party enter the country.[21]

When the Japanese ambassador presented his case in Moscow, he stressed:

> I should like the Russian Government to bear particularly in mind the fact that the present Special Envoy will be of an entirely different character from the Special Envoy I have discussed with Molotov three times in the past; this time the Envoy will be sent at the particular desire of his Majesty.[22]

The overall trend of these developments is not in question. On the other hand, there was a difference between what was known inside the U.S. government and what was said to the public. By and large the various peace feelers were publicly discounted by officials. However, even at the time, Washington reporters with close government connections understood that something more important was afoot than officials would acknowledge. As early as May 1945, for instance, the well-informed business publication *The Kiplinger Washington Letter* began advising its readers:

> It is a fact, not mere rumor, that Japan has made peace feelers. There are two of which we know, perhaps others of which we do not know. The first sought too much for Japan, the second less but still too much.
>
> Others will follow them and undoubtedly will shrink toward less & less. The Japs will expect to save something, but not as much as they hoped. Thus a whole series of peace feelers or peace offers is coming along.[23]

In mid-July, *The Kiplinger Washington Letter* provided more detail—and underscored another important distinction for its readers:

Our military men do NOT think in terms of an early Jap end. They say it will take at least a year more, and perhaps even longer.

But they talk only of MILITARY operations for outright DEFEAT, whereas current peace moves involve DIPLOMATIC operations for SURRENDER. Note the distinction when you read the news, the rumors, the denials.[24]

The distinction pointed out by *The Kiplinger Washington Letter* was, of course, crucial—and as we shall explore, understood as such. However, the intercepts alone could only give a general sense of Japan's situation. With the publication and discovery of a range of other documents during the late 1970s and 1980s, it was possible to make judgments as to the meaning and significance U.S. officials attached to the various developments.

The first significant reference made to the simple fact that the United States had broken Japan's diplomatic code—and had intercepted messages which indicated Japan's desire to end the war—appeared in a brief paraphrase in the edited version of the diary of Secretary of the Navy James V. Forrestal. This was published six years after the war's end, in 1951.[25]

Virtually the same information appeared in 1954, in Robert J. C. Butow's *Japan's Decision to Surrender*, along with portions of the Japanese cables. (Butow had arranged for special access to Japanese archival material.)[26]

The existence of the MAGIC diplomatic intercepts was formally confirmed by the U.S. government in 1960. Texts of a number of the documents were released at this time. That Truman and his close advisers at Potsdam had not only received but actually read the most important MAGIC intercepts also was not disclosed until 1960. At this time it was officially reported (in the government's *Foreign Relations* volume on the Potsdam conference) that in 1956 the president had privately confirmed to State Department historians that he had seen the intercepts in 1945.[27]

The bulk—but still not all—of the actual intercept texts were released to the National Archives in 1978; and the documents were then made available to researchers. Still, very large gaps in the record remained. Finally, in 1993, after a Freedom of Information Act challenge by Sanho Tree and the Public Citizen Litigation Group, the National Security Agency released roughly another eight hundred pages of the 1945 intercept documents. The remaining texts were released only in early 1995.

As noted above, a previously declassified intercepted Japanese message of May 5, 1945 suggested that "large sections of the Japanese armed forces would not regard with disfavor an American request for capitulation even if the terms were hard, provided they were halfway honorable."[28] The following item related to this intercept had been prepared by intelligence analysts in 1945 and was buried among the eight hundred pages of documents released only in 1993:

> Note: Previously noted diplomatic reports have commented on signs of war weariness in official Japanese Navy circles, but have not mentioned such an attitude in Army quarters.[29]

What position the Japanese military—and, in particular, army leaders— would take was, of course, absolutely critical, both at the time and in subsequent interpretations. That a decision had been made to suppress even fragmentary information in this connection was obvious: The "Note" was a single blocked-out paragraph surrounded by text which had long since been declassified.

Quite apart from the significance of this rather minor report on the attitude of army leaders in May, a decision to isolate a carefully defined passage of this kind points beyond general classification procedures to specific choices by specific officials as to what the public could and could not be permitted to know about the events of 1945.

PART I

Unconditional Surrender

. . . one point was clear to senior U.S. officials regardless of where they stood on war termination. . . . the critical condition for Japan's surrender was the assurance that the throne would be preserved.

—Leon V. Sigal, *Fighting to a Finish*

Chapter 3

APRIL–MAY 1945

> *The greatest obstacle to unconditional surrender by the Japanese is their belief that this would entail the destruction or permanent removal of the Emperor and the institution of the Throne. If some indication can now be given the Japanese that they themselves, when once thoroughly defeated and rendered impotent to wage war in future, will be permitted to determine their own future political structure, they will be afforded a method of saving face without which surrender will be highly unlikely. . . .*
>
> *The President said that he was interested in what I said because his own thoughts had been following the same line.*
>
> —Memorandum by Acting Secretary of State
> Joseph C. Grew, May 28, 1945

The now plentiful documentation that U.S. officials understood the unmistakable trajectory of Japan's decline is not the same thing as evidence that American leaders knew the war could be ended without either an invasion or use of the atomic bomb. A general trajectory is just that—an overarching trend which points in an obvious direction but does not permit a precise assessment of shifts in conditions, timing, and political mood. And these, of course, are the essential ingredients in any appraisal of whether the atomic bomb had to be used.

Evidence of the growing frequency and intensity of peace maneuvering also tells us only so much without much more detailed information about how U.S. officials judged the meaning of opportunities presented by the increasingly persistent Japanese efforts.

Over the years historians have endlessly dissected the options available to policy-makers. By far the most commonly discussed possibility relates to the U.S. demand for "unconditional surrender"—a matter, again, concerning

which we now have far more information than at the time the official justification for the bombings was presented to the public in 1945.

In the early years after World War II, a number of observers pointed out
that the only thing which appeared to have stood in the way of an end to the
war was the "formality" of the U.S. demand for unconditional surrender. It
was repeatedly noted that well before Hiroshima some U.S. officials had
urged that the rigid surrender formula be modified—and that as early as May
1945 they had argued that a slight change might well stop the fighting.[1]

Several of the decision-makers themselves also focused on the "unconditional surrender" formula after the war. These men, however, gave the argument a somewhat different twist from that of the early critics: If only the
Japanese government had not demanded that the terms be changed, things
might well have been different. For instance, in his 1947 book *Speaking
Frankly*, James F. Byrnes declared without qualification: "Had the Japanese
Government listened to [Ambassador to the Soviet Union] Sato and surrendered unconditionally, it would not have been necessary to drop the atomic
bomb."[2]

Subsequent historical discussions often echoed these early arguments and
counterarguments. With the documents presently available it is clear that
both formulations were, in fact, substantially beside the point. Indeed, they
are, and were, quite misleading—and, as we shall see, in some instances purposely so.

The reality is that as the summer of 1945 progressed, most U.S. leaders
fully realized that the only serious condition Japan's leaders sought was an
assurance that the Emperor would not be eliminated. For this reason all but
one presidential adviser urged that to secure a surrender the Japanese must
be assured of the safety of the Emperor (perhaps that he be allowed to remain in a figurehead role like that of the king of England).

Moreover, it is now known that well before the atomic bomb was used, no
close presidential adviser believed that providing Japan assurances on this
matter presented insuperable political problems—a point not widely understood among some scholars even today. Although a few saw some advantage
in temporizing for a brief period, maintaining the rigid formula was certainly
not worth risking American lives in an invasion. In any event, ultimately the
Emperor was the only one who could order an end to the fighting. Most important, we know now that the president himself repeatedly indicated that
these were his own views.

The evidence now in hand, in fact, shows that Truman was directly urged
to clarify the surrender terms by Cabinet or sub-Cabinet officials, and by
Prime Minister Churchill, on at least a dozen separate occasions. With the
sole exception of Byrnes, by early July every important Administration political and military adviser sufficiently influential to have regular direct

access to the president on the matter—including all of Roosevelt's top advisers—supported a clarification.

Furthermore, by this time these advisers agreed that it was essential to give Japan significant time to digest the implications of such a move. In no case was the period proposed less than five to six weeks before the new atomic weapon would be ready for use.

Again, the record also documents Truman's general support for an initiative of this kind—and that he personally saw little difficulty with modifying the surrender terms. There appears to be no evidence that Truman ever expressed serious fears of being criticized politically for any such change in terms.

And, of course, after using the atomic bomb the president *did* allow Japan to keep the Emperor. Hirohito, the man who became Emperor in 1926 and sat on the throne through World War II, remained titular head of the Japanese nation until his death in 1989.

The question is: Why did the president ultimately reject an approach which at the time to many appeared reasonably likely to end the war?

The significance of the Emperor in Japanese society was no secret to American leaders: The Japanese regarded the Emperor as a deity, a god—more like Jesus or the incarnate Buddha than an ordinary human being. Until the surrender occurred, the Japanese people at large had never been allowed to hear the Emperor's voice; many were moved to tears when, on the radio, they first listened to their deity speaking directly to them.

The godhood of the Emperor was a tradition which traced back to 660 B.C. and the first Japanese emperor, Jimmu, who was, according to legend, a descendant of the sun goddess Amaterasu, making him and all of his successors also divine beings. The reigning Emperor, Hirohito, was by Japanese reckoning the 124th in direct line of descent. Like his predecessors, he was customarily referred to as *Tenno Heika*, the "Son of Heaven."[3]

The tradition of zealous piety and reverence for the Emperor had also been shrewdly reinforced by the Japanese government. Official publications regularly promoted the imperial cult, which was further strengthened by repeated ceremonial events. In 1937, fearful that traditional values of loyalty and devotion might be displaced by Western immorality, the Thought Bureau of the Ministry of Education issued a document titled "Cardinal Principles of the National Polity" which defined and celebrated a "national character that is cloudless, pure, and honest."[4] The "Cardinal Principles" emphasized that "our country is a divine country governed by an Emperor who is a deity incarnate."[5]

In August 1941 the Ministry of Education distributed a publication entitled "The Way of Subjects" to Japanese schools and adult organizations for the guidance of all citizens.[6] This, too, minced few words about the Emperor or about the duty of the citizen:

> The Imperial Family is the fountain source of the Japanese nation, and national and private lives issue from this. . . . The Imperial virtues are so great and boundless that all are assimilated into one. Here is the reason for the present glorious state, in which the Emperor and his subjects are harmonized into one great unit. That the myriad subjects with one mind are glad to be unified to the Throne is the substance of the Imperial subjects.[7]

Filial piety, selflessness, and loyalty were stressed above all else:

> The way of subjects is to be loyal to the Emperor in disregard of self, thereby supporting the Imperial Throne coextensive with the Heavens and with the Earth.[8]

The standing U.S. demand for "unconditional surrender" directly threatened not only the person of the Emperor but such central tenets of Japanese culture as well. Because of the Emperor's unique political and religious status, U.S. leaders were repeatedly advised of three related but quite distinct points:

First, a surrender would likely be accepted only if the Japanese people were assured the Emperor-God would neither be removed from his throne nor harmed (or tried and possibly hanged as a war criminal, as German leaders were about to be tried).

Second, even more important, U.S. leaders were advised that if such assurances were not given, the Japanese would likely fight to the last man. Very few Japanese units had surrendered in the bloody island fighting, and there was ample evidence that the Japanese soldier was prepared to die for the Emperor. The U.S. military understood that if no assurances for the Emperor were given—whether called "conditions" or not—it would almost certainly mean a struggle to the death.

Third, the president and his chief advisers were counseled that the Emperor would play a critical role in maintaining internal order in postwar Japan—and, indeed, in helping head off the possibility of chaos or even Communist-inspired revolutionary attempts.[9]

The "unconditional" language had originally been adopted almost accidentally by Roosevelt at the January 1943 Casablanca conference. Cordell Hull recalled that it had not, in fact, originally been part of State Department strategy: "We were as much surprised as Mr. Churchill when, for the first time, the President, in the Prime Minister's presence, stated it suddenly to a press conference."[10]

The formula proved to be controversial not only because of its uncompromising tone but also, ironically, because of its ambiguity. At Casablanca, Roosevelt seemingly qualified his position at the same time he defined it when he stated that "unconditional surrender" did not mean the destruction of the peoples of Germany, Japan, and Italy; rather, it meant the destruction of the "philosophy" which had brought about world war. Given the importance of religious ideas in their political culture, of course, this was equally threatening to Japanese leaders.

Roosevelt further complicated matters when in an address to White House press correspondents on February 12, 1943, he affirmed the policy in a way which now seemed to threaten the Emperor's person:

> The only terms on which we shall deal . . . are the terms proclaimed at Casablanca: "unconditional surrender." In our uncompromising policy we mean no harm to the common people of the Axis nations. But we do mean to impose punishment and retribution in full upon their guilty, barbaric leaders.[11]

The original announcement of the surrender demand had jolted not only Japan but many knowledgeable American policy-makers. Japanese propaganda had moved quickly to rally support for the war by predicting Japan's complete and absolute destruction under "unconditional surrender." Numerous officials in Washington understood the difficulties the formula presented, and several actively began to search for ways to modify and soften its impact.

A report by the Joint Intelligence Committee, for instance, observed in March 1944—sixteen months before Hiroshima—that the

> course of conduct of Japanese armed forces deployed in the areas under consideration, to a large extent, will depend upon the Japanese political situation as of the time that our peace terms are enforced. The crux of the political situation will lie in the all-important status of the Japanese Emperor.[12]

The JIC stressed that without the Emperor's support it would be difficult to bring about a meaningful surrender; it predicted that if peace terms were not backed up by "Imperial Sanction," "many major units of the Japanese armed forces deployed outside of Japan proper would continue to offer resistance in varying degrees. Probably only those units which are completely dependent upon the homeland for supplies or completely dominated by the regime in power would surrender. . . ."[13]

General MacArthur's Southwest Pacific Command prepared a "restricted" background study in the summer of 1944 which emphasized:

In spite of heavy inroads on their shipping and major military reverses in the Central and Southwest Pacific, today [1 July 1944] the Emperor, the military gangsters, the armed forces, and the entire population are united as one, determined to fight until final victory or death. . . . They know their war has a divine mission because it has Imperial Sanction. This is sufficient to give Tojo absolute control, to lead the soldier to fanatical battlefield performance, the people to extreme fortitude, all to self-destruction if necessary.[14]

The study argued that, although there should be no weakening of the peace terms,

to dethrone, or hang, the Emperor would cause a tremendous and violent reaction from all Japanese. Hanging of the Emperor to them would be comparable to the crucifixion of Christ to us. All would fight to die like ants. The position of the gangster militarists would be strengthened immeasurably. The war would be unduly prolonged; our losses heavier than otherwise would be necessary.[15]

Specialists at the Office of War Information (OWI) had also long recognized the significance of the Emperor's position and had purposely avoided direct threats to his person. A representative OWI directive from late 1944, for instance, warned that

. . . we must refrain from attacking the Emperor as a person or as an institution except as in its spiritual aspects. To do so would be to provide Japan's propagandists with excellent material for unifying the people behind the militarists and for whipping up their fighting spirit.[16]

At Yalta, in February 1945, Churchill had also taken up this general theme, and in fact, even at this early date had proposed some modification of the surrender language. A four-power ultimatum might be issued, he proposed, "calling upon Japan to surrender unconditionally. . . ." In accepting it Japan might ask what "mitigation of the full rigour of unconditional surrender would be extended to her." He acknowledged that the decision would be up to the United States, but went on to urge that "some mitigation would be worth while if it led to the saving of a year or a year and a half of a war in which so much blood and treasure would be poured out."[17]

Although there was no sign that the president was willing to bend the Japanese surrender formula, that nothing was ever frozen in concrete in the Roosevelt era seemed obvious from the fact that FDR himself had easily sidestepped his own uncompromising rhetoric when a conditional "unconditional surrender" was negotiated with Italy in the fall of 1943, only eight months after the Casablanca statement.

Within parts of the Office of War Information and sections of the State Department, some officials argued that bending the surrender formula was the equivalent of "appeasement." In particular, two assistant secretaries of state not directly involved with the Far East raised objections in internal State Department discussions later in the summer. How the most important officials judged the matter, however, began to be tested almost immediately after Roosevelt's death on April 12, 1945.

Truman's succession to the Presidency came at an extraordinary time: The U.S. landing on Okinawa (April 1), the replacement of the Koiso government (on April 5), the announcement that the Soviet Union would not renew its Neutrality Pact with Japan (also on April 5), and Hitler's suicide (April 30) produced a radically new situation.

Predictably, Truman's initial moves emphasized continuity with his predecessor's policy. Immediately upon taking office, he reasserted the traditional formula, declaring in a speech before Congress on April 16: "Our demand has been and it remains—unconditional surrender. We will not traffic with the breakers of the peace on the terms of peace."[18]

This statement—which was met with enthusiasm, and by some accounts with a standing ovation[19]—has often subsequently been cited as a clear indication of Truman's personal position, and of the overwhelming political support for a continuation of the traditional formula which existed at the time. The evidence now available, however, makes it difficult to sustain such a view and readily puts this first speech in understandable historical perspective.

We know, of course, that in the end, Truman did not hesitate to modify the "unconditional surrender" policy after the atomic bomb was used. In fact, the president began to shift his personal stand within three weeks after his initial declaration. In a tightly worded statement released at the time of Germany's surrender on May 8, the president gave a much more carefully focused meaning to "unconditional surrender":

Our blows will not cease until the Japanese military and naval forces lay down their arms in *unconditional surrender*.

Just what does the unconditional surrender of the armed forces mean for the Japanese people?

It means the end of the war.

It means the termination of the influence of the military leaders who have brought Japan to the present brink of disaster. . . .

Unconditional surrender does not mean the extermination or enslavement of the Japanese people.[20]

Scholars have paid relatively little attention to this early indication of new presidential policy: a call for "unconditional surrender" *of the military*, of

course, was in no way unusual in the history of warfare; and the new, carefully drawn public distinction was absolutely critical.

Statements of high policy, especially at the presidential level, do not
simply happen. Modern records confirm that the May 8 demand for "unconditional surrender" of the Japanese military had its origins in an initiative of
the Office of War Information and the office of Secretary of the Navy
Forrestal.[21] A key actor was Navy Captain Ellis Zacharias, a specialist who
had been working on psychological-warfare ideas in cooperation with the
Overseas Branch of OWI, which was responsible for propaganda policy for
the Far East.

Zacharias had been brought to Washington by Forrestal to prepare a fully
developed proposal. His work—"A Strategic Plan to Effect the Occupation
of Japan," together with a tactical plan for the psychological campaign, "Operation Plan 1-45"—was delivered on March 19, 1945.[22] It received Forrestal's quick approval—and that of the commander in chief of the U.S. Fleet,
Admiral Ernest King, and of Elmer Davis, director of OWI. A presidential
statement explaining the meaning of "unconditional surrender" was prepared,
and the statement was headed for Roosevelt's approval when he died on
April 12.[23]

During the three weeks between Roosevelt's death and the eve of the German surrender, the statement was apparently temporarily lost.[24] Eventually it
was designated an OWI initiative by Davis and forwarded to the State Department and the Joint Chiefs of Staff for comment and recommendations.
On May 6, Admiral Leahy expressed his approval of the proposed statement
to Truman:

> I have discussed with the Acting Secretary of State and with the Joint
> Chiefs of Staff the proposal made by Mr. Elmer Davis that you issue a
> statement that can be used by the Office of War Information as a key
> document in a new undertaking of psychological warfare against Japan.
> Both Under Secretary Grew and the Joint Chiefs of Staff prefer the
> modified statement at a suitable time to be issued as a press release.

Although the Joint Chiefs of Staff wished to delay release of the statement
until the end of the battle for Okinawa, Leahy's own position was different:

> In view of the slowness with which our operations in Okinawa are pro-
> ceeding, it is my opinion, and I recommend, that the "modified state-
> ment" proposed by Mr. Elmer Davis should be issued as a press release
> at an early date subsequent to the announcement of the surrender of the
> German armies.[25]

The statement was, in fact, finally released as a press statement just after
Truman gave his V-E Day address of May 8.

Immediately—the same day and only a few hours after Truman's announcement—Captain Zacharias, designated "official U.S. spokesman," began a series of Japanese-language broadcasts urging surrender.[26] Based on Truman's statement, the Zacharias broadcasts reassured the Japanese that "unconditional surrender" did not mean "the extermination or enslavement of the Japanese people," and stressed that unconditional surrender of the Japanese military was at the heart of the U.S. demand.[27]

The effort in the early Truman Administration to begin to modify the rigid demand for "unconditional surrender" did not go unnoticed in the press. Indeed, some influential representatives of the national media urged much faster action. An editorial in the *Washington Post* on the day after the president's statement, for instance, advocated scrapping the surrender formula entirely:

> Japan should be told her fate immediately so that she can be encouraged to throw up the sponge. Up till now all she knows is what she hears from [the] fire-eaters. . . . The extermination ideas of men like these . . . have doubtless been spread through Japan by the Japanese themselves in order to ginger up a last-ditch fight. Better to die fighting than surrender to be destroyed!
>
> What we are suggesting, to be sure, is conditional surrender. What of it? Unconditional surrender was never an ideal formula. . . .
>
> We urge, therefore, that the task of compiling the terms for Japan and informing the Japanese of them should not be delayed.[28]

The British Foreign Office had long since concluded that a modification of the surrender formula was essential, and that the rigid demand for unconditional surrender would prolong the war. Fearing that the United States might make Britain the "scapegoat" for a modification, however, no one in London wanted to push forcefully for the change. Nonetheless, British diplomats were watching American public opinion closely for signs of shifting political mood. In his May 13 weekly report to London, British Ambassador Lord Halifax cited the *Post* editorial as an early indication of support—"not merely in the ex-isolationist press"—for some modification of unconditional surrender. He also pointed to "optimistic speculation of likelihood of her early surrender when she perceives the hopelessness of her case."[29]

The *Post* editorial found its way into the files of the War Department's Operations Division (OPD), where a shift in policy was also moving forward: Lieutenant Colonel Hugh Sawyer, Executive Officer of the Strategy and Policy Group, scrawled a handwritten note across the top of the clipping: "Someone has been reading our mail."[30]

Sawyer's comment was an understatement. Several of the intelligence reports had already begun to challenge the formula. Since the language was

Roosevelt's, officials understandably avoided a head-on assault on the word "unconditional." Instead, various groups focused on how to clarify the actual conditions demanded without (at least for the moment) seeming to alter the general tone.

On April 18—two days after Truman's initial statement but three weeks before his May 8 change—the previously cited Joint Intelligence Committee study judged that "clarification of Allied intentions with regard to the Japanese nation might bring nearer the possibility of unconditional surrender." Even at this early date it observed that "some constitutional Japanese central government, backed by the Emperor, may seek and accept a rationalized version of 'unconditional surrender' before the end of 1945." Beyond this, the report concluded:

> [W]e believe that the Japanese Government will endeavor to find some formula for ending the war, without having the stigma of absolute "unconditional" surrender attached to it. If such a formula can be found which would be acceptable to the Allies, we believe that Japan might surrender without the invasion of Japan proper.[31]

In an April 25 review of Pacific strategy, the Joint Staff Planners had gone even further in their critique of the existing language:

> It is by no means certain . . . that "unconditional surrender" can be brought about by any means. . . .
> In no case to date in this war have organized Japanese units surrendered. The concept of "unconditional surrender" is foreign to the Japanese nature.

The report's recommendation was forceful:

> Therefore, "unconditional surrender" should be defined in terms understandable to the Japanese, who must be convinced that destruction or national suicide is not implied. This could be done by the announcement on a government level of a "declaration of intentions" which would tell the Japanese what the future holds. . . .
> Unless a definition of unconditional surrender can be given which is acceptable to the Japanese, there is no alternative to annihilation and no prospect that the threat of absolute defeat will bring about capitulation.[32]

A significant point which has often been confused in subsequent studies of World War II was also highlighted in this Joint Staff Planners report. Despite these recommendations, the Planners' conclusion was that "the invasion of Japan is considered the most suitable strategy to accomplish unconditional surrender or ultimate defeat."[33] Whatever the feelings of lower-level officials, of necessity all military policy had to assume the continuation of the officially stated presidential policy of "unconditional surrender."

Put another way, until and unless the president changed the policy, the military had to assume the worst. Hence the judgment—in fact, the obvious reality—that to obtain "unconditional surrender" would require an invasion. In particular, as long as the "unconditional surrender" formula seemed to threaten the Emperor as man and as institution, military planners had no choice but to base their plans on a fight to the finish.

The Joint Chiefs of Staff, in fact, noted the Planners' report and made it the basis for future planning on May 10. However, they also followed up on the Planners' recommendation that a careful study of the surrender terms be made; and they began a major push to develop a proposal to clarify the "unconditional" language. A draft of a proposed demand for immediate surrender (JCS 1340) was simultaneously sent to the Planners and the Joint Intelligence Committee for comment and recommendations.[34] While differences of opinion arose as to timing, by May 12 there was general agreement that "unconditional surrender" should refer explicitly to the armed forces of Japan and that explicit reference should now also be made to the authority of the existing Imperial Institutions.[35]

That changing the surrender terms slightly might speed an end to the war was also strongly suggested in several of the "peace feelers" which flowed into Washington—especially after Germany's May 8 collapse. For instance, the previously cited May 12, 1945, memorandum from Donovan to Truman detailing an approach by the Japanese minister to Switzerland, noted that Kase reportedly

> believes that one of the few provisions the Japanese would insist upon would be the retention of the Emperor as the only safeguard against Japan's conversion to Communism. Kase feels that Under Secretary of State Grew, whom he considers the best US authority on Japan, shares this opinion.[36]

A number of leading Republicans also began to urge a clarification of terms. Former president Herbert Hoover met with Truman on May 28, and they discussed how to end the war. We do not have precise information on Truman's expressed views, but at his request Hoover prepared a memo urging a clarification of terms and the president subsequently circulated this memo among his advisers. In it, Hoover listed the following factors which favored an early surrender:

> (a) The appointment of Suzuki, a one-time anti-militarist elder-statesman, as Prime Minister;
>
> (b) The desire of the Japanese to preserve the Mikado who is the spiritual head of the nation;

(c) The sense they showed after the Russo-Japanese war of making peace before Russia organized her full might;

(d) The fear of complete destruction which by now they must know is their fate;

(e) The fact that there is a large middle class in Japan which was the product of industrialization, who are liberal-minded, who have in certain periods governed Japan and in these periods they gave full cooperation in peaceful forces of the world. That this group again exert itself is the only hope of stable and progressive government.

An essential point in Hoover's recommendation was that the United States clarify that

the Allies have no desire to destroy either the Japanese people or their government, or to interference [*sic*] in the Japanese way of life. . . .[37]

On June 9, Truman passed Hoover's memorandum to Grew and Stimson for comment. Stimson in turn referred it to staff for review. A week later, on June 14, a staff assessment of Hoover's paper came back. It observed:

The proposal of a public declaration of war aims, in effect giving definition to "unconditional surrender," has definite merit if it is carefully handled.[38]

The staff report was given to Stimson with a cover note from General Marshall stating:

There is attached a memorandum by the Staff, with which I am in substantial agreement, containing analysis of and comment on the paper on "ending the Japanese war," which you gave to General Handy.[39]

After his meeting with Truman, Hoover dined with several leading Republican senators, including Robert Taft and Harlan Bushfield, and (according to the diary of William Castle) then perhaps eight others were present for a discussion—among them, Senators Wiley, Shipstead, Moore, Hickenlooper, and H. Alexander Smith. The Republican senators had sought a meeting with Hoover to hear his thinking on the war and related issues in Asia. In a free and open discussion Hoover presented what he saw as some of the main elements of an appropriate strategy for the Far East. Above all, the war had to be ended. There was at least a possibility a surrender could be arranged if the United States and Britain stated specific terms. Among the most important were that Manchuria had to be restored to China; and Japan, of course, would have to withdraw from all invaded countries. (She might, however, be allowed to hold on to Formosa and Korea.) A key point was that Japan must be informed that the United States would not interfere with the Emperor or try to shape the form of its government in a manner which did not accord with the desires of the Japanese people.[40]

As we shall see, these May discussions were hardly the only indications that Republican political leaders not only would not oppose modifying the "unconditional surrender" formula, but would welcome—indeed, were beginning to push for—a clarification of terms. As Japan's deterioration continued, moreover, they also became increasingly confident of the likely success of such an effort.*

What can be ascertained of the attitude of the president himself? That Truman's own views, so far as we can tell, continued to be in the direction he had begun to establish in his May 8 statement can be documented in connection with a major push which was made to modify the formula within the government at this time.

The suggestion that the president should follow up his May 8 statement with another, further clarification was not simply the idea of the *Washington Post*, the Joint Chiefs of Staff, and leading Republicans like Herbert Hoover. It was pressed with particular vigor at the highest level by the acting secretary of state and former ambassador to Japan, Joseph C. Grew.

With Secretary of State Edward Stettinius frequently away from Washington in connection with the founding of the United Nations, Grew was the day-to-day manager of the State Department for much of the critical period from December 1944 to July 1945. Now, on May 28—shortly after Truman met with Hoover on the same day—Grew stressed to the president that

> . . . the Japanese are a fanatical people and are capable of fighting to the last ditch and the last man. If they do this, the cost in American lives will be unpredictable.
>
> The greatest obstacle to unconditional surrender by the Japanese is their belief that this would entail the destruction or permanent removal of the Emperor and the institution of the Throne. If some indication can now be given the Japanese that they themselves . . . will be permitted to determine their own future political structure, they will be afforded a method of saving face without which surrender will be highly unlikely.

"It is believed," Grew stressed, "that such a statement would have maximum effect if issued immediately following the great devastation of Tokyo which occurred two days ago." Another round of post-bombing fires, fed by high winds, had just leveled massive additional areas of the Japanese capital.

*See below, pp. 228–29.

"The psychological impact of such a statement at this particular moment would be very great."[41]

The response Grew recorded, in the formal memorandum he prepared after this meeting, gives us the following indication of the president's personal attitude at this time:

> The President said that he was interested in what I said because his own thoughts had been following the same line.[42]

Chapter 4

TO JUNE 18, 1945

It was an awkward meeting because there were people present in the presence of whom I could not discuss the real feature which would govern the whole situation, namely S-1.

—Secretary of War Henry L. Stimson, diary,
May 29, 1945

Grew was a cautious man. Earlier in the war the former ambassador to Japan had drawn criticism for a speech which seemed to indicate "softness" toward the enemy. As late as May 3, 1945, Grew had objected to a statement addressed directly to the Japanese people because a "derisive response" might impair U.S. prestige in Asia.[1] More than one observer has been puzzled by Grew's sudden late May effort to modify the surrender terms.

Two scholars, Makoto Iokibe and Nakamura Masanori, have pointed to a passage in Stimson's diary of May 8 as a possible clue to Grew's behavior. The Committee of Three—Stimson, Forrestal, and Grew—had met at 11:00 a.m., and Stimson recorded:

> After the normal business was over . . . I shooed out everybody except Forrestal and Grew and told them of the Interim Committee for S-1 that I am forming and what its purposes were . . . and we had a little short discussion about the function of the Committee.[2]

Iokibe suggests that "one cannot persuasively explain Grew's behavior unless 'S-1,' i.e., the atomic bomb, is taken into account." In the first instance, he notes, Grew's ten years in Japan had given him a real fondness and feeling for the people. Ending the war by modifying the surrender formula rather than using the atomic bomb not only would be humane, it would avoid alienating Japan as the struggle for influence in postwar Asia began. Moreover, Iokibe points out, if the liberals close to the Emperor, "to whom Grew would willingly entrust Japan's surrender and reconstruction, were killed in the bombings, what would happen?"[3] Masanori suggests that "Grew felt there was not a moment to lose, and he spent the last weeks of May and the first half of June attempting to secure a rapid end to the war."[4]

Within a few days of discussing the new weapon with Grew, Stimson described the atomic bomb as a "master card" to be played in connection with a whole complex and "tangled wave" of Asian problems. These included—but went far beyond—the surrender itself. It is quite possible that some intimation of his strategic thinking may also have been given to Grew on May 8 and may have helped stir him into action.

Whatever the source of Grew's newfound energy, there is no doubt about the next steps in the story. At the close of his May 28 review of the surrender formula with Truman, Grew recorded that the president·

> asked me to arrange for a meeting to discuss this question in the first instance with the Secretaries of War and Navy, General Marshall and Admiral King and that after we had exchanged views he would like to have the same group come to the White House for a conference with him.[5]

We are now about to enter murky waters. As noted, there are gaps in the record concerning how a number of key decisions were arrived at during the summer of 1945. What the president requested was essentially an informal meeting of the Committee of Three—i.e., the top Cabinet officers concerned. However, as Milton Gustafson of the National Archives has pointed out, even as late as 1977

> . . . no one [had] seen the minutes of all of the meetings. Most of the minutes were originally classified as Top Secret. . . . Most of the minutes were not declassified until 1974, and portions of the minutes of two meetings [not related to Japan] are still classified today. . . . Today there is no complete set anyplace.[6]

Even the minutes of this high-level group's discussion that are available are cursory in style, and often yield only the most general insight into what actually happened.

Although we often know a final decision "outcome" with certainty, the available evidence contains numerous puzzles about why specific things were done at specific points in time. In connection with the next phase of policy toward "unconditional surrender," these include the following:

First: Why was the then-developing course of policy abandoned by the president?

Second: Who was the central presidential adviser on this matter?

Third: Why was the emerging policy thrust not only abandoned but publicly reversed?

Since on all three of these questions there has been considerable controversy and confusion in the historical literature, it is necessary to proceed slowly and carefully, day by day, especially in regard to events which occurred in the middle of the Memorial Day period (May 29–June 1, 1945).

At one level of understanding there is no mystery and no disagreement. A meeting of the top-level group did in fact take place in Stimson's office at the Pentagon the next day, May 29. According to Grew's records, those present were:

Mr. Stimson, Secretary of War;
Mr. Forrestal, Secretary of the Navy;
General Marshall, Chief of Staff;
Mr. Elmer Davis, Director of OWI;
Judge Samuel Rosenman, Counsel to the President;
Mr. Eugene H. Dooman, Department of State;
Joseph C. Grew, Acting Secretary of State.[7]

Various accounts of this meeting have come to light over the years. One of the first—reprinted seven years after World War II in Grew's 1952 memoirs—runs as follows:

The purpose of the meeting . . . was to discuss whether the President, in his forthcoming speech about our war with Japan, should indicate we have no intention of determining Japan's future political structure . . . in the thought that such a statement . . . might render it easier for the Japanese to surrender unconditionally instead of fighting fanatically for their Emperor. The meeting lasted for an hour and in the course of the discussion it became clear that Mr. Stimson, Mr. Forrestal, and General Marshall were all in accord with the principle but for certain military reasons, not divulged, it was considered inadvisable for the president to make such a statement just now. The question of timing was the nub of the whole matter. . . .[8]

Forrestal's published diary account (1951) includes the following, slightly more explicit information:

I asked whether it would not suffice to say that our view of unconditional surrender meant that it was the unconditional surrender of the Japanese military power, that we did not propose to destroy Japan as a nation. Mr. Dooman [Eugene H. Dooman, then a special assistant in the

State Department, who had been counselor in the Tokyo Embassy under
Grew before the war and had an intimate knowledge of Japan] said this
would not cover, that he believed that if the Japanese became imbued
with the idea that the United States was set on the destruction of their
philosophy of government and of their religion we would be faced with
a truly national suicidal defense. He said assurances on our lack of desire to destroy them physically and industrially would not suffice.[9]

Forrestal, too, noted:

> It was agreed that the time was not appropriate for [the president] to
> make such a pronouncement.[10]

Similarly, in a speech delivered in 1960, Eugene Dooman recalled:

> A meeting was held [on May 29, 1945] in Mr. Stimson's office in the
> Pentagon which was attended by Forrestal, McCloy, along with all the
> highest officials, both civil and military, of the armed forces. Grew and
> I were there representing the State Department. The [proposed] paper
> was approved for publication by each of those present, but General Mar-
> shall who was the last to speak said that the publication of this paper at
> this time would be premature.[11]

Finally, Stimson's diary (opened in 1959) records:

> . . . I had in Joe Grew the Acting Secretary of State, Jim Forrestal of
> the Navy, Marshall the Chief of Staff, and some assistants of each one
> of them. This meeting was called by Grew on the suggestion of the
> president and its purpose was to decide upon an announcement to the
> Japanese which would serve as a warning for them to surrender or else
> something worse would happen to them.

Stimson's diary also raises the point of principal significance:

> [Grew] read [the draft] and then called for our comment. I told him that
> I was inclined to agree with giving the Japanese a modification of the
> unconditional surrender formula without the use of those words.

However,

> I told him that I thought the timing was wrong and that this was not the
> time to do it. After a discussion around the table I was backed up by
> Marshall and then by everybody else.

In the Stimson diary there is explicit evidence of what Grew called "certain military reasons, not divulged"—and as to why it was considered pre-

mature for the president to make such a statement, why "the timing was wrong":

> It was an awkward meeting because there were people present in the presence of whom I could not discuss the real feature which would govern the whole situation, namely S-1.

Once everyone had left, however, Stimson records:

> After that meeting was over Marshall and McCloy and I stayed and discussed the situation of Japan and what we should do in regard to S-1 and the application of it.[12]

In his own diary (opened in the late 1980s) McCloy also notes that in this discussion:

> The Secretary of War referred to the earlier meeting with the Acting Secretary of State and Mr. Forrestal on the matter of the President's speech and the reference to Japan. He felt the decision to postpone action now was a sound one. This only postponed consideration of the matter for a time, however, for we should have to consider it again preparatory to the employment of S-1.[13]

Most scholars now accept that the Stimson-McCloy account probably explains why a statement clarifying the surrender terms was put off at this point in time: it had something to do with the atomic bomb.* However, there are two small gaps in the evidentiary trail. First, we do not really know what Stimson (and Marshall) were thinking about in proposing to delay the statement. Did they wish to clarify the Emperor's position (as Stimson seems to imply) and then be ready to use the bomb if this failed to bring an end to the war? Did they wish to issue a statement only a brief time before the bomb was ready? Did they have other ideas?

Second, it is one thing to know that this high-level group reached this conclusion at this time (probably) for a reason related to the atomic bomb—but it is quite another to argue that a decision to put off a clarifying statement was shortly made by President Truman because of the advice of this group.

To be sure, there is a reasonable presumption that having asked Grew to arrange the high-level meeting, Truman was interested in and may have followed its recommendations. Yet doubts remain. The fact is the president did not simply delay further clarification of the meaning of unconditional surrender in the speech he made just after Memorial Day; he substantially reversed the thrust of the approach he had initiated in his May 8 statement specifying

---

*See below, pp. 55–57, for other considerations put forward at other levels.

surrender in more carefully defined military terms. The Japanese military
leaders, he now suggested on June 1:

> hope that our desire to see our soldiers and sailors home again and the
> temptation to return to the comforts and profits of peace will force us
> to settle for some compromise short of unconditional surrender.
>   They should know better. . . .
>   We are resolute in our determination—we will see the fight through
> to a complete and victorious finish.[14]

The tone of this speech was not merely forceful, it appeared designed
explicitly to be uncompromising. A June 3 *Washington Post* editorial
commented:

> The winning powers should tell the Japanese in simple and positive
> terms what they must do to stop the slaughter of their people and the de-
> struction of their homeland.

On June 6 the *Post* stated:

> Every Japanese in authority must have read the President's account of
> our war preparations with a sinking feeling about the future of Japan.
> The lesson must be rubbed in. But it cannot lead to surrender unless we
> spell out our war aims against Japan. . . .[15]

Little scholarly attention has been paid to this modification in presidential
position—even though the administration subsequently referred inquiries to
this speech (along with the May statement) as the definitive U.S. position.
  Although the main substantive point of the speech was a report on the
progress of the war—and thus was almost certainly drafted with the help of
the Pentagon—the new language on surrender was also a surprise to War Department officials. On June 7, for instance, General George A. Lincoln sent
an angry memorandum to the Policy Section of the Operations Division
which he headed:

> Let's get this unconditional surrender paper of G-2's [Military Intelli-
> gence Division's] straight. [Admiral] Duncan thinks that it is dead as
> door nail because the president has already published [a statement on]
> it. I haven't seen anything on it. If it has been published why didn't
> somebody bring it in to me?[16]

It may be useful to note another important intersection of events and dates:
The meetings during Memorial Day week on unconditional surrender and the
new presidential statement occurred during precisely the period (May 28–
June 1) that the Interim Committee—set up to make recommendations cov-

ering a variety of atomic issues—formally completed its most important recommendations.

Another note of caution: In connection with the May 29 meeting in Stimson's office, we have just seen that the secretary of war was evasive in discussing his real motives even with other government officials. We shall shortly review several well-documented instances in which the president himself also invented misleading, even dishonest cover stories in connection with his own strategic thinking on the relationship of the atomic bomb to diplomacy.

Many of the documents currently available provide what appears to be "evidence" for why certain decisions were made. But given what we know about the atmosphere of secrecy, precisely what is and is not a true representation of motives is not certain in many instances. The documentary trail is complex; and confusion awaits unwary lay persons and expert scholars alike.

Especially what the president himself was thinking—step by step—when he made key decisions is even less clear during this period and must be deciphered (whenever possible) with full recognition of the limits of the available evidence and of the prevarications and evasions we know to have been common in the pervasive atmosphere of secrecy surrounding the atomic bomb.

It is possible, however, to piece together fairly solid information on the views of some of the important figures at this precise moment. Further aspects of Marshall's personal opinion, for instance, are revealed by other reports of the second, follow-up discussion which took place after the first May 29 meeting was over. A memorandum by McCloy states:

> General Marshall said he thought these weapons might first be used against straight military objectives such as a large naval installation and then if no complete result was derived from the effect of that, he thought we ought to designate a number of large manufacturing areas from which the people would be warned to leave—telling the Japanese that we intend to destroy such centers. . . . Every effort should be made to keep our record of warning clear. We must offset by such warning methods the opprobrium which might follow from an ill-considered employment of such force.[17]

From this memorandum it appears that one of Marshall's reasons for wishing to delay a statement was related to the idea that the bomb would first be used against a military target. Thereafter a clear "warning" would be issued—including, specifically, a warning to Japanese citizens to leave any targeted cities or population centers. Only then would the bomb be used against an urban center. (As previously noted, reports of the first May 29 meeting and other evidence of his—and the Joint Chiefs of Staff's—thinking also suggest Marshall's support for a modification of the unconditional-surrender formula in any warning statement at this point.)

It is often suggested that a so-called "demonstration" of the atomic bomb was not seriously discussed at the highest levels (except once, informally over lunch, by the Interim Committee on May 31)—and, further, that a "demonstration" was impractical. In subsequent discussions the idea of a desert island explosion has often emerged (and been discounted). It may therefore be important to note that Marshall—one of the most respected military figures in modern history—apparently did not see insuperable obstacles to a carefully designed "demonstration"—against a military target.

Marshall strongly emphasized the importance of offsetting the "opprobrium" which might follow what he called "an ill-considered employment of such force." And, as he noted, if the "strictly military demonstration" did not achieve results, a city could be attacked thereafter in any event.

Also related to these matters is the fact that at this time too—on May 31 and June 1—the Interim Committee reached certain conclusions. The most important was the formal recommendation that the weapon should be used as soon as possible, rather than in the two-step fashion outlined by Marshall; that it should be used against an industrial target surrounded by workers' homes, rather than against a strictly military target; and that it should be used without specific warning. Stimson chaired the committee and its most prominent member was James F. Byrnes, representing the president.

Our primary concern at this point is with the matter of what the Japanese would be told about the fate of the Emperor and the meaning of "unconditional surrender." We do not have detailed information like the memorandum outlining Marshall's thinking which permits us to document the precise views of many top officials about the relationship of a warning statement to the new weapon at this moment. However, a great deal of evidence is available on the fundamental point: It is clear that whatever their tactical views, virtually every American leader was quite aware that modifying the terms was almost certainly the only way a surrender could ultimately be achieved.

Intercept reports, for instance, detailed a discussion between Soviet Foreign Minister Molotov and Ambassador Sato on May 29, the same day as the meeting in Stimson's office. Molotov asked Sato's view of how long the Pacific War would last, and Sato replied:

> Japan follows Russia's example in her desire to end hostilities as quickly as possible. The Pacific War, however, is a matter of life and death for Japan and, as a result of America's attitude, we have no choice but to continue the fight.[18]

Commenting on the intercept, U.S. intelligence experts singled out for special emphasis Sato's statement that "America's attitude" gave Japan "no choice but to continue the fight."[19]

Roosevelt's former aide Harry Hopkins, on a presidential mission to Moscow at this time, reported Stalin as saying, along similar lines, that "according to his information the Japanese would not accept unconditional surrender," and that "if we stick to unconditional surrender the Japs will not give up and we will have to destroy them as we did Germany."[20]

We have previously noted an OSS report to President Truman of a late May meeting with a Japanese representative in Portugal. This actually reached the Oval Office at precisely this time—on June 2, 1945—and stated that peace terms were unimportant as long as the term "unconditional surrender" was avoided.[21]

On June 22 the Joint Chiefs of Staff received an update concerning the previously noted peace feeler in Switzerland which also stated: "According to source, Fujimura insists that the Japanese, before surrendering, would require assurances that the Emperor would be retained."[22]

Just as modern scholarship has documented the complex and nuanced maneuvering in connection with efforts to alter the surrender formula at secondary levels of government during April and May, much has also been written about internal bureaucratic infighting in June.[23] Given that the "official" policy of the government had still not been relaxed—indeed, on June 1 had been formally stiffened by the president—understandably, many mid-level bureaucrats were cautious in their various approaches to the issue.

At the highest level, however, the picture was once again much more straightforward. Stimson and Marshall exchanged several memoranda on the subject of unconditional surrender. On May 30, Stimson wrote:

> As you know, I have been thinking about this matter for some time. . . .
> In place of the proposed statement of the overall objective, I am inclined to favor something as follows: "The complete defeat and permanent destruction of the war making power of Japan."[24]

On June 9, Marshall responded that "this seems acceptable from the strictly military viewpoint"—and went on to suggest

> that we take action to discourage public use of the term "unconditional surrender," which we all agree is difficult to define, and encourage instead more definitive public statements concerning our policy and war aims. We should cease talking about unconditional surrender of Japan and begin to define our true objective in terms of defeat and disarmament.[25]

At the same time Marshall also advised the Joint Chiefs that

> in drawing up terms of surrender, we should be careful not so to crys-
> tallize the phraseology "Unconditional Surrender" as to preclude the
> possibility of changing this terminology to something which might be
> psychologically more conducive to the earliest defeat of Japan.[26]

Another memorandum, responding to Stimson's "latest note . . . on the
subject of the use of the term 'unconditional surrender,' " finds Marshall urging that the definition should be

> along the lines of that already initiated by the President in his statement
> to the Japanese people on 8 May 1945. . . . [Y]ou no doubt recall that
> in it he said,—"our blows will not cease until the Japanese military and
> naval forces lay down their arms in *unconditional surrender*," and that
> he then went on to define what the unconditional surrender of the armed
> forces means to the Japanese.[27]

Similarly, on June 9 the Joint Chiefs approved and sent to the State-War-
Navy Coordinating Committee (to be presented to the secretary of state) the
final draft of JCS 1340, the proposal for an "Immediate Demand for the Unconditional Surrender of Japan," which had been prepared following its
earlier, May 9 decision. It began with this judgment:

> The full impact of the German debacle and the isolation of Japan's po-
> sition are presumed now to be recognized by informed Japanese, includ-
> ing the military elements, both in the homeland and in Asia. Uncertainty
> of Russia's future actions is the cause of considerable anxiety to the Jap-
> anese leaders.

It suggested, further, that "[w]ithin the next few months Japan may seek
a termination of hostilities on any terms provided that Allied occupation of
the home islands is not required and that Japan is allowed to retain Korea
and the Kuriles in the eventual settlement. Possibly the only terms insisted
upon would be assurance that the home islands would not be occupied."

Partly to pre-empt any such initiative by the Japanese, the document recommended that "a strong demand for the unconditional surrender [be made]
at the time the Okinawa operation has progressed sufficiently to insure its
success." (Okinawa was about to fall, and did so twelve days later, on
June 21.) It also emphasized, again, that "unconditional surrender" should be
defined as applying to the Japanese military, as Truman's May 8 statement
had indicated—and then went on to propose a new formulation which went
beyond this language to implicitly acknowledge the legitimacy of the imperial regime. A proposed draft of the surrender demand addressed "To the Imperial Japanese Government" stated:

Nothing will deflect us from our determination to prosecute the war except the unconditional capitulation of the Japanese military forces. . . .

In the interest of common humanity, we call upon you to proclaim now the unconditional surrender of all the Japanese armed forces under the authority of the Imperial Japanese Government and High Command.[28]

Another indication: Herbert Hoover had been in touch not only with Truman but also with Stimson (who had served as Hoover's secretary of state) and on May 16 had sent him a report outlining his views on the war.* Together with McCloy, the two men met during the Memorial Day week as well—on May 29. Three days later Stimson noted:

I also had a talk with General Handy [Deputy Chief of Staff of the U.S. Army] on the subject of unconditional surrender and handed him the paper which Mr. Hoover had sent me on the possibility of shortening the war and the losses if a fight to a finish could be avoided.

A June 4 OPD staff review concluded that it "would seem desirable to pursue further the thought contained in the memorandum . . . with a view to formulating the conditions incidental to Japanese complete defeat or specific terms of unconditional surrender. . . ."[29] Meanwhile, at the president's request the State Department had reviewed Hoover's May 30 memorandum. This analysis stated:

There is much with which we would agree in the brief discussion by Mr. Hoover of the factors favorable to the acceptance by the Japanese of the terms proposed by him. Every evidence, without exception, that we are able to obtain of the views of the Japanese with regard to the institution of the throne, indicates that the non-molestation of the person of the present emperor and the preservation of the institution of the throne comprise irreducible Japanese terms. . . . We are disposed to agree with the view that failure on our part to clarify our intentions in this regard, or the proclamation of our intention to try the emperor as a war criminal and to abolish the institution of the throne, will insure prolongation of the war and cost a large number of human lives.[30]

Once more the complexity of the situation needs to be underscored: Since official U.S. policy was still publicly and formally committed unyieldingly to "unconditional surrender," all military and other planning necessarily contin-

*This was distinct from the one given to Truman and especially emphasized concern about Soviet objectives in Asia. See Hoover to HLS, May 15, 1945, Stimson Papers, YUL.

ued to proceed on this basis. Moreover, as noted, the Joint Chiefs had begun to worry that the Japanese might take the initiative and independently offer an unsatisfactory form of conditional surrender which might be positively received by the U.S. public. Indeed, far from worrying that the public would criticize a modification of the surrender terms (as some writers were later to urge), the Joint Chiefs feared that a war-weary American citizenry might jump at a Japanese offer of a conditional surrender in the absence of a prior U.S. statement.

Grew also addressed these points in his response to the president:

> It is our intention, of course to further in every practical way any measures which the Joint Chiefs of Staff may consider necessary to maintain the morale of the American people. It is our view, however, that a mere call on the Japanese to surrender, in whatever terms it might be couched but without clarification of "unconditional surrender," is not likely to bring any affirmative response.

Along with his comments, Grew enclosed a draft proclamation which presented some points "designed to allay certain fears of the Japanese and to meet their basic position, that the United Nations shall not molest the person of the emperor or disestablish the institution of the throne."[31]

On June 12 the Committee of Three—the secretaries of war, navy, and state (acting)—also discussed "unconditional surrender." Again the formal minutes record:

> Mr. Forrestal said he thought the note we should take was one of avoiding a frozen position which might result in our not being able to take advantage of results in Japan; that the question of issuing warnings to Japan of what the continuation of the war would mean was a matter of coordination and timing. He felt that real thought should be given to the matter so that we did not find ourselves in the position where we might be encouraging the militant group in Japan to build up strength for themselves amongst the populace. He had in mind the somewhat mystical relationship of the people to the Emperor and the general religious background of some of the Japanese nationalism.
>
> The Secretary of War said this matter was occupying his mind; that he had talked with General Marshall about the subject. Thereupon, some discussion ensued as to the wisdom of the continuation of the phrase "unconditional surrender." He said he felt that if we could accomplish all of our strategic objectives without the use of this phrase, we should have no hesitation in abandoning it. . . .[32]

On June 15 Stettinius (in San Francisco at the United Nations founding meetings) telegraphed his views:

If the Joint Chiefs feel that a demand for unconditional surrender is in any case advisable on the occasion of the termination of the Okinawa operation, I suggest that it be made unilaterally by the President in such a way so as not to prejudice any action which the Big Three may desire to take.[33]*

By June 18 events had progressed to the point where Admiral Leahy was able to note privately in his personal diary:

It is my opinion that at the present time a surrender of Japan can be arranged with terms that can be accepted by Japan and that will make fully satisfactory provision for America's defense against any future trans-Pacific aggression.[34]

(Subsequently, when Leahy discussed this entry in his 1951 memoirs, he wrote: "Naturally, I had acquainted President Truman with my own ideas about the best course to pursue in defeating Japan as fully as I had done with President Roosevelt."[35])

At this juncture, Grew decided to make another move. In a letter to the president's special counsel, Judge Samuel I. Rosenman, following up on the Joint Chiefs' recommendation, Grew proposed that a statement calling upon Japan to surrender be timed to coincide with the collapse of Okinawa (now only five days off):

I am not convinced that there is any good reason to defer such action until the meeting of the Big Three [scheduled for later in July at Potsdam], and in my opinion the sooner we can get the Japanese thinking about surrender the better it will be and the more lives of Americans may ultimately be saved.

Grew was clearly beginning to have strong feelings on the issue:

. . . I think it will be a matter of plain common sense to give the Japanese a clearer idea of what we mean by unconditional surrender. The President has already stated that this does not mean extermination or enslavement, but there are two further points which would make it vastly easier—if they could be specifically announced—for a peace movement to get started in Japan, and I have no doubt that there are elements in Japan today who clearly realize that they have everything to lose and nothing to gain by continuing the war.

---

*Stettinius also urged: "You might also consider whether it would be useful to couple such a demand with some assurances to the Japanese regarding their future." (FRUS, Pots. I, p. 173.) See below, p.378, for Stettinius' views concerning the importance of Russia joining in such a declaration.

In addition to assurances that "we have no intention . . . to deprive the Japanese of a reasonable peacetime economy," what was essential was a clarification

> . . . that once we have rendered the Japanese incapable of again building up a military machine and once they have convinced us of their intention to fulfill their international obligations . . . the Japanese will then be permitted to determine for themselves the nature of their future political structure.[36]

Grew's initiative illuminates another aspect of the timing issue—and another gap in the record: clearly sometime during the two and a half weeks between Grew's May 28 meeting with Truman and this June 16 initiative, the idea that the statement might now be put off until the mid-July Big Three meeting had surfaced at the presidential level. Again, we do not know precisely who advised the president to do this, or precisely why. Moreover, as is evident—and as we shall shortly explore in detail—the thinking of virtually all of the other advisers seems clearly to have been moving in the direction of a statement timed to coincide with the fall of Okinawa.

This new postponement was a matter of considerable concern: Grew pointed out not only that a clarifying statement was needed, but that continued delay would present major difficulties. He urged an early statement and for a particular reason—so that "we can get the Japanese thinking about surrender" sooner rather than later. Grew and other officials knew that it would take time for Japanese leaders to digest the implications of any U.S. move. An early statement was needed "for a peace movement to get started. . . ."

Grew arranged to see Truman the morning of June 18. He told the president:

> I wanted to see every appropriate step taken which might encourage a peace movement in Japan and while it was all guesswork as to whether such a statement would have that effect I nevertheless felt very strongly that something might be gained and nothing could be lost by such a step and in my opinion the sooner it was taken the better.

Truman, however, had made a definite if somewhat puzzling decision:

> The President said that he had carefully considered yesterday the draft statement which I had given to Judge Rosenman calling on Japan for unconditional surrender to be considered for release at the moment of the announcement of the fall of Okinawa but that while he liked the idea he had decided to hold this up until it could be discussed at the Big Three meeting.

Grew continues that he pressed the president further, that he

> wished to square my own conscience at having omitted no recommendation which might conceivably result in the savings of lives of thousands of our fighting men so long as we did not recede an inch from our objectives in rendering Japan powerless to threaten peace in the future.

Finally, a discouraged Grew concludes:

> The President having ruled against the step at this time, there was of course nothing more to be done but I felt that this question should be kept prominently in mind. The President asked me to have the subject entered on the agenda for the Big Three meeting. . . .[37]

Chapter 5

JUNE 18, 1945

. . . so I said, "Well, I do think you've got an alternative; and I think it's an alternative that ought to be explored and that, really, we ought to have our heads examined if we don't explore some other method by which we can terminate this war than just by another conventional attack and landing." . . .

And the President said, "Well, that's what I've been thinking about. I wonder if you could put that down and give it to the Secretary of State and see what we can do from that."

—Former Assistant Secretary of War John J. McCloy,
recalling his advice to President Harry S Truman,
and the president's reaction, June 18, 1945

Although some things are quite clear, we do not know precisely what President Truman had in mind in making his decision to delay clarifying the surrender terms. Why did he choose to wait until the Big Three meeting rather than act on the dramatic occasion of the fall of Okinawa—as Grew, Stettinius, and, most significantly, the Joint Chiefs of Staff recommended?

Truman's after-the-fact statement of his reasoning runs as follows (as presented in his 1955 memoirs):

> It was my decision then that the proclamation to Japan should be issued from the forthcoming conference at Potsdam. This, I believed, would clearly demonstrate to Japan and to the world that the Allies were united in their purpose. By that time, also, we might know more about two matters of significance for our future effort: the participation of the Soviet Union and the atomic bomb.[1]

There is no reason to doubt this statement. However, it also seems clear that it is not the whole story. Aside from the fact that the president's explanation sidesteps the specific question of whether the proclamation would, in fact, modify the surrender formula, it does not explain specifically why the thinking of the president's top military advisers—who also knew of the bomb and the likelihood of Russian help—was rejected.

In this connection, too, it appears especially unlikely that a decision of this magnitude by a new and inexperienced president would have been made without consulting high-placed advisers. Moreover, it is plain that in addition to Stettinius and Grew, both Stimson and Marshall almost certainly can also be eliminated as advisers counseling the president on this matter.

Contemporaneous documents concerning Truman's attitude at this time are scarce. We have far fewer hard facts illuminating his calculations than we have concerning the thinking of Marshall, Stimson, and Grew. Several fragments of information are nonetheless quite suggestive, not only of the president's ambivalence and seeming uncertainty as to how to handle the central question but also of other advice he seems to have been getting (and listening to) at this time.

Things came into relatively sharp (if temporary) focus a few hours after the president's meeting with Grew when Truman held a major White House review of military planning with the Joint Chiefs of Staff. In preparation for this meeting on the afternoon of June 18, Truman had instructed Leahy to inform the military leaders:

> It is [the President's] intention to make his decisions on the campaign with the purpose of economizing to the maximum extent possible in the loss of American lives.
>
> Economy in the use of time and in money cost is comparatively unimportant.[2]

This seemingly obvious point actually represented a considerable—and revealing—change. Although the terrible costs of Okinawa were on everyone's mind at this time, the minimization of casualties was not, in fact, the basic criterion governing the war. To the contrary: On May 25 the Joint Chiefs had already formally approved an overall plan for the Pacific War and had ordered the next stage of military operations against Japan. Moreover, a directive for a landing on Kyushu had already been issued to MacArthur, Nimitz, and Arnold which for planning purposes set the landing's target date at November 1, 1945.

The surprise of top military planners on learning of Truman's new emphasis is revealed in a June 14 telephone conversation between Admiral Duncan, the senior navy member of the Joint War Plans Committee, and his opposite number General Lincoln, chief of Strategy and Policy Group, OPD:

> *D:* One thing about this that is a little disturbing. You will pick it up when you read the printed paper. There is a statement in here which

says, "It is his intention" (meaning the President) "to make his decisions on the campaign with the purpose of economizing to the maximum extent possible in the loss of American lives." Now, of course, it
is a little late in the day to be making decisions on the campaign when
there is a firm directive to do certain things.

L: We have already committed ourselves to an operation, as a matter of
fact.

D: That's right. I don't know whether this directive, which they are operating under now, cleared with the President or not. It was recommended by somebody or other that it be cleared by the President. I think
it was agreed by the Chiefs, but whether that got done or not, I don't
know. However, the Heads of State did approve the over-all strategic
concept, which this directive support [*sic*].[3]

Truman's emphasis on minimizing casualties accords with his support for
a clarification of the surrender formula (including his morning statement to
Grew that "he liked the idea . . ."). His priorities at this time, similarly, are
also suggested by Leahy's report to the Joint Chiefs that in the president's
view "economy in the use of time and in money cost is comparatively
unimportant"—a principle which, if followed, would clearly permit delay of
military operations if a diplomatic initiative were undertaken.

Although Truman's June 18 meeting with the Joint Chiefs was narrowly
focused on military issues, the possibility of ending the war "through other
means" was also raised at several points. When the president asked the secretary of war for his views, for instance, Stimson replied that:

He felt that he was personally responsible to the President more for political than for military considerations. It was his opinion that there was
a large submerged class in Japan who do not favor the present war and
whose full opinion and influence had never yet been felt. He felt that
this submerged class would fight and fight tenaciously if attacked on
their own ground. He was concerned that something should be done to
arouse them and to develop any possible influence they might have before it became necessary to come to grips with them.[4]

Stimson's caveat about "political" rather than military advice was appropriate—and Truman's initial response was not especially surprising (another
indication he was discussing such questions elsewhere with other advisers):
"The President stated that this possibility was being worked on all the
time."[5]

Another question raised by Truman further underscored his personal concern about the military versus political choice: "The President asked if the
invasion of Japan by white men would not have the effect of more closely

uniting the Japanese." Stimson replied that "he thought there was every prospect of this," and that while he agreed with the strictly military plan proposed by the Joint Chiefs of Staff, "he still hoped for some fruitful accomplishment through other means."[6]

McCloy also urged the possibility of a political solution—and the importance of acting promptly:

> Mr. McCloy said he felt that the time was propitious now to study closely all possible means of bringing out the influence of the submerged group in Japan which had been referred to by Mr. Stimson.[7]

Similarly, the president's chief of staff also pressed the political issue:

> Admiral Leahy said that he could not agree with those who said to him that unless we obtain the unconditional surrender of the Japanese that we will have lost the war. He feared no menace from Japan in the foreseeable future, even if we were unsuccessful in forcing unconditional surrender. What he did fear was that our insistence on unconditional surrender would result only in making the Japanese desperate and thereby increase our casualty lists. He did not think that this was at all necessary.[8]

Although Forrestal's published diary contains no mention of the June 18 meeting, his unpublished diary provides an even more graphic sense of Leahy's strong feelings:

> . . . our determination to stick to the unconditional surrender position [would possibly produce the] result that every living person in Japan would prefer to die fighting rather than accept military defeat. . . .[9]

To this Truman responded:

> that it was with that thought in mind that he had left the door open for Congress to take appropriate action with reference to unconditional surrender. However, he did not feel that he could take any action at this time to change public opinion on the matter.[10]

The president's endorsement of Leahy's view that "our insistence on unconditional surrender would result in making the Japanese desperate and thereby increase our casualty lists," is perfectly consistent with what we know of his views up to this point. However, something strange also seems to be going on—especially with regard to Truman's suggestion that he had left the door open "for Congress to take appropriate action. . . ."

Truman's previous public statements reveal no indication that he ever expected Congress to take the lead on this matter. Indeed, the idea makes no sense in terms of the events of the day; nor is there any evidence the president ever alerted Congress or its leaders to their influence in the matter. (Possibly, the recording secretary misheard the president—and that what he said was something to the effect that he had left the door open "before" Congress.)

Again, especially in light of his May 8 initiative, Truman's suggestion that he did not feel able to take any action to help alter public opinion also has a rather hollow ring. The May 8 statement sharply focusing "unconditional surrender" on the Japanese military had been precisely such an action. And just two and a half weeks earlier, in his May 28 meeting with Grew, Truman had indicated general approval of the idea of clarifying the unconditional-surrender formula; he had not indicated any problem with issuing a statement which would begin to mold public opinion. (What he asked Grew to check did not concern politics but rather how the military leaders felt about a statement.)

Truman's reply to Leahy may merely indicate his unwillingness to discuss the real issue with this particular group. Perhaps—as we shall see in connection with several other instances at this time—the president simply preferred not to reveal his hand in this setting. (Though the point at issue is not easily documented, a rather complex related strategy was in the process of formulation in other discussions on the Far East and elsewhere in mid-June.*)

As to the immediate concern of the meeting: We have already noted that the essential directive to Pacific commanders has been approved on May 25, 1945. After a good deal of interservice struggle, it had been decided that neither the navy notion of "strangling" Japan through blockade nor the air force concept of bombing Japan into submission would suffice. The idea of landing first on the Chinese mainland had also been essentially bypassed. It had been determined that a 1946 invasion would be necessary if "unconditional surrender" were to remain the goal set by the president. As noted, this would be preceded by an initial landing in November 1945 on Kyushu.[11] At the end of the June 18 meeting, Truman confirmed his approval of this first step:

> The President said he considered the Kyushu plan all right from the military standpoint and, so far as he was concerned, the Joint Chiefs of Staff could go ahead with it; that we can do this operation and then decide as to the final action later.[12]

Despite this confirmation, there is ample evidence of the inevitably contingent nature of any decision made at this point in mid-June. Marshall observed, for instance, that "Kyushu having been arranged for, the decision as to further action could be made later." Admiral King was explicit:

*See below, pp. 182–84.

So far as preparation was concerned, we must aim now for Tokyo Plain; otherwise we will never be able to accomplish it. If preparations do not go forward now, they cannot be arranged for later. Once started, however, they can always be stopped if desired.[13]

Although these comments related to the overall effort, as McCloy was later to recall, Truman indicated that he wanted the Joint Chiefs to "return for further instructions before the preparations arrived at a point beyond which there would not be further opportunity for a free choice on the part of the President."[14]

Four and a half months still remained before a November landing could begin, even in theory.

We have repeatedly noted the need for extreme care in the use of documents which "seem" to indicate the views of officials at a time when secrecy was the rule. A particularly significant illustration of the problem we face—and of our limited knowledge even today—concerns an important exchange which appears to have occurred at the end of the June 18 meeting.

The formal minutes of the White House meeting were made public in a 1955 Department of Defense report, *Entry of the Soviet Union into the War Against Japan: Military Plans, 1941–1945*—a document which provided the public with the first official information on this critical discussion, ten years after the fact.

Five years later, in 1960—fifteen years after the event—when the full minutes were finally made public, they included this rather enigmatic sentence at the very end of the text:

THE PRESIDENT and the Chiefs of Staff then discussed certain other matters.[15]

A brief footnote states:

This paragraph may refer to discussion of a suggestion that the Japanese should be warned, before an atomic bomb was dropped on Japan, that the United States had such a weapon.[16]

No further official information is given concerning what went on at the end of the June 18 meeting. There is not much doubt, however, that the subject discussed at this point involved the two matters which are referred to in a somewhat confused manner in the footnote: a "warning" (almost certainly including consideration of modifying the surrender formula); and the atomic bomb. Additional information provided by McCloy, however, has helped illuminate the next step in the development of policy, and, too, the president's personal viewpoint.

Over the years it has become increasingly clear that McCloy played a major role in connection with the "unconditional surrender" issue. His biographer, Kai Bird, writes that he was the "leading oarsman" drafting the main proposals on this subject.[17] Various documents show that he had concluded that the phrase "unconditional surrender" should be dropped altogether. Writing to Stimson in late May, for instance, he urged: "I feel that today Japan is struggling to find a way out of the horrible mess she has got herself into; . . . I wonder whether we cannot accomplish everything we want to accomplish in regard to Japan without the use of that term."[18]

McCloy later recalled that the day before the June 18 White House meeting:

> . . . I said, Mr. Stimson, it seemed to me that we were now at a point where our superiority was so vast over the Japanese; there were no more cities to bomb, no more carriers to sink or battleships to shell; we had difficulty finding targets; we had this tremendous moral and physical ascendancy which resulted from our win in Germany and our moving across the Pacific from the treachery of Pearl Harbor to the very doors of Japan; and I thought there must be some other means that ought to be explored in terminating the war without further bloodshed. . . . he said he was inclined to think that this was right.[19]

On several occasions before his death in 1989, McCloy provided detailed recollections of the discussion which occurred at the end of the June 18 meeting. The following is based on in-depth interviews done in connection with a 1965 NBC White Paper documentary on the occasion of the twentieth anniversary of the bombing:

> . . . as we were picking up our papers, President Truman noticed me again; . . . and Mr. Truman said, "McCloy, you didn't express yourself, and nobody gets out of this room without standing up and being counted. Do you think I have any reasonable alternative to the decision which has just been made?" And I looked at the Secretary and he said, "Say what you feel about it," and so I said, "Well, I do think you've got an alternative; and I think it's an alternative that ought to be explored and that, really, we ought to have our heads examined if we don't explore some other method by which we can terminate this war than just by another conventional attack and landing."

The president then asked (McCloy went on): "What do you mean by a political solution?"

> Well, I said, "Some communication to the Japanese government which would spell out the terms that we would settle for"—there would be a

surrender; I wouldn't use again the term "unconditional surrender," but it would be a surrender that would mean that we would get all the important things that we were fighting for; . . . that now if we could accomplish our objectives without further bloodshed, there was no reason why we shouldn't attempt to do it; and I thought this was a good opportunity.

Thereupon—McCloy continued—Truman

asked me to spell out what the terms were, and I, just off the top of my head, said that I would tell him [*sic*] that we've got all this—we've got this massive Air Force and Navy and we have no more targets, and we would be quite prepared to permit Japan to continue to exist as a nation, as a viable nation, that we would permit them to choose their own form of government, including the retention of the Mikado, but only on the basis of a constitutional monarchy, give them access to, if not—rather than control over raw materials outside their borders, and so on I spelled the thing out.

"And," McCloy concluded, "the President said,"

"Well, that's just what I've been thinking about. I wonder if you could put that down and give it to the Secretary of State and see what we [can] do from that."[20]

In a separate statement for the NBC White Paper, McCloy was even more explicit:

When asked for what my terms for surrender would be, I said a specific offer of the retention of the Mikado as a constitutional monarch if they wanted him; a specific promise of an opportunity for a viable economy by giving Japan access to, but not control over, raw materials, and I also urged a specific reference to the bomb itself by way of threat—not by indirection or circumlocution.

McCloy also expressed his personal conviction on the central issue: "I am disposed to think this sort of message transmitted in good time might have produced surrender without the bomb and I am disposed to think that this would have been better than dropping the bomb."[21]

Similar statements were made regularly and consistently to different interviewers and in different situations over time. In a discussion with Marshall's biographer, Forrest Pogue, in 1959, McCloy reported:

The President said that is just what I have been thinking about. "Why don't you draft something."[22]

In a 1984 interview with Kai Bird, McCloy recalled the president saying:

> "That's exactly what I've been wanting to explore. . . . You go down to Jimmy Byrnes and talk to him about it."[23]

McCloy was also to report on other occasions that he did indeed go to see James F. Byrnes—the man about to become secretary of state—but that he found Byrnes unwilling to consider the idea: "He said," McCloy recalled, "my proposal was not possible."[24] In an unpublished memoir, an excerpt from which was made public in James Reston's 1991 book *Deadline*, Mc-Cloy writes:

> The president indicated that what I had said was in the nature of what he was seeking. He asked me to elaborate further on my suggestion and to take the matter up with Mr. Byrnes, who was then acting as the assistant to the president. . . .
> I immediately called upon Mr. Byrnes. He told me that he would have to oppose my proposal because it appeared to him that it might be considered a weakness on our part. Mr. Byrnes inferred he might not insist on treating the emperor as a war criminal, but he would oppose any "deal" as a concomitant of a demand for surrender.[25]

In his interview with Pogue in 1959, McCloy reported, similarly: "Then we had this debate about the Mikado. Jimmy Byrnes was a little unhappy later on that he hadn't been included in the meeting. . . ."[26]

Modern documentary discoveries leave no doubt that in general Byrnes was, in fact, the adviser who was closest to Truman in 1945—and that in general he consistently opposed any modification of the surrender formula. However, the date here has a special significance: McCloy's report suggests that the person the president was relying on for advice on the surrender terms—already, in mid-June (and probably earlier)—was Byrnes.

There is indisputable evidence that Byrnes was privately advising Truman on other important issues well before this time; and although there is no direct proof, it is a reasonable supposition that the two men considered this matter well before June 18. The president had, in fact, asked Byrnes to become secretary of state in mid-April, and Byrnes was already hard at work preparing for Truman's diplomatic encounter with Stalin at Potsdam, now just one month off. Of critical importance was the fact that on May 3 Truman had also asked Byrnes to represent him on the Interim Committee considering the atomic bomb.

Given what we know of Byrnes' rigid attitude overall—and in particular his well-documented unwillingness to modify the unconditional surrender formula at other points throughout the spring and summer—it also seems reasonable to surmise that it was he who influenced Truman to reverse the thrust of his May 8 softening of the surrender formula, and to adopt the "no-compromise" position of his June 1 speech.

No significant element of the historical debate over the decision to use the atomic bomb turns on a final answer to this question. Still, given what we know of the thinking of the other advisers Truman was talking to at this time, it is difficult to imagine any of them as the source of change. Indeed, it would be surprising if the man about to become secretary of state had been entirely out of the picture in the period just prior to his meeting with Stalin and the culmination of World War II—especially since Byrnes was well known for insisting on direct and personal control of all major decisions in his area of concern.

One final reflection on Truman's attitude at this time: As we have seen, during his morning meeting the president told Grew "he liked the idea" of modifying the terms.[27] Moreover, in the afternoon when confronted by Leahy, and in a more extensive discussion with McCloy, Truman twice appears to have reiterated his general support for a clarification of the surrender terms. The limited information we have suggests the president may well have been having second thoughts about the idea of delaying a statement. It is quite possible that in sending McCloy to see Byrnes, Truman agreed with the overwhelming consensus of his other top civilian and military advisers, and thought someone else needed convincing.

It has been suggested that McCloy's repeated reports of these events were inaccurate or misremembered.[28] McCloy seems to have anticipated such subsequent questioning, for he apparently made an immediate record:

> There is somewhere in the bowels of the Pentagon archives a contemporaneous report of the meeting which I dictated to John Stucchio after my return from the meeting. I did not take it with me when I left the Pentagon and I told him to keep it in my most secret files.[29]

However, when McCloy tried to hunt down this document in 1947, Rudolph A. Winnacker, editorial chief of the War Department Historical Division, reported to him that:

> A careful perusal of the relevant folders in your voluminous files in the War Department reveals no trace of your memorandum on the White House meeting. To the best of my knowledge no copy of this memorandum is in your files, unless Miss Wehner filed it in a folder whose nomenclature did not make me think that it dealt with Japan, Surrender, or the White House.[30]

In 1965 McCloy explained that neither Stucchio nor he knew

> where one could put their [*sic*] hands on it. The essence of it is as I have
> stated here. The minutes of the meeting as it was kept by one of the sec-
> retaries of the Chiefs of Staff does not record anything but the Presi-
> dent's decision—perhaps because he thought the meeting as such was
> over before the President called on me to state my views.[31]

In the decades since 1965 this document, like so many others, has remained undiscovered. On the other hand, McCloy's reputation for integrity
and honesty on such matters—and his self-evident concern to set the record
straight—strongly suggest the general accuracy of his various reports. Moreover, Forrestal's unpublished diary for the June 18 meeting notes: "McCloy
said he thought we should exhaust every effort and have our minds alert to
finding a method of energizing these elements in Japan to the point of effective political influence."[32] So far as can be determined, none of those present
at this meeting ever challenged McCloy's oft-repeated account, although
most were alive throughout at least the first postwar decades.

A handwritten note found in the papers of War Department historian
Rudolph A. Winnacker—opened only in January 1995—indicates that during
a trip to New York on April 30–May 1, 1946, Winnacker met with McCloy
and discussed the June 18 meeting. His notes, though cryptic, offer additional
confirmation (at this early date) of McCloy's recollection of the exchange,
and, importantly, of Truman's agreement: "*JJMcC.* meeting with HST. Approved Kyushu not yet Tokyo plain. Agreed at end HST 'what about your
comment McC?' 'Time for political action: GCM agreed. HLS backed it.
King [approved]. HST yes, for me to handle. Go to Potsdam. . . .' "[33]

Chapter 6

FROM JUNE 18
TO JULY 2, 1945

---

*. . . Mr. Forrestal favored such an approach to the Japanese.
Stimson and Grew further pointed out that Leahy, King and
Nimitz were all in favor of some such approach being made
to the Japanese.*
> —Notes taken June 19, 1945, by Matthias F. Correa,
> Assistant to Secretary of the Navy Forrestal

John McCloy also subsequently reported that (like Marshall on May 29) he
urged a specific warning to the Japanese about the new atomic weapon:

> . . . I had raised the question whether we oughtn't to tell them that we
> had the bomb and that we would drop the bomb.

And, too, his recollection that

> . . . as soon as I mentioned the word "bomb"—the atomic bomb—even
> in that select circle—there was nothing but Joint Chiefs of Staff and se-
> curity and Presidents [*sic*] and Secretaries of War around—it was sort of
> a shock. You didn't mention the bomb out loud; it was like, as I said on
> another occasion—it was like mentioning skull and bones in polite so-
> ciety at Yale; it just wasn't done. Well, there was a sort of gasp at that.
> But I said, "I think our moral position would be better if we gave them
> a specific warning of the bomb."[1]

Elsewhere McCloy reports that at this meeting he urged that after offering a
clarification of the terms,

> we should notify the Japanese of our possession of a weapon of revo-
> lutionary proportions and so devastating in its effect that it could de-

stroy a city at one blow; that we would be compelled to employ it if they did not surrender. I said I was prepared to use the term *atom bomb* but realized there was such an air of secrecy about it that we could use other words to describe its effect but they had to be graphic enough to be more compelling than the threat of Hitler's secret weapons had been.[2]

There are additional pieces of important contemporaneous information on the president's personal attitude—and on the attitudes of his other advisers—regarding the unconditional-surrender formula.

On June 19, the day after the White House gathering, the main Cabinet members involved met again.[3] An edited version of notes taken by Forrestal's assistant, Major Matthias F. Correa, appeared in 1951 in Forrestal's published diary—Correa's complete notes (in an entry specially designated "Top Secret") were subsequently made available in the unpublished diary.

The published diary contains this report:

> *Surrender terms:* Grew's proposal, in [*sic*] which Stimson most vigorously agrees, that something be done in the very near future to indicate to the Japanese what kind of surrender terms would be imposed upon them and particularly to indicate to them that they would be allowed to retain their own form of government and religious institutions while at the same time making it clear that we propose to eradicate completely all traces of Japanese militarism. Both Stimson and Grew most emphatically asserted that this move ought to be done, and that if it were to be effective at all it must be done before any attack was made upon the homeland of Japan.[4]

It would appear that in 1951 there was some fear of disclosing the extent of backing for such an approach, for the published diary omits the next sentence:

> Grew stated that he had addressed a letter to Judge Rosenman on Saturday last [June 16] embodying his views and that Judge Rosenman had said he would take it up with the President on Sunday last [June 17].[5]

That support for the move among very high-level officials was not limited to Grew and Stimson is again confirmed by the following sentence concerning Forrestal and the key military leaders (also cut from the published diary):

> Mr. Gates stated that while he could not speak for Mr. Forrestal he felt that in general Mr. Forrestal favored such an approach to the Japanese. Stimson and Grew further pointed out that Leahy, King and Nimitz were all in favor of some such approach being made to the Japanese.[6]

The published meeting notes also state:

> Mr. Grew was of the impression that the President had indicated that he was not in accord with this point of view.

However, this comment was immediately challenged as inaccurate:

> Mr. Stimson said that that was not his understanding but rather he felt that the President did not want to proceed with such a plan at this moment and in particular did not want the Departments to abate in any way their preparations for the ultimate attack because of the existence of such a plan.[7]

Grew, too, later emphatically challenged the initial characterization of his views, writing in his 1952 memoirs: "Mr. Forrestal was clearly mistaken in this conception of what I had said."

> I made it quite clear in the meeting in Secretary Stimson's office on May 29, 1945, attended by numerous witnesses, that on this point the President had assured me that "his own thinking ran along the same lines as mine" but that he wished me to consult our military and naval authorities.[8]

Stimson's diary entry for this day also contains a corroborating report concerning the overall thrust of the meeting:

> . . . there was a pretty strong feeling that it would be deplorable if we have to go through the military program with all its stubborn fighting to a finish. We agreed that it is necessary to plan and prepare to go through, but it became very evident today in the discussion that we all feel that some way should be found of inducing Japan to yield without a fight to the finish and that was the subject of the discussion today. Grew read us a recent report he had made to the President on the subject in which he strongly advocated a new warning to Japan as soon as Okinawa has fallen. . . .[9]

The collapse of Okinawa was imminent—and occurred two days later on June 21. As we shall see, a statement issued at this time would have preceded the first possible use of atomic weapons by five and a half weeks and the actual use by slightly more than six weeks.

There is one additional instructive comment in Stimson's diary description of the June 19 meeting. The secretary of war goes on:

> . . . but apparently that does not meet with the President's plans in respect to the coming meeting with Churchill and Stalin.[10]

What is interesting here is the acknowledgment that the president's decision about timing seems to have been made elsewhere. Not only do none of the people at this meeting evidence desire to put things off for so long, but it is clear that they are not the ones advising Truman directly on the matter. It is also obvious that Stimson himself was not fully informed of White House thinking. Even in his private diary, he writes only that "apparently" an early statement was not in accord with the president's plans.

A week later, on June 26, still another meeting of the Committee of Three was held. At this time a subcommittee was appointed to draft an explicit warning statement.[11] Within a few days the statement, together with an explanatory memorandum, was completed and submitted to Stimson, who was shortly expected to meet with the president.

During this same period, on June 30, Grew sent Truman a State Department briefing book paper which formally recommended a modification of the surrender formula. The paper stressed that a primary objective was "to eliminate the most serious single obstacle to Japanese unconditional surrender, namely, concern over the fate of the throne. . . ." (Moreover, far from worrying that domestic politics made such a statement difficult, the paper urged that clarifying the terms would tend "to satisfy a growing body of opinion in United States which is demanding that we endeavor to hasten the end of the war in the Pacific by stating definitely our war aims."[12])

Stimson met with the president on July 2—only five days before Truman's departure for his Potsdam meeting with Stalin and Churchill. Stimson gave him the memorandum which had been drafted following the decision of the Committee of Three, together with a cover letter which stated:

> . . . I have consulted with the Secretary of the Navy and the Acting Secretary of State each of whom has approved the tenor of the memorandum and has subscribed to the recommendations contained in it.[13]

The memorandum itself posited the following question:

> Is there any alternative to such a forceful occupation of Japan which will secure for us the equivalent of an unconditional surrender of her forces and a permanent destruction of her power again to strike an aggressive blow at the "peace of the Pacific"?

Stimson's response was clear about the answer—and about the issue of timing:

> I am inclined to think that there is enough such chance to make it well worthwhile our giving them a warning of what is to come and a definite

opportunity to capitulate. As above suggested, it should be tried before the actual forceful occupation of the homeland islands is begun and furthermore the warning should be given in ample time to permit a national reaction to set in.

Nor is there any question about the official assessment he offered (with emphasis) to the president as to the likelihood of success:

I believe Japan *is* susceptible to reason in such a crisis to a much greater extent than is indicated by our current press and other current comment.

Stimson elaborated on the reasoning behind his assessment:

My own opinion is in her favor on the two points involved in this question:

a. I think the Japanese nation has the mental intelligence and versatile capacity in such a crisis to recognize the folly of a fight to the finish and to accept the proffer of what will amount to an unconditional surrender; and

b. I think she has within her population enough liberal leaders . . . to be depended upon for her reconstruction as a responsible member of the family of nations.

Equally important, Stimson stressed, was what intelligence analysts had long been stressing would happen if no offer were made:

On the other hand, I think that the attempt to exterminate her armies and her population by gunfire or other means will tend to produce a fusion of race solidity and antipathy which had no analogy in the case of Germany.

Just as McCloy had proposed on June 18, Stimson now formally urged that a "carefully timed warning" be given—that it should contain a threat of overwhelming force, but that it should also include "[t]he disavowal of any attempt to extirpate the Japanese as a race or to destroy them as a nation."[14]

The text of the proposed draft declaration which Stimson gave to the president stated explicitly that a postwar Japanese government could include

a constitutional monarchy under the present dynasty if it be shown to the complete satisfaction of the world that such a government will never again conspire to aggression.[15]

(Without this clause, McCloy had advised Stimson on June 29, "those who seem to know most about Japan feel there would be very little likelihood of acceptance."[16])

The draft also explicitly returned to the position Truman had announced on May 8—and, indeed, like the Joint Chiefs of Staff draft surrender demand, it went one step further by using language which not only emphasized a military surrender but explicitly acknowledged the authority of the existing Japanese government:

> We call upon those in authority in Japan to proclaim now the unconditional surrender of all the Japanese armed forces under the authority of the Japanese Government and High Command. . . .[17]

Finally, Stimson told Truman: "I personally think that if in saying this we should add that we do not exclude a constitutional monarchy under her present dynasty, it would substantially add to the chances of acceptance."[18]

Stimson's diary for July 2, 1945, states:

> The President read my memorandum to him which we had discussed last Tuesday at the Committee of Three and evidently was impressed with it. . . . He also examined the draft warning which, as I pointed out, was merely a tentative draft and necessarily could not be completed until we knew what was going to be done with S-1. . . .
>
>   His attitude throughout was apparently very well satisfied with the way in which the subjects were presented and he was apparently acquiescent with my attitude towards the treatment of Japan and pronounced the paper which I had written as a very powerful paper.[19]

Our primary interest, of course, is with the presidential level of decision-making. We shall shortly note one additional occasion when President Truman was directly urged to offer Japan assurances concerning the Emperor before his departure for Potsdam. It may be useful at this point, however, to reflect on the little-noted fact that by this time all of the major officials formally involved—the secretary of state, the acting secretary of state, the secretary of war, the assistant secretary of war, the secretary of the navy, Admiral Leahy, General Marshall, all the members of the Joint Chiefs of Staff—had in one way or another proposed a clarification of the surrender formula. Along with Joseph Grew the Joint Chiefs of Staff, in particular, had recommended that a statement be issued to coincide with the fall of Okinawa.

The essential momentum of the U.S. government, in short, was moving forward in an unmistakable direction. James Forrestal's diary records that on July 6, just before Truman left Washington to meet Churchill and Stalin,

> I talked . . . to Joe Grew. He expressed satisfaction that we had finally whipped into shape the draft of the proposed message to the Japanese

by the President, the aim of which is to make more specific what we mean by the phrase "unconditional surrender."[20]

Most important—as we have seen—there is also not much doubt about the general thrust of the president's own views at this point in time.

It appears that only Byrnes, who formally took office on July 3, was opposed to modifying the surrender formula.

PART II

The Russian Option

The increasing effects of air-sea blockade, the progressive cumulative devastation wrought by strategic bombing, and the collapse of Germany (with its implications regarding redeployment). . . . The entry of the U.S.S.R. into the war would, together with the foregoing factors, convince most Japanese at once of the inevitability of complete defeat.

—The Joint Intelligence Committee,
to the Joint Chiefs of Staff, April 29, 1945

Chapter 7

PHASE I: FROM PEARL HARBOR
TO THE DEATH OF ROOSEVELT

We desire Russian entry at the earliest possible date consistent with her ability to engage in offensive operations.
—Report of the Joint Staff Planners to the Joint Chiefs of
Staff, "Russian Participation in the War Against Japan,"
November 23, 1944

Modern documentary discoveries make it clear that modifying the unconditional surrender formula was not the only option which appeared to offer reasonable hope of bringing about a Japanese surrender in the summer of 1945. The most obvious way to do so seemed simply to wait for the Soviet Union to declare war on Japan—an event which was expected to occur in early August.

Given the rise of the Cold War, the growth of anti-Soviet sentiment, the Truman administration's effort to play down the Russian factor, and the paucity of documents for so many years, the "Russian option" has been the least discussed of the available alternatives in most accounts written since World War II. One of the very few exceptions is a 1955 study by Harvard historian Ernest R. May. Among other things, May (who had previously been a Defense Department historian) noted that the "Japanese die-hards . . . had acknowledged since 1941 that Japan could not fight Russia as well as the United States and Britain. . . ." Studying the actual surrender, May also concluded that since Moscow had been the outlet for numerous Japanese peace feelers, the Russian declaration of war, when it finally occurred, "discouraged Japanese hopes of secretly negotiating terms of peace," and that in the end,

The Emperor's appeal [to end the war] probably resulted, therefore, from the Russian action, but it could not in any event, have been long in coming.[1]

Forty years after this study it has become possible to demonstrate that this essential point was understood well before the bombings. By midsummer of 1945 intelligence experts, military and other officials, and the president himself, seem clearly to have recognized that the impact of a Red Army attack on the isolated and rapidly deteriorating Japanese would almost certainly precipitate a surrender either on its own or when combined with assurances for the Emperor.

One reason "the Russian option" received so little serious attention during most of the postwar years is that official government materials concerning this alternative were tightly guarded for a long period. Moreover, important gaps appear in certain files. There are suggestions that during the McCarthy era and the early 1950s controversy concerning who "lost" China, some officials may have suppressed documents which might have evidenced an interest in securing help from the Soviet Union.

Furthermore, many leaders—fearing communist influence in Asia—did not really wish to exercise the option of ending the war with a Soviet attack if they could avoid doing so. This consideration, too, undoubtedly influenced and limited the discussions reported in the available records. There has also been considerable confusion because the specific role a Soviet declaration of war might play changed several times during mid-1945 as the Japanese military and political situation itself changed. Finally, many historians have not caught up with the flow of recent documents concerning the issue.

An instructive introduction to this alternative is an official U.S. intelligence study first discovered, so far as I have been able to determine, only in 1989.* Prepared by the Intelligence Group of the War Department's Military Intelligence Division between late January and late April 1946, the study attempted to answer the question of what might have happened on "the assumption that the U.S. did not use, and had not the capability of using, atomic bombs in the war against Japan."[2]

Like the official Strategic Bombing Survey of 1946, the internal War Department report concluded the atomic bomb had not been needed to end the war. Its assessment of the impact of the Soviet declaration of war paralleled that of Ernest May: It was a "disastrous event which the Japanese leaders re-

---

*This study was declassified and technically available in the 1970s, but was filed within materials on postwar atomic tests in the Pacific and appears to have been overlooked or at least not cited by historians of the decision to drop the bomb. It was brought to my attention in 1989 by Dr. Juan Garces.

garded as utter catastrophe and which they had energetically sought to prevent at any cost. . . ."[3]

Had the atomic bomb not been available or not been used, the study concluded, it is "almost a certainty that the Japanese would have capitulated upon the entry of Russia into the war. . . ."

> The Japanese leaders had decided to surrender and were merely looking for sufficient pretext to convince the die-hard Army Group that Japan had lost the war and must capitulate to the Allies. The entry of Russia into the war would almost certainly have furnished this pretext, and would have been sufficient to convince all responsible leaders that surrender was unavoidable.[4]

Furthermore, Japan was in such difficulties by midsummer 1945 that "Coronet"—the planned full invasion of Japan—"would not have been necessary." Even a preliminary November landing on Kyushu was judged to have been only a "remote" possibility; the fighting "would almost certainly have terminated when Russia entered the war against Japan."[5]

This internal intelligence study, of course, is an after-the-fact assessment. On the other hand, it was undertaken when events were fresh in the minds of the people involved, and, as newly released documents show, drew upon otherwise unavailable intelligence materials.[6]

For our purposes the study's particular value is that it brings into focus several issues of importance not only to a retrospective understanding, but to a comprehension of how American leaders formed their own judgments on this critical question as their policies steadily evolved during the late spring and summer of 1945.

Scholars have long known that for most of World War II U.S. leaders urgently desired Soviet entry into the war against Japan—the sooner, the better. However, exploiting the extraordinary political-military "shock" of a Red Army attack in order to force a surrender before an invasion—as underscored by the War Department study—was not the initial reason. Earlier in the war—before Japan began its accelerating downward spiral—the desire for Soviet help flowed from different considerations.

U.S. officials initially wanted the Red Army to attack as soon as possible in order to pin down the vaunted Japanese Kwantung Army on the China mainland—and thus prevent it from reinforcing the home armies when the U.S. began its invasion. In a message sent to Marshall on December 10, 1941—only three days after Pearl Harbor—General Douglas MacArthur urged "that every possible effort be made to obtain immediate entry of Russia into the war."

[D]efinite information available here shows that entry of Russia is en-emy [*sic*] greatest fear. Most favorable opportunity now exists and immediate attack on Japan from the north would not only inflict heavy punishment but would at once relieve pressure from objectives of Jap drive to southward. . . . Golden opportunity exists for a master stroke while the enemy is engaged in over-extended initial air efforts.[7]

Although U.S. military planning went through several subsequent phases, the primary role assigned to the Red Army did not significantly change from this fundamental position from late 1941 to the death in 1945 of Franklin D. Roosevelt.

MacArthur was undoubtedly right about the strategic realities. However, given the all-out struggle with Hitler's armies U.S. leaders realized a Red Army attack was extremely unlikely during the early period. On Decem-ber 11, Soviet Ambassador Maxim Litvinov informed Hull that because of the extraordinary demands of the war in Europe, Russia would not, in fact, be able to join the war against Japan in the immediate future.[8] Stimson's di-ary of December 10, 1941, notes that "I went over to the State Department and talked it over with Hull. We both agreed that the chances of getting the Russians to do much is small."[9]

This judgment did not reflect Moscow's priorities alone. U.S. policy-makers themselves had good reason not to want to spread the Russians too thin by taking on the Japanese. Navy leaders in particular—as Chief of Naval Operations Admiral Harold Stark informed Roosevelt on December 18—questioned "the wisdom of Russia's entering the war against Japan at this time." Stark urged that any "Soviet effort to reconstitute their Far Eastern forces might . . . result in weakening their European defenses and lead to de-feat by Germany."[10]

Roosevelt decided to follow the Navy's recommendations and not pressure Stalin, and with the German invasion of Russia center-stage throughout 1942 and into 1943 the main focus continued to be the European war. (An impor-tant concern, indeed, was that the Japanese might attack the Russians.) At the same time, the Joint Chiefs of Staff continued to emphasize the ultimate de-sirability of Russian assistance against Japan. In preparation for the October 1943 Moscow meeting of foreign ministers, for instance, the Joint Chiefs prepared instructions to guide Brigadier General John R. Deane (who accom-panied the U.S. delegation and remained as head of the American Military Mission). These stressed

The great importance to the United States of Russia's full participation in the war against Japan after the defeat of Germany as essential to the prompt and crushing defeat of Japan at far less cost to the United States and Great Britain.[11]

Nor—once the battle of Stalingrad had been won—did the Russians offer reason to doubt their eventual participation. Indeed, especially after the Red Army's decisive victory at Kursk (in August 1943), the Russians began to give quite clear indications that they would attack Japan. At the final banquet of the foreign ministers conference in October 1943, Hull sat next to Stalin and was "astonished and delighted" when the Soviet premier told him "clearly and unequivocally that, when the Allies succeeded in defeating Germany, the Soviet Union would then join in defeating Japan."[12] Deane provided the Joint Chiefs with a similar report on October 31:

> The atmosphere was one of complete desire for cooperation. . . . It was significant that after the dinner we were shown a lengthy picture of Japanese penetration in Siberia in 1921. It was distinctly anti-Japanese propaganda and we all felt it was an indirect method of telling us their attitude with regard to Japan. In private conversations with Molotov, Vashinsky [*sic*] and others we have heard more direct statements indicating that they will join in the Pacific war as soon as Germany is defeated.[13]

Deane was certain "the Russians will go to war with Japan when they have finished with Germany. There was no question in his mind about this."[14]

Just before the Big Three met at Teheran (one month after the Moscow foreign ministers meeting) the U.S.–British Combined Chiefs of Staff approved an overall plan for the Pacific War which projected the possibility that Germany might be defeated in 1944—and that the Soviet Union would enter the Japanese war shortly thereafter.[15] A related study by the U.S. Joint Chiefs (also approved subsequently by the Combined Chiefs of Staff) stated: "We are agreed that every effort should be exerted to bring the U.S.S.R. into the war against Japan at the earliest practicable date, and that plans should be prepared in that event."[16] And once at Teheran Stalin again confirmed—explicitly—that:

> Our forces now in the East are more or less satisfactory for defense. However, they must be increased about three-fold for purposes of offensive operations. This condition will not take place until Germany has been forced to capitulate. *Then* by our common front we shall win.[17]

Military planning with regard to Russian participation in the Pacific war also remained grounded in this now familiar assumption throughout 1944.

However, it is important to note the specific reasoning of U.S. military planners. The Joint Chiefs put the central point this way:

> A Russian drive into Manchuria coincident with or prior to our invasion of Kyushu would prevent any appreciable movement of Japanese forces southward into Korea and North China and would necessitate retention of all Japanese forces on the Asiatic mainland. Such action by Russia would facilitate our invasion of Kyushu and our ultimate invasion of the heart of Japan.[18]

Although there was continuing debate over the amount of aid the U.S. could afford to give Russia—and about the possibility of ending the war by blockade and bombardment alone—American officials in Moscow continued to seek Stalin's assurances. They also began focusing on practicalities. In June 1944 Harriman reported to Roosevelt:

> In my talk with Stalin yesterday evening (10 June) we discussed in considerable detail the participation of the Soviet Union in the Japanese war. . . . I brought up the question of the basing of our bombers in the Soviet Far East and stated that you and our Chiefs of Staff believed no time should be lost in coming to an agreement and in working out necessary plans for supplies. He agreed that this was desirable and stressed the necessity for Utmost secrecy.[19]

Partly because of the intensity of the ongoing battle against Hitler, partly because of Stalin's extreme fears about secrecy (and his worry that Japan might attempt a pre-emptive strike) practical arrangements for U.S.-Soviet military coordination stalled somewhat during the summer of 1944. However, a meeting on September 23 between Stalin and the British and American ambassadors left little doubt about the main issue. Harriman once more told Roosevelt that "there was no change in [Stalin's] attitude as he had expressed it to you at Teheran. Russia is ready to participate in the war against Japan after Germany is defeated."[20]

Churchill visited Moscow in October 1944, and during his stay Harriman and Deane were able to discuss further details. Deane reported on October 16 that although Stalin did not specifically commit himself as to how soon operations could start after the defeat of Germany, he "said it would be three months or 'several months' before the Soviets would be ready to strike a blow at Japan."[21]

At roughly this time, too, new political-military thinking began to emerge—at least on the British side of the Alliance. During the Quebec conference (a few weeks before his October trip to Moscow) Churchill had assured Roosevelt that he was certain Stalin would enter the Pacific War after Germany's defeat—and, moreover, that at that point, when "Japan was confronted with the three most powerful nations in the world, she would undoubtedly think twice about continuing the fight."[22]

On the eve of his departure for Moscow (on September 27, 1944) Churchill expanded upon this point in a direct cable to Stalin:

> From all I have learnt about the internal state of Japan and the sense of hopelessness weighing on their people, I believe it might well be that once the Nazis are shattered a triple summons to Japan to surrender, coming from our three Great Powers, might be decisive.[23]

In identifying the potential "shock value" of a statement which merely pledged Soviet entry, the Prime Minister was ahead of American leadership—but only, as we shall see, by a few months.

As 1944 drew to a close—and with Germany's defeat seemingly imminent—U.S. military planners began to focus more attention on questions of timing. A November 23 study by the Joint Staff Planners, approved by the Joint Chiefs of Staff on December 5, argued that while Russia's interests and postwar politics would undoubtedly bring her into the war, the United States could influence the date of Soviet entry through logistical and operational support. The goal was an early Red Army attack well before an invasion:

> . . . the timing of Russia's entry is so important that it may be decisive in determining whether the result will be to our advantage. . . . In order to provide maximum support for our main effort the Russian offensive into Manchuria and her aerial attack on Japan should be launched at least three months prior to our invasion of Kyushu.[24]

Again, the central issue for the U.S. planners at this point was pinning down Japanese troops: They judged that if the Russian attack were to come simultaneously with or after an invasion, "the enemy [would] retain to some extent the capability of reinforcing the homeland." The JPS study concluded:

> We desire Russian entry at the earliest possible date consistent with her ability to engage in offensive operations and are prepared to offer the maximum support possible without prejudice to our main effort against Japan.[25]

Japanese officials in Tokyo and elsewhere were also focusing their attention on the status of the still-neutral Soviet Union—a fact not lost on American leaders. After reading recently intercepted cables Secretary of the Navy Forrestal recorded the following in his diary for December 7, 1944:

> Dispatches today from Japan indicate their awareness of the increasing difficulty of their situation. Indications that they count on possible differences between Russia and Anglo-American interests to facilitate their

position should they ask for a negotiated peace. Indications also [*sic*] they are fully aware of possibility of Russia joining the war against them at the proper time.[26]

Another critical political-military fact also slowly began to be clarified: A Russian attack would be of supreme importance, above all, in weakening the position and resolve of the hard-line Japanese army leaders. On January 29, 1945, the MAGIC Summary of intercepted cables posted a front-page commentary about a remarkable Japanese message:

> *Gloomy forecast by Vice Chief of Japanese Army General Staff:* On 27 January the Vice Chief of the Japanese Army General Staff sent to Military Attaches in Europe a "forecast of the situation up to about the middle of 1945." The circular which is headed "Personal" (i.e., intended for the Military Attache only) displays an unrelieved pessimism on all aspects of the war which is entirely without precedent in available traffic out of Tokyo. . . .

The intercepted cable included the following prediction:

> [On or before 25 April] Russia will probably announce her intention to abrogate the Neutrality Pact with Japan, but "for a while" thereafter will probably remain neutral. However, "if developments in the Greater East Asia war make it favorable for her to do so (particularly if the strength of the [Japanese] Empire should be considerably diminished) and if the progress of the European situation permits, Russia is very likely to commence armed warfare against Japan in the latter half of this year."*

Comment on this intercept by U.S. intelligence analysts stressed:

> There seems to be no reason to doubt that the foregoing circular is genuine and represents the sincere views of at least some members of the Army General Staff. While it may not have been personally written by the Vice Chief of the General Staff, Lt. Gen. Hikosaburo Hata, it could scarcely have gone out without his approval.[27]

It was obvious to U.S. leaders that Red Army help could not be expected unless there was something in it for the Soviets. Some of Russia's political interests in the Far East had begun to be defined at the 1943 Teheran Conference. Indeed, during one Big Three discussion of various Soviet concerns Roosevelt himself proposed that the Manchurian port of Dairen might be given over in some manner to provide the U.S.S.R. with an ice-free port.[28] A December 1944 meeting between Stalin and Harriman brought this further

---

*Brackets and parentheses in original.

report to Roosevelt: "In my talk with Stalin last night I said that you were anxious to know what political questions he had indicated in October should be clarified in connection with Russia's entry in the war against Japan"—and that Stalin proposed:

that the Kurile Islands and the lower Sakhalin should be returned to Russia. He explained that the Japanese now controlled the approaches to Vladivostok, that we considered that the Russians were entitled to protection for their communications to this important port and that "all outlets to the Pacific were now held or blocked by the enemy." He drew a line around the southern part of the Liaotung Peninsula including Port Arthur and Dairen saying that the Russians wished again to lease these ports and the surrounding area.

Harriman continued:

Stalin said further that he wished to lease the Chinese-Eastern Railway. . . . He answered affirmatively when I asked if these were the only railroad lines in Manchuria in which he was interested. In answer to my question he specifically reaffirmed that he did not intend to interfere with the sovereignty of China in Manchuria. . . . He said the only consideration he had not mentioned at Teheran was the recognition of the status quo in Outer Mongolia—the maintenance of the Republic of Outer Mongolia as an independent identity.

He concluded:

This latter did not surprise me as I have been convinced for many months that this would be the Soviet attitude because of their desire for protection for their long southern Siberian boundary.[29]

As the Yalta Conference approached, the first principle of U.S. policy (as defined by the Joint Chiefs) remained: "We desire Russian entry at the earliest possible date consistent with her ability to engage in offensive operations."[30] At the conference itself Stalin's promise to join the Allies in the Pacific three months after the defeat of Germany was confirmed. The specific political issues which had been raised were also settled. State Department Russian expert Charles E. Bohlen's minutes of the February 8, 1945, Roosevelt-Stalin meeting offer a clear sense of the relaxed U.S. attitude:

The PRESIDENT said he had received a report of this conversation [between Harriman and Stalin], and he felt that there would be no difficulty whatsoever in regard to the southern half of Sakhalin and the Kurile Islands going to Russia at the end of the war. He said that in regard to a warm water port in the Far East for the Soviet Union, the Marshal re-

called that they had discussed that point at Tehran. He added that he had
then suggested that the Soviet Union be given the use of a warm water
port at the end of the south Manchurian railroad, at possibly Dairen on
the Kwantung peninsula. The President said he had not yet had an opportunity to discuss this matter with Marshal Chiang Kai-shek, so therefore he could not speak for the Chinese.[31]

A secret accord signed by Roosevelt, Stalin, and Churchill on February 11
provided that the Red Army would enter the war on condition that "[t]he
former rights of Russia violated by the treacherous attack of Japan in 1904"
were restored. Specifically, the southern half of Sakhalin would be returned
to the Soviet Union; the Manchurian port of Dairen would be international-
ized ("the pre-eminent interests of the Soviet Union in this port being safeguarded"); Port Arthur would be leased to the Soviet Union as a naval base;
and the Chinese Eastern Railroad and the South Manchurian Railroad,
"which provides an outlet to Dairen," would be operated by a Soviet-Chinese
company ("it being understood that the pre-eminent interests of the Soviet
Union shall be safeguarded"). Additionally, Roosevelt promised American
support to preserve the status quo in Outer Mongolia. Finally, the Kurile Islands would be handed over to the Soviet Union.[32]

Since it was understood that the agreement concerning these matters (and
Outer Mongolia) would require the concurrence of Chiang Kai-shek, Roosevelt agreed to "take measures" on "advice from Marshal Stalin" to obtain
Chiang's approval so that the claims of the Soviet Union would be "unquestionably fulfilled" after the defeat of Japan.[33]

Roosevelt endorsed the accord with little hesitation. The concessions con-
stituted little more than the restoration of Russia's pre-1905 rights in the
area. Harriman later stated that the Yalta agreement usefully defined and limited Soviet claims: "It would have been a simple matter for the Soviets to
give expression to popular demand by establishing People's Republics of
Manchuria and inner Mongolia."[34] Since the area had not been controlled by
Chiang Kai-shek for many years, Admiral Leahy also believed that in exchange for Soviet support in the war, Stalin had received only "misnamed"
concessions.[35]

At Yalta Roosevelt and Churchill also met with the Combined Chiefs of
Staff—and Churchill again "expressed the opinion that it would be of great
value if Russia could be persuaded to join the United States, the British Empire, and China in the issue of a four-power ultimatum calling upon Japan to
surrender unconditionally, or else be subjected to the overwhelming weight
of all the forces of the four powers."[36]

Although the Yalta agreement was secret, the emerging possibilities were not lost on the U.S. press. On February 10, the *Army and Navy Journal* commented: "It is apparent from the Big Three communique that the discussions of the conferees are confined officially to matters relating to Europe. However, the Japanese know perfectly well that there is occurring an unofficial exchange of views to develop the prospects of Russia's entrance into the war against them. . . ."[37]

Similarly, Hanson Baldwin—military affairs correspondent for *The New York Times*—observed on February 14 that the Yalta "communique did not speak of the Pacific war, but the Pacific war lies behind many of the agreements made."

> It now seems certain that Russia will enter the Pacific war, though almost certainly not until after the final defeat of Germany.
>
> The negotiations looking toward Russia's participation in the war against Japan started at Teheran and have been carried on since with a view to delimiting and defining the extent, in terms of bases, forces, etc., to which she would participate in that war.[38]

On February 25 Sidney Shalett, also writing in the *Times*, reported:

> At least 1,000,000 Russian troops—and that figure probably is low—are facing a like number of Japanese troops, including a large number of Manchurians of doubtful fighting quality. Russia, victorious in Europe, could exert pressure on Japan that, taken in combination with the powerful blows we are capable of dealing, could be quickly fatal to the enemy.[39]

The possibility that an arrangement had been concluded with the Russians also was not lost on the Japanese. On January 21, even before the Big Three meeting, MAGIC summaries reported a January 10 cable from Japan's ambassador in Moscow warning that the upcoming Yalta conference "certainly merits our closest attention since it may lead to the worst eventualities for Japan."[40] Similarly, just before the conference actually opened, MAGIC intercepts included a cable from Major General Shimizu, the Japanese military attaché in Northern Italy. While Shimizu hoped that the Allies still might be split, he also warned:

> Japan is now facing unprecedented difficulties. If Germany fails, we will have to face alone the full strength of Britain and America. * * * If a false step on our part should then bring Russia into the war against us we face absolute destruction.[41]*

* "* * *" in original.

As the Yalta Conference came to an end, Foreign Minister Shigemitsu instructed Sato to seek an interview with Molotov as soon as possible:

> I should like you to make a regular practice of ascertaining Russia's policy toward Japan from now on, and also on some appropriate occasion to sound out her feeling about the continuance of the Neutrality Pact.[42]

The Russians were clearly not responsive to Japan's concerns—and Sato's frustration was soon obvious: a February 10, 1945, cable responding to Shigemitsu anxiously reported:

> . . . I think even you will agree that, with the war situation becoming more serious both in the East and the West, our chances of obtaining renewal of the Neutrality Pact are becoming fainter and fainter. May I reiterate that at such a time as this it is absolutely imperative that I should be informed of my Government's real intentions.

Sato requested instructions "at once," noting apologetically:

> If these were normal times, I would request your opinions in a rather more gentlemanly fashion, but there is not sufficient time for courtesy in this day of crisis and pressure.[43]

Even as the Japanese hoped against hope, U.S. military planners consolidated their positions. On February 10 a team left Yalta to inform commanders in the field of the outcome of the talks, and on February 13 Generals Marshall and Hull received the following "Eyes Only" report of discussions held in the Pacific theater by Colonel Paul L. Freeman, Jr. General MacArthur, Freeman stated,

> was apprehensive as to the possibility of the movement of the bulk of the Manchurian army and other Japanese forces from China to the defense of the homeland. He emphatically stated that we must not invade Japan proper unless the Russian army is previously committed to action in Manchuria. He said this was essential, and that it should be done without the three month's delay upon the conclusion of the defeat of Germany as intimated by Marshall Stalin to the President. [MacArthur] said that it was only necessary for action to commence in Manchuria to contain that force of Japanese in order to make possible our invasion of Japan and the rapid conclusion of the war.[44]

General George A. Lincoln also reported from the Pacific that:

> Concerning overall plan General MacArthur considers it essential that maximum number of Jap divisions be engaged and pinned down on Asiatic mainland, before United States forces strike Japan proper.[45]

Upon returning to Washington (on March 8) Lincoln provided additional details:

> As to Russia, General MacArthur pointed out that politically they want a warm water port which would be Port Arthur. He considered that it would be impracticable to deny them such a port because of their great military power. Therefore, it was only right they should share the cost in blood in defeating Japan. From the military standpoint we should make every effort to get Russia into the war before we go into Japan, otherwise we will take the impact of the Jap divisions and reap the losses, while the Russians in due time advance into an area free of major resistance. General MacArthur stated he considered the President should start putting pressure on the Russians now.[46]

Chapter 8

PHASE II: APRIL 1945

---

*Because of our estimated ability to interdict Japanese move-
ment between the Asiatic mainland and Japan proper, early
Russian entry into the war against Japan and attendant containing of the Kwantung army is no longer necessary to make
invasion feasible.*
> —The Joint Staff Planners to the Joint Chiefs of Staff,
> April 25, 1945

Ample records concerning "the Russian option" are available for the period
December 1941 to March 1945—and for several important developments
during the month of April 1945 they are at least adequate. The months from
April to July 1945, however, present major documentary problems for
historians.

First, in general, even at the time documents related to Russian military
possibilities were tightly segregated in a specially controlled series of papers
code-named LOCKUP.[1] Only a very limited number of officers had access to
these files. Subsequent accounts rarely even acknowledged the existence of
these special files (or the codeword), much less explained the highly restricted nature of the information they contained. Security was so tight that
when Cordell Hull reported from Moscow on Russian plans concerning the
war, he sent half his message to Washington using navy codes and half using
army codes.[2]

Second, the longstanding MAGIC classification "void" also explains a
good deal of the silence of many postwar accounts concerning the key issues.
Not until 1978, when the bulk of the MAGIC materials were opened to the
public did researchers and writers have access to the intercepted Japanese
messages and related intelligence assessments that had been informing top
U.S. officials on issues surrounding Japan and the Russian option.

Third, it is quite clear that some officials were unwilling to commit themselves in writing in connection with the controversial Russian questions. In early April 1945, for instance, a memorandum from Vice Admiral C. M. Cooke to Admiral Ernest King states:

> In making an outline of the factors bearing on our strategy against JAPAN, I have not included very much about RUSSIA. In this there are so many political aspects that it seems better for them not be be [*sic*] included in a Joint Chiefs of Staff paper, but, nevertheless, they should be borne in mind in any oral conversations with the President.[3]

Fourth, it is also possible to demonstrate that evidence concerning some of the most important discussions relating to this issue was expressly destroyed. For instance, the Russian issue was a central concern during an important May 15, 1945, meeting of the secretary of war, secretary of the navy, acting secretary of state, and Ambassador Averell Harriman. Summary minutes by John J. McCloy note that the very first matter taken up was a memorandum by Joseph Grew on the "Yalta Agreements relating to the Soviet Union and the possible entry of that country into the Japanese war." It was, Stimson observed, a "red hot session."[4]

Although a sketchy report is contained in the brief minutes prepared by McCloy, his recently opened diary indicates that a much more specific discussion of some kind was recorded but that it was decided this could not be allowed to remain in the written record. On May 18, 1945, McCloy noted:

> 10:30 Joseph Grew (Under Secretary of State) telephoned re Committee of Three Minutes – asked that one page be briefed for the record and that part of the original report [be] destroyed.[5]

Like Cooke's memorandum to King, the McCloy diary suggests that some of the most important issues concerning Soviet entry into the war at this time were (and still are) shrouded in secrecy. It is a reasonable assumption that other sensitive discussions either were kept at the "oral" level, or if recorded, may have been similarly destroyed.

Fifth, until very recently key components of the top-secret records of the Military Intelligence Division (MID—also known as G-2) for World War II in general—and for this period in particular—could not be located. Sanho Tree investigated this matter in depth over a long period and found that although some administrative papers, publications, and some "ULTRA" material (i.e., intelligence derived from intercepted enemy codes and ciphers) had been released, officials at the National Archives, U.S. Army historians, and personnel at INSCOM (the Army's Intelligence and Security Command) all stated that they simply did not know the whereabouts of many of the G-2 records. As late as November 1994—as this study was nearing completion—Clifford L. Snyder of the National Archives staff wrote: "We searched the records of the Records of the Army Staff (Record Group 319) but were unable to locate" the high-level G-2 Papers of World War II which had been requested.[6] At the very end of 1994 some of the files were located. But given the classified nature even of the index, only a long and tedious process is likely to fully illuminate their contents. (Fortunately, as we shall see, other evidence leaves little doubt as to the general understanding of intelligence specialists—and some of the new documents which have begun to surface help round out the general picture.*)

Sixth, at the very highest level—and even on its own terms—there is something odd about information we have concerning the way President Truman reached his judgments on this issue during the critical months of May and June 1945, when several major decisions were made and consolidated. In general, we know that the president was understandably very deliberate about military-related matters. Not only was he new to his job, he was especially new to the many complex considerations involved in decisions which could mean life or death for thousands of American servicemen. Furthermore, minimizing casualties was one of Truman's highest priorities, and, as we have seen, he clearly sought all the military advice he could get.[7] Given all this, it is peculiar that we do not have any documents which record the specific discussions which must have taken place when the president decided to revise major military judgments concerning the role of the Soviet Union during this period.

Finally, subsequent suppression of specific evidence related to this matter can also be documented—especially during the Cold War. Many earlier studies which cover these events, for instance, rely on a 1955 Defense Department publication, *The Entry of the Soviet Union into the War Against Japan: Military Plans, 1941–1945*. This official report published for the first time excerpts from many important 1945 documents concerning the role Russian participation in the Pacific War played in U.S. military planning. That the report was "sanitized"—and that references to certain documents were eliminated—is evident when it is compared with a recently discovered

---

*With the assistance of Archivist Carey Conn of the National Archives branch at Suitland, MD, many "finished" reports and lower-level administrative papers of the Military Intelligence Division (MID) have been located. However, most of the top-secret and ULTRA-level (cryptographically derived) supporting materials are missing. Some ULTRA-related material can be found in Record Group 457 (Records of the National Security Agency), but this does not account for the "missing mass" of the G-2 papers. For example, the top-secret office papers of Major General Clayton L. Bissell, the head of MID, have never been found. The same is true for the office papers of Brigadier General Carter Clarke, the "king of MAGIC." Thus, we know very little about the high-level inner workings of Army Intelligence or even about the general operations of the "specialists" who produced many of the estimates cited in this book. Even a cursory study of the Intelligence "P" files in Record Group 319 shows that many, many thousands of person-hours went into the production of these reports, but very little supporting documentation has been located.

unpublished version of the same document. For instance, the top-secret version (entitled *United States Interest in the Entry of the USSR in the War Against Japan*, and made available only in 1991) contains a section on Japanese peace feelers not included in the 1955 publication, and also contains the previously cited unedited minutes of the June 18, 1945, White House military planning meeting which, as we have seen, ends with a cryptic sentence almost certainly referring to the atomic bomb:

> The president and the Chiefs of Staff then discussed certain other matters.[8]

Evidentiary details of this kind are often left unstated, or relegated to technical reference notes. They are important reminders, however, that some early accounts of the president's strategy toward the Russians after March 1945 relied more on guesswork than on documentary evidence—and, too, that it was apparently felt that something quite sensitive had to be kept under wraps.

Franklin Delano Roosevelt died on April 12, 1945. Seemingly, U.S. policy was then clear: Soviet help against Japan was essential—especially to pin down the Japanese armies operating in Manchuria so as to make it impossible for them to reinforce the home islands when a U.S. invasion began.

Something very strange, however, happened at the end of April and during May and June 1945—something noticed by only a handful of insiders at the time and only occasionally acknowledged in subsequent reports: The United States Government, which had been ardently pressing for Red Army help to support an invasion—"a prerequisite to a landing" that year, Marshall called it as late as April 12—suddenly reversed field and appeared to lose interest in a Soviet declaration of war.

Then, just as suddenly, the United States reversed itself again, and once more began pressing intensely—including a special effort managed at the presidential level—for an early Soviet attack.

Why?

We know something about how this double reversal of emphasis occurred (and, too, how yet another reversal was subsequently to take place in late July), but there are once more important gaps in the record—especially concerning Truman's precise views through the course of the various shifts. It is possible, however, to document the most important general factors that informed U.S. decision-making—beginning with the April "about-face."

In the rapid decline of Japanese military power, as we have noted, April 1945 was an especially cruel month. A substantial change in Japan's internal politics was signaled when the nine-month-old Koiso government fell and Admiral Baron Kantaro Suzuki was appointed premier.[9] The previously cited OSS study observed: "Admiral Suzuki's appointment strongly suggests that Japan is laying the groundwork for a peace offensive."[10]

The Soviet decision not to renew its Neutrality Pact was especially important. It was impossible to mistake the implications of an official Soviet note in early April which now—after four full years of war—suddenly declared that "Japan, an ally of Germany, helps the latter in her war against the U.S.S.R."—and that "Under these circumstances the neutrality pact between Japan and the U.S.S.R. has lost its sense and a prolongation of this pact is impossible."[11]

Clearly Stalin planned to honor his pledge to enter the war roughly three months after the defeat of Germany. There would be no other reason to make a declaration of this kind—especially since it sent a message which could easily lead to a pre-emptive Japanese strike before Soviet troop strength had been fully established in the Far East.

A related OSS research report pointed out that throughout the summer and fall of 1944 "the Soviet press and public lectures devoted increasing attention to the war between Japan and Russia's Western allies, stressing Allied victories and Japan's weakness as though preparing the Soviet public for a radical change in Russo-Japanese relations."

> Then came Stalin's speech on the 27th Anniversary of the Revolution (November 6, 1944) in which he specifically labelled Japan an aggressor nation. Nine days after this first open denunciation of Japan, a Soviet military commentator, pointing out that Japan was heading for defeat, reminded his audience that Japan had attacked and raided the USSR several times.[12]

Still another April 1945 OSS study noted that under the terms of the Neutrality Pact hostilities could not begin until April 25, 1946, but suggested the rather obvious point that "the Russians may prefer to enter the war against Japan before then. . . ."[13] (OSS analysts, of course, did not know of Stalin's secret pledge.)

MAGIC intercept summaries contributed additional information on Japanese concerns. One observed that on "April 6—the day after the blow fell—[Japan's Ambassador] Sato insisted that Russia's move might well be only a gesture crudely designed to placate America and England, . . . but by [April] 8th he had apparently been compelled to view the matter as 'something more fundamental.' "[14] An intercepted message from the vice chief of the Japanese Army General Staff to Tokyo's military attaché in Berlin judged that the Soviet Union "will carefully gauge the decline in Japan's military strength and at an appropriate stage of the American offensive will probably seize some pretext or other to enter the war against our country."[15]

Although Japanese diplomats continued to hope for a substantial delay in a Red Army attack, military intelligence officers monitoring Soviet troop movements could hardly ignore the obvious transfers to the Far East: Reports of such shifts also began appearing frequently in the MAGIC intercepts being read by U.S. officials. An April 14 message from Sato, for instance, noted that

A courier who arrived here [Moscow] on the 11th reports that during his journey across Siberia he observed some 25,000 men, 540 to 550 planes, 150 tanks, and about 540 to 550 motor vehicles being transported eastward.[16]

The assessment of the chief of intelligence in Mountbatten's South East Asia Allied Headquarters was that:

In view of Japan's fear of RUSSIA's military might and of communism, the denunciation of the Pact is likely to hasten Japan's preparations for a peace move. It would be to Japan's advantage to capitulate before RUSSIA is ready to join in the war, which may not be until the Autumn of 1945.[17]

One did not need access to special intelligence materials, however, to understand the meaning of the Soviet decision to publicly renounce the neutrality pact; it was self-evident to any serious observer—inside or outside the government. *The New York Times* put it this way:

A double blow as staggering as any military defeat she has suffered, and in its cumulative effect perhaps even more devastating to her hopes, has been inflicted on Japan by Moscow's curt denunciation of the Russo-Japanese neutrality pact, and the resignation of the Koiso Cabinet. . . . [T]hese two events . . . tell the Japanese people beyond all prevarication of propaganda that they have lost the war.[18]

On April 15, Stalin again explicitly confirmed both his intention to enter the war two to three months after the defeat of Germany and his willingness to support Chiang Kai-shek. At this time, a specific understanding to implement the details of the accord negotiated at Yalta was worked out in conversations with General Patrick J. Hurley, the U.S. Special Representative and Ambassador to China: Truman would arrange to have Chinese Foreign Minister T. V. Soong come to Moscow and at that time treaties embodying Stalin's support for Chiang and Chiang's approval of the Yalta understanding would be negotiated. Then Stalin would declare war.[19]

At almost exactly the same time these arrangements were being completed, a quiet reassessment of basic assumptions was slowly beginning to develop at various lower levels within the U.S. government. The new thinking was often only fragmentarily reported (and, too, poorly understood) in subsequent accounts—in part because many relevant documents were kept classified for so long. However, it is quite clear that a very different strategic understanding steadily began to influence political-military thinking at this time. Eerily, it occurred at almost the precise moment Harry Truman took over the Oval Office on Roosevelt's death.

One aspect of the decline of Japanese power in particular had taken on special significance: the U.S. Navy gained sufficient control of Japanese waters so that it would soon be feasible to cut off all troop movements between the Chinese mainland and the home islands. On April 25 the Joint Staff Planners reported to the Joint Chiefs of Staff:

> Because of our estimated ability to interdict Japanese movement between the Asiatic mainland and Japan proper, early Russian entry into the war against Japan and attendant containing of the Kwantung army is no longer necessary to make invasion feasible.[20]

An April 25 intelligence report concerning Japanese shipping losses also noted

> a Tokyo broadcast on 17 February, in which the Japanese forces in China and other overseas garrisons were warned that they might have to operate without help from the homeland.[21]

What had previously been deemed a critical function of Russian military assistance now appeared to be essentially beside the point. Although it had been hoped the Red Army would pin down the Japanese armies in Manchuria so as to prevent them from reinforcing the home islands during an invasion, this now no longer seemed necessary. The U.S. Navy would make it just about impossible for reinforcements to return from the mainland in any event.

Other changes in the military situation also began to impact earlier assessments of the value of Soviet assistance. Originally it had been thought important to use Siberian air bases to launch long-range heavy-bomber attacks against Japan. However, as an official War Department historian—Louis Morton—later noted: "What had appeared extremely desirable at the beginning of the year, by late spring was appearing less so. . . . The B-29s from the Marianas, with fighter support from Iwo Jima, were proving so effective that the need for bases in Siberia seemed less pressing than before."[22] A study directed by General John Deane, chief of the military mission to Moscow, concluded that the Siberian air bases would not be worth their cost.

Furthermore, planners under Deane's direction also concluded that the United States should not make a major effort to keep a Pacific supply route to Russia open. In any event "there would be enough supplies on hand to maintain Russian military forces for three to six months."

According to Premier Stalin a three-month supply would suffice, for he had estimated that the Japanese war would last only two and a half to three months after the Soviet Union entered the conflict. In addition, the victories of American forces in the Pacific made it unlikely that the Japanese would be able to engage in extended counter operations against the Red Army in the Far East.[23]

A psychological fact of some significance also began to impact planning. Relations with the Russians, always somewhat rocky, deteriorated after Yalta—at both the personal and the political level. By his own admission, Deane had "become gradually nauseated by Russian food, vodka, and protestations of friendship."[24] The difficulties he had encountered negotiating Siberian air bases and Pacific supply routes had convinced him that it was not in the interest of the United States to establish full military links with the Soviet Union. "Soviet demands on our resources," he complained to the Joint Chiefs of Staff in mid-April, "have been honored wherever possible and without requiring supporting facts. . . ."

It would seem that a program such as ours could have resulted only in the gratitude and friendship of the Soviet Union. Such has not proven to be the case. Russian officials have a historic and inherent distrust of foreigners, Americans included.[25]

Deane believed that after her extraordinary victories against Hitler's armies Russia had become "so sure of her strength as to assume an attitude of dominance with respect to her allies." Judging that "[a]t this stage of the war, military collaboration with the Soviet Union is not vital to the United States," he recommended that the United States "cease forcing ourselves on the Soviet Union"—and instead "wait for the Soviet authorities to come to us on matters which require collaboration."[26]

On April 16, four days after Roosevelt's death, Deane, back from Moscow, made his recommendations to the Joint Chiefs. The Chiefs in turn canceled the Siberian air base project and postponed work on the Pacific supply route. In addition, they decided to slow down and limit general military collaboration with the Soviets, and they ordered that no additional non-essential personnel join the U.S. Military Mission in Moscow.[27]

While some military planners still felt Soviet help might be useful in connection with an invasion—particularly if there was no change in the "unconditional surrender" demand—the dominant view was no longer what it had been only a few months earlier. Precisely how different officials at various levels of government felt about these matters at different points in time

is difficult to determine. It is, however, quite clear that the military shifts—
and the reduced dependence on the Soviet Union—in turn permitted a series
of major diplomatic changes.

By this time Averell Harriman had also become increasingly fed up with
Russian bureaucracy and negotiating tactics—indeed, with Russia in general.
A draft April cable found in Harriman's recently opened papers (1986)—
marked "Not Sent" (but taken to Washington as a memorandum)—gives a
sense of his personal frustration:

> I sincerely believe that one of our underlying difficulties in our relations
> with the Soviet Union since the war is that our decisions in connection
> with the Soviet Union have been influenced by a sense of fear on our
> part. . . .
>   I recommend in the strongest terms that I can express that I be given
> some concrete means of showing the Russian officials that their outra-
> geous actions against us are affecting their vital interests. The longer we
> wait the more difficult it will be and the more drastic the action on our
> part will have to be.[28]

Recent research by Professor Diane Clemens has added considerable illumination to an additional factor which contributed to the atmosphere in
which this level of frustration developed. During March 1945 secret OSS negotiations with Nazi-related intermediaries in Berne, Switzerland, gave rise
to intense Soviet suspicions. Harriman had initially told Molotov the talks
were about surrender. However, on March 15 Molotov was informed that the
purpose of the talks was only to make contact with a view to bringing German military representatives to Allied headquarters. The Russians were obviously dubious and feared the West might be negotiating an arrangement
which would stiffen German resistance on the Soviet front in order to allow
the West to gain greater control of German territory. "In this instance the
Soviet Government sees not a misunderstanding," Molotov declared on
March 21, "but something worse."

> [N]egotiations have been going on for two weeks at Bern, behind
> the back of the Soviet Union which is bearing the brunt of the war
> against Germany. . . . The Soviet Government considers this absolutely
> impermissible. . . .[29]

Molotov's statement, in turn, touched off a high-level exchange between
Roosevelt and Stalin. The president continued to deny Soviet participation in
the talks but promised that if a meeting to discuss surrender details were arranged, Soviet representatives would be welcome. At this, Stalin replied:

the Germans have already taken advantage of the talks . . . to move three divisions from Northern Italy to the Soviet front. . . . This circumstance irritates the Soviet Command and engenders distrust. . . . In a situation of this kind Allies should have nothing to conceal from each other.[30]

Both Stalin and Roosevelt were obviously disturbed by the charges and countercharges which OSS maneuvering had produced. It is Clemens' thesis that Harriman took advantage of tensions arising out of the "Berne incident" to press arguments for a "reversal" of policy he had long been wanting to make in any event.[31] An early April cable from Harriman recommended that U.S. leaders "clearly recognize that the Soviet program is the establishment of totalitarianism, ending personal liberty and democracy as we know and respect it."[32]

The most obvious leverage the United States had was economic assistance, and Harriman now urged that "we face the realities of the situation and orient our foreign economic policy accordingly." Friendly relations and cooperation with the Soviet Union were important, but things should be "on a *quid pro quo* basis."[33] Another cable argued that "the time has come when we must by our actions in each individual case make it plain to the Soviet Government that they cannot expect our continued cooperation on terms laid down by them." Though at first there may be "adverse repercussions,"

. . . on the other hand we have evidence that in cases where they have been made to feel that their interests were being adversely affected we have obtained quick and favorable action.[34]

Harriman, who had not received much encouragement from Roosevelt, jumped at the opportunity presented by Truman's succession to the presidency. In an exhausting forty-nine-hour flight he rushed home to press his argument for a tougher line.[35] He met with Truman for the first time on April 20 and thereafter began a round of consultations to urge a reorientation of policy throughout the government.[36]

Our interest at this point is not so much with Harriman's specific diplomatic concerns (which centered particularly on Eastern Europe and Poland).* It is with how U.S. leaders weighed the importance of a Russian declaration of war—as revealed by their willingness to get tough with the Russians about such issues.

Poland in particular was a test case. At Yalta the Big Three had signed a confusingly worded agreement which provided for the establishment of a "new government" in Poland. This seemed to indicate that the existing gov-

---

*See below, pp. 174–81, for a discussion of Harriman's related worries about Asia.

ernment (which was sympathetic to the Soviets) would be changed. However, the agreement also stated that it would simply be "reorganized" on a broader democratic basis "with the inclusion of democratic leaders from Poland itself and from Poles abroad."[37] What this really meant was by no means obvious and a commission made up of Harriman, Molotov, and the British ambassador to the Soviet Union, Sir A. Clark Kerr, began consultations in Moscow to try to implement the understanding. After a fairly harmonious beginning the discussions ran into problems, and by April had more or less reached a stalemate.[38]

Harriman and others feared a government composed primarily of politicians favorable to Moscow would set a precedent for other regimes to be established throughout Eastern Europe. In his April 20 meeting with Truman, Harriman warned that what "we were faced with was a 'barbarian invasion of Europe' . . ."—and recommended that Truman take a tough stand:

> He said that he thought the Soviet Government did not wish to break with the United States since they needed our help in order to reduce the burden of reconstruction and that he felt we had nothing to lose by standing firm on issues that were of real importance to us.[39]

Harriman strongly urged that Truman reconsider Roosevelt's conciliatory policies. Above all, he wanted an early confrontation with Stalin over Eastern Europe—before the U.S. Army left the Continent to fight in the Pacific.

There was, of course, a significant risk that a tough line with the Russians over Poland would jeopardize what had formerly seemed absolutely critical—early Red Army help against Japan.

In the very first days of his presidency, Truman did nothing to alter the understanding which had been reached at Yalta. On April 19, a week after taking office—and one day before his first meeting with Harriman—he told T. V. Soong that he should go to Moscow "as soon as he could, so that relations between China and Russia could be established on a firmer basis. . . ."[40] On April 22, he also reaffirmed Roosevelt's Far Eastern pledges in a discussion with Molotov:

> The President said he stood squarely behind all commitments and agreements taken by our late great President and that he would do everything he could to follow along that path. . . .
>
> Mr. Molotov then inquired whether the agreements in regard to the Far Eastern situation made at Yalta still stood. The President replied that they did and repeated that he intended to carry out all of the agreements made by President Roosevelt.[41]

Despite such statements, it is obvious that the new hard line of advice had reached—and impacted—the new president. Moreover, Truman was personally more in tune with the tougher approach than Roosevelt had been. In his April 20 meeting with Harriman, for instance, Truman told the ambassador that "in his considered opinion unless settlement of the Polish question was achieved along the lines of the Crimean decision that the treaty of American adherence to a world organization would not get through the Senate"—and that "he intended to tell Molotov just this in words of one syllable":

> The President said that he was not in any sense afraid of the Russians and that he intended to be firm but fair since in his opinion the Soviet Union needed us more than we needed them. . . . The President again repeated that he intended to be firm with the Russians and make no concessions from American principles or traditions for the fact of winning their favor.[42]

On April 23, Truman called in his top advisers for a strategy session in preparation for a second meeting with Molotov. The president's general attitude—only eleven days after taking office—has been well documented. Again, of particular interest is how—at this point—he (and his advisers) judged the specific value of Soviet assistance in the war against Japan.

The diplomatic dispute continued to revolve around the potentially precedent-setting composition of the government to be established in Poland. As Truman had stated in his meeting with Molotov, "In its larger aspects, the Polish question [has] become for our people the symbol of the future development of our international relations." Secretary of State Edward Stettinius opened the strategy session with a report on Molotov's arrival and his activities in Washington. Truman followed with a summary of his first meeting with Molotov, and almost immediately stressed that

> he felt our agreements with the Soviet Union so far had been a one way street and that could not continue; it was now or never. He intended to go on with the plans for San Francisco and if the Russians did not wish to join us they could go to hell. . . .

A survey of his advisers produced these opinions:

> Mr. Stimson . . . said that without fully understanding how seriously the Russians took this Polish question we might be heading into very dangerous water.
>
>   Mr. Forrestal said that he felt that this difficulty over Poland could not be treated as an isolated incident. . . . He said it was his profound conviction that if the Russians were to be rigid in their attitude we had better have a showdown with them now than later.

Ambassador Harriman . . . said obviously we were faced with a possibility of a real break with the Russians but he felt that if properly handled it might be avoided. . . .

Admiral Leahy said . . . that he felt that it was a serious matter to break with the Russians but that we should tell them that we stood for a free and independent Poland.

General Marshall . . . said from the military point of view the situation in Europe was secure but that they hoped for Soviet participation in the war against Japan at a time when it would be useful to us. The Russians had it within their power to delay their entry into the Far Eastern war until we had done all the dirty work. . . .

General Deane said that he felt that the Soviet Union would enter the Pacific war as soon as it was able irrespective of what happened in other fields.

Just before dismissing his advisers, Truman made his own views crystal-clear. The president stressed that in his judgment

from a military point of view there was no reason why we should fail to stand up to our understanding of the Crimean agreements [on Eastern Europe and Poland]. . . .[43]

In his private diary, Leahy summed up the discussion in regard to the military situation in similar terms:

It was the consensus of opinion of the conferees that the time has arrived to take a strong American attitude toward the Soviet, and that no particular harm can come to our war prospects even if Russia should slow down or even stop its war effort in Europe and in Asia.[44]

At 5:30 the same day, Truman went into a second meeting with Molotov as he had said he would—uncompromising, and on the offensive. In candid language (which, Leahy observed, was "not at all diplomatic"),

The President [stated] with great firmness that an agreement had been reached on Poland and that it only remained for Marshal Stalin to carry it out in accordance with his word.

In response, Molotov stated that he could not understand why an agreement on Poland could not be made along the same lines as that which had been made on Yugoslavia (where roughly four out of five Cabinet posts went to officials "friendly" to the Soviet Union), and the minutes again note:

The President replied sharply that an agreement had been reached on Poland and that it only required carrying out by the Soviet Government.

To this Molotov again said that he could not see how his government had broken any agreement, and "he added that surely the Polish question involving a neighboring country was of very great interest to the Soviet Government."

At the end of the meeting—having reached no accord—Truman

> repeated that as he had said last night the United States Government was prepared to carry out loyally all the agreements reached at the Crimea and he only asked that the Soviet Government do the same. The President said that he desired the friendship of the Soviet Government, but that he felt it could only be on the basis of mutual observation of agreements and not on the basis of a one way street.[45]

Although contemporaneous documents do not record it, Truman later recalled in his memoirs that at this Molotov declared, "I have never been talked to like that in my life." Truman also reports that he then responded, "Carry out your agreements and you won't get talked to like that."[46]

Harriman had stressed that given the Soviet Union's huge needs, the leverage of U.S. economic assistance could be substantial.[47] In his meeting with Molotov, Truman hinted broadly

> that in his last message to Marshal Stalin on April 1 President Roosevelt had made it plain in that no policy in the United States whether foreign or domestic could succeed unless it enjoyed public confidence and support. He said that this applied of necessity to economic collaboration as well as political. The President added that legislative appropriation was required for any economic measures in the foreign field and that he could not hope to get these measures through Congress unless there was public support for them.[48]

Within less than three weeks this essential message was reinforced when—on May 11—the U.S. cut off lend-lease assistance to the Soviet Union. Ships at sea carrying supplies to Russia were immediately halted and even turned back. Historians have debated whether the lend-lease cutoff was explicitly designed to put pressure on the Soviet Union—or whether it was simply (or partly) the result of overly zealous lower-level officials.[49] Even Harriman came to feel the move was too abrupt.[50]

Lost in much subsequent discussion was an obvious point: If U.S. leaders had still felt strongly that Soviet help was absolutely essential for an invasion, it would be difficult to imagine any responsible official urging or permitting so significant an alliance-jeopardizing move—especially since it might result in the loss of American lives in the war against Japan.

Nor is there much doubt about the fundamental point: A very different conception of the value of Soviet military assistance had now become the basis of official U.S. policy. Truman himself had been explicit about the matter, and it is especially instructive to note the official military judgments made at this time.

Earlier, as we have seen, the Joint Chiefs of Staff had expressed a strong desire for Russian entry at the earliest possible date.[51] On April 25—two days after the president's meeting with Molotov—the Joint Staff Planners forwarded the detailed report on invasion strategy we noted above to the Joint Chiefs. Even though the Planners were still able to assume no change in the demanding unconditional surrender formula, in their overall recommendations for Pacific strategy they advised that "Because of our estimated ability to interdict Japanese movement between the Asiatic mainland and Japan proper, early Russian entry into the war against Japan . . . is no longer necessary to make invasion feasible."[52]

On May 10 the Joint Chiefs officially noted the Planners report, making it the basis for future U.S. military planning.[53]

Chapter 9

PHASE III: THE NEW REALITY

An important point about Russian participation in the war is that the impact of Russian entry on the already hopeless Japanese may well be the decisive action levering them into capitulation at the time or shortly thereafter if we land in Japan.

—General George C. Marshall, June 18, 1945

There is a certain irony—or perhaps amnesia—in much postwar historical reporting of these developments. This is especially the case with regard to the April military judgment: Over the years many writers were to note the tough diplomatic line taken by Truman in the last week of April—and some observed in passing that U.S. military leaders no longer felt Soviet help was necessary for an invasion.[1] A very few acknowledged that the president's ability to be so forceful with Molotov on the Polish problem was related to the new military situation—"that no particular harm could be done to our war prospects. . . ."[2]

For the most part, however, writers commonly treated the revised military assessment superficially. Typical accounts of this period reported in very general terms that the United States sought Soviet help during the summer of 1945; there was little pause to examine critical shifts in position. Most simply ignored the huge fact that at this particular juncture Soviet help simply was no longer deemed essential.

In fairness, for much of the postwar era quite understandable complications clouded the situation. For one thing, within a very short time the president once more actively began to seek Soviet help. It was relatively easy to miss the double shift in his attitude during a period of less than four weeks—especially for historians writing in the years before some of the most important documents were declassified. (That the president altered his view once again several weeks later—on the basis of a still different military analysis—was also not always easy to discover from the early documents.)

Some confusion can also be traced to the difference between "evidence" found at different levels of government. For most of the summer of 1945 the officially stated policy was still "unconditional surrender"—a demand which virtually guaranteed a long, long fight.[3] It is thus not surprising that despite the clear late April presidential judgment, several documents suggest that the Red Army could continue to play an important role in forcing the surrender of Japanese soldiers in Manchuria: The idea makes a good deal of sense if one assumes no change in the surrender terms.

On the other hand, one of the specific advantages of allowing Japan to keep the Emperor was precisely that he could order troops in Manchuria and elsewhere to lay down their arms, whether or not the Red Army intervened. At the highest level of government, as Leahy subsequently remarked, "We were certain that the Mikado could stop the war with a royal word"—and in a 1954 interview Truman forcefully recalled Marshall's similar advice that

> the million two hundred thousand Japanese in China . . . would never surrender unless the Emperor of Japan ordered it and he was of the opinion that if the Emperor made such an order we could get complete surrender—that was the only way we could get it.[4]

Another source of confusion in some accounts derives from a failure to clearly distinguish between several rather complicated tactical changes in the president's overall diplomatic approach to the Soviet Union at this time.

Still, there is no question about the main issue—and, too, about the beginning and end points of the story. Although in late April Soviet help was no longer deemed essential, within a few weeks, securing Stalin's cooperation and assistance once more became a primary objective. Why did what was not deemed important in late April become very important again as the summer progressed?

The most obvious reason the shift occurred is that although Red Army help for an invasion was no longer required, it now increasingly appeared that a Russian declaration of war might well make an invasion unnecessary. A recent assessment is that of John Ray Skates:

> [By the summer of 1945] Soviet entry was no longer needed to assure the success of OLYMPIC [the Kyushu landing]. Nonetheless, a Soviet declaration of war against Japan might provide the shock that would bring the Japanese leaders to accept unconditional surrender. . . .[5]*

---

*Note that the objective here is still "unconditional surrender." Skates also observed that "Soviet participation would preclude the necessity for landing American forces on mainland Asia." (Skates, *The Invasion of Japan*, p. 227.)

As we have seen, the previous September Churchill had suggested the mere announcement of Soviet intentions might precipitate a surrender. As Japan's situation further deteriorated, related judgments began to appear at various levels throughout the U.S. government.[6] Especially important in this regard were assessments made by staff specialists for the Joint Chiefs. Immediately after the collapse of the Koiso government and Stalin's announcement that the Neutrality Pact with Japan would not be renewed, the Joint Intelligence Committee addressed the issue in response to the following questions posed as "a matter of priority" by the Joint War Plans Committee:

a. At what stage of the war will the Japanese realize the inevitability of absolute defeat?
b. Will such realization result in their unconditional surrender, passive submission without surrender, or continuing resistance until subdued by force?[7]

After consulting with the Joint Intelligence Staff, the Joint Intelligence Committee forwarded its response to the Chiefs in the form of an April 29 "Memorandum for Information." This pointed out that increasing "numbers of informed Japanese, both military and civilian, already realize the inevitability of absolute defeat." It noted, however, that the still indeterminate nature of relations among the Big Three—and of Russia's role—played a critical role in Japanese judgments. Thus,

military and political authorities, as well as the people generally, may retain the desperate hope that continued resistance will permit the development of such disunity and war-weariness among the United Nations as to enable them to obtain peace without unconditional surrender.

The "Japanese will realize that absolute defeat is inevitable," the committee advised, "when they perceive that their armed forces are incapable of arresting the progressive destruction of their basic economy." The committee further advised that:

The increasing effects of air-sea blockade, the progressive and cumulative devastation wrought by strategic bombing, and the collapse of Germany (with its implications regarding redeployment) should make this realization widespread within the year.

A Russian decision to join with the United States and Britain, however, would have enormous force and would dramatically alter the equation:

The entry of the U.S.S.R. into the war would, together with the foregoing factors, convince most Japanese at once of the inevitability of complete defeat.[8]

The Joint Intelligence Committee was still, of course, working within the confines of "unconditional surrender." It pointed out that "the Japanese have never been forced to accept a national unconditional surrender to a foreign power. Japanese behavior in the circumstances envisaged cannot, therefore, be predicted with assurance." Even so, Japan's situation was so desperate that although "individual Japanese willingly sacrifice themselves in the service of the nation,"

> we believe that the nation as a whole is not pre-disposed toward national suicide. Rather, the characteristic fanaticism of the Japanese seems based upon a strong concept of national survival as the supreme desideratum, regardless of the fate of individuals. In this concept, national survival, even through surrender, would be preferable to virtual extinction. . . .

The central conclusion flowing from these considerations—and highlighted by the Joint Intelligence Committee—was a kind of "two-step logic":

> If . . . the Japanese people, as well as their leaders, were persuaded both that absolute defeat was inevitable and that unconditional surrender did not imply national annihilation, surrender might follow fairly quickly.[9]

Put simply, the "two-step logic" involved what in retrospect seems a rather obvious (though little discussed) strategic judgment which may be stated as follows: There must first be a "realization of the inevitability of defeat"—which, as noted, the JIC judged a Soviet declaration of war would produce; and, second, a clarification of the unconditional surrender language (so it would not imply "national annihilation") would then likely bring about a fairly quick surrender.

Some of the drafts leading up to this final paper contain additional language which gives a feel for the developing sense of Japan's impending collapse among intelligence specialists. For instance, the initial April 11 response of the Joint Intelligence Staff (a first draft of what became the April 29 Committee report) pointed out that a large number of informed Japanese realized the inevitability of defeat—despite the fact that it was "only very recently that the full power and potential of Allied capabilities are being brought home to the masses of Japanese living in the home islands."

> By the autumn of 1945, we believe that the vast majority of Japanese will realize the inevitability of absolute defeat regardless of whether the U.S.S.R. has actually entered the war against Japan.

And, again, of course: "If at any time the U.S.S.R. should enter the war, all Japanese will realize that absolute defeat is inevitable."

This paper, too, offered a clear statement of the "two-step logic": "by mid-summer or certainly before the end of 1945, we anticipate that the Japanese government will seek ways and means to accomplish surrender without the stigma of admitting that it is 'unconditional.' "

> If the Japanese can find the means or method to rationalize surrender, we believe that they are capable of discontinuing the war and doing their utmost to comply with Allied terms.[10]*

These reports, of course, represent intelligence advice as of April 1945. More than six months were still available before an initial landing could possibly occur; there were roughly ten months yet to go before the 1946 invasion of Japan proper might take place—even on paper. During the weeks and months after these assessments were made Japan's desperate situation became even worse and brought with it further internal pressures for ending the war.

Insight into this matter is also provided by other documents released in recent decades. For instance, the specialist in charge of military intelligence, Major General Clayton Bissell, also stressed the growing political-military shock value of a Russian declaration of war. Bissell's view echoed Churchill's 1944 sense that all that might be needed for the war to end was for the Japanese to believe the Russians would attack. In the previously cited May 15 memorandum to General John E. Hull (in which Bissell recommended that a surrender demand be made at once), Marshall's top intelligence adviser went so far as to suggest:

> The Japanese are gravely concerned about the future attitude of Russia. If they are convinced that Russia will enter the war against them, as some of their leaders are, the present moment will be an excellent one for an unconditional surrender demand upon Japan when she can be assured that surrender would be made to the Anglo-Americans only.[11]

Again note the "unconditional" objective.

Perspective may also be gained by recalling some rather well known facts about internal Japanese political-military relationships. Studies of the Hiroshima decision often observe that although there was a peace faction within the Japanese government, it was opposed by a strong army faction

---

*The JIS also suggested in this draft that if the Japanese were not assured that "unconditional surrender" did not mean national annihilation, "even after the inevitability of absolute defeat becomes apparent to practically all Japanese, it is probable that resistance will continue until subdued by force."

which wished to continue the war at almost any cost. The strength of this group within the Cabinet, however, depended upon three rather distinct factors:

First, of course, was the military, economic, and political situation—which was moving steadily against those who wished to continue the war.

A second factor strongly bolstered the Japanese military: So long as the U.S. continued to demand unconditional surrender, the diehards possessed an all-but-unanswerable argument. To surrender would mean to jeopardize the position of the nation's deity, and perhaps even to place the Emperor at risk of being tried and hanged as a war criminal. (Depriving the diehards of this argument, of course, was at the core of the strategy urged by Grew, Stimson, and others.)

A third factor also sustained the position of the diehards, and although obvious, has rarely been adequately emphasized: As the Joint Intelligence Committee noted, Japanese hopes rested in significant part on the outside possibility of continued Allied disunity. What was true for the government as a whole was particularly true for the Japanese military—who understood only too well what the meaning of a Red Army attack would be. So long as the Soviet Union remained neutral, the Japanese Army especially could continue to argue that all was not lost.

The force of the central point concerning Russian intervention is confirmed by evidence from both old and new Japanese sources. Keeping the Russians out of the battle was a primary objective which dated to the period before Pearl Harbor—and was so defined, for instance, at the Imperial Headquarters' Liaison Conference of November 1941.[12] It was reconfirmed at the 1942 Liaison Conference and—as Japanese historian Tadakichi Tanaka has noted—was a major goal from the beginning to the end of the war.[13] Seizaburo Shinobu notes that the "plan of the decisive battle for the homeland prepared by the Imperial Headquarters . . . required Soviet neutrality or even their favorable moves."[14]

In concrete military terms, the Japanese Army's essential strategy was to fight a massive battle for the homeland. This could not be sustained for long if the Soviet Union declared war and Japan was forced simultaneously to fight the United States in the home islands and the Russians in Manchuria.[15] Since the broad picture from 1941 on is not in doubt, we may note that by April 1945—with the Russian military buildup on the Manchurian border becoming obvious—Japan's Imperial General Headquarters had included the following statement in its overall plan:

The Greater East Asiatic War has now reached such a critical point [that] it was definitely beyond the power of military strategy alone to save the situation.[16]

A "Secret Record" kept by Admiral Sokichi Takagi reveals that in mid-May Navy Minister Admiral Yonai noted: "It seems that the army is losing confidence in the war situation. The army is very afraid of how the Soviets will move. Therefore, they want to

(1) prolong the Neutrality Pact [with the Soviets];
(2) ask the [Soviets] to be an intermediary;
(3) end the Great Asian War."[17]

In fact, the only way Japanese Army leaders could argue the slim hope that the war might continue for more than a short while was to suggest it would somehow be possible to keep the Soviet Union neutral. Which is why, conversely, American officials believed that when the Russians declared war, the "political-military" shock impact would be so great.

Numerous studies undertaken since World War II have analyzed Japanese attempts to keep the Russians out of the war by offering various diplomatic concessions.[18] A 1993 account by Shigehiko Togo (grandson of 1945 Foreign Minister Shigenori Togo) offers a clear analysis, especially of spring maneuvering by army leaders. On April 22, General Kawabe, Vice-Chief of the Army General Staff, and General Arisuye, Chief of the Second Unit (Information Unit) of the General Staff, approached Foreign Minister Togo to ask that he attempt to prevent the U.S.S.R. from ending its neutrality.[19] Shigehiko Togo shows Kawabe addressing the foreign minister with great urgency:

I desperately request you to engage in a once in a lifetime diplomatic *demarche* by offering the Soviets favorable conditions so that they will not change their [neutral] position.[20]

Within the next few days, the Vice-Chief of Navy Staff, Ozawa, and General Umezu, the Chief of the General Staff, also paid separate visits to Togo to urge that the Japanese government undertake a diplomatic initiative to keep Russia neutral.[21]

By April 29, "The Plan to Negotiate with the Soviets," produced by Colonel Tanemura—Chief of the Planning Bureau of the General Staff—stated: "Needless to say, moves of Soviets could be fatal in continuing the Great Asian War, and this has been the matter of greatest concern in planning of the war since before the beginning of the war. . . ."

Even though Japan may have to give up Manchuria, South Sakhalin, Korea, Taiwan, Okinawa, [w]hich means reverting to the borders before the Sino-Japanese War, Japan has to avoid the Soviet entry into the war no matter what, and has to accomplish fighting with the U.S. and U.K.[22]

Although Tanemura's plan did not go forward at this point, at a meeting of the Supreme Council for the Direction of the War held on May 11, 12, and 14, Umezu urged the central importance of preventing a Russian attack.[23] A formal Council decision taken at this time stated:

> While Japan is fighting with the U.S. and U.K., once the Soviets enter the war Japan will face inevitable defeat; therefore, whatever happens in the war with the U.S. and U.K., Japan has to try as much as possible to prevent the Soviet Union from entering the war.[24]

Nor was the central point lost on American officials. In fact, there is evidence that U.S. intelligence experts had intercepted cable traffic between Tokyo and Moscow which revealed Japanese attempts to improve relations between Japan and Russia as early as August 1943.[25] By 1945, one of many broad indications was an intercepted cable from Minister Kase in Berne warning Tokyo on May 14 that "[i]f Russia were to attack us, the situation facing the Empire would get completely out of hand."[26]

As we have noted, at least some intelligence information related to the attitude of the hard-line army group—and what U.S. officials knew of this— was excised from MAGIC reports (and made available in 1993 only after FOIA pressure). This related to a previously released report which, to recall, shows that on May 5, 1945, the following message—sent from the German naval attaché in Tokyo to Admiral Doenitz in Berlin—was intercepted and reported in MAGIC on May 11:

> An influential member of the Admiralty Staff has given me to understand that, since the situation is clearly recognized to be hopeless, large sections of the Japanese armed forces would not regard with disfavor an American request for capitulation even if the terms were hard, provided they were halfway honorable.[27]

We have also noted that oral reports were favored over written reports, and that some documents were destroyed. There is undoubtedly much we do not know concerning these matters—and, especially, how they were evaluated. On the other hand, Japanese proposals for delaying Russian entry or for appeasing the Soviets were the subject of numerous intercepted cables by early 1945. The April announcement that the Soviet Union would not renew its Neutrality Pact produced especially intense activity—and, too, intense efforts to try to pin the Russians down. Instructions on April 24 from Togo to Sato, for instance, stressed:

> Since Japan is facing a grave situation which permits no delay, it is urgently necessary that we should sound out Russia's real intentions

[toward Japan] and exhaust all possibilities of bringing about a new turn in the situation. . . .[28]*

On May 2, in response to growing Japanese-Russian tensions in Manchuria, Togo sent a similar, equally urgent message to his representative in Hsinking (the Japanese administrative center in Manchuria):

it is impossible to exaggerate the importance of our diplomatic policy toward Russia and, needless to say, we must strive to maintain neutrality at all costs.[29]

An intercept from Army Vice Chief of Staff Kawabe to Japanese military attachés in Stockholm and Lisbon (reported in MAGIC May 10 under the heading "Japanese fear of attack by Russia") stated:

Russia's anti-Japanese attitude has clearly become more vigorous since her recent action with respect to the Neutrality Pact. Particularly since late February or mid-March there has been a steady increase in the concentration—[place missing] of Soviet troops, particularly air personnel, which have been transferred from European Russia.†

Kawabe concluded: "We must view with alarm the possibility of future military activity against Japan."[30]

And on May 24, U.S. intelligence analysts noted that Japan's ambassador to Moscow (Sato) "expects Russo-Japanese crisis by mid-summer." Summing up an earlier "gloomy message," the analysts observed:

Sato advised Tokyo that Russia, now having an unprecedented opportunity to "settle her accounts with Japan," might well either enter the war or else seek to mediate a peace which "would be very close to unconditional surrender" and would involve substantial concessions—territorial and otherwise—to Russia.[31]

Roughly the same estimate of how long it would take the Russians to prepare for an attack that Stalin and U.S. officials had agreed upon now also appeared in the intercepts. On May 25 a cable from Togo to Sato summed up the views of Lieutenant Colonel Hamada, an intelligence officer on the Kwantung Army staff, as follows:

The Russians at present have about 40,000 trucks in that area and will need another 60,000 for an invasion of Manchukuo. . . . they will

---

*Brackets in original.
†Brackets in original.

need at least three months to transport the necessary troops and armaments. . . .[32]

As we have noted, several important decisions were made by U.S. officials during the 1945 Memorial Day period. In addition to deferring a clarification of the surrender terms, fundamental recommendations concerning the use of the atomic bomb were also consolidated at this time. At the end of May, too, Roosevelt's aide Harry Hopkins went to Moscow on a special presidential mission and met with Stalin. Reliable information on all the considerations which led to the Hopkins mission, like documents concerning the Russian option during the month of May, is very difficult to come by. We do know, however, that also at this time the Stalin-Hopkins talks reached a critical point—especially concerning Red Army help against the Japanese:

First, Stalin strongly reaffirmed his pledge to enter the war at an early point. Second, on May 30—contrary to the hard-line position it had adopted in April—the United States now essentially agreed to accept the Russian demand for a Polish government dominated by officials friendly to Moscow.

Though it is impossible to prove precisely what happened, it is reasonable to assume these two developments were not completely unrelated. The essential point for our purposes concerns Russian help: Hopkins met with Stalin on the evening of May 26 and—in stark contrast to the president's late April position—at Truman's behest told the Soviet premier that among other things "he wished to discuss" the Pacific War and the future relations of the United States and Soviet Union with China.

> He said that although he realized the answer would depend on a good many considerations it would be most useful to the American military authorities if he could take back some idea of the approximate date of the entry of the Soviet Union into the war in the Pacific.[33]

On May 28, Stalin reaffirmed his pledge that the Red Army would be prepared to march by August 8 (three months after Germany's May 8 collapse). He stated, however, that no troops would be committed until final agreement on the Yalta accord had been reached with China. Stalin suggested that T. V. Soong come to Moscow "possibly the first part of July."[34] On May 29 Hopkins advised Truman: "[T]his procedure seems most desirable from our point of view. . . . He left no doubt in our mind that he intends to attack during August. It is therefore important that Soong come here not later than July 1st."[35]

Hopkins also assured the president that "Stalin made [sic] categorical statement that he would do everything he could to promote unification of China under the leadership of Chiang Kai Shek [sic]. . . . He repeated all of his statements made at Yalta, that he wanted a unified and stable China and wanted China to control all of Manchuria as part of a united China."[36]

Also in contrast to the president's tough April position on Poland, Hopkins was allowed to say "he knew that President Roosevelt and now President Truman had always anticipated that the members of the present Warsaw regime would constitute a majority of the new Polish Provisional Government." Hopkins "said he wished to state that without equivocation."[37]

On June 7, Marshall approved and passed along to Stimson a memorandum prepared by the Strategy and Policy Group of the War Department Operations Division. This advised that a Russian declaration of war, either alone or in combination with a landing or "imminent threat of landing," might be enough "to convince [the Japanese] of the hopelessness of their position."[38]

On the same day this memorandum was actually written (June 4), an intercepted cable from the Japanese Foreign Minister in Tokyo—"Togo on Japan's policy toward Russia"—found him again urging his ambassador that

> it is a matter of the utmost urgency that we should not only prevent Russia from entering the war but should also induce her to adopt a favorable attitude toward Japan. I would therefore like you to miss no opportunity to talk to the Soviet leaders.[39]

In another (June 7, 1945) intercept summary—"Japanese report of continued Soviet military movements in the Far East"—MAGIC analysts noted:

> In recent weeks Japanese diplomats and couriers traveling in Siberia have been reporting substantial eastward movements of Soviet troops and military supplies. The latest such report—prepared by a courier who arrived in Moscow on 1 June, and forwarded to Tokyo by Ambassador Sato on the 4th—states that "the Red Army seems to be continuing mass shipments to the Far East. . . ."

This intercept indicated that:

> . . . the courier had seen—during a 68-hour period from 26 May to 29 May—about 200 "transport trains," carrying 1,149 trucks and other vehicles, 435 fighter planes, 98 attack bombers, 391 medium tanks, 66 light tanks, 88 field guns, and 211 small caliber guns.[40]

Again, a June 11 intercept—"Substance of Ambassador Sato's 8 June message to Foreign Minister Togo"—contained the following passage:

> [I]f Russia by some chance should suddenly decide to take advantage of our weakness and intervene against us with force of arms, we would be in a completely hopeless situation. It is clear as day that the Imperial

Army in Manchukuo would be completely unable to oppose the Red Army which has just won a great victory and is superior to us on all points.

Sato as yet saw no definitive sign that Russia intended to intervene. However, he observed that if the Red Army were brought together with Anglo-American air power, "the disparity and strength between the two sides would indeed be so great that there would be no hope at all of saving the Empire." If Russia were to intervene,

> I think that we would have no choice but to reach the decision quickly and, resolving to eat dirt and put up with all sacrifices, fly into her arms in order to save our national structure.[41]

One further item: A June 13, 1945, MAGIC report included a cable sent to Tokyo by the Japanese Counsellor of Naval Affairs in Berne, Captain Nishihara, which indicated that Japanese intelligence had gotten wind of the Yalta agreements and estimated the Russians would declare war in late August. The cable concluded: "Russia's entry into the war would probably bring about the very quick surrender of Japan. . . ."[42]

On June 14—in preparation for the June 18 White House military planning meeting—Truman instructed Admiral Leahy to tell the Joint Chiefs of Staff that "He desires to be informed as to exactly what we want the Russians to do."[43] The main purpose of the June 18 meeting was to discuss plans for the overall military campaign. At the meeting itself the president stated that he wanted to get Russian assistance in the war against Japan.[44]

As we have noted, explicitly excluded from the military discussions was consideration of a political solution to the war; this matter was being handled elsewhere, the president stressed. For planning purposes, "unconditional surrender" was still the objective.

As part of his presentation on military plans during the June 18 meeting, Marshall assessed developments which might bring the Japanese to "capitulate short of complete military defeat . . ." Adopting language very similar to that previously developed by the Operations Division's Strategy and Policy Group, he stated that if a surrender were to occur prior to complete military defeat, it would be because Japan was faced by "the completely hopeless prospect occasioned by"

> (1) destruction already wrought by air bombardment and sea blockade, coupled with (2) a landing indicating the firmness of our resolution, and also perhaps coupled with (3) the entry or threat of entry of Russia into the war.[45]

Marshall subsequently added a further clarification concerning the last issue—one which clearly reflects the changes in April and May. He advised the president directly that:

> An important point about Russian participation in the war is that the impact of Russian entry on the already hopeless Japanese may well be the decisive action levering them into capitulation at that time or shortly thereafter if we land in Japan.[46]

Marshall is here essentially conflating the intelligence advice developed in April with the stream of intercepts and other information which flowed into the Pentagon in the succeeding weeks. It is accordingly useful to examine the advice given to Truman with some care:

First, note carefully the word "if"—a U.S. invasion was clearly not a certainty.

Second, note several other phrases: (1) "the already hopeless Japanese," (2) Russian entry as possibly "the decisive action," (3) "levering them into capitulation."

Third, the attack alone "may well" lever them into capitulation "at that time."

Fourth, note Marshall's recognition that in any event a long invasion involving massive casualties hardly appears to be inevitable ("or shortly thereafter").

Fifth, remember this advice was given on the demanding assumption that the existing official policy of "unconditional surrender" would remain in force. The obvious "two-step logic"—first a Russian attack, then a clarification of the terms—which as early as April had been urged as likely to end the war, was simply not considered in the military planning discussions.

Sixth, and most important, is the date: June 18, 1945—seven weeks before Hiroshima, and four and a half months before a Kyushu landing could begin. During the intervening period much more dramatic evidence of the deterioration of Japanese morale, and of their desire to end the war, poured into Washington (and, soon, Potsdam).

Along these same lines, the next day the OSS Research and Analysis Division produced a sixteen-page "Estimate of the Japanese Economic and Political Situation" which concluded with still another explicit statement of the "two-step logic":

> . . . a realization [of the inevitability of complete defeat] may come after the completion and consolidation of a major landing in Japan Proper; with Russian entrance into the war; or after a protracted seige [*sic*] of intensive bombing. When the inevitability of total defeat is clear to the military, a decision to surrender may be expected, particularly if suffi-

cient assurance has been given of a tolerable post-surrender role for
Japan.[47]

(Here note especially the word "or," indicating the significance of each of
the possible and quite separate factors.)

On June 19—just after he, Forrestal, and Grew discussed Grew's proposal
for a warning to be issued on the fall of Okinawa—Stimson met with Marshall. His diary records:

> He is suggesting an additional sanction to our warning in the shape of
> an entry of the Russians into the war.

Stimson himself goes on to observe: "That would certainly coordinate all the
threats possible to Japan."[48]

In his 1994 study *The Invasion of Japan: Alternative to the Bomb*, John
Ray Skates makes an obvious connection between the evidence we have
of Marshall's viewpoint as expressed on these two succeeding occasions
(June 18 and June 19):

> Marshall . . . pointed out to Stimson the shock value of Soviet entry. It
> might, Marshall pointed out, prove to be the decisive blow to force a
> Japanese surrender. . . .
>
> Stimson and Marshall believed . . . that it could prove to be a heavy
> psychological blow to Japan's political and military leadership.[49]

On June 30, in their "Estimate of the Enemy Situation," the War Department's Intelligence division offered its continuing assessment that:

> It is believed that many Japanese now consider defeat to be probable.
> The increasing effects of sea blockade and the cumulative devastation
> wrought by strategic bombing should make this realization increasingly
> general. The entry of the Soviet Union into the war would finally con-
> vince the Japanese of the inevitability of complete defeat.[50]

In his 1955 memoirs—and on many other occasions—Truman stated that
his "immediate purpose [in going to Potsdam] was to get the Russians into
the war against Japan as soon as possible. . . ."[51] In a little-noticed comment
he also offered a quite specific reason why he judged it essential to do this:

> If the test [of the atomic bomb] should fail, then it would be even more
> important to us to bring about a surrender before we had to make a
> physical conquest of Japan.[52]

PART III

Atomic Diplomacy

I told him that my own opinion was that the time now and the method now to deal with Russia was to keep our mouths shut and let our actions speak for words. The Russians will understand them better than anything else. It is a case where we have got to regain the lead and perhaps do it in a pretty rough and realistic way.
—Secretary of War Henry L. Stimson after a meeting with Assistant Secretary of War John J. McCloy, diary, May 14, 1945

Chapter 10

PRELIMINARIES:
APRIL AND MAY 1945

If expectations were to be realized, [Stimson] told me, the atomic bomb would be certain to have a decisive influence on our relations with other countries. . . . [Byrnes had already told me] that in his belief the bomb might well put us in a position to dictate our own terms at the end of the war.
—Harry S. Truman, *Year of Decisions*

We need to consider a complex series of events which most historians now acknowledge were connected in one way or another with the decision to use the atomic bomb: the obvious impact the new weapon—if it worked—would have on diplomacy in general, and on diplomacy towards the Soviet Union in particular.*

It still surprises many Americans to think that there might be a relationship between the bombing of Hiroshima and diplomatic strategy towards the Soviet Union. Few, for instance, have heard of Albert Einstein's 1946 judgment that the bombing flowed from "a desire to end the war in the Pacific by any means before Russia's participation." (Nor, of course, do many know of Einstein's feeling that "if President Roosevelt had still been there, none of that would have been possible. He would have forbidden such an act."¹)

Also in 1946, the editor of the *Saturday Review of Literature*, Norman Cousins—writing together with former assistant secretary of state and, subsequently, secretary of the air force Thomas K. Finletter—suggested that:

*Selected portions of the following chapters draw upon the argument of my 1965 *Atomic Diplomacy*, where a more extended discussion of some points may be found. This account integrates research findings of the last thirty years as well as new evidence discovered in the course of preparing this book.

The first error was the atomic bombing of Hiroshima. Not the making of the atomic bomb; that we were forced to do out of sheer national preservation, for the enemy was working on atomic weapons as well. It was what we did with the atomic bomb after we made it that was a mountainous blunder. . . .

Can it be that we were more anxious to prevent Russia from establishing a claim for full participation in the occupation against Japan than we were to think through the implications of unleashing atomic warfare?[2]

Similarly, an important essay by left-leaning British Nobel Prize–winning physicist P. M. S. Blackett concluded: ". . . the dropping of the atomic bombs was not so much the last military act of the second World War, as the first major operation of the cold diplomatic war with Russia. . . ."[3]

Although the suggestion that there was a relationship between U.S. diplomatic strategy and the destruction of Hiroshima and Nagasaki was not something most people took seriously in the early postwar decades, this is no longer the case. A major turning point was the release of the full Stimson diaries and the Potsdam papers at the end of the 1950s and beginning of the 1960s. By 1974 a survey of the expert literature by historian Barton J. Bernstein concluded:

> . . . analysts had still not agreed on the major issues raised nearly three decades earlier about the atomic bomb and American foreign policy. . . . Yet, the published studies of the past few years have been more willing to engage in a dialogue . . . and the distance between rival interpretations appearing in the past six years does not seem as great. . . . Ironically, perhaps, Stimson's own . . . belated admission of the great importance of Russia to policymakers and its connection to their wartime thinking about atomic energy, helped ultimately to narrow the gap.[4]

A decade later—in 1985—diplomatic historian Gaddis Smith concluded: "It has been demonstrated that the decision to bomb Japan was centrally connected to Truman's confrontational approach to the Soviet Union."[5] And in 1990 the previously cited Walker review of recent studies reported:

> nearly all students of the events leading to Hiroshima agree that, in addition to viewing it as the means to end the war quickly, the political implications of the bomb figured in the administration's deliberations.[6]

The public at large, many journalists, and some historians have not entirely caught up with modern research. Moreover, although numerous studies have demonstrated that there was, indeed, a relationship between diplomacy and atomic bomb decision-making, it was complex and in many areas is still clouded. Our interest, however, is not to attempt to resolve the many issues of emphasis which are still in dispute in the scholarly literature.* It concerns the question of context.

The primary focal point of the following discussion is the fact that throughout the spring and summer of 1945 American officials developed their thinking on the use of the atomic bomb in close relationship to the planning of U.S. diplomacy towards the Soviet Union. It is also important to note that the public was not aware of this fact at the time or for a very substantial period thereafter.

Beginning in late April 1945 and carrying on with growing clarity in May and June—and then with increasing force on into July and early August—the same people who were involved in atomic-bomb decision-making were also simultaneously engaged in intense discussion of the role the new weapon would play in diplomatic strategy.

At one level, the initial discussions of the Interim Committee established to consider atomic bomb issues took place in an environment heavily influenced by other, more far-reaching debates. At another—and more generally—the record also suggests that at precisely the time it seemed increasingly evident that the war might well be ended by modifying the surrender terms and/or by awaiting the Russian attack, officials steadily became involved with a "second track" of policy development based on the notion that the atomic bomb would likely strengthen the United States against Russia.

A useful way to begin a review of the 1945 policy-making context is to note two "coincidences"—one having to do with the atomic bomb and European diplomacy vis-à-vis the Soviet Union; the other having to do with diplomatic issues in Asia.

• The first atomic test occurred at the Trinity test site in Alamogordo, New Mexico, on July 16, 1945. The next day, July 17, President Truman sat down for his first and only face-to-face meetings with Soviet Premier Joseph Stalin in Babelsberg, Germany, a suburb of Berlin near Potsdam.

• The bombing of Hiroshima took place on August 6. Two days later, on August 8, as previously agreed, the Soviet Union declared war on Japan three months to the day after Germany's surrender. Early the next morning the Red Army rolled across the Manchurian border.

That the close relationship between the two July dates and the two August dates did not occur by mere chance is no longer a matter of dispute. Nor is there any longer much serious argument that the actual decision to use the atomic bomb was made by people innocent of all considerations of power politics.

*See the Afterword for a review.

* * *

The initial phase of the "second track" of thinking about the atomic bomb can be traced to an entirely different set of concerns from those we have so far considered. Indeed, the central focal point could not have been further from the debate over policies related to Japan and the Asian war.

The first detailed information on the atomic bomb, in fact, was not brought to the attention of President Truman in connection with the war against Japan.[7] His initial full briefing on the new weapon came about in the context of a diplomatic confrontation with the Soviet Union. Moreover, the questions in dispute involved Europe, not Asia.

On April 24, 1945, at the height of the tense stand-off with Moscow over Poland—indeed, the day after Truman's White House session with his top advisers and his "showdown" with Molotov—Stimson sent the following letter to Truman:

> Dear Mr. President:
>
>   I think it is very important that I talk with you as soon as possible on a highly secret matter.
>
>   I mentioned it to you shortly after you took office but have not urged it since on account of the pressure you have been under. It, however, has such a bearing on our present foreign relations and has such an important effect upon all my thinking in this field that I think you ought to know about it without much further delay.
>
>   Faithfully yours,
>   Henry L. Stimson
>   Secretary of War[8]

When Stimson's diaries were opened for public inspection, they showed that at the previous White House meeting on Poland he had been troubled, as he wrote, because "I could not point out to [the president] what I thought were the real difficulties of the situation without apparently reflecting on my colleague in the State Department or the young men who were urging him on."[9]

Stimson's note was published in the president's 1955 memoirs. Although Truman explicitly recalled that Stimson wanted to talk with him "about the effect the atomic bomb might likely have on our future foreign relations,"[10] for decades the fact that the first extended discussion of the weapon by the president came up in this connection was largely ignored by most historians. Stimson's acknowledgment that the bomb had "such an important effect upon all my thinking in this field," moreover, was an understatement. The next day, April 25, Truman met with the secretary and with the head of the Manhattan Project, General Leslie R. Groves. In his memoirs Truman writes that Stimson told him that if expectations were realized, the atomic bomb would be certain to have a "decisive" influence on relations with other countries.[11]

Although some points about the meeting are still not clear, Stimson's diary provides a feel for the general atmosphere and for the extreme secrecy—and is worth quoting at some length:

> At twelve o'clock noon I went over for my conference with the President at the White House over S-1. General Groves was to meet me there, but he had to take a secret road around because if the newspaper men, who are now gathered in great numbers every morning in the President's anteroom, should see us both together there they would be sure to guess what I was going to see the President about. So Colonel McCarthy, the Secretary of the General Staff, arranged to have General Groves conducted around through underground passages to a room near the President and there wait till I had got far on in my talk with the President. The talk worked very well indeed. First of all I showed the President the paper that I had drawn yesterday and this morning. It is on the political aspects of the S-1 performance and the problems which are involved with the public. He read it carefully and was very much interested in it. I then produced General Groves and his account of the manufacturing operation, and Groves and I and this report explained the matter to the President. The President took one copy and we took the other and we went over it. . . .[12]

The first paper Stimson mentions—"on the political aspects"—was made public along with the secretary's diaries when they were opened in 1959. Among its dramatic points:

> Within four months we shall in all probability have completed the most terrible weapon ever known in human history, one bomb of which could destroy a whole city.
>
> Although we have shared its development with the UK, physically the US is at present in the position of controlling the resources with which to construct and use it and no other nation could reach this position for some years.
>
> Nevertheless it is practically certain that we could not remain in this position indefinitely. . . .
>
> . . . the future may see a time when such a weapon may be constructed in secret and used suddenly and effectively with devastating power by a wilful [*sic*] nation or group against an unsuspecting nation or group of much greater size and material power. With its aid even a very powerful unsuspecting nation might be conquered within a very few days by a very much smaller one, although probably the only na-

tion which could enter into production within the next few years is Russia.

The world in its present state of moral advancement compared with its technical development would be eventually at the mercy of such a weapon. In other words, modern civilization might be completely destroyed.

. . . in the light of our present position with reference to this weapon, the question of sharing it with other nations and, if so shared, upon what terms, becomes a primary question of our foreign relations. Also our leadership in the war and in the development of this weapon has placed a certain moral responsibility for any disaster to civilization which it would further.

On the other hand, if the problem of the proper use of this weapon can be solved, we would have the opportunity to bring the world into a pattern in which the peace of the world and our civilization can be saved.[13]

The slightly dismissive tone of Truman's subsequent report of the discussion at this point in his memoirs may be revealing: Stimson, Truman recalled, "seemed at least as much concerned with the role of the atomic bomb in the shaping of history as in its capacity to shorten this war."[14]

Other detailed information concerning the April 25 discussion only surfaced much later. Groves, for instance, prepared a "MEMO TO FILES"* after meeting with the president which was made available to researchers in the 1970s. At one level the purpose of the meeting, Groves noted, "was to disclose to the president all of the facts with respect to the Manhattan Engineer District. . . ." However, Groves' memo also states:

A great deal of emphasis was placed on foreign relations and particularly on the Russian situation.[15]

Groves' report of "the manufacturing operation" was based on the second, longer memorandum mentioned by Stimson. This, Groves noted, "was read by the president and the president asked questions concerning various items."[16] The report explained the basic facts of nuclear fission, outlined the development of operations in the United States, and gave an overview of the current and future plans for the production of atomic bombs. (Truman, Groves noted, "did not keep the report as he felt it was not advisable."[17])

This memorandum/report was only declassified and made available to researchers some forty-five years after the fact, in 1990.[18] Some of the information it contained concerned the atomic bomb schedule—and also U.S.

*Capitalized in original.

maneuvering to attempt to achieve a global monopoly over important raw materials. Stimson's point that "physically the US is at present in the position of controlling the resources"[19] was spelled out in considerable detail:

Our operation plans are based on the gun type bomb, the first of which, without previous full scale test (and we do not believe this will be necessary), should be ready about 1 August 1945. . . .

We should have sufficient material for the first implosion type bomb to be tested in the United States in the early part of July. . . .

Uranium is not a widespread element in recoverable amounts. . . .

In furtherance of their policy of gaining control of uranium ores throughout the world, the Governments of the United States and the United Kingdom entered into an agreement with the Government of Belgium [regarding the Belgian Congo] in September 1944. . . .

Thorium, another of the elements, has properties similar to uranium. Consequently, several new agreements to obtain complete control of thorium ores are presently anticipated.[20]

The longer memorandum also offered a number of important recommendations—including:

There must be continuous, vigorous and extensive research and development of the possibilities of atomic energy including the use of radioactive substances. This will entail:

a. Full cooperation with the United Kingdom.
b. The continued procurement and movement to American and British control of available world supplies of uranium and thorium.
c. The improvement and operation of the most efficient manufacturing processes.
d. The improvement of the bomb. . . .
h. Fundamental research so as to retain our present lead in the field.[21]

The report also proposed that a committee be established to make further recommendations for the postwar period,* and it discussed security considerations, the atomic activities of England, France, Germany, and Japan, and the monitoring of Soviet intelligence operations. An additional point concerning postwar plans was noted in Groves' "MEMO TO FILES":

The President approved our ideas about taking a few members of the Congress to Tennessee and concurred in the advisability of leaving

---

*This was the first mention to the president of what was to become the Interim Committee.

the choice to the Speaker for the House and to Senator Barkley for the Senate.[22]

None of these documents gives us much detailed information on this first discussion in the Oval Office—and especially what was meant by the statement that "a great deal of emphasis was placed on foreign relations and particularly on the Russian situation." However, Truman also subsequently reported that he had previously been told about the bomb by James F. Byrnes. Byrnes, he states in his memoirs (and in transcribed interviews upon which they were based), had

> told me that the weapon might be so powerful as to be potentially capable of wiping out entire cities and killing people on an unprecedented scale. And he had added that in his belief the bomb might well put us in a position to dictate our own terms at the end of the war.[23]

Byrnes was later to indicate that he had this discussion with the president during the latter's first days in office, just about the time he asked him to become secretary of state.[24] We know few details about what happened in this (and many) private meetings between Truman and Byrnes (and the precise meaning of "dictate our own terms at the end of the war" is clearly indeterminate). However, it is clear from other evidence that Byrnes believed the atomic bomb would add powerful leverage to his diplomacy towards Russia, especially in Europe.* Though we have no direct proof, Peter Wyden suggests that the tough line Truman took with Molotov on April 23 may already have derived from the enthusiasm which Byrnes had conveyed to the president concerning the power the new weapon would add to his diplomacy—a reasonable possibility, given other things we have learned over the years of Byrnes' attitude, the timing of his meetings with Truman, and the spring confrontation with the Soviet Union.[25]†

The above information offers a tantalizing and suggestive—though limited—glimpse into initial thinking about the "second track" of strategic development which began to evolve during the early Truman administration. However, precisely what went on at this moment in time is difficult to verify.[26] We shall shortly note unmistakable evidence that the president also had additional discussions of atomic bomb strategy with one of his advisers, but there is no record identifying the time or exact content of this discussion.

Fortunately, we know considerably more about thinking elsewhere in the U.S. government prior to this time (and after) concerning the new weapon— and, too, about high-level discussions after April.

---

*See below, especially pp. 146–47, 281–82, 429–34.

†Also see below, p. 209, for Brown's report that Byrnes instructed Truman on how he should speak to Molotov at this time.

* * *

To fully grasp the context in which various "second track" atomic bomb policy discussions took place, it is necessary to recall the situation confronting U.S. leaders at the end of World War II. As Germany disintegrated, the entire structure of power relationships seemed to be up for grabs—especially as the Red Army marched relentlessly into Eastern and Central Europe. The previously cited War Department staff report on Hoover's proposals put it this way:

> In destroying Germany, the nation which set out to dominate Europe using force, we have made Russia, a nation with an economic system of national monopoly, the unquestionably dominant power in Europe.[27]

Just before his death even the usually conciliatory Roosevelt reportedly banged his fist on his wheelchair and said, "Averell is right. We can't do business with Stalin."[28] U.S. officials especially feared that a state-run Soviet bloc in Eastern Europe would weaken the overall Continental economy and thereby undercut postwar global economic stability. Moreover, unrest was a serious prospect throughout Europe—quite apart from whether or not the communists tried to take advantage of the dislocations. Stimson informed Truman on May 16 that all "agree as to the probability of pestilence and famine in central Europe next winter. This is likely to be followed by political revolution and Communistic infiltration. . . . It is vital to keep those countries from being driven to revolution or Communism by famine."[29]

One question confronting both the United States and Britain—particularly during April and May—was what would happen when the bulk of U.S. and British forces withdrew from Europe and proceeded to the other side of the globe to join the war in the Pacific?

Worries about this prospect, in turn, began to impact calculations concerning the forms of power the United States could use to influence Soviet behavior in Europe. And this began to bring the potential role the atomic bomb might play into much sharper focus.

Americans tend to be naïve about "power." As we look back on much-admired figures in earlier periods of history (like Truman), we like to think that American diplomacy might somehow have been above such questions. In some part of our awareness, of course, most of us know this is unlikely. Still, we need to be reminded that leaders of all nations think and reason about their real-world capacity to achieve their ends.

As we have seen, the showdown Truman attempted over Poland was regarded not simply as a fight over specific problems arising in this one nation, but as a test case which might force a clarification of policy throughout Eastern and Central Europe. It is accordingly instructive to revisit these events briefly from the perspective of power politics.

In deciding to force the issue, Truman and his advisers initially believed

that they had ample leverage to achieve a favorable outcome. The main form
of power seemed obvious: The Russians had requested a postwar credit to
help rebuild their war-devastated country, a credit which, it was estimated,
might amount to six billion dollars—an extraordinary amount in 1945.[30] In
his April 20 meeting with the president Harriman had reasoned that the Soviet government would yield to the American position, "since they needed
our help in order to reduce the burden of reconstruction. . . ."[31] Truman himself also believed that what Forrestal termed "a showdown" would risk very
little—and probably for very similar reasons.[32] According to notes taken at
the meeting, "The President said that . . . he intended to be firm but fair since
in his opinion the Soviet Union needed us more than we needed them."[33]

That the U.S. exercised power in this way has often been downplayed
in accounts of the early Truman era. Accordingly, perhaps it is important
also to recall that Secretary of State Stettinius reinforced the same message,
emphasizing to Molotov (now in San Francisco at the United Nations
meetings) that future economic aid would depend entirely upon the attitude of the American people.[34] In his diary entry of April 24, a leading
Republican—Senator Arthur Vandenberg—notes that Stettinius had arrived
with a "thrilling message" about the firm stand that Truman had taken with
Molotov—and that according to Vandenberg

> Stettinius added that he explained to Molotov that future Russian aid
> from America depends entirely upon the temper and the mood and the
> conscience of the American people—and that Frisco is his last chance
> to *prove* that he deserves this aid.[35]

Our main concern so far has been with the president's military judgment—i.e., whether at the time he forced a showdown over Poland he believed he still needed Russian help for an invasion. Here, our focus is
somewhat different; one lesson concerning the power relationships is clear:
The president's initial effort failed to move the Russians. On April 24 Stalin
had sent parallel messages to Truman and Churchill which rejected proposals
to significantly change the composition of the Polish government. He also
angrily charged that it was most

> unusual when two governments—those of the United States and Great
> Britain—beforehand settle with the Polish question in which the So-
> viet Union is first of all and most of all interested and put the govern-
> ment of the USSR in an unbearable position trying to dictate to it their
> demands.[36]

By April 29, Stettinius reported that the Polish negotiations had reached a total impasse.[37] Moreover, the Russians had arrested sixteen underground Polish leaders, and there was danger of a major stalemate at the founding

meetings of the United Nations. "[L]ess than a week after V-E Day," as Robert E. Sherwood was to observe, "it seemed that the San Francisco Conference was going on the rocks."[38] And despite the pressure the May 11 cutoff of Lend-Lease put on them, the Russians did not yield in the diplomatic confrontation.

The renewed deadlock—and the failure of economic pressure—forced U.S. policy-makers to carefully consider their strategy. To the participants involved, the fate of Europe seemed to be involved in this first litmus test of the post-Hitler world—along with the momentous question of whether World War II's enormous costs in lives and resources would produce a meaningful and peaceful new world.

Deeply concerned, the same advisers who had urged the president to force the issue to a showdown in April now argued that a face-to-face meeting with the Russian leader—the sooner the better—was the only way to confront the central issue.

Moreover, time seemed to be of the essence, for an obvious reason: American and British troops were about to be withdrawn from the Continent.

No one stated the issues facing Western leaders more clearly—or more bluntly—than Winston Churchill. When Anthony Eden reported the breakdown of negotiations with Molotov and urged that the Soviet Union should now be "brought up sharply against realities," Churchill responded forcefully that the relationship with the Russians could now "only be founded upon their recognition of Anglo-American strength."[39] Above all, what he later termed "the decisive, practical points of strategy" required "that a settlement must be reached on all major issues . . . *before the armies of democracy melted.* . . ."[40]

On May 6 Churchill proposed an immediate heads-of-government meeting to Truman.[41] On May 11 and May 12 he sent further pleas: "Surely it is vital now to come to an understanding with Russia . . . before we weaken our armies mortally. . . ."[42] To Eden—using the same term previously used by Forrestal—he confidentially advised: "It is to this early and speedy showdown and settlement with Russia that we must now turn our hopes."[43]

It is difficult for Americans today to fully appreciate the depth and significance of the early 1945 crisis in relations with the Soviet Union; it seems so distant and far away. It is also difficult to grasp the intensity and subtlety of the internal administration debate over tactics which took place in the wake of the deadlock.

But it was in the context of the profound diplomatic crisis—and the initial effort to utilize one form of power—that the "second track" of U.S. strategy relating to the new atomic weapon began to take much more specific form.

Chapter 11

POSTPONING A CONFRONTATION
WITH STALIN

. . . the greatest complication was what might happen at the meeting of the Big Three. He told me he had postponed that until the 15th of July on purpose to give us more time.
—Secretary of War Henry L. Stimson, after meeting
with President Harry S. Truman, diary, June 6, 1945

One reason Churchill urged his case with such intensity is that some time during the first eight or nine days of May Truman seems clearly to have reappraised his basic posture. Most significantly, on May 9 the president had responded to Churchill's plea for an early meeting with Stalin with a cable stating that he did not feel able to leave Washington until after June 30:

> I am in agreement with your opinion that a meeting of the three heads of government would be desirable. . . .
> [However, i]n regard to timing, it will be extremely difficult for me to be absent from Washington before the end of the fiscal year (June 30). . . .[1]

In view of the issues at stake such an excuse seemed strange to the hard-headed prime minister—to say the least. On May 11 Churchill cabled back: "I would have suggested the middle of June but for your reference to your fiscal year (June 30) because I feel that every minute counts."[2] On May 13, he again urged:

> . . . I am for the conference of three as soon as possible and wherever possible.
> In this case I consider that we should try to bring the meeting off sometime in June, and I hope your fiscal year will not delay it. . . .[3]

To Churchill, delay seemed all but incomprehensible—first, because of the importance of the issues at stake; second, because it flew in the face of what seemed to be critical and obvious power realities.[4] One of the prime minister's cables (on May 12) was almost strident:

> I am profoundly concerned about the European situation. . . . Anyone can see that in a very short space of time our armed power on the Continent will have vanished. . . .
> . . . this issue of a settlement with Russia before our strength has gone seems to me to dwarf all others.[5]

Joseph Grew also challenged the president, urging (on May 15) that "we all felt in the Department of State that it was of the utmost importance that the Big Three meeting should take place as soon as possible and not be postponed until July."[6] Averell Harriman put it this way: "The problem of our relations with Russia is the number one problem affecting the future of the world and the fact was that at the present moment we were getting farther and farther apart. . . ."

> [Harriman] said he felt that the establishment of a basis for future relations with Russia and the settlement of these immediate issues could only be done at a tripartite meeting, that the longer the meeting was delayed the worse the situation would get, and that while he assumed of course that we were not prepared to use our troops in Europe for political bargaining nevertheless if the meeting could take place before we were in large measure out of Europe he felt the atmosphere of the meeting would be favorable and the chances of success increased.[7]

Grew's feelings were running so high that at 5:00 a.m. on May 19, after a sleepless night, he penned a memorandum which stated in part:

> Already Russia is showing us—in Poland, Rumania, Bulgaria, Hungary, Austria, Czechoslovakia and Yugoslavia—the future world pattern that she visualizes and will aim to create. With her certain stranglehold on these countries, Russia's power will steadily increase and she will in the not distant future be in a favorable position to expand her control, step by step, through Europe.

The conservative and anti-communist Grew, in fact, was already convinced that "a future war with Soviet Russia is as certain as anything in this world can be certain."[8] However, Truman quite clearly had made up his mind—and, again, for the seemingly odd reason he had given Churchill. The memorandum of his conversation with Harriman and Grew (Charles Bohlen was also in attendance) notes:

THE PRESIDENT said that he . . . felt that a meeting as soon as possible was most desirable. He added that he agreed with what the Ambassador said but that his difficulty was that he had a number of pressing domestic questions particularly the preparation of a budget message before the end of the fiscal year which made it difficult for him to leave before then.

Harriman's response—"the President would be confronted with a much more difficult situation two months from now than he would if the meeting could be arranged within the next few weeks"—made no apparent impression.[9] Moreover, a week later the president was still clearly stalling. On May 21 he told Churchill:

I may, within the next two weeks, have more information bearing on a date and location for the proposed tripartite meeting if Stalin agrees to participate.[10]

When Harry Hopkins cabled from Moscow on May 28 that Stalin, too, favored an early meeting, he asked:

Do you want me to tell him that you would like to meet around the 15th of July. I think Stalin would like to have the meeting at an earlier date because of the many pressing problems to be decided.[11]

At this point Truman at last responded, and confirmed still another two-week delay: "about the fifteenth of July appears to be a practicable date for me."[12] The peculiarity of the president's continued stalling now struck the Russians as well. When Hopkins informed Stalin of Truman's position (on May 30):

Marshal Stalin and Mr. Molotov inquired was this [July 15] not a mistake and was not June 15th meant, since June 15th had been the date suggested by Prime Minister Churchill in a very recent message to Stalin.
    Mr. Hopkins assured them that there was no mistake and that the President had about 15 July in mind.[13]

On June 1, Truman reported to Churchill:

Marshal Stalin has informed me that he is agreeable to having our forthcoming meeting in the vicinity of Berlin about July fifteenth, which date also seems to be possible from the point of view of my domestic duties.[14]

Churchill's exasperation is evident even in his official cable:

. . . I consider that July 15, repeat July the month after June, is much too late for the urgent questions that demand attention between us. . . . I have proposed June 15, repeat June the month before July, but if that is not possible why not July 1, 2, or 3?[15]

Truman replied coolly and definitively on June 5:

. . . in regard to the forthcoming meeting, I find, after full consideration, that July 15 is the earliest date that is practicable for me to attend.[16]

The above excerpts are reproduced at length because for a long time after World War II the intensity of the diplomatic debate involving power was simply not discussed—or was treated only very superficially. Only if the essential logic of the power issue confronting the president is fully understood is it possible to grasp the significance of the first major decision Truman made regarding the atomic bomb.

As new documents slowly surfaced over the years, it became quite obvious not only that the president was quite hardheaded but that he was following other advice. He knew exactly what he was doing; to Truman the question of power had now moved well beyond the initial discussions of financial leverage, and, too, beyond the conventional troop arguments of most of his advisers and of Churchill. The official 1962 history of the U.S. Atomic Energy Commission, *The New World*, described the president's end-of-May decision this way:

Truman was pleased with the news Hopkins cabled from Moscow. He accepted Berlin as a site for the meeting and, thinking of the latest estimates from Los Alamos, suggested July 15.[17]

In short, Truman had decided to put off meeting Stalin until the new weapon was proven.

The possibility that the first decision concerning the atomic bomb was related to Truman's strategy toward Russia would not have occurred to most Americans in 1945. Nor, given that the basic documents were simply not available, is it entirely surprising that many resisted the idea that officials might have considered the bomb in connection with power politics in Europe. The simplistic picture many had of Truman (either as too green and inexperienced or as too straightforward and candid) also made a clear-eyed view of his strategy difficult for many to attain.

Indeed, even after the official Atomic Energy Commission history and other related works appeared in the early and mid-1960s, some officials ridiculed the idea that the president might have delayed his meeting with Stalin until the atomic bomb had been tested. In his 1975 memoirs, Harriman, for instance, commented acidly that:

it is nonsense to believe—as some historians apparently do—that Truman postponed the Potsdam Conference in order to have the bomb go off before the end of his meeting with Stalin.[18]

(Harriman also went on to say that the "idea of using the bomb as a form of pressure on the Russians never entered the discussions of Potsdam"— another statement which has been disproved by modern researchers.[19]*)

We now know far more about the president's decision. Although the most important source of early information once more was the diary of Henry L. Stimson, a steady stream of documentary releases and discoveries, together with other reports, has yielded specific insight into several distinct points.

To begin with: In connection with the politics of the troop issue, a formal May 16 memorandum included in Stimson's diary shows him reassuring the president that the "work of redeploying our forces from Europe to the Pacific will necessarily take so long that there will be more time for your necessary diplomacy with the other large allies than some of our hasty friends realize."[20] In short, no need to worry about troop withdrawals for the moment.

The next two sentences in the same memorandum are crucial window-openers on presidential thinking about power by mid-May 1945:

> Therefore I believe that good and not harm would be done by the policy towards your coming meeting which you mentioned to me. We shall probably hold more cards in our hands later than now.[21]

The only "card" which would be added to the U.S. hand was the atomic bomb.†

A second, equally revealing point in the Stimson memorandum: the "policy towards your coming meeting" is one which (as Stimson writes) "you mentioned to me." The president had clearly already decided on an approach to the meeting with Stalin based on having "more cards" later—and is here informing Stimson of the plans he has in mind by May 16.

If, as it seems, Stimson was not the source of policy advice "towards your coming meeting," then either Truman made his first major decision related to the atomic bomb on his own, or some unidentified adviser helped him formulate a strategy which ran directly counter to that of other advisers like

---

*See Part V.

†The many "card" images concerning the atomic bomb also found in the Stimson diary at this time almost certainly come from conversations with Truman. Although it is difficult if not impossible to find Stimson himself ever employing such language independently, the poker-playing president did so on many occasions. Indeed, within a few days he used almost exactly the formulation found in this memorandum and in the Stimson diary of May 14 with Treasury official Bernard Bernstein: ". . . we had all the cards and . . . the Russians had to come to us . . ."; ". . . he felt he had the cards in American hands, and he made very clear that he proposed to play them as American cards. . . ." See below, pp. 283–84.

Grew and Harriman—to say nothing of Churchill—who were pressing for an early meeting.

It is also important to note the date of this memorandum and the meeting with Truman to which it refers. This is almost exactly the same time—one day after—the meeting of the Committee of Three (on May 15) for which McCloy's notation suggests minutes were destroyed.

Other fragments of information which have emerged over the years help clarify related issues. The Stimson diary also reports a private meeting followed by a lunch just one day earlier (on May 14) with British Foreign Minister Anthony Eden (along with Marshall and McCloy):

> I had about forty-five minutes with [Eden] on general matters but especially S-1. He brought me messages of congratulations from the Prime Minister and said that he would be very glad to convey to him anything that I wanted to tell him about S-1 in which he was deeply interested.

Stimson continues that, specifically,

> I then outlined to him the progress which we have made and the timetable as it stood now, and told him my own feeling as to its bearing upon our present problems of an international character.[22]

Eden reported back to Churchill that evening:

> I had a talk with Stimson this morning at his request followed by a lunch with him at which Marshall and McCloy were present.
>
> The earlier part of the conversation concerned special subject. This was satisfactory and I will give you a full report on my return.[23]

After the lunch with Eden, Stimson met alone with Marshall and McCloy to discuss several questions which the State Department had raised concerning Russia and the Far Eastern understanding. The following diary entry describes Stimson's own views—as presented to McCloy—and further illuminates the general tone of discussions at this point in mid-May:

> I told him that my own opinion was that the time now and the method now to deal with Russia was to keep our mouths shut and let our actions speak for words. The Russians will understand them better than anything else. It is a case where we have got to regain the lead and perhaps do it in a pretty rough and realistic way. They have rather taken it away from us because we have talked too much and have been too lavish with our beneficences to them. I told him this was a place where we really held all the cards. I called it a royal straight flush and we mustn't be a fool about the way we play it. They can't get along without our help

and industries and we have coming into action a weapon which will be unique. Now the thing is not to get into unnecessary quarrels by talking too much and not to indicate any weakness by talking too much; let our actions speak for themselves.[24]

This oft-cited passage is worth careful scrutiny and sober reflection. Note each of the following points:
(1) "[T]he time now and the method now" to deal with Russia was for the moment to "keep our mouths shut"; (2) also—but separately—later the United States should "let our actions speak for words. The Russians will understand them better than anything else."
Further, (3) the problem facing the United States is "to regain the lead." This, in turn, will perhaps require (4) doing "it in a pretty rough and realistic way. They have rather taken it away from us. . . ."
Apart from having "talked too much," (5) one reason has to do with the way U.S. economic power had been used: "[We] have been too lavish with our beneficences to them." Stimson, however, was extremely confident (6):

I told him this was a place where we really held all the cards. I called it a royal straight flush and we mustn't be a fool about the way we play it.

Finally, (7) they "can't get along without our help and industries and we have coming into action a weapon which will be unique." Accordingly, (8):

Now the thing is not to get into unnecessary quarrels by talking too much and not to indicate any weakness by talking too much; let our actions speak for themselves.

Stimson is commonly portrayed as one of the more moderate policy advisers, urging that the United States search for "quid pro quos" which the Russians might concede to be allowed to join the U.S./U.K. atomic partnership. Aside from the fact of his apparently limited influence with Truman, the tone of even Stimson's thinking at this juncture is quite revealing—especially his argument that the United States might have to regain the lead "in a pretty rough and realistic way" and (in light of the expected power of the new weapon) his repetition twice that the thing to do was "let our actions speak for words . . ."; "let our actions speak for themselves."
Further insight into the atmosphere in which policy was developed in the first two weeks of May is available in a Stimson diary entry for May 10:

I invited Harriman to stay and lunch with McCloy, Bundy, and myself in my room. I wanted to get his views on the situation in Russia and the chances of getting a Russia we could work with. It was rather a gloomy

report that he gave us. . . . Yet he thought that Russia would be afraid
to throw down the Dumbarton Oaks plan [for the United Nations] or the
associations with us altogether. He thinks that Russia is really afraid of
our power or at least respects it and, although she is going to try to ride
roughshod over her neighbors in Europe, he thought that she really was
afraid of us.

Stimson concludes this entry concerning European issues with an additional,
suggestive sentence about his meeting with Harriman:

I talked over very confidentially our problem connected with S-1 in this
matter.[25]

Another diary entry shows that in discussing these questions (on May 15)
Stimson was personally still under the impression that

the President has now promised apparently to meet Stalin and Churchill
on the 1st of July . . . yet we will not know until after that time probably, until after that meeting, whether this is a weapon in our hands or
not.[26]

Here, once more, the additional point to note (e.g., "apparently") is that
the secretary of war does not seem to be fully informed of what the president
has decided. On the other hand, as we have seen, the next day Stimson came
away from his meeting with Truman generally reassured as to his overall
strategy. And on June 6 he recorded the following after another meeting with
the president:

. . . the greatest complication was what might happen at the meeting of
the Big Three. He told me he had postponed that until the 15th of July
on purpose to give us more time.[27]

Concrete information on Harry Truman's personal views at this time is limited. We know that he began to engage the strategy issues early on—and we
can mark off a preliminary discussion of some kind with Byrnes prior to
April 25, a major discussion with Stimson and Groves on April 25, the appointment of Byrnes as his personal representative on the Interim Committee
on May 3, a decision on or around May 9 to put off a meeting with Stalin,
a further clarification that his policy revolved around having "more cards
later than now" by May 16, instructions to Harriman on May 21 to discuss the possibility with Stalin of the Big Three Conference "at a later date,"
and a decision on May 28 to agree to "about July 15" as the meeting
date.

We also know that during his June 6 meeting with Stimson the president briefly mentioned a satisfactory settlement of the Polish problem as one of the quid pro quos Russia might possibly be asked to offer in exchange for being allowed to join the U.S./U.K. atomic monopoly.[28]*

Beyond this however, specific details concerning the president's viewpoint are largely lacking for May and June. Again, a reasonable question is why we know so little about Truman's views when he was certainly thinking about the critical issues and discussing them with Byrnes.

On the other hand, for a man who had upped the ante in a high-stakes poker game with Stalin over Poland and run into a brick wall, Truman certainly did not seem very worried. Indeed, he exhibited enormous confidence about his ultimate power to achieve his goals in Europe. On June 4, for instance, he met with Arthur Bliss Lane, the new American ambassador to Poland. Lane urged that "our attitude toward Soviet Russia in connection with the Polish issue should be integrated with the many other issues in Central Europe, particularly the Soviet blackouts in the Balkan states and the states of Central Europe." The president responded that "he had precisely the same opinion and that this would be the fundamental subject which he intended to discuss at the Big Three meeting." Joseph Grew (who was also present) noted that Truman left no doubt "as to his intention to insist on the eventual removal of the Soviet blackout in the countries mentioned."

The president told Lane, however, that for the moment "it would be desirable not to exert too much pressure. . . ."[29]

A related point concerns the attitude of Byrnes. During the June 6 meeting at which Truman said he had postponed the Big Three conference "to give us more time," Stimson also informed him of the Interim Committee's recommendations concerning the atomic bomb. When he did, however, Truman "said that Byrnes had reported to him already about it and that Byrnes seemed to be highly pleased with what had been done."[30] Precisely what Byrnes said to the president is not known. However, we do have some additional evidence concerning Byrnes' thinking about the atomic bomb and Europe at this time.

On May 28, three scientists—Leo Szilard, Walter Bartky, and Harold C. Urey—met with Byrnes to discuss atomic bomb–related issues at his home in Spartanburg, South Carolina. Szilard subsequently reported that at their meeting,

*There is very little evidence that this idea was ever anything more than a passing thought for Truman. Much more likely, the president believed that the force of the new weapon would simply make the Russians more amenable in general to U.S. concerns. (For an insightful perspective, see Michael B. Stoff, Jonathon F. Fanton, R. Hal Williams, eds., *The Manhattan Project: A Documentary Introduction to the Atomic Age* (Philadelphia, 1991), pp. 11–12.)

Mr. Byrnes did not argue that it was necessary to use the bomb against the cities of Japan in order to win the war. He knew at that time, as the rest of the government knew, that Japan was essentially defeated and that we could win the war in another six months. At that time Mr. Byrnes was much concerned about the spreading of Russian influence in Europe; . . . [Mr. Byrnes' view was] that our possessing and demonstrating the bomb would make Russia more manageable in Europe. . . .[31]

Byrnes' statement to the scientists in connection with European issues appears to have put into only slightly different form the same general idea Stimson had expressed privately to McCloy two weeks earlier—that the United States had "coming into action a weapon which will be unique," that the "method now to deal with Russia was to . . . let our actions speak for words"—and that the United States might have to "do it in a pretty rough and realistic way."[32]

Indeed, taken together, the information we have on Stimson's views and Byrnes's views—when added to the evidence we have that Truman's "policy towards [his] coming meeting" was based on the notion that the United States would "have more cards later than now"—suggests that the three most important officials in the U.S. government, broadly speaking, shared a very similar strategic conception at this time.[33]

The report that Byrnes did not argue the bomb was necessary to end the war also accords with previous evidence concerning the likelihood that a change in surrender terms plus a Russian attack might stop the fighting. The six-month estimate of late May would have meant an end to the fighting sometime in November, or a few weeks after the first possible landing on Kyushu and many months before the full invasion of Japan could begin in the spring of 1946.*

An additional aspect of the president's thinking—and the source of the "fiscal year" excuse—was clarified in 1962 when some of the papers of Joseph E. Davies were opened. Truman met privately with the former ambassador to Moscow on May 21 and in passing explained why he had postponed his meeting with Stalin. In one version of his diary Davies writes:

He did not want to meet until July. He had his budget (*) on his hands. He also told me of another reason, etc. The test was set for June, but had been postponed for July.

In a footnote related to the asterisk, Davies writes: "The atomic bomb. He told me then of the atomic bomb experiment in Nevada [*sic*]. Charged me with utmost secrecy."[34] In another version of his diary, Davies writes:

*See below, pp. 227, 242, 246, for changes in such estimates as Japan's position deteriorated in June and July.

To my surprise, he said he did not want [the heads-of-government meeting] until July. The reason which I could assign was that he had his budget on his hands, and had to get that out. "But," he said, "I have another reason (*) which I have not told anybody."

He told me of the atomic bomb. The final test had been set for June, but now had been postponed until July. I was startled, shocked, and amazed.

In the footnote referred to by this asterisk, Davies adds: "Uranium—for reason of security, I will have to fill this in later."[35]*

Although it is obvious that the president was briefed more than once on the date for the test—and considered the dates carefully in scheduling his meeting—it is difficult to find detailed specific documentary evidence of how, when, or by whom he was informed as the various dates shifted. That he was so briefed—and that we do not know much else—further attests to the likelihood that other unrecorded high-level White House discussions went on at this time.

As is also evident, Truman was quite willing to distort the facts when he thought there were important reasons to do so. As we shall see, the point has broader implications, for despite his reputation as a straight-shooter, this is only one of several documented instances in which for reasons he thought valid the president clearly bent the truth concerning matters related to the atomic bomb.

Further insight into the relationship of the new weapon to the forthcoming Potsdam Conference is also available in the recollections of the men who were responsible for testing the atomic bomb. Although the Manhattan Project had been launched out of fear that Nazi Germany might build a bomb, J. Robert Oppenheimer later recalled that "I don't think there was a time where we worked harder at the speedup than in the period after the German surrender and [before] the actual combat use of the bomb." Oppenheimer was quite candid about the fact that we "were under incredible pressure to get it done before the Potsdam meeting. . . ."[36]

For most of the spring it had been hoped that the test would occur around July 4. In mid-June (when certain technical delays occurred), this was pushed up to July 13, and then—after a June 30 review—the date was again pushed "to July 16 or as soon thereafter as weather conditions permitted."[37] Tele-

---

*The diaries of Joseph Davies present something of a problem to researchers. Davies kept a journal but he also edited, improved, and rewrote the text over the years. Various versions of the same entry are on file at the Library of Congress, and although the general thrust of most variations is similar, it is impossible to know exactly which is the most accurate. Whenever citing Davies materials, I have attempted to select versions which represent themes common to most or all variations on file.

phone transcripts found in Groves' papers indicate that just after noon, at 12:50 p.m. on July 2, he called Oppenheimer in Santa Fe, New Mexico:

> Oppie said they . . . scheduled [the test] for the 17th. Dr. O said that the 14th was possible but was not sure. Dr. O thought the wisest thing was to schedule it for the 17th in which case they would be fairly sure of getting the thing done within a few days of that day. . . . GG [General Groves] said that he did not like the idea of a later date because of the various things that were involved. GG also said that it was extremely important that it be completed by the earlier date, because of the various things that were involved. . . . GG then told Dr. O the reason why the earlier date had to be. Dr. O said that they would meet the earlier date but it went against his own feeling. . . .

The cryptic report—"the various things that were involved"—though suggestive of higher purpose, is not definitive. At 3:30 p.m. the same day Groves called James B. Conant, chairman of the National Defense Research Committee, about the same matter:

> Dr. Conant said that the Gen had done right to stay along with the earlier date. Dr. C suggested that GG get in touch with [physicist Richard C.] Tolman and request him to exert his efforts in getting Oppy and the men persuaded to the earlier date.

An hour later, Groves called Stimson's assistant (and alternate chairman of the Interim Committee) George Harrison "with respect the [*sic*] first date":

> Gen Groves said that he had a very strong urging from the people in charge at the site to postpone the date for four days. Gen Groves said that he had told Oppy that they had to have the first date because of things beyond his control. Mr. Harrison said that was a sound decision. . . . Mr. H then told Mr. Bundy of the situation and Mr. B said that other things were involved and the earlier date was the one.

Finally, at 5:45 p.m., Groves got a call from Tolman. Groves told him that "the upper crust wanted [the test] as soon as possible. . . ."

> GG said he was not in agreement with the upper crust. GG said he wanted Tolman to stress to the people out there that he was not needling them but there was nothing he could do about it. . . . Tolman transferred GG to Oppie. . . . GG stressed on Oppie the importance of trying to arrange for the 14th and he also told Oppie to tell his people that it wasn't his fault but came from higher authority.[38]

Among Groves' papers is a letter from U.S. Air Force General B. G. Holzman. Holzman (who helped manage meteorological problems at Los Alamos) recalled why it was also decided to reject the recommendations of the specialists who, as the time approached, urged delaying the atomic test because of bad weather:

> The reason for this was quite clear. The shot had to go in time to furnish the information to President Truman who was to attend the Potsdam Conference.
>
> The scientists all wished for as much time as possible but the 24th of July would obviously not be acceptable for the information on the success or failure of the operation had to be furnished to the President.

Holzman was quite specific about the precise issue of timing:

> It was evident that the information had to be available by the 16th or immediately thereafter. . . . Since the 16th was the earliest possible date that the scientists could be ready, and the final date on which the information had to be available, the 16th was chosen as the firing date.[39]

The following confirming notation—dictated subsequently by Groves—is on file among his papers at the National Archives: "[T]his is a quite accurate account."[40] Groves also noted a few months after receiving this letter that when he arrived at the test site on July 15 he found that a "large group of excited scientists . . . were urging that the tests should be called off" because of weather. However, "the situation in Potsdam was such that we simply could not delay if it was at all possible to go on."[41]*

Related to all of this—and overlapping in time—was the mission of Harry Hopkins to Moscow. Hopkins' May negotiations with Stalin—and a parallel mission to London by Davies—now seem minor historical footnotes. However, over the years there has been a steady trickle of information which also suggests a connection between the two initiatives and the "second track" of policy concerning the atomic bomb and the Soviet Union.

As we have noted, Hopkins' mission was related substantively both to the deadlock over Poland and the spring crisis in U.S.-Russian relations—and to the president's renewed interest in Russian participation in the war against

---

*For the record, in this same set of comments Groves notes that security "requirements were such that written records were kept to a minimum and almost nothing was written that could not be handled verbally"—still another indication of the limitations of available documents. (LRG comments on "Reach to the Unknown," February 25, 1966, Box 6, Entry 10, Groves Papers, RG 200, NA.)

Japan. In the end, it resulted in conceding dominant influence in the new Polish government to Soviet-oriented politicians—and a confirmation from Stalin that Russia would join the war at an early point.[42]

Some historians have thought that Hopkins was sent to Moscow because an inexperienced new president had mistakenly gotten himself into a jam by getting tough with Molotov—and that he decided upon the symbolic gesture of sending one of Roosevelt's "conciliatory" advisers to smooth things over with Stalin. Others have noted evidence of Harriman's role in suggesting the trip. Not meeting first alone with Churchill would also show American evenhandedness.

Perhaps there was nothing more to the initiatives. There is no question that Truman's first months in office were characterized by vacillation and indecision. Moreover, other discussions with Davies suggest Truman's interest in Davies' more conciliatory advice on how to deal with Moscow.[43] However, a number of puzzling questions concerning the timing, origin, and meaning of the Hopkins mission point in a different direction.* For one thing the initial cable stalling a Big Three meeting until after the "fiscal year" went out before Truman had his discussions with Davies.

For another, Truman was quite secretive about preparations for both the Hopkins and Davies missions. He did not consult the secretary of state, the acting secretary of state, the Polish experts in the Department of State, or Admiral Leahy until the very eve of the trips—well after he had initially contacted Hopkins and Davies. James Forrestal did not learn of the trips until May 20—the same day the president told his chief of staff.[44] Leahy's diary on this day says simply:

> Yesterday evening the President, without consulting me, informed Stalin that he is sending Harry Hopkins to Moscow to discuss some of the important questions that now confront the two countries.[45]

All that was known in the Department of State—as Ambassador Lane observed—was that "suddenly and secretly, in the last days of May," Harry Hopkins left for Moscow.[46]

It is also peculiar—again, if the mission was simply a gesture of goodwill by a president who had made a mistake—that we have no record of the specific instructions given Hopkins. We also have Bohlen's report that when he and Harriman met with Hopkins in early May to discuss going to Moscow, "Hopkins mentioned the 'big bomb' " in the course of the conversation.[47]

When the McCloy diary was opened in 1990 further fragmentary evidence of a possible connection between the diplomatic issues and the second

---

*See Appendix V of the 1985 edition of my *Atomic Diplomacy* for an extended discussion.

atomic track also surfaced. McCloy saw Hopkins two days before his departure to discuss questions related to Soviet entry into the war and the Yalta
Far East agreements (and, too, the administration of Germany). McCloy's diary states:

> We also talked a bit about the big bomb—what its effect will be—when
> it should be employed and how—the moral position of the U.S. and its
> responsibilities.[48]

There is also the timing of the events in question. It was on the same day
(May 21)—during his discussion with Davies about his decision to send
Hopkins to Moscow and Davies to London—that Truman stated that he did
not want to meet Stalin until mid-July because of "another reason which I
have not told anybody"—the delay of the atomic bomb test until July.[49]
May 21 was also the day that Truman met with Harriman to give him "further and final instructions in connection Conversation [*sic*] with Stalin" and
they "discussed possibility of a meeting between Stalin, Churchill and myself at a later date. . . ."[50]

It seems clear that Truman had decided on a mission of some kind by
May 13—four days after his May 9 cable putting off the Big Three meeting
until after his "fiscal year." His first choice also appears to have been Davies
(who was unable to undertake the trip because of his health). Hopkins
was a second choice (following an earlier thought of Harriman's, and probably, too, at the suggestion of Cordell Hull). Truman's journal records:
". . . Hopkins is the best bet from our standpoint and from a political
one . . ." and that he "told Jimmie [Byrnes] I thought I would send him. No
need for anyone else to get any credit but the President."[51]

Aside from the fact that Truman's decision to dispatch a mission followed
shortly upon his decision to postpone his meeting with Stalin, the most important thing to note is that this sequence overlaps the period during which
the president told Stimson that his strategy was based upon having "more
cards later than now."[52] It is also when Stimson noted that "the time now and
the method now to deal with Russia was to keep our mouths shut. . . . Now
the thing is not to get into unnecessary quarrels by talking too much and not
to indicate any weakness by talking too much. . . ."[53] Again, it is the time
of the Committee of Three meeting, the minutes of which appear to have
been partly destroyed.[54] It is also only a few days after Stimson's discussion
with Harriman about Russia's riding "roughshod over her neighbors in
Europe"—a meeting in which they also "talked over very confidentially our
problem connected with S-1 in this matter."[55]

Finally, new evidence made available only in late 1994 from previously
restricted portions of the Davies papers provides further illumination of the

reasons behind the mission to see Churchill. Most historians accept that an important part of this initiative was to indicate that the United States and Britain were not "ganging up" on Russia. An unpublished text in the Davies papers, however, states explicitly that Truman sent him to London because he "wanted me, he said, to explain to the Prime Minister that the date suggested for the Potsdam Conference would have to be postponed from June to July, and to explain the reasons to the Prime Minister. . . . He didn't want to go to Potsdam and meet Stalin until he knew the exact outcome of the test."[56]

There has been resistance to the idea that the Hopkins and Davies missions were in any way related to the developing second-track atomic bomb strategy. Presently available evidence and what we know of the emerging policy context suggest that in all likelihood Hopkins was sent to pin down an early Soviet declaration of war; and that both men were to quiet things down for a while on the theory that the United States would be in a far stronger position once the bomb had been tested.

Once the president decided that Soviet help against the Japanese was again important—and, indeed, that if need be a Soviet declaration of war might well jolt Japan into surrender without an invasion—some way of cooling things off until the atomic test was essential. Moreover, having pushed the Polish issue to a crisis level, after Truman decided to wait for the atomic bomb he almost had to find some way of temporizing.

The Hopkins mission in particular accomplished these objectives. It did, in fact, defuse the May crisis and it did buy time until the atomic test and the Potsdam conference. It also gave the president the insurance policy he needed—in the form of confirmation by Stalin that the Red Army would enter the war roughly three months after Germany's surrender.

If one conceives the Hopkins mission only as a gesture of goodwill by an inexperienced president who had made a mistake, it also is not easy to explain the most important and commonly overlooked fact about the initiative. In accepting Stalin's demand that politicians favorable to Russia would dominate the new Polish government, Truman completely backed down from a position he had taken only a few weeks earlier with unusual personal involvement and force. In short, when the president rejected the advice of Churchill, Harriman, Grew, and others for an early meeting with Stalin, the price he paid for delay was not small.

It is not necessary, however, to resolve all the remaining questions concerning the Hopkins mission to come to terms with many crucial aspects of the second track of policy which brought together thinking about the atomic bomb and diplomatic strategy towards the Soviet Union. It is simply important (minimally) to offer a cautionary note about interpretations which gloss over some of the known facts and remaining puzzles.

On the other hand, if the pattern of occasional but regular documentary finds of the last half century continues, it would not be surprising were the Hopkins and Davies missions one day to be illuminated as fully and clearly as have the once equally puzzling reasons for the president's decision to postpone his meeting with Stalin.

Chapter 12

THE INTERIM COMMITTEE

Mr. Byrnes recommended, *and the Committee* agreed, *that the Secretary of War should be advised that, while recognizing that the final selection of the target was essentially a military decision, the present view of the Committee was that the bomb should be used against Japan as soon as possible; that it be used on a war plant surrounded by workers' homes; and that it be used without prior warning.*

—Notes of Interim Committee meeting, Thursday, June 1, 1945

The fact that the development of strategies towards the atomic bomb and towards the Soviet Union inevitably overlapped during the summer of 1945 is nowhere more evident than in connection with the deliberations of the Interim Committee—the body set up to focus specifically on issues connected with the new weapon.

A great deal of information has become available in recent decades on the Interim Committee and on matters closely related to its deliberations. In addition to the Stimson diaries, the official history of the Atomic Energy Commission, *The New World*, published in 1962, offered some of the first details of Interim Committee discussions and decisions. However, the most important sources are to be found in the Harrison-Bundy files (made available in the early 1970s). These include minutes of the committee meetings and several critical memoranda by Harvey H. Bundy and George L. Harrison, two assistants to Secretary of War Stimson. (Harrison also chaired the Interim Committee in Stimson's absence.) Between 1973 and 1979 the National Archives reviewed and declassified documents of the Manhattan Engineer District Records which had not been declassified in earlier reviews by the Atomic Energy Commission and the Department of the Army.[1] In 1985

Vincent Jones published an official U.S. Army history of the Manhattan Project which contained some additional information.

Several first-rate books and articles have drawn upon these materials to provide detailed studies of a number of questions concerning the Committee's overall work and there is no need to review many well-known points.[2] Certain issues, however, are of particular importance—both in connection with decisions made by the U.S. government and with how information was (or was not) made available to the public.

We have noted that during Stimson's April 25 meeting with the president, the formation of what became the Interim Committee was proposed. A week later—after securing General Marshall's agreement—Stimson asked Truman to authorize a committee to include the following members:

The Secretary of War (with Mr. George L. Harrison as his alternate)
Dr. James B. Conant, Chairman, National Defense Research Committee
Dr. Vannevar Bush, Director, Office of Scientific Research and Development
Dr. Karl Compton, Chief, Office of Field Service, Office of Scientific Research and Development
Honorable William L. Clayton, Assistant Secretary of State
Honorable Ralph A. Bard, Under Secretary of Navy[3]

The adjective "Interim" is accurate. First, the committee was designed to function in the interim between early May and the actual use of the weapon (and hence the end of total secrecy). Second, the committee was also to be an interim effort in the sense that it would propose policies and legislative authority for management of nuclear development before the question was posed for congressional decision.[4]

Stimson's diary indicates that he also recommended that Truman appoint "a personal representative of himself."

I said I should prefer to have such a representative and suggested that he should be a man (a) with whom the President had close personal relations, and (b) who was able to keep his mouth shut.[5]

On May 3, Stimson noted:

. . . I called up the President to suggest that Jimmy Byrnes would be a good man to put in the position on the committee for S-1 that I had told the President about when I saw him yesterday, and late in the afternoon the President called me up himself and said that he had heard of my suggestion and it was fine. He had already called Byrnes up down in South Carolina by telephone and Byrnes had accepted. So my committee is now complete.[6]

The appointment was to have momentous implications—especially in connection with the second track of policy development. The president had already asked Byrnes to become secretary of state and (as we have noted), according to Truman, Byrnes had long since determined that the atomic bomb would be crucial in international relations. The discussions reported by Leo Szilard suggest something of Byrnes' apparent hard-line view of the weapons possibilities. It seems clear that Byrnes began early on to develop his diplomatic strategy on the basis of the as yet somewhat vague but critical notion that his hand as secretary of state would be enormously strengthened once the power of the new weapon was demonstrated.

That the Interim Committee and its advisory panels did not operate in a vacuum—and that it is artificial to attempt to isolate its work from the overarching context of diplomatic confrontation with the Soviet Union as the European War ended—has long been evident. A brief review of selected calendar dates suggest why:

May 2, 1945: Appointment of Interim Committee approved.

May 5, 1945: American and British government jointly announce they will not continue discussions of the Polish issue until receiving a full explanation of the arrests of certain Polish underground leaders.[7]

May 9, 1945: First meeting of the Interim Committee.

Secretary Stimson outlined the nature of the project and expressed his views as to the purposes and function of the Committee.[8]

May 11/12, 1945: Lend-Lease cutoff orders radically reduce economic assistance to the Soviet Union.[9]

May 14, 1945: Second meeting of the Interim Committee.

The international aspects of the program were discussed at some length, the Quebec Agreement and the operations of the Combined Development Trust [for global control of resources] being stressed.[10]

May 14, 1945: Stimson diary after meeting with McCloy:

The time now and the method now to deal with Russia was to keep our mouths shut and let our actions speak for words. The Russians will understand them better than anything else. It is a case where we have got to regain the lead and perhaps do it in a pretty rough and realistic way. . . .[11]

May 18, 1945: Third meeting of the Interim Committee.

The consensus of the Committee relative to the proposed statement to be made by the President after a successful test was that the President should make only a short announcement over the radio, or possibly to the Congress, concerning the general nature of the weapon and its military and international implications.[12]

May 19, 1945: Truman dispatches a message to Moscow suggesting the Hopkins mission.[13]

May 26–June 6, 1945: Hopkins negotiates with Stalin over Poland and issues related to Russian participation in the war.[14]

May 31, 1945: Fourth meeting of the Interim Committee.

Mr. Byrnes expressed the view, *which was generally agreed to by all present*, that the most desirable program would be to push ahead as fast as possible in production and research to make certain that we stay ahead and at the same time make every effort to better our political relations with Russia.[15]

Before turning to the committee's recommendations on the bomb's actual use (a subject which was not included in its initial mandate[16]), it is worth reflecting upon the significance of the last extract from the committee minutes cited above. Byrnes is here formally stating what is at once the most important and the most obvious single point to note about both the Interim Committee and the 1945 context.

To fully grasp the decision-making environment in the spring and summer of 1945, it is necessary to come to terms with the fact that at the heart of operational activities throughout the period—day by day as tensions with the Soviet Union mounted in Europe—the U.S. government was systematically organizing its work (and money) to insure that nuclear production would continue in the period after Germany and Japan were defeated.

Truman's decision to reverse field and postpone serious negotiations with Stalin until the atomic test is his most revealing of the spring of 1945. Equally instructive is that by May of that year, U.S. leaders were moving full steam ahead with plans to build more nuclear weapons in the post–World War II period.

Fifty years after the fact we take for granted the decision to push production and "stay ahead," hardly pausing to consider its momentous implications both for a future in which a race to develop arms would be all but inevitable, and, more immediately, for what it reveals about how U.S. leaders thought about strategy toward Russia before the bomb was actually used.

Stimson and Groves—at this point, near the war's end—had also already proposed to take leading members of Congress on a tour of the atomic facilities. Stimson's diary offers an obvious reason. On May 3 he recorded as part of his day's work:

I also took up the question of arranging an appointment with Speaker Rayburn in respect to appointing a legislative committee to go down and see the Tennessee project. . . . Our object is to get him to take the responsibility of picking out the Committee to go.[17]

The next day, Stimson reached the speaker and made his intention clear:

I called Speaker Rayburn on the telephone and told him of my proposals for sending three or four Congressmen to see the manufacturing of S-1 prior to the coming up of the appropriations bill which is going to ask for more money for the same project.[18]

On May 17, the "principal thing this morning was arranging for the visit to Tennessee of the members of the House Appropriations Committee in order that Groves may show them the installation for S-1 that is there. . . ."

I told them in outline what it was all about and they seemed to be very favorably impressed with it and I told them that the meeting was on my own initiative because we were going to have to ask them for more money and we wanted them to know what it was all about.[19]

Within another two weeks (on May 30), "Groves gave me an account of his trip to Tennessee with the five Congressmen and it seems to have been very successful. They have made themselves our friends in that matter."[20]

In short, at the time the crisis with Russia was center stage—and the Interim Committee began initial discussions of the atomic bomb's use—the secretary of war and Groves were skillfully maneuvering to obtain postwar funding.

Nor was the effort to secure ongoing appropriations for the atomic bomb an afterthought. As Groves noted after the April 25 White House meeting, "[t]he President approved" the idea of involving the key congressmen less than two weeks after taking office.[21]

An emphasis on continuing production for the period beyond 1945 also stands out at numerous points in the Interim Committee's deliberations. At its first meeting, for instance, Stimson stressed that in addition to reviewing temporary wartime controls and the preparation of publicity, the committee was to "make recommendations on post-war research, development, and control . . ."[22] One—and only one—decision was taken at this very first meeting, but it was clear, unanimous, and forceful:

In discussing the nature and functions of the Combined Development Trust, the Committee strongly expressed the view that all possible steps should be taken as promptly as possible to build up our supplies of uranium and thorium.[23]

During the committee's May 31 meeting (with the Scientific Panel) Stimson similarly stressed "the implications of the project [which] went far beyond the needs of the present war." Then, "*Dr. A.H. Compton* explained the various stages of development. The first stage involved the separation of uranium 235. The second stage involved the use of 'breeder' piles to produce enriched materials from which plutonium or new types of uranium could be obtained."

> Production of enriched materials was now on the order of pounds or hundreds of pounds and it was contemplated that the scale of operations could be expanded sufficiently to produce many tons.

"While bombs produced from the products of the second stage had not yet been proven in actual operation, such bombs were considered a scientific certainty."

> It was estimated that from January 1946 it would take one and one-half years to prove this second stage in view of certain technical and metallurgical difficulties, that it would take three years to get plutonium in volume, and that it would take perhaps six years for any competitor to catch up with us.[24]

Later in the meeting the committee reviewed the "domestic program." The minutes read:

> *Dr. Lawrence* . . . expressed a view that if the United States were to stay ahead in this field it was imperative that we knew more and did more than any other country. He felt that research had to go on unceasingly. There were many unexplored possibilities in terms of new methods and new materials beyond thorium and uranium. . . .
>
> Dr. Lawrence *recommended* that a program of plant expansion be vigorously pursued and at the same time a sizable stock pile of bombs and material should be built up.

Following further discussion: "*The Secretary summarized the views of the group concerning our domestic program as follows:*

> 1. *Keep our industrial plant intact.*
> 2. *Build up sizable stock piles of material for military use and for industrial and technical use.*
> 3. *Open the door to industrial development.*"[25]

Though the point that operationally U.S. policy was moving ahead full force at this time is obvious, only in the recent decades have researchers realized the scope, scale, and larger meaning of the decision to "stay ahead." As early as the spring of 1943, Groves had launched an effort to gain as "complete control as possible" over the uranium resources of the entire world.[26] The Combined Development Trust was created in June 1944 (following the August 1943 Quebec Agreement between the United States and Great Britain) "to handle the procurement of fissionable elements not within the territorial limits of the contracting powers."[27]

Historian Gregg Herken was one of the first scholars to analyze fully the deeper significance of the Trust. As he observes, the personal contribution of Manhattan Project director Groves was "to be strategic rather than scientific—not only to supervise the building of the weapon,"

> but to retain control over it subsequently by keeping the necessary ingredients for its construction from other nations. This was to be accomplished by a monopoly of the world's atomic raw materials, a monopoly that was meant to be—in Groves' term—"preclusive," insofar as the Russians would be unable to build atomic bombs until they had somehow gained, or been given, access to such raw material.[28]

Important raw material sources were initially believed to be located in the United States, Canada, the Belgian Congo, and (Groves learned later) Sweden—and, as Herken stresses, the goal was truly to attempt to achieve a near-total worldwide monopoly.

Indeed, at the end of World War II Groves envisioned nothing less than

> an American-administered Pax-Atomica—an atomic league of nations, founded upon the West's supposed technological superiority and the secret, preclusive monopoly of atomic raw materials.[29]

It appears that Truman was given to believe this was a reasonable prospect. On April 25, Stimson had assured the president that "physically the US is at present in the position of controlling the resources with which to construct and use it and no other nation could reach this position for some years."[30] In the report Groves and Stimson reviewed with Truman, the president was also advised that the Combined Development Trust, with "available funds in the sum of $25,000,000.00," had been created to manage the effort.[31] He was told, further, that

> With few exceptions, the United States and the United Kingdom will have exclusive control of all essential patents in the entire field and non-exclusive rights to all non-essential patents.[32]

On May 18, the Interim Committee discussed the question of how long the United States could keep its nuclear monopoly. Byrnes had read a September 30, 1944, memorandum prepared by Bush and Conant which estimated that from a technical point of view Russia might catch up in three to four years.[33] Groves countered with a twenty-year estimate.[34] Herken's analysis suggests that it was essentially because of his confidence in the global resource control effort that Groves believed the United States could maintain a monopoly of nuclear weapons for so long.[35]

Nor does it seem that the notion of controlling world uranium and other resources appeared in any way farfetched to the most important single member of the Interim Committee. Szilard reports that at the meeting with the three atomic scientists on May 28,

> the first thing that Byrnes told us was that General Groves had informed him that Russia had no uranium. Of course, if Russia did not have any uranium then she would not be able to participate in an atomic-arms race, but to me this seemed to be an exceedingly unlikely assumption.[36]

That Byrnes appears to have been impressed with Groves' general assessment is also evident from other documents. Later, at the September 1945 London Conference of Foreign Ministers—partly on the basis of a previous suggestion by Stettinius—Molotov raised the question of a possible Russian trusteeship over Tripolitania (part of modern Libya).[37] British Foreign Minister Ernest Bevin thought the Russians were after the uranium in the Belgian Congo. "We have a contract for this uranium," Walter Brown noted in his diary, "but as JFB [Byrnes] says this contract is no stronger than the battleship that guards it."[38] Upon returning to Washington, Byrnes met with Joseph Davies—who offered an explanation of the Soviet position and met with what he called a "heated" reply from Byrnes:

> [Byrnes] said that the Russians wanted Libya and Tripolitania because of the Belgian Congo, and its mineral deposits, etc.; that the Uranium deposits in the Congo was what they were after and he went over to the map to point them oout [sic]. . . .[39]

Similarly, during an October 16 Committee of Three meeting,

> MR. BYRNES remarked that in his opinion the principal reason Russia wants Libya has to do with uranium. He pointed to the map how a Soviet base in Libya would facilitate their access right down to the Belgian Congo.

Secretary of War Patterson* asked Byrnes "whether the Russians are really serious with regard to Libya." Byrnes "replied emphatically in the affirmative. He said it was the cause of all his troubles. . . ."[40]

Despite the skepticism of the scientific experts, by December 1945 Groves reported to the new secretary of war, Robert Patterson, that from "present

---

*Robert P. Patterson replaced Stimson as secretary of war in September 1945.

knowledge, it appears that the Trust group of nations controls 97% of the world's uranium output from presently producing countries."[41]

Scholars and journalists seeking answers to the question of why the atomic bomb was used have scrutinized the records of the Interim Committee with extreme care since they were first released in the 1970s. The only formal body considering the atomic bomb seemed an obvious locus of policy development, and many early accounts portrayed the committee as the center of serious thinking about the decision to use the weapon. Moreover, the committee did, in fact, recommend using the bomb—and in a particular way.

But was this important group a serious institutional and policy force in connection with the key question? The length of time between its May 31–June 1 recommendations and August 6 alone suggests its distance from presidential decision-making when it counted. And in the "two months and six days afterwards," as Navy representative, Undersecretary Ralph Bard later stressed, "a lot . . . happened. . . ."[42]

A good deal of writing on this period—and on the Interim Committee's role—is now known to be seriously flawed. Most knowledgeable experts no longer credit the Interim Committee per se with significant influence on the decision to use the atomic bomb. Misconceptions still exist in some modern accounts, but as time has passed our understanding has become somewhat more sophisticated about where real power lay in Washington during the summer of 1945.[43]

In fact, so far as we know the question of whether the atomic bomb should or should not be used was never seriously discussed by the Interim Committee. Historians pondering this point have suggested that the committee simply assumed the bomb would be employed; the only thing it apparently discussed during its May 1945 deliberations was "how" to use it, not "whether."[44] Moreover, even these questions were an afterthought: As we have seen, legislative and other recommendations for the postwar period—together with what we would now call the preparation of a public relations strategy for the bomb—were its primary initial concerns.*

During the Interim Committee discussions a brief exploration of alternatives to the use of the bomb against a city apparently did take place—but it was seemingly both very brief and quite informal: So far as we can tell from memoirs and after-the-fact recollections the subject came up on May 31. Over lunch, Byrnes apparently asked one scientist, Dr. Ernest O. Lawrence, about a suggestion he had made during the morning that the Japanese might be given a demonstration of the bomb's force before it was employed in a

---

*For a review of its work preparing legislation, see Hewlett and Anderson, *The New World*, pp. 353–54, 360, 367–69, 408–14, 425, 453.

way that would result in heavy casualties.[45] (Arthur Compton indicates in his memoirs that he was the one who raised the issue over lunch. Unfortunately, there are no "lunchtime" minutes and the official minutes, which clearly omit many things, do not mention any discussion of a demonstration—another gap in the record.[46])

According to Lawrence, the idea was explored for "perhaps ten minutes." It was pointed out that the deaths resulting from a city attack "would not be greater in order of magnitude than the number already killed in fire raids." There was also the possibility that the Japanese might attack the bomber—or even bring American prisoners onto the site. In any case, J. Robert Oppenheimer could think of no demonstration "sufficiently spectacular" to produce surrender. Also, if the demonstration were to fail, the opportunity to cause maximum shock with a surprise assault would be lost.[47]

When the Interim Committee resumed its formal deliberations later in the afternoon, the minutes simply record the following concerning the bomb's use:

> After much discussion concerning various types of targets and the effects to be produced, *the Secretary expressed the conclusion, on which there was general agreement, that we could not give the Japanese any warning; that we could not concentrate on a civilian area; but that we should seek to make a profound psychological impression on as many inhabitants as possible.*[48]

The Interim Committee minutes also record that:

> *At the suggestion of Dr. Conant the Secretary agreed that the most desirable target would be a vital war plant employing a large number of workers and closely surrounded by workers' houses.*[49]

Stimson was later to suggest that there was a more deliberative and thoughtful discussion of whether the atomic bomb should or should not be used against Japan. However, the minutes do not hint at this and few scholars credit the idea. When queried about the specific point by historian Alice Kimball Smith, Ralph Bard also recalled no such serious exploration of the question of the bomb's use as Stimson subsequently maintained. "In fact," Smith writes, "he has the impression that the Committee approved a decision that had already been made."[50]

That the bomb would be used was essentially taken for granted at the time when the Interim Committee did its main work is also suggested by the way Stimson reported its recommendations to Truman.[51] The secretary did not (so his diary suggests) discuss the question of whether to use the bomb or, indeed, how. The main point of concern in the first week of June was that there be no revelation to Russia or anyone else until "the first bomb had been successfully laid on Japan. . . ."[52] The formal recommendations of the Interim Committee as to how the bomb should be used do not appear to have warranted specific presentation to the president.

It is also worth noting that at the time of the committee's deliberations not only did it not have formal access to the intelligence information reviewed earlier, but many of the key events occurred after the committee completed its main work—including: the crisis in Japanese politics (leading to the late June Supreme War Council decisions); the collapse of Okinawa; intercepts showing Tokyo's intense effort to find some way to work a negotiation with Russia; and, above all, the mid-July personal intervention of the Emperor to try to end the fighting. As J. Robert Oppenheimer was subsequently to recall:

> We didn't know beans about the military situation in Japan. We didn't know whether they could be caused to surrender by other means or whether the invasion was really inevitable. But in backs of our minds was the notion that the invasion was inevitable because we had been told that.[53]

Oppenheimer's remark, of course, did not apply to all of those involved in the committee's discussions. Stimson was fully informed of intelligence findings and MAGIC intercepts. Marshall (who was present for the key May 31 and June 1 discussions by invitation) also knew everything there was to know.* It also appears that Bard was well informed. Although it is possible that in May these men still believed a bloody invasion fight to the finish was the only alternative to using the bomb, evidence that a modification of terms plus the Russian attack seemed likely to stop the fighting was already quite impressive. For one thing, at precisely this point the president himself made a successful all-out effort to nail down the Soviet option in case the test should fail. That the intelligence and other information in hand significantly impacted other formal recommendations, in connection with clarifying the surrender formula and the Russian option by the end of the first week of June also points to the prior development of a considerable degree of common understanding among the main players in the policy process.†

The Interim Committee itself recognized that Japan's situation had so deteriorated that all that was needed was a massive "shock." Contrary to some sketchy evidence we have that earlier on there had been some thought given to using the weapon militarily—i.e., as supportive tactical bombardment directly related to an invasion assault—now the psychological shock of its impact was deemed all that was needed to force Japan to surrender.[54] It is also

---

*Marshall was absent on the afternoon of May 31.
†Or to be exact in the case of clarifying the surrender terms, impacted policy by June 9.

of interest that Stimson, Marshall, and Bard—the men most closely connected with the military who had access to solid information—each were to
propose strategies which they apparently believed reasonably likely to end
the war without bombing an urban center.

Perhaps most telling is that so sophisticated a military figure as Marshall
clearly felt Japan was in such dire straits that an alternative was worth considering. The notion of attacking a "war plant employing a large number of
workers and closely surrounded by workers' houses" was by no means the
position of all the officials concerned. Marshall had already cut through objections to a "demonstration" by suggesting that the first attack be a very
large military target like a naval installation. This would demonstrate the
weapon, but do it in a way which did not incur massive civilian casualties.
If it did not work, a city could be attacked subsequently.* Nor would such
an approach be any more subject to worries about the bomber being shot
down or the weapon failing than attacking a city.

The weakness of the evidence needs to be acknowledged. Contrary to
some accounts, which by their tone or authoritative stance seem to imply real
knowledge, the truth is that we do not know a great deal about many details
of what went on in the Interim Committee meetings.[55] Between May 9 and
July 19, the committee deliberated for a total of more than thirty hours (including lunchtime discussions on three occasions). The "notes" available
compress this into some 59 pages—i.e., about two typed pages for each full
hour of discussion.[56] Moreover, subsequent reports suggest the discussion of
topics which are not mentioned in the minutes or referred to only in very
general terms.

We do not know, for instance, the specific meaning of the following general phrase in the minutes preceding the key recommendation: "after much
discussion concerning various types of targets and the effects to be
produced. . . ."[57] Again, Bard subsequently reported something of a renewed
debate over whether a warning should be given—and a discussion of his
June 27 memorandum on the subject: "It did take place and the majority of
the Committee felt that we should go ahead on the program as voted on
June 1st."[58] No official record of this exists, however.

Political scientist Leon V. Sigal has examined the functioning of the Interim Committee from the point of view of institutional and bureaucratic politics. His analysis is that the committee "was not an action channel. . . ."[59]
He suggests that its "consideration of how to use the bomb in the war was
instead a maneuver to influence a decision made elsewhere in the policy
process."

*See above, pp. 53–54.

It became part of the bureaucratic strategy of a handful of senior American officials with a stake in dropping the bomb on Japan to head off opposition in the scientific community, lest that opposition succeeded in widening the range of options before the president on wartime use.[60]

Sigal argues that the bureaucratic process which set the terms of reference for subsequent approval was controlled by Groves. "The action channels for selecting targets for the bomb were the Military Policy Committee and the Target Committee."[61] Thereafter, the Interim Committee, which "began as an interagency committee to reach agreement on postwar plans, added a panel of surrogates for the scientific community to bless an option for using the bomb already chosen in military channels."[62]

Perhaps it is not surprising that Groves was later to comment privately:

. . . the story as to the Interim Committee having any influence on [the decision to use the atomic bomb] . . . is just plain bunk.[63]

Groves was also quite clear:

The committee was selected very carefully—the first decision was whether or not there should be any military people in it, in particular, whether I should be on it. And it was decided that it should be all civilian. That was something that I was very much in favor of, I don't know whether I recommended it or not but it was set up so that there would be no possibility of any legitimate claim of the military trying to run the country.[64]

However one assesses the specific reasons the Interim Committee was established, the most important shift in modern understanding of the only formal government body to deliberate over the atomic bomb has come about in regard to its relative power vis-à-vis one specific member—the man who represented the president personally, and who was about to become secretary of state, James F. Byrnes.

The work of several scholars has demonstrated that, far from formulating policy independently and upon due deliberation, the Interim Committee as a body responded for the most part to the interventions of its most important member when any significant difference of opinion arose: *Byrnes spoke for the president.*[65]

The other members of the committee were men of far less influence—and, in all but one case, less stature—than Byrnes. The only other Cabinet-level member, the secretary of war, was a man known to be in ill health and, unlike Byrnes, not very close to Truman. Moreover, Stimson attended the meetings only sporadically: He was not there on May 14, May 18, or

June 21, and he missed a significant part of the committee's discussions on May 31 and June 1.[66]

What is important about the documentation offered by the committee records is the contemporaneous evidence of Byrnes' general attitude—as well as the fact that as Truman's personal representative he was in position to dominate the committee's discussion and did not hesitate to do so.

Since there was general agreement on the need to push production and on the bomb's use, the committee records suggest there was really only one issue where any serious question arose in connection with the questions we are considering. It was an important matter, however, and one in which Byrnes' role was crucial—indeed, decisive.

To many at the time the period leading up to the test of the first nuclear weapon was portentous—weeks, days, hours when a die might be cast which could easily determine what Jonathan Schell was later to call "The Fate of the Earth."[67] The new development involved not only the current war but perhaps the future of the planet itself. A central issue was: Once nuclear weapons were proven to be a possibility, was there any conceivable way to avoid a catastrophic global arms race?

No one knew where it might end.

And this, of course, brought the question of Russia sharply to the fore: How should that dictatorial, enigmatic nation, and its dictatorial, enigmatic leader, be approached?

Excellent studies of the complex ins and outs of policy discussions leading up to May 1945 are now available.[68] Broadly, a number of scientists both in and outside of government urged what seemed to be a prudent course.

It was impossible to know whether a worldwide arms race could be headed off. Perhaps perfection could not be achieved; but since all nations would face the same danger, it was not unreasonable to hope that at least some form of what later came to be called "arms control" (if not total international management of nuclear weapons) might be feasible.* Given the stakes, a serious attempt had to be made; even partial control of the new weapon would clearly be impossible if an attempt were not made.

The first point of any such effort also seemed obvious: It required what today is called "trust-building." And the initial trust-building question was whether or not to inform Stalin—at the time a valued ally in the fight against Hitler—of the existence of the atomic bomb before it was used. There was widespread recognition that to simply spring the weapon on the world—and

---

*There is, of course, a substantial difference between the idea of attempting to reach some kind of control agreement (especially in the era before complex ballistics delivery systems were in place)—and the notion that Russia could have been persuaded not to build nuclear weapons at all if the United States had them. Although the two issues often have been confused in subsequent discussions, they are obviously not the same.

on Stalin—risked launching the nuclear era in a manner likely to produce maximum distrust. Since the weapon was obviously going to be revealed to the world when it was used on Japan, there seemed little to lose by communicating its existence beforehand.[69]

Various forms of this argument were urged at various times, notably early on by the eminent Danish physicist Niels Bohr, who in April 1944 believed that without an agreement to outlaw atomic weapons "any temporary advantage, however great, may be outweighed by a perpetual menace to human security."[70] On July 3, 1944, Bohr had urged Roosevelt directly that:

[We must seek] an initiative aiming at forestalling a fateful competition about the formidable weapon, [an initiative which] should serve to uproot any cause of distrust between the powers on whose harmonious collaboration the fate of coming generations will depend. . . .[71]

In a memorandum to Stimson dated September 30, 1944, Vannevar Bush, the director of the Office of Scientific Research and Development, and James B. Conant, the chairman of the National Defense Research Committee, also noted that while the United States and Britain were at a great advantage, other nations could eventually build a bomb.

Bush and Conant had suggested that there be a demonstration before using the bomb, and that information might be released at that time:

[I]t is our strong recommendation that plans be laid for complete disclosure of the history of the development and all but the manufacturing and military details on the bombs as soon as the first bomb has been demonstrated. This demonstration might be over enemy territory, or in our own country, with subsequent notice to Japan that the materials would be used against the Japanese mainland unless surrender was forthcoming.[72]

Bush and Conant also emphasized the potential for an arms race:

It is our contention that it would be extremely dangerous for the United States and Great Britain to attempt to carry on in complete secrecy further developments of the military applications of this art. If this were done Russia would undoubtedly proceed in secret along the same lines and so too might certain other countries, including our defeated enemies.[73]

They proposed that "free interchange of all scientific information on this subject be established under the auspices of an international office deriving its power from whatever association of nations is developed at the close of the present war."[74]

Similarly, on the eve of the critical May 31 Interim Committee meeting,

Stimson sent Marshall "a remarkable document"—a letter he had just received and which "I should like you to read before tomorrow's meeting," from O. C. Brewster, an engineer working on the project with the Kellex Corporation of New York.[75] Brewster's deferentially worded plea stressed that:

> Our best friends could not permit us to be the only possessor of this thing. How could they know where our friendship might be five, ten, or twenty years hence? Others, not our best friends, would be still more anxious for their own legitimate self protection to prepare themselves. I submit that we, the United States, could not rest complacently if, say, Mexico, France, or Russia, or even Britain were the sole possessor of this means of sudden destruction.[76]

Brewster was particularly worried that some production facilities were clearly oriented to post-1945 output, and hence were bound to cause concern about the future. He urged that the United States take the initiative to establish an international commission to control nuclear weapons—and that as a demonstration of good faith it temporarily halt production. The United States could announce that it would resume work on production "if world agreement is not reached."[77]

The fundamental question inherent in all of this was formally posed at the May 31 meeting by Oppenheimer and Marshall. Key passages of the minutes capture the flow of the argument:

> In considering the problem of controls and international collaboration the question of paramount concern was the attitude of Russia. *Dr. Oppenheimer* pointed out that Russia had always been very friendly to science and . . . suggested that we might open up this subject with them in a tentative fashion and in the most general terms without giving them any details of our productive effort. He thought that we might say that a great national effort had been put into this project and express a hope for cooperation with them in this field. He felt strongly that we should not prejudge the Russian attitude in this matter.
>
> At this point *General Marshall* discussed at some length the story of charges and countercharges that have been typical of our relations with the Russians, pointing out that most of these allegations have proven unfounded. The seemingly uncooperative attitude of Russia in military matters stemmed from the necessity of maintaining security. . . . With regard to this field he was inclined to favor the building up of a combination among like-minded powers, thereby forcing Russia to fall in line by the very force of this coalition. General Marshall was certain that we need have no fear that the Russians, if they had knowledge of

our project, would disclose this information to the Japanese. He raised the question whether it might be desirable to invite two prominent Russian scientists to witness the test.[78]

At this point Byrnes forcefully intervened to present what in fact was the polar-opposite position—namely, that nothing should be done which in any way might allow the Russians advance knowledge of the weapon:

> *Mr. Byrnes* expressed a fear that if information were given to the Russians, even in general terms, Stalin would ask to be brought into the partnership. He felt this to be particularly likely in view of our commitments and pledges of cooperation with the British.[79]

Dr. Bush objected that "even the British do not have any of our blue prints on plants."[80] However, the argument did not impress Byrnes; it was at this point that the previously cited conclusion was reached:

> *Mr. Byrnes* expressed the view, *which was generally agreed to by all present*, that the most desirable program would be to push ahead as fast as possible in production and research to make certain that we stay ahead and at the same time make every effort to better our political relations with Russia.[81]

The dynamics which led from the first part of the discussion to the final conclusion are obvious even from the dry minutes. Robert Messer's characterization is that "Byrnes's influential opposition to any prior disclosure succeeded in reversing the entire tenor of the committee's discussion."[82] The official historians of the U.S. Atomic Energy Commission put it this way: "Such a strong statement by a man of Byrnes's prestige was not to be dismissed lightly. All present indicated their concurrence."[83]

Another initiative taken by Byrnes during the Interim Committee deliberations of June 1 is also instructive. The day after the above discussion the committee returned to the "use of the bomb" question:

> *Mr. Byrnes recommended*, and the Committee *agreed*, that the Secretary of War should be advised that, while recognizing that the final selection of the target was essentially a military decision, the present view of the Committee was that the bomb should be used against Japan as soon as possible; that it be used on a war plant surrounded by workers' homes; and that it be used without prior warning.[84]

It is unclear why the committee should have felt it necessary essentially to repeat what it had decided the previous day. Richard Rhodes suggests that while "Stimson was away Byrnes swiftly and decisively co-opted the committee."[85] He cites the view of committee secretary R. Gordon Arneson that

"Mr. Byrnes felt that it was important there be a final decision on the question of the use of the weapon."[86]

It is also unclear why the new phrase "as soon as possible" was introduced by Byrnes. Possibly this was simply an obvious point (though, if so, it is odd it was not mentioned on the previous day).*

One final point concerning the power of the man who spoke for the president—and about the climate of opinion regarding what sociologists sometimes call "status deference": Stimson's diary reveals the concern even of the eminent secretary of war about how he was regarded, personally, by both Truman and Byrnes. After his meeting with Truman on June 6 we find Stimson writing: "His manner was so friendly and confident that it was a great reassurance to me as to our relations and cheered me up throughout the day."[87] And just before Potsdam Stimson notes: "I have been anxious about not having talked with Jimmy Byrnes over my trip to Berlin for I fear that he might think that I was encroaching on his ground."[88]

An obvious question is why—so far as the currently available records show—Marshall did not press the argument after May 29 that the atomic bomb should first be used on a military installation. One answer seems plain: if, as Ralph Bard subsequently reported, it was pretty well understood that the essential decision had already been made, this could only mean made by the president. Marshall was known for his professional determination to follow—not buck—directions which came from the ultimate civilian authority. In later years he often stressed that he advised mainly on the strictly military aspects of the problem—that the basic atomic bomb decision was not made by the military.

A perhaps equally likely explanation why Marshall's demonstration proposal does not appear in subsequent records, however, may well be the simplest. During the morning meeting of May 31, as we have just seen, Marshall made a rather forceful trust-building argument for inviting Russian scientists to witness the test—and had been essentially cut down, his argument bluntly dismissed by Byrnes. Knowing where Byrnes was coming from, it would be a rather foolish military bureaucrat indeed who would challenge the president's personal representative directly a second time on the even more important matter of the bomb's use. Especially if it was obvious to everyone that the essential decisions were being made elsewhere.

---

*June 1 is also the same day that, as we have seen, a new hard-line presidential statement was issued which backtracked from Truman's May 8 statement defining unconditional surrender as applying to the Japanese military. For a discussion of certain other aspects of the Interim Committee's position at this point and late in June, see below, pp. 524–25, 528.

Chapter 13

THE "SECOND TRACK" AND ASIA

[I]t may be necessary to have it out with Russia on her relations to Manchuria and Port Arthur and various other parts of North China, and also the relations of China to us. Over any such tangled wave of problems the S-1 secret would be dominant and yet we will not know until after that time probably, until after that meeting, whether this is a weapon in our hands or not. We think it will be shortly afterwards, but it seems a terrible thing to gamble with such big stakes in diplomacy without having your master card in your hand.
—Secretary of War Henry L. Stimson, diary, May 15, 1945

Two additional fragments of information regarding Byrnes' views at this time are worth noting; the first is contemporaneous: on June 4, Admiral Leahy's diary records that

> At 5:30 Mr. Justice Byrnes called at the house to discuss some results of his study of Dr. Busch's [*sic*] super explosive. He is more favorably impressed than I am with prospects of success in the final development and use of this weapon.[1]

The second document is after-the-fact: In a December 31, 1946 letter to the now retired secretary of war, President Truman recalled the atomic bomb committee Stimson had chaired:

> Shortly after I succeeded to the Presidency the matter [of the atomic bomb] was explained to me and I appointed a Commission consisting of Mr. Byrnes, Vannevar Bush and someone else, whose name I have forgotten.[2]

Perhaps it is not surprising that Truman seems to have forgotten Stimson's own role and recalled little about the actual functioning or membership of the

Interim Committee—except that Byrnes (together with Bush) was on it. It is also an indication of 1945 power realities that when Stimson first told Truman the committee's recommendations, as we have seen, the president responded that Byrnes had already reported to him.[3]

Let us quickly round out a few additional well-known facts related to the committee. In accordance with the Quebec agreement signed by Roosevelt and Churchill in August 1943 the United States was required to seek Britain's consent before using the new weapon.[4] At the July 4, 1945 Combined Policy Committee meeting this was done and Britain officially agreed to using the atomic bomb against Japan.[5]

Again, the committee discussed (on June 21) "the question of Clause Two of the Quebec Agreement which provides that the signatories may not use the weapon against a third country except by mutual consent." After some discussion it was moved

> that the Secretary of War be advised that the Interim Committee favored revocation of Clause Two by appropriate action. The motion was unanimously carried.[6]

The United States wished to have the unilateral option to use the new weapon as it saw fit after the war.

There is one final important area in which second-track thinking about the new weapon and diplomacy towards Russia directly intersected planning for the use of the atomic bomb—and again, where the simultaneity of decision-making on several fronts at once stands out:

Once the Russians declared war and the Red Army crossed into Manchuria, political relationships in north China and Korea could not help but be affected. Accordingly, even those who still wished for Russian help (to say nothing of those who opposed it) began to see the atomic bomb as a way not only to end the war, but perhaps to end it as soon as possible—preferably before the Russians attacked, and certainly, if feasible, before the Red Army got very far in its assault.

Harriman again was among the officials most concerned about Russian political influence. In meetings with State Department officials on April 19, he worried that Stalin would eventually support the Chinese communists against Chiang Kai-shek's Nationalists.[7] On April 21, at the secretary of state's staff meeting

> Mr. Harriman suggested Soviet policies might cause further trouble [in] Macedonia, Turkey, and especially China. If Chiang does not make a

deal with the Communists before the Russians occupy Manchuria and North China, they are certainly going to establish a Soviet-dominated Communist regime in these areas and then there will be a completely divided China, much more difficult of uniting. The extent to which the Soviets will go in all directions will depend on the extent of our pressure.[8]

George F. Kennan, the chargé d'affaires in Moscow, also sent a troubled cable concerning Asian matters. A State Department summary presented to the president on April 24 stated:

Kennan is convinced that Soviet policy will remain a policy aimed at the achievement of maximum power with minimum responsibility and will involve the exertion of pressure in various areas. He recommends that we study with clinical objectivity the real character and implications of Russian Far Eastern aims. . . .

"It would be tragic if our anxiety for Russian support in the Far East were to lead us into an undue reliance on Russian aid," Kennan urged.[9]

Political issues in Asia were also on the minds of military specialists. In their April 25 report, "Pacific Strategy," the Joint Staff Planners advised the Joint Chiefs of Staff:

If Russia enters the war her forces will probably be the first into Manchuria. This will raise the question of introducing at least token U.S. forces into Asia.[10]

Finally, concern about Russia's intentions was also obvious among Republican leaders. We have noted that this was one of the main reasons former President Hoover wished to clarify the unconditional-surrender formula and halt the fighting as soon as possible. After the Soviet Union announced it would not renew its Neutrality Pact with Japan, *The New York Times* quoted another leading Republican—Senator Robert A. Taft—as questioning Russian interests "in some parts of China" and commenting:

It does not clear up the recent impression of Russia's non-cooperation in international matters. This thing can be done for her own interests. There is no question but that Russia is interested in some parts of China now occupied by Japan.[11]

A May 10 cable from U.S. Ambassador to China Patrick J. Hurley brought the issues into sharp relief. Hurley reported his belief that Chiang Kai-shek already knew most of the terms of the Far Eastern understanding with Stalin—and that he was certain the Chinese leader would agree in substance to the major provisions. Chiang had received reports of large-scale Soviet troop movements across the Trans-Siberian Railroad, and with speculation rife in Chungking Hurley advised that it was time that he be allowed to reveal the Yalta agreements.[12]

The next day, Harriman told a meeting of navy officials gathered in Forrestal's office that "it was time to come to a conclusion about the necessity for the early entrance of Russia into the Japanese war . . . ." "[I]f China continued weak," he argued, "Russian influence would move in quickly and toward ultimate domination. . . . [T]here could be no illusion about anything such as a 'free China' once the Russians got in, . . . the two or three hundred millions in that country would march when the Kremlin ordered."[13] Later the same day Harriman pressed the same argument with Leahy: Russia would enter the war "and will in the end exercise control over whatever government may be established in Manchuria and Outer Mongolia."[14]

On May 12, Forrestal and Harriman met again for a Saturday morning discussion, this time with Joseph Grew, John McCloy, Charles Bohlen, and Stettinius' assistant William Phillips. As McCloy's diary notes, they discussed the "general subject of the policy this country should pursue with Russia . . . and more particularly the need for reviewing the so-called Yalta Agreements with Russia."

> Apart from the Polish question, there was the question of Russian participation in the Japanese War. Did we want them in, and if so, did we want them occupying a part of Japan? Did we feel the time had come to review the Yalta Agreements? These and other questions it was thought ought to be considered before Mr. Harriman returned to Russia.[15]

Forrestal's published diary states that one of the questions they grappled with was: "How urgent is the necessity for quick Russian participation in the war against Japan?"[16] His unpublished diary notes further that "[Harriman's] conduct toward Stalin . . . would obviously be greatly conditioned by the degree of urgency."[17] McCloy's diary records:

> After discussion on the significance of some of these items particularly those in which China was deeply containing, the meeting broke up with the understanding that Mr. Bohlen and Mr. Harriman would present a memorandum concerning certain questions which should be considered by the Army and Navy authorities preparatory to final determination of policy being made by the Secretary of State in consultation with the President.[18]

Following the discussion, Grew sent parallel memoranda to the secretaries of war and navy indicating that before fulfilling the Yalta agreement the State Department thought it "desirable" to obtain additional commitments and clarifications from Stalin: The Soviet government should agree not only to support Chiang Kai-shek, but also to influence the Chinese communists to yield to the Nationalist government; the Soviet government should reaffirm support for Chinese sovereignty in Manchuria and for a four-power trusteeship for Korea; the Soviet government should agree to grant emergency landing rights for commercial flights in the Kurile Islands. The State Department wished to delay fulfilling the Yalta accord until such issues were clarified and wanted to know whether the military had any objections:

> Is the entry of the Soviet Union . . . of such vital interest to the United States as to preclude any attempt . . . to obtain Soviet agreement to certain desirable political objectives in the Far East prior to such entry?
>
> Should the Yalta decision in regard to Soviet political desires in the Far East be reconsidered or carried into effect in whole or in part?
>
> Should a Soviet demand . . . for participation in the military occupation of the Japanese home islands be granted . . . ?[19]

Stimson immediately recognized the intimate relationship of Grew's memorandum to the atomic bomb. On May 13 he noted: "These are vital questions and I am very glad that the State Department has brought them up and given us a chance to be heard on them."

> The questions cut very deep and in my opinion are powerfully connected with our success with S-1. Certainly they indicate a good deal of hard thinking "before the early part of this week" when they are to be discussed.[20]

The next day, Stimson went over the matter with Marshall, also confiding to his diary: "we both decided that [the questions from the State Department] were rather impractical to discuss now with anyone."[21] After Marshall left, Stimson spoke with McCloy. It was in the context of this discussion that Stimson observed that the time now was to "keep our mouths shut and let our actions speak for words."[22]

At the "red hot session" (Stimson's words) of the Committee of Three the next day, May 15, Stimson, Grew, Forrestal, Harriman, Phillips, and McCloy grappled with the questions again—primarily, the minutes note, "the matter of our attitude toward the so-called Yalta Agreements relating to the Soviet Union and the possible entry of that country into the Japanese war."[23] Stimson's diary again notes that he "tried to point out the difficulties which existed and I thought it premature to ask those questions; at least we were not yet in a position to answer them." It continues:

The trouble is that the President has now promised apparently to meet Stalin and Churchill on the first of July and at that time these questions [relating to the Yalta Far East agreements and Russian participation in the Pacific War] will become burning and it may be necessary to have it out with Russia on her relations to Manchuria and Port Arthur and various other parts of North China, and also the relations of China to us. Over any such tangled wave of problems the S-1 secret would be dominant and yet we will not know until after that time probably, until after that meeting, whether this is a weapon in our hands or not. We think it will be shortly afterwards, but it seems a terrible thing to gamble with such big stakes in diplomacy without having your master card in your hand. The best we could do today was to persuade Harriman not to go back until we had had time to think over these things a little bit harder.[24]

The Committee of Three minutes for May 15 record that it "was the consensus of the meeting that further study would be given to the subject and that in the meantime Mr. Harriman should be asked to stay on."[25] Since the minutes of this meeting appear to have been partly destroyed, precisely what was discussed is impossible to know. Grew's sleepless-night memorandum of May 19, however, gives a vivid sense at least of his worries: "Once Russia is in the war against Japan, then Mongolia, Manchuria, and Korea will gradually slip into Russia's orbit, to be followed in due course by China and eventually Japan."[26]*

Earlier, our central concern was focused on two questions: (1) when and whether Soviet help in the war against Japan was deemed to be important (especially if the atomic test should fail)—including shifts of U.S. policy back and forth at different points in time; (2) why this help was felt to be important—especially the "two-step logic" that a Russian declaration of war plus a clarification of the surrender terms might end the fighting.

Here our concern is slightly different: As the above documentary excerpts so clearly suggest, questions about the political implications of Russian entry into the war now also become inextricably involved with questions about the actual use and timing of the atomic bomb. Although some minor points in this regard have yet to be understood, there is no longer much doubt about how the overall process unfolded.

In general, it was still U.S. policy at this point to seek Soviet entry. On the other hand, on May 21, Stimson formally responded to Grew's questions that "Military considerations . . . do not preclude an attempt by the United States

---

*McCloy's diary shows, further, that in the long get-together he had with Harry Hopkins on May 21, the two also talked of "Russia in Asia–Manchuria–Port Arthur, Dairen, etc. etc." (McCloy Diary, May 21, 1945.)

Government to obtain Soviet agreement to desirable political objectives in the Far East prior to the entry of the Soviet Union into the Pacific War." He also observed, however, that the United States was in a relatively weak bargaining position: "The concessions . . . are generally matters which are within the military power of Russia to obtain regardless of U.S. military action short of war." At the moment, Stimson suggested, "it appears we can bring little, if any, military leverage to bear on the Russians in so far as the Far East is concerned, unless we choose to use force." Although the War Department had no objection to beginning an exploration of the Soviet position, and, in fact, felt that from "the military point of view it would be desirable to have a complete understanding and agreement with the Russians concerning the Far East," Stimson did not believe "that much good will come of a rediscussion at this time."[27]

It is possible to trace the following outlines of policy development: Hurley's May 10 cable came in one day after Truman had decided to postpone meeting Stalin—and also the day after the first Interim Committee meeting. The Lend-Lease cutoff orders went out on May 11. The president was sympathetic to Harriman and others who were generally worried about Soviet intentions and it appears clear that his initial response was to temporize. On May 12, Truman cabled Hurley rejecting his request for permission to discuss the Far Eastern understanding with Chiang Kai-shek, deeming it "not appropriate at the present time for you to give any information to the Chinese Government."[28]

In a talk with T. V. Soong on May 14, the president offered no information on the Yalta agreement. Soong—anxious for Stalin's help against the Chinese communists—told the president he thought it very important that he (Soong) should "proceed to Moscow to discuss this situation with the Soviet authorities . . ." after the San Francisco United Nations meetings. When they had met on April 19, Truman had actually advised Soong to leave for Moscow "as soon as he could," but this position had clearly been revised. Also, as Grew summarized the discussion of May 14, the question of whether Soong would be transported to Moscow by the United States, "was left open."[29]

When Harriman met with the president on May 15, he also expressed concern about the agreement on the Far East. Once more, however, Truman took no stand on the questions involved, saying only that "provided the Ambassador was not delayed too long it would be wise for him to go back to Moscow with clarity on those subjects."[30]

On May 16 Stimson met with the president to discuss a variety of issues—and, in particular, the question of timing. This is the day that Truman informed Stimson of his general strategy. We do not know to what extent Stimson expressed the views recorded in his previous day's diary entry—that it would be "a terrible thing to gamble with such big stakes in diplomacy without having your master card in your hand"; or to what extent he urged that the discussions with Stalin be postponed beyond the first of July. His memorandum to the president shows, however, that by the end of the conversation, in general Stimson's fears had been dispelled—and that, as indicated, the strategy Truman had determined upon was one which Stimson found to be good.

There was very little the president needed to do at this time with regard to the Far East: He simply had to continue to withhold instructions to fulfill the Yalta conditions of Soviet entry into the war (and to refuse the State Department's suggestion that the threat of a "rediscussion" be used to try to obtain new Soviet concessions). In fact, Hurley received no instructions to inform Chiang of the Yalta agreement, and the State Department was not allowed to initiate a new démarche.

When Harry Hopkins met with the president on May 19 to discuss his mission to Moscow, Truman's journal records only that he told him "to go to Stalin . . . and tell him just exactly what we intended to have in the way of carrying out the agreements, purported to have been made at Yalta. . . ."[31] As we have seen, two days later the president met with Harriman to go over instructions for the meeting.[32] Only at the end of May did the president take a further step. He did so in connection with his decisions—first, to secure a Soviet commitment to enter the war; second, to yield to Stalin's demands on Poland; and, third (after receiving precise information on the timing of the atomic test), to nail down July 15 as the time he would meet Stalin.

On May 28, Hopkins and Harriman sought a clarification of the Soviet attitude from Stalin on the future treatment of China, Manchuria, and Korea.[33] Hopkins' report to the president summarized the favorable results of the discussion:

> The Soviet Army will be properly deployed on the Manchurian positions by August 8th. . . .
> [Stalin] stated for the first time that he was willing to take [the Yalta proposals] up directly with Soong when he comes to Moscow. He wants to see Soong not later than July first and expects us to take matter [sic] up at the same time with Chiang-Kai-shek. . . .
> Stalin made categorial statement that he would do everything he could to promote unification of China under the leadership of Chiang-Kai-shek. . . . He proposes to back the Generalissimo in spite of the reservations he expressed about him.
> He repeated all his statements made at Yalta, that he wanted a unified and stable China . . . to control all of Manchuria. . . . He stated categor-

ically that he had no territorial claims against China and mentioned specifically Manchuria and Sinkiang and that he would respect Chinese sovereignty in all the areas his troops entered to fight the Japanese.

Stalin stated that he would welcome representatives of the Generalissimo to be with his troops entering Manchuria in order to facilitate the organization of Chinese administration in Manchuria.*

Stalin agreed with America's "open door" policy and went out of his way to indicate that the United States was the only power with the resources to aid China economically after the war. He observed that Russia would have all it could do to provide for the internal economy of the Soviet Union for many years to come.

Stalin agreed that there should be a trusteeship for Korea. . . .[34]

These assurances were all that could be asked. Although it was impossible to know whether Stalin would honor his pledges, both Hopkins and Harriman were optimistic. "We were very encouraged by conference on the Far East," Hopkins cabled. Harriman added:

> The talks about the Far East, I feel, were of real value, particularly Stalin's agreement to take up with Soong in the first instance the political matters affecting China in the Yalta agreement, and also his agreement to allow the Generalissimo's representatives to go into Manchuria with the Russian troops. . . .[35]

Truman was delighted with the report. Stimson's diary entry of June 6 records the enthusiasm conveyed to him by the president at their meeting earlier that day:

> He then asked me if I had heard of the accomplishment which Harry Hopkins had made in Moscow and when I said I had not he told me there was a promise in writing† by Stalin that Manchuria should remain fully Chinese except for a ninety-nine year lease of Port Arthur and the settlement of Dairen which we had hold of.[36]

At this same meeting, as noted, among the quid pro quos also vaguely discussed for taking the Russians into partnership in connection with the atomic bomb was a settlement of the Manchurian problem.[37]

Although Stalin had reaffirmed his pledge that the Red Army would be

---

*This was a critical point and would give the Nationalists a substantial advantage over the Chinese communists. (FRUS, Pots. I, p. 62.) Harriman, for one, had argued that it would be to Chiang Kai-shek's advantage to negotiate a clear understanding with Stalin.

†This is apparently an exaggeration. No record of a written agreement has been found, nor does such an agreement reappear in later negotiations on these points.

prepared to march by August 8 no troops would be committed, of course, until final agreement had been reached between the U.S.S.R. and China interpreting the remaining points of the Yalta record. Hopkins advised:

> It is therefore important that Soong come here not later than July 1st. Stalin is ready to see him any time now.[38]

The next step of the policy process at the top of the U.S. government is also fairly clear, but a bit complex. The president's renewed interest in securing Soviet help was clearly genuine. However, scholars of the Hiroshima decision have long known that Truman's position was not nearly as straightforward as it once appeared to be.

The available evidence suggests that U.S. policy from late May to mid-July sought simultaneously to insure that the Soviet Union would enter the war *if needed* and to delay a final decision on Soviet entry until the results of the atomic test were known.

On June 4 the president informed Hurley that a number of problems related to the Far East would be dealt with only when the heads of government met.[39] He also agreed to send Soong to Moscow. Five days later the Chinese foreign minister met with Truman and Grew, along with Leahy, and Soong was informed of the details of the Yalta agreements and of Stalin's promises to Hopkins. When Truman and Soong met again on June 14, the president explained that "his chief interest now was to see the Soviet Union participate in the Far Eastern war in sufficient time to be of help in shortening the war and thus save American and Chinese lives." He also made it quite clear that although this was

> his chief preoccupation at the moment he said he wished to assure Dr. Soong that he would do nothing which would harm the interests of China since China was a friend of the United States in the Far East.[40]

When Soong reached Moscow on June 30, he pressed Harriman for an elucidation of certain specific details of the agreement.[41] However, the time for this had clearly not arrived.* In one of his first acts after being sworn in as secretary of state on July 3, Byrnes cabled Harriman that "the president and I feel it would be unwise for this Government to attempt to act as inter-

---

*It is difficult to determine from present sources the nuanced meaning of Truman's personal tactical understanding as it developed in June (e.g., on the 4th, 14th, and 30th)—as compared with the rather obvious positions taken a couple of weeks later (*e.g.* July 3 and July 6) after Soong actually got to Moscow. Byrnes later suggested the U.S. posture in this connection was part of a delaying tactic before as well as after the atomic test. See below, p. 585.

preter on this or any other point of the Yalta Agreement in connection with the present bi-lateral Chinese-Soviet talks." Byrnes added:

> you may informally confirm to Soong your understanding that in so far as this Government is concerned there was no discussion of interpretation on the sentence of the Yalta decision relating to the status of Outer Mongolia and that in the absence of such discussion the accepted meaning of the words as written would be that the present factual and juridical status of Outer Mongolia are to be preserved.[42]

On July 6—the day the U.S. delegation set sail for Europe aboard the *Augusta*—Byrnes further instructed Harriman to "inform both the Soviet Government and T. V. Soong that as a party to the Yalta Agreement we would expect to be consulted before any arrangement is concluded between the Soviet and Chinese Governments. . . ."[43]

The United States was clearly not anxious to put the final touches on an understanding which would trigger a Soviet declaration of war.* The president had postponed the Potsdam meeting until sometime after June 30, then until mid-July, "to give us more time."[44] The first combat-ready atomic bombs were expected to be ready two weeks later, roughly the same time (or perhaps a few days before) the Red Army was expected to march.[45]

The unavoidable reality was that although the scientists were confident, the atomic bomb at this point in time was still a theoretical construct. In connection with planning for June 18 White House military discussions, we have previously noted a mid-June telephone transcript between the top navy and army planners, Rear Admiral Donald B. Duncan and General George A. Lincoln. Additional portions of this conversation capture the odd situation in which a Russian declaration of war might be crucial and yet—given the likely diplomatic costs—was not really wanted:

> *L:* We are committed to the Russians, also . . .
> *D:* Here is one thing I want to check with you. We haven't talked about it.
> [At this point, the transcript goes blank. When it picks up again, Duncan is speaking.]

---

*According to Harriman, the Chinese had to be held back: "I found that Soong was not at all concerned with some of the things that worried us. He felt it was a tremendous achievement to have Stalin recognize the sovereignty of Chiang Kai-shek's National Government over Manchuria. He was far less concerned than we had been about such details as whether Chinese or Russian troops would guard the railroad or who would be the Port Master of Dairen. I saw him almost every day and urged him to be more firm." (Harriman and Abel, *Special Envoy*, p. 483.)

D: . . . opposed going tearing in and badgering the Russians to do thus and so. I think in consonance with our policy, which has lately been adopted, that we probably shouldn't even raise the question with the Russians. Let them bring it up.

L: Well, I think on the Russian angle that all we will say is that we want them to fight.

D: We want the Russians to do one thing. I think it would be good for us, probably, if we got a quick ending of this thing and we got the Japanese capitulation before the Russians came in. I mean if that happened in that way, it would be good.

L: We have to plan as if it is not going to happen.[46]

It is also clear that every effort was made to speed the production of the atomic bomb. "I can testify personally," physicist Philip Morrison later recalled, "that a date near August tenth was a mysterious final date which we, who had the daily technical job of readying the bomb, had to meet at whatever cost in risk or money or good development policy."[47]

Byrnes, as noted, had also made sure that the Interim Committee's final recommendation stressed the new weapon should be used "as soon as possible."

Chapter 14

THE CONCERNED SCIENTISTS

If the United States were to be the first to release this new means of indiscriminate destruction upon mankind, she would sacrifice public support throughout the world, precipitate the race for armaments, and prejudice the possibility of reaching an international agreement on the future control of such weapons.

Much more favorable conditions for the eventual achievement of such an agreement could be created if nuclear bombs were first revealed to the world by a demonstration in an appropriately selected uninhabited area.

—Committee on Social and Political Implications
("The Franck Committee"), June 1945

Although a great deal is now known about the efforts to influence events by a number of the people directly involved in the Manhattan Project, the scientists have been largely absent from this account because they had virtually no impact on government decisions.[1]

This is not to say the key scientists here and elsewhere were not active. We have noted Niels Bohr's attempt to convince Churchill and Roosevelt of the need to head off an arms race with the Soviet Union (and the attempts of Vannevar Bush and James Conant to take steps in this direction as well).[2] Indeed, Leon Sigal and others have argued that one reason the Interim Committee—and especially its Scientific Panel—was established was to placate the scientists.[3]

Conant biographer James Hershberg underscores the importance of this motive as well. Conant advised Stimson, Hershberg writes, that it was "essential" that "the government have full support of the scientific community," and that it was important "there be no public bickering among experts after the bomb became public knowledge."[4]

One senses the same concern in a memorandum prepared for Stimson on May 30 before a meeting with the Scientific Panel. It was an opportunity, the secretary was advised, "through them to express appreciation to the whole scientific group who have done so much to develop and make the project possible."

> . . . the meeting is to give the scientists an opportunity on their side to tell the Committee whatever they may have on their mind and to give the Committee also an opportunity to ask questions so as to increase their knowledge of the project from the scientific standpoint.[5]

After the meeting a pleased Stimson noted:

> I think we made an impression upon the scientists that we were looking at this like statesmen and not like merely soldiers anxious to win the war at any cost.[6]

The Scientific Panel, of course, represented the top echelon of scientist-administrators managing the Manhattan Project. The situation among most of the people working day-to-day in the field was not so simple: Most had initially joined the project out of fear that Hitler might build an atomic bomb—and as it became increasingly evident that there was no Nazi bomb, a number began to worry about the implications of what they were doing. Several—especially among the Chicago-based scientists—tried to make their concerns heard by the men making the decisions in Washington.

The most energetic and innovative efforts were clearly those of Leo Szilard, the iconoclastic Hungarian physicist. Szilard had played a pivotal role in initiating the American atomic bomb project, convincing Albert Einstein in 1939 to put his name to a now-famous letter urging President Roosevelt to create what ultimately became the Manhattan Project.[7] As we have seen, in late May 1945 Szilard, together with two other scientists—Harold Urey and Walter Bartky—met with James F. Byrnes. In part, their purpose was to discuss

> the psychological advantages of avoiding the use of atomic bombs against Japan and, instead, of staging a demonstration of the atomic bombs at a time which appears most appropriate from the point of view of its effect on the governments concerned. . . .[8]

As Szilard subsequently remarked, he was concerned that "by demonstrating the bomb and using it in the war against Japan, we might start an atomic arms race between America and Russia which might end with the destruction of both countries."[9]

The meeting with Byrnes was an eye-opener—albeit a depressing one—and apparently a spur to further activism. Szilard, shaken by the realization that the man about to take over the direction of foreign policy saw the new weapon primarily in terms of its utility as a diplomatic threat, returned to Chicago determined to urge some form of collective protest.

A good deal of soul-searching had already taken place among the atomic scientists at the Chicago-based Metallurgical Laboratory. Now, in June, a committee on "Social and Political Implications" headed by the Nobel Prize–winning physicist James Franck was appointed to put the views of a significant group in writing. The central recommendations of the Franck Committee were against a surprise attack on Japan and for a demonstration in an uninhabited area. The two were not quite the same; nor were the rationales.

The negative recommendation had at its core the committee's strong plea that the number-one priority of U.S. policy should be to avoid an arms race:

> If the United States were to be the first to release this new means of indiscriminate destruction upon mankind, she would sacrifice public support throughout the world, precipitate the race for armaments, and prejudice the possibility of reaching an international agreement on the future control of such weapons.[10]

Beyond this:

> Russia, and even allied countries which bear less mistrust of our ways and intentions, as well as neutral countries may be deeply shocked. It will be very difficult to persuade the world that a nation which was capable of secretly preparing and suddenly releasing a new weapon, as indiscriminate as the rocket bomb and a thousand times more destructive, is to be trusted in its proclaimed desire of having such weapons abolished by international agreement.[11]

A third "fall-back" argument bolstered the two basic points:

> It must be stressed that if one takes the pessimistic point of view and discounts the possibility of an effective international control over nuclear weapons at the present time, then the advisability of an early use of nuclear bombs against Japan becomes even more doubtful—quite independent of any humanitarian considerations. If an international agreement is not concluded immediately after the first demonstration, this will mean a flying start toward an unlimited armaments race. If this race is inevitable, we have every reason to delay its beginning as long as possible in order to increase our head start still further.[12]

The positive formulation stressed the trust-building value of putting off an attack against Japan:

Much more favorable conditions for the eventual achievement of such an agreement could be created if nuclear bombs were first revealed to the world by a demonstration in an appropriately selected uninhabited area.[13]

In any event, an attack could always take place later if need be:

After . . . a demonstration the weapon could be used against Japan if a sanction of the United Nations (and of public opinion at home) could be obtained, perhaps after a preliminary ultimatum to Japan to surrender or at least to evacuate certain regions as an alternative to the total destruction of this target.[14]

The Franck Report was completed on June 11. On June 12, Arthur Compton met with R. Gordon Arneson, the Interim Committee secretary, to discuss it. He also sent the document to the "Secretary of War—*Attention: Mr. George Harrison*" with a cover letter stating that he was "submitting this at the request of the Laboratory, for the attention of your Interim Advisory Committee."

The memorandum has not yet been considered by other members of the "Scientific Panel." This will be done within a few days, and a report by the panel dealing with the matter in question will be submitted. In the meantime, however, because time is short for making the necessary decisions, I have personally taken the liberty of transmitting this memorandum to you for the consideration of your committee. . . .

Compton made his own opinion quite clear by noting that "two important considerations have not been mentioned:"

(1) that failure to make a military demonstration of the new bombs may make the war longer and more expensive of human lives, and
(2) that without a military demonstration it may be impossible to impress the world with the need for national sacrifices in order to gain lasting security.[15]

On June 16 the Scientific Panel as a whole considered the matter, and Arthur Compton, Lawrence, Oppenheimer, and Fermi concluded that ". . . we can propose no technical demonstration likely to bring an end to the war; we see no acceptable alternative to direct military use."[16] In a letter to Groves' deputy Kenneth D. Nichols on July 24, Compton further stated: "The opinion which they expressed was that military use of such weapons should be made in the Japanese War." He went on, however:

There was not sufficient agreement among the members of the panel to unite upon a statement as to how or under what conditions such use was to be made.[17]

Partly in response to the growing agitation (and probably also partly to demonstrate additional scientific support), it appears that Groves also asked Compton to further assess the feelings of the Chicago scientists. Here the meaning of "military use" came up again. Compton asked chemist Farrington Daniels to survey responses to the question: "Which of the following five procedures comes closest to your choice as to the way in which any new weapons that we may develop should be used in the Japanese war?"

1. Use them in the manner that is from the military point of view most effective in bringing about prompt Japanese surrender at minimum human cost to our armed forces.
2. Give a military demonstration in Japan to be followed by renewed opportunity for surrender before full use of the weapons is employed.
3. Give an experimental demonstration in this country, with representatives of Japan present; followed by a new opportunity for surrender before full use of the weapon is employed.
4. Withhold military use of the weapons, but make public experimental demonstration of their effectiveness.
5. Maintain as secret as possible all developments of our new weapons and refrain from using them in this war.

More than half of those working at the Chicago facilities—150 scientists—were polled. The results were as follows:

Procedure indicated above	1	2	3	4	5
Number voting	23	69	39	16	3
Per cent of votes	15	46	26	11	2

Note that No. 1—use of the weapons in a manner that is militarily "most effective"—was supported by only 15 percent. Note also the ambiguity of No. 2—"a military demonstration in Japan" to be followed by renewed opportunity for surrender "before full use of the weapon is employed." Seemingly No. 2 was different from No. 1, but what precisely did a "military demonstration" mean? Was targeting a naval facility, as Marshall had proposed, the meaning? Certainly the implication was that a "military demonstration" was different from No. 1—use in the militarily most effective way—and different, too, from "full use," which No. 2 suggested would follow only if Japan failed to surrender after a "military demonstration" and a renewed warning. As Compton and Daniels noted in a subsequent article: "These five procedures were undoubtedly interpreted differently by different scientists, as they undoubtedly will be by present readers, but no definition or amplification of these procedures was made at the time of the poll."[18]

In the cover letter sent with the poll results, Compton stated that the second option of a "military demonstration" was his own preference, and that it was "the strongly favored procedure . . . [and] the procedure that has found most favor in all informed groups where the subject has been discussed."[19] He subsequently argued with little qualification that although a few scientists preferred not to use the bomb at all, "87 per cent voted for its military use, at least if after other means were tried this was found necessary to bring surrender."[20]

The Farrington Daniels poll was sent to Groves as a document accompanying a petition to the president from a significant group of scientists (and quite probably it was designed to help offset it). With few illusions that the concerns of many participants were being taken seriously, Szilard had decided to record scientific opinion against what he believed to be the ill-considered use of the atomic bomb through a direct appeal to Truman:

> [W]e, the undersigned, respectfully petition: first, that you exercise your power as Commander-in-Chief, to rule that the United States shall not resort to the use of atomic bombs in this war unless the terms which will be imposed upon Japan have been made public in detail and Japan knowing these terms has refused to surrender; second, that in such an event the question whether or not to use the atomic bombs be decided by you in the light of the consideration presented in this petition as well as all other moral responsibilities which are involved.[21]

(The "considerations" spelled out in the petition were similar to those contained in the Franck Report.)

Szilard's petition received the signatures of sixty-nine scientists at the Chicago Metallurgical Laboratory. Several others who apparently agreed with it declined to sign out of fear that doing so might detract from the effectiveness of Franck's effort. Szilard also tried to circulate the petition among scientists at other Manhattan Project facilities but met with little success. (For instance, after consulting with Oppenheimer, Edward Teller decided against circulating it at Los Alamos.)[22] At Oak Ridge the petition reportedly received eighty-eight signatures before its circulation was stopped by Groves' staff.[23]

It seems clear that Szilard fully understood that a petition would change few minds. By this time, however, his motives were different. In a letter to Oppenheimer he observed:

> I hardly need to emphasize that such a petition does not represent the most effective action that can be taken in order to influence the course of events. But I have no doubt in my own mind that from a point of

view of the standing of the scientists in the eyes of the general public one or two years from now it is a good thing that a minority of scientists should have gone on record in favor of giving greater weight to moral arguments and should have exercised their right given to them by the Constitution to petition the President.[24]

Szilard gave the petition to Arthur Compton for delivery to Washington on July 19. "Since the matter presented in the petition is of immediate concern," Compton's cover letter to Nichols noted, "the petitioners desire the transmittal to occur as promptly as possible."[25] It took six days, however, to go from Compton's office to Groves' office.[26] After receiving the petition on July 25, Groves held it several more days (until August 1), whereupon it was finally passed along to Stimson's Washington office as Truman was about to leave Europe on the return voyage home from Potsdam. So far as we know the petition was never seen by the president.[27]*

*See below, pp. 606–07, for postwar developments in this regard.

PART IV

James F. Byrnes

Despite the enormous quantities of documentation available to historians of this last World War, the real reasons behind many of our decisions are comparatively obscure. For many of our most important moves were decided upon at informal conferences where no memoranda were kept.
—General Omar Bradley, *A Soldier's Story*

Chapter 15

"A VERY MACHIAVELLIAN CHARACTER"; "AN OPERATOR"

[Byrnes had an] almost pathological obsession with concealing his thoughts from public and even possible historical exposure. . . .
—Robert Messer, "The Making of a Cold Warrior"

For almost two decades following World War II, most historians believed that Henry Stimson was President Truman's closest adviser on atomic bomb matters.[1] The impression was understandable but wrong: Stimson was the Cabinet official ultimately responsible for the Manhattan Project, but when Truman became president Stimson was seventy-seven years old and, as we have noted, in poor health.

A major reason historians (including this one) initially judged Stimson to have played a central role is that his diary provides much more detailed information than any other single source for the period. This fact should have been a warning: One of the reasons the diary is so extensive is that Stimson (unlike many busier officials) had time to dictate long entries almost every day.

Stimson had to invite himself to the Potsdam Conference, even though the climax of the Manhattan Project would occur as it opened.[2] Once in Germany he did not attend the main meetings, nor participate in many strategy sessions with the president. Stimson complained bitterly that he was being denied access to the president—by the man who had almost total access: Byrnes.[3] Averell Harriman later recalled that Stimson "had plenty of free time. So we sat in the sun together outside his villa talking. . . ."[4] During an off-the-record discussion at Harriman's home in 1967, John J. McCloy was less charitable. The situation, he observed, was "pathetic."[5]

Another reason Byrnes' powerful role in the early Truman administration was commonly missed is that Truman and Byrnes subsequently had a major falling-out: Byrnes was replaced as secretary of state by George Marshall in January 1947, and after he and Truman parted ways Byrnes seemed to fade in significance.[6] Byrnes was, in fact, secretary for under nineteen months (and only a brief six weeks before Japan surrendered). As the Cold War got under way, he was largely forgotten as public and scholarly attention came to focus on the Marshall Plan, the Berlin Airlift, the Korean War, and many events seemingly far more dramatic than those (always excepting Hiroshima) which took place in the last months of 1945 and during 1946.

As we have seen, when Stimson met with the president on June 6 to convey the Interim Committee's recommendations, Truman responded that he had already heard from Byrnes.[7] However, although the official White House schedule records many presidential visitors, it does not record a private meeting with James F. Byrnes between the May 31 Interim Committee decisions and the June 6 meeting with Stimson.[8]

That there is no official record of Truman's discussion with Byrnes (or, it appears, of many other such meetings) points to a fundamental challenge: Throughout this period Byrnes spoke with the authority of—and personally represented—the president of the United States on all atomic bomb–related matters in the Interim Committee's deliberations. It is also quite clear that by early July 1945 when he was sworn in as secretary of state, Byrnes was firmly in control of U.S. foreign policy. It is obvious that Byrnes and the president—two very old friends—must have discussed the extraordinarily important issues under consideration. Yet we have almost no information concerning Byrnes' private meetings with Truman, what they talked about— nor for that matter about any form of communication between the two men on numerous critical developments during the spring and early summer months.

Indeed, our records are fragmentary concerning Byrnes' activities for the entire period between Roosevelt's death on April 12, 1945, and the beginning of the Potsdam Conference on July 17, 1945. Moreover, as we shall see, there are problems with the integrity of some of the records we do have.

Given Byrnes' central role—and the importance of the period in question—how are we to understand the influence and involvement of perhaps the most important presidential adviser in the critical period leading up to the final atomic bomb decisions?

At the outset of his administration Harry Truman regarded Byrnes as at least an equal. He had, in fact, been a mentor to Truman: when the newcomer from Missouri first arrived in the Senate in 1935, the far more experienced

Byrnes had taken him under his wing and made him something of a protégé. "[I]n terms of political knowledge and skill," Byrnes scholar Robert Messer observes, "Truman held him in the sort of awe a young sibling feels toward a more experienced and more talented older brother."[9]

A revealing moment during Byrnes' swearing-in ceremony as secretary of state offers insight into the relationship: The diary of Byrnes' friend and assistant Walter Brown records that when "the oath was completed, the President said, 'Jimmy, kiss the Bible.' He did and then handed it over to the President and told him to kiss it too. The President did so as the crowd laughed."[10]

One of Truman's close friends and advisers, his appointments secretary Matthew Connelly, later recalled that Truman "had a great deal of confidence in Mr. Byrnes because of their association in the Senate." That the president's former mentor did not entirely reciprocate Truman's feelings is also suggested by Connelly:

> Mr. Byrnes came from South Carolina, and talked to Mr. Truman and immediately decided that he would take over. Mr. Truman to Mr. Byrnes, I'm afraid, was a nonentity, as Mr. Byrnes thought he had superior intelligence. . . . Mr. Truman was completely loyal to Senator Byrnes because of their Senate association. . . .[11]

Similarly, Robert G. Nixon—who served as White House correspondent for the International News Service at the time—would later remark that "Byrnes looked down on Truman. He had a superior attitude. . . . He, in a sense, despised Truman . . . he looked upon Truman as an accident of history and not a very good accident at that." The same term Connelly used also came naturally to mind: "Byrnes' attitude seemed to be that Truman was a nonentity, with no abilities to speak of, no knowledge of how to conduct foreign policy, or much else for that matter."[12]

Especially in connection with international issues—as David McCullough has observed—Truman

> didn't know the right people. He didn't know Harriman. He didn't know his own Secretary of State [Edward Stettinius], more than to say hello. He had no background in foreign policy, no expert or experienced advisers of his own to call upon for help.[13]

Almost immediately after taking office, Truman demonstrated his great trust in Byrnes by informing him of his intention to appoint him secretary of state sometime that summer—as, of course, he did. It should be kept in mind that the position of secretary of state carried far more weight in 1945 than it does today. At the time, before the post of national security adviser was established, it was the premier Cabinet office. Under then-existing law—with no vice president in office once Truman succeeded Roosevelt—the secretary of state was next in line of succession. If anything happened to Truman, Byrnes would become president.[14]

That Truman should choose Byrnes for a position of such responsibility—and that the choice was universally acclaimed and unanimously approved by the Senate[15]—points to a major source of Byrnes' personal influence and power. In 1945, Byrnes was an imposing political figure in his own right—far better known and more highly regarded than Truman, the moderately influential Missouri senator Roosevelt had selected as his compromise running mate in 1944. Not only had Byrnes served as congressman, senator, and Supreme Court justice—but also (stepping down from the Court at FDR's request) as director of the Office of War Mobilization (OWM), he had acted as Roosevelt's "Assistant President for the homefront," essentially in charge of running the entire domestic economy with unprecedented authority while the president looked after the war.[16]*

On April 15, 1945—only three days after Roosevelt's death—the *Washington Post* reported a consensus that "James F. Byrnes, former director of War Mobilization and Reconversion, could have any job he wanted."[17] Reflecting upon Byrnes' unusual stature in a July 1945 editorial just before he was officially sworn in, *The New York Times* declared enthusiastically:

> The appointment of James F. Byrnes as Secretary of State will bring almost universal satisfaction. Like Mr. Hull, he will come into his new office with the confidence of Congress. He has had a rich and varied experience. He has spent thirty years in the House and Senate, and will know how to get their cooperation. He has filled with distinction a position as a member of the Supreme Court. As Director of War Mobilization he successfully held the most responsible and difficult of all administrative posts in the economic field. His long record in Congress has made his views on a wide range of subjects well known to the public. In the Democratic party he has been described as standing about midway between the conservative Southern Democrats and the New Dealers, and this record will help him to enlist maximum party support.[18]

In recent years scholars have also come to understand a fair amount about the personal chemistry between Truman and Byrnes—at least from the president's perspective. The same day it reported Roosevelt's death *The New*

---

*According to Brown, Roosevelt went so far as to give Byrnes blank executive orders, signed by the president, which permitted him "to do anything he thought necessary under the War Powers Act to promote the prosecution of the war" in the event of an emergency arising when the president was out of the country. [Walter Brown, *James F. Byrnes of South Carolina* (Macon, Ga.: Mercer University Press, 1992), p. 206.]

York Times also reported that Byrnes was "known to be one of President Truman's warmest friends in Washington. . . ."[19] The newspaper added that "President Truman's admiration of former Justice Byrnes is well known here."[20] Within two days of Truman's succession the paper's correspondent was describing Byrnes as the president's "confidant."[21]

Stimson's April 27–29 diary account of an important matter unrelated to our immediate concern offers further insight into the relationship:

> [Under Secretary of War Robert P.] Patterson brought up the question of advising the President to veto the bill increasing the scope and power of the deferments of men in agriculture. It is a most vicious bill in every respect and I told Patterson that I would certainly be against it. I advised him to call up Jimmy Byrnes who is now away in South Carolina and who has a good deal of influence over Truman and to get him to join in urging the President to veto it.[22]

Beyond the fact that the two men were long-time political associates, Truman felt deeply indebted to Byrnes. Many commentators had, in fact, expected Roosevelt to choose Byrnes, rather than Truman, to replace Henry Wallace as his running mate in 1944. (Truman had been expected to nominate Byrnes at the Democratic Convention in Chicago.) However, in a surprise decision just before the convention, Roosevelt selected Truman as a middle-of-the-road candidate whose state (and views) fell roughly between the liberal Wallace wing of the party and the Southern conservatives who felt more comfortable with Byrnes.[23]

Walter Brown recalls that on the two-hour flight to Washington for Roosevelt's funeral

> Byrnes was visibly upset. Of course, in the back of both our minds was the one fact neither of us mentioned—by all the rules of the game, he, not Harry Truman, should have now been president and at this critical hour the nation would have had someone more ably equipped and experienced to take over the tremendous duties that now rested in the office of the Presidency.[24]

Charles Bohlen was one of many observers to note that "Truman felt that he owed Byrnes, his political senior in the Democratic party, a political debt."[25] (Significantly, Bohlen added: "Thus began a relationship between the President and Byrnes which turned out to be less than perfect. . . ."[26]) Truman himself acknowledged his feelings of debt and embarrassment concerning the nomination. "Byrnes, undoubtedly, was deeply disappointed and hurt," he later recalled. "I thought that my calling on him at this time [to become secretary of state] might help balance things up."[27]

In appointing Byrnes to high office, Truman not only recognized him as something of an equal but—as Brown's diary indicates—agreed to give him much greater autonomy in the post than had been enjoyed by former secretary of state Cordell Hull.[28] *The New York Times* even reported publicly that after

> an hour's conference, it was understood that Mr. Byrnes would, in effect, replace Harry Hopkins as Presidential confidant, and, it was asserted, receive far more authority than a President has yet yielded to any man.[29]

Truman, the *Times* emphasized, had "unqualified confidence" in Byrnes.[30]

In addition to his respect for and sense of indebtedness to Byrnes, Truman badly needed help from someone with national standing who knew what he was doing. At the outset of his presidency—and for a substantial period of time thereafter—it seemed obvious to many observers that the new president deferred to the judgment of his far more worldly mentor on numerous issues of foreign policy.

Nonetheless, information on Byrnes' policy role during the summer preceding the use of the atomic bomb is extremely sketchy. Nor was this an accident.

The most obvious reason the record is so fragmentary during these three months is that Byrnes held no formal position other than his membership on the Interim Committee. There was a second difficulty, however: Although Truman asked Byrnes to become secretary of state very shortly after he became president, neither man wished to embarrass Edward Stettinius, the former steel executive whom Roosevelt had selected to replace Hull. Stettinius was preparing for the first conference of the United Nations Organization, scheduled to open in San Francisco on April 25. It was agreed that for a short while Byrnes would maintain a low public profile—and considerable secrecy—until he was officially sworn in.[31] Publicly, Byrnes remained a private citizen, informing the press that he was returning to South Carolina and that he "had no plans to come back into the government."[32]

There was also the nature of the relationships involved. General Omar Bradley stated the general issue in his 1951 memoirs:

> Despite the enormous quantities of documentation available to historians of this last World War, the real reasons behind many of our decisions are comparatively obscure. For many of our most important moves were decided upon at informal conferences where no memoranda were kept.[33]

The essential informality of the really important 1945 relationships has been documented time and again—and should always be kept in mind when attempting to decipher the truth from "official" papers of the period. At the moment Truman received the call summoning him to the White House to be told of Roosevelt's death, for instance, he was enjoying a "libation" with Lewis Deschler, the House Parliamentarian, and White House aide James M. Barnes in the private office of the Speaker of the House of Representatives, Sam Rayburn.[34] One imagines many such informal meetings, typical of insider Washington of a half-century ago, between Truman and Byrnes. Walter Brown records this August 1944 talk between the two "old friends":

> At the conclusion, I rejoined them and we "struck a blow for liberty." I remember Truman's taking a large tumbler and pouring it half full of Byrnes' good bourbon which he drank without a pause with no chaser.[35]

A few items selected from Truman's personal journal add to our feel for how the president related to close associates in general:

> *May 27, 1945:* Went upstairs and found that Steve Early, Scott Lucas and Jack Nichols had arranged a poker game. They expected me to get into it. To be fair I announced that I'd leave at midnight because I didn't want to stay out after 1 a.m. and it would be that time when I "hit the hay."
> For some reason I was lucky enough not to lose any money. . . .[36]
> *May 30, 1945:* Took a day off Memorial Day (May 30) and went down the Potomac on the [presidential yacht] "Potomac." . . . Had Steve Early, George Allen, Ed McKim, John Snyder, Harry Vaughan, J.K. Vardaman, Russell Stewart of Chicago Times and Shay Minton along. . . . We organized a low limit poker game and the wise cracks would make Bob Hope laugh. My sides are sore. We make George Allen a "whipping boy" most of the time—and can he take it! . . .[37]
> *June 5, 1945:* Took Ross, Snyder and Rosenman to the "House" for lunch. Had 'em upstairs in my so called "Study" and gave them a libation before we went to the family dining room for lunch.[38]

The way things really worked in the 1945 White House is also suggested by a passage from Brown's book in which he explains why Byrnes eventually fell from Truman's favor:

> I believe the nature of the Truman-Byrnes relationship changed after the first meeting of the [September 1945] Foreign Ministers in London. The chief reason for this change was that Byrnes had to spend so much of his time away from Washington, that he was unable to join the President at the end of the day at "bullbat" time for a drink of bourbon. This gave "the Palace Guard," including Admiral Leahy, Harry Vaughan, Jim Vardaman and others of Truman's drinking and poker-playing coterie

at the White House the opportunity to hammer away at Byrnes'
independence.[39]

Such evidence reminds us how misleading it is to think of this period—
and these men—only in terms of formal policy considerations and classified
government papers. Another reason our records are so poor is even more
challenging: Throughout his entire career Byrnes was compulsive about controlling access to information; the secrecy with which he operated during the
summer of 1945 built upon and intensified his lifelong practices.

Byrnes commonly conducted business in private meetings or on the telephone.[40] Greatly fearful of leaks from the bureaucracy, he operated as much
as possible at arm's length from the State Department.[41] Brown notes that he
had a pronounced "passion for anonymity"—that his preferred role was always that of the "behind-the-scenes broker."[42] Byrnes even invented a private stenographic note-taking code which to this day has only been partially
deciphered.[43] A recent biography by David Robertson observes:

> This secretive part of his nature was so distinct from his personality as
> a whole that to onlookers there appeared at times to be almost two sep-
> arate individuals named Jimmy Byrnes. The first was the public Byrnes,
> whom everyone knew and most men liked. . . . Then, in an instant,
> Byrnes would become the other: snappish, wounded, self-protective.[44]

Even after leaving office, Byrnes was adept at what is today called "spin
control." He wrote (or had "ghosted") two books concerning his tenure as
secretary of state—*Speaking Frankly* (1947), and his autobiography, *All in
One Lifetime* (1958).[45] Seven years after the latter book was published an assessment of his service as secretary of state appeared in a historical series of
scholarly studies. It was written by George Curry, whom Byrnes had hired to
help write *All in One Lifetime*.[46] "It might be argued that 'Jimmy' Byrnes has
been assured of a prominent place in cold war history," Gregg Herken has
observed, "simply by the fact that there are so many of him."[47]

A final reason scholars have had so much difficulty piecing together
Byrnes' activities adds an even greater layer of complexity to any serious attempt to find out what actually happened during the critical period between
April and July 1945. To put it bluntly, by virtually all accounts Byrnes was
a very devious politician. Although Truman had regarded him highly for
many years, even at the outset of his administration he was quite clear about
Byrnes' character. On several occasions the president privately referred to
Byrnes as his "conniving" secretary of state—a person who found ways, often unprincipled, to work things around in a complex manner to achieve his
goals.[48]

Matthew Connelly later described Byrnes without reservation as "a very

Machiavellian character," adding that "I never trusted him."[49] Samuel I. Rosenman, special counsel to both Roosevelt and Truman, recalled advising the president against appointing Byrnes as secretary of state:

> I had had some rather bad experiences with Byrnes in the White House under President Roosevelt. Being a kind of a "no" man, I said to President Truman, "I don't think you know Jimmy Byrnes, Mr. President. You think you do. In the *bonhomie* of the Senate, he's one kind of a fellow; but I think you will regret this, and if I were you, I wouldn't do it."[50]

Historian Arthur Schlesinger, Jr., who liked Byrnes and found him personally charming, nevertheless had no illusions about him: "He was an operator. He was a kind of prior Lyndon Johnson."[51] John J. McCloy's recollection was that Byrnes

> was an absolutely adroit, unbelievably adroit manipulator of majorities and votes on the floor of the Senate. He had a real instinct for that and was very good at it. But it was quick little intuitiveness without any conception of the imponderables, without any conception of the long-range.[52]

After an extended 1959 interview (which Byrnes would not permit to be quoted for publication)* historian Forrest Pogue noted his "affability" and, yet, a sense of how it was that "he was called a fixer."

> I didn't get the impression he was a man of enormous power. There was no element of the aura of power, no tremendous personality thing there which you get from talking to some of the other men of this era.[53]

According to Clark Clifford, Leahy, who initially was favorably disposed towards Byrnes,[54] came to regard him as a "horse's ass."[55] Bernard Baruch, the financier who presented Truman's first nuclear arms control proposal at the United Nations in 1946, regarded his friend Byrnes as "power-crazy—that he wants to decide everything himself. . . ."[56] Averell Harriman recalled that after Potsdam, "I was through with Jimmy Byrnes . . . I didn't want to have anything more to do with him."[57] Even admirers like journalists Joseph Alsop and Robert Kintner saw him as both "sly and able"—hence the title David Robertson chose for his biography.[58]

---

*Pogue's interview comments note that "He [Byrnes] talked to me about an hour and three-quarters, but declined to record the early part of his discussion, at last he did agree to say something about the General [Marshall] in the nature of a tribute, provided it were not printed, so I have done that here." (Byrnes interview with Forrest C. Pogue, November 16, 1959, p. 1, Pogue Papers, GCMRL.)

Robert Messer, a close student of Byrnes' activities during the 1945–46 period, observes that "Byrnes was congenitally uncandid."[59] He had an "almost pathological obsession with concealing his thoughts from public and even possible historical exposure. . . ."[60] "Byrnes' constant sensitivity to the public, political implications of virtually everything he said or did is evident. . . ."[61] The lengths to which Byrnes apparently went to control information related to his activities as secretary of state are extraordinary:

> Byrnes' efforts at manipulating history include his deliberate editing, altering and at times even fabricating evidence of his past as it is recorded in the documents and other manuscript sources. . . .
>
> Byrnes' manipulation of his personal papers goes beyond the normal limits of genteel dishonesty. Extensive research of these archival records leads unavoidably to the conclusion that they have been systematically doctored. . . .[62]

For instance:

> Correspondence that for years was meticulously collated and preserved with an attached carbon copy of Byrnes' response suddenly begins to include incoming letters and memoranda on sensitive subjects from which Byrnes' reply has been detached.[63]

And:

> In 1954 the persistent scholars at the Department of State approached Byrnes' former associates . . . for any records they might have relating to the Potsdam Conference of July, 1945. One such associate was Walter Brown, Byrnes' long time friend. . . . Byrnes did not know that during the conference Brown had kept a detailed daily journal recording Byrnes' activities and his private utterances concerning the negotiations. . . .
>
> Byrnes was at first furious when he learned of the existence of such a diary.* However, Byrnes' initial anger soon subsided and he eventually turned this record, too, toward his own uses.
>
> The edited "excerpts" of Brown's diary entries for July 1945 that Byrnes eventually sent the State Department alter the meaning and substantially destroy the significance of Brown's diary. . . . The alterations and deletions indicated in Byrnes' own hand throughout the copy of the diary sent him by Brown, distort and at times totally reverse the meaning of the actual contemporary record.[64]

---

*Other evidence suggests Byrnes learned of Brown's journal earlier than this. It confirms his anger, however. See below, p. 760.

"Having made certain that the State Department would no longer trouble with the Brown diary," Messer observes,

> Byrnes sent what he titled "Excerpts From Notes of Walter Brown" to the State Department with his "best wishes."
>
> In manipulating evidence in this way Byrnes was able to extend his control over the historical record beyond his personal manuscript collection to influence the official documentary histories compiled by the Department of State. These official sources in turn have been relied on by scholars throughout the world. When asked directly by individual private scholars for information on some of the same subjects for which he had sent the State Department his own manipulated evidence, Byrnes with the straightest of faces politely referred the inquiring historian to the official State Department record.[65]

Although many of the changes made by Byrnes seem to have been designed to protect him from conservative attack in the years after he left office, there is evidence that during the summer of 1945 he was even more secretive than his normal pattern.[66]

Most of his closest associates, men who were usually kept abreast of his dealings, were not informed of much of the work Byrnes had undertaken for Truman in connection with diplomatic strategy—to say nothing of his role in shaping the president's policy towards the atomic bomb. Even Brown, his personal assistant, neighbor, and close friend, was unaware of many of his activities at this time.[67]

Chapter 16

SLY AND ABLE POLICIES

Justice Byrnes has been directed by the President to make a study of this project on which some two billion dollars has already been spent. He, Byrnes, seems to be favorably impressed with the possibilities of the new explosive. . . .
—Admiral William D. Leahy, chief of staff to the president,
diary, May 20, 1945

Modern accounts of the first months of the Truman administration commonly fall into two distinct classes. On the one hand, the new president is portrayed as frightened, ill-informed, and indecisive. "Insecure and uncertain," Melvyn Leffler writes, "he sought help from advisers and friends, but they, too, were divided. . . . Truman in fact personified the ambivalence that prevailed throughout his administration."[1] An oft-quoted line is Truman's plea to a group of reporters:

> if you ever pray, pray for me now. I don't know whether you fellows ever had a load of hay fall on you, but when they told me yesterday what had happened, I felt like the moon, the stars, and all the planets had fallen on me.[2]

A rather different picture—presented most recently by biographers David McCullough and Robert Ferrell—suggests only a very brief moment of understandable confusion followed by clarity and decision: "The first test was his address to Congress the afternoon of Monday, April 16, and he passed with flying colors," McCullough writes. "Indeed, for days, for weeks, he seemed to do nearly everything right."[3] Ferrell emphasizes a theme that has become legend: Truman "had a tenacious ability to focus on a problem and make a decision."[4]

Neither portrayal conveys calculation, sophistication, or shrewdness. These, however, are precisely the qualities most often associated with Byrnes.

They also are a reasonable characterization of some of the subtle atomic strategies we have reviewed—and there are reasons to believe that Byrnes played a far more active (and far earlier) behind-the-scenes role in developing the summer policies than has commonly been assumed.

Given the relationship between Truman and Byrnes—and the president's agreement to cede substantial control over foreign policy—it would have been surprising if Byrnes had not kept close tabs on what was going on in the short period before he formally took over as secretary of state. However, the scarcity of direct information during the period when Byrnes was playing a low-profile role forces us to assemble whatever information we can from indirect, secondhand, and after-the-fact evidence.

We have previously noted an unrecorded visit to the White House on April 25 by General Groves. John W. Snyder, Truman's director of the Office of War Mobilization and Reconversion, also recalled: "Although I frequently saw the president every week, I had an arrangement with his appointments secretary, Matt Connelly, to keep my name off the visitors' list except when appearing officially with the president and others."[5] How often Byrnes slipped into the White House for discussions over a "libation" of bourbon with his friend the president we may never know. We do know in general, however, that Byrnes began advising Truman almost from the beginning.

"Immediately upon becoming President, I sent for him because I wanted his assistance," Truman later recalled;[6] indeed, the two men met privately on the first full day of his presidency, April 13.[7] The president's journal records that they "discussed everything from Tehran to Yalta, law of individual who had public office, and everything under the sun."[8]* Similarly, Brown recalls that

> The president and Byrnes talked for an hour and it was apparent Truman was looking to Byrnes for guidance. . . . Truman said he considered Byrnes one of his best friends and realized that he knew more about government than anyone else around and, therefore, he wanted Byrnes' help.[9]†

Truman spoke with Byrnes later the same day by telephone.[10] Although he held no formal office, the next day, April 14, Byrnes accompanied Truman and Henry Wallace, now secretary of commerce, to Union Station to meet the train bringing Roosevelt's body back from Georgia.[11] Byrnes' prominence and relationship to Truman were unmistakable: Although at the time

---

*"[L]aw of individual who had public office" may well be a reference to the Presidential Succession Act. See reference note number 14 of Chapter Fifteen.

†Brown also reports that Byrnes came back from this meeting "feeling very low and fearing for the country, because Roosevelt had not confided in Truman and he was thus ill-prepared for the job." (Brown, *James F. Byrnes*, p. 256.)

only a private citizen, he rode with the president and Wallace in the funeral procession up Pennsylvania Avenue to the White House.[12]

The same afternoon—April 14—Byrnes met with Truman and Leahy "regarding messages passing back and forth from Churchill and Stalin," adjourning (according to Truman's journal) to attend the White House funeral service.[13] That night Byrnes accompanied Truman when the president went by special train to Hyde Park for Roosevelt's burial.[14] En route, Brown—employing the same phrase Truman had used—indicates that the president and Byrnes

> discussed almost every other subject under the sun. They were together continually from the time they left Washington until they returned, even to the extent of Byrnes' riding with the President out to Truman's apartment before Byrnes returned to the Shoreham [Hotel] to join us.[15]

The New York Times also reported that Truman and Byrnes were "in constant consultation"—especially about foreign policy issues—during the April 14–15 Hyde Park trip:

> Mr. Byrnes, more than any other man, is considered to be informed on the details of Mr. Roosevelt's negotiations with the chiefs of Allied States. . . . Mr. Byrnes returned to Washington to offer counsel and information to the friend who now takes up the heavy responsibilities of carrying through the proposed conference of United Nations at San Francisco and of entering on the unfamiliar ground for him of all the intricacies of world affairs.[16]

The day after Roosevelt's burial, April 16, Byrnes met alone with Truman from 11:00 a.m. until sometime before the president gave his first address to Congress, at 1:00 p.m.[17] According to Brown, Byrnes and his assistants largely redrafted this first presidential speech:

> The President had asked Byrnes to look over his speech to Congress, which had been prepared by George Allen and others. Byrnes turned it over to us, saying we should have seen it before he got hold of it. He had worked on it all day and improved it, but it certainly was not in keeping with an occasion when the whole world would be listening to the new president. . . . Ben Cohen and I went to my home in Foxhall Village and worked on the speech until three o'clock in the morning. In fact, we practically rewrote it![18]

Brown continues that before it was given,

> . . . I met Byrnes and Cohen at the White House and after Byrnes made some changes, we had it retyped. He took the speech over to the Pres-

ident, read it to him three times for gestures and points to emphasize and Truman was well pleased. Then the speech was sent out to be mimeographed.[19]

Finally, on April 17, also according to Brown's records,

> . . . Byrnes again met at length with Truman. . . . After a more general discussion on appointments, carried over from the previous day, Byrnes told the President how he should speak to Molotov when he arrived in Washington Friday. Then Byrnes said he was flying to Spartanburg but that he could be reached whenever he could be helpful.[20]

After a brief return to South Carolina in late April, it appears that Byrnes shuttled back and forth between Spartanburg and Washington during May and June, quietly slipping into the capital to attend high-level policy discussions at the White House and elsewhere.[21] At this time Byrnes was also regularly briefed by White House and State Department officials. George M. Elsey—later assistant to the naval aide to the president, and then a naval intelligence officer working in the White House Map Room—subsequently recalled:

> The new president, no secret to anyone, was woefully unprepared. My assignments from Leahy piled up. Short, to-the-point synopses of all kinds of issues were needed in a hurry. Soon there was another "customer." Leahy called me in one day and said that Truman was going to replace Secretary of State Edward R. Stettinius with James F. Byrnes as soon as the United Nations Conference in San Francisco was over. Would I start work on briefing materials for Byrnes?[22]

James W. Riddleberger, chief of the State Department Division of Central European Affairs during this period, also later recalled numerous late-night sessions in Byrnes' Shoreham Hotel apartment which were never officially recorded:

> We all knew that Byrnes was to be the next Secretary of State, in fact arrangements were made within the State Department for the principal chiefs of divisions to go out and brief him before he became Secretary of State, and he in turn was trying to keep Truman informed about the principal issues that would arise [at the Potsdam conference] . . . several of the principal divisions chiefs in the State Department would go out to the what is now—what is now this hotel . . . [t]he Shoreham, and we'd go out at night and we'd spend hours briefing Jimmy Byrnes on all the aspects of the current international situation.[23]

Unfortunately, available records contain very little about private, personal meetings like the ones described by Elsey and Riddleberger (except that they occurred)—and even less about Byrnes' private, off-the-record discussions with the president. Two reports of specific discussions which have survived, however, are highly suggestive: as noted, on April 17, according to Brown, "Byrnes told the President how he should speak to Molotov when he arrived in Washington Friday."[24] This was the time of the first major confrontation. We also noted the president's private journal report that they "discussed everything from Tehran to Yalta."[25] Truman later recalled that he had "wanted to get [Byrnes'] firsthand account of what had gone on at Yalta":

> I asked him to transcribe his notes for me, especially since he had indicated that there were no available stenographic or official transcripts of the Yalta meetings. It was not until some ten days later that I received from him a typed and leather-bound transcript of his notes, which bore a title, "The Crimean Conference, Minutes of Meetings, prepared by James F. Byrnes."[26]

A combination of direct and indirect evidence helps clarify some aspects of Byrnes' specific role. Stimson's June 6 report that Truman had already heard the Interim Committee's recommendations is elaborated upon by at least two accounts. In his 1958 book *All in One Lifetime*, Byrnes recalled very generally that the "day the [Interim] committee reached agreement, I communicated its decision to President Truman."[27] In an interview with Fred Freed for a 1965 NBC television "White Paper," Byrnes also stated:

> The day that the committee decided to make that recommendation [concerning the use of the bomb] to the president, I went by the White House in the afternoon and told President Truman of the final decision of his Interim Committee.[28]

Integrating various pieces of evidence also offers perspective on some issues. For instance, Byrnes is a prime candidate for the adviser who helped Truman draft his still-unexplained June 1 no-compromise stand on "unconditional surrender"—a substantial retreat from the May 8 statement which had carefully defined "unconditional surrender" as applying to the Japanese armed forces. So far as we can tell Byrnes was the only adviser whose views were fully compatible with this position at this time; everyone else involved supported the general principal of modifying the terms. Grew, of course, wished to move forward immediately, and although Stimson wanted a brief delay, given what we know of their views it is difficult to believe Stimson, Forrestal, Leahy, or Marshall would likely have urged a retreat from the May 8 language, nor is there any evidence that they did so.

We also know that Byrnes had a major hand in writing the president's initial April 16 speech affirming "unconditional surrender"—going so far, apparently, as to coach Truman on forceful gestures (in the end Truman pounded his fist on the podium as he declared: "Our demand has been, and it remains—unconditional surrender!").[29] Moreover, Byrnes was in Washington for Interim Committee meetings on May 31 and June 1 and he met (as he reports) with Truman at the White House the same day the June 1 statement was issued. It also appears clear that Byrnes continued to maintain a hard-line position on the surrender formula later in June (apparently blocking McCloy). In July, as we shall see, he was responsible for advising Truman to remove explicit assurances for the Emperor from the Potsdam Proclamation. (Indeed, in general Byrnes stood virtually alone in consistently opposing any softening of the surrender formula.)

There are also reasons to believe Byrnes may have been the presidential adviser who helped persuade Truman to reverse his position on Poland in May. Indeed, all the other advisers directly involved were strongly on the other side of the issue, here wishing to maintain a hard line. Modifying the U.S. stance on Poland was clearly an element in at least temporarily improving relations with the Soviet Union and perhaps in securing the insurance policy of an early Red Army declaration of war should the atomic test fail. (In this regard, it also appears that Byrnes was instrumental, perhaps along with Marshall, in convincing Truman once more to seek Russian help in the war—reversing the late-April judgment that "no particular harm can now be done to our war prospects even if Russia should slow down or even stop its war effort in Europe and in Asia."[30*]) We also know that Byrnes participated in White House discussions with the president on the Polish issue on May 18—just as Hopkins was about to leave.[31] On June 6, moreover, Byrnes felt a need to defend the decision to retreat on Poland—and to tell Davies that there was "no justification under the spirit or letter of the [Yalta] agreement" for insisting on an entirely new government in Poland (he compared the Polish settlement to a "political compromise where the party in the commanding position, for the sake of cooperation, included the other elements which were agreed upon").[32] In his post-Yalta press conference, Byrnes had also explicitly defined Poland as a "compromise," saying:

Whenever you have three great powers seeking to stand in unity to win a war and to promote peace, and two of them are recognizing one gov-

---

*Forrestal's diary of March 8, 1947, notes that according to McCloy, before the atomic test it was "under the pressure of Secretary Byrnes" that Truman made it a "principal mission" to actively seek Soviet assistance against Japan. (Forrestal, *The Forrestal Diaries*, ed. Millis, p. 70.) Similarly Brown's diary notes that before the test Byrnes "had hoped Russian declaration of war would come out of this conference." (WB's Book, July 18, 1945, Folder 602, Byrnes Papers, CUL.)

ernment and one of them is recognizing another government, there must be a reconciliation of views.[33]*

That Byrnes was deeply involved in policy-making throughout the spring and summer seems plain, too, from his decisive first acts as secretary of state. For instance, his agreement to recognize the new Polish government two days after taking office, on July 5,[34] seems inconceivable unless one assumes a deep previous involvement with the issue—especially as it involved a potentially explosive and controversial public reversal (and, too, because one of the leading Republican foreign policy spokesmen, Senator Arthur Vandenberg of Michigan, represented a large and vocal Polish constituency).[35] Similarly, Byrnes' confident demand on July 6 that he and Truman be consulted before any decisions were made in the Soong-Stalin negotiations on the Far East bespeak the actions of a man who was clearly on top of his job and knew what he wanted to do, and why, well before he actually took office on July 3.

Byrnes also appears to be a logical candidate for the adviser who convinced Truman to postpone meeting Stalin until the atomic bomb had been tested—one of the truly fundamental strategic decisions of the spring and summer. Although our information is even more sketchy in this area, we have seen that his mandate—and his alone—included both atomic and diplomatic issues. Moreover, all the other top advisers directly involved in diplomacy were pressing for an early meeting with Stalin. Thus, either Truman made the decision against their advice on his own or some other highly placed adviser concerned with the atomic bomb convinced him the new weapon would be critical in his approach to Stalin. Byrnes is the only such counsellor other than Stimson—and Truman appears clearly to have made this decision by early in the second week of May (before Stimson advised delay). Furthermore, Byrnes was in Washington and in close communication with Truman when the first major cable beginning the stalling process was sent. Indeed, Byrnes and Truman met for substantial discussions during the period immediately before the decision to put off a meeting with Stalin was implemented. Stimson's diary for May 4 records:

> After Cabinet I asked the President for the details of the J. F. Byrnes acceptance of membership on my committee and he said that he had accepted; that he was coming here tomorrow, May 5th; would be here over Sunday [May 6], Monday, Tuesday, and Wednesday [May 9]. I told the President that we were at work on the agenda so as to get the thing

---

*Surprisingly few scholars have probed to search for the specific source of advice behind Truman's radical policy reversal and his late-May acceptance of Stalin's proposal for a pro-Soviet majority in the new Polish government.

started as soon as Byrnes was available. He said something which indicated that he was going to talk with Byrnes in the first part of his stay.[36]

Churchill's cable requesting an early meeting came in on May 6[37]—and Truman's response delaying the meeting until after June 30 because of his "fiscal year" went out on May 9.[38] Truman met with Byrnes for over two hours on May 7, and perhaps at other points during the weekend of May 5–6.[39] (Stimson—the only other possible adviser in this instance—so far as we can tell, did not meet with the president at this time. Furthermore, six days later, on May 15, Stimson can record only that "apparently" the president had now promised to meet Churchill on July 1.[40])

That the policy had been decided elsewhere is also evident from the fact that on May 16 Stimson informed Truman he agreed with the strategy the president delineated concerning the Big Three meeting based on the calculation that the U.S. would be in a better position later.[41]*

Intimately related to all of this, of course, is the strategic perspective which informed the advice Byrnes gave Truman—especially as it relates to atomic bomb matters. A variety of pieces of information help provide a general sense of the secretary of state's overall stance. In addition to Truman's statement that at one of their first meetings Byrnes told him the atomic bomb might put the United States in position to "dictate" terms at the end of the war,[42] we have previously noted Leo Szilard's report that at their May 28 meeting the secretary of state–designate did not argue the bomb was needed to bring about a Japanese surrender, but that it would make Russia more "manageable" in Europe.[43]

The record of Byrnes' Interim Committee interventions at this time also suggests a hard-line attitude—especially his May 31 opposition to Marshall's proposal to invite Russian scientists to the atomic test, his strong opposition to any prior disclosure of the weapon's existence, and his June 1 modification of the Interim Committee's recommendation (so as to emphasize using the bomb "as soon as possible").

It seems obvious that Byrnes saw the atomic bomb as important bar-

---

*Byrnes' role in connection with the related Hopkins mission to Moscow is even more difficult to pin down. The general strategy—and especially the extreme secrecy—seem consistent with everything we know of Byrnes' style and views. Also, according to Truman's journal Byrnes was consulted about the mission (and advised against sending Hopkins). His objection is sometimes seen as opposition to the mission. More likely, it was opposition to Hopkins—an old rival who had played a role in denying Byrnes the vice-presidency as well as an earlier possible appointment as secretary of state. As noted, Davies, who was close to Byrnes, was asked first—but declined because of ill health. (See Sherwin, *A World Destroyed*, p. 184n.; Truman, *Off the Record*, pp. 30, 35; Journal, May 13, 1945, Chrono File, Box 16, Davies Papers, LC; Robertson, *Sly and Able*, p. 293; Brown, *James F. Byrnes*, pp. 95–96, 263; Wallace, *The Price of Vision*, pp. 418–19. For an extended discussion, see Appendix V of the 1985 Viking Penguin edition of my *Atomic Diplomacy: Hiroshima and Potsdam*.)

gaining leverage, potentially useful in all manner of international negotiations. The Memorial Day period in particular appears to have been a time when a cluster of decisions were made. The range of issues then decided suggests the likelihood of a series of discussions between Byrnes and Truman ranging from Poland and Russian participation in the war to the unconditional-surrender language and the use of the bomb without warning and as soon as possible. It was during this brief period, too, that the final date for the Potsdam meeting was set on the basis of the latest estimate for the Alamogordo test.

Just prior to this time, on May 20, Byrnes met with Leahy (according to Leahy's diary) to discuss "the status and prospects of a new explosive that is in process of development 'Manhattan Project.' " Leahy observed:

> Justice Byrnes has been directed by the President to make a study of this project on which some two billion dollars has already been spent. He, Byrnes, seems to be favorably impressed with the possibilities of the new explosive. . . .[44]

In general it appears that Byrnes not only regarded the atomic bomb as extremely important to his diplomacy towards Russia, but that in advising Truman he took a very narrow view of its role. Minimally, he seems to have seen it from the very beginning as leverage to help American diplomacy and, more likely, as the critical factor which—if shrewdly handled—would allow the United States to impose its own terms once its power was demonstrated.

Chapter 17

THE SHADOW OF YALTA

. . . OWMR boss Jimmy Byrnes suddenly reappeared in Washington, having made the 6,700 mile trip from Yalta in 38 hours. Without wasting a minute, he called a press conference. It appeared that Jimmy Byrnes' role was to be the official interpreter of the Crimea Charter to the U.S. people and Congress.

—*Time* magazine, February 26, 1945

It is worth pausing briefly to reflect upon the fact that Truman made Byrnes both his secretary of state and simultaneously his personal representative on the Interim Committee. The choice of a person connected first and foremost with diplomacy, particularly diplomacy towards the Soviet Union (rather than, for instance, a military specialist), to represent the president on the committee concerned with the atomic bomb highlights the early and deep connection of the new weapon with foreign affairs.

At the upcoming Potsdam conference Byrnes would be under intense public scrutiny. In his debut as secretary of state he would be the de facto master of ceremonies at the first Big Three meeting after the defeat of Hitler. The meeting with Stalin and Churchill, moreover, would establish a basic framework and set the terms of reference for Byrnes' next major moves—and perhaps shape his entire subsequent period in office.

At Potsdam, too, issues well beyond Europe would be on the agenda; the negotiations would range over the entire gamut of postwar questions—from the future of Asia to the fate of key areas of the Middle East. Indeed, the possibility of world peace itself might be decided in the meeting amidst the ruins of Nazi Germany.

Perhaps the simplest point concerning Byrnes' deep involvement with both atomic bomb and diplomatic planning is the most obvious: any man about to become secretary of state—particularly so seasoned and sophisticated a politician—would have to have been rather dense not to have seen the new weapon as intimately related to his foreign policy objectives.

Beyond this, we now also know that Byrnes had a special relationship to the famous (and controversial) provisions of the Yalta agreement which seemed to promise "democracy" in Eastern Europe. During the entire 1945 period we are considering, as Robert Messer has demonstrated, Byrnes was personally identified in American politics as the foremost spokesman for (and defender of) Yalta.[1]

Byrnes' public identification with Yalta stemmed from the fact that Roosevelt had sent him back ahead of the delegation as his personal representative to sell the understanding with Stalin to the American public. ". . . OWMR boss Jimmy Byrnes suddenly reappeared in Washington, having made the 6,700 mile trip from Yalta in 38 hours," *Time* magazine reported on February 26, 1945. "Without wasting a minute, he called a press conference. It appeared that Jimmy Byrnes' role was to be the official interpreter of the Crimea Charter to the U.S. people and Congress."[2] As David Robertson notes, "[M]uch of the initially favorable public reaction to the Yalta agreements and Byrnes' reputation as an expert on Yalta originated in this first, successful news conference."[3]

At Yalta, moreover, Byrnes had a hand—together with Alger Hiss (at the time, deputy director of the State Department Office of Special Political Affairs)—in drafting the "Declaration on Liberated Europe" which vaguely promised consultation on how to achieve future free elections in Eastern Europe, but did not include any enforcement procedures.[4] (The original copy of this draft bears the following notation in Hiss' handwriting: "1st redraft after talking to Justice Byrnes."[5]) Even the weak enforcement "machinery" contemplated in the initial U.S. draft—eliminated when Stalin and Molotov objected[6]—would have been subject to Soviet veto.

Byrnes' public defense of the Yalta language was nonetheless unqualified: "The declaration as to the liberated areas is a proposal of the President's. To my mind, it is of the greatest importance."[7]

> That declaration, re-affirming the Atlantic Charter, will give hope to small nations, but it will be effective, too, in contributing to the adoption of the United Nations organization.[8]

After attending an off-the-record briefing given by Byrnes, a reporter in the *New York Sun*'s Washington bureau went further: "Like everyone who has returned from Russia, [Byrnes] has been tremendously impressed by Joseph Stalin."[9] Indeed, on the Polish issue

[Byrnes] said that time after time Stalin proved his readiness to compromise; that throughout he proved to be tractable and to possess a malleable mind. He made concession after concession.[10]

He points out that Russia will come out of this war as the most powerful nation in the world. Stalin has definite plans in the Pacific, he reported, but apart from that wants only to rebuild Russia and to bring it to the standard of living that it ought to enjoy with its vast resources. He believes that once Stalin has settled with the Japs, we can trust him to keep the peace.[11]

In addition to promoting the Yalta agreement with the press, Byrnes was assigned the job of privately explaining and lobbying for it with Congressional leaders.[12] Shortly after his return, he had lunch and a two-hour discussion of Yalta with fifteen Senators.[13] He also met with the Senate Foreign Relations Committee at the home of its chairman, Tom Connally of Texas.[14] Byrnes also lunched with Republican Congressional leaders, and thereafter undertook a steady round of discussions with individual senators and various interested groups. *Newsweek* columnist Ernest K. Lindley called him the "Persuasive Reporter"; another report called him the "Yalta Legman."[15]

Byrnes, a one-time court stenographer, had actually taken detailed notes in shorthand on a number of important discussions during the conference.[16] Although they were far from complete, the notes—combined with the general belief that Byrnes enjoyed Roosevelt's deep confidence—enabled him to represent himself as having a unique understanding of what had really happened among the Big Three.[17] We have noted Truman's interest in these materials; the president, in fact, told South Carolina Senator Olin Johnston that he picked Byrnes to become secretary of state because "it's the only way I can be sure of knowing what went on at Yalta."[18] He called upon Byrnes immediately after becoming president, he later recalled, because he "wanted to get his firsthand account of what had gone on" during Roosevelt's last meeting with Stalin and Churchill.[19]

It is clear that Byrnes used the fact that he had what seemed the only direct, verbatim account of several Yalta conversations to cement his early relationship as chief adviser on foreign policy. That his role was not without certain political dangers, however, was obvious—as the cover note he sent to Truman along with his "Minutes" suggests:

> When you read this you will immediately see reasons why it should be kept under lock and key. Should it fall into the hands of anyone close to the columnists, it could start a war on several fronts.[20]

The Yalta agreement hung over Byrnes' head throughout the period we are considering (and beyond). As Edmund Preston observes, he was "[p]ersonally identified with the Yalta accords," and as he prepared to take over as secretary of state, clearly his own political position would become increasingly dependent on the daunting fact that he would now be personally responsible for fulfilling the Yalta promises he had sold for Roosevelt.[21] Recent scholarship on Byrnes demonstrates that, given his somewhat compromised position, the secretary of state–designate followed a highly complex strategy during the spring and summer of 1945.

Publicly, he had given assurances that democracy and free elections would be held in Eastern Europe, and that Roosevelt had made no concessions to Stalin that would result in a dominant Soviet sphere of influence in that region. At his February press conference, even as he affirmed the principle of compromise, he had stated that "what is done by this document is to say [the existing Polish government] must be reorganized and must be placed—replaced by a new government."[22]

Privately, however, Byrnes carefully acknowledged to a very few key people that in some areas his public statements were different from the specific understandings he knew Roosevelt had reached. (He told Davies, for instance, that there "was no justification under the spirit or the letter of the [Yalta] agreement for insistence by Harriman . . . that an entirely new Government should be created and that members of the London Emigré Polish Government should be included.[23]) At the same time, Byrnes began preparing recommendations to Truman for the forthcoming Potsdam conference which urged a tough line toward the Soviet Union in much of Eastern Europe that was generally consistent with his public assurances that democracy would prevail throughout the liberated areas.

Byrnes also was simultaneously trying to impress upon influential columnists and other important public figures worried about the deterioration of relations with Moscow that his attitude toward the Russians was one of cooperation. On April 30, for instance, he wrote Walter Lippmann:

> Peace in the future will not depend on what is written in any document at the conference. It will depend upon what is in the hearts of the people of Russia, Britain and the United States. We cannot promote it by promoting distrust of the Soviets. We must have confidence in each other. . . .[24]*

---

*Later, in August, Byrnes flattered Lippmann by offering him the position of assistant secretary of state. Lippmann declined, but was clearly very moved by the offer: "Your invitation caught me so completely unprepared that I know I did not find words to say on the telephone how much it will always mean to me," adding that ". . . I hope you will believe that I shall always be grateful and deeply honored that the President and that you thought of me at all. . . ." (Lippmann to Byrnes, August 23, 1945, Folder 355, Box 59, Lippman papers, YUL.)

It was, as Messer has observed, an "elaborate international masquerade"[25]—even more convoluted in its details than this summary can suggest. We can understand why Byrnes was anxious that his notes on Yalta not fall into the hands of the columnists—as well as why Truman privately judged his new secretary of state to be "conniving."[26]

Critics of some earlier accounts of the Potsdam meeting have sometimes felt that Byrnes was represented as being too devious.[27] We have noted his unvarnished dishonesty in manipulating the historical record in connection with the diaries of his assistant, Walter Brown. Evidence compiled over the last two decades on his intricate political manipulations suggests that, if anything, earlier accounts provided a less-than-adequate description of the unbelievably complicated manner in which the "sly and able" James F. Byrnes actually operated.

Here the significant point to note is that beyond his official concern Byrnes had a direct stake in these issues. Dimly recalled 1945 events in Hungary, Bulgaria, and Rumania today seem distant relics of a time long past. To Byrnes they were important personal issues. Especially after—and perhaps in part because of—the decision to back down in Poland, his own political standing was directly linked to his capacity to make good on his publicly proclaimed pledge that no fundamental concessions had been made, that the United States had not and would not concede Soviet domination of Eastern Europe, and that democracy would ultimately prevail in the Soviet border regions.

PART V

Potsdam

When in July the Big Three met . . . at Potsdam, outside Berlin, the Americans remained as anxious as ever to have the Red Army in the Pacific.

Then came the successful test of the first atomic bomb. It inaugurated a new era in the world's history and in the tools of American foreign policy. No longer—or so it seemed— would the United States have to rely on mass armies, either those of its allies or its own. The atomic bomb had the great advantage of being cheaper than mass armies—and much quicker. The Americans immediately began to use the bomb as an instrument of diplomacy. . . .

—Stephen E. Ambrose, *Rise to Globalism*

Chapter 18

TO THE BIG THREE MEETING

Saturday, July 7th:
The President, accompanied by members of his party, went aboard the Augusta at 0601. . . .

Sunday, July 8th:
At 0930, The President met with Secretary Byrnes, Admiral Leahy and State Department advisers Cohen, Matthews and Bohlen in the Secretary's cabin in the first of a series of daily pre-conference business conversations. . . .

—Excerpts from log compiled by
Lieutenant William M. Rigdon, U.S.N.,
personal secretary to the president

The weeks prior to the first days of August when the president met with Stalin and Churchill (and, after the British elections, Churchill's successor as prime minister, Clement Attlee) are a special time: The Potsdam meetings constitute the approach period to the final decisions concerning the use of the atomic bomb. Writing about the period in later years, Byrnes observed that the "events which looked to the end of the Pacific War" and the Big Three discussions "were so intertwined in the making they cannot easily be separated in the telling."[1] Moreover, with the president and Byrnes away from Washington—isolated in the high-pressure cocoon of a top secret "summit" meeting—things happened with a certain emotional intensity different from business-as-usual in Washington. It would have been all but impossible to avoid bringing decisions about diplomacy together with decisions about the new weapon's use during the period when the stage was set for the final go-ahead choice.

Numerous accounts of the Potsdam conference have appeared in the last half century—especially since 1960, when the first important documents concerning the Big Three meeting were initially made public.[2] Early in the post-war period—ten to fifteen years before the major documentary releases—the conference was commonly treated strictly as a diplomatic occasion. Little attention was paid to the "coincidence" that produced the atomic test on July 16 and the meeting with Stalin on July 17. The obvious possibility that top American officials might have thought their hand would be strengthened by the new weapon was not discussed.

Although there are still differences of opinion as to the precise role the new weapon played in U.S. diplomatic thinking at Potsdam, most scholars now recognize that the atomic bomb powerfully impacted attitudes in connection with both Europe and Asia.[3] Equally important, many also understand that this fact, in turn, began to influence thinking about the actual use of the weapon.

Broadly speaking, whereas earlier in the summer the "second track" idea that the bomb would strengthen U.S. diplomacy had been quite general, at Potsdam—after the bomb was proven to work—a number of developments advanced the strategy and gave it specific content.

First, the successful test transformed abstract theory into potent immediate reality. "The bomb as a merely probable weapon had seemed a weak reed on which to rely," Stimson later recalled, "but the bomb as a colossal reality was very different."[4] "It has taken a great load off my mind," Truman told Joseph Davies.[5]

Second, once the full report arrived, the test proved to be far more dramatic than anyone had expected. It impressed American leaders with the extraordinary power now at their disposal in a way that had not previously been imagined.

Third, not only was the bomb no longer a merely theoretical possibility, it also now seemed probable—again, in reality rather than in theory—that the bomb would actually be *used*.

Fourth, as a result of these developments, American leaders now began to assume and rely upon the expected demonstration of the new weapon at the very same time they fashioned specific diplomatic strategies for Europe and Asia.

Fifth, by all accounts, U.S. (and British) leaders became quite excited. The emotional impact of the new development added a special psychological dimension to their confidence—and to expectations of a future in which the atomic bomb would play a major role in world affairs. J. R. Parten, chief of staff to the United States Delegation to the Allied Commission on Reparations, later observed that "everyone was pretty high."[6]

Put another way, during the brief period Truman, Byrnes, and other top American leaders were at Potsdam, the assumption that the actual use of the bomb would, in fact, add powerfully to their diplomatic hand was confirmed in their own thinking—and then became deeply embedded in the basic approach and specific negotiating positions which defined their overall diplomatic stance. In the environment shaped by these realities, several crucial decisions were made with regard to alternative ways to end the war and to the actual use of the atomic bomb.

Truman and Byrnes now made a conscious decision not to provide Japan with the specific assurances that had been sought for the Emperor (aware, in so doing, that a surrender was not likely to occur).

They also made a conscious decision not to encourage Soviet participation in the war. Indeed, they attempted to delay the Red Army's attack to the extent feasible, thereby hoping to limit Soviet political influence in Asia. They did so at a time when the impact of a Russian declaration of war had been greatly enhanced by Tokyo's approach to Moscow. Indeed, as we are about to see, some of the most important documentary discoveries of the postwar era illuminate more clearly than had previously been possible just how the men at the top of the U.S. government now understood the great power a Red Army attack would have.

Ralph Bard—who represented the Navy Department on the Interim Committee—is the only person known to have formally dissented from the use of the atomic bomb without advance warning. In a June 27, 1945, memorandum Bard declared:

> Ever since I have been in touch with this program I have had a feeling that before the bomb is actually used against Japan that Japan should have some preliminary warning for say two or three days in advance of use. The position of the United States as a great humanitarian nation and the fair play attitude of our people generally is responsible in the main for this feeling.
>
> During recent weeks I have also had the feeling very definitely that the Japanese government may be searching for some opportunity which they could use as a medium of surrender. Following the three-power conference emissaries from this country could contact representatives from Japan somewhere on the China Coast and make representations with regard to Russia's position and at the same time give them some information regarding the proposed use of atomic power, together with whatever assurances the President might care to make with regard to the Emperor of Japan and the treatment of the Japanese nation following unconditional surrender. It seems quite possible to me that this presents the opportunity which the Japanese are looking for.[7]

Although Bard's dissent is well known, it is seldom noted that he, too, proposed a modified version of the "two-step logic" which, in the period leading up to the president's departure for Potsdam, had become common ground in policy discussions at high levels of the U.S. government: Not only would information on the bomb be given to the Japanese, but after the Big Three Conference the United States could (1) "make representations with regard to Russia's position" and (2) provide Japan with "assurances" regarding the Emperor.

> I don't see that we have anything in particular to lose in following such a program. The stakes are so tremendous that it is my opinion very real consideration should be given to some plan of this kind. I do not believe under present circumstances existing that there is anyone in this country whose evaluation of the chances of the success of such a program is worth a great deal. The only way to find out is to try it out.[8]

Bard's memorandum was delivered by courier to Stimson on June 28 and given also to Byrnes on July 2.[9] Bard later reported that it was discussed by the Interim Committee as well, although the terse minutes and logs of the committee do not register this.[10]

Bard also arranged to see the president just before he left to meet Churchill and Stalin. Although we do not have a contemporaneous record of the conversation, in a subsequent interview with historian Alice Smith, Bard indicated that he wished "to make his dissent from the Interim Committee recommendation as emphatic as possible"—and that the views he outlined to Truman were similar to those stated in his memorandum.[11] Bard explained to another investigator (Nuel Pharr Davis) that he told the president: "For God's sake, don't organize an army to go into Japan. Kill a million people? It's ridiculous."[12]

Bard's efforts met with little enthusiasm. Truman appears simply to have assured him that questions concerning an invasion and a possible warning had been given careful attention and thanked him for his interest.[13]

The text of Bard's memorandum was published in 1960 by Fletcher Knebel and Charles W. Bailey II in their book *No High Ground.*[14] In a private letter to Admiral Lewis L. Strauss—special assistant to Forrestal in 1945, later chairman of the Atomic Energy Commission—Bard subsequently offered this additional information concerning his motivation:

> such a warning as I proposed would have been a wonderful thing as at that time we had not made a final deal with Russia, and we would not have had to do so because the Japanese were looking for an out, and it is almost certain that they would have used such a warning to make peace.[15]

Bard also stated (in a second letter to Strauss): ". . . I believed the situation at that time was such that our warning would end the war and we would not have to drop the bombs."[16]

Bard left government on July 1. As we shall explore in Part VII, important questions remain concerning the extent to which he acted solely on his own or was reflecting the views of Forrestal (who, so far as we can tell from other evidence, also sought to end the war by clarifying the surrender terms).

At the time Bard was meeting with Truman—just prior to his departure for Potsdam—the U.S.–British Combined Intelligence Committee (CIC) completed a pre-conference "Estimate of the Enemy Situation." As noted in Chapter 1, this high-level report, too, confirmed the continuing assessment:

> We believe that a considerable portion of the Japanese population now consider absolute military defeat probable. The increasing effects of sea blockade and the cumulative devastation wrought by strategic bombing, which has already rendered millions homeless and has destroyed from 25% to 50% of the builtup areas of Japan's most important cities, should make this realization increasingly general.

The CIC also stressed the judgment that:

> An entry of the Soviet Union into the war would finally convince the Japanese of the inevitability of complete defeat.[17]

Related to this was the other element of the "two-step logic:" "The Japanese . . . are becoming increasingly desirous of a compromise. . . ."[18] To avoid foreign occupation and custody of the Emperor if possible,

> and in any event, to insure survival of the institution of the Emperor, the Japanese might well be willing to withdraw from all the territory they have seized on the Asiatic continent and in the southern Pacific, and even to agree to the independence of Korea and to the practical disarmament of their military forces.

The committee also was quite clear about what would happen if the surrender terms were not clarified: The Japanese believe "unconditional surrender would be the equivalent of national extinction."

> There are as yet no indications that the Japanese are ready to accept such terms.[19]

A few days after this "estimate" was submitted, the War Department's Operations Division (OPD) also advised (on July 12):

There is much to be gained by defining as completely as possible, the detailed war aims in Japan. . . .

Japanese surrender would be advantageous for the U.S., both because of the enormous reduction in the cost of the war and because it would give us a better chance to settle the affairs of the Western Pacific before too many of our allies are committed there and have made substantial contributions towards the defeat of Japan. . . .

The present stand of the War Department is that Japanese surrender is just possible and is attractive enough to the U.S. to justify us in making any concession which might be attractive to the Japanese, so long as our realistic aims for peace in the Pacific are not adversely affected.[20]

As Potsdam approached there were also a number of additional calls for clarification of the surrender terms by high-ranking Republicans. These expanded upon the theme which Herbert Hoover had discussed with Truman in May. On July 3, for instance—the very day Byrnes was sworn in as secretary of state—*The New York Times* reported that

Senator White of Maine, the minority leader, declared that the Pacific war might end quickly if President Truman would state, specifically, in the upper chamber just what unconditional surrender means for the Japanese.[21]

Although White indicated he was speaking as an individual, the move by so important a political figure could hardly be ignored.* Moreover, White's move was supported immediately by Senator Homer Capehart of Indiana— who called a press conference the same day to state:

It isn't a matter of whether you hate the Japs or not. I certainly hate them. But what's to be gained by continuing a war when it can be settled now on the same terms as two years from now?[22]

Five days later, Lord Halifax—the British ambassador to the United States—privately reported to London that Capehart had:

stirred up discussion about peace terms for Japan by asserting that he had heard from an unimpeachable administration source that about a month ago Japan had made a definite offer of conditional surrender which the State Department had kept from Congress and the public. After a denial by Grew, Capehart asserted that it was nevertheless the

---

*It may possibly be significant that the Senate minority leader was one of the very few members of Congress who had previously been informed of the Manhattan Project. (Memorandum for the Secretary of War, *Atomic Fission Bombs*, from LRG, April 23, 1945, p. 13, Military Reference Branch, NA.)

truth. His general thesis was that unconditional surrender was not necessarily the best weapon for compassing Japan's downfall, and that conditions existed and could be formulated on which the United States could and should be prepared to end the Japanese war.

Halifax also reported that there were increasing demands for a clarification of the surrender terms by such important radio and other commentators as Raymond Swing, ABC's highly popular broadcaster. "Even [Walter] Lippmann warns against suicidal slaughter." The ambassador's conclusion was straightforward: A "fairly strong trend against the purely unqualified 'unconditional surrender' formula is thus now under way."[23]

On July 13 *The New York Times* reported a further, more formal public move:

> Senator Homer E. Capehart, Indiana Republican, expressed the hope in a speech on the Senate floor today [July 12] that the Allied leaders at their Potsdam meeting would define "unconditional surrender" so that the Japanese would know exactly the price they must pay for peace.

Capehart's position now, as described by the *Times*, was that

> the publication of a definition of "unconditional surrender" for the Japanese not only would have the effect of shortening the war in the Pacific materially, saving numerous American lives, but also would mean that "those who hereafter must die will know exactly what is to be accomplished by their sacrifice.". . .
>
> "With an abiding conviction that I am right, I submit, Mr. President, that our nation, in cooperation with her Allies, should proceed to formulate, and when formulated, announce to the world, the exact minimum terms required of Japan."[24]

As we have previously noted, several newspapers had also begun to urge a clarification of terms in the late spring. Here, too, there were further developments. The *Washington Post*, for instance, challenged the "unconditional surrender" formula head-on in a June 11, 1945, editorial entitled "Fatal Phrase."

> President Truman, of course, has already stated that there is no thought of destroying the Japanese people, but such assurances, even from so high a source, are negated by that fatal phrase.

The *Washington Post* stressed that the two words "remain a great stumbling block to any propaganda effort and the perpetual trump card of the Japanese die-hards for their game of national suicide."

Let us amend them; let us give Japan conditions, harsh conditions certainly, and conditions that will render her diplomatically and militarily impotent for generations. But also let us somehow assure those Japanese who are ready to plead for peace that, even on our terms, life and peace will be better than war and annihilation.[25]

On July 2, *Newsweek* columnist Raymond Moley also weighed in with a report (perhaps of Hoover's effort) that the "desirability of clarifying our aims in the Japanese war was brought to the attention of President Truman a month ago by a well-known American, who is thoroughly familiar with the Far East."

It was suggested then that unconditional surrender be defined as applying to the army and navy . . . in the postwar era, they might continue to enjoy the paternal rule of the emperor.[26]

In a June 6 broadcast, Raymond Swing had proposed that "our psychological warfare against Japan . . . should enter a new phase."[27] Swing was personally opposed to continuance of the Japanese imperial system. Nonetheless, by July 3 he was reporting that the "pressure for a definition of peace terms to Japan has mounted in Washington in recent days"—and that the present moment "would be an appropriate time to proclaim the terms."[28]

On July 13 the *Washington Post* ran two separate columns on the issue. "[T]here might be great saving of American lives," Mark Sullivan argued, "if we would make perfectly clear to the Japanese people just what we mean, and do not mean, by an unconditional surrender." Ernest K. Lindley addressed the Emperor question directly:

. . . if adequate steps are taken to disarm Japan and to prevent its rearmament, the type of government which the Japanese have after the war will become a matter of secondary importance.[29]

On July 16, *Time* magazine chimed in. Calling for statesmanship, *Time* urged that the U.S. make a "clear and positive statement of U.S. aims toward Japan. . . ."

U.S. military policy is clear: blow upon blow until all resistance is crushed. But the application of shrewd statesmanship might save the final enforcement of that policy—and countless U.S. lives.

Time stressed above all that:

the Japanese have never been told, even in general terms, that such a restricted life need not mean U.S. domination of their every affair, need not mean everlasting international disgrace.

The conclusion seemed irresistible:

> A statement beyond "Kill Japs—unconditional surrender" was awaited by Americans from Berlin to Okinawa.[30]

Finally—to cite one further example—on July 16 *Life* declared: "The big problem confronting the U.S. with regard to Japan is no longer a military problem; it is now essentially a problem in statesmanship. . . ."

> Out of [Japan's] tragic turmoil there may come no emperor at all, or an emperor of purely religious and no political significance, or even a "constitutional monarchy." In any case, the intelligent thing for us to do is to let the Japs figure it out for themselves.[31]*

Several religious journals also urged a clarification of terms. *The Christian Century* called upon its readers to sign a petition to the president "asking him to make public the basis on which peace will be restored with Japan after the surrender of that nation."[32] Similarly, *Christianity and Crisis*—with the specific endorsement of theologian Reinhold Niebuhr—also expressed concern

> over the interpretation of the slogan "unconditional surrender." Surrender is a military act. The demand that it be unconditional in no way precludes' a statement by our government in explicit terms of what the economic and political consequences of surrender for the Japanese people will be. The failure to make such a statement prompts the Japanese to delay an ultimately inevitable decision through fear of unnamed consequences.[33]

Such statements of military, political, media, and religious opinion, of course, were not universal. There was still great hatred for the Japanese—and strong sentiment against softening the terms, particularly in the liberal press and among Democratic congressmen. *The Nation* warned regularly against a "soft peace" which would allow the big-business groups—"the Zaibatsus"—to remain in control.[34] The *New York Times* editorial board also urged great caution in connection with a clarification of the surrender formula. The *Times* worried that any change might result in stiffening Japanese resistance. On the other hand, it also stated:

> If such measures could really shorten the Pacific war and make Japan harmless for the future, they might, indeed, be worth considering.[35]†

---

*See below, pp. 328, 331–32, 635–36, for further discussion of the views of Time-Life publisher Henry R. Luce at this time.

†The *Times'* news reports and commentators were even more optimistic than its editorial board about a negotiated end to the war. (See Uday Mohan and Sanho Tree, "The Ending of

From the vantage point of fifty years it is difficult to gauge nuances of public sentiment as it began to shift after Germany's defeat and the possibility of a bloody invasion slowly sank in. Plainly the call for a clarification of the surrender terms did not constitute an overwhelming chorus, but—contrary to many subsequent accounts—neither is it true that by this point in the summer Truman and Byrnes were confronted with an unyielding wall of public opinion demanding rigid allegiance to "unconditional surrender."

An instructive and balanced assessment is contained in a detailed internal government study, "Current Public Attitudes Toward the Unconditional Surrender of Japan," prepared at this time. This pointed out that despite continued support for "unconditional surrender,"

> Influential press and radio commentators are increasingly calling for a statement to supplement—or to succeed—the "unconditional surrender" formula; and public opinion polls indicate considerable willingness to accept less than unconditional surrender, since nearly a third of the nation would "try to work out a peace" with Japan on the basis of Japanese renunciation of all conquests.[36]

On July 13—while the president and Byrnes were at sea—Joseph Grew cabled the secretary that he had released a general statement to the press denying that any serious "peace feelers" had reached Washington. He went on, however, to offer his assessment, too, that

> if the President, either individually or jointly with others, now conveys the impression that unconditional surrender may not be as bad a matter as they had first believed, the door may well be opened to an early surrender. This of course is guesswork but it seems to us to be sound guesswork.[37]

The date of Grew's cable is important. His assessment that "the door might well be opened to an early surrender" was made at almost exactly the same time that a major and dramatic shift in Japan's political-military stance occurred. On June 22, during a meeting with the Supreme Council for the Direction of the War, Emperor Hirohito had declared that although war planning had to continue, it was also "necessary to have a plan to close the war at once. . . ."[38] Now, on July 12, as the *Augusta* reached mid-Atlantic, an "extremely urgent" intercepted cable from Foreign Minister Togo to Ambassador Sato in Moscow revealed that

World War II: Media Perspectives in the 1940s–1960s and early 1990s," paper presented at the conference of the American Historical Association, Chicago, IL, January 6, 1995.)

We are now secretly giving consideration to the termination of the war because of the pressing situation which confronts Japan both at home and abroad.[39]

The following day the United States intercepted the explosive "very urgent" cable from Togo we cited at the outset which documented by far the most important diplomatic development of the summer—the direct intervention of Emperor Hirohito:

His Majesty the Emperor, mindful of the fact that the present war daily brings greater evil and sacrifice upon the peoples of all belligerent powers, desires from his heart that it may be quickly terminated.

The main obstacle to peace, Togo's cable went on, was that

so long as England and the United States insist upon unconditional surrender the Japanese Empire has no alternative but to fight on with all its strength for the honor and the existence of the Motherland.

Togo requested that Moscow receive a personal representative of the Emperor who would bring with him proposals for Soviet help in terminating the conflict:

It is the Emperor's private intention to send Prince Konoye to Moscow as a Special Envoy with a letter from him containing the statements given above.[40]

Sato was instructed to meet with Foreign Minister Molotov as soon as possible to make the necessary arrangements. When Sato finally saw Molotov's deputy, Vice Commissar Solomon Abramovich Lozovsky, at 5:00 p.m. on July 13 (reported in MAGIC on July 15), he stressed:

I should like the Russian Government to bear particularly in mind the fact that the present Special Envoy will be of an entirely different character from the Special Envoy I have discussed with Molotov three times in the past; this time the Envoy will be sent at the particular desire of his Majesty.[41]

Hirohito's move was no small development. Even though the precise negotiating position a special envoy would bring with him to Moscow was still unclear, American officials recognized the momentous nature of the Emperor's personal involvement. Unlike the various "peace feelers" in Switzerland, Portugal, and through the Vatican which had appeared at regular intervals throughout the spring and early summer, this was clearly an "official" move—and at the very highest level. At the cautious end of the spectrum was this preliminary (July 13) assessment by Forrestal:

The first real evidence of a Japanese desire to get out of the war came today through intercepted messages from Togo, Foreign Minister, to Sato, Jap Ambassador in Moscow, instructing the latter to see Molotov if possible before his departure for the Big Three meeting and if not then immediately afterward to lay before him the Emperor's strong desire to secure a termination of the war.

Nor was there much question in Forrestal's mind about the central issue:

Togo said further that the unconditional surrender terms of the Allies was [sic] about the only thing in the way of termination of the war and he said that if this were insisted upon of course the Japanese would have to continue to fight.[42]

A July 14 paper prepared by the Pacific Strategic Intelligence Section (PSIS)—the navy's top Pacific intelligence group—took Forrestal's assessment a step further:

Although the above [intercepted cable] traffic does not reveal definitely whether or not the Japanese Chiefs of Staff participated with the Foreign Office in "secretly giving consideration to termination of the war", the fact that the move is stated to be an expression of "the Emperor's will", would appear to be of deep significance.[43]

Neither Stimson nor McCloy had been invited to accompany the president on the *Augusta*, and they apparently received word of the Emperor's move only on their arrival at Potsdam on July 16 after taking a ship to Gibraltar and flying separately to the meeting site. Both, however, immediately grasped the fact that a major turning point had been reached. Stimson's diary of July 16 notes: ". . . received important paper in re Japanese maneuverings for peace."[44] McCloy—less restrained than the aging secretary of war—was exuberant:

News came in of the Japanese efforts to get the Russians to get them out of the war. Hirohito himself was called upon to send a message to Kalinin and Stalin. Things are moving—what a long way we have come since that Sunday morning we heard the news of Pearl Harbor![45]

As we have seen, Stimson and McCloy had for some time been quite clear about the importance of clarifying the surrender terms; only the matter of timing had been in doubt (for a brief few weeks prior to the collapse of Okinawa). Sometime before July 15—probably en route to Potsdam—they had begun work on yet another memorandum to the president.[46] Now news of Hirohito's initiative spurred them into immediate action. Forwarding to

Truman the latest memorandum the two had developed just after his arrival in Potsdam, Stimson advised (on July 16):

> It seems to me that we are at the psychological moment to commence our warnings to Japan.

The secretary pointed out the obvious situation facing Japan—and, like Bard, noted the Russian factor as well:

> The great marshalling of our new air and land forces in the combat area in the midst of the ever greater blows she is receiving from the naval and already established Army forces, is bound to provoke thought even among their military leaders. Added to this is the effect induced by this Conference and the impending threat of Russia's participation, which it accentuates.

The truly critical development, however, was the Emperor's move:

> Moreover, the recent news of attempted approaches on the part of Japan to Russia, impels me to urge prompt delivery of our warning.

Stimson concluded:

> I would therefore urge that we formulate a warning to Japan to be delivered during the course of this Conference, and rather earlier than later, along the lines of the draft prepared by the War Department and now approved, I understand, by both the State and Navy Departments.[47]

The draft statement, of course, included explicit assurances for the Emperor.[48]

As we have seen, in his July 2 memorandum Stimson had already stated his belief that the Japanese would react favorably to a warning which also offered appropriate assurances for the Emperor. Now, in a cover letter, he told the president:

> . . . we have enormous factors in our favor and any step which can be taken to translate those advantages into a prompt and successful conclusion of the war should be taken. I have already indicated in my memorandum to you of 2 July 1945, the reasons which impel me to urge that warnings be delivered to Japan, designed to bring about her capitulation as quickly as possible.[49]

Stimson's assessment of the situation at this point in time is also suggested by another passage in his memorandum which recommended that "*if* the Japanese persist"—and, it appears, only in this event—"the full force of our newer weapons should be brought to bear. . . ."* Moreover, he also suggested an intervening step—"a renewed and even heavier warning, backed by the power of the new force and possibly the actual entrance of the Russians in the war. . . ."⁵⁰

Stimson's July 16 memorandum to the president urged a double warning: the first he thought might well bring surrender; the second would be issued if it did not. Only if both failed would the bomb be used.

McCloy's sense of the new possibilities opened up by the Emperor's intervention is also reasonably well documented. On June 29, he had sent Stimson a memorandum which—following the familiar "two-step logic"—suggested that the best time to issue a clarifying statement would be after a Russian declaration of war.⁵¹ Now his position had changed dramatically. On July 17, McCloy's diary notes:

> Conferred with the Secretary of War, and with Harvey Bundy immediately after breakfast, preparatory to the visit of the Secretary of War to the Secretary of State. More in this morning re the Japanese approaches to Russia. The delivery of a warning *now*† would hit them at *the* moment.⁵²

Now McCloy's judgment is to take action long before a Russian attack has occurred or even been explicitly threatened. His diary also states:

> The Secretary [of War] went off to the President's for dinner, but I gather that it was rather difficult for him to find a satisfactory opportunity to talk with the President. That was unfortunate as the Japanese matter is *so* pressing. There are so many things to do if the Japanese collapse should come suddenly.⁵³

The presently available evidence contains a variety of other direct and indirect indications of how the Emperor's July move impacted high government officials. We have previously noted Eisenhower's stated opposition to the use of the atomic bomb. In the following excerpt from notes taken by historian Herbert Feis during a 1960 interview with then President Eisenhower, the role of the intercepted cables is also evident:

> The President said that his first quick thought was to the effect that he hoped we would not have to use this new awesome weapon, since Japan was so nearly beaten by then. This view of the prospect he had in part

*Emphasis added.
†Emphasis added.

derived from the intercepts of messages between the Japanese government in Tokyo and its Ambassador in Moscow.[54]

Hirohito's initiative also forcefully impacted Byrnes. Although it appears from the following report that the secretary of state kept the fact that Japanese codes had been broken secret from some of his aides, the essential point is not in doubt. Like McCloy's diary entry of July 17, Brown's of the same day notes:

> JFB encouraged over early ending of Japanese war as a result of message given him by Churchill. This message apparently came to Churchill from his Ambassador in Moscow, telling of the overtures being made by Japan for an armistice.[55]

One additional indication of U.S. reactions: When the papers of Lewis L. Strauss were opened in the early 1980s, they contained handwritten notes of a discussion held on September 29, 1946, at the home of the *New York Times* publisher Arthur Sulzberger. Stimson's aide, George Harrison, had reported that the four scientists consulted by the Interim Committee had approved the bomb's use. The note in Strauss' papers raises an obvious point:

> Question: Had the 4 [Oppenheimer, Lawrence, Fermi, and Compton] been told of the intercepted messages from the Japanese Foreign Minister & Premier to Moscow.[56]

This document also reminds us of the limited information upon which the Interim Committee and its advisory panel made recommendations. What stands out in general, however, is the significance top officials attached to the first messages revealing the personal intervention of the Emperor.

The understanding that something momentous had occurred has often been missed in accounts of this phase of 1945 development. It is true that the precise negotiating posture of the Japanese government was not yet clear. However, almost certainly other factors were at work which account for the limited nature of the reporting in some subsequent accounts—especially in the early postwar decades.

For one thing, since the intercepts came in while Truman and Byrnes were away from Washington, very little solid information is available concerning discussions which almost certainly took place over the meaning of the new development—especially while they were at sea aboard the *Augusta*.

Moreover, it was not until 1951 that the fact that U.S. officials knew firsthand of the Emperor's initiative was made public. Even then, only a little-noticed mention of the intercepts appeared in *The Forrestal Diaries*.

That some historians subsequently simply reported the intercepts—but gave less than full emphasis to the impact made at the time—also can almost certainly be traced to the fact that evidence of Truman's personal knowledge of them was simply not available. "What did the president know; and when did he know it?"—the famous question of the 1970s and 1980s—could not be answered definitively for most of the early postwar years. Only in 1960, when the official Potsdam Papers were published, did the public learn that Truman had been fully aware of the key intercepts (something he had privately confirmed to State Department interviewers four years earlier, in January 1956).[57]

However, it was almost another decade and a half before the "discovery" in 1979—thirty-four years after the fact—of the president's handwritten journal. This provided researchers with Truman's personal characterization of the cable intercepted while he crossed the Atlantic. On July 18, a handwritten entry shows the president referring to the intercept after a conversation with Churchill as the "telegram from Jap Emperor asking for peace."[58]

Chapter 19

CLEAR ALTERNATIVES;
FIRST DECISIONS

---

*He'll be in the Jap War on August 15th. Fini Japs when that
comes about.*
> —President Harry S. Truman, journal, after a meeting
> with Premier Joseph Stalin, July 17, 1945

*Byrnes was opposed to a prompt and early warning to
Japan. . . .*
> —Secretary of War Henry L. Stimson, diary,
> July 17, 1945

Three brief documents offer a revealing glimpse of the attitudes of President
Truman and Secretary Byrnes on the eve of the Potsdam conference. The
first comes from Jonathan Daniels—a man who had worked on Truman's
1948 campaign staff and was close to the president. According to notes Daniels
made after a 1949 discussion of the atomic bomb, Truman explained that
as the meetings were about to begin he felt:

> "If it explodes as I think it will I'll certainly have a hammer on those
> boys."[1]

The metaphor is different, but the "hammer" image suggests the same general
point Truman expressed in indicating that he would "have more cards"
in his hand later in the summer. Daniels confirmed and expanded on the
above note in his book *The Man of Independence*: The president "seemed to
be referring not merely to the still unconquered Japs but to the Russians with
whom he was having difficulty in shaping a collaboration for lasting peace."[2]
(Daniels also noted that, in general, material in his book "was in effect later
checked by the President himself."[3])

The second piece of evidence is from a journal entry the president wrote just before the first plenary session at Potsdam got under way:

> I told Stalin that I am no diplomat but usually said yes & no to questions after hearing all the argument. It pleased him. I asked if he had the agenda for the meeting. He said he had and that he had some more questions to present. I told him to fire away. He did and it is dynamite—but I have some dynamite too which I'm not exploding now.[4]

Finally, the full entry from his previously mentioned July 7 journal—made after a pre-Potsdam discussion during the Atlantic crossing—which reads as follows:

> Had a long talk with my able and conniving Secretary of State. My but he has a keen mind! And he is an honest man. But all country politicians are alike. They are sure all other politicians are circuitous in their dealings. When they are told the straight truth, unvarnished, it is never believed—an asset *sometimes*.[5]

At this moment, though he was most impressed with the secretary's "keen mind," something about Byrnes' dealings, about "country politicians" who are all alike, clearly worried Truman. Precisely what the "straight truth" was which Byrnes would not accept ("an asset *sometimes*"), we cannot know. That the president's feelings of concern about his closest adviser's attitude at this time were real, however, also cannot be ignored—especially since Truman was later to charge Byrnes with duplicity.*

The first successful test of a nuclear device occurred at 5:29:45 a.m. on July 16, 1945, at a site code-named Trinity in the New Mexico desert 200 miles south of Los Alamos and 60 miles northwest of Alamogordo. The now-famous first report sent to Secretary Stimson by his assistant George L. Harrison was cryptic:

> Operated on this morning. Diagnosis not yet complete but results seem satisfactory and already exceed expectations. . . . Dr. Groves pleased.[6]

This message arrived at 7:30 p.m. on July 16, 1945, and was taken immediately to the president and Byrnes at the "Little White House" in the Berlin suburb of Babelsburg by Stimson.[7]

A further cable arrived on the morning of July 18 which confirmed the great success and provided significant additional information:[8]

---

*For example, in an (unsent) 1957 letter to Dean Acheson, Truman declared that at Potsdam "I trusted him implicitly—and he was then conniving to run the Presidency over my head!" (Truman, *Off the Record*, ed. Ferrell, p. 348.)

Doctor has just returned most enthusiastic and confident that the LIT-TLE BOY is as husky as his big brother.* The light in his eyes discernible from here to Highhold and I could have heard his screams from here to my farm.[9]

The informal code meant that the explosion could be seen for 250 miles and heard 50 miles away.[10]

Truman's calculated decision had paid off: The president would have his initial encounter with Stalin at noon on July 17—twenty-one hours and thirty minutes after the actual test.[11]

Just before the formal opening of the conference the potential options for ending the war came into sharp focus. Most important to the president himself was confirmation that Stalin would declare war upon Japan in the first half of August.

Truman's personal attitude has been emphasized for three specific reasons. First, many earlier researchers did not know of (or ignored) the modern evidence which shows that securing a Red Army attack was the most important objective the president had in mind in going to Potsdam. Second, even some studies which recognize the importance of the Russians fail to give adequate attention to evidence which suggests the reason Truman made this such a high priority: that "if the test should fail, then it would be even more important to us to bring about a surrender before we had to make a physical conquest of Japan."[12]

The third reason is that modern evidence confirms that once at Potsdam the president was tremendously encouraged by the assurances he received that Russia would join the war; this same evidence confirms the reasons why he felt so pleased: Contrary to many earlier accounts, the documents we now have indicate that Truman's personal judgment now appears to have been essentially the same as that reached in military planning circles beginning in April—namely, that there was a very good chance the shock of a Russian attack would end the war on its own without an invasion.

Two of the most important documentary "finds" bear directly on this issue: the discovery in 1979 of the president's personal journal for the Potsdam conference period and the release in 1983 of his private letters to his wife.

After his initial pre-conference meeting with Stalin on July 17—and after Stalin reported on his negotiations with Chinese Foreign Minister T. V. Soong on the Yalta understandings concerning the Far East—the president observed:

Most of the big points are settled.

---

*Which was to say, the gun-type uranium bomb would be as powerful as the implosion plutonium bomb.

He then went on to record Stalin's confirmation that:

> He'll be in the Jap War on August 15th.

Finally, the president noted his own judgment:

> Fini Japs when that comes about.[13]

The next day Truman further clarified his sense of the new realities—and his happiness—in a private letter to his wife:

> . . . I've gotten what I came for—Stalin goes to war August 15 with no strings on it. He wanted a Chinese settlement—and it is practically made—in a better form than I expected. Soong did better than I asked him.[14]

The letter to Bess continues:

> I'll say that we'll end the war a year sooner now, and think of the kids who won't be killed! That is the important thing.[15]

Joseph Davies' (July 18) diary also notes:

> The President said he could go home now if he had to, for he had obtained from Stalin a commitment that he would fight the Japs as he had agreed with [Roosevelt] to do. He told me of his visit with Stalin in detail, in reply to my question that regardless of how the conference came out, Stalin had said "Yes" unequivocally; that he would come in to fight Japan.[16]

It is useful to underscore the above dates—July 17 and July 18. Not only did additional information on Japan's deterioration reach the president during the next weeks, but (as we have noted) planning did not allow for even the first stage of a landing until November 1—still three and a half months off.

It is also instructive to recall that the previously cited U.S./British Combined Intelligence Committee's "Estimate of the Enemy Situation"— including the judgment that an "entry of the Soviet Union into the war would finally convince the Japanese of the inevitability of complete defeat"[17]—was, like several other estimates, prepared *before* the intercepted messages revealed the Emperor's personal attempt to end the war.

The other major option which had emerged earlier in the summer also became even more clearly defined a few days after Hirohito's move—namely the strong possibility that a modification of the rigid surrender terms might also end the war.

An intercepted cable of July 17 bears directly on these issues: in it Foreign Minister Togo expressed the Japanese position regarding the surrender terms in this way:

If today, when we are still maintaining our strength, the Anglo-Americans were to have regard for Japan's honor and existence, they could save humanity by bringing the war to an end.[18]

Togo also stressed to Ambassador Sato that, conversely:

If, however, they insist unrelentingly upon unconditional surrender, the Japanese are unanimous in their resolve to wage a thorough-going war.

The Emperor himself has deigned to express his determination and we have therefore made this request of the Russians. Please bear particularly in mind, however, that we are not asking the Russians' mediation in anything like unconditional surrender.[19]

The next day, July 18, Churchill met with Truman for lunch. As he observed in a note to the Cabinet, the prime minister told Truman he believed "that the Japanese war might end much quicker than had been expected."[20] Churchill, too, urged a clarification of terms:

I imparted to the President the disclosure about the offer from the Mikado, made to me by Marshal Stalin the night before; . . .

The President also thought the war might come to a speedy end. Here I explained that Marshal Stalin had not wished to transmit this information direct to him for fear he might think the Russians were trying to influence him towards peace. In the same way I would abstain from saying anything which would indicate that we were in any way reluctant to go on with the war against Japan as long as the United States thought fit. However, I dwelt upon the tremendous cost in American life and, to a smaller extent, in British life which would be involved in forcing "unconditional surrender" upon the Japanese. It was for him to consider whether this might not be expressed in some other way, so that we got all the essentials for future peace and security, and yet left the Japanese some show of saving their military honour and some assurance of their national existence, after they had complied with all safeguards necessary for the conqueror.[21]

Churchill went on to note Truman's initial and then more extended reaction:

The President countered by saying that he did not think the Japanese had any military honour after Pearl Harbour. I contented myself with saying that at any rate they had something for which they were ready to face certain death in very large numbers, and this might not be so important to us as to them. He then became quite sympathetic, and spoke, as Mr. Stimson had to me two days earlier, of the terrible responsibilities that rested upon him in regard to the unlimited effusion of American blood.[22]

To this Churchill added:

My own impression is that there is no question of a rigid insistence upon the phrase "unconditional surrender," apart from the essentials necessary for world peace and future security, and for the punishment of a guilty and treacherous nation.[23]

Churchill's assessment of U.S. attitudes at this point in time is also revealing:

It has been evident to me in my conversations with Mr. Stimson, General Marshall and now with the President, that they are searching their hearts on this subject, and that we have no need to press it.[24]

(We shall return to his further observation at this point that: "We know of course that the Japanese are ready to give up all conquests made in this war."[25])

The president's journal entry of July 18 concerning this discussion with Churchill contains the characterization of the Japanese intercept we have previously cited, and, too, his own sense of the emerging situation:

P.M. [Churchill] & I ate alone. Discussed Manhattan (it is a success). Decided to tell Stalin about it. Stalin had told P.M. of telegram from Jap Emperor asking for peace. Stalin also read his answer to me. It was satisfactory. Believe Japs will fold up before Russia comes in.[26]

Here two additional points must be noted with some care. First, Stalin's July 18 response to the Emperor's initiative was a very noncommittal cable which stated in part:

. . . the intentions expressed in the Japanese Emperor's message are general in form and contain no specific proposals. It is the Soviet Government's view that the mission of Prince Konoye, the Special Envoy, is in no way made clear and that it is therefore impossible for the Soviet Government to give a definite reply to the Japanese Emperor's message or in regard to the [proposed mission of the] Special Envoy, Prince Konoye, mentioned in your letter of 13 July.[27]

Many writers have noted that Stalin may have had his own reasons for not wanting to follow up on the Japanese initiative: If the war ended immediately, the Red Army might not get into Manchuria.[28] In approving as "satisfactory" Stalin's response to the Emperor's initiative, however, the president also made it clear he had no desire to follow up on this possibility at this time.

The second point refers to Truman's belief at this point that Japan will "fold up" before Russian entry. Let us simply note his judgment here; we shall attempt to assess its precise meaning after exploring several other pieces of evidence.

The Hiroshima decision is often said to have been one of military necessity. Although we shall examine this question at considerable length in the next Part, one important development at the outset of the conference bears directly on the issue. On July 16, 1945, a remarkable initiative by top U.S. and British military leaders brought together the two basic options clarified earlier in the summer in a fresh presentation of the "two-step logic."

During a meeting of the Combined Chiefs of Staff the first day at Potsdam Britain's Field Marshal Sir Alan Brooke, chief of the Imperial General Staff, called attention to the July 8, 1945, Combined Intelligence Committee estimate "where the survival of the institution of the Emperor was mentioned."[29] Sir Alan Brooke then asked the U.S. Chiefs of Staff if they had given thought to "the question of interpretation of the term 'unconditional surrender.' "

From the military point of view it seemed to the British Chiefs of Staff that there might be some advantage in trying to explain this term to the Japanese. . . . If, for instance, an interpretation could be found and communicated to the Japanese which did not involve the dissolution of the Imperial institution, the Emperor would be in a position to order the cease-fire in outlying areas whereas, if the dynasty were destroyed, the outlying garrisons might continue to fight for many months or years.[30]

The official minutes record the following response by U.S. military leaders:

The United States Chiefs of Staff explained that considerable thought had been given to this subject on the political level. One suggestion was that some form of agreed ultimatum might be issued at the correct psychological moment, for example, on Russian entry into the war, the idea being to explain what the term "unconditional surrender" did not mean rather than what it did mean.[31]

Then—having delineated the "two-step logic" in this fashion—in an extraordinary maneuver, Admiral Leahy (who, as we have seen, had been urging a modification of terms within the U.S. government), proposed what in modern times is sometimes termed an "end run": The American military leaders urged the British military leaders to try to get their prime minister to push the idea with the American president.

> Admiral Leahy suggested that as the matter was clearly a political one primarily, it would be very useful if the Prime Minister put forward to the President his views and suggestions as to how the term "unconditional surrender" might be explained to the Japanese.[32]

Nor was this a casual suggestion; a formal decision was taken and recorded in the official minutes:

> The Combined Chiefs of Staff:—
> a. Took note of the estimate of the enemy situation. . . .
> b. Invited the British Chiefs of Staff to consider the possibility of asking the Prime Minister to raise with the President the matter of unconditional surrender of Japan.[33]

The next day, July 17, General Sir Hastings Ismay, chief of staff to the minister of defence,* also strongly underscored the "two-step logic" in a Minute given directly to Churchill:

> 1. The Combined Chiefs of Staff at their first meeting had under consideration a paper prepared by the Combined Intelligence Staffs on the enemy situation, in which it was suggested that if and when Russia came into the war against Japan, the Japanese would probably wish to get out on almost any terms short of the dethronement of the Emperor.

Ismay explained that:

> This led to a discussion on the interpretation to be placed on the term "Unconditional Surrender". It was generally agreed that, if this involved the dissolution of the Imperial Dynasty, there would be no one to order the cease fire in outlying areas, and fighting might continue in various British and Dutch territories, and also in China for many months or years. Thus from the military point of view, there was a good deal to be said for the retention in Japan of some central authority who would command obedience.

Finally, he told Churchill:

> 2. The United States Chiefs of Staff said that they had had considerable discussion on this point among themselves, and suggested that it ought to be considered at the highest level during "Terminal" [the Potsdam

---

*Prime Minister Churchill was acting simultaneously as minister of defence at this time.

Conference]. They asked whether you yourself would be prepared to raise the point with the President.

3. We replied that, as the Americans were so very much the predominant partner in the war against Japan, you might feel reluctant to take the lead in this matter; but we agreed to inform you at once of what had taken place.[34]

It appears clear that Ismay was wrong about Churchill's reluctance, and that the end run which began with Leahy's suggestion stimulated the approach he made to Truman on July 18.

Taken together, these various initiatives just after the Emperor's *démarche* defined the possibilities which seemed available as the Potsdam Conference opened. Simultaneously they underscored three clear questions and decision points: first, whether to issue an early warning statement; second, whether to continue to seek an early Russian declaration of war; and third, whether to offer explicit assurances to the Emperor by clarifying the "unconditional surrender" language.

It is no longer difficult to trace the way in which decisions on the three key points were made during the July 17–August 6 period—or whose influence was dominant on all three. For the moment, however, only one decision absolutely had to be made at the outset of the Potsdam period: whether to issue a statement immediately or whether to wait.

We have seen how quickly Stimson and McCloy responded after learning of the Emperor's initiative—and, specifically, that in a memo of July 16 Stimson urged an immediate warning to Japan (including assurances for the Emperor). Modern documents make it clear that the question of timing involved one of the important contested issues and decision points of the Hiroshima bombing. However, the significance of the issue—and the choice made—has seldom been adequately explored:

As we have seen, for a statement to do any real good, adequate time would have to be allowed for the Japanese to digest its meaning ("to let the yeast work," as the War Department Strategy and Policy group put it).[35] Anything else would simply be, in modern parlance, a public relations gesture. Indeed, by June 18 Stimson, Forrestal, Grew, Leahy, and McCloy had all recommended an early statement. Stimson had put it this way at the June 18 meeting with the president:

> It was his opinion that there was a large submerged class in Japan who do not favor the present war and whose full opinion and influence had never yet been felt. He felt sure that this submerged class would fight and fight tenaciously if attacked on their own ground. He was concerned that something should be done to arouse them and to develop any pos-

sible influence they might have before it became necessary to come to grips with them.[36]

Similarly, Stimson's July 2 memorandum to Truman had stated: "the warning should be given in ample time to permit a national reaction to set in. . . ."[37]

Now, just after the messages concerning the Emperor's intervention were intercepted, a decision had to be made. On July 16 Stimson sent Byrnes his "we are at the psychological moment" memorandum to the president, saying the subject was "of supreme importance."[38] Stimson's diary records on July 17 that "I went to the 'White House' for a conference with Byrnes early in the morning"—but he found that

Byrnes was opposed to a prompt and early warning to Japan. . . .[39]

Stimson records further that Byrnes then

outlined a timetable on the subject warning which apparently had been agreed to by the President. . . .[40]

Since the American delegation had only recently arrived at Potsdam, it is reasonable to assume that the "timetable" must have been worked out at least in part during the trans-Atlantic crossing.

The concluding phrase in Stimson's diary entry records something more than the fact that a clear decision had already been made. It bespeaks as well the truth that there was no longer any question about power roles, or about Byrnes' dominant relationship with the president:

. . . so I pressed it no further.[41]

Chapter 20

REMOVING
THE SOVIET BLACKOUT
FROM EUROPE

"Now I know what happened to Truman yesterday. I couldn't understand it. When he got to the meeting after having read this report he was a changed man. He told the Russians just where they got on and off and generally bossed the whole meeting". Churchill said he now understood how this pepping up had taken place and that he felt the same way. His own attitude confirmed this admission.

—Secretary of War Henry L. Stimson,
diary, July 22, 1945

The advent of the atomic bomb was a truly extraordinary event, one which affected attitudes on virtually every issue. Stimson's diary for July 16 records that when he took the first message telling of the Alamogordo success to the president's house and showed it to Truman and Byrnes, they "of course were greatly interested, although the information was still in very general terms."[1]

The same day Joseph Davies' diary contains the following report:

When the President came down and joined us, I asked him, "Is everything all right?" He said, "Yes, fine!" I said, "Over here (Soong's Conference going on in Moscow) or back home?" He said, "Back home," and laughingly remarked, "It has taken a great load off my mind." . . . He had told me that he would have the final results of the Nevada [*sic*] experiment (atomic bomb) at about this time. The visit of Stimson and Marshall was to report its complete success. So he told me later, when he described the details of this "terrible success."[2]

On July 18 Stimson's diary notes that when Harrison's second message came in, "giving a few of the far reaching details of the test," he at once took it to the President, "who was highly delighted. . . . The President was evidently very greatly reinforced over the message from Harrison. . . ."[3]

While these conversations were taking place at Potsdam, in Washington General Groves was drafting a detailed account of the test to be sent to the president and his advisers.[4] Many scholars have noted that the arrival of Groves' full report by special courier on July 21 was the psychological turning point of the conference.[5] "It was an immensely powerful document, clearly and well written and with supporting documents of the highest importance," Stimson observed. "It gave a pretty full and eloquent report of the tremendous success of the test and revealed far greater destructive power than we expected. . . ."

> I then went to the "Little White House" and saw President Truman. I asked him to call in Secretary Byrnes and then I read the report in its entirety and we then discussed it. They were immensely pleased. The President was tremendously pepped up by it and spoke to me of it again and again when I saw him.[6]

The secretary of war goes on:

> He said it gave him an entirely new feeling of confidence. . . .[7]

Recently released materials from McCloy's papers add to the overall picture, particularly his diary entry of July 21, 1945:

> The report came in today of the catasclysmic event at Albuquerque [sic]. . . . the description of it leaves little doubt that we are on the edge of a new world—that of atomic force. It is probably of greater significance than the discovery of electricity. The phenomena of the explosion were so vivid that words seem to fail those who described it.[8]

Truman's journal for July 25 adds his belief that:

> We have discovered the most terrible bomb in the history of the world. It may be the fire destruction prophesied in the Euphrates Valley Era, after Noah and his fabulous Ark.
>
> Anyway we "think" we have found the way to cause a disintegration of the atom. An experiment in the New Mexico desert was startling—to put it mildly. Thirteen pounds of the explosive caused the complete disintegration of a steel tower 60 feet high, created a crater 6 feet deep and 1,200 feet in diameter, knocked over a steel tower ½ mile away and knocked down men 10,000 yards away. The explosion was visible for more than 200 miles and audible for 40 miles and more.[9]

Even now, 50,000 nuclear weapons later, the language of the report which Stimson read to Truman and Byrnes conveys the extraordinary nature of what had just occurred:

[I]n a remote section of the Alamogordo Air Base, New Mexico, the first full scale test was made of the implosion type atomic fission bomb. For the first time in history there was a nuclear explosion. . . . The test was successful beyond the most optimistic expectations of anyone. . . . I estimate the energy generated to be in excess of the equivalent of 15,000 to 20,000 tons of TNT; and this is a conservative estimate. . . . There were tremendous blast effects. . . . there was a lighting effect within a radius of 20 miles equal to several suns in midday; a huge ball of fire was formed which lasted for several seconds. This ball mushroomed and rose to a height of over ten thousand feet. . . .[10]

The feeling of the entire assembly was . . . profound awe.[11]

Included with Groves' report was the description of Brigadier General Thomas F. Farrell:

The effects could well be called unprecedented, magnificent, beautiful, stupendous, and terrifying. . . . Thirty seconds after the explosion came first, the air blast pressing hard against the people and things, to be followed almost immediately by the strong, sustained awesome roar which warned of doomsday and made us feel that we puny things were blasphemous to dare tamper with the forces heretofore reserved to The Almighty.[12]

Physicist Ernest O. Lawrence also described his experience of a

gigantic ball of fire rising rapidly from the earth. . . . The grand, indeed almost cataclysmic proportion of the explosion produced a kind of solemnity in everyone[']s behavior immediately afterwards. There was restrained applause, but more a hushed murmuring bordering on reverence in manner as the event was commented upon. . . .[13]

The main reason a meeting of the Big Three had initially seemed important, of course, had been the need to discuss problems arising out of the collapse of Axis power and the defeat of Nazi Germany. "We anticipated little discussion at Potsdam about the Japanese phase of the war," Byrnes later recalled. ". . . [In preparation] we concentrated on the subjects incident to winding up the European conflict. . . ."[14] An extensive literature now touches upon various aspects of the negotiations among the Big Three. Our particular interest is the impact which the atomic bomb had on the general posture and psychology of the key figures involved (and—in turn—the reverberations in connection with subsequent decisions concerning the weapon).

It would have been surprising if the news of the successful test had *not* influenced American diplomatic attitudes. Just how extraordinary the general impact was—even on the most sober and cautious members of the U.S. delegation—is suggested by the secretary of war's personal reaction.

Stimson, who had been worried about the dangers the atomic bomb presented to world peace—and who was soon to urge a direct initiative to control the new weapon in cooperation with the Soviet Union—was momentarily so moved by the initial indications of its power that he advised Truman the weapon might enable the United States to force the Soviet Union to abandon or radically alter its entire system of government.[15]

Similarly, according to one high-ranking member of the delegation, even on the basis of the first fragmentary news of the New Mexico test, Truman told reparations chief negotiator Edwin Pauley that the bomb "would keep the Russians straight."[16] This, however, only hints in the most general terms at the kind of thinking which now began to appear at Potsdam.

As we have noted, it is often forgotten that the first documented presidential discussion of the atomic bomb after Roosevelt's death was not occasioned by military concerns—or, indeed, by anything to do with the war against Japan. What first stirred Stimson to speak to Truman about the atomic bomb was the tense April confrontation with Stalin over Poland.[17]

That top policy-makers early on saw the atomic bomb as central to their diplomacy toward the Soviet Union was also obvious in the decision to delay a meeting with Stalin and to put several matters on hold until the Alamogordo test. Many scholars now recognize that the atomic bomb was connected to diplomacy concerning Europe in general and Eastern Europe in particular.[18]

The president's overall posture is quite clear: Leahy's June 15 diary entry indicates that Truman directed him to prepare an agenda for Potsdam—and that it would now be time "to take the offensive. . . ."[19] A War Department memorandum the next day by Colonel Kenneth W. Treacy also notes that "the President feels the U.S. is by far the strongest country in the world and he proposes to take the lead at the coming meeting" and that in "this connection he proposes to raise all the controversial questions. . . ."[20]

Precisely what this meant is now also plain regarding a number of issues. As we have previously noted, during a June 4 presidential meeting with Joseph Grew and the U.S. ambassador to Poland, Arthur Lane, concerning Soviet actions in the Balkan states and the states of Central Europe, Truman said "this would be the fundamental subject which he intended to discuss at the Big Three meeting."

> The President . . . left Mr. Lane in no doubt as to his intention to insist on the eventual removal of the Soviet blackout in the countries mentioned.[21]

Similarly, on the eve of Hopkins' conciliatory May visit to Moscow, according to physicist Leo Szilard, Byrnes was quite open about his view that Eastern Europe was not to be abandoned—and, that, indeed, the atomic bomb would play a central role in making Russia more "manageable" in the area. Poland had been viewed as a test case in April. Now, at Potsdam, the area of immediate concern was the Balkans.[22] The State Department recommended that it "be made clear to Stalin that we cannot accord diplomatic recognition to regimes such as those in Bulgaria and Rumania until they have been fundamentally changed in line with the [Yalta] Declaration on Liberated Europe."[23]

Although the Russians were clearly violating the essence of the Declaration, a difficulty facing policy-makers was that when the United States and Britain had endorsed the late 1944 and early 1945 armistice agreements for the defeated Axis satellite nations, they had formally conceded almost total control to the Red Army commander in each country. Russian generals were in charge, and Western representatives had only a modest advisory role—a pattern which paralleled the situation favoring the United States in Italy and subsequently in Japan.[24]

The armistice agreements, in turn, had essentially put a Stalin-Churchill "percentages" arrangement negotiated in late 1944 into specific language.[25] Under this "deal" Russian influence had been defined as 90 percent in Rumania, 75 percent in Bulgaria, and 50 percent in Hungary. Britain, in turn, was to have 90 percent influence in the country which mattered most to it in the eastern Mediterranean—Greece—and 50 percent also in Hungary.[26]

Since the Yalta declaration promising democracy in Eastern Europe was very general (and contained no serious implementation mechanism), and since the armistice agreements were very specific—in essence a policy challenging Soviet dominance in the area (as Melvyn Leffler has observed) would be a reversal of "the real meaning of the Churchill-Stalin agreement, the armistice accords, and the Yalta compromises."[27] A related problem involved the general principle of "spheres of influence" and the new U.N. charter. A late-June briefing paper advised Truman:

> In view of the actual Eastern European sphere and the Western Hemisphere bloc . . . we are hardly in a position to frown upon the establish-

ment of measures designed to strengthen the security of nations in other areas of the world.[28]

A telephone transcript found in the Stimson papers offers this additional insight as the United Nations negotiations began:

MCCLOY: . . . I've been taking the position that we ought to have our cake and eat it too; that we ought to be free to operate under this regional arrangement in South America, at the same time intervene promptly in Europe; that we oughtn't to give away either asset. . . .
STIMSON: I think so, decidedly. . . .
MCCLOY: Now, she [Russia] will say, "All right, we'll give you that, but give us the same thing in Europe and in Asia." If we do that I do think there's an argument that we cut the heart out of the whole world organization—is it worth doing that? . . .
STIMSON: Well, you don't think that Russia is going to give up her right to act unilaterally in those nations around her which she thinks so darned—are useful, like Romania, and Poland. . . .
MCCLOY: Uh, no . . .[29]

Despite awareness of such difficulties—and despite the fact that communist armies found themselves working with monarchies in Rumania and Bulgaria—throughout the spring and summer U.S. policy-makers at various levels had become increasingly concerned about Russian domination. In an interview with the president on May 2, for instance, Brigadier General Cortlandt Schuyler—the American representative on the Allied Control Commission in Rumania—urged that

Rumania and Bulgaria were test cases and if the Soviets were able to get away with their program in those countries they would be encouraged to try the same game in every other country in Europe as far as they could penetrate.[30]

Similarly, on June 22, Grew's Staff Committee recommended

that the principles of the [Yalta] Declaration [on Liberated Europe] should be reaffirmed and agreement of the British and Soviet Governments should be sought on procedures for its application, including the supervision of elections.[31]

The committee also urged that "the agreement of the Soviet Government should be sought on the admission of American and other press correspondents into these countries. . . ."[32] This was not only a matter of lofty principle but of cold politics. Another briefing paper observed that our effort to bring about the establishment of more representative governments in eastern Europe is hampered by the American public's lack of knowledge of developments there. If the United States is to be in a position to exert its influence in this direction, it must have the full backing and understanding of the American people, who can be properly and adequately informed only by our press and radio. . . . With the spotlight trained on these areas through the stories of American correspondents, the Soviet Government might be constrained to modify some of its more drastic policies and to become more amenable to our suggestions for the establishment of more representative regimes in the countries concerned.[33]

To carry through on all of this, Grew sent the president a list of suggested actions just before his departure for Potsdam—including a proposal

That provision be made for tripartite consultation [on the Control Commissions] . . . to work out any procedures . . . for the reorganization of the governments to include representatives of all significant democratic elements. . . .

That the three Allied governments consider how best to assist the local governments in the holding of . . . elections. . . .[34]

As Potsdam approached, the immediate question was whether to recognize the governments established under Red Army auspices in each country. The Russians wanted formal recognition so as to stabilize the new governments; a U.S. decision not to recognize would inevitably invite destabilizing political activity of the kind we today sometimes term "contra." Michael Boll notes, further, that

Until recognition and the subsequent peace treaties were granted the former Nazi satellites, these countries would remain outside the normal economic and political intercourse of nations, denied participation in formulating the rules and organizations that would eventually constrict or facilitate national development. Refusal of recognition meant that the trade embargoes invoked during the war would continue to wreak havoc with domestic plans for economic recovery. Nonrecognized regimes would be denied an official role in future peace conferences with the major Axis states, severely limiting any claims regarding border modifications or reparations.[35]

In early June a series of probes on the basic issues was authorized. Harriman was allowed to protest Soviet procedural violations and to urge that the United States and Britain be given veto power over the work of the Control Commissions.[36] At the same time, the president sent Stalin a message complaining that governments in the Soviet sphere were "neither representative of [n]or responsive to the will of the people."[37]

The U.S. ambassador in Britain reported that the British Foreign Office thought the Allied Control Commissions initiative "useless" (". . . Moscow would never allow itself to be maneuvered into position where Brit and AmReps would be able to outvote Soviets on matters dealing with reparations and requisitions").[38] Surprisingly, however, the mid-July Soviet response was relatively conciliatory, although seemingly shaded in different ways in line with the "percentages" involved: the U.S.S.R. would allow a veto "on questions of principle" in Hungary and it would permit representatives on the commissions in all three Balkan countries the right of prior consultation on "the most important problems. . . ."[39]

The State Department regarded the Hungarian development as particularly significant. H. Freeman Matthews, director of European affairs, received a July 16 memorandum on Hungary from his special assistant Samuel Reber which concluded: "We believe Soviet note offers real basis for agreement on reorganized ACC [Allied Control Commission]. . . . agreement in principle on truly tripartite ACC . . . [might be] . . . reached at Potsdam."[40]

On the other hand, the acting U.S. representative in Rumania, Roy M. Melbourne, cabled that even with the concessions "virtually every difficulty encountered by the American representation upon the ACC since its beginnings to date could have occurred. . . ."[41] Similarly, Maynard Barnes, the U.S. representative in Bulgaria, urged:

"Consultation" . . . could in my opinion only make our representation and that of the British on the Allied Control Commission even more effective as a tool of Russian policy than has been the case hitherto. If we accept the procedure outlined, the Russians will be able to contend with better face than ever that directives of the Commission are Allied in character.[42]

The next stage of policy development presents several features of particular interest from the perspective of our overall inquiry. The first concerns the U.S. proposal to establish a Council of Foreign Ministers to begin meeting soon after the Heads of Government Conference had concluded.[43] All unfinished business would be referred to this group, and as a June 28 State Department briefing paper explained: "Such a Council would . . . serve as a useful interim means through which the United States would work for the liquidation of spheres of influence."[44]

We know that the proposal for a Council of Foreign Ministers was especially important to Byrnes. On the eve of his departure for Potsdam he privately dubbed the recommended council "the Executive Committee" and indicated that the real action would take place there.[45] Robert Messer observes that the council would provide Byrnes with "the vehicle and the forum in which to operate as Truman's 'assistant president' in charge of the peace."[46] It would also establish an international public setting where Byrnes could personally take center stage—especially since the critical Yalta issues which were so much his personal domain would inevitably come into focus at the initial meetings.

Most important, the negotiations would take place after the atomic bomb had been publicly demonstrated.

It is clear that in general Byrnes was quite happy to delay a variety of major decisions until the first post-Hiroshima meetings (soon set for September). Details of the calculation that waiting for the weapon's demonstration would help his Balkan diplomacy are not available, but the overall strategy is rather obvious from the evidence we have from before, during, and after Potsdam that Byrnes regarded the bomb as especially important vis-à-vis Eastern Europe. Furthermore, a number of considerations make it all but impossible to believe that Truman and Byrnes did not discuss the implications of the atomic bomb as they considered the matter during the summer:

First, Poland (and Eastern Europe generally) had been Truman's initial and most widely publicized personal diplomatic effort; second, as we have repeatedly noted, the issues were central to Byrnes' personal interest; third, in preparation for the meeting (according to White House aide George Elsey) Truman made a specific point of directing that Byrnes be given a complete account of the Yalta discussions;* fourth, according to Szilard's report, Byrnes emphasized the Balkan issues in discussing the new weapon; and, fifth, Truman specifically mentioned Poland, Rumania, and Yugoslavia in discussions of the bomb with Stimson.†

There is no question, of course, that materials prepared specifically for the Potsdam conference urged an active initiative—and we know from various sources that Byrnes conferred extensively with Matthews on the ship, and, too, with the president and Leahy.[47] ("At least once a day during the entire trip," Byrnes later recalled, "the President and I would go over [recommendations on various issues]. . . ."[48]) In any case, whether the president made the decision to challenge the Russians in their area of Europe on his own or (as seems likely) was following Byrnes' advice, it is evident that his state-

*See p. 576, below.
†Stimson's diary records that in a meeting with Truman on June 6: "We then also discussed further quid pro quos which should be established in consideration for our taking them into partnership [with regard to the weapon]. [Truman] said he had been thinking of that and mentioned the same things that I was thinking of, namely the settlement of the Polish, Rumanian, Yugoslavian, and Manchurian problems. (Stimson Diary, June 6, 1945.)

ments to Grew, Lane, and Leahy that he "planned to take the offensive" were an accurate report of his planned strategy.

That the new weapon added to his confidence is also quite clear. At Potsdam's opening plenary session on July 17, Stalin suggested that Truman take the chair. Before the Yalta conference Roosevelt had sent the Soviet premier a letter saying: "We understand each other's problems and, as you know, I like to keep these discussions informal, and I have no reason for a formal agenda."[49] Truman, however, wasted no time in stating his full position. "[S]eizing this hoped for opportunity* to take the offensive," Leahy noted (using exactly the same language he had recorded in his diary a month earlier) Truman "presented at once, without permitting any interruption, the . . . proposals for the agenda which we had prepared on the ship while enroute across the Atlantic."[50] Taking up Eastern Europe, the president asserted that the obligations of the three governments undertaken in accord with the Yalta declaration had not been fulfilled—and he went on to demand:

> 1. . . . the immediate reorganization of the present governments in Rumania and Bulgaria . . .
>
> 2. . . . immediate consultations to . . . include representatives of all significant democratic elements. . . .
>
> 3. That . . . the three governments consider how best to assist any interim government in the holding of free and unfettered elections. Such assistance is immediately required in the case of Greece, and will in due course undoubtedly be required in Rumania and Bulgaria, and possibly other countries.[51]

"The boys say I gave them an earful," Truman wrote his wife, Bess, on July 18. "I hope so. Admiral Leahy said he'd never seen an abler job and Byrnes and my fellows seemed to be walking on air."[52]

The Balkan questions were referred to the foreign ministers' meetings, where only brief agenda-related discussions took place on July 18 and 19.[53] At a dinner meeting between Churchill and Stalin (on July 18), the Soviet Premier expressed concern about the new U.S. position. (Churchill replied noncommittally that he had not yet seen the U.S. proposals.)[54] Then, on July 20, at the third meeting of the foreign ministers, Byrnes became much more specific. Complaining that restrictions on the movement of U.S. representatives and the press ". . . had become a source of great irritation among our people . . . ," Byrnes made it clear that "[i]n view of the attitude of the governments concerned, we could not recognize them at this time."[55] Furthermore, "if elections are held without asking for supervision by the Big

---

*The phrase "hoped for opportunity" also seems clearly to point to an idea discussed prior to the meeting, probably aboard the ship.

Three, and governments were established which were distrusted generally by the people of our country, it will affect our relations."[56]

The next day Byrnes offered a new proposal which bypassed the demand for reorganization of the Balkan governments, but carried the same force as the one the president had previously submitted. Truman's July 17 statement had not included Hungary and had called upon "the three governments [to] consider how best to assist any interim governments in the holding of free and unfettered elections."[57] Now Byrnes proposed that "the three Governments agree . . . to provide for observation of elections in Italy, Greece, Bulgaria, Rumania, and Hungary. . . ."[58] Free elections, besides being an end in themselves, would, of course, almost certainly produce a reorganization of the governments in question. He further demanded that the Control Commissions "henceforth operate on a tri-partite basis. . . ."[59]

The next stage was dramatic—and intimately linked to the atomic bomb. As we have seen, Groves' full report of the successful Alamogordo test also came in on this day, July 21. It was at this specific juncture that Stimson observed:

> The President was tremendously pepped up by it and spoke to me of it again and again when I saw him. He said it gave him an entirely new feeling of confidence and he thanked me for having come to the Conference and being present to help him in this way.[60]

McCloy's diary, too, records that "[t]hroughout it all the 'big bomb' is playing its part—it has stiffened both the Prime Minister and the President" and specifically that

> After getting Groves' report they went to the next meeting like little boys with a big red apple secreted on their persons.[61]

The fifth plenary session began almost immediately after Stimson brought the report in, at 5:00 p.m. At this time Stalin proposed an amendment which asked recognition of the governments of the former Nazi satellite countries.[62] The confidence which Truman told Stimson the bomb had given him—and, indeed, his extraordinary bluntness—are apparent even in the official third-person report of the discussion:

> The president stated that the American Government was unable to recognize the governments of the other satellite countries. When these countries were established on a proper basis, the United States would recognize them and not before. The President stated that the meeting would proceed and that this question would be passed over.[63]

"I was getting tired of sitting and listening to endless debate on matters that could not be settled at this conference yet took up precious time,"

Truman later recalled. "I was becoming very impatient, and on a number of occasions I felt like blowing the roof off the palace."[64]

Churchill was struck by Truman's forceful attitude throughout the plenary session, and the next morning—after the Prime Minister himself had read Groves' full report—Stimson's diary records:

[He] told me that he had noticed at the meeting of the Three yesterday that Truman was evidently much fortified by something that had happened and that he stood up to the Russians in a most emphatic and decisive manner, telling them as to certain demands that they absolutely could not have and that the United States was entirely against them. He said, "Now I know what happened to Truman yesterday. I couldn't understand it. When he got to the meeting after having read this report he was a changed man. He told the Russians just where they got on and off and generally bossed the whole meeting." Churchill said he now understood how this pepping up had taken place and that he felt the same way. His own attitude confirmed this admission.[65]

Stimson's diary continues that Churchill "now not only was not worried about giving the Russians information of the matter but was rather inclined to use it as an argument in our favor in the negotiations."[66]

The diary of Sir Alan Brooke, chief of the British Imperial General Staff, provides further insight into Churchill's state of mind on the same day (July 22)—and also offers additional indirect illumination of American attitudes.

First:

[The Prime Minister] had absorbed all the minor American exaggerations

Second:

and, as a result, was completely carried away. It was now no longer necessary for the Russians to come into the Japanese war; the new explosive alone was sufficient to settle the matter. Furthermore, we now had something in our hands which would redress the balance with the Russians. The secret of this explosive and the power to use it would completely alter the diplomatic equilibrium which was adrift since the defeat of Germany. Now we had a new value which redressed our position (pushing out his chin and scowling); now we could say, "If you insist on doing this or that, well . . . And then where are the Russians!"[67]

Brooke subsequently commented that Churchill

was already seeing himself capable of eliminating all the Russian centres of industry. . . . He had at once painted a wonderful picture of himself as the sole possessor of these bombs and capable of dumping them where he wished, thus all-powerful and capable of dictating to Stalin!*[68]

Of particular interest, of course, is Sir Alan Brooke's phrase "American exaggerations."

At the afternoon plenary meeting later this same day (July 22) Truman's new confidence was again striking. At the outset of a debate over the western frontier of Poland the president declared that he "had already stated the case so far as the United States was concerned."[69] He was not prepared to settle the question at this time and said so again and again through the course of the meeting. Indeed, as Churchill and Stalin attempted to discuss the issue, Truman interrupted:

"THE PRESIDENT proposed to proceed to the next question"[70]; "THE PRESIDENT said that the question could be brought up again at any time while they were in session"[71]; "THE PRESIDENT said that doing this [sending the issue to the Foreign Ministers] would not prevent further discussion at this meeting. They could not agree now and he proposed that they take up something else"[72]; "THE PRESIDENT said he did not see the urgency of the matter. It would be helpful to have a preliminary discussion and the matter would not finally be settled until the peace conference."[73]

When Stalin and Churchill persisted, Truman finally declared that he had already stated his views: "That was his position yesterday, that was his position today, and that would be his position tomorrow."[74]

A Stimson diary entry concerning a meeting with Truman the next day (July 23) states explicitly: he "told me that the United States was standing firm and he was apparently relying greatly upon the information as to S-1. He evidently thinks a good deal of the new claims of the Russians are bluff, and told me what he thought the real claims were confined to."[75]

That evening, another cable from Washington provided dates when the bomb was expected to be ready:

Operation may be possible any time from August 1 depending on state of preparation of patient and condition of atmosphere. . . . some chance August 1 to 3, good chance August 4 to 5 and barring unexpected relapse almost certain before August 10.[76]

---

*On July 23, Admiral of the Fleet Sir Andrew Cunningham noted in his diary: "PM now most optimistic, and placing great faith in the new bomb. He now thinks it a good thing that the Russians should know about it and it may make them a little more humble." (Cunningham Diary, July 23, 1945, Cunningham Papers; cited in Martin Gilbert, *"Never Despair,"* p. 90.)

Stimson reported the message to Truman the next morning and noted that the president "said that was just what he wanted, that he was highly delighted."[77]

Churchill's admission to Stimson that he "couldn't understand" what happened to Truman at the fifth plenary session illuminates a particular facet of U.S. policy. It also suggests one useful litmus test of the bomb's specific impact on diplomacy. Earlier in the year, in May, Stimson had advised Truman that the United States had long since

> made up our minds on the broad policy that it was wise not to get into the Balkan mess . . . I said that the American people in my opinion would not like to get mixed up in the Balkans and we had taken that policy right from the beginning, Mr. Roosevelt having done it himself or been a party to it himself.[78]

Now, however, things had changed dramatically. What was once a very distant problem had become an immediate American concern.

Before the atomic bomb, British policy was also based on the assumption that there was no point in pressing Stalin in an area vital to Soviet security. Not only did Churchill have little capacity to affect events deep within the Soviet sphere,[79] but he wanted Stalin's support in the area that mattered most to him. Although the prime minister was "deeply disturbed" by the February 1945 Soviet-backed coup in Rumania, for instance,

> [w]e were hampered in our protests because Eden and I during our October visit to Moscow had recognised that Russia should have a largely predominant voice in Rumania and Bulgaria while we took the lead in Greece. . . . if I pressed him too much he might say, "I did not interfere with your action in Greece; why do you not give me the same latitude in Rumania?"[80]*

As we have seen, even on July 18—after the vague first report of the test had come in—the prime minister had replied noncommittally to the Soviet premier's complaints about the new U.S. position when they dined together. As the reports of the successful test arrived, however, Churchill's reservations disappeared. The Foreign Office abandoned a previously planned effort to try to convince the United States to recognize the Bulgarian and Rumanian governments, and at the July 21 plenary—reversing field entirely—Churchill began to support the American demands.[81]

---

*In Greece, according to Churchill, Stalin "kept very strictly to this understanding during the six weeks fighting against the Communists . . . in spite of the fact that all this was most disagreeable to him and those around him." (Churchill, *Triumph and Tragedy*, p. 420.)

Churchill's unhesitating breach of the spheres of influence agreements he himself had originally proposed neatly documents the impact of the atomic bomb upon the power realities. From London's perspective the Balkans, which had seemed beyond the reach of Western diplomacy, now appeared accessible. Still, perhaps the most important thing to understand about the Potsdam negotiations in regard to most Eastern Europe and Balkans matters is that nothing much happened at this point in time.

In reporting the Interim Committee recommendations to the president on June 6, Stimson had urged "there should be no revelation to Russia or anyone else of our work in S-1 until the first bomb had been successfully laid on Japan."[82] In many respects the Big Three conference was still two weeks too early; in several instances Truman stated his case at Potsdam but did not press matters further.

Indeed, Truman's July 21 declaration that the United States would not recognize these countries until they were "established on a proper basis" and that "this question would be passed over" precisely defined the president's basic position.[83] He would not agree to the Soviet position; he had stated his own demand; and he was quite prepared to pass over anything in dispute . . . for the moment.

Several analysts have recognized that the delaying strategy rested fundamentally on the expectation the new weapon would shortly greatly strengthen U.S. diplomacy. Robert Messer, for instance, writes that Byrnes probably concluded that "the overriding significance of the atomic bomb would only sink into the remarkably obtuse Soviet consciousness after its power had been demonstrated in combat against Japan."[84]*

Moreover, as William H. McNeill has noted, much of the remainder of the conference was "conducted under the threat of imminent American departure, with or without agreement."[85] On July 24, 1945, Stimson's diary notes:

> The President was frank about his desire to close the Conference and get away. He told me Churchill was going away Wednesday and was coming back Friday, and that he hoped to get the whole thing closed up and get away either Sunday or Monday.[86]

In what appears to have been a coordinated effort, at the morning foreign ministers' meeting Byrnes stated that the "United States Delegation wants to dispose of pending matters so that the Conference can end."[87] At the afternoon plenary session the same day—even though no agreements had as

---

*Similarly, Melvyn Leffler observes that Truman "was satisfied with the establishment of the Council of Foreign Ministers as an ongoing institutional arrangement for the negotiation of the peace treaties. Other matters could be deferred until he observed the Russian reaction to the atomic bomb." (Leffler, *A Preponderance of Power*, 38.)

yet been reached on the Balkans—Truman also informed Stalin that "when there was nothing more upon which they could agree he was returning home."[88]

Since Stalin and Truman both held their ground, in fact, little further substantive progress was made on the Balkans. The final protocol recorded an agreement for modestly improved control commission procedures, and stated that "[t]he Three Governments have no doubt that . . . representatives of the Allied Press will enjoy full freedom to report. . . ."[89] The stalemate on the fundamental issue was diplomatically papered over: "The Three Governments agree to examine each separately in the near future, in the light of the conditions then prevailing, the establishment of diplomatic relations. . . ."[90]

The attitude of the U.S. delegation at this moment is highly instructive: On July 24 Stimson recorded that the president "told me about the events of yesterday's meeting with which he seemed to be very well satisfied."[91] Harriman also "commented on the increasing cheerfulness evidently caused by the news from us [of the atomic test]. . . ."[92] The American delegation was, indeed, quite pleased with an overall outcome which to the uninformed observer must have seemed essentially a stalemate. (In his memoirs Charles de Gaulle recalled his impression, on reading the final communiqué, that the Potsdam conference "had concluded in a kind of uproar."[93])

The U.S. feeling of cheerfulness rather than frustration makes little sense unless one realizes that top policy-makers were thinking ahead to the time when the force of the new weapon would be displayed. The growing probability (and then, after the test, the *reality*) of the new weapon gave U.S. leaders a steadily deepening sense of confidence that they could manage things quite well—with or without an understanding with the Soviet Union.

This, in turn, suggests one additional perspective on their thinking. There is, in fact, strong evidence that Truman did not really want to go to the Potsdam meeting. We have noted that in July his primary concern had been to secure Russian help against Japan in case the atomic test should fail. However, if the test should succeed, as expected, the Russians might not be needed at all. Certainly their help would be far less important—and probably not worth a trip by ship across the Atlantic, since most believed that they would enter the war shortly for their own reasons anyway.[94]

Furthermore, the meeting would take place before the weapon was actually used; hence, before it could be expected to enhance the U.S. bargaining position. Truman was thus committed to a meeting which would take place a scant two weeks too early to be decisive.

The hobbles placed upon the president's diplomacy by the technological timetable must have been frustrating. In a letter written on July 3, Truman made no attempt to hide his feelings: "I am getting ready to go see Stalin & Churchill, and it is a chore. . . . Wish I didn't have to go, but I do and it can't be stopped now."[95] On the voyage to Europe he wrote to complain again: "I wish this trip was over. I hate it. But it has to be done."[96]

Only a few months earlier a conference to work out European matters with Stalin before the United States withdrew its troops from the Continent had been an urgent necessity. Now it was a tiresome bore. What was important was not a series of agreements negotiated before the United States had shown the "master card" it now held in its diplomatic hand. What was important was to get on home.

Chapter 21

SECOND DECISION

JFB still hoping for time, believing after atomic bomb Japan will surrender and Russia will not get in so much on the kill, thereby being in a position to press for claims against China.
—Walter Brown, diary, July 24, 1945

We need to pause briefly to consider the strategic posture of the U.S. delegation as it evolved during the Potsdam meeting. In developing their diplomacy vis-à-vis Eastern Europe and the Balkans on the assumption that the atomic bomb would be used, American leaders put themselves in a rather tenuous position. If for any reason they now were to decide not to use the new weapon, the strategy of delaying agreements on European matters would backfire. Minimally, there would be complications and embarrassing reversals.

This is not to say they chose—consciously or unconsciously—to employ the atomic bomb for this reason (a complex question we shall explore in the Afterword). However, even scholars who have stressed traditional interpretations of the Hiroshima decision have noted that such diplomatic bonuses, as Barton Bernstein has put it, "undoubtedly impeded leaders from reconsidering their assumptions and from revising their policy. The combat use of the bomb might greatly impress the Soviets and make them more tractable in the postwar period."[1]

It is also a matter of record that as soon as the atomic bomb was publicly demonstrated, U.S. diplomacy did actively and urgently begin to press aggressively for major changes in the Balkans.[2] Not only had the weapon given American leaders "an entirely new feeling of confidence" during the Potsdam negotiations,[3] but the very day Nagasaki was destroyed (August 9) President Truman declared of Rumania, Bulgaria, and Hungary that "These nations are not to be spheres of influence of any one power."[4]

* * *

Just before the president made it clear that he was prepared to leave Potsdam without reaching agreement, a second major decision point was reached with regard to the atomic bomb's use. Before the new weapon was successfully tested, Truman had urgently sought Russian assistance against Japan. Did the president still wish to continue to urge an early Russian declaration of war? Did he wish to do nothing to encourage Stalin? Did he wish actively to stall a Russian attack?

There is no doubt that a choice of options was available—and there is no doubt what decision was made, why it was made, or on whose advice. We also now know a fair amount about the precise timing of the advice the president received, and of how his own thinking evolved.

Very early on—after news of the Emperor's effort and of the successful test, but before Groves' powerful report—Byrnes' own judgment shifted. Walter Brown's diary of July 18 reports:

> JFB had hoped Russian declaration of war against Japan would come out of this conference. No[w] he thinks United States and United Kingdom will have to issue joint statement giving Japs two weeks to surrender or fac[e] destruction. (Secret weapon will be ready by [t]hat time.)[5]

On July 20, Brown's diary is even more explicit. Byrnes, he noted

> [h]opes Soong will stand firm and then Russians will not go in war.[6]

This entry goes on to note, further:

> Then he feels Japan will surrender before Russia goes to war and this will save China. If Russia goes in the war, he knows Stalin will take over and China will suffer.[7]

Three days later, Stimson's diary indicates:

> At ten o'clock [on July 23] Secretary Byrnes called me up asking me as to the timing of the S-1 program. I told him the effect of the two cables, and that I would try to get further definite news. I dictated a cable to Harrison asking him to let us know immediately when the time was fixed.[8]

As we have noted, Harrison replied that the operation would be possible between August 1 and August 10.[9]

Most important in terms of the decision point we are here considering, Brown's diary records on July 24:

> Truman has wired Chiang-Kai-Shek in response to his telegram that he (Truman) does not expect China to yield further than terms of Yalta

agreement. Hopes Soong will return to Moscow and agreement can be reached with Stalin.[10]

On the surface of it this cable seems merely a statement of general support. However, there is no doubt about U.S. strategy at this point, about why this particular cable was sent, or about who had advised the president. Brown's diary continues:

> JFB still hoping for time, believing after that atomic bomb Japan will surrender and Russia will not get in so much on the kill, thereby being in a position to press for claims against China.[11]

Similarly, Byrnes subsequently explained to historian Herbert Feis that "he was trying to encourage Soong to prolong the negotiations until after the United States ended the war."[12]

The cable Byrnes wrote for Truman was actually sent on July 23.[13] Thus, it appears that as the reports of the successful test came in, an explicit decision was made to attempt to use the Soong negotiations to delay a Russian declaration of war.

Although this broad picture is no longer disputed by most scholars, some additional points concerning the evolution of the decision are quite revealing. We have noted that Byrnes' views concerning Soviet participation in the war had changed by July 18 and that Truman had agreed to the new strategy by July 23 when his cable was sent.

There is confusion, however, about the exact timing of the president's reversal in the period between these dates:

As we have seen, in his letter to his wife, Bess, the president was still enthusiastic about Russia's expected participation in the war on July 18 (at a point when Byrnes was not). Similarly, on July 20, the president wrote his wife:

> We had a tough meeting yesterday. I reared up on my hind legs and told 'em where to get off and they got off. I have to make perfectly plain to them at least once a day that so far as this President is concerned Santa Claus is dead and that my first interest is U.S.A., then I want the Jap War won and I want 'em both in it.[14]

Moreover, two days later on July 22, again writing to Bess, the president seems to refer to his happiness with Stalin's pledge to enter the war:

> Some things we [Stalin and I] won't and can't agree on—but I have already what I came for.[15]

On the other hand, there are also some clear hints that Truman's attitude may have begun to shift at just about the same time Byrnes' did. On July 18, as noted, he had already observed in his journal: "Believe Japs will fold up before Russia comes in." (He had added: "I am sure they will when Manhattan appears over their homeland.")[16] And during the plenary meeting of July 19 the following exchange took place over the disposition of the German merchant and naval fleet:

> THE PRESIDENT said he would be agreeable to a three-way division of the German merchant and naval fleets but that he should like it to be done after the Japanese war. We needed these ships not only for the conduct of the war but also to haul food and supplies for rehabilitation of Europe. . . .
>
> THE PRESIDENT said that we will need every bomb and every ton of food.
>
> STALIN said what about the navy?
>
> THE PRESIDENT said he was ready to dispose of them now. He added that when the Japanese war was over, the United States would have merchant and naval ships for sale but he did not want to upset our war against Japan now.
>
> STALIN inquired, "Are not the Russians to wage war against Japan?"[17]

The president's reply—"that when Russia was ready to fight Japan, she would be taken in the shipping pool the same as the others"—was hardly a satisfying response.[18] The record goes on to say that the president "added that we wanted them in the pool."[19]

Though this lukewarm reply suggests the president's interest in Soviet help may have been fading, almost certainly he had not yet fully made up his mind. On July 23, Stimson noted:

> The President had told me at a meeting in the morning that he was very anxious to know whether Marshall felt we still needed the Russians in the war or whether we could get along without them, and that was one of the subjects we talked over.[20]

Stimson goes on to report on the following discussion he had with Marshall after lunch the same day:

> Of course Marshall could not answer directly or explicitly. We had desired the Russians to come into the war originally for the sake of holding up in Manchuria the Japanese Manchurian Army. That now was being accomplished as the Russians have amassed their forces on that border, Marshall said, and were poised, and the Japanese were moving up positions in their Army. But he pointed out that even if we went ahead in the war without the Russians, and compelled the Japanese to

surrender to our terms, that would not prevent the Russians from march-ing into Manchuria anyhow and striking, thus permitting them to get virtually what they wanted in the surrender terms. Marshall told us dur-ing our conference that he thought thus far in the military conference they had handled only the British problems and that these are practically all settled now and probably would be tied up and finished tomorrow. He suggested that it might be a good thing, something which would call the Russians to a decision one way or the other, if the President would say to Stalin tomorrow that "inasmuch as the British have finished and are going home, I suppose I might as well let the American Chiefs of Staff go away also" that might bring the Russians to make known what their position was and what they were going to do, and of course that indicated that Marshall felt as I felt sure he would that now with our new weapon we would not need the assistance of the Russians to con-quer Japan.[21]

The next morning, July 24, at 9:20 a.m., Stimson met with Truman and

> told him of my conference with Marshall and the implication that could
> be inferred as to his feeling that the Russians were not needed. I also
> told the President of the question which Marshall had suggested might
> be put to Stalin as to the Americans going home, and he said that he
> would do that this afternoon at the end of the hearing, but he told me
> that there had been a meeting called by Leahy of the Military Staffs to
> meet either this afternoon or I think tomorrow morning.[22]

A number of studies have taken the above Stimson diary entries as evi-dence of the president's attitude at this particular moment.[23] However, we know from many sources that Stimson was generally out of the loop of top information for most of the Potsdam Conference; and the evidence, in fact, indicates that in sending his cable to Chiang Kai-shek the day before, July 23, Truman had already decided in favor of Byrnes' strategy of at-tempting to hold off Russian entry into the war.

British documents, too, indicate that the president made his decision be-fore receiving Stimson's report of Marshall's views, and possibly even before he asked about them: in a July 23 minute to Sir Anthony Eden, the foreign secretary, for instance, Churchill reported:

> Mr. Byrnes told me this morning that he had cabled to T.V. Soong ad-
> vising him not to give way on any point to the Russians, but to return
> to Moscow and keep on negotiating pending further developments.

It is quite clear that the United States do not at the present time desire Russian participation in the war against Japan.[24]*

Several additional points related to the president's reversal and his and Byrnes' decision to attempt to hold off a Russian declaration of war may also be noted.

This decision marked the third shift in the U.S. attitude (and the fourth policy) toward Soviet participation in the war within the space of little more than three months' time: (1) Until sometime in mid-April, Soviet help had been deemed absolutely essential *for an invasion to take place*; (2) then, once it was clear the U.S. Navy could prevent Japanese troops in Manchuria from returning to reinforce the home lands, Soviet help was no longer deemed essential *for an invasion*; (3) thereafter, Japan's deterioration had so accelerated that it now seemed that the massive shock of a Russian declaration of war might "lever" Japan into surrender *without* an invasion; and now (4) the president and Byrnes had clearly decided that they preferred not to utilize this method of attempting to end the war—and actively sought to delay a Red Army attack.

Even today many studies miss all of these changes in position and instead suggest in very general terms that the United States sought Russian assistance during the summer of 1945. As we have observed in connection with other controversial aspects of the atomic bomb story, the idea that U.S. strategy might have been so complex—even Machiavellian—was sometimes decried as being excessively critical of American leaders. The notion that a tactic based on the simple ploy of delaying final negotiations until the bomb had been demonstrated was not seriously entertained by most journalists and scholars for a substantial period.

Related to this is the fact that articles by Stimson and his 1948 memoirs, *On Active Service in Peace and War*, make no mention of the strategy.[25] Nor do many early historical accounts report the deliberate use of the Soong negotiations as a delaying tactic.[26] There seems to have been a general unwillingness among scholars and journalists to face up to the fact that politicians in power—especially Byrnes—were often quite shrewd and wily or, to use Truman's term, "conniving."

The situation has changed considerably in recent years. The following representative statements by important modern scholars bespeak a now well-understood consensus:

• Marc Gallicchio:

*The morning reference suggests the actual decision may well have been made the evening before, on July 22.

Stalin had told Truman and Byrnes that the Soviets would not enter the war until they had a firm agreement with the Chinese. To prolong the talks, Byrnes sent a cable to Chiang over Truman's signature in which he advised the Chinese not to make any concessions in excess of the Yalta agreements.[27]

· Melvyn Leffler:

Since the Soviets had stated that they would not go to war until the Chinese accepted the substance of the Yalta agreement, Truman and Byrnes now hoped that a stalemate in the Chinese-Soviet talks would delay Soviet intervention. . . .[28]

· McGeorge Bundy:

[Byrnes] . . . somewhat naively hoped that he could keep Stalin out of the war by encouraging Chinese delay in negotiations with Russia on the execution of the Yalta terms. . . .[29]

· Barton Bernstein:

Byrnes purposely impeded Sino-Soviet negotiations in order to *prevent* the Soviets from entering the war.[30]

It is important to understand that only in the mid- and late 1950s—more than a decade after the fact—did some of the documents which permitted the new understanding begin to become available. Before that time—throughout the decade when the official explanation of the Hiroshima decision was consolidated and became deeply embedded in American popular consciousness—this facet of the story was not a matter of public record.

A second point related to the decision to attempt to delay or avoid a Russian declaration of war involves a certain problem of nuance which was also commonly missed in early accounts (and still often confused):

There is no doubt that Truman and Byrnes were interested in and concerned about Soviet political influence in Asia—and that they wished to end the war as quickly as possible in order to limit that influence. We have also seen that as early as May 15 Stimson had come to see the atomic bomb as the "master card" of diplomacy which would be dominant in connection with the "tangled wave" of Far Eastern diplomatic objectives.[31]

It is sometimes thought that because the substantive issues involved were so important, the decision—on the one hand to try to stall the Russians; on the other to rush the atomic bomb—had to be made. However, a close reading of the evidence also challenges so simple an argument.

In the first place, U.S. control of the seas made it obvious that Russia would not have the power to share in the actual occupation of Japan if the United States chose otherwise.[32] Moreover, the Red Army, as Marshall pointed out, was likely to enter and dominate Manchuria in any event, if Stalin so chose. Little was likely to change in connection with these fundamentals.

In the second place, by this point the matters in dispute in the Soong negotiations were no longer world-shaking. The remaining issues—precisely how power would be shared on the management board of the Manchurian railroad and how a "free port" in the city of Dairen would be administered— had a certain significance, but, as Truman himself made clear in several different contexts, they were relatively minor problems:[33]

Truman, indeed, had told Stimson as early as June 6 of his satisfaction with the Hopkins negotiations; he was similarly pleased about the Manchurian situation when he and Stimson dined together on July 17 at Potsdam. Stimson, worried about economic matters, the same day had "impressed on [Byrnes] the importance of the Open Door policy in connection with Stalin's new pressure for commercial rights in Manchuria."[34] Now, the president "told me briefly of his first meeting with Stalin"—and that he had "said he thought that he had clinched the Open Door in Manchuria."[35]*

The next day—after Stimson gave Truman more details from the second message on the atomic test—"The President again repeated that he was confident of sustaining the Open Door policy. . . ."[36]† And—writing to his wife on July 18—Truman had also confirmed his judgment that significant substantive issues no longer presented major problems in the negotiations.

Although there is little doubt that some U.S. officials felt continuing concern about these matters, in light of such evidence it is difficult to argue that the importance of the railroad and port management issues were the reason the president and Byrnes dug in their heels in connection with the Soong negotiations. More reasonable is the suggestion that these issues were emphasized almost entirely as a tactic to delay the Russian attack.

Viewed in broader historical perspective, the way information and understanding changed over time in connection with this issue offers an illuminating case study of how early myths were slowly punctured; how occasional broad hints were followed by hard information until old beliefs finally col-

---

*The same day, July 17, as we have seen, Truman also noted in his journal: "Most of the big points are settled. . . ." (Truman, *Off the Record*, p. 53.) The "open door" policy for U.S. goods and investment had been the economic centerpiece of U.S. free trade strategy on the Asian mainland from the turn of the century on.

†Stimson goes on to say: "and I took the occasion to emphasize to him the importance of going over the matter detail by detail so as to be sure that there would be no misunderstanding over the meaning of the general expressions." Given Truman's confidence in this connection, it is worth recalling that the very next line in this diary entry is the previously quoted statement: "The President was evidently very greatly reinforced over the [atomic test] message from Harrison and said he was very glad I had come to the meeting."

lapsed. A few (selected) milestones usefully trace the slow unfolding of information and nuanced understanding of tactics vis-à-vis the Far Eastern diplomatic issues:

• *1947:* In his book *Speaking Frankly*, Byrnes hints: "As for myself, I must frankly admit that . . . I would have been satisfied had the Russians determined not to enter the war."[37]

• *1951:* In *The Forrestal Diaries* on July 28, an entry states: "Byrnes said he was most anxious to get the Japanese affair over with before the Russians got in, with particular reference to Dairen and Port Arthur. Once in there, he felt it would not be easy to get them out."[38]

• *1953:* In his memoirs, *Triumph and Tragedy*, Churchill reports the previously noted July 23 "minute" to Eden: "It is quite clear that the United States do not at the present time desire Russian participation in the war against Japan."[39]

• *1955:* In his memoirs, *Year of Decisions*, Truman writes: "Anxious as we were to have Russia in the war against Japan, the experience at Potsdam now made me determined that I would not allow the Russians any part in the control of Japan."[40]

• *1957:* As we have seen, in notes taken during an interview by historian Herbert Feis (opened to the public in 1971), Byrnes is recorded as stating that "he was trying to encourage Soong to prolong the negotiations until after the United States had ended the war."[41]

• *1958:* In his book *All in One Lifetime*, Byrnes now explicitly acknowledged that he had wanted "to encourage the Chinese to continue negotiations after the adjournment of the Potsdam Conference. I had some fear that if they did not, Stalin might immediately enter the war. . . . On the other hand, if Stalin and Chiang were still negotiating, it might delay Soviet entrance and the Japanese might surrender. The President was in accord with that view."[42]

• *1960:* In an August 15, 1960, issue of *U.S. News and World Report*, Byrnes was asked, "Was there a feeling of urgency to end the war in the Pacific before the Russians became too deeply involved?"—and responded: "There certainly was on my part, and I'm sure that, whatever views President Truman may have had of it earlier in the year, that in the days immediately preceding the dropping of that bomb his views were the same as mine—we wanted to get through with the Japanese phase of the war before the Russians came in."[43]

• *Early 1970s:* The full diaries of Walter Brown show him writing on July 24, 1945: "JFB still hoping for time, believing after atomic bomb Japan will surrender and Russia will not get in so much on the kill, thereby being in a position to press for claims against China."[44]

That we are in the presence of a process guided not by the vagaries of the inevitable march of time through history—but rather by conscious human attempts to control information—is illuminated, finally, by comparing the published 1951 version of the July 28, 1945, Forrestal diary account of these matters with the full unpublished account. The 1951 diary extract, as noted, reports in general that

> Byrnes said he was most anxious to get the Japanese affair over before the Russians got in, with particular reference to Dairen and Port Arthur. Once in there, he felt, it would not be easy to get them out.[45]

The next sentence, documenting not only Byrnes' general attitude but the specific tactics he used to achieve his goal, is to be found only in the original unpublished diary:

> With all this in mind, he was in favor of Soong's return to Moscow, which he proposes to do, in order to keep the conversation on this subject going.[46]

One final point is of interest in connection with these matters: The decision to attempt to delay "the Russian Option" for ending the war can hardly be called a military decision. Every strictly military consideration pointed to the use of as much force as possible so as to get as speedy a surrender as possible and thereby save as many lives as possible.

The decision to attempt to put off this readily available option was a decision to reduce, not add to, the force available to achieve the earliest possible surrender.

Chapter 22

THE BOMB AND GERMANY

[Byrnes] was still having a hard time over Reparations. The details as to the success of the Atomic Bomb, which he had just received, gave him confidence that the Soviets would agree as to these difficulties.

—Ambassador Joseph Davies, diary, July 28, 1945

There is other evidence concerning how various officials assessed the emerging situation in Japan after Emperor Hirohito's intervention—especially during the specific period when the decision to put off a Russian declaration of war was made.

As we have seen, Walter Brown's diary on July 17 noted that Byrnes' feeling of encouragement "over early ending of Japanese war" came "as a result of" the message concerning the Emperor's intervention. It is especially significant that this entry describing Byrnes' attitude was written before Groves' full report came in (and before Harrison's second preliminary report arrived on July 18). Although he knew from the first cable that the test had succeeded, Byrnes' encouragement at this point cannot as yet have derived from knowledge of the truly extraordinary power of the new weapon. His level of confidence is particularly striking when one further considers that there is no indication that Byrnes expected to alter the demanding unconditional-surrender language at this point.

A similar sense of optimism is also evident in reports of Eisenhower's assessment of the situation. Although the following is taken from a meeting recorded in Forrestal's postwar diary and is not contemporaneous, it points in exactly the same direction as Brown's report:

When President Truman came to Potsdam in the summer of 1945 he told Eisenhower he had as one of his primary objectives that of getting

Russia into the Japanese war. Eisenhower begged [Truman] at that time not to assume that he had to give anything away to do this, that the Russians were desperately anxious to get into the Eastern war and that in Eisenhower's opinion there was no question but that Japan was already thoroughly beaten. When the President told him at the end of the Conference that he had achieved his objectives and was going home, Eisenhower again remarked that he earnestly hoped the President had not had to make any concessions to get them in.[1]

The significance of this report is underscored because numerous accounts indicate that Eisenhower was against using the atomic bomb.* His assessment that an early surrender was likely seems clearly to have been based on the judgment that Japan was in such serious trouble the war could be ended without either the Russians or the bomb.

As in the Balkans, a strategy which in many ways relied for its ultimate success on demonstrating the weapon's power was also adopted in connection with the two truly central issues of the postwar world discussed at Potsdam: Germany and the future of the European economy. Here, however, not only did the fact of the bomb's existence serve to stiffen the U.S. negotiating position but—far more significantly—it directly solved the most important problem facing American diplomacy, and it greatly alleviated a tremendous burden placed on U.S. policy by Roosevelt's pre-atomic strategy. So important—indeed, radical—were the weapon's implications in these areas that it is not too much to say that the atomic bomb quite literally revolutionized the fundamental assumptions of U.S. policy.

There is very little dispute that throughout World War II the central postwar issue facing U.S. leaders was that of security—above all, how to control Germany. The obvious problem was how to insure that Germany would not start yet another, third world war in one century. The German question, as Herbert Feis observed, boiled down to: "What measures, acceptable to the conscience of our times, could eliminate the chance that they might rise from the rubble and strike out again?"[2]

Put another way, as McCloy noted in his diary, Germany was the "cockpit of our policy. . . ."[3]

Although the "German problem" was extremely important, the choices available were far more constrained than is commonly realized. The main difficulty was that no American president could count on the public allowing him to keep a significant number of troops in Europe for very long after the

*See below, pp. 352–58.

war. "[D]omestic political realities," as Stephen Ambrose has noted, simply "precluded the maintenance of a large, conscripted, standing army in postwar Europe."[4]

Indeed, as early as November 1943 at the Teheran conference FDR had informed Stalin that U.S. forces would be withdrawn from Europe within one to two years after victory over the Nazis.[5] Similarly, Roosevelt told Churchill in late 1944: "You know, of course, that after Germany's collapse I must bring American troops home as rapidly as transportation problems will permit."[6] A few months later, at Yalta, the president told both leaders "that he did not believe that American troops would stay in Europe much more than two years."[7]*

In these circumstances the question facing U.S. leaders was what—specifically—was there to guarantee U.S. security against a revival of Germany? Furthermore, what answer to this question might a president give to the American people which could survive political challenge?

At the time of Roosevelt's death the only concrete strategy available to any president was the consolidation of an alliance with the other great power which had an equally strong interest in keeping Germany down—namely, the Soviet Union: "It is by now a commonplace," Willard Thorp, deputy to the assistant secretary of state for economic affairs, characteristically noted, "that Germany cannot commit another aggression so long as the Big Three remain united."[8] The essence of the U.S. pre-atomic security policy for Europe was just that—an agreement, sealed at Yalta, for joint control of Germany by the United States and the Soviet Union (together, of course, with the lesser great power, Britain, and with the then still lesser power, France). "It is our inflexible purpose," Roosevelt, Stalin, and Churchill proclaimed, "to destroy German militarism and Nazism and to ensure that Germany will never again be able to disturb the peace of the world."[9]

Since the Soviet Union desperately needed help in rebuilding its devastated society, the Yalta understanding that "to the greatest extent possible" there would be large-scale reparations taken out of the German economy—in the neighborhood of $20 billion, half to go to the Soviet Union—completed the deal.[10] At the same time, the extraction of "industrial reparations" was also understood as a way to weaken Germany's "military-industrial complex." In fact, the Yalta protocol stated that it was

---

*Moreover, in very short order there were riots in Europe as U.S. soldiers demanded repatriation: in January of 1946, four thousand GI demonstrators in Frankfurt marched on the Supreme Commander, General Joseph T. McNarney, demanding, "We want to go home!" (Richard Barnet, *The Rocket's Red Glare*, p. 249.) (See also R. Alton Lee, "The Army 'Mutiny' of 1946," *The Journal of American History*, Vol. 53, No. 3, [December 1966], pp. 555–71.)

"to be carried out chiefly for purpose of destroying the war potential of Germany."[11]

This overall strategy was later misleadingly lumped together with oversimplified notions of making Germany into a "pastoral" society.[12] In essence, however, the plan was a commonsense accommodation to the fact that specific measures to control Germany were essential.

Nor at the time did the arrangement seem utopian. An early 1945 War Department memorandum stressed:

> While the United States can afford to make no concessions which leave its security or vital national interests at the mercy of the Soviet Union, there is almost no other concession which it can afford not to make to assure Soviet collaboration in the maintenance of security.[13]

Before the atomic bomb was successfully tested, Byrnes was clear about the central issue (or so it appears he told Davies). Six weeks before the test (on June 6, 1945), Davies' diary records that Byrnes "discussed the entire Russian situation at great length":

> It was clear that without Russian cooperation, without a primary objective for Peace, another disastrous war would be inevitable. . . . Nor did he think that our people on sober second thought would undertake fighting the Red Army and Russia for a hopeless cause of attempting to control the ideology or way of life which these various rival groups wished to establish in the various countries.[14]

In 1945 even hard-line U.S. officials did not view Russia as a major military threat to the West. Far from worrying about a Russian attack, as we have seen, a number of policy-makers believed they had sufficient power to challenge Russian influence in Eastern Europe. The intervening Cold War years have served to confuse many accounts of this period. It is therefore useful to note that at this time even Harriman stressed (to the secretary of state's staff committee on April 21, 1945):

> [I]t was important not to overestimate Soviet strength. The Army is an extraordinarily effective but disorganized mass of human beings. Almost all of the Army's transport equipment and much of its food is supplied by us. The country is still fantastically backward. There is no road system, railroad mileage is very inadequate, and ninety percent of the people of Moscow live in a condition comparable with our worst slum areas.[15]

Roughly half the Soviet army's transport in 1945 was reportedly still horse-drawn (and would remain so until 1950).[16] A memorandum recently discovered by Frank Kofsky records President Truman being briefed even at the height of the 1948 Berlin crisis that

> the Russians have dismantled hundreds of miles of railroads in Germany and sent the rails and ties back to Russia. There remains, at the present time . . . only a single track railroad running Eastward out of the Berlin area and upon which the Russians must largely depend for their logistical support. The same railroad line changes from a standard gauge, going Eastward to a Russian wide gauge in Poland, which further complicates the problem of moving equipment and supplies forward.[17]

Most close students of this period also agree that for a substantial period the Russians kept to the agreements ultimately reached on Germany—for the good reason that they, too, needed the Americans. As General Lucius Clay, the U.S. military commander in Germany after the war, repeatedly told Washington, it was the French under de Gaulle—not the Russians—who regularly threw monkey wrenches into the Allied Control Council operations in Germany.[18] A recent authoritative study by Jean Smith goes so far as to conclude that Clay "believed that Washington was being duped by the British and French into taking unwarranted anti-Soviet positions."[19]

In short, given the complementary U.S.–U.S.S.R. interest in holding down the common enemy, in 1945 to many there seemed to be a reasonable chance that the "German problem" could be solved—and that whatever irritations might develop between Moscow and Washington, common need would serve to sustain practical big power relations (if not amicable cooperation) in Germany.

As Truman privately explained to reporters in April 1946:

> What you have to remember about Russia and its fear of another war is that the Germans slaughtered 25,000,000 people not connected in any way with the military. They ruthlessly wiped out everybody from the Polish border to Leningrad and Moscow.[20]

Numerous studies have documented the obvious fact that the atomic bomb radically altered general U.S. conceptions of national security strategy in the postwar era.[21] However, few have fully grasped the fact that at one stroke the new weapon also altered the entire basis of American policy toward the number-one security problem—Germany. The bomb not only made Russian help to control Germany totally irrelevant, it also rendered secondary the idea of extracting industrial reparations as a way to weaken Germany's military-industrial potential (and cement the deal with Russia).

Moreover, it did so in a manner that at the time was extraordinary to the individuals involved—wiping away in one sudden blast the entire framework they had previously taken for granted. The bomb simply bypassed the central consideration which had dominated Roosevelt's German security policy— awareness that the American people were not likely to allow U.S. troops to remain in Europe.

Once again, the formal official records do little to illuminate the impact of the changed power-diplomatic relationships. The fact that the atomic bomb revolutionized the assumptions of postwar U.S. security policy—and of its approach to Germany—is nowhere explicitly mentioned in the official documents. However, other evidence—especially from private diaries opened to researchers from the mid-1960s to the late 1980s—provides insight into the thinking of the time.

The fundamental question in dispute at Potsdam was a seemingly arcane matter which actually penetrated to the heart of virtually all the other issues—whether to fulfill Roosevelt's Yalta understanding whereby the Soviets were to receive reparations of roughly ten billion dollars from Germany. To do so would be to continue the basic approach and implement the U.S.– U.S.S.R. arrangement to jointly hold down Germany and simultaneously "industrially disarm" the common foe.

The position the U.S. delegation now took was: "No." The basic Rooseveltian posture was simply abandoned. As Melvyn Leffler has observed, not only did American officials "distance themselves from the position on reparations taken by Roosevelt at Yalta," they also thereby almost certainly committed what the Russians saw as an "overt violation of the meaning and spirit of the Yalta compromises."[22]

Indeed, although Red Army help to control Germany had once seemed absolutely essential, the United States now became quite cavalier in its negotiations. The United States also was now more than willing to accept a far more powerful industrial basis for the German economy than had previously been assumed. Moreover, once again U.S. leaders were quite willing to leave Potsdam with no agreement—and to await the development of events.

Nor is there any doubt about what produced this revolution. At Potsdam, U.S. leaders explicitly stated their private judgment that the atomic bomb had given them power to control all security problems—including the once-central German threat.

The new assumptions of policy were illuminated in two conversations between Byrnes and Davies. A diary entry by Davies on July 28, 1945, reports Byrnes' sense of the diplomatic leverage the bomb now offered:

[Byrnes] was still having a hard time over Reparations. The details as to the success of the Atomic Bomb, which he had just received, gave him confidence that the Soviets would agree as to these difficulties.[23]

(Davies notes further that "Byrnes' attitude that the atomic bomb assured ultimate success in negotiations disturbed me more than his description of its success amazed me. I told him the threat wouldn't work, and might do irreparable harm."[24])

The specific argument concerning the bomb and security was stated the following day, July 29. First, the secretary of state's view that

> Because of New Mexico development . . . [Byrnes] felt secure anyway. He elaborated upon the extent of the power of the atomic bomb.[25]

Beyond this Davies notes that

> SECRETARY BYRNES suggested that the New Mexico situation had given us great power, and that in the last analysis, it would control.[26]

As in the case of the Balkans, it is also possible to chart the general evolution of U.S. policy over the summer. At Yalta the Big Three had agreed to establish a Reparations Commission charged with creating a detailed plan and the fixing of the total sum of reparations payments to be made by Germany. Roosevelt's commitment to twenty billion dollars was not a definitive statement of policy. Nevertheless, it established a clear, if rough, order of magnitude for reparation withdrawals.*

After Yalta, Roosevelt appointed Dr. Isador Lubin to head the American delegation to the Allied Commission on Reparations, which was about to meet in Moscow.[27] The choice seemed a clear confirmation of Roosevelt's basic intent: Lubin was known to be sympathetic to Secretary of the Treasury Henry Morgenthau's views concerning a radically weakened postwar Germany, and could be expected to support large-scale reparations and a substantial deindustrialization of the German economy.[28]

There is no doubt that Roosevelt's essential policy was disturbing to some State and War Department officials who were concerned about the consequences of drastic surgery on the German economy. It is also clear that Truman shared this concern; more specifically, he feared that the United States might ultimately be forced to finance German reparations costs (as had happened after World War I).[29] In any event, only fifteen days after Roosevelt's death Lubin was replaced by a new appointee, Edwin W. Pauley, an oilman—in the words of a State Department colleague: "a very picturesque

---

*Leffler notes that "throughout the Crimean deliberations Roosevelt did not contest the amount of reparations with Stalin. . . ." (Leffler, "Adherence to Agreements," p. 104). Moreover, precisely because the British Cabinet would not concur in the general commitment recorded in the protocol Churchill refused to endorse this aspect of the agreement. (FRUS, Malta and Yalta, p. 983.)

character; a great big, tough guy . . . he got things done."[30] Pauley also happened to be a Democratic fundraiser who had played an important role in the selection of his friend Harry Truman for the national ticket in 1944.[31]

There was more to Pauley's appointment than the mere payback of a political crony, however. As *U.S. News and World Report* noted, it was also "evidence of this country's changing attitude towards Russia"; that now "almost every detail of the peace is to be a matter of sharp, shrewd bargaining."[32] Truman told Lubin by way of explanation that this was "the most important job in the United States as of the moment . . . and I want somebody as head of the delegation who can throw his weight around."[33] (After the war he remembered Pauley as one of the few "hard boiled hard hitting anti-Russian advisers" he had at Potsdam.[34]) He also made Pauley an ambassador and gave him the right to report directly to the president.[35]

As we have seen, the stop-start tactics of tough and then accommodating negotiations with the Russians over various issues—plus the absence of documentary evidence at numerous points—make it difficult to pin down precise details in several areas. Nonetheless, the overall pattern in connection with the German security-reparations issues, like that in connection with the Balkans, is clear.

There is little question either about Pauley's general viewpoint or his sense of what the president ultimately wanted. For instance, as early as May 22—while meeting with British officials en route to Moscow for the initial reparations talks—Pauley privately stated that the United States "had no idea of signing a hard and fast agreement at Moscow. In particular . . . they could not agree to the 20 billion dollar figure."[36]

(Pauley did not convey this basic stance to the Russians. Almost a month later, when Ivan Maisky—his Soviet counterpart on the Reparations Commission—raised the twenty-billion-dollar figure, Pauley told the State Department that "Inasmuch as Roosevelt, Stalin and Churchill agreed at Yalta to use this as a basis of discussion, I have not officially resisted this basis."[37] His personal opinion, however, was that "a formula [should] be adopted which will emphasize percentages, rather than dollars. . . ."[38])

We also know something about Truman's sense of the situation. In early June, at just about the same time the president confidentially told Ambassador Lane that he intended to remove "the Soviet blackout" from Eastern Europe, Bernard Bernstein of the U.S. Group Control Commission for Germany also met with Truman. Bernstein reported to Morgenthau that the president

didn't seem at all pessimistic about his relations with the Russians because he felt that we held all the cards and that the Russians had to come to us. . . . He said Russia was pretty much destroyed from Poland,

and that unless they did something to remedy that situation promptly, they would have extensive starvation. That was why he felt he had the cards in American hands, and he made very clear that he proposed to play them as American cards.[39]

Nevertheless, there was no major shift in the stated U.S. position on the reparations-security issues during May and June. Despite the fact that numerous State and War Department officials ardently wished a stronger German economy (and therefore less reparations)—and even though there was concern about Russian machinery removals from Eastern Germany—the United States did not officially break with the Yalta reparations understanding during the summer.[40]* Indeed, on July 2, Joseph Grew went so far as to cable Pauley that

> the [State] Department is not opposed to the discussion of an amount of reparations. While it is felt that a figure of twenty billion dollars is too high and that one approaching twelve or fourteen billion dollars would be more appropriate, the twenty billion dollar figure may be adopted as a starting point for exploration and discussion.[41]

Just as a policy began to take on tougher dimensions in the Balkans once the president departed for Potsdam, it similarly began to shift in connection with Germany. Pauley sent Byrnes a cable on July 5 that ignored the State Department message of July 2[42]—and contemplating the situation aboard the *Augusta* two days later (July 7), Truman noted in his journal:

> Byrnes & I discussed Pauley's plans on reparations. The smart boys in the State Department, as usual, are against the best interests of the U.S. if they can circumvent a straightforward hard hitting trader for the home front. But they are stymied this time. Byrnes & I shall expect our interests to come first. Pauley is doing a job for the United States.[43]

The time was not yet quite ripe for changing course, however. The next day Grew conveyed Byrnes' response for the time being: "Instead of replying now to the questions raised in your [cable]," Pauley was notified, "Secretary suggests that these issues be discussed and decided when you join President at Berlin."[44] Even as late as July 17—the first day of the conference—the agreed principles governing reparations still began:

---

*The much-discussed U.S. policy in connection with the related question of troop withdrawals was similarly conciliatory at this point. Briefly, extended positions were maintained until after Hopkins' successful negotiations over Poland—and Russia's renewed promise to enter the Pacific war. On June 12, the president proposed to Churchill that all troops be pulled back into their respective zones. Actual withdrawal of Western troops was set for the beginning of July. (See Alperovitz, *Atomic Diplomacy*, p. 131.)

Removal of property for reparations shall be primarily such as to assist in bringing to an end the war-making power of Germany by eliminating that part of Germany's industrial capacity which constitutes war potential.[45]

Interpreting such broad language, of course, was the basic issue as the Potsdam conference convened. Almost immediately the president telegraphed his general inclinations by singling Pauley out for special attention and a show of personal support: The reparations negotiator was invited to join Truman and Byrnes in the president's car on the drive from Gatow airport to Potsdam after their arrival on July 15.[46]

It was also clear that Byrnes was now at the center of policy-making; and almost immediately the new confidence and tremendous assertiveness which had appeared in connection with Balkan issues began to characterize the American attitude towards Germany.

The actual reparations negotiations focused around two quite specific questions: first, whether to set any fixed target for reparations; and, second, if a target were set, what would it be? If a target were set—and if the figure was large—the essence of Roosevelt's policy would be continued. If no target were set—or if a small figure were set—the new view would be implemented.

These questions first received serious consideration at lower levels on July 19.[47] For three difficult days the Economic Subcommittee skirmished over such issues as the U.S. insistence that "the necessary means must be provided for payment of imports . . . *before reparation deliveries are made*" (i.e., there ought to be a "prior charge" on the German economy to pay for imports *before* the calculation of reparations).[48] The U.S.S.R., for its part, attempted to justify seizures of material in eastern Germany as "war booty" (as opposed to "reparations")—so that no charge against its ultimate claims would occur.[49]

Only minimal progress had been made by the evening of July 21.[50] However, sometime during the thirty-six hours between the evening of July 21 and the morning of July 23—the same time the decision to attempt to delay a Russian attack against Japan appears to have been consolidated—the official position of the U.S. delegation became clear.

A post-Potsdam report to the president provides this cool summary:

> . . . the US Delegation to the Allied Commission on Reparations came to the conclusion that an "overall percentage" allocation of shares as between the Big Three was no longer feasible. The division of reparations . . . would have to be abandoned for some less controversial method of dividing what would be removed as reparations. . . .[51]

Put baldly, the Yalta agreement—with its stipulation of 50 percent of a fixed sum in the range of twenty billion dollars to go to the Soviets—was simply abandoned. The United States now suggested that reparations essentially be taken from each zone by each occupying power rather than collectively from Germany as a whole. Since the Russians occupied predominantly agricultural areas while the West had the lion's share of industry, the implications were obvious.[52]

The new stance was far tougher than anything even Pauley had initially proposed. Not only would there be no "fixed target," but even the idea of "percentages" was now gone. As Carolyn Eisenberg has noted, the decision was "an open break with Yalta"[53]—and as many others have observed, the idea that each side would simply focus on its own zone also inevitably implied that four-power control of a unified German economy was largely, if implicitly, laid to rest.

Subsequently, the State Department produced a variety of "reasons" for the U.S. reversal.[54] The fact is, however, reparation issues had not even been seriously discussed at the foreign ministers' level when the new position was put forth. And, as we have seen, Byrnes was quite explicit about the source of his new confidence in private discussions with Joseph Davies: ". . . details as to the success of the Atomic Bomb . . . gave him confidence that the Soviets would agree as to these difficulties. . . ."[55] Much more fundamentally, he also was no longer worried about the security problem: "[I]n the last analysis, it [the atomic bomb] would control."[56]

Once more, a brief review of the timetable at Potsdam helps suggest the relationships between various developments:

JULY 21, 1945, 11:35 a.m.—General Groves' dramatic report of the Alamogordo test arrives.[57]

JULY 22, 1945, 11:10 a.m.—Following disagreement in the Economic Subcommittee, the reparations question is referred to the Foreign Ministers and put on the next day's agenda by Byrnes.[58]

JULY 23, 1945, 10:00 a.m.—Byrnes telephones Stimson and asks for further information "as to the timing of the S-1 program."[59]

JULY 23, 1945, 10:30 a.m.—Byrnes meets with Molotov and informally indicates the new U.S. reparations position ("under the circumstances he wondered whether it would not be better to give consideration to the possibility of each country taking reparations from its own zone").[60]

JULY 23, 1945, 11:00 a.m.—at the Foreign Ministers' meeting Byrnes declares: ". . . the American position is clear. It is the position of the United States that there will be no reparations until imports in the

American zone are paid for. There can be no discussion of this matter."[61]

As John Lewis Gaddis has commented: "News of the secret explosion in the New Mexico desert . . . greatly cheered Truman and his advisers, contributing to their firm stand on German reparations. . . ."[62] An entry in the diary of General Henry H. Arnold, Commander of the U.S. Army Air Forces, in the midst of this period (after a dinner on July 22, 1945) is also suggestive: "Byrnes—what we must do now is not make the world safe for democracy, but make the world safe for the U.S.A."[63]

As Byrnes made his new position explicit, Molotov backed down from a "fixed figure" of 10 billion dollars for reparations to 9.7 billion, then to 9 billion, then to 8.5 billion, and finally to 8 billion.[64] The latter was only 1 billion more than the acceptable figure suggested in the State Department instruction to Pauley of July 2, but Byrnes was simply not interested.[65]

At the foreign ministers' meeting of July 27 Molotov demanded to know "if the decision with regard to reparations which was taken at the Crimea Conference remained in force. . . ."[66] Byrnes replied that the United States had never agreed to 20 billion dollars. "All that was done was to accept the proposal as a basis for discussion. If he were asked for a million dollars and he said he would discuss it, this did not mean that he would write a check for it."[67] Molotov then said that he

> understood Mr. Byrnes' proposal to be that each country should take reparations from its zone. He pointed out that if they failed to agree on reparations the result would be the same as under Mr. Byrnes' plan. Each would draw reparations from their respective zones.[68]

Two days later Assistant Secretary of State William L. Clayton privately cautioned Byrnes that

> any decision to exclude them from any participation in the distribution of the heavy equipment in the Ruhr as reparation, would be considered by the Russians as a reversal of the Yalta and Moscow position, since no Allied understanding would be necessary to enable them to get reparations from their own zone.[69]

Byrnes, however, was unyielding—and with Molotov continuing to insist on the Yalta terms and Byrnes completely unwilling to establish a firm target, very little progress was made.[70] As in the case of the Balkans, U.S. officials were more than willing to hold the line and accept a (temporary) stalemate on these matters at Potsdam. On July 24 both Truman and Byrnes had already made it quite clear that the United States was prepared to end the conference when no further agreements could be reached. On July 26 Admiral Leahy noted in his diary: "The President today decided to depart for home at the earliest practicable date. . . ."[71] The next day, Truman conferred with both Leahy and Byrnes "on prospects and methods of bringing this conference to an end at an early date."[72]

Byrnes told Molotov directly on July 29 that it was time to wind up the negotiations and on July 30 he put the final U.S. position on the table. Now the proposal that each side satisfy its reparations requirements from its own zone (with a certain modest percentage to be transferred to the Soviet zone from the West) was to be "conditional upon agreement on two other proposals. . . ." Byrnes brought forward a paper relating to the treatment of Italy and another concerning the satellite nations and the proposed new western border of Poland (the Oder-Neisse line).[73] All would have to be accepted as a package. If Molotov did not agree, Byrnes "was willing to report to the Big Three and they could decide whether to continue the discussion or refer the matter to some future conference."[74] The following day, as Byrnes later recalled, he was blunt: "I told him we would agree to all three or none and that the President and I would leave for the United States the next day."[75]*

Again, there is little doubt about the source of such confidence. Employing the same characteristic poker imagery he had used in connection with the atomic bomb earlier in the summer, Truman wrote his wife, Bess, on July 31: "[Stalin] doesn't know it but I have an ace in the hole and another one showing—so unless he has threes or two pair (and I know he has not) we are sitting all right."[76]

The tough stance worked—probably because the Russians had little alternative—and in the end Byrnes' "package deal" became one of the very few substantive agreements reached at Potsdam. Stalin accepted the West's de facto abandonment of the Yalta reparations accord[77] (and, as we have seen, some minor alterations in the situation in the Balkans); and the United States and Britain accepted the Polish border understanding† (with the pro-

---

*In a related move, Byrnes also rejected the suggestion of his special assistant Benjamin Cohen for four-power international control of the Ruhr as another means of controlling Germany's "military-industrial complex." (WB's Book, July 17, Folder 602, Byrnes Papers, CUL; Brown, *James F. Byrnes of South Carolina*, p. 275.) At Teheran in November of 1943, FDR had outlined a tentative plan for division of Germany into several parts which also included some kind of international trusteeship for the Ruhr. See, for instance, Diane Clemens, *Yalta*, p. 32.

†See above, p. 261. At Yalta, the Big Three had agreed that "Poland must receive substantial accessions of territory in the North and West." In the interim the Soviet Union had unilaterally shifted the border westward to the Oder-Neisse region. See FRUS, Malta and Yalta, p. 980. For more details, see FRUS, Pots. I, pp. 743–47, 750–54, 757–59, 777–81; also Leffler, *A Preponderance of Power*, p. 38.

viso that "the final delimitation of the western frontier of Poland should await the peace settlement"[78]).

The atomic bomb also helped diminish the other truly fundamental difficulty facing the United States in Europe: economic chaos. Reducing the amount of reparations extracted from Germany was part and parcel of an effort to strengthen Germany's contribution to Continental economic stability—and, as we have just seen, the bomb was pivotal in this connection.

Throughout the spring and summer of 1945, U.S. leaders had been deeply worried about the European economy, and about social and political unrest. After visiting Germany in April, McCloy had brought back reports of "chaos" and utter devastation: "something that is worse than anything probably that ever happened in the world."[79] In a report to the president he observed:

> There is complete economic, social, and political collapse going on in Central Europe, the extent of which is unparalleled in history unless one goes back to the collapse of the Roman Empire, and even that may not have been as great an economic upheaval.[80]

Similarly, Grew wrote Stimson on June 8: "I am deeply concerned over conditions in Western Europe and the possibility that serious disorders may develop during the coming months."[81] An internal State Department document at this time warned that

> unless immediate and drastic steps are taken, there will occur in North West Europe and the Mediterranean next winter a coal famine of such severity as to destroy all semblance of law and order, and thus delay any chance of reasonable stability.[82]

Truman himself wrote Churchill (on June 24): "From all the reports which reach me, I believe that without immediate concentration on the production of German coal we will have turmoil and unrest in the very areas of Western Europe on which the whole stability of the continent depends."[83]

Roosevelt, too, had worried about the European economic situation. However, the fact is FDR needed Soviet help to control Germany. Once the atomic bomb was tested, this was no longer so and important ongoing concerns over the future of the European economy could take precedence. It is true that Roosevelt's strategy towards the German issues and the Soviet Union was based on a somewhat more flexible and cooperative personal style than Truman's, but the new weapon made what had once been a profoundly serious policy dilemma into an easy decision.

"The problem which presents itself," Stimson wrote just before details of the atomic test arrived, "is how to render Germany harmless as a potential aggressor, and at the same time enable her to play her part in the necessary rehabilitation of Europe."[84] This defined in precise terms the question confronting U.S. policy. Within hours of Stimson's statement, however, the problem had been resolved in a radical and dramatic way. Although Truman continued to endorse "industrial disarmament" as a way to achieve European security, after the atomic test the issue took on a distinctly secondary importance. By March 1946 U.S. Military Government officials in Germany were urging that few if any additional economic controls were needed because Germany presented no significant conventional military threat—and could not possibly produce nuclear weapons without being detected.[85]

The ongoing consequences of the long-forgotten dispute over "reparations" at Potsdam are difficult to overstate.* The dominant U.S. interest continued to be overall economic stability in Europe, and in the period following Potsdam the complexities of the reparations/economic conundrum unfolded in fits and starts—a tale well beyond our period of concern. (An especially important milestone was the May 1946 U.S. decision to halt even modest industrial shipments from the West.)[86] From the perspective of our current inquiry it is important simply to note that, as in the Balkans, U.S. leaders now largely rested their strategy towards Germany on the assumption that the atomic bomb would, in fact, be demonstrated. Whatever course they subsequently chose—and for whatever reason—if the power of the bomb were not now shown, the fundamental basis of the new position they had taken would largely disappear.

And just as modern diaries and other documentary evidence confirm the post-Hiroshima shift in U.S. policy towards the Balkans, so, too, there is explicit confirmation that the Potsdam accounts of Byrnes' general views on Germany and security were not mistaken. Charles de Gaulle met with Truman and Byrnes at the White House on August 22 to press his own concerns about Germany. A memorandum documenting the meeting shows Truman and Byrnes responding that "the German danger should not be exaggerated. . . ."[87] But de Gaulle—who had no atomic bomb—continued to stress the gravity of French fears after the experience of World War II. He also emphasized the necessity of concrete security measures and specific policies similar to those proposed by Stalin and (before the atomic bomb) contemplated by Roosevelt: De Gaulle urged that in addition to large-scale reparations, preventing a resurgence of the German threat required international control of the Ruhr and severing the west bank of the Rhine.[88]

Impatient with such arguments—and apparently irritated by the French

---

*For a broader discussion, see Gar Alperovitz and Kai Bird, "The Centrality of the Bomb," *Foreign Policy*, No. 94 (Spring 1994), pp. 3–20.

leader's persistence—Truman and Byrnes coolly stated what to them had become obvious as they contemplated the security problem. Germany (as well as any other potential enemy) was now of little concern: ". . . the atomic bomb will give pause to countries which might be tempted to commit aggressions."[89]

Chapter 23

THIRD DECISION

General Marshall cautioned against any move to oust the Emperor because it would lead to a last-ditch defense by the Japanese. . . .
—Charles H. Donnelly, secretary of the Joint Chiefs of Staff,
diary, July 18, 1945

We have noted a series of Japanese peace feelers in Switzerland which OSS Chief William Donovan reported to Truman in May and June. These suggested even at this point that the U.S. demand for unconditional surrender might well be the only serious obstacle to peace. At the center of the explorations, as we also saw, was Allen Dulles, chief of OSS operations in Switzerland (and subsequently director of the CIA).

In his 1966 book *The Secret Surrender*, Dulles recalled that

On July 20, 1945, under instructions from Washington, I went to the Potsdam Conference and reported there to Secretary Stimson on what I had learned from Tokyo—they desired to surrender if they could retain the Emperor and the constitution as a basis for maintaining discipline and order in Japan after the devastating news of surrender became known to the Japanese people.[1]

Stimson's contemporaneous July 20 diary also notes: "Late in the afternoon Allen Dulles turned up and I had a short talk with him. He has been in the OSS in Switzerland and has been the center of much underground information." Stimson's next sentence is cryptic: "He told us about something which had recently come into him with regard to Japan."[2]

It appears that McCloy had arranged for Dulles' trip to Potsdam and his diary for the same day also records: "Allen Dulles came in . . . today with reports of tentative approaches made to him by the Japanese through Jacobsen [*sic*]."[3] McCloy—deeply impressed at just this moment by the new

MAGIC intercepts showing the Emperor seeking a direct negotiating channel through Moscow—was not sure how much reliance to place on Dulles' contacts in Switzerland:

> I gather that there is something behind it, but just how substantial I do not know—it apparently operates through the International Bank of Settlements. . . .[4]

Probably thinking of both initatives, McCloy noted in his diary on July 27: "Maybe the Secretary's big bomb may not be dropped—the Japs had better hurry if they are to avoid it."[5]

OSS papers concerning these matters were slowly declassified during the 1980s. Dulles' papers were made available to researchers in 1974, with certain restrictions that were lifted in 1992. However, information we have from these documents and from the Stimson and McCloy diaries is less than totally enlightening. A major difficulty is that what Dulles wrote and what the documents "say" often is obviously not the whole story of what went on.

Reliable evidence relating to OSS activities, like materials relating to its successor agency the CIA, is very difficult to come by even today. Moreover, we know that Dulles was exceedingly deceptive: The record shows that he lied blatantly even in face-to-face meetings with the president's chief of staff. When Dulles was in Washington in early June, Leahy's diary of June 14 records that at the very time of his negotiations, Dulles simply denied that anything at all was going on:

> Mr. Allen Dulles, O.S.S. representative in Berne, called at the office at my request. I told him that reports have been received to the effect that some of his agents are endeavoring to arrange for conversations with Japanese officials regarding peace terms with Japan.
>
> He replied that he has no knowledge of any such activity and that he does not believe any of his group are involved. He is returning to Switzerland tomorrow where he will, upon arrival in Berne, make a personal investigation of the matter.[6]

In fact, we do not know all the reasons why Dulles was called back to Washington. Did he meet only with OSS officials? With McCloy? Possibly even with Byrnes and the president?

Furthermore, Dulles was a professional in the intelligence business—which meant, among other things, that there was often a very considerable gap between what he was doing and what he was saying. He openly—even proudly—admitted as much:

> An intelligence officer in the field is supposed to keep his home office informed of what he is doing. That is quite true, but with some reserva-

tions, as he may overdo it. If, for example, he tells too much or asks for instructions, he is likely to get some he doesn't relish, and, what is worse, he may well find headquarters trying to take over the whole conduct of the operation. Only a man on the spot can really pass judgment on the details as contrasted with the policy decisions, which, of course, belong to the boss at headquarters.[7]

The trick in any complex negotiation at the margins of "official" legitimacy is to offer your contact sufficient solid information that he can wheedle a bit more of a response from his superiors—which you can then use to entice *your* superiors to take another step. If you are shrewd—like Dulles—you end up in the catbird's seat by virtue of having created a slow mating dance (largely with mirrors) of two constrained bureaucracies. If you are clumsy, everything evaporates into thin air.*

As is obvious, the most important single piece of ammunition Dulles or anyone needed to open a serious channel of communication was solid evidence that the United States would modify the surrender formula sufficiently to give Japan assurances for the person and at least nominal position of the Emperor.

We are here again, of course, in the presence of the familiar problem of "estimation." There is no doubt that the group Dulles was in contact with did not represent the full Japanese government. (So far as we can tell, the main connections were to high-ranking Japanese navy officials.)[8] On the other hand Dulles was a seasoned professional who had, in fact, succeeded in completing the complex negotiations which on May 2, 1945, produced the surrender of German Army Group C, responsible for defending the southern approaches to the Third Reich.[9] His assessment of how to judge the overall significance of the approaches being made—as well as the specific proposals—could not easily be dismissed.

When we turn to the contemporaneous written documents now available, it is obvious that they are carefully drawn. They do not promise that a negotiation can succeed, or that Dulles is sure of the possibilities and connection of his contacts. On the other hand, on July 13, the acting director of the OSS, Charles S. Cheston, informed Byrnes that the Japanese officials Dulles was in touch with clearly "implied that the only condition on which Japan would insist with respect to surrender would be some consideration for the Japanese Imperial family."[10] Three days later, on July 16, Donovan himself informed Byrnes that according to Dulles

---

*As we have seen, some of Dulles' independent surrender explorations with Nazi contacts contributed to U.S.-Soviet recriminations and tension in March.

these two Japanese are insisting on the retention of the Emperor because they feel that he alone can take effective action with respect to surrender and that some hope of survival must be held out to him in order to gain his support for unconditional surrender.[11]

On July 18, Donovan reported that

Mr. Dulles believes that for the next few days important developments in this matter are not likely, but that a line is being opened which the Japanese may use when the situation in Tokyo permits Japan to accept unconditional surrender.[12]

It is a reasonable question whether Dulles may have been called to Potsdam—perhaps before the Emperor's messages were intercepted and before the atomic test—on the idea that his post in Switzerland might offer one possible channel through which to arrange a surrender. As we have seen, by the time of Potsdam several top U.S. officials believed that it might be feasible to end the war not only without the atomic bomb but also even before the Russian attack in early August. Given his track record of success with the Italian surrender, Dulles was an obvious candidate to handle things when the moment arrived.

The "channel" Dulles was working on in Switzerland was not the only serious negotiating venue available, however. Although it may have been considered a serious option, so far as we can tell by late July it was not even the channel preferred by the U.S. government. Much more interesting—and, given the gaps in the record, much more intriguing—was the situation in Sweden, where not one but three channels had begun to open up.

The first was through the Swedish minister in Tokyo, Widar Bagge, who had close contacts with Mamoru Shigemitsu, foreign minister in the Koiso government, and other high-ranking Japanese officials. Initially, as we saw in Chapter 2, Bagge's reports reached the United States through the British Foreign Office. As early as September 24, 1944, one of his forwarded telegrams stated:

I learn from a very reliable source that in important civilian circles in Japan the peace problem is being discussed with increasing anxiety. A speedy German collapse is expected and it is not believed that Japan can then continue the war.[13]

By the spring of 1945 Herschel V. Johnson, the U.S. minister in Stockholm, reported (on April 6) that Bagge's sources believed it "probable that very far-reaching conditions would be accepted by the Japanese by way of negotiation."[14] However:

There is no doubt that unconditional surrender terms would be unacceptable to the Japanese because it would mean dishonor. Application of such terms would be fatal and lead to desperate action on the part of the people. . . . The Emperor must not be touched.[15]

Recent research by Justin H. Libby confirms that after Bagge returned to Stockholm in early May, he opened a second channel involving Suemasa Okamoto, the Japanese minister to Sweden.[16] Okamoto in turn cabled home for instructions, but was told that Tokyo would study the situation—undoubtedly because of the internal debates at this time and because Tokyo favored a démarche through Moscow, not Stockholm.[17] On July 21, however, MAGIC intercepts revealed Okamoto again urging Tokyo "to consider the welfare of the Imperial Family and the future of our nation," and recommending that the government seek a way out of "an impossible, unreasonable war which has made practically the whole world our enemy. . . ."[18]

The third channel involved the Japanese military attaché in Stockholm, General Makoto Onodera, who appears to have been put in charge of Japanese intelligence for the whole of Europe at the end of 1944.[19] Onodera was in touch with the Swedish royal family, and through Prince Carl Bernadotte, also connected with the American Legation in Stockholm. On May 11, 1945, Johnson reported that Onodera had told his contact:

. . . it is realized that Japan cannot win and that the best possible solution would be to prevent the destruction of its cities and places of culture. He stated that he was authorized to arrange for a member of the Swedish Royal Family to approach the Allies for some settlement. . . .[20]

As in the case of Dulles' exploratory talks, the question of whether Okamoto or Onodera could produce any serious results was dependent upon what either could bring back to his superiors in Tokyo. By now the overwhelmingly obvious issue, as Johnson observed in the same cable, involved the rigid formula: "Onodera pointed out the necessity of this not being unconditional surrender. . . ."[21] By July 6, Johnson was cabling the following "substance of report given Leg[ation] by Prince Carl Bernadotte following a conversation with Jap Military Attaché" (a brief excerpt of which we cited at the outset):

Major General Onodera, Jap Mil Attaché, stated that Japs know war has been lost and when right time comes they will make direct contact with King of Swed. Onodera said this would be done by him and he emphasized that he and not Jap Minister [Okamoto] has authorization from Emperor and Jap Govt to enter into negotiations. Onodera referred to Emperor and pointed out that by reason of Emperor's position contact will have to be made by Swed King. He further stated that Emperor must be maintained in his position after the capitulation. No other conditions of surrender were specified.[22]

The ins and outs of feints, shadowboxing, and intrigues related to all of this have been explored by several scholars and need not be detailed here, except—once more—to state the need for caution in evaluating specific conclusions: We have just seen an important U.S. intelligence operative—Dulles—secretly working from one set of orders all the while denying this was so at the highest level. A reasonable question is whether Onodera, too, had independent orders through his army intelligence network. Apart from such complexities—and beyond the obviously important "unconditional surrender" issue—five points should be noted:

First, clearly a turf battle was going on between Okamoto and Onodera. Okamoto, in particular, appears to have been disturbed by Onodera's involvement in diplomatic affairs.[23]

Second, as noted, once Tokyo had decided to concentrate its efforts on the Moscow channel—and on a special imperial envoy—a decision was apparently made to dampen down the possible Swedish channels.[24]

Third, Onodera is particularly interesting on other accounts: As a high Japanese military intelligence official in Europe, he was clearly in communication with Japanese army (not navy or Foreign Ministry) operations—the army being the real locus of power in Japan.

Fourth, the notion of using a person of royalty—the king of Sweden—as a contact with Japanese royalty—the Emperor—had a certain appeal.

The fifth point may well be the most important. One person in particular was clearly impressed with the possibilities of a Swedish channel. President Truman referred to Sweden twice during the period immediately before the atomic bombs were dropped. In the Potsdam Papers released in 1960, for instance, we find the following (in Charles Bohlen's notes concerning a discussion of peace feelers during the Truman-Stalin talk of July 18): "PRES—we had indicati[on] from Sweden. . . ."[25] The "lost" memorandum Bohlen made from these notes (recently found in the Harriman papers) states: "THE PRESIDENT observed that we had received some indication of a Japanese desire to negotiate through a source in Sweden."[26]*

The various possible negotiating channels which came into focus at the time of the Potsdam conference—along with the repetitive nature of Japanese statements that the central issue was assurances for the Emperor—bring us to the third and final major choice related to the use of the atomic bomb. This, of course, was the considered decision not to alter the unconditional

*See below, p. 415, for another indication of Truman's interest in the Swedish channel.

surrender formula so as to offer Japan the specific assurances she sought. Far more thoughtful attention has been paid to this decision over the last fifty years than to the decision to shorten the time Japan was given to consider a warning and the decision to attempt to stall a Russian attack. It is now possible to isolate some of the truly critical issues:

The decision not to alter the unconditional surrender formula was clear, forceful, unequivocal. Moreover, it was a contested decision, one which reversed the dominant thrust of policy development and of numerous specific cabinet-level and military recommendations.

This point must be emphasized because many studies all too easily skip over the specific nature of the choice which was made at this point in time. Especially problematic in this regard are various accounts which propose theories that an unconscious "momentum" simply carried events along.* In fact, the essential reality is in many ways 180 degrees the reverse of such theories: We now have overwhelming evidence that the momentum of government analysis, recommendation, and policy was almost entirely in the direction of an early clarification of the surrender terms—and it was this momentum which had to be interrupted and reversed.

Leaving aside for the moment the numerous recorded initiatives noted in Part I, evidence of ongoing concern by both civilian officials and military officials is abundant. On June 30, to recall, the State Department recommended that "the principal United Nations at war with Japan issue a joint statement outlining the program for the treatment of a defeated Japan. . . ."[27] "Such a statement of war aims would tend"

(1) to dissipate the present Japanese fear of the unknown, (2) to combat the Japanese domestic propaganda to the effect that unconditional surrender means the extinction of the Japanese state and the enslavement of the people, (3) to create a conflict in Japan between the die-hard militarists and those who wish to end the war before all of Japan is destroyed, (4) to eliminate the most serious single obstacle to Japanese unconditional surrender, namely, concern over the fate of the throne. . . .[28]

Stimson, of course, had forcefully pressed his own strong recommendation on the matter on July 2, just before the president boarded the *Augusta*. The recommended draft proclamation which had been worked out by a joint committee of the State, War and Navy Departments—and approved by Forrestal and Grew—contained the critical paragraph twelve assurances:†

---

*See the Afterword for a discussion of "momentum" theories at various levels of bureaucratic decision-making.
†The draft also contained one line referring to the "unconditional surrender of all the Japanese armed forces" which survived until the end.

The occupying forces of the Allies shall be withdrawn from Japan as soon as our objectives are accomplished and there has been established beyond doubt a peacefully inclined, responsible government of a character representative of the Japanese people. This may include a constitutional monarchy under the present dynasty if it be shown to the complete satisfaction of the world that such a government will never again aspire to aggression.[29]

In presenting it to the president, Stimson had stressed his belief that "Japan *is* susceptible to reason in such a crisis . . . ," and that his "own opinion" was that she had "the intelligence and versatile capacity in such a crisis to recognize the folly of a fight to the finish and to accept the proffer of what will amount to an unconditional surrender."[30]

We have also noted Stimson's July 16 initiative following news of the Emperor's personal intervention. This had urged immediate issuance of a warning statement and proposed that if this failed it would then be followed by a second warning—and only then would the bomb be used. (The warning, he had also explicitly recommended, should be "along the lines of the draft prepared by the War Department and now approved . . . by both the State and Navy Departments"—that is, one containing assurances for the Emperor.[31])

Again, we have noted that on July 16 the Joint Chiefs of Staff felt so strongly about the matter that they arranged for the British Chiefs of Staff to persuade Churchill to approach Truman to urge a change. Churchill did just that on July 18.[32] As John Ray Skates has recently observed, from the perspective of the Joint Chiefs, "The emperor's status was no small matter."[33] "[T]he Joint Chiefs argued that for military reasons alone the emperor's position should be protected."[34]

Related to this was a parallel independent effort to clarify the terms by the Joint Chiefs: The diary of the secretary of the Joint Chiefs, Charles H. Donnelly, indicates that at a July 17 meeting "General Marshall cautioned against any move to oust the Emperor because it would lead to a last-ditch defense by the Japanese. . . ."[35] Indeed, advised by another Pentagon group* studying the matter that the Japanese might possibly misunderstand the wording of the key paragraph in the draft proclamation, the Joint Chiefs proposed what they considered even more effective language.

The problem was that there was a chance that the crucial sentence of paragraph twelve as drafted—"[t]his may include a constitutional monarchy under the present dynasty"—could just possibly be "misconstrued as a commitment by the United Nations to depose or execute the present Emperor and

---

*The Joint Strategic Survey Committee (JSSC), a military advisory committee made up of "elder statesmen" of the War and Navy departments.

install some other member of the Imperial family."[36] A more neutral formulation could still give Japan the required assurances without raising this fear. In a memorandum to the president of July 18, the Joint Chiefs recommended the following way of stating the same point:

> Subject to suitable guarantees against further acts of aggression, the Japanese people will be free to choose their own form of government.[37]

This language, as we shall shortly explore, was almost precisely the same as had been used in the Atlantic Charter statement of war aims issued by Roosevelt and Churchill on August 14, 1941 (and ultimately subscribed to by twenty-six nations).

What is striking about the modern evidence is that every top presidential civilian and military adviser up to this point in time except Byrnes—as well as Prime Minister Churchill and the top British military leadership—clearly and directly urged a clarification of the unconditional surrender formula.

Indeed, it is possible to identify more than a dozen separate occasions on which Truman was personally approached in one way or another on this matter prior to the issuance of the Potsdam Proclamation:

(1) by Acting Secretary of State Grew on May 28, 1945[38];
(2) by former President Herbert Hoover in a May 30, 1945, memorandum[39];
(3) by Grew again on June 13, 1945[40];
(4) by Counsel to the President Samuel I. Rosenman on June 17, 1945[41];
(5) by Grew once more on June 18, 1945[42];
(6) by Assistant Secretary of War McCloy on June 18, 1945[43];
(7) by Admiral Leahy on June 18, 1945[44]*;
(8) by the State Department in a formal recommendation of June 30, 1945[45];
(9) by Under Secretary of the Navy Ralph Bard on July 1, 1945[46];
(10) by Secretary of War Stimson (with the support of Secretary of the Navy Forrestal and Grew) on July 2, 1945[47];
(11) by Stimson again on July 16, 1945[48];
(12) by Churchill on July 18, 1945[49];

---

*We may also note that on May 6 Leahy urged Truman to release the " 'modified statement' proposed by Mr. Elmer Davis," which called specifically for the "unconditional surrender of the armed forces." (Memorandum for the President, from WDL, May 6, 1945, Chairman's File, Admiral Leahy 1942–48, File 125, box 19, RG 218, NA.) Leahy also states in his memoirs: "Naturally, I had acquainted President Truman with my own ideas about the best course to pursue in defeating Japan. . . ."—which, as we have seen, included clarifying the unconditional surrender language. (Leahy, I Was There, p. 385.)

(13) by the Joint Chiefs of Staff on July 18, 1945[50];

(14) by Stimson on July 24, 1945[51].

In addition to these direct approaches to the president, Edward Stettinius had recommended a clarification of the formula on June 15, and the Joint Chiefs had done so on June 9 (and, as noted, had done so again, indirectly through the British Chiefs of Staff and Churchill in the July 16–18 time frame).[52] As Leon V. Sigal has observed:

> one point was clear to senior U.S. officials regardless of where they stood on war termination. . . . U.S. senior officials knew that the critical condition for Japan's surrender was the assurance that the throne would be preserved.[53]

The question is: Why did Truman and Byrnes decide to reverse the momentum of policy development and eliminate from the warning statement the kind of specific assurances for the Emperor recommended by every other significant figure involved?

Chapter 24

THEORIES AND CHOICES

I then spoke of the importance which I attributed to the reassurance of the Japanese on the continuance of their dynasty, and I felt that the insertion of that in the formal warning was important and might be just the thing that would make or mar their acceptance, but that I had heard from Byrnes that they preferred not to put it in, and that now such a change was made impossible by the sending of the message to Chiang.

—Secretary of War Henry L. Stimson, diary report of a meeting with President Truman, July 24, 1945

It is helpful to clear away one bit of sometimes confusing evidentiary underbrush: There is little dispute that in making the decision to excise the recommended language concerning the Emperor, American officials understood that the warning to Japan (which soon came to be known as the Potsdam Proclamation) almost certainly could not be accepted—and that therefore the atomic bomb would be used. Thus, in choosing to eliminate assurances for the Emperor, Truman and Byrnes with full awareness decided also to eliminate the one remaining option (other than the Russian attack) which in the judgment of their advisers might have produced a surrender.*

We have noted that at least two quite distinct but closely associated issues were involved in the Emperor question: first, assurances were needed in order to secure a surrender; but, second—a slightly different and quite separate matter—if such assurances were not given, the Japanese would not surrender.

Although some analysts were later to question whether assurances alone would have produced a rapid surrender, none has ever argued that a surren-

*Leaving aside the "two-step logic" of a Russian attack *plus* a modification of terms.

der was likely so long as the position of the Emperor was threatened. Given the unanimity of judgment, it would be surprising if Truman had not understood this central point as well; indeed, the available evidence is quite clear that he did. As we have noted, he subsequently observed that General Marshall had told him that if the Emperor ordered it "we could get complete surrender—that was the only way we could get it." His journal of July 25 also states:

> we will issue a warning statement asking the Japs to surrender and save lives. I'm sure they will not do that. . . .[1]

The evidence concerning Byrnes' attitude—and especially the way the warning statement was characterized during this period—is also instructive. Walter Brown's diary of July 26 puts it this way:

> Joint message to Japan released. This was prelude to atomic bomb. . . .[2]

We have seen that Byrnes had no interest in issuing a warning well in advance so as to give Japanese officials time to digest its meaning; on July 17 he had rejected Stimson's urgent plea that this be done. There is little evidence that Byrnes ever saw the Potsdam Proclamation as anything but a "prelude" to the bombing rather than a serious effort to obtain a surrender. From Byrnes' perspective the proclamation seems to have been largely a public relations tactic. "Neither a gesture of conciliation, nor an ultimatum," Leon Sigal observes, "it was reduced to mere propaganda."[3]

There is little doubt that the advice to eliminate the recommended assurances came from Byrnes; and so far as we can tell it was advice which (though accepted) ran contrary to the president's personal inclinations. Moreover, there are reasons to believe Byrnes was involved at a very early point in connection with the surrender issue.

Throughout the late spring and early summer Truman's personal preference appears to have been to clarify the terms. He had moved in this general direction with seemingly little hesitation only three and a half weeks after taking office, with his May 8 statement indicating unconditional surrender was to be applied to the Japanese military. And, as we have noted, virtually every extant fragment of contemporaneous evidence concerning his personal views in May and June also suggests flexibility.

Nevertheless, the president obviously chose not to clarify the surrender terms during this period and he took a very strong new "no compromise" position in his public Memorial Day week statement of June 1. Thereafter he continued to hold to this policy even though by the third week of June all the president's official advisers—his chief of staff, the secretary of war, the secretary of the navy, the secretary of state, the acting secretary of state, the Joint Chiefs of Staff—favored some form of clarification.

Given what we know of Truman's personal sense of insecurity during his first months in office—especially about foreign and military affairs—it is difficult to believe he would have done this on his own.

That someone else whom the president respected must have advised him against making the change during this period seems obvious. As we have noted, so far as we can tell, James F. Byrnes—though not yet officially in office—was, in fact, the only person at a level of high influence and access to the president generally opposed to such a change.

We also can document that by the time of Potsdam Byrnes and Truman together struck out the key language—even though all the other top officials disagreed. Byrnes must therefore be regarded as the prime (probably the only) candidate as the adviser upon whom Truman relied in making his earlier spring and summer decisions as well.

We can also piece together some additional fragments concerning timing. It seems clear that the policy of not clarifying the terms must have been discussed aboard the *Augusta*—both before and after the intercepted message showing the Emperor's intervention. Several pieces of indirect evidence point to a decision having been made (or confirmed) sometime during the trans-Atlantic crossing.

We noted above that the day after the presidential party arrived at Potsdam (on July 17)—when Stimson urged the immediate issuance of a warning—Byrnes not only rejected the proposal but gave Stimson to understand that the "timetable on the subject warning . . . [already] apparently had been agreed to by the President. . . ."[4]

Indirect evidence of a decision already having been made (or confirmed) by the president also comes from the July 16 Combined Chiefs of Staff meeting. The unusual proposal by the U.S. Chiefs to try to get Churchill to turn Truman around not only suggests the frustration of the U.S. military leaders but also indicates their sense that the president had already taken a stance against making a change.

Furthermore, at the July 17 meeting of the U.S. Joint Chiefs, Admiral Leahy pointed out that "this matter had [*already*] been considered on a political level and consideration had been given to the removal of the sentence in question"[5]—probably on board the *Augusta* and/or the first day at Potsdam prior to this meeting.

As we have seen, Truman's apparent decision not to modify the terms also seems evident in his evasive response to Churchill's proposal the next day, July 18:

The President countered by saying that he did not think the Japanese had any military honour after Pearl Harbour.[6]*

Again—also on July 18—the president's reply when Stalin discussed the Emperor's initiative with him (and read Truman his proposed response) was apparently instantaneous—thereby suggesting prior consideration of his position. When Stalin gave him a copy of his draft message to Japan—"the equivalent of a definite refusal"—the president immediately "said that the reply was entirely satisfactory."[7] Had the president not considered the issue of how to respond prior to this time, the logical and traditionally accepted reply would simply have been to take Stalin's proposed message under advisement for a day or two to study the matter.

A specific item suggesting Byrnes' attitude just as the Potsdam conference opened is a cable he sent on July 17 to Grew (to pass on to former secretary of state Cordell Hull). This, too, stated his agreement with the idea that no assurances for the Emperor be given.[8]

There is no doubt that the decision to eliminate the recommended language was confirmed and implemented by July 24 when the final version of the Potsdam Proclamation was sent to Chiang Kai-shek for approval. There is also additional evidence on how both Truman and Byrnes understood the implications. Stimson's diary for July 24 records, first, that when he read Harrison's cable to the president outlining the latest timetable for using the atomic bomb, Truman said "that was just what he wanted, that he was highly delighted and that it gave him his cue for his warning" (another indication that he, too, apparently understood the proclamation as a "prelude" to the bombing).[9]

Stimson goes on to record that Truman "said he had just sent his warning to Chiang Kai-shek to see if he would join in it, and as soon as that was cleared by Chiang he, Truman, would release the warning and that would fit right in time with the program we had received from Harrison."[10] Again, note: the warning "would fit right in time with the program. . . ." Here, too, there is every expectation that the bomb will be used and that the proclamation will not be accepted.

Stimson's diary continues:

> I then spoke of the importance which I attributed to the reassurance of the Japanese on the continuance of their dynasty, and I felt that the insertion of that in the formal warning was important and might be just

---

*Still, Churchill's impression at this point was that "there is no question of a rigid insistence upon the phrase 'unconditional surrender,' apart from the essentials necessary for world peace and future security, and for the punishment of a guilty and treacherous nation." (Ehrman, *Grand Strategy*, pp. 302–03.)

the thing that would make or mar their acceptance, but that I had heard from Byrnes that they preferred not to put it in, and that now such a change was made impossible by the sending of the message to Chiang.[11]

Words to note here are: "they"—Byrnes and the president—"preferred not to" and "might be just the thing that would make or mar their . . . acceptance." Also, by this time Stimson had already heard from Byrnes that the decision had been made.

That Byrnes was the key—indeed, only—figure involved seems beyond dispute. The remaining issues are obvious.

Why, on the one hand, did Byrnes reject the advice of the best experts in the U.S. government and all the other top civilian and military officials involved? Much more important, why did Truman accept Byrnes' advice?

Even today, fifty years after the fact, all attempts to answer these questions are necessarily speculative: records of what Byrnes and Truman actually discussed between themselves simply do not exist (or have yet to be found).

The weakness of the underlying documentary evidence must be emphasized because some writers have asserted as if fact that decisions by the president were made for one or another imputed reason. Although fragments of evidence exist suggesting why some other officials (and ex-officials) urged specific positions at this time, it is all but impossible to define clear and explicit linkages between their expressed views and the motives of Byrnes—and even more difficult to demonstrate direct linkages to the motives of Truman.

What the documentary record does permit is a careful narrowing of the field of candidate theories, as well as a fair degree of certainty about interpretations which are not supported by the available evidence:

The most commonly suggested theory as to why Byrnes and Truman reversed the thrust of ongoing policy and eliminated the recommended clause offering assurances concerning the Emperor is that they feared political criticism if they were to show any "softness" toward Japan. A representative view is that of Ronald H. Spector—who states without qualification:

> Byrnes was convinced that a retreat from unconditional surrender could
> have devastating political consequences for the president, since the vast
> majority of the public was still opposed to retention of the Emperor. At
> Byrnes's urging, Truman agreed to a rewording of the surrender de-
> mand.[12]*

---

*Spector also notes: "Army polling of soldiers, however, revealed that few fighting men cared whether the Emperor remained or not so long as surrender could be quickly achieved." (Spector, *Eagle Against the Sun*, p. 563.)

That certain evidence points in the direction of this theory in the case of Byrnes is not in dispute. Some writers, for instance, have argued that Byrnes was influenced by Cordell Hull on the matter: first, when he met with the hospitalized former secretary of state on July 6, and subsequently, when he received a cable from him via Grew on July 16.[13] The record shows that Hull feared "terrible political repercussions" might result if assurances were offered and this failed to produce a surrender.[14]

Did the opinions of Hull have anything to do with the decisions of the highly independent Byrnes? Although as a political and personal matter he undoubtedly wished to show concern for Hull's views, it is difficult to believe that Byrnes had any real interest in the ideas of this rather discredited, aging, and ailing man. Averell Harriman reminds us that "Jimmy Byrnes, the damn fool, never consulted anybody. . . . If anybody disputes that, I will be glad to document it."[15]

The fact is, Hull was something of an anachronism who had rarely been taken seriously even during the Roosevelt era. FDR's low opinion of Hull is legendary. Similarly, Byrnes told John Foster Dulles in August 1945: "Cordell Hull was 'My dear friend' but was never Secretary of State."[16] In a 1964 NBC interview with Fred Freed, Byrnes did not even "remember that Cordell Hull took any active position [on unconditional surrender] after I became secretary." Indeed, Byrnes' recollection was that Hull "shared the views of—in great part of Undersecretary Grew who believed firmly . . . that it would be unwise for us to insist upon the ousting of the emperor."[17]

Even more important, those who believe Hull to have had significant influence with Byrnes commonly ignore his central argument: Hull's objection was not, in fact, put forward as opposition to a clarification of the terms in principle. The advice he gave to Byrnes was to delay issuing an ultimatum with explicit assurances for the Emperor. What he proposed was: "Would it be well first to await the climax of allied bombing and Russia's entry into the war?"[18]

As we have repeatedly seen, such advice was in no way unusual. It was by now close to conventional wisdom among top policy-makers. In essence it followed exactly the same two-step logic which had been put forward at various levels of the government beginning in April: first, a Russian declaration of war would convince Japan of the inevitability of defeat; then clarification of the surrender terms might bring about a quick end to the fighting.

The only ambiguity in Hull's position is one which reinforces a point we have previously noted: Hull's statement seems to imply (as Marshall had suggested a month earlier) that the Russian attack might even be sufficient to end the war on its own—and thus possibly make a change in terms unnecessary. Amplifying his views in a telephone conversation with Grew the next day, Hull said he had thought the point over and "suggested that we wait for other developments, to see if something wouldn't happen."[19] To Hull and others not privy to the most tightly held secrets concerning the atomic bomb, the only other serious "development" which might "make something happen" in Japan was "Russia's entry into the war."[20]

Finally, any specific link between the advice of Cordell Hull and President Truman's decision is even more difficult to demonstrate—nor has anyone ever attempted to demonstrate (rather than simply assert) the connection. The understanding of General Groves is instructive: in a personal letter responding to an article in *Air Force Magazine* by Major Kenneth Moll, Groves was almost adamant that "Secretary Hull had been out of the picture for a long time and I doubt if his advice received much consideration from Mr. Truman."[21]

Although, strictly speaking, their arguments were not about politics, the suggestions of two sub-Cabinet State Department officials are also sometimes cited to explain Byrnes' views and, by implication, the president's decision to eliminate assurances for the Emperor from the Potsdam Proclamation. Assistant secretary of state for public and cultural relations Archibald MacLeish and assistant secretary of state for congressional relations Dean Acheson also expressed concern about a modification of the surrender terms. For instance, MacLeish sent Byrnes a memorandum on July 6 in which he expressed his fear (after characterizing himself as a "non-expert" on Japan) that "[w]hat has made Japan dangerous in the past and will make her dangerous in the future if we permit it, is, in large part, the Japanese cult of emperor worship. . . ."[22] Similarly, the minutes of the secretary of state's staff meeting of July 7 note:

> MR. MACLEISH referred again to his feeling that the institution of the Emperor was an implement which the military machine had found useful in controlling the Japanese people. MR. ACHESON said he could not understand why, if the Emperor had no importance in Japanese warmaking capacity, the military element in Japan should be so insistent on retaining the Emperor.[23]

Despite the opinions held by MacLeish and Acheson, the evidence that their views actually affected decision-making is all but nonexistent. Both men were later to become rather well known, and perhaps had some degree of influence in certain circles even at the time. However, there is no contemporaneous record of either having significant influence with Byrnes—and none, so far as we know, indicating more than passing access to the president during this period. The dates of both of the above documents, for instance, coincide with Truman's and Byrnes' departure for Potsdam.

Again, from everything we know of Byrnes' style and personality, the idea that he would be influenced by the opinions of sub-Cabinet-level State Department officials is questionable. A widely quoted comment Byrnes made a few weeks later captures his attitude only too well: "I might tell the president sometime what happened, but I'm never going to tell those little bastards in State Department anything about it."[24] Byrnes' feelings also seem clear from a 1952 letter he sent to Groves:

> Of course, you are right about some of my subordinates. When I became Secretary, I found in the Department a heated controversy, the left-wingers arguing that under no circumstances could we accept a surrender of the Japanese unless they agreed that Japan would no longer have an emperor. Without the emperor we would have found it a more difficult task to secure the surrender. . . .[25]

Beyond the fact that MacLeish and Acheson were far removed from the White House decision-making process, a careful reading of their actual positions—and the minutes of the staff meetings involved—indicates that the arguments of these two men were far less definitive than is sometimes suggested. In his memorandum to Byrnes, MacLeish did not challenge the basic point. Like Hull, he recommended a delay in issuing a statement containing assurances until the policy had been further clarified internally. MacLeish was quite explicit that he was not "raising the question of whether we should accept the irreducible Japanese terms" (that is, "the nonmolestation of the person of the present Emperor and the preservation of the institution of the throne") but rather,

> . . . the question whether, if we do, we should not state explicitly what it is we are doing. If we are modifying the announced policy of unconditional surrender to a new policy of surrender on irreducible Japanese terms, the American people have a right to know.[26]

It is also important to recall that the arguments of MacLeish and Acheson date from the period before the Emperor's intervention made it clear that a significant turning point had been reached within Japan.[27]

There is little direct evidence that fear of political criticism was a significant factor in Truman's mind in connection with the decision to remove the critical language from the Potsdam Proclamation. What is striking, in fact, is that not even those who believe the president must have made his decision for political reasons claim unqualified evidence for such a concern.[28]

Indeed, the preponderance of contemporaneous evidence we have of the president's own inclinations during the summer suggests not only that he did not regard clarifying the terms as presenting overwhelming political difficulties, but that he seemed to favor such a move.

It would also be extremely surprising—giving the close-in atmosphere of

the much smaller and informal White House of 1945—if every major adviser
other than Byrnes would have pressed so hard to modify the terms had they
sensed the president felt this to be politically impossible. That they did urge
such a change—repeatedly—points to their sense, too, that the president's
mind was quite open on the subject, that he did not feel trapped by political
considerations.

Perspective on this matter also again comes from Groves, one of the most
ardent defenders of the decision to use the atomic bomb. In his letter to
Major Moll, Groves also took up the suggestion that Truman's advisers
feared a change "might arouse a terrible political storm." "As to the emperor
issue . . ." Groves stated:

> Personally I doubt whether despite the Rooseveltian influence which
> was still existent that there would have been any protest on the part of
> the American people over the abandonment of this idea. I believe the
> average American understood full-well that the idea of unconditional
> surrender had prolonged the war in Europe and would undoubtedly pro-
> long the war in the Pacific.[29]

Recent research suggests, furthermore, that if political considerations were
the central factor influencing the president, by the time of Potsdam the trend
was beginning to move in the direction of support for (even demand for) a
change of terms.

As we have seen, various Republican leaders had long since begun to send
the president direct and indirect signals that he could expect strong support
from the opposition party if he were to modify the surrender formula. Now,
as the decision time was reached, additional voices were heard.

Senator Homer E. Capehart's call for a definition of " 'unconditional surrender' so that the Japanese would know exactly the price they must pay for
peace," was followed by the previously cited *Time* magazine report on Republican Senator Wallace White's demand for a redefinition of "unconditional surrender." Truman had begun to move in this direction, *Time* noted:

> But patently he had not said enough. What was needed now, more than
> anything else, was a clear and positive statement of U.S. aims toward
> Japan, of U.S. policy after Japan succumbs to inevitable defeat.[30]

In his July 25 column the *New York Times*' Washington correspondent Arthur
Krock also noted "demands from members of Congress and publicists now
coming almost daily, that the President make clearer to the Japanese people
what unconditional surrender does *not* mean, as well as what it does."[31]

One of the reasons cited in the State Department's June 30 recommendation was that a clarification of terms would not only "eliminate the most serious single obstacle to Japanese unconditional surrender," but also "satisfy

a growing body of opinion in United States which is demanding that we endeavor to hasten the end of the war in the Pacific by stating definitely our war aims."[32]

We do not, in fact, need to look much further than two pieces of contemporaneous evidence to see that neither Truman nor Byrnes seemed overwhelmingly worried about political criticism in connection with assurances for the Emperor. Stimson's diary for July 24 shows that after he had expressed the hope "that the President would watch carefully so that the Japanese might be reassured verbally through diplomatic channels if it was found that they were hanging fire on that one point [the maintenance of the dynasty],"

[Truman] said that he had that in mind, and that he would take care of it.[33]*

Recalling the events at Potsdam in his diary a few days later, Stimson again noted that when Byrnes and Truman "struck out" assurances for the Emperor from the Potsdam Proclamation, they were hardly "obdurate" about the main substantive point at issue, and were more than willing to allow Japan to keep the Emperor if this became a problem.[34]

*Note again Stimson's own attitude: Having failed to secure a public statement assuring the position of the Emperor before the bomb was used, he is here offering still another tactical option (which Truman and Byrnes obviously seem to prefer). Stimson's diary entry of this day also states: "I then spoke of the importance which I attributed to the reassurance of the Japanese on the continuance of their dynasty, and I had felt that the insertion of that in the formal warning was important and might be just the thing that would make or mar their acceptance. . . ." (Stimson Diary, July 24, 1945.)

Chapter 25

UNANSWERABLE QUESTIONS

---

*It is quite possible that it was thought the proof of the power
of the weapon, as demonstrated in actual warfare, might be
an effective source of added authority to the American Government in the settlement of matters at issue with the Soviet
Union.*

— Herbert Feis, "Discussion of the Question of Whether
It was Essential to Use the Atomic Bomb Against Japan"

None of this, of course, is to suggest that no consideration of the political
problems involved in modifying the terms entered into decision-making prior
to July 24 when the section of the Potsdam Proclamation offering assurances
regarding the Emperor was finally eliminated. It is simply to observe that the
evidence commonly cited does not establish this as a dominant consideration
in the minds of the men who actually made the decision at the time.

Few authors who have urged that "politics" explains why Byrnes and
Truman eliminated the critical portion of paragraph twelve have openly confronted the implications of their theory—namely, that for (possibly modest)
domestic political gains (not for military reasons or to save lives) 200,000 or
more people, mostly civilians, may ultimately have been sacrificed. (And, of
course, if saving U.S. lives was the primary objective, the decision, as the
Joint Chiefs made clear, only added to the obstacles standing in the way of
an end to the fighting.)

With little hesitation on August 11, President Truman (and Secretary
Byrnes) did, in fact, offer implicit assurances regarding the Emperor of essentially the kind Japan had been seeking throughout the summer. (At that
time, Truman had to be reminded of the position taken at Potsdam!*)

The United States did so, of course, all the while holding on to the rheto-

---

*See below, pp. 417–18.

ric of "unconditional surrender"—an obvious way to finesse the issue which could be traced back to advice given since the early spring and to the precedent Roosevelt himself had set in connection with the Italian surrender.

The elapsed time between the moment assurances for the Emperor were finally removed from the draft Potsdam Proclamation and the moment they were put forward on August 11 was eighteen days. (The "secret" option Truman said he would pursue if Japan seemed to be "hanging fire" on the Emperor issue was not, in fact, exercised.) Had bad weather not intervened to delay the bombing, the time might well have been little more than a week. This latter fact—together with some of the previously cited evidence—suggests one of the most troubling questions left unanswered by the currently available evidence.

Quite apart from the issue of whether Japan would, in fact, have surrendered if assurances had been given for the Emperor (with or without the Russian attack), we have seen that the president was repeatedly advised that Japan would not (could not) surrender in the absence of such assurances. In light of the evidence on this point, it is difficult to believe that Truman and Byrnes ever really judged that in the end a surrender would be feasible without ultimately offering some protection for the person and position of the Emperor. If they knew they would almost certainly have to provide assurances shortly in any event, the question of why, specifically, they put things off is even more puzzling—especially given the strong advice to act by every other official involved.

Furthermore, on numerous occasions an even more forceful third military argument had been strongly urged in favor of the Emperor. Top service leaders believed, first, that the Japanese would not likely surrender unless the position of the Emperor was assured; second, that such assurances would help produce a surrender decision; but that, third, the Emperor was the only one who actually could order men in the field to lay down their arms. For instance, at the July 17 Joint Chiefs of Staff meeting:

> General Marshall stated that from a purely military point of view he considered that the attitude of the Joint Chiefs of Staff should be that nothing should be done prior to the termination of hostilities that would indicate the removal of the Emperor of Japan, since his continuation in office might influence the cessation of hostilities in areas outside of Japan proper.[1]

The next day Leahy advised Truman directly:

> From a strictly military point of view the Joint Chiefs of Staff consider it inadvisable to make any statement or take any action at the present time that would make it difficult or impossible to utilize the authority of

the Emperor to direct a surrender of the Japanese forces in the outlying areas as well as in Japan proper.[2]

Similarly, Byrnes made the connection in the previously cited letter to Groves. Without the Emperor, it would have been more difficult "to secure the surrender of the Japanese Army on the various islands of the Pacific and the task of General MacArthur would have been a more difficult one."[3]

In short, the rapidity with which the Emperor's position was assured after the bombings, the fact that Truman and Byrnes almost certainly must have understood that ultimately the change would be made in any event, and, finally, the strong military advice that the Emperor was absolutely essential—all these add to the considerations which challenge easy acceptance of "politics" as an explanation for the crucial decision.*

Three other indirect-candidate theories have been offered to attempt to explain the lack of assurances for the Emperor, and why, specifically, Truman and Byrnes eliminated the critical recommended portion of the Potsdam Proclamation. The first is implicit in the general idea that the president was following the momentum of events, a theory which we have seen is challenged by the fact of a major debate and the reversal of the recommended policy.

A second indirect-candidate theory has also already been noted in passing—namely that Truman and Byrnes became so involved in the belief the atomic bomb would help their diplomacy that they became psychologically blinded to the possibilities for surrender. A version of this theory was put forward by an official Army historian even before most of the modern documentation became public. Writing in the February 1959 *Marine Corps Gazette*, Louis Morton observed:

> Although no first-hand evidence is available, the fact cannot be ignored that certain responsible officials feared the political consequences of Soviet intervention and hoped that ultimately it would prove unnecessary. This feeling may perhaps unconsciously have made the atomic solution more attractive. For some officials believed that the bomb would serve as a deterrent to Soviet expansion in Europe, an expansion that had already engulfed Rumania, Bulgaria, Yugoslavia, Czechoslovakia and Hungary.[4]

---

*A speculative idea as to why the president and Byrnes waited is that they may have thought there could be some tactical advantage in holding to a firm line as long as possible. Although such a view was urged by the Joint Chiefs of Staff in early June before the fall of Okinawa, to my knowledge there is no contemporaneous evidence that any responsible official still held this view in July. Most important, of course, U.S. military leaders—who might have been expected to urge a tough line—advised just the opposite strategy.

The theory of "unconscious" influences, like the momentum theory, does not readily explain the specific and quite openly discussed explicit (conscious) choice which was made to eliminate the recommended language.

A final significant candidate theory is a troubling explanation suggested by former Undersecretary of State William R. Castle. This is that Truman and Byrnes, in fact, wished to use the atomic bomb—preferred to demonstrate its power—and therefore explicitly chose not to end the war by offering assurances to the Emperor.

Castle had served as Stimson's deputy when the latter was Herbert Hoover's secretary of state, and he had kept in close touch with emerging events and with many old friends like Grew who were still important State Department officials. His diary—opened in 1985—includes several important references concerning the key questions.* Perhaps the most significant entry is one written on February 9, 1947, in which he speculates openly as to whether Stimson and Marshall really wanted the war to continue long enough to give the United States an opportunity to test the new weapon on various Japanese cities.[5] Although it is clear that the President and Byrnes (not Stimson and Marshall) were at the center of decision-making at this time, the critical issue is here sharply defined. Castle's basic question was put this way by a Japanese investigator in a recent interview: "Might they simply have been trying to delay the surrender for two weeks until the bomb could be shown?"[6]

Castle does not specify exactly why a decision might have been made along these lines, but his theory is compatible with an implicit or explicit argument that Truman and Byrnes felt that it was important to demonstrate the bomb to the Russians.

The possibility that impressing the Russians was an explicit goal of policy troubled another conservative who—like Castle—was also close to the men who made the decision. Historian Herbert Feis had been a consultant to four different Cabinet secretaries and was a good friend of Stimson's. He was also a friend of Harriman (and helped him prepare his personal papers in connection with his memoirs).

That Feis understood the end was very near is indicated in many texts but perhaps nowhere more graphically than in a private comment recorded during an interview he had with President Eisenhower in 1960:

> Professor Feis said that reading intelligence reports at that time gave a very clear impression the Japanese were defeated. Even a careful reading of the New York Times would make it completely evident.[7]†

*See also pp. 44–45, 476–77.

†Similarly, another memorandum to himself states: "Was it a mistake not to try to get the Soviet Government to join in a Potsdam declaration, or at least allowed to be know [*sic*] that it agreed to these proposals? Might that have swayed the debates in the Japanese Government towards acceptance?" ("Chapters 16 and 17 notes," Box 65, Feis Papers, LC.)

Feis' papers at the Library of Congress (opened in 1971) show that he struggled mightily with the evidence confronting him on the question of why the bomb had been used—first during the late 1950s, and then again in the mid-1960s. A memorandum to himself entitled "Discussion of the Question of Whether It Was Essential to Use the Atomic Bomb Against Japan" notes that "the effort to make the bomb, the zeal for bringing it to the test, and the arrangements for using it were all marked by an intense sense of urgency and impatience." Apart from military reasons, Feis observes, "It is virtually certain that one of the reasons for haste and impatience was the thought that if we knew we were going to have this new weapon, the American position in the matters to be thrashed out at the Potsdam Conference could be the more confident and stubborn."[8]

In the same memorandum to himself Feis also states: "Similarly, it is entirely possible that the eagerness to put the bomb to use as soon as possible was affected by the thought that it would be advantageous if this demonstration of our power and possibly the resultant quick termination of the war came about before Soviet advances into Manchuria had gone too far."[9]

Finally, among the "complimentary thoughts and supplementary purposes" Feis noted was that: "It is quite possible that it was thought the proof of the power of the weapon, as demonstrated in actual warfare, might be an effective source of added authority to the American Government in the settlement of matters at issue with the Soviet Union."[10]

One draft of Feis' major book on the atomic bomb decision included this key judgment: "It may be inferred that the political leaders of the western world probably valued this new means of impressing the Russians. . . ."

> And I think it may be inferred further that they wished the impression to be sure and strong; and that it could only be so if the might of the bomb was registered in the awful register of the dead and dying.[11]

When Feis' book *Japan Subdued: The Atomic Bomb and the End of the War in the Pacific* appeared in 1961, this language was dropped and a much softer formulation substituted:

> It may be also—but this is only conjecture—that Churchill and Truman and some of their colleagues conceived that besides bringing the war to a quick end, it would improve the chances of arranging a satisfactory peace. For would not the same dramatic proof of Western power that shocked Japan into surrender impress the Russians also?[12]

However, this was not the end of the matter: Feis republished his book in 1966 (under the new title *The Atomic Bomb and the End of World War II*) and once more revised his position to explicitly state:

It is likely that Churchill and probably also Truman, conceived that besides bringing the war to a quick end, [use of the bomb] would improve the chances of arranging a satisfactory peace both in Europe and in the Far East. Stimson and Byrnes certainly had that thought in mind. For would not the same dramatic proof of Western power that shocked Japan into surrender impress the Russians also?[13]

One scholar has pointed to the significance of a specific passage in General Groves' memoirs in this regard. A 1979 study by Edmund R. Preston notes Groves' clear statement that officials were awaiting the results of the atomic test in order to know how to complete the final wording of the Potsdam Proclamation:

I was extremely anxious to have the test carried off on schedule. One reason for this was that I knew the effect that a successful test would have on the issuance and wording of the Potsdam ultimatum.[14]

If the report in Groves' memoirs is accurate, it suggests, too, the possibility of a choice of options and of preferences: before the test, the most obvious option was a modification of the surrender terms—together possibly with the shock of a Russian declaration of war; once the test succeeded, this option was dropped because the atomic bomb was preferred. Had the atomic test failed, Preston observes, "Truman would probably have issued a more readily acceptable ultimatum, containing assurances about the monarchy and perhaps other concessions."[15]

These difficult issues clearly troubled Morton, Castle, and Feis. Because we do not know what Truman and Byrnes actually discussed privately when they made their decision, and although the presently available evidence permits us to discount certain theories, none can be proved definitely at this stage of our knowledge.*

As previously noted, a final and unqualified answer as to why the atomic bomb was used is neither essential nor possible. What is important is whether, when the bomb was used, the president and his top advisers understood that it was not required to avoid a long and costly invasion, as they later claimed and as most Americans still believe.

In connection with this question, evidence accumulated over the last five decades has even more to suggest—both about additional views of "military necessity" and about developments subsequent to the July 26 issuance of the Potsdam Proclamation.

---

*See the Afterword for a detailed analysis of various theories.

PART VI

"Military Necessity"

The Japanese were already defeated and ready to surrender. . . .

—Admiral William D. Leahy,
Chief of Staff to the President, *I Was There*

Chapter 26

NAVY LEADERS

I didn't like the atom bomb or any part of it.
—Fleet Admiral Ernest J. King,
Commander in Chief of the U.S. Fleet
and Chief of Naval Operations, July 4, 1950

The issue of military necessity—like the issue of surrender in general—cannot be discussed purely in the abstract without consideration of exactly what question is being asked. Thus, if the question were: "How could Japan be made to surrender unconditionally with no assurances whatsoever for the Emperor?" the answer would inevitably have been: "It would take a great deal of force over a very long period of time."

It would have been surprising had U.S. military leaders said the use of the atomic bomb was totally unnecessary in this situation. In such circumstances one would not have expected any but the most independent-minded and secure in their positions to challenge the atomic bomb's use.

Once the president had determined there would be no modification of the surrender formula, that is the way the question, in fact, was posed. What is interesting and unexpected is that many military leaders seem nevertheless (even in these circumstances) to have felt the use of the atomic bomb was not dictated by military necessity.

It is useful in this regard to recall the two after-the-fact official studies which were done closest to the actual events. As we have seen, the U.S. Strategic Bombing Survey concluded that Japan would in all probability have surrendered by November and the War Department's Military Intelligence Division judged that it was "almost a certainty that the Japanese would have capitulated upon the entry of Russia into the war."[1]

The question is whether—at the time—military considerations in general, and military advice in particular, were responsible for the decision to use the atomic bomb.

Prior to Potsdam (and even before July's Emperor-related intercepts), Stimson, Forrestal, Leahy, Marshall, McCloy, Bard—as well as Arnold, King, and Nimitz—had all in various ways urged that the surrender terms be clarified. And at Potsdam the Joint Chiefs of Staff twice tried to find a way to clarify the surrender formula.

Were the military leaders directly involved in the actual decision to use the atomic bomb? Did they favor and advise its use?

The order to use the atomic bomb was issued to Spaatz by General Handy on July 25, the day before the Potsdam Proclamation was issued (an important point of chronology we shall take up shortly).[2] However, there is little contemporaneous evidence that military leaders had any direct formal involvement in the decision-making process. Indeed, not a shred of serious deliberative work concerning options and decisions appears in any Joint Chiefs record. As JCS official historian Grace Person Hayes notes:

> During the war years the Joint Chiefs of Staff had been generally aware of the development of atomic research, although this very secret project was not under their authority and JCS discussion of it, if there was any, was never recorded.[3]

Every major official and unofficial study done on this matter—and nearly every statement touching on it by the military leaders involved—has underscored this point.[4] No record exists of the kind of careful staff work and policy development which routinely goes into serious military decision-making. There is no sophisticated paper trail like the complex series of surrender-related staff and other documents known as the "J.C.S. 1340 series" which we reviewed in Part I.

There is no doubt, as Hayes also acknowledges, that President Truman talked informally about the atomic bomb with military leaders.[5] Even here, however, the method and degree of consultation are very much in question. A specific instance where a "claim" of serious consultation has been made involves a possible brief meeting at Potsdam. This paragraph appears in Margaret Truman's 1972 biography, *Harry S. Truman*:

> The following day [July 22] my father convened a conference of his chief advisers in the little White House at Babelsberg [near Potsdam] to make the final decision about the use of the bomb. More than two months of thought by the best available minds was at his fingertips. Once more [since the White House meeting of June 18] he polled the men in the room. Only one man had changed his mind. Commander of the Army Air Force General Hap Arnold now thought Japan could be bombed into submission with conventional weapons. . . . But none of

the other military men—especially General Marshall—concurred with General Arnold.[6]*

Similar general statements appear in another book edited by Truman's daughter and in *Mr. President*, a book written with the president's help by his journalist friend William Hillman.[7]

But there is little contemporaneous evidence that a meeting of this kind ever occurred. Barton Bernstein, who has searched the record thoroughly, observes:

> Probably Truman would have mentioned it in his own diary but did not, and the quasi-official record also did not mention it. Certainly Stimson, Leahy, or Arnold, all of whom kept diaries for the period and later published memoirs, would have put it into a diary or memoir. None of them did. Nor did Marshall ever mention it in later interviews. Nor did Byrnes in his two memoirs. And Admiral King, who also published a post-war memoir and questioned the military necessity of the A-bomb in that book, never mentioned such a meeting.[8]

Given the momentous nature of the decision under consideration, it is reasonable to assume that at least one of the participants would have marked the event.

Margaret Truman's report is particularly intriguing because it seems to offer specific information on the views of Arnold and Marshall; details of this kind often suggest the writer is working with a specific document in hand. However, she has repeatedly failed to reply to letters of inquiry from various historians (including myself) on this point.[9]

Even the above account does not state explicitly that the military leaders recommended, positively, in favor of the bomb. Nor are the alternatives of modifying the terms or awaiting the Russian declaration of war even mentioned. What is said explicitly is that no one concurred with General Arnold that Japan could be bombed into (at this point, "unconditional") submission by conventional air attacks.

David J. Williams has compared the various after-the-fact accounts with the detailed hour-by-hour (indeed, often minute-by-minute) log of the Potsdam Conference. He concludes that if a meeting actually occurred, July 22 is indeed the most plausible date. Comparing what is known of the schedules of the suggested participants with the log of the president's schedule, Williams further states that the most likely and perhaps only time

---

*According to Margaret Truman, atomic weapons were not discussed at the June 18 meeting. When she writes, "Only one man had changed his mind," she is referring to the decision to invade. (M. Truman, *Harry S. Truman*, pp. 261–62.)

a meeting might have occurred on that day is after the president had attended both Protestant church services at 10:00 a.m. (accompanied by his military and naval aides, as the log states) and Catholic mass at 11:30 a.m.—but before 12:15 p.m. (when he had lunch with Churchill and Arnold is reported to have seen Stimson).[10]

As Williams writes: "It was either a short mass or the president left early"; in either case the meeting would have been extremely brief.[11]

When we turn to the testimony of the top military leaders themselves, the evidence not only confirms that their advice was not seriously sought, but also (with one possible, somewhat ambiguous exception) strongly suggests that none believed the use of the atomic bomb was dictated by overwhelming military considerations. Several expressed deep revulsion at the idea of targeting a city.

The documentary record is sketchy, and we are forced to piece together whatever fragments of information can be found to form even a partial picture of what actually happened. In the end, however, it is extremely difficult to accept easy claims of the "military necessity" of the atomic bombing. This is true, moreover, even though—again—modifying the surrender formula and awaiting the Russian attack are rarely included in the specific statements made by military leaders.

We may also observe that if America's top military leaders either recommended or supported the use of the atomic bomb as militarily necessary, they gave very little evidence of such convictions in almost everything most were to say thereafter, both publicly and privately.

Among the leadership of the U.S. Navy, we have already noted the strong feelings of Fleet Admiral William D. Leahy, the man who chaired meetings of the Joint Chiefs of Staff. ("The Japanese were already defeated and ready to surrender. . . .")[12] We have also noted Leahy's advice to Truman to clarify the surrender formula on June 18—almost a month before the Emperor's July intervention and seven weeks before the atomic bomb was used. The same day, recall also, Leahy recorded in his private diary:

> It is my opinion at the present time that a surrender of Japan can be arranged with terms that can be accepted by Japan and that will make fully satisfactory provisions for America's defense against future trans-Pacific aggression.[13]

The July 16, 1945, minutes of the Combined Chiefs of Staff at Potsdam also record Leahy as urging the British Chiefs of Staff

> that as the matter was clearly a political one primarily, it would be very useful if the Prime Minister put forward to the President his views and

suggestions as to how the term "unconditional surrender" might be explained to the Japanese.[14]

In his memoirs Leahy describes the views of the Combined Chiefs of Staff in these terms:

We felt it would be helpful and wise to explain to Tokyo that unconditional surrender did not mean the complete destruction of the Japanese Government.[15]

(It is in this context that he added: "We were certain that the Mikado could stop the war with a royal word."[16])

Leahy was an extremely discreet adviser, and other than his June 18 recommendation we do not have contemporaneous records detailing the specific counsel he gave to Truman on issues related to the use of the atomic bomb. However, the two men met routinely every morning at 9:45 a.m. for discussions which were not recorded (or only briefly noted in Leahy's diary).[17] Numerous other unrecorded meetings undoubtedly occurred. As Robert Ferrell notes, Leahy was "constantly by [Truman's] side in the White House. . . ."[18]) Although it appears that no notes of conversations between Truman and Leahy have survived concerning this issue, we know a fair amount about the admiral's candor. When Truman told Leahy he wanted him to stay on after Roosevelt's death, for instance, his chief of staff

reminded Truman that when I disagreed with Roosevelt, I told him so very frankly, and that Roosevelt had seemed to like that way of doing business. "If I am to remain as your Chief of Staff," I said, "it will be impossible for me to change. If I think you are in error I shall say so."[19]

According to Leahy, Truman replied:

That is exactly what I want you to do. . . . I want you to tell me if you think I am making a mistake. Of course, I will make the decisions, and after a decision is made, I will expect you to be loyal.[20]

Did Leahy tell the president directly that he thought the atomic bomb was unnecessary and should not be used? It is impossible to know for certain. Given what we know of his strong views, however, it is difficult to believe that he did not argue his case with the president.* Leahy's own recollection is understated but quite clear:

Naturally, I had acquainted President Truman with my own ideas about the best course to pursue in defeating Japan as fully as I had done with President Roosevelt.[21]

---

*It appears that Leahy may, in fact, have put his views in writing. In 1971 Brigadier General Sidney F. Giffin recalled: "I remember his opposition to the concept of using atomic weapons

Other corroborating evidence of Leahy's general viewpoint comes from well-informed journalists, his private secretary, and friends and writers who were close to the conservative admiral. Hanson Baldwin, the *New York Times* military writer, recalled in an oral history interview that Leahy "thought the business of recognizing the continuation of the Emperor was a detail which should have been solved easily."[22] Leahy's secretary, Dorothy Ringquist, remembered vividly that the day Hiroshima was bombed he said: "Dorothy, we will regret this day. The United States will suffer, for war is not to be waged on women and children."[23] And in 1949, presidential biographer Jonathan Daniels recorded that Leahy complained bitterly: "Truman told me it was agreed that they would use it, after military men's statements that it would save many, many American lives by shortening the war, only to hit military objectives."

> Of course, then they went ahead and killed as many women and children as they could which was just what they wanted all the time.[24]

Leahy's disgust at the idea of attacking "women and children" is consistently stated in virtually every report we have of his attitude. It is also worth noting that he was a friend of Truman's—and continued to be regarded as such by the president. Cabell Phillips has observed that Leahy was one of the two advisers (along with Marshall) whom Truman "revered almost without limit."[25] In his memoirs, the president writes that "he typified the Navy at its best. . . ."[26] The memoirs in which Leahy characterizes the use of the atomic bomb as "barbarous" contain an introductory note by Truman praising his "long and brilliant career."[27]*

The remarkable thing is not simply that Leahy had very strong feelings about the issue, but that he put his views forward so forcefully and publicly.

It is important in all of this to keep in mind a point which has often been confused in subsequent studies: Earlier in the war navy leaders had argued that Japan could be forced to surrender through a policy of blockade, which would slowly "strangle" Japan's supply lines.[28] They had also recommended a blockade as an alternative to invasion—if that were the choice (which, to

was in a very brief memo, on the basis that they simply were not right. They in no way accorded in notions of chivalry, something, words like this. But the chivalry was in there, if they didn't accord with the idea of chivalry he was against it." Giffin interview with Dr. Murray Green, August 10, 1971, Box 50, 8.76, Murray Green Collection, USAFAL. (No document of this kind, however, has as yet turned up.)

*Leahy also told the press that Truman had read portions of the manuscript before it was published, and was pleased with it. (WDL, Press Conference, March 14, 1950, " 'I Was There' Press Conference, 1950," Box 10, Leahy Papers, LC.)

be sure, it almost certainly was so long as the rigid demand of "unconditional surrender" remained unchanged).[29]

However, as his private diary and the other contemporaneous documents we have noted suggest, by mid-June—and certainly by the time of Potsdam—the real issue for Leahy and many naval leaders was no longer the old question of blockade versus invasion. That was largely past.

In the case of Leahy we have both contemporary evidence of his judgments and corroborating after-the-fact information. A similar balance exists in connection with several other navy leaders, but in some cases the mix is different. What stands out in both the contemporaneous and after-the-fact evidence, however, is the remarkable consistency of attitudes at the top.

In his 1952 "third person" autobiography (co-authored with Walter Muir Whitehill), the commander in chief of the U.S. Fleet and chief of Naval Operations, Ernest J. King, states:

> The President in giving his approval for these [atomic] attacks appeared to believe that many thousands of American troops would be killed in invading Japan, and in this he was entirely correct; but King felt, as he had pointed out many times, that the dilemma was an unnecessary one, for had we been willing to wait, the effective naval blockade would, in the course of time, have starved the Japanese into submission through lack of oil, rice, medicines, and other essential materials.[30]

Although King registers his dissent from the bombing in this passage, he is here stating the early 1945 navy view that a blockade would have brought about surrender. Other evidence suggests that by late June, King had come to the same conclusion as Leahy—namely, that the war could be ended well before a November invasion, and that therefore use of the atomic bomb was both unnecessary and immoral. For instance, King's deputy chief of staff, Rear Admiral Bernhard H. Bieri, recalled in a 1969 oral history interview that by late spring of 1945 he and his colleagues were quite clear that there would be no invasion:

> There were certain of us [on King's staff] that felt that [an invasion] was never going to be undertaken or necessary. . . . [O]nce the Japanese fleet was defeated, that they were unable to get material from overseas, maintain their industry, maintain their shipbuilding, and carry on their commercial life such as it had, their connection to the continent was broken; there would be nothing left for them to do but call it off. Especially if their principle [*sic*] allies—Germany had been defeated.[31]

Bieri went on: "I was quite sure that they wouldn't want to get mixed up with the Russians at that stage of the game. . . ."—a judgment which both accords with many such statements we have noted and helps clarify the issue of timing.* Bieri added that although this was not the official agreed position of the Joint Chiefs of Staff, King also privately shared his staff's view to a very large extent.[32] In fact, King writes openly that

> . . . in June 1945 he [King] concurred in the majority decision of the Joint Chiefs to make plans for the invasion and seizure of objectives in the Japanese home islands without sharing the Army conviction that such operations were necessary.[33]

Bieri's testimony points to the considerable gap between what was put on paper at various points in 1945—the information commonly cited by historians—and what top officials actually believed and discussed privately among themselves. The difference is particularly interesting in regard to King and those who worked with him. An April 26 memorandum from General Hull to Marshall reports: "Messages initiated by Nimitz, which are available to us, indicate that there is considerable doubt in the minds of his staff that we really intend to carry through with the invasion program."[34] Similarly, Henry Luce, the publisher of *Time* and *Life* magazines, visited the Pacific in the spring of 1945 and realized that navy leaders there had few illusions about Japan's situation:

> A few months before Hiroshima, I was with Admiral Halsey's Navy as it assaulted the coast of Japan. Two things seemed clear to me—as they did to many of the top fighting men I talked to: first, that Japan was beaten; second, that the Japanese knew it and were every day showing signs of increasing willingness to quit.[35]

The naval historian E. B. Potter, who was close to many top officers, points out that at the end of June—before the July intercepts showing the Emperor's intervention (and before the Alamogordo test):

> . . . Admiral Nimitz flew to San Francisco for what proved to be his final wartime meeting with Admiral King. At this conference, which lasted only one day, King informed Nimitz that President Truman had approved Operation Olympic and that the Joint Chiefs recommended that preparations be made for the subsequent Operation Coronet. The

*As early as March, Bieri told King: "I am inclined to believe that if we have Japan completely 'ringed in' and under constant assault from air and sea with threat of invasion imminent, that she may seek peace on our terms when Germany collapses, and if Russia comes into the war. . . ." He made clear at this point, moreover, that "our terms" meant unconditional surrender. (Bernhard H. Bieri to EJK, "Subject: Far East Strategy," March 1945, Military Operations and Planning—Pacific Theater, Vol. III, May 22, 1944–March 1945, Box 22, Cooke Papers, HIA.)

briefness of the meeting may well have reflected the near-conviction in the minds of both Nimitz and King that neither Olympic nor Coronet would ever take place.[36]*

In a 1987 oral history Captain Robert Dornin, King's aide and flag lieutenant, stated:

> Well, I do know how Admiral King felt. We had them on their knees and why not wait for three or four months and then if they didn't [surrender], drop the bomb. I mean, why do it now? . . . Admiral King said, "I don't think we should do it [drop the bomb] at this time. It is not necessary."[37]

In addition to all this, of course, there is the matter of "unconditional surrender." King, along with Forrestal, supported the general efforts of Captain Ellis Zacharias to clarify the surrender formula.[38] The minutes of the June 19, 1945, (State-War-Navy) Committee of Three meeting also state: "Stimson and Grew further pointed out that Leahy, King, and Nimitz were all in favor of some such approach [as that urged by Grew] being made to the Japanese."[39]

Private interview notes jotted down by Walter Whitehill report King's feelings quite simply as: "I didn't like the atom bomb or any part of it."[40]

Below King in the chain of command was Fleet Admiral Chester W. Nimitz, commander in chief of the Pacific Fleet. On September 22, 1945, *The New York Times* reported on a Nimitz press conference at Pearl Harbor:

> The admiral took the opportunity of adding his voice to those insisting that Japan had been defeated before the atomic bombings and Russia's entry into the war.[41]

Subsequently, in a public address given at the Washington Monument on October 5, 1945, Nimitz stated: "The Japanese had, in fact, already sued for peace before the atomic age was announced to the world with the destruction of Hiroshima and before the Russian entry into the war."[42] A year later, Nimitz declared in a speech to the National Geographic Society: "The atomic bomb merely hastened a process already reaching an inevitable conclusion."[43]

---

*As we saw in Part I, at the June 18 White House meeting King emphasized the difference between planning for an invasion and actually carrying it out: "If preparations do not go forward now, they cannot be arranged for later. Once started, however, they can always be stopped if desired." (DoD, *Top Secret Entry*, Sec. V, p. 24; DoD, *Entry*, p. 81.)

I am convinced that the complete impunity with which the Pacific Fleet pounded Japan at point-blank range was the decisive factor in forcing the Japanese to ask the Russians to approach us for peace proposals in July.

Meanwhile, aircraft from our new fields in the Okinawa group were daily shuttling back and forth over Kyushu and Shokoku [sic] and B-29s of the Twentieth Air Force were fire-bombing major Japanese cities. The pace and the fury were mounting and the government of Japan, as its official spokesmen have now admitted, were [sic] looking for a way to end the war.[44]

Admiral Harry W. Hill, commander of the Fifth Amphibious Force, subsequently recalled that "neither Admiral Nimitz or Spruance [Vice Admiral Raymond A. Spruance, commander of the Fifth Fleet] considered that it would ever be necessary to invade the homeland of Japan."[45]

As noted above, the June 19, 1945, Committee of Three meeting report indicates that Nimitz, too, was among those who clearly supported clarifying the unconditional surrender formula in connection with Grew's proposed statement. E. B. Potter—who interviewed Nimitz at length in connection with his biography—observes that

Nimitz considered the atomic bomb somehow indecent, certainly not a legitimate form of warfare.[46]

Potter's interview notes contain the following Nimitz quotation:

It is [an] indiscriminate killer and I am hopeful that it will be dropped as an inefficient weapon. Poison gas and bacteriological weapons are in the same category.[47]

Rear Admiral E. B. Fluckey, who commanded a submarine during the war and was subsequently personal aide to Nimitz, also recalled: "I don't think that Admiral Nimitz thought it probably saved many many lives to blow up the Japanese like that."[48] And in a 1969 oral history interview Nimitz's widow observed that her husband "always felt very badly over the dropping of that bomb because he said we had Japan beaten already."[49] She added that he told her explicitly:

. . . I felt that that was an unnecessary loss of civilian life. . . . We had them beaten. They hadn't enough food, they couldn't do anything.[50]

Nimitz is also on record as emphasizing that the decision to use the bomb was not primarily a military decision. In a 1946 letter to Walter Michels of the Association of Philadelphia Scientists, he observed that it was his understanding that "the decision to employ the atomic bomb on Japanese cities was made on a level higher than that of the Joint Chiefs of Staff."[51]

Similar views also appear to have been dominant among other top-ranking navy officials. Admiral William "Bull" Halsey's Third Fleet was meeting almost no resistance as it bombarded Japanese coastal installations. Halsey made this public statement in 1946:

> The first atomic bomb was an unnecessary experiment. . . . It was a mistake to ever drop it. Why reveal a weapon like that to the world when it wasn't necessary? . . . [the scientists] had this toy and they wanted to try it out, so they dropped it. . . . It killed a lot of Japs, but the Japs had put out a lot of peace feelers through Russia long before.[52]

Again, in the early 1970s, Admiral Robert Lee Dennison, a special adviser to the undersecretary of the navy and a member of the Joint War Plans Committee, noted that in announcing the surrender doctrine President Roosevelt

> wanted to make it perfectly clear that we were fighting for total victory. But the thing became outmoded, of course, as time went on. . . . It was perfectly obvious in the case of Germany or Japan we couldn't and didn't have an unconditional surrender. It would be unthinkable to destroy a country. We would have ruined our own.[53]

Dennison, who became Truman's naval aide after 1948, added that in any case, "[I]t was pretty obvious that Japan was going down the drain. It was just a question of when."

> Admiral Leahy, for one, felt and quite rightly so that Japan had already been defeated by being cut off from her sources of supply, food, products, and it was only a matter of a relatively short time before the country would collapse. . . .
> I basically agreed with Admiral Leahy's views because we had plenty of intelligence to show what straits Japan was in.[54]

Henry Luce also reported that on his May–June tour of the Pacific theater:

> . . . I spent a morning at Cavite in the Philippines with Admiral Frank Wagner in front of huge maps. Admiral Wagner was in charge of air search-and-patrol of all the East Asian seas and coasts. He showed me that in all those millions of square miles there was literally not a single target worth the powder to blow it up; there were only junks and mostly small ones at that.
> Similarly, I dined one night with Admiral [Arthur] Radford [later

Joint Chiefs Chairman, 1953–57] on the carrier *Yorktown* leading a task force from Ulithi to bomb Kyushu, the main southern island of Japan. Radford had invited me to be alone with him in a tiny room far up the superstructure of the *Yorktown*, where not a sound could be heard. Even so, it was in a whisper that he turned to me and said: "Luce, don't you think the war is over?" My reply, of course, was that he should know better than I. For his part, all he could say was that the few little revetments and rural bridges that he might find to bomb in Kyushu wouldn't begin to pay for the fuel he was burning on his task force.[55]

In 1952, Rear Admiral Richard Byrd wrote privately to King to praise his memoirs—and also expressed his own view:

Especially it is good to see the truth told about the last days of the war with Japan. . . . I was with the Fleet during that period; and every officer in the Fleet knew that Japan would eventually capitulate from . . . the tight blockade.

I, too, felt strongly that it was a mistake to drop the atom bombs, especially without warning.[56]

In short, at the very top of the U.S. navy—among those with access to the best information—it is difficult to find a knowledgeable World War II officer who is on record as supporting the idea that use of the atomic bomb was militarily required. Indeed, although some may have supported the president in general, many, like Leahy, were revolted at the slaughter of noncombatants.

Navy leaders—partly because of their experience in Japanese waters, partly because Navy intelligence was responsible for a good deal of the intercept work—were well informed on other surrender-related issues as well. In Part V we noted that some also made an effort to get their views heard at the top. To recall, the undersecretary of the navy, Ralph Bard, formally dissented from the Interim Committee's recommendations for using the bomb and secured a meeting with Truman to express his dissent.[57]

Rear Admiral Lewis L. Strauss, special assistant to the secretary of the navy from 1944 to 1945 (and later chairman of the Atomic Energy Commission), replaced Bard on the Interim Committee. After the war, he, too, repeatedly stated his belief that the use of the atomic bomb "was not necessary to bring the war to a successful conclusion. . . ."

It seemed to me not only that it was a sin—to use a good word—[a word that] should be more often used—to kill non-combatants, but that if such a weapon could be made it would be better that it not be used in a war which was ending in order that we might reserve to ourselves the knowledge of its construction and its use in the event that some day we might need it to preserve our government and our safety.[58]

In the mid-1960s Strauss also recalled that if it was used at all

I proposed to Secretary Forrestal at that time that the weapon should be demonstrated before it was used. . . . Primarily, it was because it was clear to a number of people, myself among them, that the war was very nearly over. The Japanese were nearly ready to capitulate. . . . My proposal to the Secretary was that the weapon should be demonstrated over some area accessible to the Japanese observers, and where its effects would be dramatic. I remember suggesting that a good place—satisfactory place for such a demonstration would be a large forest of cryptomaria [*sic*] trees not far from Tokyo. The cryptomaria tree is the Japanese version of our redwood. . . . I anticipated that a bomb detonated at a suitable height above such a forest . . . would [have] laid the trees out in windrows from the center of the explosion in all directions as though they had been matchsticks, and of course set them afire in the center. It seemed to me that a demonstration of this sort would prove to the Japanese that we could destroy any of their cities, their fortifications at will. . . .[59]

Strauss added that "Secretary Forrestal agreed wholeheartedly with the recommendation. . . ."[60]

In all of this we have so far not distinguished between general judgments made at various points throughout the summer of 1945 and specific judgments made after the July 12–13 MAGIC intercepts revealed the Emperor's personal bid to attempt to end the war. Information from this latter period, as we shall shortly see, further illuminates the thinking and related initiatives of top navy leaders in the final weeks before the atomic bombs were used.

Chapter 27

AIR FORCE LEADERS

LeMay: *The war would have been over in two weeks without the Russians entering and without the atomic bomb.*
The Press: *You mean that, sir? Without the Russians and the atomic bomb?*
LeMay: *The atomic bomb had nothing to do with the end of the war at all.*

—September 20, 1945, press conference by
Major General Curtis E. LeMay, U.S. Army
Air Forces

High-ranking air force leaders also expressed judgments similar to those of their naval counterparts. Indeed, public statements made by a number of air force generals after the war helped stimulate a steady buildup of public questioning of the Hiroshima decision in late 1945 and on into 1946.

The commanding general of the U.S. Army Air Forces, Henry H. "Hap" Arnold, gave a strong indication of his views in a public statement only eleven days after Hiroshima was attacked. Asked on August 17 by a *New York Times* reporter whether the atomic bomb caused Japan to surrender, Arnold said:

From the Japanese standpoint the atomic bomb was really a way out. The Japanese position was hopeless even before the first atomic bomb fell, because the Japanese had lost control of their own air.[1]

In his 1949 memoirs Arnold observed that "it always appeared to us that, atomic bomb or no atomic bomb, the Japanese were already on the verge of collapse."[2]

At Potsdam, Arnold read into the record of the July 16 Combined Chiefs of Staff meeting his judgment that by October Japan would have "tremendous difficulty in holding her people together for continued resistance to our terms of unconditional surrender."[3]

This assessment was almost certainly prepared before the July intercepts regarding the Emperor were in hand, and did not assume the impact of a Soviet declaration of war. Nor, significantly, did Arnold assume modification in the unconditional-surrender terms.

Other well-informed sources also confirm the basic thrust of Arnold's position. His deputy, Lieutenant General Ira C. Eaker, summed up his understanding this way in a 1962 official oral history interview:

Arnold's view was that it [the dropping of the atomic bomb] was unnecessary. He said that he knew the Japanese wanted peace. There were political implications in the decision and Arnold did not feel it was the military's job to question it.[4]

Since the 1947 enactment of the National Security Act the air force has been an independent service, but in 1945 it was still operating within the structure of the army. Although Arnold was technically a member of the Joint Chiefs, he was subordinate to (and reported to) Marshall. Eaker reports that Arnold told him:

When the question comes up of whether we use the atomic bomb or not, my view is that the Air Force will not oppose the use of the bomb, and they will deliver it effectively if the Commander in Chief decides to use it. But it is not necessary to use it in order to conquer the Japanese without the necessity of a land invasion.[5]

Given Arnold's subordinate position, the public statements he made beginning in 1945 are perhaps even more significant indications of the strength of his conviction. As Herman S. Wolk, the senior historian for the Air Force Historical Support Office in Washington, D.C., has observed, quite simply, Arnold "thought it was not necessary to drop the A-bomb." Another Arnold observation—that the "surrender of Japan was not entirely the result of the two atomic bombs"—is a laconic understatement of attitudes common throughout the upper ranks of the U.S. Air Force leadership.[6]

Nor was Arnold the only high-ranking air force official to claim publicly, in the immediate aftermath of the attacks on Hiroshima and Nagasaki, that the use of the bomb had been unnecessary. Six days after Nagasaki was bombed, on August 15, 1945, *The New York Times* reported the views of Major General Claire Chennault, founder of the American Volunteer Group (the famed Flying Tigers) and former U.S. Army Air Forces commander in China:

Russia's entry into the Japanese war was the decisive factor in speeding its end and would have been so even if no atomic bombs had been dropped. . . .[7]

Even more forcefully, on September 20, 1945, the famous "hawk" who commanded the Twenty-first Bomber Command, Major General Curtis E. LeMay (as reported in *The New York Herald Tribune*) publicly

said flatly at one press conference that the atomic bomb "had nothing to do with the end of the war." He said the war would have been over in two weeks without the use of the atomic bomb or the Russian entry into the war.[8]

The verbatim transcript of the press conference provides these details:

LeMay: The war would have been over in two weeks without the Russians entering and without the atomic bomb.
The Press: You mean that, sir? Without the Russians and the atomic bomb?
LeMay: Yes, with the B-29. . . .
The Press: General, why use the atomic bomb? Why did we use it then?
LeMay: Well, the other people were not convinced. . . .
The Press: Had they not surrendered because of the atomic bomb? . . .
LeMay: The atomic bomb had nothing to do with the end of the war at all.[9]

LeMay did not leave it at one press conference. In a November speech to the Ohio Society of New York City he added that it was "obvious that the atomic bomb did not end the war against Japan. Japan was finished long before either one of the two atomic bombs were dropped. They gave the Japanese an opportunity to surrender without losing too much face."[10]

The strong public statements made by men like Arnold, Chennault, and LeMay were not simply off-the-cuff reactions. Within the air force the idea that the war would likely end before an invasion could begin was very widespread in 1945. Eaker, for instance, later stated unequivocally: "I knew nobody in [the] high echelons of the AAF who had any question about having to invade Japan."[11]

General George C. Kenney, who commanded Army Air Forces units in the Southwest Pacific, was asked (in 1969): "Both militarily and politically do you believe it was a wise decision to use the atomic bomb on Hiroshima and Nagasaki? . . ." Kenney's response was representative: "No! I think we had the Japs licked anyhow. I think they would have quit probably within a week or so of when they did quit."[12]

Dictated notes found in the recently opened papers of Averell Harriman provide additional insight. After a November 1965 dinner with General Carl "Tooey" Spaatz, who in July 1945 was commander of the Pacific-based U.S. Army Strategic Air Forces (USASTAF), and subsequently chief of staff of the U.S. Air Force—together with Spaatz's one-time deputy commanding general in Europe Frederick L. Anderson—Harriman observed:

Both men were quite critical of Gen. Marshall's rigidity about Japan— they both felt Japan would surrender without use of the bomb, and neither knew why the second bomb was used.[13]

Harriman's private notes also recall his own 1945 understanding:

I know this attitude is correctly described, because I had it from the Air Force when I was in Washington in April '45.[14]

In subsequent years some air force leaders began to modify their positions slightly—either to express support "for the president" or support "in general" for the bombing. Although statements taken out of context have sometimes caused confusion—especially some made at the height of the Cold War—a careful examination of the record underscores the 1945 consensus.

Because of his subsequent fame, the quality and depth of information we have on the views of General Curtis E. LeMay permit us to document variations over time which are not as easily detected in the much more limited record left by less well-known officials:

As early as April 15, 1945, the Associated Press carried a story quoting LeMay as stating publicly that the "destruction of Japan's industry by air blows alone" was possible.[15] In an interview in the mid-1960s, LeMay subsequently explained why he and others judged very early on that the war would likely end before a November 1945 landing could begin:

General Arnold made a visit to our headquarters in the late spring of 1945 and he asked that question: When is the war going to end? . . . We went back to some of the charts we had been showing him showing the rate of activity, the targets we were hitting, and it was completely evident that we were running out of targets along in September and by October there wouldn't really be much to work on, except probably railroads or something of that sort. So we felt that if there were no targets left in Japan, certainly there probably wouldn't be much war left.[16]

LeMay's after-the-fact recollection is supported by this entry in Arnold's June 1945 diary:

. . . LeMay's staff showed how Japan's industrial facilities would be completely destroyed by October 1st. 30 large and small cities, all to go, then Japan will have none of the things needed to supply an Army, Navy or Air Force. She cannot continue her fighting after her reserve supplies are gone. October 1st—we will see. We did it in Germany with much more difficult targets and much more intense antiaircraft. Why not in Japan? We will see.[17]

Additional confirming evidence of LeMay's 1945 thinking comes from Brigadier General Roscoe C. Wilson, chief of staff of the 316th Bomb Wing (which, as of June 1945, was based at Okinawa as part of the XXI Bomber Command). In a 1961 interview Wilson recalled

that LeMay said just before the end of the war, "just give me another month and I'll destroy Japan." LeMay felt, as did the Navy, that an invasion of Japan wasn't necessary. He saw that we had the Japanese licked. His planes were encountering little or no air opposition because the Japanese fighters were out of fuel. Without the bomb LeMay could have destroyed all the Japanese cities anyway.[18]

Another wartime subordinate, Lieutenant General Glen Martin, operations officer of the 20th Air Force (interviewed in 1978), summed up LeMay's 1945 views this way:

. . . LeMay saw the end of the war coming as a result of concentrated airpower. He had seen enough of the mining to know—as it turned out, it cut the intercoastal shipping down by 90 percent. Fantastic. He had seen enough of the bombing particularly after the low-level raids to know that the Japanese were just going to have no place to hide. They weren't going to be able to have any fighters. They weren't going to be able to have any fuel to put them in. They weren't going to have any industry. He saw what happened a few months later well in advance.[19]

After the war, LeMay became one of the nation's leading proponents of nuclear deterrence as commander of the U.S. Strategic Air Command (SAC). As his status changed he temporarily reversed his previous public and private statements somewhat—especially in situations where his own straightforward language could be tempered by editorial assistants. Even as he did, however, he commonly hedged his position, arguing not that the bomb had been needed to end the war before an invasion could begin, but rather that if it shortened the war at all (even "a few days") he believed it had been a good thing to do. Here, for instance, is a statement taken from *Mission with LeMay: My Story*, the book he wrote with MacKinlay Kantor in 1965:

Certainly I did not and do not decry the use of the bomb. Anything which will achieve the desired results should be employed. If those bombs shortened the war only by days, they rendered an inestimable service, and so did the men who were responsible for their construction and delivery. There was no transgression, no venturing into a field illicit and immoral, as has so often been charged.[20]

LeMay's next sentence points to a rather different issue—that of ultimate responsibility:

Soldiers were ordered to do a job. They did it.[21]

LeMay also argued that

If a nuclear weapon shortened the war by only a week, probably it saved more lives than were taken by that single glare of heat and radiation.[22]

In an extended 1965 interview LeMay offered the following slightly different variation:

I guess I was one of many who didn't actually realize the explosive power and potential of the bomb. However, I agreed then with dropping it, and still believe the decision to drop it was correct. . . . While the war with Japan could have been won without dropping either of the two atomic bombs, I am certain in my own mind that they significantly shortened the war and, therefore, saved lives in the long run. We all wanted to end the war before an invasion of Japan became necessary.[23]

Here the explicit 1945 statements are simply abandoned and the phrasing "by a few days" or "only a week" becomes "significantly shortened the war." In *Mission*, LeMay also asks himself a series of questions in a mock interview:

Do you think that by relying solely on incendiary attack, you could have knocked Japan out of the war, thus precluding any invasion of the Japanese homeland until after the collapse came?

Yes. I think it could have happened.

Then it would have been possible to force Japan out of the war, and thus end the conflict, without actually employing atomic weapons?

It might have been possible.

I don't want to be a Monday morning quarterback. Never did. I'll say it again: *I think it might have been possible.*[24]

By 1970—having made a foray into politics as George Wallace's 1968 vice-presidential running mate—LeMay's position was revised (slightly) again. In an interview on file at the U.S. Air Force Academy Library, LeMay expressed his support for the decision to use the atomic bomb, but then went on to explain:

> There were less people killed than if we had to invade, and I do think it shortened the war a little bit. True, the war had been won with conventional weapons; true, we probably could have eventually got out of the war, Japan would have capitulated without dropping. . . . We didn't know exactly how long it would take if we let nature take its course with the normal weapons. By dropping it, I think, we probably speeded things up just a little bit. So my point was that I thought by dropping it, even though it was a potent weapon, we would probably save lives in the long run by doing it, by shortening the war.[25]

The language here now is "probably speeded things up just a little bit." (In the same interview, LeMay also stressed that "It was [a] civilian decision all the way through."[26])

By 1985 LeMay had retired, and his (unedited) emphasis had shifted yet again. Now there was no longer any significant attempt to justify the bombings. In a frank interview published in the *Omaha World-Herald* he returned to the position he had stated openly in 1945: "I felt there was no need to use them [atomic weapons]."

> We were doing the job with incendiaries. We were hurting Japan badly. . . . We went ahead and dropped the bombs because President Truman told me to do it. . . .
> All the atomic bomb did was, in all probability, save a few days.[27]

One final shift was to come in 1988. Now in his early eighties, LeMay stated (with editorial assistance) an even more complex and somewhat confusing position in *Superfortress*, a book he wrote with Bill Yenne. He first pointed out, "Throughout the rest of the world it was clear that the nuclear strikes were the straw that broke the camel's back" and he then continued:

> They were, however, merely straws among straws. They were part of the mix of ordnance—high explosive, incendiary, mines, *and* nuclear— that together proved to be Japan's undoing, all of which was delivered onto Japan *from the air* by the B-29s of the U.S. Twentieth Air Force.[28]

LeMay (and Yenne) then endorsed the decision in the following language:

> Even given that strategic bombing could have ended the war without the atomic bomb, I think it was a wise decision to drop the bomb because

this action *did* hasten the surrender process already underway. . . . What guided me in all my thinking, and guided all our efforts—the reason the Twenty-First Bomber Command worked like no other command during the war and the thing that kept us going—was the million men we were going to lose if we had to invade Japan. That says nothing of the Japanese losses, although we didn't give a damn about them at the time. We were worried primarily about our own people. . . . The atomic bomb probably saved 3 million Japanese, and perhaps a million American casualties.[29]

Here "just a little bit" has become the "surrender process already underway" which is "hastened"—and what LeMay and Yenne say guided LeMay was the expectation that an invasion would otherwise occur which would have cost one million American lives (or—it is unclear—casualties) and three million Japanese casualties.

Although a careful tracing of the variations in statements made by LeMay and others during the Cold War helps clear up the confusion which selective citation has sometimes created, our central concern is with the position air force leaders took in 1945; in particular, with whether at the time they believed the use of the atomic bomb was militarily necessary and so advised President Truman. The evidence so far reviewed makes it difficult to believe that leading generals like Arnold and LeMay made an argument to the president based on overriding military necessity.

That air force leaders did not think the use of the atomic bomb was militarily dictated is even more striking when we reflect on the problem not as it was stated in general terms in subsequent years, but as it was actually posed at the time of the Potsdam Proclamation. We have so far touched only in passing on the two central issues studied at length in Parts I and II—"unconditional surrender" and the Russian option.

What is particularly noteworthy about all the statements made by air force leaders suggesting the war could have been ended before an invasion is that none seems even to have assumed a change in the surrender formula and only one acknowledges the force of a Russian declaration of war.*

Although the two additional strategies could only have enhanced any bid for surrender, they are rarely hinted at in the statements of air force leaders, even though there is little doubt that the issues were clearly understood at the very top. We have mentioned that on June 9 Arnold joined the other members of the JCS to recommend that a statement clarifying unconditional sur-

---

*Chennault's reported view that Russia's declaration of war was decisive is the only statement I have seen by an air force general which discusses the availability and power of this option. (*The New York Times*, August 15, 1945, p. 13.)

render be made at the time of the fall of Okinawa. And on July 16 he joined with the other U.S. Chiefs in urging the British to ask Churchill to speak with Truman about a clarification of the surrender formula.[30]

There is also the matter of whether conventional bombing on its own could have ended the war—a general question much debated in subsequent accounts and post–World War II discussions. Not surprisingly—given the way air force leaders themselves commonly formulated the issue—the question has often been stated in a confusing manner which clouds rather than illuminates the real choices available in 1945.

Discussions of the efficacy of conventional bombing seldom stress the fact that once Truman had chosen not to modify the surrender terms, the problem facing planners was much greater and the length of time conventional bombing might require was much longer. But the evidence we possess nonetheless suggests that in 1945 Arnold and others appear to have argued that conventional bombing on its own would bring surrender even without considering the possibilities presented by modifying the terms (and/or awaiting the Russian attack). LeMay's chief of staff, Brigadier General August Kissner, reports that after his June briefing by LeMay, Arnold exclaimed: "Why can't I have this information in Washington? . . . I've got to have Marshall hear this information. This is all fact and all verified; it's right here."[31]

Arnold, indeed, sent LeMay back to the JCS to give the same briefing he had received in the Pacific, predicting that the air force would run out of targets in September.*

It has been argued in this connection that using the atomic bomb was less costly in human life than the continuation of conventional bombing would have been.[32] Apart from the fact that accounts which urge such a view commonly leave aside questions concerning the surrender formula and the impact of the Russian attack, by early August 1945 very few significant Japanese civilian targets remained to be bombed. Moreover, on July 25 a new targeting directive had been issued which altered bombing priorities.

After consultation with Paul Nitze and other directors of the Strategic Bombing Survey who had studied the results in Europe, city bombing was downplayed in favor of targets that were essential to Japan's war machine.[33] Attacks on urban centers became only the fourth priority, after railway targets, aircraft production, and ammunition depots.[34]†

---

*However, LeMay's report failed to impress Marshall, who, LeMay reports, was exhausted and dozed off during their June meeting. (LeMay and Yenne, *Superfortress*, p. 143.)
†Spaatz carried the new directive out to the Pacific when he assumed command of USASTAF, and although existing procedures, staffing, and ammunition stockpiling kept the city bombing momentum going for a while the new directive (as the U.S. Strategic Bombing Survey noted) "was about to be implemented when the war ended." (The United States Strategic Bombing

* * *

Some additional insight into the thinking of top air force leaders may also be gained from the more limited information we have on the views of Generals Eaker and Spaatz. In a 1959 interview with Marshall biographer Forrest Pogue at the height of the Cold War, Eaker stated: "The Air view was that [the Japanese] were finished. That they had had it."[35] He then went on to add, however:

> Now looking back on it I still feel the war would have been finished without an invasion but I feel very strongly the wisdom of having dropped the bomb at Nagasaki and Hiroshima to insure that we would arrive at a proper posture with this tactic of atomic weapons. I think the Russians now have them and we wouldn't have made that initial [word missing in transcript]. . . .[36]

Here Eaker's clear reaffirmation that the war would in any event have ended without an invasion must be carefully distinguished from his additional after-the-fact argument that using the bomb helped in some way with postwar tactics connected with the Russians.

Eaker did not back away from his most important judgment. In 1974 the previously cited air force historian Herman Wolk wrote asking him to confirm that "as you told me, the AAF view was that militarily it was not necessary to drop the atomic bomb."[37] That conclusion was "valid," Eaker replied.[38] In a similar vein a year later he confirmed to another air force interviewer that his view had been that the atomic bomb "would have little effect and was little needed to finish this war."[39]

General Spaatz's command included the 509th Composite Group, the specialized B-29 unit which dropped the atomic bombs. He arrived in the Pacific theater on July 29,[40] and after an initial review quickly cabled Washington that "unless Japan desires to commit national suicide, they should quit immediately."[41] A few days after the bombing of Hiroshima and Nagasaki, on August 11, 1945, he wrote the following in his diary:

> When the atomic bomb was first discussed with me in Washington I was not in favor of it just as I have never favored the destruction of cities as such with all inhabitants being killed.[42]

Survey, *The Effects of Strategic Bombing on Japan's War Economy*, p. 65, fn. 13.) At the time of the surrender, however, bombing had not yet shifted away from area assaults on population centers. (Michael Sherry, *The Rise of American Air Power*, p. 309.) See also the table of incendiary missions against secondary cities found in Wesley Craven and James Cate, eds., *The Army Air Forces in World War II, Volume V, The Pacific: Matterhorn to Nagasaki, June 1944 to August 1945*, pp. 674–75. Related to this is the obvious point that since the new policy had been approved on military grounds, its implementation could have been speeded had U.S. officials so ordered.

Using somewhat formal language (which may perhaps have been aimed at future writers of history), he continued:

> It was pointed out to me however that the use of the atomic bomb would certainly mean that an invasion would be unnecessary and that thousands of American lives would be saved.[43]

In a far less formal letter written to his wife nine days after Nagasaki was bombed, Spaatz observed:

> The excitement of the atomic bomb almost made the news of the surrender an anti-climax. I am not sure that the former had anything to do with the latter, but we are proud and happy that Japan was brought to her knees with no need for an invasion.[44]

In a 1959 oral history Spaatz stated:

> I didn't think the atomic bomb was necessary on the other hand I didn't think enough about it except to say oh, what the hell this was going to be a terrific black mark on our character the rest of the—to me war is war no matter how you kill them.[45]*

And in 1962 he added that the "idea I had was that if we were not going to have this invasion of Honshu I felt that conventional bombing would do the job."[46]

In 1965 Spaatz emphasized that the mere statement of a threat of continued conventional bombing would have had enormous force:

> I think that had the Japanese been told that we would continue our present bombing until they surrendered and would not invade, but would just keep up this present bombing, that they would have surrendered without the atomic bomb.[47]

In all of this perhaps one of the most telling facts is that at the time, in 1945, Spaatz refused to go forward with the bombings without the direct written order noted earlier. Years later Lieutenant General Thomas Handy, Marshall's deputy chief of staff, recalled:

> Well, Tooey Spaatz came in . . . he said, "They tell me I am supposed to go out there and blow off the whole south end of the Japanese Islands. I've heard a lot about this thing, but my God, I haven't had a

---

*However Spaatz biographer David R. Mets writes that his family recalled that one reason he had been reluctant "to take command of USASTAF in the first place arose from his revulsion over what had happened to the cities of Germany and his expectation of doing even worse to the Japanese." (David R. Mets, *Master of Airpower: General Carl A. Spaatz*, pp. 302–03.)

piece of paper yet and I think I need a piece of paper." "Well," I said, "I agree with you, Tooey. I think you do," and I said, "I guess I'm the fall guy to give it to you."[48]

In his 1962 oral history, Spaatz himself recalled that he gave "notification that I would not drop an atomic bomb on verbal orders—they had to be written—and this was accomplished."[49] And in his 1965 interview—responding to the question, "Did you have any difficulties, for instance, in connection with the dropping of the atomic bomb?"—Spaatz stated: "Well, I had no difficulty in that. I ordered the drop. I first had verbal orders but I insisted on written orders."[50]

Having ensured that written records would clearly define where ultimate responsibility for the decision lay, on various occasions Spaatz stressed:

> The dropping of the atomic bomb was done by a military man under military orders. We're supposed to carry out orders and not question them.[51]

He made the same point in his 1965 interview: "That was purely a political decision, wasn't a military decision. The military man carries out the orders of his political bosses."[52]

Finally, there are indications that Spaatz explicitly challenged the Nagasaki bombing. In his 1962 oral history he told air force interviewers:

> I thought that if we were going to drop the atomic bomb, drop it on the outskirts—say in Tokyo Bay—so that the effects would not be as devastating to the city and the people. I made this suggestion over the phone between the Hiroshima and Nagasaki bombings and I was told to go ahead with our targets.[53]

Glen Martin offered this related report in 1978 concerning Spaatz's August 1945 views:

> I think the recommendation attributed to "Tooey" Spaatz . . . was to drop the first atomic bomb as a *demonstration* rather than on a target. . . . I can't vouch for it. I didn't hear him say it, but my understanding is that he did make that recommendation.[54]

As noted, Spaatz—the commanding general of the U.S. Army Strategic Air Forces—later told Ambassador Harriman that even he did not know why a second bomb had been used against Nagasaki.*

---

*Once the presidential go-ahead decision was made, Spaatz also recommended the vicinity of Tokyo for a possible third bomb. (Kirkpatrick to Nimitz and Spaatz, August 9, 1945, "August 1–15, 1945 official," Box 24, Spaatz Papers, LC; Spaatz to Norstad, August 10, 1945, "August 1945," Box 21, Spaatz Papers, LC; Special Radio Teletype Conference, August 14, 1945,

* * *

Two significant puzzles in the record must be mentioned. We have noted that Arnold's deputy, Ira C. Eaker, represented the air force at the June 18 White House planning meeting with President Truman. The full minutes of this meeting released in 1960 end with the enigmatic statement: "THE PRESIDENT and the Chiefs of Staff then discussed certain other matters,"[55] almost certainly meaning (as we have seen) the atomic bomb issue.

The following exchange took place in the middle of the 1959 interview Eaker had with Marshall biographer Forrest Pogue:

> *Eaker:* The President . . . was to make the decision about whether to drop the atom bomb at Hiroshima. Mr. Truman turned to Gen. Marshall as the dean of the meeting and asked his view and was apparently prepared to make a decision and Gen. Marshall said, "Mr. President, the new junior member of our group is the airman present. I think we ought to hear his view." It was always that way. Gen. Marshall always made it a point that the Air people although junior at least got to say their pieces.
>
> *Pogue:* This was at Potsdam.
>
> *Eaker:* No, this was
>
> *Pogue:* Oh, before you left to go to Potsdam. I didn't realize that that decision had been made just before you left, but the actual test was not made untill [sic] you were on the high seas.[56]

As Pogue's question suggests, the idea that Truman made the decision to use the atomic bomb *at this time* is not at all established by other reports. On the other hand, as we have repeatedly noted, there are numerous gaps throughout the record, and secrecy about such matters in 1945 was extraordinary. Eaker, however, did not let the matter drop; he reiterated his report and added further details in subsequent comments. In 1972, for instance, he told an air force interviewer:

> . . . I went as the Air Force representative with General Marshall to the conference in President Truman's office and I heard the conversation,

---

"August 1945," Box 21, LC.) Subsequently he stated that "in case" a third bomb was used, a strike on the capital would "impress the top political and military leaders. . . ." (Spaatz interview with Len Giovannitti for NBC White Paper, p. 8, 1964, Box 103, Feis Papers, LC.) Spaatz tried to hold down conventional city bombing during the war's final days, and on August 14, after seeing pictures of Hiroshima, he cabled, "Hope there is never occasion to use another [bomb]. . . ." (Telecon Conference, August 14, 1945, "August 1945," Box 21, Spaatz Papers, LC.) That same day, in reply to Arnold's overall comment that AAF "operations have been coordinated with all my superiors all the way to the top," Spaatz replied, "Thank God." (Special Radio Teletype Conference, August 14, 1945, "August 1945," Box 21, LC.) See also Michael S. Sherry, *The Rise of American Air Power,* p. 345.

the recommendations and decision announced by the President. The President asked me to remain behind and when I did so, he said, "Here is a letter to General Spaatz directing him to drop the atom bomb and I trust you to deliver it."[57]*

In a 1974 article in *Air Force Magazine* on the occasion of Spaatz's death, Eaker also stated simply that "When President Truman decided to drop the atomic bombs, he handed me a letter directing General Spaatz to carry out that mission."[58] (In 1959 Eaker told Pogue: "It was plain obvious to everybody at that time that the President had made up his mind. . . ."[59])

In this vein, too, in 1983 Eaker's former aide-de-camp James Parton sent Eaker a letter containing information based on a conversation with Colonel Lou Cummings, ex–base commander at Andrews Air Force Base:

He [Cummings] said that you once told him that you were in President Truman's office, representing the Air Force since General Spaatz† was in the Pacific, when Truman made the decision to drop the A-bomb on Hiroshima.[60]

Parton's own question to Eaker remains:

True? Who else was there? Was it truly a meeting to make the decision, or was it ceremonial? Any details would be grist for the mill.[61]

If Eaker's recollection of the June 18 meeting is accurate, it would mean the decision to use the atomic bomb had been firmly made (and a letter to this effect possibly written) by this time—a view which accords with the report given by Ralph Bard to historian Alice Smith: "he has the impression that the Committee approved a decision that had already been made."[62]

As to the second puzzle: Numerous accounts make it clear that given the position of the air force in 1945, Arnold regularly supported Marshall in meetings of the Joint Chiefs of Staff. Air Force Brigadier General Laurence Kuter put it this way in a 1974 oral history:

*The interviewer, Lieutenant Colonel Joe B. Green, proceeded to ask Eaker whether he would describe the meeting in any more detail. Eaker replied, "It has been done and it is in my files and my records. I believe that it is obtainable elsewhere and I am not at all sure of the classification status of it. So I think that it would be better to get it from that earlier record. I was asked that question by the Air Staff and it is in their record. I would be happy to do it after we have checked the classification because I remember very well the nature of the meeting." (Eaker interview with Lieutenant Colonel Joe B. Green, March 20, 1972, p. 42, Senior Officers Oral History Program, Eaker Papers, USAMHI.) To my knowledge, no such document has ever been found.

†Parton apparently means General Arnold.

Arnold was Marshall's subordinate, and there was never a minute's doubt about it on King's part. Marshall never made a point of it. At the same time, Arnold never differed with Marshall at the Joint table. He may have privately, I rather doubt that, but never at the Joint table.[63]

A particular aspect of this situational logic bears on issues directly related to the Hiroshima decision.

Despite the fact that top air force leaders—especially Arnold—did not believe the use of the atomic bomb was militarily necessary, we know that Arnold instructed "Eaker to support the position taken by General Marshall" at the June 18 meeting.[64] Historians are also aware that something else, something beyond the fact of the subordinate position of the air force, was involved. As Paul Nitze has pointed out,

> [Arnold] had made an agreement with General Marshall that . . . if General Marshall backed the air force on having an independent strategic air command [during the war] and that after the war would support a separate air force, separated from the army, that then General Arnold would always vote with General Marshall in this meeting of the . . . Joint Chiefs. So General Arnold was silenced by that agreement, so he agreed with General Marshall and General Marshall insisted as I say, upon the army invading the home island of Japan.[65]

Furthermore, that this "arrangement" was generally understood within air force leadership circles is confirmed by many other reports. For instance, in his 1980 book *Strategic Air War Against Japan*, Brigadier General Haywood S. Hansell (who commanded the Twenty-first Bomber Command until his replacement by LeMay in January 1945) describes Arnold as believing that

> this policy position [of supporting invasion planning, and being prepared to support the actual invasion] would be an expression of loyalty to General Marshall, who had stood "in loco parentis" behind the birth and growth of the Army Air Forces and who had given evidence of supporting a separate Air Force, coequal with the Army and Navy after the war.[66]

All of this, of course, was earlier in the summer, during the "planning" phase (and specifically at the June 18 meeting). In 1990 Paul Nitze was interviewed about the general understanding and its relationship to the specific decision to use the atomic bomb. He was asked about

> some sort of understanding that Arnold would support Marshall in general but also in specific on the nuclear weapon decision, and either implicitly or explicitly Marshall would support also the buildup of the

postwar independent air force. Is that something that you recollect as well or have I stated it inaccurately?[67]

Nitze commented:

That's my recollection. I don't know who told me that or why or how but that's my recollection, the lay of the land.[68]

That Arnold did not believe the use of the atomic bomb was necessary—and that in general he supported Marshall in exchange for Marshall's support for an independent air force—are matters of record. That despite his own views on the subject he supported the bombing of Hiroshima in part for the latter reasons, as Nitze's statement suggests, is a logical if as yet unproven hypothesis.*

*In connection with the "deal," see also Wolk, "The B-29, the A-Bomb, and the Japanese Surrender, p. 60.

Chapter 28

ARMY LEADERS

---

*[General Douglas] MacArthur once spoke to me very elo-
quently about it, pacing the floor of his apartment in the
Waldorf. . . . MacArthur, you see, was a soldier. He believed
in using force only against military targets, and that is why
the nuclear thing turned him off, which I think speaks well
of him.*

—Former President Richard M. Nixon, July 1985

With one possible exception, the judgment that use of the atomic bomb was
not dictated by considerations of military necessity also appears to have been
widely shared by army leaders. On numerous occasions after the war, for instance, the man in charge in the Pacific, General Douglas MacArthur, stated
his military judgment that the bomb had been unnecessary. MacArthur, however, was never asked for a formal military review of the issue; nor was he
asked his informal advice as to whether the bomb was needed.* Indeed, he
was only apprised of the new weapon's existence after Spaatz briefed him on
August 1.[1]

The day after Hiroshima was bombed MacArthur's pilot, Weldon E.
Rhoades, privately noted in his diary:

> General MacArthur definitely is appalled and depressed by this Frank-
> enstein monster [the bomb]. I had a long talk with him today, necessi-
> tated by the impending trip to Okinawa. He wants time to think this
> thing out, so he has postponed the trip to some future date to be decided
> later.[2]

Herbert Hoover met with MacArthur alone for several hours on a tour of
the Pacific in early May 1946. His private diary states:

---

*See below for Truman's subsequent claims, p. 548.

I told MacArthur of my memorandum of mid-May 1945 to Truman, that peace could be had with Japan by which our major objectives would be accomplished. MacArthur said that was correct and that we would have avoided all of the losses, the Atomic bomb, and the entry of Russia into Manchuria.[3]

In his 1987 book *The Pathology of Power*, Norman Cousins also recalled that during a postwar interview with MacArthur, "I was surprised to learn he had not even been consulted." Moreover:

he saw no military justification for the dropping of the bomb. The war might have ended weeks earlier, he said, if the United States had agreed, as it later did anyway, to the retention of the institution of the emperor.[4]*

Undoubtedly if MacArthur's "opinion had been requested before the Potsdam ultimatum," writes military historian D. Clayton James, "he would have strongly urged an assurance to the Japanese that the Emperor would be retained."[5] In a 1974 oral history interview Marshall's deputy, Lieutenant General Thomas Handy, also recalled 1945 discussions with MacArthur's staff along the same lines—especially concerning whether Japanese units would surrender: "They said, MacArthur's people and they were right as it turned out, 'If they got the word from the Japanese Emperor they would.' "[6]

Although MacArthur's views were to shift during the Korean War, at this time he clearly had reservations about the bombing of civilians. In his recent study of strategic bombing, Conrad C. Crane points out that MacArthur "adhered to the most restrictive bombing policy concerning civilians" and that, as a matter of principle, he took the laws of war very seriously. On one occasion when Japanese commanders at Rabaul complained that a hospital had been bombed, MacArthur went so far as to provide the Japanese command structure with maps (via a neutral embassy) to support his staff's claim that the real target was an anti-aircraft battery situated next to the hospital.[7]†

---

*The judgment not only that the atomic bomb was not needed, but that the war could have been concluded earlier if the Emperor's position had been clarified, points to a much larger issue. Since a clarification of the unconditional surrender formula was delayed in significant part because of the atomic bomb, as we shall see, some analysts have suggested that the new weapon itself may well have prolonged the war and therefore cost, rather than saved, lives.

†Crane notes that MacArthur never had "to deal directly with the issue of bombing Japanese civilians during his operations. . . ." (Conrad C. Crane, *Bombs, Cities, and Civilians: American Airpower Strategy in World War II* [Lawrence, 1993], p. 123.) On the other hand, following a June meeting with MacArthur, Arnold noted that he generally supported AAF bombing efforts, and the Fifth Air Force under MacArthur's command hit cities on Kyushu near the end of the war. (Arnold Diary, June 17, 1945, "Pacific Trip," Box 272, Arnold Papers, LC; William M. Leary, ed., *We Shall Return!: MacArthur's Commanders and the Defeat of Japan, 1942–1945* [Lexington, 1988], p. 205.)

Similar views appear to have been common among top officers who had MacArthur's confidence. An internal June 1945 memorandum by Brigadier General Bonner Fellers describes LeMay's firebomb raids as "one of the most ruthless and barbaric killings of non-combatants in all history."[8] In a postwar article copyrighted by the Veterans of Foreign Wars and reprinted in *Reader's Digest*, Fellers also stated: "Obviously . . . the atomic bomb neither induced the Emperor's decision to surrender nor had any effect on the ultimate outcome of the war."[9]

As many writers have noted, MacArthur was later to express contradictory views on some World War II issues (particularly concerning Russian entry into the war).[10] However, his public and private statements concerning the atomic bomb were generally consistent.[11] Perhaps the best insight into MacArthur's view comes from a surprising source. In a long 1985 interview on the occasion of the fortieth anniversary of the Hiroshima bombing, former president Richard Nixon recalled that

> MacArthur once spoke to me very eloquently about it, pacing the floor of his apartment in the Waldorf. He thought it a tragedy that the Bomb was ever exploded. MacArthur believed that the same restrictions ought to apply to atomic weapons as to conventional weapons, that the military objective should always be limited damage to noncombatants. . . . MacArthur, you see, was a soldier. He believed in using force only against military targets, and that is why the nuclear thing turned him off, which I think speaks well of him.[12]

During the course of the Cold War, as we have seen, some military leaders altered their public statements, backtracking slightly on their clearly stated 1945 views. In one important case, the high-level officer in question was at first apparently reluctant to criticize the Hiroshima decision in public—only allowing himself to do so many years after the fact. Perhaps it is understandable, for the issue involved not only his personal opinion but the question of the direct advice he gave to Stimson—and, more important, to Truman himself—before the atomic bomb was used.

As we have repeatedly noted, there is no dispute about Eisenhower's continuing judgment that the use of the atomic bomb was completely unnecessary. However, only one small hint of his thinking appears to have surfaced in 1945. Visiting Moscow shortly after Hiroshima, Eisenhower is reported to have "answered a private question privately" as follows:

> Before the bomb was used, I would have said yes, I was sure we could keep the peace with Russia. Now, I don't know. I had hoped the bomb

wouldn't figure in this war. Until now I would have said that we three, Britain with her mighty fleet, America with the strongest air force, and Russia with the strongest land force on the continent, we three could have guaranteed the peace of the world for a long, long time to come. But now, I don't know. People are frightened and disturbed all over. Everyone feels insecure again.[13]

Though the comment that "I had hoped the bomb wouldn't figure in this war" suggests something less than enthusiastic approval, Eisenhower was very circumspect in his public comments for several years—especially while he still held important official positions. He was chief of staff of the U.S. Army from November 20, 1945, until February 7, 1948, and later (after a brief stint as president of Columbia University) was named the first Supreme Commander of NATO in December 1950, a post he held until 1952. After his election as president of the United States, of course, Eisenhower held an office of even greater public responsibility until January 20, 1961.[14]

Only very slowly during this period—as time passed and once controversial events became matters of history—did Eisenhower offer specific information on his actual feelings, and on discussions he had while at Potsdam in 1945. At first, even his private remarks were guarded. As we have noted, following a "reminiscent luncheon gathering" with top military leaders at the Pentagon in 1947, James Forrestal noted that Eisenhower said he had "begged" Truman not to give anything away to get the Russians into the war because in his opinion "there was no question but that Japan was already thoroughly beaten."[15]

Among Eisenhower's papers is a copy of the powerful July 16, 1945, memorandum Stimson wrote for Truman urging multiple warnings before the atomic bomb was used.[16] It is unclear when this was given to him. In his 1948 book *Crusade in Europe*, however, Eisenhower included the following brief account of his "personal and immediate" reaction on hearing of plans for the atomic attack from Stimson:

> I expressed the hope that we would never have to use such a thing [the atomic bomb] against any enemy because I disliked seeing the United States take the lead in introducing into war something as horrible and destructive as this new weapon was described to be. . . .[17]

Additional information also comes to us from two documents from Eisenhower's presidential years. In a letter of April 9, 1955, from him to businessman William D. Pawley, the president recalled a recent dinner discussion in which he apparently had made comments similar to those noted by Forrestal in 1947:

. . . I think I said that I recommended strongly that we not *ask* the Russians to come into the Far Eastern War.[18]

He then went on to explain:

One of the reasons I gave was that in my opinion it was impossible to keep them out of that war—another was that they were not needed . . .
      . . . as we neared the end of the European war and during the weeks following thereon, my staff and I became convinced that the Japanese were on their last legs. (I assume that a lot of other people, by that time, believed the same thing.)[19]

Eisenhower elaborated further:

On the other hand, when I suggested to Secretary of War Stimson, who was then in Europe, that we avoid using the atomic bomb, he stated that it was going to be used because it would save hundreds of thousands of American lives.[20]

Although this carefully worded presidential letter confirms (and makes more explicit) that Eisenhower had urged that the bomb not be used, he also quickly defended Stimson (albeit in somewhat confused wording which seems to contradict his own statement that the atomic bomb was not necessary):

So that [*sic*] I suppose that as far as I was concerned I still believed in the difficulty of any assault against Japan. But you must remember that there had been many bloody battles in the Pacific and certainly you cannot blame anyone for wanting to save American lives.[21]

The second document from this period is a White House memorandum written by Brigadier General Andrew Goodpaster (at the time staff secretary and defense liaison officer to the president), based on an interview with Herbert Feis on April 6, 1960:

Professor Feis next asked the President what he knew about the atomic weapon and what his views were on that in the late days of the war. The President said he had Secretary Stimson to dinner the same day, during the Potsdam meetings, of the report that the "baby was born." Mr. Stimson told him about the weapon. The President said he told Mr. Stimson that he hoped his country would not be the first to use this weapon. He recalled that Mr. Stimson really hit the ceiling over this. The President said he knew from intelligence reports that the Japanese were at that moment trying to surrender.* The Japanese in Tokyo were in communication with their Ambassador in Moscow about this.[22]

The Goodpaster memorandum also notes that Eisenhower said that because of this,

> He did not think there was anything like the value in bringing the Russians into the Pacific war or the need for doing so which others seemed to feel.[23]

The first full public statement by Eisenhower (beyond the brief mention in *Crusade in Europe*) is contained in the book the president wrote immediately after leaving office, his 1963 *Mandate for Change*. In it Eisenhower also recalled the meeting at which Stimson told him about plans to use the bomb, and, as we have seen, added the following information:

> During his recitation of the relevant facts, I had been conscious of a feeling of depression and so I voiced to him my grave misgivings, first on the basis of my belief that Japan was already defeated and that dropping the bomb was completely unnecessary, and secondly because I thought that our country should avoid shocking world opinion by the use of a weapon whose employment was, I thought, no longer mandatory as a measure to save American lives. It was my belief that Japan was, at that very moment, seeking some way to surrender with a minimum loss of "face." The Secretary was deeply perturbed by my attitude, almost angrily refuting the reasons I gave for my quick conclusions.[24]

Nor did Eisenhower leave it at that. In an interview with *Newsweek* he elaborated on his meeting with Stimson and provided still more details:

> We'd had a nice evening together at headquarters in Germany, nice dinner, everything was fine. Then [Secretary of War Henry L.] Stimson got this cable saying the bomb had been perfected and was ready to be dropped. The cable was in code, you know the way they do it, "The lamb is born" or some damn thing like that. So then he told me they were going to drop it on the Japanese. Well, I listened, and I didn't volunteer anything because, after all, my war was over in Europe, and it wasn't up to me. But I was getting more and more depressed just thinking about it. Then he asked for my opinion, so I told him I was against

---

*Feis adds, specifically, that this "he had in part derived from the intercepts . . . ." Also, fifteen years after the fact, Eisenhower seems possibly to have scrambled the dates a bit. We know he definitely met with the secretary of war on July 20 and July 27; the "Baby" message came in on July 16.

it on two counts. First, the Japanese were ready to surrender and it wasn't necessary to hit them with that awful thing. Second, I hated to see our country be the first to use such a weapon. Well . . . the old gentleman got furious. And I can see how he would. After all, it had been his responsibility to push for all the huge expenditure to develop the bomb, which of course he had a right to do and *was* right to do. Still, it was an awful problem.[25]

It may perhaps be relevant to note that Eisenhower began work on *Mandate for Change* in early 1961 shortly after he decided to speak out publicly on another controversial matter. His famous Farewell Address—warning against the dangers of the "military-industrial complex"—was delivered on January 17, 1961:

In the councils of government, we must guard against the acquisition of unwarranted influence, whether sought or unsought, by the military-industrial complex. The potential for the disastrous rise of misplaced power exists and will persist.

We must never let the weight of this combination endanger our liberties or democratic processes. We should take nothing for granted. Only an alert and knowledgeable citizenry can compel the proper meshing of the huge industrial and military machinery of defense with our peaceful methods and goals, so that security and liberty may prosper together.[26]

In the same speech Eisenhower also felt it important to declare:

. . . in holding scientific research and discovery in respect, as we should, we must also be alert to the . . . danger that public policy could itself become the captive of a scientific-technological elite.[27]

Although some were later to question Eisenhower's memory and the accuracy of his many statements recalling discussions of the atomic bomb in 1945,[28] confirming evidence also comes from a 1967 oral history interview conducted with his son John:

The story has been told, I'm sure, of Dad's reaction to the atomic bomb, when Stimson told him about it, at the time of the Potsdam conference. Stimson told Dad about this thing, and Dad was very depressed about this new bomb, although its possibility had been at the back of everybody's mind. There'd been special efforts to hit heavy water plants in Trondheim in the bombardment programs. The idea of Hitler developing a bomb that could have turned the tide in this European war was not to be sneezed at completely. So Dad had some idea of it, but he was sorry that it had been developed, and was against its being used.

Stimson was one of the few people who had known about it early. As a matter of fact, when Truman was a Senator, Truman and his investigating committee had allowed Stimson to spend a considerable amount of money, pots full of it, without question, based on Stimson's good word, and Truman had not investigated what this money was going for. It was going for the Manhattan Project. So Stimson had a tremendous personal investment in this atomic bomb.

Dad said, "Well, again, it's none of my business, but I'd sure hate to see it used, because Japan's licked anyway, and they know it."[29]

In his 1974 book *Strictly Personal*, John Eisenhower provided this personal recollection of another specific (and to him highly important) moment at the time of Potsdam:

> From my point of view, however, the most significant part of the Potsdam Conference occurred after we had returned to Bad Homburg, Dad's residence outside Frankfurt. Just before going to bed that evening the two of us sat and visited for a few minutes in his bedroom. He was sitting on the edge of his single bed, up against the wall, his .32-calibre pistol lying on the side table. The room was dim, with only the reading light on. He had something on his mind, and finally he came out with it: "John," he said, "Secretary Stimson told me something today. He says that they've now developed a new bomb, based on splitting the atom, that'll be so powerful that it exceeds the imagination of man. They're thinking very seriously about using this against the Japanese. This is, of course, highly secret."
>
> The news was too much for me to comprehend, and I could make no comment. I doubt that I could say anything very helpful, because Dad's reaction was obviously one of depression. He talked quietly and softly, shaking his head slowly as he spoke.[30]

One of Eisenhower's most intimate associates was his brother Milton, president of Johns Hopkins University. In *Mandate for Change*, Eisenhower emphasizes "the close relationship between us for a matter of sixty years"—and recalls especially that "during the entire period of my two administrations" his brother was a "constant adviser, a confidant and, at times, a personal representative."[31]

In his own 1974 book *The President Is Calling*, Milton Eisenhower also discusses the decision to use the atomic bomb. Although he presents only his personal opinion, his own thinking may reflect understandings he arrived at in conversations with the president. For instance, the book contains one very candid passage which brings to mind Eisenhower's more nuanced 1945 observation in Moscow that "before the bomb was used . . . I would have said yes, I was sure we could keep the peace with Russia. Now I don't know. . . .

Everyone feels insecure again. . . ."[32] Milton Eisenhower puts a related point more forcefully:

> Our employment of this new force at Hiroshima and Nagasaki was a supreme provocation to other nations, especially the Soviet Union. . . .[33]

He then continues with an explicit condemnation of the bombings:

> Moreover, its use violated the normal standards of warfare by wiping out entire populations, mostly civilians, in the target cities. . . . Certainly what happened at Hiroshima and Nagasaki will forever be on the conscience of the American people.[34]

There is finally the question of the advice Dwight Eisenhower gave directly to Truman. On the basis of numerous private interviews historian Stephen Ambrose reports the following in his biography of Eisenhower:

> There was one additional matter on which Eisenhower gave Truman advice and was ignored. It concerned the use of the atomic bomb. Eisenhower first heard of the bomb during the Potsdam Conference; from that moment on, until his death, it occupied, along with the Russians, a central position in his thinking. . . .
>
> When Stimson said the United States proposed to use the bomb against Japan, Eisenhower voiced ". . . my grave misgivings. . . ." . . . Three days later, on July 20, Eisenhower flew to Berlin, where he met with Truman and his principal advisors. Again Eisenhower recommended against using the bomb, and again was ignored.[35]*

The views of the chief of staff, George Marshall, present a puzzle to modern researchers. The contemporaneous documentary evidence strongly suggests that before the atomic bomb was used Marshall understood the war could likely be ended through a combination of altering the surrender formula and awaiting the Russian shock. Thus, to recall:

• On May 29, 1945, Marshall joined with Stimson and Forrestal in approving Grew's proposal that the unconditional surrender language be clarified (but, with Stimson, proposed a delay in timing).

• On June 9, 1945, along with the other members of the Joint Chiefs of

---

*In a letter to me dated July 30, 1993, Ambrose stated: "In the interviews, he [Eisenhower] frequently expressed his disagreement with the use of the bomb—he almost always referred to the bomb as 'that awful thing.' " In a letter to me dated January 28, 1993, Ambrose stressed: "In conversation with me he was insistant [sic] that he advised HST [Harry S. Truman] it was not necessary." In a further letter to me dated May 27, 1995, however, he said that he now doubted "that [Eisenhower] spoke directly to HST. . . ."

Staff, he recommended that a statement clarifying the surrender terms be issued on the fall of Okinawa (which occurred on June 21).

• On July 16, 1945, at Potsdam—again along with the other members of the Joint Chiefs—Marshall urged the British to ask Churchill to approach Truman about clarifying the terms,[36] and on July 18 he led the Chiefs in recommending appropriate language to the president directly.

Related to this is evidence we have of Marshall's awareness that if the terms were not changed, the Japanese would fight to the finish. Again, to recall: In a 1954 interview Truman described a

> conversation I had with Marshal [*sic*] in which he made the statement that if the million two hundred thousand Japanese in China were able to be supplied without reference to Japan it [*sic*] would never surrender unless the Emperor of Japan ordered it and he was of the opinion that if the Emperor made such an order we could get complete surrender— that was the only way we could get it.[37]

Marshall is also on record as having felt strongly that the atomic bomb should not be used without warning against a city.

Finally, as early as June 18, 1945—well before the dramatic news that the Emperor had personally intervened to attempt to end the war—Marshall advised President Truman that the Russian declaration of war could be decisive.

Evidence from Marshall's top staff points in this same direction:

As we have noted, Colonel Charles "Tick" Bonesteel, 1945 chief of the War Department Operations Division Policy Section, subsequently recalled: "[T]he poor damn Japanese were putting feelers out by the ton so to speak, through Russia. . . ."[38] Brigadier General Carter W. Clarke, the army officer in charge of preparing the MAGIC summaries in 1945, stated (in a 1959 historical interview):

> we brought them [the Japanese] down to an abject surrender through the accelerated sinking of their merchant marine and hunger alone, and when we didn't need to do it, and we knew we didn't need to do it, and they knew that we knew we didn't need to do it, we used them as an experiment for two atomic bombs.[39]

On July 10, 1945—again, even before the Emperor's initiative—Brigadier General George A. Lincoln, chief of the Strategy and Policy Group of the Operations Division, wrote Lieutenant General Albert C. Wedemeyer, the commander of U.S. forces in China:

> The B-29s are doing such a swell job that some people think the Japs will quit without an invasion. This may be so providing we can get an

adequate formula defining unconditional surrender. That we have attempted to do, and it has gone from this group through channels to the
President. My personal opinion, which isn't much, is that there are two
psychological days in this war; that is, the day after we persuade Russia
to enter, if we can, and the day after we get what the Japs recognize as
a secure beachhead in Japan. Around either of those times we might get
a capitulation, providing we have an adequate definition of what capitulation means.[40]

Finally, there is this suggestive fragment from Telford Taylor's 1992 book
The Anatomy of the Nuremberg Trials: A Personal Memoir. Taylor, who was
a Nuremberg prosecutor, recalled that as a 1945 reserve colonel in the intelligence branch of the Army he had returned to Washington "about May 22"
and

discussed the situation in the Pacific theater with my superiors in the intelligence division, particularly with Colonel Alfred McCormack, in
peacetime a law partner of John J. McCloy, the Assistant Secretary of
War. I knew that McCormack was as well informed and otherwise
equipped as anyone to assess the prospects of the war against Japan.
Whether or not he was in on the secret of the atom bomb I do not
know,* but he told me categorically that the Japanese military situation
was hopeless, that the Emperor's advisers knew it, and that intercepted
Japanese diplomatic messages revealed their anxiety to make peace. He
thought it highly unlikely that an invasion of the Japanese mainland
would be necessary or that the war would last much longer.[41]†

On the other hand, Marshall gave two interviews in the 1950s, shortly before his death, which run directly contrary to the thrust of the 1945 evidence.
In the first—an extended 1957 discussion with Forrest Pogue, the historian
preparing his biography—Marshall stated:

There were hundreds and hundreds of thousands of American lives
involved in this thing, as well as hundreds of billions of money. They
[the Japanese] had been perfectly ruthless. We had notified them
of the bomb.‡ They didn't choose to believe that. And what they
needed was shock action, and they got it. I think it was very wise to
use it.[42]

*He was not, so far as is known.
†On the basis of this information, Taylor altered his own plans and did not request a transfer to
the Pacific.
‡To my knowledge, no evidence of this exists.

Marshall then reiterated his judgment that:

> We had to end the war. We had to save American lives. We had to halt
> this terrific expenditure of money which was reaching a stupendous to-
> tal. And there was no way to economize on it until we stopped the war.
> The bomb stopped the war. Therefore, it was justifiable.[43]

In the second set of mid-1950s interviews, with John P. Sutherland of *U.S.
News and World Report* in 1954 and 1955,* Marshall was only slightly less
forceful:

> When we got the bombs we had to use them in the best possible way
> to save American lives. . . . I heard all kinds of discussions on how we
> should use the first one. Some wanted to drop it on the Sea of Japan.†
> But we didn't know how it would work in water. It might be a dud or
> get out of control. We just didn't know.
>
> Others wanted to drop it in a rice paddy to save the lives of the Jap-
> anese. But we only had two, and the situation demanded shock action.
> After using these two bombs against Japan, there would be nothing in
> reserve. . . .
>
> We had to assume that a force of 2.5 million Japanese would fight to
> the death, fight as they did on all those islands we attacked. We figured
> that in their homeland they would fight even harder. We felt this despite
> what generals with cigars in their mouths had to say about bombing the
> Japanese into submission.‡ We killed 100,000 Japanese in one raid in
> one night, but it didn't mean a thing insofar as actually beating the
> Japanese.[44]

One possible explanation of the difference between the thrust of the contemporaneous documents and the after-the-fact interviews is that the chief of
staff was extremely cautious—that he did not want to take any chances, that
as the top army planner he always had to assume worst-case possibilities.
The heavy casualties the Japanese took at Okinawa may also have influenced
his opinion—and in the end he may have disagreed with the military judgments of Leahy, King, Arnold, Eisenhower, and the others.

Also, of course, the Manhattan Project was Marshall's direct responsibility.
Groves reported to the chief of staff, who personally signed for the vast expenditures needed to build the bomb.[45]

Another possible explanation is that Marshall did not wish to criticize

---

*But not made public until November 2, 1959, after Marshall's death.
†This may possibly be a reference to a suggestion Spaatz claimed to have made for a water-
targeting in Tokyo Bay in lieu of a second city attack before Nagasaki was bombed. See
above, p. 345.
‡This would seem to be an obvious reference to LeMay.

Truman or take public issue with so momentous an official decision. The chief of staff was widely recognized to be a soldier's soldier—and an extremely discreet official.* Marshall served under both Roosevelt and Truman and in 1947 was named secretary of state. It would have been totally out of character for him to have publicly criticized Harry Truman, directly or indirectly—especially at the height of the Cold War.[46]

A contributing factor may also have to do with a particular facet of Cold War political history. During the 1950s, ardent anti-communist politicians—especially Senator Joseph McCarthy—targeted Marshall as one of the men who "lost" China. Marshall had undertaken a postwar mission to attempt to arrange a compromise between the communist forces under Mao Tse-tung and Nationalist forces under Chiang Kai-shek; one of McCarthy's charges was that Marshall (together with Secretary of State Dean Acheson) had "created the China policy which, destroying China, robbed us of a great and friendly ally, a buffer against the Soviet imperialism with which we are now at war."[47]

Criticism that Marshall was "soft on Communism" also can be traced to the fact that he had strongly urged the importance of Russian participation in the war. He did so initially, as noted, to pin down the Japanese armies in Manchuria; and, subsequently—as Japan's situation worsened—to shock Japan into surrender. A McCarthy ally—anti-communist journalist Walter Trohan—claimed in the *American Mercury* that at "the Yalta Conference in February 1945 General Marshall helped to deliver Asia to Russia just as he had helped to deliver Europe at Teheran."[48] This was part and parcel of what McCarthy castigated as "the carefully planned retreat from victory."[49]

The situational logic created by the political atmosphere of the 1950s may have made it all but impossible for Marshall to argue publicly what he had argued privately in 1945—namely, that there was a good chance a Russian attack would end the war. Not only would this have played directly into the hands of McCarthy and others, it would also have undermined the Truman Administration's public argument that the atomic bomb was the only way an invasion could have been avoided.

Marshall apparently never spoke to these issues on the record. Privately, however, he is reported to have stated to columnist Clayton Fritchey: "if I have to explain at this point that I am not a traitor to the United States, I hardly think it's worth it."[50]

That the two unqualified endorsements of the Hiroshima decision Marshall

---

*A typical instance: In 1974, when Army Air Force Brigadier General Laurence Kuter recalled which of the participants at the Yalta conference wrote books about their experience, he observed that "Marshall, of course, wrote nothing." (Kuter interview with Hugh N. Ahmann and Tom Sturm, September 30–October 3, 1974, p. 344, United States Air Force Oral History Program, AFHRA.)

made at the height of the Cold War did not represent his entire viewpoint is suggested by careful scrutiny of the 1950s texts themselves. Here is an additional excerpt from one of the interviews with Sutherland:

> I think the surrender was brought about by the helplessness of the situation—the defeat in Okinawa, the destruction of practically all shipping in the China, Yellow, and Japan Seas, the elimination of the Japanese Navy, the isolation of the Japanese forces in North China by the loss of sea control and by the intervention of the Russian forces in Manchuria, with the destruction of that [Kwantung] Army, the bombardment of the Japanese land installations by Admiral Halsey's Fleet [Admiral William F. Halsey Jr., Commander, U.S. Third Fleet], the terrific bombing of Japanese cities by our Air Force and, finally, by the explosions of the atomic bombs at Hiroshima and Nagasaki.
>
> The last-mentioned, in my opinion, precipitated the surrender by months.[51]

The ambiguity of the phrase "by months" is noteworthy after the long list of other factors deemed responsible for the Japanese collapse—and, too, when it is remembered that a first landing was still months away, in November. How quickly a surrender could have been achieved was also obviously dependent on whether assurances for the Emperor were offered (a point which is notably absent from this listing).*

Keenly aware of the issues, Pogue asked Marshall directly whether or not he tried to get the unconditional surrender formula "dropped." Contrary to the evidence—or at least contrary to the overriding thrust of the evidence (since here the word "dropped" may be ambiguous)—the usually forthright Marshall responded: "I don't recall that I did."[52]

Recently discovered 1949 interview notes made by Dr. Edward P. Lilly for a JCS history of psychological warfare also record that

> He [Marshall] stated that the military did not have any responsibility along this line, that the civilians, especially the President, decided if the bomb would be used and the military decided where and when, with the civilian advisers having the right to make additional recommendations regarding both the where and the when.[53]

---

*Another formulation in Marshall's interview with Pogue is: "I think it was quite necessary to drop the bomb in order to shorten the war." (Pogue, *George C. Marshall Interviews and Reminiscences for Forrest C. Pogue*, p. 391.) The last three words are undeniable: how could the bombs not have "shortened the war?" Again, with months to go before a possible first landing, this obviously is not the same as arguing that the bomb was needed to end the war without an invasion.

Corroborating evidence on this point comes from Pogue's additional research suggesting that "when Marshall was asked to make a recommendation, [John J.] McCloy says that he was struck by Marshall's resistance to
making a final decision"[54]—and that McCloy reported Marshall as declaring:
"Don't ask *me* to make the decision. . . ."[55] Writing to Fred L. Hadsel,
Director of the George C. Marshall Foundation, in 1985, McCloy himself
elaborated on an incident that was

> very vivid in my mind. . . . I can recall as if it were yesterday, [Mar-
> shall's] insistence to me that whether we should drop an atomic bomb
> on Japan was a matter for the President to decide, not the Chief of Staff
> since it was not a military question . . . the question of whether we
> should drop this new bomb on Japan, in his judgment, involved such
> imponderable considerations as to remove it from the field of a military
> decision.[56]

In a letter-memorandum to William Parsons the same year, McCloy recalled: "General Marshall was right when he said you must not ask me to declare that a surprise nuclear attack on Japan is a military necessity. It is not
a military problem. It is a problem of deeply significant imponderables."[57]

Further, in a text made public after his death (in journalist James Reston's
1991 *Deadline: A Memoir*), McCloy wrote that

> General Marshall was anxious to leave the main questions regarding the
> use of the bomb to the president. He treated it as a matter involving the
> highest form of policy for which he looked to political leaders for direc-
> tion. He believed that the decision should not be left to the military
> leaders. He never indicated to me that he opposed the use of it, but the
> general is on record as favoring that warning of some kind should
> be given in advance to the Japanese before any atomic bomb would be
> dropped.[58]

Finally, there is this report in the previously cited oral history interview
with General Eisenhower's son John:

> I'm quite sure also, although I'm not in a position to say so, that Mar-
> shall felt the same way [as Eisenhower]—that the bomb did not need to
> be used because the Japs were licked.[59]

At present, there is no satisfactory way to resolve the contradictions in the
evidence concerning Marshall's views. Given the 1945 documentary record,
however, it is difficult to believe that Marshall advised Truman that using the
atomic bomb without warning against an urban population center was the
only option available.

Perhaps the simplest explanation is the most obvious: Although Marshall had ardently sought to change the surrender formula, once Truman rejected his advice and decided not to offer assurances concerning the Emperor, then the only plausible way to achieve the commander in chief's stated objective of "unconditional surrender" was, indeed, to use the atomic bomb.

Chapter 29

ADDITIONAL PERSPECTIVES

---

*The Japanese were already on their last legs; but if they were
given to think that a rigid interpretation would be placed
on the term "Unconditional Surrender," and that their Emperor—to them the Son of Heaven—would be treated as a
war criminal, every man, woman, and child would fight on
till Domesday. If, on the other hand, the terms of surrender
were phrased in such a way as to appear to preserve the right
of their Emperor to order them to lay down their arms, they
would do so without a moment's hesitation.*

—British Major General Sir Hastings Ismay,
chief of staff to the minister of defence, *Memoirs*

U.S. military figures—especially Marshall—were not ignorant of the
political-diplomatic calculations being made by James Byrnes and Harry
Truman in connection with the atomic bomb. For instance, a memorandum
declassified in the 1980s from General Groves to Marshall—dated July 30,
shortly after the Potsdam Proclamation was issued—discusses a possible improvement in the atomic bomb which might take ten days to implement. In
language which seems clearly to reflect other understandings at this level,
Groves then goes on to advise the chief of staff:

> From what I know of the world situation, it would seem wiser not to
> make this change until after the effects of the present bomb are
> determined.[1]

Despite all that has been written in the last fifty years, that so many military leaders expressed themselves as critical of the use of the atomic bomb
is simply not realized by the American public. Nor have the implications
been faced of the fact that almost every prominent military leader seems

clearly to have understood the atomic bomb was not needed to achieve a Japanese surrender without an invasion.

Something about the way we have been willing to think about this issue, it appears, has led to avoidance and oversimplification. Few accounts even mention such basic information as the comments contained in the published memoirs of Arnold, King, Leahy, and others. Hardly any point out that strictly military judgments of "necessity" must in any event turn in significant part on how the issue of unconditional surrender is treated—and whether or not the massive shock of a Russian declaration of war is assumed.

Some who acknowledge the dissenting views of military figures attempt to dismiss their arguments by reference to secondary issues. The air force, it is said, did not like the atomic bomb because it might diminish the role of the B-29; Leahy, it has been noted, was always a skeptic about the new atomic technology; Eisenhower was not directly involved in planning for the Far East; et cetera.

It is possible or even likely that the views of one or another of the military chiefs were tainted by such considerations. That most of the main figures understood the use of the atomic bomb was not a military necessity, however, cannot easily be brushed aside by reference to secondary matters. Nor, as we have seen, does the modern evidence indicate they were offering only after the fact judgments for public consumption.

Confusion over the question of "military necessity" has sometimes arisen because careful attention has not been paid to the difference between "planning" for the invasion and its actual authorization at various times during the spring and summer of 1945.

Throughout the spring a high-level debate took place over whether to go forward with an all-out exercise aimed at the ultimate invasion.[2] An agreed plan was endorsed by the Joint Chiefs on May 25 and, after high-level review, accepted by the president on June 18.[3] However, as we have seen, even as planning continued, the day after the White House meeting, at the Cabinet-level (State, War, and Navy) Committee of Three meeting,

> there was a pretty strong feeling that it would be deplorable if we have to go through the military program with all its stubborn fighting to a finish. We agreed that it is necessary now to plan and prepare to go through, but it became very evident today in the discussion that we all feel that some way should be found of inducing Japan to yield without a fight to the finish. . . .[4]

Since it was impossible to be certain when the war would end, planning was simply prudent. As Lieutenant General John E. Hull subsequently observed: "[W]e could stop that plan [for invasion] at anytime in its execution by just a signal out of Washington to the troops to change their destination."[5]

At Potsdam the U.S. and British Joint Chiefs consolidated specific arrangements which left the control of "operational strategy" in the Pacific "in the hands of the United States Chiefs of Staff."[6] In addition, command zones for British and American operations in East Asia and the Western Pacific were delineated.[7] At the same time, however, on July 21, orders were sent to MacArthur and the U.S. commander in China, Lieutenant General Albert Wedemeyer,

> to make plans to take immediate advantage of favorable circumstances such as the sudden collapse or surrender of Japan, at present there are increasing indications that it may prove necessary to take action within the near future on the basis of Japanese capitulation, possibly before Russian entry.[8]

Five days later, on July 26, the Joint Chiefs sent MacArthur and Nimitz an urgent cable stating: "Coordination of plans for the procedure to be followed in the event of Japanese governmental surrender is now a pressing necessity."[9]

Confusion in subsequent discussions can also be traced to factors intimately related to the planning effort. Quite apart from the need to prepare for all contingencies, it was necessary, in order to keep the pressure on, to make every effort to convince Japan that an invasion was, in fact, inevitable; there was to be no let-up in public appearances. This inevitably also involved convincing lower-level military planners, U.S. troops, and the U.S. public of this idea.

As we have seen, a memorandum of April 26 from General Hull to Marshall had warned that there was "considerable doubt in the minds of his [Nimitz's] staff that we really intend to carry through with the invasion program. . . ." Hull therefore had urged:

> It is most desirable that at an early date this decision as to the course we are to adopt be firmed and announced to all concerned.[10]

At the June 18 White House meeting, Marshall declared that "every individual moving to the Pacific should be indoctrinated with a firm determination to see it [the invasion] through."[11] Truman also made every effort to indicate that there would be no compromise, that U.S. intentions were firm.

Further perspective on the issue of "military necessity" is also offered by considering from a slightly different angle the two official studies of the decision we have previously cited:

To recall, the U.S. Strategic Bombing Survey concluded the war would have ended ". . . certainly prior to 31 December and in all probability prior to 1 November 1945 . . ."[12]; and the 1946 War Department Military Intelligence Division study judged that the "Japanese leaders had decided to surrender and were merely looking for sufficient pretext to convince the die-hard Army Group that Japan had lost the war. . . ."

> The entry of Russia into the war would almost certainly have furnished this pretext, and would have been sufficient to convince all responsible leaders that surrender was unavoidable.[13]

Quite apart from the substance of such official evaluations, it is a commonplace among students of bureaucracy that important studies which contradict the views of top officials rarely see the light of day—or even get beyond the initial stages. That these two studies progressed to these conclusions (one publicly, the other within the government) suggests a continuing climate of opinion within the U.S. military that the atomic bombings were, at the very least, not absolutely essential.

A similar conclusion is suggested by the fact that several high-level journalists with close ties to leading military figures also commonly expressed critical judgments after the war—judgments that almost certainly reflected conversations they had had with important military sources. We noted that Hanson Baldwin of *The New York Times* understood that Leahy viewed a clarification of the surrender terms as a "minor detail." In his 1950 book *Great Mistakes of the War* Baldwin, himself an Annapolis graduate, argued that in using "the atomic bomb against a prostrate and defeated Japan . . ."

> We were . . . twice guilty. We dropped the bomb at a time when Japan already was negotiating for an end of the war but before those negotiations could come to fruition. We demanded unconditional surrender, then dropped the bomb and accepted conditional surrender, a sequence which indicates pretty clearly that the Japanese would have surrendered, even if the bomb had not been dropped, had the Potsdam Declaration included our promise to permit the Emperor to remain on his imperial throne.[14]

Another journalist close to military thinking—Carl W. Borklund—reported in his book *Men of the Pentagon* that Secretary of the Navy Forrestal "believed, and wanted to convince Truman, that the Japanese were anxiously looking for a face-saving way to surrender, that bringing Russia in would accomplish nothing except to extend Communist tentacles in the Far East, and that killing thousands of helpless civilians on the Japanese mainland was a brutal, and probably unnecessary, act."

Much better, thought Forrestal, to drop the bomb on a solely military target, or, at least, on a sparsely populated area and then issue a warning. That, he believed, might be all the face-saving excuse a desperate Japanese Government would need to surrender.[15]

Further evidence has also emerged over the last fifty years concerning the thinking of top British leaders present at Potsdam. Most of these officials also clearly did not believe use of the atomic bomb was dictated by military necessity—and several offered at least indirect reports of the thinking of American leaders with whom they were in day-to-day contact.

Sir Alan Brooke, for instance, chief of the Imperial General Staff, was adamant on the significance of the surrender formula. On July 11, 1945, he wrote:

[U]nconditional surrender was an objective which we did not require and which, if achieved, might even impede the liberation of territory now occupied by the Japanese, as it appeared likely that the Japanese forces in those territories would only capitulate if instructed to do so by the Emperor.[16]

As we have noted, during the July 16 Potsdam discussions with the U.S. Joint Chiefs of Staff, Brooke and the other British military leaders strongly urged a modification of the surrender formula, and the next day General Ismay reported to Churchill that intelligence estimates had concluded that if this were done the war would likely end when Russia attacked. Ismay put it this way in his 1960 memoirs:

The Japanese were already on their last legs; but if they were given to think that a rigid interpretation would be placed on the term "Unconditional Surrender," and that their Emperor—to them the Son of Heaven—would be treated as a war criminal, every man, woman, and child would fight on till Domesday. If, on the other hand, the terms of surrender were phrased in such a way as to appear to preserve the right of their Emperor to order them to lay down their arms, they would do so without a moment's hesitation.[17]

On hearing that the atomic test was successful, Ismay's first reaction was one of "revulsion."[18]

And shortly after the bombing of Hiroshima, J. C. Stearndale-Bennett, the head of the Far Eastern Department of the Foreign Office, observed (in language reminiscent of Marshall's May 29 recommendation):

The present tactics in the employment of the bomb . . . seem likely to do the maximum damage to our own cause. . . . A more intelligent way of proceeding would surely have been to have given publicity to the discovery and its possible effects, to have given an ultimatum with a time limit to the Japanese before using it, and to have declared the intention of the Allies to drop a bomb on a given city after a given date by way of demonstration, the date being fixed so as to give time for the evacuation of the city.[19]

Perhaps the last word on British views of the atomic bomb is best left to Churchill—both because of his clarity and because of what he has to teach us of American attitudes he sensed at Potsdam.

Churchill, as we have seen, seems to have judged that a combination of the Russian threat and a modification of the surrender formula would be likely to end the war. As early as September 1944 he had argued that merely announcing Russia would join the Allies in the Pacific "might be decisive";[20] in February at Yalta he had suggested that modifying the surrender formula might save a year and a half of war.[21] At Potsdam on July 18 he had raised the surrender issue directly with Truman:

> I dwelt upon the tremendous cost in American life and, to a smaller extent, in British life which would be involved in forcing "unconditional surrender" upon the Japanese. It was for him to consider whether this might not be expressed in some other way, so that we got all the essentials for future peace and security, and yet left the Japanese some show of saving their military honour and some assurance of their national existence, after they had complied with all safeguards necessary for the conqueror.[22]

After the war Churchill was nonetheless to write that "the decision whether or not to use the atomic bomb to compel the surrender of Japan was never even an issue." One reason may perhaps be that he clearly became convinced of its other advantages. As we have noted, five days after he failed to get Truman to modify the surrender terms, Brooke's diary records that Churchill—having read Groves' full report of the atomic test—"had absorbed all the minor American exaggerations . . . now we could say, 'If you insist on doing this or that, well. . . . And then where are the Russians!' "[23]

Churchill's reversal of attitude—both in private and then in public statements—anticipates and helps illuminate how quickly and easily a different gloss can be put on historical events in general and issues of military necessity in particular. Despite what we now can document of the prime minister's actual 1945 views, within a week after the atomic bombs were used Churchill attacked critics in a House of Commons speech in uncompromising terms. The only alternative to the atomic bomb, he now claimed, would have been to sacrifice "a million American, and a quarter million British lives in the desperate battles and massacres of an invasion of Japan."[24]

PART VII

Endgame

At present, in accordance with the Imperial will, there is a unanimous determination to seek the good offices of the Russians in ending the war. . . .

—Foreign Minister Togo
to Ambassador Sato, August 2, 1945

Chapter 30

RELATIONS OF FRANKNESS

---

*I recall your telling me with considerable relish, after your
return, just how the possibility [of the forthcoming use of the
atomic bomb] had been broken to Stalin. . . .*
　　　—Leslie R. Groves to James F. Byrnes, April 28, 1952

The publication of the Potsdam Proclamation on July 26, after deletion of the
paragraph twelve assurances for the Emperor, was a major turning point.
From this time forward the terms of reference facing Japan were firmly set
and the remaining days of the Big Three Conference flowed quickly over
into the first week of August and the run-up to the atomic bombings on August 6 and August 9.

The dominant preoccupation of the Potsdam meeting itself, of course, still
had to do with diplomatic matters in Europe and Asia; and it is important to
keep in mind that the man closest to President Truman throughout this period
was not a military adviser but Secretary of State James F. Byrnes.

By all accounts not only was Byrnes the central figure, he also was extremely adept at controlling access to the president—thereby keeping other,
contending advice at a distance. We have noted Stimson's complaint about
this in his diary entry of July 19. Four days later, on July 23, he wrote: "I
am finding myself crippled by not knowing what happens in the meetings in
the late afternoon and evening. . . ."[1]

Joseph E. Davies noted that "Stimson said, frankly, that he regretted that
he did not have more to do here. He had been the head, he said, of three
delegations to three international conferences of this kind."[2] And McCloy
later recalled "Stimson sitting there in the garden excluded from all the
interviews."[3]

Not only were Truman and Byrnes at sea together on the way to Potsdam,
their staterooms separated only by a narrow passageway, on arrival the two
men and Leahy, along with their aides, shared a villa at Potsdam: The pres-

ident had a suite on the second floor, Byrnes the suite just below, on the first floor.

It is also clear that Byrnes was not much interested in advice from those with long experience in the key areas. State Department Far Eastern expert Eugene H. Dooman was queried about his experiences with Byrnes by historian Herbert Feis in 1960:

> I have nothing to offer on the Potsdam conference. I might as well have stayed in Washington for all the use I was. The Department sent over a fairly large crowd of specialists, [John Carter] Vincent, George Allen and myself among others, and so far as I know none of us was ever consulted by Byrnes or Truman for that matter.[4]

Averell Harriman later recalled that Byrnes "though[t] he could deal with all these things off his cuff, you know." (Harriman added: "He's my candidate for the worst Secretary of State during an important period of the life of our Republic.")[5]

There are also huge, easily identifiable but commonly overlooked gaps in the materials we have at our disposal, even at this late date. At the most obvious level, the official log refers to meetings involving Byrnes and Truman on July 16, 17, 18, 21, 24, 27 and 28—for which few records have so far appeared.[6]

Futhermore, the government editors of the Potsdam papers long ago pointed out that they had "found no complete record . . . of those messages and memoranda copies of which were forwarded by air pouch to the Delegation at Babelsberg."

> It was standard practice, however, for the Department of State to forward by daily pouch information copies of important incoming telegrams, airgrams, and despatches, as well as carbon copies of certain memoranda prepared in Washington, so that the United States Delegation to the Berlin Conference was fully informed of world developments taking place during the Conference.[7]

Again, Byrnes and Truman undoubtedly had numerous unrecorded private talks in the evenings and at meals, and as they were driven back and forth to the conference.[8] From what we know of their warm and informal relationship at this point in time—and from reports of similar relationships between presidents and very close associates—almost certainly some of the most important thinking and talking went on at these times rather than at meetings where formal notes were being taken.[9]

Also among the important documents concerned with this period which are still not available to the public are the full diaries of Walter Brown—the man who kept such close tabs on Byrnes' daily activities that Byrnes felt compelled to radically edit (and even rewrite) the materials which were passed on to government archivists. The Brown diary excerpts reworked by Byrnes pertain especially to the Potsdam time frame.

Truman himself, as we shall explore more fully in Book II, suppressed important information concerning this period as well; and there are also significant gaps in material in the president's personal journal which became available after his death.

With these reminders of where real power lay at Potsdam—and, given our lack of evidence, the need for extreme care in attempting to reconstruct the conversations Truman and Byrnes may have had privately—several aspects of the atomic bomb story as it unfolded in the final period may be briefly noted. Especially important are instances where modern documents shed new light on old issues. In this order, they are: the question of whether to include the Russians in a warning—and whether (and what) to tell them about the bomb; two highly important but little discussed initiatives by navy officials; the confused response of the Japanese to mixed signals sent from Washington and Potsdam; and the additional decisions made by Truman and Byrnes in the last weeks before the new atomic weapons were used.

The emerging context was set by several obvious and continuing realities as the Potsdam Conference drew to a close: the unwavering U.S. demand for unconditional surrender still hampered open peace maneuvering within the Japanese cabinet. The position gave hard-line army leaders a trump card against early surrender proposals. The army could continue to argue that the Emperor-god might be removed, perhaps tried as a war criminal, possibly even hanged.

Related to this was another decision which set the terms of reference for the use of the atomic bomb: We have noted Churchill's suggestion that merely including the Soviet Union in the warning proclamation would have enormous impact. At Yalta he had also emphasized the importance of a "four-power ultimatum."[10]* Records on the narrow question of precisely how Washington officials estimated the impact of having Russia join in as one of the powers issuing the ultimatum are very skimpy. We do know, however, that the proposed warning taken by the U.S. delegation to Potsdam began with this heading: "DRAFT PROCLAMATION BY THE HEADS OF STATE, U.S.—U.K.—[U.S.S.R.]—CHINA." A brief follow-on note stated:

[Delete matters inside brackets if U.S.S.R. not in war]

The opening passages of the draft Proclamation read:

*See above, p. 92.

We,—the President of the United States, the Prime Minister of Great Britain, [the Generalissimo of the Soviet Union] and the President of the Republic of China; . . ."[11]

In June, Secretary of State Stettinius had advised Grew that "The four power ultimatum suggested by the Prime Minister at Yalta seems well worth our careful consideration at this time. Certainly, if there is any chance of success, we should explore every possibility at the Big Three meeting, and make a real effort to get the Russians to agree to join us. . . ."[12]

It appears that initial guidance on the inclusion of Russia was set at the June 26 meeting of the Committee of Three. Here again, however, difficulties with the record have caused confusion over the years. For instance, a related section of the Forrestal diary was also eliminated from early materials. The published diary contains the following passage concerning this meeting:

> The question of a public statement to the Japanese people outlining the terms of surrender was discussed. Mr. Stimson read a memorandum which he proposed to send to the President.* It was agreed by all present that such a statement should be made before the actual invasion of the homeland of Japan was begun. . . . Suggestion was made that Berlin [the Potsdam Conference] might be an appropriate platform.[13]

"A public statement" in this context appears in no way unusual and would hardly catch the eye, since a presidential statement had been under consideration for some time. When the full text of the diary became available, however, it was found that the material italicized below had been deleted from this passage—material which suggests that quite another specific possibility had also been under consideration:

> The question of a public statement to the Japanese people outlining the terms of surrender was discussed. Mr. Stimson read a memorandum which he proposed to send to the President. It was agreed by all present that such a statement should be made before the actual invasion of the homeland of Japan was begun. *It was further agreed that such a statement should emanate from the President, either alone or possibly in conjunction with the chiefs of state of the British and the Russians.* Suggestion was made that Berlin [Potsdam] might be an appropriate platform *from which to issue such a statement*.[14]

Both versions also include the following language: "McCloy stated that Stalin would definitely raise the question at the Berlin meeting. He stated

---

*This became the memorandum that Stimson gave to the president on July 2. See above, pp. 76–78.

that Stalin had no strong views on the subject either way but was prepared to follow our leadership in the matter."[15]

The term "either way" in McCloy's statement is interesting: with the underscored materials, it is obvious the meaning is that Stalin could accept a statement with or without Russia as a signatory. Without the excised material the passage appears to suggest, vaguely, that Stalin would have little objection to a presidential statement either sometime generally before an invasion or, specifically, at Potsdam.

The important point, of course, is the material alluding to possible Russian participation in the statement has simply been eliminated.

This passage, of course, also points to the fact that a warning issued from a gathering of the Big Three would likely have a more powerful impact on the Japanese than a statement issued simultaneously from Washington and London by the United States and Great Britain alone, as was common in other instances during the war.

Clearly a political decision as to whether to include the Russians had not as yet been made on this date. That the issue was still open at this point in time is also suggested by Grew's notation on June 18 that the "President asked me to have the subject [of the warning] entered on the agenda for the Big Three meeting. . . ."[16] Similarly, the next day, June 19, Stimson's diary records that Marshall reminded him of "an additional sanction to our warning in the shape of an entry by the Russians into the war."[17]

Finally, both the draft approved in principle on June 26 by the Committee of Three and Stimson's formal July 2 memorandum to Truman recommending the (undiluted) version of what became the Potsdam Proclamation also state:

> It is therefore my conclusion that a carefully timed warning be given to Japan by the chief representatives of the United States, Great Britain, China and, if then a belligerent, Russia, calling upon Japan to surrender and permit the occupation of her country in order to insure its complete demilitarization for the sake of the future peace.

In the body of his memorandum Stimson notes that "if Russia is part of the threat" the Red Army attack "must not have progressed too far," but allows, too, that the attack may not, in fact, be "actual" at the time the proclamation is released.[18]

Similarly, the subcommittee appointed by the Committee of Three to study terms and timing (headed by McCloy) concluded that "if possible U.S., U.K. and China should join in the declaration and, if Russia was then or about to become a belligerent, it should also join."[19]

As promised, Grew sent Truman a memorandum dated June 30 on "Sub-

jects for Discussion at the Meeting of the Three Heads of Government." Item
three on this "agenda" reads: "Unconditional Surrender of Japan and Policy
toward Liberated Areas in the Far East." The State Department recommended the following for Big Three discussion:

> (a) That the principal United Nations at war with Japan issue a joint
> statement outlining the program for the treatment of a defeated Japan in
> the hope that Japan will be more inclined to accept unconditional sur-
> render if the Japanese people know what their future is to be.[20]

It appears that striking this item was one of Byrnes' first official acts. In
a memorandum sent to the British and Soviet governments on July 5, two
days after he became secretary of state, Byrnes provided a "list of topics
which the President may wish to raise for discussion at the forthcoming
meeting of the Heads of Government." The memorandum covered the same
points on Grew's agenda with one exception: point 3, "Unconditional Surrender of Japan and Policy toward Liberated Areas in the Far East," had been
eliminated. In its place was the following vague and noncommittal sentence:

> It is likewise expected that there will be some discussion of policy with
> respect to the Far East.[21]

Indeed, the government editors of these documents subsequently noted that:

> This entire item is deleted in pencil in [Assistant Secretary of State
> James C.] Dunn's copy of the Briefing Book.[22]

From the perspective of our inquiry, the significant point is that sometime
before it was issued, all mention of the Soviet Union was dropped from the
Potsdam Proclamation. At the least, this weakened the threat and potential
impact of the ultimatum—and, if we are to accept Churchill's judgment, may
have effectively eliminated one promising option for ending the war.

It also caused considerable confusion in Japan.*

We have seen that the Emperor's initiative had stirred Stimson to urgently
press for an immediate release of the proclamation. As he put it in his
July 16 memorandum to the president: "[W]e are at the psychological moment to commence our warnings." In this same memorandum he explicitly
raised the question of "whether the Russians are to be notified of our intentions in advance in this regard."[23] (The question itself suggests that the idea
of including the Russians—as opposed to simply notifying them—had been

---

*See below, pp. 404–07.

dropped by now.*) The answer to Stimson's question is that the Russians were not notified; the proclamation was simply issued from the site of the Big Three meeting with no advance notice given.

This lack of candor was clearly irritating to the Russians: the Potsdam Proclamation was hardly a matter which could be kept secret. That it had been prepared while Truman and Byrnes were at Potsdam—and the fact kept from them—was self-evident the day it was made public. When Stalin brought the latest Japanese proposals to the president's attention on July 28, Walter Brown notes, "There was reason to detect [in his remarks] . . . a mild reflection on the United States for not consulting Russia before sending the joint proclamation to Japan."[24] The plenary session minutes record Stalin as saying:

> Although the Soviet Delegation had not been informed when the [Potsdam Proclamation] document was drawn up against Japan they, nevertheless, were informing the other countries of this approach.
>   The translator then read the communications from Ambassador Saito [*sic*]. . . .

Truman's response to the information provided by the Soviet premier at this point is also of interest in its own right. The minutes report that after the translator read the Japanese message:

> THE PRESIDENT thanked Marshal Stalin. The President added that he understood the Soviet Delegation had two questions to take up this evening.[25]

He was obviously uninterested in following up on the Japanese overtures.

Given Truman's intense interest in Soviet help prior to the full news of the atomic test—and given his marked disinterest thereafter—it is difficult to believe the Russians did not suspect something peculiar was afoot during this period. Nor was this the only reversal of presidential attitude during the conference.

In fact, the odd situation vis-à-vis the Russians gave rise to a number of minor tactical problems at Potsdam. We have noted that after the Groves report came in the Soong negotiations were used to stall the Red Army attack—even though the United States "officially" was simultaneously urging Soviet entry into the war. On July 29, the day after the above exchange,

---

*We noted above Stimson's advice on July 2 that he believed the Japanese would listen to reason, and his sense in the same memorandum that an early warning which clarified the terms might end the war. Note here that the assumption that the Russians were not, in fact, needed further indicates Stimson's seeming confidence that the war could probably be ended without either the bomb or the Russians.

Molotov asked the president for some kind of letter stating formally what the United States had been privately urging for almost two years—that it would like the Soviet Union to join the conflict:

> Mr. Molotov said that in conclusion he had one other matter that the Marshal wished him to take up and that was the immediate cause of the Soviet entry into the Far Eastern war. He said that the Soviet government considered that the best method would be for the United States, England and the other allies in the Far Eastern war to address a formal request to the Soviet government for its entry into the war. He said that this could be based on the refusal of the Japanese to accept the recent ultimatum to surrender and made on the basis of shortening the war and saving of lives. He added, of course, that the Soviet government was assuming that the agreement with the Chinese would be signed before the Soviet Union entered the war.[26]

Now clearly unwilling to commit such a request to paper, Byrnes and his assistant Benjamin Cohen spent the better part of the afternoon trying to devise a response to the Soviet request. "We had, of course, begun to hope that a Japanese surrender might be imminent and we did not want to urge the Russians to enter the war," Byrnes subsequently recalled.[27]

Two days later, on July 31, Truman sent Stalin a legalistic letter which in the words of Walter Brown "was not a rejection of the Russian proposal but neither was it a warm request that the Soviet Union enter the war."[28] Truman stated that under the terms of the Moscow Declaration and of Articles 106 and 103 of the new United Nations Charter (although not yet ratified), "it would be proper for the Soviet Union to indicate its willingness to consult and cooperate with other great powers now at war with Japan with a view to joint action. . . ."

Undoubtedly aware of the limitations of this document, in a covering note Truman told Stalin: "If you decide to use it, it will be all right. However, if you decide to issue a statement basing your action on other grounds or for any other reason prefer not to use this letter, it will be satisfactory to me."[29]

We can imagine the Soviet leader's puzzlement upon receiving so circuitous a letter from an American president who had been urgently seeking Red Army help only a few days earlier. Moreover, as what Robert Messer has called "a game of cat and mouse" went forward with Stalin to delay a declaration of war, at quite another level U.S. military officials were allowed to encourage a sense of cooperation with Moscow's top military leaders.[30] Thus, at the same time Byrnes and Truman actively attempted to stall the Russians, on July 24 the Combined Chiefs of Staff formally agreed to "encourage Russian entry into the war against Japan," and to provide "such aid to her war-making capacity as may be necessary and practicable in connection therewith."[31] On the same day, the Combined Chiefs met with their Soviet counterparts and exchanged information on future operations. Two days later—on July 26—the Soviet and American Chiefs met again, this time to discuss precise coordination of Allied operations. The meeting was amicable, and agreement was quickly reached on all subjects under discussion.[32]

A specific development which occurred during the military discussions allows further insight into Byrnes' tactics and sense of timing. It is sometimes thought that his attempt to hold off a Russian attack until Japan surrendered was foolhardy. (McGeorge Bundy, for instance, has written that "he somewhat naively hoped that he could keep Stalin out of the war. . . ."[33]) Careful examination of the dates involved, however, suggests that whatever one thinks of Byrnes' calculation it was not without foundation.

Originally Stalin had promised to enter the war three months after Germany's May 8 defeat, which would have meant August 8. On July 17, Stalin amended this slightly, telling Truman the Red Army would be ready to roll on August 15 if the Soong negotiations were completed.[34] During the July 24 meeting of the Combined Chiefs of Staff, however, the minutes state:

> General [of the Army] Antonov said that Soviet troops were now being concentrated in the Far East and would be ready to commence operations in the last half of August. The actual date, however, would depend upon the result of conferences with Chinese representatives which had not yet been completed.[35]

Byrnes' idea that the Soong negotiations might possibly delay a Red Army attack long enough to end the war fits reasonably well with the "second half of August" timetable indicated by the Soviet military leaders. In the end, of course, Japan's surrender was put forward on August 10 and, after being accepted on August 11, was officially proclaimed on August 14.

Documents found in General Groves' papers during the 1970s also suggest that another well-known related "event" which occurred during the Potsdam meetings may have had a slightly different meaning than has commonly been thought. This involved the moment when Truman approached Stalin to tell him "something" about the atomic bomb.

At the urging of Byrnes, the Interim Committee had recommended there be no disclosure whatsoever of the new weapon. Byrnes' specific worry had been that "if information were given to the Russians, even in general terms, Stalin would ask to be brought into the partnership."[36]

A further development had, however, occurred after these discussions. On June 16, under pressure from scientists in Chicago, the Scientific Panel of the Interim Committee had reconsidered the matter, and now recommended that:

before the weapons are used not only Britain, but also Russia, France, and China be advised that we have made considerable progress in our work on atomic weapons, that these may be ready to use during the present war, and that we would welcome suggestions as to how we can cooperate in making this development contribute to improved international relations.[37]

The full Interim Committee had then met on June 21 to consider the matter, and in turn decided to revise its earlier recommendation. A major problem was the extremely tight schedule. If the Russian allies were kept in the dark and the bomb was simply sprung on them almost immediately after the Potsdam Conference, severe repercussions might occur. Any hope of building the trust needed for postwar control might be lost.

In the hope of securing effective future control and in view of the fact that general information concerning the project would be made public shortly after the Conference, the Committee unanimously agreed that there would be considerable advantage, if suitable opportunity arose, in having the President advise the Russians that we were working on this weapon with every prospect of success and that we expected to use it against Japan.[38]

When George Harrison reported on the meeting to Stimson (who was absent on June 21), he made the committee's reasoning somewhat clearer:

This matter of notice to the Russians was made a subject of thorough discussion at the last meeting of the Interim Committee on June 21. It was unanimously agreed that in view of the importance of securing an effective future control, and in view of the fact that most of the story, other than production secrets, will become known in ——— in any event, there would be considerable advantage, if a suitable opportunity arises at the "Big Three" meeting, in having the President advise the Russians simply that we are working intensely on this weapon and that, if we succeed as we think we will, we plan to use it against the enemy.* Such a statement might will [sic] be supplemented by the statement that in the future, after this war, we would expect to discuss the matter further with a view to insuring that this means of warfare will become a substantial aid in preserving the peace of the world rather than a weapon of terror and destruction.

The central point seemed obvious:

*Blank in original.

Not to give them this prior information at the time of the "Big Three" Conference and within a few weeks thereafter to use the weapon and to make fairly complete statements to the world about its history and development, might well make it impossible ever to enlist Russian cooperation in the set-up of future international controls over this new power.[39]

Just before the president boarded the *Augusta*, Stimson reported the Interim Committee's new recommendation directly: ". . . if [Truman] found that he thought that Stalin was on good enough terms with him, he should shoot off at him what we had arranged, George Harrison and I, in the aide memoire."

> In other words, simply telling him that we were busy with this thing working like the dickens and we knew he was busy with this thing and working like the dickens, and that we were pretty nearly ready and we intended to use it against the enemy, Japan; that if it was satisfactory we proposed to then talk it over with Stalin afterwards, with the purpose of having it make the world peaceful and safe rather than to destroy civilization. If he pressed for details and facts, Truman was simply to tell him that we were not yet prepared to give them.

Stimson's diary continues: "The President listened attentively and then said that he understood and he thought that was the best way to do it."[40] At a Combined Policy Committee meeting the next day (July 4) Stimson explained that "[h]is own opinion had been very much influenced by probable use within a few weeks after the meeting. If nothing was said at this meeting about the T.A. weapon,* its subsequent early use might have a serious effect on the relations of frankness between the three great Allies."[41]

Stimson also discussed the matter with Churchill at Potsdam. Although at first he met with some resistance, after Groves' full report was read the prime minister quickly came around. On July 22, Stimson noted:

> [Churchill] now not only was not worried about giving the Russians information of the matter but was rather inclined to use it as an argument in our favor in the negotiations. The sentiment . . . was unanimous in thinking that it was advisable to tell the Russians at least that we were working on that subject and intended to use it when it was successfully finished.[42]

Churchill and Truman also talked over the question of what to tell Stalin during a lunch meeting on July 18. In a note to the War Cabinet Churchill wrote:

---

*"Tube Alloys," the British code for the atomic bomb.

The President showed me telegrams about the recent experiment, and asked what I thought should be done about telling the Russians. He seemed determined to do this, but asked about the timing and said he thought that the end of the Conference would be best. I replied that if he were resolved to tell it might well be better to hang it on the experiment, which was a new fact on which he and we had only just had knowledge. Therefore he would have a good answer to any question, "Why did you not tell us this before?" He seemed impressed with this idea, and will consider it.[43]

We do not know precisely how or exactly when the president made his decision. However, on July 24, three days after receiving Groves' report, Truman approached Stalin at the end of the day's plenary session. The subsequent report in his memoirs is terse:

I casually mentioned to Stalin that we had a new weapon of unusual destructive force. The Russian Premier showed no special interest. All he said was that he was glad to hear it and hoped we would make "good use of it against the Japanese."[44]*

Several other reports of what happened are also available. Byrnes, for instance, recalled the event in the following way (and that it came about as a result of a conversation he had with Truman):

The President and I discussed whether or not we were obligated to inform Stalin that we had succeeded in developing a powerful weapon and shortly would drop a bomb in Japan. Though there was an understanding that the Soviets would enter the war with Japan three months after Germany surrendered, which would make their entrance about the middle of August, with knowledge of the Japanese peace feeler and the successful bomb test in New Mexico, the President and I hoped that Japan would surrender before then. However, at luncheon we agreed that because it was uncertain, and because the Soviets might soon be our allies in that war, the President should inform Stalin of our intention, but do so in a casual way.

He then informed the British of our plan, in which they concurred. Upon the adjournment of the afternoon session, when we arose from the table, the President, accompanied by our interpreter, Bohlen, walked

---

*In the interviews transcribed while the memoirs were being prepared, Truman states: "He didn't know what I was talking about. I told him that we had been experimenting with this tremendously high explosive in New Mexico and that it had been successful. . . . [H]e had a pleasant expression on his face, and I don't think he knew what I was talking about, and I didn't care whether he did or not." (HST, "Discussion [with Hillman and Noyes]," February 18, 1954, HST Quotes File, Box 9, Post-Presidential-Memoirs, HSTL.)

around to Stalin's chair and said, substantially, "You may be interested to know that we have developed a new and powerful weapon and within a few days intend to use it against Japan." I watched Stalin's expression as this was being interpreted, and was surprised that he smiled blandly and said only a few words. When the President and I reached our car, he said that the Generalissimo had replied only, "That's fine. I hope you make good use of it against the Japanese."[45]

Churchill's report is slightly different:

I was perhaps five yards away, and I watched with the closest attention the momentous talk. I knew what the President was going to do. What was vital to measure was its effect on Stalin. I can see it all as if it were yesterday. He seemed to be delighted. A new bomb! Of extraordinary power! Probably decisive on the whole Japanese war! What a bit of luck! This was my impression at the moment, and I was sure that he had no idea of the significance of what he was being told.

Churchill added:

As we were waiting for our cars I found myself near Truman. "How did it go?" I asked. "He never asked a question," he replied.[46]

Charles Bohlen, the president's interpreter, adds these details:

Three days after the successful test blast, after consulting his advisers and Churchill (the British had cooperated in the project), Truman decided it would be wise to tell Stalin the news. Explaining that he wanted to be as informal and casual as possible, Truman said during a break in the proceedings that he would stroll over to Stalin and nonchalantly inform him. He instructed me not to accompany him, as I ordinarily did, because he did not want to indicate that there was anything particularly momentous about the development. . . .

Across the room, I watched Stalin's face carefully as the President broke the news. So offhand was Stalin's response that there was some question in my mind whether the President's message had got through.[47]

It appears that Truman felt that if he held back all information from Stalin—still an ally—it might jeopardize future relations and, most important, the possibility of some form of international control of nuclear weapons. However, it is also clear that the president did not wish to tell him anything of importance, and if engendering trust was the primary U.S. motive it almost certainly failed—indeed, probably furthered suspicions, since the Russians would learn of the new development soon enough.

The Soviet Union, of course, had long since begun work on its own version of a Manhattan Project—and was making substantial progress (partly as a result of information provided by Klaus Fuchs and other spies). Both Molotov and Marshal Georgi K. Zhukov were later to report that Stalin fully understood Truman's meaning. However, recent research in Soviet archives by David Holloway suggests that while Stalin undoubtedly knew about the Manhattan Project, what "is less clear is what he understood the significance of Truman's remark to be"; only after Hiroshima did he order a speed-up of the Soviet atomic effort.[48]

One possible explanation for Truman's maneuver—and his decision not to follow the June 21 Interim Committee "trust building" recommendation— finds its source in the previously cited minutes of the initial May 31 Interim Committee meeting and Byrnes' fear that "Stalin would ask to be brought into the partnership." This explanation, however, seems lame, for as Stimson subsequently observed: "If he pressed for details and facts, Truman was simply to tell him that we were not yet prepared to give them."

A more revealing—and probably much more accurate—understanding appears in a private 1952 letter from Groves to Byrnes (marked "Confidential" "because I do not feel that any benefit would result if it should become public at this time"):

> You may recall various discussions that I had with you directly and indirectly about my very strong recommendations that we should not tell Mr. Stalin about our anticipated use of the atomic bomb. The reason for this was a desire [sic], which I had every reason to believe you shared, that any such knowledge would make Russia's entry into the war more certain and that we all wanted to avoid. I recall you telling me with considerable relish, after your return, just how the possibility had been broken to Stalin. . . .

Byrnes replied: "Your recollection is right. . . . I did my best to have him informed in such a manner that the importance of the information would not impress him."[49]*

Almost certainly related to this was Truman's rush to leave the Big Three meeting. We have seen that on July 24, "[t]he president was frank about his desire to close the Conference and get away."[50] In an oral history conducted

---

*Similarly, the interview notes of Herbert Feis dated February 27, 1958, state: "Byrnes said that, after rather intense thinking over of what our duty was . . . he reached the conclusion that it would be a disaster for the United States and China if the Soviet Union entered the Pacific war. This led to the thought that it would be just as well, if not better, if Stalin were not too fully aware of the potentialities of the atomic bomb, for otherwise he might hasten Soviet entry into the war." (Notes on Herbert Feis' meeting with Byrnes, 2/27/58, Byrnes draft Manuscript File, Box 65, Feis Papers, LC.)

for the Truman Library in 1969, George M. Elsey, Truman's naval aide and a Map Room officer at Potsdam, recalled that

> in no circumstances did [Truman] want the bomb to be dropped until af-ter he had left Potsdam. He wanted to be away from the Russians and on his way home before the actual dropping of the first bomb. You may recall that the bomb was dropped a couple of days after we left Potsdam.[51]

In his book on Byrnes, drawing on his personal diaries, Walter Brown re-ports that "[w]hen Truman learned that the atomic bomb targets and the time of attack were agreed upon, he told Secretary Byrnes that they should speed up their work and get ready to depart."

> Truman hastened to meet the *Augusta* so that he would not have to deal further with the Russians or have to explain to Stalin why he had not been kept fully informed of the success of the bomb.[52]

The president had been less than forthright with Stalin when the Potsdam Proclamation was released. Now, under Byrnes' continuing guidance, he had moved still more deeply into an awkward and uncomfortable position, jeop-ardizing the possibility of what Stimson had called "relations of frankness." Truman knew full well that in speaking to Stalin of "the new weapon" he had hardly been forthcoming about its nature.

The actual explosion, now only a few days off, would reveal just how lacking in candor the various maneuvers had been.

Chapter 31

NAVY INITIATIVES

*The fact that the Americans alluded to the Atlantic Charter is
particularly worthy of attention at this time. It is impossible
for us to accept unconditional surrender, no matter in what
guise, but it is our idea to inform them by some appropriate
means that there is no objection to the restoration of peace
on the basis of the Atlantic Charter.*
—Foreign Minister Togo to Ambassador Sato, July 25, 1945

One of the most intriguing features of the atomic bomb story involves the
U.S. navy—for it appears that most of the top leadership not only felt
strongly about the issue, but in one way or another tried to do something
about ending the war by clarifying the surrender formula. Undersecretary
Ralph Bard's pre-Potsdam approach to Truman was only the first of three
navy initiatives which occurred in July and August during the last weeks before the bombings.

Viewed in any serious historic perspective, in fact, it seems fairly obvious
that Bard's effort to end the war without bombing a city grew out of ideas
which had been developing within high-level navy circles for some time.
When Bard chose to challenge the Interim Committee recommendation that
the atomic bomb be used without warning, it is not likely that he was contradicting the views of the man he not only worked for but regarded as a
close friend, Secretary of the Navy James V. Forrestal.[1] Bard did not represent that he was offering an "official" opinion—at least according to a report
of a June 26, 1945, telephone discussion he had with George Harrison.[2] But
aside from the fact that it would be surprising if any high navy official had
taken so important a position without the knowledge and prior approval of
his superior, the modern evidence strongly suggests that before acting Bard
had in fact received the support of Forrestal.

Historian Alice Kimball Smith interviewed Bard on precisely this question before his death. She reports that it was "at Secretary of the Navy Forrestal's suggestion" that he obtained an interview with Truman to urge "that because of the bottling up of Japan, already effected by the Navy, an all-out invasion would not be necessary."[3]

A similar report comes from naval historian Robert G. Albion (who was close to Forrestal and his staff). On the basis of his independent research Albion concluded:

> Strong dissent [from the Interim Committee's June 1 decision to bomb without warning] quickly came from those in [on] the secret. Scientists by the score who had been working on the project voiced their opposition. So, too, did some of the Air Forces and Navy leaders, as part of their belief that the Kyushu invasion was unnecessary. . . . As for Forrestal's feelings about [Bard's and Strauss's recommendations], what indirect evidence there is, seems to indicate he shared the views of Bard and Strauss.[4]

A recent biography of Forrestal by Townsend Hoopes and Douglas Brinkley also concludes that the "strong inference is that Forrestal agreed with Bard. . . ."[5] Strauss—Forrestal's special assistant and intimate associate—put the obvious point with a certain understated force: "Had Forrestal disagreed with the position taken by Undersecretary Bard and by me, I feel sure that I should have made a note of that."[6]

A poignant moment at Forrestal's May 25, 1949, funeral also points to the close connection between navy thinking, the previously noted Republican interest in ending the war quickly, the Russian problem, and attempts to bring about surrender without the bomb. ". . . Herbert Hoover came over to talk to me," Bard later recalled in a private letter to Lewis Strauss, "and said as a student of American history he wanted me to know how important he thought my recommendation had been, and how sorry he was it had not received the approval of the [Interim Committee]. He felt it would have been a great thing for this country if my advice had been followed."

Bard continued in a tone which once more suggests the common—and confident—judgment we have noted all along among those in the navy inner circle: "From the standpoint of what has happened, of course, such a warning as I proposed would have been a wonderful thing as at that time we had not made a final deal with Russia, and we would not have to do so because the Japanese were looking for an out, and it is almost certain that they would have used such a warning to make peace."[7]

The impending Russian attack, as Bard's letter again reminds us, cannot be separated from the judgments made at this time. Hoopes and Brinkley also suggest that strictly humanitarian concerns were not central in Forrestal's thinking. Rather,

Forrestal, whose overriding concern at this juncture was to develop strategic counterweights to what he foresaw as burgeoning Russian/Communist power in Asia, may have feared that using the atomic bomb would aggravate the problems of Japan's economic recovery and produce hatred of America for years to come.[8]

That navy leaders in general—and the secretary in particular—felt strongly about the atomic bomb's use is further suggested by a growing, if still incomplete body of evidence concerning a special trip Forrestal took to the Big Three meeting on his own initiative.

Forrestal had not been invited to the Potsdam conference. However, he scheduled an inspection trip to Europe at this time which conveniently permitted him to drop in on the meeting. Whether (as seems likely) this was his private intention all along or an afterthought is impossible to determine. In *Forrestal and the Navy*, Albion writes:

> Concerned anyway about the ways matters would probably be handled [at Potsdam], Forrestal had become really disturbed by July 13, when he learned that "The first real evidence of a Japanese desire to get out of the war came today through intercepted messages" from the Japanese foreign minister to his Ambassador in Moscow. . . . On July 25, still more urgent Tokyo messages were picked up; and he decided to fly to Potsdam with these himself and "crash" the conference.[9]

Hoopes and Brinkley, among others, note that at Potsdam Forrestal "seems to have argued for a formula that would induce Japanese surrender without need for either the bomb or invasion."[10] The previously cited report by C. K. Borklund (to recall) adds that "Forrestal believed, and wanted to convince Truman, that the Japanese were anxiously looking for a grace-saving way to surrender, that bringing Russia in would accomplish nothing except to extend Communist tentacles in the Far East, and that killing thousands of helpless civilians on the Japanese mainland was a brutal, and probably an unnecessary, act."[11]*

We do not have evidence that Forrestal directly challenged the use of the atomic bomb. Moreover, he arrived in Germany just after the Potsdam Proclamation had been issued without the key clause offering assurances for the Emperor—not a particularly good moment to challenge a decision now firmly set by the president himself. We do know that Forrestal had dinner with Truman on July 28 and breakfast on July 30[12]; and in general, there is

---

*Another Forrestal concern is also evident—namely "that if possible, we should find some other way of communicating with Japan rather than Russia, and I suggested the possibility of the King of Sweden. . . ." (Unpublished Forrestal Diary, July 30, 1945.) See below, p. 415, for evidence of presidential concern about this question as well.

not much doubt about the secretary's views.* At the same time Strauss linked Bard's effort to Forrestal, for instance, he provided Albion (in somewhat stilted but unmistakable terms) with the following additional details:

> The fact that . . . [Forrestal] took the Japanese messages with him to Potsdam leads me to believe that he hoped their collective impact might result in a realization on the part of the conferees there that the war was essentially over and that little more than a question of semantics separated the terms which the victors would impose and those which the vanquished were eager to accept.

Strauss' letter also recalls explicitly that:

> Joseph C. Grew, and Forrestal had prepared with Secretary Stimson's concurrence a pronouncement to be made to Japan by the President and calling upon Japan to surrender but it would have permitted the retention of the institution of the Imperial house.

The letter to Albion then goes on to state matter-of-factly:

> This was omitted from the Potsdam declaration and as you are undoubtedly aware was the only reason why it was not immediately accepted by the Japanese who were beaten and knew it before the first atomic bomb was dropped.[13]

The unabashed and unqualified tone of Strauss' private letter (like the tone of Bard's letter to Strauss) offers additional indirect evidence of the confidence high-level navy leaders had in their assessment of the realities. It, too, adds to the picture of Forrestal in all probability having made a last-minute attempt to head off use of the atomic bomb by urging a clarification of terms.

On many occasions after the war, Strauss stated his position quite openly. Here, for instance, is how he put it in an NBC interview in the mid-1960s:

> it was clear to a number of people, myself among them, that the war was very nearly over. The Japanese were nearly ready to capitulate.[14]

In his letter to Albion, Strauss added that the historian might find that for "authoritative statements as to the condition of Japan in the late spring, at least from the Navy's point of view, there are statements by Admiral King,

---

*McCloy's diary of July 30 also notes: "Harriman had a long talk with Jim Forrestal about the Japanese business, particularly the Emperor's position. He says, as I thought, that Jim feels we may need the Emperor to stabilize things in Japan and bring about peace on the continent. If the Emperor does not go along with what we feel is a complete demobilization of Japan, we can unseat him. If he does, he may be an asset to a liberal element." (McCloy Diary, July 30, 1945.)

Admiral Halsey, Admiral Radford, Admiral Nimitz and others who expressed themselves to the effect that neither the atomic bomb nor the proposed invasion of the Japanese mainland were necessary to produce the surrender."[15]

Since there was later to be considerable confusion about the matter, note carefully that in his letter and elsewhere Strauss is primarily discussing the late-summer judgment that a change of terms would now likely have ended the war—not the navy view earlier in 1945 that an extended blockade would have been preferable to an invasion.

The Forrestal trip appears to have been closely connected with another important navy-related initiative which occurred during the final pre-Hiroshima period. This involved a public radio broadcast made by Captain (later Rear Admiral) Ellis M. Zacharias four days after the Potsdam conference began. The broadcast had continuing ramifications throughout the next two weeks.

We have previously noted a link between the initial spring 1945 launching of Zacharias' radio series and the statement made by Truman on May 8 which drew a sharp distinction between "unconditional surrender" in general and "unconditional surrender" of the Japanese "armed forces." It is clear that Zacharias received approval for his overall psychological warfare campaign from Forrestal and (although again the record is incomplete), that coordination with the White House of some kind seems obvious from the fact that the first radio address was aired only two hours after Truman's statement was released. Moreover, before making his statement Truman was specifically advised that it was to be the kick-off to a continuing psychological warfare campaign.[16]

Zacharias' initial broadcast was followed by thirteen weekly transmissions in both Japanese and English. Number twelve—on July 21, 1945—Zacharias later termed the "decisive" one of the series. Again, although some details are uncertain, modern sources strongly suggest coordination with the Department of the Navy and in all probability, as Zacharias subsequently claimed, specific approval by Forrestal himself. (In any event, the importance of the effort far transcended the precise conditions of its origin.)

Zacharias began his July 21 broadcast with a declaration to the Japanese people that defeat was inevitable:

> Japan has already lost the war. Your progressive defeats and our progressive victories have brought the war to Japan's very doorstep.

He then went on to urge "Japan's greatest need at this crucial hour is for *loyal*, *intelligent*, and *inspired* leadership"—and proceeded to offer an "analysis" of the "unconditional surrender" formula in terms which had highly significant implications:

As you know, the Atlantic Charter and the Cairo Declaration are the sources of *our* policy, and both begin with the categorical statement that we seek no territorial aggrandizement in *our* war against Japan. Are the leaders of Japan really so short-sighted that they cannot see the possible complications which they may have to face if they fail to act, and act promptly?

In a key paragraph Zacharias declared:

the Japanese leaders face two alternatives. One is the virtual destruction of Japan followed by a dictated peace. The other is unconditional surrender with its attendant benefit as laid down by the Atlantic Charter.[17]

The last phrase was extraordinary—especially since Zacharias was designated an "official spokesman" of the United States. As previously noted, the Atlantic Charter referred to the declaration of peace aims set forth by Roosevelt and Churchill on August 14, 1941, and later affirmed by representatives of twenty-six nations (in January 1942). Its key passage and promise lay in the third point—a declaration that the signatory nations

respect the right of all peoples to choose the form of government under which they will live; and they wish to see sovereign rights and self-government restored to those who have been forcibly deprived of them.[18]

A peace based on the Atlantic Charter also would preclude territorial changes without the consent of the people involved; insure access by all states to trade and raw materials; and require movement towards general disarmament, guaranteed by the establishment of a permanent system of global security.[19]

For Japan, of course, the right to choose its own form of government would guarantee the preservation of the Emperor. The Zacharias offer as tendered opened the door to an "honorable peace" as defined by the Allies.

The broadcast was important, and although many subsequent accounts have ignored it, close observers in 1945 did not. In a move that was unusual at the time, the full text of Zacharias' broadcast was simultaneously released to the press (for the first time in the series). Not surprisingly, it received extensive coverage. *The New York Times*, for instance, carried a front-page story under the headline: "Japan Is Warned to Give Up Soon: U.S. Broadcast Says Speed Will Bring Peace Based on Atlantic Charter." The *Times* story opened with the following lead:

A peace on the basis of the Atlantic Charter was promised last night to Japan if she surrendered unconditionally soon.[20]

Zacharias' broadcast was also prominently featured in the *Washington Star*, the *Washington Post*, the *Baltimore Sun*, the *New York Herald Tribune*, and numerous other papers. Like the *Times*, the *Herald Tribune* headline also stressed: "Japan Told to Surrender Unconditionally or Face Inevitable Destruction: Official Broadcast Bids Enemy Leaders Yield Under Atlantic Charter."[21] In the same vein, the *Washington Post* also noted in its report that "CBS commentator [Tris] Coffin predicted that the Potsdam announcement on Japan would promise the Japanese freedom of religion and the right to choose whatever form of government they want."[22]

Zacharias' broadcast was complemented by an apparently authoritative report on the subject of U.S. intentions which appeared on the same day in the *Army and Navy Journal*, a prominent magazine of military opinion. "[T]he signs point to a declaration of our Pacific war aims," the *Journal* noted, "perhaps [to be announced] at the end of the [Potsdam] Conference."

> Mr. Truman has been urged to make such a declaration and the understanding is that he has been disposed to make it but that he would prefer to give it to the world from the background of the Big Three conference rather than of Washington.
>
> He has already announced, through his statement on VE-Day, that unconditional surrender will not mean enslavement for the Japanese people. A further exposition of our aims conceivably might encourage the Japanese to discuss peace seriously.

The *Journal*, too, understood that the central question was the future of the Emperor:

> Chief interest in the expected declaration of Pacific War aims will be directed to what may be said about Emperor Hirohito. Will there be no mention of him, or will his punishment be demanded as a war criminal?[23]

The *Army and Navy Journal* article was itself treated as hard news by the *Times* and other papers.[24] The *Times*, in fact, quoted extensively from the *Journal* in its July 22 story on the Zacharias broadcast, "noting" that the "*Journal* commented that the chief interest in the declaration would center on what it said about Emperor Hirohito."[25]

Joseph Grew, reporting on all this to Byrnes in Potsdam, cabled:

> Particular importance is attached by U.S. press to [the] statement in release that Captain Zacharias broadcast as "an official spokesman of the U.S. Government," and to the fact that the Atlantic Charter commits the signatory governments to permit peoples to select their own form of

Government. This was interpreted as indicating formulation of American policy with reference to the Emperor.

Grew informed Byrnes of the official position taken by the State Department:

Department has been asked if broadcast was cleared with the Department. Our answer has been that all major propaganda themes are discussed by the Department and other interested Government Agencies and the broad policy under which the OWI would conduct the campaign has been laid down. In no case, however, has the Department cleared any individual propaganda broadcast and was not informed that this broadcast was to be given to the American press.[26]

The obvious question was what relationship the Zacharias broadcast had to the negotiations under way at Potsdam. The answer came in two parts.

In a story published on July 23 (filed on July 22) under the headline "Truman Approved Warning to Japan," the Associated Press reported from Potsdam that the Zacharias statement had been approved by the president himself. According to the report,

The American warning to Japan calling for immediate surrender, broadcast from Washington by a naval officer, was viewed tonight as part of President Truman's strategy here to secure American aims in the Far East.

The radio broadcast to Japan, it stated, "was known to have been made with the President's full knowledge."[27]

The next day (July 24) Arthur Krock of *The New York Times* reported authoritatively (but with less specificity) that:

[Zacharias] is an officer of the Navy, but his work is with the Office of War Information, to which he is accredited and which has responsibility for what he had been beaming to Japan and, in this instance, to the American people as well. He knows the President and has been one of his consultants on this propaganda. Also, the OWI would not have passed the broadcast, or released it for home attention, on its own decision. Approval undoubtedly was given at Potsdam.[28]

There are a number of unresolved puzzles related to the Atlantic Charter initiative. It is still unclear, for instance, whether Zacharias acted entirely on his own or with the full approval of the Office of War Information and the Navy Department. Zacharias subsequently wrote that offering the Japanese a surrender based upon the Atlantic Charter was an initiative that he and his team carried out "almost singlehanded." However, he also stated explicitly that "Secretary Forrestal was behind us," and that the effort was taken "with his help. . . ."[29] Given what we know of Zacharias' relationship to Forrestal, of Forrestal's interest in assurances for the Emperor, and of his wish to end the war before the Russians got into Manchuria—it is difficult to believe that the secretary did not give Zacharias at least some nod of indirect approval. Futhermore, the presently available evidence strongly suggests that Forrestal was the source of the follow-up *New York Times* story by his close friend Arthur Krock.* According to Zacharias:

> Forrestal came to our aid. He told Arthur Krock, Chief of the New York *Times* Washington bureau, that I did have the authority to make the statement I had made in the broadcast and that it did indeed reflect the President's opinion.
>
> Forrestal then called Potsdam and requested Presidential approval (after the fact) for our "deliberate indiscretion." Finally he dropped everything in Washington and flew to Potsdam himself.
>
> Our nerves were on edge as we waited for word from Potsdam. Then came the Associated Press flash saying the President would stand by my reference to the Atlantic Charter.[30]

Aside from some apparent confusion in the dates—in fact, the A.P. story came first, the Krock story second, and Forrestal's arrival at Potsdam third—a similar general report is provided by Ladislas Farago (who worked closely with Zacharias on the Navy's psychological warfare team):

> We were still apprehensive that Truman, who was maintaining ominous silence at Potsdam, might yet disavow us. Forrestal sought to prevent this. He asked Commodore Vardaman, the President's Naval Aide, to brief Truman on the issue. This intervention saved the day for us. While the President continued to refrain from taking a direct part in the controversy, he authorized Anthony Vaccaro, White House correspondent of the Associated Press covering him at Potsdam, to report that the President "tacitly approved the Zacharias broadcast."[31]

None of these accounts is definitive. However, even without the indication of "tacit" approval, of critical importance is the fact that there was no official rejection from Potsdam of the Atlantic Charter proposal.

Had Truman and Byrnes so desired, it would have been an easy matter to

---

*Phone logs found in the Forrestal Papers indicate that Forrestal called Krock on July 23 at 12:50 p.m.; and that Krock called him back at 2:45 p.m.; that Zacharias called Forrestal at 2:52 p.m. on July 24; and that Forrestal called Krock again 11:59 a.m. on July 26, the day he left for Europe (at 11:57 p.m.). See Phone Log 1945, Box 130, Forrestal Papers, Princeton University Archives.

knock down the broadcast as not having been officially sanctioned. That they did not—especially given the A.P. report of Truman's direct involvement—could not help but be a signal of some form of presidential support for the Atlantic Charter offer.

Nor did the Japanese miss the significance of the broadcast. On July 25 (reported in MAGIC on July 26), an intercepted message from Japanese Foreign Minister Togo to Ambassador Sato in Moscow cited Zacharias' broadcast—and stated without reservation:

> The fact that the Americans alluded to the Atlantic Charter is particularly worthy of attention at this time. It is impossible for us to accept unconditional surrender, no matter in what guise, but it is our idea to inform them by some appropriate means that there is no objection to the restoration of peace on the basis of the Atlantic Charter.[32]

Chapter 32

"MOKUSATSU"

[*"Mokusatsu"*] *might be translated roughly as "to be silent"
or "to withhold comment" or "to ignore." "To withhold comment" probably comes the closest to its true meaning, implying that something is being held back, that there is something
significant impending. Certainly that is what the Japanese
government meant.*
> —Kazuo Kawai, " 'Mokusatsu,' Japan's Response
> to the Potsdam Declaration," November 1950

To insiders at the Potsdam conference it appeared obvious that the position
taken in regard to the Zacharias broadcast was related to the question of
when—or whether—the Soviet Union would enter the war. The July 23 A.P.
story on Truman's approval of the Atlantic Charter language, for instance,
also reported from Potsdam that

Observers saw in this broadcast a thinly veiled warning that Russian
participation in the war against Japan might be imminent, especially in
[Zacharias'] question: "Are the leaders so short-sighted that they cannot
see the possible complication that they may have to face if they do not
act promptly?"

The story also reported growing fear among officials in the president's party
that Russian entry would entangle postwar power negotiations in the Pacific:

Observers here believe that, unless the Japanese act quickly, important
developments may be forthcoming in a Russian announcement, the
price of which may complicate peace settlements when eventually they
are made.[1]

In his July 24 *New York Times* column, Krock also stated:

What no official would admit was the widespread surmise that another purpose of this broadcast was to end the war before Soviet Russia enters it and avoid the complications of this victorious partnership.[2]

Whatever the precise motivations of the various parties at the time—day by day, as information relating to the bomb, the Japanese, and the Russians shifted and was continually updated—it is important to note that another decision was taken at this time: Truman and Byrnes decided not to pursue the obvious possibilities suggested by Japan's response to the Atlantic Charter proposal. They did so even though the seemingly acceptable Charter language affirming the "right of all peoples to choose the form of government under which they will live" was virtually the same as that which the Joint Chiefs had urged on July 18: "the Japanese people will be free to choose their own form of government."*

The decision not to follow up on the Japanese intercepts at this time was also made in the face of intelligence and other information which added force to the intercept's essential message. For instance, evaluating the July 25 cable from Togo to Sato, the navy's highly respected Pacific Strategic Intelligence Section (PSIS)—a group similar to the War Department's team of MAGIC analysts—advised:

With regard to terminating the war, Japan, though still balking at the term "unconditional surrender," has reached the point where she "had no objection to the restoration of peace on the basis of the Atlantic Charter."[3]

Additional confirmation of Japanese interest also came from an English-language Tokyo radio statement. In a page-one July 26 story, *The New York Times* reported the broadcast (made two days earlier) as saying:

Should America show any sincerity of putting into practice what she preaches, as for instance in the Atlantic Charter, excepting its punitive clause, the Japanese nation, in fact the Japanese military, would automatically, if not willingly, (several words missing) follow in the stopping of the conflict and then and only then will sabers cease to rattle both in the East and in the West. . . .[4]

Given Japan's exceedingly tight internal press and radio controls, a formal public statement that "the Japanese nation, in fact *the Japanese military*" would stop the conflict spoke volumes. To be sure, objection to the punitive clause of the Atlantic Charter had been expressed, but taken together with the

*See above, pp. 299–300.

secret intercepts, such a public declaration—considered as a possible "initial bid" in negotiations—was extraordinary.

Despite these additional signals, there is no evidence that Truman or Byrnes ever wished to follow up on the intercepted July 25 message; if anything, Byrnes sought to avoid and downplay the Atlantic Charter initiative. For instance, Forrestal's unpublished diary for July 28 notes the following (in the course of the previously cited discussion on the use of the T. V. Soong negotiations to stall the Russians):

> Talked with Byrnes: *We agreed that Zacharias should cease his use of the phrase "official spokesman" in his broadcasts to Japan because of the delicacy of current negotiations.* Byrnes said he was most anxious to get the Japanese affair over with before the Russians got in, with particular reference to Dairen and Port Arthur. Once in there, he felt it would not be easy to get them out.[5]

The language here italicized, again, was left out of the published version of the diary. That Byrnes had in mind some (unexplained) tactical connection between how the Zacharias–Atlantic Charter issue was handled and the Russian attack seems obvious from the sequence of sentences. However, precisely what his motives were in lowering Zacharias' profile "because of the delicacy" of the situation remains unclear.*

What about the reaction of Japanese leaders to the Potsdam Proclamation itself? How Japanese officials understood the warning statement—and how U.S. officials "read" the meaning of Japan's response—cannot easily be judged without first recognizing the extraordinary complexity of the "signals" that were being sent from Washington and Potsdam in the final weeks before Hiroshima was bombed.

Many accounts of the Japanese response to the Proclamation were—and often still are—almost unbelievably oversimplified. (For instance, as we have noted, in *Speaking Frankly* Byrnes writes simply that had the Japanese government "surrendered unconditionally, it would not have been necessary to drop the atomic bomb."[6]) Similarly, in an important 1947 article (to which we shall return) Stimson stated:

> On July 28 Premier Suzuki rejected the Potsdam ultimatum by announcing that it was "unworthy of public notice." In the face of this rejection we could only proceed to demonstrate that the ultimatum had meant exactly what it said. . . .[7]

---

*One possibility may have been fear that if the Japanese made a positive public response to Zacharias' Atlantic Charter offer, this would lead to time-consuming negotiations—which in turn might allow the Russians to enter the war.

However, all along it had been clear to top U.S. officials that the war would almost certainly continue if the unconditional surrender formula were maintained; Truman himself was fully aware that as written the Potsdam Proclamation was unlikely to be accepted. Indeed, so long as the U.S. position could be construed as threatening the person of the Emperor, the army faction had an almost unanswerable response to any internal cabinet proposal to end the war.

Furthermore, as we have noted, there had been widespread discussion in the U.S. press of an expected "new statement" on war aims. In this environment the decision not to include specific assurances for the Emperor meant that the Potsdam Proclamation did not, in fact, move significantly beyond what had already been said on the key issue in the president's May 8 and June 1 statements.

In this important sense the proclamation appeared not as something new, but as official confirmation that there would be no significant change in the basic U.S. position. Moreover, it was a retreat from the Atlantic Charter "offer." (It was also an implicit rejection of the favorable signal Togo had sent Sato in response.) Though unconditional surrender of the armed forces (as stated on May 8) was reaffirmed in the proclamation, the ambiguity and threatening tone of the following passage was particularly problematic:

> There must be eliminated for all time the authority and influence of those who have deceived and misled the people of Japan into embarking on world conquest. . . .[8]

Even supporters of the Administration's position, like *The New York Times*, pointed out that the phrase was "broad enough to include not only the military caste, but though he is not mentioned by name, the 'God-Emperor' whose authority and influence have been used at every stage to lead the Japanese people into conquest."[9]

Intercepted Japanese cables make it clear that the proclamation's failure to clarify the crucial issue was causing major problems—and that U.S. officials knew this. An intercepted cable sent on July 28, for instance, showed Ambassador Sato stressing:

> The important point in connection with the Joint Proclamation is that America and England have demanded Japan's immediate unconditional surrender and have stated clearly that they have no intention of softening the terms set forth in the Proclamation.[10]

In reporting on a discussion of the proclamation he had with Soviet Vice Commissar Alexander Lozovsky on July 30, Sato also noted that he had reminded the Russians that "the Japanese Government is completely unable to surrender unconditionally." At the same time, however, Sato had emphasized that

> the Japanese Government—which is taking a very broad and concilia-
> tory attitude so long as its own honor and existence are guaranteed—
> hopes to bring the war to an end and for this reason has requested the
> good offices of the Russian Government.[11]

Another problem with the warning was its public nature and the publicity given to it. Zacharias later complained bitterly that the handling of the Potsdam Proclamation "wrecked everything we had been working for. . . ." Especially troubling was that "[i]nstead of being a diplomatic instrument, transmitted through regular diplomatic channels and giving the Japanese a chance to answer, it was put on the radio as a propaganda instrument pure and simple. The whole maneuver, in fact, completely disregarded all essential psychological factors [for] dealing with Japan."[12]

Modern documents show that Japanese officials were mystified by the juxtaposition of the Atlantic Charter broadcast (together with the signal of presidential "approval") and the Potsdam Proclamation. They also demonstrate that here, too, U.S. officials were fully aware of this fact.

Intercepted cables indicated that Sato, for instance, was all over the map in his analysis. On July 29, he noted, first, that "Although the American 'spokesman' [word in English] spoke firmly for an unconditional surrender he certainly hinted that if we were to agree to this the terms would in actual practice be toned down. . . ."* However, Sato was then unsure "to what extent the statements of Captain Zacharias in his recent broadcast were authoritative. . . ." On the other hand,

> the principle enunciated by him—that Japan can reap the benefits of the
> Atlantic Charter—differs from the attitude which the Allies took toward
> Germany before her capitulation.

But "the fact remains that [the Potsdam Proclamation] is . . . the basis of the statement made by Captain Zacharias." To be sure, however, "It is true that there are discrepancies in some of the important points in the Ultimatum [presumably: between it and the Atlantic Charter]."[13]†

When the Potsdam Proclamation was issued "on top of" the Atlantic Charter proposal, so to speak, an already complicated situation became further confused in Japan. Which American message was the American message?

A third—and even more fundamental—complication involved the strange position of the Russians. Many accounts of the final weeks before the atomic

---

*Brackets in original.
†Brackets in original.

bomb was used have excessively compressed time in this regard, skipping over important stages of the complex interaction. Evidence now available, however, makes it obvious that Japanese leaders were understandably confused by the issuance of the Potsdam Proclamation from the site of a meeting of the Big Three—but not signed by Stalin. In Moscow, Sato expected the worst, cabling Togo on July 27:

> The joint ultimatum . . . seems to have been intended as a threatening blast against us and as a prelude to a Three Power offensive. As might have been expected, any aid from the Soviet Union has now become extremely doubtful and there can be little doubt that this ultimatum was meant to serve as a counter-blast to our peace feelers.[14]

In fact, as we have seen, the proclamation was in no way connected to Japan's approach to Russia. From Tokyo's perspective things also were not obvious; it was essential to get more information rather than speculate. Togo acknowledged on July 28 that "I think it would be hard to believe that the Russians were not also aware in advance of the present Joint Declaration." However, he stressed to Sato:

> What the Russian position is with respect to the Potsdam Joint Declaration made by England, America and Chungking is a question of extreme importance in determining our future counter-policy.[15]

If the proclamation had been issued with Russian agreement, there was little hope for the future. If not, however—if the absence of Stalin's signature was a sign of continuing Soviet neutrality or possibly even of conflict among the Big Three—perhaps Japan might have a chance to avoid the worst. An official report by General MacArthur's staff (made public in 1966) offered this assessment of the situation facing Japanese officials:

> It was . . . essential, first, not to reject the Allied declaration, which would at once close the door to further peace negotiations, and second, to await Russia's final answer on the Konoye mission.[16]

The decision to exclude the Russians—and the confusion caused by the uncertain relationship of the Soviet Union to the proclamation—also inevitably helped bolster the position of army leaders in the Japanese Cabinet. For months the hope that Russia just possibly might be kept at bay had been at the heart of the army's argument that a continuation of the war was feasible. Now not only could army leaders continue to stress that "unconditional surrender" threatened the Emperor, but so long as Russia's position remained undefined, they could also continue to argue that the situation was not totally hopeless.

A specific unresolved issue involved the Emperor's request that Moscow receive a negotiating team headed by Prince Konoye. Togo's July 28 cable noted that since the Potsdam Proclamation "happened" while

> we were awaiting the Russian answer in regard to sending a Special Envoy, the question arises as to whether there is not some connection between this Joint Declaration and our proposal. Obviously we are deeply concerned as to whether there is such a connection, that is to say, whether the Russian Government communicated our proposal to the English and the Americans. . . .[17]

In the same July 30 cable in which he noted the uncompromising U.S. position on unconditional surrender, Sato stated his own (misinformed) opinion, first, that "The Potsdam Proclamation must certainly have been communicated to Stalin, etc., beforehand"—and, second, that "the Joint Proclamation was issued in order to make clear the attitude of America, England, and China in response to our proposal." To Sato it seemed obvious that

> If it is to be understood that Stalin was completely unable to influence the intentions of America and England on this point, it follows that he will be unable to accept our proposal to send a Special Envoy. However much we may exert ourselves to prevent Stalin from entering the war . . . we shall have no particular success.[18]

The Japanese foreign minister was not convinced. Nor—as recent Japanese writers have shown—given the power of the army faction, was he in a position to be fully explicit about his own views and tactics.[19] In the absence of any formal indication of Soviet involvement in the Potsdam Proclamation the situation at least admitted of another possible interpretation. On August 2, Togo cabled Sato that although it was "difficult to decide on concrete peace conditions here at home all at once. . . ."

> At present, in accordance with the Imperial will, there is a unanimous determination to seek the good offices of the Russians in ending the war, to make concrete terms a matter between Japan and Russia, and to send Prince Konoye, who has the deep trust of the Emperor, to carry on discussions. . . .

The cable stressed, finally, that "we are exerting ourselves to collect the views of all quarters on the matter of concrete terms"; hence

> Whatever happens, if we should let one day slip by, that might have – – – – – [word uncertain probably "results"]* lasting for thousands of years. Consequently, if the Soviet Government should reply in the neg-

*Brackets in original.

ative . . . I urge you to do everything possible to arrange another interview with Molotov at once.[20]

The crucial issue, of course, is how U.S. leaders understood what was going on at the time—and, as a consequence of their understanding, how they
assessed the likelihood of a surrender. Obviously, the idea that Japan was still
totally committed to an all-out fight to the finish was less and less credible.
A threshold question was the relationship between various public statements
made by Japanese officials and the intercepted messages secretly being read
by American officials.

On July 27 the Domei News agency (a propaganda vehicle of the Japanese
Army) had announced that the Potsdam Proclamation "would be ignored. . . ."[21] The next day Suzuki had read the following prepared statement
at a Tokyo press conference:

> I consider the joint proclamation of the three powers to be a rehash of
> the Cairo Declaration. The government does not regard it as a thing
> of any great value; the government will just ignore ["*mokusatsu*"] it.
> We will press forward resolutely to carry the war to a successful
> conclusion.[22]

Did Suzuki mean what he seemed to say? How explain this language when
the intercepted messages suggested something rather different? Early in the
postwar era, scholars began to probe well beyond superficialities to illuminate several important issues connected with these key questions.

In 1950 one knowledgeable Japanese writer, Kazuo Kawai, suggested (in
the *Pacific Historical Review*) that a close reading of the various statements
indicated that Japan had *not*, in fact, rejected the Potsdam Proclamation as
the conventional wisdom held. Kawai emphasized that in his statement of
July 28 Suzuki had used the Japanese term "*mokusatsu*" to describe the government's position—and that the term had several possible meanings:

> It might be translated roughly as "to be silent" or "to withhold com-
> ment" or "to ignore." "To withhold comment" probably comes the clos-
> est to its true meaning, implying that something is being held back, that
> there is something significant impending. Certainly that is what the Jap-
> anese government meant.

Given the complex political situation and the confusing signals it was receiving, Kawai suggested that the Japanese government had used the term
"*mokusatsu*" in order to avoid committing itself one way or the other. "Obviously the enemy's demand for surrender could not be praised, but equally
obviously the government did not want it criticized inasmuch as tentative
moves toward its conditional acceptance were being contemplated."[23]

As Kawai pointed out, one indicator of Japanese attitudes was the performance of the Tokyo stock exchange. Dormant throughout the war, the market showed a sudden spurt of activity the day after the Potsdam Proclamation was announced—and on August 2 registered an average jump of three points. It was well known that Japanese business leaders commonly had inside information—and the greatest gains were made in such peacetime consumer industries as beer, tobacco, paper, and textiles. "The more perceiving sections of the Japanese public had no difficulty in understanding what the government's attitude was," Kawai observed. "The announcement of the Potsdam terms raised perceptible hopes that peace was near."[24]

Nonetheless, "[t]he Japanese government soon discovered to its dismay . . . that the meaning of its policy of 'mokusatsu' had been completely misinterpreted by the outside world."[25] Kawai's overall conclusion was judicious:

> The subsequent course of events predicated on the assumption that Japan had rejected the Potsdam Declaration represents a tragedy of errors for which the major responsibility must be attributed to the inexcusable bungling of the Japanese officials. . . .

Kawai also cautiously observed, however, that

> some measure of responsibility also rests upon the more excusable but unfortunate deficiency in perception on the part of the Western allied leaders and upon the calculated reluctance of the Russian authorities to share their information with their Western Allies.[26]

As is obvious from the last sentence, Kawai's early postwar study was written before information on two key points had been made available to scholars: He assumed the Allies knew nothing of the Japanese peace initiatives; and his criticism of the Russians for their "calculated reluctance" to share information also clearly assumed Western ignorance of the approaches to Moscow.

The American historian Robert J. C. Butow followed up on Kawai's study in his 1954 book *Japan's Decision to Surrender*. Like Kawai, Butow also noted that *mokusatsu* had several possible meanings—literally to "kill with silence," and more idiomatically, to "take no notice of it," "treat it with silent contempt," or "ignore it." Butow suggested that initially Togo had obtained the agreement of the Cabinet (on Friday, July 27) that ". . . Japan should not issue an 'answer' to the Allied proclamation but should merely content herself with ascertaining Soviet intentions."[27]

"[S]omehow," Butow observed, "and just how, either no one knows or cares to say—the Premier's phrase, 'mokusatsu,' passed out of the conference room Friday afternoon and found its way onto the front pages of Japan's Saturday morning papers." For anyone "privy to the cabinet's decision, *mokusatsu* may have conveyed the meaning of 'withholding comment,' " he added, "but under the circumstances then prevailing the whole burden of choosing a term which not even a language-school beginner could have misinterpreted rested with the government."[28] Butow concluded:

> Perhaps Japan meant to convey that her attitude was "wait and see," but the Allied reaction to Japan's response was based on what Japan *said* and not what she *meant*.[29]

"The obvious inference, and the one drawn in Washington by the then Secretary of War, Mr. Stimson, was rejection."[30]

As with Kawai's study, the date of Butow's book is significant: The Forrestal diary was published in abridged form in 1951—three years prior to *Japan's Decision*. This indicated that at least Forrestal had seen portions of intercepts on July 13, 15, and 24. In a footnote Butow speculated: "Although Forrestal does not make it clear who—besides himself—knew about the deciphered cables, it seems logical to assume that the President and the Secretary of State were informed. This assumption is supported by the material quoted in Byrnes, *Speaking Frankly*, 211 ff., although the latter may be based on information obtained after the war and not during it."[31]

The MAGIC intercepts were not available until 1978, but in the course of his research Butow had gained access to at least some of the original cables sent and received by the Japanese Foreign Office.[32] As his note speculating that Byrnes may have based his account on postwar information suggests, Butow did not know precisely which of the original cables (or that all of them) had been intercepted. The key point is that the intercepts did indeed indicate that the Japanese government's position was far closer to "wait and see" than to a dismissal.

Other passages of Butow's study suggest he was not unaware of the central issue. Quite apart from his assessment of the final *mokusatsu* confusion, Butow's judgment of the meaning of the few intercepts available to him in 1954 (specifically, Togo's cables of July 12 and 21) was unmistakable:

> It was all there, clear as crystal:
> "Togo to Sato: . . . Unconditional surrender is the only obstacle to peace."[33]

Chapter 33

RACE TO THE FINISH

Aboard Augusta/ President, Leahy, JFB agrred [sic] Japas [sic] looking for peace. (Leahy had another report from the Pacific) President afraid they will sue for peace through Russia instead of some country like Sweden.
　　　　　　—Walter Brown, diary entry of August 3, 1945

Documents which have become available since the early 1950s, when Kawai and Butow did their studies, help clarify the critical issue of what U.S. officials actually knew at the time—and whether top American leaders truly "misunderstood" the meaning of Japanese officials as they suggested.

There is no longer much doubt that U.S. policy-makers were aware that what was going on inside the Japanese government was an intense effort to figure out just what the Potsdam Proclamation meant—and what, precisely, was being demanded of it.

That the Japanese were studying the proclamation before making a real response was self-evident. Moreover, that time had to be allowed for this to occur had been stressed repeatedly by Stimson, Grew, and others at various points throughout the spring and summer of 1945.*

There was also considerable public evidence at the time that the term *mokusatsu* was not to be regarded as a simple and straightforward rejection of U.S. terms. Well before the bombings the U.S. press had, in fact, offered much more sophisticated analyses of the Japanese response to the Potsdam Proclamation—and of Japan's internal situation—than were later to become the conventional wisdom. For instance, on July 16, just as the Potsdam con-

---

*As noted, had a statement clarifying the surrender formula been offered upon the fall of Okinawa—the time virtually every top-level military and civilian official involved except Byrnes thought appropriate—there would have been some five to six weeks of warning. Had a statement been issued at the end of May, as Grew first proposed, there would have been roughly nine weeks of warning.

ference was about to get under way, *Newsweek* contributing editor Compton Pakenham pointed out that a public dialogue with Japan on the surrender issue would be unimaginable since "the civilian government is flanked by the Japanese Army. . . ." Only a private diplomatic effort could be taken seriously:

> For a civilian government to give a hint that it proposed throwing in the sponge would likely be the same as actual suicide.[1]

Again, on July 30—just after the proclamation was issued—another *Newsweek* story underscored the difference between public statements coming out of Tokyo and private negotiations:

> As Allied air and sea attacks hammered the stricken homeland, Japan's leaders assessed the war situation and found it bordering on the disastrous. . . . As usual, the nation's propaganda media spewed out brave double-talk of hope and defiance.

However, the article also reported the inside information that:

> Behind that curtain Japan had put forward at least one definite offer. Fearing the results of Russian participation in the war, Tokyo transmitted to Generalissimo Joseph Stalin the broad terms on which it professed willingness to settle all scores.[2]

Again, although a number of editorials simply supported the Administration without qualification, on August 1 the *Washington Post* stated: "It was to be expected that Premier Suzuki would reject the terms of surrender outlined in the Potsdam communication. . . ."[3] And the *Army and Navy Journal* believed it obvious that "the announcement by Premier Suzuki that the Japanese cabinet was ignoring the Potsdam ultimatum for unconditional surrender cannot be accepted on face value as a rejection. . . ."

> It was to be expected that some such statement would be made by the Premier, if serious consideration was to be given to the ultimatum. It would be natural for Japan or any other power in her position, to throw a cloak over her study of the ultimatum and such efforts as might be desirable in the direction of ascertaining more explicitly the implications of some of the proffered terms—the prospective status in a defeated Japan, for example, of Emperor Hirohito, who was not mentioned in the proclamation of the Allied leaders.[4]*

---

*Similarly, Ernest K. Lindley commented in *Newsweek*: "It was not to be expected that the Japanese Government would instantly accept the proposals. Even if it had already decided to surrender, it could be expected to angle a little longer for better terms." (Lindley, "The Value of the Potsdam Terms," *Newsweek*, August 6, 1945, p. 22.)

Some important evidence bearing on this matter was made available in 1969. We now know that on August 2 the acting director of the OSS, Charles Cheston, also reported to Truman on an initiative taken by Japanese officials in Switzerland which urged that:

> The Allies should not take "too seriously" what was said over the Tokyo Radio about the tripartite proclamation. This radio comment was merely "propaganda to maintain morale in Japan." The real reply will be given through some "official channel", possibly by Minister Kase or General Okamoto, if an official Government reply is not made over Tokyo Radio.[5]

Other information reported to the president also strongly suggested that Japanese officials were not "rejecting" the Potsdam Proclamation, but rather that they were trying to decipher its meaning along with all the other signals Tokyo was receiving—that is, studying the terms. Indeed, U.S. experts framed the issue precisely this way: War Department intelligence analysts presented cable summaries between Togo and Sato in the July 29 MAGIC intercepts under the heading: *"Tokyo 'studying' Allied ultimatum."*[6]

Perhaps the most important information reaching Truman and Byrnes, however, was contained in messages which arrived on August 2 and August 3—just as the *Augusta* began the return voyage home from Potsdam. We noted above that the August 2 MAGIC report suggested the "unanimous determination" of top leaders in Tokyo that Japan should seek peace. The decision to send a special envoy to Russia, Togo had also stressed, had been made "in accordance with the highest leaders of [this] Government." And, further, that:

> (Under the circumstances there is a disposition to make the Potsdam Three Power Proclamation the basis of our study concerning terms.)[7]

The MAGIC report of August 3 contained a second, delayed portion of the same cable which was even more specific. Under the subheading, *"Japanese Army's interest in peace negotiations,"* War Department intelligence analysts stressed that

> The second half of Foreign Minister Togo's 2 August message to Ambassador Sato—now available—contains the first statement to appear in the traffic that the Japanese Army is interested in the effort to end the war with Soviet assistance.

A segment of Togo's message, as noted, was quite explicit about this critical point: "The Premier and the leaders of the Army are now concentrating all their attention on this one point."[8]

Although there was obviously still room for considerable debate about final terms, several strands of development now came together with dramatic urgency. All along it had been clear that a surrender could be achieved only with the support of the Japanese military leadership. The personal intervention of the Emperor had been a major development in this regard, since the traditionalist army was sworn to obey his order. As yet, however, only fragmentary reports of the army's involvement or support of the actual surrender process had emerged.

It had also been plain that the shock of a Soviet declaration of war would likely have extraordinary impact—especially on the army's position. Moreover, the Emperor's attempt to secure Moscow's help had greatly enhanced the potential significance of a Red Army attack: Russian assistance with the negotiations represented Japan's last (distant) possibility of ending the war on honorable terms; if this tiny fragment of hope were shattered, there would be nothing left. With the army now focused explicitly on Moscow, the point was even more obvious. Appropriately, the July 30 *Newsweek* story was headlined: "Heavy Allied Blows, Fear of Reds Make Jap Leaders Seek Way Out."[9]

Truman, Byrnes, and top advisers now faced still another choice. The president had gone to Potsdam expressly to obtain a Russian declaration of war. "Fini Japs when that comes about," he had noted in mid-July before there were indications that the Japanese Army leaders had fallen into line behind the Emperor's initiative.[10] A Russian declaration of war could now only be more potent.

The question was what to do about Russia.

The answer given by the president and his advisers is not in doubt. As previously noted, documents made public in 1960 show that on July 23 Truman had sent a cable drafted by Byrnes to Chiang Kai-shek requesting that he not make any further concessions to Russia.[11] As Byrnes subsequently explained, the goal was

> to encourage the Chinese to continue negotiations after the adjournment of the Potsdam Conference. I had some fear that if they did not, Stalin might immediately enter the war. . . . On the other hand, if Stalin and Chiang were still negotiating, it might delay Soviet entrance and the Japanese might surrender. The President was in accord with that view.[12]

We have also noted that the full Forrestal diary of July 28 provides this contemporaneous confirmation:

> Byrnes said he was most anxious to get the Japanese affair over with before the Russians got in, with particular reference to Dairen and Port Arthur. Once in there, he felt it would not be easy to get them out. With all this in mind, [Byrnes] was in favor of Soong's return to Moscow,

which he proposes to do, in order to keep the conversation on this subject going.[13]

Now, apparently worried that Stalin might become impatient with the continued stalling, or that Soong might yield, on August 5 Truman and Byrnes
sent further instructions to Harriman requesting that "no agreement be made
involving further concessions by China. . . ."[14]

On July 17, in his journal Truman had privately noted that "[m]ost of the
big points are settled"—and the next day, writing to his wife, that "Soong did
better than I asked him."[15] Clearly now, however, there was no interest in using the shock of Russian entry to speed a surrender—even though its value
had become much greater. Quite the contrary.

Indeed, the first days of August now took on the air of a frenzied race for
time. As Soong prepared to meet with Stalin on August 7, the specially
trained 509th Composite Group of the 20th Air Force waited for the weather
to clear over target cities in Japan. The July 25 order to General Spaatz had
set the bombing for "after about" August 3.[16]*

How long could the Red Army be stalled on the Manchurian border? If the
weather cleared, long enough for the weapon to be used against Hiroshima
on August 6.

New evidence bearing on the atomic bomb story has come to light in a variety of different ways over the last fifty years. Most important is that official
records have been declassified—either as a matter of routine (or special) declassification procedures, or in response to Freedom of Information Act challenges. In some cases, after many years private citizens involved at the
time—or their heirs—have decided to open personal papers for public inspection and historical research. Accidental "finds" have also produced discoveries of historical importance.

In connection with evidence concerning Truman's attitude at this time,
none of the above occurred. Certain critical evidence concerning the president's personal understanding of the situation when he authorized the use
of the atomic bomb has been available for roughly three decades. As in the
case of many things in life, it appears that its significance was simply overlooked.

We noted above that parts of the diaries of Byrnes' assistant Walter Brown
were made available in the 1960s. Many scholars have studied these papers
and have found them particularly illuminating in connection with Byrnes'
strategy towards the Russians during the Potsdam conference.

---

*The weapon used against Hiroshima was assembled on the island of Tinian. With the excep-
tion of three critical elements which were flown in separately, the bomb was transported to
Tinian aboard the cruiser *Indianapolis*, arriving on July 26. It was ready for use on July 31.

Just after the conference, however, in his diary entry of August 3, Brown described how Truman, Byrnes, and Leahy viewed the situation when they received the key intercepts we have just reviewed. Three days prior to the bombing of Hiroshima, Brown noted:

> Aboard Augusta/ President, Leahy, JFB agrred [*sic*] Japas [*sic*] looking for peace. (Leahy had another report from Pacific) President afraid they will sue for peace through Russia instead of some country like Sweden.[17]

It is commonly held that Truman simply had no choice except to use the atomic bomb—or that he did not understand the emerging reality.

This contemporaneous diary report—together with the wide range of other evidence this and numerous other studies have reviewed—strongly suggests otherwise.

Chapter 34

THE END OF THE WAR

The sky filled with black smoke and glowing sparks. Flames rose and the heat set currents of air in motion. . . . Pieces of flaming wood soared and fell like fiery swallows. . . .

The streets were deserted except for the dead. . . .

Hiroshima was no longer a city, but a burnt-over prairie. To the east and to the west everything was flattened. The distant mountains seemed nearer than I could ever remember. The hills of Ushita and the woods of Nigitsu loomed out of the haze and smoke like the nose and eyes on a face. How small Hiroshima was with its houses gone.

—From the diary of a Hiroshima resident,
Dr. M. Hachiya, August 6, 1945

Hiroshima was destroyed at 8:15 a.m., on August 6, 1945. Still concerned about what Russia would do some thirty-four hours after the bombing, Japanese officials urgently sought clarification of the Soviet position. On August 7, MAGIC intercepts revealed Foreign Minister Togo cabling Ambassador Sato:

> The situation is becoming more and more pressing, and we would like to know at once the explicit attitude of the Russians. So will you put forth still greater efforts to get a reply from them in haste.[1]

At 5:00 p.m. Moscow time on August 8—although Chinese Foreign Minister Soong and Molotov had not reached final agreement on the Yalta terms—the Soviet Union declared war on Japan.[2] Units of the Red Army crossed the Manchurian border at 12:10 a.m. (local Manchurian time) on the morning of August 9.[3]

Later that morning, shortly after 11:00 a.m., Nagasaki was bombed.

At an afternoon Cabinet meeting on August 10 (according to the diary of Commerce Secretary Henry Wallace), "Truman said he had given orders to stop atomic bombing. He said the thought of wiping out another 100,000 people was too horrible. He didn't like the idea of killing as he said, 'all those kids.' "[4]

On hearing of the Hiroshima bombing, Togo requested a meeting with the Emperor—who agreed the time had come to surrender. A conference of the top six officials (the Big Six) was called for August 8, but army leaders indicated they were "too busy" to attend. A meeting was then scheduled for August 9 and at 10:30 a.m.—a few hours after receiving news of the Soviet declaration of war—the Japanese leaders sat down to discuss surrender.

While the meeting was in progress, news of the Nagasaki bombing was received. However, after an entire day of meetings—including an almost eight-hour Cabinet session—no decision was reached. Finally Premier Suzuki took the unprecedented step of requesting the Emperor's views. Hirohito "swallow[ed] [his] own tears and [gave his] sanction to the proposal to accept the Allied proclamation on the basis outlined by [Togo]."[5] On the morning of August 10, the Japanese Foreign Ministry sent a surrender offer to its representatives in Stockholm and Berne.

The offer accepted the Potsdam Proclamation with one sole condition—the now familiar (and continued) requirement that the Emperor be protected:

> The Japanese Government are ready to accept the terms enumerated in the Joint Declaration which was issued at Potsdam on July 26 . . . with the understanding that the said Declaration does not comprise any demand which prejudices the prerogatives of His Majesty as a sovereign ruler.[6]*

Truman, on the advice of Leahy (supported by Stimson), favored immediate acceptance of the offer.[7]† However, Byrnes—who joined the White House gathering late—was irked with Leahy. (Byrnes told Brown that Leahy still "thought he was Secretary of State, just as he was under Roosevelt, and [I] had to show him differently. . . ."[8]) Byrnes pointed out that "the big-3 [sic] said 'unconditional surrender' " at Potsdam; this was before the bomb and the Russian attack. "Truman asked to see statement," Brown reports—continuing:

---

*See the Afterword for a discussion of the complex evidence on the internal Japanese process leading to this and the subsequent surrender decision—and for further references.
†Again, note the president's apparent lack of concern about political criticism. It is sometimes held that at this meeting Byrnes objected to offering assurances for the Emperor. More likely, as his quoted comments suggest, he was primarily upset by the draft cable Leahy had prepared (which apparently downplayed the phrase "unconditional surrender"). Brown's report that Leahy's message "would have led to the crucifixion of the president" has also sometimes been cited as opposition to keeping the Emperor rather than concern about the specific language of Leahy's draft—a view that is difficult to sustain given that the cable sent on August 11 allowed for the Emperor's continued presence. It is also unclear if the word "crucifixion" is Brown's or Byrnes'. See WB's Book, August 10, 1945, Folder 602, Byrnes Papers, CUL.

JFB cited page, paragraph and line of Potsdam declaration. Forrestal spoke up for JFB's position. Truman swung over. . . . JFB had lunch with the president and said that the two of them had to decide the question and there could not be so many cooks. Truman agreed and JFB message as written was sent.[9]

On August 11 (after receiving the approval of Great Britain, China, and the Soviet Union) a carefully worded response accepted Japan's surrender. The key clause artfully finessed the central issue. Although it held to the rhetoric of "unconditional surrender," it also implicitly recognized the Emperor's position:

> From the moment of surrender the authority of the Emperor and the Japanese Government to rule the state shall be subject to the Supreme Commander of the Allied powers who will take such steps as he deems proper to effectuate the surrender terms.[10]

As American officials now impatiently awaited Tokyo's acceptance, the Red Army advanced rapidly into Manchuria. Virtually unopposed by the once formidable Japanese Kwantung Army (now "bled white of trained units and of first-line equipment," as Raymond Garthoff has written), Russian troops covered some twenty-five miles in the first day of their offensive.[11] "Never have I known time to pass so slowly," Byrnes later recalled.[12] (In Japan, Suzuki is reported to have said: "Is the Kwantung Army that weak? Then the game is up."[13])

On August 13—even as Tokyo struggled to devise a final response—intercepted MAGIC cables reported a "Japanese Army General Staff statement on surrender." The text (dated August 12) from the vice chief of the Army General Staff to Japan's military attachés in Sweden, Switzerland, and Portugal, included two main points. The first concerned the cause of the surrender negotiations:

> As a result of Russia's entrance into the war, the Empire, in the fourth year of its [war] endeavor, is faced with a struggle for the existence of the nation.

The second used a traditional formula to make clear the one critical point which would not be given up:

> You are well aware of the fact that as a final move toward the preservation of the national structure [i.e., the Emperor and the Imperial system], diplomatic negotiations have been opened. . . . Unless the aforementioned condition is fulfilled, we will continue the war to the bitter end.[14]

The atomic bomb was neither mentioned in the army message nor cited as reason for the surrender negotiations.*

On August 14 at 2:49 p.m. local time (1:49 a.m. August 14, Washington time), Radio Tokyo announced that Japan's surrender would shortly be forthcoming in accord with the new U.S. terms implicitly assuring the position of the Emperor.[15]

Previously, while discussing the Japanese surrender offer and possible responses during the morning meeting of August 10, Truman, Byrnes, Stimson, Forrestal, and Leahy—together with director of War Mobilization and Reconversion John Snyder, the president's military aide General Harry Vaughan, and the president's naval aide Captain James K. Vardaman—had also discussed military strategy. Stimson's diary records that in addition to pointing out that the Emperor would be useful in achieving surrender, he suggested that something like an armistice over the settlement of the

> question was inevitable and that it would be a humane thing and the thing that might effect the settlement if we stopped the bombing during that time—stopped it immediately.[16]

Forrestal, who agreed with Stimson, recorded in his own diary that Stimson had also "cited the growing feeling of apprehension and misgiving as to the effect of the atomic bomb even in our own country."[17]

Stimson's diary reports that his suggestion to stop conventional bombing "was rejected on the ground that it couldn't be done at once because we had not yet received in official form the Japanese surrender. . . ." The entry continues: "This of course was a correct but narrow reason, for the Japanese had broadcast their offer of surrender through every country in the world."[18]

Truman did, in fact, order conventional military operations halted after the Japanese message of August 10. However, on August 14, Generals Kenney and Spaatz received orders to continue their efforts full force.[19] After Radio Tokyo had broadcast that Japanese surrender was forthcoming (1:49 a.m., Washington time, August 14) but before the message had reached Washington through official channels, Arnold (who wished to stage as big a finale as possible) was permitted to launch a massive bombing raid in which 1,014 aircraft dropped six thousand tons of conventional explosives on Honshu.[20]

The formal surrender reply broadcast by Radio Tokyo earlier in the day was received from Tokyo through Switzerland at 6:00 p.m. (Washington time). Its essential paragraphs stated:

*See the Afterword for a review of the ongoing debate concerning the army's role at this point—and over whether the bombs or the Red Army, or both, brought the surrender.

With reference to the Japanese Government's note of August 10 regarding their acceptance of the provisions of the Potsdam declaration and the reply of the Governments of the United States, Great Britain, the Soviet Union, and China sent by American Secretary of State Byrnes under the date of August 11, the Japanese Government have the honor to communicate to the Governments of the four powers as follows:

1. His Majesty the Emperor has issued an Imperial rescript regarding Japan's acceptance of the provisions of the Potsdam declaration.

2. His Majesty the Emperor is prepared to authorize and ensure the signature by his government and the Imperial General Headquarters of the necessary terms for carrying out the provisions of the Potsdam declaration. His Majesty is also prepared to issue his commands to all the military, naval, and air authorities of Japan and all the forces under their control wherever located to cease active operations, to surrender arms and to issue such other orders as may be required by the Supreme Commander of the Allied Forces for the execution of the above-mentioned terms.[21]

The final result was greeted with wild enthusiasm throughout the United States. There was virtually no criticism from important political figures or the mainstream press of the fact that the Emperor's position had been maintained.

In the early 1970s, Thomas G. Paterson—a historian studying the papers of Vermont's Republican Senator Warren R. Austin—found a memorandum dated August 20, 1945, which recorded a meeting with James F. Byrnes. It stated in part:

Secretary Byrnes had hoped that we could finish up with the Japanese *without* participation by the Russians. . . .

Premier Stalin early indicated to Secretary Byrnes that he intended to come in, but he said he could not mobilize before the 15th of August. Secretary Byrnes was very anxious that this be true. He hoped that the Russians could not mobilize until that time because he knew of the development of the atomic bomb and the probability of its being effective.[22]

Book Two

THE MYTH

That evening we were all very quiet as we gathered in the wardroom for dinner. We knew that even before the bomb was dropped the enemy had been defeated and seeking peace. There was an air of sadness at the thought of Hiroshima's needless destruction. Finally one of our officers broke the silence. "Why?" was all he said. . . .

When I returned home after the war and told my story, people would look at me in complete disbelief. They all seemed totally convinced by the media and governmental pronouncements that the dropping of the bombs was absolutely essential to ending the war.

—Former Navy Chaplain Willard H. Reeves,
"Remembering Hiroshima"

How is it that so many people should be so ignorant of important facts a half century after Hiroshima?

In one sense, of course, everything was self-evident. The atomic bombs fell; the war ended.

On August 14 the president announced: "I have received this afternoon a message from the Japanese Government. . . . I deem this reply a full acceptance of the Potsdam Declaration which specifies the unconditional surrender of Japan. In the reply there is no qualification."[1]

What was there to discuss?

Moreover, the boys were coming home. Millions of young men and women were thrilled: the bomb had saved their lives. "[W]e cried with relief and joy. . . . We were going to grow up to adulthood after all," Paul Fussell later wrote.[2] Another responded: "I did not cry when I heard the news, I just got drunk with happiness. . . . My luck would have run out, I am convinced, if I had been a part of the invasion of Japan. . . ."[3]

Perhaps fifty million Americans—the fathers and mothers and wives and children and brothers and sisters of the men and women in uniform—"knew," too, that a loved one had been saved from possible death.

If aunts, uncles, cousins, grandparents, and close friends were included, virtually every individual in American society knew someone personally whose life, it appeared, had been saved or might possibly have been saved by the extraordinary new weapon.

Rarely has so powerful a cultural transmission belt for so seemingly obvious an idea existed in history.

And, of course, the descendants of all these Americans passed on the memory and the "knowledge" of these events to the next generation, to our own time in history.

It would be quite understandable if the idea that the use of the atomic bomb was necessary lingered for a very long time—quite apart from efforts that were made to persuade Americans of this conclusion.

On the other hand, it would be surprising if what most Americans have been taught to believe about the Hiroshima story were simply an accident.

PART I

Henry L. Stimson

. . . this deliberate, premeditated destruction was our least abhorrent choice.

—Henry L. Stimson, 1947

Chapter 35

A DIRECT APPROACH
TO RUSSIA

. . . I think the bomb . . . constitutes merely a first step in a new control by man over the forces of nature too revolutionary and dangerous to fit into the old concepts.
—Secretary of War Henry L. Stimson
to President Harry S. Truman, September 11, 1945

Polls taken in August 1945 indicate that an amazing 85 percent of Americans approved the use of the atomic bomb. Many believed that regardless of how destructive the new weapon was, the Japanese got what they deserved.[1]

American newspaper editorials almost unanimously applauded the attacks.[2] According to one study, only 1.7 percent of 595 newspaper editorials surveyed opposed using the atomic bomb.[3] *The New York Times* put it succinctly: "By their own cruelty and treachery our enemies had invited the worst we could do to them."[4] The *Atlanta Constitution* editorialized:

> If it were not for the treachery of Pearl Harbor; the horrible cruelties of the Death March of Japan [*sic*]; the stories told by the starved, filth-encrusted, dazed American prisoners coming out of Japanese prison camps, we might feel sorrow for the Japanese who felt the atomic bomb.[5]

Initial radio coverage—as Michael Yavenditti has observed—"implicitly and explicitly justified the bomb's use by emphasizing the military value of Hiroshima; by claiming that Japan had sufficient warning through the Potsdam Declaration; by reminding listeners of Japan's atrocities; or by arguing that, because Japan never signed the Hague Convention, she was not entitled to claim immunities under its terms."[6]

Nor were such views restricted to mainstream opinion. Paul Boller, who surveyed responses to the bombing on the part of the "American left," observes: "To say that the *Nation*, the *New Republic*, and *PM* supported the bombing of Hiroshima and Nagasaki is to understate the matter. All three publications took for granted, from the beginning, the necessity and desirability of the bombings."[7] On August 9 John P. Lewis—managing editor of the very liberal newspaper *PM*—wrote: "While we are dropping atomic bombs why not drop a few on Tokyo, where there's a chance to run up our batting average on the royal family—and clear the bases for democracy after the war."[8]*

A strong strand of racism also could be detected in many of the affirming judgments. In his book *War Without Mercy: Race and Power in the Pacific War*, John Dower has shown how Americans during World War II created and accepted an image of the Japanese as being so different from Americans as to be less than human. The same month the air force began low-altitude incendiary bombing of Japanese cities, for instance, a cartoon of a slant-eyed, buck-toothed insect appeared in the U.S. Marine monthly *Leatherneck*. Titled "Louseous Japanicas," the cartoon caption proclaimed:

> The first serious outbreak of this lice epidemic was officially noted on December 7, 1941. . . . To the Marine Corps . . . was assigned the gigantic task of extermination. . . . But before a complete cure may be effected the origin of the plague, the breeding grounds around the Tokyo area, must be completely annihilated.[9]

A significant portion of the American public went so far as to favor a policy of genocide toward the entire Japanese people. According to a December 1944 Gallup poll, 13 percent of those surveyed urged the extermination of all Japanese.[10]

Whatever the quality of his private, somewhat limited influence with President Truman, Henry L. Stimson was far and away the most prominent American official publicly identified with the building and use of the atomic bomb. Moreover, he was to become *the* spokesman for the decision.

It is not surprising, however—given the response to the bombings—that at the outset the man who bore public responsibility for creating the atomic bomb was little worried about criticism of its use. Initially, other—related, but quite different—problems filled his mind.

---

*Far less visible were the writings of such radicals as Dwight Macdonald, editor of *Politics*. Unlike the larger liberal papers and magazines, Macdonald believed Hiroshima to be a fundamental turning point: "[S]uch atrocities as The Bomb and the Nazi death camps are *right now* brutalizing, warping, deadening the human beings who are expected to change the world for the better. . . ." (Dwight Macdonald, "The Bomb," *Politics*, Vol. 2, No. 9 [September 1945], p. 258.)

We do not know all the political and moral themes which dominated Stimson's thinking in the late summer and early autumn of 1945. However, it is clear from his diaries that he began to have second thoughts about a number of issues. McCloy joined him twice at his Adirondack Mountain retreat during the initial weeks. Stimson later recalled that their talks involved "long and painful thoughts about the atomic triumph"—and about the dangers of an arms race.[11] Above all, Stimson was deeply concerned by the approach James F. Byrnes had taken to the new weapon.

Shortly after Hiroshima, McCloy had met with Byrnes and reported to Stimson that the secretary of state was "quite radically opposed to any approach to Stalin whatever. He was on the point of departing for the foreign ministers' meeting and wished to have the implied threat of the bomb in his pocket during the conference."[12]

Stimson himself also had a highly disturbing conversation with Byrnes following a September 4 White House meeting:

> . . . I took up the question which I had been working at with McCloy up in St. Hubert's, namely how to handle Russia with the big bomb. I found that Byrnes was very much against any attempt to cooperate with Russia. His mind is full of his problems with the coming meeting of the foreign ministers and he looks to having the presence of the bomb in his pocket, so to speak, as a great weapon to get through the thing he has.[13]

This particular conversation made a lasting impression on Stimson. Byrnes went off to the September meeting of foreign ministers in London, and a few weeks later Stimson's diary again records:

> . . . I was much worried over what Secretary Byrnes had said to me about his coming conference with the Foreign Ministers at which he proposed to keep the bomb, so to speak, in his hip pocket without any suggestion of sharing it with Russia.[14]*

Byrnes' concern with Eastern Europe had become a centerpiece of official U.S. policy. As we have noted, Truman declared that Rumania, Bulgaria,

---

*On October 19, Robert Oppenheimer met with Secretary of Commerce Henry Wallace. Wallace's diary states: "I never saw a man in such an extremely nervous state as Oppenheimer. He seemed to feel that the destruction of the entire human race was imminent. . . . He wanted to know if I thought it would do any good for him to see the President. I said yes. . . . He says that Secretary Byrnes' attitude on the bomb has been very bad. It seems that Secretary Byrnes has felt that we could use the bomb as a pistol to get what we wanted in international diplomacy. Oppenheimer believes that that method will not work. . . . He thinks the mishandling of the situation at Potsdam has prepared the way for the eventual slaughter of tens of millions or perhaps hundreds of millions of innocent people." (Wallace Diary, October 19, 1945; in Wallace, *The Price of Vision*, ed. Blum, pp. 496–97.)

and Hungary were "not to be spheres of influence of any one power" on August 9—the day of the Nagasaki bombing.[15] In the same speech the president also indicated his opposition to any early attempt to achieve international control of atomic weapons. The United States, he announced, would "constitute ourselves trustees of this new force—to prevent its misuse, and to turn it into the channels of service to mankind."[16]

Nine days after this presidential statement, Stimson gave a brief talk to friends at the Ausable Club in the Adirondacks—a talk that, as Godfrey Hodgson has noted, manifests more than a hint of his growing "moral unease"[17]—concerning the "forces of terrific destructiveness" which the United States had "been compelled to invent and unleash."

> Unless we now develop methods of international life, backed by the spirit of tolerance and kindliness, viz: the spirit of Christianity, sufficient to make international life permanent and kindly and war impossible, we will with another war end our civilization.[18]

World War II had left Stimson exhausted and in poor health, "nearing the limits of his strength."[19] For several months during the spring and summer he had increasingly frequent heart attacks.[20] "I am much gratified that I was able to outlast both the Germans and the Japs, but my victory on V-J Day was a pretty narrow one," he later wrote Herbert Hoover.[21] Two days after the bombing of Hiroshima, Stimson appears to have suffered still another mild attack.[22]

Despite his precarious health and doctors' orders to get complete rest, sometime during this period Stimson concluded that he had to make at least one attempt to challenge Byrnes' general approach to the new weapon. Assisted by McCloy, he decided to draft a memorandum to Truman urging a radically different approach.

The memorandum was to become a historic statement of Stimson's considered judgment of the choices available a half century before 50,000 nuclear warheads came to be dispersed across the globe—and a document which offered revealing insight, too, into how other top U.S. policy-makers viewed the atomic bomb at the time.

Henry L. Stimson has come down to us in history as a revered figure, almost too perfect in character ever to be judged. As scholars like Richard Current and Richard W. Van Alstyne have shown, such a picture is flawed. Though dignified and austere, Stimson was quite human—and a shrewd political strategist to boot. His career as Taft's secretary of war, as Coolidge's special emissary in Nicaragua, as governor general of the Philippines, and as Hoover's secretary of state suggests that he was also quite willing occasionally to cut corners, trim the truth, and use "spin control" to manipulate the press.*

What marked Stimson as different was a remarkable quality which he now exhibited in dramatic form.

The cover letter he sent to Truman with his memorandum was something exceedingly rare in politics. It was a frank admission to the president of the United States of Stimson's belief that the advice he had given him only a few weeks earlier concerning the atomic bomb's future role in American diplomacy was wrong.

As we have noted, while at Potsdam Stimson had advised Truman that he believed the United States might use the new discovery to help bring the Soviet Union to abandon its system and perhaps become something of a Western-style democracy.[23] "I still recognize the difficulty," he now wrote, "and am still convinced of the ultimate importance of a change in Russian attitude toward individual liberty but I have come to the conclusion that it would not be possible to use our possession of the atomic bomb as a direct lever to produce the change."[24] To attempt to pressure the Russians, he now felt, was likely to produce just the opposite of what the United States desired. It would be "so resented that it would make the objective we have in view less probable."[25]

The real danger—the one which could potentially shatter all of human civilization—was the bomb itself, and Byrnes' attitude toward it. At the heart of Stimson's memorandum to the president was an urgent plea for an immediate private approach to the Russians to attempt to head off an arms race of potentially world-destroying proportions:

> In a world atmosphere already extremely sensitive to power, the introduction of this weapon has profoundly affected political considerations in all sections of the globe. . . .
>
> If the atomic bomb were merely another though more devastating military weapon to be assimilated into our pattern of international relations, it would be one thing. We could then follow the old custom of secrecy and nationalistic military superiority relying on international caution to prescribe the future use of the weapon as we did with gas.

"But I think the bomb instead constitutes merely a first step in a new control by man over the forces of nature too revolutionary and dangerous to fit into the old concepts."[26]

---

*Van Alstyne notes that in connection with Manchuria during the 1930s, Stimson's carefully considered written statements, in particular, often were difficult to "reconcile" with "the documented record"—an opinion echoed by Current in connection with Nicaragua. (Richard W. Van Alstyne, cited in Current, *Secretary Stimson*, p. 14.)

The atomic bomb was clearly playing a critical role as Byrnes prepared for his first post-Hiroshima negotiations. Focusing specifically on this immediate question, Stimson noted that in "many quarters it has been interpreted as a substantial offset to the growth of Russian influence on the continent."[27] The problem was that the implications were not being faced. What had to be squarely addressed, Stimson argued, was that:

> We can be certain that the Soviet government has sensed this tendency and the temptation will be strong for the Soviet political and military leaders to acquire this weapon in the shortest possible time. Britain in effect already has the status of a partner with us in the development of this weapon. Accordingly, unless the Soviets are voluntarily invited into the partnership upon a basis of co-operation and trust, we are going to maintain the Anglo-Saxon bloc over against the Soviet in the possession of this weapon.

"Such a condition will almost certainly stimulate feverish activity on the part of the Soviet toward the development of this bomb in what will in effect be a secret armament race of a rather desperate character."[28]*

Nor, contrary to some later accounts, was Stimson simply making an abstract and general argument. He turned to the specific issue at hand—Byrnes' view of the bomb as leverage to help solve European problems in the context of the evolving peace treaty deliberations:

> If we feel, as I assume we must, that civilization demands that some day we shall arrive at a satisfactory international arrangement respecting the control of this new force, the question then is how long we can afford to enjoy our momentary superiority in the hope of achieving our immediate peace council objectives.[29]

Stimson had no doubt about where wisdom lay—and he now penned several lines which were to be cited time and again over the next half century: "To put the matter concisely, I consider the problem of our satisfactory relations with Russia as not merely connected with but as virtually dominated by the problem of the atomic bomb."

> Except for the problem of the control of that bomb, those relations, while vitally important, might not be immediately pressing. The establishment of relations of mutual confidence between her and us could

---

*On August 20, 1945, the State Defense Committee of the Soviet Union established a Special Committee on the Atomic Bomb. Under the chairmanship of Stalin's notorious secret-police chief Lavrentii Beria, the Special Committee was charged with overseeing a crash program to build a Soviet bomb. (Holloway, *Stalin and the Bomb*, pp. 116, 134.)

afford to await the slow progress of time. But with the discovery of the bomb, they became immediately emergent.[30]

In his memoirs Stimson subsequently underscored the next sentence to emphasize what he saw as the most urgent and immediate problem. Repeating the same phrases which had leapt to mind in his September 4 White House meeting with Byrnes, he stressed:

> *Those relations may be perhaps irretrievably embittered by the way in which we approach the solution of the bomb with Russia. For if we fail to approach them now and merely continue to negotiate with them, having this weapon rather ostentatiously on our hip, their suspicions and their distrust of our purposes and motives will increase.*[31]

Stimson's concrete policy recommendations in connection with what we today call the "proliferation" problem were straightforward. He proposed a serious effort "to enter an arrangement with the Russians, the general purpose of which would be to control and limit the use of the atomic bomb as an instrument of war. . . ."

Such an approach might more specifically lead to the proposal that we would stop work on the further improvement in, or manufacture of, the bomb as a military weapon, provided the Russians and the British would agree to do likewise. It might also provide that we would be willing to impound what bombs we now have in the United States provided the Russians and the British would agree with us that in no event will they or we use a bomb as an instrument of war unless all three Governments agree to that use.[32]

In his memoirs, Stimson called the following passage "the most important point of all":[33]

> *I emphasize perhaps beyond all other considerations the importance of taking this action with Russia as a proposal of the United States— backed by Great Britain but peculiarly the proposal of the United States. Action of any international group of nations, including many small nations who have not demonstrated their potential power or responsibility in this war would not, in my opinion, be taken seriously by the Soviets.*[34]

Not only does this document give us a glimpse into Stimson's thinking in the late summer of 1945, but it also provides firsthand confirming documentation of the central thrust of U.S. strategy as it appeared to a highly informed insider just after the atomic bomb was demonstrated.

Stimson's initiative was a last-ditch attempt to challenge the overall policy approach adopted initially by Byrnes during the summer, carried forward at Potsdam, and now backed openly by Truman.

Nor did he leave much doubt what was worrying him most:

> It is my judgment that the Soviet would be more apt to respond sincerely to a direct and forthright approach made by the United States on this subject than . . . if the approach were made after a succession of express or implied threats or near threats in our peace negotiations.[35]

The argument that a highly publicized proposal involving many small nations would not be taken seriously by the Russians also stands as a backdrop to the 1946 Baruch Plan for controlling atomic weapons—a proposal put forward in precisely the manner Stimson thought could not possibly be effective.

Stimson presented his memorandum to Truman on September 12. The president read the paper in Stimson's presence: "He said step by step as we went through it that he was in full accord with each statement that I made and that his view on the whole thing was in accord with me. He thought that we must take Russia into our confidence."[36]

It is highly doubtful that Truman actually agreed with Stimson's proposals even at the time. As Gregg Herken has noted, "Truman had with equal facility agreed to Stimson's assessment some six weeks earlier that the Russians were not to be trusted. It is likely, instead, that the President . . . saw no point in challenging the advice of an elder statesman approaching retirement."[37] (Nor, as we shall see, was this the only time Truman demonstrated a willingness to conceal or offer misleading statements about how he really felt about atomic bomb matters.)

The president did arrange for Stimson to present his ideas at one last full Cabinet meeting. This gathering—on September 21—was Stimson's final appearance as secretary of war. (His resignation took effect later that same afternoon.) A highly confusing discussion took place, followed by equally confusing and misleading leaks to the press. Stimson's proposal, for instance, was mistakenly called the "Wallace plan" by *The New York Times*—after Henry Wallace. Someone—perhaps Forrestal—privately told selected reporters that the plan would give away the so-called secret of the atomic bomb to the Russians, and the press was filled for weeks thereafter with fearful speculation about this danger.[38]

Seventeen days later Truman left no doubt whatsoever that this would not be done—and about which side of the Byrnes-Stimson divide he had chosen. Speaking to reporters on October 8 near Tiptonville, Tennessee, the president made it absolutely clear that the United States would keep control of all technological information. "Well, I don't think it would do any good to let them in on the know-how," he commented, "because I don't think they could do it, anyway."[39] Nor did Truman undertake to launch a private diplomatic initiative as urged by Stimson.

A few days after his Tennessee news conference an old friend asked Truman point-blank: "Then, Mister President, what it amounts to is this. That the armaments race is on, is that right?" Truman assured him that, indeed, it was—but he "added that we would stay ahead."[40]

Stimson now was totally out of the policy-making picture. About the time of Truman's press conference he privately noted: "I have sought the seclusion of my home in Huntington and have been virtually put to bed by my doctors under strict orders to take absolute rest for the recuperation of a very tired heart."[41]

A month after leaving office, Stimson suffered another massive coronary occlusion, which kept him in bed until Christmas.[42] Even after the turn of the new year he was still weak, his level of activity greatly limited.[43] We know very little about this period—except that sometime during the next months Stimson made a modest attempt to put his thoughts into the public arena. In March 1946 a one-page, much-watered-down article based on his September memorandum to the president (prepared with the help of George Harrison and Gordon Arneson and cleared for publication by McCloy) appeared in *Harper's*.

In sharp contrast with the September memorandum, the essay made only passing reference to political power, no mention of the Soviet Union and the "Anglo-Saxon bloc over against the Soviet," no mention that the weapon was being carried "ostentatiously on our hip," none that the bomb might lead to the permanent embitterment of relations with Russia or that a private and direct approach to the Soviets needed to be made, and none that the United States should stop work on the bomb and impound weapons already produced.

Although Stimson made an abstract case for the importance of swiftness, transparency, and open dealing with other nations, he had obviously chosen not to present any of the specific policy recommendations for public debate which he had privately felt to be so urgent.

(He had not, however, altered his views. On May 28, 1946, Stimson sent a copy of his September memorandum to Bernard Baruch with a letter which reads in part: ". . . I find I have not changed my opinions as there expressed as to the general principles under which we should deal with this problem."[44])

By the spring of 1946, Stimson's health was somewhat improved. With his limited energy—and given the experience of several heart attacks—it was time for him to think of final things, in particular the writing of his memoirs.

Although he had resisted numerous requests from publishers—and as late as March 13 had informed War Department historian Rudolph Winnacker that he did not intend to write an autobiography—Stimson's former associates urged him on.[45]

His old friend, next-door neighbor, and sometime publicist, Arthur Page (himself a consultant for the Manhattan Project on press matters), spoke to the aide who had been directly responsible for helping Stimson with atomic bomb matters throughout the war, Harvey Bundy. Bundy, in turn, talked to Winnacker; in March and April 1946, both exchanged correspondence with Stimson directly.[46] By May the three men had settled on a logical candidate to assist Stimson with his memoirs, someone they all knew could be trusted to work with great discretion, Harvey Bundy's twenty-seven-year-old son, McGeorge Bundy.[47]

By late May, Page was actively seeking a publisher; "Mac" Bundy moved into a little red cottage on Stimson's Highhold estate and began work.[48] Each morning, accompanied by his longtime secretary, Elizabeth Neary, Stimson would come by for extensive talks. The main source for the memoir was to be his lengthy diary, to which Bundy was given exclusive access. Winnacker occasionally passed along secret War Department documents, but no systematic attempt was made to search the archives for relevant materials. Bundy's job was not to dig for the story beneath the story, but to tell Stimson's story from his perspective.

Although, as we shall see, Stimson continued to worry about Byrnes' attitude, the issue of defending the decision to use the atomic bomb, so far as we know, had not arisen in any serious way as the summer of 1946 got under way. Nor had any of the real decisions about what could and could not be made public from Stimson's diary yet been made.

Chapter 36

A THIN LINE OF CRITICISM

[T]he surprise bombings of Hiroshima and Nagasaki are morally indefensible. . . .

Both bombings, moreover, must be judged to have been unnecessary for winning the war. . . .

As the power that first used the atomic bomb under these circumstances, we have sinned grievously against the laws of God and against the people of Japan.
—Commission on the Relation of the Church to the War
in the Light of the Christian Faith, Federal Council
of the Churches of Christ in America, March 1946

To understand the context which produced the first postwar effort to manage public perception of the atomic bomb decision we need to note what at first blush seems a tiny eddy in a much more powerful flow of American cultural history.

A small but steady stream of criticism began to achieve a modest momentum almost immediately after the bombings. Although the critics made little detectable impact on the general public, they were by no means restricted to the margins of American society. The interesting question is not only what happened, but why it ultimately became sufficiently important to worry some of the nation's leaders—and to disturb the peaceful writing process in which Stimson and Bundy were engaged at Highhold.

One of the first to express concern was John Foster Dulles, at the time a leading Presbyterian layman and subsequently a 1950s Cold War secretary of state noted for his nuclear "brinkmanship." On August 9, Dulles—together with the president of the Federal Council of the Churches of Christ, the

Methodist bishop G. Bromley Oxnam—appealed directly to Truman to show "restraint" by temporarily suspending "our program of air attack on the Japanese homeland to give the Japanese people an adequate opportunity to react to the new situation. . . ." Such an act, they pleaded, "would be taken everywhere as evidence not of weakness but of moral and physical greatness."[1]

A number of other religious spokesmen were also deeply upset—especially Catholic leaders. "[W]e, the people of the United States of America . . . have struck the most powerful blow ever delivered against Christian civilization and the moral law," Father James M. Gillis, editor of *Catholic World*, declared:

> I would call it a crime were it not that the word "crime" implies sin and sin requires consciousness of guilt. . . . [T]he action taken by the United States Government was in defiance of every sentiment and every conviction upon which our civilization is based.[2]

An essay published in the September 1 issue of another leading Catholic publication, *America*, concluded that "Facts now available indicate that . . . surrender had been under preparation for some time before the exciting events of early August."[3]

Several Protestant leaders besides Dulles and Oxnam also raised their voices in protest. The *Christian Century*, for instance, editorialized: "It is our belief that the use made of the atomic bomb has placed our nation in an indefensible moral position."[4] Writing in *Christianity and Crisis*, theologian Reinhold Niebuhr observed:

> [A]mong the more sober and thoughtful sections of our nation the victory over Japan leaves a strange disquiet and lack of satisfaction.
>
> There are many reasons for this. The most obvious one is that the victory was secured, or at least hastened, by the use of the atomic bomb. . . . we used more terrible instruments against the Japanese than they used against us. . . .[5]

Dissent, though limited, was not restricted to the churches. On August 17, David Lawrence, the conservative owner and editor of the *United States News* (soon to change its name to *U.S. News and World Report*) published a strongly worded two-page editorial:

> Military necessity will be our constant cry in answer to criticism, but it will never erase from our minds the simple truth that we, of all civilized nations, though hesitating to use poison gas, did not hesitate to employ the most destructive weapon of all times indiscriminately against men, women and children.[6]

Similarly, Felix Morley, editor of the conservative *Human Events*, asked: "If December 7, 1941, is 'a day that will live in infamy', what will impartial history say of August 6, 1945?"[7] Morley was particularly disturbed by the "floodgates of official publicity" that followed the Hiroshima bombing:

> Rivers of racy material prepared in our various agencies of Public Enlightenment poured out to the press and radio commentators whose well-understood duty it is to "condition" public opinion. . . .
> Never has any totalitarian propaganda effort fallen more flat.[8]

These critical statements were not, however, indications of anything that can be called American public opinion in general—especially the kind that can be detected by such instruments as polls and surveys of newspaper editorials. Still, most intriguing from the vantage point of a half century was the continuing stream of conservative criticism. Lawrence, for instance, published an irregular but ongoing series of public challenges in his magazine. Thus:

> • *October 5:* If the right to use the atomic bomb is sanctioned, then the right to invent weapons that will deal a so-called merciful death—indeed as quick and instantaneous as the lethal chambers of Buchenwald—is also sanctioned.
> . . . the United States should be the first to condemn the atomic bomb and apologize for its use against Japan. Spokesmen of the Army Air Forces say it wasn't necessary anyway and that the war had been won already. Competent testimony exists to prove that Japan was seeking to surrender many weeks before the atomic bomb came.[9]

> • *November 2:* Is idealism losing ground in America and especially in high places in our Government? Did Hitler really win the war?[10]

> • *November 23:* The truth is we are guilty. Our conscience as a nation must trouble us. We must confess our sin. We have used a horrible weapon to asphyxiate and cremate more than 100,000 men, women and children in a sort of super-lethal gas chamber—and all this in a war already won or which spokesmen for our Air Forces tell us could have been readily won without the atomic bomb. . . .
> We ought, therefore, to apologize in unequivocal terms at once to the whole world for our misuse of the atomic bomb.[11]

Lawrence, who had been one of the first important radio commentators (at NBC, 1929–1933), was well connected. Obituaries on his death in 1973 noted that he "not only wrote about but knew 11 Presidents, from William Howard Taft to Richard M. Nixon."[12] He was particularly close to Nixon, who awarded him the Medal of Freedom on April 22, 1970.[13]

United States News was not, however, an organ of the mass media. One of the first critical articles to reach a broad middle-class readership was the previously cited essay by Captain Ellis Zacharias published in the *Saturday Evening Post*. Zacharias, as we have seen, had had access to at least some inside official sources. His November 1945 article stated that U.S. leaders had

> had definite information from inside Japan that since early 1945 a powerful group of Japanese leaders discussed in almost daily meetings the ways and means by which Japan could best extricate herself from a war which they had all regarded as inevitably lost.[14]

Without directly challenging the decision to use the atomic bomb, Zacharias nevertheless indicated that Japan's surrender was "imminent" during the summer of 1945. Furthermore, he stated that the only sticking point was the definition of "unconditional surrender" and the status of the Emperor. Japan's July 24 reply to Zacharias' "Atlantic Charter" broadcast, he told *Saturday Evening Post* readers, "was conclusive evidence of Japanese decision to terminate the war then and there. . . ."[15]

The audience addressed by ABC radio commentator Raymond Swing also was not inconsequential. During the war Swing—a respected and popular broadcaster often compared to Edward R. Murrow—was heard regularly by fifteen million people over 120 stations in the United States alone; his worldwide audience was more than twice this number.[16]

Swing reported that prior to the Hiroshima attack a number of atomic scientists had "addressed to President Truman a plea that the bomb itself should not be dropped over Japan before a test demonstration had been arranged . . . which would convince the Japanese of our power, and so impel them to end the war."[17] He was particularly disturbed that even though the war was long over, information about the scientists' dissent was still being kept from the American people:

> There is no conceivable consideration of genuine security for keeping that document a secret, nor for withholding from the public the reasons which prompted President Truman's advisers to argue the immediate use of the bomb.[18]

Although he had been concerned that "we stepped over the line that divides bombing of a military objective from the bombing of civilians," Swing had not been among the early critics of Truman's decision.[19] As late as September 28—and despite his prediction that the president "may be criticized as long as the history of these times is written"—Swing had stated his belief that in the end Truman would "be justified by the consideration that he was responsible for the lives of Americans in war time. . . ."[20]

By the end of November, however—and with the report that a number of scientists had urged a demonstration—Swing began to become more critical. Specifically, he now questioned rather directly why the bomb had been used without a prior demonstration:

> One reason suggests itself. We had completed the bomb just in time to use it a week *before* the Russians were due to enter the Japanese war. Had time been taken out to stage the humanitarian demonstration the scientists urged, we should not have been able to say that the bomb played the part we can now ascribe to it in Japan's surrender.[21]

That the critics were a minority was abundantly clear from a December 1945 Roper poll published in *Fortune* magazine. This showed that more than half of the American public still believed we "should have used the two bombs on cities, just as we did."[22] Indeed, at year's end an additional 23 per cent believed that we "should have quickly used many more of them [atomic bombs] before Japan had a chance to surrender."[23]

A somewhat different order of attack began to mount in early 1946. Lewis Mumford's *Values for Survival* allowed that "even before the atomic bomb had been used, we had accepted, as a normal instrument of warfare, the practice of exterminating civilians." Mumford went on to suggest that "as with the Nazis, our lack of a sense of guilt was almost as great a sin as the sin itself."[24]

In the business and popular press Lawrence continued to publish his irregular series, proposing in March 1946 that the United States should rebuild Hiroshima: "our people and our government—must accept responsibility for the destruction we have wrought. . . ."[25] Swing also continued his series of regular critiques, raising pointed questions in Friday broadcasts on the atomic bomb.[26]

On March 6, 1946, representatives of a significant institution issued a challenge: a high-level Federal Council of Churches* commission made up of twenty-two leading Protestant clergy and educators issued a report which concluded that the use of the atomic bomb was both militarily unnecessary and ethically unjustifiable:

> [T]he surprise bombings of Hiroshima and Nagasaki are morally indefensible. . . .
>   Nagasaki was bombed . . . without specific warning, after the power of the bomb had been proved but before the Japanese government and high command had been given reasonable time to reach a decision to

---

*The predecessor to today's National Council of Churches.

surrender. Both bombings, moreover, must be judged to have been unnecessary for winning the war. . . .

As the power that first used the atomic bomb under these circumstances, we have sinned grievously against the laws of God and against
the people of Japan.[27]

The strong language of the Calhoun Commission* was signed by such
leading Christian thinkers as Reinhold Niebuhr, John Bennett, Henry P. Van
Dusen, and Georgia Harkness, and was given front-page attention by *The
New York Times* and other papers.[28] The religious leaders, moreover, went beyond mere criticism to urge that the United States halt the production of nuclear weapons, publicly adopt a "no first use" policy, and work to establish
international control of atomic research.[29] As an act of "active penitence"
they called upon the nation's churches to "provide special aid for the survivors of those two murdered cities. . . ."[30]

On May 1, 1946, the *Bulletin of the Atomic Scientists* published the June
1945 Franck Report† of the Chicago atomic scientists we have previously reviewed. Written almost two months before Hiroshima but only made public
now, the Report offered a forceful argument, first, against the surprise use of
the bomb against Japan; and, second (implicitly), against its use on Japanese
civilian population centers. The likely consequences of a surprise attack, the
Franck Report urged, would be a nuclear arms race which would begin "in
earnest not later than the morning after our first demonstration of the existence of nuclear weapons."[31]

Much more favorable conditions for the eventual achievement of such
an agreement could be created if nuclear bombs were first revealed to
the world by a demonstration in an appropriately selected uninhabited
area.[32]

The *Bulletin of the Atomic Scientists* was not a mass-circulation journal,
and publication of the Report did not at first cause a major stir. However, a
June 1946 article in the influential *Saturday Review of Literature* (which we
have briefly noted in Book I) introduced a much broader public to the Franck
Report. The *Review*'s editor, Norman Cousins—writing together with
Thomas K. Finletter, a former assistant to the secretary of state and, subsequently, secretary of the air force—termed the Report "one of the most important American documents of recent years—even though it is virtually
unknown to the American people."[33]

Cousins and Finletter noted with approval the Franck Report's conclusion

*After its chairman, Yale University theologian Robert L. Calhoun.
†See above, pp. 187–88.

that "the military advantages and the saving of American lives achieved by the sudden use of atomic bombs against Japan may be outweighed by the ensuing loss of confidence and by a wave of horror and repulsion sweeping over the rest of the world."[34] As we have seen, they, too, posed the nagging questions which had bothered Swing and others: Why hadn't the United States devised a way to demonstrate the bomb to the Japanese? Why hadn't the Soviet Union been informed about the new weapon before it was used?

> Why, then, did we drop it? Or, assuming that the use of the bomb was justified, why did we not demonstrate its power in a test under the auspices of the UN. . . . ?[35]

Cousins and Finletter suggested these questions pointed to the plausibility that the use of the atomic bomb had been shaped by American diplomatic strategy towards the Soviet Union rather than by purely military concerns:

> Can it be that we were more anxious to prevent Russia from establishing a claim for full participation in the occupation against Japan than we were to think through the implications of unleashing atomic warfare? . . . [A]ny test would have been impossible if the purpose was to knock Japan out before Russia came in—or at least before Russia could make anything other than a token of participation prior to a Japanese collapse.[36]

Shortly after the Cousins-Finletter article was published, front-page stories across the country describing the July 1 and July 25 Bikini atoll atomic tests reminded the public of the awesome power of the new weapon. As Jonathan Weisgall notes in his recent history of Operation Crossroads:

> The media attention given the tests was phenomenal. Nearly 2.5 million words and 400 photographs were transmitted by radio from Bikini to newspapers and magazines, together with 615 radio broadcasts. "As for fanfare," the *New York Times* observed, "Operation Crossroads has been one of the most thoroughly press-agented shows in modern history, aside from war itself." . . . In fact, in the days immediately following each test, more than 20 percent of front-page U.S. newspaper articles were devoted to Operation Crossroads.[37]

"The apocalyptic sight of an atomic explosion and mushroom cloud," Weisgall notes, "was indelibly seared into the public's conscience."[38]

Significantly, the tests had been allowed to go forward at almost precisely the same time when, at the United Nations, the United States was offering its Baruch Plan for controlling nuclear weapons.

Those who raised questions were still isolated voices. Indeed, a survey of fourteen leading syndicated columnists from August 1945 through December 1948 concluded that the widely read writers "shared the common predispositions of the American people," and that "only fleeting mention was made by the columnists of the opinion that the bombing of Japanese cities had been an immoral act, or that it might be so regarded by others."[39]

Even the July 1 publication of *Japan's Struggle to End the War*, one of the most important of the reports of the U.S. Strategic Bombing Survey, did not generate much of a reaction, even though its conclusion tended to confirm the line of argument developing among the critics.

Still, here was yet another piece of evidence suggesting that something did not quite ring true about the official rationale. Picking up on the survey in a July 12 broadcast, Swing, for instance, observed that the Japanese government "was looking for an opportunity to surrender, and the testimony of various Japanese leaders indicates that some other excuses would have been found at an early date even if the atomic bomb had not been dropped."—exactly the point stressed in the War Department study completed only a few months earlier but not available to the public.[40]

On August 19, 1946, another front-page headline in *The New York Times* brought one of the world's most respected scientists back into public awareness. The headline announced: "Einstein Deplores Use of Atom Bomb." The *Times'* story reported Albert Einstein's view that "a great majority of scientists were opposed to the sudden employment of the atom bomb." As we have seen, Einstein's judgment also was that political-diplomatic rather than military motives had been dominant: "I suspect that the affair was precipitated by a desire to end [the] war in the Pacific by any means before Russia's participation."[41]

Then, on August 31, an explosive piece of reporting, John Hersey's *Hiroshima* was published as an entire issue of *The New Yorker*. Hersey's moving description of the human consequences of the destruction of Hiroshima shifted the atomic bomb story away from such abstractions as "mushroom" clouds. "For perhaps the first time since Pearl Harbor," as Michael J. Yavenditti notes, "thousands of Americans confronted Japanese who were ordinary human beings. . . ."[42]

Hersey told the stories of six survivors of the Hiroshima bombing, recounting their experiences—both bizarre and mundane—in the initial moments and days following the attack. A representative passage catches the horror of Hersey's report:

Mr. Tanimoto found about twenty men and women on the sandspit. He drove the boat onto the bank and urged them to get aboard. They did not move and he realized that they were too weak to lift themselves. He reached down and took a woman by the hands, but her skin slipped off in huge, glovelike pieces. He was so sickened by this that he had to sit down for a moment. . . . He had to keep consciously repeating to himself, "These are human beings."[43]

Americans were clearly more ready for some human sense of what the bomb signified than the polls seemed to suggest. The newsstand issue of *The New Yorker* quickly sold out and requests for thousands of reprints poured into the magazine's offices. Many newspapers carried the thirty-thousand-word essay in its entirety, and in early September ABC radio broadcast the full text in four half-hour commercial-free readings. By early fall the article had been republished in book form and the Book-of-the-Month Club distributed hundreds of thousands of free copies to its members.[44]

On September 9, another military voice was added to the arguments of the air force leaders and the Strategic Bombing Survey. Admiral William F. Halsey, commander of the Third Fleet, was publicly quoted as stating his view, as we have seen, that the atomic bomb was used because the scientists had a "toy and they wanted to try it out. . . ." "The first atomic bomb was an unnecessary experiment. . . . It was a mistake to ever drop it."[45]

Almost immediately Norman Cousins followed up with a new editorial in the *Saturday Review of Literature* which now attacked the "crime of Hiroshima and Nagasaki" head-on. Cousins asked: ". . . now that we have learned from a Navy spokesman that Japan was ready to quit even before Hiroshima, what happens to the argument that numberless thousands of American lives were saved?" Furthermore, why hadn't the government heeded the scientists' pleas that the bomb be first demonstrated to the Japanese?[46]

The September *Saturday Review* editorial struck a nerve—not so much with the general public as with one of the government scientist-administrators who had been responsible for building the atomic bomb.

James B. Conant, the president of Harvard University, was a prominent scientist. After having initially made his mark as a chemist working on poison gas during World War I, Conant had gone on to a distinguished private and public career. During the war, he chaired the National Defense Research Committee from the summer of 1941 on. He was also deputy director of the Office of Scientific Research and Development under Vannevar Bush and chairman of its S-1 Executive Committee. Conant was one of the central figures overseeing the Manhattan Project.[47]

The Harvard president's views on the atomic bomb were complex. Early on, he saw the need for international control of nuclear weapons, but he also believed a real-world demonstration of the bomb was essential—in part, it seems, as a way to force the world to face the need for control. As we have seen, Conant had proposed to the Interim Committee that the best target would be an important production facility surrounded by workers' homes.[48]

Recent research by James Hershberg and Barton Bernstein has demonstrated that Conant more than any other leading official found the steady growth of criticism deeply troubling.[49] In March 1946, for instance, he had been especially unsettled to note that Reinhold Niebuhr—a favorite Christian theologian and a man who had long impressed Conant with his political "realism"—had signed the Federal Council of Churches report criticizing the bombing.

"At the risk of having this letter considered a highly personal reaction by one who has a guilty conscience," a protest sent to the respected theologian began. Conant went on to note that the bombing had overwhelming public support, and pointedly expressed "the strange feeling that I have that by taking this stand the leaders of the Protestant churches are cutting themselves off from a vast body of American opinion."

> I think a poll of opinion of citizens with high standards of moral responsibility and upright conduct would show only a small percentage taking the point of view presented in your document. I think a very large majority would follow the line of argument which is implied in my criticism, namely, that the atomic bomb was, from the point of view of its use in the last war, part and parcel of the total operation of that war.[50]

Niebuhr responded that: "The position taken was that we would have been in a stronger moral position had we published the facts about this instrument of destruction, made a demonstration of its effects over Japan in a non-populated section, and threatened the use of the bomb if the Japanese did not surrender."[51]*

Conant was also disturbed by the Strategic Bombing Survey conclusion. ". . . I doubt if anyone in the United States or Great Britain," he wrote a Buffalo newspaper editor, "was in a position to find out the facts which the United States strategic bombing survey found out after the war was over."[52] It was, he felt, "Monday morning quarterbacking."[53] Similarly, Conant was upset by Halsey (who, as noted, had publicly stated that the scientists had a "toy and they wanted to try it out").[54] But it was Cousins' September editorial which convinced the Harvard president that decisive action needed to be taken to prevent the growing criticism from gaining real force.[55]

The key to halting the critics in their tracks, Conant decided, was to ar-

---

*He added: ". . . it seems to me there is too general a disposition to disavow guilt because on the whole we have done good—in this case defeated tyranny. I was ready to sign the report on the expression of guilt—particularly because I thought it important from the Christian standpoint to admit the moral ambiguity of all righteous people in history. . . ." (Reinhold Niebuhr to James B. Conant, March 12, 1946, Box 3, Niebuhr Papers, Library of Congress.)

range to have a highly respected public figure—someone above political question—explain authoritatively, once and for all, how and why the decision to use the bomb had been made. Perhaps it would be possible to have someone so convincingly set the record straight that "sentimental" and "verbally minded" critics of the bomb would be left speechless—or at least without a receptive audience.[56]

The obvious candidate for the job was the esteemed Republican statesman and former secretary of war, Henry L. Stimson.

Chapter 37

"A MERE RECITAL OF THE FACTS"

. . . I think we deserve some sort of medal for reducing these particular chatterers to silence.
> —McGeorge Bundy to Henry L. Stimson,
> February 18, 1947

The full tale—or rather, the full tale so far as we now know it—of how Conant and others maneuvered to arrange for Stimson to present a full-scale defense of the bombing of Hiroshima shares one major feature with the story of the decision itself: It was not known—indeed, not even knowable—for much of the early postwar period when the Hiroshima story, as most Americans understand it, was consolidated.

Only with the opening of the Stimson papers at Yale in 1959, the Frankfurter papers at the Library of Congress in 1967, and some of the Conant papers at Harvard in the 1960s and 1970s, was it possible for scholars to assemble the basic facts. Much of what can now be documented was pieced together over a twelve-year period by James G. Hershberg, the director of the Cold War International History Project at the Woodrow Wilson International Center for Scholars—first in a 1989 Ph.D. dissertation, then with the 1993 publication of the first major biography of Conant.[1] Hershberg's work, in turn, is augmented by a long, deeply researched essay by Barton Bernstein, and by additional research done in the course of writing this book.[2] As in connection with so many other aspects of the atomic bomb story, however, there still is also a good deal that is not known about these events. Harvard's fifty-year rule governing closed archives, for instance, is even more restrictive than that of the U.S. government. Most of Harvey Bundy's personal papers either are not available or, perhaps, no longer exist. Nor has McGeorge Bundy given scholars access to his own papers.

There is little doubt about the overall picture, however. In general, the Conant-Stimson-Bundy effort provides a case study in how the world worked during an era, as Hershberg puts it, when "the consolidated voice of the establishment could effectively shape mass opinion. . . ."[3] High-level strategizing to promote a particular version of the history of the atomic bomb, we now know, began with the Harvard president but eventually involved many of America's most important leaders at the time.

On September 23, 1946, Conant sent a letter to Harvey Bundy, including with it a copy of Cousins' editorial. The letter was an outpouring of concern about the growing criticism:

> You may be inclined to dismiss all this talk as representing only a small minority of the population, which I think it does. However, this type of sentimentalism, for I so regard it, is bound to have a great deal of influence on the next generation. The type of person who goes in to [sic] teaching, particularly school teaching, will be influenced a great deal by this type of argument. We are in danger of repeating the fallacy which occurred after World War I. You will recall that it became accepted doctrine among a group of so-called intellectuals who taught in our schools and colleges that the United States had made a great error in entering World War I, and that the error was brought about largely by the interests of the powerful groups. Of course, there is little relation between these two types of fallacies, but I mention the history after World War I only to emphasize that a small minority, if it represents the type of person who is both sentimental and verbally minded and in contact with our youth, may result in a distortion of history.[4]

Conant reminded Bundy that he, Conant, had recommended using the bomb "on the grounds (1) that I believed it would shorten the war against Japan, and (2) that unless it was actually used in battle there was no chance of convincing the American public and the world that it should be controlled by international agreement."[5]

He was, he stressed, "quite unrepentant" for having taken this line. A demonstration of the new weapon before Japanese observers would not have been "realistic," and "much Monday morning quarterbacking is now involved in the statements that Japan would have surrendered anyway." In particular, Conant felt that the impression created by some atomic scientists that they had not supported the use of the bomb needed to be countered:

> . . . I think it is important to show that while there was a small group of scientists who protested, that the scientific leaders of the movement, including the members of that scientific panel who met with Mr. Stimson in May or June, raised no protest against the proposed plan.[6]

It was time to reveal the still-classified information that the Interim Committee's advisers—Oppenheimer, Lawrence, Fermi, and Arthur Compton—had all signed off on using the bomb. "I think it [is] unfair for the scientists by implication to try to dodge the responsibility for this decision," Conant declared. (He acknowledged, however, that "of course they were not in a position to influence greatly whatever was done at Potsdam."[7])

Above all, Conant emphasized that: "It seems to me of great importance to have a statement of fact issued by someone who can speak with authority. There is no one who could do this better than Mr. Stimson."[8] Would it be possible for Harvey—together perhaps with Stimson's other good friend George Harrison—to persuade the retired secretary of war to write "a short article . . . pointing out the conditions under which the decision was made and who made it?"[9]

It did not take very much to persuade Harvey Bundy, the man who helped Stimson supervise the Manhattan Project. After discussing the matter with Harrison, he informed Conant: "He [Harrison] is also interested and will get in touch with me further."[10]

We do not know for certain if Harvey Bundy was in contact with his son McGeorge (though it seems likely), nor when Stimson agreed to undertake an article. Within a very few weeks, however, a decision had been made. On November 4, McCloy informed Secretary of War Patterson that "Harvey Bundy and George Harrison are preparing, I believe, a draft of a statement for Mr. Stimson . . . which may cast some light on the political decisions which were taken in connection with the manufacture of the bomb."[11] On November 10, Stimson met with Rudolph Winnacker and several others to outline his thoughts in a brainstorming session.[12] Before the month was out he conferred again with Harvey Bundy and Harrison, and also at some point (so his correspondence files indicate) with Byrnes.[13]

The real work of preparing the article would of necessity be left to "young Bundy." Educated at Groton and Yale, McGeorge Bundy had been trained at Fort Monmouth as a cryptographer and had been assigned as personal aide to Admiral Alan G. Kirk, commander of the Allied amphibious forces in the Atlantic. The Bundys were old family friends of the Stimsons, and "Mac" was well aware that his father had been part of the inner circle of men who had contributed to the decision to use the atomic bomb. (The younger Bundy, of course, was later to become National Security Adviser to presidents Kennedy and Johnson during the 1960s.)

Although McGeorge Bundy clearly understood the special nature of the assignment, and though he had been relying largely on Stimson's own recollections for the longer memoir, he was hardly operating on his own in connection with the article. For one thing, of course, he was in regular and close communication with the eminent scientist who was president of Harvard Uni-

versity. For another, many of the top officials involved in the decision offered suggestions. Bundy was soon to be in correspondence with such figures
as George Kennan and Supreme Court Justice Felix Frankfurter on various
related issues in connection with the memoirs.

From the documents now available it seems clear that an important source
for many of the arguments initially considered in drafting Stimson's article
almost certainly was a memorandum written by Harvey Bundy, on September 25, 1946. "Notes on the Use by the United States of the Atomic Bomb"
was completed within a day or two of his receiving Conant's letter and six
weeks before the November 10 brainstorming session Stimson held with
Winnacker and the others. The senior Bundy urged the following points:

· That the atomic bombing was ordered "primarily on the belief that the
use would save American lives by terminating the War as rapidly as possible."[14] Otherwise possibly "thousands and perhaps hundreds of thousands
of American soldiers might be killed or permanently injured in continuing
hostilities."[15]

· That "nobody in authority in Potsdam was satisfied that the Japanese
would surrender on terms acceptable to the Allies without further bitter fighting, even though they were aware through secret sources of Japan's attempt
to terminate hostilities through the good offices of Russia."[16]

· That the Interim Committee had rejected using the bomb on targets
"where the destruction of life and property would be the very greatest" in
favor of "a target primarily military in character but where the nature of
the building construction would show completely the devastating effect
of the bomb."[17]

· That the Interim Committee had "discussed intensively . . . whether
the bomb should be used at all." "These discussions included lengthy deliberations on the problem of whether the bomb should be used by the United
States."[18]

· That the Interim Committee also deliberated over whether a demonstration of the bomb could be held before Japanese observers.[19]

Harvey Bundy also claimed that "in the minds of at least some of the
Advisory [Interim] Committee and possibly in the minds of the executive authorities in Potsdam was the thought that unless the bomb were used it would
be impossible to persuade the world that the saving of civilization in the future would depend on a proper international control of atomic energy."[20]

Finally, he held that the timing of the Hiroshima bombing was in no way
tied to Russian entry into the war:

The time was not set with reference to any attempt to keep Russia from
entering the War in the Far East. No doubt those in executive authority
saw large advantages in winning the Japanese War without the aid of

Russia, but the time schedule was set by the military with sole reference to using the earliest moment that all preparations would be ready for the effective use of the weapon.[21]

As we have seen (and shall further explore), the evidence now available provides little support for many of these arguments. Nonetheless, the broad overview Bundy proposed seems clearly to have provided several of the main girders of the article ultimately drafted for Stimson by his son.

Other materials which directly or indirectly contributed to the effort include a draft article prepared by General Groves' office and sent to Harvey Bundy.[22] This suggested additional arguments and variations on the essential themes "which could be released over the signature of Mr. Stimson"—for instance:

• That "those in charge . . . gave full opportunity to representative scientists to present their views and gave careful consideration to these views."[23]

• That the Interim Committee recommended that the bomb "should not be dropped upon a preponderantly civilian area but preferably upon a target such as a vital war plant."[24]

• That "the war, although it would have been won without the bomb, was shortened by its use probably by many months, and the terrific sacrifice in human lives which the planned invasion of Japan would have exacted was averted."[25]

Groves also proposed to assure readers of the Stimson article that

Major General L. R. Groves, who had been in continuous charge of the project as a whole, . . . perhaps more than any other man, had had opportunity to consider in detail the potentialities and implications of the new weapon, not only from the military and national, but also from the social and international, point of view.[26]

Additional advice came from Winnacker, who sent Stimson a letter and several enclosures on November 12. Among them was a "still highly classified" memorandum on "Strategic Plans for the Defeat of Japan," which held that "the only possible conclusion in July 1945 was that the immediate use of a decisive weapon would shorten the war, at least by months, possibly by years." Winnacker also sent a "rough draft of your thoughts as you outlined them to us last Sunday." These included arguments that: "a stubborn, bloody fight loomed up, which might last a year and a half," that efforts were made to "confine damage to military target[s] as far as possible," that "if atomic bomb works, might save hundred thousands [sic] of American lives," and that "full demonstration of [the] power of [the] new weapon might convert nations to accept peaceful solutions of conflicts in the future."[27]

Within a week Winnacker followed up with two more letters and accompanying enclosures.[28] One of these was the Summary Report of the U.S. Strategic Bombing Survey, which, as we have seen, reached an official conclusion quite different from the line of argument being assembled by "Mac" Bundy (and which was ignored in the final article).

By the end of November 1946, Bundy had prepared an initial draft of the proposed article on the basis of these various materials. We do not know if Stimson himself edited or approved this draft, or precisely how deeply he was involved in the actual writing during the initial period. The evidence suggests that he gave general guidance on certain key points, but was not continuously and directly involved in day-to-day editing. There is no doubt about the next step in the crafting of the article, however—nor about whose hand was most important in giving the argument its real focus.

On the afternoon of November 29, Bundy left Stimson's estate for Cambridge to deliver the draft to Conant for review.[29] Within a day the Harvard president had blue-penciled the article, added paragraphs, deleted whole pages, and generally revised its tone. The edited version was promptly mailed back to Bundy, accompanied by an eight-page explanatory letter. Among Conant's most important proposed revisions were:

· That "the statement about the various alternatives considered by the Interim Committee should be amplified by the insertion of a paragraph. . . . I have in mind the fact that the Interim Committee and its advisers certainly considered the practicability of (a) giving warning, and (b) giving a demonstration. Since both these points are stressed strongly by the people we are trying to impress with this article, I think they should be dealt with at greater length."[30]

· That "even the success of the test at Alamogordo Proving Grounds did not give 100% assurance that the first bombs used in combat would actually be successful. . . ."[31]

· That "the number of bombs which were at our disposal before the invasion was not unlimited. Therefore, a maximum effect had to be obtained with the few at our disposal. Nothing would have been more disastrous than a prior warning followed by a dud, and this was a very real possibility."[32]

· Conant also urged Bundy to emphasize that the bomb was a weapon like any other weapon:

> There is just one point that I think should be inserted somewhere in the document which I have not covered in this letter or in my notations, and that is a sentence or two pointing out the similarity in destruction brought about by the fire raids over Tokyo and the damage done by the atomic bomb.[33]

Conant's suggested deletions were as illuminating as his proposed additions. Most significantly, he urged Bundy to eliminate all discussion of the issue of "unconditional surrender" and of the fate of the Emperor—and whether decision-makers had debated a modification of surrender terms:

"Particularly I feel that the introduction of the problem of the Emperor diverts one's mind from the general line of argumentation." Conant even proposed eliminating one of Stimson's main contemporaneous briefs to the president in this connection: "I do not think the memorandum of July 2 is sufficiently closely related to the point at issue to be included."[34]

Conant also drew attention to the Interim Committee recommendations of May 31 and June 1 to suggest that "the story is unnecessarily complicated by bringing in both sets of recommendations, and in the interests of brevity and clarity the recommendations of May 31 might be omitted."[35]*

Finally, Conant suggested deleting the entire last five pages of the draft manuscript:

> in essence the materials . . . are either summaries of what has preceded or concerned with the problem of the Emperor (which I consider irrelevant for this discussion, interesting though it is), or in the nature of an argument on the Secretary's part of why he acted as he did. I think the argumentation is unnecessary and unwise. . . .[36]

"I think Mr. Stimson's position is such that it is quite unnecessary for him to take an argumentative line. Indeed I feel it would be unwise, if I may say so. To me a mere recital of the facts speaks for itself." This would make it difficult for critics to "attack Mr. Stimson in such a way as to make him feel that he should reply."[37]†

Within a week, McGeorge Bundy wired Conant that he was "personally delighted" with his suggestions[38]—and (as Hershberg writes) "a fortnight later, like a student handing in a revised term paper, he [Bundy] returned to Cambridge bearing a new draft that incorporated most of Conant's ideas."[39] Conant in turn was greatly pleased with this nearly polished draft; on December 14 he wrote Stimson:

> Mr. Bundy has just showed me the revised manuscript which you have prepared. I have read it with great interest and enthusiasm. I do hope

---

*To recall, the May 31 Interim Committee recommendation states explicitly: "At the suggestion of Dr. Conant the Secretary agreed that the most desirable target would be a vital war plant employing a large number of workers and closely surrounded by workers' houses." In contrast, Conant's name was not specifically attached to the June 1 recommendation in the official minutes.

†In his cover letter Conant stated: "I hope you will express my apologies to Mr. Stimson in case he should see this mutilated manuscript. I trust he will not think it presumptuous of me to tell him how he should present his material or write a paper." (James B. Conant to McGeorge Bundy, November 30, 1946, p. 2, Stimson Papers, Sterling Library, Yale University.)

that you will publish it in Harper's as you plan as soon as possible. I feel certain that it will accomplish a great deal of good.

. . . I have found the line of argumentation which you have set forth so ably in your document to be convincing. I know there has been a great deal of misinformation widely circulated in the United States on this point and, therefore, I feel it is of great importance that this misinformation be corrected. You are the only one who can do it properly and I am delighted that you propose to publish the article I have just seen.[40]

Stimson and Bundy also shared the near-final draft with Groves, Frankfurter, Patterson, and Bernard Baruch.[41] Groves, for one, replied with pages of "corrections," some of which Bundy and Stimson were also to adopt in the final version, others of which they ignored.[42] It is also known that Bundy received unrecorded suggestions by telephone.[43] In early December, Stimson was able to write Patterson: "Our statements in it have passed the scrutiny of so many actors in this drama that I think you will not find any matter which should be excised for lack of security or other official reason."[44]

The article appeared in the February 1947 issue of *Harper's*. It was, to say the least, an extraordinary success. Recognizing its unusual significance, *The New York Times* treated the essay as front-page news,[45] reprinted a substantial excerpt, and praised it in a lead editorial: "There can be no doubt that the President and Mr. Stimson are right when they maintain that the bomb caused the Japanese to surrender."[46]*

The article was also reprinted in the *Washington Post*, the *St. Louis Post-Dispatch*, the *Omaha World Herald*, the *Infantry Journal*, *Reader's Digest*, the *Bulletin of the Atomic Scientists*, and many other media outlets. Excerpts appeared in *Time*, *U.S. News*, and an indeterminate number of newspapers throughout the United States and in several other countries. Editorial comment was decidedly uncritical and, indeed, often effusive in praise.

NBC radio commentator Lowell Thomas informed Stimson that "I was enormously impressed by the article . . . I myself am planning to say something about it within a few days in the hope that my remarks will cause a million or two Americans to read it. . . ."[47] Major portions of the essay were also broadcast by ABC, and it was given extensive coverage by other radio outlets. (Rudolph Winnacker wrote Stimson: "When the story broke a week ago Monday night, the radio newsmen gave it full play, and all the radio commentators—and I tried to listen to all of them—got the spirit and message of your story."[48])

Part of the response, of course, was inevitable, given the nature of the sub-

---

*Even so, the *Times* wondered whether in deciding "to drop the first bomb without warning or previous demonstration, this notice [the Potsdam ultimatum] was adequate." ("War and the Bomb," *The New York Times*, January 28, 1947, p. 22.)

ject and the prestige of the author. However, another part was the result of careful planning and hard work. Indeed, that widespread promotion was intended for the essay from the start is readily apparent. This unusual note, for instance, appeared at the end of the article in *Harper's*:

> In view of the exceptional public importance of this article, permission is given to any newspaper or magazine to reprint it, in part or (preferably, since its effect is cumulative) in full, with credit to *Harper's Magazine* but without charge.—The Editors[49]

Harper's editor, Frederick L. Allen, also reported to Stimson:

> You may be interested to know that we mailed out at appropriate intervals before the publication date some four hundred copies of the article to press associations, radio networks, columnists and commentators, and a long list of newspapers; that the more important newspapers got two copies, one for the managing editor and one for the editor; that we called up the press associations and networks, the New York *Times* and New York *Herald Tribune* news desks the day before the release date to make sure that they had the material and were all set; and that we wired thirty or forty of the out of town papers to remind them that the material had been sent to them and was important.[50]

Stimson also took the initiative and personally contacted several key people. A letter to Henry Luce, the publisher of *Time* and *Life*, for instance, runs: "Now that I have been through the trials of preparing the article, I am naturally anxious that it should be widely noticed. . . ."[51] (In response, Luce informed Stimson that he had "expedited your article on The Bomb to the Managing Editor of TIME and I am happy to say that he agrees it is a sound and powerful work. It is proposed to run a considerable part of the text in the next issue."[52])

Clearly seeking to blunt Raymond Swing's criticism, Stimson sent the broadcaster an advance copy with a note stating: "I am sorry to hear that you have been disturbed about the wisdom of this decision since I have always respected your judgment and have felt that your work as a radio commentator was on an unusually high level. I hope that this article may show you the reasons for our course of action."[53]

After the article's publication a large number of letters of congratulations poured in—especially from many of the officials who had been involved. Conant himself, for instance, declared: "It seems to me just exactly right, and I am sure will do a great deal of good."[54] Under Secretary of State Dean Acheson wrote that:

General Marshall [who a few days earlier had taken over as secretary of state] had spoken to me with enthusiasm about the article and I was looking forward eagerly to reading it. I did so with mounting enthusiasm. The simplicity and power with which you presented the essential facts and considerations . . . leave no doubt as to the wisdom of the decision. This exposition was badly needed and it is superbly done.[55]

Karl Compton, the president of MIT (and member of the Interim Committee), was also full of praise. The article "will prove to be one of the most important of statements made by public servants. Certainly no one can read your article and not be tremendously impressed by the care, thoughtfulness, and highminded consideration which led to the atomic bomb decisions."[56]

Even Ralph Bard, the sole dissenter on the Interim Committee, applauded the piece in a letter which betrayed no sign of discomfort at the contradiction between the views he urged privately in 1945 and repeatedly thereafter: ". . . it was an exceptionally well-done job. It covered the subject fully, clearly and precisely, and gave a most accurate account of what transpired."[57]

During a return trip to Harvard in February 1947, McGeorge Bundy wrote a happy note to Stimson:

Boston I find humming with activity and interest—the Harper's article has been read by everyone I meet, and it seems to have covered the subject so well that I find no follow-up work needed. This is of particular interest in the case of one or two of my friends who certainly fall in Mr. Conant's unkindly classification of the "verbal-minded"—I think we deserve some sort of medal for reducing these particular chatterers to silence.[58]

Chapter 38

"AN EXACT DESCRIPTION"

There was no mention of postwar relations with the Soviets as a consideration in the calculations and deliberations preceding the bomb's use; no mention of the Strategic Bombing Survey's claim that Japan would have surrendered even without the bomb or an invasion; no explicit mention of the arguments raised against the decision; only the barest grazing of the issue of why Truman rejected proposals to modify unconditional surrender so as to leave the Emperor on his throne. . . .

—James G. Hershberg, *James B. Conant*

Bundy was right to be pleased. As several scholars have noted, the essay he drafted for Stimson essentially shut down all but the most independent-minded critics for most of the early postwar era. It was, in Hershberg's words, a "preemptive strike" carefully plotted against potentially important criticism—a "first and seemingly definitive account of the atomic bomb decision [which] stood for almost two decades. . . ."[1] ". . . Stimson's explanation of the use of the bomb," Bernstein observes, ". . . helped to block a probing dialogue among plain citizens and foreign policy analysts too, about why the bombs were dropped, whether their use was ethically justified, and what role the bombs' use and America's related policy had on the Cold War."[2]

A great deal of the authority of Stimson's 1947 *Harper's* article derived from the simple fact that he had the only byline. Bundy's authorship and the deep involvement of others, especially Conant, would be unknown to the public at large.[3] Challenging a man of Stimson's character and reputation gave many writers pause in 1947—and, indeed, continues to do so even today.

Moreover, Stimson was a Republican. Truman was not likely to be criticized by his own party, and the Republican leaders who had early on urged a modification of the surrender formula were not likely to attack an eminent and aging national statesman of their own. In a note to John O'Laughlin, publisher of the *Army and Navy Journal*, Herbert Hoover declared that "the use of the atomic bomb, with its indiscriminate killing of women and children, revolts my soul."[4] However, though he continued to criticize the decision in off-the-record statements, Hoover said little publicly.

Although scholars who have studied the origins and impact of the *Harper's* article are unanimous that it played a critical role at a moment when opinion was beginning to shift—or at least beginning to be open to more discriminating questions—they have been puzzled by a related issue: the intensity of concern evidenced by Conant, Stimson, and other American leaders that autumn.

The fact is criticism of the Hiroshima decision, though growing among selected groups, had hardly become widespread among the public at large. Even the extraordinary attention given to John Hersey's *New Yorker* article, as Paul Boyer has observed, "neither reenergized the international-control movement nor launched a vigorous public debate over the bombing of Hiroshima and Nagasaki."[5]

Hershberg has speculated that guilt may have had something to do with the intensity of Conant's feeling: ". . . the criticism of Hiroshima rubbed a raw nerve in this usually unemotional man."[6] Conant, indeed, did not stop at one article; he stimulated a parallel defense of the bombing in *The Atlantic Monthly* by Karl Compton which went even further in its claims:

> . . . I believe, with complete conviction, that the use of the atomic bomb saved hundreds of thousands—perhaps several millions—of lives, both American and Japanese. . . .[7]

Something besides possibly guilty consciences was also at work. Conant, for one, was quite open about his own larger strategic and political concerns. Writing to Stanford University president Donald Tresidder on January 22, 1947, he stressed that what was important was that "*the American people stay tough* in regard to the use of the bomb. . . ." If this could be assured, "I think we may be in for a period of peace. . . ."[8] To Stimson he explained that

> if the propaganda against the use of the atomic bomb had been allowed to grow unchecked, the strength of our military position by virtue of having the bomb would have been correspondingly weakened, and with this weakening would have come a decrease in the probabilities of an international agreement for the control of atomic energy.[9]

Hershberg has studied the context of these events as carefully and closely as any scholar. His summary observation is that

> Conant's reaction . . . and that of others around him, revealed the depth of the fear among those responsible for the birth and maintenance of America's nuclear policy that the lurking, inchoate, anomic terror of living in the strange new atomic age might coalesce into an unstoppable demand for the elimination of America's nuclear arsenal—or, almost as damaging, vitiate its diplomatic usefulness. . . .
>
> America was heading into a period marked by U.S.–Soviet rivalry, not one of unlimited global cooperation, and if the negotiations were doomed to fail, then it was time to resume the job of building atomic weapons, not dismantling them.

"Their efforts helped to reassure the American public that their leaders could handle atomic decisions morally and judiciously, and to stave off inquisitiveness about nuclear policies (which were still shrouded in secrecy)."[10]

Hershberg also points out that as the Cold War heated up, Conant developed a different rationale—to bolster support for the possible use of nuclear weapons against the Soviet Union. At a secret National War College meeting in October 1947, Conant said he had "always wished some official source would make the statement that if war occurred we should certainly order our battleships to fire and if it was militarily advisable the first thing that we would do is to drop [atomic] bombs." In this respect the Stimson article had "helped a great deal," Conant added. "You have to get the past straight before you do much to prepare people for the future."[11]

From the perspective of nearly a half century—and with the documents now available—we may examine the *Harper's* essay not only in terms of its origins, role, and extraordinary success, but also in the light of the specific choices Stimson and Bundy made when they reviewed the wide range of materials they received during the late fall of 1946.

At the heart of Stimson's essay is the contention that there was simply no other acceptable way to end the war. The article develops this argument with unusual force. Its theme is that the only alternative available—other than the use of the atomic bomb (targeted specifically against a city)—would have been an invasion which would likely have cost the United States alone over a million casualties.

That these were the only two alternatives—the bombing of a city or a massive invasion—is emphasized in several distinct ways. First, following Conant's suggestion that Stimson's prestige would allow him to state rather than argue the case, the former secretary solemnly assures the reader that this is the truth of the matter, again and again, in several different ways. Thus:

I felt that to extract a genuine surrender from the Emperor and his military advisers, they must be administered a tremendous shock which would carry convincing proof of our power to destroy the Empire. Such an effective shock would save many times the number of lives, both American and Japanese, that it would cost.[12]

Again:

. . . I have tried to give an accurate account of my own personal observations of the circumstances which led up to the use of the atomic bomb and the reasons which underlay our use of it. To me they have always seemed compelling and clear, and I cannot see how any person vested with such responsibilities as mine could have taken any other course or given any other advice to his chiefs.

And, once more:

In the light of the alternatives which, on a fair estimate, were open to us I believe that no man, in our position and subject to our responsibilities, holding in his hands a weapon of such possibilities for accomplishing this purpose and saving those lives, could have failed to use it and afterwards looked his countrymen in the face.[13]

And finally:

. . . this deliberate, premeditated destruction was our least abhorrent choice. The destruction of Hiroshima and Nagasaki put an end to the Japanese war. It stopped the fire raids, and the strangling blockade; it ended the ghastly specter of a clash of great land armies.[14]

The assertion that there was no alternative is bolstered by a number of distinct subordinate arguments.

• It was known to us that she [Japan] had gone so far as to make tentative proposals to the Soviet government, hoping to use the Russians as mediators in a negotiated peace. These vague proposals contemplated the retention by Japan of important conquered areas and were therefore not considered seriously.[15]

• In reaching these conclusions the Interim Committee carefully considered such alternatives as a detailed advance warning or a demonstration in some uninhabited area. Both of these suggestions were discarded as impractical.[16]

• . . . the Scientific Panel made a report, from which I quote the following . . . *"we can propose no technical demonstration likely to bring an end to the war; we see no acceptable alternative to direct military use.*"[17]

• These two cities [Hiroshima and Nagasaki] were active working parts of the Japanese war effort.[18]

• Had the war continued until the projected invasion on November 1, additional fire raids of B-29's would have been more destructive of life and property than the very limited number of atomic raids which we could have executed in the same period.[19]

• On July 28 the Premier of Japan, Suzuki, rejected the Potsdam ultimatum by announcing that it was "unworthy of public notice." In the face of this rejection we could only proceed to demonstrate that the ultimatum had meant exactly what it said. . . .[20]

The entire tone of the essay is authoritative, almost Olympian. It ends on a somber and moving note:

In this last great action of the Second World War we were given final proof that war is death. . . . The bombs dropped on Hiroshima and Nagasaki ended a war. They also made it wholly clear that we must never have another war. This is the lesson men and leaders everywhere must learn. . . . There is no other choice.[21]

For scholars familiar with the modern research findings, careful scrutiny of the Stimson essay has not been an uplifting experience. Contrary to the overwhelming thrust of the essay, evidence now available shows that:

• Stimson himself had repeatedly urged that the Japanese be told they could keep the Emperor; that he had reached this position as early as late May/early June; that he had formally recommended it to the president with the support of Forrestal and Grew in early July; that he had especially pressed this point just after the July 12–13 intercepts revealing the Emperor's initiative; and that he urgently reiterated it as late as July 24.

Moreover, contrary to some accounts, Stimson's contemporaneous advice to Truman—and his considered written opinion—was that a clarification of terms was likely to work. To recall, as early as June 2 he wrote:

I think the Japanese nation has the mental intelligence and versatile capacity in such a crisis to recognize the folly of a fight to the finish and to accept the proffer of what will amount to unconditional surrender. . . .[22]

• Again, as we have seen, modern research has shown that intelligenc assessments beginning in April suggested—even before the Emperor'

July 12–13 intervention—that, in line with the "two-step" logic, the war would likely end once the Red Army attacked and the Emperor's position was assured. When General Marshall gave similar advice directly to the president on June 18, he did not even specify the second step; his advice that the war might end cited only the impact of the Russian attack.

· As noted, the president went to Potsdam expressly to secure a Russian declaration of war, later stating quite openly that he did so because "if the [atomic] test should fail, then it would be even more important to us to bring about a surrender before we had to make a physical conquest of Japan."[23] His journal and letters to his wife indicate a similar understanding.

The significance of the Russian option, however, is not discussed.

· Modern research has also demonstrated that so far as we can tell—and, again, contrary to the impression left by the *Harper's* article—with the possible exception of Marshall every top U.S. military leader doubted the military necessity of the bombing. Nor does it appear the military leaders were seriously consulted; the U.S. Chiefs of Staff felt they had to urge the British Chiefs of Staff to try to get Churchill to persuade the president to modify the terms after the July 12–13 intercepts came in.

· Despite Stimson's assertion that the Interim Committee "carefully considered . . . alternatives," no evidence has ever been adduced that the committee, in fact, did seriously review alternatives. Nor was its Scientific Panel given any substantial information about the actual course of the war—and of Japanese attempts to end it—so as to be able to judge whether using the bomb was the only option. Its advice concerning "military use," as we have seen, was given with the express reservation that full agreement on what targeting would be appropriate had not been reached.[24]

· Nor, contrary to Stimson's specific statement, is there evidence that the Interim Committee had "carefully considered . . . a detailed advance warning or a demonstration"—or that consideration was ever seriously given to Marshall's proposal in discussions with Stimson that the bomb be used against a naval base, and that only if this failed to produce a surrender should an urban center be attacked—and then only after residents had been warned to leave.

· While Stimson implied that Hiroshima and Nagasaki were significant military production centers, there is no evidence that these cities were targeted primarily for this reason (a poorly understood matter we shall explore at some length in Chapter 42).

· Stimson's argument that if the "fire raids" had continued until November 1 far more lives would have been lost than if further "atomic raids" had been "executed" in the same period, is misleading on at least three counts:

First, Stimson himself had been repulsed by the conventional bombing of cities and only accepted the tactic, he stated,[25] because he believed it was re-quired to destroy significant Japanese industry located in cities (which by August was no longer a central consideration since most of the important in-dustrial centers had by then been destroyed). On July 2, moreover, Stimson had specifically recommended to Truman that "our own bombing should be confined to military objectives as far as possible."[26]

Second, on the basis of a high-level review of European bombing expe-rience, a directive had been issued not to concentrate on urban centers. Instead, railways, aircraft production, ammunition supplies, and urban indus-trial concentrations had been given priority—in that order. Although, as the Strategic Bombing Survey noted, the momentum of city bombing continued, this directive "was about to be implemented when the war ended."[27]

Third, and most important, as we have seen, the fundamental choice avail-able was hardly between firebombing and the atomic bomb, but between its use and, as Stimson urged, clarifying the surrender terms (and/or awaiting the Russian attack).

• Despite Stimson's argument that Tokyo's approaches to Moscow were not seriously considered because they contemplated retention of important conquered areas by the Japanese: (1) the approaches did not, in fact, include such conditions; (2) moreover, other intercepted messages—in particular those expressing no objection to a surrender based on the Atlantic Charter—suggested this was hardly a problem (since the charter's specific provisions prohibited continued occupation of conquered territory); (3) in any event, British and U.S. analysts—as Churchill pointed out on July 18—fully under-stood this was not a serious problem ("We know of course that the Japanese are ready to give up all conquests made in this war");[28] and (4) finally, Stimson himself had urgently advised Truman to try to end the war on July 16 (and had not raised this issue as a significant problem).

Foreign Minister Togo's "extremely urgent" intercepted July 11 cable to Ambassador Sato in Moscow put it this way:

> Japan . . . has absolutely no idea of annexing or holding territories which she occupied during the war.[29]

As important as these various misleading assertions are, even more trouble-some are other points which are simply not mentioned at all in the article:

• Nothing is said, for instance, about diplomacy towards the Russians even though we now know that throughout the summer Byrnes in particular—and Stimson and Truman as well—had come to see the atomic bomb as central to their diplomatic strategy in both Europe and Asia. It was "the master card" of diplomacy, as Stimson had put it.[30] It was needed to make the Russians "more manageable," Byrnes told Szilard.[31] At Potsdam, it was "tying in what we are doing in all fields."[32]

· Nor does Stimson tell the reader that once the atomic test had proven the efficacy of the new weapon, the United States actively attempted to delay a Russian declaration of war—even though this could only have helped speed a surrender (and thereby save lives). While every effort was made to rush the atomic test, Byrnes was "hoping for time," so that "Russia will not get in so much on the kill. . . ."[33]

· Nor would a reader of the essay know that U.S. leaders had broken Japan's codes and were reading all of the intense diplomatic traffic of the period—nor, specifically, that the thrust of this traffic indicated the main obstacle to peace to be the "unconditional surrender" formula.

· Stimson also neglects to mention the specific point that the cables stated that Japan was prepared to surrender on the basis of the Atlantic Charter.

· Nor does Stimson acknowledge the official finding of the U.S. Strategic Bombing Survey that the war would likely have ended before November in any event (which had been publicly quoted in *The New York Times*).

· Nor is the conclusion of the 1946 War Department Operations Division study cited (which Stimson may or may not have known about, but which is likely to have been available to Secretary of War Robert Patterson and others who reviewed the draft): "The war would almost certainly have terminated when Russia entered the war against Japan."[34]

In all of this, the two most important omissions are critical: first, that the issue of surrender turned in large part on the threatened position of the Emperor; second, that the expected shock of a Russian attack on its own—or in "two-step" fashion followed by assurances for the Emperor—seemed highly likely to end the war well before the planned November landing.

Particularly disturbing in this connection is what the evidence shows not only about the basic facts, but about Stimson's personal knowledge of them (as, for instance, indicated by Stimson's July 2 and July 16 arguments and recommendations). The *Harper's* article does mention Stimson's views on the question of the Emperor. However, the issue is discussed only briefly and its significance would be lost to all but the most careful reader.[35] Meanwhile, as Conant had urged, the essay as a whole essentially ignored the problem of unconditional surrender and the Emperor's status. The overall effect is to reinforce the idea that neither was of any real significance.

No reader of the *Harper's* article would have any idea that every important member of the U.S. government involved except Byrnes favored a clarification of the surrender formula by early June—or, for that matter, that

Stimson's urgent advice had been ignored both before the Potsdam Proclamation was issued and after when the available cable traffic suggested that
the Japanese (as he had worried) were, in fact, "hanging fire" on this point.[36]

Henry Stimson must also have known of the early intelligence advice concerning the likely impact of a Russian declaration of war; and he was present
at the June 18 meeting when Marshall advised Truman directly that "the impact of Russian entry on the already hopeless Japanese may well be the decisive action levering them into capitulation at that time or shortly thereafter
if we land in Japan"—a judgment made almost a month before the Emper-
or's intervention signaled Japan's strong interest in an early end to the fighting.[37]* He would have had to be extremely obtuse or disinterested—which he
was not—not to have understood the importance of all this as well.

Perhaps the most enduring single obfuscation created by the *Harper's* article, however, is the notion—still prevalent—that the atomic bomb was used
because the alternative would likely have cost the United States alone "a million casualties." This specific estimate is offered not once but twice. Stimson
states that had the bomb not been used, "the major fighting would not end
until the latter part of 1946, at the earliest. I was informed that such operations might be expected to cost over a million casualties, to American forces
alone."[38]†

The "over a million" claim became the essential source for a myth which
has been repeated with only occasional challenge for much of the last half
century. Modern scholarship has nevertheless demonstrated the estimate to be
without any serious foundation in the documents of the period. It is also clear
from the evidence now available that at the time Stimson was personally informed of figures radically different from the "over a million" estimate he
put forward in his essay.

In the mid-1980s the research of two scholars in particular subjected the
casualty estimate to intense scrutiny. A 1985 study by Rufus E. Miles, Jr.,
concluded that "the number of American deaths prevented by the two bombs
would almost certainly not have exceeded 20,000 and would probably have
been much lower, perhaps even zero."[39] At virtually the same time Barton
Bernstein demonstrated in greater detail that a November Kyushu landing,
had it actually occurred—and, moreover, continued without interruption to
the end—might have cost a maximum of 20,000 deaths.[40] The highest estimate discovered in the various planning reports—assuming both the 1945

---

*Indeed, in the article Stimson explicitly refers to his diary entry of June 19 concerning possi-
ble sanctions to a warning, but omits both Marshall's specific suggestion on that date of the
additional sanction of Soviet entry—and his own response: "That would certainly coordinate
all the threats possible to Japan." Stimson Diary, June 19, 1945.

†At another point he states: "Enemy armies still unbeaten had the strength to cost us a million
more." Stimson, "The Decision," p. 106.

landing and the full-scale 1946 invasion to have taken place—was in the range of 40,000 to 46,000 deaths.[41]

On July 9, furthermore, the Joint Staff planners reaffirmed Marshall's essential conclusions of June 18 and these figures.[42] The planners added that if a spring 1946 invasion of the Tokyo plain were to occur, because of the favorable terrain and the superiority of American equipment "this invasion . . . should be relatively inexpensive."[43]

Again, it is not only the facts that are important, but evidence of Stimson's personal knowledge of them. In the absence of an invasion, of course, there would have been no such casualties—and, to repeat, there is substantial evidence that by July, Stimson himself had come to believe (and advise Truman) that altering the surrender terms stood a good chance of ending the war even without the Russians. Moreover, we know that not only was Stimson present when Marshall stated that a Russian declaration of war might "lever" Japan into surrender immediately "or shortly thereafter *if* we land in Japan" but at this time, too, Marshall gave the president his estimate of what might happen "shortly thereafter" even if a Kyushu landing occurred: Casualties for the first thirty days were not expected to exceed those experienced in Luzon—that is, a combined total of 31,000 wounded, missing, and dead (or roughly 7,000 to 8,000 deaths).* Indeed, at this critical meeting there was no discussion of large casualty figures anywhere near the *Harper's* estimate—even though, as we have noted, the president had stressed that consideration of possible casualties was his highest priority.

A recent detailed study by John Ray Skates confirms that however Stimson and Bundy arrived at their figure, "similar estimates did not emerge in the 1945 Joint Chiefs' debates about the invasion, nor did the planners ever cite such high numbers."[44]†

Where did Stimson and Bundy get their "over a million" estimate? We do not know. According to Winnacker's notes, during a brainstorming session on November 10, 1946, one point Stimson said he wanted to make was: ". . . if atomic bomb works, might save hundred thousands [*sic*] of American lives."[45] This, of course, is different from the "over a million" figure, but even this number has no basis in the planning documents.

---

*Emphasis added. Leahy's diary of June 18 suggests that if the Kyushu campaign were actually to have continued, Marshall estimated 63,000 casualties (i.e., 12–16,000 deaths), still less than the planning estimate of 20,000. For further discussion, see pp. 515–20 and, in the notes section, note 44 of chapter 38 and note 7 of the Afterword.

†In evaluating the issue of casualty estimates, note also that policy-makers expected *by July and August* that the shock of the Russian attack would occur in mid-August; second, that the president had made it clear that if the Japanese were "hanging fire" on the question of the Emperor, he would offer the necessary assurances; and that for these additional reasons the likelihood was even higher of the war ending without incurring casualties of the scale assumed in the various planning scenarios presented in June.

It is possible, of course, that Stimson simply forgot the information presented in 1945, and that neither Bundy nor the others who helped prepare the *Harper's* article had the correct figures available to them. However, the record shows that Stimson and Bundy specifically asked Winnacker for casualty estimates—and that Winnacker wrote to them on November 12 to say that he was "trying to obtain the Surgeon General's estimates. . . ."[46] Moreover, we also know that other numbers (such as estimated Japanese strength) cited in the article were carefully checked prior to publication.[47] Also, on November 12 Winnacker wrote Stimson that "I will have the [redeployment] figures checked and, if possible, obtain more pertinent data for the entire problem, such as estimated casualties."[48]*

No supporting document has been found in the Stimson papers—in itself, something of a puzzle. Given the care taken in the preparation of the essay, the extraordinary involvement of numerous high-level officials with access to all the relevant documents, and, too, that the finished draft was sent out for review to Groves and Stimson's successor, Patterson—we are left to wonder how so crucial a piece of information in so important a public statement could be included without specific substantiation and careful checking.†

Given Stimson's reputation and personal integrity, perhaps it is not surprising to find him writing Justice Felix Frankfurter on December 12, 1946: "I have rarely been connected with a paper about which I have so much doubt at the last moment."[49] Rather than publish the article at this time, Stimson sug-

---

*A December 10, 1946, letter from Bundy to War Department historian Rudolph Winnacker, however, asked him among other things to generally check all of the figures in the draft essay. On a related issue, in a November 18, 1946, letter to Stimson, Winnacker cautioned against using nonbattle casualty estimates since "these figures are rather deceiving and include anybody admitted to hospitals or quarters even for the treatment of a sore throat." Attachments also noted that "casualty" figures are actually "admissions" to hospitals and quarters—and thus frequently count the same person more than once. (McGeorge Bundy to Rudolph A. Winnacker, December 10, 1946 and Rudolph A. Winnacker to Henry L. Stimson, November 18, 1946, Stimson Papers, Sterling Library, Yale University.)

†Recently, Bundy stated that the estimate in the *Harper's* article "comes from the call I made to the Pentagon, but I don't remember who I called." He added that he would most likely have talked to Winnacker, and that the figure referred to what might have happened had the United States been forced to fight the five-million Japanese army to the very end. "If you say to me," Bundy noted, " 'But it's a bit of a lawyer's question,' I would say, 'Yes, it's about his nightmare.' " Bundy clearly indicated, however, that Stimson did not believe such an extreme possibility was likely following the policy he urged. (McGeorge Bundy interview with author, April 6, 1995.) In a subsequent letter Bundy amplified a comment he made in the interview, noting that the article stated that the figure came from Stimson himself, and that neither of them would have invented it; his call was probably to check Stimson's memory. Bundy said he did not remember discussing with Stimson whether the war would, in fact, have lasted so long without the bomb, but he was sure Stimson would have felt it important to assess the bomb's use against the full possible cost of the overall effort. (McGeorge Bundy to author, April 21, 1995.)

gested that he might "hold it until the subject comes up in my book where proper explanation and background can be given, showing how the art of war has deteriorated during the 20th century and particularly under the influence of the abolition of all the restrictions of international law by the Nazis."[50]

Frankfurter, however, urged immediate publication: "The longer a sentimentally appealing error is allowed to make its way, the more difficult it is to overtake it"[51]—and Bundy soon informed the Justice that his urging had done the trick. Still, "it really was touch and go whether he would go ahead with the article on the afternoon he decided to write you. . . ."[52]

McCloy, who perhaps had been closer to Stimson than anyone at the time, later told biographer Kai Bird: "I knew Stimson as well as any man alive and while after the war he wrote an article for *Harper's* defending his decision, I know in his soul there were doubts. He lay awake at night before the decision thinking about the consequences of dropping it on a civilian target, a city of that size."[53]

Martin Sherwin has observed that, in general, "The manipulation of the estimated casualty figures, and thereby the history of the decision-making process that led to the atomic bombings of Hiroshima and Nagasaki, has masked an important lesson. The choice in the summer of 1945 was not between a conventional invasion or a nuclear war. It was a choice between various forms of diplomacy and warfare."[54] Barton Bernstein adds that the myth "helped deter Americans from asking troubling questions about the use of the atomic bombs. The destruction of this myth should reopen these questions."[55] Skates is less circumspect: ". . . prophecies of extremely high casualties only came to be widely accepted after the war to rationalize the use of the atomic bombs."[56]

Apart from the specific problem of the casualty figure, we may also ask in general what led a man of Henry Stimson's standing to sign his name to the kind of essay which appeared in *Harper's* in early 1947?

It may be that in connection with the article's many misstatements of fact, Stimson truly did not recall precisely what happened during the summer of 1945, or what the record shows him to have known and said. During the final months of the war he experienced several heart attacks and suffered from migraines, insomnia, and arthritis. Over much of that year he had to rest during each busy workday, and he often left Washington on weekends to recuperate at his Highhold estate. He was not present, in fact, at several important Interim Committee meetings and other discussions concerning the atomic bomb.

Stimson would not be the first or the last person who after the fact convinced himself of a comforting version of reality different from what actually had occurred—and who subsequently came honestly to believe what now seemed to be an accurate recollection. For instance, one transcribed conversation with McGeorge Bundy in the summer of 1946—a conversation clearly not designed to convince the public—seems to indicate that despite what the record shows, he may genuinely have come to believe that "the American attack [was] moving along on a certain basis which would have produced and carried through in the way it was planned and was giving so many million casualties."[57]

A related possibility is that he was manipulated to an extent by Conant, Bundy, and others. We know that Stimson was susceptible to pressure from his friends; his papers show that he did not initiate the March 1946 *Harper's* article, the 1947 *Harper's* article, or even the writing of his memoirs. In each case, in varying degrees, Stimson was convinced to participate in writing projects that were initially the ideas of friends and associates. Bundy told Frankfurter: "Now your letter has been reinforced by others . . . and the Colonel is in full fighting trim, waiting for the article to appear and the fun to begin."[58]

A more calculated and self-conscious possibility cannot be excluded. Scholars have documented earlier instances in his career when Stimson was less than fully forthright in his public statements. Bernstein suggests that Stimson was not consciously "seeking to distort history." More likely, he was probably "seeking to reveal enough of the past, and to present it in a framework, that it would justify recent decisions on the A-bomb, advance American policy, and maintain calm patriotism."[59]

Another reason the *Harper's* essay took the form it finally did almost certainly is that Stimson felt personal loyalty to the president and his advisers, and loyalty to the process of statecraft itself.* We know from transcripts of other 1946 discussions that even though Stimson had strong feelings about Byrnes' hard-line approach to the atomic bomb and diplomacy, he had qualms about making his real thoughts public. As he and Bundy considered what to say in the memoirs concerning the control of nuclear weapons, Stimson commented at one point: "I don't think I can make those [my views on the need to control the bomb] public more than what I did make public in the Harper's statement."[60] (He was here referring not to the 1947 essay on the atomic bomb, but to the March 1946 condensation of his memo urging Truman to seek an agreement with the Russians to control nuclear weapons.)

> The very fact that I had such a part in it [the debate over how to approach the atomic bomb and Russia] would make the smallest statement by me subject to possible misinterpretation and would be given a greater effect than it should and would very likely embarrass Byrnes. The one

---

*"This is a public man making a statement on a public issue . . . ," Bundy recently stated. "The article has a political purpose. . . ." (McGeorge Bundy interview with author, April 6, 1995.)

thing I cannot do is to embarrass the President and Byrnes in their efforts to work that problem out and I would shy away from it rather than do that.[61]

Related to this, it may also be that Stimson was so worried about the possible impact of the developing criticism of the Hiroshima decision that he simply felt there was no alternative. He may have shared Conant's view that "if the propaganda against the use of the atomic bomb had been allowed to grow unchecked, the strength of our military position by virtue of having the bomb would have been correspondingly weakened. . . ."[62]

It is impossible to know precisely what mix of conscious and unconscious motives produced the *Harper's* article. We are left to struggle with the disturbing facts before us. We are also left to ponder the unqualified assurances with which Stimson (and Bundy) introduced the famous essay. Stimson informed readers of the *Harper's* article that it was "an exact description of our thoughts and actions as I find them in the records and in my clear recollection."[63]

Chapter 39

"WE HAVE FOLLOWED
THE RECORD"

I am afraid that if these statements were now to appear in an official biography of Mr. Stimson, a part of the reading public might conclude that the hope of influencing Russia by the threat of atomic attack had been, and probably remained, one of the permanent motivating elements of our foreign policy.
— George F. Kennan to McGeorge Bundy,
December 2, 1947

One of the truly fundamental misconceptions created by the *Harper's* article is perhaps the most obvious: simply by virtue of writing the essay, Stimson appeared to have been the primary source of advice to Truman on the use of the atomic bomb. Moreover, he said as much:

> For nearly four years . . . I was directly connected with all major decisions of policy on the development and use of atomic energy, and from May 1, 1943, until my resignation as Secretary of War on September 21, 1945, I was directly responsible to the President for the administration of the entire undertaking. . . . At the same time I was the President's senior adviser on the military employment of atomic energy.[1]

Though this was technically true, in fact, it completely misrepresented the actual reality: As we have seen, Byrnes, not Stimson, was the president's closest adviser on the atomic bomb—from at least early May on, when he joined the Interim Committee as Truman's personal representative. Stimson himself had been only too aware that on the really important points— especially assurances for the Emperor and the timing of the warning— Byrnes had rebuffed him at every turn.

Despite Stimson's eminence and the widespread praise the article received in the press, support for the *Harper's* essay was not unanimous. Most reviewers did not question the kinds of arguments and "facts" which during this period were subject to merciless attack in the work of critics of the decision.[2] But not all the "chatterers" were silenced.

The *Washington Post*, for instance, was "not convinced that in July, 1945, there was no sign of any 'weakening of the Japanese determination to fight.' "[3] As we have seen, very early on the *Post* had urged a modification of the unconditional-surrender formula. Although it agreed with much of Stimson's argument, it now also noted that the *Strategic Bombing Survey* "confirms the judgment of the proponents of psychological warfare (of which we were one) that 'the level of confidence was quite low in Japan well before the time of the atomic bombing.' "[4]

The *Post*'s criticism was itself given additional publicity in an article terming it a "rebuttal" in *Human Events*[5]; and Raymond Swing worried: ". . . I am not sure that sufficient weight was given [to] the effect on the future of using such a weapon. The decision to drop the bomb was perhaps the most fateful of our time. . . . in using the bomb we became the most ruthless nation in warfare on earth."[6] In a similar vein, the *Christian Century* thought the findings of the Strategic Bombing Survey would "stand the test of history better than the statements of President Truman and Secretary Stimson."[7]

For the most part, however, it was plain that anyone who wished to challenge the former secretary of war would have to do so with all the evidentiary cards stacked against him. "Your article gives only the views of a small committee of scientists," Swing wrote Stimson. "We know that many others had views that they carried to you and the White House."[8] Stimson (and Bundy)—for better or worse—had access to many still-classified facts.[9] The critics had access to none.

Except, that is, for those who had themselves also been insiders—or very close to high-level officials on the inside.

A handful of people with special knowledge of the events in question knew that Stimson and Bundy had not been straightforward with the facts. For instance, Alexander Leighton, formerly co-chief of OWI's Foreign Morale Analysis Division, wrote an article for syndication which stressed that the "whole story . . . of what we knew when it was decided to use the atomic bomb" had not been told:

> *The fact is that as early as May, 1945 it was perceived in Washington that the Japanese determination to fight had become seriously undermined and most of the morale findings ultimately made by the Strategic Bombing Survey were explicitly described at that time.*[10]

Joseph Grew also immediately grasped that the *Harper's* article had sidestepped the central question of whether the war could have been brought to a close by clarifying the terms of surrender. A close friend observed in his diary that Grew was quite upset about the *Harper's* piece.[11] On February 12, 1947, Grew wrote Stimson, zeroing in on the fact that the essay contained no real discussion of the Emperor issue or the many conversations the two men had had about it in 1945:[12]

> The main point at issue historically is whether, if immediately following the terrific devastation of Tokyo by our B-29s in May, 1945, the President had made a public categorical statement that surrender would not mean the elimination of the present dynasty if the Japanese people desired its retention, the surrender of Japan could have been hastened.
>
> . . . I myself and others felt and still feel that if such a categorical statement about the dynasty had been issued in May, 1945, the surrender-minded elements in the [Japanese] Government might well have been afforded by such a statement a valid reason and the necessary strength to come to an early clear[-]cut decision.[13]

The implications were obvious, and Grew stated them in no uncertain terms:

> If surrender could have been brought about in May, 1945, or even in June or July, before the entrance of Soviet Russia into the war and the use of the atomic bomb, the world would have been the gainer.[14]

And he concluded:

> . . . I and a good many others will always feel that had the President issued as far back as May, 1945, the recommended categorical statement that the Japanese dynasty could be retained if the Japanese people freely desired its retention, the atom bomb might never have had to be used at all.[15]

These paragraphs of Grew's letter were reprinted five years later in his published 1952 memoirs. A portion of the letter not subsequently published, and made available in 1959, sheds light on why Grew went to the trouble of writing Stimson. Even today, the diplomat's somewhat formal language seems barely to conceal a quiet frustration, even despair, at what Stimson had done:

> The almost unique position which you enjoy before the American people gives any statement of yours a conclusive character and crystallizes history as your statements may shape it. History is necessarily built on a mosaic of contemporary comment, and I believe, as I am sure you believe, that all the pieces should be available to produce the complete picture, thus supplementing your historically-important article in Harper's Magazine.[16]

Grew's cool challenge required some kind of response. However, Stimson sat on the communication from his former colleague for more than four months. Only on June 19, 1947, did he finally reply to what he called "your very interesting letter about the Japanese surrender." The essence of the matter, he explained, was that:

> The Harper's article did not seem the place for any discussion as to what might have happened if the position you so early and ably urged had been adopted sooner than it was or stated more clearly in the Potsdam ultimatum. My own views, as you know, were very much in accord with yours all the way through, with perhaps the small exception that in May 1945 I was not convinced that the right moment for a strong public statement on the Emperor had yet come. As I recall it, the difficulty at the time was that we were having considerable trouble with the Japanese in the land campaign on Okinawa and some of us were afraid that any public concession at that time might be taken as an indication of weakness.[17]

Stimson's acknowledgment that his views "were very much in accord with yours all the way through . . ." spoke volumes: It would have been impossible not to acknowledge to so intimate a colleague as Grew what both knew to be the obvious truth.

Stimson's recollection of what he called "perhaps the small exception" about timing was contradicted by many documents (especially in connection with his own views at the time)—including Stimson's diary and the minutes of at least two high-level meetings. As we have seen, the first delay in clarifying the surrender terms, Stimson noted, had occurred not because of Okinawa, but because of the desire to coordinate a clarifying statement with the atomic bomb, which would not be tested until mid-July. His diary of May 29, 1945, states:

> . . . I had in Joe Grew the Acting Secretary of State, Jim Forrestal of the Navy, Marshall the Chief of Staff, and some assistants of each one of them. . . . It was an awkward meeting because there were people present in the presence of whom I could not discuss the real feature which would govern the whole situation, namely S-1. . . . I told him [Grew] that I was inclined to agree with giving the Japanese a modification of the unconditional surrender formula and some hope to induce them to practically make an unconditional surrender without the use of those words. I told him that I thought the timing was wrong and that this was not the time to do it.[18]

To be sure, a second reason for delay had involved Okinawa (at least in the thinking of some advisers). However, Stimson's argument concerning the

Okinawa campaign was misleading even on its own terms. The issue was not simply what happened in May; the Okinawa campaign ended on June 21. Why had a clarification not been put forward at that time, as the Joint Chiefs and others recommended, if this had been the problem?

Even allowing for such misstatements, Stimson's letter to Grew was an astonishing admission—especially considering what he had recently published in *Harper's*. Essentially, Stimson acknowledged that he had all but eliminated from his essay the central fact that as secretary of war he personally had favored a course of action which at the time, like Grew, he believed had a high likelihood of ending the war without the atomic bomb.

To be sure, within the seven-thousand-word article Stimson had included one mention of his position. However, given the overall thrust of his essay, he did not even attempt to suggest that this was a serious presentation of the argument. Instead, he assured Grew that he would be addressing the Emperor issue more fully in his forthcoming memoirs. In it he and "young Bundy" were trying "to make clear in some detail the cross currents which put so much difficulty in the way of the course you and I advocated before it was finally and clearly accepted by the President."[19]

The most revealing portion of Stimson's letter to Grew, however, was the former secretary of war's rather forthright explanation as to why he had not told the real story:

> This is a difficult and rather touchy business because, as you know, feelings ran high and there were very fine men, who should have known better, working on the other side.[20]

It is very easy to miss the brief five-word phrase sandwiched between commas in the above sentence. Given Henry L. Stimson's stature and the public argument he had so successfully just put forward in defense of the use of the atomic bomb, however, one is jolted to reflect upon this statesman's terse, private bottom-line judgment. After having said he agreed with Grew's views "all the way through," his observation that those who had opposed their joint effort to end the war by modifying the surrender terms *"should have known better"* stands as a punctuation mark to an entire era of history.

Grew was not the only conservative insider diplomat who was shocked by the *Harper's* article. William R. Castle—who knew Stimson well and had served directly under him in the Hoover Administration—was another nonbeliever. Castle privately fumed at several specific distortions of fact, and at what he regarded as a blatant misrepresentation of history by an important public official.[21]

Noting in his diary in January 1947 that Stimson's essay argued the use of the atomic bomb against Japan had been absolutely essential to achieve a surrender, Castle acidly observed that—as in many Stimson articles—careful omissions disguised the true picture. One thing in particular bothered him: that Stimson had suppressed (or simply failed to mention) the fact that before the decision to use the bomb had been made, the United States had heard from Russia that Japan was seeking peace. The essay seemed a rather desperate and inappropriate effort to obtain credit—and to protect Stimson from charges that the use of the atomic bomb had been unnecessary. The whole episode had larger implications. Castle disliked seeing historical matters sullied at their very source—and Stimson was a primary source of information on this issue. Castle noted that he himself had never believed the atomic bombings were justifiable, and the more he found out about the situation the clearer he was in his own mind that the decision was mistaken.

Two weeks later, on February 9, 1947, Castle got together with former State Department Far Eastern expert Eugene Dooman, and the old friends together discussed errors in the *Harper's* essay. Two related aspects of the essay appeared to be blatantly dishonest: the first was what looked like an attempt by Stimson to claim that he had personally authored the Potsdam Proclamation; the second involved the general view taken in the essay that there were few signs Japan was faltering. It seemed obvious to Castle that Stimson knew Japan had been attempting to end the war and that its economy was in ruins. Undoubtedly he must also have known of navy information suggesting surrender was only days off.*

As we noted in Book I, at this time, too, Castle privately speculated as to whether Stimson and Marshall actually wished the fighting to go on for a sufficiently long period that they could test the new weapon on Japanese cities. The more he reflected on the atomic bombing, the more he became convinced that it had been a terribly brutal and indefensible act. (Castle informed Dooman that President Hoover wished to see him; and Dooman indicated he would return if it was important.)[22]

What other high-level and well-informed insiders felt about the Stimson article we do not know. What did those involved with the preparation of the Strategic Bombing Survey think or say at the time? Although the available documents tell us very little, we do know the overall opinion of one leading member of the *Survey*, Paul Nitze. Often considered a hard-line cold warrior, Nitze nonetheless writes in his memoirs: "Even without the attacks on Hiroshima and Nagasaki, it seemed highly unlikely, given what we found to have been the mood of the Japanese government, that a U.S. invasion of the islands would have been necessary."[23]

---

*The vague reference in Castle's diary may be to various MAGIC intelligence intercepts processed by the navy.

Except for Stimson's belated letter to Grew and his February 4 response to Raymond Swing, there is no record of his replying to any of the critical letters he received in the wake of the *Harper's* article. (There are, in fact, very few critical letters of any kind on file in the Stimson papers, and only a handful of responses by ordinary citizens objecting to the atomic bomb decision.)

We know just a bit more about Stimson's own feelings about all of this, however. The *Harper's* essay was essentially an interruption in the work Stimson and Bundy were doing on the memoirs. The decision to use the atomic bomb obviously had to be dealt with here, too, and the question of how this should be done came up not once but at least twice (so far as we know)—first, before the *Harper's* essay was undertaken; second, after it was published.

When they actually got down to deciding what to include in the memoirs, Stimson—perhaps embarrassed by Grew's reminder of his own efforts to modify the surrender terms—decided to make an alteration in the position he had stated in his essay. The final text of Stimson's memoir contained a strange admission. Bundy was authorized to state (in the somewhat stilted third-person voice adopted for their collaboration) that:

> Only on the question of the Emperor did Stimson take, in 1945, a con-
> ciliatory view; only on this question did he later believe that history
> might find that the United States, by its delay in stating its position, had
> prolonged the war.[24]

Although this statement never received the publicity given the *Harper's* article, Stimson was here acknowledging that the war might well have been ended without the atomic bomb had the surrender formula been modified early on as he, Grew, and others had urged. Something more, however, was also being said.

Since from his perspective the main reason a modification of the terms had been delayed was because of a wish to wait for the atomic bomb test, Stimson was acknowledging in essence that the advent of the new weapon itself may well have "prolonged the war"—and hence cost lives rather than saved them.[25]

Martin Sherwin was one of the first scholars to grasp what really was being acknowledged. Despite the fact that Stimson continued, simultaneously, to argue that the atomic bomb saved lives, "a considerable body of evidence suggests that the decision to use the bomb, which involved a decision to reject another recommended initiative, *delayed* the end of the war." "[T]he point that is relevant here is that many more American soldiers and Japanese of all types might have had the opportunity to grow old if Truman had accepted Grew's advice"[26]—and, we may add, Stimson's.

Reading the memoirs, Joseph Grew recognized that Stimson had not found it in himself to continue flatly to assert that the use of the atomic bomb had been necessary to end the war. His acknowledgment that "history might find that the United States . . . had prolonged the war" stood out like a sore thumb if you knew what to look for. Writing to Eugene Dooman about the difference between the 1947 *Harper's* article and the passage in the memoirs, Grew observed:

> On the basis of this admission I believe that some day in [the] future— not now—[there] should be published the record of my talk with the President on May 28, 1945, my letter to Stimson of February 12, 1947, and his reply to me of June 19, 1947, with which you are familiar.[27]

It is a measure of the temper of the era that although Grew fully realized the significance of the documentary materials in his possession—and although he clearly wanted them to come eventually to light—he, too, decided to suppress information he felt was somehow not suitable to be laid before the American people at that time.[28]

Certain other aspects of the Stimson memoirs (published in 1948 under the title *On Active Service in Peace and War*) are also significant—especially as they concern Stimson's treatment of the "Russian problem" and his general attitude towards the disclosure of potentially embarrassing information in his possession.

Stimson, to recall, on July 9, 1946, had explained his reluctance to criticize Byrnes' approach to the atomic bomb as a diplomatic weapon to Bundy: "I end on what I said in September. Even the memorandum I made in September I assume is still top secret. I doubt whether we had better try to unravel Jim Byrnes' problems now. I think it would be rather improper for me to forecast in what way the problem should be worked out, how Russia should be handled and what she should do."[29]

After gently pressing Stimson to see if there was anything else that could safely be written about the atomic control issue, Bundy finally concluded: "Maybe the thing to do is just reprint the Harper['s] article. . . ."[30] (the one-page March 1946 essay on international control, not the 1947 article on the Hiroshima decision). Stimson agreed. Nonetheless, in the end—perhaps because Byrnes had left office in January 1947, replaced as secretary of state by George Marshall—a decision was made (we do not know exactly how or when) to reprint Stimson's powerful September 1945 memorandum to Truman.

However, along with the text of Stimson's plea for an immediate approach to the Russians ("the chief lesson I have learned in a long life is that the only way you can make a man trustworthy is to trust him. . . ."[31]) was a new explanation. This both qualified the force of the original argument and shifted the blame away from Byrnes. "As an expression of his [Stimson's] views in 1947," Bundy now wrote of the ideas expressed in the September plea to Truman,

> they were seriously incomplete. . . . what if the man whose trust you sought was a cynical "realist" who did not choose to be your friend? . . .
> It was a daring and imaginative democrat indeed who could ignore in 1947 the mountain of evidence supporting the hypothesis that Stalin and his associates were committed to a policy of expansion and dictatorial repression. In so far as it insufficiently emphasized this aspect of the Russian problem, Stimson's September memorandum was dangerously one-sided.[32]

Stimson, it appears, either fully agreed with this view or, minimally, allowed his name to be attached to it. In mid-1947 he wrote George Roberts that "we should stand by with all the bombs we have got and can make . . . until Russia learns to be decent."[33] On the other hand, a certain ambivalence seems clearly to be indicated by the fact that at this same time he emphasized (by newly italicizing specific materials in the memoirs) that he considered the following previously noted passage "the heart of the memorandum":

> *Those relations may be perhaps irretrievably embittered by the way in which we approach the solution of the bomb with Russia. For if we fail to approach them now and merely continue to negotiate with them, having this weapon rather ostentatiously on our hip, their suspicions and their distrust of our purposes and motives will increase.*[34]

And, again—at this same time—he also newly stressed as "the most important point of all":

> *I emphasize perhaps beyond all other considerations the importance of taking this action with Russia as a proposal of the United States— backed by Great Britain but peculiarly the proposal of the United States. Action of any international group of nations, including many small nations who have not demonstrated their potential power or responsibility in this war would not, in my opinion, be taken seriously by the Soviets.*[35]

Other more recently discovered documents suggest just how difficult it is to tell precisely how Stimson felt about the central issues (as opposed to whether he again did not wish to embarrass U.S. government leaders with whom he had served so long). Letters found by McCloy's biographer Kai Bird at the George C. Marshall Library in Lexington, Virginia, show that after Bundy and Stimson had agreed upon a draft manuscript of the memoir, they sent the chapters concerning the war years to Marshall. Although Marshall was extremely preoccupied with official duties, he began reading the chapters (usually between the hours of 11:00 p.m. and two or even three in the morning).[36] On November 7, 1947, he wrote Bundy a three-page letter with preliminary comments on all but the final three chapters of the book, including one titled "The Bomb and Peace with Russia."

As to this chapter, he said: "I am giving very careful consideration to the chapter on the atomic bomb in relation to the Soviets because the question of its publication at the present time is a very critical matter."[37] The date of Marshall's letter is important. In the early winter of 1947 the Cold War had only recently moved into its initial post–Truman Doctrine public phase. Congress and the American people were debating economic aid to noncommunist Europe through the Marshall Plan. What was said—or not said—in the memoirs of so important a figure as Henry L. Stimson could be significant, especially since Stimson's draft included an explicit attack on Byrnes' hard-line approach.

Bundy responded to Marshall almost immediately (on November 10) that:

> I quite understand that Chapter XIII, on the bomb and Russia, may present problems of present importance in diplomacy; we have tried to state the issues as they presented themselves to Mr. Stimson, mainly with the idea of showing how even a very experienced statesman had to wrestle for a long time and with the gravest worry before reaching a balanced conclusion. . . . Whether it is wise to present this problem from Cabinet documents of 1945 is of course another question, although I admit that I am not clear as to the dangers of this course. In any case, you must know that you are the sole judge of that, and that Mr. Stimson will accept your advice without question.[38]

In short, although Bundy doubted the necessity of eliminating the material, the secretary of state need not worry: Stimson would defer to Marshall's wishes "without question."

A few days later Marshall met with George Kennan—then serving as director of the Policy Planning Staff at the State Department—and made a point of reading the draft aloud to the diplomat. However, after going over the first part of the chapter—about which Kennan "expressed no concern over its publicity"—the two men were interrupted by other business.[39] Thereafter, Marshall inadvertently sent the manuscript back to Bundy without comment. Bundy's letter apparently reminded Marshall that he had not obtained Kennan's reaction to the entire chapter, and he wrote Bundy again asking him to send it directly to Kennan to "get his reaction to the effect of its publication under present circumstances."[40] When he in turn wrote Kennan, Bundy attached another conciliatory letter of explanation:

I suppose that the principal difficulty or possible difficulty that might arise in publication is that Mr. Stimson's memorandum urging a direct approach, in September, 1945, might seem to be an implied criticism of what was actually done during those months. We have however tried to hedge any implied criticism with a recognition of the difficulties involved in Mr. Stimson's recommendation.

As I have explained to the Secretary, Mr. Stimson is wholly determined not to publish any material which would be regarded as unhelpful in your Department, and he is therefore delaying final approval of this chapter until he hears again from Secretary Marshall. Any changes or amendments which seem necessary to you, and which Mr. Stimson can conscientiously make, he will make—and if we cannot amend, we can always delete.[41]

Bundy's concern about what might constitute the "principal difficulty" in publishing this material was misplaced. Upon reading the remainder of the chapter, Kennan was not greatly worried by Stimson's treatment of the post-Hiroshima debate over how to establish international control of the atomic bomb and energy. He was, however, alarmed by Stimson's reference to the atomic bomb as a diplomatic weapon.

Stimson had clearly not forgotten his basic disagreement with Byrnes; nor, at least as of this date, did he wish to soft-pedal it (whatever was later said). Bundy and Stimson had, in fact, included the following statement in the text concerning the post-Potsdam period (based obviously on the diary entries we have previously reviewed):

. . . the War Department civilian staff was thinking long and painful thoughts about the atomic triumph. Meanwhile in the State Department there developed a tendency to think of the bomb as a diplomatic weapon. Outraged by constant evidence of Russian perfidy, some of the men in charge of foreign policy were eager to carry the bomb for a while as their ace-in-the-hole.[42]

At another point in the draft Bundy and Stimson had also stated that Stimson's September memorandum urging a direct approach to Russia to control nuclear weapons had been ". . . [p]resented at a time when some American statesmen were eager for their country to browbeat the Russians with the atomic bomb 'held rather ostentatiously on our hip.' "[43] The draft had observed, finally, that Stimson's September recommendation that the Russians be approached directly, openly, and privately, "was not adopted, even partially, until the passage of several months in which an exactly contrary course was pursued, with resulting serious changes in the whole atmosphere."[44]

Kennan considered these three passages nothing short of inflammatory. "I do not know to what officials of the Department of State these passages refer," he wrote Bundy, "and I have no wish to start a discussion of the attitudes of individual officials at that time. I am sure, however, that the responsible heads of the Department did not hold the views described. . . ."[45]

It is—to say the least—highly doubtful that Kennan was unaware of Byrnes' attitude (as subsequent documents also show). However, the important point is that the director of the Policy Planning Staff did not want the text published in its present form:

> I am afraid that if these statements were now to appear in an official biography of Mr. Stimson, a part of the reading public might conclude that the hope of influencing Russia by the threat of atomic attack had been, and probably remained, one of the permanent motivating elements of our foreign policy. Such an impression would play squarely into the hands of the Communists, who so frequently speak of our "atomic diplomacy" and accuse us of trying to intimidate the world in general by our possession of the bomb.[46]

Kennan added that he would share the correspondence with Marshall, noting: "I believe that he, too, had some misgivings about the passages I have cited."[47]

Bundy immediately replied and agreed that "the language you question was incautious and exaggerated." He assured Kennan that he would bring his criticism to Stimson's attention and that the two of them would likely rework the offending passages; he had "little doubt that he [Stimson] will agree with your *central* criticism. . . ." Perhaps because he was aware of Stimson's strong feelings on the subject, however, Bundy did not concede the main point at issue. The truth of the matter, he wrote Kennan, was that the "divergence between Mr. Stimson and Mr. Byrnes in September 1945 was a real one, and Mr. Byrnes' *reported* attitude (for purely short-term negotiating purposes) was not far from the one described. . . ."

> It is also my feeling, however, that the basic *attitude* of Mr. Stimson's September paper was not shared at the highest levels in the direct line of foreign-policy making, and I wonder whether we may not in the end have to face a serious question as to the intensity and skill of our effort to educate the Russians.[48]

Bundy assured Kennan that "in any event, the situation now has changed, and we do not want to play into the hands of the Kremlin's hired liars. We will try again. . . ."[49] Soon he and Stimson had redrafted the text to exclude the troublesome material[50]—specifically, to omit the language about the bomb being "a diplomatic weapon" and an "ace-in-the-hole." The phrase "some American statesmen" became "some Americans." In addition, the statement that "an exactly contrary course was pursued, with resulting serious changes in the whole international atmosphere" was changed in order to soften Stimson's disagreement with Byrnes. The new text read:

> Stimson had no desire to criticize the course actually followed by the United States between September and December, 1945, but he did not believe that this course represented precisely the policy and method he had in mind in presenting his September memorandum. This was not by any means the result of a purely American decision; the Russians continued to make it extremely difficult for any American negotiator to conduct the sort of bed-rock discussion of fundamental problems which Stimson was advocating. The good faith and honorable intentions of those charged with American policy in this period seemed to Stimson unquestionable. If he had a difference with them, it was in method and emphasis, and not in basic purpose.
>
>   Nor could he claim with any certainty that his own policy would have been more successful. If there had been an immediate and direct effort, in September, 1945, to reach agreement with Russia on the control of atomic energy, would it have been successful? He could not say. Much would have depended on the manner in which the attempt was made. . . .[51]

Whatever the softened language stated, the sting in the last sentence— "much would have depended on the manner in which the attempt was made"—suggests that Stimson's essential position had not changed. However, the problem was now solved. Kennan sent the revised language to Marshall with the following cover note:

> At your request, I read over the section of Mr. Stimson's manuscript on the atomic bomb. I suggested two changes to Mr. Bundy, and as a consequence, Mr. Stimson has agreed to make the changes indicated. . . . If you concur in these changes, Mr. Bundy would appreciate being notified at once.[52]

Marshall's handwritten response on the memorandum reads simply: "I concur," and Kennan lost no time in giving Bundy the go-ahead: "The changes which are suggested in your letter meet entirely the points that I had in mind, and I appreciate deeply Mr. Stimson's understanding and helpfulness in making these changes."[53]

Bundy concluded by thanking Kennan for his letters and noted:

> It is good to know that the suggested revisions meet your requirements and that the Secretary concurs. I do not feel that they affect what

Mr. Stimson wants said in any material way. In effect, you have merely improved our manners, and I am grateful.[54]

To the modern reader reviewing these documents, two related statements published in the memoirs give a certain pause. A particularly jarring passage is Bundy's assertion (in a concluding "note of explanation and acknowledgment") that in preparing the memoirs "We have . . . tried to make a clear distinction between his [Stimson's] views as they were during any given period and his present opinions, and wherever memory or desire has conflicted with the written record, we have followed the record."[55]

Similarly, Stimson himself explains to the reader at the outset that what he and Bundy have assembled is presented "as clearly and as honestly as we can." Although the text may perhaps contain some understandable errors, "it is as accurate as Mr. Bundy and I can make it. . . ."[56]

Chapter 40

"OMISSIONS MERELY
FOR BREVITY"

*Unfortunately I have lived long enough to know that history
is often not what actually happened but what is recorded
as such.*
   —Henry L. Stimson, *On Active Service in Peace and War*

Clearly, fear—explicit, but only privately acknowledged—of undercutting
U.S. policy in the early Cold War years was at work as Stimson and Bundy
prepared the memoirs for publication. It is also helpful to remember something about the human relationships involved. Scattered throughout the
Stimson diaries are entries noting informal occasions with associates at his
home enjoying games of bowls, deck tennis, horseback riding, and fishing
outings. The people we are remembering were not just government officials
and historical personages; they were intimate associates and friends.

The emerging Cold War environment and loyalty to close colleagues do
not, however, tell us the entire story. Even as we attempt to understand context and relationships, it is important not to lose sight of what might fairly
be called the existential issue: The simple fact is Stimson (and Bundy) chose
to revise what both had initially believed it appropriate to say in their draft
chapter, and what both knew to be the truth.[1]

This point is emphasized because accounts of choices by various American leaders made during these years sometimes seem to "explain" the actions
of individuals as "caused" by the Cold War culture. Yet, another choice—
hence human responsibility—was also possible: Leahy's and Eisenhower's
public criticisms of the bombing of Hiroshima (among others) stand as alternative positions—and as reminders that not everything which can seemingly
be "explained" in history is also inevitable.

The point is especially important because the personality, integrity, and character of the men involved have so often been made central to the analysis of this period. A recent account of early Cold War policy-making, for instance, emphasizes the historical importance of *The Wise Men* (as its title reads).[2] But clearly conscious decisions were made to mislead the American people, and it cannot be denied that the decisions were made with full awareness of what was being done.

What we now know about other decisions to exclude materials from the memoirs—especially materials related to the context in which the final decision to use the atomic bomb was made—further illuminates this critical point. In the note with which he ended the memoirs Bundy stated:

> For the periods it fully covers, the [Stimson] diary is the basic document; it shows what was really in Mr. Stimson's mind at any given time as no files or correspondence can do. . . .
>
>   The diary has been liberally quoted. . . . Omissions are indicated by the usual dots; in most cases the omissions are merely for brevity; in a few, they involve comments or expressions which Mr. Stimson does not now wish to publish, either because he no longer agrees with himself or because they might cause unnecessary pain to men who were his associates and are his friends.[3]

In fact, however, in connection with virtually all of the critical issues surrounding the atomic bomb story, the diary is quoted only in very minor ways. When the memoir narrative comes close to the most telling issues related to the actual decision—and to discussions of the relationship of the bomb to diplomacy towards the Soviet Union during the summer of 1945—almost none of the information which modern historians have found so illuminating (and so different from the thrust of the *Harper's* article) is presented.

The memoirs reprint the September memorandum and (within the reproduced *Harper's* essay) the April 25 and July 2 memoranda which had previously been published. However, the diary itself is actually explicitly drawn upon in this connection on only three occasions: March 15, June 19, and August 10, 1945.[4] The quoted material includes:

• *March 15, 1945:* Information concerning Stimson's last meeting with President Roosevelt. This suggests Stimson's general thinking about postwar international control of atomic technology as of this date: "the implications of success in terms of its long-range postwar effect."[5]

> I went over with him [Roosevelt] the two schools of thought that exist in respect to the future control after the war of this project, in case it is successful, one of them being the secret close-in attempted control of the project by those who control it now, and the other being the international control based upon freedom both of science and of access. I

told him that those things must be settled before the first projectile is used and that he must be ready with a statement to come out to the people on it just as soon as that is done. He agreed to that.[6]

• *June 19, 1945:* A discussion of when a warning should be given to Japan. Stimson is quoted as saying "the last chance warning . . . must be given before an actual landing of the ground forces in Japan, and fortunately the plans provide for enough time to bring in the sanctions to our warning in the shape of heavy ordinary bombing attack and an attack of S-1."[7]

Omitted, however, are the preceding sentences in which he reports on the consensus reached after the critical June 18 meeting with the President, the Joint Chiefs of Staff, McCloy, and Forrestal:

> The Chiefs of Staff had taken their position at the meeting on Monday, and Forrestal and I have agreed to it as far as the purely military side of it goes. But there was a pretty strong feeling that it would be deplorable if we have to go through the military program with all its stubborn fighting to a finish. We agreed that it is necessary now to plan and prepare to go through, but it became very evident today in the discussion that we all feel that some way should be found of inducing Japan to yield without a fight to the finish and that was the subject of the discussion today. Grew read us a recent report he had made to the President on the subject in which he strongly advocated a new warning to Japan as soon as Okinawa has fallen, but apparently that does not meet with the President's plans in respect to the coming meeting with Churchill and Stalin.[8]

(A related, shorter diary item from the previous day, June 18, is also not used. In it Stimson reports discussing with Truman "the big political question lying apart from the military plans, namely as to whether we had grounds for thinking that there was a liberal-minded section of the Japanese people with whom we can make proper terms for the future life of Japan."[9])

• *August 10, 1945:* The excerpt printed in the memoirs shows Stimson advising the president to agree to give the Japanese assurances for the Emperor at this point in time:

> The President then asked me what my opinion was and I told him that I thought that even if the question hadn't been raised by the Japanese we would have to continue the Emperor ourselves under our command and supervision in order to get into surrender the many scattered armies of the Japanese who would own no other authority and that something like this use of the Emperor must be made in order to save us from a score of bloody Iwo Jimas and Okinawas all over China and the New

Netherlands. He was the only source of authority in Japan under the Japanese theory of the State.[10]

Left out of the text of the same diary entry, however, are passages in which Stimson states:

> . . . I read the messages. Japan accepted the Potsdam list of terms put out by the President "with the understanding that the said declaration does not comprise any demand which prejudices the prerogatives of his majesty as a sovereign ruler". It is curious that this [the status of the Emperor] was the very single point that I feared would make trouble. When the Potsdam conditions were drawn and left my office where they originated, they contained a provision which permitted the continuance of the dynasty with certain conditions. The President and Byrnes struck that out.[11]

Some of the other important diary and related materials concerning surrender and the use of the atomic bomb which a reader would simply not know had been omitted from the memoirs, include:

- *May 29, 1945:* I told him [Grew] that I was inclined to agree with giving the Japanese a modification of the unconditional surrender formula and some hope to induce them to practically make an unconditional surrender without the use of those words.
- *July 2, 1945:* He [Truman] . . . said that he . . . wanted my views. I then took out this bunch of papers which I had been preparing during the past week and started on the problem of, first, whether it was worthwhile to try to warn Japan into surrender.
- *July 17, 1945:* Byrnes was opposed to a prompt and early warning to Japan which I had first suggested. He outlined a timetable on the subject warning which apparently had been agreed to by the President, so I pressed it no further.
- *July 24, 1945:* I then spoke [to Truman] of the importance which I attributed to the reassurance of the Japanese on the continuance of their dynasty, and I had felt that the insertion of that in the formal warning was important and might be just the thing that would make or mar their acceptance, but that I had heard from Byrnes that they preferred not to put it in, and that now such a change was made impossible by the sending of the message to Chiang. I hoped that the President would watch carefully so that the Japanese might be reassured verbally through diplomatic channels if it was found that they were hanging fire on that one point. He said that he had that in mind, and that he would take care of it.[12]

* * *

A similar pattern of omissions is apparent in connection with diary entries which bear on the context in which decisions were made in the summer of 1945—and, particularly, the developing "second track" understanding of the atomic bomb as what Stimson termed the "master card" of diplomacy.[13] In this area the material which was omitted is so extensive (and has previously been quoted at length) that brief excerpts will suffice to illustrate the point.

None of the information indicated by the following excerpts appears in the memoirs. Indeed, not a single diary entry concerning the atomic bomb and the Russians is reproduced in the text:

· *May 10, 1945:* He [Harriman] thinks that Russia is really afraid of our power or at least respects it and, although she is going to try to ride roughshod over her neighbors in Europe, he thought that she really was afraid of us. I talked over very confidentially our problem connected with S-1 in this matter.

· *May 14, 1945:* I then outlined to him [British Foreign Minister Anthony Eden] the progress which we have made [on the atomic bomb] and the timetable as it stood now, and told him my own feeling as to its bearing upon our present problems of an international character.

· *May 14, 1945:* I told him [McCloy] that my own opinion was that the time now and the method now to deal with Russia was to keep our mouths shut and let our actions speak for words. The Russians will understand them better than anything else. It is a case where we have got to regain the lead and perhaps do it in a pretty rough and realistic way. . . . I told him this was a place where we really held all the cards. I called it a royal straight flush and we mustn't be a fool about the way we play it. They can't get along without our help and industries and we have coming into action a weapon which will be unique. Now the thing is not to get into unnecessary quarrels by talking too much and not to indicate any weakness by talking too much; let our actions speak for themselves.

· *May 15, 1945:* The trouble is that the President has now promised apparently to meet Stalin and Churchill on the first of July and at that time these questions will become burning and it may be necessary to have it out with Russia on her relations to Manchuria and Port Arthur and various other parts of North China, and also the relations of China to us. Over any such tangled wave of problems the S-1 secret would be dominant and yet we will not know until after that time probably, until after that meeting [the Potsdam conference], whether this is a weapon in our hands or not. We think it will be shortly afterwards, but it seems a terrible thing to gamble with such big stakes in diplomacy without having your master card in your hand.*

• *June 6, 1945:* . . . the greatest complication was what might happen at the meeting of the Big Three. He [Truman] told me he had postponed that until the 15th of July on purpose to give us more time [to complete work on the atomic bomb].

• *July 22, 1945:* Churchill read Groves' report in full. He [Churchill] told me that he had noticed at the meeting of the Three yesterday that Truman was evidently much fortified by something that had happened and that he stood up to the Russians in a most emphatic and decisive manner, telling them as to certain demands that they absolutely could not have and that the United States was entirely against them. He said "Now I know what happened to Truman yesterday. I couldn't understand it. When he got to the meeting after having read this report he was a changed man. He told the Russians just where they got on and off and generally bossed the whole meeting". Churchill said he now understood how this pepping up had taken place and that he felt the same way.

• *July 23, 1945:* We had a brief discussion about Stalin's recent expansions. . . . But he [Truman] told me that the United States was standing firm and he was apparently relying greatly upon the information as to S-1.

• *July 23, 1945:* . . . Marshall felt as I felt sure he would that now with our new weapon we would not need the assistance of the Russians to conquer Japan.[14]

We have already noted important omissions from the post-Hiroshima period. These include McCloy's August conversation with Byrnes (noting that he "was on the point of departing for the foreign ministers' meeting and wished to have the implied threat of the bomb in his pocket"[15]) and Stimson's September 4 conversation with Byrnes on "how to handle Russia with the big bomb": ". . . Byrnes was very much against any attempt to cooperate with Russia. His mind is full of his problems with the coming meeting of the foreign ministers and he looks to having the presence of the bomb in his pocket, so to speak, as a great weapon to get through the thing he has."[16]

Not one of these diary entries concerning the bomb and Russia is quoted in the memoirs.[17] The contrast with the rest of Part III of Stimson's memoirs

---

*Also omitted is Stimson's May 16, 1945 memorandum to the president, included in his diaries, which states: ". . . I believe that good and not harm would be done by the policy towards your coming meeting which you mentioned to me. We shall probably hold more cards in our hands later than now."

(covering 1940 to the end of the war) is striking. Leo C. Maley III notes that in the ten chapters preceding "The Atomic Bomb and the Surrender of Japan"—all of which cover Stimson's tenure as secretary of war—the diary is quoted more than 120 times. However, in this key chapter the diary is cited only three times, and in the chapter titled "The Bomb and Peace with Russia" the diary is not quoted at all—the only one of the final thirteen chapters for which this is the case.[18]

Though it is possible to debate individual instances, it is obviously doubtful—as Bundy states—that "in most cases the omissions are merely for brevity." Nor is it likely, in the "few" cases where this is not the rationale, that the only other reasons for suppressing the material were that Stimson no longer agreed with himself or that the information might possibly "cause unnecessary pain to men who were his associates and are his friends."[19]

Henry Stimson died in 1950. As Godfrey Hodgson, his most recent biographer, notes, the former secretary "took unusual care concerning what might be written about him and the great causes in which he had served. . . . Like the prudent lawyer he was, in fact, Colonel Stimson made provision not only for his financial but for his political testament, and his reputation was left safe in friendly hands."[20]

Stimson assigned McGeorge Bundy and Arthur Page control over his literary estate; and, in early 1948, as the memoirs were about to be published, Stimson also asked Bundy to be his literary executor. We know something, though not a very great deal, about some of the things which took place over the next decade. For instance, Cass Canfield of Harper & Brothers approached Bundy in March 1951 about possibly publishing an abridged volume of Stimson's diaries. Bundy, however, replied that "until a few more people are no longer alive, and until a few more quarrels cool, the whole cannot be published."[21]

When University of Illinois historian Richard Current decided to write a biography of Stimson in the early 1950s, he also applied to Bundy. In his *Secretary Stimson: A Study in Statecraft* (1954), Current thanks Bundy for allowing him access to some of the Stimson diaries.[22] However, his bibliography states that he was not permitted to see any material after 1933.[23]

Current relied largely on Grew's memoirs in connection with the critical 1945 surrender issues. On the basis of this and other published sources Current suggested that the atomic bombing of Hiroshima and Nagasaki had probably not been needed to end the war:

> . . . there was a strong possibility that Japan might have been brought to surrender, in 1945, by the pressure of the sea-air blockade alone. There was an even stronger possibility that Russian entry into the war,

expected by the end of the first or second week in August, would quickly have applied the final coup to Japan. There was also the probability, not stressed in the Strategic Bombing Survey's report, that a modification or definition of the surrender terms would have hastened the end of the fighting, even without Russian participation in it.[24]

Current also noted that Stimson's memoirs "hint[ed] that Russia and not Japan was the real target of the bomb," that using the bomb had something to do with an American desire to "check the Russians in the Far East." (He adds, however: "If the purpose really was to check the Russians in the Far East, the destruction of their historic enemy in that area must seem, in retrospect, like a peculiar way to go about it. A quick peace with Japan, short of complete humiliation, might have been a more sensible expedient."[25])

Current's book also raised serious questions about discrepancies between Stimson's public statements and documents covering the secretary of war's earlier, prewar career (where he had more contemporaneous information to work with). We do not know to what degree Bundy was disturbed by such criticism or by Current's work in general. (Current mentions a "challenging and stimulating" correspondence between the two men.[26]) However, as the biography was nearing completion—possibly as a result of inferences drawn from the correspondence—Bundy and Page agreed that it was time for someone else to take up the story.[27]

In the introduction to the memoirs Stimson states that a major reason he and Bundy had made "an earnest effort to make an accurate and balanced account" was that he wished "to forestall possible biographies written without the careful aid of my papers or myself."[28] Now Bundy wrote Felix Frankfurter (in March 1953) that it was Mrs. Stimson who wished to push the matter, and that she "has had no other interest in life than to press forward for a full biography of the Colonel, and under this pressure Arthur Page and I, after much questioning, settled upon Elting Morison to do a full length portrait."[29]

Morison was both a good and a safe choice. The volume he produced in 1960, *Turmoil and Tradition: A Study of the Life and Times of Henry L. Stimson*, offers the reader a very favorable account of Stimson's life and career. Although Morison had privileged access to Stimson's full diary, he neglected to quote from the important material cited earlier in this chapter. Morison acknowledges that the book "was written at the suggestion of Arthur W. Page and McGeorge Bundy, the trustees of the papers of Henry L. Stimson"—and that "the expense of its preparation was defrayed by grants from the Stimson estate and the Carnegie Corporation of New York."[30]

On a couple of points, however, *Turmoil and Tradition* anticipates modern research findings. In his assessment of the significance of the Interim Committee, Morison shrewdly observes: "The Interim Committee, insofar as the special matter of using the bomb was concerned, was, in a sense, a symbolic act to demonstrate with what care this enormous conclusion had been considered."[31]

In one of Morison's footnotes there is also an acknowledgment (but no detail) that "in the pages of the Diary is a clear indication of how much the news of the Alamogordo test cheered everybody up and made Truman a 'changed man' who 'stood up to the Russians in a most emphatic and decisive manner.' "

> This would appear to justify the decision, rarely noticed in accounts of Potsdam, to postpone the conference for two weeks so that the United States representatives could negotiate with greater confidence that the bomb would work.[32]

Richard Hewlett, co-author of the U.S. Atomic Energy Commission study, *The New World*, later recalled that even for this official history Bundy would not allow access to the Stimson diaries until Morison had finished his book.[33] As Morison's volume was going to press in 1959, Bundy finally opened the Stimson papers, which had been deposited at Yale University. The official Potsdam papers which include portions of the diaries appeared in 1960; Volume I of the Atomic Energy Commission history, which also draws on the diaries, was published in 1962.

Bundy himself went on to become a government professor and then dean of the Harvard faculty. In 1961 he was appointed National Security Advisor to President Kennedy, and he held that post also under President Johnson in the opening period of the Vietnam War. Subsequently, he became president of the Ford Foundation and then a professor at New York University. He is currently a scholar in residence at the Carnegie Corporation of New York.

Four decades after the *Harper's* article and publication of Stimson's memoirs, McGeorge Bundy returned to the issues he had addressed as a young man, and although our concern is with Stimson, not Bundy, some points he made in subsequent statements and his 1988 book, *Danger and Survival: Choices About the Bomb in the First Fifty Years*, help round out the story.

Interviewed in 1985 on the "MacNeil/Lehrer NewsHour" on the fortieth anniversary of the bombing, Bundy stated: ". . . I am not disposed to criticize the use of the existence of the bomb to help to end the war, but it does seem to me, looking back on it, that there were opportunities for communication and warning available to the United States government which were not completely thought through by our government at that time."

In July and early August, 1945, the United States government knew three things that the Japanese government did not. One was that the bomb was coming into existence, had been successfully tested. One was that the United States government was prepared to allow the emperor to remain on his throne in Japan, and the third was that the Russians were coming into the war. And the question, it seems to me, that was not fully studied, fully presented to President Truman, was whether warning of the bomb and assurance on the emperor could not have been combined in a fashion which would have produced Japanese surrender without the use of the bomb on a large city, with all of the human consequences that followed.[34]

In his book Bundy defends the decision and the role of Stimson (and implicitly of his father, Harvey Bundy)—or, more precisely, he says that "The bomb did not win the war, but it surely was responsible for its ending when it did.* To those who cheered at the time—and they were the vast majority—that was what mattered most."[35] However, another measured comment also suggests his doubts:

Whether broader and more extended deliberation would have yielded a less destructive result we shall never know. Yet one must regret that no such effort was made.[36]†

Still, of the 1947 *Harper's* article, Bundy openly states: "After the war Colonel Stimson, with the fervor of a great advocate and with me as his scribe, wrote an article intended to demonstrate that the bomb was not used without a searching consideration of alternatives."[37]

Of Stimson's subsequent acknowledgment that "history might find that the United States, by its delay in stating its position [on the Emperor], had prolonged the war,"[38] Bundy writes: "Grew and McCloy always thought an earlier statement might well have brought victory without the use of the bomb, and Stimson later came to think that judgment might be right."[39] Bundy claims—contrary to Stimson's July 2 memorandum to Truman ("I think the Japanese nation has the mental intelligence and versatile capacity

*Bundy acknowledges that many specialists believe the Russian attack helped trigger the Japanese surrender: "The Japanese decision for surrender came less than twenty-four hours later. Efforts to measure the two shocks against each other are futile; both were powerful, and different Japanese advisers weighed them differently. . . . Even today we cannot know *by how much* this extraordinary set of events shortened the war—whether by days, weeks, or months." (Bundy, *Danger and Survival*, p. 93.)

†In a 1991 *Newsweek* essay, Bundy went further, stating that the decision to use the atomic bomb was "debatable." (McGeorge Bundy, "Pearl Harbor Brought Peace," *Newsweek*, December 16, 1991, p. 8.)

. . . to accept the proffer . . ."[40])—that "Stimson . . . did not truly expect that an assurance on the emperor would in fact bring a quick surrender before the bomb was used; the 'substantially improved' chances that he thought such an assurance would give were still small."[41]

(In a recent recorded discussion, however, Bundy stated that Stimson believed assurances would have ended the war before an invasion—and perhaps "had he [Stimson] been five years younger he would have fought harder" and in the right circumstances his views might have prevailed.)[42]

Directly related to this, of course, is the issue of casualty estimates—and the quite untenable "over a million" figure he and Stimson had put forward with such success. Nothing is said about this in the body of Bundy's long text. However, a reference note at the end of the volume (on page 647) acknowledges that "defenders of the use of the bomb, Stimson among them, were not always careful about numbers of casualties expected. Revisionist scholars are on strong ground when they question flat assertions that the bomb saved a million lives."[43]

On the significance of Byrnes' influence on Truman, Bundy holds: "At the most the opinions of Byrnes deprived Truman of the different advice that he might have heard from a different secretary of state." Moreover,

> [The atomic bomb] decision belonged, by all the accepted practices of wartime Washington, in the hands of the commander in chief and the Pentagon; Byrnes supported it, but he did not originate it or modify it in any way.[44]

On the issue of the secretary of state's general attitude, Bundy writes: "Byrnes appeared to believe that the existence of the American weapon might make the Russians more tractable on other issues." (He adds that "Stimson and his associates, most notably McCloy, disagreed.")[45] "It is also true that Byrnes in particular was eager to get the war in Japan over before the Russians came in, thinking quite wrongly that their moves on the mainland might thus be forestalled."[46]

Finally, Bundy writes that "When the full report from Alamogordo arrived in Potsdam on July 21 he [Truman] asked for Marshall's opinion and found that the general, whom he greatly respected, no longer thought it urgent to have Soviet help."

> Byrnes was even more emphatic; fearing Soviet intentions in Asia, he somewhat naively hoped that he could keep Stalin out of the war by encouraging Chinese delay in negotiations with the Russians on the execution of the Yalta terms. Stimson, more realistic, saw no way to prevent Russian entry, but he now hoped for an early surrender, induced

by the bomb, that would limit the weight of the Russian claim to a share in the occupation of Japan itself.

"These emerging opinions made it entirely natural for the Americans not to consider using the Soviet plan to attack as a means of inducing Japanese surrender."[47]

In short, the Russian shock option as an approach to ending the war was dropped for political-diplomatic reasons.

PART II

President Harry S. Truman

The dropping of the bombs stopped the war, saved millions of lives. . . .

—Harry S. Truman, 1959

Chapter 41

THE MAN FROM MISSOURI

[Truman] is the part Jimmy Stewart plays in American movies.
                                    —David McCullough, author of *Truman*

At the start of this research project I shared the popular perception of Truman as a down-home sort of character with a refreshing honesty that seems absent from politics today. After going into the matter thoroughly I now view him as a professional big-city machine politician, involved in shady personal and political dealings.
                                    —Richard Miller, *Truman: The Rise to Power*

It will not do to ask which was the real Harry Truman. Both were the real Harry Truman.
                                    —Alonzo Hamby, "An American Democrat"

In late 1984 two old Truman Administration "hands"—John J. McCloy and Clark M. Clifford—met at a luncheon given by the ambassador to the United Nations, Jeanne Kirkpatrick. The occasion was the commemoration of the one-hundredth anniversary of the late president's birth.

McCloy, after 1945, had served as president of the World Bank, high commissioner of Germany, chairman of the Ford Foundation, and chairman of the Council on Foreign Relations.[1] So unquestioned was his reputation that John Kenneth Galbraith and Richard Rovere both dubbed him "chairman" of the American Establishment—a tag which stuck for the rest of his life.[2]

Clifford had been an assistant to the White House naval aide in 1945. However, in short order he became special counsel to the president, and went on to play a major role in the strategy which produced Truman's 1948 election win. He spent the intervening years as a Washington lawyer-lobbyist and friend and adviser to presidents. Not only had he been John F. Kennedy's personal lawyer, he had been tapped by Lyndon Johnson to become secretary of defense at the height of the Vietnam war.[3] Until his image was tarnished by the B.C.C.I. banking scandals of the 1990s, Clifford was regarded as one of the nation's most eminent and influential patriarchs.

The two old friends (McCloy was eighty-nine, Clifford seventy-seven at the time) got to talking after the luncheon.[4] McCloy felt he had been misunderstood about something he had said in the brief talk he had given about his wartime association with Truman. He felt it was important enough to take the time to write Clifford both a formal seven-page memorandum and a personal letter.

The subject was the atomic bomb.

The thing to understand, McCloy wrote in his memorandum, was that by mid-June 1945 Japan was collapsing and—having given "much thought to the subject"—by the critical June 18, 1945 White House military planning meeting, McCloy

> had reached the conclusion that the time was propitious to attempt a political solution of the war. . . . I urged that the attempt be made. I believed we should give warning to Japan of the tremendous power of the bomb, whose secret we now possessed. We should warn Japan that we would have no alternative but to use it in the war unless Japan completely surrendered and disbanded its Armed Forces. In connection with such a surrender, we would not insist on treating the Emperor as a war criminal but would be prepared to preserve the institution of the Emperor as the leader of a democratic constitutional monarchy.[5]

Clifford had been uneasy with this argument, and McCloy's memorandum went on to explain more fully his reasoning and his belief in the likelihood of success. In general:

> This was a very rough outline of the basis on which I believed a complete surrender could be achieved and many further casualties on both sides could be avoided.

The key political judgment involved the role of the Emperor and the need to mobilize internal Japanese efforts to end the bloodshed:

> I became well convinced by our experienced Ambassador James [sic] Grew that such a procedure would receive the support of the large body of moderate and responsible opinion present in Japan to which Grew constantly referred.

McCloy observed of Stimson's personal understanding:

I also gained the strong impression that Mr. Stimson seemed willing to give favorable consideration to this means of achieving peace without the necessity of first exploding the bomb on Japan. He indeed asked me to bring the proposal up for discussion at the June 18 meeting. . . .[6]

As we have seen, throughout his life McCloy returned time and again to the June 18 meeting—and, especially, to Truman's reaction to his proposal. His memorandum to Clifford went on to recap events McCloy tried to explain to interviewers, television audiences, book writers, and friends—many of whom, it seemed, couldn't quite get the point:[7]

Mr. Truman expressed his interest in the proposal and he directed me to take it up with Mr. Byrnes . . . as it was an alternative he wished to have carefully considered.

When McCloy met with Byrnes, however, he "expressed some opposition to it on the grounds that the proposal might be taken as a suggestion of weakness on our part."

McCloy reminded Clifford of his great admiration for Truman—especially for his willingness to explore every possible option. Nonetheless:

I have always regretted that we had not at least tried out this attempt, for even though the offer to preserve the institution of the Emperor might not have been taken up, we had nothing to lose since all we needed to do was to go on with the bomb.

And, he reiterated,

I have the firm opinion that if the retention of the Emperor on the basis stated had been proposed, a full surrender could have been achieved.[8]

Possibly McCloy thought his formal memorandum might be circulated to others, for he reserved a few additional points for his separate, private letter to Clifford. First, when the president

sensed . . . that he would have to meet the opposition of Jimmy Byrnes and that he might later even find that influential and prominent liberals such as Dean Acheson and Archie MacLeish were disposed to take somewhat the same point of view as Byrnes he succumbed to the so-called hard liners.

Second:

He then authorized the dropping of the bombs and stoutly took full responsibility for doing so.[9]

Was McCloy's basic insight into what happened correct? Did Truman give in to Byrnes—the only really influential "hard-liner"—on the critical issue? We will never know what went on in the mind of the thirty-third president, of course; however, as we have seen, there is no question that Truman was profoundly influenced by Byrnes—and the preponderance of modern evidence suggests that "succumbed to" is, in fact, an appropriate formulation.

On the other hand, Truman was not without his own, independent view of how to play atomic poker with the Russians. Nor is there much doubt that after receiving confirmation that the Red Army would march in mid-August, he was aware that the war would almost certainly be over well before a landing on Kyushu. In the end, as he so often said, "the buck stops here."

As to McCloy's suggestion that having made his decision, Truman "stoutly" took full responsibility, the evidence at one level again seems clear: He adamantly and unwaveringly defended the decision until his death in 1972.

At another level, however, there are odd signs of anguish, doubt, and defensiveness in his position—indications, perhaps, that McCloy's choice of the word "stoutly" may carry with it a profound insight.

The word suggests that Truman's firm stand was a matter of principle and character and that he defended his use of atomic weapons whatever the facts might have been. It also suggests that Truman may have been defensively covering over whatever lingering doubts may have remained concerning a decision that caused the deaths of many thousands of noncombatants.

We must push beyond the conventional portrait of the simple, straightforward, always-truthful president from Independence, Missouri, that so many Americans have come to revere if we are ever to understand Harry Truman as a real flesh-and-blood human being.

And we must assemble and scrutinize the facts about his own role in creating the Hiroshima myth carefully, if we are ever to make sense of Truman's "stout" defense of the decision to drop the atomic bomb.

Americans have to confront something about themselves in regard to Harry Truman: They want him to be something no person could possibly have been.

Indeed, as historian Alonzo Hamby has observed, the nation seems to need Truman. "To a generation in which individuality was all but smothered by bigness, bureaucracy, and impersonality," Hamby notes, "he represented an era of small communities, sincere relationships, and elemental values."[10] The shared mental picture of Harry Truman allows Americans to imagine a better, simpler time when straightshooting was the coin of the realm, and honest men took honest stands against unmistakable evil.

"The thought of honesty and simplicity in high office has a special attraction," another historian, Robert Griffith, stresses—especially "in an age grown weary and disillusioned by the piety and pretense which has surrounded the presidency in recent decades."[11]

Journalist Tris Coffin, who knew Truman well, once put it bluntly: "Harry S. Truman is the great American dream. He is the country boy who worked reasonably hard, made friends, didn't get into any serious trouble, and grew up to be President. It was as simple as that."[12]

In point of fact, during his lifetime Truman was largely regarded as a failed president. When he left the White House in 1953, his Gallup Poll approval rating was 31 percent—the lowest of any departing president since Roosevelt until Richard Nixon departed in disgrace during the Watergate scandal. Indeed, Truman had the dubious distinction of scoring the lowest Gallup popular-approval rating ever accorded a president (23 percent)—lower even than Nixon's 24 percent.[13]

Nor do the private observations of many officials who dealt with Truman resonate well with the modern image. The following, written after an intimate conversation with General Lucius Clay, is to be found in McCloy's diary of April 24, 1945:

> . . . Clay seems to have known the new President for a long time. A number of years ago he worked with him on Rivers and Harbors matters and during this war he saw much of him in connection with the Truman Committee. His chief impression of him is as a politician. Clay said his instinct is to react to political pressures and usually to the pressures of some individual who is apt to be influencing him at the time. While naturally very guarded in expressing any judgment Clay gave me the impression that he felt he was not a strong man in his own right.[14]

Henry Wallace's diary gives the president this faint praise: Truman is "a small man of limited background who wants to do the right thing."[15]

How are we to explain the discrepancies between these judgments and the popular image? Several scholars have studied how the modern conception of the man actually came into being. For one thing, Truman's death in 1972 came at almost the perfect time for making comparisons—just as the dishonesty of Nixon's Watergate scandal (to say nothing of anguish over the drawn-out Vietnam war) had created deep public concern with the character of the man who was then president. In significant part because it contrasted an honest, down-to-earth Truman with the "slippery" politicians of the Watergate era, Merle Miller's *Plain Speaking*—an oral biography of Truman published in 1973—achieved phenomenal status, selling over two and a half million copies by mid-1975.[16] Miller noted at the beginning of his book:

It has been good to think about Harry Truman this spring and summer, the twentieth summer since he left the White House, the summer after his death, the summer of Watergate. The memory of him has never been sharper, never brighter than it is now, a time when menacing, shadowy men are everywhere among us.[17]

Margaret Truman's loving biographical portrait of her father, also published shortly after his death, added to the glow. "I asked Dad if he wanted to say anything special, to close this book," she recalls. In reply he offered his personal assessment of the lives of Andrew Jackson, James K. Polk, and Andrew Johnson. There was a point he wanted to leave in the minds of readers concerning these men—and by strong implication himself: "Do your duty and history will do you justice."[18]

Also in the mid-1970s, a successful one-man play, *Give 'Em Hell Harry* (constructed from Truman's own words), left audiences calling for more of the warm feelings one could now begin to associate with the steadily refurbished image of the late president. Actor James Whitmore presented the Truman of *Give 'Em Hell* as a man whose self-confidence was matched only by his folksy wisdom. The play got the full Washington buildup: Margaret Truman endorsed it, President Gerald Ford attended its premiere, the script was published as a paperback, an excerpt appeared in *Reader's Digest*, and when it was made into a film *Give 'Em Hell Harry* opened across the country simultaneously in fifteen hundred theaters.[19]

Time magazine discovered what it called a new "Trumania"—and *Newsweek* quipped that "Everyone's Wild About Harry."[20] The rock group Chicago got into the act with a hit titled "Harry Truman"—and the president's likeness soon even began to appear on T-shirts. "If a beneficent Providence would grant us, say, two-thirds of the clear vision with which Truman saw what he ought to do," a *New Republic* essay intoned, "and even half of the courage he needed to do it, the republic would be safe."[21]

Historian Allen Weinstein has observed that there is "a normal rhythm to the manner in which Americans respond to their presidents once out of office . . . a period of rejection, followed by one of reconciliation and, finally, by one of admiration." However, Weinstein marvels, in death Truman graduated to a "fourth phase, one of sanctification or hero worship," a status achieved only by "a select few."[22]

"Sanctification" seems a strong term, but Weinstein is not alone in finding religious terminology somehow appropriate. Garry Wills put it this way: "The Truman religion has its bible as well as its shrine—Merle Miller's *Plain Speaking* is the sacred word. . . . And the cult has a liturgy—the James Whitmore show, repeated in person or on film."[23]

Perhaps it is not surprising that politicians of every stripe responded to Truman's new popularity by styling themselves after the plain-spoken man of the people—and this further added to Truman's image. In 1976 President Ford kept a copy of *Plain Speaking* in clear view when reporters came to see him in the Oval Office.[24] During the final stages of the 1988 campaign, Michael Dukakis also began to suggest a connection, and traveled to Independence, Missouri, for a major appearance.[25] The 1992 presidential campaign found both George Bush and Bill Clinton shamelessly wrapping themselves in Truman. Indeed, during his acceptance speech at the Republican National Convention, Bush went so far as to recall of the highly partisan Democrat: ". . . Harry Truman knew the freedom I know this evening, the freedom to talk about what's right for America, and let the chips fall where they may."[26] Clinton, for his part, mentioned Truman fully a dozen times in a speech in Independence on September 7, 1992—all the while standing under a huge statue of Truman in front of the Jackson County courthouse where he had once served as an administrator.[27]

By the early 1990s, in fact, there was virtual unanimity: Liberal political columnist Mary McGrory observed that Truman was "someone we would love to be able to vote for today," and conservative William Safire commented that President Bush had " 'redefined' himself as Harry Truman because he could not define himself as George Bush."[28]

The publication in 1992 of David McCullough's biography of Truman gave the president's image a final boost. Ronald Steel, the distinguished biographer of Walter Lippmann, termed the book a "1,000 page valentine,"[29] and *Truman* was selected by *Time* magazine as one of the best books of 1992.[30] The man from Missouri of McCullough's biography is the construct of a writer who openly acknowledges his lack of objectivity and his personal admiration for Truman. "I don't see myself as a historian," McCullough told one interviewer. "I'm a writer and a storyteller—and 'Truman' is the story of 'everyman' in trouble. . . . He is the part Jimmy Stewart plays in American movies."[31]

Indeed, in McCullough's hands Truman achieves almost mythical stature—"the kind of president the founding fathers had in mind for the country. He came directly from the people. He *was* America."[32]

Given the extraordinary buildup of the popular image of President Truman, we obviously need a more balanced sense of the man if we are to understand his decisions. To grasp the complexity of his own role in creating the popular view of the Hiroshima decision, it is also useful to gain perspective on how he commonly dealt with other difficult issues.

There is little doubt that on the whole Harry Truman was an honest, hard-working, and decent man. But there is also little doubt that he was a far more complex person than the modern mythology suggests. Robert Griffith notes that Truman was

> a complicated, not a simple, man; a man at times both diffident and aggressive, capable of both humility and arrogance; a man who could leap to decisions quickly, and perhaps impulsively, but who could also be vacillating and indecisive; a man who always seemed to know his own mind, yet who appears in retrospect to have been highly dependent on those who advised him; a man who valued honesty and plain speaking, but who was also capable of contradiction and deception, including and perhaps especially, self-deception. . . .[33]

Alonzo Hamby makes a similar point this way:

> On the one hand, he was a faithful husband and loving father, a man who lived according to a simple and virtuous ethic built on concepts of personal honesty, loyalty, and dedication to the public welfare. . . .
>
> On the other hand, he often damaged his public image by appearing petty. As a county administrator, he was in many respects a typical machine politician loading down the public payrolls with patronage henchmen, indulging in nepotism, and using his public office to evade payment of lawful debts. As a senator he refused to renounce a corrupt organization. As president he maintained associations with some of the more disreputable elements of the world of professional politics. . . .
>
> It will not do to ask which was the real Harry Truman. Both were the real Harry Truman.[34]

As Hamby reminds us, Truman had some obvious and very glaring faults along with his strengths. For one thing, he was the handpicked choice of the notorious Pendergast organization of Kansas City, Missouri. The machine thrived on bribes, protection money, and lucrative government contracts—all of which derived, directly or indirectly, from victory at the polls. Election fraud was rampant. Richard Miller writes that since "ballot secrecy was a joke, the machine could determine if the family voted as instructed."

> You could fear that your brother-in-law's vote might endanger your job even if you worked in private industry. If you complained you might suddenly have trouble with city water or might find your house or factory reassessed and taxes doubled. If a small business could no longer afford to pay bribes it could lose its city license or be wrecked by thugs. . . . Voices raised in protest were silenced by anonymous threats. Some Jackson County politicians were kidnapped and murdered.[35]

Truman could not have helped but be aware of operations of the organization which put him in office. So powerful was the machine that even fifty years later, in the 1980s, some Kansas City residents still feared retribution for revealing what Pendergast had done.[36] McCullough notes that because of the pressures of his job—and the moral turmoil caused by having to compromise with "no account sons of bitches"[37]—Truman "suffer[ed] from disillusionment and pangs of conscience such as he had never before known, all of which may have had a great deal to do with his headaches."[38]

During his early career Truman would disappear for days at a time to the seclusion of a local hotel where he drafted page after page of autobiographical reflection—arguably an effective form of self-therapy. Some of Truman's private writings help illuminate his understanding of the "machine." They also offer insight into his way of dealing with difficult facts. The following was written in the privacy of Kansas City's Pickwick Hotel in the early 1930s:

> The Boss wanted me to give a lot of crooked contractors the inside and I couldn't. He got awful angry at me but decided that my way was best for the public and the party. But I had to compromise with him. . . . This sweet associate of mine, my friend, who was supposed to back me had already made a deal with a former crooked contractor, a friend of the Boss's who had robbed Jackson County. . . . I had to compromise in order to get the voted road system carried out all because of my associate. I had to let a former saloon keeper and murderer, a friend of the Big Boss, steal about $10,000. . . .[39]

Truman's public version of the same events—written and published when he was president—took the following form:

> . . . Mr. Pendergast called me and told me that he was in trouble with the local road contractors and would I meet and talk with them. I told him I would. I met them with T.J.P. [Thomas J. Pendergast] present. They gave me the old song and dance about being local citizens and taxpayers and that they should have an inside track to the construction contracts. I told them that the contracts would be let to the lowest bidders wherever they came from and that the specifications would be adhered to strictly. T.J. turned to his friends and said "I told you that he's the contrariest man in the county. Get out of here." When they were gone he said to me "You carry out your commitments to the voters." I did just that. . . . Tom Pendergast was always a man of his word with me. My handling of the county business became a credit to the Democratic organization.[40]

Richard Miller, who researched Truman's early career in great detail, goes so far as to conclude that "Truman played a key role in maintaining the Pendergast control of life in Jackson County after 1926. He not only knew of the machine's illegalities but participated in some of them."[41] Even *Time*'s admiring review of *Truman* made the obvious point that "the old machine worked pretty well if it could start a man who was an unsuccessful farmer and failed haberdasher on the road to the White House. . . ."[42] As Miller suggests, the fact is that "to win elections he had to be part of the Pendergast machine."

> Truman was a practical man and used the machine to get what he wanted. His private memoranda of that era show a troubled conscience praying that the ends would justify the means.[43]

"A troubled conscience praying that the ends would justify the means." The words linger, as does the public gloss Truman put on his relationship to Pendergast. This was neither the first nor the last time an uneasy combination of private knowledge of difficult facts and public misinformation were to appear in the Truman record.

McCullough also acknowledges that on close inspection many of Truman's personal dealings do not jibe with the modern myth. During World War II, for instance, Truman put his wife, Bess, on his Senate payroll, paying her $4,500 a year, the highest salary paid to a Senate office clerk.[44] That Mrs. Truman was not expected to do any real work is suggested in this April 1942 letter from her husband: "I'm sure glad you went to the office. It's much better for you to go there a few days a week and see what goes on. . . . You don't have to say a word only just drop in and do some signing. It helps all concerned."[45] At the time Truman was making a national reputation as chairman of a special Senate committee set up to investigate inefficiency and waste in the government's defense effort.

Of particular concern to the Hiroshima story is Truman's apparent general willingness consciously or unconsciously to bend the truth—to tell people what they wanted to hear. The way he handled difficult facts in situations like that of the Pendergast bribe was matched by an odd capacity to ignore contradictions in his own pronouncements. The problem troubled associates on both sides of the political aisle. Henry Wallace's diary recalls one of numerous instances (this one from mid-1946):

> The President spoke very vigorously in one part of the meeting about the necessity of cutting down on the budget, saying that he had already pruned it about $3 billion. He said the place to cut was in the askings of the Army and Navy. This agreed completely with conversations I had

had with him earlier. But within half an hour he was saying that after the last war we had cut our Navy too much; that we had to be careful not to cut our Army and Navy; that if we had not cut our Army and Navy after the last war there would not have been World War II. I was utterly amazed that he could go two different directions within the hour. It reminded me of Tuesday when within the hour he spoke about being patient with Russia to me and then at the cabinet luncheon agreed completely with Jimmie Byrnes in a number of cracks he took against Russia. I suspect there has never been a President who could move two different directions with less time intervening than Truman. He feels completely sincere and earnest at all times and is not disturbed in the slightest by the different directions in which his mind can go almost simultaneously.[46]

Henry Stimson jotted the following in his private journal a year before Truman became president: "Truman is a nuisance and a pretty untrustworthy man. He talks smoothly but he acts meanly."[47]

Such "corrections" of the popular image are required not because of any need to sully the reputation of the president, but because we must attempt to see him as he was—a man with strengths and weaknesses, faults and virtues. For better or worse, it is perhaps inevitable that politicians must learn to bend the truth and speak in "different directions." The complaints about Truman are neither extreme nor unusual for his time.

But, of course, that is precisely the point. It was in no way unusual for the truth to suffer when it caused problems. That the general rule might also apply to the specific case of Hiroshima is an obvious possibility, especially since Truman had a lifelong personal interest in history—and how he would be remembered by history.

"[T]he one great external influence which, more than anything else, nourished and sustained that interest in government and public service," he emphasized in *Year of Decisions*, "was the endless reading of history which I began as a boy and which I have kept up ever since."[48] Indeed, Truman had thought seriously of becoming a history teacher before going into politics.[49] His concern with how he would be remembered resulted in the construction of the Truman Presidential Library—still something of an innovation at the time. (The Roosevelt Library at Hyde Park, New York, was a precedent.) Lacking the personal income necessary even to store his papers, Truman's determination to have a library built for himself required that he put together a highly organized effort to raise money from a wide range of sources to begin construction in Missouri.[50]

Something of the president's desire to be remembered favorably by history is also revealed in the following (unsent) letter to Roy Roberts, editor of the

Kansas City Star, written in response to a seventieth-anniversary edition published in 1950:

> [There is no] mention in your whole edition of the most convenient and efficient Court House in the county, no mention of the Andrew Jackson Statue by the greatest sculptor of our time, no mention of the planned road connections to the County and to Kansas, no mention of the attempted interstate plan which would make the region the greatest in the country. To do this you'd have to give a little, backward county judge and a knownothing U.S. Senator from Missouri some mention. He wants no mention from your lousy sheet! History will tell the tale and you and Big Palefaced Bill [Nelson]* won't even be mentioned.
>
> Ain't it hell for a prophet to be without honor in his own home county, where he made his reputation that caused him to be Senator twice, Vice President and President in *his own right* of this Republic?[51]

The concluding lines of another version of the same unsent letter remind us that his interest was not simply passive:

> I'm sure history will take care of that. In fact I'll see to it that it does.[52]

The president's concern with how he would be remembered by history is widely recognized. However, something more must be said about his approach to how history would understand his decision to use the atomic bomb. We know that, in fact, Truman lied—directly, repeatedly, and without apparent hesitation—about some of the most important aspects of the Hiroshima story. At the outset two examples which have come to light over the years serve as a cautionary warning about other statements the president was to make.

As we have seen, Truman postponed the Potsdam conference in order to await the outcome of the July 16 atomic test. However, he told Churchill and others that the reason for the delay was the "end of the fiscal year."[53] This minor bit of dishonesty is fully understandable: The country was at war and the bomb was an extraordinary secret. There were very good "reasons of state" why any president might prevaricate under the circumstances.

Again, however, given that he was willing to bend the truth for "reasons of state," the question becomes whether other ongoing "reasons of state" (good or bad) guided him in subsequent statements. And, minimally, of course, this small lie contradicts the image of a man who always told the unvarnished truth. One option he had—which any president always has—was simply to say nothing about his reasons.

*Roy Roberts' predecessor as managing editor of the *Star*.

A second incident leads us to a more difficult confrontation with the inherited image of the man. We know from several accounts that Truman's first reaction to news of the bombing of Hiroshima was one of extreme excitement and pleasure: "I telephoned Byrnes aboard ship to give him the news," he was later to recall, "and then said to the group of sailors around me, 'This is the greatest thing in history. It's time for us to get home.' "[54] A United Press reporter on the *Augusta* at the time wrote, "the President afterward said he had never been happier about any announcement he had ever made."[55]

When the official White House files were opened in the late 1950s, among them was an exchange with Lew Wallace, a Democratic National Committeeman from Portland, Oregon. Wallace had read about the president's reaction in the August 7 *Oregon Journal* under the headline, "Truman, Jubilant Over New Bomb, Nears U.S. Port."[56] Much disturbed, he telegrammed:

> We on the Pacific Coast and all Americans know that no president of the United States could ever be jubilant over any device that would kill innocent human beings. Please make it clear that it is not destruction but the end of destruction that is the cause of jubilation. This is very important. Headlines do not reflect your true sentiment.[57]

Two days later, on August 9, 1945, Truman sent a letter back to Wallace replying:

> I appreciated your telegram very much but I think if you will read the paper again you will find that the good feeling on my part was over the fact Russia had entered into the war with Japan and not because we had invented a new engine of destruction.[58]

Truman's claim that the Russian declaration of war had caused his "good feeling" on August 6, of course, is simply not possible. Russia did not declare war until the day after the *Journal* story had run. The news was first announced to the American people by the president at 3:00 p.m. on August 8.[59] It is also difficult to dismiss the incident as a lapse in Truman's memory: His reply to Wallace was sent on August 9, the next day. Furthermore, of course, we know that Truman was hardly "jubilant" about Russian entry.[60]

The general record is also replete with evidence suggesting a great deal of confusion, honest self-deception, and mere forgetfulness in the way Truman conveyed the Hiroshima tale to the American people. For instance, there is the matter of what kind of decision it really was. At a 1959 Columbia University symposium Truman was asked about his "greatest decisions," and in particular:

Mr. President, are there any decisions that you made while you were in the White House that you have regrets about, do you think, seeing them in retrospect?

Truman replied, "The great decisions, I think, in no way need to be changed."[61] Not surprisingly, an immediate follow-up question raised the issue of Hiroshima—and brought this reply:

The atom bomb was "no great decision." . . . It was merely another powerful weapon in the arsenal of righteousness. . . . It was a purely military decision to end the war.[62]

In quite another setting—as he considered how he wished to be portrayed for history in the MGM film *The Beginning or the End*—the president's view was rather different. Truman objected to one scene portraying his decision because "it appeared to have been a snap judgment program. It was anything but that—the use of the atomic bomb was deliberated for long hours and many days and weeks. . . ."[63]

The subject also came up during a private 1951 meeting with William Hillman, the journalist friend who helped him with his memoirs. Notes of their meeting record the following exchange:

Q. What was your feeling in general about the atom bomb at the time it struck? There has been so much discussion since, that the atomic bomb was the worst—
THE PRESIDENT: (interposing) It was, in my opinion, just another weapon of war, that's all.[64]

Such illustrations of the easy way in which alternative explanations of the decision itself were offered by the president point to a pattern which appears in connection with virtually every significant facet of the atomic bomb story.

Chapter 42

MAIN ELEMENTS
OF THE OFFICIAL RATIONALE

I think it is important that the President's casualty figure be changed to conform with that of Secretary Stimson.
    —Kenneth W. Hechler, White House special assistant, to David D. Lloyd, administrative assistant to the president,
January 2, 1953

There are many ways to explore Harry Truman's role in the creation of the Hiroshima myth. The most illuminating, however, has to do with the central claim: Throughout the half century since World War II, the single most important argument in defense of the use of the atomic bomb has been that it saved a very large number of lives—perhaps even as many as a million.

It is instructive at the outset to note the language of Truman's brief August 9, 1945, statement to "the men and women of the Manhattan Project," one of his earliest public comments on the point:[1]

Atomic bombs have now been successfully employed against the enemy.

A grateful nation, hopeful that this new weapon will result in the saving of thousands of American lives, feels a deep sense of appreciation for your accomplishment.[2]

This general formulation, in fact, is not far from what might have been the truth—that is, if the atomic bomb had been the only alternative to invasion. As previously noted, at the time the number of lives it was estimated that avoiding a full 1946 invasion (by whatever means) might save was in the range of 46,000.

The president's initial formulation of "thousands," however, was clearly not his final statement on the matter, to say the least. The following are only a few of numerous subsequent public estimates President Truman made or approved after August 9, 1945.

· To the annual Gridiron Dinner on December 15, 1945, in Washington, D.C., he explained that at the time he made the decision to use the atomic bomb:

> It occurred to me that a quarter of a million of the flower of our young manhood was worth a couple of Japanese cities, and I still think they were and are.[3]

· Roughly a year later the critical "decision" scene in the previously noted MGM film on the bombing, *The Beginning or the End*, was approved a year later during a meeting with Truman.[4] In it "The President" offers the following explanation for the decision:

> A year less of war will mean life for three hundred thousand—maybe half a million—of America's finest youth. Not only that, but it will mean life to untold numbers of Russians, of Chinese, of Japanese. These were the decisive considerations in my consent.[5]

· In October 1948, at a speech in Toledo, Ohio, Truman stated that his civilian and military chiefs had advised him that

> while we might find it necessary to wipe out a couple of Japanese cities devoted entirely to munitions manufacture, in the long run we would save a quarter of a million young Americans from being killed, and we would save an equal number of Japanese young men from being killed.[6]

· On April 6, 1949, the president told a group of new Democratic senators and representatives that he

> made that decision because I thought 200,000 of our young men would be saved by making that decision, and some 3[00,000] or 400,000 of the enemy would be saved by making that decision.[7]

· Only seven months later, the president told biographer Jonathan Daniels that he

> . . . asked Marshall and Eisenhower specifically how many American casualties a landing on the Toyko [sic] plane [sic] would involve. Marshall said it would take a million men for the landing and a million to hold it and that he thought such a landing would involve half a million casualties.[8]

· In a January 12, 1953, letter to Professor James L. Cate, Truman stated that at a special meeting at Potsdam,

I asked General Marshall what it would cost in lives to land on the Tokio [*sic*] plain and other places in Japan. It was his opinion that such an invasion would cost at a minimum one quarter of a million casualties, and might cost as much as a million, on the American side alone, with an equal number of the enemy. The other military and naval men present agreed.[9]

• And on April 28, 1959, Truman told students at Columbia University simply that "the dropping of the bombs stopped the war, saved millions of lives."[10]

What are we to make of the discrepancies between Truman's various statements? Is there more at work here than faulty memory, self-deception, and the all-but-inevitable tendency on the part of most people to exaggerate in their own defense?

We now know something about how at least one of these estimates was made. It is an example worth examining in some detail both for its own sake and as an illustration of the day-to-day functioning of the Truman White House.

Documents related to the January 1953 letter from Truman to Professor Cate became available at the Truman Library in the late 1970s. In connection with work he was doing on an official U.S. Army Air Forces history, Cate had written the president to ask about the precise timing of his order to drop the atomic bomb (a matter we shall take up shortly).[11]

Truman's initial thought—and his idea of what to tell Cate—was set down in a handwritten draft response dated December 31, 1952:

I asked Gen. Marshall what it would cost in lives to land on the Tokio plane [*sic*] and other places in Japan. It was his opinion that 1/4 million casualties would be the minimum cost as well as an equal number of the enemy. The other military and naval men present agreed.[12]

As he reworked the draft, a White House aide, Kenneth W. Hechler, noticed an obvious problem with the response: Truman's estimate of "1/4 million casualties" was considerably different from the "over a million casualties" estimate previously published by Stimson in his 1947 *Harper's* article (and repeated in his memoirs).[13] Hechler brought the problem to the attention of another White House aide, David D. Lloyd, in a January 2, 1953, memorandum:

On page 2, it is stated: "I asked Gen. Marshall what it would cost in lives to land on the Tokio plane [*sic*] and other places in Japan. It was his opinion that 1/4 million casualties would be the minimum cost as well as an equal number of the enemy." Stimson says in his book *On Active Service*, p. 619: "We estimated that if we should be forced to carry this plan to its conclusion, the major fighting would not end until the latter part of 1946, at the earliest. I was informed that such operations might be expected to cost over a million casualties, to American forces alone." I think it is important that the President's casualty figure be changed to conform with that of Secretary Stimson, because presumably Stimson got his from Gen. Marshall; the size of the figure is very important.[14]

Lloyd promptly prepared a memorandum to Truman on the basis of Hechler's observations which pointed out:

> In your draft, you state that General Marshall told you that a landing in Japan would cost a quarter of a million casualties to the United States, and an equal number of the enemy. Mr. Stimson, in his book written by McGeorge Bundy, says that Marshall's estimate was over a million casualties. Your recollection sounds more reasonable than Stimson's, but in order to avoid a conflict, I have changed the wording to read that General Marshall expected a minimum of a quarter of a million casualties and possibly a much greater number—as much as a million.[15]

Although neither Hechler nor Lloyd seems to have checked any actual records of casualty estimates ("your recollection sounds more reasonable")—and although Stimson's estimate appears to have had no documentary basis whatsoever—Truman approved Lloyd's revision as if it were historical fact. A photostatic copy of the final version of the president's letter was reproduced and published as an authoritative source in the official U.S. Army Air Forces history.[16]

As we have seen, modern research has demonstrated that both of the estimates contained in Truman's letter to Cate are grossly exaggerated. Furthermore, the only estimate we can prove that was actually presented personally and directly to the president—on June 18 by General Marshall—was 31,000.[17] On the basis of ratios then common in the Pacific campaign, this in turn would translate into 7,000–8,000 deaths.

As we also have noted, no historian has been able to find solid contemporaneous evidence that Truman's meeting with his military advisers at Potsdam (where the president says the estimates were offered) actually occurred. There is no corroborating documentation of the kind which regularly precedes or follows such meetings in the official record, in Truman's personal diary, or in the numerous diaries of the officials concerned.

All of this, however, only touches the surface of the problem. The various estimates we have reviewed, of course, are of losses which might possibly have occurred if either a November 1945 Kyushu landing were to take place, or if a March 1946 invasion of the main Japanese island of Honshu were to occur. It is here that all of the presidential estimates—including his response to Cate—are even more problematic. To take them at face value is to avoid dealing with some of the central findings of the past five decades of historical research.

In the first place, the mid-June estimates given to the president were made before the July intercepts revealed the Emperor's intervention.

By early in the third week of July, when the Emperor's messages had been intercepted and Stalin had confirmed his intention to enter the war—and certainly by early August, when the intercepts which Truman, Byrnes, and Leahy reviewed on the return voyage home came in—it was clear to all concerned that a spring 1946 invasion was now unlikely.

That the Russian attack would almost certainly have obviated the 1946 invasion is a virtually unassailable point. And it is this all-out engagement, of course—and not simply the smaller projected November 1945 landing on Kyushu—that is referred to in connection with very large estimates.

All of Truman's claims—however exaggerated—about the numbers of lives that might have been lost had the atomic bomb not been used can only have been in reference to the full invasion (as he regularly stated or implied).

A more reasonable but also still problematic question is how many lives might have been lost in Kyushu. Marshall's estimate of 31,000 casualties was for the first thirty days of a Kyushu landing, and so far as the records we have indicate, this was the only one he presented to Truman at the June 18 meeting.[18] Since the president was seeking advice as to whether or not to approve the Kyushu landing, it may be asked why the readily available total estimated cost of the full operation was not given him. Marshall had with him elaborate longer-term estimates.[19] Truman not only had asked for casualty estimates, but had emphasized that they were his primary concern.[20]

Furthermore, there is no indication in the minutes that Truman requested estimates beyond the first thirty days or was in any way dissatisfied by Marshall's presentation. It may perhaps be that Marshall wanted to play down casualties, but this does not explain Truman. An explanation consistent with the modern documents is that neither Truman nor Marshall really expected the war to go on beyond thirty days after a landing (if it got to that point at all). Viewed in this light, Marshall's statement that a Russian declaration of war "may well be the decisive action levering" Japan into surrender "at that time or shortly thereafter if we land in Japan" suggests that even as early as mid-June Truman and his advisers may have considered thirty days a worst-case scenario once the Russian attack was confirmed.[21]*

*For further discussion of subsequent developments in light of ULTRA intercepts concerning Japanese deployments, see endnote 7 for the Afterword.

A careful consideration of the casualty issue, in short, adds to the steady accumulation of evidence which helps explain why Truman felt so strongly (before the bomb was tested) that he had to meet with Stalin to secure the Russian declaration of war. And, of course, mid-June was not the final point of judgment. By early July, as we have seen, the Combined Intelligence Committee had concluded—again, even before news of the Emperor's move was received—that the combination of a Russian attack and a change of terms appeared likely to bring an end to the fighting. (Four months still remained before troops would be committed in a November landing.) As we have also seen, in his journal and letters—and explicitly in his memoirs—the president himself suggests that the Russians were wanted in the Pacific War (before the results of the atomic bomb test came in), because the shock of a Red Army attack seemed likely to end the war before an invasion would have to be undertaken.[22]

The war might have continued until a November Kyushu landing, of course, had Truman been unwilling to alter the surrender formula to safeguard the Emperor. But it is also abundantly clear that he had no fundamental objection to doing this if it meant avoiding casualties.

Two final footnotes may be added to this discussion. Most of the estimates of large numbers of lives saved by the atomic bomb were made after 1946—that is, at times when Truman did not lack for considerable additional information on this subject. For instance, it is unlikely Truman was unaware of the widely quoted conclusion of the United States Strategic Bombing Survey that "certainly prior to 31 December 1945, and in all probability prior to 1 November 1945, Japan would have surrendered even if the atomic bombs had not been dropped, even if Russia had not entered the war, and even if no invasion had been planned or contemplated."[23]

We do not know whether he read the 1946 War Department study which concluded that "the war would almost certainly have terminated when Russia entered. . . ."[24]

In his widely read biography of Truman, David McCullough states that "a memorandum of June 4, 1945, written by General Thomas Handy of Marshall's staff," estimated America "would save no less than 500,000 to 1 million lives by avoiding the invasion altogether—which shows that figures of such magnitude were then in use at the highest levels."[25]

This document was actually an analysis made by the War Department staff of the memorandum former president Herbert Hoover sent to Stimson on May 15.[26] In it Hoover had suggested that a clarification of terms might possibly save "500,000 to 1,000,000 [American] lives. . . ."[27] However, the internal staff memorandum cited in McCullough's book does not support Hoover's estimate. In fact, it states rather bluntly:

It is obvious that peace would save lives and resources, but the estimated loss of 500,000 lives due to carrying the war to conclusion under
our present plan of campaign, is considered to be entirely too high.[28]*

Close examination of a second aspect of Truman's explanation of the decision to use the atomic bomb provides additional perspective on the president's personal role in the creation of the modern myth.

The public statement Truman made on August 6, 1945, calls Hiroshima
"an important Japanese Army base," implying that this was a major reason
why it was attacked.[29]

Three days later, in his August 9 report on the Potsdam conference, the
president offered a similar explanation:

> The world will note that the first atomic bomb was dropped on Hiro-
> shima, a military base. That was because we wished in this first attack
> to avoid, in so far as possible, the killing of civilians.[30]

Mr. President, a 1952 book by his journalist friend William Hillman, includes the following statement:

> I . . . asked Stimson to indicate on the map what cities the military
> would favor as targets, if Japan did not surrender, and we had to use the
> bomb. Among the targets was Hiroshima, an army center and military
> supply port; and, Nagasaki, a major seaport containing large industrial
> establishments.
>
> I then agreed to the use of the atomic bomb if Japan did not yield.[31]

In Truman's 1955 memoir, *Year of Decisions*, the president also refers to
Hiroshima in a similar, if very general, fashion: "With this order [the July 25
order to bomb from Handy to Spaatz] the wheels were set in motion for the
first use of an atomic weapon against a military target."[32]

Modern documentary discoveries provide a great deal of information on
precisely what kind of city Hiroshima was (and was not)—and on why it and
other cities were selected for targeting. They make it quite clear that it was
hardly accurate to characterize the city of Hiroshima primarily as "an important Japanese Army base"—or, to imply that it had been attacked mainly because it was a "military base" or a "military supply port."

It is true that the headquarters of the Fifth Division, the Second Army, and
the Chugoku regional army were located in Hiroshima. A significant number
of military personnel were stationed in the city. However, the notion that the

---

*McCullough has recently acknowledged his error in response to an inquiry from *Defense
Week*. (See Tony Capaccio, "Truman Author Errs on Japan Invasion Casualty Memo," *Defense Week*, October 11, 1994, pp. 1, 8–9.)

city was selected primarily because of its great military importance at this point in the war is difficult to sustain. (One of the reasons Hiroshima had not been bombed earlier, in fact, was that it had been judged to be of low priority.)[33]

The second rationale—that Hiroshima was bombed because it was "a military supply port," as proposed in *Mr. President*—also finds little support in the documentary record. Aside from the fact that Japanese shipping was already extremely crippled, Hiroshima harbor had been successfully mined during Operation Starvation.[34] On June 18 Marshall had informed Truman not only that U.S. air and sea power had already "greatly reduced movement of Jap shipping south of Korea," but that it "should in the next few months cut it to a trickle if not choke it off entirely."[35]

Truman's statement at Columbia University that "the objective [in dropping the bombs] was, as nearly as we possibly could determine, to shut off the supplies to the Japanese" in China is simply false.[36] As indicated, there was very little threat of Japanese supplies crossing the sea from Hiroshima to China—even if significant supplies were being produced. There also is no indication that at the time the president was advised—or believed—that a serious goal in using the atomic bombs was to "shut off the supplies to the Japanese" in China.

Truman also often gave another rationale for bombing Hiroshima. In his December 31, 1946, letter to Stimson—which urged that he "get out an article for the record on the facts regarding the atomic bomb and the procedure that was followed before it was dropped"—the president wrote:

> If you will remember our conversation in Potsdam, we came to the conclusion that the bomb should be dropped on a town which was engaged almost exclusively in war work. Hiroshima was the town picked out and then Nagasaki was the second one.[37]

Similarly, in an October 1951 background interview with William Hillman, he stated:

> He [Stimson] brought me the message [on the successful Alamogordo test], and we got an asiatic map with Japan enlarged on it, and I asked him to point out to me the cities that were entirely devoted to war work in Japan; and he pointed out Hiroshima—whatever you call it—Nagasaki.[38]

In Truman's initial December 1952 handwritten letter to Professor Cate (as noted), he also wrote:

> I asked Sec. Stimson which cities in Japan were devoted exclusively to war production. He promptly named Hiroshima and Nagasaki.[39]

And, again, in his 1955 memoir Truman stressed:

> In deciding to use this bomb I wanted to make sure that it would be used as a weapon of war in the manner prescribed by the laws of war. That meant that I wanted it dropped on a military target. I had told Stimson that the bomb should be dropped as nearly as possible upon a war production center of prime military importance.[40]

Finally, the following exchange took place at his Columbia University lectures in 1959:

> *Student:* . . . it seemed to me the second bomb came pretty soon after the first one, two or three days.
> *President Truman:* That is right. We were destroying the centers, the factories that were making more munitions. Just a military maneuver, that is all.[41]

The modern evidence also directly contradicts Truman's third rationale for Hiroshima's selection as a target. The city was not deemed important because it was a war production center. Indeed, as the U.S. Strategic Bombing Survey was to point out, "all major factories in Hiroshima were on the periphery of the city—and escaped serious damage. . . ."[42] The location of industry, we now also know, was fully understood *before* the bombing occurred.

Such largely ignored facts point to a deeper set of questions, first, about the president's various statements; second, about his own actual understanding of the central issue at the time.

Hiroshima would not likely have been allowed to remain as it was, unblemished, waiting to be the target chosen for a new, untested, experimental weapon if it had been deemed important for any of the reasons cited by President Truman. Indeed, when the Target Committee first met in late April, Hiroshima was not even on the Twenty-first Bomber Command priority list.[43] When the committee convened to select cities for atomic attack in May, it included Hiroshima among those which not only were still largely intact but which were also "likely to be unattacked by next August"—and, further, "which the Air Forces would be willing to reserve for our use unless unforeseen circumstances arise."[44]

The official notes of the initial April 27 meeting of the Target Committee are especially illuminating on this point: "It should be remembered that in our selection of any target, the 20th Air Force is operating primarily to laying waste all the main Japanese cities, and that they do not propose to save some important primary target for us if it interferes with the operation of the war from their point of view."[45]

Why Hiroshima had been selected involved quite different reasons. Target Committee files declassified in the 1970s record discussions delineating these initial criteria for determining possible targets:

(1) they be important targets in a large urban area of more than three miles diameter, (2) they be capable of being damaged effectively by a blast, and (3) they are likely to be unattacked by next August.[46]

In addition to these factors, the committee also agreed

that psychological factors in the target selection were of great importance. Two aspects of this are (1) obtaining the greatest psychological effect against Japan and (2) making the initial use sufficiently spectacular for the importance of the weapon to be internationally recognized when publicity on it is released.[47]

One of the reasons the city of Hiroshima initially seemed a good choice was that it had "the advantage of being such a size and with possible focusing from nearby mountains that a large fraction of the city may be destroyed."[48] This advantage was later discounted because the hills were too remote.[49] However, Hiroshima still remained high on the list because it met the other criteria.

Target Committee minutes also show that Kokura Arsenal, the most obvious military-industrial target on its list, was initially given the lowest priority—even though it fulfilled the Interim Committee's formal June 1 recommendation of "a vital war plant" almost perfectly. Previously the Target Committee had noted:

This is one of the largest arsenals in Japan and is surrounded by urban industrial structures. The arsenal is important for light ordnance, anti-aircraft and beach head defense materials.[50]

Nor, of course, had direct military significance or even industrial production been the central concern of the Interim Committee. As we have noted, the committee recommended on May 31, 1945, "that we should seek to make a profound psychological impression on as many of the inhabitants as possible." (To achieve this objective, it was agreed "that the most desirable target would be a vital war plant employing a large number of workers and closely surrounded by workers' houses.")[51]

Few analysts have noticed that the Interim Committee's formal recommendations of May 31 and June 1 were not actually followed. In fact, the way in which the bombing was planned—and carried out—specifically avoided significant war plants.

The subject came up at the Target Committee meeting of May 28—and, as the minutes show:

Dr. Stearns presented data on Kyoto, Hiroshima and Niigata and the following conclusions were reached:

(1) not to specify aiming points, this to be left to later determination at base when weather conditions are known.

(2) To neglect location of industrial areas as pin point target, since on these three targets such areas are small, spread on fringes of cities and quite dispersed.

(3) to endeavor to place first gadget in center of selected city; that is, not to allow for later 1 or 2 gadgets for complete destruction.[52]

The points to note carefully are "(2) . . . *industrial areas . . . are small, spread on fringes*"—and, the conclusion, therefore, "(3) to endeavor to place first gadget *in center of selected city. . . .*"* These criteria run directly counter to the Interim Committee's charge that the target should be "a vital war plant."

On June 21 the Interim Committee modified its earlier position, and now recommended that the atomic bomb "be used on a dual target, namely, a military installation or a war plant surrounded by or adjacent to homes or other buildings most susceptible to damage."[53]†

There is no specific information in the minutes as to why the Interim Committee altered its initial targeting recommendation. Perhaps it was realized that the May 31 "vital war plant" criterion simply could not be met in Hiroshima without shifting the aiming point away from the city center.‡ On the other hand, as we have seen, the Interim Committee was not really a serious locus of decision-making. (To recall, as Leon Sigal observes, "The action channels for selecting targets for the bomb were the Military Policy Committee and the Target Committee." Essentially, the Interim Committee "added a panel of surrogates for the scientific community to bless an option for using the bomb already chosen in military channels."[54])

Given the extraordinary implications—and the fact that the major new sci-

---

*Emphasis added.

†Although not in the formal "notes" of the Interim Committee, on June 6, a memorandum from R. Gordon Arneson to George Harrison also states: "The notes of the Thursday and Friday [May 31 and June 1] meetings of the Interim Committee" include the recommendation that the bomb "be used on a dual target, that is, a military installation or war plant surrounded by or adjacent to homes or other buildings most susceptible to damage." (R. Gordon Arneson to George Harrison, June 6, 1945, File 100, Harrison-Bundy Files, Roll 8, M1108, National Archives.)

‡This—together with further discussions with Marshall and others—may account for a slight difference between the May 31 and June 1 committee recommendation. The recommendation that a "war plant" be the target was qualified by a statement saying that this was "the present view of the Committee" and that "the final selection of the target was essentially a military decision. . . ." (Notes of the Interim Committee Meeting, Friday, June 1, 1945, File 100, Harrison-Bundy Files, Roll 8, M1108, National Archives.)

entific and military breakthrough would receive massive worldwide attention and scrutiny—it is difficult to believe that the leaders of the U.S. government were ignorant of the actual targeting goals for the new weapon. Unfortunately, however, the information we have concerning Truman's personal knowledge is both spotty and contradictory. Furthermore, at the center of the available information there is a very obvious and glaring hole—and explicit evidence of a key document having been destroyed.

It is possible (though questionable) that in connection with Truman's claim that the target cities were selected because of war production facilities, the president was confused for good reason: This, at least in part, was what the Interim Committee had initially recommended. On the other hand, Stimson's diary entry describing his June 6 meeting with the president indicates a rather broader understanding of what was being planned:

> I told him that I was busy considering our conduct of the war against Japan and I told him how I was trying to hold the Air Force down to precision bombing but that with the Japanese method of scattering its manufacture it was rather difficult to prevent area bombing. I told him I was anxious about this feature of the war for two reasons: first, because I did not want to have the United States get the reputation of outdoing Hitler in atrocities; and second, I was a little fearful that before we could get ready the Air Force might have Japan so thoroughly bombed out that the new weapon would not have a fair background to show its strength. He laughed and said he understood.[55]

In *Year of Decisions* Truman characterizes the Interim Committee's recommendation only very generally as that the bomb be "used without specific warning and against a target that would clearly show its devastating strength."[56] He quotes the recommendation of the committee's panel of scientific advisers urging—very generally—the "direct military use" of the bomb.[57] Truman also states:

> Four cities were finally recommended as targets: Hiroshima, Kokura, Niigata, and Nagasaki. They were listed in that order as targets for the first attack. The order of selection was in accordance with the military importance of these cities, but allowance would be given for weather conditions at the time of the bombing. Before the selected targets were approved as proper for military purposes, I personally went over them in detail with Stimson, Marshall, and Arnold, and we discussed the matter of timing and the final choice of the first target.[58]

At the outset of the Target Committee meetings, Groves had emphasized that the decision on actual use would be made by "higher authority,"[59] and the above extract from the memoirs suggests that the president almost certainly was briefed in detail before the bomb was used.

At Potsdam on July 25, Truman wrote the following in his journal:

> This weapon is to be used against Japan between now and August 10th. I have told the Sec. of War, Mr. Stimson, to use it so that military objectives and soldiers and saliors [*sic*] are the target and not women and children. Even if the Japs are savages, ruthless, merciless and fanatic, we, as the leader of the world for the common welfare cannot drop this terrible bomb on the old Capitol [*sic*] or the new.
>
> He & I are in accord. The target will be a purely military one. . . .[60]

It is possible that when he wrote this journal entry the president was unaware of all the facts we now have which directly contradict this statement. However, given what we now know, it is difficult to continue to give Truman the benefit of the doubt. Perhaps he may simply have been writing with an eye to "history"—a reasonable possibility, given his deep concern with how he would be remembered. At this point, however, the statement must simply stand as another of the many unexplained puzzles in the Hiroshima record.

There is not much doubt about the president's understanding of the essential issue in the weeks following, however. To recall, Truman told his Cabinet on August 10 that he stopped the bombing after Nagasaki because "the thought of wiping out another 100,000 people was too horrible."[61]

As to the hole in the record, there is little doubt that the president was briefed on the basis of a written document, not simply informally and orally. As he himself notes: "Before the selected targets were approved . . . I personally went over them in detail. . . ."[62] We know from Groves that a specific and detailed memorandum was sent to Marshall with page-long descriptions of each target city—and, furthermore, that the memorandum was then destroyed. This was done, Groves says, "to avoid any chance of breach of security"[63]—an explanation which is hard to accept, given that numerous Potsdam documents of equal security importance were not destroyed.*

Given that the modern documentary record demonstrates that Hiroshima was of low direct military priority, that it was not a significant operating port, and

---

*Related to this: Truman later assigned White House aide Eben A. Ayers the task of assembling his papers on the atomic bomb. A one-page description dated July 2, 1945, and titled simply "Hiroshima"—quite possibly a copy of this briefing paper—was recently located in the Ayers papers at the Truman Library. Among other things it states: "The leading industrial and military storage districts are located outside the heavily built up regions, to the SSE and E of the city proper." There also is no mention of any army headquarters in the city. ("Hiroshima," July 2, 1945, Atomic, Box 4, Eben A. Ayers Papers, HSTL.)

that it was specifically targeted in a way designed to avoid major industrial installations, we need to consider once more the specific language of Truman's August 9 statement—namely that Hiroshima was selected to avoid the killing of civilians.[64]

But of course, precisely the opposite was the explicit recommendation of the Interim Committee—and the essential aim of the Target Committee. Although on May 31 the Interim Committee suggested that "we could not concentrate on a civilian area," its recommended target, in fact, was "a vital war plant employing a large number of workers and closely surrounded by workers' houses."[65] Nor did the central idea change when a military installation was substituted for a war plant. Without question the primary and continuing interest of both the Interim Committee and the Target Committee both before and after the June 21 modification was to make as large a "psychological" impact as possible[66]*—a goal quite different, for instance, from destroying a military installation (or, as Marshall proposed on May 29, destroying a naval installation).[67]

This meant targeting large numbers of civilians.

It is possible that the president was unaware of the fact that making a massive psychological impact was the primary aim. It is, however, extremely doubtful that the manner in which the first atomic bomb was to be used was not fully explained to him.

Did Truman simply forget the details of what he had been advised? Perhaps. Over the years he may have convinced himself of many things the documentary record now shows not to have been true. However, it is difficult to believe that at the outset—so close to the events—he did not know that the various claims he made about why Hiroshima was bombed, and which set authoritative presidential terms of reference for all subsequent public debate, were simply false.†

There is one final, even more problematic point. As noted, this formulation appears in the president's memoirs:

*The Interim Committee's language is: "to make a profound psychological impression on as many of the inhabitants as possible." (Notes of the Interim Committee Meeting, Thursday, May 31, 1945, p. 14, File 100, H-B Files, Roll 8, M1108, NA.) The Target Committee minutes, as noted, put it this way: "It was agreed that psychological factors in the target selection were of great importance." (Summary of the Target Committee Meetings on May 10 and 11, 1945, p. 6, File 5D [Selection of Targets], Roll 1, M1109, Top Secret Correspondence of the MED, NA.)

†Related to this: Explaining how Hiroshima and Nagasaki came to be "wiped out" during the transcribed discussions as the memoirs were being prepared, Truman stated: "The civilian population is treated as a military asset in (modern) wars. And the destruction of manufacturing plants is war on civilians." ("Discussion," February 11, 1954, p. 5, Box 9, Post-Presidential File, HSTL.)

In deciding to use this bomb I wanted to make sure that it would be used as a weapon of war in the manner prescribed by the laws of war. That meant that I wanted it dropped on a military target.[68]

If the target was not primarily a military target—if the goal was psychological (a "terror bombing," as Barton Bernstein has put it)[69]—then, as the president suggests, serious legal questions may indeed arise.[70] Moreover, handwritten notes he made for a December 1945 speech—though misleading as to casualty estimates—seem quite accurate as to his reasoning and the essential reality of what was done: he believed it "worth a couple of Japanese cities. . . ."[71]

The only time the Hiroshima decision was actually judged in a court of law was in the 1963 Shimoda case. In this instance, a Tokyo district court (which had residual jurisdiction under provisions of the 1951 U.S.–Japanese Peace Treaty providing for Japan's legal responsibility in such cases) found a direct violation of international law.[72]

There is no evidence that legal issues were ever seriously considered in connection with the atomic bombings in 1945. However, the following points may be of possible relevance to future research—when and if further evidence on this point is discovered:

First, Admiral Leahy reports that he strongly urged President Roosevelt and others that the use of bacteriological agents or poison gas "would violate . . . all of the known laws of war. It would be an attack on the noncombatant population of the enemy"—and that in his opinion, "the atomic bomb belongs in exactly the same category."[73]

Second, in 1942 the Army's Judge Advocate General held that use of liquid agents to destroy Japan's rice crop "would not violate any rule of international law prohibiting poison gas . . . ," with the significant proviso, intimately related in law to the bomb's radioactive poisoning properties, that "such chemicals do not produce poisonous effects upon enemy personnel. . . ."[74]

Third, at the time he made his decision Truman was not without access to some of the most eminent legal talent in the world: James F. Byrnes, of course, had been a Supreme Court Justice; and Henry L. Stimson was one of the nation's leading international lawyers.

Fourth, Truman himself—as an active duty and reserve officer—was at least somewhat familiar with the laws of war.

Fifth, the treaty establishing the legal basis for both the Nuremberg and Tokyo War Crimes trials was signed in London on August 8, 1945. Although many have questioned the applicability of ex post facto law in the case of Germany and Japan, this happened one day before Nagasaki was destroyed. Professor Francis Boyle has suggested that the treaty's provisions make the second bombing (and probably also the first, if the Nuremberg standard is accepted) not only illegal but within the treaty's definition of a crime.[75]

Sixth, by chance one of the assistants who helped Truman with his memoirs—Morton Royse—was a scholar who had written a book on the law of aerial warfare.[76] It is possible that the president's awareness of this point of law derives from Royse's advice.

Again, however, we do not know whether Truman's statement that he understood and considered the legal issues involved in 1945 is accurate or was added subsequently when his memoirs were being written in the mid-1950s.

Chapter 43

NAGASAKI AND
"YEAR OF DECISIONS"

The president would come in about 8:30 in the morning from
Independence. . . . Then we just went through this word by
word, comma by comma, semicolon by semicolon and it
was really at these extended conferences that the President
molded the book into the final form he wanted it in.

—Professor Francis H. Heller,
Address before the Jackson County Historical Society,
Independence, Missouri, May 18, 1958

The city of Kyoto (the "old Capitol" in Truman's July 25 journal entry) was
spared from attack. The story has intrinsic interest, and seems clear evidence
of humanitarian concern. In fact, it is even more illuminating in connection
with the larger "second track" diplomatic issues we have reviewed.

When the Target Committee initially prepared its list of selected cities,
Kyoto was among them. It was a particularly good selection from the committee's (and General Groves') point of view. Kyoto, the committee minutes note,

> is an urban industrial area with a population of 1,000,000. It is the
> former capital of Japan and many people and industries are now being
> moved there as other areas are being destroyed. From the psychological
> point of view there is the advantage that Kyoto is an intellectual center
> for Japan and the people there are more apt to appreciate the signifi-
> cance of such a weapon as the gadget.[1]

We know from many sources—including his diary, his 1947 *Harper's* article, and his 1948 memoirs—that Henry Stimson strongly objected to the
bombing of Kyoto.[2] Truman explains in his memoirs that the city, "though

favored by General Arnold as a center of military activity, was eliminated when Secretary Stimson pointed out that it was a cultural and religious shrine of the Japanese."[3]

What is missing from this explanation is the specific concern central to the discussions throughout the summer of 1945—the Soviet Union. Stimson's diary of July 24, however, clarifies both his reasoning and (in response) the president's own emphasis and understanding:

> We [Stimson and Truman] had a few words about the S-1 program, and I again gave him my reasons for eliminating one of the proposed targets. He again reiterated with the utmost emphasis his own concurring belief on that subject, and he was particularly emphatic in agreeing with my suggestion that if elimination was not done, the bitterness which would be caused by such a wanton act might make it impossible during the long post-war period to reconcile the Japanese to us in that area rather than to the Russians. It might thus, I pointed out, be the means of preventing what our policy demanded, namely a sympathetic Japan to the United States in case there should be any aggression by Russia in Manchuria.[4]

Related to this issue is the question of Nagasaki. Why was a second city attacked so quickly? Why weren't the Japanese given additional time to evaluate the results of the first bombing? Was the decision-making process a serious and thoughtful one?

Even those who believe the Hiroshima bombing was justified have had difficulty with this issue. McGeorge Bundy, for instance, writes in *Danger and Survival*:

> . . . Hiroshima alone was enough to bring the Russians in; these two events together brought the crucial imperial decision for surrender, just *before* the second bomb was dropped. . . . There can be little doubt that the news of a second terrible attack strengthened the peace party and further shook the diehards, but the degree of this effect cannot be gauged. . . . a delay would have been relatively easy, and I think right.[5]

Victor Weisskopf, a Manhattan Project physicist, is more adamant: "On some occasion I ventured to say that the first bomb might have been justifiable, but the second was a crime."[6]

Truman rarely addressed the question of Nagasaki directly. But he was extremely sensitive about the intimately related question of whether the atomic bomb decision had been a hasty one, made without careful consideration of all the consequences. When he asked Stimson to "straighten out the record on it," one of his main concerns was that there "has been a great deal of conversation about how the conclusion was reached to drop the bomb and there has been some indication that the decision was arrived at hurriedly and without consideration."[7]

On one of the few occasions when Truman was confronted with a direct question about Nagasaki in a public situation which demanded a response, the answer he gave raises considerable doubt about his actual view—and his memory or truthfulness. At Columbia University, the following exchange (portions of which we have previously noted) took place:

> *Student:* Mr. President, would you be willing to explain to us what led you to believe that the first atomic bomb had failed to achieve peace with Japan and made it necessary to drop the second one?
> *President Truman:* It was a military procedure, under which the armed forces decided that it would be necessary to destroy both towns, the manufacturing towns for raw materials which were being sent to the Japanese in China; and the objective was, as nearly as we possibly could determine, to shut off the supplies to the Japanese.[8]

In this instance the president simply evaded the direct question—and, at the same time, offered information which is not supported by the record. In his October 1951 background interview with William Hillman for *Mr. President* Truman erroneously mentioned Nagasaki briefly along with Hiroshima as "entirely devoted to war work."[9]*

By late July, Nagasaki was the fourth city on the target list (after the deletion of Kyoto). Only because of an accident of weather which closed in Kokura Arsenal (Niigata was too distant to be a backup target) did it become the second city to be bombed.

At the Manhattan Project level, General Groves' goal had always been to use two of the new weapons—one plutonium bomb ("Fat Man") employing a complex "implosion" mechanism; the other a uranium bomb ("Little Boy"), utilizing a fairly simple "gun-type" design.[10]

General Handy's July 25 order to Spaatz provided that "Additional bombs will be delivered on the above targets as soon as made ready by the project staff."[11]

The Nagasaki field order designated the Mitsubishi Steel and Arms Works on the east bank of the Urakami river as the aiming point.[12] There is some confusion about this, however, since an undated Mission Planning Summary for Nagasaki states the primary purpose as follows:

> In accordance with the plans expressed in Report Number 1C, 509th Composite Group . . . the effort would be made to launch two Atomic

*See above, p. 522.

attacks within a short period of time for psychological as well as tactical reasons.[13]

The Mission Planning Summary then lists three specific reasons for selecting Nagasaki: "1. Industrial importance. 2. Undamaged, totally virgin territory. 3. Size of the city." It adds: ". . . commercial and public buildings are concentrated along the eastern and central parts of the city. Densely-grouped houses crowd these buildings and extend in an almost solid mass to the hills."[14] That said, the Summary coolly notes: "The aiming point was placed east of Nagasaki Harbor in the commercial district of the city."[15]

In other words, if the mission report is accurate, the Nagasaki bomb was also explicitly targeted in a manner designed to destroy large numbers of workers' homes.*

Why didn't President Truman pause to see if the August 6 bombing of Hiroshima—in conjunction, too, with the Soviet declaration of war—might end the fighting, as his journal indicates he seemed clearly to understand? Why did Truman conclude, as he told his Cabinet on August 10, that "the thought of wiping out another 100,000 people was too horrible" only after the second bomb was used?[16]

There are no clear answers to these questions in the available records. What is plain is that there was an intense, almost frenzied desire to end the war very quickly in the period following the Potsdam conference.

The goal was not merely to halt the fighting before an Allied landing, but instantly—before August 15, the earliest date the Red Army was expected to cross the border into North China and Manchuria. As we have seen, American leaders wanted the war to end *immediately.*[17]

Although it is impossible to know for sure, the real answer to the question of why no one at the highest level of the U.S. government thought to take the time to investigate or reflect is almost certainly to be found in the ur-

---

*In general, the Nagasaki attack did not go smoothly. Luis Alvarez (a scientist who had flown on the Hiroshima raid) later stated his belief that Nagasaki was bombed by radar—not visually, as orders specified and as the officers on the Nagasaki mission claimed. The aiming point designated in the Mission Planning Summary was missed by almost two miles. (Mission Planning Summary, Report Number 9, 509th Composite Group, Box 6, Entry 1, Groves Papers, RG 200, NA; Luis W. Alvarez to LRG, Box 1, Entry 10, Groves Papers, RG 200, NA.) Although major portions of the Mitsubishi arms plant and steel works were destroyed, "shortage of raw materials had [already] reduced operations at these . . . plants to a fraction of their capacity" before they were bombed. Unlike Hiroshima, only 150 Japanese military personnel are estimated to have been killed. (United States Strategic Bombing Survey, *The Effects of Atomic Bombs on Hiroshima and Nagasaki*, pp. 13, 15; United States Strategic Bombing Survey, *Summary Report* [*Pacific War*], p. 24; and The Committee for the Compilation of Materials on Damage Caused by the Atomic Bombs in Hiroshima and Nagasaki, *Hiroshima and Nagasaki: The Physical, Medical, and Social Effects of the Atomic Bombings*, trans. Eisei Ishikawa and David L. Swain [New York: Basic Books, 1981], p. 367.)

gency officials felt in connection with diplomatic-political concerns. In the tense early-August atmosphere, it seems evident that the decision not to pause, not to reflect, not to think, became natural—even normal—for American leaders.

We have seen that President Truman took an active interest in contributing to the way the story got out to the public. He also signed his name to a letter to Karl Compton, part of which appeared in the February 1947 issue of the *Atlantic Monthly* in support of Compton's defense of the atomic bombing.[18] On the basis of his experience as a war-time adviser to Stimson and a two-month stint with MacArthur's staff after the Hiroshima bombing (including a month in Japan), Compton concluded "with complete conviction, that the use of the atomic bomb saved hundreds of thousands—perhaps several millions—of lives, both American and Japanese. . . ."[19] Truman's letter endorsing Compton's article—published in larger-than-usual type, and on the magazine's title page—affirmed that

> Your statement in the *Atlantic Monthly* is a fair analysis of the situation except that the final decision had to be made by the President, and was made after a complete survey of the whole situation had been made. The conclusions reached were substantially those set out in your article.[20]

In the previous chapter we examined several statements taken from Truman's personal writings (or from transcripts of background discussions used in the preparation of his writings). A review of a wide range of similar materials by Edward Winstead has documented numerous additional errors, omissions, and misstatements of fact related to several other important issues connected with the bombings.[21] Many discrepancies are also evident when various articles, speeches, and related books by Truman are compared with the presently available documents. The following examples, taken from Truman's memoirs, *Year of Decisions*, serve to illustrate a clear and consistent pattern:

• *On Japan's deterioration:* Truman makes only passing reference to the extraordinary destruction and industrial collapse of Japan. Indeed, his memoirs contain only one specific mention of the subject—a statement from roughly mid-June: "Our air and fleet units had begun to inflict heavy damage on industrial and urban sites in Japan proper."[22]

None of the reports, memoranda, intelligence estimates, and other documents surveyed in Chapter 1 are drawn upon to any significant extent or quoted in the memoirs. One would not know from reading *Year of Decisions* that in July 1945 the United States controlled the seas surrounding Japan and dominated the sky over Japan, and that shipments of food and essential raw materials to the home islands had been almost entirely cut off.

(By way of comparison, Leahy reported in *I Was There* that as early as the summer of 1944 "a large part of the Japanese Navy was already on the bottom of the sea. The same was true of Japanese merchant shipping. There was every indication that our Navy would soon have the rest of Tokyo's warships sunk or out of action."[23])

• *On the "MAGIC" intercepts:* Truman does not tell the reader that the United States had broken the Japanese codes and all along was reading the crucial intercepted cables. He makes no mention of MAGIC anywhere in his memoirs. From reading the book it would be impossible to discern that the president and his advisers had independent knowledge of all the key Japanese moves. Most significantly, one would not be aware of the Emperor's personal bid to end the war.

Nor can "security" be claimed as an important reason for the president's silence on this issue. By 1955 it was no secret that the United States had broken the Japanese codes. Not only were Truman's memoirs published a full decade after the war's end, but the Pentagon had cleared *The Forrestal Diaries* for publication in 1951,[24] and, as we have seen, they include direct references to the Japanese intercepts.[25] Furthermore, all pre–Pearl Harbor MAGIC intercepts had been made available to Congress and discussed in the press in late 1945 and 1946.

• *On altering the unconditional surrender formula:* In his memoirs Truman provides only a very brief, superficial (and misleading) treatment of the advice he received regarding unconditional surrender. He mentions only one of the more than a dozen (known) occasions in which he was advised by U.S. officials and Prime Minister Churchill to clarify the surrender terms.

One would not know that Truman himself had initiated a modification of the surrender terms in his May 8 public statement, that he had substantially retreated from this position on June 1, and that, following Byrnes' advice, he had resisted all proposals for change thereafter.

Nor does the president reveal to the reader the related but slightly different point that U.S. experts also had advised him repeatedly that unless the Japanese were given assurances for the Emperor, the war would likely continue indefinitely.

Truman also does not explain why he accepted Byrnes' advice not to modify the terms as against the position of almost every other top administration adviser and Prime Minister Churchill. Nor (except for a brief passing acknowledgment of his support for Grew on May 28) does the president indicate that he personally had no serious objection to such changes, as several documents show.[26]

Indeed, in the five chapters he devotes to the Potsdam conference in *Year of Decisions* Truman reports nothing about the debate over unconditional surrender. It is not until after he discusses the atomic bombings that he mentions the role of the Emperor in achieving surrender.[27]

(In this regard Truman offered the following striking explanation during the discussions which were transcribed as the memoirs were being prepared: "It was because of the unconditional surrender policy against Japan that Hiroshima and Nagasaki were wiped out. . . .")[28]

• *On the specific issue of the Potsdam Proclamation and its relationship to the surrender formula:* Truman presents a misleading account which confuses the issue of whether to offer a general warning to Japan with the critical question of whether to clarify the specific terms of surrender concerning the Emperor.

For instance, Truman reports (correctly) that Grew's proposal of May 28 would "urge the Japanese to surrender but would assure them that we would permit the Emperor to remain as head of the state." However, he then skips over the central point at issue—whether or not the Potsdam Proclamation would contain assurances concerning the Emperor—and goes on to say in the most general terms that Grew "favored issuing the proclamation at once." Again, once more ignoring the critical point at issue, he goes on to observe simply that "It was my decision then that the proclamation to Japan should be issued from the forthcoming conference at Potsdam."[29]

Furthermore, Truman also writes: "If the test of the bomb was successful, I wanted to afford Japan a clear chance to end the fighting before we made use of this newly gained power."[30] Here and elsewhere the implication is that the Potsdam Proclamation was such a chance.[31] Yet, as we have seen, the president was fully aware it was highly unlikely Japan could accept the vague Potsdam Proclamation as written.

Nowhere does Truman inform the reader that language assuring the continuance of Japan's Imperial tradition was present in the Potsdam Proclamation when it reached his desk. Nor does he report that he and Byrnes cut the crucial sentences out of the draft.[32] Truman omits this entire sequence of events from his memoirs, his personal papers, his diary, and his public statements, as though it never happened.

• *On the timing of what became the Proclamation:* As noted, at Truman's suggestion, Grew took his May 28 proposal to a meeting of Stimson, Marshall, and Forrestal the next day. Many documents record that these officials shared Grew's general view but decided to postpone a statement (according to Grew) "for certain military reasons, not divulged."[33]

Truman writes in his memoirs that "the service chiefs were of the opinion that we should wait until we were ready to follow a Japanese refusal with the actual assault of our invasion forces."[34] On the contrary, the chiefs sought a public statement timed to coincide with the fall of Okinawa. In any event,

U.S. troops would not be positioned to invade Japan until November, and no one advised waiting that long to define the terms. Indeed, at Potsdam the Chiefs urged that clarifying language be included in the July 26 Proclamation.

• *On Japan's reaction to the Potsdam Proclamation:* In his August 6 announcement, quoted in *Year of Decisions*, Truman suggests he decided to use the bomb only after Tokyo "rejected" the Potsdam Proclamation. "It was to spare the Japanese people from utter destruction that the ultimatum of July 26 was issued at Potsdam. Their leaders promptly rejected that ultimatum."[35]

However, as we have noted, on July 28, the Japanese government told the press that it had decided to *"mokusatsu"* the proclamation—a term which could mean "to kill with silence," "take no notice of," or "withhold comment."[36] As we have seen, whatever the ambiguities of the public language, intercepts make it clear that privately U.S. officials knew Japan had not, in fact, rejected the proclamation out of hand but were studying it with a view to clarifying a response. In particular, Brown's diary of August 3 records Truman's personal sense that Japan was seeking peace.

• *On the surrender terms ultimately accepted: Year of Decisions* reprints the following statement made by the president on August 14, 1945:

> I have received this afternoon a message from the Japanese Government in reply to the message forwarded to that Government by the Secretary of State on August eleventh. I deem this reply a full acceptance of the Potsdam Declaration which specifies the unconditional surrender of Japan. In the reply there is no qualification.[37]

But, in fact, as *Life* magazine (among many others) noted on August 20, 1945: "The Japs . . . agreed to the Potsdam ultimatum, with one condition."[38] As is obvious, in the end, the president accepted the critical condition which had been under discussion all summer: He allowed Japan to retain the Emperor (with the stipulation that he would rule subject to the guidance of the Supreme Allied Military Commander). Indeed, Emperor Hirohito reigned for forty-four more years until his death in 1989.

The reprinting of the August 14 statement, in fact, implicitly distorts reality twice—first in 1945, second when reproduced in the memoirs. Truman fully understood that Japan's surrender was conditional, as was quite clear from his August 10, 1945, journal.[39]

• *On the expected impact of a Soviet attack:* In his memoirs, Truman repeatedly states that he went to Potsdam to get assurances that the Russians would enter the war against Japan.[40] He allows that this was important since if the atomic test were to fail, the Russian declaration of war could be instrumental in making it unnecessary to undertake the physical conquest of Japan. However, he does not discuss the implications of this statement; nor does he report on any of the 1945 intelligence estimates or other advice suggesting that the shock of Russian entry, together with a change in terms, would likely end the war.[41]

Finally, Truman also fails to report his own sense of exultation when on July 17 Stalin confirmed that he would, in fact, enter the war.[42]

• *On the desire to delay a Russian declaration of war once the successful atomic test had been carried out:* As we have seen, U.S. policy after the full impact of the atomic test had been digested reversed course entirely and now actively attempted to stall the Red Army attack for as long as possible. In *Year of Decisions*, Truman provides no indication of the concerted effort to delay the Soviet attack. Nor does he mention the specific tactic of prolonging the Sino-Soviet negotiations in the hope of ending the war before Russian troops entered Manchuria.

• *On the many issues related to the atomic bomb and diplomacy toward the Soviet Union:* With two very general exceptions, Truman does not reveal anything about the numerous "second track" strategic considerations which have been documented over the years. The exceptions include, first, the April 24, 1945, note from Stimson to the president during the intense diplomatic confrontation with Molotov over Poland. This shows that Stimson asked to see the president to talk to him in depth about the atomic bomb for the first time not in connection with the war in the Pacific but because of diplomatic concerns related to Russia.

Second, Truman recalls a discussion—portions of which we have previously quoted—with Stimson and Byrnes during his first weeks in office:

> If expectations were to be realized, he [Stimson] told me, the atomic bomb would be certain to have a decisive influence on our relations with other countries. And if it worked, the bomb, in all probability, would shorten the war.
>
> Byrnes had already told me that the weapon might be so powerful as to be potentially capable of wiping out entire cities and killing people on an unprecedented scale. And he had added that in his belief the bomb might well put us in a position to dictate our terms at the end of the war. Stimson, on the other hand, seemed at least as much concerned with the role of the atomic bomb in the shaping of history as in its capacity to shorten this war.[43]

Aside from these statements, the memoirs provide the reader with no information concerning a variety of many other now well-understood facts concerning the weapon's relationship to diplomacy. For instance, they do not explain that the president intentionally postponed meeting Stalin until after the bomb had been tested. In this connection the memoirs mislead the reader by quoting—as if it were an accurate statement—Truman's May 9 message to Churchill saying that he had to delay Potsdam because of his "fiscal year."

Nor do the memoirs give any indication that Truman personally was involved in a strategy of delay on the explicit expectation that his diplomatic hand would be stronger once the bomb was tested. The memoirs also do not mention that Truman believed that the atomic bomb might help resolve many of the Far Eastern and Eastern European diplomatic issues then in dispute. Nor is there any hint of the fact that the president not only knew Japan was on the verge of surrender, but that he was worried that a surrender might occur through the Soviet Union—and that he anxiously wished to avoid this in the period just before Hiroshima was bombed.

The reader of *Year of Decisions* would find nothing about any of these and many other facts concerning the atomic bomb story which have been documented over the last half century.

In short, what we now know about the 1945 decision-making process makes it obvious that the historical accuracy of much of Truman's memoir is questionable.[44] Skeptics often suggest that statements made in the memoirs of important officials are never to be taken too seriously, that we should simply accept routine distortions in such accounts as an inevitable malady of the political world. Moreover, in most cases, we are reading ghostwritten words, and we should perhaps not expect real accuracy.

Our concern here, however, is not with the general accuracy of the memoirs but with a much more specific matter: It is with the role the president played in personally crafting the message concerning the atomic bomb decision contained in his account—and, too, with his relationship to the writers who assisted him in the process.

In the first paragraph of *Year of Decisions*, Truman writes: "A vast amount of research of my personal papers and documents was necessary in my efforts to achieve a true and accurate picture."[45] He also states:

> For the last two and a half years I have checked my memory against my personal papers, memoranda, and letters and with some of the persons who were present when certain decisions were made, seeking to recapture and record accurately the significant events of my administration.[46]

The documents now available allow us to understand in great detail the specific process by which the memoirs were written—and the president's direct role in the enterprise. These show that Truman carefully scrutinized and personally approved, page by page, line by line, each and every statement included in his memoirs.

Among the most important sources are typed transcripts of daily meetings with the president concerning how each issue should be presented, articles written by several assistants who worked with him on the memoirs, and interviews with some of the same people.

Contemporary accounts indicate that Truman "worked on the memoirs full time, from 9 until 4, five days a week, for thirty months."[47] His chief aides were journalist William Hillman and David Noyes, an advertising executive and longtime Democrat. Hillman and Noyes were responsible for hiring the project's actual writers.[48]

Truman took a "hands-on" approach to the effort from the beginning. Dissatisfied with the first writer hired—journalism professor Robert E. G. Harris—he fired him in November 1953 after Harris had worked for five months and generated a draft of 150,000 words.[49] (Truman found his style too anecdotal.[50])

A second writer, Morton Royse, a former adjunct professor at Georgetown University, lasted until the spring of 1954. Here the problem was just the reverse. Royse apparently was too painstaking; he irritated the president by persistently questioning him when he found Truman's responses incomplete.[51] An example from a February 1954 transcript shows Royse pressing for clarification about various attempts to get Truman to alter the surrender terms:

> *Mr. Royse:* There was one item that indicated Churchill wanted to vary unconditional surrender. There's a report from Winant . . . that the British were under pressure from Canada which wanted surrender arrangements made, and Winant says the way it was drafted left it vague about unconditional surrender.
> *Mr. Truman:* I don't think there could have been a surrender that wasn't unconditional.
> *Mr. Royse:* Leahy said that Churchill was pushing for something not less than unconditional surrender but at variance with it, with you.
> *Mr. Truman:* I don't remember that.[52]

Frustrated by two false (and expensive) starts, Truman personally took over the search for a third writer. Calls to the president of the University of Missouri and the chancellor of the University of Kansas turned up Herbert Lee Williams, a doctoral candidate in journalism, and Dr. Francis H. Heller, an associate professor of political science. Both were hired, and in short order the manuscript began to take shape.

Williams later recalled an "elaborate rewrite method" in which he would regularly meet with Truman, Hillman, and Noyes to review the narrative:

> . . . it was in these get-togethers that the memoirs got on true course. As my manuscript was read aloud, usually by Hillman, the ex-president would listen intently. His approval or criticism was solicited almost

paragraph by paragraph. The whole idea was to jog the memory of the man who had been there, to add the auto to the biography.[53]

A stenographer using a stenotype machine produced a verbatim transcript of the discussions to expedite rewrites.

"It was my job to put it down the way I found it," noted Williams (who was also soon to leave). "[H]is prerogative, of course, was to put it the way he wanted it left."[54]

In December 1954, Heller assumed full responsibility for completing the job:[55]

. . . One of my first queries was to find out where [Truman's previous assistant] had gone wrong. The explanation given me provided an excellent introduction to Truman's thinking: the professor simply refused to accept Truman's statement to him that he, Truman, had seen the employment of the atomic bomb solely in terms of weaponry and not of ethics. . . .[56]

At this point Truman was taking home a draft chapter each night in a small aluminum carrying case to read over with Mrs. Truman. The next day the drafts were returned to Heller with handwritten notes marked in pencil in the margins.[57] By May 1955, the final stage in preparing the manuscript—"a close, word-for-word reading" in Truman's office—was reached.[58]

"The President, Hillman, Noyes, and I each had a copy before us and we would take turns reading the manuscript out loud," Heller recalled.[59] Here, too, a stenographer recorded the discussion so Heller could incorporate the changes into the manuscript. Heller was later to stress that Truman paid "close attention to the process," adding: "If anything, I would give even greater credit to Mr. Truman: there simply is not a word in his memoirs that he did not personally review."[60]

In a 1958 address before the Jackson County Historical Society in Independence, Missouri, Heller recalled that he will "always remember" the "last few weeks" spent working on the memoirs:

The President would come in about 8:30 in the morning from Independence and we would settle down in his office, he behind his desk and Mr. Noyes, Mr. Hillman and I and [stenographer] Gene Bailey, each of us with a copy of the draft in front of us, along with notes that had been made by several other people who had seen copies of the draft beforehand and had been asked to comment on it. Then we just went through this word by word, comma by comma, semicolon by semicolon and it was really at these extended conferences that the President molded the book into the final form he wanted it in.[61]

Chapter 44

CERTAIN CLASSES OF PAPERS

He confirmed, rather testily in the end, what the librarian had told me: There were certain classes of papers that were "his" and he didn't plan to relinquish them "until I'm good and ready."

—Cabell Phillips, *The Truman Presidency*

We have seen that Harry Truman stated that "as much as a million" American casualties were prevented by the use of the atomic bomb, modifying his own unsubstantiated quarter-of-a-million estimate so as to be in line with the equally unsubstantiated Stimson-Bundy figure. Another question involving the atomic bomb decision was also taken up in the president's exchange with James L. Cate. Here, too, the response prepared for the Army Air Forces history helped perpetuate additional misleading elements of the tale.

Once again, the actual process by which the misleading information was developed can also be studied in some detail.[1] The main reason Cate had written Truman was that he was puzzled by what seemed an inconsistency: In his first public statement on the atomic bomb the president had said that "it was to spare the Japanese people from utter destruction that the ultimatum of July 26 was issued at Potsdam. Their leaders promptly rejected that ultimatum."[2] In his published letter to Karl T. Compton in February 1947, Truman had also stated that "the Japanese were given fair warning. . . ."[3]

These two statements clearly implied that Truman made the decision to use the atomic bomb only after Premier Suzuki "rejected" the Potsdam Proclamation. However, Cate or perhaps an observant editor had noticed that the actual order to bomb Japanese cities was dated July 25. The Potsdam Proclamation was issued on July 26. Did it follow, then, that "the decision to use the bomb had been made at least one day before the promulgation of the Potsdam Declaration and two days before Suzuki's rejection thereof on 28 July, Tokyo time"?

> Such an interpretation is in flat contradiction to the explanation implicit in the published statements, that the final decision was made only after the Japanese refusal of the ultimatum.[4]

Cate also noted that General Henry "Hap" Arnold's memoirs seemed to suggest that the July 25 order was not directly authorized by the president:

> According to General Arnold's statement elsewhere [H. H. Arnold, *Global Mission* (New York, 1949), p. 589], this directive was based on a memorandum dispatched by courier to Washington after a conference on 22 July between himself, Secretary Stimson, and General Marshall.*

Cate concluded:

> Your well-known interest in history has encouraged me to seek my information at the source, as the historian should, without apology other than for having intruded on your crowded schedule with a letter made overly long by my desire to state the problem accurately.[5]

Along with his letter to Truman, Cate enclosed a copy of the July 25 order from the War Department in Washington (signed by Thomas T. Handy while Marshall was at Potsdam). Nothing in the order appeared to suggest the president's direct involvement:

25 July 1945

> TO: General Carl Spaatz
>   Commanding General
>   United States Army Strategic Air Force
>   1. The 509 Composite Group, 20th Air Force will deliver its first special bomb as soon as weather will permit visual bombing after about 3 August 1945 on one of the targets: Hiroshima, Kokura, Niigata and Nagasaki. . . .
>   2. Additional bombs will be delivered on the above targets as soon as made ready by the project staff. . . .
>   3. Dissemination of any and all information concerning the use of the weapon against Japan is reserved to the Secretary of War and the President of the United States. . . .
>   4. The foregoing directive is issued to you by direction and with the approval of the Secretary of War and of the Chief of Staff, USA. It is desired that you personally deliver one copy of this directive to

---

*Bracketed text in original.

General MacArthur and one copy to Admiral Nimitz for their information.

> /S/   Thos. T. Handy
> THOS. T. HANDY
> General, G.S.C.
> Acting Chief of Staff[6]

Papers also on file at the Truman Library show that the president's initial draft reply to Cate's inquiry was curt: "We sent an ultimatum to Japan. It was ignored. I ordered atomic bombs dropped on the two cities named on the way back from Potsdam when we were in the middle of the Atlantic Ocean."[7]

Kenneth W. Hechler, the same White House aide who helped "revise" upward the president's casualty estimates, reviewed Truman's longhand draft and decided to consult Rudolph Winnacker, historian of the Office of Secretary of Defense. Hechler's memorandum for his immediate superior, David D. Lloyd, indicated that according to Winnacker.

> it is clear that the Gen. Handy order could have been countermanded in the event Japan had responded to the Potsdam ultimatum—just as any military order can be countermanded. The fundamental decision to use the bomb preceded the Gen. Handy letter, and the decision to "trigger" its use and define the targets was made by the President as indicated in his memorandum. I do not feel this needs elaboration.[8]

On the basis of this information Lloyd in turn told Truman that he had

> inserted a paragraph explaining why the orders to General Spaatz were dated July 25 rather than after the ultimatum. This has been checked with the historian of the Department of Defense.[9]

The text of the final letter Truman sent to Cate (including the rewritten paragraph) reads as follows:

> We sent an ultimatum to Japan. It was rejected.
>
> I ordered atomic bombs dropped on the two cities named on the way back from Potsdam, when we were in the middle of the Atlantic Ocean.
>
> In your letter, you raise the fact that the directive to General Spaatz to prepare for delivering the bomb is dated July twenty-fifth. It was, of course, necessary to set the military wheels in motion, as these orders did, but the final decision was in my hands, and not made until we were returning from Potsdam.[10]

Neither Hechler nor Lloyd had any evidence, of course, that the July 25 order was given with the thought that it was understood as a preliminary command to be followed by another order. Moreover, neither did they have any evidence that the final decision was made—or that Truman actually issued an order to drop the bombs—on his way back from Potsdam. Nonetheless, typed on White House stationery and signed by the president himself, Truman's letter gave credibility to this account when it appeared in the official history. Shortly thereafter, the University of Chicago Press began to utilize the new information to publicize its book.[11]

In a further round of confusion, the unsubstantiated information then apparently became in part the basis for the following in Truman's memoirs:

> In order to get preparations under way, the War Department was given orders to instruct General Spaatz that the first bomb would be dropped as soon after August 3 as weather would permit. . . .
>
> With this order the wheels were set in motion for the first use of an atomic weapon against a military target. I had made the decision. I also instructed Stimson that the order would stand unless I notified him that the Japanese reply to our ultimatum was acceptable.[12]

The result was that three distinct explanations from the president himself began to circulate concerning the timing of the decision to use the atomic bomb and the specific order given to the Air Force.

First, from Truman's August 6, 1945, statement: "It was to spare the Japanese people from utter destruction that the ultimatum of July 26 was issued . . .": when they "rejected" the Potsdam Proclamation on July 28, the decision was made.[13] Second, the president's letter in the official Army Air Forces history: During the first week of August, he "ordered atomic bombs dropped . . . when we were in the middle of the Atlantic Ocean."[14] Third, *Year of Decisions* repeats the claim that the July 25 order set the "wheels . . . in motion," but now adds that the president "instructed Stimson that the order would stand unless I notified him that the Japanese reply to our ultimatum was acceptable."[15]

Prior to 1979, when the president's Potsdam journal was discovered, historians lacked contemporaneous evidence concerning the timing of the critical decision. We now know that Truman wrote the following in his private journal on July 25, the same day the Handy order was dated—one day before the Potsdam Proclamation and three days before the first Japanese response: "This weapon is to be used against Japan between now and August 10th."[16]

Truman's July 18 journal entry—"I am sure they will ["fold up"] when Manhattan appears over their homeland"—adds further contemporaneous evidence suggesting that he had essentially decided to use the atomic bomb against Japan well before he issued the Potsdam Proclamation.[17]

It is also clear that in any event the president understood there was little chance Japan would accept the Potsdam Proclamation in the form it was finally issued. (To recall, on July 25, 1945, he also noted that ". . . we will issue a warning statement asking the Japs to surrender and save lives. I'm sure they will not do that, but we will have given them the chance."[18])

A decade later, examining the same question which had bothered Cate, historian Herbert Feis also contacted the president to request detailed information on the timing of the decision—and of the specific order. Feis had been a friend of Stimson's; he had also been an adviser to four Cabinet officers.[19] Truman, however, was clearly irritated at being questioned even by a friendly insider about the Hiroshima decision. The following letter was drafted in reply to Feis (but in the end not sent):

> My dear Mr. Feis:
>
> You write just like the usual egghead. The facts are before you but you'd like to garble them. The instruction of July 25th, 1945 was final. It was made by the Commander in Chief after Japan refused to surrender.
>
> Churchill, Stimson, Patterson, Eisenhower and all the rest agreed that it had to be done. It was. It ended the Jap War. That was the objective. Now if you can think of any other, "if, as, and when" egghead contemplations, bring them out.
>
> You get the same answer—to end the Jap War and save ¼ of a million of our youngsters and that many Japs from death and twice that many on each side from being maimed for life.
>
> It is a great thing that you or any other contemplator "after the fact" didn't have to make the decision.
>
> Our boys would all be dead.[20]

Feis did not give up his attempt to pin down the actual facts. In a letter to General Groves a few months later, however, he noted that

> all my subsequent efforts to find any other instructions later than that of June [sic] 25—from General Hardy [sic]—have come to nought; no message from President Truman sent from the USS AUGUSTA has yet been found.[21]

Groves's reply was straightforward:

> With reference to your hunt for a message from President Truman from the U.S.S. Augusta prior to Hiroshima, I doubt if any will ever be found no matter how hard you search for none reached me. I am sure if one had come to the War Department it would have been addressed either to Mr. Stimson, General Marshal [sic], General Handy, or myself. It [sic] it had been sent to one of the others it would have been referred to me.

I will add that if it had gone to any of them except on an "eyes only" basis it would have created quite a stir in the operations Division of the General Staff and I would certainly have learned of this. In short, I cannot help but feel that such a message was never actually sent from the Augusta. I would point out too that it would have been unnecessary as the proposed plan of action was definitely approved in a cable from Pottsdam [sic]. Mr. Truman was not one to repeat an approval previously given.[22]

The following exchange (which occurred during a presidential press conference on October 26, 1950) added one final bit of confusion:

Q.— . . . John Gunther has written an article, in which he said that General MacArthur knew nothing about plans for dropping the atomic bomb on Japan. Do you have any comment, or can you throw any light on that?
The President. It just isn't true.
Q. Not true?
The President. It's just not true.
Q. He did know?
The President. Of course he did. He had to make the order. I gave the order to him and he gave the order to the men to drop the bomb. How do you suppose you transact business militarily? [Laughter][23]

As we have seen, so far as historians have been able to determine—and as the Handy order suggests—MacArthur knew nothing about advance planning for the atomic bomb's use until almost the last minute. Nor was he personally in the chain of command in this connection; the order came straight from Washington. Indeed, the War Department waited until five days before the bombing of Hiroshima even to notify MacArthur—the commanding general of U.S. Army Forces in the Pacific—of the existence of the atomic bomb.[24]

That Truman was loose with the facts in his various public explanations of the decision to use the atomic bomb should now be obvious. Beyond this it is also clear that he actively suppressed some of the most crucial information which might have challenged his account.

Experts familiar with the way important and potentially embarrassing records were managed by Truman are unanimous in agreeing that he was extremely reluctant to provide anyone access to certain critical documents—and that as a rule he maintained personal control over information which he did not wish to be made public.

White House aide Eben Ayers later recalled that even though he was acting on the president's direct request—and even though Truman told him that he would have access to everything he needed to assemble the president's papers on a number of key events—in fact, Ayers was not allowed to see certain documents:

> He [Truman] had in his own office, or more properly, the office of his secretary, Miss Rose Conway, personal files which I do not believe were accessible to or seen by anyone other than Miss Conway and the President. I know that in my work on the President's papers, during 1951 and 1952, I found it practically impossible to get from Miss Conway anything from these files for my use, despite the President's having assured me that everything was to be available to me.[25]

Other examples abound. In background conversations on his memoirs with one of his first ghostwriters, Robert E. G. Harris, the president referred to the "secret file" he kept in his office. The following transcribed exchange concerns papers related to arrangements for the Potsdam Conference:

> *Mr. Harris:* How should we go about getting these secret papers?
> *Mr. Truman:* I will have to go look at them myself. They may be in the secret file we have right here, but if they're not, I'll go over there . . . and pull them out. They will have to be put back, of course. . . .[26]

In this case, it is not clear exactly which papers were finally used, only that certain highly secret ones were "over there" (almost certainly a reference to Rose Conway's office).

In another background conversation with Hillman and Noyes, on May 24, 1954, Truman also made it clear that he intended to maintain control of certain documents until he alone decided to release them (in this case, notes made by Benjamin Cohen at Potsdam):

> *Truman*–[Cohen's] is a very accurate report. It is a good thing we have it because there are a few things in each [version] missing apparently. You can't remember day by day without a record.
> *Noyes*–that is why the State Department are [*sic*] after this stuff.
> *Truman*–they are not going to get it until we are through with it.[27]

Truman also refused Feis access to other papers he sought for his research—in this case concerning events at Potsdam. Robert H. Ferrell reports that in 1957

> Feis inquired through [former Secretary of State] Dean Acheson if it would be possible to see Truman's private papers pertaining to the Potsdam Conference—Feis was writing a book which eventually received the Pulitzer Prize in history. Acheson spoke with Truman, who mulled

over the possibility of Feis's use of the papers and eventually decided against it.[28]

A few years later, in 1964, Averell Harriman also wrote urging the president to release certain secret materials:

Dear Harry:

. . . I was talking the other day with Dr. Franklin in charge of our Historical Office [at the State Department]. He tells me that they need only seven papers from you to complete their work on the "Foreign Relations" volumes for the year 1945. . . .

Your hesitation about letting any unofficial researchers into your private papers is very understandable, but the State Department's "Foreign Relations" series is official and is in a class by itself. My feeling is that if you made these seven papers available for reproduction in "Foreign Relations," no private researcher could possibly claim that this gave him any right or reason to ask access to papers in your office.[29]

Considering the sophistication of the man he was addressing, the president's reply was somewhat strained:

I have the list of papers which are wanted and I am considering the matter. The main difficulty with me is that I have been handicapped by the fact that some of the papers are top secret and I have no right to give them out, but I will help in any way I can.[30]

Harriman forwarded a copy of Truman's letter to the head of the State Department Historical Office—and received the following reply:

He must realize, if he stops to think about it, that we have been declassifying and publishing hundreds of top-secret documents and that he himself gave us some of the top-secret documents that are published in the Potsdam volumes. Perhaps he is merely stalling us off again, but I do not think that we should let his excuse go uncorrected.[31]

There are numerous additional illustrations of Truman's unwillingness to release information he did not wish made public. Indeed, fully 2,700 linear feet of material were off limits to researchers and even to the Truman Library staff until after his death.[32]

Three additional reports help fill out the picture—and, too, the essential continuity over time:

In 1959 Richard G. Hewlett, who was then working on the official history of the U.S. Atomic Energy Commission, interviewed the former president at the Truman Library, and thereafter noted for his files: "I explained to Mr.

Truman the general purpose of our history and pointed out to him that this was an official history and therefore we were not trying to make an extensive amount of interpretation but were mainly interested in the putting down the cold hard facts. Mr. Truman agreed that this was the only way it could or should be done."[33] Hewlett's notes reveal the frustration he felt at his inability to get solid information—and, indeed, at Truman's seeming desire to give him stock answers of little value. For instance:

> I asked him whether there was any truth to the argument that the bomb had been used to keep Russia out of the war. Here again his reaction was automatic. He said absolutely not; that that [*sic*] was his primary reason for going to Potsdam to get the Russians in the war. He never for a moment considered trying to keep them out.[34]

On a specific point of substantial interest, Hewlett notes:

> I, at once, asked him the main question—whether there had been any consideration of putting a specific warning of the weapon in the Potsdam Declaration. His reply was immediate and positive. He said that certainly the Potsdam Declaration did not contain such a warning but that the Japanese had been warned through secret diplomatic channels by way of both Switzerland and Sweden. He said that this warning told the Japanese that they would be attacked by a new and terrible weapon unless they would surrender.[35]

Apparently taken aback by this bit of totally new information, Hewlett goes on:

> I am sure that he could sense my surprise at this astounding statement. I again reviewed with him the facts of his statement. I asked him to confirm that this was a secret communication through diplomatic channels; that it had nothing to do with the Potsdam Declaration itself. He assured me that this was true. I asked him if he had copies of this diplomatic message. He said he did not but he was very such [*sic*] they could be found in the records of the State Department or perhaps in CIA. He gave me the impression that this message was drafted in Potsdam, but he steered away from all questions regarding the specific[s] of the matter.[36]

No record or any other indication of a specific warning of this kind has ever been found.

In 1966 Cabell Phillips, a Washington journalist, published a book on the Truman presidency. In a concluding "Word About Presidential Libraries," Phillips recalled:

Throughout his tenure in the White House I had enjoyed an amicable if not intimate professional relationship with him. . . . [He] told me: "Come out to the Library. Everything I did as President is there, and you are welcome to all of it."

I went to the Harry S. Truman Memorial Library at Independence, Missouri, in the spring of 1962, prepared to stay a month or two. In less than two weeks I was disillusioned and on my way back home. The bulk of its claimed "five million papers on the Presidency" turned out to be largely routine public correspondence, printed reports, and documents available almost anywhere in the government, mimeographed speeches and statements issued through the White House Press Secretary, and Mr. Truman's office files while he was a Senator. When I asked for the working papers and other documents relating to such major policy matters as the Marshall Plan, NATO, the veto of the Taft-Hartley Act, and the loyalty investigations, I was told with evident embarrassment by the Library's director: "Well, you see, they are in Mr. Truman's wing of the Library. He regards those as his personal papers and we have never been permitted to examine or catalogue them."

A few days later I brought this matter up with Mr. Truman himself. He confirmed, rather testily in the end, what the librarian had told me: There were certain classes of papers that were "his" and he didn't plan to relinquish them "until I'm good and ready."[37]

Finally, Samuel I. Rosenman, Truman's close friend and counsel during the war, expressed real concern (in an oral history interview conducted for the Library) that Truman would not get the historical recognition he deserved because—as late as 1969—

so many of his papers have not been made available. I don't agree with that. He has kept them under his own supervision. . . .[38]

There thus can be no question about Truman's basic attitude. Even so admiring a historian as Robert H. Ferrell has observed that he did not give researchers access to many of his papers: "Other than using his private papers for the memoirs, and allowing some use by his friend William Hillman for a coffee table book entitled *Mr. President* . . . and use by his daughter, Margaret, for a biography entitled *Harry S. Truman* . . . other than for these three books, the papers remained closed."[39]

Perhaps the single most important set of documents relating to the atomic bomb decision kept under tight control were Truman's Potsdam journals.

As we have seen, these contemporaneous "Fini Japs" records, together with the letters he wrote to his wife, Bess, reveal his 1945 views concerning the coming end of the war.

Robert Messer has observed that the

> implications of these passages from Truman's diary and letters for the orthodox defense of the bomb's use are devastating: if Soviet entry alone would end the war before an invasion of Japan, the use of atomic bombs cannot be justified as the only alternative to that invasion. This does not mean, of course, that having the bomb was not useful. But it does mean that for Truman the end of the war seemed at hand; the issue was no longer when the war would end, but how and on whose terms. If he believed that the war would end with Soviet entry in mid-August, then he must have realized that if the bombs were not used before that date they might well not be used at all.[40]

Minimally, these journal entries, together with the letters to his wife, raise the most serious questions about the credibility of the president's claim that the atomic bomb was used because it was the only way to save "a quarter million," "a half million," or "millions" of casualties or lives.

How is it that these documents—especially the president's journals—were made public only three and a half decades after the fact?

In the case of the letters to Bess it appears (as Ferrell writes) that "she casually secreted them in her bedroom, perhaps, or carted them (once the mass reached inconvenient proportions) to some storage room. Her filing system was haphazard, but she evidently threw very little away."[41] Shortly after Bess Truman's death in 1982, her daughter Margaret turned the letters over to the Truman Library, where they were opened for inspection in March 1983.[42]

The story of why the president's private journal was not disclosed until 1979 is more complex and involves conflicting opinions on several basic points. One possibility, of course, is that the journal was simply misplaced. This is the belief of Robert H. Ferrell, the historian who edited *Off the Record: The Private Papers of Harry S. Truman:*

> The President's diary entries for the Potsdam conference itself—his experiences in the former German capital—were not discovered until 1979. Press Secretary Charles G. Ross borrowed the account, perhaps in 1945 or 1946, hoping to write a story of the conference, but never got around to it, and after his death in 1950 the diary sheets and other miscellaneous materials in Ross's White House office were given to Rose Conway, who put them away in a file labeled "Ross, Mr. and Mrs. Charles G." in the President's personal file. Miss Conway appears to

have stapled the sheets hurriedly, out of sequence. The archivists of the Truman Library who organized the President's Secretary's Files did not notice them, even though the handwriting was that of the President.[43]

That there is considerably more to this story is revealed by a series of other documents on file at the Truman Library, and by other research undertaken in the course of writing this book.

There is clear evidence that the Potsdam journal in Ross' file was not the only copy of the journal—and, furthermore, that the president not only had not forgotten it, but was fully aware of its existence. Indeed, it was one of the general sets of documents he specifically refused to allow researchers to see—including those on his personal staff whom he had asked to assemble information pertaining specifically to the atomic bomb.

Before he left the White House, Truman assigned Eben Ayers the task of pulling together the record concerning the atomic bomb decision.[44] As Ayers began to search for information, he, in turn, contacted Ross' widow and discovered that she had "an envelope of what was evidently secret material about the atom bomb which Charlie had put together and left in his safe deposit box" and also "a record of some notes" Truman had made while at Potsdam.[45]

Mrs. Ross, however, informed Ayers that "Charlie's instructions were that this [the "secret material"] was to be given only to the President . . . ,"[46] and before providing him with any of the papers, she checked with Truman. A letter to the president dated October 16, 1951, explains:

> Over the phone yesterday . . . Mr. Ayers asked [about] any notes he [Charlie Ross] may have had on the atomic bomb explosion. There is one envelope of notes marked "Private and Confidential", a typed copy of some personal notes of your own of the Potsdam trip you had loaned him. He had these typed from your own notes by his secretary . . . and—so the accompanying note says—returned the original to you. Part of it is in diary form.
>
> Also, as you may recall, I still have where he placed it in our safety deposit box, the story Charlie wrote—while it was fresh in his mind—of the decision to use the bomb.[47]

The 1951 letter provides evidence, first, of the existence of the president's journal concerning the Potsdam period; and, second, that there was apparently at least one typed copy of the journal—plus the original handwritten notes.

Far from wanting Mrs. Ross to give the journal notes to Ayers for use in his work—or, for that matter, asking her to return them to his files where they would be available for future historical research—the next day, October 17, 1951, Truman replied:

> I think you had better keep those private papers of Charlie's in the safety deposit vault because I am sure we have all the information that was contained in them.[48]

Nor did the president appear interested in the fact that Mrs. Ross had a copy of "the story Charlie wrote—while it was fresh in his mind—of the decision to use the bomb."[49] Quite the contrary, disregarding her explicit statement, Truman allows that although he has "had Eben Ayers collecting information on what took place with regard to the atomic bomb . . . I knew that Charlie had intended to assemble and write the history of what did take place. I suppose he [Charlie] never did get around to [writing] it."[50] Truman then told Ayers "to drop the matter as far as Mrs. Ross is concerned."[51]

Ayers may not have been aware that the president was directly blocking his access to documents in Mrs. Ross' safe deposit box. However, it became obvious to him that in general Truman was not giving him access to the complete file on the atomic bomb decision. In an oral history interview, Ayers later recalled:

> I think Charlie Ross had made some notes, which I believe are at the Library, but I don't believe they are available to anybody yet; and I never was able to get at any records the President had on the atomic bomb, although he said I could see anything I wanted to, but I couldn't get by Miss Conway on that. I don't know that I ever asked her specifically for anything on the atomic bomb because I knew I wouldn't get it out of her.[52]

That Ayers was right to doubt that the president was giving him access to everything he might need to write the account he had been asked to prepare—and, too, that the president had a copy of the critical materials in his own files—is also suggested by a memorandum to Truman dated nine months earlier, January 12, 1951, from Ross' former secretary, Myrtle Bergheim. This states:

> The attached envelope contains the President's handwritten notes, which were made at the time of the Potsdam meeting in 1945. I know that Mr. Ross borrowed these notes a long time ago and that it was his intention to return them to the President.[53]

Further reasons to doubt that the president simply forgot the existence of the critical Potsdam journal is suggested by materials connected with the preparation of *Mr. President*. Billed as "The first publication from the personal diaries, private letters, papers and revealing interviews of Harry S. Truman," *Mr. President* was unusual in that it involved a sitting president and drew heavily on his confidential files.[54] (Ayers' diary of March 6, 1952, notes that "the President indicated to me, he . . . believed it would be helpful in this campaign year."[55])

Mr. President repeats essentially the same arguments concerning the atomic bomb decision that the president offered elsewhere. The text quotes liberally from President Truman's personal journal in numerous places—a point of considerable significance at the time. "That a President of the United States while in office during an election year should allow a reporter to base a book upon his private diaries and letters," *The New York Times* observed, "is enough to make 'Mr. President' important as news."[56]

In his Foreword, Hillman explains that "the President made available to me all his diaries, his private papers and correspondence."[57] He goes on to state that "the reading of the complete diaries and personal notes reveals a man sure of his purpose . . ."[58]—and to stress that "the President himself had forgotten many of the hand-written memoranda which I found among his papers, turned over to me by his private secretary. Where they were used he requested that they not be changed nor edited in any way."[59]

Mr. President also ends with this personal declaration from Truman to Hillman:

> The White House, Washington
> October 1, 1951
>
> Dear Bill:
>   I have thought long and hard about making available to you my private notes and papers for publication. As you will judge from reading them, nearly all were intended to remain in my personal files. But I have concluded that for the historical record and a broader comprehension by the public of their thirty-second President and the Presidency I should release some of them to you for publication now. . . .
>   Within the bounds of the Nation's security, public interest, and good taste as the only restrictions I would impose, I hand you these private papers with every confidence. With this letter I also give you full authority to publish this material in any manner you deem suitable and useful.[60]

Hillman's private papers also show that the president personally read, approved, and initialed each section of *Mr. President* before it was published.[61] Given these assurances and this level of involvement it is worth noting three striking facts concerning the Potsdam journals as reported in *Mr. President*:

Mr. President quotes directly from Truman's journal during the voyage to Potsdam (July 7), during the voyage back from Potsdam (August 5), and, too, during the time of the Japanese surrender offer (August 10 and 11).[62] With one exception (which we shall explore below) there is a gap between July 17 and August 2, the time of the Potsdam conference and the critical atomic bomb decisions.

Some of the quotes are slightly doctored; in others, the treatment of important substantive issues is modified. For instance, the original August 10 diary reads:

> Ate lunch at my desk and discussed the Jap offer to surrender which came in a couple of hours earlier. They wanted to make a condition precedent to the surrender. Our terms are "unconditional." They wanted to keep the Emperor. We told 'em we'd tell 'em how to keep him, but we'd make the terms.[63]

This journal entry is changed in *Mr. President* to downplay Truman's implicit acceptance of the essential condition:

> Ate lunch at my desk and discussed the Japanese offer to surrender which came in a couple of hours earlier. They wanted to make a condition precedent to the surrender. Our terms were "unconditional." They wanted to keep the Emperor. We told them we would make the terms.[64]

In addition to minor but perhaps revealing editing of this kind, *Mr. President* contains one journal excerpt dated July 19, 1945:

> Stalin was a day late in arriving. It was reported that he was not feeling up to par. He called on me as soon as he arrived. It was about 11 A.M. He, Molotov, Vishinski and Pavlov stayed for lunch. We had a most pleasant conference and Stalin assured me that Russia intended to carry out the Yalta agreements and to enter the war against Japan in August. Mr. Churchill had arrived on time the day set for the conference. He had called on me as soon as he arrived in Berlin. . . .[65]

The entry is particularly intriguing because it seems to suggest that Hillman had the full Potsdam journal in hand as he was editing but that he chose to print only this one entry.

More puzzling still—at least at first blush—is the fact that the president's handwritten Potsdam journal "discovered" in 1979, contains only the following dates: July 16, 17, 18, 20, 25, 26, and 30.* Is the July 19 entry published in *Mr. President* a missing piece of the president's Potsdam journal? If so, this itself would be of considerable historical interest. It might also indicate that still more dates may possibly once have existed:

Neither *Mr. President* nor the presently available Potsdam journal includes

---

*Truman's journal also contains entries for August 5, 10, and 11.

other pages for July 21, 22, 23, and 24—indisputably some of the most important days at Potsdam when, as we have seen, the full report of the atomic test came in and so strongly impacted the attitude of the key figures involved and when the final decisions concerning the Potsdam Proclamation were made.

It was also during these four days that Byrnes instructed T. V. Soong to continue negotiations in Moscow in order to stall Russian entry; also at this time the final draft of the proclamation (without assurances for the Emperor) was sent to Chiang Kai-shek for formal approval before release. After writing in his journal for five consecutive days, did Truman stop keeping a written record during what were by far the most critical days of the conference?

Nor are there entries in either the available handwritten journal or in *Mr. President* for July 27, 28, and 29, the dates immediately following the issuance and "rejection" of the Potsdam Proclamation.

Margaret Truman's book on her father includes detailed passages that strongly suggest she or the writer assisting her is working directly from original documents which contain information no other author has seen. However, this may be based on oral or other information given to her privately by her father[66]; and we may never know whether the gap in the record is the result of a deliberate decision to suppress documents or simply of the president's having insufficient time to write in his journal.*

The direct evidence available concerning the July 19 entry points to another equally interesting possibility: Given that Truman did not wish to open even the known Potsdam journal papers for inspection—and given that this inevitably left a large hole in *Mr. President*'s account of a very important event—it may simply be that the president invented (or misdated) an entry for July 19 so as to have something with which to fill the gap.

It is impossible to know for sure what actually happened. However, the source of what became the July 19 entry can be traced following a paper trail which involves a similar difficulty in the work being done for the president by Ayers.[67] The fact is the July 19 journal entry printed in *Mr. President* is not taken from the Potsdam journal at all; it is lifted verbatim from a memorandum prepared by the president in the fall of 1951 to help Ayers fill out an account of the Potsdam Conference he was preparing at the president's request. On September 22, Ayers reported to Truman that he had

> nearly complete[d] a piece dealing with the Potsdam Conference which, although rather lengthy, seems to me lacking in one thing that should be

---

*As noted in Book I, Margaret Truman has failed to respond to inquiries on various questions from this writer and from other historians on numerous occasions.

a part of it, i.e., something of your own impressions of the other participants and of the conference itself. . . .

I have found no notes by you and I believe that the value of this
record, particularly for the future, would be greatly enhanced by the
inclusion of something, if only a few lines, of your impressions of
Stalin—and Churchill, too. . . . If you could find opportunity to jot
down some of your thoughts for this record I know it would be tremendously worth while.[68]

Ayers seems clearly to have asked privately not only for "impressions of
the other participants" but also, as he says, "of the conference itself"—and
Truman replied with a handwritten four-page "Note for Mr. Ayers" concerning Potsdam.[69] Apparently without Ayers' knowledge, the president also gave
the same memorandum to Hillman—and, in turn, the first two and a half
paragraphs were reprinted in *Mr. President* without change (or comment)
under the erroneous heading "Potsdam, July 19, 1945."

The simplest thing the president might have done to fill in the gaps in both
Mr. President and the Ayers account, of course, was to hand over the file
containing the known items in the Potsdam journal from July 17 to July 30.
That he did not simply forget these materials, but instead made a clear and
conscious decision to suppress them, is obvious: Hillman was working on
Mr. President in October 1951, and Truman, in fact, met with him on October 10. Had the president so wished, there would have been little difficulty
in providing materials both to Hillman and Ayers. (Ayers contacted Mrs.
Ross on October 15; she wrote Truman on October 16, asking whether he
wanted the journals and article in her husband's safe deposit box; Truman replied on October 17, asking her to keep them.)

It may even be that in preparing his "Note" for Ayers, and then giving this
to Hillman, the president actually had his private journal before him and
drew directly on it as he wrote. With regard to the Yalta understanding, for
instance, the actual July 17, 1945 entry reads: "Most of the big points
are settled," and then goes on to say "He'll be in the Jap War on August 15th."[70] The Ayers' memorandum and Hillman's "July 19" version
states: "We had a most pleasant conference and Stalin assured me that Russia
intended to carry out the Yalta agreements and to enter the war against Japan
in August."[71]

Additional evidence that the suppression of "difficult facts" related to the
central issue is not accidental but a matter of deliberate intent is also to be
found in *Mr. President*. The critical point addressed in Truman's July 17 private journal entry, of course, is his sense of the enormous likely impact of
the now confirmed Russian declaration of war. If Truman had allowed Hill-

man to publish a journal entry suggesting his own awareness that there were reasons to believe the war might end after the Russian attack—and well before an invasion—then, obviously, the basic rationale for using the atomic bomb would be called into question.[72]

Although the reader of *Mr. President* is assured that Truman requested that his papers "not be changed nor edited in any way"—and although he reviewed the publication personally page by page—the editing of a related letter written by Truman on August 9, 1945, also attests to a very specific concern. *Mr. President* presents the following Truman quote:

> I know that Japan is a terribly cruel nation in warfare but I can't bring myself to believe that, because they are cruel, we should ourselves act in the same manner. For myself, I certainly regret the necessity of wiping out whole populations because of the "pigheadedness" of the leaders of a nation and, for your information, I am not going to do it unless it becomes absolutely necessary. My object is to save as many American lives as possible but I also have a humane feeling for the women and children in Japan.[73]

This paragraph—in a book put forward as containing original material "not changed nor edited in any way"—actually condenses three paragraphs of a letter written by Truman (to Senator Richard Russell) into one. In the process, one sentence—and only one—has been eliminated:

> It is my opinion that after the Russians enter into [the] war the Japanese will very shortly fold up.[74]

Though it is impossible to tell for certain, the available evidence also suggests that the president may possibly have had his Potsdam journal in hand in the period 1953–55 when he was working on his memoirs. At one level, for instance, a careful reading of *Year of Decisions* suggests that certain passages seem to follow a word pattern similar to that of the journal. By way of illustration, Truman's actual journal for July 16 reads:

> We reviewed the Second Armoured [*sic*] Division. . . .
> Then we went on to Berlin and saw absolute ruin. Hitler's folly. He overreached himself in trying to take in too much territory. . . .
> We saw old men, old women, young women, children from tots to teens carrying packs, pushing carts, pulling carts, evidently ejected by the conquerors and carrying what they could of their belongings. . . .[75]

In comparison, a similar passage in *Year of Decisions* reads:

> About halfway to the city we found the entire American 2nd Armored Division. . . .

Our motorcade then drove to the center of Berlin. . . . I never saw such destruction. "That's what happens," I said, "when a man over-reaches himself."

. . . A more depressing sight than that of the ruined buildings was the long never-ending procession of old men, women, and children wandering aimlessly along the autobahn and the country roads carrying, pushing, or pulling what was left of their belongings.[76]

Since, with certain clear exceptions, language similar to the above is found in other published accounts, it is impossible to say to what extent the journal was the basis for this report.[77] However, in a (taped) interview on the subject of the writing process with the author, Truman's main assistant at the time—Francis Heller—confirmed that in general the journal was being used as the memoirs were being prepared:

I had the journal there and I had the letter file there, and obviously I used them and obviously [writing assistant Herbert Lee] Williams used them.[78]

Nor can there be any doubt that in general the president chose to keep such material from the public with a clear understanding of exactly what he was doing:

Francis Heller: I think that certainly there are instances, and I'm sure there are instances in the parts that I have worked on, in which we took Truman language out of essentially the materials that Bob [historian Robert Ferrell] pulled together, and essentially converted it into recollections rather than direct quotes. . . . I know that I did this on several occasions. In part, because at that stage of the game, for one reason or the other, the existence of a diary-type journal was being denied.
GA: Oh, it was? . . . I didn't know that.
FH: Truman was asked on several occasions whether he had kept a diary and he denied it.
GA: Around this period of time?
FH: Yes.[79]

Chapter 45

"THE MOST TERRIBLE BOMB,"
"THE MOST TERRIBLE THING"

When they think this is just another bomb, they are making a very serious mistake. . . . But this isn't just another weapon . . . not just another bomb. People make a mistake about that when they talk that way.
    —President Truman, as recorded by David E. Lilienthal,
                        February 14, 1949

We have seen how John J. McCloy explained his sense of what actually happened when the decision to use the atomic bomb was made: Truman "succumbed" to the "hard-liners," he told Clark Clifford, and for the rest of his life "stoutly took full responsibility" for the bomb's use.[1]

As one reflects upon the numerous documents which have come to light over the last five decades, the evidence suggests that in all probability Truman himself may have understood what McCloy was getting at.

If the decision to use the bomb had really been as simple and straightforward as the president often maintained, why not complete openness? Why not allow all the pages of his private journal to be examined? If there were nothing to hide—if the president were totally confident of his position—this would have been the normal and obvious course. The evidence would simply bear out and further document his story.

Another question concerns how the president dealt with the material in his journal. Did he simply ignore it? Did he rationalize it away? When the key passages were suppressed in *Mr. President* and during the writing of his memoirs, was he oblivious to what was going on?

Truman cannot have been unaware that information which raised severe doubts about his argument was being withheld from these semi-official accounts. What, then, could have been his state of mind when he made his subsequent public statements?

At another level the president was clearly informed of the U.S. Strategic Bombing Survey. How did he handle the conclusion of this official study?

Related to this is the question of whether Truman was briefed on the 1946 War Department study which concluded that the invasion of Japan had been only a "remote" possibility and that the war would almost certainly have ended when the Russians came in. And if he was briefed (or simply knew in general of the study, as seems plausible), how did he square this—personally and psychologically—with his repeated public statements that the bomb had been necessary to avoid the loss of thousands and perhaps even a million lives?

The lingering question here is how a man who knew what had actually happened felt about his public stance. Possibly McCloy's phrase—"stoutly took full responsibility"—also speaks directly to the president's private way of handling such difficult facts.

Truman's sensitivity to being asked probing questions about the decision also suggests some underlying uneasiness. Outbursts similar to his reply to Herbert Feis occur in various documents, diaries and letters.[2] The record is also replete with efforts by Truman to explain and justify himself—sometimes in extreme ways or by reference to notions of revenge, sometimes "out of the blue" without being asked. Three days after Hiroshima was bombed, the president received this telegram from Samuel McCrea Cavert, general secretary of the Federal Council of Churches:

> Many Christians deeply disturbed over use of atomic bombs against Japanese cities because of their necessarily indiscriminate destructive efforts [*sic*] and because their use sets extremely dangerous precedent for future of mankind. . . . Respectfully urge that ample opportunity be given Japan to reconsider ultimatum before any further devastation by atomic bomb is visited upon her people.[3]

Truman's irritated reply was blunt:

> Nobody is more disturbed over the use of Atomic bombs than I am but I was greatly disturbed over the unwarranted attack by the Japanese on Pearl Harbor and their murder of our prisoners of war. The only language they seem to understand is the one we have been using to bombard them.
>
> When you have to deal with a beast you have to treat him as a beast. It is most regrettable but nevertheless true.[4]

Similar explanations based on revenge also appear in other responses. In a December 1946 letter to Roman Bohnen (the actor who played the president in MGM's *The Beginning or the End*), Truman explained that he had "no qualms about it whatever"; the Japanese "in their conduct of the war had been vicious and cruel savages. . . ."[5] An (unsent) 1963 letter to Chicago *Sun Times* columnist Irv Kupcinet—drafted after reading a favorable column on his decision—states:

You must always remember that people forget, as you said in your column, that the bombing of Pearl Harbor was done while we were at peace with Japan and trying our best to negotiate a treaty with them.[6]

A related episode occurred in connection with the filming of a 1958 CBS "See It Now" television report. Here the president also said that he had "no qualms" in ordering the use of the atomic bomb against Japan—and added that "if the world gets into turmoil . . . it will be used [again]. You can be sure of that."[7] When his comments were reported in Japan, the Hiroshima City Council—writing on behalf of "The citizens of Hiroshima who have led their life in tribulation of more than two hundred thousand lives taken in sacrifice . . ."—sent a declaration which stated that

If . . . the statement made by Mr. Truman, former President of the United States, that he felt no compunction whatever after directing the atomic bombing of Hiroshima and Nagasaki, and that hydrogen bombs would be put to use in future in case of emergency be true, it is a gross defilement committed on the people of Hiroshima and their fallen victims.

We, the City Council, do hereby protest against it in deep indignation shared by our citizens and declare that in the name of humanity and peace we appeal to the wisdom of the United States and her citizens and to their inner voice for peace that said statement be retracted and that they fulfil their obligations for the cause of world peace.[8]

It was now almost thirteen years after the fact. Nevertheless, instead of simply ignoring the letter, Truman felt it somehow important to call a press conference at which he formally read a prepared reply to the assembled newspaper, radio, and television representatives[9]:

it becomes necessary for me to remind the City Council, and perhaps you also, of some historical events. . . .

After a long conference with the Cabinet, the military commanders and Prime Minister Churchill, it was decided to drop the atomic bomb on two Japanese cities devoted to war work for Japan. The two cities selected were Hiroshima and Nagasaki.

When Japan surrendered a few days after the bomb was ordered dropped, on August 6, 1945, the military estimated that at least a quarter of a million of the invasion forces against Japan and a quarter of a million Japanese had been spared complete destruction and that twice that many on each side would, otherwise, have been maimed for life.

As the executive who ordered the dropping of the bomb, I think the sacrifice of Hiroshima and Nagasaki was urgent and necessary for the prospective welfare of both Japan and the Allies.

The need for such a fateful decision, of course, never would have arisen, had we not been shot in the back by Japan at Pearl Harbor in December, 1941.

And in spite of that shot in the back, this country of ours, the United States of America, has been willing to help in every way the restoration of Japan as a great and prosperous nation.[10]

Truman succeeded in getting the press's attention. *The New York Times*, for instance, ran a front-page story under the headline: "Truman, in Letter to Hiroshima, Defends His Atom Bomb Order," and it reprinted Truman's entire reply.[11] Within a week, Tsukasa Nitoguri, Chairman of the Hiroshima City Council, sent back "A Protest against Mr. Truman's Reply to the Resolution passed by Hiroshima City Council":

Do you consider it a humane act to try to justify the outrageous murder of two hunred [*sic*] thousand civilians of Hiroshima, men and women, young and old, as a countermeasure for the surprise attack? . . .

At this very moment when I am appealing to you, someone may be dying somewhere in Japan, in Hiroshima, or on the bed in the hospital for the atomic bomb victims. How do you feel about it?[12]

(Truman's handwritten note across the top of this letter reads: "File it. No answer.")

Hiroshi Wakiyama, Speaker of the Nagasaki Municipal Assembly, also wrote to the former president:

We can understand how concerned you must have been, as the Supreme Commander of the United States of America, with the problem of bringing hostilities to an end as quickly as possible. We find it difficult to understand, however, your ultimate decision to use that genocidal weapon on innocent non-combatants wiping out in an instant hundreds of thousands of lives in the greatest tragedy in recorded history. . . .

. . . we deeply regret the war-crimes committed by our nation during the last World War, and today we rejoice that we have developed a friendly understanding toward Your Excellency and the American people. Nevertheless, we cannot remain silent in the face of your persistent attempt to justify the atomic raids.[13]

(Truman's note on this reads: "File with [Hiroshima] statement.")

Truman's press conference also brought this March 29, 1958, editorial comment from William F. Buckley's *National Review*:

> . . . the occasion calls for thoughtfulness, magnaminity [*sic*], and gallantry. . . .
>
> . . . [Yet there was] not one word of sympathy (we think of it as Lincoln might have written it) for the survivors of Hiroshima's dead; not one grave word of regret that Hiroshima's dead should have had to die; not one gentle turn of phrase that might suggest to the people of Hiroshima that the man who ordered the bombing suffered, perhaps even prayed, before making the decision, and carries within him a deep sense of its awfulness; and not one ray of recognition of the question that must be at the back of the minds of the people of Hiroshima, and that ought to haunt Harry Truman: "Was it *really* necessary? Might a mere demonstration of the bomb, followed by an ultimatum, have turned the trick?"
>
> If there is a satisfactory answer to that question, the people of Hiroshima *and* the people of the United States have a right to hear it.[14]

Whether the question "haunted" Harry Truman we do not know. However, there is a strong thread of ambivalence and even horror running through many of the president's references to the atomic bomb. Despite his lifelong defense of the Hiroshima attack, there also is evidence of discomfort and concern with the human implications of the decision.

On July 25, 1945—two weeks before the bombing—his journal records: "We have discovered the most terrible bomb in the history of the world. It may be the fire destruction prophesied in the Euphrates Valley Era. . . . It seems to be the most terrible thing ever discovered. . . ."[15]

Truman was shown pictures of the first bomb's effects on August 8. That he was only too aware of the weapon's meaning in human terms is evident from the Cabinet discussion which took place two days later (and one day after Nagasaki), when he declared there would be no more atomic bombing, that the idea of killing another 100,000 people was too horrible.[16]

The president returned to these themes repeatedly at various points throughout the remainder of his life. In handwritten notes for a December 15, 1945, speech, for instance, he put it this way:

> You know that the most terrible decision a man ever had to make was made by me at Potsdam. . . . It was a decision to loose the most terri-

ble of all destructive forces for the wholesale slaughter of human beings. . . . I couldn't help but think of the necessity of blotting out women, children and noncombatants.[17]

Describing a July 21, 1948, White House meeting to discuss the custody of atomic weapons, Lewis L. Strauss noted:

The President indicated that he was not going to have "some trigger-happy Colonel" using atomic bombs—that they were not weapons in the ordinary sense, but the liberation of a great natural force which killed women and children and old people indiscriminately.[18]

Six months later, in a private conversation recorded by Atomic Energy Commission chairman David E. Lilienthal on "what we were capable of doing in terms of wartime destruction, which I shan't write down here but which I shall never, never forget,"[19] Truman stressed:

When they think this is just another bomb, they are making a very serious mistake. . . . But this isn't just another weapon . . . not just another bomb. People make a mistake about that when they talk that way.

"The President said solemnly" (Lilienthal records), " 'Dave, we will never use it again if we can possibly help it.' "[20]

A few years later, during the Korean War, the following exchange occurred at a White House press conference:

Q. Mr. President, you said every weapon we have. Does that mean that there is [currently] active consideration of the use of the atomic bomb?
A. He said that there has always been active consideration of its use. He said that he does not want to see it used. He added that it is a terrible weapon and it should not be used on innocent men, women and children who have nothing to do with this military aggression—that happens when it is used.[21]*

Replying in early 1953 to a letter on his Farewell Address from Thomas E. Murray (a commissioner of the Atomic Energy Commission), Truman urged:

I rather think you have put a wrong construction on my approach to the use of the Atomic bomb. It is far worse than gas and biological warfare because it affects the civilian population and murders them by the wholesale.[22]

*Indirect quotation of the president was the standard rule for press conferences.

A year later in a memorandum apparently written for his personal file on the decision not to use atomic weapons in Korea, Truman privately reasoned,

> Now suppose, for speculative purposes, the C in C [Commander in Chief] had yielded to his locally minded and in most cases locally mis-informed field Generals. What would have happened[?] The Generals say that a few bombs on airfields in Manchuria would have caused a Korean victory to the Yalu.
>
> To have been effective Peking, Shanhai [*sic*], Canton, Mukden, Diarien [*sic*], Vladivostok and Central Siberia at Ulan-Ude on Lake Balkal [*sic*] would have had to be destroyed. It would have been a uni-lateral action by the U.S.A.
>
> . . . we would have wiped out those great Chinese cities and have killed some 25,000,000 innocent women, children and noncombatants.[23]

There is also this concerning atomic weapons during the Korean War from a background discussion for the memoirs with Hillman and Noyes:

> We had time for very serious thought, and I was always of the opinion that if they can carry atomic fission in uranium—the whole thing at one time was atomically fused—and continuing it all the time might create a reaction or fission that would turn the earth into a ball of fire, and that's what the Bible says will happen. There is that possibility; this is just opening the door. I thought about it all the time.[24]

In late 1961 filmmaker Robert Arthur (who calls himself "the participant" in the following recollection) discussed various movie ideas with Truman—and also asked him to go to Hiroshima to make a film:

> When I went into my outline of the Korean film, he stared at me, un-blinking, his face, deeply lined, set in Rushmore-like granite, and all at once the participant realized whom he was conning, what this man was and what he had been, and the words sounded trivial, the idea infantile. But when I finished, Mr. Truman nodded sharply once, saying, "All right, sounds pretty good," and I knew Noyes and Hillman had already briefed him and gotten his approval.
>
> "Just one thing," Mr. Truman warned, "don't try to make a play-actor out of me."
>
> Swearing this was the last intention possible, the participant needed only to flee, but Hillman held me back. "Tell the President your idea for the atom-bomb film," he said.
>
> Mr. Truman looked at me with quick suspicion; this was something

he hadn't been told. No way out for me; I explained my desire to film the basic framework for the hour in Hiroshima.

It was the only time I ever saw him blink. He was silent for a moment as Noyes studied the rug pattern and Hillman shuffled some papers, and then he said something surprising to me, if not to Noyes and Hillman.

"I'll go to Japan if that's what you want," he said. "But I won't kiss their ass."[25]

Truman enjoyed a lifelong love affair with Bess Wallace, the woman from a "better" family he wooed and finally wed. It may therefore also be of interest to note that Margaret Truman recalls John Snyder's report that although her mother "accepted the explanation" that the bomb was needed to save lives "without comment," she was "deeply disturbed" by the new weapon.[26]*

We will never know what personal doubts the president may have experienced in the quiet of his own heart. Two final observations, however, suggest a strange—even moving—sense of the burden he may have carried as he "stoutly took full responsibility" for his decision. The first is a report of the experience of a former Cabinet member and U.S. ambassador to Poland, John A. Gronouski—an experience which "made such an impression on me."[27]

In 1964 Gronouski had to come to Independence, Missouri, to speak at a campaign fundraising dinner for a local member of Congress:

After the afternoon tour of the Library I dropped him [Truman] off at his home and agreed to pick him up in time to have a couple of drinks at the Country Club bar. . . .

We stood at the bar and Mr. Truman ordered us each a double shot of Southern Comfort neat. (Not my favorite drink, but when drinking with ex-Presidents you do as...............!) After ordering each of us another of same he began about a ten minute monologue on his decision to drop the first atomic bomb on Hiroshima. He did not ask me whether he did the right thing—he simply was explaining to me and me alone his rationale for deciding to drop the bomb. He did not address the question of the second bomb—I interpreted his explanation as his justification for dropping both bombs.

His reasoning was that with which we are all familiar: he talked about the heavy loss of American (and Japanese) lives that resulted from the storming of the Japanese held Pacific Islands. He added that on the basis of his best information an invasion of Japan could have cost as many as one million American lives and casualties and an untold number of

*Snyder was director of the Office of War Mobilization and Reconversion.

Japanese lives. He said that he regretted the loss of lives at Hiroshima (and Nagasaki, I presumed) but pointed out that the Japanese would have had many more dead and wounded resisting an American invasion and again referred to the saving of American lives. He noted that the best intelligence available to him was of the strong opinion that Japanese morale was high and that dropping a bomb off the coast rather than in a populated area would not have induced the Japanese to surrender. As I say, he went on in this vein for about ten minutes. At no time did he seem defensive nor did he solicit my opinion as to the merits of his decision.

"What fascinated me," Gronouski emphasized, ". . . is the fact that he out of the blue brought up the subject in conversation with an almost total stranger (I had been one of dozens who shook hands with him on a previous occasion several years earlier, but otherwise I had no previous contact with him)."

At the time and when I thought about it later I was struck by the fact that this man, who had a reputation of putting out of mind the consequences of tough decisions once he had made them, would spend ten minutes explaining his actions to a virtual stranger almost twenty years after the event. I surmised that he had been troubled by criticism of his decision all of those years and surmised that the exercise he went through with me was probably one of countless times he had done the same thing with others. However, he gave no indication that he regretted his decision; only that he felt it necessary to point out to me the reasons why, in his mind, it was the right decision.[28]

Finally, there is this "oral history" recollection by former Attorney General and Supreme Court Justice Tom Clark of a visit with Truman as he neared the end of his life:

. . . I talked with him about four or five months before he died. I had to be over in Kansas City and he was in the hospital. I think I called up after I got there—I went out to the University of Missouri—and I went over to the hospital. The doctor said I could stay about five minutes, but the President wouldn't let me go and I stayed there about forty-five minutes, and we got . . .
[Interviewer]: What did he talk about?
Oh, we got to talking about various things, all the way from playing poker to the atomic bomb. He sat in a chair, and I didn't notice any weakness at all, and his mind was just like a steel trap, and he was very forceful and he didn't pull any punches. Typical Truman appearance. He defended his dropping the bomb. . . .[29]

PART III

James F. Byrnes

There was nothing left to do but use the bomb. . . .
—James F. Byrnes, 1947

Chapter 46

DISAPPEARING FROM—
AND REVISING—HISTORY

---

*. . . it is very disquieting to see the Secretary of State trying
to play both ends against the middle.*
——*Commonweal*, September 14, 1945

Although modern historians agree that James F. Byrnes was at the heart of
the decision process, he and his central role were simply not much discussed
in most early postwar accounts. Even observers who sensed that diplomatic
factors were involved somehow lost sight of the man in charge of U.S. diplomacy. The 1946 *Saturday Review of Literature* article by Norman Cousins
and Thomas K. Finletter which asked: "Can it be that we were more anxious
to prevent Russia from establishing a claim for full participation in the occupation against Japan . . . ?" did not even mention Byrnes.[1]

Stimson's 1947 *Harper's* essay did cite Byrnes—but only to list him as
Truman's representative on the Interim Committee.[2] MGM's film *The Beginning or the End* did not include a Byrnes character.[3] Nor did Ellis M. Zacharias name names in a 1950 *Look* magazine article in which he declared that
"the A-bombing of Japan is now known to have been a mistake" (adding, as
we have noted: "The Potsdam Declaration . . . wrecked everything we had
been working for to prevent further bloodshed and insure our postwar strategic aims").[4] P.M.S. Blackett's 1948 argument that the Hiroshima decision
marked the earliest point of the Cold War similarly offered no suggestion that
Byrnes was in any way responsible for U.S. strategy.[5]

In *Great Mistakes of the War* (1950) Hanson W. Baldwin wrote: "Not only
was the Potsdam ultimatum merely a restatement of the politically impossible—unconditional surrender—but it could hardly be construed as a direct
warning of the atomic bomb and was not taken as such by anyone who did

not know the bomb had been created."[6] However, Baldwin also did not associate the secretary of state with the key decisions which produced this result.

I have mentioned a book I wrote as a Cambridge University doctoral dissertation more than thirty years ago. I would not ordinarily cite my own early
work; however, in keeping with the general form of this study I believe it is
valid to note (without attempting to assess degrees of emphasis) that, as the
most recent scholarly literature review judged, after the publication of *Atomic
Diplomacy* "a broad consensus viewed diplomatic considerations as an important part of the administration's view of the bomb's value."[7] Earlier
studies by Blackett, William Appleman Williams, and Louis Morton had anticipated my own and subsequent findings.[8] The essential point, however, is
that with the recognition that diplomatic issues were involved also came a
new view that Byrnes was important: J. Robert Oppenheimer, for instance,
wrote me that much of what I had written in *Atomic Diplomacy* had "been
largely unknown to me . . ." —and then went on to observe: "but I do recognize your Byrnes, and I do recognize your Stimson."[9]

How did Byrnes—in many ways the central figure in the Hiroshima
story—keep himself out of the picture for so long? How was he able to avoid
both scholarly and public attention?

How was it possible for the views he represented to disappear for virtually
the entire postwar era in which most Americans consolidated their understanding of the Hiroshima bombing?

And what was Byrnes' own role in helping create the Hiroshima myth?

Byrnes was able to disappear from the atomic bomb story for a long while
for several reasons:

The first is that he simply was out of office after January 1947. Following
a rather unpleasant break with Truman, Byrnes left the spotlight of the national press corps. He moved back to Spartanburg, South Carolina (keeping
his Washington apartment until the summer of 1948 in order to return to the
city to represent legal clients).[10] Meanwhile, the new secretary of state,
George Marshall, took center stage as the major events of the Cold War unfolded after 1947.

Byrnes initially threw himself into writing a book on his period as secretary of state. (But, as Walter Brown was to note, "it was obvious . . . he was
unhappy out of the limelight."[11] Although often invited to speak, he rarely
accepted.)[12] When he again turned his attention to politics, in the main it was
not at the national level. Instead, he moved aggressively to rebuild his Southern political base. Fellow South Carolinian Strom Thurmond's 1948 Dixie-
crat break with Truman's Democratic party stirred powerful new forces, and
in 1950 Byrnes ran successfully for governor of South Carolina on a segre-
gationist, anti–civil rights platform.[13] Biographer David Robertson observes

that "Byrnes intended by winning the governorship of South Carolina in 1950 to become that southern leader who, like John C. Calhoun, could direct his region as a bloc to exercise a political veto over the policies of [Truman's] Fair Deal."[14]

A second reason the national public lost sight of Byrnes was the extraordinary success of Stimson's *Harper's* article. His departure from the Washington political scene occurred just weeks before Stimson's account of the atomic bomb decision captured national attention. Quite apart from the fact of its triumph in the nation's media, the essay inevitably focused attention on Stimson—not Byrnes—even though the realities of influence were quite the reverse. As we have seen, Stimson and Bundy also took great pains to eliminate references to Byrnes' "atomic diplomacy" attitude from Stimson's memoirs after Kennan and Marshall objected.

A third reason for Byrnes' absence from the drama is that there was very little information available to document his activities. This is true in general—and especially in connection with some of the most controversial issues connected with the atomic bomb and diplomacy towards the Soviet Union. Byrnes did not become secretary of state until July 3—and, as we have seen, most of his informal work for the president in the preceding months produced very little in the way of official documents.

Fragments of information on truly important points, moreover, appeared only intermittently: Leo Szilard's report that Byrnes did not argue the bomb was needed to end the war but rather that he wanted it to "make Russia more manageable" was published only in 1949.[15] The first real evidence that Byrnes tried to end the Pacific War before the Russians got in came with the 1951 publication of the Forrestal diary.[16]

The opening of the Stimson diary occurred only in 1959. Especially significant in connection with Byrnes was evidence the diary revealed concerning the pre-Hiroshima period—and the decisions not to provide a reasonable period between the Potsdam Proclamation and the bombings for Japan to consider the matter and to eliminate the recommended assurances for the Emperor from the proclamation. The diary also confirmed that Stimson had virtually no influence at this point—and that Byrnes was dominant.

The year after the Stimson diary was opened the State Department published its official documentary record of the Potsdam conference. This provided much more detail on the proclamation, the views of the Combined Chiefs of Staff, and many other matters. More fragments of information on Byrnes' own role were added when portions of the papers of Ambassador Joseph Davies were opened in the mid-1960s—and especially (in stages)—as the diary of Byrnes' assistant Walter Brown began to appear.

The most important reason why so little was known about Byrnes' role for so long a period of time, however, is that Byrnes seems clearly to have wanted it that way. Besides his general penchant for extreme secrecy, there is ample evidence that Byrnes was more than willing to bend the truth in connection with his own 1945 role when he felt it useful to do so. We have noted his rewriting of Walter Brown's diary. Another specific instance concerns his treatment of the Yalta agreement on the Far East:

At various points after World War II Byrnes simply denied that he knew of the Yalta agreement—a denial which most authorities regard as a blatant lie. In fact, as George M. Elsey—Truman's naval aide and a Map Room officer at Potsdam—has recently noted:

> Byrnes had the full text of the agreement by which Stalin, in return for territorial concessions in China and Japan, pledged to enter the war against Japan within ninety days after the German surrender, as well as all other Yalta texts, in his Shoreham Hotel apartment well before he became secretary. I know, because I provided them to him in a typed, loose-leaf briefing book, a copy of which I still have.[17]

Herbert Feis was one of the first to note that a July 4, 1945, cable from Byrnes to Harriman also reveals his clear awareness of the agreement[18]—and Athan Theoharis (who has traced Byrnes' various postwar statements) observes:

> To preserve his reputation and relations with Congress, Byrnes dissembled in January 1946. (His memory would suffer drastically with the passing years. By 1958, Byrnes would assert that he learned of the Far Eastern agreements only on February 10, 1946.) . . . In December 1945 Byrnes knew of the Yalta Far Eastern agreements but deliberately feigned ignorance.[19]

The various written accounts Byrnes produced after the war also commonly avoided the most important issues in connection with critical aspects of the story as we now know it. For instance, in his book concerning his time in office, *Speaking Frankly* (1947), Byrnes both kept back important information and affirmed all the now-familiar elements of the official rationale:

• *On MAGIC and Japanese Attempts to End the War.* Byrnes does not tell the reader that he and Truman had been reading intercepted Japanese cables during the summer of 1945. He reports that "Stalin told the President and me that the Japanese Ambassador in Moscow had asked whether the Soviet Union would agree to act as a mediator to bring about the settlement of the war."[20] The reader is allowed to believe that it was only from Stalin—and only after the U.S. delegation had arrived at Potsdam—that American leaders learned anything of the Emperor's intentions and of Japan's desire to end the war.

• *On the Emperor and Unconditional Surrender.* Byrnes describes the debate over assurances for the Emperor in extremely general terms which typically confuse both the issue and his own role. He states that:

> Immediately upon becoming Secretary of State, I learned about the differences of opinion in the State Department as to whether, at the time of surrender, we should insist on the removal of the Emperor. Before we left for Potsdam, I was presented with memoranda setting forth the varying views. These went into a brief case bulging with the problems of war and peace in the Pacific.[21]

He also reports very generally that:

> Secretary of War Stimson, on July 2, had submitted to the President a wise memorandum setting forth a proposed message to Japan. Using this memorandum as a basis, the President prepared a draft of a declaration to be issued jointly by the United States, the United Kingdom and China. The President and I spent some time on it. Then Prime Minister Churchill made some suggestions which were adopted. The declaration to which Mr. Churchill agreed followed the general lines of Secretary Stimson's proposal except that it did not contain a reference to the future status of the Emperor. The proposed declaration then was sent to Chiang Kai-shek for his approval.[22]

What Byrnes does not report is the unanimity of opinion (except for himself) that assurances for the Emperor were essential—and the fact that he alone had been responsible for recommending the removal of such assurances from the Potsdam Proclamation—and that this all but guaranteed the bombing would go forward. Byrnes also implies that after the bombs were used the Japanese finally accepted the demand for "unconditional surrender," downplaying the fact that they did so only after the requisite assurances for the Emperor were implicitly given by the United States.[23]

• *On the Expected Impact of a Russian Declaration of War.* Byrnes deftly sidesteps all the critical issues regarding Russian entry. He does not say that he actively sought an early Soviet declaration of war until he learned of the successful atomic test. Nor does he report anything of the expected shock value of the attack. He also fails to tell of his effort to stall the Red Army assault via the Soong negotiations once the test succeeded. He does say, however, that "I would have been satisfied had the Russians determined not to enter the war."

> Notwithstanding Japan's persistent refusal to surrender unconditionally, I believed the atomic bomb would be successful and would force the Japanese to accept surrender on our terms.[24]

• *On the Interim Committee's Role.* Byrnes greatly exaggerates the influence of the Interim Committee in *Speaking Frankly*, and his summary of its central recommendation regarding the bomb's use is misleading. He states that the Interim Committee recommended to the President that the bomb be used against Japan without warning, adding "that the bomb should be used only where war plants or military installations were located"[25]—a report which passes over the May 31–June 1 recommendation specifying the targeting of "a vital war plant employing a large number of workers and closely surrounded by workers' houses."[26] Also, as we have seen, in the end the actual targeting did not center on industrial installations. Byrnes also downplays his own role and influence, stating simply: "As the President's representative on the committee, it was my duty to report to him the reasons for our various recommendations."[27]

• *On the Related Issue of the General Rationale for the Bombing.* Having alluded in the most cursory—indeed, misleading—fashion to the debate within the U.S. government on the importance of clarifying the unconditional surrender formula, and having failed to discuss the intelligence and other advice concerning the expected impact of a Russian declaration of war (either alone, or combined with assurances for the Emperor following the "two-step logic")—Byrnes goes on to describe the report he gave to the president on the Interim Committee's work in these terms:

> Throughout our deliberations, I told him, we relied on the estimates of the military situation presented by the Joint Chiefs of Staff. Their plans called for an invasion of Kyushu, the southernmost island of the Japanese homeland, on November 1. This was to be followed by an invasion of the main island on Honshu in the spring of 1946. The Joint Chiefs anticipated that more than five million of our armed forces would be engaged. The Japanese armies were then estimated at about five million—an estimate we later found was quite accurate.[28]

He then states that:

> The military experts informed us that, from the facts at their disposal, they believed our invasion would cost us a million casualties, to say nothing of those of our Allies and of the enemy.[29]

Little evidence has ever been found that the Interim Committee reviewed the military's plans or casualty estimates in any serious way—and, of course, as we have seen, there is no documentary basis for the one-million figure in any event. Byrnes' statement that the Interim Committee's recommendation was based on this seems to be a pure invention.

Byrnes writes that he "reported these conclusions to the President. I also told him what the scientists, engineers and industrialists, who had come before the committee, had to say"[30]—and then states that Truman decided to use the bomb after considering the Interim Committee's recommendations: "He expressed the opinion that, regrettable as it might be, so far as he could see, the only reasonable conclusion was to use the bomb."[31]

In all of this the fact that the Interim Committee's main decisions were made on May 31 and June 1—and that many important developments occurred in the months before Hiroshima was bombed—is also sidestepped. Few would likely have caught the fact that the invasion which might possibly have cost major casualties could not have taken place before the spring of 1946, and that when the Interim Committee met there were still five months left before even a November landing might possibly occur on Kyushu.

In 1958 Byrnes published *All in One Lifetime*, an autobiographical book which covered both his period as secretary of state and other facets of his long career. Although the standard account is essentially presented here as well, a few new points are acknowledged. For the first time Byrnes states that government officials were reading Japanese intercepts at the time. In one reference to MAGIC he writes that

> as late as July 21 the Japanese militarists caused their government to wire the Ambassador [Sato], "We cannot consent to unconditional surrender under any circumstances. Even if the war drags on, so long as the enemy demands unconditional surrender we will fight as one man against the enemy in accordance with the Emperor's command."[32]

Although Byrnes avoids discussing the specific issue of assurances for the Emperor, he also indirectly indicates his full awareness that "unconditional surrender" was the critical question. He says that because of the importance attached to this matter, the

> cable, which we intercepted, depressed me terribly. It meant using the atomic bomb; it probably meant Russia's entry into the war.[33]

In another reference to MAGIC, Byrnes now says that two days after the Potsdam Proclamation was issued—nine days before Hiroshima was bombed—"Secretary Forrestal arrived and told me in detail of the intercepted messages from the Japanese government to Ambassador Sato in Moscow, indicating Japan's willingness to surrender."[34]

In the end, *All in One Lifetime* is somewhat equivocal and evasive in regard to Byrnes' own position on the surrender terms. He concedes that he understood that the rigid terms were the main obstacle to peace, but he also claims he saw no alternative. The book all but ignores the fact that he and Truman removed assurances from the proclamation and that Stimson's diary also indicates that neither felt strongly or was "obdurate" about the issue.[35]

Only a passing vague phrase—"I finished drafting the warning"[36]—hints at Byrnes' own central role. On the other hand, a careful reading of the text clearly shows Byrnes implicitly acknowledging that he changed his position on the Emperor after the atomic bombings and Russian entry.[37]

All in One Lifetime also does not report any information on the expected shock impact of the Soviet attack. It does not acknowledge Byrnes' own initial desire to have the Russians enter the war.* Instead, the matter is approached indirectly—with the added implication that Byrnes was in a position to understand the issue more fully than Roosevelt and Churchill had been at Yalta:

> When I read the signed [Yalta Far Eastern] agreement, I was troubled by the specific pledge given by the United States and the United Kingdom that "these claims of the Soviet Union shall be unquestionably fulfilled after Japan has been defeated." The record shows that Roosevelt and Churchill acted because their military advisers told them the invasion of Japan planned for the following fall would result in a million casualties.† Their decision was made early in February when the German army was still fighting, but in the six months that followed our enemies surrendered in Europe and in the Pacific. Today many will say that Churchill and Roosevelt should have had the foresight to anticipate these events and should have refused to woo the Soviets. This is not written in their defense, but we must remember that hindsight has some advantage over foresight.[38]

Perhaps not surprisingly—since it was published at the height of the Cold War—*All in One Lifetime* reveals more of Byrnes' hard-line attitude toward the Soviet Union. He now states that the July 23 cable to Chiang Kai-shek which he drafted for Truman in connection with the Soong negotiations was sent

> to encourage the Chinese to continue negotiations after the adjournment of the Potsdam Conference. I had some fear that if they did not, Stalin might immediately enter the war. . . .[39]

As to likely casualties, Byrnes claims that his own support for the Interim Committee's unanimous‡ June 1 recommendation was based on a specific assessment of alternatives:

---

*Byrnes does allow that *Truman* may have felt this way. Noting that Forrestal reported Eisenhower as saying Truman told him "his principal objective at Potsdam would be to get Russia in the war," Byrnes states: "I told him it was most probable that the President's views had changed; certainly that was not now my view." (Byrnes, *All in One Lifetime*, p. 297.)
†This estimate is again stated as fact without further documentation.
‡ Byrnes neglects to mention Bard's subsequent dissent. (Byrnes, *All in One Lifetime*, p. 285.)

. . . the imperial armies remained intact, and were estimated by our General Staff to number over five million effective troops. At least that number of United States soldiers, sailors, and airmen would be involved in the attack on the Japanese homeland, and a fifth of these, it was thought, would be casualties.[40]

In connection with both *Speaking Frankly* and *All in One Lifetime*, it can be demonstrated that Byrnes and his assistants* had certain key documents before them—and that they did not choose to cite (or wished to suppress) important evidence. Most significant were some of the highly revealing passages of the Brown diary we have previously noted.[41]

In less formal postwar statements Byrnes also commonly repeated the familiar elements of the traditional rationale with only a few noteworthy variations. He granted two major interviews during the 1960s—one to *U.S. News and World Report* and another to television journalists Fred Freed and Len Giovannitti for an NBC "White Paper" on the atomic bomb decision. In the first Byrnes was asked specifically:

Q. Before drawing up the Potsdam Declaration, there were some suggestions that the Japanese be given assurance that the Emperor would be retained. Why did the Potsdam Declaration omit this proposal regarding the Emperor?

In this instance Byrnes simply denied this was so:

A. The draft given to me by the President, and which I now have, does not contain any such assurance. It did not refer specifically to the status of the Emperor. I know that in the State Department there was some division of sentiment among officials as to whether there should be specific mention of the status of the Emperor, but in the draft which Secretary of War Henry Stimson first gave to the President, and he gave to me, there is no statement.

U.S. News pressed Byrnes further:

Q. Do you recall any discussions at Potsdam with President Truman and/or Mr. Stimson on the question of whether the proclamation to Japan should include a categorical undertaking that unconditional surrender would not mean the elimination of the dynasty, if the Japanese people desired its retention?

Here again—although the record is clear both that Stimson raised the issue directly with him and the president, and that Stimson's draft contained such assurances—Byrnes replied:

*Porter McKeever assisted with *Speaking Frankly*; George Curry with *All in One Lifetime*.

A. Mr. Stimson did not talk to me at any time about the Emperor, and the first draft of the Declaration which was given to me by the President—and which had been given to him by Mr. Stimson—has no reference to what should be the future status of the Emperor.

U.S. News then asked how Truman's other top advisers viewed the decision to omit assurances from the Potsdam Proclamation:

Q. Was there full concurrence in the decision by President Truman's top advisers, including Mr. Stimson?
A. It was my understanding President Truman did not discuss the Declaration with anyone other than Mr. Churchill, General Marshall, Admiral Leahy [military adviser to the President],* Stimson and me. If Stimson did not approve, the President did not so advise me.

The evidence we have is that each person cited favored clarifying the terms—and so advised the President. Moreover, the statement concerning Stimson's view ignores the July 2 memorandum—and Stimson's draft proclamation—which Byrnes himself had noted in *Speaking Frankly* included assurances for the Emperor. That Truman did not tell him of Stimson's position is doubtful and—in light of Byrnes' own discussions with Stimson—quite beside the point.

The *U.S. News* interviewer did not let up on the subject of assurances:

Q. In retrospect, might it have been possible to avoid using the atom bomb by offering Japan a chance to keep the Emperor, as Joseph Grew [U.S. Ambassador to Japan before World War II] has stated?†
A. That's dealing in the realm of speculation. Later, on August 11, in drafting the message to Japan replying to their surrender message, I wrote that Japan would have the right to determine the form of government under which its people wished to live. It was approved by the President and by Stimson.

U.S. News also pressed Byrnes on the final resolution of the issue:

Q. But in our final acceptance of their offer of surrender, didn't we agree to retain the institution of the Emperor? Wasn't that a change from the Potsdam Declaration?
A. No. When the Japanese Government submitted its agreement to surrender, provided the surrender did not envisage the insistence upon the

*Bracketed phrase in the original.
†Bracketed phrase in the original.

removal of the Emperor, we replied that "from the moment of surrender the authority of the Emperor and the Japanese Government to rule the state shall be subject to the Supreme Commander of the Allied Powers who will take such steps as he deems proper to effectuate the surrender terms."

Q. Did this represent any change of view on our part?

A. No, it did not. It was a requirement that the Emperor, as head of the Japanese Government, should agree to the terms of surrender. Then we added that it was for the people of Japan to determine the form of government under which they would live.

Byrnes was now almost boastful about another aspect of his strategy:

Q. Did we want to drop the bomb as soon as possible in order to finish the war before Russia got in?

A. Of course, we were anxious to get the war over as soon as possible.

Q. Was there a feeling of urgency to end the war in the Pacific before the Russians became too deeply involved?

A. There certainly was on my part, and I'm sure what, whatever views President Truman may have had of it earlier in the year, that in the days immediately preceding the dropping of that bomb his views were the same as mine—we wanted to get through with the Japanese phase of the war before the Russians came in.[42]

Given what we now know of Byrnes' view of the atomic bomb's relationship to diplomacy, one other comment made in this interview may possibly shed additional light on his motives. Asked: "Did our use of the atom bomb weaken our standing in world opinion?" Byrnes replied:

When we speak of "world opinion," of course that covers a lot of territory. Certainly it did not affect our prestige with the free nations of the world that are today our Allies. I don't think that it has affected our prestige with the neutrals. And certainly, so far as the Soviet Union is concerned, they respect only power.[43]

In his interview with *U.S. News* Byrnes also repeated the claim that we "were told by the military advisers that we should anticipate a million casualties . . ."[44] An innovation here, however, is his suggestion that this would occur "when we invaded the mainland in the fall."[45] (As we have seen only a preliminary landing on Kyushu would have occurred in 1945; an assault on the main Japanese island might have begun only in the spring of 1946.)

Byrnes' subsequent interview with NBC involved an unusual—and even more revealing—mixture of candor and dissembling. Asked by Fred Freed about the Emperor, Byrnes now replied:

> There were a number of people [in the State Department], splendid officials, who . . . [were] . . . demanding unconditional surrender, we should insist that the Emperor be ousted. I didn't agree with them. . . . As a matter of fact, the Japanese presented an unusual problem in that respect because with them their devotion to the Emperor was a part of their religious . . . they would have fought to the death for the Emperor.[46]

Later in the interview Byrnes added:

> We knew that the Japanese Army was scattered around on islands in the Pacific and if we attempted to enforce peace [without the Emperor], that these Japanese soldiers all around the Pacific, we'd have had a terrible time. We'd have lost a lot of men. But the emperor could accomplish a lot in bringing about the prompt surrender and again I say that's what we were after.[47]

Freed also asked Byrnes about the relationship of the Potsdam Proclamation to the use of the bomb—and, specifically, about the matter of timing:

> There is another point which I would like to ask you about which there has sometimes been some confusion and that is the order to go ahead with the preparation to drop the bomb on Hiroshima and the Potsdam Declaration went out almost simultaneously. In a sense it almost seems as if you had a very strong feeling the Japanese would not surrender.[48]

Byrnes' response was odd—especially in view of the argument he made to Freed that the Japanese "would have fought to the death" in the absence of assurances for the Emperor (which the Proclamation, of course, lacked):

> Well, I do not know that to be the fact. . . . I do not know that I did not have any hope that they would hearken to our warning.[49]

Freed attempted to clarify the point about timing:

> Well, I was simply talking in terms of the time being so short . . . from the time of the Potsdam Declaration there was only little more than a week when the first bomb was dropped.[50]

To which Byrnes replied:

> Yes, but really that . . . I do not know that it was more than a coincidence. We were fighting for the development of the use of the bomb at

the earliest possible date, embarking on an entirely new field. That was an uncertain date and when on the other hand we reached full agreement as to the declaration, it was simply a coincidence.[51]

Byrnes also repeated the claim—in connection with the casualties issue—that "it was General Marshall's opinion, based upon the knowledge of the terrain and of the Japanese in the spirit of suicide that they had shown in their air attacks, their willingness to make suicidal attacks—that we would suffer a million casualties."[52]

Finally, he again asserted that this was the basis of the Interim Committee's resolution:

> It was the consensus . . . that with the terrific losses that we had that we could not justify risking the loss of a million men when we had the means or we thought we had the means to bring about an immediate ending of the war.[53]

(He also again stated that only when the committee "had exhausted all the alternative plans that had been suggested, the committee voted unanimously that the bomb should be dropped. . . ."[54])

In connection with the Russians Freed asked: "Did it also seem, Governor, that there seemed an additional possible advantage in the fact that you might be able to end the war before the Russians became . . . deeply involved?"[55]—and Byrnes replied:

> Oh, it was ever present in my mind. I cannot speak for the others but it was ever present in my mind that it was important that we should have an end to the war before the Russians came in.[56]

Later in the interview Byrnes observed that "neither the President nor I were anxious to have them enter the war after we had learned of this successful test. . . ."[57] He also openly discussed the use of the Soong negotiations to hold off a Red Army attack: "It was my thought that the Chinese would see that we were not bringing any pressure to bear on them and that they might stall a little more and if they did this bomb might be tested, prove to be successful, bring about the end of the war and save a lot of trouble."[58]

When Freed asked: "Was there any advantage to knowing about the bomb in dealing with the Russians at Potsdam?" Byrnes replied: "Yes, it was. It undoubtedly gave to us a greater confidence than we otherwise would have had."[59] However, he denied there was any link between the timing of the July 16 test and the July 17 opening of the Potsdam conference; it was again, only a "coincidence."[60]

* * *

As we have seen, one of the most important sources of contemporaneous information on Byrnes' personal activities is the diary of his friend and assistant Walter Brown. Considering the significance of this document, it is important to note that we still do not have full information on its contents. In point of fact, only twenty-nine pages of actual text covering 1945 have been opened for inspection by researchers.

Two fragments of the diary for the period—on file at the Strom Thurmond Institute at Clemson University—comprise twenty-seven pages. However, the fragments—one of fourteen and the other of thirteen pages—differ only very slightly concerning the period of interest.[61] (Close textual analysis by David J. Williams, moreover, reveals that one contains information for some dates, such as the results of the British election, which can only have been added after the fact.[62])

A third fragment—only two pages—is the one Byrnes passed on to the State Department after editing out key segments.[63] A fourth fragment consists of an interview done in 1972 by Robert Messer in which Walter Brown read certain passages of the original diary text into a tape recorder.[64] What may be termed a fifth version of the diary is Brown's friendly and protective 1992 book based generally upon the original text, *James F. Byrnes of South Carolina: A Remembrance.*

Brown has refused all requests that the full original diary be opened for scholarly inspection and research;[65] a comparison of the fragments we have with the published version indicates discrepancies which can only be resolved when the actual diary is made public.[66]

An important exception—or possible slip in Byrnes' reporting—must also be noted. Very early on (three weeks after the bombing, on August 29, 1945)—long before any serious controversy arose—Byrnes answered questions in a revealing manner at a partly off-the-record press conference. His emphasis was reflected in a front-page *New York Times* headline the next day which read: "Japan Beaten Before Atom Bomb, Byrnes Says, Citing Peace Bids."[67] The article reported that the secretary of state "cited what he called Russian proof that the Japanese knew they were beaten before the first atomic bomb was dropped on Hiroshima."[68]

The report also went on to state that "the Berlin declaration for unconditional surrender put an end" to the Japanese proposal that "Prince Fujimaro Konoye head a delegation to seek Russia's mediation."[69] Byrnes' reported formulation concerning the bomb's significance was somewhat oblique: "To the extent that the bomb had facilitated the surrender, he said, it saved the lives of hundreds of thousands of American soldiers. . . ."[70]

The unpublished transcript of the critical portion of the press conference includes this statement:

. . . OFF THE RECORD from previous questions. . . .

I will tell you something for the record* about the atomic bomb since the Japanese announced that the surrender was brought about by the atomic bomb. I would not attempt to say what motivates any individual to certain actions but history will record that at Potsdam, we were informed by Marshal Stalin that he received a request to admit to the Soviet Republic a delegation for the purpose of requesting the Soviet Government to act as an intermediary to bring about the end of the war, it being the desire of the Emperor to bring about an end to the bloodshed. . . . It was evident, of course, that what they were seeking was a negotiated peace. In that interim, the Potsdam Declaration was made public. And as you know, it was subsequent to this desire for peace that the atomic bomb was dropped in Japan and subsequent to the Potsdam Declaration. . . .[71]

The text then continues:

. . . so I only say that the United States, having been the most aggressive and having borne the brunt of the fighting, that before the atomic bomb was heard of by Japan, they were seeking peace and to bring it about through the Soviet Republic.[72]

(On September 14, 1945—noting Byrnes' simultaneous claim that the atomic bomb saved "the lives of hundreds of thousands of American soldiers"—the Catholic weekly *Commonweal* commented: "[I]t is very disquieting to see the Secretary of State trying to play both ends against the middle. . . ."[73])

One possible additional insight into Byrnes' overall view of the atomic bomb and diplomacy comes from George F. Kennan. In 1965 Kennan wrote the present author to say that although he had been Harriman's deputy in Moscow in 1945—and that "in such a position one sees only a small part of what is occurring, particularly in one's own government"—nonetheless:

. . . I never, at any time, attached any importance to our possession of the atomic bomb, as a weapon of diplomacy or a means of pressure on the Russians. I tended rather to agree with Stalin's view that this was something you used, if you liked, to frighten people with weak nerves.

Kennan's intriguing next sentence confirmed his own sense of—and disagreement with—Byrnes' general approach:

*It seems clear from the context that at this point Byrnes is speaking in a figurative rather than literal sense, and that this portion of the August 29 press conference is therefore still off the record. ("Sec. Byrnes Verbatim Report of Press Conference at Dept. of State," Vol. XVI, August 29, 1945, pp. 17–19, RG 59, NA.)

All this being so, you can see that I was not uncritically disposed towards the policies that were being pursued at that time. . . .

This letter also adds a bit more to our understanding of how important
evidence was sometimes dealt with during the Cold War. Having offered this
report of his views from Moscow in 1945, Kennan added that he "would not
wish that anything said in this letter should be published."[74]*

---

*The document was deposited with his papers at Princeton University's Seeley G. Mudd
Library, in 1968—but can be cited only with Kennan's permission.

PART IV

Managing History

The evolution of government secrecy proceeds in phases. In the beginning, it is threat-driven; it starts with the belief that disclosure of certain information could compromise national security. Controls are instituted to prevent that disclosure. But subsequently, the controls become bureaucratized and various categories of information are reflexively classified. In its latter, decadent phase, government security bears little or no relation to any identifiable threat.
—Steven Aftergood, "The Perils of Government Secrecy,"
Issues in Science and Technology, Summer 1992

Chapter 47

LESLIE R. GROVES

The files contain highly classified information concerning the Manhattan District. Some of this information is of considerable historical importance and should be preserved for that purpose. Other parts of the files are of particular value for protecting the interests of the War Department, General Groves and General Nichols.

—Major General Kenneth D. Nichols
to the Adjutant General, "Subject: Custody of
Manhattan District Classified Files," October 27, 1953

It would be surprising—given the way Stimson, Truman, and Byrnes treated the Hiroshima tale—if lesser officials were not found to have acted in a similar manner. It is impossible to catalogue, let alone know, the many other ways information was quietly suppressed and favorable versions of events promoted after the bombing of Hiroshima and Nagasaki. Nor is it necessary, given the evidence we have previously reviewed, to document all the many additional activities by different men and women which have contributed to the Hiroshima myth over the past fifty years.

A few additional aspects of the story are important to consider, however—either because of their inherent significance or because they point to ongoing problems which can be traced to the early history of the atomic bomb. There is no way to grasp the full picture of how information regarding the Hiroshima decision was controlled and manipulated, for instance, without some understanding of the role played by the man who directed the Manhattan Project, General Leslie R. Groves. It is also useful to scan through a disturbing mix of practices at various levels of government, many still common, which helped produce distortions and misinformation which were widely circulated and are still commonly believed. Excessive government secrecy and the routine classification of documents, for instance, obviously contributed

to—still contribute to—the suppression of information important to an understanding of these and many other events.

In the following pages we shall briefly review certain aspects of Groves'
unique role in the story and then take up a selection of important, other
(known) efforts to "manage" the Hiroshima tale. The public officials involved range from Stimson's successor as secretary of war, Robert P. Patterson, and members of the Joint Chiefs of Staff, to other authorities concerned
with reporting radiation information or editing the U.S. Strategic Bombing
Survey reports. We shall also consider how privileged access to information
was arranged so as to allow "friendly" writers to set the first terms of reference for the public reporting of key issues.

By all accounts Groves—the official most responsible for making the atomic
bomb—was a caricature of the tough army officer of the old school. He was
"the biggest sonovabitch I've ever met in my life," according to his deputy,
Kenneth D. Nichols, "but also one of the most capable individuals."

> He had an ego second to none, he had tireless energy—he was a big
> man, a heavy man but he never seemed to tire. He had absolute confi-
> dence in his decisions and he was absolutely ruthless in how he ap-
> proached a problem to get it done.[1]

Groves, an engineer, had been brought in to oversee the Manhattan Project
because of his successful record in building the Pentagon—one of the largest
construction projects in American history when it was completed in January 1943. In his new assignment, huge facilities had to be erected from
the ground up especially for the isolation and purification of uranium and
plutonium. Moreover, the lives and work of hundreds of scientists, including five Nobel laureates, had to be directed ("by fiat," as one physicist later
put it).[2]

Contrary to his own self-image and the opinion of some writers, modern
documents show that Groves' contribution did not impinge directly on many
of the issues we have been considering; in the end his influence on the fundamental Hiroshima decision was far more constrained than is sometimes
thought. So far as we can tell, for instance, Groves was not privy to most of
the May, June, and July high-level White House maneuvering regarding Japan's attempt to surrender. Nor did he participate in the debate over clarifying the Emperor's role which went on at various levels throughout the
summer. He did not receive MAGIC intercept briefings, and, so far as we
know, was not informed of MAGIC.[3] (Groves later stated that he had not
been told of the Japanese peace feelers.[4]) There also is no extant evidence indicating knowledge on Groves' part of the specific intelligence estimates
concerning the likely impact of a Russian declaration of war.

Most important, Groves played no part in discussions of strategy during the Atlantic crossing aboard the *Augusta*. Nor was he present at the Big Three meeting. Indeed, he was totally out of the inner policy loop for the full month the president and Byrnes were away from Washington. Finally, Groves had no involvement in the rejection of the Atlantic Charter option, or in the decision not to follow up the additional important intercepts received during the final pre-Hiroshima days.*

It is true that Groves desperately wanted to see the atomic bomb used (indeed, to see *two* bombs used). Fearing the war would end before the weapons were ready, he put intense pressure on Hanford and Los Alamos officials to speed up production—often at the cost of important resource efficiencies.[5] (A number of reports indicate that Groves was worried there would be a Congressional investigation of the huge sums spent if, in the end, the Manhattan Project made no contribution to the war effort.[6]) Groves also played a significant role in structuring the Target Committee's recommendations and he was a meaningful presence at the May and early June Interim Committee meetings.[7]

However, aside from some esoteric and much-publicized theoretical physics, the fact is that the bulk of the day-to-day work of the Manhattan Project was construction and production, pure and simple. That is why an engineer was put in charge.[8]

Groves was at the center of many other things directly related to our present concern, however. He was an expert public relations artist and news "spin" master long before these terms came into common usage. Early on, Groves determined to take as much control of information as he could within the Manhattan Project—and, critically, in preparation for public disclosure of the weapon as the time for its use approached.

There were several interrelated problems: First, a presidential statement had to be developed to announce and explain the use of the atomic bomb. Second, the public would have to be informed of the huge, previously secret effort which had produced the weapon. Third, a host of scientific and technical questions would have to be dealt with.

Groves was not the only one concerned with these matters, of course. Manhattan Engineer District (MED) records make it clear that planning to "position" the atomic bomb story began long before work on the weapon was completed. Among the other officials involved were Stimson, Harvey Bundy, James B. Conant, George Harrison, R. Gordon Arneson, and members of the Interim Committee.[9] Only Groves, however, had a fully professional staff operation at his disposal dedicated specifically to protecting and

---

*See the Afterword for an evaluation of alternative theories of Groves' influence at various points in time.

enhancing the image of the atomic bomb project—and as the summer progressed, it took ever greater control.

A March 26, 1945, memorandum from Groves to Marshall marks the formal initiation of one level of press planning. Groves pointed out that serious news breaks would almost inevitably occur "after the initial use" of the weapon. Also, unless advance thought were given to the problem, follow-up stories after an initial presidential statement "could well be ruinous."

> These breaks may well develop into situations beyond our control, particularly if scientific claims of discovery are made to the credit of individuals. At that time, it may be necessary to control the situation by the issuance of carefully written press releases. Background for such releases would necessitate study for several months.[10]

In early April Groves hired William L. Laurence, a journalist who had initially come to his attention with a 1940 *Saturday Evening Post* article on the possibilities of atomic power. Laurence was a science reporter working for *The New York Times*, and in an unusual understanding which transgressed all lines of established tradition, he was secretly hired but also remained on the *Times'* payroll.[11]* His job was to help with official statements and press releases.

A sense of the process which produced the presidential statement—especially as it relates to the more controversial issues—is readily apparent from various Manhattan Project papers. Laurence's first draft of the presidential statement was rejected and this writing responsibility was turned over to Stimson's friend, Arthur Page—with Laurence playing a supporting role.[12] Accompanying one draft of the statement written on or near May 29 is a brief memorandum listing the following among the key "objectives":

> Notify world we have atomic bomb.
>
> 1000 to 1.
> . . . wiser not to mention that bigger ones will follow for we want to have our acts more dreadful than our words to the Japs.
> Call on the Japs to surrender.
> Making it clear that if they do not all subsequent slaughter is their guilt.
> Making it clear that also we do not count on the bomb alone but intend to follow it with the foot soldiers and fleet. . . .

---

*Groves later explained that it "seemed to us . . . that it would be much better to bring in an outside newspaperman who would have a more objective touch." (Groves, *Now It Can Be Told*, p.325.) Peter Wyden is less oblique; Laurence, he suggests, acted simply as a "government propagandist. . . . His warmly admiring dispatches . . . displayed no reservations about anything he saw or heard." (Wyden, *Day One*, p. 212 n.)

Notify the Russians that they do not get the secret for nothing but might
  if a proper international organization were effected. . . .
Hold the second story so it won't compete with the president's message.
Choose a military target like a naval base if possible so that wholesale
  killing of civilians will be on the heads of the Japanese who refused
  to surrender at our ultimatum.[13]

The last point—which parallels Marshall's recommendation of May 29—
was, of course, dropped. However, its inclusion here again suggests that the
proposal of a strictly military "demonstration" was not Marshall's idea alone.
Indeed the coincidence of dates suggests some form of active consideration
in more than one office—another puzzle and gap in the record.

The draft statement to which the above notes were attached also included
this language: "Two hours ago an American airplane dropped a bomb on the
Nagasaki Naval Base and the Naval Base ceased to exist." From June 7 until
July 23 all drafts began with a slight variation: "Two hours ago an American
airplane dropped one bomb on the Nagasaki Naval Base and destroyed its
usefulness to the enemy." Thereafter, the name of the target was left blank
until August 6. (As we have seen, the field order for the Nagasaki bombing
placed the target at the Mitsubishi Steel and Arms Works in the northern section of the city, while the mission planning summary stated that the target
was the commercial district of the city. In fact, there were no significant military installations at Nagasaki.)[14]

On another important issue the draft statement of June 7 had the president
saying: "I shall . . . consider the possibility of an international agreement, the
purpose of which shall be to insure an effective international control of this
power . . ."[15] This language, however, was struck from subsequent drafts. Ultimately Truman's August 6 statement concluded with only a vague allusion
to the possibility of international control:

I shall give further consideration and make further recommendations to
the Congress as to how atomic power can become a powerful and forceful influence towards the maintenance of world peace.[16]

By the June 21 Interim Committee meeting, "The draft statement for the
President was approved with minor changes."[17] (At this time, it was also
"agreed that releases that would be necessary after the statement of the S/W
was made public should be handled by Groves' organization in cooperation
with Page."[18])

With Harrison's approval Arneson and Page subsequently revised the draft
to reflect events at Potsdam, and to produce what was expected to be the final revision at the end of July, Stimson also met with Bundy, Harrison, Page,
and Groves to fine-tune it again.[19] (Stimson's diary notes: "I did not realize

until I went over these papers now what a great change [the successful test] had produced in my own psychology.")[20] The sentence "Their leaders promptly rejected that [Potsdam] ultimatum" was among the additions.[21]

Finally, on July 31, 1945, the secretary of war sent Truman the following note:

> Dear Mr. President:
> Attached are two copies of the revised statement which has been pre-pared for release by you as soon as the new weapon is used. This is the statement about which I cabled you last night.
>   The reason for the haste is that I was informed only yesterday that, weather permitting, it is likely that the weapon will be used as early as August 1st, Pacific Ocean Time, which as you know is a good many hours ahead of Washington time. . . .
>
>   Faithfully yours,
>   Henry L. Stimson
>   Secretary of War[22]

Later the same day—July 31, 1945—a cable from Truman to Stimson stated: "In reply to your [31 July message], suggestions approved. Release when ready but not sooner than 2 August."[23]

Finally, on the morning of the announcement Groves—acting on his own authority—hedged his bets in case the destruction was not as thorough as an-ticipated and had the first paragraph of the president's statement rewritten. Thus "an American airplane dropped one bomb on ———* and destroyed its usefulness to the enemy" was changed to "an American airplane dropped one bomb on Hiroshima, an important Japanese Army base"—language which, as we have seen, the president was also to make his own in his radio broadcast and on many other occasions thereafter.[24]†

Stimson's statement was the most straightforward and least controversial in terms of framing the atomic bomb story for the American public. Here Arneson was assigned the drafting duties (by Harrison on May 19).[25] Page evidently helped in the revisions (to what extent is unclear) and Colonel William A. Consodine—the man Groves put in charge of his overall public relations effort—monitored the process.

A day after he received the draft Stimson statement (on June 19), Conso-dine sent Page a series of proposed changes. Among the most illuminating were:

---

*Blank in original.
†For further details on the role of the Interim Committee and other, more routine aspects of the public relations effort, see Vincent C. Jones, *Manhattan: The Army and the Atomic Bomb* (1985), pp. 554–56.

I question whether . . . the specific information regarding the agreement between the United States and the United Kingdom should be mentioned. Every executive agreement represents a potential attack on the floor of the Congress for the evasion of the Senate ratification clause of the Constitution.[26]

Again:

. . . It is my opinion that no mention should be made of the Belgian Agreement [regarding uranium] at all for the reason that there are certain international treaties which give equal rights to other nations in the resources of the Congo. It seems to me that this would simply precipitate the first case for the new World Court, and Russia might well be the plaintiff.[27]

Finally:

There is too great a stress on the scientists as a whole. The job was finished because of the complete coordination of the Army, industry and the scientists. There is too little mention of the part played by the Army. I believe that industry has been given proper attention and that the scientists have been given absolutely too much attention.[28]

Stimson's statement was also considered by the Interim Committee on June 21, and after incorporating various technical and other modifications suggested by Consodine, the British, and others, a near-final version was accepted on July 6.[29] The final statement described the development of the bomb and the organizational infrastructure behind it (i.e., the scientific and army effort, the Interim Committee, Scientific Panel, etc.). It reported on the overall project, reviewed the state of the atomic energy research prior to World War II, explained why the effort had been kept secret, discussed agreements with the British, and opened a general perspective on the long-range potential of atomic energy.[30]

Paul Boyer has observed that once the weapon was disclosed, technical issues almost immediately blanketed—even masked—all other issues:

Within hours of the White House announcement, newspapers and magazines were offering detailed explanations of nuclear physics, long self-congratulatory histories of the Manhattan Project, and euphoric discussions of an atomic energy utopia of limitless power, atomic cars and planes, medical wonders, boundless leisure, and revolutions in agriculture.

"That the response of most Americans to Hiroshima and Nagasaki froze immediately at the surface level," Boyer suggests, ". . . is surely attributable in large part to the fact that the nation's media and opinion molders quickly turned to other aspects of the atomic energy story. . . ."

> That this latest scientific wonder had burst upon the world's conscious-
> ness through the obliteration of a city seemed merely a regrettable piece
> of bad luck—rather as though electricity had first become known
> through the mass electrocution of several hundred thousand people.[31]

In one sense, the outpouring of technical and scientific stories was clearly inevitable given the extraordinary nature of the new development. It was also, however, the result—indeed a major achievement of—Groves' hard work and what the Interim Committee called "Groves' organization." A team effort similar to that which produced the main statements also operated here—but in this instance Groves had full control of all the key issues.

The essential strategy was to saturate what would be a huge market hungry for information with officially approved material from the only authoritative source available. An internal June 6, 1945, memo from public relations officer Lieutenant George O. Robinson pointed out that "immediately after the President's original announcement, a wild rush will develop among the press to develop additional stories."

> This will mean that with the lid off they can interview anyone, quote
> anyone for reactions, comment as freely as they see fit and otherwise
> handle the story as they want. . . . This gives added impetus to the need
> for covering the story as completely as possible ourselves in the first
> releases.[32]

What was needed was a sophisticated system to distribute and broadcast materials. On June 27 Consodine reported to Groves on "public relations recommendations" which had been generated at a New York conference held two days earlier. Among the most significant:

> • . . . The list of stories being compiled by Mr. Laurence will be made
> available to the areas after correction by you, the Interim Committee, if
> necessary, and Colonel Nichols and [Lieutenant Colonel Franklin T.]
> Matthias [commanding officer at Hanford] where necessary. They will
> be classified top secret until release. . . .
> . . . It is suggested that all material possible be released immediately af-
> ter the President's announcement, including the Laurence material and
> the background stories on you, Colonel Nichols and Colonel Matthias.
> • It is imperative that the MED public relations office be the single
> agency to handle all phases of the project's public relations to eliminate
> confusion, to insure protection of that part of the project which will not
> be releasable and to insure proper credit for the work. . . .

• It is important that every effort be made to eliminate from the picture civilian public relations men now employed by contractors at Oak Ridge. . . .
• The Air Forces should be restricted by military order from any publicity. While they will be given due credit, they will not be allowed to steal the show.[33]

General rules for press release authorization by the Interim Committee were also prepared so that the committee would not be put in the position of having to review each individual story.[34] When he approved the final public relations plan, Groves also banned "extemporaneous" broadcast interviews: "Radio releases must be limited to previously cleared scripts."[35] (In addition: "Handling of all public relations visitors at the areas including facilities and necessary arrangements will be a function of the local public relations organizations. Confidential funds will be used if necessary.")[36]

Laurence and other Manhattan Project officials prepared drafts which would eventually become the basic press releases[37]—including multiple stories developed before the Alamogordo test offering various options in case of major property damage or death.[38] Just prior to the test Laurence wrote to his editor at *The New York Times*, "there are at least twenty-five individual one-page stories to be given out following the break of The Big News."[39] With Groves' blessing, Laurence also witnessed the Trinity test (and the bombing run on Nagasaki, although not Hiroshima).[40]

A basic question was how to treat the fundamental science of the new weapon. Aside from Laurence's popularized accounts, something was needed which would explain the scientific facts sufficiently well so as to manage the debate but also sufficiently carefully so as not to give away important discoveries. An authoritative official statement was needed to envelop other discussions.

What became known as the "Smyth report" (after its principal author, Professor Henry D. Smyth of Princeton University) was the result—a highly detailed 264-page effort to "officially" set the terms of reference for the discussion before others even got to the starting line.[41] Almost a year and a half before it was released—in April 1944—Groves (acting on the advice of Conant, Vannevar Bush, Arthur Compton, and Smyth himself) selected Smyth to write a report covering the technical achievements of the Manhattan Project.[42] Criteria for the information which could be cited included:

(A) That it is already known generally by competent scientists or (B) That it can be deduced or guessed by competent scientists from what is already known, combined with the knowledge that the project was in the overall successful. . . .[43]

Although in the end the fact-filled final document had the look of real authority, Groves likened it "to instructions given people going west years ago when they were told that they should go to a water hole about 30 miles away and that if it was dry they should go to one about 10 miles beyond that."[44] He told Marshall: "This release contains no information which will be of real value to any competitor nation."[45]

Laurence's press releases and the Smyth report were the only serious sources of authoritative scientific and other information on an extraordinary—indeed world-shaking—development. Not surprisingly, reporting in most parts of the nation was almost uniformly the same. As Groves later recalled, "most newspapers published our releases in their entirety."[46] Media critic Robert Manoff points to the effect, too, of wartime habit: ". . . after years of operating under voluntary censorship guidelines which discouraged initiative by prohibiting even the mention of atomic energy, uranium, or Los Alamos, the [New York] *Times*—and, it should be said, the rest of the press—simply went with what the government gave it."[47]

These judgments were confirmed by a survey of fourteen selected newspapers by Louis Liebovich which found that most of the initial stories drew directly on the explanations of the bomb project provided by Laurence. Liebovich concluded that "the news organizations . . . questioned neither the propriety of bombing Hiroshima and Nagasaki nor the motives behind the destruction."[48]

Responding openly to a subsequent Army research inquiry as to his overall public relations strategy, Groves suggested it could "best be divided into three phases:"

a. The immediate effect upon the Japanese people and the resultant effect upon their rapid and complete surrender.

b. The immediate effects on the American people.

c. The future effects on the American people and upon international relations and enduring peace.

"The first two dealt with immediate problems. The third dealt with the international situation of the future [,] with the future attitude of the people of the United States [,] and particularly with the influence which the people would bring to bear upon the Congress and upon the type of legislation which would be passed."[49]

Groves also played a significant role in the development of the MGM film *The Beginning or the End*. Indeed, after MGM won White House approval for the project, one of its first moves was to hire Groves as a primary consultant—for the then-unheard-of fee of $10,000, MGM was authorized to depict Groves' role in the film and Groves agreed to offer his "best cooperation" in the production of the picture.[50] At the same time, with apparently few questions asked about conflict of interest—and little embarrassment— Groves remained as head of the Manhattan Project. He also continued to receive the pay of a major general.

Some of the changes Groves urged (and did not urge) in reviewing the film are instructive. Upon reviewing the script, for instance, he did not object to the film's misleading presidential "decision scene"*—and on April 15, 1946, he recommended that one of his own speeches read:

> The minimum estimate of our losses is a half million men. If the Japs do have suicide planes we will lose a lot more than that.[51]

Two other inaccuracies which survived into the final film which Groves also did not find objectionable were:

> • a portrayal of planes dropping leaflets on Hiroshima warning of atomic attack "for ten days." (In a *Bulletin of the Atomic Scientists* film review, Harrison Brown called this the "most horrible falsification of history . . . that Hiroshima had been warned of the approaching attack.")[52]
> • a portrayal of death by radiation as relatively painless (in contrast to the excruciating death known to have been suffered by one Los Alamos scientist—Harry Daghlian—in September 1945).[53]

After seeing a preview of the uncut version of the film, columnist Walter Lippmann complained to James McGuinness of Loew's Inc. and MGM. Lippmann found the White House decision scene especially worrisome, and in a further letter to Frank Aydelotte at the Institute of Advanced Studies at Princeton he observed:

> All the political part of the film, which has to do with the decisions to make it, and the decisions to use it, are melodramatic simplifications and, indeed, falsifications of what actually took place. The scene between General Groves and President Truman is, of course, an outright fabrication. . . .[54]

(In the end modifications of the scene were agreed upon; the inflated casualty estimate, however, remained.[55])†

Throughout the war Groves was understandably extraordinarily protective of information and almost paranoid in his efforts to prevent leaks both to the

---

*See above, p. 516.
†For further information on the MGM film, see Michael Yavenditti, "Atomic Scientists and Hollywood: *The Beginning or the End?*," *Film and History*, Vol. 8, No. 4 (Dec. 1978), pp. 73–88; Nathan Reingold, *Science, American Style* (New Brunswick, N.J., 1991), pp. 334–50; and Hershberg, *James B. Conant*, pp. 287–91.

enemy and to the American public. We know in considerable detail, for instance, that almost from the outset he ordered an extreme form of "compartmentalization"—the rigid segregation of information, projects, and people. Only those with a demonstrated "need to know" were allowed even the most rudimentary information on aspects of the project not deemed relevant to their own narrowly defined concerns. An undated note to himself found among Groves' personal papers offers this sense of his mind-set:

> . . . I often had to carry highly secret papers. Invariably these were carried in a plain brown government envelope with my name and War Department address underneath. I never separated myself from these papers. If I was in a dining car or a restaurant I would invariably sit on the envelope. At night in a train I would place them under my mattress. I always carried a small automatic pistol in my trousers pocket where it did not show. I also always traveled in closed space on trains and invariably before going to bed would tie the door handle so that anyone coming in would make sufficient noise to awaken me. On airplanes I normally clutched the envelope in one hand or held it in my lap.[56]

As a matter of policy, Groves also avoided committing anything to writing whenever possible. When Marshall asked him to take over foreign intelligence on atomic energy matters in the fall of 1943, for instance, "as was customary, nothing was put in writing."[57] Groves also developed a "custom" in which memoranda for Marshall were read in his presence and then immediately returned for safekeeping.[58] Similarly, the "use of officer messengers on highly secret missions, carrying no papers or very limited ones, was common practice in the Manhattan Project. . . . Every written message increased the chances of disclosing information to outsiders."[59]

In a 1959 letter to Groves one Army Air Forces liaison officer (Lieutenant General Roscoe C. Wilson) recalled that when he first began working with the project,

> . . . I was explicitly directed not to keep records. . . . I was told to report to you for instructions; to share no confidences with anyone; to keep no records; to report to no one in the AAF [Army Air Forces] except [General Oliver P. Echols] and [Air Forces Commander] General Arnold: my reports were to be verbal or in my own handwriting.[60]

The sketchiness of Groves' personal diary also was "due, in large part, to our general practice to minimize written records, particularly those that would give an overall picture of the operation and its state of progress."[61] Nor was the policy restricted to technical secrets and administrative issues; in another private letter Groves also explained that "Many key decisions were never put in writing," and that "very seldom were any papers prepared which would indicate the background on which our decisions were based."[62]

The impact of such practices on our knowledge of many important issues regarding the atomic bomb is certainly considerable—and by definition, impossible to define. Here, too, there are undeniable gaps in the record.

Much more active control of information is also clear. In the spring of 1945 the Manhattan Project began to document its activities. A representative memorandum prepared under Groves' direction—"Some Notes for Guidance to Writers of Basic Data Books on DSM Project"*—established the terms of reference for the official internal history of the Manhattan Project. A copy sent to an officer at Oak Ridge, Major Harry S. Traynor, states:

> Extreme care should be exercised not to emphasize unduly any point on which the War Department may be, or may be thought to be, somewhat sensitive of criticism or in a somewhat weak position.

And . . .

> The writer should bear in mind at all times that the books, while intended to be used by General Groves, may also be seen and studied by persons who are antagonistic or hostile to him, the War Department, or the project. . . .

"Nor does it do any harm to permit the reader occasionally to reach his own conclusions, provided the steps leading up to them render these conclusions inescapable."[63]

An example of how potentially damaging information was actively suppressed involves the July 1945 scientists' petition which urged Truman not to use the atomic bomb until full and explicit terms of surrender had been explained to the Japanese. As we have seen, physicist Leo Szilard had given the petition to Arthur Compton, director of the University of Chicago Metallurgical Project, who in turn had forwarded it to Groves' deputy, Nichols, who had then sent it on to Groves. Truman was in Potsdam at the time, and Groves had deftly and easily stalled the paper flow.

Following procedures common at the time, at the request of Manhattan Project officials Szilard had initially classified the petition himself—and two days after Nagasaki was bombed he similarly wrote a letter declassifying the document. Within a few days Manhattan Project intelligence officer Captain James A. Murray confirmed that this was acceptable.[64] Szilard then wrote to Truman's White House appointments secretary, Matthew Connelly,

*D.S.M. = Development of Substitute Materials, an early alternative designation for the Manhattan Project.

asking permission to publicize the petition[65]; he also sent a copy to the editors of *Science* magazine—as he explained, so that the public might be aware of "the attitude of at least a substantial minority of scientists engaged at present in this work at one of the atomic power projects."[66]

Although the war was over, on August 25 Groves told Murray that he wanted the petition again classified "secret." Unable to order compliance at this point, Murray first telephoned Szilard and then urged him in writing to reclassify the petition. Szilard could choose not to do so; however, he was warned that there could be consequences:

It appears unnecessary to point out to you that any information considered "secret" by the highest authority which you divulge to persons unauthorized to receive it will be in violation of [a signed agreement to preserve secrecy] and of the Espionage Act. . . .[67]

In a follow-up on August 28, Murray also strongly implied that Szilard would be fired if he did not comply with the "request" to reclassify the petition. This letter reminded him of Paragraph 7 of his contract with the Metallurgical Laboratory and the University of Chicago:

[T]he Laboratory reserves the right and privilege to terminate this contract of employment immediately, for good and sufficient cause, including but not limited to incompetency, neglect of duty, violation of the applicable rules and regulations of the Laboratory or of the United States Government, or conduct inimical to the interests of the United States Government.

"In my opinion the portion of the contract quoted above," Murray stated, ". . . specifically puts you on knowledge [*sic*] of the necessity for compliance with the regulations of the United States Government concerning disclosures of classified military information . . . [S]uch commitments . . . preclude the disclosure by you of any information considered secret by the head of the Manhattan District, Major General L. R. Groves."[68]

Since the war was over and since the petition disclosed no scientific or other secret information, Szilard had asked Murray for an explanation during their telephone conversation. His written response—itself designated "secret" at the time or shortly thereafter—stated:

You asked me to point out certain passages in your petition which might be considered as justification for General Groves [*sic*] belief that it should be classified secret. The opinions which I give you are my own. . . . In my opinion, then, every paragraph of the petition either contains some information or implies "inside" information, i.e.—

information gained through employment, which, when linked with the
purpose of the petition, implies that internal dissention [*sic*] and fundamental differences in point of view disrupted the development and fru-
ition of the District's work. . . .

This implication, Murray urged, "if released at this time, might well cause
'injury to the interest or prestige of the nation or governmental activity.' "[69]

In the end either the pressure worked or (the record is not clear) Groves
simply took charge. The petition was reclassified "secret" and *Science* magazine was informed that it could not be made public.[70]

When the Atomic Energy Commission was established in January 1947
an executive order provided for the transfer to it of most of the Manhattan
Project files.[71] However, Groves himself retained custody of seventy-
two linear feet of special files—primarily those documenting significant
policy issues and military operations. Included were files concerning the
petition.[72]

The petition's suppression now became tied to the fate of the entire special
collection. Not only did Groves maintain these "top secret" files under close
personal control while he was in charge of the atomic project, but he continued to do so after his retirement in 1948. When Nichols prepared to succeed
Groves as chief of the Armed Forces Special Weapons Project (established in
1947 to oversee military participation in the development of atomic weaponry), Groves informed him of an arrangement he had negotiated with Eisenhower, the first postwar chief of staff: Certain papers "were to be under my
complete control subject to the written orders of the Chief of Staff or the
Secretary of War":

There were two files set up for the War Department; one a secret file
and one a non-secret. These files are designed primarily to preserve
those papers which pertained to strictly military operations and those
without which it would be difficult to disprove unjust attacks on the
reputation of the War Department and of its responsible officers, particularly Secretary Stimson, yourself and me.

Nichols was authorized to examine the papers, "provided they are not permanently removed from the files." He was also informed that as "various
matters are declassified, I have planned on removing these papers to my personal control."[73]

In October 1953, as Nichols himself prepared to retire from the army,
Groves—at this point five years out of uniform—contacted him to urge that
the special files now should be transferred "to the physical custody of the
Adjutant General."

This action would mean that the contents of these files would be accessible to you and to me, and to such persons as were specifically designated in writing from time to time by either you or myself, and, of course, subject to any written instructions of the Chief of Staff, U.S. Army.[74]

Nichols' memorandum to the adjutant general, in turn, explained:

The files contain highly classified information concerning the Manhattan District. Some of this information is of considerable historical importance and should be preserved for that purpose. Other parts of the files are of particular value for protecting the interests of the War Department, General Groves and General Nichols.

The documents were indeed transferred to the adjutant general (in 1953), and in 1958 they were finally turned over to the National Archives and Records Service.[75]

Included in the collection were papers showing how the scientists' petition had been sidetracked and effectively withheld from Truman in July 1945. Also included was a copy of the petition's text, which had been separately declassified (although not published) by the Atomic Energy Commission in 1957.[76]*

During the final years of the Eisenhower Administration journalists Fletcher Knebel and Charles W. Bailey—who ultimately broke the story— were amazed to find that "the Army still stands on a letter written by General Dwight D. Eisenhower, when he was Chief of Staff, putting the Manhattan papers in the personal custody of General Groves and requesting future Chiefs of Staff to continue this arrangement."

Thus, to all intents and purposes the records of the Manhattan project remain totally inaccessible until General Groves chooses to allow them to be inspected. Such a policy not only frustrates legitimate research on a vital subject but also flies in the face of a basic principle: that in a democracy the public has an inherent right to inspect the records of the public's business.[77]

Only in 1963—after a long declassification battle involving security clearances by the Defense Department, the State Department, and the Atomic Energy Commission—was the full petition story made public.

The article Knebel and Bailey published in *Look* magazine—cleared by

---

*The existence of the petition—but not its text—was reported in the *Bulletin of the Atomic Scientists*, May 1, 1946, and as we have seen, discussed in very general terms in a broadcast by Raymond Gram Swing.

the Kennedy Administration a year and a half after it had been written—reported the broad outlines of the 1945 events and stated:

> President Truman, faced with one of the great moral decisions of human history, was denied access to the petitions of many American nuclear scientists who opposed the dropping of the atomic bomb on Hiroshima without warning.[78]*

In a personal letter to Truman which did not directly deny that he had simply pigeonholed the petition—and, indeed which did not explicitly acknowledge the petition's existence—Groves presented seemingly related but largely irrelevant information concerning the general charge

> that I withheld from Secretary Stimson, and hence from you, the fact that some of the scientists felt that the bomb should not be used. Their feelings were thoroughly discussed with Mr. Stimson at a meeting of the Interim Committee at which the Scientific Panel was also present, as were General Marshall and myself. Previous to this meeting Mr. Stimson had been kept fully informed by me at all times of these attitudes. I am sure he passed all pertinent information on to you.[79]

This statement, of course, is not a direct falsehood; it simply avoids the fact that Groves withheld the petition until the document could have no impact. Interviewed by *The New York Times* at this time, Groves stated that the petition was "given to Mr. Stimson; I don't know just when. . . . I think it's reasonable to say that Stimson was fully aware of the proposal; and that Truman, presumably, was informed."[80]

The petition tale stands as an illustration of how difficult information in general was managed. Other reports of Groves' approach—including the intimidation of various scientists and reporters—have been documented in a number of accounts.[81] Given what we know of Groves' overall public relations efforts and his attempts to guide history, it is instructive to return to the central question of the Hiroshima myth.[82]

Throughout his life Groves repeatedly claimed that the atomic bomb saved huge numbers of lives—indeed, perhaps half a million lives.[83] Documents found in Groves' personal papers from the period shortly after Hiroshima reveal a rather different possible understanding—and something perhaps of Groves' sense of just how close Japan was to surrender at the time the atomic bomb was actually used.

An October 10, 1945, letter to Dr. Robert S. Stone provides this suggestive

---

*The full text of the petition was published the same year (1963) in *The Atomic Age*, edited by Morton Grodzins and Eugene Rabinowitch.

insight into Groves' personal judgment as to whether the early August bombing had in fact been needed to avoid a November landing (let alone a full-scale invasion in 1946):

> [S]urrender was of course an ultimate certainty anyway, but it is indisputable that the war would have continued for weeks and perhaps months longer had it not been for the timely knock-out blow. . . .[84]

Chapter 48

CENSORSHIP AND SECRECY: RULES AND EXCEPTIONS

The records of this period are not normally available to non-governmental researchers. Exceptions to the rule will be limited in general to mature scholars undertaking research regarded by the Department as desirable in the national interest.

—"Regulation Concerning Non-Official Research in the
Unpublished Records of the Department of State,"
January 1951

Actions taken by American officials thousands of miles away from Washington also helped control how important aspects of the atomic bomb story were managed. In Japan, American censorship picked up where Japanese wartime controls left off. On September 18, 1945, a restrictive Press Code established guidelines which included such extremely general rules as: "Nothing shall be printed which might, directly or by inference, disturb public tranquility" and "There shall be no false or destructive criticism of the Allied Powers."[1]

The Japanese press was required to walk a tightrope. On the one hand, "Minor details of any news story must not be overemphasized to stress or develop any propaganda line." On the other, "No news story shall be distorted by the omission of pertinent facts or details."[2] The Civil Censorship Division of the Occupation followed up by decreeing that the fact of censorship itself was to be censored. The Division prohibited "any traces, such as blank spaces, dots, circles, or blacked-out portions, that would imply censorship deletions," notes one scholar, Monica Braw.[3]

Two of the earliest instances of direct censorship—a twenty-four-hour ban on the Domei news agency and a two-day suspension of one of Japan's largest newspapers, *Asahi Shimbun*—were occasioned by coverage of the Hiroshima bombing.[4] A Domei report had stated that "Japan might have won the war but for the atomic bomb, a weapon too terrible to face and one which only barbarians would use."[5] The offending article in *Asahi Shimbun* had stated that so "long as the United States advocates 'might is right,' it cannot deny that the use of the atomic bomb and the killing of innocent people is a violation of international law and a war crime worse than an attack on a hospital ship or the use of poison gas."[6] At this time, too, George Weller of the *Chicago Daily News* filed a series of stories on hospital patients in Nagasaki—but made the mistake of sending his only copies to Tokyo for clearance by U.S. officials. The stories were neither approved nor returned.[7]*

As the broad structure of censorship took hold, other materials—including books, textbooks, motion pictures, and even private mail—were put under controls. By the summer of 1946 the Civil Censorship Detachment employed over 8,700 people and was examining thousands of newspaper and magazine issues.[8] Robert Manoff recalls that one writer whose work on Hiroshima ran afoul of the censors—Sadako Kurihara—was especially disturbed that "the American democrats" had developed a more sophisticated censorship system "than had the Japanese militarists they replaced."[9]

Occupation authorities suppressed various accounts of the atomic bombings. A noteworthy instance involved the denial in late 1946 of a request by the *Nippon Times* to publish John Hersey's *Hiroshima* (in English); the widely read American book was not brought out in Japan until 1949. (MacArthur denied *Hiroshima* had actually been banned. Technically the Civil Information and Education Section had not censored *Hiroshima* but simply had not approved the *Nippon Times*' request. However, the *Times* had also been informed that signing an agreement with the original U.S. source—*The New Yorker*—would be a violation of the Trading with the Enemy Act.)[10]

American and Japanese films of Hiroshima and Nagasaki—still photographs as well as movies—were also confiscated, and, indeed, some of the people involved taken into custody.[11] One of the Japanese cameramen, Sueo Inoue, remembered it this way:

> Our team also belonged to an academic investigation group doing research about the effects of the bomb. We were thirty-two or thirty-three persons. On September 16 we started filming in Nagasaki. We contin-

---

*A left-wing journalist, Wilfred Burchett, was the first Western reporter to reach Hiroshima. Following his September 5 story in the London *Daily Express* detailing deaths from "an unknown something which I can only describe as the atomic plague," the U.S. Army declared Hiroshima out of bounds for non-approved journalists. (Burchett, *Shadows of Hiroshima*, pp. 11–24. See also, Richard Tanter, "Voice and Silence in the First Nuclear War: Wilfred Burchett and Hiroshima," in *Burchett Reporting the Other Side of the World, 1939–1983*, Ben Kiernan, ed. (London, 1986), pp. 13–40.)

ued until October 24, when we were arrested by American military police. . . .

The films were taken to America—everything we had shot and edited, even the small cuts. All in all it was 30,000 feet of film.[12]

Team leader Akira Iwasaki recalled that the Strategic Bombing Survey decided that "they wanted to have a film of Hiroshima and Nagasaki. . . . [so] they allowed me or better ordered me to continue and complete the film."[13] In the end, the confiscated film—including negatives, positives, and outtakes—was classified "Secret" and not released to the Japanese government for more than two decades. A condensed version was first shown to an American audience in 1970.[14]

Working under orders of the Occupation, an American film crew also took pictures at Hiroshima and Nagasaki, but this material, too, was immediately confiscated. One of the men involved—Herbert Sussan—subsequently fought for the films' declassification and public release. Greg Mitchell reports that finally, "in the late-1970s, after the 90,000 feet of raw film had been placed in the National Archives, Herb alerted the Japanese public to its existence (inspiring a mass movement for the purchase of the film)."[15*]

John Dower has observed that the rationale for such censorship was twofold: "American occupation authorities feared that unrestrained discussion of the effects of the bombs might incite 'public unrest' against them. . . ." There was also fear a campaign might develop which might call attention to Allied atrocities "exemplified by the nuclear destruction of the two essentially civilian targets."[16] The specialist whose study was cited above—Monica Braw—adds that "there were many reasons why the United States suppressed publication in Japan of material about the atomic bombings of Hiroshima and Nagasaki. The security of the United States, which, it was said, demanded secrecy about the bomb, was one. Fear of criticism of the United States by Japanese was another. The campaign of impressing war guilt on the Japanese was also involved."

> But above all there was concern about the reputation of the United States. An often-stated reason for suppression was that the material gave the impression that the United States was inhumane or barbaric in using the atomic bomb.[17]

* * *

*Another instance of suppressed photographs is also cited by Mitchell: "In the mid-1970s the U.S. Army sent to Japan photographs taken in Hiroshima and Nagasaki following the bombing. . . . They were virtually the first color photographs of the aftermath of the bombing anyone in Japan had ever seen. Many showed victims—some badly burned, others bald and afflicted with radiation disease—posing with impossible dignity for the American photographers." (Greg Mitchell, "August 6/August 9," *Nuclear Times*, March 1985, p. 22.)

The work of many researchers was required to force the disclosure of information concerning American servicemen killed by the atomic bomb.

The first public indication that Americans had been killed at Hiroshima came in a July 1970 United Press International report. A former Japanese warrant officer, Hiroshi Yanagida, told reporters he had been in charge of twenty-three American POWs held in three locations near where the bomb fell. Yanagida said the prisoners' dogtags, saved by the Japanese, had been handed over to the American occupation authorities. (A Department of Defense spokesperson claimed to know nothing about the deaths.)[18]

However—perhaps inspired by Yanagida's report—a National Archives employee began searching through the records and discovered a document dated September 23, 1945, indicating that the American Red Cross had informed the War Department that Sergeant Ralph J. Neal, of the 866th Bomb Squadron, had been "wounded by the atomic bomb on 6 August . . . and subsequently died on 9 August. Apparently two or possibly three more airmen of the same crew [the *Lonesome Lady*, a B-24 shot down on July 28] who are now missing possibly died as a result of the Hiroshima bombing."[19] A Sixth Army message of October 9 confirmed that "Neal, one Norman Roland Brisset, one Blankbek, and 17 other Americans (names unknown) were being held in Hiroshima at the time of [the] atomic bombing. All except Neal and Brisset were killed instantly, [and these two died] as a result of wounds sustained in [the] bombing."[20]

Subsequently, in 1975 and 1976 three American fliers reported that they had seen dying U.S. airmen on August 16, 1945, when they briefly shared a cell with two American survivors.[21] One of the pilots, Walter Ross, described what appeared to be the lingering pain of radiation poisoning: "These two fellows were really dying a very horrible death. You could tell that just by looking at them."[22]

In 1977 a Japanese list (in English) of twenty American POWs killed in Hiroshima was found and made public by Satoru Ubaki, a Japanese professor.[23] (Subsequently, it was shown that nine of the Americans were not actually in Hiroshima when the bomb fell.[24])

Throughout this period no official information was given to the families of the servicemen. In 1973 a fire at a St. Louis army records warehouse destroyed many personnel files—and this in turn was offered as a reason why it was impossible to assemble the remaining records of individual servicemen thought to have died in the bombing.[25]

Although the army maintained that these were the only records which could confirm whether individual Americans had died in Hiroshima, a Veterans Administration employee tipped off documentary filmmaker Gary DeWalt to the existence of another set of records concerning the identification and burial of dead American soldiers. DeWalt, in turn, used the Freedom of Information Act to force the release of documents confirming that the government had records indicating that American servicemen had, in fact, been killed at Hiroshima on August 6, 1945.[26]

An eerie sidelight—probably the result of bureaucratic ineptitude—was thrown on the deaths by a military memorial service held in 1949 at the Jefferson Barracks Army Cemetery in St. Louis. A tombstone for eight servicemen gives the names of each and lists their common date of death as August 6, 1945.[27]*

By far the most obvious way in which information related to the decision to use the atomic bomb was kept from the public was at once the most general and the simplest: government "classification" of information—the ongoing, routine denial of official documents to the citizenry. The Hiroshima story is hardly an exception to a very old and deeply entrenched rule, the "normal" functioning of which is even more effective than the occasional excesses which make the headlines.

Thomas G. Paterson, a former president of the Society for Historians of American Foreign Relations, looked into the functioning of the overall system in the late 1980s:

> . . . I found myself descending into a dark cavern of executive orders, legislative acts, executive directives, proposed amendments, letters of explanation, secret guidelines, and court rulings. I am sure I do not understand all of it, and I am assured by archivists and historians in the government that they have not mastered the rules either.[28]

The regulations and rules governing "confidential," "restricted," "secret," "top secret," and other materials are often so byzantine and complex—revised and re-revised over time—that no brief account can possibly do jus-

---

*It is now also known that U.S. officials understood that American and other servicemen were almost certainly being held in the target cities. Although officials in the Pacific thought (erroneously as it turned out) that there were no prisoners in Hiroshima, a War Department telegram dated July 31, 1945, informed them: "if you consider your information reliable Hiroshima should be given first priority. . . ." It added, however, "Information available here indicates that there are prison camps in practically every major Japanese city." (H. M. Pasco to General Spaatz, Commanding General, U.S. Strategic Air Forces, Guam, July 31, 1945, File 5D, Roll 1, M1109, Top Secret Correspondence of the MED, NA.)

There were also over three thousand other American citizens in Hiroshima, and additional American citizens in Nagasaki at the time of the bombings—to say nothing of thousands of resident nationals of other countries. For the most part, the Americans were children born in the United States and the wives of Americans of Japanese descent who had been visiting Japan and were trapped when the war broke out. (Hiroshima in particular was at the center of a region from which many Japanese families had come to the United States.) (Rinjiro Sodei, "Were We the Enemy? A Saga of Hiroshima Survivors in America," unpublished manuscript, 1982.)

tice to the system.[29] Not only were limited numbers of documents available for a very long period after the war, but at times materials which had been released were reclassified when they were found to be embarrassing.[30]

The rules governing atomic bomb related issues were (and are) even more stringent than those of the general classification system. Specific provisions of the Atomic Energy Act of 1946 established a separate category of classified information—"restricted data"—which exists parallel to the system of national security information set by executive order. According to the act:

> The term "restricted data" . . . means all data concerning the manufacture or utilization of atomic weapons, the production of fissionable material, or the use of fissionable material in the production of power, but shall not include any data which the [Atomic Energy] Commission from time to time determines may be published without adversely affecting the common defense and security.[31]

A person shown to have acquired or disseminated "any document, writing, sketch, photograph, plan, model, instrument, appliance, note or information involving or incorporating restricted data" with the "intent to injure the United States" can face life imprisonment or death.[32] Atomic energy related information is "born secret." The general rule is that a positive decision is required to declassify restricted data; in other areas of government a positive decision is needed to classify and control information. A recent report estimated that there were 32 million pages of classified Department of Energy documents alone—the equivalent, it noted, of 32 Washington Monuments or 3.3 miles![33]

As modern disclosures ordered by Energy Department Secretary Hazel O'Leary concerning human radiation experiments suggest, such classification provisions helped foster a climate in which government officials were virtually exempt from public accountability. A March 18, 1947, Atomic Energy Agency memorandum illustrates the "public relations" and other motives at work behind some of the information management strategies. It recommended that

> release of "Studies of Human Exposures to Uranium Compounds" would be *unwise* because it reflects a fatal accident involving uranium hexafluoride. Certain law suits, it is felt, could be effected by free publication of such a document.
>
> . . . release of "Distribution and Excretion of Plutonium" would be *unwise* since it reflects experiments on human beings.
>
> . . . release of "Uranium Excretion Studies" would be *unwise* because it reflects hospitalization of certain personnel and possibly could have an effect on certain lawsuits.[34]

A month later, on April 17, another AEA memorandum, titled "Medical Experiments on Humans," stated:

> It is desired that no document be released which refers to experiments with humans and might have adverse effect on public opinion or result in legal suits. Documents covering such work field should be classified "secret". . . . It is understood that three documents in this field have been submitted for declassification and are now classified "restricted". It is desired that these documents be reclassified "secret" and that a check be made to insure that no distribution has inadvertently been made to the Department of Commerce, or other off-Project personnel or agencies.[35]

By definition, of course, it is impossible to know to what degree the provisions of the Atomic Energy Act have been misused in connection with the Hiroshima tale. What is secret remains secret. What *is* known, however, does not give rise to great confidence in the integrity of the overall system.*

The general government classification system works to suppress information far beyond any reasonable national security needs—for most people. However, that is not the way it works (or worked) for everyone—especially in connection with various facets of the Hiroshima decision. The fact is, if you had the right connections, there were ways to get around substantial portions of the system.[36]

An important instance concerns Herbert Feis—a well-connected historian regularly granted privileged access to secret government documents. During the early 1930s a book Feis wrote brought him to the attention of Henry Stimson, at the time Herbert Hoover's secretary of state. Feis was offered an appointment as economic adviser to the State Department—a post he held for thirteen eventful years, first under Stimson, then under Roosevelt's secretary of state, Cordell Hull. In late 1943 Feis became a special assistant to Stimson

---

*Despite the Clinton Administration's efforts at greater "openness," its first annual report on overall government classification noted that total classifications had actually increased by 1 percent in 1993 (for a total of 6.4 million new classification actions). Declassification actions decreased by 30 percent. (See [Steven Aftergood,] "Classified Universe Still Expanding," *Secrecy & Government Bulletin*, No. 36, June 1994.) Only recently, on November 14, 1994—almost fifty years after the Hiroshima period—did a new Presidential Executive Order specifically authorize the declassification of 43.9 million pages held at the National Archives, 21.0 million of which were from World War II or earlier. "Bulk" (all at once) declassification of most World War II documents was mandated, but the requirement that "sources and methods" be protected meant that important categories of intelligence information could only be declassified after a time-consuming, page-by-page review process, if at all. Atomic-energy-related information was also largely exempted. As this study was going to press—on April 17, 1995—a new comprehensive executive order—requiring further openness in many areas was announced.

(now secretary of war). Feis continued in the position under Stimson's successor, Robert Patterson, remaining until 1947.* Thereafter, arguably he became the leading historian of recent American foreign relations. The prefaces to Feis' numerous books stand as milestone markers illustrating the way government information could be managed in favored cases:

• *The Road to Pearl Harbor: The Coming of the War Between the United States and Japan* (1950). Feis states directly that "the State Department granted me full access to all pertinent records."[37] He also notes that he was given access to "the full private diaries of the former Secretary of War, Henry L. Stimson, the former Secretary of the Treasury, Henry Morgenthau, Jr., and the former Ambassador to Japan, Joseph C. Grew."[38]

• *The China Tangle: The American Effort in China from Pearl Harbor to the Marshall Mission* (1953). "This work was made possible only by the wish of the State Department to have this historical experience as fully explored and objectively told as it could be at this time. . . . For this reason the former Secretary of State, Dean G. Acheson, encouraged the enterprise, and the competent Departmental Committee authorized me to consult the official files. From beginning to end many members of the Division of Historical Policy Research in the State Department aided me in locating the pertinent records and gave me the benefit of their own knowledge . . ."[39]

• *Churchill-Roosevelt-Stalin: The War They Waged and the Peace They Sought* (1957). Again, Feis notes: "The State Department permitted me to utilize its records," and that he was allowed to read draft chapters of one of the official army histories of World War II.[40] Feis acknowledges former President Truman "for permitting me to examine the collection of his correspondence with Churchill and Stalin during the spring of 1945" and he thanks Allen Dulles, then head of the CIA, for "the loan of a manuscript of an unfinished narrative telling of the secret attempt to arrange for the surrender of German forces in Italy in March–April 1945."[41] George Kennan shared "papers written while he was Counsellor of the American Embassy in Moscow during the war. . . ."[42] "The Honorable W. Averell Harriman encouraged and aided the effort throughout, sharing, in fact, in its origination. He has allowed me to use the records of, and connected with, his many assignments during the war, particularly as Ambassador to the Soviet Union beginning October 1943."[43]

Of particular relevance to our concern, of course, are the two books Feis wrote on the events of 1945:

• *Between War and Peace: The Potsdam Conference* (1960). Feis offers thanks to "the Department of State for enabling me to consult the collection of records on the Potsdam Conference which are being prepared for publica-

---

*Feis stayed on for a brief period after Kenneth C. Royall replaced Patterson.

tion, and to members of its Historical Office . . . for guidance in their use. . . ." The Department of the Army also made "available selected files. . . ."[44] "With patient kindness, former Secretary of State Byrnes put at my disposition many papers having to do with his participation in the Conference at Potsdam, and freely reviewed that experience with me. Similarly, the Undersecretary of State, Joseph C. Grew, was good enough to allow me to read and use his diary and memoranda."[45]

• *Japan Subdued: The Atomic Bomb and the End of the War in the Pacific* (1961). Feis repeats

> the acknowledgment made in *Between War and Peace* of the opportunity to consult the collection of papers regarding the Potsdam Conference which have been assembled by the State Department, and to express thanks for assistance in their use to members of the Historical Division, particularly Dr. J. [*sic*] Bernard Noble, Dr. E. Taylor Parks, and Dr. G. M. R. Dougall. I am also indebted to the Department of the Army, which permitted me to consult various records, including segments of the file on the Manhattan Project (the atomic bomb). . . .[46]

Again, the records which Averell Harriman ". . . with steadfast generosity, allowed me to draw on were of much value."[47]

A related aspect of the information access story takes us beyond such general support for favored writers. A close reader of Feis' 1957 *Churchill-Roosevelt-Stalin* might have wondered—since no source was cited or mentioned in the foreword—how the author knew what was in Henry L. Stimson's mind on May 15, 1945, when he wrote on page 640:

> As Stimson saw the situation, the atomic bomb project might well be the dominant factor in the tangled mass of considerations before them. But the outcome of the test would not be known for weeks, and it seemed a terrible thing to gamble such high stakes in diplomacy without having the master card securely in hand.[48]

It was not until two years after this book was published that the Stimson diaries were opened for general researchers and one could read the entry (noted in Book I) which Feis had obviously softened and paraphrased:

> The trouble is that the President has now promised apparently to meet Stalin and Churchill on the first of July and at that time these questions will become burning and it may be necessary to have it out with Russia on her relations to Manchuria and Port Arthur . . . Over any such tangled wave of problems the S-1 secret would be dominant and yet we will not know until after that time probably, until after that meeting,

whether this is a weapon in our hands or not. We think it will be shortly afterwards, but it seems a terrible thing to gamble with such big stakes in diplomacy without having your master card in your hand.[49]

There is no mystery how Feis managed to get advance access to the Stimson diaries for the 1945 period*: McGeorge Bundy, the man who had penned Stimson's *Harper's* defense of the bombing and who was now Stimson's literary executor, had given it to him. On March 3, 1958, as he prepared for further research, Feis wrote Bundy:

It will not surprise you to learn that I am engaged in preparatory work for a continuation of my study of wartime strategy and diplomacy—this time to carry on for a much briefer period from May 1945 through the Japanese surrender in September 1945.

So once again I wish to petition the privilege of consulting Mr. Stimson's diary. . . . If it isn't there [in Cambridge], I presume I shall have to use the microfilm at the Yale library, and would you give the necessary signal for that.[50]

Throughout this period—as we saw in the case of Richard Current—Bundy continued to deny others access to relevant portions of the diary. In 1956 he also refused a request by Roberta Morgan, a Rand Corporation researcher working on the Pearl Harbor story—despite Felix Frankfurter's personal intervention on her behalf. Bundy could not "make exception to rule *not* to open [the] papers," states a note in the files of the Supreme Court Justice.[51]

That McGeorge Bundy saw Feis as an ally and a friend is obvious throughout their correspondence; a casual, easy relationship with Stimson is also evident. Feis recalls at one point in his papers "those late afternoons when I went to Woodley to play deck tennis or bowl with him, McCloy, [Harvey] Bundy, or one or other of his military aides"[52]—and Stimson's diary of May 30, 1945, notes: "I then came home and had a game of bowls with Kyle, Herbert Feis, and Arthur Page."[53] Excerpts from letters from Bundy to Feis from as early as 1949 confirm the tone of the relationships involved:

Fortunately, his [Stimson's] friends have long since learned to ride with his ways, and as his associate biographer, I know very well how much he counts you as a friend.[54]

In general, I have nothing but admiration for your handling of Col. Stimson's material, and I have from him a blanket authorization to settle directly with you the exact uses you propose to make. . . .

---

*As we have noted, Feis had acknowledged access to Stimson's diaries for the earlier period covered by his book *The Road to Pearl Harbor*. See above, p. 616.

Thank you again for your patience in bearing with our rather cumbersome procedure. I look forward enormously to the pleasure of reading the whole as a student. . . .[55]

It is also instructive to read the extraordinary review Feis did for the *American Foreign Service Journal* of the Stimson-Bundy memoir, *On Active Service*: ". . . written with graphic lucidity by Mr. McGeorge Bundy," the memoir, Feis suggests, is "another act of instruction and leadership," indeed, a "book [of] lasting significance" which "will give meaning and sustaining faith to . . . efforts to deal with the doubts and dangers of our present days." The Foreign Service officer would do well to "keep this book at his bedside, especially when the night's news is bad."[56]

Our interest is neither with Feis nor with Bundy per se. Nor is it even with the fact that Feis was given special access to the Stimson diaries before other scholars. What is of considerable relevance is that McGeorge Bundy became National Security Adviser to presidents Kennedy and Johnson during the early 1960s—and at this point was in a powerful official position where he could help Feis with government rather than private documents. Again, simply by way of illustration of how the system now worked:

In August 1965 Feis contacted Bundy to ask if he could help arrange access to portions of the still "top secret" Manhattan Project files. Bundy replied on August 24, 1965, that he had "checked into your problem . . . the clearance has been approved and . . . the letter so advising you should have been dispatched by the Adjutant General's office either last night or early this morning. If you run into any more difficulty, please let me know."[57]

The documentary record generated in the wake of Feis' request indicates the unusual steps which were taken to expedite his case. For instance, a subsequent memorandum to the chief of staff of the U.S. Army from Major General J. C. Lambert reported that:

To facilitate a review of the notes by Army, OSD [Office of the Secretary of Defense], State and the Atomic Energy Commission, NARS [National Archives and Records Service] performed a service for Dr. Feis and typed his handwritten notes. . . . they were handcarried to TAGO [The Adjutant General's Office] to eliminate normal mailing time. . . . TAGO personnel hand delivered two sets of typed notes to OCINFO [Office of the Chief of Information], recommending that the notes be declassified and that expeditious action be taken to review and clear the notes.

Lambert continued: "Since the notes are taken from security classified records relating to international aspects of the development and use of the atomic bomb, they require internal Army coordination and formal coordination with OSD, State, and AEC. This is a time consuming process."[58]

On August 28 Feis wrote Bundy with a further problem:

> Thanks for responding to my request so quickly and effectively. I have heard from General Lambert that I will be able to pore through most, if not all, of the Bundy-Harrison files about S-1. But the permission is based on such various conditions that I don't know whether I will be able to use any information I may find in time for printing the revision. Notes and manuscript [are] to be inspected for "security" reasons.[59]

Feis' worry that there might be delays and limitations placed on his use of the "Harrison-Bundy" files was not misplaced. On September 13 he again wrote the National Security Adviser at the White House:

> In your note [of August 24] you were good enough to say that if I had any further trouble about obtaining and using any information that I might find in the Harrison-Bundy files about S-1 to let you know. Reluctantly I am appealing to you again. . . .
>
> Could you possibly have someone again make inquiry of the Adjutant General's office or the Administrative Officer of the Army and see if he can spur the review and clearance of these notes? Let them blue pencil anything about which they have doubt, but get them back to me quickly![60]

On September 16, the general counsel of the Department of the Army, Alfred B. Fitt, informed Feis that the "staff officer told me that McGeorge Bundy had also called asking for expedition of the clearance process. I will keep after the Army people, but it may be a little while yet before they can round up OSD, State and AEC clearances."[61]

The difference between access available to men like Feis and ordinary researchers is further illustrated by another important relationship: for a significant period—especially in the early years when he began work on his book *Churchill-Roosevelt-Stalin*—Feis was on Averell Harriman's personal payroll. A September 1, 1953, letter of agreement from the former ambassador and Truman Administration Cabinet member specified:

> I am anxious to record my wartime experiences, particularly as they relate to the historic implication of those affairs with which I was involved. In this you are undertaking for a period of one year beginning September 1, 1953 to help me in a manner to be worked out as we go along. It is understood that this will not be full time and that you are free to undertake other matters that interest you. . . .

In full compensation for your services, I agree to pay you a total of nine thousand dollars. . . .[62]

What Feis termed the "Harriman Project" also required office space and clerical support. A November 5, 1954, letter from Feis to J. D. Powell, of Brown Brothers Harriman & Company, describes in some detail the relationship between Feis and his employer—including the sharing of office rent and secretarial costs.[63]

Working for and with Harriman not only gave Feis privileged access to information in his private files, it also put him in a position to do favors for the people within the government he regularly asked to help with documents. A March 2, 1956, letter from G. Bernard Noble, Chief of the State Department Division of Historical Policy Research, for instance, thanks Feis for getting Harriman to focus on a matter related to the Potsdam conference he was trying to pin down for the Department's historical series—and then goes on to ask: "Do you think there is any point in raising with Governor Harriman once more the question of access to his files on Potsdam?"[64]

Feis' books on the Potsdam conference and the decision to use the atomic bomb were the first major studies written on the basis of a great deal of newly available government information and, accordingly, had enormous impact. They got ahead of—and for many years set the terms of reference for—modern historical understanding of the critical events of 1945. The final conclusion Feis reached concerning the decisions made by men he had known, worked for, and befriended was straightforward: The use of the atomic bombs had been impelled by military concerns and "the decision to drop the bombs upon Hiroshima and Nagasaki ought not to be censured."[65]

By all accounts, Feis was a man of high integrity. He felt that as a Jew he could not give fair and unbiased advice concerning Germany—and therefore turned down an offer to become economic adviser to Eisenhower as the supreme Allied commander prepared to invade France and occupy western Germany.[66] On the other hand, it would take an extraordinary human being indeed to write objectively on an extremely controversial subject which involved old friends and professional colleagues, an eminent friend and Cabinet member who had successfully promulgated the dominant national theory of why the atomic bomb had been used, his close associate in that project who had also helped the writer himself gain access to important information and now held the powerful position of National Security Adviser to the president of the United States, and, finally, another friend who was a former ambassador to the Soviet Union who played a central role in the American establishment and who had paid the writer to help organize his most confidential personal papers.

In theory, Feis might possibly have been critical of Stimson, McGeorge Bundy's father, Harvey, and Harriman, but in practice . . . ? Normally, even the most scrupulous scholar working in such circumstances would be open to the obvious charge of "conflict of interest"—and only the naïve would fail to raise an eyebrow at the "history" produced in such circumstances.[67]

The wonder, indeed, is not that Feis concluded that the use of both atomic bombs was justified. It is that he also was so candid in discussing some of the difficult and "troubling" questions which still worried him.

Feis explicitly stated his firm opinion, for instance, that the use of the atomic bomb was not essential.[68] Furthermore, he allowed that more warning time probably should have been given—and also argued specifically that information about the new weapon should have been announced and that information on the impending Russian attack should have been made public. In one of his research memoranda he wrote that "the view continued to prevail that Soviet entry would under all the circumstances be an added adverse fact that would compel Japan to accept surrender; and in the event that the bomb did not go off, Soviet action in Manchuria would remain very important in producing the surrender that it was hoped to get without invasion. So much can be affirmed with certainty."[69]

Feis also pointed out in his published account that by—or it appears possibly before—July there was a very good chance the war could have been ended without the bombs had the United States followed a variation of the "two-step logic": "I think it may be concluded that . . . the fighting would have continued well into July at the least, *unless* . . ."

the American and Soviet governments together had let it be known that unless Japan laid down its arms at once, the Soviet Union was going to enter the war. That, along with a promise to spare the Emperor, might well have made an earlier bid for surrender effective.[70]

We may regard it as a final sign of Feis' integrity that despite his friendship and access he even allowed himself to waver back and forth, in the end concluding:

It is likely that Churchill, and probably also Truman, conceived that besides bringing the war to a quick end, it [using the bomb] would improve the chances of arranging a satisfactory peace both in Europe and in the Far East. Stimson and Byrnes certainly had that thought in mind. For would not the same dramatic proof of western power that shocked Japan into surrender impress the Russians also?[71]

Chapter 49

FINAL PERSPECTIVES

---

*The implication that the atomic bombs were dropped on a
people who had already sued for peace should not be in-
cluded in a paper prepared for release to the public.*
—Memorandum to General Dwight D. Eisenhower,
Chief of Staff, from General George A. Lincoln,
April 2, 1946

As noted, even Herbert Feis was not always successful in gaining access to
all the official documents he sought; he, too, became progressively more and
more frustrated by excessive government secrecy, both before but especially
after some of his friends and former colleagues were no longer in government.[1] In a 1967 *Foreign Affairs* article entitled "The Shackled Historian"
Feis observed:

> Let the historian try to get from the authorities all the extant records,
> unedited, of what was said and done during the past two decades from
> 1945 to 1965! He will find out that he cannot. If he persists, eventually
> doors may be closed to him. Now and then he may manage to hasten
> the process of declassification. But only exceptionally so.[2]

In this essay, Feis also presented a classic description of the experience most
researchers have had for most of the postwar period:

> It takes just one quick, easy and safe movement of the wrist to place the
> stamp of secrecy on a document or communication. But ordinarily that
> stamp cannot be removed until committees of cautious officials have
> long pondered the wisdom or utility of doing so. Few of those I have
> known were disposed to take even faint risks that by declassifying a
> document they might be exposing their country, department or superiors
> to controversy and jeopardizing their own jobs.[3]

The situation Feis describes, of course, concerns the most general—and often indiscriminate—ways information has been (and continues to be) controlled. Perhaps it may therefore be useful to close with two final reminders of the deliberate and purposive nature of information management at certain points in connection with the Hiroshima tale.

We have noted the conclusion of the Strategic Bombing Survey that Japan would almost certainly have surrendered in any event even if the atomic bombs had not been used. As the survey's report was being readied for publication in June 1946, Secretary of War Robert Patterson received word of what he regarded as worrisome language from Groves.[4] In turn Patterson advised Eisenhower (now army chief of staff) that he was "disturbed by the section on the Japanese decision to surrender, pages 27–29. The statement is made at the outset that the Japanese decision to surrender was taken 'at least as early as 26 June. . . .' "

> We have no responsibility for what is contained in the report. But it is passing through my mind that the War Department may come in for severe criticism, on account of the statement in the report that the Japanese had decided to surrender as early as June 26, for having advised that the atomic bombs should be launched against Japan in August.[5]

On the bottom of Patterson's file copy a typed postscript states: "Have since spoken to Strategic Survey and they are toning down their statement."[6] The next day another memorandum to Eisenhower reported that the Strategic Bombing Survey draft definitely had been changed:

> The statement to the effect that the Japanese decision to surrender was made as early as June 26 has been eliminated. In its place a sentence has been inserted that the Japanese were looking for ways and means to end the war as early as May.
> This removes the objectionable material.[7]

Similarly, we have noted a top-secret 1946 War Department study which concluded that even if there had never been an atomic bomb a full-scale invasion of Japan would not have occurred—indeed, that even a November 1945 landing on Kyushu had been only a "remote" possibility:

> The Japanese leaders had decided to surrender and were merely looking for sufficient pretext to convince the die-hard Army Group that Japan had lost the war and must capitulate to the Allies.[8]

As we have seen, the study pointed out that although the "dropping of the bomb was the pretext seized upon . . . it [is] almost a certainty that the Japanese would have capitulated upon the entry of Russia into the war."[9]

The top-secret study did not come out of the blue. It was ordered by the

War Department in connection with a statement on atomic weapons being developed for presentation to Congress by the Joint Chiefs of Staff.[10] Eisenhower had requested preparation of the statement because, as he noted on December 20, 1945, it "appears that early in 1946 the Congress will give serious consideration to the effect of developments in the field of atomic energy on U.S. military organization and military requirements for the future."[11]

The "Statement of Effect of Atomic Weapons on National Security and Military Organization" went through many drafts. It is impossible to tell from available documents to what extent the conclusions of the War Department study were discussed in its preparation.[12]* From the point of view of our current concern, however, the process by which other critical aspects of the statement were prepared—and in the end revised—is of equal interest:

As the statement neared completion—on February 23, 1946—the commander of the Army Air Forces, General Carl Spaatz, objected to the vague wording of the opening sentence. The draft language stated very generally: "The atomic bombs dropped on Japan had two primary effects: first, the accelerated ending of the war with the probable saving of thousands of lives; and second, a profound revolution in military thought."[13] Spaatz urged, instead, that the opening sentence should be made to read:

> The atomic bombs dropped in Japan had two primary effects: first, although the Japanese had already initiated diplomatic action leading to surrender, the actual ending of the war was accelerated with the probable saving of thousands of lives; and second, a profound revolution in military thought has resulted.[14]

The chief War Department Operations Division Planner, General Lincoln, noted the same day: "It appears that [this and two other of] General Spaatz's amendments are not essential but do strengthen the paper."[15] With the concurrence of Manhattan Project and other officials, the Operations Division recommended approval of Spaatz's proposed change. Similarly, on March 12, 1946, Admiral Nimitz, the Chief of Naval Operations, recommended a similar change.[16] His reason: "I believe the proposed wording more nearly expresses the fact." A subsequent memo includes the additional notation: "Admiral Leahy concurs."[17]

There is little doubt that one of Spaatz's concerns was to emphasize that conventional bombing (rather than the new weapon) had played a central role

---

*The date of the study in its final form supersedes by one month the date of the final statement. However, preliminary drafts of such studies commonly circulated informally well in advance of the final dates.

in the prior (late June) Japanese decision to seek a way out of the war. None-theless, the new language was accurate—as navy leaders also agreed—and, as Lincoln noted, it helped "strengthen the paper." There was one major difficulty with the text, however.

As Lincoln pointed out in a further top-secret memorandum of February 27, when his "attention was called to *the possible implication to be drawn by the public that the atomic bombs were dropped on a people who had already sued for peace*, Spaatz agreed to the inadvisability of using the quoted phrase."[18] Lincoln put the essential point even more explicitly in a follow-on report to Eisenhower:

> The implication that the atomic bombs were dropped on a people who had already sued for peace should not be included in a paper prepared for release to the public.[19]

At this time Lincoln also reported that General Spaatz had now "agreed to the deletion of the phrase." The April 2, 1946, memorandum to Eisenhower concluded formally:

> OPD [THE OPERATIONS DIVISION] RECOMMENDS:
> . . . *That the objectionable phrase in paragraph 1 of JCS 1477/8 (underlined above and marked in attached paper) be eliminated. No difficulty is anticipated in reaching agreement on this point.*[20]

The final form of the Joint Chiefs of Staff statement prepared for presentation to Congress, like the Strategic Bombing Survey report, did not include the troublesome language.

Conclusion

THE COMPLICITY OF SILENCE

[T]he readiness to use nuclear weapons against other human beings—against people whom we do not know, whom we have never seen, and for whose guilt or innocence it is not for us to establish—and, in doing so, to place in jeopardy the natural structure upon which all civilization rests . . . this is nothing less than a presumption, a blasphemy, an indignity—an indignity of monstrous dimensions—offered to God!

—George F. Kennan,
"A Christian's View of the Arms Race"

Repeated polls over the years have shown that the vast majority of Americans have raised very few questions about the bombing of Hiroshima and Nagasaki.[1] The conventional wisdom that the atomic bomb saved hundreds of thousands—perhaps a million—lives persists.

It is certainly the case that we Americans have been badly served by our leaders in connection with the promulgation of various Hiroshima myths—that we were systematically misled about many of the basic facts. Furthermore, an entire generation of soldiers, sailors, airmen, and marines (and through them, their families and friends) were taught that their lives were saved by the atomic bomb; their understandable relief based on this false information has added to the strength of the myth.

The general rule of press and other reporting throughout this fifty-year period also has commonly been to repeat without challenge (or even a minimal amount of research) "facts" which have long since been shown to be either questionable or false. Although there have always been exceptions, the myth of a half-million or a million casualties, for instance, was often reported as fact during the 1994–95 controversy over the Smithsonian Institution's exhibit of the *Enola Gay*.[2]

Beyond all this, however, it is also quite clear that we Americans did not wish to probe for the truth—or even ask tough questions about what we were being told. We seem to have preferred the myth.

Few wished even to see whether there might be something behind the troubling information which somehow kept seeping out over the half century—and it is obvious that we have found it very, very difficult to confront even the most basic and well-documented facts.

Over fifty years we often also seem to have felt a strong need to justify the bombings by reference to what can only be called notions of "revenge." Time and again, the question of whether the use of the atomic bomb was militarily required has become entangled with the quite separate issue of our anger at Japan's sneak attack and the brutality of her military. The Japanese people have a great deal of ugly history to confront—including not only Pearl Harbor but the bombings of Shanghai, the rape of Nanking, the forced prostitution of Korean women, the human experiments of the notorious Unit 731, the horror of the Bataan death march, and the systematic torture and murder of prisoners of war.

Even so, the question of Hiroshima remains.

Again, we have often allowed ourselves to confuse the discussion of the modern research findings with criticism of American servicemen. This is—or should be—even less justified (as the statements of so many World War II generals and admirals should suggest). The men serving in the Pacific in 1945 were prepared to risk their lives for their nation. By this most fundamental test they can only be called heroes.

The fact that policy-makers in Washington were advised there were alternatives to the atomic bomb is no reflection on the troops who knew nothing of the MAGIC cables, the Russian option, or the Emperor's intervention. Quite the contrary. This was neither the first nor the last time that people on the ground were misinformed about what the higher-ups knew.

Unfortunately, our reluctance to ask questions about the received wisdom has not dissipated over time. Indeed, although the information now available is more plentiful than it once was, in many ways public discussion has become less rather than more thoughtful. A recent survey of the press concluded that "present media coverage is worse than it was in the euphoric aftermath of World War II—the media now ignore, with limited exceptions, an impressive body of evidence and argument that run counter to the official line. . . ."

> in the earlier [1945–1950] period 1) some journalists and editors themselves questioned the decision to use the bomb, in ways that are strikingly similar to the current scholarly consensus, and 2) journalists understood that the Russian entry into the Pacific war played an important part in ending the war. . . .[3]

We have lost an older generation of military leaders who in the earlier period served as alternative sources of authoritative information for the press and who spoke from personal experience and conviction on the subject. It is not the case, however, that some of the most important facts have been impossible to discover—or, minimally, that the remaining unresolved questions could not be defined with honesty. Nor, indeed, is it impossible to state and face the fundamental moral issues even on the basis of traditional versions of the events of 1945.

Throughout the entire half-century since Hiroshima, in fact, individuals of all ideological and religious persuasions have repeatedly demonstrated that it was always possible to find out a very great deal—and always possible, too, to raise obvious questions about what was not known if one so desired.

As we have extensively shown in this narrative, if Americans had wished to know more than the official myth—or had merely wished even to ask hard questions—it is quite clear they could have done so.

Some of the unresolved issues of the 1945 record—particularly those related to the precise weight to attach to diplomatic considerations in the Hiroshima decision—are explored in the Afterword. It is not necessary, however, to answer all the remaining questions to confront the most important issue.

Quite simply, it is not true that the atomic bomb was used because it was the only way to save the "hundreds of thousands" or "millions" of lives as was subsequently claimed. The readily available options were to modify the surrender terms and/or await the shock of the Russian attack. Three months remained before a November Kyushu landing could take place even in theory; there were six to seven months before the spring invasion of Honshu could begin under the existing planning assumptions.

If we accept the conclusion of either the U.S. Strategic Bombing Survey (which did not even assume a modification of the unconditional surrender formula or the impact of a Russian declaration of war) or the War Department study which judged the war would almost certainly have ended when the Red Army attacked—then in retrospect, minimally, the bombings were, as Hanson Baldwin put it, a "mistake."[4]

However, the evidence—especially from the MAGIC intercepts, the records of the Joint Chiefs of Staff, the 1945 intelligence studies, numerous statements by military leaders close to the decision process, and the Leahy, Stimson, Forrestal, McCloy, and Brown diaries—allows us to go beyond this. It is impossible to peer into the hearts and minds of men fifty years after the fact. Nevertheless, although matters of nuance and degree can be endlessly debated, it is quite clear that alternatives to using the bomb existed—and that the president and his advisers were aware of them.[5]

One of the charges about which Truman was most sensitive was that the use of the atomic bomb was rushed, that it did not flow from a careful and thoughtful consideration of all the available alternatives. His feeling is understandable.

Modern evidence—reinforced, again, by the information which has been discovered in the course of research for this book—suggests not only that the president and Byrnes knew Japan was on the verge of surrender, but that once the new weapon had been successfully tested, rushing to end the war before an expected mid-August Red Army attack was indisputably a major concern.

That the decision was something less than thoughtful is also suggested by the fact that on August 10 Truman had to have his memory refreshed concerning the passage in the Potsdam Proclamation issued only two weeks earlier which used the critical phrase "unconditional surrender."

It is sometimes held that there is little difference between the atomic bombing of Hiroshima and Nagasaki and the conventional attacks which killed more than 100,000 people in Tokyo on the night of March 9–10, 1945—and continued in many cities thereafter.

As John Dower has recently observed, the actual numbers are often not considered. Modern estimates, he points out, suggest that roughly as many or more deaths—ultimately, possibly 300,000—were caused by the atomic bomb as were produced by all the conventional city-bombing combined.[6] Precise data are, of course, impossible to determine, but the orders of magnitude are clearly similar. Even more significant, it is not the case that the conventional bombing of cities would have continued unabated had the atomic bombs not been used: As we have seen, a new directive had been issued (and was about to be implemented as the war ended) to concentrate first on such priority military targets as railroads and aircraft production facilities.

The judgments expressed by the various military leaders also help clarify this issue. Most important is the fact that the dramatic bombing of Tokyo and many other major Japanese cities occurred before information was received showing the Emperor's intervention to attempt to end the war. What men like Eisenhower and Leahy were saying was not only that it was both ineffective and wrong to target what were primarily civilian population concentrations, but that to do this when the Japanese seemed plausibly on the verge of surrender was an uncalled-for violation of traditional norms.[7]

There was also a strong sense, as Eisenhower put it, that "our country should avoid shocking world opinion. . . ."[8] Similarly, on May 29, 1945, Marshall proposed that "these weapons might first be used against straight military objectives such as a large naval installation."[9] If cities ultimately were attacked, he also suggested that they be given very clear warning to evacuate so as to avoid "the opprobrium which might follow from an ill considered employment of such force."[10]

It is sometimes held that no real "decision" to use the atomic bomb ever took place, that the "momentum" of war (or of bureaucracy, etc.) produced the bombings—and that, besides, there is no surviving contemporaneous evidence that anyone directly challenged the decision.

As a historian who once subscribed to—indeed, helped launch—one version of the "no-decision," momentum theory, I know the temptation this view offers: Among other things, if there was no human decision, no burden of judgment must be borne—and no human responsibility is to be assigned.

Moreover, there is a good deal of apparent support for one or another theory of momentum. For instance, there is very little sign* that the question "Should the atomic bomb be used? Or should it not be used?" was posed directly and squarely at the highest level of government. Hence, the empty silence of the documentary record makes it appear as if no real "decision" was made, that momentum governed.

The modern evidence makes it obvious that things were not so simple.

The truth is that at least three very clear and explicit decisions (and probably more) were made which set the terms of reference for the bomb's subsequent seemingly "inevitable" use. Indeed, once they were made, they so tightly framed the remaining issues as to make it all but impossible thereafter to oppose the bombings.

The first decision involved rejection of the recommendation that to offer any meaningful possibility of surrender a statement to Japan would have to allow enough time for the development of a serious response. As we have seen, a conscious choice not to allow a meaningful interval was made early on—and explicitly reaffirmed at Potsdam.

The second and more fundamental choice was the decision not to offer Japan assurances for the Emperor. Once this decision had been made—and the Japanese were allowed to believe the Emperor might be removed and possibly hanged as a war criminal—it was obvious to all concerned that the fighting would continue.

In this area there was, in fact, a certain "momentum" at the top levels of the U.S. and British governments—but it was moving powerfully in a direction quite opposite to the automatic use of the bomb. As we have seen, the president was advised to clarify the surrender terms on more than a dozen occasions—and by virtually the entire U.S. and British leadership. The sole exception among presidential advisers was James F. Byrnes.

The decision to eliminate the critical paragraph-twelve assurances of the Potsdam Proclamation was a move to oppose—not go with the flow of—the then ongoing policy momentum. It was also the central decision—and was so understood, as the conflict and concentration on it suggests.

*But not none. See below, p. 633.

We must also note that all along—as Truman subsequently acknowledged on many occasions—it appears to have been clear to those concerned that in the end the Emperor would in any event almost certainly have to be retained to command a cessation of the fighting and to maintain internal order. (And, of course, five days after the bombing of Hiroshima, his position was in fact assured by the president.)

That the documentary record shows little direct challenge to the idea the atomic bomb would be used is understandable, once one grasps the implications of these facts.

The decision to delete assurances for the Emperor from the Potsdam Proclamation was one relegated to political authority. Once the president had made his choice on this matter—and since it was known that therefore the fighting would now unquestionably continue—the basic military options were narrowed to two: The only choice now was to use the bomb or go forward with an invasion.

In this situation the silence and seeming momentum of events is not difficult to comprehend. For any official—military or civilian—to oppose the bombing in these circumstances would have been absurd. It would have been equivalent to arguing for a bloody invasion. It would also have been to challenge the president after he had made his decision quite clear.

The third fundamental choice has now also been fully documented. It was the decision not to test the impact of the Russian declaration of war—indeed, to weaken the military challenge posed to Japan by attempting to put off an event which all understood would have extraordinary impact. This decision, too, was made at the political level.

In connection with recommendations to modify the terms, as we have seen, virtually all the president's advisers except Byrnes were essentially in accord. However, no one really wanted the Russians in the war if it could be concluded without them. (Indeed, some, like Grew—and probably Forrestal—had urged a change in terms precisely because they thought this on its own could end the fighting before August.) Hence, on this issue there was very little reason to wish to challenge the president and Byrnes—despite the fact that intelligence and other advice even before the Emperor's intervention strongly suggested "the Russian option" seemed likely to end the war alone or as part of the "two-step logic" in combination with a modification of the surrender terms.

The sense of a process seemingly governed by a silent momentum—of no explicit decision about whether to use the bomb being made—is a natural result of the fact that there really was very little to talk about after the critical framing decisions had been made. Indeed, once the obvious alternatives had been eliminated by presidential decree, to challenge the bombing would have seemed ridiculous.

Perhaps only a victorious Supreme Commander who had just presided over the defeat of Hitler, a man Truman understood to be a great national hero (and whom at Potsdam Truman personally offered to support for president in lieu of himself in 1948), could halt this "momentum."[11]

Although it is impossible to know for certain, if we are to accept the word of the man himself, on or about July 20, 1945, Eisenhower did urge Truman directly not to use the atomic bomb.

Beyond this, further explicit decisions were made subsequently by the president and Byrnes—particularly the decisions not to follow up on the Japanese responses to the Atlantic Charter broadcast; and, most importantly, not to follow up on the early August intercepts.

Finally, the idea that no real decision took place—or that no one understood that the decision not to change the terms and to put off the Russian attack were serious decisions—is also belied by Stimson's private acknowledgment to Grew that "as you know, feelings ran high and there were very fine men . . . working on the other side."[12]

It is thus not the case that some inevitable force of history, of momentum, tied everyone's hands. Eisenhower's straightforward assessment stands: "[I]t wasn't necessary to hit them with that awful thing."[13] It also wasn't necessary to "succumb" to Byrnes.

"To use the atomic bomb, to kill and terrorize civilians, without even attempting [negotiations]," Michael Walzer writes, "was a double crime."[14] The point Eisenhower and others made repeatedly was that choice was possible—that the advisers who had lost the battle to Byrnes over modifying the terms—and the military leaders who later spoke out critically on the subject—were right to suggest there had been good reason to believe the war could have been ended otherwise, and that the attempt should have been made.

All of this also obviously bears on the issue of the number of lives which may possibly have been saved by the atomic bomb. As we have seen, over the last decade scholars working in very different fields—Barton Bernstein, Rufus E. Miles, Jr., and John Ray Skates—all separately have demonstrated that even if the first landing and subsequent invasion had gone forward, at the time it was officially estimated that the number of lives which might have been lost (and therefore possibly saved by the atomic bomb) was of the order of magnitude of 20,000 to 26,000 for Kyushu, and a maximum of 46,000 in the unlikely event of a full invasion in 1946.[15]

However, even these numbers confuse the central issues (as do other nonofficial estimates). The fact is if the war could have been ended by clarifying the terms and/or the Russian shock, there would have been no lives lost in an invasion. Fighting was reduced as both sides regrouped, and the most that may be said is that the atomic bombs may have saved the lives which might have been lost in the time it would have taken to arrange the final surrender terms.

That saving lives was not the very highest priority, however, seems obvious from the three choices made in July: If one really wished to end the war as fast and surely as possible—and save as many men as possible—then as Marshall had pointed out as early as June, the full force of the Russian shock plus assurances for the Emperor could not be left out of the equation.

Moreover, if we accept Stimson's judgment that "history might find" that the decision to delay assurances for the Emperor "had prolonged the war," then—as Martin Sherwin has stressed—the atomic bomb probably cost U.S. lives (since the delay was occasioned by the decision to wait for the Alamogordo test).[16] As many as five thousand American men in arms may have lost their lives between Grew's May 28 recommendation that the "unconditional" terms be clarified and the final surrender.[17]

In the decades since World War II, writers who have defended the bombings have repeatedly pointed to the hard-line Japanese army faction which was opposed to surrender and which was clearly preparing to defend against a possible invasion. Some have even offered dramatic, detailed descriptions of battles which in theory might possibly have been fought. The intricacies of various arguments are taken up in the Afterword, but the essential points to note here are rather straightforward:

In the first place it is an obvious non sequitur to argue from the fact that preparations were going forward that what was "planned" was also what, in fact, was likely to happen. The U.S. military, after all, was also engaged in preparations and plans for an invasion. It is quite clear that the Japanese both wished to be prepared for an invasion and wanted to make sure U.S. officials believed they would fight to the death if invaded.

Much more important, no knowledgeable historian would dispute the idea that so long as the Emperor's position was in doubt—as it was throughout this entire period—the Japanese would likely have resisted to the end. The army faction held all the cards so long as the Emperor was threatened. And so long as the Russians were neutral they could also argue it was not totally insane to continue the war.

Nor is it surprising that after the war some Japanese leaders honestly recalled that they had planned to fight on. That is, in fact, what they had expected to do, given that U.S. policy continued to threaten the Emperor. This was what the fundamental debate was all about inside the U.S. government—and precisely why American military leaders urged the president to offer Japan assurances for the Emperor.

Put another way, eliminating the political-psychological props holding up the army faction and securing the shock of a Red Army attack were the central thrust of top intelligence and other advice throughout the summer. That even without such changes so many U.S. military leaders felt the war could have been ended before a November landing only underscores the narrow focus of some arguments which point to opposition to surrender within Japan yet ignore or downplay the options available to U.S. leaders at the time.

Nor, contrary to some theories, did political considerations compel the president's choices. *The New York Times* ran this suggestive headline on page one of its August 12, 1945, edition: "GI's in Pacific Go Wild With Joy; 'Let 'Em Keep Emperor,' They Say." It was always known, to repeat, that in the end the terms would almost certainly have to be modified so that the Emperor could order troops in the field to lay down their arms. There may possibly have been some modest political advantage in postponing a clarification of terms for a few days. However, as we have seen, several of the president's private contemporaneous comments make it obvious that political considerations were hardly overriding for him personally.

Moreover, the pressure from leading Republicans was all in the direction of offering a clarification of terms sooner rather than later. From Herbert Hoover's private discussions with the president in May to public statements by the Senate minority leader in June and July, Republicans had begun to signal quite clearly that the president could expect support from the opposition party if he were to negotiate an end to the war.

This, in turn, may help explain why some of the most powerful early criticism of the Hiroshima bombing came from conservative Republicans. Indeed, the day before Nagasaki was destroyed Hoover could not contain his feelings. As we have noted, in a memorandum sent to the publisher of the *Army and Navy Journal*, Colonel John Callan O'Laughlin, he exclaimed: "The use of the atomic bomb, with its indiscriminate killing of women and children, revolts my soul."[18]

Similarly, before news of the bombing of Nagasaki had been publicly announced, John Foster Dulles joined Methodist Bishop Oxnam to appeal for at least a temporary halt in the attacks:

One choice open to us is immediately to wreak upon our enemy mass destruction such as men have never before imagined. That will inevitably obliterate men and women, young and aged, innocent and guilty alike, because they are part of a nation which has attacked us and whose conduct has stirred our deep wrath. If we, a professedly Christian nation, feel morally free to use atomic energy in that way, men elsewhere will accept that verdict.[19]

Henry Luce, the publisher of *Time* and *Life*, also subsequently recalled his trip to the Pacific a few months before Hiroshima—and observed:

Two things seemed clear to me—as they did to many of the top fighting men I talked to: first, that Japan was beaten; second, that the Japanese knew it and were every day showing signs of increasing willingness to quit. If, instead of our doctrine of "unconditional surrender," we had all along made our conditions clear, I have little doubt that the war with Japan would have ended soon without the bomb explosion which so jarred the Christian conscience.[20]

The language used in some of these statements must be confronted. Almost certainly it was because many knowledgeable conservatives had judged early on that the war could be ended on virtually the same terms as were ultimately accepted that they felt strongly about the matter—about what the bombings really meant. Hoover's characterization of the primary victims was exactly the same as Leahy's: "women and children."[21] It was also close to Truman's post-Nagasaki acknowledgment to his Cabinet on August 10 that he had halted the bombing because he didn't like the idea of killing so many ordinary people—especially the children.[22]

Perhaps it is here, most poignantly, that we confront our own reluctance to ask the difficult questions—for even if one were to accept the most inflated estimates of lives saved by the atomic bomb, the fact remains that it was an act of violent destruction aimed deliberately at large concentrations of noncombatants.

We do not like to speak of such things. "The knowledge of horrible events periodically intrudes into public awareness," professor of psychiatry Judith Herman observes, but it "is rarely retained for long. Denial, repression, and dissociation operate on a social as well as an individual level."[23]

Indeed, fifty years after the fact we have so abstracted Hiroshima from direct human experience that it appears mostly to us (if at all) symbolically—as a "mushroom cloud."[24] Even a writer—this writer—who has lived with the subject on and off for more than thirty years has trouble penetrating the dumb wall of inherited abstraction.

There is thus something further to reflect upon in the responses of leading American conservatives and, too, of military men who spoke out after the decision—something important, something which lingers. To point to the fact of choice is to realize that some men grasped the human realities of the decision—and some did not.

More than most Americans, it appears that some military leaders recognized that a line had been crossed, a transgression had occurred. Military men of the World War II generation knew what the bombing of a city meant.

If we wish ever to truly come to terms with Hiroshima, we must penetrate to the truth behind these feelings. I visited Hiroshima in the mid-1980s. What struck me was the same thing which apparently struck Harry Truman on August 10, 1945—the inevitable ordinariness of a city of this kind. Here a young uniformed schoolgirl, perhaps nine years old, walks past hand in hand with a friend. There two older women, perhaps sisters, return from shopping. A garbage man of indiscernible age makes his rounds. A daughter-in-law, it seems, helps an elderly mother-in-law across the street.

For the most part, these were by far the vast majority of people who were incinerated by the atomic bombs or penetrated with radiation, tortured, perhaps for years, to die a slow agonizing death.

The gritty human truth behind the abstract atomic cloud which some of the military leaders understood so well does not come into consciousness easily. It is too painful to look at up close. Years later the Catholic Bishop of Seattle, Raymond Hunthausen, recalled that in 1945 he simply "could not then put into words the shock I felt from the news that a city of hundreds of thousands of people had been destroyed by a single bomb."

> That awful event and its successor at Nagasaki sank into my soul, as they have in fact sunk into the souls of all of us, whether we recognize it or not.[25]

To poke through these old ashes obviously raises the most troubling kinds of questions about the nature of decision-making in our democracy, the quality of our leaders, even the moral integrity (or superiority?) of our nation.[26]

None of the officials who made the decision to use the atomic bomb did so out of evil intent. Their motives, broadly speaking, were good; their intentions well-meaning. Mainly they were people who had experienced two world wars in one generation who did not want to see a third war occur—and who believed the new weapon gave them the power to shape events so as to achieve a truly enduring peace.

Given that this is so—and, too, that so much time has passed—is it really necessary for us to return to reflect, now, today, on this fifty-year-old tragedy? The great majority of Americans alive today had not been born in 1945, or were children at the time. Those who were adults had little access to critical information and virtually no access to decision-making. Why should this generation, in particular, care? *What has any of this to do with us?*

One answer—quite simply—is that perhaps we can learn something from experience. Stimson's observation about those who made the Hiroshima decision was not simply that they were "very fine men"—but also that they "should have known better. . . ."[27]

There is, too, the matter of how we understand ourselves in relationship to others. Around the world Americans are famous for a certain naive self-righteousness, even arrogance. We like to see ourselves as possessed of special, unique virtue.

Ours is a great nation. So long as we accept a distorted, overly idealized image of ourselves and of our society, however—so long as we see all "good" here and all "evil" elsewhere—I believe we must inevitably err in our relationships with others. Many of the excesses of the Cold War—and the overreaching that produced the Vietnam War—can be traced in part to such attitudes.

No nation can claim perfect virtue or absolute moral superiority. An honest confrontation with Hiroshima is important for its own sake, and as a way to help us achieve a better understanding of ourselves—one which may be the precondition to a different, better form of global understanding in the new century. Reinhold Niebuhr was right in 1946 to insist that we must "admit the moral ambiguity of all righteous people in history. . . ."[28]

In all of this, too, at bottom there is the question of our human capacity to pierce through to the implications of how we have thought about the enormity of nuclear weapons now for half a century. We are so used to the all-too-conventional language of nuclear strategy—of "deterrence"—that most of us have lost any real sense of what it is we have been saying (and listening to) for so many years.

In "A Christian's View of the Arms Race" George F. Kennan has sharpened the point for those who take their moral and religious questions seriously:

> [T]he readiness to use nuclear weapons against other human beings—against people whom we do not know, whom we have never seen, and for whose guilt or innocence it is not for us to establish—and, in doing so, to place in jeopardy the natural structure upon which all civilization rests, as though the safety and perceived interests of our own generation are more important than everything that has ever taken place or could take place in civilization: this is nothing less than a presumption, a blasphemy, an indignity—an indignity of monstrous dimensions—offered to God![29]

Are we really so surprised when we observe violence and threats of violence all around us in our communities? We as a nation have been threatening unbelievable violence—without fully grasping the implications—for fifty years. To penetrate to the human truth, in all its pain, of Hiroshima may also be a way to help undo some of our own numbness to the meaning of our words. The chief cost of Hiroshima, Hanson Baldwin also felt, was suffered "in our own souls."[30]

We are not the only people who have struggled with questions of this nature about the past. None have found them easy. We recognize quite easily, however, that it is important for modern Germans, Japanese, Russians, and others—people who themselves also had little to do with decisions made by earlier leaders—to acknowledge their past, to learn from it, even to make reparation. Some Germans today have come to admit the (far greater) evils of their past. The Japanese have a long way to go but many also have begun to realize some of the all too many outrages committed during World War II. Russians—recently even in the case of the Katyn massacres—have sometimes acknowledged crimes from the past committed by another generation. Perhaps one day we Americans will come to terms with Hiroshima.

In 1983 the U.S. Catholic bishops urged that after the passage of many decades

> and a concomitant growth in our understanding of the ever growing horror of nuclear war, we must shape the climate of opinion which will make it possible for our country to express profound sorrow over the atomic bombings in 1945. Without that sorrow, there is no possibility of finding a way to repudiate future use of nuclear weapons. . . .[31]

We are about to enter a new century, a time to rethink our assumptions. A reconsideration of the central features of the Hiroshima story points forward, not back. Indeed, viewed in any serious perspective, none of the central issues really concern the past.

We have toyed with the question of nuclear arms control for decades—and even achieved what some call "progress" in recent years. The number of weapons has been scaled back. However, enough warheads still exist to destroy most life on the planet many times over. As many former Cold War leaders—from Paul Nitze to Robert McNamara—have argued, simply to insure our own security in an era of cheap plutonium and easy proliferation, it is time to reappraise our fundamental assumptions. There is no good reason why in the new century nuclear weapons should not be relegated to that category of weaponry which, like poison gas, is beyond the pale of civilized consideration or use.

We also need to confront the profound challenge such weapons pose to our most basic ideas of governance. What does it mean, really—for a democracy—if one person literally has the power to order the destruction of the entire planet? For decades, we as a nation have been lax about the Constitutional requirement that Congress must declare war.[32] But we have entirely ignored the central challenge which so great a delegation of power as nuclear decision-making presents to democratic principles.

Finally, there is the matter of secrecy and public deception. We have learned all too many other ways that officials involved with nuclear weapons have deceived the public in recent years—injecting unknowing children, patients, and workers with plutonium; feeding them radioactive food; allowing radioactive materials to escape into the environment for "test" purposes; irradiating men in prison.

Hiroshima teaches that even the best leaders will lie to their people about the most fundamental issues if they are not constrained by effective checks and balances. Perhaps the fifty-year deception that is Hiroshima can also prod us to develop specific new policies, measures, laws, even Constitutional requirements, to assure the public availability of critical information. Without openness—without access to information needed for thoughtful decision-making—there can be no democratic accountability. Indeed, there can be no democracy.

To propose a reappraisal of fundamental assumptions is to suggest that we accept the need for a profound national questioning, for a deep public dialogue, for an extended probing to root causes and basic issues. How even to begin is not obvious; nor is it obvious that what one citizen may say or do matters.

Perhaps we can learn one more lesson from military men like Leahy and Eisenhower.

To some it is strange, even ironic, that the military culture of the World War II era was characterized by a measure of ethical restraint—at least for some leaders.[33] It was, after all, a period of racism and jingoism—especially among men who had lost friends and comrades-in-arms in the war. Even so, "I was not taught to make war in that fashion," Leahy stressed, "and wars cannot be won by destroying women and children."[34] So, too, Richard Nixon, recalling MacArthur's distress, underscored tradition and culture: "MacArthur, you see, was a soldier. He believed in using force only against military targets, and that is why the nuclear thing turned him off. . . ."[35]

Despite its many strengths, the culture which set the terms of reference for Harry Truman—and especially James Byrnes—obviously did not include ethical restraints sufficient to give serious pause to their decision-making. They drew their ideas and vision—good and bad—from the culture, ethics, morality we all imbibe. Had that been different, they might have been different.

So, too, do we today largely imbibe our ideas and vision from the culture, ethics, morality we all inherit. However, we also create the culture of the future—the culture which restrains or permits—by our own action or inaction. Indeed, the culture of the future will only be what we make it.

How, precisely, do we "make a culture"? Where do we begin? I believe we do so, first, by that which we accept silently—and above all by our own acts of language. We have a role in producing that which becomes beyond the pale—culturally, morally.

Perhaps, in the end, this may be why some of the military leaders chose to break with the customary practices of silence. The lesson to learn from men like Leahy and Eisenhower is that the place to begin is with a personal choice.

The chief of staff to the president, an admiral and a good friend of Truman's, decides publicly to state that in using the atomic bomb, the United States "adopted an ethical standard common to the barbarians of the Dark Ages."[36] A president of the United States—even in the midst of the Cold War—decides publicly to state his continuing judgment that: ". . . it wasn't necessary to hit them with that awful thing."[37]

These men, it seems, somehow could not maintain the usual polite silence about what they believed. At some point, they clearly came to the conclusion that it was important to speak out.

To be silent about the past is to accept the decision silently, with no challenge. It is thereby also to sustain and silently nurture the idea that nuclear weapons can and should be used or threatened to be used.

To confront Hiroshima requires that if we choose to be silent we know what it means to be silent—to be acquiescent.

This in the end also may well be precisely why we have avoided that confrontation for so many years and decades.

If we hope to change the future we, too, are complicit to the extent we do not confront our common history and then speak what we know. Not simply—or even—to criticize. There is no healing without forgiveness (including, importantly, of ourselves), and no new future.

Perhaps enough time has passed for us to openly face the Hiroshima decision. A poll taken in 1991 at the time of the fiftieth anniversary of Pearl Harbor reported that roughly half of those surveyed felt that both sides should apologize for the respective acts which marked the beginning and the end of World War II.[38]

Afterword

QUESTIONS, ISSUES, AND MAJOR THEORIES CONCERNING THE USE OF THE ATOMIC BOMB

Several matters remain to be discussed, including: the significance of different questions asked in the historical controversy over Hiroshima; a few problems concerned with evidence; some related comments on the tentative nature of much historical proof (and on one or two important speculative issues); finally, a broader discussion of critical issues of interpretation—and major theories and theorists—concerning why the atomic bomb was used.

Among experts it is a commonplace that discussion of the atomic bomb decision has often confused rather than clarified differences of viewpoint. A recurrent problem even among the most thoughtful commentators* is that contending arguments often emphasize different kinds of evidence—in large part because different writers ask different questions. As analysts ignore evidence related to questions asked by others, warring historians sail along on their own trajectories, and like ships passing in the night never quite confront each other directly.

I have suggested that by July 1945 a combination of assurances for the Emperor and the shock of a Russian declaration of war appeared quite likely to bring about surrender long before an invasion could begin. Many historians have long since understood the significance of the Emperor issue. However, the fact is this broader argument has rarely been fully analyzed in the

---

*Especially at the height of the Cold War, debate over the use of the atomic bomb was often lacking in balance. Angry exchanges were common and critics were regularly attacked as unpatriotic. Even in recent times large errors in favorable treatments—such as McCullough's mistake concerning a 500,000-casualty estimate—were passed over by reviewers, while small details were seized upon in critical writing. From the vast Hiroshima literature, I have attempted to select recognized authorities who are acknowledged representatives of major interpretive positions. (For commentary on the uglier side of the debate, see Warren F. Kimball, "The Cold War Warmed Over," *American Historical Review*, Vol. 79, No. 4 [October 1974], pp. 119–36; and Peter Novick, *That Noble Dream: The Objectivity Question and the American Historical Profession* [New York, 1988, pp. 450–52].)

literature. The reasons are understandable: With the exception of Marshall's June 18 advice that the shock of a Russian declaration of war might well "lever" Japan into surrender, significant evidence related to the additional power the Russian shock option offered was simply not available for much of the first quarter century after the war.

Only with the release of intelligence studies in the 1970s outlining the "two-step logic," the discovery of the president's Potsdam journal in 1979, and the opening of his letters to his wife in 1982—together with further research in Japanese sources—has it been possible to clarify the significance of the strategy. This in turn has also allowed us to understand more clearly why—having first been quite cavalier about Russian assistance—the president suddenly ardently sought a Red Army attack in case the atomic test should fail.

In this instance much of the literature simply did not discuss—and for a long while could not have adequately explored—the specific questions involved. (However, as we have noted, Herbert Feis recognized that by July, coupling assurances for the Emperor with even the mere announcement of Russia's intentions appeared to be a reasonable way to end the war; and even earlier Ernest May also was quite clear about the power of a Russian declaration of war.)

That American leaders had options available which seemed likely to end the fighting well before a November landing when they made their decision opens the door to—but does not directly address—what is in fact a very different question: Why was the atomic bomb used? Before assessing what can be said with confidence and what is still speculative concerning motivation and historical dynamics, it is useful to examine other related but also quite separate questions: 1) Would Japan likely have surrendered anyway? 2) What did Japanese leaders tell interrogators after the fact? 3) Was the use of the atomic bomb without warning against urban populations justified under any circumstances?

It often surprises nonspecialists to learn that many experts and others judge that the bombings were, in fact, almost certainly unnecessary—and that a surrender would probably have occurred in any event before November. We have already noted: 1) Walker's summary of the expert consensus in the modern literature; 2) the conclusion of the Strategic Bombing Survey; 3) the conclusion of the 1946 War Department Military Intelligence Division study; 4) the forceful statements of Eisenhower and Leahy; 5) the evidence that Arnold, Spaatz, LeMay, Nimitz, King, Halsey, MacArthur, Strauss, Bard, McCloy, and many other insiders believed the war could almost certainly have been ended without using the atomic bomb.[1] In addition, there is the evidence from contemporary journalists with close ties to U.S. military leaders of the period—from Hanson Baldwin to Henry R. Luce.

Similarly, we have noted the judgment of the most important early postwar authority—a man who also personally knew many of the participants intimately. Feis, for one, believed that: "by far the easiest [question] to answer, is whether it was *essential* to use the bomb in order to compel the Japanese to surrender on our terms within a few months. It was not."

. . . There can hardly be a well-grounded dissent from the conclusion reached by the members of the U.S. Strategic Bombing Survey . . . "that certainly prior to 31 December 1945, and in all probability prior to 1 November 1945, Japan would have surrendered even if the atomic bombs had not been dropped, even if Russia had not entered the war and even if no invasion had been planned or contemplated."[2]

Moreover, as time passed and he gathered and reflected upon further evidence, Feis eliminated all shreds of ambiguity from this assessment. When he revised his initial 1961 language in 1966, he first made the question tougher—and then made the answer more explicit. Instead of asking whether the bomb was essential to compel "surrender on our terms within a few months," he now clarified that he meant "before [Japan] was invaded." And instead of the formulation "There can hardly be," he now wrote: "There cannot be a well-grounded dissent from the conclusion reached as early as 1945 by members of the U.S. Strategic Bombing Survey. . . ."[3]

There are, of course, historians who still disagree with the judgment that the war would have ended in any event before an invasion. Also, some general scholars have not as yet caught up with the modern expert research findings. However, it is difficult to believe that Japan would have fought on once the Russians actually attacked and once assurances for the Emperor were actually given. And it is very difficult—given what we now know—to believe that in the end assurances would not have been given if the alternative was an invasion. Truman and Byrnes, as Stimson noted, were hardly "obdurate" about the point.[4]

Several scholars specializing in military matters have examined Japanese decision-making and added to the modern understanding. A recent study by Robert A. Pape, for instance, offers details concerning the central reality of Japan's extreme military vulnerability—and shortages of everything from ammunition and fuel to trained personnel. He suggests that: "Japan's military position was so poor that its leaders would likely have surrendered before invasion, and at roughly the same time in August 1945, even if the United States had not employed strategic bombing or the atomic bomb."[5] In this situation:

The Soviet invasion of Manchuria on August 9 raised Japan's military vulnerability to a very high level. The Soviet offensive ruptured Japanese lines immediately, and rapidly penetrated deep into the rear. Since the Kwantung Army was thought to be Japan's premier fighting force, this had a devastating effect on Japanese calculations of the prospects for home island defense.

"If their best forces were so easily sliced to pieces, the unavoidable implication was that the less well-equipped and trained forces assembled for [the last decisive home island battle] had no chance of success against American forces that were even more capable than the Soviets."[6]*

As we have observed, a quite different question, of course, is what Japanese leaders subsequently told interrogators they were planning to do if the war actually were to have continued. It is easy to find statements by Japanese generals and others which indicate they would have fought to the death. And there is no doubt that plans were being laid to do so if necessary. Moreover, as several military analysts have suggested, ULTRA intercepts of tactical military communications indicate a considerably increased Japanese buildup on Kyushu in July and early August.[7] However, it is one thing to note such statements and such plans—and it is quite another to accept them as prima facie evidence that this was also what would in fact have happened.

The Japanese military leaders who told their American captors they would not likely have surrendered were not lying. They were reporting what they had been feeling and planning—*given the context they faced*. In its most significant aspect, the Potsdam Proclamation—without the key element of paragraph 12—appeared as a reaffirmation of the rigidity of the continuing U.S.

---

*"In comparison to the Soviet entry," Pape also stresses, "the atomic bomb had little or no impact on the Army's position. First, the Army initially denied that the Hiroshima blast had been an atomic bomb. Second, they went to great lengths to downplay its importance. When Togo raised it as an argument for surrender on August 7, General Anami explicitly rejected it. Finally, the Army vigorously argued that minor civilian defense measures could offset the bomb's effects." (Pape, "Why Japan Surrendered," p. 187.) See also the official British history: "The Russian declaration of war was the decisive factor in bringing Japan to accept the Potsdam declaration, for it brought home to all members of the Supreme Council the realization that the last hope of a negotiated peace had gone and that there was no alternative but to accept the Allied terms sooner or later." (Major General S. Woodburn Kirby, *The War Against Japan*, Vol. 5: *The Surrender of Japan* [London, 1969].) This view is also common in Japanese studies. See Shinichi Arai, *Genbaku Toka eno Michi* [The Road to the Atomic Bombing]; Ariatsu Nishijima, *Genbaku ha Naze Toka Saretaka* [Why Were the Atomic Bombs Dropped?]; Seizaburo Shinobu, *Sengo Nihon Seiji Shi I* [Political History of Japan After the War]; Tadashi Motohashi, "Daresu Kikan wo Tsuzuru Wahei Kosaku" [Peace Negotiation Through the Dulles Agency], and Tadakichi Tanaka, "Tai So Kosaku: Taiheiyo Senso Chu ni Okeru Nisso Kosho" [Maneuvering with the Soviets: Negotiations Between Japan and the Soviets During the Pacific War], in Nihon Gaiko Gakkai, ed., *Taiheiyo Senso Shuketsu Ron* [Some Discussions on the Ending of the Pacific War].

demand for unconditional surrender. The idea that they wanted to fight on—that they would not likely have surrendered—is exactly what one would expect them to have felt, and believed (and psychologically continued to believe), since at the time they formed their views the United States had not given them any reason to believe the Emperor would be protected.

Again, throughout the period when Japanese leaders were developing their thinking, the Russians had not as yet declared war.*

Unfortunately U.S. military interrogators rarely asked carefully focused questions about the Russians or about the contingent nature of Japanese feelings and plans. When they did, however, the answers were often quite direct. During the Strategic Bombing Survey interrogations, for instance, Imperial Envoy Prince Konoye recalled that the "army had dug themselves in the mountains and their idea . . . was fighting from every little hole or rock in the mountains." However, when asked specifically (in the very next question): "Would the Emperor have permitted them to do that?"—Konoye responded immediately: "I don't think the Emperor would have let them go that far. He would have done something to stop them."[8]†

Similarly, Navy Chief of Staff Admiral Toyoda stated: "I believe the Russian participation in the war against Japan rather than the atom bombs did more to hasten the surrender."[9] Army Vice-Chief of Staff Kawabe, too, observed that "Since Tokyo was not directly affected by the bombing, the full force of the shock was not felt. . . . In comparison, the Soviet entry into the war was a great shock when it actually came. . . . It gave us all the more severe shock and alarm because we had been in constant fear [that] the vast Red Army forces in Europe were now being turned against us."[10]

In this connection some authors have simply argued that since the Japanese were unwilling to surrender unconditionally, the atomic bomb had to be

---

*In general, of course, psychologists have long since noted the extreme difficulty almost all individuals have in subsequently articulating views different from those they once held, expressed, and—especially—acted upon.

†Several scholars (Pape among them) have recently criticized the work of the Strategic Bombing Survey—and especially its conclusion that the war would have ended through air power alone. The central issue, of course, is not whether the Survey was right or wrong—especially since it did not directly take up the impact of the Russian attack or a clarification of the Emperor's role. Unlike Pape, some analysts have implied without warrant that weaknesses in the Survey's methods undermine the more fundamental judgment that one way or another Japan would likely have surrendered before November. (See for instance, Robert P. Newman, "Ending the War with Japan: Paul Nitze's 'Early Surrender' Counterfactual," paper presented to the Modern History Faculty, Oxford, May 25, 1994.) Other sections of the Strategic Bombing Survey suggest that if the Japanese railroad system had been attacked together with cities, the war might well have ended even earlier. (The United States Strategic Bombing Survey, *The Effects of Strategic Bombing on Japan's War Economy*, p. 64; and The United States Strategic Bombing Survey, *The War Against Japanese Transportation 1941–1945*, pp. 10–12.)

used. But few scholars of this period would disagree that—given the unconditional demand and especially the continued threat to the Emperor—the
Japanese were preparing to fight on. Changing these conditions—and in particular offering assurances for the Emperor—was what the debate was about.
As the Joint Staff Planners had put it in April 1945:

> Unless a definition of unconditional surrender can be given which is ac-
> ceptable to the Japanese, there is no alternative to annihilation and no
> prospect that the threat of absolute defeat will bring about capitulation.[11]

A different question still is whether the bombings were justified. This, in
turn, involves at least three quite distinct issues. The first is whether at the
time U.S. leaders believed they had no choice but to use the atomic bomb;
the second is whether the weapon had to be used without notification and
against cities; the third is whether the bombing of two cities was necessary.
Beyond these specifics, of course, is the question of whether the bombing of
civilian populations can ever be justified.

The evidence we have reviewed makes it clear that U.S. leaders were
aware they could almost certainly end the war before an invasion and without the new weapon—and that there was plenty of time to test whether this
was so. As Eisenhower, Leahy, Bard, and many others were repeatedly to
state, the hurried use of the atomic bombs was not dictated by overwhelming
military necessity.

Second, it would have been possible to issue a much more explicit warning and to attack a non-urban target first, as George Marshall proposed.
Third, had there been a less intense rush to end the war before the Russians
came in, the issue of a second city might well have been posed more
thoughtfully. Along with McGeorge Bundy, many have urged not only that
the bombing of Hiroshima is "debatable" but that the bombing of Nagasaki
was "unnecessary."[12]

Some historians who acknowledge that the war would probably have
ended before a November landing suggest that the bombing of Hiroshima
was nonetheless understandable. For instance, Barton Bernstein argues that at
the time "the so-called alternatives generally looked too risky; therefore, the
alternatives were not pursued. In that context, virtually any risk was too
great."[13] Related to this, it is often claimed that American leaders were
guided solely by a determination to save as many lives as possible by ending
the war as surely and quickly as possible.

The modern evidence challenges such interpretations as well. Indeed, both
the issue of "risk" and the issue of saving lives point in quite a different direction. The real risk—as the Joint Chiefs of Staff urged—was in not telling
Japan they could keep the Emperor. "Marshall, who believed that retention

[of the Emperor] was a military necessity," John Ray Skates notes, "asked that the members [of the Joint Chiefs of Staff] draft a memorandum to the president recommending that the Allies 'do nothing to indicate that the emperor might be removed from office upon unconditional surrender.' "[14] Downplaying and stalling the Red Army attack involved further risks. As Marshall also urged on June 19, the most effective way to achieve surrender was to "coordinate all the threats possible to Japan"—which, of course, meant (as Stimson's diary notes) the "additional sanction to our warning in the shape of an entry by the Russians into the war."[15]

Put another way, it is difficult to reconcile the decision to eliminate the recommended assurances for the Emperor with a risk-avoidance strategy—at least as regards military considerations. And given the decision to delay the impact of a Russian declaration of war, it is all but impossible to argue that the only concern was doing everything to end the fighting as surely and quickly as possible so as to save as many lives as possible.

That the war was close to being over—and that many thought it might well have been ended—is sometimes acknowledged by those who recognize the significance of the Emperor issue but then go on to explain that assurances could not have been given because of political considerations. Robert Newman, for instance, writes that "the unconditional surrender policy was so strongly supported by the American electorate that Truman would not have dared at this stage of the war to scuttle it overtly."[16]

Over the years several quite distinct theories of the role of politics in the decision have been offered. The most extreme or "determinist" view is that American political culture—as Newman contends—was so powerfully anti-Japanese that it was literally impossible for the president to clarify the position of the Emperor. Some who agree that this position is untenable nevertheless hold that anger at the Japanese simply made it very difficult for the president.* A third view is that although there may possibly have been some political gains to be had in temporarily withholding assurances, they were hardly overwhelming.

That there may have been some slight advantage—or, rather, that Byrnes may have urged some slight advantage—in not clarifying the Emperor's role is a reasonable position. However, as Truman's own less than forceful views on the issue suggest—and given Republican support for a clarification of terms—the advantages do not appear to have been very great. Minimally, there clearly was ample room for political maneuver. In any case, it was all

---

*However, as I have indicated, even among analysts who argue such a view, if the question is put clearly and explicitly only a minority holds that the war would inevitably have continued once assurances for the Emperor were given (and the Russians attacked)—and an even smaller number would likely contend that in the end assurances would not have been given, and therefore, the use of the atomic bomb was the only option available.

but certain, as we have repeatedly noted, that in the end the Emperor would be needed to command a surrender and maintain order.*

It is also important to emphasize again that little direct evidence has been found—e.g., a clear, direct, contemporaneous report—that either Byrnes or Truman privately or publicly explicitly stated political worries as a major reason for not clarifying the position of the Emperor before the bomb was used. Moreover, the direct reports we have after Hiroshima was bombed also strongly suggest Truman's lack of concern about political criticism. Indeed, the evidence is that he was not much troubled by the issue. Finally, the contemporaneous reports of Byrnes' possible views even at this time are ambiguous on the critical distinction between altering the rhetoric of unconditional surrender (which he did not wish to do) and offering assurances for the Emperor (which he did on August 11).†

Contrary to those who agree the war could likely have been ended had the president offered assurances for the Emperor—but that politics interfered—it has been argued that Japanese officials sought only mediation, that they were opaque about the conditions they sought, and that in any event the Army leaders were adamantly opposed to surrender. Here the issues often arise in connection with what Japan had in mind in the July approach to Moscow and in its response to the Potsdam Proclamation.

It is especially important in this connection to distinguish between stated positions and the "bottom line" of what American leaders believed Japan might have been willing to accept. There was certainly vagueness in the Emperor's request for Soviet mediation—and in the *"mokusatsu"* statement. On the other hand, Truman told Stimson he was quite clear which of Stalin's demands were "bluff" and which were real, and it is highly doubtful that the poker-playing president took the initial general positions put forward by Japanese officials any more at face value than he did those of the Russian leaders.[17] A large literature on labor, marital, political, and many other areas of conflict negotiation—as well as common sense—has taught the same lesson the president seems to have learned playing poker. As Robert J. C. Butow noted more than forty years ago:

> The mere fact that the Japanese had approached the Soviet Union with a request for mediation should have suggested the possibility that Japan, for all of her talk about 'death to the last man,' might accept the Allied demand for unconditional surrender if only it were couched in more

---

*David Robertson, who recognizes the Republican pressures for an early end to the war, thinks Byrnes saw the bomb as a way to avoid both their criticism and attacks from those who urged a continued hard line. (Robertson, *Sly and Able*, p. 415.)
†See above, pp. 417–18.

specific terms than those which Washington was already using to define its meaning.[18]

War crimes trials were about to begin in Germany; hanging the Emperor was a real possibility. What Japanese leaders were being asked in the Potsdam Proclamation was: *Are you willing to surrender unconditionally given this reality?* What is surprising is not that they did not leap forward to embrace the surrender demand; it is that the intercepted cables registered such desperation despite the rigidity of the U.S. position. Had the proclamation been accepted it would have been truly surprising (but, as we have seen, Truman himself understood this was unlikely).

As to the degree of military opposition: It had long since been agreed that a plan for surrender was necessary. Furthermore, the August intercepts which now showed "unanimous determination" to seek surrender through Moscow were an important new signal of the army's position—a point explicitly noted by U.S. intelligence at the time. That the president recognized the game was essentially up as well is further indicated, as we have seen, in his comments on the August 2–3 intercepts.[19]

All of this, of course, relates to the situation before the bombings and before the Red Army attack. Some feel that what Japanese military leaders said they wanted in internal discussions after August 9 also makes it difficult to believe a surrender could have been achieved on terms acceptable to the United States. The Japanese military wish-list included preservation of the imperial system, no postwar occupation, self-disarmament, and self-management of war-crimes trials. The question is what weight to assign the wish-list in after-the-fact assessments.

A "literalist" approach would suggest that since the list and U.S. desires differed, no surrender could have taken place. But such an uncritical or literalist reading of the texts sidesteps the central issues presented by the logic of the fast-changing situation—and, in August, the military vulnerability exposed by the rapid Red Army advances in Manchuria. It also again abstracts from everything we know about the psychology and practice of negotiations in general: Few observers would rest a judgment on the likely outcome of a hard-fought labor negotiation on a comparison of the proposals stated by the contending parties before the beginning of bargaining. Leahy's private judgment as early as June 18 that he believed it possible to achieve satisfactory terms is a useful reminder in connection with all arguments that U.S.-Japanese differences were insurmountable. The same may be said of Ismay's summary for Churchill of U.S.-British intelligence: After the Russian attack "the Japanese would probably wish to get out on almost any terms short of the dethronement of the Emperor."[20]

A related point was made on June 30 by the War Department's Military Intelligence Division (G-2):

> it is apparent that the Japanese leaders feel that they may get better terms from the Allies if they give the impression that the people are determined to fight to the last man rather than accept unconditional surrender.[21]

Further light is thrown on the weight army leaders attached to the three second-order items on their wish-list by Pape's examination of what happened after the Red Army began its assault and after the Emperor called for a halt in the fighting. Since all the top leadership—including the army—had already agreed in principle on surrender, the only question was whether to fight on to attempt to secure improved conditions. Many analysts have pointed out that the Japanese Emperor—though symbolically important—was politically weak. As Pape notes:

> [War Minister] Anami could simply have refused to endorse the emperor's decision since, under the Meiji constitution, cabinet decisions required unanimous consent. Alternatively, Anami could have resigned, which would have dissolved the government, effectively vetoing the decision for surrender, because a new government could not be formed without the Army's approval of a new war minister.

Instead of standing firm on their demands when the Emperor intervened to call for a halt in the fighting on August 9, however, army leaders, Pape writes, "no longer blocked the civilians' efforts to make peace, which they had the power to do."[22]

A related issue concerns the brief attempt by lower-level Japanese officers to block the surrender broadcast—which has led some writers to suggest in sometimes highly dramatic terms that an early end to the fighting was not assured. It is never possible to be absolutely certain about such matters, of course, but the short-lived uprising—which was put down without much difficulty—has been exaggerated in some accounts. Historians who vary widely in their conclusions as to the possibilities for surrender have pointed out that this effort did not enjoy the support of military officials with real power—and was hardly a serious threat to the surrender. Bernstein, for instance, calls it "virtually stillborn."[23] John Toland—who devotes a chapter to the attempted coup in *The Rising Sun*—acknowledges that the disruption "had one positive effect: it unified the Army leaders. . . ."

> At 3:30 p.m. [August 14] Anami climbed a small platform. "The Emperor has decided to end the war," he told the standing audience. "It is, therefore, proper that we abide by the imperial wish."

"Anami's speech," Toland observes, "destroyed the possibility of any coup involving high-rank officers."[24] Leon Sigal points out that Anami, Chief of Staff General Umezu, and the third-highest-ranking officer, General Kenji Doihara, ordered their principal subordinates to pledge that "the Army will act in obedience to the Imperial decision to the last."[25]

There is, of course, little evidence that American decision-makers based their judgments on—or even seriously worried about—such challenges; the question comes up mainly in after-the-fact arguments. Here Leahy's observation, "We were certain that the Mikado could stop the war with a royal word" is telling.[26] It is also relevant to recall that a major reason Grew and Stimson urged that a statement clarifying the surrender formula be issued well in advance was to give the peace faction time to organize support for a surrender bid and thereby be in a better position to deal with challenges.

Finally, there is the question of the relationship of the uprising to the central issue: The Kyushu landing could not begin for almost another three months. The junior officers' group clearly did not hold sufficient power to prolong the war against the opposition of the generals for long enough to force an invasion.

The recent discovery of a telephone transcript and a related memorandum exploring the possible use of atomic bombs, tactically, in support of an invasion has led to some speculation that U.S. leaders—or, rather, possibly General Marshall—also thought the war might continue for a longer period.[27] No analyst has attempted to claim that this evidence reveals attitudes at the level of Truman and Byrnes. Even in the case of the chief of staff, as Marc Gallicchio observes, "[g]iven Marshall's overall responsibility . . . it is not surprising that he desired to be prepared for every contingency."[28] Actually, it has long been known that some discussion of a possible tactical use of the new weapon took place early in 1945. (Documentation, however, is very thin.) In 1965 Herbert Feis wrote to Defense Department historian Rudolph Winnacker to ask him whether there were any documents in air force files which might illuminate Marshall's strategy. Winnacker's search turned up nothing. At that time Feis concluded—in all likelihood, correctly—that: "Probably the idea of using them had not yet found its way into any plan or document, but was merely an idea in Marshall's head"—a comment which seems reasonable in connection with the more recent discoveries as well.[29]

If military reasons were not overriding—and political reasons less than overwhelming—how are we to explain the bombings? Why the atomic bombs were used is not the same question as whether they were needed. Among historians who implicitly or explicitly acknowledge that the war could in any event have been ended well before the Kyushu landing, a variety of nonmilitary factors have been adduced to explain the decision.

Similar to the theory that political fears were critical is an argument about money. Some analysts have emphasized Groves' incessant worrying about Congressional criticism of the huge cost of the Manhattan Project—and also noted Stimson's comment to Harvey Bundy that "I have been responsible for spending two billions of dollars on this atomic venture. Now that it is successful I shall not be sent to prison in Fort Leavenworth."[30] Stanley Goldberg writes:

> The bomb dropped on Hiroshima, a uranium bomb, justified the more than $1 billion investment in isotope separation at Oak Ridge. The bomb dropped on Nagasaki justified the more than $400 million spent on Hanford. It seems clear today that the rush to produce the active material and to drop the bombs on Japan as soon as possible was driven largely by a fear that the war might end before both types of fission bombs could be used.[31]*

Although statements of concern about costs are to be found in the record, it is much more difficult to show a direct line of causation between such concerns and the actual decision—especially at the very highest level. Groves, as we have seen, was out of the loop on the critical Emperor-related issues; moreover, he was not present when the final conversations and decisions occurred on the *Augusta* and at Potsdam. Stimson—financial worries notwithstanding—made an all-out effort to clarify the surrender terms before the bomb was used.

Szilard reported Byrnes as saying in late May that the administration would have to answer to Congress about nuclear expenditures—and in arguing that domestic political concerns were "primary" in the decision to use the atomic bomb, David Robertson states: "Congress would 'expect results' for the two billion dollars invested for the secret weapon of the Manhattan Project. . . ."[32] Here the question is not just past money spent, however. Although he may have been worried about such costs, Byrnes' stated concern about future funding of atomic development cannot be separated from his strategic concerns. In the same conversation he made it clear that what he sought was the ongoing capacity to make Russia more "manageable."[33]

Most important, there is little evidence that the president was seriously

---

*Elsewhere Goldberg has written that the three most important factors were: "Momentum, protection of the reputations of the civilian and military leadership of the project, and the personal ambitions of some, especially General Leslie R. Groves." Goldberg makes clear, however, that the last two factors were intimately related to the money question. (Stanley Goldberg, "Racing to the Finish," p. 4, paper presented at the American Historical Association conference, January 6, 1995.)

concerned about money or worried about criticism of costs when he made his decision. Despite his general oversight role in the Senate, Truman was in a rather secure position in this regard since he had not been personally responsible for ordering the expenditures. In fact, Groves noted during his April 25 meeting with Truman and Stimson: "The President did not show any concern over the amount of funds being spent. . . .[34] (There also is little evidence that Byrnes returned to the argument he made to Szilard as indications of Japan's desperation flowed in during the succeeding months.)

Finally, arguments that fear of criticism about costs were a significant determining factor imply this as the reason for the deaths of two hundred thousand people (and possibly more). As Kai Bird has recently observed in connection with Robertson's argument: "Surely, the notion that 200,000 Japanese civilians were incinerated for [such] domestic political reasons is far more shocking than anything contained in the scholarly literature which has so far inflamed critics of the Smithsonian Museum's planned exhibit on the Enola Gay."[35]*

There is also the question of racist attitudes. It is certainly possible that racial stereotypes and virulent anti-Japanese sentiment built up during the war influenced the decision. However, the fact is it is all but impossible to find specific evidence that racism was an important factor in the decision to attack Hiroshima and Nagasaki. It is also significant that so many American military leaders seem not to have felt the bomb's use was essential: Such officials knew well the terrible brutality their men had suffered at the hands of the Japanese military. If racism were a central factor, one would expect to find it strongly expressed here.

For race to have played a determining role it would also be necessary to show that U.S. leaders would not have been likely to use the atomic bomb in Germany against Europeans had it been available. This is difficult to do. True, the conventional city-bombing of Japan was a departure from the general rule of at least attempting to "precision-bomb" in Europe. However, U.S. leaders were quite prepared to bomb European cities and Caucasian civilian populations as a matter of policy when they deemed it to be of special significance. Aside from the role the air force played in the bombing of Dresden, at almost the same time that the United States began major Japanese city-bombing with the March 9–10 destruction of Tokyo, it launched a massive attack on Berlin in the hope of speeding the Nazi collapse.[36]

This is not to deny that racism was widespread. In connection with both

---

*James B. Conant argued another nonmilitary reason—namely that a demonstration of the weapon was needed to warn the world of the need for international control. However, there is little evidence that this was a significant factor in decision-making at the highest level at the time. (See Hershberg, *James B. Conant*, pp. 228–29.)

the financial and the racial arguments, however, it is important to distinguish between such attitudes—and causation. Alternatively—as in the case of "political factors"—an observable tendency of indeterminate weight and force is sometimes transformed without adequate argument into a determining factor.

Great care must also be taken with regard to analyses which assert that a combination of factors—political, military, racial, financial—produced the decision. It is easy to assemble fragments of evidence and mechanically add them up, as it were, and then suggest that taken together they explain the final result. It is even possible that the cumulative impact of several factors tipped the balance for one or another adviser. However, given the details now available in the modern evidence, to jump from the assembling of fragments to an explanatory conclusion about decision-making at the very top of the U.S. government is suspect.

A different class of explanatory theories involve various forms of a momentum argument. I have already indicated why in general I no longer believe such theories offer an adequate explanation of the events of 1945. The earlier tradition represented by Stimson, Baldwin, and Feis—that a *decision* was made—finds strong support in recent research discoveries. Once we reach the presidential level—and the July–August time frame—any careful dissection of the process, day by day, adviser by adviser, makes it clear that well-defined choices were available and considered. Moreover, the most important decision concerning the Emperor was highly contested: All of Truman's top advisers except Byrnes urged a course of action which was specific—and the opposite of what one would expect if momentum theories were valid.

The decision not to allow Japan significant time to consider a warning and the decision to stall a Russian declaration of war were also the result of considered and active choice. We may add, too, the decisions to pass over the Atlantic Charter option and to ignore the early August intercepts. None of these choices is easily explained by the simple idea of "going with the flow."

On the other hand, the appearance of no atomic decision, yes or no, is easy to understand. As we have noted, after the fundamental framing decisions were set in concrete the sense of a process going forward—with no choice points—is a natural result. There was little to decide once the president opted to continue the implied threat to the Emperor. The war would then go on unless some other development—the bomb, the Russians, or a change in terms—intervened. "The Japanese believe . . . that unconditional surrender would be the equivalent of national extinction," the Combined Intelligence Committee stressed on July 8. "There are as yet no indications the Japanese are ready to accept such terms."[37]

Several distinct momentum theories have been put forward over the years. One of the most abstract and popular derives from Groves' rather catchy August 1963 suggestion that Truman "was like a little boy on a toboggan. . . ."[38] Although Groves subsequently backed away from this statement, undoubtedly from his particular vantage point ("looking up," as it were), it probably seemed that everything flowed inexorably from the vast bureaucratic effort he commanded.[39] The "toboggan" metaphor, of course, is so vague as to be impossible to refute; the related argument that Truman's only choice was to say no ignores the specific issues involved in the three key decision points.* Moreover, the real decisions did not involve Groves.

It has also been suggested in broad-brush terms that "the momentum of war" governed events. Such general arguments can have an odd feeling of seeming plausibility about them. However, not only do the specifics of the decision-making details as we now know them bring all abstract notions down to earth, but here especially the attitudes of the military leaders seem particularly significant indicators.

If the momentum of war was what forced things to happen, why is it that so many military men in particular urged a prior clarification of terms and appear to have had so many doubts about the decision? "Momentum of war" theories resemble "heat of battle" theories which sometimes employ general slogans to "explain" all unnecessary deaths as somehow "inevitable." War is hell, of course, but as serious military leaders have always emphasized, the distinction between violent combat and the planned and systematic destruction of large numbers of civilians is critical—and not to be papered over with comforting rhetoric.

Another broad theory is that the Hiroshima and Nagasaki bombings were the logical (and it is sometimes implied, "inevitable") culmination of the development of twentieth-century air power in general—and of the heavy bomber in particular.[40] Related to this is the argument that Truman and his advisers had become inured to the mass killing of civilians, and therefore did not stop to think about the consequences of using the new weapon.[41]†

Here, too, the modern evidence suggests reasons to discount such theories. If the momentum of air power was what forced things to happen, why is it that so many air force leaders seem to have had so many doubts—and to have expressed them both privately and publicly?

(On the other hand, it is certainly true that in a very general sense the delivery of an atomic bomb by airplane was the culmination of a long twentieth-century trend—even if the actual decision cannot be said to have been controlled by this trend and appears not to have been warmly re-

*Gabriel Kolko's 1968 argument may also be read this way. See Kolko, *The Politics of War*, pp. 538–43.
†McGeorge Bundy recently noted that the "standards of bombing criteria at the end of World War II . . . are obviously a given for Groves. . . ."—and went on to ask: "But should they have been a given for anyone else? I don't understand it." (Interview with author, April 6, 1995.)

ceived by those who guided the trend through to its World War II air power peak.)

A more sophisticated category of momentum theories attempts to explain the decision through an analysis of bureaucratic and organizational dynamics. In *Fighting to a Finish*, Leon Sigal argues that "neither the states' acts nor the organizational interests that motivated them are the product of conscious calculation. . . ."[42] The analysis is explicitly antirational; Sigal suggests that the specific bureaucratic interests of various agencies and departments interacted—almost as in a physical weighing of vectors of force—to produce the outcome we observe. He writes:

> Seldom did conscious strategic calculation guide the United States. Seldom too did the politics of war termination in Japan enter explicitly into American deliberations.[43]

The modern evidence suggests several difficulties with such an approach. First, as a matter of direct observation the expected one-to-one relationships are not, in fact, present. Earlier in the war there is evidence that the navy wished a naval solution to the war; the air force an air power solution; and the army a ground invasion. However, after June—as the critical point of no return approached—things began to change rapidly. Each military group still privately probably favored its approach if the war were to continue. But as the evidence concerning the attitudes of army, air force, and especially navy leaders reveals, they did not urge their expected bureaucratic positions to the end. And they were united in strongly recommending a clarification of the position of the Emperor.

At a higher level the anomalies increase rapidly. For instance, the War Department—which might perhaps have been expected to urge a continuation of the military effort—was for a clarification of terms. So were the Navy Department and the Joint Chiefs of Staff. On the other hand, the State Department under secretary of state Byrnes was against, not for, a diplomatic solution. (But up until June 30 the Department formally and officially urged a clarification of terms—as did both Stettinius and Grew. A change in personalities at the top, not inherent institutional interests, produced the new position after Byrnes took office on July 3.)

Sigal's suggestion that the organizational interests of the Manhattan Project (and Groves) controlled Truman's ultimate choice fails to explain the intense July and early August dynamics. His conclusion that Groves "saw to it" that Truman never heard a full debate of alternatives is difficult to fathom.[44] Both of Groves' superiors—Stimson and Marshall—strongly urged the president to clarify the surrender terms, and far from having no decisions to make, Truman had to reverse the formal recommendations concerning the Emperor.

Sigal is undoubtedly right that Groves essentially controlled the Target

Committee's recommendations and indirectly strongly influenced the Interim Committee. However, had Byrnes not dominated the Potsdam as well as the Interim Committee decisions, it seems doubtful that assurances for the Emperor would have been pulled back. Indeed, they would probably have been put forward—or, minimally, the process of clarifying the surrender formula would have been initiated at the time of the fall of Okinawa, as the Joint Chiefs and virtually everyone else urged.

Even on its own terms, there is an unexplained imbalance in Sigal's overall analysis. Within Japan considerable attention is given to the Palace (and the Emperor) as an institutional locus of power. However, the structural analysis on the American side of the equation all but ignores the presidency and White House as institutions. A representative illustration is a chart on pages 313–14 of his book, where the Imperial Palace is located but the White House is not even mentioned. The asymmetrical analysis is particularly odd given that the American presidency is commonly regarded as a uniquely powerful institution compared with the leadership structures of most other nations. Furthermore, in the period under consideration—and given the unusual Byrnes-Truman relationship—decision-making in connection with the bomb seems to have been even more concentrated in the presidency. Indeed, with the representatives of virtually all the other major government entities urging a clarification of surrender policy, the extraordinary institutional power of the presidency (guided by Byrnes) is illuminated by the capacity to resist bureaucratic pressures.

A modern comparison is also instructive. Several analysts have noted that at the time of the 1991 Persian Gulf War, President George Bush and a small group of White House advisers pushed through the decision for war against the advice (or with only the lukewarm acquiescence of) the State Department, the Defense Department, and the Joint Chiefs of Staff. In his book *The Commanders*, Bob Woodward observes that "the Pentagon is not always the center of military decision making. . . . When the President and his advisers are engaged, they run the show."[45] By virtually all accounts, the Hiroshima decision was similar in this essential respect.

A final point is highlighted by the statements of Leahy, Eisenhower, and many others: Even the most rigorous structural analysis must allow for some degree of human choice. None of the actors involved—especially Byrnes and Truman—can be regarded as mere automatons responding in mechanical fashion to institutional forces.*

* * *

---

*Curiously, in passing, Sigal also writes that "[o]rganizational considerations rather than national purpose dominated the planning, *if not the decision*, to use the atomic bomb. . . ." Emphasis added (Sigal, *Fighting to a Finish*, pp. 218–19.)

A rather different class of momentum arguments derive from Marxist theories which explain the decision in terms of the inevitable thrust of American capitalist expansion. Related to these are the arguments of Thomas McCormick, who—following the work of Immanuel Wallerstein—also urges that the dynamic of central concern is economic.[46] In both cases America's political-economic interests in Europe and Asia are understood as the key factors generating all but inevitable pressures (the word "momentum" is rarely used, but the idea is similar) which produced the bombing.

A more nuanced argument was that of the late William Appleman Williams. This emphasized the development of a shared long-term ideological framework in which U.S. free-market and open-trade interests are understood as deeply connected with freedom and democracy. Hence an "open door" for American economic policies was judged important not only because of capitalist concerns but because of the moral importance of achieving and maintaining the "free world." Within this framework Williams concluded that the "United States dropped the bomb to end the war against Japan and thereby stop the Russians in Asia, and to give them sober pause in eastern Europe."[47]*

There is no doubt that U.S. leaders were explicitly and deeply concerned about their economic interests. Stimson, for instance, repeatedly discussed these in connection with Asia (e.g., on July 17, "The President . . . told me briefly of his first meeting with Stalin and said he thought that he had clinched the Open Door in Manchuria"[48]). It is also plain that in any serious historical perspective the projection of U.S. economic concerns across the Pacific to Asia cannot be separated from the history of capitalist global economic expansion. Finally, U.S. leaders were indisputably worried about establishing a capitalist market-oriented postwar Europe—including Eastern Europe.

It is one thing to acknowledge such historic factors, however, and quite another to argue a determinist theory either of momentum or of the inherent dynamics of world system conflict leading to the inevitability of the bombing of Hiroshima and Nagasaki. To do so is to ignore the evidence—and, again, the reality of choice. Most policy-makers (including Stimson, the senior official most worried about the "Open Door") urged a course of action which held the potential of ending the war without the bomb. Grew may well have been worried that using the bomb would damage—rather than improve—U.S. political and economic relationships in Asia in general and in Japan in particular.

---

*Williams also argued that "It was not the possession of the atomic bomb which prompted American leaders to get tough with Russia but rather their open-door outlook which interpreted the bomb as the final guarantee that they could go further faster down that path to world predominance." (Williams, *The Tragedy of American Diplomacy*, p. 229.)

In general, virtually all momentum theories beg certain key questions—especially why urban populations had to be attacked and why a second city had to be destroyed. Similar to momentum arguments—but somewhat more specific—are "inherited assumption" theories. According to these, the use of the atomic bomb was the result of assumptions and policies carried forward from the Roosevelt era. Bernstein offers this general interpretation:

> The momentum of assumptions initiated under FDR and inherited by Truman, the easy shift of targets to Japan, the quest to save American lives by ending the war speedily, and the unwillingness to take risks to avoid use of the bombs, together substantially explain why these weapons were dropped on Japan.[49]

We have seen how the last two factors in this list—ending the war as fast as possible to save lives and the unwillingness to take risks (at least in connection with military considerations)—are contradicted by modern evidence. There also is little real evidence to indicate that there was a coherent policy on the use of the bomb inherited from Roosevelt. Indeed, what we actually know of Roosevelt's own understanding points in a somewhat different direction. In the Hyde Park Agreement initialed by Roosevelt and Churchill in September 1944 very tentative and careful language was used:

> [W]hen a "bomb" is finally available, it might perhaps, after mature consideration, be used against the Japanese, who should be warned that this bombardment will be repeated until they surrender.[50]

Four days after endorsing this agreement the president discussed atomic issues with Vannevar Bush, Leahy, and Churchill's science adviser Lord Cherwell. In a letter to James Conant the next day, Bush noted "one other matter which came up. . . ."

> At one time in the conversation the President raised the question of whether [the bomb] should actually be used against the Japanese or whether it should be used only as a threat with full-scale experimentation in this country.[51]

As McGeorge Bundy observes, "There are several tantalizing hints that Franklin Roosevelt was troubled about the basic question of using the weapon against Japan in a way that his successor never was. . . . twice in less than a week Roosevelt thought about *whether* and *how* to use the bomb."[52]

Indications that Roosevelt appears to have been thinking about a warning and possibly a demonstration also come from Alexander Sachs, a well-known economist and one of the organizers of the initial effort to interest FDR in atomic research. According to Sachs, Roosevelt told him a few months after signing the Hyde Park understanding that he agreed a warning should be given before using the bomb and that it should be dropped on an area from which humans and animals were evacuated.[53]

At best Roosevelt's position was ambiguous, and if anything the record suggests that he had considerable doubts about attacking a city. (Bernstein describes Roosevelt's policy as "clearly defined," but at the same time concedes, "Actually there is some spotty evidence that Roosevelt was mulling over the possibilities of not using the bomb in combat or of using it only after a warning or demonstration."[54]) As we have seen, moreover, even when Truman did inherit a specific policy from Roosevelt (as in the case of reparations policy), he did not hesitate to make substantial and lasting changes.

The most important point, however, is that whatever thoughts Roosevelt may have had about the use of the weapon, the real-world situation changed radically in the final months before Hiroshima. Roosevelt died as virtually everything—in Europe, in the Far East, and at Los Alamos—reached simultaneous turning points. A week before his death the Russians publicly announced their intention not to renew their Neutrality Pact and—at virtually the same time—the Japanese government collapsed; Germany was about to surrender—and did so twenty-six days later; the Manhattan Project neared its climax and would reach it at Alamogordo in July. And during the final weeks before Hiroshima, of course, the evidence concerning Japan's disintegration flowed in with steadily increasing force.

In 1973 Martin Sherwin also urged an "inherited assumption" theory (". . . Truman was bound to the past by his own uncertain position and by the prestige of his predecessor"[55]). In light of more recent evidence, however, Sherwin modified his earlier view, concluding in 1987 that it was

> not the lack of an alternative that might induce Japan's surrender that led to the use of atomic bombs. It was the undesirability of relying on the available alternatives *given the nuclear option*. The nuclear option was preferred because it promised dividends—not just the possibility that it would end the war but the hope that it would eliminate the need to rely on one of the other alternatives.[56]

For Sherwin, too, that a real decision had been made now seemed inescapable. The "choice in the summer of 1945 was not between a conventional invasion or a nuclear war. It was a choice between various forms of diplomacy and warfare."

> While the decision that Truman made is understandable, it was not inevitable. It was even avoidable.[57]

All of this also relates to the speculation as to whether Roosevelt would have used the atomic bomb. Although the question is impossible to answer, reflection on several factors related to the change-over from the Roosevelt to Truman presidency is instructive.

Those who believe that Roosevelt would likely have used the weapon—against a city without warning—appear mainly to feel that once the bomb was built it would inevitably have been employed. Aside from the fact that what we actually know of Roosevelt's own thinking suggests different possibilities, the post-April developments clearly involved major shifts in the situational logic of the war. We can only speculate for instance, as to what Roosevelt's response would have been to the Emperor's July 12 intervention. FDR's general approach to the Soviet Union also was both more subtle and more oriented to cooperation—and it is reasonable to assume that arguments against surprising and thereby indirectly threatening the Soviet ally might well have been more favorably received.

The most important point, however, is the most obvious: *Had Roosevelt lived, James F. Byrnes would not have become secretary of state.* Since by the time of Potsdam all of Roosevelt's civilian and military advisers (with Churchill) favored a clarification of the surrender terms—and since only Byrnes stood strongly in the way of the recommended policy—there is a reasonable likelihood that the assurances in paragraph 12 of the Potsdam Proclamation would not have been eliminated (and that the assurances it contained would have triggered the surrender process).

Moreover, as we have seen, not only did Roosevelt's secretary of state, Edward Stettinius, agree with all of the other advisers about the importance of giving Japan assurances, but he also recommended that the U.S. government should "explore every possibility . . . and make a real effort" to get the Soviets to be one of the signatories of the Potsdam Proclamation.[58]

Roosevelt may have wished to hold to the formal language of "unconditional surrender," but it had long since been clear that this issue could be finessed by focusing the demand on the Japanese military. FDR himself had demonstrated how easy it was to bend the "unconditional" language in Italy—and so crafty a politician would not likely have had much difficulty with the tactical problems involved, especially since, to repeat, leading Republicans were largely for a change in terms.[59]

As we have noted, Albert Einstein for one was very clear about the question. He judged—and stated publicly in 1946—that the decision to use the atomic bomb "was precipitated by a desire to end the war in the Pacific by any means before Russia's participation. I am sure that if President Roosevelt had still been there, none of that would have been possible."[60]

A final group of questions concern the influence of diplomatic considerations on the decision. This issue became especially heated in the mid-1960s (as

Gaddis Smith has observed) because of the intense debate over general questions of American foreign policy during the Vietnam War.* Even Herbert Feis, as we have seen, judged that it was "likely that Churchill, and probably also Truman, conceived that besides bringing the war to a quick end, [using the bomb] would improve the chances of arranging a satisfactory peace both in Europe and in the Far East."[61]

As noted, by the beginning of the 1990s, Samuel Walker's review of the modern literature concluded that although many writers judged military factors to be critical, "nearly all students of the events leading to Hiroshima agree that, in addition to viewing it as the means to end the war quickly, the political implications of the bomb figured in the administration's deliberations." He also observed that "a broad consensus viewed diplomatic considerations as an important part of the administration's view of the bomb's value."[62] Gregg Herken put it this way: "Responsible traditional as well as revisionist accounts of the decision to drop the bomb now recognize that the act had behind it *both* an immediate military rationale regarding Japan and a possible diplomatic advantage concerning Russia."[63] Assessing the president's role in the timing and approval of the atomic test, Department of Energy historian Roger M. Anders wrote: ". . . Truman seems to have focused directly on the Trinity test. . . ."

> The importance to the president of estimates about the size of the implosion bomb was obvious: the larger the bomb, the greater was its potential as a diplomatic weapon.[64]

With the Cold War over, it is reasonable to expect that the trend towards increasing understanding of the role of diplomatic factors in the decision is likely to continue. Given the gaps in the record, however, it is not surprising that scholars continue to debate matters of emphasis and degrees of influence. Anders' further observations on the sketchiness of our information concerning Truman's April meeting with Stimson and Groves is applicable to many other records on this subject:

> Because Truman knew little about the atomic bomb project, tended to ask direct questions, sought direct advice, needed ammunition for the forthcoming diplomatic tilts with the Soviets, and examined Project Trinity much closer to the scheduled test date, it is almost inconceivable that he did not discuss it in some detail with Stimson and Groves. By not reflecting this, the existing documentation is somewhat misleading.[65]

---

*To recall, although my *Atomic Diplomacy* was written before the Vietnam War, when it was published in 1965 numerous caveats (e.g., "at present no final conclusion can be reached on this question. . . .") were ignored (Alperovitz, *Atomic Diplomacy*, p. 289).

At one end of the range of modern judgments on diplomatic factors (as he himself has noted) is the position of Barton Bernstein. Although Bernstein has acknowledged that "impressing the Soviet Union did constitute a subtle deterrent to reconsidering combat use of the bomb and to searching for alternative means of ending the war," he believes that the expected effect of the atomic bomb on the Soviet Union was viewed only as a "bonus."[66]*

However, the modern evidence does not support the view that diplomatic considerations were merely a "bonus" in the minds of top U.S. officials. Although it is impossible to reach a full and final answer to the question of emphasis, what we now know even more strongly suggests—but does not as yet definitively prove—that diplomatic factors were of far greater significance. The most important points concern Byrnes' attitude and his influence on the president—especially when compared with virtually all the other top advisers (and Churchill). Some matters are no longer in doubt:

First, in general Byrnes clearly saw the weapon as important to his diplomacy vis-à-vis the Soviet Union.

Second, of particular significance are features of the context established during the two weeks in Germany. It is no longer seriously disputed that Byrnes and the president took a hard-line position on a variety of issues during the Potsdam discussion because of—in anticipation of—the atomic bomb. This fact itself set the terms of reference for the next stage of decision-making: Having developed a negotiating position based upon the expected force of the new weapon, to have immediately thereafter taken action to avoid demonstrating its power obviously would have been extremely difficult, consciously or unconsciously.

Third, it was in this specific context—and at this specific time—that Byrnes arranged for the elimination of language offering assurances for the Emperor.†

Fourth, it is beyond question that once the atomic bomb was successfully tested, Byrnes saw it as a way to end the war before the Red Army entered

---

*He has also written that for "policy makers, the atomic weapons scheduled for combat use against Japan were intimately connected with the problem of Russia." (Bernstein, "Roosevelt, Truman and the Atomic Bomb," p. 42.) In addition, as previously noted, he has stated: ". . . undoubtedly [diplomatic factors] impeded leaders from reconsidering their assumptions and from revising their policy. The combat use of the bomb might greatly impress the Soviets and make them more tractable in the postwar period." (Bernstein, "Triumph and Tragedy," p. 262.)

†In this regard it is of some significance that although there are no direct contemporaneous reports that either Byrnes or the president ever expressed clear and explicit concerns about political criticism in connection with the Emperor issue prior to Hiroshima, there *are* several clear and direct contemporaneous reports that they both viewed the atomic bomb as important to their diplomacy vis-à-vis the Soviet Union.

Manchuria—and urgently attempted both to get a surrender and to stall the Russians.

Finally, the evidence from Walter Brown's journal illuminates a slightly different diplomatic factor—agreement that Japan was looking for peace but fear that the war might end in a manner which would make Moscow the peacemaker.

How much weight should be accorded such factors? How much was conscious and how much unconscious? On the basis of presently available evidence, where is it most appropriate to place the greatest emphasis?

The evolution of Sherwin's position is again instructive. In 1973 he believed that "if the assumption that the bomb might bring the war to a rapid conclusion was the principal motive for using the atomic bomb, the expectation that its use would also inhibit Soviet diplomatic ambitions clearly discouraged any inclination to question that assumption." At this time, too, he stressed that given "the ambiguity of the available evidence the question defies an unequivocal answer. . . ."

> What can be said with certainty is that Truman, Stimson, Byrnes, and several others involved in the decision consciously considered two effects of a combat demonstration of the bomb's power: first, the impact of the atomic attack on Japan's leaders, who might be persuaded thereby to end the war; and second, the impact of that attack on the Soviet Union's leaders, who might then prove to be more cooperative.[67]

Eight years later—in 1981—as he attempted to further understand the decision to eliminate assurances for the Emperor, Sherwin moved beyond this position. One possible explanation may have been fear of the political consequences of changing the unconditional surrender language. The second possibility, Sherwin pointed out, was "that [Truman] preferred to use the atomic bomb." Although the conclusion that the bomb was used for diplomatic reasons ("to establish clearly America's postwar international position and strategic supremacy in the anticipated cold war setting"), he noted, "is difficult to 'prove,' "   ,

> any serious effort to interpret Truman's motives must confront the significant evidence in Stimson's diaries, in the Manhattan Project files and in the President's papers that supports it. "The bomb as a merely probable weapon had seemed a weak reed on which to rely," Stimson wrote in his memoir . . . "but the bomb as a colossal reality was very different." This expected difference, it must be recognized, may have made *the* difference when Truman chose between unconditional surrender and the atomic bomb.[68]

My own view has shifted slightly in recent years. By the early 1960s it was clear that the Potsdam conference had been postponed in order to have the weapon tested before negotiating with Stalin. It was also obvious from the Stimson diaries that as early as May 16 Truman himself believed that the United States would "hold more cards in our hands later than now"—and that by June 6 the president had "postponed [the Big Three meeting] . . . on purpose to give us more time." Stimson had first brought information to the president about the atomic bomb because of its bearing on the crisis over Poland.[69] And at the end of May, according to Szilard, Byrnes saw the bomb as a way to make Russia more manageable in Europe.[70]

Furthermore, having discussed "very confidentially" with Harriman the relationship of the atomic bomb to problems with Russia in Europe, Stimson also noted a few days later that "we have a weapon coming into action which will be unique," and argued that the United States should "let our actions speak for words. . . ."[71] European issues, of course, were also the primary questions facing the foreign ministers immediately after Hiroshima; at this time Stimson "found that Byrnes was very much against any attempt to cooperate with Russia. His mind is full of his problems with the coming meeting of foreign ministers and he looks to having the presence of the bomb in his pocket, so to speak, as a great weapon to get through the thing. . . ."[72]

In the early 1980s I was impressed by the research Robert Messer had done on Byrnes' concerns—especially his demonstration that having been sent by Roosevelt to sell the Yalta agreement to the Senate and to the American public, Byrnes had a strong interest in achieving a satisfactory settlement in Eastern Europe.[73] Moreover, Byrnes' personal political stature now rested almost entirely on his performance as secretary of state—and in general it is evident that the bomb appeared critical in this regard as well.*

Although it still seems clear that considerations related to Europe established key aspects of the diplomatic context as Potsdam and the Alamogordo test approached, there was considerable uncertainty until the force of the test was actually experienced. Byrnes seems genuinely to have wanted Russia to enter the war prior to mid-July. Almost surely the combination of news of the Emperor's intervention (July 13) with the news of the successful test im-

---

*Quite apart from the diplomatic questions themselves, the broad argument that Byrnes was overwhelmingly oriented to domestic politics is far more persuasive here than in relation to the Emperor issue. As Stimson noted, neither Byrnes nor Truman was adamant about the paragraph 12 assurances for the Emperor. However, as Messer points out in connection with the Yalta issues, "Byrnes knew that his domestic audience would measure his success as Secretary in terms of that mythical reality [concerning the future of Eastern Europe] he had helped to create . . . ." (Messer, "The Making of a Cold Warrior," p. 253.)

mediately thereafter (July 16) crystallized the final decisions: Now the bomb might end the war not only before an invasion but also before the Red Army moved into Manchuria.

In this regard, Truman's strong interest in the Manchurian question— perhaps partly because of its importance to many Republicans—probably also played a role. In any event, both European and Asian issues appear to have weighed heavily on the minds of American leaders in the final weeks before Hiroshima. However, we simply do not have enough information to make a final judgment as to emphasis—and we will probably never know what passed between Truman and Byrnes in their unrecorded private discussions.[74]

Appendix

BYRNES' ACTIVITIES: APRIL TO JULY 1945

To get a better grasp of Byrnes' activities during the period when he was maintaining a low profile, David J. Williams (with the help of Kathryn C. Morris, J. P. Rosensweig, Sanho Tree, and Edward Rouse Winstead) has assembled information from a variety of sources on known—but in most instances, unrecorded—meetings and discussions in which Byrnes was involved from mid-April to his formal assumption of office in early July. It can be demonstrated that Byrnes was in Washington on the following dates:

April 13, April 14, April 15, April 16, April 17;[1,2,3,4,5]
May 5, May 6, May 7, May 8, May 9; and again on May 14, May 17, May 18, May 20, May 31;[6,7,8,9,10,11,12,13,14,15]
June 1, June 4, June 5, June 6; and again on June 16, June 21;[16,17,18,19,20,21]
July 3, July 4, July 5, July 6.[22,23,24,25]

In addition to the discussions directly with Truman already noted on April 13, 14, 15, 16 and 17,* we can also document (known) presidential meetings or discussions on:

May 2 or May 3: Byrnes was telephoned by Truman and asked to represent him on the Interim Committee;[26]
May 7: Byrnes met with Truman, 3:15 p.m.;[27]
May 18: Byrnes met with Truman, 5:00 p.m.;[28]
June 1: Following the Interim Committee meeting, Byrnes went to the White House to tell Truman what was decided;[29]
June 5: Byrnes was present when Joseph Davies made his report on London meetings to Truman;[30]
July 3: Byrnes was sworn in as secretary of state in the Rose Garden with Truman present.[31]

*See above, pp. 207–09.

Beyond this, of course, Byrnes discussed the atomic bomb with the Interim Committee at length on:

May 9:   9:30 a.m.–12:30 p.m.;[32]
May 14:   10:00 a.m.–12:30 p.m.;[33]
May 18:   2:30 p.m.–4:30 p.m.;[34]
May 31:   10:00 a.m.–1:15 p.m.;
            luncheon; 2:15 p.m.–4:15 p.m.;[35]
June 1:   11:00 a.m.–12:30 p.m.;
            luncheon; 1:45 p.m.–3:30 p.m.;[36]
June 21:   9:30 a.m.–1:15 p.m.;
            luncheon; 2:00 p.m.–4:15 p.m.[37]

Almost certainly discussions occurred before, during, and after these meetings. For instance, Byrnes reported that Groves at some point told him that Russia had no uranium;[38] and, as we have noted, Groves later also reported conversations concerning Byrnes' reasons for not telling the Russians about the new weapon.

The record also indicates many informal and other high-level meetings with various officials at this time:

April 16: At a dinner in honor of Sir Anthony Eden at the British Embassy, Byrnes had informal discussions with Ambassador Halifax, Eden, Secretary of War Henry Stimson, and Chief of Staff William Leahy;[39]

May 8: Byrnes met with Stimson at the Pentagon. Immediately thereafter Groves, Bundy, and Harrison joined them to discuss Interim Committee matters;[40]

May 17: Byrnes met with Harry Hopkins;[41]

May 18: Byrnes met with McCloy;[42]

May 20: Byrnes met Leahy to discuss the Manhattan Project;[43]

May 28: Byrnes met with atomic scientists Leo Szilard, Walter Bartky, and Harold Urey in Spartanburg;[44]

June 4: Byrnes met with Leahy to discuss the Manhattan Project again;[45]

June 6: Byrnes met privately with Davies;[46]

June 13: Byrnes met with Interim Committee Secretary Gordon Arneson regarding the Quebec Agreement;[47]

June 16: Byrnes met with Harry Hopkins;[48]

June 25: Byrnes met with Harry Hopkins.[49]

There are also indirect indications of discussions concerning the atomic bomb. We have noted McCloy's report that at Truman's request he discussed altering the unconditional-surrender formula with Byrnes after June 18. That other, similarly undated and unrecorded policy discussions occurred is likely.

Notes

List of Abbreviations

Individuals

EJK	Admiral Ernest J. King, Commander in Chief, U.S. Fleet, Chief of Naval Operations
FDR	Franklin D. Roosevelt, President, 1933–April 12, 1945
GCM	General George C. Marshall, Chief of Staff, U.S. Army
HHA	General Henry H. Arnold, Commanding General, U.S. Army Air Forces
HLS	Henry L. Stimson, Secretary of War
HST	Harry S. Truman, President; Commander in Chief of the Army and Navy
JBC	James B. Conant, Chairman, National Defense Research Committee
JCG	Joseph C. Grew, Under (and Acting) Secretary of State
JFB	James F. Byrnes, Secretary of State
JJMc	John J. McCloy, Assistant Secretary of War
JVF	James V. Forrestal, Secretary of the Navy
LRG	General Leslie R. Groves, Commanding General, Manhattan Engineer District
WAH	W. Averell Harriman, U.S. Ambassador to the Soviet Union
WDL	Admiral William D. Leahy, Chief of Staff to the Commander in Chief of the Army and Navy
WSC	Winston S. Churchill, British Prime Minister

Institutions

ACA	Amherst College Archives, Amherst, MA
AFHRA	Air Force Historical Research Agency, Maxwell Air Force Base, AL
CUL	Clemson University Library, Clemson, SC
CMH	Center for Military History, Washington, D.C.
DDEL	Dwight D. Eisenhower Library, Abilene, KS
GCMRL	George C. Marshall Research Library, Lexington, VA
HHPL	Herbert Hoover Presidential Library, West Branch, IA
HIA	Hoover Institute Archives, Stanford, CA
HSTL	Harry S. Truman Library, Independence, MO
HUA	Harvard University Archives, Cambridge, MA
LC	Manuscript Division, Library of Congress, Washington, D.C.
NA	National Archives, Washington, D.C., Suitland, MD, and College Park, MD
NHC	Naval Historical Center, Navy Yard, Washington, D.C.
NHCNWC	Naval Historical Collection, Naval War College, Newport, RI
USAFAL	United States Air Force Academy Library, Colorado Springs, CO

USAMHI   U.S. Army Military History Institute (Carlisle Barracks), Carlisle, PA
USMAL   United States Military Academy Library, West Point, NY
YUL   Yale University Library, New Haven, CT

Miscellaneous

FRUS   U.S. State Department, *Foreign Relations of the United States* series
H-B   Harrison-Bundy
MED   Manhattan Engineer District
OPD   Operations Division, War Department General Staff
OSS   Office of Strategic Services
OWI   Office of War Information
Pots. I U.S. State Department, *Foreign Relations of the United States: Conference of Berlin (Potsdam)*, Vol. I
Pots. II U.S. State Department, *Foreign Relations of the United States: Conference of Berlin (Potsdam)*, Vol. II
RG   Record Group

Introduction: A Personal Note

1. William D. Leahy, *I Was There: The Personal Story of the Chief of Staff to Presidents Roosevelt and Truman, Based on His Notes and Diaries Made at the Time* (New York, 1950), p. 441.

2. Leahy, *I Was There*, p. 4.

3. Dwight D. Eisenhower, *Mandate for Change 1953–1956* (Garden City, NY, 1963), pp. 312–13.

4. Paul Boyer, "The Cloud over the Culture: How Americans Imagined the Bomb They Dropped," *New Republic*, August 12 and 19, 1985, pp. 26–31, cited material from p. 26.

5. Boyer, "The Cloud over the Culture," pp. 28, 26.

6. Diaries of Henry L. Stimson (hereafter, Stimson Diary), May 15, 1945, Manuscripts and Archives, YUL. Also available on microfilm at the Manuscript Division of the Library of Congress.

7. Stimson Diary, May 14, 1945.

8. Gar Alperovitz, *Atomic Diplomacy: Hiroshima and Potsdam* rev. ed. (New York, 1985), p. 290. Originally published by Simon and Schuster, 1965. All references in this book are to the 1985 revised edition. Cited material from Leo Szilard, "A Personal History of the Atomic Bomb," *University of Chicago Roundtable*, No. 601 (September 25, 1949), pp. 14–15.

9. Alperovitz, *Atomic Diplomacy*, pp. 284, 289, 64.

10. Gaddis Smith, "Was Moscow Our Real Target?," *The New York Times Book Review*, August 18, 1985, p. 16.

11. Also, written originally as a Cambridge University Ph.D. thesis, the book often referenced British editions of various books, and hence indicated different page numbers for sources than did U.S. editions.

12. J. Samuel Walker, "The Decision to Use the Bomb: A Historiographical Update," *Diplomatic History*, Vol. 14, No.1 (Winter 1990), pp. 97–114, cited material from p. 110.

13. Robert L. Messer, "New Evidence on Truman's Decision," *Bulletin of the Atomic Scientists*, Vol. 41, No. 7 (August 1985), pp. 50–56, cited material from p. 55.

14. Walker, "The Decision to Use the Bomb," p. 110.

15. A Gallup poll from August 1945 showed 85% of those polled approved the use of atomic bombs on Japanese cities. George H. Gallup, *The Gallup Poll: Public Opinion, 1935–1971*, Vol. I: *1935–1948* (New York, 1972), pp. 521–22. A survey published in De-

cember 1945 indicated 53.5% of Americans agreeing with the decision to drop bombs on Japanese cities, with an additional 22.7% believing the United States should have dropped *more* bombs. Only 4.5% believed no atomic bombs should have been dropped at all, while 13.8% believed a demonstration bomb should have been dropped on an unpopulated region, with an actual strike against a Japanese city only if the demonstration failed to induce surrender. "The Fortune Survey," *Fortune*, December 1945, p. 305. See also Lillian Wald Kay, "Public Opinion and the Bomb," *Journal of Educational Sociology*, Vol. 22 (January 1949), pp. 357–60, cited in Paul Boyer, *By the Bomb's Early Light* (New York, 1985), p. 183. Polls from 1988, 1982, and 1971 showed 65%, 63%, and 64% of Americans felt it was "Necessary to drop bombs on Japan" and only 26%, 26%, and 21% agreeing that "We were wrong to drop the bombs." See Alan Kay, *Americans Talk Security* (Winchester, MA: October 19, 1989), Appendix: "Public Opinion on Nuclear War and Weapons," Fig. 33. Polls taken in 1990 showed 53% of Americans approving the atomic bombing of Japanese cities in 1945, with 41% disapproving. See "Only Half of Americans Now Approve of the Atomic Bombing of Japan," *The Gallup Poll Monthly*, No. 299 (August 1990), p. 33.

16. See, for example, Richard Rhodes, *The Making of the Atomic Bomb* (New York, 1986); Leon V. Sigal, *Fighting to a Finish: The Politics of War Termination in the United States and Japan, 1945* (Ithaca, NY, 1988); Alice Kimball Smith, *A Peril and a Hope: The Scientists' Movement in America, 1945–1947* (Cambridge, MA, 1971); Martin Sherwin, *A World Destroyed: Hiroshima and the Origins of the Arms Race* (New York, 1987). See the Bibliography of this book for a listing of related works.

17. ABC News, *Nightline*, "What If . . . We Hadn't Dropped the Bomb," (August 5, 1985), Transcript of show No. 1096, p. 2.

18. Martin J. Sherwin, "The Atomic Bomb and the Origins of the Cold War: U.S. Atomic Energy Policy and Diplomacy, 1941–1945," *The American Historical Review*, Vol. 78, No. 4 (October 1973), pp. 945–68, cited material from p. 965.

19. Barton J. Bernstein, "Roosevelt, Truman and the Atomic Bomb, 1941–1945: A Reinterpretation," *Political Science Quarterly*, Vol. 90, No. 1 (Spring 1975), pp. 23–69, cited material from p. 48.

20. The Legacy of Strategic Bombing Lecture Series, "The Atomic Bombing of Japan," National Air and Space Museum, Washington, D.C., July 12, 1990. Recorded on videotape, available at the National Air and Space Museum Film Archive. Panel including Richard Cohen, Gen. David Birchnall, Barton Bernstein, and Paul Fussell, with additional comments by Gen. Andrew Goodpaster.

21. Stephen Ambrose to author, January 28, 1993.

22. See David McCullough, *Truman* (New York, 1992).

23. HLS to JCG, June 19, 1947, Grew Papers, Houghton Library, Harvard University.

24. Eisenhower, *Mandate for Change*, p. 312; Leahy, *I Was There*, p. 441.

25. Maya Angelou, *The Inaugural Poem: "On the Pulse of Morning"* (New York, 1993). Read by the poet at the Inauguration of President William Jefferson Clinton.

Book One: The Decision

Chapter 1: The Trajectory of Japan's Decline

1. Robert J. C. Butow, *Japan's Decision to Surrender* (Stanford, CA, 1954), p. v.

2. Lt. Gen. George C. Kenney to Gen. Arnold, September 17, 1944, "McCormack Papers," Part 2, SRH-141, RG 457, NA.

3. Herbert Feis, *Japan Subdued: The Atomic Bomb and the End of the War in the Pacific* (Princeton, NJ, 1961), p. 3.

4. For details on Suzuki's nomination, see Butow, *Japan's Decision to Surrender*, pp. 61–67.

5. Memorandum for Information, Subject: Fall of Koiso Cabinet and Naming of Adm. Baron Kantaro Suzuki to Form a New Government, April 5, 1945, OSS, Folder 696 – "Japan – Cabinet," Box 57, Entry 136, RG 226, NA.

6. JIC 266/1, "Defeat of Japan by Blockade and Bombardment," April 18, 1945, "ABC 387 Japan (15 Feb. 45) Sec 1-a," Box 504, Entry 421, RG 165, NA.

7. The five-year Neutrality Pact between Japan and the Soviet Union was signed on April 13, 1941. Under the terms of the pact, renewal for another five years would occur automatically in April 1946 unless one of the parties gave a year's notice that it did not desire renewal. The Soviet denunciation of the pact on April 5, 1945, fulfilled this requirement. See U.S. State Department, *Bulletin*, Vol. XII (April 29, 1945), p. 812.

8. U.S. intelligence summaries of intercepted and decrypted Japanese diplomatic communications—otherwise known as "MAGIC" intercepts—were reported daily and designated "Eyes Only" for the very top political and military officials in the U.S. government. See below, p. 29, for details.

9. MAGIC, No. 1076, March 6, 1945, RG 457, NA. See also MAGIC No. 1061, February 19, 1945, No. 1070, February 28, 1945, and No. 1087, March 17, 1945.

10. MAGIC, No. 1131, April 30, 1945, RG 457, NA.

11. Memorandum for Information, Subject: Fall of Koiso Cabinet, April 5, 1945, OSS, Folder 696—"Japan—Cabinet," Box 57, Entry 136, RG 226, NA.

12. JIS 143/2, "Unconditional Surrender of Japan," April 11, 1945, "CCS 387 Japan (4-6-45)," JCS Geographic Files 1942–45, RG 218, NA.

13. MAGIC, No. 1143, May 12, 1945, RG 457, NA.

14. Memorandum for Assistant Chief of Staff, OPD, from Clayton Bissell, May 15, 1945, "ABC 387 Japan (15 Feb 45)," Box 504, Entry 421, RG 165, NA.

15. Ibid.

16. Office of War Information, "Current Psychological and Social Tensions in Japan," Special Report V: 1 June 1945, in Alexander H. Leighton, *Human Relations in a Changing World* (New York, 1949), pp. 72, 257.

17. Butow, *Japan's Decision to Surrender*, p. 94.

18. HLS to HST, July 2, 1945, enclosure: *Proposed Program for Japan*, "White House Correspondence," Box 15, Stimson Safe File, Entry 74A, RG 107, NA; also in Stimson Diary, July 2, 1945, and U.S. Department of State, *Foreign Relations of the United States: Conference of Berlin (Potsdam), 1945* (hereafter cited as FRUS, Pots. I) (Washington, D.C.: U.S. Government Printing Office, 1960), pp. 890–93.

19. CCS 643/3, "Estimate of the Enemy Situation (as of 6 July 1945)," July 8, 1945, pp. 9–10, "CCS 381 (6-4-43), Section 2, Part 5," JCS Decimal Files 1942–45, RG 218, NA.

20. Raymond Swing broadcast, July 3, 1945, Box 27, Swing Papers, LC.

21. *The New York Times*, July 23, 1945, p. 4.

22. Ibid.

Chapter 2: General Efforts to End the War

1. MAGIC, No. 869, August 11, 1944, RG 457, NA.

2. Ibid.

3. U.S. Department of State, *Foreign Relations of the United States: Diplomatic Papers* (hereafter cited as FRUS), 1944, Vol. V (Washington, D.C.: U.S. Government Printing Office, 1965), p. 1184.

4. FRUS, 1944, Vol. V, p. 1185.

5. Ibid.

6. See memo to Leahy, FRUS, 1944, Vol. V, p. 1186.

7. MAGIC, No. 944, October 25, 1944, RG 457, NA.

8. Ibid.

9. FRUS, 1945, Vol. VI (Washington, D.C.: U.S. Government Printing Office, 1969), p. 475. The negotiations at the Vatican were ultimately unsuccessful. For details, see Martin S. Quigley, *Peace Without Hiroshima: Secret Action at the Vatican in the Spring of 1945* (New York, 1991).

10. MAGIC, No. 1051, February 9, 1945, RG 457, NA.

11. FRUS, 1945, Vol. VI, p. 477.

12. Ibid.

13. MAGIC, No. 1142, May 11, 1945, RG 457, NA.

14. Memorandum for the President, from Donovan, May 12, 1945, "Rose Conway File," Papers of Harry S. Truman, HSTL; also in FRUS, 1945, Vol. VI, p. 481.

15. FRUS, 1945, Vol. VI, pp. 485–86.

16. Memorandum for the President, from G. [*sic*] Edward Buxton, June 4, 1945, Rose Conway File, Papers of Harry S. Truman, HSTL; also in FRUS, 1945, Vol. VI, p. 486. "[?]" in original.

17. FRUS, 1945, Vol. VI, pp. 487–88.

18. Ibid.

19. Memorandum for the President, from Donovan, July 16, 1945, Rose Conway File, Papers of Harry S. Truman, HSTL; also in FRUS, 1945, Vol. VI, pp. 489–90.

20. Gen. Bonesteel interview with LTC Robert St. Louis, 1973, p. 187, Charles H. Bonesteel III Papers, USAMHI. Note: In 1945 Bonesteel held the rank of colonel.

21. MAGIC, No. 1205, July 13, 1945, RG 457, NA.

22. MAGIC, No. 1207, July 15, 1945, RG 457, NA.

23. *Kiplinger Washington Letter*, May 12, 1945, "34-1-3," Forrestal Papers, RG 80, NA.

24. *Kiplinger Washington Letter*, July 21, 1945, "34-1-3," Forrestal Papers, RG 80, NA.

25. See James V. Forrestal, *The Forrestal Diaries*, ed. Walter Millis (New York: Viking Press, 1951), p. 74.

26. See Butow, *Japan's Decision to Surrender*, pp. 130–31; also, Butow interview with Kathryn C. Morris, August 23, 1994.

27. At a conference with members of his staff and Department of State historians in 1956, Truman acknowledged that he was familiar with the contents of the July 12 cable before Stalin mentioned it to him at their July 18 meeting at Potsdam, and that he was familiar with the contents of the July 25 cable before Stalin mentioned it on July 28. FRUS, Pots. I, p. 873.

28. MAGIC, No. 1142, May 11, 1945, RG 457, NA.

29. Ibid.

Part I: Unconditional Surrender

Chapter 3: April–May 1945

1. Early studies, mainly by politically conservative authors, that examine the problem of the unconditional surrender formula include: Forrest Davis, "Did Marshall Prolong the Pacific War?," a two-part article in *The Freeman*, November 5, 1951, pp. 73–75, and November 19, 1951, pp. 112–15; Harry Elmer Barnes, "Hiroshima: Assault on a Beaten Foe," *National Review*, May 10, 1958, pp. 441–43; Anthony Kubek, "How We Lost the Pacific War: The Soviets Reaped the Benefits of U.S. Fighting," *Human Events*, Vol. XV, No. 48 (December 1, 1958), pp. 1–4; Elizabeth Churchill Brown, *The Enemy at His Back* (New York: Distributed by The Bookmailer, 1956).

2. James F. Byrnes, *Speaking Frankly* (New York, 1947), p. 211.

3. See John W. Dower, *War Without Mercy: Race and Power In the Pacific War* (New York, 1986); Otto Tolischus, *Tokyo Record* (New York, 1943); Also see the English trans-

lation by John O. Gauntlett, edited by Robert K. Hall, of *Kokutai no Hongi: Cardinal Principles of the National Entity of Japan* (Boston, 1949) especially pp. 54, 66, 79, 82, 91, 100, 101, 120–40, 105.

4. See Dower, *War Without Mercy*, p. 221.

5. Dower, *War Without Mercy*, pp. 221–22.

6. See Tolischus, *Tokyo Record*, pp. 405–27.

7. Tolischus, *Tokyo Record*, p. 424.

8. Ibid.

9. See OSS reports of May 12 (in FRUS, 1945, Vol. VI, p. 481), and June 4 (in FRUS, 1945, Vol. VI, p. 486). Also see Stimson Diary, August 10, 1945; and Joseph C. Grew, *Turbulent Era: A Diplomatic Record of Forty Years 1904–1945*, Vol. II (Boston, 1952), p. 1411.

10. Cordell Hull, *Memoirs of Cordell Hull*, Vol. II (New York, 1948), p. 1570.

11. Hull, *Memoirs*, Vol. II, pp. 1570–71.

12. JIC 181, "Japanese Surrender – Postwar Resistance," March 29, 1944, "JIC by No. 175-189," ACSI "P" Files, Box T-164, Entry 82, RG 319, NA.

13. Ibid.

14. "Answer to Japan" Booklet, pp. 20–21, Box 2, Dr. Edward P. Lilly Papers, JCS Historical Section, RG 218, NA.

15. "Answer to Japan" Booklet, pp. 22–23, Box 2, Lilly Papers, JCS Historical Section, RG 218, NA.

16. "Annex on Treatment of Japanese Emperor," Nov. 28–Dec. 5, 1944, O.W.I. – Office of Policy Coordination, November 1945, Record Central Directors, Nov.–Dec. 1944, Box 819, Entry 359, RG 208, NA.

17. FRUS, *The Conferences at Malta and Yalta, 1945* (hereafter cited as Malta and Yalta) (Washington, D.C.: U.S. Government Printing Office, 1955), p. 826.

18. *The New York Times*, April 17, 1945, p. 12.

19. Truman writes in his memoirs that in his first address to Congress on April 16, 1945, "I reaffirmed our demand for unconditional surrender and expressed my full confidence in the grand strategy of the United States and our allies. . . . There were many indications of approval of what I said. I was applauded frequently, and when I reaffirmed the policy of unconditional surrender the chamber rose to its feet." Harry S. Truman, *Memoirs of Harry S. Truman*, Vol. I: *Year of Decisions* (New York, 1955), p. 42. Similarly, on April 17, *The New York Times* reported, "He received an ovation both when he entered the House chamber and when he departed after his appeal for national support. . . ." The *Times* and Bundy both make reference to Truman banging on the table before him. *The New York Times*, April 17, 1945, p. 1. See also McGeorge Bundy, *Danger and Survival* (New York, 1988), p. 59.

20. Statement by the President, May 8, 1945, Confidential Files, White House Central Files, HSTL; also in "ABC 387 Japan (15 Feb. 45)," Box 505, Entry 421, RG 165, NA. For details on the evolution of this statement, see Davis to HST, April 26, 1945, and Davis to HST, May 2, 1945, "OWI," Box 30, Confidential Files, White House Central Files, Papers of Harry S. Truman, HSTL.

21. See "Sec. II, Chp. V – Unconditional Surrender," Box 16, Lilly Papers, JCS Historical Section, RG 218, NA. See also Zacharias, *Secret Missions: The Story of an Intelligence Officer* (New York, 1946); Zacharias, "We Did Not Need to Drop the A-Bomb," *Look*, Vol. 14, No. 11 (May 23, 1950), pp. 29–35; and Zacharias, "How We Bungled the Japanese Surrender," *Look*, Vol. 14, No. 12 (June 6, 1950), pp. 12–21.

22. For copies of "A Strategic Plan to Effect the Occupation of Japan," and "Operation Plan 1-45," See Zacharias, *Secret Missions*, pp. 336–40, and pp. 342–45. Some controversy later arose concerning Zacharias' role, and most historians have neglected the origin of the carefully planned psychological warfare campaign which Truman's May 8 speech initiated. The recent research by Sanho Tree on the unpublished work of Dr. Edward Lilly on psychological warfare in World War II helps illuminate this development. See "Sec. II,

Chp. V – Unconditional Surrender," Box 16, Lilly Papers, JCS Historical Section, RG 218, NA.

23. Zacharias, *Secret Missions*, pp. 341–47.

24. Zacharias, *Secret Missions*, pp. 347–48; and "Sec. II, Chp. V – Unconditional Surrender," p. 149, Box 16, Lilly Papers, JCS Historical Section, RG 218, NA.

25. Memorandum for the President, May 6, 1945, from WDL, File 125, Box 19 (U.S. Joint Chiefs of Staff), Chairman's file Admiral Leahy, 1942–1948, RG 218, NA.

26. See Zacharias, *Secret Missions*, pp. 332–50.

27. Zacharias, *Secret Missions*, pp. 399–401.

28. "Now Japan," *Washington Post*, May 9, 1945, p. 6.

29. Halifax weekly political report, May 13, 1945, Document 1641, Reel 3, F.O. 371, Great Britain Foreign Copying Program, LC Manuscript Division.

30. "Now Japan," *Washington Post*, May 9, 1945, copy in "ABC 387 Japan (15 Feb. 45)," Entry 421, RG 165, NA.

31. JIC 266/1, "Defeat of Japan by Blockade and Bombardment," April 18, 1945, "ABC 387 Japan (15 Feb. 45) Sec 1-A," Entry 421, RG 165, NA.

32. JCS 924/5, "Pacific Strategy," April 25, 1945, pp. 244–45, "ABC 384 Pacific (1-17-43), Sec. 9," Entry 421, RG 165, NA.

33. JCS 924/5, "Pacific Strategy," April 25, 1945, p. 245, "ABC 384 Pacific (1-17-43), Sec. 9," Entry 421, RG 165, NA.

34. JPS 675/D, "Immediate Demand for the Unconditional Surrender of Japan," May 9, 1945, "ABC 387 Japan (15 Feb. 45)," Entry 421, RG 165, NA. See also "Terms of Japanese Surrender, Chronology," "ABC 387.2 Japan (15 Feb. 45)," Entry 421, RG 165, NA.

35. JPS 675/1, "Immediate Demand for the Unconditional Surrender of Japan," May 12, 1945, "ABC 387 Japan (15 Feb. 45)," Box 504, Entry 421, RG 165, NA.

36. FRUS, 1945, Vol. VI, p. 481.

37. Memorandum for the Secretary of War, from HST, enclosure: Memorandum on Ending the Japanese War, June 9, 1945, "Japan (After Dec. 7/41)," Box 8, Stimson Safe File, Entry 74A, RG 107, NA.

38. Memorandum of Comments on "Ending the Japanese War," June 14, 1945, "ABC 387 Japan (15 Feb. 45)," Entry 421, RG 165, NA.

39. Memorandum for the Secretary of War, from GCM, June 15, 1945, "Japan (After Dec. 7/41)," Stimson Safe File, Entry 74A, RG 107, NA.

40. William R. Castle Diaries (hereafter, Castle Diary), May 29, 1945, MS Am 2021, Houghton Library, Harvard University.

41. Joseph C. Grew, *Turbulent Era*, Vol. II, pp. 1429–31.

42. Grew, *Turbulent Era*, Vol. II, p. 1431.

Chapter 4: To June 18, 1945

1. JCG to WDL, May 3, 1945, "OWI," Box 30, Confidential Files, White House Central Files, Papers of Harry S. Truman, HSTL.

2. Stimson Diary, May 8, 1945; Forrestal, *The Forrestal Diaries*, ed. Millis, p. 54.

3. Makoto Iokibe, "American Policy Toward Japan's 'Unconditional Surrender,'" *The Japanese Journal of American Studies*, No. 1 (1981), pp. 19–53, cited material from pp. 46, 47.

4. Nakamura Masanori, *The Japanese Monarchy: Ambassador Joseph Grew and the Making of the "Symbol Emperor System," 1931–1991* (New York, 1992), p. 70.

5. Grew, *Turbulent Era*, Vol. II, p. 1431.

6. Milton O. Gustafson, "The Committee of 3: The Origins of the National Security Council, 1944–1947," p. 3, part of a panel on "The National Security Council and Planning for Defense," The Citadel, Conference on War and Diplomacy, The Citadel, March

10–12, 1977. 1974 correspondence between Gustafson and John J. McCloy found in the McCloy Papers offers further details about the workings of the Committee of Three in 1944–45. See Gustafson to McCloy, October 16, 1974, and McCloy's reply of November 7, 1974, Folder 34, COR 3, McCloy Papers, ACA.

7. Grew, *Turbulent Era*, Vol. II, p. 1434. It is likely that McCloy was present as well.

8. Ibid.

9. Forrestal, *The Forrestal Diaries*, ed. Millis, p. 66.

10. Ibid.

11. Eugene H. Dooman, Speech to St. Michael's Church Men's Club, January 12, 1960, Litchfield, Conn., p. 6, File—"The A-bomb and American Foreign Policy," Box 1, Dooman Papers, HIA.

12. Stimson Diary, May 29, 1945.

13. Diaries of John J. McCloy (hereafter, McCloy Diary), Memorandum of Conversation with General Marshall and the Secretary of War, May 29, 1945, DY1, McCloy Papers, ACA.

14. Message of the President to the Congress, June 1, 1945, *Department of State Bulletin*, Vol. XII, No. 310 (June 3, 1945), p. 1000.

15. *Washington Post*, June 3, 1945, p. 1; June 6, 1945, p. 10.

16. Memo for the Policy Section, from Lincoln, June 7, 1945, "ABC 387 Japan (15 Feb. 1945)," Entry 421, RG 165, NA.

17. McCloy Diary, Memorandum of Conversation with General Marshall and the Secretary of War, May 29, 1945.

18. MAGIC, No. 1163, June 1, 1945, RG 457, NA.

19. Ibid.

20. FRUS, Pots. I, p. 44; U.S. Department of Defense, *The Entry of the Soviet Union into the War Against Japan* (hereafter, DoD, *Entry*), (Washington, D.C.: U.S. Government Printing Office, 1955), p. 74. Stalin's official position on whether or not the Allies should try to obtain unconditional surrender at this point was open—and his intentions were ambiguous. See FRUS, Pots. I, p. 44.

21. FRUS, 1945, Vol. VI, p. 485.

22. Memorandum of Information for the Joint Chiefs of Staff, "Japanese Peace Feelers," "CCS 387 Japan (10-3-44)," JCS Geographic File, 1942–45, RG 218, NA.

23. See, for example, Brian L. Villa, "The U.S. Army, Unconditional Surrender, and the Potsdam Proclamation," *The Journal of American History*, Vol. 63, No. 1 (June 1976), pp. 66–92; Sigal, *Fighting to a Finish*; Ray S. Cline, *Washington Command Post: The Operations Division* (Washington, D.C.: Department of the Army, Office of the Chief of Military History, 1951); Grace Pearson Hayes, *The History of the Joint Chiefs of Staff in World War II: The War Against Japan* (Annapolis, MD, 1982).

24. Memorandum for the Chief of Staff, from HLS, May 30, 1945, "Japan (After Dec. 7/41)," Box 8, Stimson Safe File, Entry 74A, RG 107, NA.

25. Memorandum for the Secretary of War, from GCM, June 9, 1945, "ABC 337 11 Jan 45) Sec 1-A," Entry 421, RG 165, NA.

26. Memorandum by the Chief of Staff, Undated—June 1945, "ABC 387 Japan (15 Feb. 45)," Entry 421, RG 165, NA.

27. Memorandum for the Secretary of War, from GCM, Undated—June 1945, "ABC 387 Japan (15 Feb. 45)," Entry 421, RG 165, NA.

28. SWNCC 149, "Immediate Demand For the Unconditional Surrender of Japan," June 9, 1945, "ABC 387 Japan (15 Feb. 45)," Entry 421, RG 165, NA.

29. Stimson Diary, June 1, 1945; Memorandum for General Hull, from Lincoln, June 4, 1945, "ABC 387 Japan (15 Feb. 45)," Box 504, Entry 421, RG 165, NA.

30. Memorandum for the President, from JCG, June 13, 1945, "Japan," Stimson Safe File, Entry 74A, RG 107, NA.

31. Ibid.

32. Committee of Three Minutes, June 12, 1945, RG 59, NA.

33. FRUS, Pots. I, p. 173.

34. Diaries of William D. Leahy (hereafter, Leahy Diary), June 18, 1945, on microfilm at the Manuscripts Division of the Library of Congress.

35. Leahy, *I Was There*, p. 385.

36. JCG to Rosenman, June 16, 1945, "Japan (After Dec. 7/41)," Stimson Safe File, Entry 74A, RG 107, NA; see also Grew, *Turbulent Era*, Vol. II, pp. 1435–36.

37. Grew, *Turbulent Era*, Vol. II, 1952, p. 1437.

Chapter 5: June 18, 1945

1. Truman, *Year of Decisions*, p. 417.

2. DoD, *Entry*, p. 76.

3. Telephone conversation, June 14, 1945, Adm. Duncan and Gen. Lincoln, "ABC 384 Japan (3 May 44) Sec. 1-B," Box 428, Entry 421, RG 165, NA.

4. DoD, *Entry*, p. 83.

5. Ibid.

6. Ibid.

7. Ibid.

8. DoD, *Entry*, p. 84.

9. Diaries of James V. Forrestal (hereafter, Unpublished Forrestal Diary), June 18, 1945, Mudd Library, Princeton University Archives.

10. DoD, *Entry*, p. 84.

11. For detailed studies of JCS planning at this time, see Charles F. Brower, "The Joint Chiefs of Staff and National Policy: American Strategy and the War with Japan, 1943–1945," Ph.D. Dissertation, University of Pennsylvania, 1987; Cline, *Washington Command Post*; DoD, *Entry*; Hayes, *The History of the Joint Chiefs of Staff in World War II*; John Ray Skates, *The Invasion of Japan: Alternative to the Bomb* (Columbia, SC, 1994).

12. DoD, *Entry*, p. 84.

13. DoD, *Entry*, p. 81.

14. John J. McCloy, *The Challenge to American Foreign Policy* (Cambridge, MA, 1953), p. 41.

15. FRUS, Pots. I, p. 910.

16. FRUS, Pots. I, p. 910, footnote 8.

17. See Kai Bird, *The Chairman: John J. McCloy, the Making of the American Establishment* (New York, 1992), p. 247.

18. Memorandum for Colonel Stimson, from McCloy, May 28, 1945, "Japan," Stimson Safe File, Entry 74A, RG 107, NA.

19. McCloy interview with Fred Freed for NBC White Paper, "The Decision to Drop the Bomb" (interview conducted sometime between May 1964 and February 1965), Roll 1, p. 11, File 50A, Box SP2, McCloy Papers, ACA.

20. McCloy interview with Freed, pp. 15–18.

21. Questions from NBC For Mr. McCloy Re: NBC White Paper on "The Decision to Surrender," circa 1965, pp. 5–6, File 50A, Box SP2, McCloy Papers, ACA.

22. McCloy interview with Forrest C. Pogue, March 31, 1959, p. 7, Tape 65, Pogue Interview Tapes (McCloy), Pogue Papers, GCMRL.

23. Bird, *The Chairman*, p. 246; see also p. 694, endnote 30.

24. Bird, *The Chairman*, p. 694, endnote 30.

25. James Reston, *Deadline: A Memoir* (New York, 1991), p. 499.

26. McCloy interview with Pogue, p. 7. For further indications of Byrnes' opposition to giving assurances, see McCloy interview with Fred Freed, pp. 21–22, and McCloy to Clark Clifford, September 17, 1984, enclosure: "President Truman & the Atom Bomb," Box 1, Records of the Truman Centennial Committee, HSTL. In the late 1950s and early

1960s (in interviews with Pogue and NBC), McCloy said that he had not been familiar firsthand with Byrnes' views, but that Byrnes' opposition to assurances "had been reported" to him. In later years, particularly after Byrnes' death, he stated that he met personally with Byrnes to discuss the question of issuing a warning with assurances. For McCloy's recollections of meeting with Byrnes, see Bird, *The Chairman*, pp. 246, 694; McCloy interview with Walter Cronkite, undated, courtesy of Milton Leitenburg; Reston, *Deadline*, p. 499.

27. Grew, *Turbulent Era*, Vol. II, p. 1437.

28. See, for example, p. 62, fn. 105, in Barton J. Bernstein, "Seizing the Contested Terrain of Early Nuclear History: Stimson, Conant, and Their Allies Explain the Decision to Use the Atomic Bomb," *Diplomatic History*, Vol. 17, No. 1 (Winter 1992), pp. 35–72.

29. McCloy's Comments for National Broadcasting Company on "The Decision to Drop the Atom Bomb," p. 10, File 50A, Box SP2, McCloy Papers, ACA.

30. R. A. Winnacker to McCloy, August 1, 1947, File 47, Box PA1, McCloy Papers, ACA.

31. McCloy's Comments for National Broadcasting Company on "The Decision to Drop the Atom Bomb," pp. 10–11.

32. Unpublished Forrestal Diary, June 18, 1945.

33. Handwritten note by Winnacker, Apr. 30, May 1 '46, "Surrender of Japan Notes," Box 69, Office of Chief of Military History Papers, RG 319, NA. Additional confirmation seems to be indicated by a July 22, 1947 letter from Winnacker to McCloy which states (on the basis of his review of classified documents and private diaries and notes): "The White House meeting at which the political offensive against Japan was decided upon occurred on June 18 [1945]." Winnacker to McCloy, July 22, 1947, File 47, Box PA1, McCloy Papers, ACA.

Chapter 6: From June 18 to July 2, 1945

1. McCloy interview with Fred Freed, p. 18.

2. Reston, *Deadline*, p. 498.

3. Though Secretary of the Navy Forrestal did not attend this meeting, he was represented by Under Secretary of the Navy Artemus L. Gates and Forrestal's assistant, Matthias F. Correa. See Unpublished Forrestal Diary, June 19, 1945.

4. Forrestal, *The Forrestal Diaries*, ed. Millis, p. 69.

5. Unpublished Forrestal Diary, June 19, 1945.

6. Ibid.

7. Unpublished Forrestal Diary, June 19, 1945, and Forrestal, *The Forrestal Diaries*, ed. Millis, pp. 69–70.

8. Grew, *Turbulent Era*, Vol. II, pp. 1423–24, footnote 10.

9. Stimson Diary, June 19, 1945.

10. Ibid.

11. See the minutes of the Committee of Three meeting, June 26, 1945, RG 59, NA.

12. FRUS, Pots. I, p. 884.

13. HLS to HST, July 2, 1945, "White House Correspondence," Box 15, Stimson Safe File, Entry 74A, RG 165, NA; also in FRUS, Pots. I, p. 888.

14. HLS to HST, July 2, 1945, enclosure: *Proposed Program for Japan*, "White House Correspondence," Box 15, Stimson Safe File, Entry 74A, RG 107, NA; also in Stimson Diary, July 2, 1945, and FRUS, Pots. I, pp. 889–92.

15. HLS to HST, July 2, 1945, enclosure: *Proclamation by the Heads of State* (draft of 1 July 1945), "White House Correspondence," Box 15, Stimson Safe File, Entry 74A, RG 107, NA; also in Stimson Diary, July 2, 1945, and FRUS, Pots. I, p. 894.

16. Memorandum for Colonel Stimson, from McCloy, June 29, 1945, "Japan (After 7/41)," Box 8, Stimson Safe File, Entry 74A, RG 107, NA.

17. HLS to HST, July 2, 1945, enclosure: *Proclamation by the Heads of State* (draft of 1 July 1945), "White House Correspondence," Box 15, Stimson Safe File, Entry 74A, RG 107, NA; also in Stimson Diary, July 2, 1945, and FRUS, Pots. I, p. 894.

18. HLS to HST, July 2, 1945, enclosure: *Proposed Program for Japan*, "White House Correspondence," Box 15, Stimson Safe File, Entry 74A, RG 107, NA; also in Stimson Diary, July 2, 1945, and FRUS, Pots. I, p. 892.

19. Stimson Diary, July 2, 1945.

20. Forrestal, *The Forrestal Diaries*, ed. Millis, p. 73. Forrestal's diary also records that Grew "was afraid [the draft] would be ditched on the way over [to Potsdam] by people who accompany the President," such as Charles Bohlen, "among others."

Part II: The Russian Option

Chapter 7: Phase I: From Pearl Harbor to the Death of Roosevelt

1. Ernest R. May, "The United States, the Soviet Union, and the Far Eastern War, 1941–1945," *Pacific Historical Review*, Vol. 24, No. 1 (February 1955), pp. 153–74, cited material from pp. 172–73.

2. Memorandum for Chief, Strategic Policy Section, S&P Group, OPD, from Ennis, Subject: Use of Atomic Bomb on Japan, April 30, 1946, "ABC 471.6 Atom (17 Aug. 45), Sec. 7," Entry 421, RG 165, NA.

3. Ibid.

4. Ibid.

5. Ibid.

6. The Intelligence Group, of course, undoubtedly had access to all intelligence (G-2) materials, some of which are still unavailable today. Documents obtained by a Freedom of Information Act request in 1995 show that this study was commissioned in conjunction with the proposed JCS statement before Congress on atomic weapons. (For details on this statement, see below, pp. 624–26.) Also, it can now be shown that the study's author, Col. Riley Ennis, then Chief of the Intelligence Group, was responsible for many of the high-level intelligence studies produced during the immediate postwar period. See Post-War Studies Book, ID 961275, ACSI, RG 319, NA.

7. MacArthur to GCM, December 10, 1941, Box 254, WPD 4544-26, RG 165, NA; see also, DoD, *Entry*, p. 1.

8. Hull, *Memoirs*, Vol. II, p. 1111; also, DoD, *Entry*, p. 2.

9. Stimson Diary, December 10, 1941.

10. Memorandum for the President, from Stark, December 13, 1941, Box 255, WPD 4557-32, RG 165, NA; see also JCS Historical Section, *United States Interest in the Entry of the USSR in the War Against Japan*, April 25, 1995, unpublished manuscript, formerly Top Secret (hereafter, DoD, *Top Secret Entry*), Sec. I, p. 5, JCS Historical Section, Department of Defense.

11. DoD *Top Secret Entry*, Sec. III, p. 11; also, DoD, *Entry*, p. 21.

12. Hull, *Memoirs*, Vol. II, pp. 1309–10.

13. DoD, *Top Secret Entry*, Sec. III, p. 12; also, DoD, *Entry*, p. 22.

14. DoD, *Top Secret Entry*, Sec. III, p. 16.

15. DoD, *Top Secret Entry*, Sec. III, p. 15; also, DoD, *Entry*, p. 26.

16. CCS 397, "Specific Operations for the Defeat of Japan, 1944," December 3, 1943, *Sextant Conference, November–December 1943, Papers and Minutes of Meetings, Sextant and Eureka Conferences*, (Washington, D.C.: Office U.S. Secretary, Office of the Combined Chiefs of Staff, 1943), p. 66; also, DoD, *Top Secret Entry*, Sec. III, p. 16; DoD, *Entry*, p. 27.

17. Eureka Conference, Minutes of the First Plenary Session (USA, UK, USSR), *Sex-*

tant Conference, November–December 1943, p. 516; also DoD, *Top Secret Entry*, Sec. III, p. 18; DoD, *Entry*, p. 24.

18. JCS 924, "Operations Against Japan Subsequent to Formosa," June 30, 1944, p. 36, "CCS 381 Pacific Ocean Area (6-10-43), Sec. 5," Box 164, RG 218, NA; also, DoD, *Top Secret Entry*, Sec. IV, p. 2.

19. DoD, *Top Secret Entry*, Sec. IV, p. 6; DoD, *Entry*, p. 32.

20. DoD, *Top Secret Entry*, Sec. IV, p. 11; DoD, *Entry*, p. 34.

21. DoD, *Top Secret Entry*, Sec. IV, p. 20.

22. Winston S. Churchill, *Triumph and Tragedy* (Boston, 1953), p. 154.

23. Churchill, *Triumph and Tragedy*, p. 215.

24. JCS 1176, "Russian Participation in the War Against Japan," November 23, 1944, p. 7, "CCS 381 Japan (10-4-43), Sec. 3," Box 124, RG 218, NA; also, DoD, *Top Secret Entry*, Sec. IV, p. 28; DoD, *Entry*, p. 40.

25. JCS 1176, "Russian Participation in the War Against Japan," November 23, 1944, p. 22, "CCS 381 Japan (10-4-43), Sec. 3," Box 124, RG 218, NA; also, DoD, *Top Secret Entry*, Sec. IV, p. 28; DoD, *Entry*, p. 41.

26. Forrestal, *The Forrestal Diaries*, ed. Millis, p. 20.

27. MAGIC, No. 1040, January 29, 1945, RG 457, NA. MAGIC analysts noted, however, "On the other hand, the views expressed may well not be shared by all of Japan's top officials; in that connection, it may be noted that: Neither Ambassador Sato nor Foreign Minister Shigemitsu has displayed such complete pessimism with respect to Russia's intentions toward Japan."

28. See Herbert Feis, *The China Tangle: The American Effort in China from Pearl Harbor to the Marshall Mission* (Princeton, NJ, 1953), pp. 112–13; and Robert E. Sherwood, *Roosevelt and Hopkins: An Intimate History* (New York, 1948), pp. 791–92.

29. DoD, *Top Secret Entry*, Sec. IV, p. 34; FRUS, Malta and Yalta, pp. 378–79.

30. DoD, *Entry*, p. 43.

31. FRUS, Malta and Yalta, pp. 768–69.

32. FRUS, Malta and Yalta, p. 984.

33. Ibid.

34. Harriman Statement, *Congressional Record*, August 27, 1951, p. A5412.

35. Leahy, *I Was There*, p. 318.

36. FRUS, Malta and Yalta, p. 826.

37. "Service News and Gossip," *The Army and Navy Journal*, February 10, 1945, p. 718.

38. Hanson Baldwin, "Long War Task Ahead," *The New York Times*, February 14, 1945, p. 10.

39. Sidney Shalett, "Manchuria Is Viewed as Japanese Bastion," *The New York Times*, February 25, 1945, p. 5.

40. MAGIC, No. 1032, January 21, 1945, RG 457, NA.

41. MAGIC, No. 1045, February 3, 1945, RG 457, NA.

42. MAGIC, No. 1051, February 9, 1945, RG 457, NA.

43. MAGIC, No. 1055, February 13, 1945 RG 457, NA.

44. Col. Paul L. Freeman, Jr., to GCM and General Hull, February 13, 1945, "Miscellany (19 Nov. 43–Dec. 1945)," Item 11, Exec. 2, Box 32, OPD Executive Files, Entry 422, RG 165, NA; reprinted in DoD, *Entry*, p. 51.

45. DoD, *Entry*, p. 50.

46. Memorandum for the Chief of Staff, March 8, 1945, "ABC 384 USSR, (25 Sept. 44), Sec. 1-B," Entry 421, RG 165, NA; reprinted in DoD, *Entry*, p. 51.

Chapter 8: Phase II: April 1945

1. For fragmentary documentation concerning LOCKUP, see GCM to Byron Price, May 8, 1945, "Miscellany (19 Nov. 43–Dec. 1945)," Item 11, Exec. 2, OPD Executive Files, Entry 422, RG 165, NA; LOCKUP cables in Item 20, Exec 5, OPD Executive files, Entry 422, RG 165, NA; "LOCKUP," Folder 79, Leahy Files 1942–48, Joint Chiefs of Staff, RG 218, NA; "US Relations (military) with U.S.S.R. – Operation LOCKUP," Box 24, Cooke Papers, HIA. For further details on LOCKUP, see unpublished memorandum by Sanho Tree, September 11, 1994.

2. See Hull, *Memoirs*, Vol. II, p. 1311.

3. Memorandum for Adm. King, April 4, 1945, "Lockup," Box 24, Cooke Papers, HIA.

4. Committee of Three minutes, May 15, 1945, RG 59, NA; Stimson Diary, May 15, 1945.

5. McCloy Diary, May 18, 1945.

6. Clifford L. Snyder to Sanho Tree, Reply #: ML94-4854-CLS, November 4, 1994, Textual Reference Division, Suitland Reference Branch (NNRR).

7. See, for example, Memorandum for the JCS, from Leahy, June 14, 1945, in DoD, *Entry*, p. 76.

8. DoD, *Top Secret Entry*, Sec. V, p. 27.

9. For details on Suzuki's appointment as premier, see Butow, *Japan's Decision to Surrender*, pp. 61–67.

10. Memorandum for Information, Subject: Fall of Koiso Cabinet and Naming of Admiral Baron Kantaro Suzuki to Form a New Government, April 5, 1945, Folder 696 – "Japan – Cabinet," Box 57, Entry 136, RG 226, NA.

11. *The New York Times*, April 6, 1945, p. 4.

12. OSS Research and Analysis Branch Situation Report: USSR, Russia Serves Notice on Japan, R & A 1785.41, April 7, 1945, p. 1, OSS R & A Reports (on microfiche), RG 59, NA.

13. OSS Research and Analysis Branch, Current Intelligence Study No. 10: Soviet Break with Japan, R & A 3039S, April 13, 1945, Folder 712 – "Japanese-Russo Relations," Box 58, Entry 136, RG 226, NA.

14. MAGIC, No. 1111, April 10, 1945, RG 457, NA.

15. MAGIC, No. 1116, April 15, 1945, RG 457, NA.

16. MAGIC, No. 1124, April 23, 1945, RG 457, NA. See also MAGIC intercepts No. 1150 (May 19, 1945), No. 1159 (May 28, 1945), No. 1169 (June 7, 1945), RG 457, NA.

17. Report of the director of Intelligence, Headquarters, Supreme Allied Commander South East Asia, Subject: Japanese Reactions to the Abrogation of the Russo-Japanese Neutrality Pact, April 12, 1945, Box 12, ID #925054, ACSI, RG 319, NA.

18. *The New York Times*, April 6, 1945, p. 14.

19. See FRUS, 1945, *Volume VII: The Far East, China* (hereafter Vol. VII) (Washington, D.C.: U.S. Government Printing Office, 1969), pp. 338–40; also Feis, *The China Tangle*, pp. 284–85.

20. JCS 924/15, "Pacific Strategy," April 25, 1945, p. 250, "ABC 384 Pacific (1-17-43) Sec. 9," Box 457, Entry 421, RG 165, NA.

21. G-2 Estimate of the Enemy Situation with Respect to an Operation Against Southern Kyushu in November 1945, April 25, 1945, p. 10, "OLYMPIC," Box 1842, Entry 418, RG 165, NA.

22. Louis Morton, "Soviet Intervention in the War with Japan," *Foreign Affairs*, Vol. 40, No. 4 (July 1962), pp. 653–62, cited material from p. 658.

23. DoD, *Top Secret Entry*, Sec. V, pp. 7–9; DoD, *Entry*, pp. 60–61. For background

details on plans for Siberian air bases, see DoD, *Top Secret Entry*, especially Sections III and IV. See also John R. Deane, *The Strange Alliance: The Story of Our Wartime Cooperation with Russia* (New York, 1947).

24. Deane, *The Strange Alliance*, p. 84.

25. JCS 1313, "Revision of Policy with Relation to Russia," April 16, 1945, "ABC 384 USSR (25 Sept. 44) Sec. 3," Box 470, Entry 421, RG 165, NA.

26. Ibid.

27. DoD, *Top Secret Entry*, Sec. V, p. 9; also, Decision on JCS 1313, April 17, 1945, "ABC 384 USSR (25 Sept. 44), Sec. 3," Box 470, Entry 421, RG 165, NA.

28. Harriman to the Secretary of State, "Not Sent," April 10, 1945, "April 10–13/45," Box 178, Harriman Papers, LC.

29. Joseph Stalin, *Stalin's Correspondence with Churchill, Attlee, Roosevelt and Truman, 1941–45*, Vol. 2 (London, 1958), p. 297.

30. Stalin, *Stalin's Correspondence*, Vol. II, pp. 200–01.

31. See Diane S. Clemens, "Averell Harriman, John Deane, the Joint Chiefs of Staff, and the 'Reversal of Co-operation' with the Soviet Union in April 1945," *The International History Review*, Vol. XIV, No. 2 (May 1992), pp. 277–306.

32. FRUS, 1945, *Volume V: Europe* (hereafter cited as Vol. V) (Washington, D.C.: U.S. Government Printing Office, 1967), p. 819.

33. FRUS, 1945, Vol. V, p. 820.

34. FRUS, 1945, Vol. V, pp. 822–24.

35. See Walter Isaacson and Evan Thomas, *The Wise Men: Six Friends and the World They Made* (New York, 1986), p. 260.

36. For details on Harriman's April 20, 1945, meeting with Truman, see FRUS, 1945, Vol. V, pp. 231–34.

37. FRUS, Malta and Yalta, pp. 973–74.

38. For details on the Polish negotiations of 1945, see Alperovitz, *Atomic Diplomacy*; Clemens, "Averell Harriman, John Deane, the Joint Chiefs of Staff"; FRUS, 1945, Vol. V, pp. 110–436; W. Averell Harriman and Elie Abel, *Special Envoy to Churchill and Stalin, 1941–1946* (New York, 1975); Arthur Bliss Lane, *I Saw Poland Betrayed: An American Ambassador Reports to the American People* (Indianapolis, 1948); Melvyn P. Leffler, "Adherence to Agreements, Yalta and the Experiences of the Early Cold War," *International Security*, Vol. 11, No. 1 (Summer 1986), pp. 88–123; Edmund R. Preston, "Prelude to Cold War: American Reactions to the Growth of Soviet Power 1944–1945," Ph.D. Dissertation, University of Virginia, 1979.

39. FRUS, 1945, Vol. V, p. 232; See also Truman, *Year of Decisions*, p. 70.

40. Truman, *Year of Decisions*, p. 66.

41. FRUS, 1945, Vol. V, pp. 235–36.

42. FRUS, 1945, Vol. V, pp. 232–33. For details on Truman's April 22 meeting with Molotov, see FRUS, Vol. V, pp. 235–36.

43. FRUS, 1945, Vol. V, pp. 252–55.

44. Leahy Diary, April 23, 1945.

45. FRUS, 1945, Vol. V, pp. 257–58. For background on the negotiations in Yugoslavia, see Alperovitz, *Atomic Diplomacy*; Preston, "Prelude to Cold War"; Gabriel Kolko, *The Politics of War: The World and United States Foreign Policy, 1943–1945* (New York, 1968).

46. Truman, *Year of Decisions*, p. 82.

47. See FRUS, 1945, Vol. V, p. 232.

48. FRUS, 1945, Vol. V, p. 256.

49. See Sherwin, *A World Destroyed*, pp. 176–85; Isaacson and Thomas, *The Wise Men*, pp. 278–80; DoD, *Top Secret Entry*, Sec. V, pp. 11–12. For background documents, see FRUS, 1945, Vol. V, pp. 994–1000.

50. Harriman and Abel, *Special Envoy*, p. 460.

51. JCS 1176, "Russian Participation in the War Against Japan," November 23, 1944, "CCS 381 Japan (10-4-43), Sec. 3," Box 124, RG 218, NA; also, DoD, *Top Secret Entry*, Sec. IV, p. 28; DoD, *Entry*, p. 41.

52. JCS 924/15, "Pacific Strategy," April 25, 1945, p. 250, "ABC 384 Pacific (1-17-43), Sec. 9," Box 457, Entry 421, RG 165, NA.

53. DoD, *Entry*, p. 68.

Chapter 9: Phase III: The New Reality

1. See, for example, Bernstein, "Roosevelt, Truman and the Bomb," pp. 23–69; Clemens, "Averell Harriman, John Deane, the Joint Chiefs of Staff," pp. 277–306; Louis Morton, "Soviet Intervention in the War with Japan," *Foreign Affairs*, Vol. 40, No. 4 (July 1962), pp. 653–62; Skates, *The Invasion of Japan*.

2. Leahy, *I Was There*, p. 351. For examples, see May, "The United States, the Soviet Union, and the Far Eastern War, 1941–1945"; William Hardy McNeill, *America, Britain, & Russia: Their Co-operation and Conflict 1941–1946* (New York, 1953); Sigal, *Fighting to a Finish*.

3. See JIC 266/1, "Defeat of Japan by Blockade and Bombardment," April 18, 1945, "ABC 387 Japan (15 Feb. 45), Sec. 1-A," Box 504, Entry 421, RG 165, NA; JCS 924/15, "Pacific Strategy," April 25, 1945, "ABC 384 Pacific (1-17-43), Sec. 9," Box 457, Entry 421, RG 165, NA; JCS 1388, "Details of the Campaign Against Japan," June 16, 1945, "ABC 384 Japan (3 May 44), Sec. 1-B," Entry 421, RG 165, NA.

4. Leahy, *I Was There*, p. 419. HST interview with David M. Noyes, April 15, 1954, "HST Quotes," Post-presidential Papers, HSTL.

5. Skates, *The Invasion of Japan*, p. 226.

6. Churchill, *Triumph and Tragedy*, p. 215.

7. Memorandum for Secretary, Joint Intelligence Committee, Subject: Unconditional Surrender of Japan, April 6, 1945, "Unconditional Surrender of Japan," Box 655, "CCS 387 Japan (4-6-45)," JCS Geographic Files, 1942–45, RG 218, NA.

8. JCS Info Memo 390, "Unconditional Surrender of Japan," April 29, 1945, "ABC 387 Japan (15 Feb. 45), Sec. 1-A," Box 504, Entry 421, RG 165, NA.

9. Ibid.

10. JIS 143/2, "Unconditional Surrender of Japan," April 11, 1945, "Unconditional Surrender of Japan," Box 655, "CCS 387 Japan (4-6-45)," JCS Geographic Files, 1942–45, RG 218, NA.

11. Memorandum for Assistant Chief of Staff, OPD, Subject: JCS 1340/1, May 15, 1945, "ABC 387 Japan (15 Feb. 45)," Box 504, Entry 421, RG 165, NA.

12. Gaimusho [Foreign Ministry], ed., *Dainiji Sekaitaisen Shusenshi Roku* [*The Record of the Ending of World War II*] (Tokyo, 1990), p. 5; Shigeru Hayashi, "Tai So Kosaku no Tenkai [The Development of Maneuvering with the Soviets]," in Nihon Gaiko Gakkai, ed., *Taiheiyo Senso Shuketsu Ron* [*Some Discussions on the Ending of the Pacific War*] (Tokyo, 1958), p. 189. All Japanese translations courtesy of Akiko Naono.

13. Tadakichi Tanaka, "Tai So Kosaku: Taiheiyo Senso Chu ni Okeru Nisso Kosho [Maneuvering with the Soviets: Negotiations Between Japan and the Soviets During the Pacific War]," in Nihon Gaiko Gakkai, ed., *Taiheiyo Senso Shuketsu Ron* [*Some Discussions on the Ending of the Pacific War*], p. 433. Tanaka also writes that even before the beginning of the Pacific War, "[a]s American-Japanese relationship got worse, keeping Russian neutrality was prerequisite for Japan's handling of the U.S. and Britain." Tanaka, p. 432. For the decision at the Liaison Conference on January 10, 1942, see "Matter in regard to plans in response to progress in war situations," "Point 5: Soviet Union," in Gaimusho [Foreign Ministry], ed., *Dainiji Sekaitaisen Shusenshi Roku* [*The Record of the Ending of World War II*], p. 7.

14. Seizaburo Shinobu, *Sengo Nihon Seiji Shi: Senryo to Minshu Shugi* [*Political History of Japan After the War*], Vol. I: *Occupation and Democracy* (Tokyo, 1966), p. 108. Similarly, Kiyoshi Inouye has concluded:

> [T]hose diehards who wanted to fight the decisive battle for the homeland planned to continue fighting at Manchuria as a last resort; however, when it became impossible [after Soviet entry], even those who did not give up fighting in response to the atomic bombing of Hiroshima and Nagasaki, lost all hope. Therefore, Soviet entry into the war forced Japan to surrender.

Ariatsu Nishijima, *Genbaku ha Naze Toka Saretaka* [*Why Were the Atomic Bombs Dropped?*] (Tokyo, 1985), pp. 186–87. Other historians who argue that Soviet neutrality was a prerequisite for the decisive battle include Tadashi Motohashi, "Daresu Kikan wo Tsuzuru Wahei Kosaku [Peace Negotiation Through the Dulles Agency]," in Nihon Gaiko Gakkai ed. *Taiheiyo Senso Shuketsu Ron* [*Some Discussions on the Ending of the Pacific War*], p. 569; Tanaka, "Tai So Kosaku: Taiheyuo Senso Chu ni Okeru Nisso Kosho [Maneuvering with the Soviets: Negotiations Between Japan and the Soviets During the Pacific War]," p. 454.

15. At the Imperial Council held on June 8, 1945, General Kawabe, who represented the Chief of General Staff, stated that "[i]n order to carry out the war with the U.S., it is needless to say that prevention of Soviet entry into the war is the essential condition." Gaimusho [Foreign Ministry], ed., *Dainiji Sekaitaisen Shusenshi Roku* [*The Record of the Ending of World War II*], pp. 498–99. Sumio Hatano observes:

> The army's hope was to prevent [Soviet] entry into the war. In carrying out "Ketsu-Go" [the decisive battle for the homeland] . . . a Soviet declaration of war against Japan was the greatest concern of the General Staff.

Gaimusho [Foreign Ministry], ed., *Dainiji Sekaitaisen Shusenshi Roku* [*The Record of the Ending of World War II*], pp. 411–12.

It was known that the Kwantung Army was not equal to combat with the Red Army, and would suffer a virtually certain and very rapid defeat if the Soviets attacked. See Takashi Nakayama, *Sorengun Shinko to Nihongun* [*The Attack of Soviet Troops and the Japanese Military*] (Tokyo, 1990), p. 32; Yomiuri Shimbun Sha [Yomiuri Newspaper], ed., *Showashi no Tenno* [*History of Showa Period and the Emperor*], Vol. 2 (Tokyo, 1967), p. 308; Seizaburo Shinobu, *Seidan no Rekishigaku* [*Historical Meaning of the Emperor's Majestic Decision*] (Tokyo, 1992), p. 294.

According to *Showashi no Tenno* [*History of Showa Period and the Emperor*], Soviet moves in Siberia made the hard-liners vulnerable. Since the Kwantung Army in Manchuria had very little strength, the army had to make any concession in order to avoid Soviet entry. See Yomiuri Shimbun Sha [Yomiuri Newspaper], ed., *Showashi no Tenno* [*History of Showa Period and the Emperor*], Vol. 2, pp. 121–22.

16. Sigal, *Fighting to a Finish*, p. 50.

17. Gaimusho [Foreign Ministry], ed., *Dainiji Sekaitaisen Shusenshi Roku* [*The Record of the Ending of World War II*], p. 460.

18. See Butow, *Japan's Decision to Surrender*; Shigehiko Togo, *Sofu Togo Shigenori no Shogai* [*The Biography of Shigenori Togo*], (Tokyo, 1993); John C. Palumbo, "Prince Konoe's Efforts for Peace, 1941–1945," Ph.D. Dissertation, St. John's University, 1972; John L. Snell, *Illusion and Necessity: The Diplomacy of Global War, 1939–1945* (Boston, 1963); "Soviet-Japanese Contacts in 1945," *Vestnik*, August 1990, pp. 64–73.

19. Togo, *Sofu Togo Shigenori no Shogai* [*The Biography of Shigenori Togo*], pp. 333–34; Sanbohonbu [The General Staff], *Haisen no Kiroku* [*The Record of Defeat*] (Tokyo, 1967), p. 343.

20. Togo, *Sofu Togo Shigenori no Shogai* [*The Biography of Shigenori Togo*], pp. 333–34.

21. Togo, *Sofu Shigenori no Shogai* [*The Biography of Shigenori Togo*], pp. 333–34;

Gaimusho [Foreign Ministry], ed., *Dainiji Sekaitaisen Shusenshi Roku* [*The Record of the Ending of World War II*], p. 454.

22. Sanbohonbu [The General Staff], *Haisen no Kiroku* [*The Record of Defeat*], pp. 343, 346–47. See also Butow, *Japan's Decision to Surrender*, p. 122.

23. Togo, *Sofu Shigenori no Shogai* [*The Biography of Shigenori Togo*], p. 335.

24. Saiko senso shido kaigi kosein kaigi iken icchi jiko [The Note of Agreement at the Supreme Council for the Direction of the War], May 11, 12, 14, 1945, cited in Gaimusho [Foreign Ministry], ed., *Dainiji Sekaitaisen Shusenshi Roku* [*The Record of the Ending of World War II*], pp. 452–53. See also MAGIC, No. 950, October 31, 1944, RG 457, NA; Louis Morton, "The Soviet Union and the War Against Japan, September 1944–August 1945," pp. 37–38, Unpublished paper drafted 1961–1962, Folder 65, Box 2, Morton Papers, Dartmouth College Library; Shigenori Togo, *Jidai no Ichimen* [*The Cause of Japan*] (Tokyo, 1952); Shinichi Arai, *Genbaku Toka eno Michi* [*The Road to the Atomic Bombing*] (Tokyo, 1985); Sanbohonbu [The General Staff], *Haisen no Kiroku* [*The Record of Defeat*].

25. See MAGIC, No. 756, April 20, 1944, RG 457, NA. For evidence of the ongoing nature of Japanese attempts to keep the Soviets neutral, see MAGIC, No. 869 (August 11, 1944), No. 892 (September 3, 1944), No. 899 (September 10, 1944), No. 904 (September 15, 1944), No. 909 (September 20, 1944), No. 950 (October 31, 1944), No. 971 (October 21, 1944), No. 977 (October 27, 1944), No. 998 (December 18, 1944), No. 1032 (January 21, 1945), No. 1045 (February 3, 1945), RG 457, NA; also, Pacific Strategic Intelligence Section Commander-In-Chief United States Fleet and Chief of Naval Operations (PSIS), "The Problem of the Prolongation of the Soviet Neutrality Pact," February 12, 1945, SRH-069, RG 457, NA.

26. MAGIC, No. 1149, May 18, 1945, RG 457, NA.

27. MAGIC, No. 1142, May 11, 1945, RG 457, NA.

28. MAGIC, No. 1131, April 30, 1945, RG 457, NA.

29. MAGIC, No. 1138, May 5, 1945, RG 457, NA. For a background study on developments in Manchuria, see PSIS, "White Russians in Manchukuo," May 8, 1945, SRH-073, RG 457, NA.

30. MAGIC, No. 1141, May 10, 1945, RG 457, NA.

31. MAGIC, No. 1155, May 24, 1945, RG 457, NA.

32. MAGIC, No. 1156, May 25, 1945, RG 457, NA.

33. FRUS, Pots. I, p. 29.

34. FRUS, Pots. I, p. 42.

35. DoD, *Entry*, p. 72.

36. DoD, *Entry*, p. 73.

37. FRUS, 1945, Vol. V, p. 305. Also during these talks, on June 6, Stalin agreed to U.S. proposals on voting procedures at the newly formed United Nations. See Sherwood, *Roosevelt and Hopkins*, pp. 910–12.

38. Memorandum for General Hull, from Lincoln, June 4, 1945, "ABC 387 Japan (15 Feb. 45)," Box 504, Entry 421, RG 165, NA; see also Cline, *Washington Command Post*, p. 344. This memorandum was the staff's review of Herbert Hoover's May 15 memorandum. For other excerpts from this review, see above, p. 57, and below, p. 135.

39. MAGIC, No. 1166, June 4, 1945, RG 457, NA. Also see the MAGIC summary of June 2, 1945—"Sato on Soviet intentions"—which stresses that the "Ambassador felt that . . . with the defeat of Germany Russia had come to feel an increased interest in the Far East . . . [and] if his 'forecast' as to Russia's attitude were correct, '*we are facing future troubles with Russia and it is absolutely essential that we take immediate steps to meet this situation.*'" (Emphasis added.) MAGIC, No. 1164, June 2, 1945, RG 457, NA.

40. MAGIC, No. 1169, June 7, 1945, RG 457, NA.

41. MAGIC, No. 1173, June 11, 1945, RG 457, NA.

42. MAGIC, No. 1175, June 13, 1945, RG 457, NA.

43. DoD, *Entry*, p. 76.

44. See DoD, *Top Secret Entry*, Sec. V, p. 25; also, DoD, *Entry*, p. 84.

45. DoD, *Top Secret Entry*, Sec. V, p. 22; also DoD, *Entry*, p. 78. General Marshall's comments were prepared by the S&P group of OPD. See Memorandum for Gen. Eaker and Gen. Handy, from Hull, enclosed: Memorandum for the Chief of Staff, Subject: "Amplifying Comments on Planners' Paper for Presentation to the President," June 17, 1945, Case 17, OPD 387.4. T.S. 1945, RG 165, NA.

46. DoD, *Top Secret Entry*, Sec. V, p. 23; also DoD, *Entry*, p. 79.

47. Office of Strategic Services, Research and Analysis Branch, R & A No. 3155, "Estimate of the Japanese Economic and Political Situation," June 19, 1945, p. 4, M1221, RG 59, NA.

48. Stimson Diary, June 19, 1945.

49. Skates, *The Invasion of Japan*, p. 238.

50. Memorandum for the Assistant Chief of Staff, OPD, from Bissell, Subject: Estimate of the Enemy Situation, June 30, 1945, "Estimate of the Enemy Situation," OPD 350.05 TS, Entry 419, RG 165, NA.

51. Truman, *Year of Decisions*, pp. 322–23.

52. Truman, *Year of Decisions*, p. 417.

Part III: Atomic Diplomacy

Chapter 10: Preliminaries: April and May, 1945

1. *Sunday Express* (London), August 18, 1946, p. 4.

2. Norman Cousins and Thomas K. Finletter, "A Beginning for Sanity," *The Saturday Review of Literature*, June 15, 1946, pp. 5–9, 38–40, cited material from pp. 6–7.

3. P.M.S. Blackett, *Fear, War, and the Bomb: Military and Political Consequences of Atomic Energy* (New York, 1949), p. 139.

4. Barton J. Bernstein, "The Atomic Bomb and American Foreign Policy, 1941–1945: An Historiographical Controversy," *Peace and Change*, Vol. 2, No. 1 (Spring 1974), pp. 1–16, cited material from p. 13.

5. Smith, "Was Moscow Our Real Target?," p. 16.

6. Walker, "The Decision to Use the Bomb," p. 111.

7. Shortly after taking office, the president had been told in passing by Stimson of the existence of the Manhattan Project. See Truman, *Year of Decisions*, p. 10.

8. HLS to HST, April 24, 1945, "White House Correspondence," Box 15, Stimson Safe File, Entry 74A, RG 107, NA; see also Truman, *Year of Decisions*, p. 85.

9. Stimson Diary, April 23, 1945.

10. Truman, *Year of Decisions*, p. 87.

11. Ibid.

12. Stimson Diary, April 25, 1945.

13. Ibid.

14. Truman, *Year of Decisions*, p. 87.

15. MEMO TO FILES, Subject: Report of Meeting with The President, April 25, 1945, Box 3, Entry 2, Groves Papers, RG 200, NA.

16. MEMO TO FILES, Subject: Report of Meeting with The President, April 25, 1945, Box 3, Entry 2, Groves Papers, RG 200, NA. For the "manufacturing" report, see Memorandum for the Secretary of War, *Atomic Fission Bombs*, from LRG, April 23, 1945, Military Reference Branch, NA.

17. MEMO TO FILES, Subject: Report of Meeting with The President, April 25, 1945, Box 3, Entry 2, Groves Papers, RG 200, NA.

18. An excerpt of this memorandum was published by Department of Energy Historian Roger Anders in *Prologue*, a publication of the National Archives. (See Roger M. Anders, "The President and the Atomic Bomb: Who Approved the Trinity Nuclear Test?" *Pro-*

logue, Vol. 20, No. 4 (Winter 1988), pp. 268–82.) The full report was declassified in June 1990 through the National Archives at the request of Sanho Tree.

19. Stimson Diary, April 25, 1945.

20. Memorandum for the Secretary of War, *Atomic Fission Bombs*, from LRG, April 23, 1945, pp. 6–17, Military Reference Branch, NA.

21. Memorandum for the Secretary of War, *Atomic Fission Bombs*, from LRG, April 23, 1945, p. 22, Military Reference Branch, NA. Other items on the list related to the use of atomic energy in engines of naval bases and commercial and industrial power, and the medical and industrial applications of radioactive substances.

22. "MEMO TO FILES," Subject: Report of Meeting with The President, April 25, 1945, Box 3, Entry 2, Groves Papers, RG 200, NA.

23. Truman, *Year of Decisions*, p. 87. In the interviews—in the sentence immediately following—Truman says: "I tried to get the Russians to go along with us and have [atomic weapons] put under international control, but I never did succeed in getting it done." HST, "Discussion with [Hillman and Noyes]," February 18, 1954, HST Quotes File, Box 9, Post-Presidential-Memoirs, HSTL.

24. Byrnes interview with Fred Freed for NBC White Paper, 1964–1965, pp. 4–5, Box 79, Feis Papers, LC; also Len Giovannitti and Fred Freed, *The Decision to Drop the Bomb* (New York, 1965), p. 28.

25. See Peter Wyden, *Day One: Before Hiroshima and After* (New York, 1984), p. 131.

26. Representative studies which explore the activities of various officials below the Cabinet and White House level include James Hershberg, *James B. Conant: Harvard to Hiroshima and the Making of the Nuclear Age* (New York, 1993); Richard G. Hewlett and Oscar E. Anderson, *The New World, 1939–1946* (University Park, PA, 1962); Richard Rhodes, *The Making of the Atomic Bomb* (New York, 1986); Sherwin, *A World Destroyed*.

27. Memorandum for General Hull, from Lincoln, June 4, 1945, "ABC 387 Japan (15 Feb. 45), Box 504, Entry 421, RG 165, NA. This was the staff's review of Herbert Hoover's May 15 memorandum. See above, p. 57.

28. Isaacson and Thomas, *The Wise Men*, p. 249.

29. Stimson Diary, May 16, 1945.

30. See FRUS, 1945, Vol. V, pp. 994–96.

31. FRUS, 1945, Vol. V, p. 232; see also Truman, *Year of Decisions*, p. 70. For a detailed study of the U.S. loan to the Soviet Union, see Thomas G. Paterson, "The Abortive American Loan to Russia and the Origins of the Cold War, 1943–1946," *The Journal of American History*, Vol. 56, No. 1 (June 1969), pp. 72–92.

32. In Forrestal's words: ". . . we had better have a show down with them now than later." See FRUS, 1945, Vol. V, p. 253.

33. FRUS, 1945, Vol. V, p. 232.

34. Arthur H. Vandenberg, *The Private Papers of Senator Vandenberg* (Cambridge, MA, 1952), edited by Arthur H. Vandenberg, Jr., p. 176.

35. Vandenberg, *The Private Papers*, ed. Vandenberg, pp. 175–76.

36. FRUS, 1945, Vol. V, pp. 263–64.

37. Truman, *Year of Decisions*, p. 109. For a recent detailed study of U.S. positioning in the controversy over Poland at this time, see Clemens, "Averell Harriman, John Deane, the Joint Chiefs of Staff," pp. 277–306.

38. Sherwood, *Roosevelt and Hopkins*, p. 885.

39. Churchill, *Triumph and Tragedy*, pp. 491–92.

40. Churchill, *Triumph and Tragedy*, pp. 456–57.

41. See FRUS, Pots. I, p. 3.

42. FRUS, Pots, I, pp. 5–9, cited material from p. 9.

43. FRUS, Pots. I, p. 7.

Chapter 11: Postponing a Confrontation with Stalin

1. FRUS, Pots. I, p. 4.
2. FRUS, Pots. I, p. 5.
3. FRUS, Pots. I, p. 10.
4. It is also possible that Churchill was anxious to settle matters before the impending British elections.
5. FRUS, Pots. I, pp. 8–9.
6. Memorandum of Conversation, May 15, 1945, "May 14–18/45," Moscow Files, Box 179, Harriman Papers, LC; also FRUS, Pots. I, p. 12.
7. Memorandum of Conversation, May 15, 1945, "May 14–18/45," Moscow Files, Box 179, Harriman Papers, LC; also FRUS, Pots. I, p. 13.
8. Grew, *Turbulent Era*, Vol. II, p. 1446.
9. Memorandum of Conversation, May 15, 1945, "May 14–18/45," Moscow Files, Box 179, Harriman Papers, LC; also FRUS, Pots. I, p. 13.
10. FRUS, Pots. I, p. 19.
11. FRUS, Pots. I, p. 86.
12. FRUS, Pots. I, p. 87.
13. FRUS, Pots. I, p. 53.
14. FRUS, Pots. I, p. 90.
15. FRUS, Pots. I, pp. 90–91.
16. FRUS, Pots. I, p. 93.
17. Hewlett and Anderson, *The New World*, p. 352.
18. Harriman and Abel, *Special Envoy*, p. 490.
19. Harriman and Abel, *Special Envoy*, p. 490.
20. Stimson Diary, May 16, 1945.
21. Ibid.
22. Stimson Diary, May 14, 1945.
23. From Washington to Foreign Office, from Eden, May 14, 1945, AP 20/13/216, Eden Papers, University of Birmingham (Edgbaston, Birmingham, Great Britain).
24. Stimson Diary, May 14, 1945.
25. Stimson Diary, May 10, 1945.
26. Stimson Diary, May 15, 1945.
27. Stimson Diary, June 6, 1945.
28. Ibid.
29. Grew, *Turbulent Era*, Vol. II, pp. 1464–65.
30. Stimson Diary, June 6, 1945.
31. Szilard, "A Personal History of the Atomic Bomb," pp. 14–15.
32. Stimson Diary, May 14, 1945.
33. Quoted material from Stimson Diary, May 16, 1945.
34. Diary, May 21, 1945, (8-10-54), Chrono File, Box 17, Davies Papers, LC.
35. Journal, May 21, 1945, (11-2-50), Chrono File, Box 17, Davies Papers, LC.
36. U.S. Atomic Energy Commission (hereafter, U.S. AEC), *In the Matter of J. Robert Oppenheimer; Transcript of Hearing before Personnel Security Board, Washington DC, April 12, 1954 Through May 6, 1954* (Washington, D.C.: Government Printing Office, 1954) pp. 32–33, 31.
37. Hewlett and Anderson, *The New World*, p. 376.
38. Groves Diary, July 2, 1945, Diaries 1940–48, Box 3, Groves Papers, RG 200, NA.
39. Brig. Gen. B. G. Holzman to LRG, April 17, 1963, Box 4, Entry 2, Groves Papers, RG 200, NA.
40. Comments on letter from Gen. Holzman dictated on October 22, 1963, Box 4, Entry 2, Groves Papers, RG 200, NA.
41. LRG Comments on "Reach to the Unknown," February 25, 1966, Box 6, Entry 10,

Groves Papers, RG 200, NA. "Reach to the Unknown" was an article published in the July 16, 1965, edition of *The Atom*, the monthly publication of the Los Alamos Scientific Laboratory; Groves made these comments and filed them in his private papers.

42. For details on the Hopkins-Stalin discussions of these matters, see FRUS, Pots. I, pp. 24–62, and FRUS, 1945, Vol. V, pp. 299–315.

43. See Journal, May 13, 1945 (11-2-50), Chrono File, Box 16, Davies Papers, LC.

44. Forrestal, *The Forrestal Diaries*, ed. Millis, p. 58.

45. Leahy Diary, May 20, 1945.

46. Lane, *I Saw Poland Betrayed*, p. 71.

47. Charles E. Bohlen, *Witness to History, 1929–1969* (New York, 1973), p. 236.

48. McCloy Diary, May 21, 1945.

49. Journal, May 21, 1945, (11-2-50), Chrono File, Box 17, Davies Papers, LC.

50. Harry S. Truman, *Off the Record: The Private Papers of Harry S Truman*, ed. Robert H. Ferrell (New York, 1982), p. 33.

51. Truman, *Off the Record*, ed. Ferrell, pp. 35, 30.

52. Stimson Diary, May 16, 1945.

53. Stimson Diary, May 14, 1945.

54. McCloy Diary, May 18, 1945.

55. Stimson Diary, May 10, 1945.

56. "The Days of Their Power," Galleys, p. 100 Box 100, Davies Papers, LC.

Chapter 12: The Interim Committee

1. Before 1973 the Atomic Energy Commission and the Department of Army granted special access to specific files in response to discrete requests. For example, Fletcher Knebel and Charles W. Bailey were granted access to certain files in the MED collection for their 1960 book *No High Ground*, as was Herbert Feis (see below, pp. 615–21). However, it was not until the general review by the National Archives that the records were made available to the public.

2. See, for example, Bundy, *Danger and Survival*; Giovannitti and Freed, *The Decision to Drop the Bomb*; Gregg Herken, *The Winning Weapon: The Atomic Bomb in the Cold War* (New York, 1980); Hewlett and Anderson, *The New World*; Jones, *Manhattan*; Rhodes, *The Making of the Atomic Bomb*; Sherwin, *A World Destroyed* and "The Atomic Bomb and the Origins of the Cold War"; Sigal, *Fighting to a Finish* and "Bureaucratic Politics & Tactical Use of Committees: The Interim Committee & the Decision to Drop the Atomic Bomb," *Polity*, Vol. 10 (Spring 1978), pp. 326–64; Smith, *A Peril and a Hope* and "Behind the Decision to Use the Atomic Bomb: Chicago, 1944–45," *Bulletin of the Atomic Scientists*, Vol. XIV, No. 8 (October 1958), pp. 288–312.

3. Stimson Diary, May 2, 1945. Memorandum for the Secretary of War, from Harrison, May 1, 1945, File 3, sub-series II, Roll 4, Top Secret Files, MED, M1109, NA.

4. See Memorandum for the Secretary of War, from Harrison, May 1, 1945, File 3, Sub-series II, Roll 4, Top Secret Files, MED, M1109, NA.

5. Stimson Diary, May 2, 1945.

6. Stimson Diary, May 3, 1945.

7. FRUS, 1945, Vol. V, p. 284; Lane, *I Saw Poland Betrayed*, p. 67.

8. Notes of an Informal Meeting of the Interim Committee, May 9, 1945, File 100, Roll 8, H-B Files, M1108, NA.

9. For documents related to the cutoff, see FRUS, 1945, Vol. V, pp. 998–1003.

10. Notes of an Informal Meeting of the Interim Committee, May 14, 1945, File 100, Roll 8, H-B Files, M1108, NA.

11. Stimson Diary, May 14, 1945.

12. Notes of an Informal Meeting of the Interim Committee, May 18, 1945, File 100, Roll 8, H-B Files, M1108, NA.

13. FRUS, Pots. I, pp. 21–22.

14. FRUS, Pots. I, pp. 21–61; and FRUS, 1945, Vol. V, pp. 299–315.

15. Notes of the Interim Committee Meeting, May 31, 1945, pp. 11–12, File 100, Roll 8, H-B Files, M1108, NA.

16. See Notes of an Informal Meeting of the Interim Committee, May 9, 1945, File 100, Roll 8, H-B Files, M1108, NA.

17. Stimson Diary, May 3, 1945.

18. Stimson Diary, May 4, 1945.

19. Stimson Diary, May 17, 1945.

20. Stimson Diary, May 30, 1945.

21. MEMO TO FILES, Subject: Report of Meeting with The President, April 25, 1945, Box 3, Entry 3, Groves Papers, RG 200, NA.

22. Notes of an Informal Meeting of the Interim Committee, May 9, 1945, File 100, Roll 8, H-B Files, M1108, NA.

23. Notes of an Informal Meeting of the Interim Committee, May 9, 1945, File 100, Roll 8, H-B Files, M1108, NA.

24. Notes of the Interim Committee Meeting, May 31, 1945, pp. 2–4, File 100, Roll 8, H-B Files, M1108, NA.

25. Notes of the Interim Committee Meeting, May 31, 1945, pp. 5–6, File 100, Roll 8, H-B Files, M1108, NA.

26. Hewlett and Anderson, *The New World*, pp. 285–86. See also Groves, *Now It Can Be Told*, pp. 180–84.

27. Memorandum for the Secretary of War, *Atomic Fission Bombs*, from LRG, April 23, 1945, p. 16, Military Reference Branch, NA.

28. Herken, *The Winning Weapon*, p. 101.

29. Herken, *The Winning Weapon*, p. 113.

30. Memorandum discussed with the President, Stimson Diary, April 25, 1945.

31. Memorandum for the Secretary of War, *Atomic Fission Bombs*, from LRG, April 23, 1945, p. 16, Military Reference Branch, NA.

32. Memorandum for the Secretary of War, *Atomic Fission Bombs*, from LRG, April 23, 1945, p. 20, Military Reference Branch, NA.

33. For details, see Memorandum for the Secretary of War, Subject: Salient Points Concerning Future International Handling of Subject of Atomic Bombs, from Bush and Conant, September 30, 1944, File 69, Roll 5, H-B Files, M1108, NA; reprinted in Stoff, Fanton, Williams, eds., *The Manhattan Project*, pp. 78–79.

34. See Hewlett and Anderson, *The New World*, p. 354.

35. Herken, *The Winning Weapon*, p. 110; see also FRUS, 1945, *Volume II, General: Political and Economic Matters* (hereafter, Vol. II) (Washington, D.C.: U.S. Government Printing Office, 1967), pp. 84–85.

36. "Was A-bomb on Japan a Mistake?" *U.S. News and World Report*, August 15, 1960, p. 69.

37. For details of this discussion, see FRUS, 1945, Vol. II, pp. 297–98.

38. WB's Book, September 24, 1945, Folder 602, Byrnes Papers, CUL.

39. Journal, October 9, 1945, Chrono File, Box 21, Davies Papers, LC.

40. FRUS, 1945, Vol. II, p. 61.

41. FRUS, 1945, Vol. II, pp. 84–85; see also Herken, *The Winning Weapon*, pp. 109–11.

42. Bard interview with Len Giovannitti for NBC White Paper, 1964, p. 12, Box 103, Feis Papers, LC.

43. An early exception is Elting Morison's *Turmoil and Tradition*, which characterizes the Interim Committee as essentially a "symbolic act." (Elting Morison, *Turmoil and Tradition: A Study of the Life and Times of Henry L. Stimson* [Boston, 1960], p. 630.) More typical is Herbert Feis' 1961 *Japan Subdued*, which attributes a highly significant role to

the committee (pp. 31–39). Giovannitti and Freed devote an entire chapter to the committee, essentially taking it at face value (pp. 97–108). The official history of the U.S. Atomic Energy Commission, *The New World*, leaves the reader with the impression that the committee's recommendations were of critical importance. (Hewlett and Anderson, *The New World*, pp. 353–61.) More sophisticated are Richard Rhodes' *The Making of the Atomic Bomb* [pp. 628, 641–51] and David Robertson's *Sly and Able: A Political Biography of James F. Byrnes* (New York: 1994), pp. 395–99, both of which show how the committee was adroitly used by Byrnes to advance his own agenda. Some of the most penetrating modern work on the Interim Committee has been done by Leon Sigal. (Leon Sigal, "Bureaucratic Politics & Tactical Use of Committees: The Interim Committee & The Decision to Drop the Atomic Bomb," *Polity*, Vol. 10, [Spring, 1978], pp. 326–64.) Stewart Udall's *The Myths of August* is similarly perceptive (Stewart Udall, *The Myths of August: A Personal Exploration of Our Tragic Cold War Affair with the Atom* [New York, 1994], pp. 89–91).

44. See, for example, Feis, *Japan Subdued*, p. 36.

45. Lawrence to Darrow, August 17, 1945, Folder 9, Box 6, Lawrence Papers, Bancroft Library Archives, University of California at Berkeley.

46. Arthur Compton, *Atomic Quest: A Personal Narrative* (New York, 1956), pp. 238–39; Notes of the Interim Committee Meeting, May 31, 1945, p. 13, File 100, Roll 8, H-B Files, M1108, NA.

47. Lawrence to Darrow, August 17, 1945, Folder 9, Box 6, Lawrence Papers, Bancroft Library Archives, University of California at Berkeley. See also James Byrnes, *All in One Lifetime* (New York, 1958), p. 261; Hewlett and Anderson, *The New World*, p. 358.

48. Notes of the Interim Committee Meeting, May 31, 1945, pp. 13–14, File 100, Roll 8, H-B Files, M1108, NA.

49. Ibid., p. 14.

50. Alice Kimball Smith, "Behind the Decision to Use the Atomic Bomb," p. 297.

51. Stimson Diary, June 6, 1945.

52. Ibid.

53. U.S. AEC, *In the Matter of J. Robert Oppenheimer*, p. 34.

54. John P. Sutherland, "The Story General Marshall Told Me," *U.S. News and World Report*, November 2, 1959, pp. 50–56, cited material on p. 53; U.S. Senate Committee on Armed Services and Committee on Foreign Relations, *Military Situation in the Far East*, Part I (Washington, D.C., 1951), p. 563. See also Forrest C. Pogue, *George C. Marshall Interviews and Reminiscences for Forrest C. Pogue: Transcripts and Notes, 1956–57* (Lexington, 1986), p. 390.

55. Hewlett and Anderson's *The New World* is a good example. See pp. 353–61.

56. Notes of an Informal Meeting of the Interim Committee, May 9, 1945, File 100, Roll 8, H-B Files, M1108, NA; Notes of an Informal Meeting of the Interim Committee, May 14, 1945; Notes of an Informal Meeting of the Interim Committee, May 18, 1945; Notes of the Interim Committee Meeting, May 31, 1945; Notes of the Interim Committee Meeting, June 1, 1945; Notes of the Interim Committee Meeting, June 21, 1945; Notes of the Interim Committee Meeting, July 6, 1945; Notes of the Interim Committee Meeting, July 19, 1945. There is also an Interim Committee Log, several pages of which deal with the meetings in summary form (and appear to be based on the "Notes.") (Interim Committee Log, File 98, Roll 8, H-B Files, M1108, NA.)

57. Notes of the Interim Committee Meeting, May 31, 1945, p. 18, File 100, Roll 8, H-B Files, M1108, NA.

58. Bard interview with Len Giovannitti for NBC White Paper, 1964, p. 16, Box 103, Feis Papers, LC.

59. Leon V. Sigal, "Bureaucratic Politics and Tactical Use of Committees," p. 329.

60. Sigal, "Bureaucratic Politics and Tactical Use of Committees," pp. 329–30.

61. Sigal, "Bureaucratic Politics and Tactical Use of Committees," p. 330.

62. Sigal, "Bureaucratic Politics and Tactical Use of Committees," p. 331.

63. Groves interview with George Carroll, June 15, 1949, p. 4, Box 1, Ent. 10, RG 200, NA.

64. Groves interview with George Carroll, June 15, 1949, pp. 6–7, Box 1, Ent. 10, RG 200, NA.

65. See, for example Messer, *The End of an Alliance: James F. Byrnes, Roosevelt, Truman and the Origins of the Cold War* (Chapel Hill, NC, 1982), pp. 87–88; Rhodes, *The Making of the Atomic Bomb*, pp. 650–51.

66. Notes of an Informal Meeting of the Interim Committee, May 14, 1945, File 100, Roll 8, H-B Files, M1108, NA; Notes of an Informal Meeting of the Interim Committee, May 18, 1945; Hewlett and Anderson, *The New World*, pp. 358–60; Notes of the Interim Committee Meeting, June 21, 1945.

67. Jonathan Schell, *The Fate of the Earth* (New York: Alfred A. Knopf, 1982).

68. See, for example, Hewlett and Anderson, *The New World*, pp. 322–46; Hershberg, *James B. Conant*, pp. 194–224.

69. That the Russians knew a substantial amount about the Manhattan Project in any case has been confirmed by modern studies. For example, see David Holloway, *Stalin and the Bomb: The Soviet Union and Atomic Energy, 1939–1956* (New Haven: 1994), pp. 106–08, 115. What U.S. officials believed the Russians knew at the time is less clear. A summary of the "Russian Situation" forwarded by Groves to Byrnes on May 13, 1945, noted: "The Soviet Union through its Embassy officials and espionage agents in the United States has been active for a long time trying to elicit as much information as possible concerning the project." [Attachment to Groves to Byrnes, May 13, 1945, "Intelligence and Security," File 12, Roll 2, M1109, NA.] See also Harvey Klehr, John Earl Haynes, and Fridrikh Igorevich Firsov, *The Secret World of American Communism* (New Haven, 1995), pp. 216–18, 222–25, 230.

70. Bohr memorandum of April 2, 1944, cited in Hershberg, *James B. Conant*, pp. 197, 812n.14.

71. Memorandum, Bohr to Roosevelt, July 3, 1944, cited in Abraham Pais, *Niels Bohr's Times: In Physics, Philosophy, and Polity* (New York, 1991), pp. 501, 508, endnote 125, material bracketed by Pais.

72. Vannevar Bush and James Conant, "Salient Points Concerning Future International Handling of Subject of Atomic Bombs," September 30, 1944, Folder 69, Roll 5, H-B Files, M1108, NA.

73. Vannevar Bush and James Conant, "Salient Points Concerning Future International Handling of Subject of Atomic Bombs," September 30, 1944, Folder 69, H-B Files, RG 77, H-B Files, MED, NA.

74. Ibid.

75. Stimson to Marshall, May 30, 1945, "Interim Comm.—Int'l Control," File 77, Roll 6, H-B Files, M1108, NA; Brewster to Truman, May 24, 1945, "Interim Comm.—Int'l Control," File 77, Roll 6, H-B Files, M1108, NA.

76. Brewster to Truman, May 24, 1945, "Interim Comm.—Int'l Control," File 77, Roll 6, H-B Files, M1108, NA.

77. Ibid.

78. Notes of the Interim Committee Meeting, May 31, 1945, pp. 10–11, File 100, Roll 8, H-B Files, M1108, NA.

79. Notes of the Interim Committee Meeting, May 31, 1945, p. 11, File 100, Roll 8, H-B Files, M1108, NA.

80. Ibid.

81. Notes of the Interim Committee Meeting, May 31, 1945, pp. 11–12, File 100, Roll 8, H-B Files, M1108, NA.

82. Messer, *The End of an Alliance*, p. 88.

83. Hewlett and Anderson, *The New World*, p. 357.

84. Notes of the Interim Committee Meeting, June 1, 1945, File 100, Roll 8, H-B Files, M1108, NA.

85. Rhodes, *The Making of the Atomic Bomb*, p. 650.

86. The Arneson interview in question is cited in Giovannitti and Freed, *The Decision to Drop the Bomb*, p. 107, and was conducted by them between May 1964 and February 1965.

87. Stimson Diary, June 6, 1945.

88. Stimson Diary, July 4, 1945.

Chapter 13: The "Second Track" and Asia

1. Leahy Diary, June 4, 1945.

2. HST to HLS, December 31, 1946, Vertical File 89, HSTL.

3. Stimson Diary, June 6, 1945.

4. For the text of the Quebec Agreement, see Stoff, Fanton, and Williams, *The Manhattan Project*, pp. 46–47.

5. FRUS, Pots. I, p. 941; also see John Ehrman, *Grand Strategy*, Vol. VI: *October 1944–August 1945* (London, 1956), pp. 275–76, 296–98.

6. Notes of the Interim Committee Meeting, June 21, 1945, File 100, Roll 8, H-B Files, M1108, NA.

7. FRUS, 1945, *Vol. VII: The Far East, China* (hereafter, Vol. VII) (Washington, D.C., 1969), pp. 341–42.

8. Minutes of the Secretary's Staff Committee meeting, April 21, 1945, "April 17–24, 1945," Box 178, Harriman Papers, LC.

9. Truman, *Year of Decisions*, pp. 84–85; see also FRUS, 1945, Vol. VII, pp. 342–44.

10. JCS 924/15, "Pacific Strategy," April 25, 1945, p. 250, "ABC 384, Pacific (1-17-43) Sec. 9," Entry 421, RG 165, NA.

11. *The New York Times*, April 6, 1945, p. 3.

12. FRUS, 1945, Vol. VII, pp. 865–68; also, Herbert Feis, *The China Tangle*, pp. 304–05.

13. Forrestal, *The Forrestal Diaries*, ed. Millis, p. 55.

14. Leahy Diary, May 11, 1945.

15. McCloy Diary, May 12, 1945.

16. Forrestal, *The Forrestal Diaries*, ed. Millis, p. 56; Unpublished Forrestal Diary, May 12, 1945.

17. Unpublished Forrestal Diary, May 12, 1945.

18. McCloy Diary, May 12, 1945.

19. Memorandum for the Secretary of War, from JCG, May 12, 1945, "ABC 336 Russia (22 Aug. 43), Sec. 3," Box 252, Entry 421, RG 165, NA.

20. Stimson Diary, May 13, 1945.

21. Stimson Diary, May 14, 1945.

22. Ibid.

23. Minutes of the Committee of Three meeting, May 15, 1945, RG 59, NA.

24. Stimson Diary, May 15, 1945.

25. Minutes of the Committee of Three meeting, May 15, 1945, RG 59, NA.

26. Grew, *Turbulent Era*, Vol. II, p. 1446.

27. HLS to the acting secretary of state (Grew), May 21, 1945, Box 12, Stimson Safe File, Entry 74A, RG 107, NA; also, Grew, *Turbulent Era*, Vol. II, pp. 1457–59.

28. FRUS, 1945, Vol. VII, p. 868; also, Truman, *Year of Decisions*, p. 266.

29. Grew, *Turbulent Era*, Vol. II, pp. 1460–61. On the April 19 Truman-Soong meeting, see Truman, *Year of Decisions*, p. 66. It is impossible to know exactly what Truman's intentions were in withholding information from Soong. On the one hand, Stalin and Roo-

sevelt had agreed that the United States would not inform the Chinese until Stalin gave the word. On the other, given the U.S. review of policy on the Yalta Agreements and Russian entry at this time, a policy on the Yalta Agreements and Russian entry at this time, a reasonable presumption is that it was convenient to not encourage an early Soong-Stalin meeting.

30. Memorandum of Conversation, the president, the acting secretary of state, Ambassador Harriman, and Mr. Bohlen, May 15, 1945, "May 14–18/45," Moscow Files, Box 179, Harriman Papers, LC.

31. Truman, *Off the Record*, ed. Ferrell, p. 31.

32. Truman, *Off the Record*, ed. Ferrell, p. 33.

33. FRUS, Pots. I, pp. 41–52.

34. DoD, *Entry*, pp. 72–73.

35. For Hopkins' comments, see DoD, *Entry*, pp. 72–73; for Harriman's report, see FRUS, Pots. I, pp. 61–62.

36. Stimson Diary, June 6, 1945.

37. Ibid.

38. DoD, *Entry*, p. 72.

39. FRUS, Pots. I, p. 162.

40. FRUS, 1945, Vol. VII, p. 902; Grew, *Turbulent Era*, Vol. II, p. 1468. See also Leahy Diary, June 9, 1945.

41. For details on the early Soong-Stalin negotiations, see FRUS, 1945, Vol. VII, pp. 910–34.

42. FRUS, 1945, Vol. VII, pp. 914–15; also JFB to Harriman, July 4, 1945, "July 1–6/45," Moscow Files, Box 180, Harriman Papers, LC.

43. FRUS, 1945, Vol. VII, p. 916; also, Truman, *Year of Decisions*, p. 317.

44. Stimson Diary, June 6, 1945.

45. Memorandum for the Secretary of War, *Atomic Fission Bombs*, from LRG, April 23, 1945, p. 6, Military Reference Branch, NA; for details on the planning dates for Soviet entry, see above, p. 120.

46. Telephone Conversation, Adm Duncan and Gen Lincoln, June 14, 1945, "ABC 384 Japan (3 May 44), Sec. 1-B," Box 428, Entry 421, RG 165, NA.

47. Phillip Morrison, "Blackett's Analysis of the Issues," *Bulletin of the Atomic Scientists*, Vol. 5, No. 2 (February 1949), pp. 37–40, cited material from p. 40.

Chapter 14: The Concerned Scientists

1. For accounts of the pre-Hiroshima activism of some of the atomic scientists, see, William Lanouette with Bela Szilard, *Genius in the Shadows: A Biography of Leo Szilard, the Man Behind the Bomb* (New York, 1992), pp. 259–76; Sherwin, *A World Destroyed*, pp. 210–19; Smith, *A Peril and a Hope*, pp. 24–74.

2. See, for example, Memorandum for the Secretary of War, Subject: Salient Points Concerning Future International Handling of Subject of Atomic Bombs, from Bush and Conant, September 30, 1944, File 69, Roll 5, H-B Files, M1108, NA; reprinted in Stoff, Fanton, Williams, eds., *The Manhattan Project*, pp. 78–79.

3. See, for example, Sigal, *Fighting to a Finish*, p. 199.

4. Hershberg, *James B. Conant*, p. 223. Hershberg is citing correspondence from Conant to Stimson, May 5, 1945.

5. Memorandum for the Secretary, May 30, 1945, File 100, Roll 8, H-B Files, M1108, NA.

6. Stimson Diary, May 31, 1945.

7. For details, see Lanouette, *Genius in the Shadows*, pp. 198–206.

8. Leo Szilard, *Leo Szilard: His Version of the Facts, Selected Recollections and Cor-

respondence, eds. Spencer R. Weart and Gertrud Weiss Szilard (Cambridge, MA, 1978), pp. 196–204, cited material from p. 202.

9. Leo Szilard, "Reminiscences," eds. Gertrud Weiss Szilard and Kathleen R. Winsor, *Perspectives in American History*, Vol. 2 (1968), pp. 94–151, cited material from p. 128.

10. Memorandum on "Political and Social Problems," from Members of the "Metallurgical Laboratory" or the University of Chicago, June 11, 1945, p. 15, File 76, Roll 6, H-B Files, M1108, NA; reprinted in Stoff, Fanton, Williams, eds., *The Manhattan Project*, pp. 140–47.

11. Ibid., p. 9.

12. Ibid., p. 10.

13. Ibid., p. 15.

14. Ibid., p. 10.

15. Arthur H. Compton to Secretary of War—*Attention: Mr. George Harrison*, June 12, 1945, File 76, Roll 6, H-B Files, M1108, NA; reprinted in Stoff, Fanton, Williams, eds., *The Manhattan Project*, pp. 138–39; see also Interim Committee Log, June 12, 1945, File 98, Roll 8, H-B Files, M1108, NA.

16. Recommendations of the Scientific Panel on the Immediate Use of Nuclear Weapons, June 16, 1945, File 76, Roll 6, H-B Files, M1108, NA; reprinted in Stoff, Fanton, Williams, eds., *The Manhattan Project*, pp. 149–50.

17. Arthur H. Compton to Col. K. D. Nichols, July 24, 1945, File 76, Roll 6, H-B Files, M1108, NA; reprinted in Szilard, *Leo Szilard*, eds. Weart and Szilard, pp. 214–15.

18. Arthur H. Compton and Farrington Daniels, "A Poll of Scientists at Chicago, July 1945," *Bulletin of the Atomic Scientists*, Vol. 4, No. 2 (February 1948), pp. 44, 63; reprinted in Smith, *A Peril and a Hope*, pp. 57–58.

19. Arthur H. Compton to Col. K. D. Nichols, July 24, 1945, File 76, Roll 6, H-B Files, M1108, NA.

20. Arthur Compton, *Atomic Quest: A Personal Narrative* (New York, 1956), p. 244.

21. A Petition to the President of the United States, July 17, 1945, File 76, Roll 6, H-B Files, M1108, NA; reprinted in Szilard, *Leo Szilard*, Weart and Szilard, eds., pp. 211–12. See also Memorandum to Maj. Gen. L. B. Groves, from Nichols, July 25, 1945, File 76, Roll 6, H-B Files, M1108, NA.

22. Teller's role in the circulation of the petition is in dispute. See Teller's own recollection in Edward Teller with Allen Brown, *The Legacy of Hiroshima* (Garden City, N.Y., 1962), pp. 13–14. For a different interpretation, see Lanouette, *Genius in the Shadows*, pp. 269–70. For Teller's initial response to the petition, see Teller to Szilard, July 2, 1945, reprinted in Szilard, *Leo Szilard*, eds. Weart and Szilard, pp. 208–09.

23. For details on scientists' reactions to the petition, see Smith, *A Peril and a Hope*, p. 55; also, Lanouette, *Genius in the Shadows*, pp. 270–73.

24. Sherwin, *A World Destroyed*, p. 217; see also Lanouette, *Genius in the Shadows*, p. 271, and Szilard, *Leo Szilard*, eds. Weart and Szilard, pp. 212–13.

25. Arthur H. Compton to Col. K. D. Nichols, July 24, 1945, File 76, Roll 6, H-B Files, M1108, NA; reprinted in Szilard, *Leo Szilard*, Weart and Szilard, eds., pp. 214–15.

26. Nichols to LRG, July 25, 1945, File 76, Roll 6, H-B Files, M1108, NA.

27. See Memorandum for the Files, by R. Gordon Arneson, May 24, 1946, File 76, Roll 6, H-B Files, M1108, NA. Here Arneson explains that the petition was "delivered by General Groves' office to the Office of the Secretary of War on August 1, 1945," and that "it was decided that no useful purpose would be served by transmitting either the petition or any of the other attached documents to the White House, particularly since the President was not then in the country."

Part IV: James F. Byrnes

Chapter 15: "A Very Machiavellian Character"; "An Operator"

1. See Giovannitti and Freed, *The Decision to Drop the Bomb*, p. 24; Feis, *Japan Subdued*, pp. 28–47.
2. Stimson Diary, July 2, 1945.
3. Stimson Diary, July 19, 23, 1945.
4. Harriman and Abel, *Special Envoy*, p. 488.
5. "Off the Record Discussion of the Origins of the Cold War," May 31, 1967, p. 71, "Memoirs—Chadwin Files—Interviews Harriman, W.A.," Box 869, Harriman Papers, LC.
6. For details on the Byrnes-Truman falling-out, see Robert L. Messer, *The End of An Alliance: James F. Byrnes, Roosevelt, Truman, and the Origins of the Cold War* (Chapel Hill, North Carolina: University of North Carolina Press, 1982), pp. 156–240; David Robertson, *Sly and Able: A Political Biography of James F. Byrnes* (New York: W. W. Norton & Company, 1994), pp. 440–510.
7. Stimson Diary, June 6, 1945.
8. White House appointments book, May 31–June 6, Daily Sheets, May, June 1945. "President's Appointment File," President's Secretary Files, HSTL. As indicated (see above, p. 210), other evidence suggests that they met on June 1. According to the log, however, Byrnes was present at a larger June 5 discussion of the Polish issue. See the June 5 entry of the appointment book; see also Diary, June 5, 1945 (1-25-54), Box 114, Davies Papers, LC.
9. Messer, *The End of an Alliance*, p. 13.
10. WB's Book, July 3, 1945, Folder 602, Byrnes Papers, CUL.
11. Connelly interview with Jerry N. Hess, November 28, 30, 1967; August 21, 1968, pp. 327–29, Oral History Collection, HSTL.
12. Nixon interview with Jerry N. Hess, October 9, 16, 19, 20, 21, 22, 23, 28, 29, 30; November 4, 5, 6, 20, and 23, 1970, p. 246, Oral History Interview Collection, HSTL.
13. McCullough, *Truman*, p. 355.
14. The Presidential Succession Act of 1886 provided for transfer of the office to the Secretary of State. "Pending a change in the law," Truman later wrote, "I felt it my duty to choose without too much delay a Secretary of State with proper qualifications to succeed, if necessary, to the presidency." Truman, *Year of Decisions*, p. 23.
15. *The New York Times*, July 3, 1945, pp. 1, 7; Robertson, *Sly and Able*, p. 414.
16. Messer, *The End of An Alliance*, p. 21.
17. *Washington Post*, April 15, 1945, p. 6.
18. *The New York Times*, July 2, 1945, p. 14, editorial.
19. *The New York Times*, April 13, 1945, p. 1.
20. Ibid.
21. *The New York Times*, April 14, 1945, p. 1.
22. Stimson Diary, April 27 to April 29, 1945.
23. On the selection of the 1944 Democratic vice-presidential nominee, see Messer, *The End of an Alliance*, pp. 11–30; Robertson, *Sly and Able*, pp. 332–64.
24. Walter Brown, *James F. Byrnes of South Carolina: A Remembrance* (Macon, GA, 1992), p. 254.
25. Bohlen, *Witness to History*, p. 224.
26. Ibid.
27. Truman, *Year of Decisions*, p. 23.
28. WB's Book, August 22, 1945, Folder 602, Byrnes Papers, CUL; see also Messer, *The End of an Alliance*, p. 79.
29. *The New York Times*, April 14, 1945, p. 1.

30. *The New York Times*, April 14, 1945, p. 3.

31. Messer, *The End of an Alliance*, p. 73.

32. *The New York Times*, April 17, 1945, p. 13.

33. Omar Bradley, *A Soldier's Story* (New York, 1951), pp. ix–x.

34. McCullough, *Truman*, pp. 340–41.

35. Brown, *James F. Byrnes*, p. 215.

36. Truman, *Off the Record*, Ferrell, ed., p. 37.

37. Truman, *Off the Record*, Ferrell, ed., pp. 38–39.

38. Truman, *Off the Record*, Ferrell, ed., p. 42.

39. Brown, *James F. Byrnes*, p. 345.

40. Robert Messer, "The Making of a Cold Warrior: James F. Byrnes and American-Soviet Relations, 1945–1946," Ph.D. Dissertation, University of California, Berkeley, 1975, pp. 12, 15.

41. Bohlen, who had been special liaison between the State Department and the White House, recalled that "[m]y job as liaison ceased when Byrnes became Secretary of State. Byrnes told me that henceforth he would be dealing directly with the President. . . ." (Bohlen, *Witness to History*, p. 225.) Daniel Yergin quotes Byrnes as telling an associate in September of 1945, "God Almighty, I might tell the President sometime what happened, but I'm never going to tell those little bastards at the State Department anything about it. . . ." (Daniel Yergin, *Shattered Peace: The Origins of the Cold War and the National Security State* [New York, 1990], p. 122.) Byrnes has also been quoted as telling State Department official Theodore Achilles, "Hell, I may tell the President sometime what happened, but I'm never going to tell the State Department about it." Achilles interview with Philip A. Crowl, May 7, 1966, p. 2, John Foster Dulles Oral History Project, PUA. See also "Off the Record Discussion of the Origins of the Cold War," May 31, 1967, p. 19; "Memoirs-Chadwin Files-Interviews Harriman, W.A.," Box 869, Harriman Papers, LC.

42. Brown, *James F. Byrnes*, pp. 181, 127.

43. Messer, "The Making of a Cold Warrior," pp. 14, 450, endnote 19.

44. David Robertson, *Sly and Able*, p. 7.

45. Byrnes, *Speaking Frankly*; Byrnes, *All in One Lifetime*.

46. George Curry, "James F. Byrnes," in *The American Secretaries of State and Their Diplomacy*, Vol. 14, eds. Robert H. Ferrell and Samuel Flagg Bemis (New York, 1965), pp. 87–317.

47. Gregg F. Herken, " 'Stubborn, Obstinate, and They Don't Scare': The Russians, The Bomb, and James F. Byrnes," in *James F. Byrnes and the Origins of the Cold War*, ed. Kendrick A. Clements (Durham, NC, 1982), pp. 49–57, cited material from p. 49.

48. See Truman, *Off the Record*, Ferrell, ed., p. 49, Messer, "The Making of a Cold Warrior," p. 205.

49. Connelly interview with Jerry N. Hess, November 28 and 30, 1967, and August 21, 1968, pp. 96–97, Oral History Collection, HSTL.

50. Rosenman interview with Jerry N. Hess, October 15, 1968, and April 23, 1969, p. 25, Oral History Collection, HSTL.

51. "Off the Record Discussion of the Origins of the Cold War," May 31, 1967, p. 25, "Memoirs-Chadwin Files-Interviews Harriman, W.A.," Box 869, Harriman Papers, LC.

52. "Off the Record Discussion of the Origins of the Cold War," May 31, 1967, p. 20, "Memoirs-Chadwin Files-Interviews Harriman, W.A.," Box 869, Harriman Papers, LC.

53. Byrnes interview with Forrest C. Pogue, November 16, 1959, pp. 1, 14, Pogue Papers, GCMRL. The interview transcript includes Pogue's post-interview comments.

54. In a diary entry of June 30, 1945, Leahy judged Byrnes' selection as secretary of state as "the best appointment made by Mr. Truman since his accession to the Presidency." (Leahy Diary, June 30, 1945.)

55. Clifford interview with Jonathan Daniels, October 26, 1949, "Jonathan Daniels' Notes, Part I," p. 44, Box 1, Jonathan Daniels Papers, HSTL.

56. Henry Wallace, *The Price of Vision: The Diary of Henry A. Wallace, 1942–1946*, John Morton Blum, ed. (Boston, 1973), p. 469. The quote is from a Wallace diary entry of July 19, 1945.

57. "Off the Record Discussion of the Origins of the Cold War," May 31, 1967, p. 22, "Memoirs—Chadwin Files—Interviews Harriman, W.A.," Box 869, Harriman Papers, LC.

58. Joseph Alsop and Robert Kintner, "Sly and Able: The Real Leader of the Senate, Jimmy Byrnes," *Saturday Evening Post*, July 20, 1940, pp. 18–19, 38–45. Kenneth Davis writes that Byrnes "was an intensely private, rather cold personality, shrewd, quick, manipulative, hard-working, the very opposite of colorful or dramatic, with a sharp eye for the main chance and a talent for seizing it." (Kenneth S. Davis, "Mr. Assistant President," *The New York Times Book Review*, December 18, 1994, pp. 31–32, cited material from p. 31.)

59. Messer, "The Making of a Cold Warrior," p. 12.

60. Messer, "The Making of a Cold Warrior," p. 15.

61. Messer, "The Making of a Cold Warrior," pp. 12–13.

62. Messer, "The Making of a Cold Warrior," p. 5.

63. Messer, "The Making of a Cold Warrior," p. 6.

64. Messer, "The Making of a Cold Warrior," pp. 10–11. Brown notes that Byrnes actually learned of the diary earlier. (Brown, *James F. Byrnes of South Carolina*, p. 332.)

65. Messer, "The Making of a Cold Warrior," p. 12.

66. Messer, "The Making of a Cold Warrior," pp. 2–3, 11.

67. Messer, *The End of an Alliance*, p. 250, endnote 20.

Chapter 16: Sly and Able Policies

1. Leffler, *A Preponderance of Power*, p. 25.

2. Truman, *Year of Decisions*, p. 19.

3. McCullough, *Truman*, pp. 358–59.

4. Robert Ferrell, *Harry S Truman: A Life* (Columbia, MO, 1994), p. 180.

5. Francis H. Heller, ed., *The Truman White House: The Administration of the Presidency, 1945–1953* (Lawrence, KS, 1980), p. 21.

6. Truman to Wehman, November 15, 1945, Folder 731, Post Presidential Files, HSTL.

7. *The New York Times*, April 14, 1945, p. 1.

8. Truman, *Off the Record*, Ferrell, ed., p. 17.

9. Brown, *James F. Byrnes*, p. 256.

10. Ibid.

11. Truman, *Off the Record*, Ferrell, ed., p. 18. Truman also indicates he talked with Byrnes—at least about the appointment of John Snyder to become Federal Loan Administrator—between 9:00 a.m. and 9:45 a.m. on this day.

12. Ibid.

13. Truman, *Off the Record*, Ferrell, ed., p. 19; "Appointments for the First Thirty Days of the Administration of President Harry S Truman," Daily Sheets, April, 1945, "President's Appointment File," "President's Secretary's Files," HSTL. In his memoirs, Truman states that he met again with Byrnes prior to the service. (Truman, *Year of Decisions*, p. 33.)

14. Brown, *James F. Byrnes*, p. 257; Truman, *Off the Record*, Ferrell, ed., p. 19.

15. Brown, *James F. Byrnes*, p. 258.

16. *The New York Times*, April 16, 1945, p. 16.

17. "Appointments for the First Thirty Days of the Administration of President Harry S Truman," Daily Sheets, April, 1945, "President's Appointment File," President's Secretary's Files, HSTL.

18. Brown, *James F. Byrnes*, pp. 258–59.

19. Brown, *James F. Byrnes*, p. 259.

20. Brown, *James F. Byrnes*, pp. 259–60.

21. Messer, *The End of an Alliance*, p. 79.

22. George M. Elsey, "Some White House Recollections, 1942–1953," *Diplomatic History*, Vol. 12 (Summer 1988), pp. 357–64, cited material on p. 361.

23. Riddleberger interview with Jerry N. Hess, April 6 and 26, 1972, pp. 23–24, Oral History Collection, HSTL.

24. Brown, *James F. Byrnes*, p. 259.

25. Truman, *Off the Record*, ed. Ferrell, p. 17.

26. Truman, *Year of Decisions*, ed. Ferrell, p. 22.

27. Byrnes, *All in One Lifetime*, p. 286.

28. Byrnes interview with Fred Freed for NBC White Paper, 1964, p. 12, Box 79, Feis Papers, LC.

29. *The New York Times*, April 17, 1945, p. 1.

30. Leahy Diary, April 23, 1945.

31. Truman, *Off the Record*, Ferrell, ed., p. 30.

32. Diary, June 6, 1945, (Journal), "Chrono File," Box 17, Davies Papers, LC.

33. "Press and Radio Conference #9," February 13, 1945, p. 9, Folder 637 (3), Byrnes Papers, CUL.

34. FRUS, Pots. I, p. 735.

35. See Vandenberg, *The Private Papers of Senator Vandenberg*, p. 148.

36. Stimson Diary, May 4, 1945.

37. FRUS, Pots. I, p. 3.

38. FRUS, Pots. I, p. 4.

39. *The New York Times*, May 8, 1945, p. 34.

40. Stimson Diary, May 15, 1945.

41. Stimson Diary, May 16, 1945.

42. Truman, *Year of Decisions*, p. 87.

43. Leo Szilard, "A Personal History of the Atomic Bomb," pp. 14–16.

44. Leahy Diary, May 20, 1945.

Chapter 17: The Shadow of Yalta

1. See Messer, "The Making of a Cold Warrior," pp. 121–99.

2. *Time*, February 26, 1945, pp. 15–16, cited material from p. 15.

3. Robertson, *Sly and Able*, p. 384.

4. Messer, *The End of An Alliance*, p. 51. See FRUS, Malta and Yalta, pp. 848, 860–63, 873, 908, 918–19, 972–73. On Byrnes' reluctance to commit the United States in this connection, see also Stettinius' account of the Yalta conference. (Edward R. Stettinius, *Roosevelt and the Russians: The Yalta Conference* [Garden City, New York: Doubleday & Company, Inc., 1949], pp. 88–89.)

5. FRUS, Malta and Yalta, p. 860, fn.

6. FRUS, Malta and Yalta, p. 873.

7. "Press and Radio Conference #9," February 13, 1945, pp. 4–5, Folder 637 (3), Byrnes Papers, CUL.

8. "Press and Radio Conference #9," February 13, 1945, p. 6, Folder 637 (3), Byrnes Papers, CUL.

9. Glen C. H. Perry, *"Dear Bart": Washington Views of World War II* (Westport, CT, 1982), p. 294.

10. Perry, *"Dear Bart,"* p. 295.

11. Perry, *"Dear Bart,"* p. 296.

12. Messer, "The Making of a Cold Warrior," p. 182.

13. Messer, "The Making of a Cold Warrior," p. 183.

14. Messer, "The Making of a Cold Warrior," p. 182.

15. Ernest K. Lindley, "Byrnes, the Persuasive Reporter," *Newsweek*, March 12, 1945, p. 42; "Yalta Legman," *Newsweek*, March 19, 1945, p. 52.

16. Messer, *The End of an Alliance*, pp. 68–69.

17. Messer, *The End of an Alliance*, pp. 53–70.

18. Cabell Phillips, *The Truman Presidency: The History of a Triumphant Succession* (New York, 1966), p. 84.

19. Truman, *Year of Decisions*, p. 22.

20. Byrnes to Truman, April 25, 1945, Folder 622, Byrnes Papers, CUL.

21. Edmund Preston, "Prelude to Cold War: American Reactions to the Growth of Soviet Power 1944–1945," Ph.D. dissertation, University of Virginia, 1979, p. 184.

22. "Press and Radio Conference #9," February 13, 1945, p. 13, Folder 637 (3), Byrnes Papers, CUL.

23. Diary, June 6, 1945, (Journal), "Chrono File," Box 17, Davies Papers, LC.

24. Byrnes to Lippmann, April 30, 1945, Folder 355, Box 59, Lippmann Papers, YUL.

25. Messer, "The Making of a Cold Warrior," p. 253.

26. Truman, *Off the Record*, ed. Ferrell, p. 49.

27. See, for example, Robertson, *Sly and Able*, pp. 425–39.

Part V: Potsdam

Chapter 18: To the Big Three Meeting

1. Byrnes, *All in One Lifetime*, p. 292.

2. A representative sample includes: Herbert Feis, *Between War and Peace: The Potsdam Conference* (Princeton, 1960); John Lewis Gaddis, *The United States and the Origins of the Cold War* (New York, 1972); Adam Ulam, *Stalin: The Man and His Era* (New York, 1972); Charles Mee, *Meeting at Potsdam* (New York, 1975); John M. Backer, *The Decision to Divide Germany: American Foreign Policy in Transition* (Durham, 1982); James L. Gormly, *From Potsdam to the Cold War: Big Three Diplomacy, 1945–1947* (Wilmington, 1990); Kolko, *The Politics of War*.

3. See Gaddis, *United States and Origins of Cold War*, p. 244; Yergin, *Shattered Peace*, p. 115; Bernstein, "Shatterer of Worlds, Hiroshima and Nagasaki," *Bulletin of the Atomic Scientists*, Vol. 31, No. 10, (December 1975), p. 16; Ambrose, *Rise to Globalism*, p. 46; Messer, *The End of an Alliance*, pp. 106–07; Forrest C. Pogue, *George C. Marshall, Vol. IV: Statesman, 1945–1959* (New York, 1987), p. 20; Leffler, *A Preponderance of Power*, p. 38.

4. Stimson and Bundy, *On Active Service*, p. 637.

5. Diary, July 16, 1945, (5-23-51), "Chrono File," Box 18, Davies Papers, LC.

6. Parten interview with author, December 26, 1984, and January 5, 1985.

7. Memorandum on the use of S-1 bomb, Ralph A. Bard, June 27, 1945, File 77, Roll 6, H-B Files, M1108, NA: reprinted in Stoff, Fanton, Williams, eds., *The Manhattan Project*, p. 162.

8. Ibid.

9. See Memorandum for the Secretary of War, from Harrison, June 28, 1945, File 77, Roll 6, H-B Files, M1108, NA, and Interim Committee Log, July 2, 1945, File 98, Roll 8, H-B Files, M1108, NA; also Hewlett and Anderson, *The New World*, p. 370.

10. In a 1960 interview with *U.S. News and World Report*, Bard was asked: "How wide a circulation did your memorandum to the Interim Committee, studying use of the bomb, actually get?" Bard responded: "The matter was discussed in the Interim Committee, and I'm quite sure it was called to the attention of Secretary Stimson. Whether it went to the President or not, I don't know." "Was A-Bomb on Japan a Mistake?," pp. 73–74.

11. Alice Kimball Smith, "Behind the Decision to Use the Atomic Bomb: Chicago,

1944–45," *Bulletin of the Atomic Scientists*, Vol. XIV, No. 8 (October 1958), pp. 288–312, see especially p. 297. Oddly, although in 1957 he told Smith that he had met with Truman, Bard denied discussing the matter with the president in the 1960 interview with *U.S. News and World Report*. (Unfortunately, it has so far not been possible to retrieve Ms. Smith's notes.) However, most historians believe that this meeting took place. See, for example, Hewlett and Anderson, *The New World*; Bundy, *Danger and Survival*; Nuel Pharr Davis, *Lawrence and Oppenheimer* (New York, 1968); Sigal, *Fighting to a Finish*; Sherwin, *A World Destroyed*.

12. Davis, *Lawrence and Oppenheimer*, p. 247.

13. Smith, "Behind the Decision to Use the Atomic Bomb," p. 297.

14. See Fletcher Knebel and Charles W. Bailey, *No High Ground* (New York, 1960), pp. 109–10. Although Alice Smith made reference to Bard's memorandum, she did not reproduce it.

15. Bard to Strauss, August 24, 1956, Strauss Papers—AEC Series—Bard, Ralph A., HHPL.

16. Bard to Strauss, September 24, 1956, Strauss Papers—AEC Series—Bard, Ralph A., HHPL.

17. CCS 643/3, "Estimate of the Enemy Situation (as of 6 July)," July 8, 1945, p. 10, "CCS 381 (6-4-43), Sec. 2, Part 5," RG 218, NA.

18. Ibid., p. 7.

19. Ibid., p. 10. The CIC added that since "the Japanese Army is the principal repository of the Japanese military tradition it follows that the Army leaders must, with a sufficient degree of unanimity, acknowledge defeat. . . . For a surrender to be acceptable to the Japanese Army, it would be necessary for the military leaders to believe that it would not entail discrediting [*sic*] warrior tradition and that it would permit the ultimate resurgence of a military Japan." Note that the point about disarmament does not appear in the very similar June 30 U.S. intelligence "Estimate of the Enemy Situation," upon which it was based; and it is almost certainly a British addition. In fact, the June 27 report of the British Joint-Intelligence Sub-committee, "The Japanese Attitude to Unconditional Surrender," contains this exact language. See Annex I of J.P. (45) 144 (Final), "Grand Strategy in the War Against Japan," 6th July, 1945, DEFEZ/1313, 196263, Public Record Office U.K., DEFEZ/1313. Even more important, this assessment was made well before MAGIC revealed the Emperor's (and later, *the Army's*) hand in the Japanese surrender approach to Moscow. We may also note that Grew, who knew Japan well and was adamant about disarmament, did not think this would be a hindrance to achieving a surrender. (See Grew, *Turbulent Era*, Vol. II, pp. 1428–30, and Memorandum for the President, from Grew, June 13, 1945, Stimson Safe File (Japan), Entry 74A, RG 107, NA.) For the June 30 American estimate, see Memorandum for the Assistant Chief of Staff, OPD, from Bissell, June 30, 1945, "Estimate of the Enemy Situation," OPD 350.05 TS, Entry 419, RG 165, NA.

20. OPD Book, title: Compilation of Subs for Possible Discussion at TERMINAL; as cited in Cline, *Washington Command Post*, pp. 345–46.

21. *The New York Times*, July 3, 1945, p. 3.

22. *Washington Post*, July 3, 1945, p. 2.

23. Halifax weekly political report, July 8, 1945, Document 2192, Reel 3, F.O. 371, Great Britain, Foreign Copying Program, LC Manuscript Division.

24. *The New York Times*, July 13, 1945, p. 3.

25. *Washington Post*, June 11, 1945, p. 8.

26. Raymond Moley, "Attacking the Jap Mentality," *Newsweek*, July 2, 1945, p. 92.

27. Raymond Swing Broadcast, June 6, 1945, Box 26, Swing Papers, LC.

28. Raymond Swing Broadcast, July 3, 1945, Box 27, Swing Papers, LC.

29. *Washington Post*, July 13, 1945, p. 6.

30. "U.S. At War," *Time*, The Nation, July 16, 1945, p. 15.

31. "Japan—An Opportunity for Statesmanship," *Life*, July 16, 1945, p. 22.

32. "A Petition to The President of The United States," *The Christian Century*, June 27, 1945, p. 762.

33. "A Statement on Our Policy Toward Japan," *Christianity and Crisis*, Vol. V, No. 11 (June 25, 1945), p. 1.

34. See, for example, *The Nation*, May 12, 1945, p. 533; June 23, 1945, pp. 683–84; July 14, 1945, p. 23.

35. *The New York Times*, July 19, 1945, p. 22.

36. Memorandum for Mr. MacLeish, "Current Public Attitudes Toward the Unconditional Surrender of Japan," July 16, 1945, Box 39, Office of Public Opinion Studies, 1943–1945, RG 59, NA.

37. FRUS, Pots. I, p. 902.

38. USSBS, *Japan's Struggle to End the War*, p. 7; also see Butow, *Japan's Decision to Surrender*, pp. 117–20.

39. MAGIC, No. 1204, July 12, 1945, RG 457, NA.

40. MAGIC, No. 1205, July 13, 1945, RG 457, NA.

41. MAGIC, No. 1207, July 15, 1945, RG 457, NA.

42. Unpublished Forrestal Diary, July 13, 1945; Forrestal, *The Forrestal Diaries*, p. 74.

43. Publication of Pacific Strategic Intelligence Section, Russo-Japanese Relations (1–12 July 1945), July 14, 1945, p. 10, SRH-084, RG 457, NA. The initial (July 12–13) assessment by Brig. Gen. John Weckerling, Deputy Assistant Chief of Staff, G-2, was more cautious than the July 14 PSIS report. See Memorandum for the Deputy Chief of Staff, from Weckerling, July 12 and July 13, Item 13, Exec. 17, Box 98, OPD Executive Files, Entry 422, RG 165, NA.

44. Stimson Diary, July 16, 1945.

45. McCloy Diary, July 16, 1945.

46. On July 15, the day he arrived in Potsdam, McCloy noted in his diary, "I worked very late on the Japanese warning paper. . . ." On the 16th he noted again, "At work on the papers again in the morning. Had a long conference with the Secretary and Harvey Bundy on the two memoranda for the President." (McCloy was simultaneously preparing a paper on issues related to U.S. German policy.) McCloy Diary, July 15 and 16, 1945.

47. FRUS, *Conference of Berlin (Potsdam)*, Vol. II (hereafter, Pots. II), p. 1266.

48. Assurances for the Emperor were given in paragraph twelve of this draft. See FRUS, Pots. I, pp. 897–99. See also p. 713, endnote 48.

49. FRUS, Pots. II, p. 1265.

50. FRUS, Pots. II, p. 1266.

51. See Memorandum for Colonel Stimson, from McCloy, and Memorandum, Subject: Timing of Proposed Demand for Japanese Surrender, June 29, 1945, "Japan (After Dec. 7/41)," Box 8, Stimson Safe File, Entry 74A, RG 107, NA.

52. McCloy Diary, July 17, 1945.

53. Ibid.

54. Unedited notes on talk with President Eisenhower, April 6, 1960, War Department Notes envelope, Box 66, Feis Papers, LC.

55. Brown Journal, July 17, 1945, Folder 54(1), Byrnes Papers, CUL.

56. Handwritten memorandum dated Sept. 29, 1946, Japanese Surrender & A-Bomb, Strauss Papers—AEC, HHPL.

57. FRUS, Pots. I, p. 873.

58. Truman, *Off the Record*, ed. Ferrell, p. 53.

Chapter 19: Clear Alternatives; First Decisions

1. Truman interview with Jonathan Daniels, November 12, 1949, "Research Notes Used in Connection with Writing *The Man of Independence*," p. 67, Part I, Notes on In-

terviews, Daniels Papers, HSTL. Daniels added that: "He was referring I think to the Russians etc. as well as the Japs."

2. Jonathan Daniels, *The Man of Independence* (Port Washington, N.Y., 1971), p. 266.

3. Cover letter by Daniels, November 27, 1962, "Research Notes Used in Connection With Writing *The Man of Independence*," Part I, Notes on Interviews, Daniels Papers, HSTL.

4. Truman, *Off the Record*, ed. Ferrell, p. 53.

5. Truman, *Off the Record*, ed. Ferrell, p. 49.

6. FRUS, Pots. II, p. 1360.

7. Stimson Diary, July 16, 1945.

8. Stimson Diary, July 18, 1945.

9. FRUS, Pots. II, pp. 1360–61.

10. Rhodes, *The Making of the Atomic Bomb*, p. 688.

11. FRUS, Pots. II, xxiii.

12. Truman, *Year of Decisions*, p. 417.

13. Truman, *Off the Record*, ed. Ferrell, p. 53.

14. Harry S. Truman, *Dear Bess: The Letters from Harry to Bess Truman, 1910–1959*, ed. Robert Ferrell (New York, 1983), p. 519.

15. Ibid.

16. Diary, July 18, 1945 (8-13-54), "Chrono File," Box 18, Davies Papers, LC.

17. CCS 643/3, "Estimate of the Enemy Situation (as of 6 July)," July 8, 1945, p. 10, CCS 381 (6-4-43), Sec. 2, Part 5, RG 218, NA.

18. MAGIC, No. 1210, July 17, 1945, RG 457, NA.

19. Ibid.

20. WSC, Note to the Cabinet, quoted in Ehrman, *Grand Strategy*, p. 302. Ehrman does not provide a source, but see Martin Gilbert, *'Never Despair'*, p. 66, fn. 5, p. 70, fn 1.

21. WSC, Note to the Cabinet, quoted in Ehrman, *Grand Strategy*, pp. 302–03.

22. WSC, Note to the Cabinet, quoted in Ehrman, *Grand Strategy*, p. 303.

23. Ibid.

24. Ibid.

25. WSC, Note to the Cabinet, quoted in Ehrman, *Grand Strategy*, p. 303.

26. Truman, *Off the Record*, ed. Ferrell, pp. 53–54. The original handwritten diary on file at the Truman Library begins a new paragraph after the sentence: "Believe Japs will fold up before Russia comes in," suggesting the possibility Truman may have believed that Japan was now so near collapse that a surrender might occur both before the Russians came in and before the atomic bomb was used. The widely cited published version of this entry shows no new paragraph break so that the next sentence mistakenly appears as a single continuation of Truman's thought: "I am sure they will when Manhattan appears over their homeland." (Truman diary, July 18, 1945, "Ross, Mr. and Mrs. Charles G.," Box 322, "Personal File," President's Secretary's Files, Truman Papers, HSTL; Truman, *Off the Record*, ed. Ferrell, p. 54.) I am indebted to Edward Rouse Winstead for pointing this out.

27. MAGIC, No. 1212, July 20, 1945, RG 457, NA. Ellipsis in original MAGIC summary.

28. See, for example, Butow, *Japan's Decision to Surrender*, p. 132; Giovannitti and Freed, *The Decision to Drop the Bomb*, p. 213.

29. FRUS, Pots. II, p. 36.

30. Ibid.

31. FRUS, Pots. II, p. 37.

32. Ibid.

33. Ibid.

34. Ismay to WSC, July 17, 1945, quoted in Ehrman, *Grand Strategy*, p. 291.

35. Memorandum, Subject: Timing of Proposed Demand for Japanese Surrender, June 29, 1945, "Japan (After Dec. 7/41)," Box 8, Stimson Safe Files, Entry 74A, RG 107, NA.

36. DoD, *Top Secret Entry*, Sec. V, p. 25; DoD, *Entry*, p. 83.

37. HLS to HST, July 2, 1945, enclosure: *Proposed Program for Japan*, White House Correspondence, Box 15, Stimson Safe File, Entry 74A, RG 107, NA; also in Stimson Diary, July 2, and FRUS, Pots. I, pp. 889–92.

38. FRUS, Pots. II, pp. 1265–67.

39. Stimson Diary, July 17, 1945.

40. Ibid.

41. Ibid.

Chapter 20: Removing the Soviet Black-out from Europe

1. Stimson Diary, July 16, 1945.

2. Diary, July 16, 1945 (5-23-51), "Chrono File," Box 18, Davies Papers, LC.

3. Stimson Diary, July 18, 1945.

4. Leslie Groves, *Now It Can Be Told: The Story of the Manhattan Project* (New York: 1962), p. 303.

5. See, for example, Yergin, *Shattered Peace*, pp. 115–16; also Sherwin, *A World Destroyed*, pp. 223–24.

6. Stimson Diary, July 21, 1945.

7. Ibid.

8. McCloy Diary, July 21, 1945.

9. Truman, *Off the Record*, Ferrell, ed., p. 55.

10. FRUS, Pots. II, pp. 1361–62.

11. FRUS, Pots. II, p. 1367.

12. FRUS, Pots. II, p. 1366.

13. FRUS, Pots. II, pp. 1366–67. Bracketed material in original.

14. JFB to Strauss, December 17, 1960, "AEC, Japanese Surrender & A-Bomb," Strauss Papers, HHPL.

15. See HLS, "Reflections on the Basic Problems Which Confront Us," attached to Stimson Diary, July 22, 1945. See above, p. 431.

16. Parten interview with author, December 26, 1984, and January 5, 1985.

17. HLS to HST, April 24, 1945, "White House Correspondence," Box 15, Stimson Safe File, Entry 74A, RG 107, NA.

18. In 1959, Louis Morton raised this issue. (See "The Decision to Use the Atomic Bomb," *Foreign Affairs*, Vol. 25 [January 1959], pp. 334–53.) See also Feis, *The Atomic Bomb and the End of World War II*, p. 194; Leffler, *A Preponderance of Power*, p. 38; Messer, *The End of an Alliance*, pp. 86–114.)

19. Leahy Diary, June 15, 1945

20. Kenneth W. Treacy, "Memorandum for General Hull: Information from the White House," June 16, 1945, Item 71, Exec. 10, Box 62, OPD Executive Files, Entry 422, RG 165, NA.

21. Grew, *Turbulent Era*, Vol. II, p. 1464. Technically, Lane was merely the "appointed ambassador" to Poland at this point. With U.S. recognition of the Lublin government in July, he became full ambassador.

22. Although the term "the Balkans" does not, strictly speaking, include Hungary, nonetheless, Hungary, Bulgaria, and Rumania were often considered as a unit by the State Department, and it is convenient to use the term "the Balkans" in a broad sense.

23. FRUS, Pots. I, p. 361.

24. As Melvyn Leffler writes, "The armistice accords denied the Soviet Union any significant influence in Italy and gave the Kremlin the preeminent role in Rumania, Finland, Bulgaria and Hungary. For all intents and purposes, Soviet officials had a legal claim to run things as they wished in Rumania and Finland until peace treaties were completed and

in Bulgaria and Hungary at least until the war was over." (Melvyn P. Leffler, "Adherence to Agreements," p. 99.)

25. FRUS, Pots. I, p. 215. Also see Leffler, "Adherence to Agreements" p. 99.

26. Churchill, *Triumph and Tragedy*, p. 227. Often overlooked is a second "deal" on Eastern European spheres of influence made by Eden and Molotov on October 11, 1944, which gave the Soviets an 80% influence in Hungary. According to Eastern European expert Charles Gati, this arrangement was "apparently accepted" by the British. (Charles Gati, *Hungary and the Soviet Bloc* (Durham: 1986, pp. 30–32.)

27. Leffler, "Adherence to Agreements," p. 100.

28. FRUS, Pots. I, p. 262.

29. "Telephone Conversation Between the Secretary of War and Mr. McCloy in San Francisco, May 8, 1945," reel 128, pp. 462, 464, 466, Stimson Papers, LC.

30. Grew, *Turbulent Era*, Vol. II, p. 1455.

31. FRUS, Pots. I, p. 189.

32. FRUS, Pots. I, pp. 189–90.

33. FRUS, Pots. I, p. 319.

34. FRUS, Pots. I, pp. 201–02.

35. Michael M. Boll, *Cold War in the Balkans: American Foreign Policy and the Emergence of Communist Bulgaria, 1943–1947* (Lexington, KY, 1984), p. 132.

36. FRUS, Pots. I, p. 364, fn.; p. 368, fn.; pp. 372–73, fn.

37. FRUS, Pots. I, p. 358, fn.

38. FRUS, Pots. I, pp. 393–94.

39. FRUS, Pots. I, p. 405; FRUS, Pots. II, pp. 691, 1494.

40. FRUS, Pots II, p. 688.

41. FRUS, Pots. II, p. 690.

42. FRUS, Pots. I, p. 407.

43. FRUS, Pots. II, pp. 52, 609–10. It was this proposal that Truman brought up first at the initial plenary session.

44. FRUS, Pots. I, p. 263.

45. Acting Director of European Affairs to British Minister Balfour, July 7, 1945, Decimal File 500. CC/7-545, Department of State Central Decimal Files, RG 59, NA; cited in Messer, *The End of an Alliance*, p. 110; p. 254 n. 39.

46. Messer, *The End of an Alliance*, p. 94.

47. FRUS, Pots. II, pp. 4–7; Byrnes, *Speaking Frankly*, p. 67.

48. Byrnes, *Speaking Frankly*, p. 67.

49. FRUS, Malta and Yalta, p. 16.

50. Leahy Diary, July 17, 1945.

51. FRUS, Pots. II, pp. 53, 644.

52. Truman, *Dear Bess*, ed. Ferrell, p. 519.

53. FRUS, Pots. II, pp. 67, 102.

54. Churchill, *Triumph and Tragedy*, p. 636.

55. FRUS, Pots. II, pp. 150–51.

56. FRUS, Pots. II, p. 152.

57. FRUS, Pots. II, p. 644.

58. FRUS, Pots. II, p. 646.

59. FRUS, Pots. II, p. 647.

60. Stimson Diary, July 21, 1945.

61. McCloy Diary, July 23 and July 24, 1945.

62. FRUS, Pots. II, p. 207.

63. Ibid.

64. Truman, *Year of Decisions*, p. 369.

65. Stimson Diary, July 22, 1945. This account has Churchill reading Groves' report on July 22, while McCloy's diary states: "After getting Groves' report [on July 21] they

[Truman and Churchill] went to the next meeting like little boys with a big red apple secreted on their persons. . . ." (McCloy Diary, July 23 and July 24, 1945.) On the other hand, Stimson's diary of July 21 notes that "I turned over the paper to Churchill and he began reading it but was interrupted a few minutes before five in order to hurry to the Big Three Conference at five o'clock." (Stimson Diary, July 21, 1945.) The next day Churchill "read Groves' report in full." (Stimson Diary, July 22, 1945.)

66. Stimson Diary, July 22, 1945.

67. Arthur Bryant, *Triumph in the West: A History of the War Years Based on the Diaries of Field-Marshal Lord Alanbrooke, Chief of the Imperial General Staff* (Garden City, NY, 1959), pp. 363–64.

68. Ibid.

69. FRUS, Pots. II, p. 247.

70. Ibid.

71. Ibid.

72. FRUS, Pots. II, p. 249.

73. Ibid.

74. FRUS, Pots. II, p. 251.

75. Stimson Diary, July 23, 1945.

76. FRUS, Pots. II, p. 1374.

77. Stimson Diary, July 24, 1945.

78. Stimson Diary, May 10, 1945.

79. Churchill had told his secretary John Colville just before Yalta, "all the Balkans, except Greece, are going to be Bolshevised; and there is nothing I can do to prevent it." (John Colville, *The Fringes of Power: Downing Street Diaries* [(London, 1985], p. 555.)

80. Churchill, *Triumph and Tragedy*, p. 420.

81. FRUS, Pots. I, pp. 413–14; FRUS, Pots. II, p. 207.

82. Stimson Diary, June 6, 1945.

83. FRUS, Pots. II, p. 207.

84. Messer, *The End of an Alliance*, p. 214.

85. McNeill, *America, Britain, and Russia*, p. 622.

86. Stimson Diary, July 24, 1945.

87. FRUS, Pots. II, p. 330.

88. FRUS, Pots. II, p. 367.

89. FRUS, Pots. II, p. 1494, p. 1492.

90. FRUS, Pots. II, p. 1492.

91. Stimson Diary, July 24, 1945.

92. Stimson Diary, July 23, 1945.

93. Charles de Gaulle, *War Memoirs*, Vol. III: *Salvation* (New York, 1951), p. 230.

94. See, for example, McCloy Diary, July 23 and July 24, 1945; Leahy Diary, July 31, 1945; Forrestal, *The Forrestal Diaries*, ed. Millis, p. 79.

95. Truman, *Year of Decisions*, p. 331.

96. Truman, *Year of Decisions*, p. 338. (From a letter of July 12, 1945.)

Chapter 21: Second Decision

1. Barton Bernstein, "Triumph and Tragedy: Hiroshima and Nagasaki—30 Years Later," *Intellect*, No. 104 (Summer, 1975), pp. 257–63, cited material from p. 262.

2. Messer, *The End of an Alliance*, pp. 126–30; Yergin, *Shattered Peace*, pp. 122–25.

3. Stimson Diary, July 21, 1945.

4. Harry S. Truman, "Radio Report to the American People on the Potsdam Conference, August 9, 1945," from *Public Papers of the Presidents of the United States: Harry S. Truman, Containing the Public Messages, Speeches, and Statements of the*

President, April 12 to December 31, 1945 (Washington, D.C. U.S. Government Printing Office, 1961), p. 97.

5. WB's Book, July 18, 1945, Folder 602, Byrnes Papers, CUL.

6. WB's Book, July 20, 1945, Folder 602, Byrnes Papers, CUL.

7. Ibid.

8. Stimson Diary, July 23, 1945.

9. FRUS, Pots. II, p. 1374.

10. WB's Book, July 24, 1945, Folder 602, Byrnes Papers, CUL.

11. Ibid.

12. Herbert Feis, "Talk with former Secretary of State *James F. Byrnes* (c. November 25, 1957) about his experience at the *Potsdam Conference*," Byrnes draft manuscript file, Box 65, Feis Papers, LC.

13. FRUS, Pots. II, p. 1241. Byrnes acknowledged the cable's authorship in *All in One Lifetime* (Byrnes, *All in One Lifetime*, p. 291.)

14. Truman, *Dear Bess*, ed. Ferrell, p. 520.

15. Truman, *Dear Bess*, ed. Ferrell, p. 521.

16. Truman, *Off the Record*, ed. Ferrell, p. 54.

17. FRUS, Pots. II, p. 120.

18. Ibid.

19. Ibid.

20. Stimson Diary, July 23, 1945.

21. Stimson Diary, July 23, 1945.

22. Stimson Diary, July 24, 1945.

23. See, for example, Sherwin, *A World Destroyed*, pp. 226–27; Bernstein, "Roosevelt, Truman and the Atomic Bomb, 1941–1945," p. 44.

24. WSC to Eden, July 23, 1945, quoted in Ehrman, *Grand Strategy*, p. 292. Ehrman does not list his source, but Gilbert, *'Never Despair'*, p. 90, indicates that the document in question was a minute from the Prime Minister to his Foreign Secretary.

25. Stimson, *On Active Service in Peace and War*; Henry L. Stimson, "The Decision to Use the Bomb," *Harper's*, Vol. 194, No. 1161 (February 1947), pp. 97–107.

26. Feis' 1953 *The China Tangle* misses the delaying tactics; Churchill's 1953 *Triumph and Tragedy* also fails to note the issue, as does Ehrman's 1956 *Grand Strategy* and Giovannitti and Freed's 1965 *The Decision to Drop the Bomb*.

27. Gallicchio, *The Cold War Begins in Asia*, p. 46.

28. Melvyn P. Leffler, "Adherence to Agreements, Yalta and the Experiences of the Early Cold War," *International Security* (Summer, 1986), pp. 88–123, cited material from p. 108.

29. Bundy, *Danger and Survival*, p. 88.

30. Barton Bernstein, "Roosevelt, Truman, and the Atomic Bomb, 1941–1945: A Reinterpretation," *Political Science Quarterly*, Vol. 90, No. 1 (Spring, 1975), pp. 23–69, cited material from p. 46.

31. Stimson Diary, May 15, 1945.

32. David Holloway has studied Soviet plans to occupy at least part of the island of Hokkaido. On August 18, Truman rejected Stalin's request to be allowed to accept the surrender of Japanese forces there. Nonetheless, the next day the 1st Far Eastern Front was ordered to go ahead with occupation of the territory—only to have the order rescinded on August 22. Holloway writes: "Stalin had evidently concluded that the attempt to land forces on Hokkaido would cause a political row—and perhaps even an armed clash—with the United States. . . . Stalin chose to be satisfied with securing the concessions he had obtained at Yalta. . . ." (David Holloway, *Stalin and the Bomb: The Soviet Union and Atomic Energy, 1939–1956* [New Haven: Yale University Press, 1994], p. 131.) See also David M. Glantz, "The Soviet Invasion of Japan," *MHQ: The Quarterly Journal of Military History*, Vol. 7, No. 3 (Spring 1995), pp. 96–97.

33. For details concerning the Soong negotiations, see FRUS, 1945, VII, pp. 932–34.

34. Stimson Diary, July 17, 1945.
35. Ibid.
36. Stimson Diary, July 18, 1945.
37. Byrnes, *Speaking Frankly*, p. 208.
38. Forrestal, *The Forrestal Diaries*, ed. Millis, p. 78.
39. Churchill, *Triumph and Tragedy*, p. 639.
40. Truman, *Year of Decisions*, p. 412.
41. Herbert Feis, "Talk with former Secretary of State *James F. Byrnes* (c. November 25, 1957) about his experience at the *Potsdam Conference*," Byrnes draft manuscript file, Box 65, Feis Papers, LC.
42. Byrnes, *All in One Lifetime*, p. 291.
43. "Was A-Bomb on Japan a Mistake?," pp. 62–78, cited material from p. 66.
44. WB's Book, July 24, 1945, Folder 602, Byrnes Papers, CUL.
45. Forrestal, *The Forrestal Diaries*, ed. Millis, p. 78.
46. Unpublished Forrestal Diary, July 28, 1945.

Chapter 22: The Bomb and Germany

1. Forrestal, *The Forrestal Diaries*, ed. Millis, pp. 78–79.
2. Herbert Feis, *Churchill, Roosevelt, Stalin: The War They Waged and the Peace They Sought* (Princeton, NJ,), p. 530.
3. McCloy Diary, April 30, 1945.
4. Ambrose, *Rise to Globalism*, p. 67.
5. Richard Barnet, *The Rocket's Red Glare: When America Goes to War—the Presidents and the People* (New York, 1990), p. 251.
6. FRUS, Malta and Yalta, p. 286.
7. FRUS, Malta and Yalta, p. 617. Also at Yalta, Byrnes is reported to have stated that "American troops wanted to go home right away, and it would be unpopular if they had to remain in Europe. . . ." (Stettinius, *Roosevelt and the Russians*, p. 89.)
8. FRUS, Pots. I, p. 504.
9. FRUS, Malta and Yalta, p. 970.
10. FRUS, Malta and Yalta, p. 971.
11. FRUS, Malta and Yalta, p. 983.
12. See the forthcoming book by Bernd Greiner, *Die Morgenthau-Legend. Zur Geschichte eines umstrittenen Plans* (Hamburg, 1995).
13. "Comments on J.S.C. Memorandum No. 362," May 8, 1945, "Outgoing Correspondence," Intelligence Group, Box 793, Entry 203, RG 165, NA. The exact date of the actual memorandum is unclear, as is the source. Probably "J.S.C." is a typographical error—in all likelihood, this is a J.C.S. document. It is also conceivable, though unlikely, that the reference is to the J.S.S.C. (i.e., the Joint Strategic Survey Committee).
14. Diary, June 6, 1945, (Journal), "Chrono File," Box 17, Davies Papers, LC.
15. Minutes, Secretary's Staff Committee, April 21, 1945, "Apr. 17–24/45," Box 178, Harriman Papers, LC.
16. Matthew A. Evangelista, "Stalin's Postwar Army Reappraised," *International Security*, Vol. 7, No. 3 (Winter 1982/1983), pp. 110–38, especially p. 121.
17. Memorandum for the President, from Col. Robert B. Landry, Sept. 28, 1948, Folder 1, Subject File, White House, Hoyt Sanford Vandenberg Papers, LC. My thanks to Professor Kofsky for bringing this to my attention. See also his *Harry S. Truman and the War Scare of 1948: A Successful Campaign to Deceive the Nation* (New York, 1993).
18. Jean Smith, *Lucius D. Clay: An American Life* (New York, 1990), pp. 280–88.
19. Smith, *Lucius D. Clay*, p. 280.
20. Notes by Felix Belair, Jr., April 29, 1946, "corresp. w/Truman file," Box 58, Krock Papers, Mudd Library, Princeton University Archives.

21. See, for example, Samuel R. Williamson and Steven L. Rearden, *The Origins of U.S. Nuclear Strategy, 1945–1953* (New York, 1993); Herken, *The Winning Weapon*, pp. 195–217.

22. Melvyn Leffler, "Adherence to Agreements," pp. 105–106. For details of the complex reparations discussions, see, for example, Bruce Kuklick, *American Policy and the Division of Germany: The Clash with Russia Over Reparations* (Ithaca, 1972); Carolyn Eisenberg, *Drawing the Line: The American Decision to Divide Germany, 1944–49* (forthcoming from Cambridge University Press); Philip A. Baggaley, "Reparations, Security, and the Industrial Disarmament of Germany: Origins of the Potsdam Decisions," Ph.D. Dissertation, Yale University, 1980.

23. "Journal," July 28, 1945 (2-1-51), "Chrono File," Box 19, Davies Papers, LC.

24. "Diary," July 28, 1945, "Chrono File," Box 19, Davies Papers, LC.

25. "Diary," July 29, 1945, "Chrono File," Box 19, Davies Papers, LC.

26. "Diary," July 29, 1945 ("Potsdam Diary"), "Chrono File," Box 19, Davies Papers, LC.

27. FRUS, 1945, *Volume III: European Advisory Commission, Austria; Germany* (hereafter cited as Vol. III) (Washington, D.C., 1968), p. 1179, Backer, *The Decision to Divide Germany*, p. 40.

28. Backer, *The Decision to Divide Germany*, pp. 40–41.

29. See Truman, *Year of Decisions*, pp. 307–09.

30. Collado interview with Richard McKinzie, July 11, 1974, pp. 33, 38, Oral History Collection, HSTL. Collado, director of the State Department's Office of Financial and Development Policy, worked with Pauley at Potsdam.

31. "Peace and Politics," *Time*, May 7, 1945, p. 21.

32. "People of the Week," *U.S. News and World Report*, May 11, 1945, pp. 62–64, cited material on p. 62.

33. *The Reminiscences of Isador Lubin*, (1957), p. 86, in the Oral History Collection of Columbia University.

34. Truman, *Off the Record*, ed. Ferrell, p. 348.

35. FRUS, 1945, Vol. III, pp. 1290–91.

36. FO 371, UE2104/624/77, May 22, 1945, PRO, cited in Baggaley, "Reparations, Security, and the Industrial Disarmament of Germany," p. 434.

37. FRUS, Pots. I, p. 510. Pauley is in error as to Churchill's position. See above, p. 282.

38. Ibid., p. 511. Material bracketed by FRUS editors.

39. "Report from Col. Bernstein," June 5, 1945, cited in the *Morgenthau Diary (Germany)*, Vol. II, prepared by the Subcommittee to Investigate the Administration of the Internal Security Act and Other Internal Security Laws of the Committee on the Judiciary, United States Senate (Washington, D.C.: U.S. Government Printing Office, 1967), p. 1555. This reference was brought to my attention by Dr. Bernd Greiner of the Hamburger Institut für Sozialforschung, Hamburg, Germany.

40. Kolko, *The Politics of War*, p. 569; Baggaley, "Reparations, Security, and the Industrial Disarmament of Germany," p. 419.

41. FRUS, Pots. I, p. 519.

42. FRUS, Pots. I, pp. 526–27.

43. Truman, *Off the Record*, ed. Ferrell, p. 49.

44. FRUS, Pots. I, p. 532.

45. FRUS, Pots. II, p. 833.

46. FRUS, Pots. II, p. 8.

47. FRUS, Pots. II, p. 110.

48. FRUS, Pots. II, p. 845. See also FRUS, Pots. II, pp. 110–11, 141–42, 942–43; FRUS, Pots. I, pp. 547–48.

49. FRUS, Pots. II, pp. 942–43.

50. FRUS, Pots. II, p. 942.

51. FRUS, Pots. II, p. 943.

52. FRUS, Pots. II, pp. 877, 900–01.

53. Eisenberg, *Drawing the Line*, p. 149.

54. FRUS, Pots. II, p. 943.

55. "Journal," July 28, 1945 (2-1-51), "Chrono File," Box 19, Davies Papers, LC.

56. "Diary," July 29, 1945 ("Potsdam Diary"), "Chrono File," Box 19, Davies Papers, LC.

57. FRUS, Pots. II, p. 1361.

58. FRUS, Pots. II, p. 232.

59. Stimson Diary, July 23, 1945.

60. FRUS, Pots. II, pp. 274–75.

61. FRUS, Pots. II, p. 279.

62. Gaddis, *The United States and the Origins of the Cold War*, p. 244.

63. Arnold journal, July 22, 1945, "Terminal Conference—July 10–30," Box 272, Arnold Papers, LC.

64. FRUS, Pots. II, pp. 296–97.

65. FRUS, Pots. II, p. 298.

66. FRUS, Pots. II, p. 428.

67. FRUS, Pots. II, p. 429.

68. FRUS, Pots. II, p. 430.

69. FRUS, Pots. II, p. 901.

70. FRUS, Pots. II, pp. 428–32.

71. Leahy Diary, July 26, 1945.

72. Leahy Diary, July 27, 1945.

73. FRUS, Pots. II, pp. 484–85.

74. FRUS, Pots. II, p. 485.

75. Byrnes, *Speaking Frankly*, p. 85.

76. Truman, *Dear Bess*, ed. Ferrell, p. 522.

77. FRUS, Pots. II, pp. 1485–87.

78. FRUS, Pots. II, pp. 1491–92.

79. Stimson Diary, April 19, 1945.

80. Truman, *Year of Decisions*, p. 102.

81. FRUS, Pots. I, p. 524, fn.

82. FRUS, Pots. I, pp. 619–20.

83. FRUS, Pots. I, p. 612.

84. FRUS, Pots. II, p. 756.

85. APO 742, "11 18-1 18," Box 95, Office of Military Government of Germany, Economics Division Industry Branch, APO 742, RG 260, NA.

86. Leffler, *A Preponderance of Power*, p. 118.

87. "Memorandum of Conversations at the White House on August 22, 1945 between the President and General de Gaulle," "France," "Subject File," President's Secretary's Files, HSTL.

88. Ibid.

89. Ibid.

Chapter 23: Third Decision

1. Allen Dulles, *The Secret Surrender* (New York, 1966), pp. 255–56. This seems to be an exaggeration—or at least different from what Dulles conveyed in written documents in 1945. See above, pp. 294–95.

2. Stimson Diary, July 20, 1945.

3. Dulles to Elliston, September 6, 1950, "Hirohito File," Box 21, Dulles papers, Mudd

Library, Princeton University Archives; McCloy Diary, July 20, 1945. Per Jacobsson, a Swedish national and economic adviser to the Bank for International Settlements.

4. McCloy Diary, July 20, 1945.

5. McCloy Diary, July 27, 1945.

6. Leahy Diary, June 14, 1945.

7. Dulles, *The Secret Surrender*, p. 87.

8. Justin H. Libby, "The Search for a Negotiated Peace," *World Affairs*, Vol. 156, No. 1 (Summer 1993), pp. 35–45, especially p. 37.

9. Dulles, *The Secret Surrender*, pp. 1, 197–238.

10. FRUS, 1945, Vol. VI, p. 488.

11. FRUS, 1945, Vol. VI, p. 490.

12. FRUS, 1945, Vol. VI, p. 492.

13. FRUS, 1944, Vol. V, p. 1184.

14. FRUS, 1945, Vol. VI, p. 477.

15. Ibid.

16. Justin H. Libby, "The Search for A Negotiated Peace," *World Affairs*, Vol. 156, No. 1 (Summer 1993), pp. 35–45, especially p. 41; Butow, *Japan's Decision to Surrender*, p. 56.

17. Libby, "The Search for a Negotiated Peace," p. 41.

18. MAGIC, No. 1215, July 23, 1945, RG 457, NA.

19. Onodera's true status is noted in a postwar U.S. Army document which observed that his position as military attaché "was a cover for his real mission which was secret intelligence of all kinds." At the end of 1944, he "was put at the head of intelligence for the whole of Europe." "Brief for the Interrogation of Major General Makato Onodera," undated but clearly postwar, "Makato Onodera," XE 154606, Box 168, "I.R.R.," RG 319, NA.

20. FRUS, 1945, Vol. VI, pp. 479–80.

21. Ibid.

22. FRUS, Pots. II, pp. 1589–90.

23. See Butow, *Japan's Decision to Surrender*, pp. 56–57.

24. In this regard, see Butow, *Japan's Decision to Surrender*, pp. 57, 76–92.

25. FRUS, Pots. II, p. 87.

26. Memorandum of Conversation, July 17, 1945 (date is apparently incorrect on memorandum), "July 16–19, 1945," Box 181, Harriman Papers, LC.

27. FRUS, Pots. I, p. 201.

28. FRUS, Pots. I, p. 884.

29. HLS to HST, July 2, 1945, enclosed: *Proclamation by the Heads of States* (draft of July 1, 1945), White House Correspondence, Box 15, Stimson Safe File, Entry 74A, RG 107, NA; also in Stimson Diary, July 2, 1945, and FRUS, Pots. I, p. 894.

30. HLS to HST, enclosed: *Proposed Program for Japan*, July 2, 1945, "White House Correspondence," Stimson Safe File, Entry 74A, RG 107, NA; also in Stimson Diary, July 2, 1945, and FRUS, Pots. I, p. 891.

31. FRUS, Pots. II, pp. 1265–67.

32. FRUS, Pots. II, pp. 36–37. On Churchill's July 18 approach to Truman, see Ehrman, *Grand Strategy*, pp. 302–03.

33. Skates, *The Invasion of Japan*, p. 239.

34. Ibid., p. 238.

35. "Autobiography by Charles Howard Donnelly, Colonel, U.S.A.R. (Retired)," copyright July 11, 1979, p. 743, Donnelly Papers, USAMHI.

36. J.C.S. 1275/5, "Military Aspects of Unconditional Surrender Formula for Japan," July 12, 1945, p. 36. "CCS 387 Japan (2-7-45) Sec. 1," JCS Geographic File, 1942–45, RG 218, NA. Unaccountably, Brian L. Villa suggests that the "JSSC specifically recommended deleting the paragraph allowing the retention of the emperor. . . ." See Villa, "The U.S. Army, Unconditional Surrender, and the Potsdam Proclamation," p. 90.

37. FRUS, Pots. II, pp. 1268–69.

38. On May 28, Grew advised the president: "The greatest obstacle to unconditional surrender by the Japanese is their belief that this would entail the destruction or permanent removal of the Emperor and the institution of the Throne. If some indication can now be given the Japanese that they themselves . . . will be permitted to determine their own future political structure, they will be afforded a method of saving face without which surrender will be highly unlikely." Grew, *Turbulent Era*, Vol. II, p. 1429.

39. In a May 30 memorandum to Truman, Hoover recommended that Japan be assured "the Allies have no desire to destroy either the Japanese people or their government, or to interference [sic] in the Japanese way of life. . . ." Memorandum for the Secretary of War, from HST, June 9, 1945, enclosed: "Memorandum on Ending the Japanese War," "Japan (After Dec. 7/41)," Stimson Safe File, Entry 74A, RG 107, NA.

40. At Truman's request, on June 13 Grew commented on Hoover's memorandum: "Every evidence, without exception, that we are able to obtain of the views of the Japanese with regard to the institution of the throne, indicates that the non-molestation of the person of the present emperor and the preservation of the institution of the throne comprise irreducible Japanese terms. . . . We are disposed to agree with the view that failure on our part to clarify our intentions in this regard . . . will insure prolongation of the war and cost a large number of human lives." Memorandum to the President, from Grew, June 13, 1945, "Japan," Stimson Safe File, Entry 74A, RG 107, NA.

41. In a June 16 letter to the president's special counsel, Judge Samuel I. Rosenman, requesting that Rosenman take the issue up with Truman, Grew restated: ". . . I think it will be a matter of plain common sense to give the Japanese a clearer idea of what we mean by unconditional surrender. . . . [that] the Japanese will then be permitted to determine for themselves the nature of their future political structure." Grew to Rosenman, June 16, 1945, "Japan (After Dec. 7/41)," Box 8, Stimson Safe File, Entry 74A, RG 107, NA. On June 17, Rosenman went out on the U.S.S. *Potomac* with the president and they discussed Grew's proposal. When Grew met with Truman on June 18, Truman "said that he had carefully considered the draft statement which [Grew] had given to Judge Rosenman" to take up with the president. Grew, *Turbulent Era*, Vol. II, pp. 1435–37.

42. On June 18, after Truman told him of his decision to put off discussion of a warning statement until the Potsdam conference, Grew noted he informed the president that he "felt very strongly that something might be gained and nothing could be lost by such a step and in my opinion the sooner it was taken the better." Grew, *Turbulent Era*, Vol. II, p. 1437.

43. McCloy recalled that on June 18 he urged Truman to let Japan know "we would permit them to choose their own form of government, including the retention of the Mikado, but only on the basis of a constitutional monarchy. . . ." McCloy interview with Fred Freed for NBC White Paper "The Decision to Drop the Bomb," 1964, Roll 1, pp. 17–18, File 50A, Box SP2, McCloy Papers, ACA. See also Bird, *The Chairman*, pp. 246, 694; Reston, *Deadline*, pp. 498–99; McCloy to Clark Clifford, September 17, 1984, enclosure: "President Truman & the Atom Bomb," Box 1, Records of the Truman Centennial Committee, HSTL.

44. On June 18, Leahy said "that he could not agree with those who said to him that unless we obtain the unconditional surrender of the Japanese that we will have lost the war. . . . What he did fear was that our insistence on unconditional surrender would result only in making the Japanese desperate and thereby increase our casualty lists." DoD, *Top Secret Entry*, Sec. V, p. 26; DoD, *Entry*, p. 84.

45. On June 30 Grew sent the president a memorandum in which the State Department officially recommended issuing a statement telling Japan "of our intention to permit them to retain their political institutions, in so far as they are not inimicable to peaceful international relations." Among the specific reasons: "to eliminate the most serious single obstacle to Japanese unconditional surrender, namely, concern over the fate of the throne. . . ." FRUS, Pots. I, pp. 201, 884.

46. On June 27, Bard urged that Japan be contacted and given "some information regarding the proposed use of atomic power, together with whatever assurances the President might care to make with regard to the Emperor of Japan and the treatment of the Japanese nation following unconditional surrender. It seems quite possible to me that this presents the opportunity which the Japanese are looking for." Memorandum on the use of S-1 bomb, Ralph A. Bard, June 27, 1945, File 77, Roll 6, H-B Files, M1108, NA; reprinted in Stoff, Fanton, Williams, eds., *The Manhattan Project*, p. 162. Historian Alice Kimball Smith, who interviewed Bard in 1957, wrote that on July 1 Bard obtained an interview with Truman and also discussed this matter with him at this time. Alice Kimball Smith, "Behind the Decision to Use the Atomic Bomb," p. 297.

47. In addition to the specific language recommended in the draft ("may include a constitutional monarchy . . ."), note, especially, Stimson's opinion that "I personally think that if in saying this we should add that we do not exclude a constitutional monarchy under her present dynasty, it would substantially add to the chances of acceptance." HLS to HST, July 2, 1945, enclosed: *Proposed Program for Japan*, "White House Correspondence," Box 15, Stimson Safe File, Entry 74A, RG 107, NA; also in Stimson Diary, July 2, 1945, and FRUS, Pots. I, pp. 888–94.

48. On July 16, Stimson urged that "we formulate a warning to Japan to be delivered during the course of this Conference, and rather earlier than later, along the lines of the draft prepared by the War Department and now approved . . . by both the State and Navy Departments." FRUS, Pots. II, p. 1266. The twelfth paragraph of this approved draft stated that a peacefully inclined Japanese government "may include a constitutional monarchy under the present dynasty if the peace-loving nations can be convinced of the genuine determination of such a government to follow policies of peace which will render impossible the future development of aggressive militarism in Japan." FRUS, Pots. I, p. 899.

49. During a July 18 lunch with Truman, Churchill reports he "dwelt upon the tremendous cost in American life and, to a smaller extent, in British life which would be involved in forcing 'unconditional surrender' upon the Japanese. It was for him to consider whether this might not be expressed in some other way, so that we got all the essentials for future peace and security, and yet left the Japanese some show of saving their military honour and some assurance of their national existence, after they had complied with all safeguards necessary for the conqueror." Ehrman, *Grand Strategy*, pp. 302–03.

50. In a July 18 memorandum for the president, the Joint Chiefs of Staff stated: "From a strictly military point of view the Joint Chiefs of Staff consider it inadvisable to make any statement or take any action at the present time that would make it difficult or impossible to utilize the authority of the Emperor to direct a surrender of the Japanese forces in the outlying areas as well as in Japan proper." They recommended offering assurances in the following way: "Subject to suitable guarantees against further acts of aggression, the Japanese people will be free to choose their own form of government." FRUS, Pots. II, p. 1269.

51. On July 24, Stimson met with Truman and recorded in his diary: "I then spoke of the importance which I attributed to the reassurance of the Japanese on the continuance of their dynasty, and I had felt that the insertion of that in the formal warning was important and might be just the thing that would make or mar their acceptance. . . ." Stimson Diary, July 24, 1945.

52. For Stettinius' June 15 recommendations, see FRUS, Pots. I, p. 173. For the Joint Chiefs' position as of June 9, see SWNCC 149, "Immediate Demand for the Unconditional Surrender of Japan," June 9, 1945, "ABC 387 Japan (15 Feb. 45)," Entry 421, RG 165, NA. For details on their "end run" at Potsdam, see above, pp. 245–47.

53. Sigal, *Fighting to a Finish*, p. 86. McCloy's diary of July 17 also contains the following entry about Stimson's proposed warning of July 16: "It would probably bring what we are after—the successful termination of the war *and* at least put them in a great dither before it was turned down." McCloy Diary, July 17, 1945.

Chapter 24: Theories and Choices

1. Truman, *Off the Record*, ed. Ferrell, p. 56.
2. WB's Book, July 26, 1945, Folder 602, Byrnes Papers, CUL.
3. Sigal, *Fighting to a Finish*, p. 130.
4. Stimson Diary, July 17, 1945.
5. FRUS, Pots. II, pp. 39–40.
6. FRUS, Pots. II, p. 81; Ehrman, *Grand Strategy*, p. 303.
7. Memorandum of Conversation, July 17, 1945 (date is apparently incorrect on memorandum), "July 16–19, 1945," Box 181, Harriman Papers, LC.
8. FRUS, Pots. II, p. 1268.
9. Stimson Diary, July 24, 1945.
10. Ibid.
11. Ibid.
12. Spector, *Eagle Against the Sun*, p. 546.
13. See, for example, Bernstein, "Roosevelt, Truman and the A-Bomb," p. 56; Morton, "The Atomic Bomb and the Japanese Surrender," *Marine Corps Gazette*, Vol. 43, No. 2 (February 1959), p. 26; Sherwin, *A World Destroyed*, p. 229; Sigal, *Fighting to a Finish*, pp. 128–29.
14. FRUS, Pots. II, p. 1267.
15. "Off the Record Discussion of Origins of the Cold War," May 31, 1967, p. 19, "Memoirs-Chadwin Files-Interviews Harriman, W.A.," Box 869, Harriman Papers, LC.
16. WB's Book, August 22, 1945, James F. Byrnes Papers, Folder 602.
17. Byrnes interview with Fred Freed for NBC Paper, 1964, pp. 20–21, Box 79, Feis Papers, LC.
18. FRUS, Pots. II, p. 1267.
19. FRUS, Pots II, p. 1268.
20. On Hull's being kept in the dark, see Hull, *Memoirs*, Vol. II, p. 1110.
21. LRG to Kenneth Moll, September 3, 1945, Box 3, Entry 10, Groves Papers, RG 200, NA. Groves was commenting on Moll's article "The Birth of the A-Bomb . . . And the Aftermath," *Air Force Magazine*, August 1965, pp. 29–36.
22. FRUS, Pots. I, p. 896.
23. FRUS, Pots. I, p. 901.
24. Yergin, *Shattered Peace*, p. 122, footnote; Messer, *The End of an Alliance*, p. 126. See also Theodore Achilles Oral History interview with Philip A. Crowl, May 7, 1966, p. 2, John Foster Dulles Oral History Project, Mudd Library, Princeton University Archives.
25. JFB to LRG, May 1, 1952, Box 5, Entry 3, Groves Papers, RG 200, NA.
26. FRUS, Pots. I, p. 895.
27. Years later, looking back on the position he took with regard to the question of assurances, Acheson wrote that he "very shortly came to see that I was quite wrong." Dean Acheson, *Among Friends: Personal Letters of Dean Acheson* (New York, 1980), David S. McLellan and David C. Acheson, eds., p. 55.
28. One fragment—Truman's comment on June 18 that "that he had left the door open for Congress to take appropriate action with reference to unconditional surrender. However, he did not feel that he could take any action at this time to change public opinion on the matter"—possibly points in this direction. It is unclear, however, whether this is a reporting error, since there are no other indications that Congress was ever expected to act in this regard. (Possibly Truman said "that he had left the door open before Congress. . . .") Moreover, this comment was made several weeks before the Emperor's personal intervention in the surrender process. Furthermore, the president had already shown his willingness to begin to take public steps in this direction with his May 8 statement

calling for the unconditional surrender of the Japanese "armed forces." See above, p. 39. See also his statements of May 28 (pp. 45–46), June 18 (p. 69), and July 24, (p. 311).

29. LRG to Kenneth Moll, September 3, 1945, Box 3, Entry 10, Groves Papers, RG 200, NA.

30. "The Nation," *Time*, July 16, 1945, p. 15. For Senator Capehart's statements, see above, p. 229.

31. Arthur Krock, " 'Soft' Peace for Japan?" *The New York Times*, July 25, 1945, p. 4.

32. FRUS, Pots. I, pp. 198–201, 884.

33. Stimson Diary, July 24, 1945.

34. Stimson Diary, August 10, 1945.

Chapter 25: Unanswerable Questions

1. FRUS, Pots. II, p. 40.

2. FRUS, Pots. II, pp. 1268–69.

3. JFB to LRG, May 1, 1952, Box 5, Entry 3, Groves Papers, RG 200, NA.

4. Morton, "The Atomic Bomb and the Japanese Surrender," p. 27.

5. Castle Diary, February 9, 1947.

6. Alperovitz interview by Masakazu Nariai of the Tokyo Broadcasting System, Inc., April 16, 1994.

7. Andrew Goodpaster, "Memorandum of Conference with the President, April 6, 1960," April 11, 1960, "Staff Notes—April 1960," Folder 2, DDE Diary Series, Box 49, Dwight D. Eisenhower papers as president, DDEL.

8. "Discussion of the Question of Whether It Was Essential to Use the Atomic Bomb Against Japan," undated, Box 66, Feis Papers, LC.

9. Ibid.

10. Ibid.

11. Feis, "Draft," pp. 8–9, Box 66, Feis Papers, LC.

12. Feis, *Japan Subdued*, p. 181.

13. Herbert Feis, *The Atomic Bomb and the End of World War II* (Princeton, NJ, 1966), p. 194.

14. Groves, *Now It Can Be Told*, p. 292.

15. Preston, "Prelude to Cold War," p. 112.

Part VI: "Military Necessity":

Chapter 26: Navy Leaders

1. Memorandum for Chief, Strategic Policy Section, S&P Group, OPD, from Ennis, Subject: Use of the Atomic Bomb on Japan, April 30, 1946, "ABC 471.6 Atom (17 Aug. 45), Sec. 7, RG 471.6, Entry 421, RG 165, NA.

2. Handy to Spaatz, July 25, 1945, "July 1945," Box 21, Spaatz Papers, LC.

3. Hayes, *The History of the Joint Chiefs of Staff*, p. 723. One document that I have seen, a July 2 memorandum to Adm. King from his Chief of Staff, Vice Adm. Charles Cooke, Jr., does refer to a JCS luncheon the next day, July 3, at which "General Marshall will bring up . . . the special bombing of JAPAN project." However, clearly implying that a decision has already been made, it goes on: "The tentative date of first bombing is August 5th." Cooke to EJK, July 2, 1945, "Naval Career Office File," Box 22, Cooke Papers, HIA.

4. See, for example, C. H. Donnelly, Memorandum for General Ward, September 1, 1949, "Background: [illegible]," Box 69, OCMH, RG 319, NA; R.A. Winnacker, "CCS

Approval of the Use of the Atomic Bomb," August 24, 1949, "Background: [illegible]," Box 69, RG 319, NA. An exception is a statement that Army Chief of Staff George Marshall made to his biographer Forrest Pogue: "I was just as responsible [for the decision to use the bomb] as [Stimson] was, because my arguments were very much for using the bomb." Forrest C. Pogue, *George C. Marshall Interviews and Reminiscences for Forrest C. Pogue: Transcripts and Notes, 1956–57* (Lexington, 1986), p. 391. See above, pp. 358–365, for a discussion of Marshall's position.

5. Hayes, *The History of the Joint Chiefs of Staff*, p. 723.

6. Margaret Truman, *Harry S. Truman* (New York, 1973), p. 273.

7. William Hillman, ed., *Mr. President: Personal Diaries, Private Letters, Papers, and Revealing Interviews of Harry S. Truman, Thirty-Second President* (New York, 1952), p. 190; Margaret Truman, ed., *Where the Buck Stops: The Personal and Private Writings of Harry S. Truman* (New York, 1989), p. 205.

8. Barton Bernstein, "Ike and Hiroshima: Did He Oppose It?" *The Journal of Strategic Studies*, Vol. 10, No. 3 (Spring 1987), pp. 377–89, cited material from p. 379.

9. Garces to Truman, October 26, 1990, in author's collection; author to Truman, February 6, 1995. Referring to an account by President Truman edited by his daughter in *Where the Buck Stops: The Personal and Private Writings of Harry S. Truman* (New York: Warner Books, 1989), Barton Bernstein has noted that "Margaret Truman has never replied to any one of my six separate letters about the origin of this A-bomb manuscript, and apparently no archivist or historian has been able to track it down." (Barton Bernstein, "Writing, Righting, or Wronging the Historical Record: President Truman's Letter on His Atomic-Bomb Decision," *Diplomatic History*, Winter 1992, Vol. 16, No. 1 (Winter 1992), pp. 163–73, cited material from p. 172, fn. 28.)

10. David J. Williams, "Did the President Consult With the JCS at Potsdam Regarding the Atomic Bomb?," February 13, 1995, unpublished memorandum in the author's collection.

11. Ibid.

12. Leahy, *I Was There*, p. 441.

13. Leahy Diary, June 18, 1945.

14. FRUS, Pots. II, p. 37.

15. Leahy, *I Was There*, p. 419.

16. Ibid.

17. Leahy, *I Was There*, p. 348.

18. Truman, *Off the Record*, Ferrell, ed., p. 11.

19. Leahy, *I Was There*, p. 347.

20. Leahy, *I Was There*, pp. 347–48.

21. Leahy, *I Was There*, p. 385.

22. Baldwin interview with John T. Mason, Jr., July 28, 1975, p. 438, U.S. Naval Institute Oral History Program, USNI.

23. Ringquist interview with Henry H. Adams, no date. Cited in Henry Adams, *Witness to Power: The Life of Fleet Admiral William D. Leahy* (Annapolis, MD, 1985), p. 299.

24. Leahy interview with Jonathan Daniels, August 31, 1949, "Research Notes Used in Connection with Writing *The Man of Independence*," p. 2, Part I, Daniels Papers, HSTL.

25. Phillips, *The Truman Presidency*, p. 63.

26. Truman, *Year of Decisions*, p. 18.

27. Leahy, *I Was There*, inscription by President Truman, October 11, 1949.

28. See Sigal, *Fighting to a Finish*, p. 102; McCullough, *Truman*, p. 400; Ronald H. Spector, *Eagle Against the Sun: The American War With Japan* (New York, 1985), p. 541.

29. See, for example, Ernest J. King and Walter Muir Whitehill, *Fleet Admiral King: A Navy Record* (New York, 1952), p. 605.

30. King and Whitehill, *Fleet Admiral King*, p. 621.

31. Bieri interview with John T. Mason, Jr., July 17, 1969, p. 221, U.S. Naval Institute Oral History Program, USNI.

32. Bieri interview with John T. Mason, Jr. July 17, 1969, p. 222, U. S. Naval Institute Oral History Program, USNI. Various members of King's staff shared Bieri's judgment. Rear Adm. Malcolm F. Schoeffel, assistant chief of staff for operations, recalled in 1974 that one of King's planners, Rear Adm. Matthias B. Gardner, "urged him to oppose [Russian entry] at Potsdam, holding even before the A-bomb that we had the Japanese beaten." (Schoeffel to Buell, September 9, 1974, File 2, Box 2, Buell Papers, NHCNWC.) Capt. William Smedberg, King's combat intelligence officer, recalled in 1975 that his subordinate, Capt. William J. Sebald, had predicted in June of 1945 that Japan would fold up within two months if it was assumed that a catastrophe (like a massive earthquake) would strike the country in the imminent future. (Smedberg interview with John T. Mason, Jr., 1975, U.S. Naval Institute Oral History Program, USNI.) Sebald, however, recalled in 1977 that in June of 1945 he gave a two-month estimate "assuming that the same pressures were applied against the Japanese as we were then applying." He added that: "I felt that Japan was on the verge of collapse . . . it seemed clear to me that everything about the situation, with the economy in a state of collapse, lack of oil, tremendous losses which they were having, and the fear that the country itself would be destroyed completely, that the Japanese would come to their senses and surrender. . . . There was no question about it, they were whipped . . . the people . . . were completely dejected. Their biggest problem was to find food. They were on a starvation diet, the entire nation." (Sebald interview with James Plehal, 1977, pp. 326–27; pp. 364–65, U.S. Naval Institute Oral History Program, USNI.)

33. King and Whitehill, *Fleet Admiral King*, p. 605, fn. 2.

34. Memorandum for the Chief of Staff from Lt. Gen. Hull, April 26, 1945, "ABC 384 (1-17-43)," Box 457, Entry 421, RG 165, NA.

35. Luce, "How China Fell," from an unfinished book Luce was working on at the time of his death in 1967, printed in John K. Jessup, ed., *The Ideas of Henry Luce* (New York, 1969), p. 297.

36. E. B. Potter, *Nimitz* (Annapolis, MD, 1976), p. 384.

37. Dornin interview by Robert E. Dornin, Jr., May 10, 1982, pp. 17–18, U.S. Naval Institute Oral History Program, USNI.

38. Zacharias, *Secret Missions*, p. 345.

39. Unpublished Forrestal Diary, June 19, 1945, Memorandum of State-War-Navy Meeting.

40. "Miscellaneous notes of conversation with Admiral King," July 4, 1950, by Walter Muir Whitehill, Folder 8, Box 6, King Papers, NHCNWC.

41. *The New York Times*, September 22, 1945, p. 3.

42. *The New York Times*, October 6, 1945, p. 6. The testimony of Nimitz's personal wartime aide, H. Arthur Lamar, also helps illuminate his view. Recalling that Adm. Halsey had made a claim that he would ride Hirohito's personal horse following the surrender, he noted: "[Nimitz] told [Halsey], if you ever again use the expression, 'I'm going to ride the Emperor's white horse through the streets of Tokyo,' he'd relieve him of his command. [Nimitz] said, because the Emperor is the only person that can save our souls after we occupied Japan—and he was so right. . . ." Lamar interview with John T. Mason, Jr., May 3, 1970, p. 35, U.S. Naval Institute Oral History Program, USNI.

43. Hanson Baldwin, *Great Mistakes of the War* (New York, 1949), pp. 93–94.

44. Baldwin, *Great Mistakes of the War*, pp. 93–94.

45. Hill memorandum, November 17, 1966, cited in George Carroll Dyer, *The Amphibians Came to Conquer: The Story of Admiral Richard Kelly Turner* (Washington, D.C., 1972), p. 1108.

46. Potter, *Nimitz*, p. 386.

47. Nimitz interview with E. B. Potter, undated "Interviews w/Nimitz Relatives," Series XV, Nimitz Papers, Operational Archives Branch, NHC.

48. Fluckey interview with John T. Mason, Jr., October 20, 1971, pp. 4–5, U.S. Naval Institute Oral History Program, USNI. Subsequently Adm. Fluckey—citing the Japanese

warrior tradition which he investigated after the war—changed his mind on the use of the bomb. In a recent letter he states: "I now believe that the atomic bomb was absolutely necessary. I believe Nimitz would think so, also. . . ." Fluckey to author, May 12, 1995.

49. Mrs. Chester W. Nimitz and Nancy Nimitz interview with John T. Mason, Jr., June 8, 1969, p. 5, U.S. Naval Institute Oral History Program, USNI.

50. Mrs. Chester W. Nimitz and Nancy Nimitz interview, p. 6. Much earlier in 1945, when Nimitz was briefed on the atomic bomb, he reportedly told Frederick Ashworth, "That sounds fine, but this is only February. Can't we get one sooner?" (Knebel and Bailey, *No High Ground*, p. 90.)

51. Nimitz to Dr. Walter C. Michels of the Association of Philadelphia Scientists, September 21, 1946, "Correspondence—Nimitz, Chester, Dec. 1943–1947 and undated," Box 15, Halsey Papers, LC. Once the presidential decision to use the bombs had been made, Nimitz concurred in the recommendation of Capt. William Parsons (who armed the bomb aboard the *Enola Gay*), Adm. William R. Purnell (in charge of coordinating the handling of the atomic bomb with U.S. naval leadership in the Pacific), and Col. Elmer Kirkpatrick and General Thomas Farrell (Groves' representatives at Tinian) to use a third bomb on the Tokyo region. For Spaatz's concurring recommendation "in case" a third bomb was needed, see above, pp. 345–46. Kirkpatrick to Nimitz and Spaatz, August 9, 1945, August 1–15, 1945 official, "Box 24, Spaatz Papers, LC. See also Jones, *Manhattan, the Army, and the Atomic Bomb*, pp. 526–27, 534–35.

52. Baruch to JVF, September 10, 1946, James V. Forrestal File, Baruch Papers, PUL. In private correspondence later in the same year Halsey called the atomic bomb an "unholy weapon"; and testifying before Congress in 1949, he stated: "I believe that bombing—especially atomic bombing—of civilians, is morally indefensible. . . . I do not have to wrestle with my conscience. I know that the extermination theory has no place in a properly conducted war. . . ." (Halsey to Cherrington, December 12, 1946, "General Correspondence 1946 Nov–Dec," Box 5, Naval Historical Foundation Collection, LC, Testimony of Adm. Halsey, September 8, 1949, File: "Congressional Hearings 1949–57," Box 35, Halsey Papers, LC.) On the other hand, a May 1944 newsreel quoted Halsey as saying, "We are drowning and burning the bestial apes all over the Pacific, and it is just as much pleasure to burn them as to drown them. . . ." Dwight MacDonald, *Memoirs of a Revolutionist: Essays in Political Criticism* (New York, 1957), p. 93. And at around this time, Halsey also told an off-the-record dinner of Washington newsmen, "I hate Japs. I'm telling you men that if I met a pregnant Japanese woman, I'd kick her in the belly. . . ." MacDonald, *Memoirs of A Revolutionist*, p. 93.

53. Dennison interview with John T. Mason, Jr., January 17, 1973, p. 80, U.S. Naval Institute Oral History Program, USNI.

54. Ibid., pp. 87, 83–84. Similarly, consider the views of Capt. Robert E. Dornin (whose report of King's position is cited above):

> The Russians had agreed to come in the war against Japan three months after the Germans had surrendered. . . . we were reading the Japanese dispatches right and left; we were breaking their codes. We knew that they had made overtures . . . to the Russians . . . for a surrender. . . . The B-29s with their fire bombs from Saipan had practically burned out Tokyo and the submarines had strangled their only pipeline for oil or any needed imports. So there they were—they were starving to death and there was nothing left. (Dornin interview by Robert E. Dornin, Jr., May 10, 1982, pp. 16–17, U.S. Naval Institute Oral History Program, USNI.) See also endnote 32, above.

55. Luce, "How China Fell," Jessup, ed. *The Ideas of Henry Luce*, p. 203.

56. Byrd to EJK, November 28, 1952, "Correspondence Richard Byrd," Box 7, King Papers, LC. Similarly, in the mid-1960s Rear Adm. Harold C. Train, a former director of Naval Intelligence, offered this judgment: "we had Japan defeated in World War II long before we dropped the atom bomb, and Russia wasn't in the war." Interview with Rear

Adm. Harold C. Train, 1965–66, p. 218, Columbia Oral History Program, Butler Library, Columbia University. And Capt. William Parsons, the naval officer in charge of the Ordnance Division at Los Alamos (best known as the man who armed the atomic bomb on board the *Enola Gay*), in 1948 wrote:

> I think the feasibility and effectiveness of a warning of atomic attack on cities, plants, etc., depends decisively on the circumstances. The conditions in Japan at the end of July 1945 were ideal for such warning. (Parsons to Livingston Hartley, December 7, 1948, "Correspondence, 1948," Box 1 Naval Historical Foundation Collection, Parsons Papers, LC.)

57. See Ralph A. Bard, Memorandum on the Use of the S-1 Bomb, June 27, 1945, File 77, H-B Files, M1108, NA.

58. Strauss interview for NBC White Paper, 1964, pp. 18–19, Box 103, Feis Papers, LC.

59. Strauss interview for NBC White Paper, 1964, pp. 13–14, Box 103, Feis Papers, LC.

60. Ibid., p. 16.

Chapter 27: Air Force Leaders

1. *The New York Times*, August 18, 1945, p. 4.

2. H. H. Arnold, *Global Mission* (New York, 1949), p. 598.

3. "Report on Army Air Operations in the War Against Japan," CCS 894, p. 8, "ABC Decimal File, 1942–1948, Japan (9 Nov. 43), Sec. 3," Box 479, Entry 421, RG 165, NA; FRUS, Pots. II, p. 38.

4. Eaker interview with Charles Hildreth and Alfred Goldberg, May 22, 1962, p. 4, U.S. Air Force Oral History Program, AFHRA.

5. Eaker interview with Hugh N. Ahmann, February 10–11, 1975, p. 559, U.S. Air Force Oral History Program, AFHRA.

6. Herman S. Wolk, "The B-29, the A-Bomb, and the Japanese Surrender," *Air Force Magazine* (February 1975), pp. 55–61, cited material from p. 60. Arnold, *Global Mission*, p. 598.

7. *The New York Times*, August 15, 1945, p. 13.

8. *The New York Herald Tribune*, September 21, 1945, p. 4.

9. Press conference of Lt. Gen. Barney Giles, Maj. Gen. LeMay, and Brig. Gen. Emmett O'Donnell, September 20, 1945, 8.76, Box 50, Murray Green Collection, USAFAL.

10. "Air Power," Speech of Gen. Curtis LeMay at the Ohio Society of New York, New York City, November 19, 1945, p. 12, File B-11, Box 41, LeMay Papers, LC.

11. Eaker interview with Dr. Charles Hildreth and Dr. Alfred Goldberg, May 22, 1962, p. 4, U.S. Air Force Oral History Program, AFHRA. Following Air Force Historical Division procedure, Eaker was given the option to make changes to the transcript; he rewrote this sentence to read: "I know nobody in high echelons of the AAF who thought it would be necessary to invade Japan"—adding, "The effectiveness of the Air Attack on Japan had already demonstrated that Japan could be destroyed by conventional bombing."

12. Kenney interview with Col. Marvin M. Stanley, January 25, 1969, U.S. Air Force Oral History Program, AFHRA. In 1967, when Arnold's former executive officer, Brig. Gen. Emmett O'Donnell, was asked "Did we have to drop the bomb?", he responded: Well, that backsight [*sic*]. I don't know. I would think not, because I think we could have run—but that was a political decision again. And these political decisions in military affairs can become very, very rough. And of course, the fact of the matter was that they are made, and you just live by them. They had $2 billion spent on the bomb, and they had

to justify it, apparently." O'Donnell interview with Murray Green, December 2, 1967, 8.76, Murray Green Collection, USAFAL.

13. Averell Harriman, "Notes on a recent dinner with Generals Spaatz and Anderson, Nov. 9," November 11, 1965, "Memoirs—Chadwin Files—Planning Notes and Outlines," Box 871, Harriman Papers, LC.

14. Ibid.

15. Quoted in Norstad to LeMay, April 17, 1945, cited by Murray Green, 8.70, Murray Green Collection, USAFAL.

16. LeMay interview with either Len Giovannitti or Fred Freed, sometime between May 1964 and February 1965, cited in Giovannitti and Freed, *The Decision to Drop the Bomb*, p. 308.

17. Arnold diary of Pacific Trip, June 13, 1945, "Pacific Trip," Box 272, Arnold Papers, LC.

18. Wilson interview with Dr. Henry L. Bower, October 13, 1961, p. 5, U.S. Air Force Oral History Program, AFHRA. See also p. 602 above for Wilson in connection with MED.

19. Martin interview with Lt. Col. Vaughn Gallacher, February 6–10, 1978, p. 104, U.S. Air Force Oral History Program, AFHRA.

20. Curtis E. LeMay with MacKinlay Kantor, *Mission with LeMay: My Story* (Garden City, NY, 1965), p. 388.

21. LeMay with Kantor, *Mission with LeMay*, p. 388.

22. LeMay with Kantor, *Mission with LeMay*, p. 381.

23. LeMay interview with U.S. Air Force Historical Division, January 12, 26, 27, 1965, p. 2, U.S. Air Force Oral History Program, AFHRA.

24. LeMay with Kantor, *Mission with LeMay*, p. 369.

25. LeMay interview with Dr. Murray Green, March 14, 1970, 8.76, Box 50, Murray Green Collection, USAFAL.

26. Ibid.

27. *Omaha World-Herald*, August 4, 1985, pp. 1–12.

28. Curtis E. LeMay and Bill Yenne, *Superfortress: The Story of the B-29 and American Air Power* (New York, 1988), p. 155.

29. LeMay and Yenne, *Superfortress*, p. 155.

30. That Arnold clearly had to have been aware of the difference between a demand for "unconditional surrender" and a surrender based upon some assurances for the Emperor, may also help explain two seeming inconsistencies in the record. In his Potsdam diary he mentions that on July 16 he bet Britain's Air Marshal Sir Charles Portal that the war would end closer to Christmas Day, 1945, than Valentine's Day, 1946. Arnold diary, Terminal Conference, July 16, "Journals—Terminal Conf.," Box 272, Arnold Papers, LC. However, at another point sometime during the first four days of the conference, he also is reported to have bet Major-General Sir Hastings Ismay two dollars that the Japanese "do not fold up this year." Hastings Lionel Ismay, *The Memoirs of General Lord Ismay* (New York, 1960), p. 401. Arnold's first wager was made the same day the U.S. and British Chiefs agreed to try to get Truman to modify the terms. The "Christmas Day" estimate may well reflect the uncertainty and ambiguity before Churchill made his approach to Truman. The second bet quite possibly reflects insider knowledge that the president had declined to alter the surrender formula and that, therefore, surrender would be far more difficult. A related point involves the distinction between the disintegration of effective resistance to the surrender demand (which on July 16 Arnold estimated would occur in October) and the actual formal end of the war on the basis of no change in the unconditional-surrender demand (which the same day he reckoned would be closer to December 25, 1945, than February 14, 1946). Though a full clarification of this issue is not possible, in either case note that Arnold judged an invasion to be unnecessary.

31. Kissner interview with Dr. Murray Green, May 21, 1972, 8.76, Box 50, Murray Green Collection, USAFAL.

32. See, for example, Truman, *Harry S. Truman*, p. 273; LeMay with Kantor, *Mission with LeMay*, p. 381.

33. Conrad C. Crane, *Bombs, Cities, and Civilians: American Airpower Strategy in World War II* (Lawrence, KS, 1993), p. 139; Paul H. Nitze, *From Hiroshima to Glasnost: At the Center of Decision, A Memoir* (New York, 1989), pp. 34–37.

34. Directive to Commanding General, United States Army Strategic Air Forces, July 25, 1945, "July 1945," Box 21, Spaatz Papers, LC.

35. Eaker interview with Dr. Forrest Pogue, July 10, 1959, p. 7, Pogue Papers, GCMRL.

36. Ibid.

37. Wolk to Eaker, October 19, 1974. In possession of Dr. Wolk.

38. Eaker to Wolk, October 22, 1974. In possession of Dr. Wolk. My thanks to Dr. Wolk for confirming this correspondence to Sanho Tree, March 31, 1995.

39. Eaker interview with Hugh N. Ahmann, February 10–11, 1975, p. 551, U.S. Oral History Program, AFHRA.

40. Craven and Cate, *The Army Air Forces in World War II*, Vol. V, p. 700.

41. Spaatz to Eaker, 020141Z August 1945, cited in Craven and Cate, *The Army Air Forces in World War II*, Vol. V, pp. 731–32.

42. Spaatz Diary, August 11, 1945, "August 1945 Personal," Box 20, Spaatz Papers, LC.

43. Ibid.

44. Carl Spaatz to Ruth Spaatz, August 18, 1945, "Private diary 1945, Jan.–Aug.," Box 20, Spaatz Papers, LC.

45. Spaatz interview with Brig. Gen. Noel Parrish and Alfred Goldberg, February 21, 1962, p. 4, U.S. Air Force Oral History Program, AFHRA.

46. Spaatz interview with Forrest Pogue, July 24, 1959, p. 13, Pogue Papers, GCMRL.

47. Spaatz interview with Alfred Goldberg, May 19, 1965, p. 22, U.S. Air Force Oral History Program, AFHRA. Spaatz goes on to say, however, that U.S. policy was committed to a landing and if it had in fact been undertaken the losses would have been heavy (pp. 22–23).

48. Handy interview with LTC Edward M. Knoff, Jr., 1974, p. 42, Senior Officers Oral History Program, Handy Papers, USAMHI.

49. Spaatz interview with Brig. Gen. Noel Parrish and Alfred Goldberg, February 21, 1962, p. 4, U.S. Air Force Oral History Program, AFHRA.

50. Spaatz interview with Alfred Goldberg, May 19, 1965, pp. 5–6, U.S. Air Force Oral History Program, AFHRA.

51. Spaatz interview with Len Giovannitti for NBC White Paper, 1964, p. 8, Box 103, Feis Papers, LC.

52. Spaatz interview with Alfred Goldberg, May 19, 1965, p. 6, U.S. Air Force Oral History Program, AFHRA.

53. Spaatz interview with Noel Parrish and Alfred Goldberg, February 21, 1962, p. 4, U.S. Air Force Oral History Program, AFHRA. According to Vice Adm. F. L. Ashworth, on hearing that the second bomb had missed the center of Nagasaki, Gen. James Doolittle observed (in a discussion on Okinawa): "Well, I think that General Spaatz will be much happier that it went off up here in this valley and not over the city." (Ashworth interview with A. B. Christman, April 1969, p. 30, Naval Weapons Center/Parsons Collection Operational Archives Branch, NHC)

54. Martin interview with LTC Vaughn Gallacher, February 6–10, 1978, pp. 144–45, U.S. Air Force Oral History Program, AFHRA. Martin offered his own view, too (in 1978), that the defeat of Japan is "generally concluded to be the result of the two atomic bombs. But that's *not* the case . . ."

it's easy to attribute the lack of an invasion necessity in Japan to this new mysterious, technological device, the nuclear weapon, and let it go at that. Essentially, the reason that an invasion was not required was because of airpower, of which the nuclear weapon was a part. But according to people like Spaatz, LeMay, Norstad, an invasion would not have been necessary anyway, without the nuclear weapons. And I am of that school of thought myself. (Martin interview with LTC Vaughn Gallacher, February 6–10, 1978, pp. 140, 143–44, U.S. Air Force Oral History Program, AFHRA.)

55. DoD, *Top Secret Entry*, Sec. V, p. 27.
56. Eaker interview with Dr. Forrest Pogue, July 10, 1959, p. 6, Pogue Papers, GCMRL.
57. Eaker interview with LTC Joe B. Green, March 20, 1972, p. 42, Senior Officers Oral History Program, Eaker Papers, USAMHI.
58. Ira C. Eaker, "Gen. Carl A. Spaatz, USAF," *Air Force Magazine* (September 1974), pp. 43–48, cited material from p. 47.
59. Eaker interview with Dr. Forrest Pogue, July 10, 1959, pp. 6–7, Pogue Papers, GCMRL.
60. Parton to Ira and Ruth Eaker, March 31, 1983, "James Parton File—Correspondence," Box 149, Eaker Papers, LC.
61. Ibid.
62. Smith, "Behind the Decision to Use the Atomic Bomb," p. 297.
63. Kuter interview with Hugh N. Ahmann and Tom Sturm, September 30–October 3, 1974, p. 355, U.S. Air Force Oral History Program, AFHRA.
64. Haywood S. Hansell, *Strategic Air War Against Japan* (Maxwell Air Force Base, AL: Air War College, 1980), p. 69.
65. Interview for the program, "Citizen Soldier: George Marshall and the American Century," p. 11, Great Projects Film Company, Inc. Copyright 1989. Transcript available at GCMRL.
66. Hansell, *Strategic Air War Against Japan*, p. 69.
67. Nitze interview with author, September 27, 1990.
68. Nitze interview with author, September 27, 1990.

Chapter 28: Army Leaders

1. Knebel and Bailey, *No High Ground*, pp. 141–42; Eaker interview with Hugh N. Ahmann, February 10–11, 1975, pp. 552–53, U.S. Air Force Oral History Program, AFHRA; Spaatz Diary, August 1, 1945, "August 1945 Personal," Box 21, Spaatz Papers, LC.
2. Weldon E. Rhoades, *Flying MacArthur to Victory* (College Station, 1987), p. 429.
3. HH Diary, 1946 Journey, May 4, 5, 6, 1946, Post-Presidential Papers, HHPL.
4. Norman Cousins, *The Pathology of Power* (New York, 1987), p. 71.
5. D. Clayton James, *The Years of MacArthur*, Vol. II: 1941–1945 (Boston, 1975), p. 775.
6. Handy interview with LTC Edward M. Knoff, Jr., 1974, p. 45, Senior Officers Oral History Program, Handy Papers, USAMHI.
7. Crane, *Bombs, Cities, and Civilians*, p. 123. For the Korean War period, see Michael Schaller, *Douglas MacArthur: The Far Eastern General* (New York, 1989), pp. 225–26; William Manchester, *American Caesar: Douglas MacArthur, 1880–1964* (Boston, 1978), p. 627.
8. Fellers, memorandum to Lt. Col. Greene, June 17, 1945, "Correspondence" Box 3, Bonner Frank Fellers Collection, HIA.
9. Bonner Fellers, "Hirohito's Struggle to Surrender," *Reader's Digest* (July 1947), pp. 90–95, cited material from p. 93.
10. In connection with postwar statements by MacArthur contradicting his 1945 recom-

mendations for Soviet help in the Pacific War, his biographer D. Clayton James states simply that ". . . MacArthur's traits included a desperate need to save face, even if it involved lying." James, *The Years of MacArthur*, p. 765. See also Manchester, *American Caesar*, p. 428.

11. In a recent letter to me, infantry veteran Robert Klein reported that MacArthur personally told him that the bomb had aborted an invasion. (Klein to author, February 28, 1995.) Undoubtedly, MacArthur—and perhaps other military leaders—offered off-the-cuff informal comments of varying degrees of precision at various times. As we have seen, however, there is little doubt about the overall thrust of statements by such leaders made in formal interviews, diaries, and private letters.

12. "What the President Saw: A Nation Coming into Its Own," *Time*, July 29, 1985, p. 48.

13. Edgar Snow, *Journey to the Beginning: A Personal View of Contemporary History* (New York, 1958), pp. 360–61.

14. Also, of course, while he held office, the credibility of America's nuclear deterrent depended heavily upon his public statements.

15. Forrestal, *The Forrestal Diaries*, Millis, ed., pp. 78–79; Unpublished Forrestal Diary, April 25, 1947.

16. HLS, "The Conduct of the War with Japan," July 16, 1945, "Stimson, Henry L.," Box 111, Pre-Presidential Papers, DDEL. For confirmation that Stimson met Eisenhower at both his office and his home, see his letter to Eisenhower of August 8. (HLS to Eisenhower, August 8, 1945, "Stimson, Henry L.," Box 111, Pre-Presidential Papers, DDEL.)

17. Dwight D. Eisenhower, *Crusade in Europe* (Garden City, NY, 1948), p. 443.

18. Eisenhower to Pawley, April 9, 1955, Roll 6, Frame 198–199, Eisenhower Papers, LC.

19. Ibid.

20. Ibid.

21. Ibid.

22. Goodpaster, "Memorandum of Conference with the President, April 6, 1960" April 11, 1960, Staff Notes—April, 1960, Folder 2, Box 49, DDE Diary Series, Dwight D. Eisenhower papers as president, DDEL.

23. Ibid.

24. Dwight D. Eisenhower, *Mandate for Change*, pp. 312–13.

25. "Ike on Ike," *Newsweek*, November 11, 1963, pp. 107–10, cited material from p. 107. See also Eisenhower to McCloy, June 18, 1965, "McA--," Box 14, Secretary's Series, Post-Presidential Papers, DDEL; John N. Wheeler's 1966 *Houston Chronicle* article. "Excerpt from an article written by John N. Wheeler (United Feature Syndicate) appearing in the *Houston Chronicle*, August 1, 1966, "Atom Bomb—Wheeler Article," Convenience File, Box 1, Post-Presidential Papers, DDEL. In addition, Eisenhower wrote his brother Milton in 1968 that "I criticized at the time, the use of that slogan [unconditional surrender] in World War II." DDE to Milton Eisenhower, January 15, 1968, "Correspondence 1968," Box 15, Milton Eisenhower Papers, DDEL.

26. Podell and Anzovia, eds., *Speeches of the American Presidents*, p. 595.

27. Ibid.

28. See, for example, Barton J. Bernstein, "Ike and Hiroshima," pp. 377–89; Robert James Maddox, "Why We Had to Drop the Atomic Bomb," *American Heritage*, May/June 1995, pp. 71–77.

29. John Eisenhower interview with Ed Edwin, February 28, 1967, DDEL.

30. John Eisenhower, *Strictly Personal* (Garden City, NY, 1974), p. 97.

31. Eisenhower, *Mandate for Change*, p. 577. In 1958 *Time* put it this way: "Dwight Eisenhower's inner circle includes many top aides. Yet none of these friends approaches Milton Eisenhower in the heart and mind of his brother Dwight." A year later a piece in the *New York Times Magazine* observed that

A President must have at least one friend, and this friend must know what he is talking about when he discusses public affairs. . . . The only person who really qualifies is Milton. . . . Theirs is a relationship in which neither has to finish a sentence.

Cited in Milton Eisenhower, *The President Is Calling* (Garden City, NY, 1974), pp. 312–13.

32. Snow, *Journey to the Beginning*, p. 360.

33. Milton Eisenhower, *The President Is Calling*, pp. 220–21.

34. Eisenhower, *The President Is Calling*, p. 220.

35. Stephen E. Ambrose, *Eisenhower*, Vol. I: *Soldier, General of the Army, President-Elect, 1890–1952* (New York, 1983), pp. 425–26. Perhaps future historians will discover contemporaneous documentary evidence which provides additional confirming details concerning the advice Eisenhower gave to Stimson and Truman. The presence of the July 16 Stimson memo in his files suggests serious discussions. Aside from the fact that he had little to gain from distorting the record—indeed, taking a hard-line view was popular and common during the Cold War—the essential consistency of statements made over many years suggests that his recollection was probably accurate in all important essentials.

In any event, of course, there is no doubt whatsoever about his personal opinion: Eisenhower, like Leahy, King, Nimitz, LeMay, Arnold, Spaatz, and MacArthur—and, as we shall see, in all probability, Marshall—did not agree with the argument later put forward, that the atomic bomb was the only way to end the war without an invasion.

36. A typical position taken by Marshall personally, as we have also seen, is the following (from a memorandum sent to Stimson on June 9) suggesting that

we take action to discourage public use of the term "unconditional surrender," which we all agree is difficult to define, and encourage instead more definitive public statements concerning our policy and war aims. We should cease talking about unconditional surrender of Japan and begin to define our true objective in terms of defeat and disarmament. "Memorandum for the Secretary of War, Subject: Basic Objective in the Pacific War," June 9, 1945, "Japan (After Dec. 7/41)," Box 8, Entry 74A, Stimson Safe File, RG 107, NA.

37. Truman interview with William Hillman and David M. Noyes, April 15, 1954, Box 9, Memoirs Collection, HSTL.

38. Bonesteel interview with LTC Robert St. Louis, November 9, 1972, p. 187, Senior Officers Oral History Program, USAMHI.

39. Clarke interview with Dr. Forrest Pogue, July 6, 1959, p. 29, Pogue Papers, GCMRL.

40. Lincoln to Wedemeyer, July 10, 1945, Wedemeyer Folder, Box 5, Lincoln Papers, USMAL. Lincoln, however, was subsequently to claim that there was no other choice but to use the bomb. (George A. Lincoln, "Memorandum for Director, Historical Division, WDSS, Subject: Comment on Study Prepared by P&O Historian Concerning Historical Facts Related to the Use of the Atomic Bomb," October 11, 1946, "ABC 471.6 Atom (17 Aug 45) Sec. 7," Entry 421, RG 165, NA.)

41. Telford Taylor, *The Anatomy of the Nuremberg Trials: A Personal Memoir* (New York, 1992), p. xi.

42. Forrest C. Pogue, *George C. Marshall Interviews and Reminiscences for Forrest C. Pogue: Transcripts and Notes, 1956–57* (Lexington, VA. George C. Marshall Research Foundation, 1986), p. 391.

43. Pogue, *George C. Marshall Interviews and Reminiscences*, p. 391. Regarding the question of peace feelers, Marshall told Pogue also that

The Japanese peace offers to the Russians—I don't know the details about that. But I had been reading all the prime minister said to the various ambassadors of Japan, and he was unable at that time to direct the army. The army was dominant in these matters and they could only apparently be slugged into submission. And we slugged them. (Pogue, *George C. Marshall Interviews*, p. 391.)

44. John P. Sutherland, "The Story Gen. Marshall Told Me," *U.S. News and World Report*, November 2, 1959, pp. 50–56, cited material on pp. 52–53. As noted, Acheson also reported that Marshall—who had just been named secretary of state—was pleased with Stimson's 1947 *Harper's* article. (See above, pp. 456–57.)

45. Ed Cray, *General of the Army: George C. Marshall, Soldier and Statesman* (New York: 1990), p. 6. Marshall's deputy, Gen. Thomas Handy—the man Spaatz forced to sign the actual order—also was to regularly defend the use of the atomic bomb during the postwar and Cold War years. On the other hand, Handy stated in 1974:

> It [the unconditional surrender formula] sounded good at the time [when Roosevelt announced it in January 1943] and nobody had ever thought the thing through. But as far as the Joint Chiefs of Staff advocating it as soon as we got round to thinking about it and particularly when we got involved with the Japs toward the end, everybody knew it was a big mistake. And furthermore, you never want to put your enemy in the position where he is a cornered rat; where it's do or die; where it's either this or absolute curtains. . . . (Handy interview with LTC Edward M. Knoff, Jr., 1974, p. 16, Senior Officers Oral History Program, Handy Papers, USAMHI.)

46. Related to this is Marshall's dislike of controversy in general: when Groves and Stimson met with Truman on April 25, Marshall, who was originally scheduled to come, backed out at the last minute. Groves made a written note to himself that "Mr. Stimson and I agreed that General Marshall's decision might have been influenced by the possibility that the meeting would be very unpleasant." William Lawren, *The General and the Bomb: A Biography of Leslie R. Groves, Director of the Manhattan Project* (New York, 1988), p. 194. (Groves had had clashes with then-Senator Truman earlier in the war over MED expenditures.)

47. *Congressional Record*, June 14, 1951, p. 6602, cited in Cray, *General of the Army*, p. 722.

48. Walter Trohan, "The Tragedy of General Marshall," *American Mercury*, Vol. LXXII, No. 327 (March 1951), p. 273.

49. Cray, *General of the Army*, p. 721. For another such attack, see Forrest Davis, "Did Marshall Prolong the Pacific War?," *The Freeman*, November 15, 1951, pp. 73–75.

50. David Ignatius, "They Don't Make Them Like George Marshall Anymore," *Washington Post Weekly Edition*, June 8, 1987, p. 25, cited in Cray, *General of the Army*, p. 723.

51. Sutherland, "The Story Gen. Marshall Told Me," *U.S. News and World Report*, p. 52.

52. Pogue, *George C. Marshall Interviews and Reminiscences for Forrest C. Pogue*, p. 386.

53. Lilly, "Memorandum of Interview with General George C. Marshall, 10 February, 1949," February 11, 1949, "Atom," Box 2, Lilly Papers, JCS Historical Section, RG 218, NA.

54. Forrest C. Pogue, *George C. Marshall*, Vol. IV: *Statesman, 1945–1959* (New York, 1987), p. 550, fn. 30.

55. Ibid.

56. McCloy to Hadsel, April 8, 1985, Series 33, Folder 46, COR4, McCloy Papers, ACA.

57. McCloy to Parsons, January 18, 1985, Folder 74, COR4, McCloy Papers, ACA.

58. John J. McCloy, unpublished memoir, in Reston, *Deadline*, pp. 494–95.

59. John Eisenhower interview with Ed Edwin, February 28, 1967, DDEL.

Chapter 29: Additional Perspectives

1. Leslie Groves, "Memorandum to the Chief of Staff," July 30, 1945, MEDTS Folder, Tab C, M1108, NA. This document was declassified after the series was microfilmed, and therefore can be obtained through the Military Reference Branch of the National Archives.

2 Skates, *The Invasion of Japan*, pp. 52–58.

3. Ibid.

4. Stimson Diary, June 19, 1945.

5. Hull interview with LTC James W. Wurman, 1974, p. 16, Senior Officers Oral History Program, Hull Papers, USAMHI, As Adm. Leahy later recalled: "The JCS did order the preparation of plans for an invasion, but *the invasion itself was never authorized*." Leahy, *I Was There*, p. 245. Adm. King put it this way with regard to the main attack at the June 18 meeting:

> . . . so far as preparation was concerned, we must aim now for Tokyo Plain; otherwise we will never be able to accomplish it. If preparations do not go forward now, they cannot be arranged for later. Once started, however, they can always be stopped if desired. . . . DoD, *Top Secret Entry*, Sec. V, p. 24; DoD, *Entry*, p. 81. See also Dennison interview with John T. Mason, Jr., November, 1972–July, 1973, p. 70, U.S. Naval Institute Oral History Program, USNI; WDL " 'I Was There' Press Conference, 1950," p. 6, Box 10, Leahy Papers, LC.

6. FRUS, Pots. II, p. 1464.

7. FRUS, Pots. II, pp. 1469–72.

8. Joint Chiefs of Staff to MacArthur, Item 11, Exec. 2, Box 32, "Miscellany (19 Nov. 1943–December 1945)," Entry 422, OPD Executive Files, RG 165, NA: for the date of this document, see DoD, *Entry*, p. 106.

9. JCS 1331/6, "Occupation of Strategic Areas in Japan Proper in Event of Collapse or Surr.," July 30, 1945, cited in Cline, *Washington Command Post*, p. 349.

10. "Memorandum for the Chief of Staff," April 26, 1945, by Lt. Gen. John E. Hull, "ABC 384 (1-17-43) Sec. 9," Box 457, Entry 421, RG 165, NA.

11. DoD, *Top Secret Entry*, Sec. V, p. 23; DoD, *Entry*, p. 80.

12. United States Strategic Bombing Survey, *Japan's Struggle to End the War*, p. 13.

13. Memorandum for Chief, Strategic Policy Section, S&P Group, OPD, Subject: Use of Atomic Bomb on Japan, April 30, 1946, p. 5, "ABC 471.6 Atom (17 Aug. 45), Sec. 7," Entry 421, RG 165, NA.

14. Baldwin, *Great Mistakes of the War*, p. 92.

15. Carl Borklund, *Men of the Pentagon* (New York, 1966), p. 20.

16. Cited in Christopher Thorne, *Allies of a Kind: The United States, Britain, and the War Against Japan, 1941–45* (New York, 1978), p. 531.

17. Ismay, *The Memoirs*, p. 375.

18. Ismay, *The Memoirs*, p. 401. Ismay went on to say that "I had always had a sneaking hope that the scientists would be unable to find a key to this particular chamber of horrors. But first thoughts were soon erased by a surge of thankfulness that the secret had eluded our enemies."

19. Cited in Thorne, *Allies of a Kind*, pp. 533–34.

20. Churchill to Stalin, September 27, 1944, in Churchill, *Triumph and Tragedy*, p. 215.

21. FRUS, Malta and Yalta, p. 826.

22. WSC, Note to the Cabinet, quoted in Ehrman, *Grand Strategy*, pp. 302–03.

23. Churchill, *Triumph and Tragedy*, p. 639; Bryant, *Triumph in the West*, pp. 363–64.

24. James, ed., *Winston S. Churchill: His Complete Speeches*, Vol. VII, p. 7210.

Part VII: Endgame

Chapter 30: Relations of Frankness

1. Stimson Diary, July 23, 1945.

2. Diary, July 21, 1945, Box 18, Davies Papers, LC.

3. Off the Record Discussion of Origins of the Cold War, May 31, 1967, pp. 70–71, "Memoirs-Chadwin Files-Interviews Harriman, W.A.," Box 869, Harriman Papers, LC.

4. Dooman to Feis, December 7, 1960, "Letters about Japan Subdued," Box 20, Feis papers, LC.

5. Off the Record Discussion of the Origins of the Cold War, May 31, 1967, pp. 19–20, "Memoirs-Chadwin Files-Interviews Harriman, W.A.," Box 869, Harriman Papers, LC.

6. See FRUS, Pots. II, pp. 10–21, fns. The meeting on July 16 also involved Leahy; the one on July 17 included Harriman and Pauley. For July 18, the log states: "The President conferred with the Secretary of State and a number of his advisers during the forenoon." The editors of FRUS note: "No reference has been found of the discussion that took place at the meeting or meetings referred to other than . . . [the Stimson Diary of July 18, relating to Harrison's second message.]" Meetings on the 21st and 24th were Byrnes/Truman discussions exclusively, and to my knowledge no record of the discussion has been found. The meetings of the 27th and 28th were with Leahy, and are mentioned briefly in his diary.

7. FRUS, Pots. I, p. xxiii.

8. See Herbert Feis, "HF mtgs w/Byrnes," February 27, 1958, Byrnes draft manuscript file, Box 65, Feis Papers, LC. Feis' memorandum includes a handwritten note by Byrnes concerning his time at Potsdam: "The Pres and I lunched together every day. . . ."

9. On similar close relationships, see Sherwood, *Roosevelt and Hopkins*; Arthur Schlesinger, Jr., *A Thousand Days: John F. Kennedy in the White House* (Boston, 1965); Rowland Evans, Jr. and Robert Novak, *Nixon in the White House: The Frustration of Power* (New York, 1971); Bob Woodward, *The Commanders* (New York, 1991).

10. See Churchill, *Triumph and Tragedy*, p. 215, and FRUS, Malta and Yalta, p. 826.

11. FRUS, Pots. I, pp. 897–98.

12. FRUS, Pots. I, p. 173.

13. Forrestal, *The Forrestal Diaries*, ed. Millis, pp. 71–72.

14. Unpublished Forrestal Diary, June 26, 1945.

15. Unpublished Forrestal Diary, June 26, 1945; also, Forrestal, *The Forrestal Diaries*, ed. Millis, pp. 71–72.

16. Grew, *Turbulent Era*, Vol. II, p. 1437.

17. Stimson Diary, June 19, 1945.

18. HLS to HST, July 2, 1945, enclosure: *Proposed Program for Japan*, "White House Correspondence," Box 15, Stimson Safe File, Entry 74A, RG 107, NA; also Stimson Diary, July 2, 1945, and FRUS, Pots. I, pp. 891–92.

19. Memorandum for Colonel Stimson, from McCloy, June 29, 1945, "Japan (After Dec. 7/14)," Box 8, Stimson Safe File, Entry 74A, RG 107, NA.

20. FRUS, Pots. I, p. 201.

21. FRUS, Pots. I, pp. 226–27.

22. FRUS, Pots. I, p. 201, fn. 7.

23. FRUS, Pots. II, pp. 1265–67.

24. Brown, *James F. Byrnes*, p. 284.

25. FRUS, Pots. II, p. 460.

26. FRUS, Pots. II, p. 476.

27. Byrnes, *All in One Lifetime*, p. 298; see also, Byrnes, *Speaking Frankly*, p. 208.

28. Brown, *James F. Byrnes*, p. 285.

29. FRUS, Pots. II, pp. 1333–34.

30. Robert Messer, "New Evidence on Truman's Decision," p. 56. For details on the Combined Chiefs' policy on Soviet Entry at Potsdam see CCS 877/5 (TERMINAL), "Basic Objectives, Strategy and Policies," July 21, 1945, "CCS 381 (5-13-45)," RG 218, NA; also, DoD, *Entry*, pp. 90–104.

31. CCS 877/5 (TERMINAL), "Basic Objectives, Strategy and Policies," July 21, 1945, "CCS 381 (5-13-45)," RG 218, NA; also, DoD, *Entry*, p. 91.

32. FRUS, Pots. II, pp. 408–17.

33. Bundy, *Danger and Survival*, p. 88.

34. FRUS, Pots. II, pp. 45, 1586.

35. FRUS, Pots. II, p. 345. Note that in his April report to Stimson and Truman, Groves had estimated that the first "gun type bomb" was expected to be "ready about 1 August 1945." However, on July 23 Harrison reported, "Operation may be possible any time from August 1 depending on state of preparation of patient and condition of atmosphere. From point of view of patient only, some chance August 1 to 3, good chance August 4 to 5 and . . . almost certain[ly] before August 10." For Groves' estimate, see Memorandum for the Secretary of War, *Atomic Fission Bombs*, from LRG, April 23, 1945, p. 6, Military Reference Branch, NA. For Harrison's cable see FRUS, Pots. II, pp. 1372–74.

36. Notes of the Interim Committee Meeting, May 31, 1945, p. 11, File 100, Roll 8, H-B Files, M1108, NA.

37. Recommendations of the Scientific Panel on the Immediate Use of Nuclear Weapons, June 16, 1945, File 76, Roll 6, H-B Files, M1108; reprinted in Stoff, Fanton, Williams, eds., *The Manhattan Project*, pp. 149–50.

38. Notes of the Interim Committee Meeting, June 21, 1945, File 100, Roll 8, H-B Files, M1108, NA.

39. Memorandum for the Secretary of War, from Harrison, June 26, 1945, File 77, Roll 6, H-B Files, M1108, NA; reprinted in Stoff, Fanton, Williams, eds., *The Manhattan Project*, pp. 156–61, cited material from pp. 160–61.

40. Stimson Diary, July 3, 1945.

41. FRUS, Pots. I, pp. 941–42.

42. Stimson Diary, July 22, 1945.

43. Churchill, *Triumph and Tragedy*, pp. 640–41.

44. Truman, *Year of Decisions*, p. 416.

45. Byrnes, *All in One Lifetime*, pp. 300–01.

46. Churchill, *Triumph and Tragedy*, pp. 669–70.

47. Bohlen, *Witness to History*, p. 237.

48. David Holloway, *Stalin and the Bomb: The Soviet Union and Atomic Energy, 1939–1956* (New Haven, 1994), p. 117.

49. LRG to JFB, April 28, 1952, Box 5, Entry 3, Groves Papers, RG 200, NA. And JFB to LRG, May 1, 1952, Box 5, Entry 3, Groves Papers, RG 200, NA.

50. Stimson Diary, July 24, 1945.

51. Fifth Oral History Interview with George M. Elsey, July 17, 1969, Vol. II, p. 344, Box 128, Oral History Interview Collection, HSTL.

52. Brown, *James F. Byrnes*, p. 293. Brown continues: "Anxious to get home, the President had given orders for the *Augusta* to pull anchor in Antwerp and sail for Plymouth, England. He had been advised that if he would fly to England to meet the ship he would save two days on the return trip." (p. 294) For further comments by Brown, see pp. 286–87 of *James F. Byrnes*.

Chapter 31: Navy Initiatives

1. For evidence of Forrestal's and Bard's friendly relationship see Letters to Ralph Bard, "Correspondence 'B' 1945," Box 62, Forrestal Papers, Mudd Library, Princeton University Archives.

2. See Memorandum for the Secretary of War, from Harrison, June 28, 1945, File 77, Roll 6, H-B Files, M1108, NA.

3. Alice Kimball Smith, "Behind the Decision to Use the Atomic Bomb," p. 297.

4. Robert Greenhalgh Albion and Robert Howe Connery, *Forrestal and the Navy* (New York, 1962), p. 175.

5. Townsend Hoopes and Douglas Brinkley, *Driven Patriot: The Life and Times of James Forrestal* (New York, 1992), p. 212.

6. Strauss to Albion, December 19, 1960, Strauss Papers—AEC, Japanese Surrender & A-Bomb, HHPL.

7. Bard to Strauss, August 24, 1956, Strauss Papers—AEC, Japanese Surrender & A-Bomb, HHPL.

8. Hoopes and Brinkley, *Driven Patriot*, p. 212.

9. Albion and Connery, *Forrestal and the Navy*, pp. 176–77. Correspondence between Forrestal and Truman's naval aide Capt. James K. Vardaman indicates Forrestal had scheduled a stop at Potsdam just after the departure of the presidential party. See Forrestal to Vardaman, July 9, 1945, and Memorandum for the Secretary of the Navy, from Vardaman, July 14, 1945, "97-3-39," Box 1140, General Correspondence, Forrestal Papers, 1940–47, RG 80, NA.

10. Hoopes and Brinkley, *Driven Patriot*, p. 213.

11. Borklund, *Men of the Pentagon*, pp. 19–20.

12. See the Unpublished Forrestal Diary, July 28 and July 30, 1945.

13. Strauss to Albion, December 19, 1960, Strauss Papers—AEC, Japanese Surrender & A-Bomb, HHPL.

14. Giovannitti and Freed, *The Decision to Drop the Bomb*, p. 145.

15. Strauss to Albion, December 19, 1960, Strauss Papers—AEC, Japanese Surrender & A-Bomb, HHPL.

16. See Davis to HST, April 26, 1945, and Davis to HST, May 2, 1945, "OWI," Box 30, Confidential Files, White House Central Files, Papers of Harry S. Truman, HSTL.

17. Zacharias, *Secret Missions*, pp. 420–21.

18. *The New York Times*, August 15, 1941, p. 1.

19. See the text of the Atlantic Charter, printed in *The New York Times*, August 15, 1941, p. 1.

20. *The New York Times*, July 22, 1945, p. 1.

21. See FRUS, Pots. II, pp. 1273–74.

22. *Washington Post*, July 22, 1945, p. 2; also noted in *Baltimore Sun*, July 22, 1945, p. 1.

23. "Service News and Gossip," *Army and Navy Journal*, July 21, 1945, p. 1426.

24. See, for example, *New York Herald Tribune*, July 22, 1945, p. 1.

25. *The New York Times*, July 22, 1945, p. 4.

26. FRUS, Pots. II, p. 1274.

27. *The New York Times*, July 23, 1945, p. 5.

28. Arthur Krock, "Objects of Our Propaganda to Japan," *The New York Times*, July 24, 1945, p. 22.

29. Rear Adm. Ellis M. Zacharias, USN [Ret.], "How We Bungled the Japanese Surrender," *Look*, Vol. 14, No. 12 (June 6, 1950), pp. 12–21, cited material from p. 19. Zacharias' claim is supported by the recollections of Ladislas Farago, who worked closely with Zacharias on the navy's psychological warfare team. See Ladislas Farago, *Burn After Reading: The Espionage History of World War II* (New York, 1961), pp. 298–300. Phone

logs from the Forrestal Papers indicate that Forrestal and Zacharias spoke regularly during this period. See Phone Log 1945, Box 130, Forrestal Papers, Mudd Library, Princeton University Archives.

30. Zacharias, "How We Bungled the Japanese Surrender," p. 19.

31. Farago, *Burn After Reading*, pp. 298–300.

32. MAGIC, No. 1218, July 26, 1945, RG 457, NA.

Chapter 32: *"Mokusatsu"*

1. *The New York Times*, July 23, 1945, p. 5.

2. Arthur Krock, "The Objects of Our Propaganda to Japan," *The New York Times*, July 24, 1945, p. 22.

3. PSIS, August 2, 1945, "Russo-Japanese Relations (21–27 July 1945)," p. 21, SRH-086, RG 457, NA.

4. *The New York Times*, July 26, 1945, p. 1; also see Zacharias, *Secret Missions*, pp. 373–74. The source of this broadcast is still something of a mystery. In *Secret Missions*, Zacharias named Dr. Kiyoshi Inouye, a prominent Japanese international-relations expert, as the voice behind the broadcast. On the other hand, research by Yomiuri Newspaper suggests that it was an unofficial and unauthorized initiative led by Isamu Inouye, a reporter at the Foreign Desk of Domei Radio. They also point out that the Japanese government was likely to be aware of the initiative—which seems to accord with the fact that the language of the broadcast largely parallels the language of Togo's July 25 cable. See Yomiuri Shinbun Sha [Yomiuri Newspaper], ed., *Showashi no Tenno* [*History of the Showa Period and Emperor*], Vol. 3, (Tokyo, 1967), pp. 196–246, especially pp. 220–21.

5. Unpublished Forrestal Diary, July 28, 1945.

6. Byrnes, *Speaking Frankly*, p. 211.

7. Henry L. Stimson, "The Decision to Use the Atomic Bomb," *Harper's*, Vol. 194, No. 1161 (February 1947), pp. 97–107, cited material from pp. 104–05.

8. FRUS, Pots. II, pp. 1474–76.

9. *The New York Times*, July 28, 1945, editorial. Note that in saying this the *Times* was not launching a critical attack. In fact, in this same editorial it called the terms of the proclamation "fair" and "as generous as they could afford to be. . . ."

10. MAGIC, No. 1224, August 1, 1945, RG 457, NA.

11. MAGIC, No. 1223, July 31, 1945, RG 457, NA.

12. Zacharias, "How We Bungled the Japanese Surrender," p. 21.

13. MAGIC, No. 1222, July 30, 1945, RG 457, NA.

14. MAGIC, No. 1221, July 29, 1945, RG 457, NA.

15. Ibid.

16. Reports of General MacArthur, *Japanese Operations in the Southwest Pacific Area*, Volume II–Part II: "Decision to Surrender," (Washington, D.C.: U.S. Government Printing Office, 1966), National Archives Library.

17. MAGIC, No. 1221, July 29, 1945, RG 457, NA.

18. MAGIC, No. 1224, August 1, 1945, RG 457, NA.

19. See, for instance, Togo, *Sofu Togo Shigenori no Shogai* [The Biography of Shigenori Togo].

20. MAGIC, No. 1225, August 2, 1945, and No. 1226, August 3, 1945, RG 457, NA. Note that this language is that of the original MAGIC intercept—translated and paraphrased by War Department intelligence analysts—which accounts for the difference from the commonly cited language from the translation of the original cable.

21. *The New York Times*, July 28, 1945, p. 1.

22. Butow, *Japan's Decision to Surrender*, p. 148.

23. Kazuo Kawai, " 'Mokusatsu,' Japan's Response to the Potsdam Declaration," *Pa-*

cific Historical Review, Vol. 19, No. 4 (November 1950), pp. 409–14, cited material from p. 412.

24. Kawai, " '*Mokusatsu*,' " p. 413.

25. Ibid.

26. Kawai, " '*Mokusatsu*,' " p. 409.

27. Butow, *Japan's Decision to Surrender*, pp. 144–45.

28. Butow, *Japan's Decision to Surrender*, pp. 146–47.

29. Butow, *Japan's Decision to Surrender*, p. 147.

30. Butow, *Japan's Decision to Surrender*, p. 149.

31. Butow, *Japan's Decision to Surrender*, p. 130, fn. 56.

32. Robert J. C. Butow interview with Kathryn C. Morris, August 1994.

33. Butow, *Japan's Decision to Surrender*, p. 130.

Chapter 33: Race to the Finish

1. Maj. Compton Pakenham, "How the Jap Will Take Final Defeat," *Newsweek*, July 16, 1945, p. 40.

2. "Heavy Allied Blows, Fear of Reds Make Jap Leaders Seek Way Out," *Newsweek*, July 30, 1945, p. 29.

3. *Washington Post*, August 1, 1945, p. 8.

4. "Service News and Gossip," *Army and Navy Journal*, August 4, 1945, p. 1482.

5. FRUS, 1945, Vol. VI, p. 493; and "Memorandum for the President," from Cheston, August 2, 1945, Rose Conway File, Papers of Harry S. Truman, HSTL.

6. MAGIC, No. 1221, July 29, 1945, RG 457, NA.

7. MAGIC, No. 1225, August 2, 1945, RG 457, NA.

8. MAGIC, No. 1226, August 3, 1945, RG 457, NA.

9. "Heavy Allied Blows, Fear of Reds Make Jap Leaders Seek Way Out," *Newsweek*, July 30, 1945, p. 29.

10. Truman, *Off the Record*, ed. Ferrell, p. 53.

11. FRUS, Pots. II, p. 1241.

12. Byrnes, *All in One Lifetime*, p. 291.

13. Unpublished Forrestal Diary, July 28, 1945.

14. FRUS, 1945, Vol. VII, pp. 955–56; Truman, *Year of Decisions*, p. 423.

15. Truman, *Off the Record*, ed. Ferrell, p. 53; Truman, *Dear Bess*, ed. Ferrell, p. 519. For details on the Soong-Stalin negotiations, see FRUS, Pots. II, pp. 1223–47, and FRUS, 1945, Vol. VII, pp. 910–74.

16. Craven and Cate, eds., *The Army Air Forces in World War II*, Vol. V, facsimile facing p. 697.

17. WB's Book, August 3, 1945, Folder 602, Byrnes Papers, CUL.

Chapter 34: The End of the War

1. MAGIC, No. 1231, August 8, 1945, RG 457, NA.

2. In the second set of Soong-Stalin negotiations (which began on August 7) the major points in dispute involved the status of Port Arthur and the port of Dairen, and control of the operations of jointly run Chinese-Soviet railroads in Manchuria. See FRUS, 1945, Vol. VII, pp. 957–74.

3. *The New York Times*, August 9, 1945, p. 1. Japanese government officials began receiving word of Soviet entry into the war at 4:00 a.m. (local time) August 9 from the Domei News agency broadcast. See Toshikazu Kase, *Journey to the Missouri* (New Ha-

ven, CT, 1950) p. 224; also, Reports of General MacArthur, *Japanese Operations in the Southwest Pacific Area*, Vol. II, Part II: "Decision to Surrender," p. 708.

4. Wallace, *The Price of Vision*, ed. Blum, p. 474.

5. Butow, *Japan's Decision to Surrender*, pp. 175–76.

6. MAGIC, No. 1233, August 10, 1945, RG 457, NA; reprinted in Butow, *Japan's Decision to Surrender*, p. 244.

7. For accounts of the August 10 morning meeting, see Stimson Diary, August 10, 1945; Unpublished Forrestal Diary, August 10, 1945 (Forrestal, *The Forrestal Diaries*, ed. Millis, pp. 82–83); Leahy Diary, August 10, 1945; WB's Book, August 10, 1945, Folder 602, Byrnes Papers, CUL; Byrnes, *All in One Lifetime*; p. 305; Truman, *Year of Decisions*, p. 428.

8. WB's Book, August 10, 1945, Folder 602, Byrnes Papers, CUL.

9. Brown Diary, August 10, 1945. This material comes from a taped interview with Walter Brown by Robert Messer in 1972, during which Brown carefully read for the record excerpts from his diary which do not appear in any of the versions available in the Byrnes papers at Clemson University. Interview tapes courtesy of Dr. Messer. For further details concerning the Brown Diary, see pp. 204–05, 581, 586.

10. Leahy Diary, August 10, 1945; also in Butow, *Japan's Decision to Surrender*, p. 245. Forrestal's diary entry of this day indicates that at one point Byrnes "spoke of Prince Chichibu, brother of the emperor. He said that the institution of the Throne could be preserved without commitment as to who should occupy it." Unpublished Forrestal Diary, August 10, 1945.

11. Raymond L. Garthoff, "The Soviet Manchurian Campaign, August 1945," *Military Affairs*, Vol. XXXIII, No. 2 (October 1969), pp. 312–36, cited material from p. 313.

12. Byrnes, *All in One Lifetime*, p. 306.

13. Sigal, *Fighting to a Finish*, p. 226.

14. MAGIC, No. 1236, August 13, 1945, RG 457, NA.

15. Butow, *Japan's Decision to Surrender*, p. 209, fn. 45. For further details on the Japanese surrender process see Butow, *Japan's Decision to Surrender*; Reports of General MacArthur, *Japanese Operations in the Southwest Pacific Area*; Kase, *Journey to the Missouri*; Sigal, *Fighting to a Finish*; John Toland, *The Rising Sun: The Decline and Fall of the Japanese Empire* (New York, 1971); Robert A. Pape, "Why Japan Surrendered," *International Security*, Vol. 18, No. 2 (Fall 1993), pp. 154–201. For a study of deliberations within both the U.S. and Japanese governments at this time, see Barton J. Bernstein, "The Perils and Politics of Surrender: Ending the War with Japan and Avoiding the Third Atomic Bomb," *Pacific Historical Review*, Vol. 64, No. 1 (February 1977), pp. 1–27.

16. Stimson Diary, August 10, 1945.

17. Unpublished Forrestal Diary, August 10, 1945; Forrestal, *The Forrestal Diaries*, ed. Millis, p. 83.

18. Stimson Diary, August 10, 1945.

19. Craven and Cate explain: "When news of the Japanese note of 10 August was broadcast, FEAF [Far Eastern Air Forces] planes continued their strikes against the home islands, but because he feared that area bombing might complicate the negotiations, Spaatz limited USASTAF operations to precision missions. This involved canceling a scheduled strike because of bad weather, and the cancellation unfortunately was interpreted by the American press as a cease-fire order. Believing that a resumption of B-29 attacks would in turn be played up as an indication that negotiations had failed, the President on 11 August ordered that USASTAF stop all strategic operations, even to the extent of recalling planes which might be in the air. FEAF held up operations on the 12th, but with negotiations still hanging fire on the 14th, both Kenney and Spaatz were ordered to resume bombing." Craven and Cate, eds., *The Army Air Forces in World War II*, Vol. V, p. 732.

20. Craven and Cate, *The Army Air Forces in World War II*, Vol. V, pp. 732–33; *The New York Times*, Aug. 15, 1945; Bernstein, "Perils and Politics of Surrender," pp. 13–17.

21. Butow, *Japan's Decision to Surrender*, pp. 245–46; Truman, *Year of Decisions*, pp. 435–36.

22. Thomas G. Paterson, "Potsdam, the Atomic Bomb, and the Cold War," *Pacific Historical Review*, Vol. 41, No. 2 (May 1972), pp. 225–30, cited material from pp. 228–29.

Book II: The Myth

1. *Public Papers of the Presidents: Harry S. Truman, 1945* (Washington, D.C.: U.S. Government Printing Office, 1961), p. 216; also cited in Truman, *Year of Decisions*, p. 436.

2. Paul Fussell, "Hiroshima: A Soldier's View," *New Republic*, August 22 and 29, 1981, pp. 26–30, cited material from p. 29.

3. John Delehanty, "Happy to be Home," *New Republic*, September 16, 1981, p. 4.

Part I: Henry L. Stimson

Chapter 35: A Direct Approach to Russia

1. George H. Gallup, *The Gallup Poll: Public Opinion, 1935–1971*, Vol. I: *1938–1943* (New York, 1972), pp. 521–22; also, *Public Opinion Quarterly*, Vol. 9 (Fall 1945), p. 385. The poll was released on August 26. The question "Do you approve or disapprove of using the new atomic bomb on Japanese cities?" was asked between August 10 and August 15, 1945. Only 10 percent of the American public disapproved of the bombing.

2. Michael J. Yavenditti, "The American People and the Use of Atomic Bombs on Japan: The 1940s," *Historian*, Vol. 36, No. 2 (February 1974), pp. 224–47, see especially p. 225.

3. National Service Board for Religious Objectors, "Public Reactions to Atomic Bomb," October 5, 1945; cited in Michael John Yavenditti, "American Reactions to the Use of Atomic Bombs on Japan, 1945–1947," unpublished dissertation (University of California, Berkeley, 1970), pp. 149–50.

4. "One Victory Not Yet Won," *The New York Times*, August 12, 1945, p. 8E.

5. *Atlanta Constitution*, September 1, 1945; quoted in Yavenditti, "The American People," p. 229. See also Boyer, *By the Bomb's Early Light*, p. 185.

6. Yavenditti, "American Reactions," p. 303.

7. Paul F. Boller, Jr., "Hiroshima and the American Left: August 1945," *International Social Science Review*, Vol. 57, No. 1 (Winter 1982), pp. 13–28, cited material from p. 17.

8. Quoted in John M. Muresianu, *War of Ideas: American Intellectuals and the World Crisis, 1938–1945* (New York, 1988), p. 368.

9. "Louseous Japanicas" is reproduced in Dower, *War Without Mercy*, p. 185.

10. Yavenditti, "The American People," p. 228.

11. Stimson and Bundy, *On Active Service*, p. 641.

12. Stimson Diary, August 12 to September 3, 1945.

13. Stimson Diary, September 4, 1945.

14. Stimson Diary, September 21, 1945.

15. *Public Papers of the Presidents: Harry S. Truman, 1945* (Washington, D.C.: U.S. Government Printing Office, 1961), p. 210.

16. *Public Papers of the Presidents: Harry S. Truman, 1945*, p. 213.

17. Godfrey Hodgson, *The Colonel: The Life and Wars of Henry Stimson, 1867–1950* (New York, 1990), p. 355.

18. "H.L.S. statement at the Ausable Club, August 18, 1945"; a copy is included in the Stimson Diary, August 12 to September 3, 1945.

19. Stimson and Bundy, *On Active Service*, p. 641.

20. HLS to John Spencer Muirhead, December 12, 1947, Stimson Papers, YUL. Since Stimson's correspondence is generally ordered chronologically on microfilm, reel numbers are generally not given in the following notes.

21. HLS to Herbert Hoover, October 5, 1945, Stimson Papers, YUL.

22. Stimson Diary, August 8, 1945.

23. "Reflections on the Basic Problems Which Confront [U]s," July 22, 1945; a copy is included in Stimson Diary.

24. HLS to HST, September 11, 1945. This cover letter is printed in Stimson and Bundy, *On Active Service*, p. 642; a copy is also included in the Stimson Diary.

25. HLS to HST, September 11, 1945; printed in Stimson and Bundy, *On Active Service*, p. 642.

26. HLS, "Memorandum for the President," September 11, 1945; printed in Stimson and Bundy, *On Active Service*, pp. 643–44; a copy is also included in the Stimson Diary.

27. HLS, "Memorandum for the President," September 11, 1945; printed in Stimson and Bundy, *On Active Service*, p. 643.

28. Ibid.

29. Ibid.

30. HLS, "Memorandum for the President," September 11, 1945; printed in Stimson and Bundy, *On Active Service*, pp. 643–44.

31. HLS, "Memorandum for the President," September 11, 1945; printed in Stimson and Bundy, *On Active Service*, p. 644. Emphasis added in *On Active Service*: "Stimson later considered those sentences and one later passage to be the heart of the memorandum." *On Active Service*, p. 644, n. 1.

32. HLS, "Memorandum for the President," September 11, 1945; printed in Stimson and Bundy, *On Active Service*, p. 645.

33. Stimson and Bundy, *On Active Service*, p. 645, n. 2.

34. HLS, "Memorandum for the President," September 11, 1945; printed in Stimson and Bundy, *On Active Service*, p. 645. Emphasis added in *On Active Service*.

35. HLS, "Memorandum for the President," September 11, 1945; printed in Stimson and Bundy, *On Active Service*, p. 645.

36. Stimson Diary, September 12, 1945.

37. Herken, *The Winning Weapon*, p. 27.

38. Henry Wallace notes in his diary that "I asked him [Dean Acheson] who he thought had leaked. He said he thought Forrestal had leaked; or those in the Navy to whom Forrestal had talked." Wallace Diary, October 1, 1945; reprinted in Wallace, *The Price of Vision*, ed. Blum, p. 487. See also Herken, *The Winning Weapon*, pp. 30–32.

39. Truman, quoted in Truman, *Year of Decisions*, p. 534.

40. Fyke Farmer; quoted in Herken, *The Winning Weapon*, p. 39.

41. HLS to Herbert Hoover, October 5, 1945, Stimson Papers, YUL.

42. Hodgson, *The Colonel*, p. 367.

43. See HLS to Felix Frankfurter, January 3, 1946, Reel 63, Frankfurter Papers, LC.

44. HLS to Bernard M. Baruch, May 28, 1946, Stimson Papers, YUL.

45. See Rudolph A. Winnacker to HLS, March 14, 1946, Stimson Papers, YUL.

46. On April 1, Harvey Bundy wrote: ". . . I have been thinking further about the record of your active life and also what could be published now with advantage to the country. I have a line on one or two young men who might fill the bill of acting as your general assistant in working on parts of the project, and will write you further about this a little later." Harvey H. Bundy to HLS, April 1, 1946, Stimson Papers, YUL. By April 29 Winnacker had a thirty-page "Skeleton Outline of Events in the Life of Henry L. Stimson." On May 1 he wrote Stimson: "Listening to your reminiscences during the last two days, I have become convinced more than ever before that some *personal* account of your active and varied life should be given to the public." Rudolph A. Winnacker to HLS, May 1, 1946, Stimson Papers, YUL. Winnacker also suggested a couple of potential assistants.

47. Harvey Bundy to HLS, April 1, 1946, and n.d. [June 1946]; Rudolph A. Winnacker to HLS, March 14, May 1, May 7, 1946; Cass Canfield to Arthur Page, June 10, 1946; all in the Stimson Papers, YUL.

48. Arthur Page to HLS, May 28, 1946; HLS to L. Ethan Ellis, July 12, 1946, Stimson Papers, YUL.

Chapter 36: A Thin Line of Criticism

1. "Oxnam, Dulles Ask Halt in Bomb Use," *The New York Times*, August 10, 1945, p. 6. See also "Churchmen Speak on Atomic Bomb," *Federal Council Bulletin*, Vol. 28, No. 7 (September 1945), p. 6.

2. James M. Gillis, "The Atom Bomb," *Catholic World* (September 1945), pp. 459–52, cited material from pp. 449–50. While not all the Catholic press was so outspoken, Michael J. Yavenditti notes that "No prominent American Catholic theologian, periodical, or newspaper endorsed the atomic bombing of Japan." Yavenditti, "The American People," p. 240.

3. Conrad H. Lanza, "The Surrender of Japan," *America*, Vol. 73, No. 22 (September 1, 1945), pp. 428–30, cited material from p. 428.

4. "America's Atomic Atrocity," *Christian Century*, Vol. 62, No. 35 (August 29, 1945), pp. 974–76, cited material from p. 974.

5. Reinhold Niebuhr, "Our Relations to Japan," *Christianity and Crisis*, Vol. 5, No. 15 (September 17, 1945), pp. 5–7, cited material from pp. 5–6.

6. David Lawrence, "What Hath Man Wrought!" *United States News*, August 17, 1945, pp. 38–39, cited material from p. 38.

7. Felix Morley, "The Return to Nothingness," *Human Events*, August 29, 1945, pp. 144–47, cited material from p. 144.

8. Morley, "The Return to Nothingness," pp. 146–47.

9. David Lawrence, "The Right to Kill," *United States News*, October 5, 1945, pp. 34–35.

10. David Lawrence, "Did Hitler Win the War?," *United States News*, November 2, 1945, pp. 34–35, cited material from p. 35.

11. David Lawrence, "Where Is the Faith?," *United States News*, November 23, 1945, pp. 34–35, cited material from p. 35.

12. "'Won Respect of Millions': Life Story of David Lawrence," *U.S. News and World Report*, February 26, 1973, p. 93.

13. Ronald S. Marmarelli, "David Lawrence," in *Dictionary of Literary Biography*. Vol. 29: *American Newspaper Journalists, 1926–1950*, ed. Perry J. Ashley (Detroit, 1984), pp. 158–67.

14. E. M. Zacharias, "Eighteen Words That Bagged Japan," *Saturday Evening Post*, Vol. 218, No. 20 (November 17, 1945), pp. 17, 117–20, cited material from p. 17.

15. Zacharias, "Eighteen Words That Bagged Japan," pp. 17, 120.

16. "Raymond Swing, Radio Commentator, Dies at 81," *The New York Times*, December 24, 1968; John A. Garraty and Mark C. Carnes, eds., *Dictionary of American Biography, Suppl. 8, 1966–1970* (New York, 1988), p. 640.

17. Raymond Swing, *In the Name of Sanity* (New York, 1945, 1946), p. 74.

18. Swing, *In the Name of Sanity*, p. 74.

19. Raymond Swing, August 13, 1945, typescript, p. 3, Box 27, Swing Papers, LC.

20. Raymond Swing, September 28, 1945, typescript, p. 1, Box 27, Swing Papers, LC; also published in Swing, *In the Name of Sanity*, p. 31.

21. Swing, *In the Name of Sanity*, p. 74.

22. "The Fortune Survey," *Fortune*, December 1945, p. 305. (The precise figure cited is 53.5%.) See also Boyer, *By the Bomb's Early Light*, p. 183; Dower, *War Without Mercy*, p. 54; and Yavenditti, "The American People," p. 225.

23. "The Fortune Survey," p. 305. (The precise figure cited is 22.7%.)

24. Lewis Mumford, *Values for Survival: Essays, Addresses, and Letters on Politics and Education* (New York, 1946), p. 93; also in Lewis Mumford, *Programme for Survival* (London, 1946), p. 19.

25. David Lawrence, "Let's Rebuild Hiroshima!," *United States News*, March 1, 1946, pp. 26–27, cited material from p. 26.

26. Swing's *In the Name of Sanity* is a collection of these Friday broadcasts.

27. Federal Council of the Churches of Christ in America, Commission on The Relation of the Church to the War in the Light of the Christian Faith, *Atomic Warfare and the Christian Faith* (New York, March 1946), pp. 11–12. See also *The New York Times*, March 6, 1946, p. 15. Substantial portions of the report were also reprinted as "Atomic Warfare and the Christian Faith," *United States News*, March 22, 1946, pp. 30–31. The full report has been recently reprinted as an appendix to Harold L. Lunger, ed., *Facing War/Waging Peace: Findings of the American Church Study Conferences, 1940–1960* (New York, 1988), pp. 299–312; and as an appendix to the 1994 edition of *Atomic Diplomacy*: Gar Alperovitz, *Atomic Diplomacy: Hiroshima and Potsdam* (London: Pluto Press, 1994), pp. 321–37.

28. The commission members were "the representative thinkers of American Protestantism," notes Edward LeRoy Long, Jr., in *The Christian Response to the Atomic Crisis* (Philadelphia, 1950), p. 14. Given their professional and public standing, the Calhoun Commission Report arguably represents the measured collective theological and ethical consideration of liberal Protestantism at that time. Only seven of the Commission's twenty-two members were pacifists, making the report's conclusions all the more striking. "Theologians Declare U.S. Bombing Morally Indefensible," *Fellowship*, April 1946, p. 64.

29. Federal Council of Churches, *Atomic Warfare and the Christian Faith*, p. 14.

30. Federal Council of Churches, *Atomic Warfare and the Christian Faith*, pp. 17, 19.

31. "A Report to the Secretary of War," *Bulletin of the Atomic Scientists*, Vol. 1, No. 10 (May 1, 1946) pp. 2–4, 16; cited material from p. 3.

32. "A Report to the Secretary of War," p. 16.

33. Cousins and Finletter, "A Beginning for Sanity," p. 6.

34. Franck Committee Report; quoted in Cousins and Finletter, "A Beginning for Sanity," p. 7.

35. Cousins and Finletter, "A Beginning for Sanity," p. 7.

36. Cousins and Finletter, "A Beginning for Sanity," pp. 7–8.

37. Jonathan M. Weisgall, *Operation Crossroads: The Atomic Tests at Bikini Atoll* (Annapolis, MD, 1994), p. 194.

38. Weisgall, *Operation Crossroads*, p. 2.

39. Janet Besse and Harold D. Lasswell, "Our Columnists on the A-Bomb," *World Politics*, Vol. 3, No. 1 (October 1950), pp. 72–87, cited material from pp. 73, 78.

40. Raymond Swing, July 12, 1946, typescript, p. 3, Box 30, Swing Papers, LC.

41. "Einstein Deplores Use of Atom Bomb," *The New York Times*, August 19, 1946, p. 1.

42. Michael J. Yavenditti, "John Hersey and the American Conscience: The Reception of 'Hiroshima,'" *Pacific Historical Review*, Vol. 43 (1974), pp. 24–49, cited material from p. 36.

43. John Hersey, *Hiroshima* (New York, 1946, 1985), p. 45.

44. See "One Thing and Another," *The New York Times*, September 8, 1946, Sec. II, p. 7; "Hiroshima," *Christian Century*, Vol. 63, No. 39 (September 25, 1946), pp. 1143–44; Charles Poore, "The Most Spectacular Explosion in the Time of Man," *New York Times Book Review*, November 10, 1946, pp. 7, 56; Joseph Luft and W. M. Wheeler, "Reaction to John Hersey's 'Hiroshima,'" *Journal of Social Psychology*, Vol. 28 (1948), pp. 135–40; and Yavenditti, "John Hersey and the American Conscience," pp. 24–49.

45. Halsey, quoted from an A.P. dispatch in Bernard M. Baruch to JVF, September 10, 1946, Forrestal Papers, Mudd Library, Princeton University Archives.

46. Norman Cousins, "The Literacy of Survival," *Saturday Review of Literature*, Vol. 29, No. 37 (September 14, 1946), p. 14.

47. See Hershberg, *James B. Conant*, especially pp. 5, 147.

48. Notes of the Interim Committee Meeting, Thursday, May 31, 1945, p. 14, File 100, Roll 8, H-B Files, M1108, NA.

49. James Gordon Hershberg, "James B. Conant, Nuclear Weapons, and the Cold War, 1945–1950," Ph.D. Dissertation, Tufts University, May 1989 (Ann Arbor, MI, University Microfilms International, 1989), especially pp. 132–94; Hershberg, *James B. Conant*, especially pp. 279–304; Barton J. Bernstein, "Seizing the Contested Terrain," pp. 35–72.

50. JBC to Reinhold Niebuhr, March 6, 1946, Box 3, Niebuhr Papers, LC.

51. Reinhold Niebuhr to JBC, March 12, 1946, Box 3, Niebuhr Papers, LC. The March 1946 exchange of letters between Conant and Niebuhr has been examined in Richard Wightman Fox, *Reinhold Niebuhr: A Biography* (San Francisco, 1985, 1987), pp. 224–25; Hershberg, *James B. Conant*, pp. 283–85; and Bernstein, "Seizing the Contested Terrain," pp. 38–39. Niebuhr acknowledged that had the U.S. failed by other means to achieve "a Japanese surrender, the bomb would have had to be used to save the lives of thousands of American soldiers who would otherwise have perished on the beaches of Japan."

52. Conant, quoted in Hershberg, *James B. Conant*, p. 292.

53. JBC to Harvey H. Bundy, September 23, 1946, "Bu-By" Correspondence Folder, 1946–47, Box 296, JBC Presidential Papers, HUA. This letter is reprinted in Hershberg, *James B. Conant*, pp. 761–62.

54. JBC to Harvey H. Bundy, September 23, 1946, "Bu-By" Correspondence Folder, 1946–47, Box 296, JBC Presidential Papers, HUA. See also Hershberg, *James B. Conant*, pp. 292–93.

55. JBC to Harvey H. Bundy, September 23, 1946, "Bu-By" Correspondence Folder, 1946–47, Box 296, JBC Presidential Papers, HUA.

56. Ibid.

Chapter 37: "A Mere Recital of the Facts"

1. Hershberg, "James B. Conant"; Hershberg, *James B. Conant*.

2. Barton J. Bernstein, "Seizing the Contested Terrain," pp. 35–72.

3. Hershberg, *James B. Conant*, p. 751.

4. JBC to Harvey H. Bundy, September 23, 1946, "Bu-By" Correspondence Folder, Box 296, JBC Presidential Papers, HUA.

5. JBC to Harvey H. Bundy, September 23, 1946, "Bu-By" Correspondence Folder, Box 296, JBC Presidential Papers, HUA.

6. Ibid.

7. Ibid.

8. JBC to Harvey H. Bundy, September 23, 1946, "Bu-By" Correspondence Folder, Box 296, JBC Presidential Papers, HUA. Vannevar Bush had already seconded Conant's choice of the ideal author. "I talked with Van Bush about this the other day and he said that I could quote him to you to the effect that he wishes Mr. Stimson would make a statement clarifying what actually happened with regard to the decision to use the bomb against the Japanese."

9. JBC to Harvey H. Bundy, September 23, 1946, "Bu-By" Correspondence Folder, Box 296, JBC Presidential Papers, HUA.

10. Harvey H. Bundy to JBC, September 24, 1946, "Bu-By" Correspondence Folder, Box 296, JBC Presidential Papers, HUA.

11. JJMc to Robert P. Patterson, November 4, 1946, File 67, Box PA1, McCloy Papers, ACA.

12. Rudolph A. Winnacker to HLS, November 12, 1946, Stimson Papers, YUL. Winnacker writes that "Enclosure V is a rough draft of your thoughts as you outlined them to us last Sunday." (November 10 was the previous Sunday.)

13. See Stimson's November 20, 1946, letter to Rudolph Winnacker: "I am very much obliged to you for these papers. They come at a timely moment for I am going to have another conference with Mr. Harvey Bundy and George Harrison this week." HLS to Rudolph A. Winnacker, November 20, 1946, Stimson Papers. When Stimson sent Byrnes a preprint of the finished article, he noted in his cover letter that "You will remember I spoke to you about this article when I first took it up." Note for HLS's file, noted on the bottom of HLS to Dean Acheson, January 20, 1947, Stimson Papers, YUL.

14. [Harvey H. Bundy], "Notes on the Use by the United States of the Atomic Bomb," September 25, 1946, p. 3, Roll 3, Top Secret Documents Files of Interest to General Groves, M1109, RG 77, NA.

15. [Harvey H. Bundy], "Notes on the Use by the United States of the Atomic Bomb," September 25, 1946, p. 4, Roll 3, Top Secret Documents Files of Interest to General Groves, M1109, RG 77, NA.

16. [Harvey H. Bundy], "Notes on the Use by the United States of the Atomic Bomb," September 25, 1946, p. 5, Roll 3, Top Secret Documents Files of Interest to General Groves, M1109, RG 77, NA.

17. [Harvey H. Bundy], "Notes on the Use by the United States of the Atomic Bomb," September 25, 1946, p. 3, Roll 3, Top Secret Documents Files of Interest to General Groves, M1109, RG 77, NA.

18. [Harvey H. Bundy], "Notes on the Use by the United States of the Atomic Bomb," September 25, 1946, p. 2, Roll 3, Top Secret Documents Files of Interest to General Groves, M1109, RG 77, NA.

19. [Harvey H. Bundy], "Notes on the Use by the United States of the Atomic Bomb," September 25, 1946, pp. 2–3, Roll 3, Top Secret Documents Files of Interest to General Groves, M1109, RG 77, NA.

20. [Harvey H. Bundy], "Notes on the Use by the United States of the Atomic Bomb," September 25, 1946, p. 5, Roll 3, Top Secret Documents Files of Interest to General Groves, M1109, RG 77, NA.

21. [Harvey H. Bundy], "Notes on the Use by the United States of the Atomic Bomb," September 25, 1946, pp. 5–6, Roll 3, Top Secret Documents Files of Interest to General Groves, M1109, RG 77, NA.

22. On November 6, 1946, Groves sent Harvey Bundy copies of "two separate drafts of an article which could be released over the signature of Mr. Stimson." One had been done by Groves' office "using [Gordon] Arneson's draft, your own notes dated September 1946, and additional information gleaned from our review of the files." LRG to Harvey H. Bundy, November 6, 1946, Roll 3, Top Secret Correspondence of MED, M1109, NA.

23. [LRG], "Preliminary Draft Decision to Use the Atomic Bomb Against Japan," p. 1, Roll 3, Top Secret Correspondence of MED, M1109, NA.

24. [LRG], "Preliminary Draft Decision to Use the Atomic Bomb Against Japan," p. 5, Roll 3, Top Secret Correspondence of MED, M1109, NA.

25. [LRG], "Preliminary Draft Decision to Use the Atomic Bomb Against Japan," p. 11, Roll 3, Top Secret Correspondence of MED, M1109, NA.

26. [LRG], "Preliminary Draft Decision to Use the Atomic Bomb Against Japan," p. 10, Roll 3, Top Secret Correspondence of MED, M1109, NA.

27. Rudolph A. Winnacker to HLS, November 12, 1946; enclosures IV, "Strategic Plans for the Defeat of Japan," and V, "Japanese Surrender and the Atomic Bomb," Stimson Papers, Reel 116, YUL.

28. Rudolph A. Winnacker to HLS, November 14, 1946; and Winnacker to HLS, November 18, 1946, Stimson Papers, YUL.

29. A copy of the first thirty pages of the thirty-one-page draft text that McGeorge Bundy presented Conant on November 29 was recently located in the McCloy Papers at the Amherst College Archives, and was brought to my attention by Leo C. Maley III. That the McCloy Papers draft is the same as the one Bundy left with Conant is shown by comparing this undated draft with the detailed suggestions Conant mailed Bundy. See "Use of the Atomic Bomb Against Japan," [undated], McCloy Papers, ACA, and JBC to McGeorge Bundy, November 30, 1946, Stimson Papers, YUL.

30. JBC to McGeorge Bundy, November 30, 1946, pp. 3–4, Stimson Papers, YUL.

31. JBC to McGeorge Bundy, November 30, 1946, p. 4, Stimson Papers, YUL.

32. JBC to McGeorge Bundy, November 30, 1946, pp. 4–5, Stimson Papers, YUL.

33. JBC to McGeorge Bundy, November 30, 1946, pp. 6–7, Stimson Papers, YUL.

34. JBC to McGeorge Bundy, November 30, 1946, p. 5, Stimson Papers, YUL.

35. JBC to McGeorge Bundy, November 30, 1946, p. 3, Stimson Papers, YUL.

36. JBC to McGeorge Bundy, November 30, 1946, p. 6, Stimson Papers, YUL.

37. JBC to McGeorge Bundy, November 30, 1946, p. 2, Stimson Papers, YUL.

38. McGeorge Bundy to JBC, quoted in Hershberg, *James B. Conant*, p. 297.

39. Hershberg, *James B. Conant*, p. 297.

40. JBC to HLS, December 14, 1946, Stimson Papers, YUL.

41. HLS to LRG, December 10, 1946, Stimson Papers, YUL (also in "Winant-Stimson Correspondence-Cables," H-B Files, M1109, NA); HLS to Felix Frankfurter, December 12, 1946, Stimson Papers, YUL; HLS to Robert P. Patterson, December 10, 1945, Stimson Papers, YUL; and HLS to Bernard Baruch, January 20, 1947 Stimson Papers, YUL (also in the Baruch Papers, Mudd Library, Princeton University Archives). The manuscript was also read by Rudolph Winnacker, Cass Canfield, and Frederick Allen. Rudolph A. Winnacker to HLS, December 13, 1946, Stimson Papers, YUL; and Cass Canfield to HLS, December 13, 1946, Stimson Papers, YUL.

42. [LRG], "Corrections," in "Winant-Stimson Correspondence-Cables," H-B Files, M1109, NA. These line-by-line "corrections" correspond with marks in the margin of Groves' December 10, 1946, copy of the Stimson draft article. See "The Atomic Bomb and the Surrender of Japan," following HLS to LRG, December 10, 1946, "Winant-Stimson Correspondence-Cables," H-B Files, M1109, NA.

43. Lewis L. Strauss, Untitled Memorandum, February 24, 1947, AEC-Memoranda to AEC Commissioners, Strauss Papers, HHPL.

44. HLS to Robert P. Patterson, December 10, 1946, Stimson Papers, YUL.

45. William L. Laurence, "Truman Used Atom Bomb to Halt War, Stimson Says," *The New York Times*, January 28, 1947, pp. 1, 15.

46. "War and the Bomb," *The New York Times*, January 28, 1947, p. 22.

47. "Message from Lowell Thomas to HLS," February 6, 1947, Stimson Papers, YUL.

48. Rudolph A. Winnacker to HLS, February 5, 1947, Stimson Papers, YUL. Portions of the essay were even broadcast in Italian by the International Broadcasting Division of the Department of State. See Sally Nash to McGeorge Bundy, February 10, 1947, Stimson Papers, YUL.

49. Henry L. Stimson, "The Decision," editors' comment, p. 107.

50. Frederick L. Allen to HLS, February 18, 1947, Stimson Papers, YUL.

51. HLS to Henry R. Luce, January 20, 1947, Stimson Papers, YUL.

52. Henry R. Luce to HLS, January 26, 1947, Stimson Papers, YUL.

53. HLS to Raymond Gram Swing, January 20, 1947, Stimson Papers, YUL. See also HLS to Raymond Swing, February 4, 1947, Stimson Papers, YUL.

54. JBC to HLS, January 22, 1947, Stimson Papers, YUL.

55. Dean Acheson to HLS, January 25, 1947, Stimson Papers, YUL.

56. Karl T. Compton to HLS, January 28, 1947, Stimson Papers, YUL.

57. Ralph A. Bard to HLS, February 7, 1947, Stimson Papers, YUL.

58. McGeorge Bundy to HLS, February 18, 1947, Stimson Papers, YUL.

Chapter 38: "An Exact Description"

1. Hershberg, *James B. Conant*, pp. 294, 299.
2. Bernstein, "Seizing the Contested Terrain," p. 69.
3. See Bernstein, "Seizing the Contested Terrain," especially p. 52 and p. 52, n. 64.
4. Herbert Hoover to John Callan O'Laughlin, August 8, 1945, O'Laughlin Correspondence File, Box 171, Post-Presidential Papers, HHPL.
5. Boyer, *By the Bomb's Early Light*, p. 209.
6. Hershberg, *James B. Conant*, p. 282.
7. Karl T. Compton, "If the Atomic Bomb Had Not Been Used," *Atlantic Monthly*, Vol. 178, No. 6 (December 1946), pp. 54–56, cited material from p. 54.
8. JBC to Donald Tresidder, quoted in Hershberg, *James B. Conant*, p. 298.
9. JBC to HLS, January 22, 1947, Stimson Papers, YUL.
10. Hershberg, *James B. Conant*, p. 304.
11. Conant, quoted in Hershberg, *James B. Conant*, p. 304.
12. Stimson, "The Decision," p. 101.
13. Stimson, "The Decision," p. 106.
14. Stimson, "The Decision," p. 107.
15. Stimson, "The Decision," p. 101.
16. Stimson, "The Decision," p. 100.
17. Stimson, "The Decision," p. 101.
18. Stimson, "The Decision," p. 105.
19. Ibid.
20. Stimson, "The Decision," pp. 104–05.
21. Stimson, "The Decision," p. 107.
22. [HLS], "Memorandum for the President: Proposed Program for Japan," July 2, 1945, copy in Stimson Diary; printed in Stimson, "The Decision," p. 103.
23. Truman, *Year of Decisions*, p. 417.
24. To recall, Robert Oppenheimer, one of the four members of the Interim Committee's panel of scientific advisers, later noted that he and his fellow panel members "didn't know beans about the military situation in Japan. We didn't know whether they could be caused to surrender by other means or whether the invasion was really inevitable. But in back of our minds was the notion that the invasion was inevitable because we had been told that." Oppenheimer, cited in *In the Matter of J. Robert Oppenheimer*, p. 34.
25. See Stimson Diary, especially June 1 and 6, 1945.
26. [HLS], Memorandum for the President, July 2, 1945, copy in Stimson Diary; printed in Stimson, "The Decision," p. 104.
27. "Directive to Commanding General, United States Army Strategic Air Forces, July 25, 1945, "July 1945" File, Box 21, Spaatz Papers, LC; United States Strategic Bombing Survey, *The Effects of Strategic Bombing on Japan's War Economy*, p. 65, n. 13.
28. WSC, Note to the War Cabinet; cited in Ehrman, *Grand Strategy*, p. 303.
29. MAGIC, No. 1204, July 12, 1945, RG 457, NA.
30. Stimson Diary, May 15, 1945.
31. Szilard, "Reminiscences," p. 127.
32. Stimson Diary, July 23, 1945.
33. WB's Book, July 24, 1945, Folder 602, Byrnes Papers, CUL.
34. Memorandum for Chief, Strategic Policy Section, S & P Group, OPD, from Ennis, Subject: Use of Atomic Bomb on Japan, April 30, 1946, p. 6, "ABC 471.6 Atom (17 Aug. 45), Sec. 7," Entry 421, RG 165, NA.
35. Stimson, "The Decision," pp. 104, 106.
36. Stimson Diary, July 24, 1945.
37. DoD, *Entry*, p. 79; DoD, *Top Secret Entry*, Sec. V, p. 23.
38. Stimson, "The Decision," p. 102. Another indication of how casually such figures

were bandied about is a private letter written by Stimson at the end of 1947: "Fortunately the atom bomb, which was in my particular charge, worked successfully and brought the war to a finish in August, *saving thereby hundreds of thousands of Americans, British, and Japs* who would have perished if the invasion that we were setting on foot had taken place." HLS to John Spencer Muirhead, December 12, 1947, Stimson Papers, YUL; emphasis added.

39. Rufus E. Miles, Jr., "Hiroshima: The Strange Myth of Half a Million American Lives Saved," *International Security*, Vol. 10, No. 2 (Fall 1985), pp. 121–40, cited material from p. 121.

40. Although Miles' article was the first to appear in a scholarly journal, Bernstein actually published his findings first (*Los Angeles Times*, July 28, 1985). His longer analysis appeared subsequently in the June/July 1986 edition of the *Bulletin of the Atomic Scientists.*

41. Barton J. Bernstein, "A Postwar Myth: 500,000 U.S. Lives Saved," *Bulletin of the Atomic Scientists*, Vol. 42, No. 6 (June–July 1986), pp. 38–40.

42. Bernstein, "A Postwar Myth," p. 40.

43. Joint Staff Planners, quoted in Bernstein, "A Postwar Myth," p. 40.

44. Skates, *The Invasion of Japan*, p. 78. Some writers have noted a chart titled "Estimated Casualties and Calculated Whole Blood Requirements, Olympic" on p. 18 of a chapter from an undated manuscript on medical services in the Pacific War (which from internal evidence was clearly written more than two decades after the fact). ("From Olympic to Blacklist," U.S. Army Center for Military History, Washington, D.C.) The chart suggests that by July 31, 1945, medical planners on MacArthur's staff assumed the possibility of 394,859 casualties for D-Day plus 120. Noting that 124,935 were battle casualties, Skates observes that assuming a 25% death ratio, "about fourteen thousand soldiers and airmen would die in the first sixty days of OLYMPIC, and approximately thirty-one thousand could die if the operation persisted until 1 March 1946" (i.e., 11,000 greater than the 20,000 JWPC estimate). (Skates, *The Invasion of Japan*, p. 79.) (If a one-in-five ratio is assumed, the figure is 25,000—i.e., one-fourth higher than the JWPC estimate.) Without claiming the 394,859 estimate is accurate, Robert Newman has argued that it "raises the question" of larger figures. (See Robert Newman, "What New Consensus?," *Washington Post*, November 30, 1994.) One writer, Robert Maddox, has gone so far as to suggest that the 384,859 figure does not include soldiers killed, since "they obviously would require no medical attention." (See Robert James Maddox, "Why We Had to Drop the Atomic Bomb," *American Heritage*, May/June 1995, p. 77.) To my knowledge, no other writer has offered such an interpretation of this document. On a related point, a G-2 estimate of almost exactly this time (August 1, 1945) took account of a larger-than-expected Japanese troop buildup on Kyushu, and may have figured in the generation of the 25,000–31,000 estimate. (See "G-2 Estimate of the Enemy Olympic Situation OLYMPIC OPERATION 1 August 1945," NA.) Bruce Lee suggests on the basis of interviews and other sources that the medical study was informed by the most recent ULTRA information concerning the Japanese buildup on Kyushu. (Bruce Lee, *Marching Orders: The Untold Story of World War II* [New York: 1995], pp. 515–16.) For further discussion of casualties and ULTRA-related issues, see pp. 518–20; also Afterword, endnote 7.

45. Enclosure V, with Rudolph A. Winnacker to HLS, November 12, 1945, Stimson Papers, YUL.

46. Enclosure II, with Rudolph A. Winnacker to HLS, November 12, 1946, Stimson Papers, YUL.

47. See Rudolph A. Winnacker to McGeorge Bundy, December 13, 1946, Stimson Papers, YUL.

48. Rudolph A. Winnacker to HLS, November 12, 1946, Stimson Papers, YUL.

49. HLS to Felix Frankfurter, December 12, 1946, Stimson Papers, YUL.

50. Ibid.

51. Felix Frankfurter to HLS, September 16, 1946, Reel 63, Frankfurter Papers, LC.

52. McGeorge Bundy to Felix Frankfurter, January 2, 1947 (misdated 1946), Reel 18, Frankfurter Papers, LC. Possibly—given its date—President Truman's December 31, 1946, letter to Stimson—"I think you know the facts of the whole situation better than anybody and I would like for you to straighten out the record on it"—was part of an effort to bolster Stimson's resolve during this period of self-doubt. (HST to HLS, December 31, 1946, Stimson Papers, YUL; copy in Vertical File, HSTL.)

53. McCloy, quoted in Bird, *The Chairman*, p. 263.

54. Sherwin, *A World Destroyed*, p. xxiv.

55. Bernstein, "A Postwar Myth," p. 40.

56. Skates, *The Invasion of Japan*, p. 78.

57. Transcript of conversation dated July 9, 1946, between Stimson and McGeorge Bundy, "Atomic Energy," Reel 136, Stimson Papers, YUL.

58. McGeorge Bundy to Felix Frankfurter, January 2, 1947 [misdated 1946], Reel 18, Frankfurter Papers, LC.

59. Bernstein, "Seizing the Contested Terrain," p. 71. Bernstein further observes: "It is tempting to speculate whether these efforts . . . also came partly out of an uneasy conscience."

60. Transcript of conversation dated July 9, 1946, between Stimson and McGeorge Bundy, "Atomic Energy," Reel 136, Stimson Papers, YUL.

61. Transcript of conversation dated July 9, 1946, between Stimson and McGeorge Bundy, "Atomic Energy," Reel 136, Stimson Papers, YUL.

62. JBC to HLS, January 22, 1947, Stimson Papers, YUL.

63. Stimson, "The Decision," p. 97.

Chapter 39: "We Have Followed the Record"

1. Stimson, "The Decision," p. 97.

2. See, for instance, the blistering criticisms of P.M.S. Blackett's *Fear, War, and the Bomb* in the *Atlantic Monthly* and the *Bulletin of the Atomic Scientists*: I. I. Rabi, "Playing Down the Bomb: Blackett versus the Atom," *Atlantic Monthly*, Vol. 183, No. 4 (April 1949), pp. 21–24; Edward A. Shils, "Blackett's Apologia for the Soviet Position," *Bulletin of the Atomic Scientists*, Vol. 5, No. 2 (February 1949), pp. 34–37; and Brian McMahon, "Comment on Blackett's Book," *Bulletin of the Atomic Scientists*, Vol. 5, No. 2 (February 1949), pp. 40–43.

3. "Why We Used the Atom Bomb," *Washington Post*, January 28, 1947.

4. Ibid.

5. See *Not Merely Gossip: A Supplement to Human Events*, Vol. 4, No. 5 (January 29, 1947).

6. Raymond Swing to HLS, January 31, 1947, Stimson Papers, YUL.

7. "Deny Atomic Bomb Use Was Atrocity," *Christian Century*, Vol. 64, No. 7 (February 12, 1947), p. 196.

8. Raymond Swing to HLS, January 31, 1947, Stimson Papers, YUL.

9. Groves supplied Bundy with classified information. A note in his papers states that "Mr. Bundy has returned the papers we sent him while he worked on the Stimson article. Among the papers are the Brewster file. . . ." Untitled office note, March 19 [1947], "201 Groves, L. R., Ltn. Gen. Correspondence 1941–47," Entry 5, Box 86, MED Decimal Files, RG 77, NA. Winnacker also supplied Stimson and Bundy with "still highly classified" information. Rudolph A. Winnacker to HLS, November 12, 1946, Stimson Papers, YUL. Also, in drafting the *Harper's* article Bundy quoted directly from two of the Interim Committee meeting minutes—documents that remained classified until the 1970s.

10. Alexander H. Leighton, "Atomic Bomb Wasn't Necessary," Science Service, April 20–26, 1947, pp. 1, 4; copy in Atomic Bomb File, Box 2, Dooman Papers, Hoover Institution on War, Revolution and Peace. Emphasis in original.

11. William R. Castle Diary, February 9, 1947, p. 28, Houghton Library, Harvard University.

12. Joseph C. Grew to HLS, February 12, 1947. This letter is found in the Grew Papers, Houghton Library, Harvard University; in the Stimson Papers, YUL; in the Eugene H. Dooman Papers, Atomic Bomb File, Box 2, HIA; and in the Groves Papers, Box 1, Entry 4, RG 200, NA.

13. Grew to HLS, February 12, 1947, Stimson Papers, YUL. See also Grew, *Turbulent Era*, Vol. II, p. 1425.

14. Grew to HLS, February 12, 1947, Stimson Papers, YUL. See also Grew, *Turbulent Era*, Vol. II, pp. 1425-26.

15. Grew to HLS, February 12, 1947, Stimson Papers, YUL. See also Grew, *Turbulent Era*, Vol. II, p. 1428.

16. Grew to HLS, February 12, 1947, Stimson Papers, YUL.

17. HLS to Grew, June 19, 1947, Stimson Papers, YUL.

18. Stimson Diary, May 29, 1945.

19. HLS to Grew, June 19, 1947, Stimson Papers, YUL.

20. Ibid.

21. Castle's diary was not opened to scholars until 1985.

22. Castle Diary, January 26, 1947, p. 19; and, February 9, 1947, p. 28. I am particularly indebted to Sanho Tree for these references.

23. Paul H. Nitze with Ann M. Smith and Steven L. Rearden, *From Hiroshima to Glasnost: At the Center of Decision* (New York, 1989), pp. 44-45.

24. Stimson and Bundy, *On Active Service*, p. 629.

25. And yet, the very next paragraph goes on: ". . . as it turned out, the use of the bomb, in accelerating the surrender, saved many more lives than it cost." Stimson and Bundy, *On Active Service*, p. 630.

26. Martin J. Sherwin, "Hiroshima and Modern Memory," *The Nation*, Vol. 233, No. 11 (October 10, 1981), 329, 349-53, cited material from p. 352.

27. Grew to Eugene H. Dooman, April 10, 1948, Atomic Bomb File, Box 2, Dooman Papers, HIA.

28. On June 9, 1948, Castle wrote Hoover that he regretted that Stimson had published an error-filled account of the decision to use the atomic bomb against Japan. Castle thought it unquestionably dishonest for Stimson to have suggested he had no inkling of Japan's desire to end the war; this, he felt, undercut his entire argument. William R. Castle to Herbert Hoover, June 9, 1948, and Hoover's handwritten reply, Castle Papers, HHPL. Hoover responded: "I could say many more violent things."

29. Transcript of July 9, 1946, conversation between HLS and McGeorge Bundy, "Atomic Energy," p. 176, Stimson Papers, YUL.

30. Transcript of July 9, 1946, conversation between HLS and McGeorge Bundy, "Atomic Energy," p. 177, Stimson Papers, YUL.

31. HLS, "Memorandum for the President," September 11, 1945; printed in Stimson and Bundy, *On Active Service*, p. 644.

32. Stimson and Bundy, *On Active Service*, pp. 646-47.

33. HLS to George Roberts, June 11, 1947, YUL.

34. HLS, "Memorandum for the President," September 11, 1945; printed in Stimson and Bundy, *On Active Service*, p. 644. Emphasis added in *On Active Service*.

35. HLS, "Memorandum for the President," September 11, 1945; printed in Stimson and Bundy, *On Active Service*, p. 645. Emphasis added in *On Active Service*.

36. GCM to McGeorge Bundy, November 7, 1947, Folder 17, Box 86, Marshall Papers, GCMRL.

37. GCM to McGeorge Bundy, November 7, 1947, Folder 17, Box 86, Marshall Papers, GCMRL.

38. McGeorge Bundy to GCM, November 10, 1947, Folder 17, Box 86, Marshall Papers, GCMRL.

39. GCM to McGeorge Bundy, November 19, 1947, Folder 17, Box 86, Marshall Papers, GCMRL.

40. Ibid.

41. McGeorge Bundy to George Kennan, November 21, 1947, Folder 17, Box 86, Marshall Papers, GCMRL.

42. Draft text from *On Active Service*, quoted in George F. Kennan to McGeorge Bundy, December 2, 1947, Folder 17, Box 86, Marshall Papers, GCMRL.

43. Ibid.

44. Ibid.

45. George F. Kennan to McGeorge Bundy, December 2, 1947, Folder 17, Box 86, Marshall Papers, GCMRL.

46. Ibid.

47. Ibid.

48. McGeorge Bundy to George Kennan, December 4, 1947, Folder 17, Box 86, Marshall Papers, GCMRL.

49. Ibid.

50. McGeorge Bundy to George Kennan, December 8, 1947, Folder 17, Box 86, Marshall Papers, GCMRL.

51. Proposed text for *On Active Service*, quoted in McGeorge Bundy to George F. Kennan, December 8, 1947, Folder 17, Box 86, Marshall Papers, GCMRL. See also *On Active Service*, pp. 647–48, which incorporates these changes almost to the letter.

52. George F. Kennan to GCM, December 16, 1947, Folder 17, Box 86, Marshall Papers, GCMRL.

53. George F. Kennan to McGeorge Bundy, December 16, 1947, Folder 17, Box 86, Marshall Papers, GCMRL.

54. McGeorge Bundy to George Kennan, December 22, 1947, Folder 17, Box 86, Marshall Papers, GCMRL.

55. Stimson and Bundy, *On Active Service*, p. 673.

56. Stimson, in Stimson and Bundy, *On Active Service*, p. xi.

Chapter 40: "Omissions Merely for Brevity"

1. "The divergence between Mr. Stimson and Mr. Byrnes . . . was a real one. . . ." McGeorge Bundy to George Kennan, December 4, 1947, Folder 17, Box 86, Marshall Papers, GCMRL.

2. Walter Isaacson and Evan Thomas, *The Wise Men: Six Friends and the World They Made: Acheson, Bohlen, Harriman, Kennan, Lovett, McCloy* (New York, 1986).

3. Bundy, in Stimson and Bundy, *On Active Service*, p. 674.

4. See Stimson and Bundy, *On Active Service*, pp. 615–16, 624, and 627. The March 15 and June 19 diary entries had also already been quoted in Stimson's *Harper's* essay. Only the August 10 quote was a new disclosure.

5. Stimson Diary, March 15, 1945; quoted in Stimson and Bundy, *On Active Service*, p. 616.

6. Ibid.

7. Stimson Diary, June 19, 1945; quoted in Stimson and Bundy, *On Active Service*, p. 624.

8. Stimson Diary, June 19, 1945.

9. Stimson Diary, June 18, 1945.

10. Stimson Diary, August 10, 1945; quoted in Stimson and Bundy, *On Active Service*, p. 627.

11. Stimson Diary, August 10, 1945.

12. Stimson Diary, May 29, July 2, July 17, and July 24, 1945.

13. Stimson Diary, May 15, 1945.

14. Stimson Diary, May 10, May 14, May 15, June 6, July 22, and July 23, 1945.

15. Stimson Diary, August 12–September 3, 1945.

16. Stimson Diary, September 4, 1945.

17. A brief chapter section, "The Emergent Russian Problem," quotes some diary material. However, none of the quoted entries refer to the atomic bomb; and the latest entry quoted is for April 23, 1945. Stimson and Bundy, *On Active Service*, pp. 605–11.

18. Leo C. Maley III, "Use of the Stimson Diary in *On Active Service*," March 1, 1995, unpublished memorandum in author's possession.

19. Bundy, in Stimson and Bundy, *On Active Service*, p. 674.

20. Hodgson, *The Colonel*, pp. 368–69.

21. McGeorge Bundy to Cass Canfield, March 19, 1951, Stimson Papers, YUL.

22. Current, *Secretary Stimson*, p. vii.

23. Current, *Secretary Stimson*, p. 251.

24. Current, *Secretary Stimson*, p. 234.

25. Current, *Secretary Stimson*, p. 237.

26. Current, *Secretary Stimson*, p. vii. Richard Current later recalled that Bundy "didn't much like what I wrote." Richard Current telephone interview with author, March 7, 1995.

27. McGeorge Bundy to Felix Frankfurter, March 24, 1953, Reel 19, Frankfurter Papers, LC.

28. Stimson, in Stimson and Bundy, *On Active Service*, p. xi.

29. McGeorge Bundy to Felix Frankfurter, March 24, 1953, Reel 19, Frankfurter Papers, LC.

30. Elting E. Morison, *Turmoil and Tradition: A Study of the Life and Times of Henry L. Stimson* (Boston, 1960), p. vii.

31. Morison, *Turmoil and Tradition*, p. 630.

32. Morison, *Turmoil and Tradition*, p. 640, fn. 34.

33. Richard Hewlett interview with Kai Bird, March 9, 1993.

34. The MacNeil/Lehrer NewsHour, August 6, 1985, Transcript No. 2572.

35. Bundy, *Danger and Survival*, p. 93.

36. Bundy, *Danger and Survival*, p. 97.

37. Bundy, *Danger and Survival*, pp. 92–93. Clearly, as we have seen, Bundy had been more than Stimson's "scribe."

38. Stimson and Bundy, *On Active Service*, p. 629.

39. Bundy, *Danger and Survival*, p. 86.

40. HLS, "Memorandum for the President: Proposed Program for Japan," July 2, 1945, copy in Stimson Diary; printed in Stimson, "The Decision," p. 103.

41. Bundy, *Danger and Survival*, p. 86. In an endnote Bundy states: "This is my reading of the Stimson diary for the whole period, and also my recollection of Stimson's retrospective view in 1946." Bundy, *Danger and Survival*, p. 650, n. 71. However, Stimson's repeated efforts and statements from the time suggest he held much stronger views. For instance, three times in three weeks Stimson approached Truman on this matter: As indicated, on July 2 he told Truman that "I think the Japanese nation has the mental intelligence and versatile capacity . . . to accept the proffer. . . ." On July 16—with the news of the Emperor's intervention—he deemed the matter of a warning to Japan "of supreme importance at the moment" and urged that Truman consider issuing two warnings: one (with assurances) to be delivered "during the course of this Conference, and rather earlier than later," and a second (backed by the "full force of our newer weapons"), only if "the Japanese persist" after the first warning. At this time he indicated his judgment that the issuance of a warning with assurances might result in a "prompt and successful conclusion of the war. . . ." On July 24 he again attempted to impress upon the president "the importance which I attributed to the reassurance of the Japanese on the continuance of their dynasty," and argued that it "might be just the thing that would make or mar their acceptance. . . ." Finally, on August 10, Stimson again confided to his diary that the ques-

tion of the future of the Emperor had been "the very single point that I feared would make trouble." Stimson Diary, July 2 memorandum, 24, and August 10, 1945. On the July 16 memorandum see FRUS, Pots. II, pp. 1265–67. As noted, in a recent interview Bundy acknowledged that Stimson believed the war could well have been ended by clarifying the surrender terms, and that Stimson might have succeeded in gaining acceptance for this policy had he been a younger man. See above, p. 496.

42. McGeorge Bundy interview with author, April 6, 1995.

43. Bundy, *Danger and Survival*, p. 647, n. 19.

44. Bundy, *Danger and Survival*, p. 89.

45. Bundy, *Danger and Survival*, pp. 137–38.

46. Bundy, *Danger and Survival*, p. 89.

47. Bundy, *Danger and Survival*, p. 88.

Part II: President Harry S. Truman

Chapter 41: The Man from Missouri

1. On McCloy, see especially Bird, *The Chairman*.

2. Richard H. Rovere, "Notes on the Establishment in America," *American Scholar*, Vol. 30, No. 4 (Autumn 1961), pp. 489–95, especially p. 491 on McCloy. Rovere revised this essay for the May 1962 issue of *Esquire*. It is reprinted as "The American Establishment," *Wilson Quarterly*, Vol. 2, No. 3 (Summer 1978), pp. 170–81; see also Rovere's accompanying "Postscript: A 1978 Commentary," pp. 182–83.

3. Clark Clifford, with Richard Holbrooke, *Counsel to the President: A Memoir* (New York, 1991).

4. At the last minute, Kirkpatrick was unable to attend the luncheon.

5. JJMc, "President Truman & The Atom Bomb," appended to JJMc to Clark M. Clifford, September 17, 1984, Box 1, Records of the Truman Centennial Commission, HSTL.

6. JJMc, "President Truman & The Atom Bomb," appended to JJMc to Clark M. Clifford, September 17, 1984, Box 1, Records of the Truman Centennial Commission, HSTL.

7. McCloy told Forrestal about his comments to the president in 1947 (published in *The Forrestal Diaries* in 1951, pp. 70–71). McCloy again recalled this meeting in his 1953 book, *The Challenge to American Foreign Policy*, pp. 42–43; see also handwritten note by Rudolph A. Winnacker, Apr. 30, May 1 '46, "Surrender of Japan Notes," Box 69, Office of Chief of Military History Papers, RG 319, NA; JJMc interview with Forrest Pogue, March 31, 1959, Tape 65, Forrest Pogue Papers, GCMRL; JJMc interview with Fred Freed for NBC White Paper, "The Decision to Drop the Bomb," (interview conducted sometime between May 1964 and February 1965), p. 11, Roll 1, File 50A, Box SP2, McCloy Papers, ACA; Giovanitti and Freed, *The Decision to Drop the Bomb*, p. 136; Questions From NBC For Mr. McCloy Re: NBC White Paper on "The Decision to Surrender," ca. 1965, File 50A, Box SP2, McCloy Papers, ACA; JJMc to McGeorge Bundy, April 30, 1985, File 3, COR2, McCloy Papers, ACA; "McCloy on the A-Bomb," appendix in James Reston, *Deadline*, pp. 498–99.

8. JJMc, "President Truman & The Atom Bomb," appended to JJMc to Clark M. Clifford, September 17, 1984, Box 1, Records of the Truman Centennial Commission, HSTL. Contrary to some speculation, this is, so far as I have been able to determine, the only specific indication in the record—forty years after the fact—that fear of looking weak might have figured in Byrnes' strategy. See above, p. 314.

9. JJMc to Clark M. Clifford, September 17, 1984, Box 1, Records of the Truman Centennial Commission, HSTL. Also, as we have noted, there is no contemporaneous evi-

dence that at the time he actually made his decision Truman was influenced by either Acheson or MacLeish. See above, pp. 308–09.

10. Alonzo L. Hamby, "The Mind and Character of Harry S. Truman," in *The Truman Presidency*, ed. Michael J. Lacey (New York, 1989), pp. 19–53, cited material from p. 52.

11. Robert Griffith, "Harry S Truman and the Burden of Modernity," *Reviews in American History*, Vol. 9, No. 3 (September 1981), pp. 295–306, cited material from p. 296.

12. Tris Coffin, *Missouri Compromise* (Boston, 1947), p. 12.

13. "Trumania in the '70s," *Time*, June 9, 1975, p. 45.

14. McCloy Diary, April 14, 1945.

15. Wallace Diary, August 3, 1944; in Wallace, *The Price of Vision*, ed. Blum, p. 374.

16. For sales figures, see: "Trumania in the '70s," *Time*, June 9, 1975, p. 45; and "Everyone's Wild About Harry," *Newsweek*, March 24, 1975, p. 28. For a recent critical review, see Robert H. Ferrell and Francis H. Heller, "Plain Faking?," *American Heritage*, Vol. 46, No. 3 (May/June 1995), pp. 14, 16.

17. Merle Miller, *Plain Speaking: An Oral Biography of Harry S. Truman* (New York, 1973), p. 15. Also quoted in Richard S. Kirkendall, "Harry Truman as National Hero," review of *Truman*, by David McCullough, *Reviews in American History*, Vol. 21, No. 2 (1993), pp. 314–19, quote from Miller on p. 314.

18. Truman, *Harry S. Truman*, pp. 580–81.

19. Samuel Gallu, *"Give 'Em Hell Harry": Reminiscences* (New York, 1975); "His Own Man," *Time*, May 12, 1975, p. 63; *Reader's Digest*, Vol. 107, No. 642 (October 1975), pp. 105–10.

20. "Trumania in the '70s," *Time*, June 9, 1975, p. 45; "Everyone's Wild About Harry," *Newsweek*, March 24, 1975, p. 28.

21. Gerald W. Johnson, "Truman Nostalgia," *New Republic*, Vol. 172, No. 22 (May 31, 1975), pp. 17–19, cited material from p. 19.

22. Allen Weinstein, "Presidential Reputations: Truman and the American Imagination," in *Truman and the American Commitment to Israel: A Thirtieth Anniversary Conference*, ed. Allen Weinstein and Moshe Ma'oz (Jerusalem, 1981), pp. 37–47, cited material from p. 40.

23. Garry Wills, "I'm Not Wild About Harry," *Esquire*, Vol. 85, No. 1 (January 1976), pp. 91–95, cited material from p. 91.

24. "Trumania in the '70s," *Time*, June 9, 1975, p. 45; "Everyone's Wild About Harry," *Newsweek*, March 24, 1975, p. 28; Wills, "I'm Not Wild About Harry," p. 91.

25. Sidney Blumenthal, "The Essential Clark Clifford," *Washington Post Magazine*, February 5, 1989, pp. 12–18, especially pp. 15–16.

26. [George Bush], "Bush Takes Off the Gloves, Comes Out Fighting," *Congressional Quarterly*, August 22, 1992, pp. 2556–59, cited material from p. 2559.

27. A. L. May, "ELECTION '92 Clinton Tries to Claim Truman Mantle: Bush Also Sees 33rd President as Inspiration," *Atlanta Journal and Constitution*, September 8, 1992, p. A5.

28. Mary McGrory, "Learning from 'Truman,' " *Washington Post*, July 7, 1992; William Safire, "Grading Bush's Speech," *The New York Times*, August 24, 1992, p. 15.

29. Ronald Steel, "Harry of Sunnybrook Farm," review of *Truman*, by David McCullough, *New Republic*, August 10, 1992, pp. 34–39, cited material from p. 34.

30. "The Best Books of 1992," *Time*, January 4, 1993, pp. 64, 66–67; *Truman* discussed on p. 66.

31. David McCullough, quoted in John Budris, "Up-Close and 'Down to the Ground,' " *Christian Science Monitor*, June 12, 1992, p. 13.

32. McCullough, *Truman*, p. 991.

33. Griffith, "Harry S Truman and the Burden of Modernity," p. 296.

34. Alonzo L. Hamby, "An American Democrat: A Reevaluation of the Personality of

Harry S. Truman," *Political Science Quarterly*, Vol. 106, No. 1 (1991), pp. 33–55, cited material from p. 37.

35. Richard Miller, *Truman: The Rise to Power* (New York, 1986), p. 167.

36. Ibid.

37. HST, quoted in McCullough, *Truman*, p. 187.

38. McCullough, *Truman*, p. 183.

39. HST, quoted in Andrew J. Dunar, *The Truman Scandals and the Politics of Morality* (Columbia, MO, 1984), pp. 9–10.

40. Hillman, *Mr. President*, p. 187. This account was adapted from a January 1952 handwritten memorandum.

41. Miller, *Truman: The Rise to Power*, p. 167.

42. "The Best Books of 1992," *Time*, January 4, 1993, p. 66.

43. Miller, *Truman: The Rise to Power*, p. 167. See also Willard B. Blanton, "Harry S Truman and Pendergast Politics," *Gateway Heritage*, Vol. 11, No. 3 (Winter 1990–91), pp. 60–69, especially p. 63; and Hamby, "An American Democrat," especially p. 42.

44. McCullough, *Truman*, p. 284. McCullough shows her salary as $2,400 a year. Additional information is provided by Robert Ferrell, who notes that "Bess went on the Senate payroll on July 1, 1941, at $2,280 per year, which increased to $4,500 in June 1942. She continued this salary in the vice president's office through March 1945." (Truman also hired his sister, Mary Jane Truman.) Robert H. Ferrell, *Harry S. Truman: A Life* (Columbia: University of Missouri Press, 1994), p. 417, n. 28. According to the *New York Herald Tribune*, Bess' $4,500 salary was the highest paid (at the time) to a Senate office clerk. "Truman's Wife Is on Pay Roll at $4,500 Plus," *New York Herald Tribune* Bureau, July 27, 1944; copy in the Vertical File, HSTL.

45. HST to Bess [Truman], April 30, 1942, Box 8, Papers Pertaining to Family Business and Personal Affairs, HSTL; see also Truman, *Dear Bess*, ed. Ferrell, p. 474.

46. Wallace Diary, July 24, 1946; in Wallace, *The Price of Vision*, ed. Blum, pp. 602–03.

47. Stimson Diary, March 13, 1944.

48. Truman, *Year of Decisions*, p. 119. Truman concluded an unsent letter to Norman Littel, a former Roosevelt Justice Department official, by noting that "I am more than happy to receive communications from you on any subject. I enjoy also 'showing off' my historical bent to one who'll read it." HST, cited in Monte M. Poen, ed., *Strictly Personal and Confidential: Letters Harry Truman Never Mailed* (Boston, 1982), p. 146.

49. Miller, *Plain Speaking*, p. 333. In an interview with William Hillman, Truman said, "If I couldn't have been a pianist, I think I would have done better as a professor [of] history." (Hillman replied, "You are a damn good professor of history right now, in my opinion.") "Mr. President" interviews, October 10, 1951, p. 4, Box 269, PSF, HSTL.

50. See, for instance, many of the 1951–52 entries in the Eben A. Ayers Diary, HSTL.

51. HST to Roy Roberts (handwritten), June 12, 1950; in Poen, ed., *Strictly Personal and Confidential*, pp. 142–43.

52. Truman, *Off the Record*, ed. Ferrell, p. 182.

53. FRUS, Pots. I, p. 4.

54. Truman, *Year of Decisions*, p. 421.

55. "Aboard U.S.S. Augusta with President Truman, Aug. 6-(UP)," Potsdam File, Box 3, Samuel I. Rosenman Papers, HSTL.

56. Copy in Official File, HSTL.

57. Lew Wallace to HST, August 7, 1945, 692-A, Official File, HSTL.

58. HST to Lew Wallace, August 9, 1945, 692-A, Official File, HSTL.

59. *Public Papers of the Presidents, Harry S. Truman, 1945*, p. 200.

60. Moreover, the papers of Truman's press secretary, Charles Ross, contain what appears to be a copy of a press release, dated August 6, stating directly that "The President was jubilant over the tremendous success attendant upon the first use of the atomic bomb." "Off the Atlantic Coast, Monday, August 6," Atomic Bomb File, Box 7, Ross Pa-

pers, HSTL. Nevertheless, Ross wrote Lew Wallace to assure him that "obviously, the President was not 'jubilant' over a device for killing." Charles G. Ross to Lew Wallace, August 20, 1945, 692-A, Official File, HSTL.

61. Harry S. Truman, *Truman Speaks* (New York, 1960), p. 66.

62. Truman, *Truman Speaks*, p. 67.

63. HST to Roman Bohnen, December 12, 1946, Atomic Energy, Box 2, PSF, HSTL. For the "new treatment and dialogue [which] was approved following a conference between Charlie Ross, Matt Connelly, Clark Clifford and the President," see "New Scene. The Beginning or the End," typescript attached to Carter T. Barron to LRG, December 9, 1946, Box 11, Entry 1, Groves Papers, RG 200, NA.

64. "Mr. President" interviews, October 10, 1951, p. 2, Box 269, PSF, HSTL.

Chapter 42: Main Elements of the Historical Rationale

1. The files of Truman's press secretary contain what appears to be a copy of an August 6 press release which states that "to the President it meant that the war must certainly end soon now, and with it the saving of the lives of perhaps a million young Americans." "Off the Atlantic Coast, Monday, August 6," Atomic Bomb File, Box 7, Ross Papers, HSTL. Although it is clearly possible, given Truman's tendency to casually throw out large (and often differing) casualty estimates, I have seen no evidence to confirm that Truman personally approved this "perhaps a million" estimate at this early date.

2. HST, "To the Men and Women of the Manhattan Project," August 9, 1945, Atom Bomb File, Box 692-A, Official File, HSTL. Also on August 9, the White House issued the president's report to the nation on the Potsdam Conference. Truman told the American people that "We have used it [the atomic bomb] in order to shorten the agony of war, in order to save the lives of *thousands and thousands* of young Americans." *Public Papers of the Presidents: Harry S. Truman, 1945*, p. 212; emphasis added. Peter Maslowski also points out: ". . . not long after Japan's formal surrender, leading figures in the U.S. military . . . proposed putting out a news release explaining that many American lives had been saved by not having to invade. But how many? The news release's first draft suggested 200,000, but Lieutenant General John E. Hull, chief of the War Department Operations Division during the war's last year, thought that figure was too high. He suggested 'tens of thousands of American lives, possibly 200,000 lives.' Lieutenant General Ira C. Eaker, deputy commander of the U.S. Army Air Forces, agreed with this language, but the army air forces chief of staff, Henry H. ('Hap') Arnold, did not. He told Eaker that 'the casualty figure you indicate is higher than that envisioned when [the] invasion was planned,' and he suggested that the statement simply read 'tens of thousands of American lives,' which was more in line with the earlier wartime estimates based on the assumption that both Olympic and Coronet would actually happen." Peter Maslowski, "Truman, the Bomb, and the Numbers Game," *MHQ: The Quarterly Journal of Military History*, Vol. 7, No. 3 (Spring 1995), pp. 103–7, material cited from p. 106. (References cited in Maslowski's original manuscript courtesy of Peter Maslowski and *MHQ*: "Hull to Eaker, 13 September 1945, Eaker to Hull, 14 September 1945, and Arnold to FEAF [Far Eastern Air Force], 14 September 1945, all in OPD Files, 1945, OPD 704 PTO. Records of the War Department General Staff, RG 165, NA.")

3. HST, handwritten speech delivered to the Gridiron Dinner, December 15, 1945, "Speeches, Longhand Notes," Box 46, PSF, HSTL. (A typed copy of this speech given by Truman to his press secretary, Charles Ross, is located in the same file.)

4. Carter T. Barron to LRG, December 9, 1946, Box 11, Entry 1, Groves Papers, RG 200, NA.

5. "New Scene. The Beginning or the End." Copy attached to letter from Carter T. Barron to LRG, December 9, 1946, Box 11, Entry 1, Groves Papers, RG 200.

6. *Public Papers of the Presidents: Harry S. Truman, 1948* (Washington, D.C.: U.S. Government Printing Office, 1964), p. 859.

7. *Public Papers of the Presidents: Harry S. Truman, 1949* (Washington, D.C.: U.S. Government Printing Office, 1964), p. 200.

8. Notes/Part 1, Interview with Harry Truman, November 12, 1949, p. 13 [also numbered p. 67], Jonathan Daniels Papers, HSTL.

9. HST to James L. Cate, January 12, 1953, Atomic Bomb, Box 112, PSF, HSTL. This letter was reproduced in Craven and Cate, eds., *The Army Air Forces in World War II*, Vol. 5, facing p. 713.

10. Truman, *Truman Speaks*, p. 67.

11. While this book was in preparation, helpful research paralleling certain aspects of this discussion was published by Barton Bernstein. See Barton J. Bernstein, "Writing, Righting, or Wronging the Historical Record: President Truman's Letter on His Atomic-Bomb Decision," *Diplomatic History*, Vol. 16, No. 1 (Winter 1992), pp. 163–73.

12. HST to James L. Cate, handwritten draft letter, December 31, 1952, Atomic Bomb File, Box 112, PSF, HSTL.

13. Stimson, "The Decision," p. 102; Stimson and Bundy, *On Active Service*, p. 619.

14. Kenneth W. Hechler to David D. Lloyd, January 2, 1953, Atomic Bomb File, Box 112, PSF, HSTL. Note, also, Stimson, "The Decision," p. 102, and Stimson and Bundy, *On Active Service*, p. 619.

15. David D. Lloyd to HST, January 6, 1953, Atomic Bomb File, Box 112, PSF, HSTL.

16. HST to James L. Cate, January 12, 1953, Atomic Bomb File, Box 112, PSF, HSTL. See also Craven and Cate, eds., *The Army Air Forces in World War II*, Vol. 5, facing p. 713.

17. DoD, *Entry*, p. 79; DoD, *Top Secret Entry*, Sec. V, pp. 22–23.

18. DoD, *Entry*, p. 79; DoD, *Top Secret Entry*, Sec. V, p. 23.

19. On the other hand, as Skates points out, "Marshall was apparently disturbed by the large number of casualties predicted for the first days of OLYMPIC, for he immediately asked MacArthur to clarify the figure. . . . He did not expect such high casualty rates, MacArthur informed Marshall, and he concluded with a strong argument in favor of OLYMPIC. . . . Marshall sent his thanks to MacArthur 'for the promptness of your reply . . . to my query regarding OLYMPIC and casualty estimates.' MacArthur's last message, Marshall noted, had 'arrived with 30 minutes to spare and had a determining influence in obtaining formal presidential approval for OLYMPIC.' " Skates, *Invasion of Japan*, pp. 80–81. See endnote 7 of Afterword.

20. DoD, *Entry*, p. 76. As we have seen, according to Leahy's diary, Marshall estimated casualties of 63,000 for the Kyushu campaign.

21. DoD, *Entry*, p. 79; DoD, *Top Secret Entry*, Sec. V, p. 23. Further indication that the thirty-day estimate might have been a worst-case scenario comes from the previously cited July 10 letter from top War Department planner Brig. Gen. George Lincoln to the Commanding General of U.S. forces in China, Lt. Gen. A. C. Wedemeyer. Lincoln judged that there were "two psychological days" around which "we might get a capitulation, providing we have an adequate definition of what capitulation means"—these were "the day after we persuade Russia to enter . . . and the day after we get what the Japs recognize as a secure beachhead in Japan." Lincoln to Wedemeyer, July 10, 1945, Wedemeyer Folder, Box 5, Lincoln Papers, USMAL.

22. Truman, *Year of Decisions*, p. 417.

23. United States Strategic Bombing Survey, *Japan's Struggle to End the War*, p. 13; and United States Strategic Bombing Survey, *Summary Report (Pacific War)*, p. 26. These findings were directly quoted at the time in *The New York Times*. "Japanese Defeat Laid to Air Attack," *The New York Times*, July 14, 1946, p. 13.

24. Memorandum for Chief, Strategic Policy Section, S & P Group, OPD, from Ennis, Subject: Use of Atomic Bomb on Japan, April 30, 1946, p. 6, "ABC 471.6 Atom (17 Aug. 45), Sec. 7," Entry 421, RG 165, NA.

25. McCullough, *Truman*, pp. 400–1.

26. G.A.L. [George A. Lincoln], to General Hull, June 4, 1945, "ABC 387 Japan (15 Feb. 45)," Box 504, Entry 421, RG 165, NA; and Pasco, "Memorandum for the Chief of Staff," June 6, 1945, Folder 29, Box 84, Marshall Papers, GCMRL. For further details of this report, see above, pp. 57, 135.

27. Hoover's May 15 memorandum is appended to Herbert Hoover to HLS, May 15, 1945, Reel 112, Stimson Papers, YUL. A copy is also appended to T.T.H. [Thomas T. Handy], "Memorandum to General Hull," June 1, 1945, File 29, Box 84, Marshall Papers, GCMRL.

28. "Memorandum," June 4, 1945, "Japan (After Dec. 7/41)," Box 8, Entry 74A, Stimson Safe File, RG 107, NA; copy also in Folder 29, Box 84, Marshall Papers, GCMRL. Marshall concurred with Lincoln's analysis: "With reference to the memorandum concerning which you asked General Handy for the reaction of the Staff, I am attaching a study with which I am in general agreement." GCM to HLS, June 7, 1945, "Japan (After Dec. 7/41)," Box 8, Entry 74A, Stimson Safe File, RG 107, NA.

29. *Public Papers of the Presidents: Harry S. Truman, 1945*, p. 197. See above, p. 596, for Groves' role in crafting this statement.

30. *Public Papers of the Presidents: Harry S. Truman, 1945*, p. 212.

31. Hillman, *Mr. President*, p. 248.

32. Truman, *Year of Decisions*, p. 421.

33. It was noted at the initial April 27 Target Committee meeting that "21st Bomber Command has 33 primary targets on their target priority list. . . . Hiroshima is the largest untouched target not on the 21st Bomber Command priority list. . . . It should be remembered that in our selection of any target, the 20th Air Force is operating primarily to laying waste all the main Japanese cities, and that they do not propose to save some important primary target for us if it interferes with the operation of the war from their point of view." Notes on Initial Meeting of Target Committee, [April 27, 1945], p. 4, File 5 (Selection of Targets), Roll 1, M1109, Top Secret Correspondence of the MED, NA.

34. The Strategic Bombing Survey noted that "an aerial mining program carried out by B-29s in the last months of the war . . . sealed off the vital Inland Sea and disrupted every major home island port." United States Strategic Bombing Survey, *Japan's Struggle to End the War*, p. 11. The official Army Air Forces history notes that Hiroshima "had been an important military port of embarkation"; however, "the mining campaign had in recent months dried up its traffic." Craven and Cate, *Army Air Forces in World War II*, Vol. 5, p. 715.

35. DoD, *Entry*, p. 77; DoD, *Top Secret Entry*, Sec. V, p. 21.

36. Truman, *Truman Speaks*, p. 73.

37. HST to HLS, December 31, 1946, Stimson Papers, YUL; copy also in Vertical File, HSTL. Six weeks earlier Truman had written Stimson: "You remember the conversation we had in the little White House in Potsdam as to whether we should drop it or not, and if we did drop it we should pick a city *entirely devoted to war work*, if we could find a city of that sort." HST to HLS, November 13, 1946, Stimson Papers, YUL; emphasis added.

38. Mr. Pres. Interviews by Hillman, October 10, 1951, p. 1, Box 269, PSF, HSTL.

39. HST to James L. Cate, handwritten draft letter, December 31, 1952, Atomic Bomb, Box 112, PSF, HSTL. Truman's sentence was changed to read: "He promptly named Hiroshima and Nagasaki, among others." See editing on the December 31 draft letter; HST to James L. Cate, Atomic Bomb, Box 112, PSF, HSTL; and Craven and Cate, *The Army Air Forces in World War II*, Vol. 5, p. 713.

40. Truman, *Year of Decisions*, p. 420.

41. Truman, *Truman Speaks*, p. 73.

42. United States Strategic Bombing Survey, *The Effects of Atomic Bombs on Hiro-*

shima and Nagasaki (Washington, D.C.: U.S. Government Printing Office, June 30, 1946), p. 41.

43. At the first meeting of the Target Committee it was noted that "21st Bomber Command has 33 primary targets on their target priority list. . . . Hiroshima is the largest untouched target not on the 21st Bomber Command priority list." Notes on Initial Meeting of Target Committee, [April 27, 1945], p. 4, File 5D (Selection of Targets), Roll 1, M1109, Top Secret Correspondence of the MED, NA.

44. Summary of Target Committee Meetings on May 10 and 11, 1945, p. 4, File 5D (Selection of Targets), Roll 1, M1109, Top Secret Correspondence of the MED, NA.

45. Notes on Initial Meeting of Target Committee [April 27, 1945], Roll 1, M1109, Top Secret Correspondence of the MED, NA.

46. Summary of the Target Committee Meetings on May 10 and 11, 1945, p. 4, File 5D (Selection of Targets), Roll 1, M1109, Top Secret Correspondence of the MED, NA.

47. Summary of the Target Committee Meetings on May 10 and 11, 1945, p. 6, File 5D (Selection of Targets), Roll 1, M1109, Top Secret Correspondence of the MED, NA.

48. Ibid.

49. At the May 28 Target Committee Meeting, Dr. John Von Neumann "gave it as his opinion that any hills in vicinity of proposed targets were too remote to have serious effect." Minutes of Third Target Committee Meeting—Washington, May 28, 1945, p. 3, File 5D (Selection of Targets), Roll 1, M1109, Top Secret Correspondence of the MED, NA.

50. Summary of the Target Committee Meetings on May 10 and 11, 1945, p. 5, File 5D (Selection of Targets), Roll 1, M1109, Roll 1, Top Secret Correspondence of the MED, NA. The minutes note that "it was the recommendation of those present at the meeting that the first four choices of targets for our weapon should be the following: a. Kyoto b. Hiroshima c. Yokohama d. Kokura Arsenal." The Kokura arsenal was later put as the first choice for the second bombing (August 9). Nagasaki was bombed instead because of last-minute weather changes over Kokura.

51. Notes of the Interim Committee Meeting, Thursday, May 31, 1945, p. 14, File 100, Roll 8, H-B Files, M1108, NA.

52. Minutes of Third Target Committee Meeting—Washington, May 28, 1945, p. 3, File 5D (Selection of Targets), Roll 1, M1109, Top Secret Correspondence of the MED, NA.

53. Notes of the Interim Committee Meeting, Thursday, June 21, 1945, p. 7, File 100, Roll 8, H-B Files, M1108, NA.

54. Sigal, "Bureaucratic Politics & Tactical Use of Committees," pp. 330, 331. For a similar understanding, see Morison, *Turmoil and Tradition*, p. 630.

55. Stimson Diary, June 6, 1945.

56. Truman, *Year of Decisions*, p. 419.

57. Ibid.

58. Truman, *Year of Decisions*, p. 420.

59. William G. Penney, quoted in Peter Wyden, *Day One: Before Hiroshima and After* (New York: Simon and Schuster, 1984), p. 194. (Penney was present at the Target Committee meetings.)

60. HST, handwritten journal, July 25, 1945, "Ross, Mr. and Mrs. Charles G.," Box 322, PSF, HSTL; see also Truman, *Off the Record*, ed. Ferrell, pp. 55–56.

61. Wallace Diary, August 10, 1945; in Wallace, *The Price of Vision*, ed. Blum, p. 474.

62. Truman, *Year of Decisions*, p. 420.

63. Groves, *Now It Can Be Told*, p. 309, n. 2.

64. *Public Papers of the Presidents, Harry S. Truman, 1945*, p. 212.

65. Notes of the Interim Committee Meeting, Thursday, May 31, 1945, p. 14, File 100, Roll 8, H-B Files, M1108, NA. The findings of the Strategic Bombing Survey are illumi-

nating in this regard: "Industry in the center of the city [Hiroshima] was effectively wiped out. Though small workshops numbered several thousand, they represented only one-fourth of the total industrial production of Hiroshima, since many of them had only one or two workers. The bulk of the city's output came from large plants located on the outskirts of the city; one-half of the industrial production came from only five firms. Of these larger companies only one suffered more than superficial damage. Of their working force, 94 percent were uninjured. Since electric power was available, and materials and working force were not destroyed, plants ordinarily responsible for nearly three-fourths of Hiroshima's industrial production could have resumed normal operation within 30 days of the attack had the war continued." United States Strategic Bombing Survey, *The Effects of Atomic Bombs on Hiroshima and Nagasaki*, p. 8.

66. "Two aspects of this are (1) obtaining the greatest psychological effect against Japan and (2) making the initial use sufficiently spectacular for the importance of the weapon to be internationally recognized when publicity on it is released." Summary of the Target Committee Meetings on May 10 and 11, 1945, p. 6, File 5D (Selection of Targets), Roll 1, M1109, Top Secret Correspondence of the MED, NA.

67. Present at the May 29 meeting were Stimson, McCloy, and Marshall. According to McCloy's notes of the meeting: "General Marshall said he thought these weapons might first be used against straight military objectives such as a large naval installation and then if no complete result was derived from the effect of that, he thought we ought to designate a number of large manufacturing areas from which the people would be warned to leave—telling the Japanese that we intended to destroy such centers. There would be no individual designations so that the Japs would not know exactly where we were to hit—a number should be named and the hit should follow shortly after. Every effort should be made to keep our record of warning clear. We must offset by such warning methods the opprobrium which might follow from an ill considered employment of such force." McCloy Diary, Memorandum of Conversation with General Marshall and the Secretary of War, May 29, 1945.

68. Truman, *Year of Decisions*, p. 420.

69. Barton J. Bernstein, "The Atomic Bombings Reconsidered," *Foreign Affairs*, Vol. 74, No. 1 (January–February 1995), pp. 135–52, cited material from p. 144.

70. Most of the currently available academic legal studies of the Hiroshima decision (pro and con) either were done before much of the modern evidence was declassified or have not involved a thorough assessment of that evidence. A study being prepared by Greg Jordan which utilizes the modern evidence concludes that there is a strong argument that the decision to drop the atomic bomb on Japan was a violation of both treaty and customary international law, as well as of U.S. military law. Jordan also cites U.S. field manuals. He stresses that the understanding that the atomic bomb was "superpoisonous," and that it would kill by radiation as well as blast, made its use a violation of the prohibition against using poisons. Additionally, the modern evidence suggests that the decision to use the bomb, when compared to the alternatives of clarifying surrender terms or waiting for Russian entry, is difficult to justify under the legal principles of necessity. Gregory M. Jordan, "But Was It Legal?: The Atomic Bomb and Hiroshima," March 1, 1995, unpublished draft essay.

71. HST, handwritten speech delivered to the Gridiron Dinner, December 15, 1945, "Speeches, Longhand Notes," Box 46, PSF, HSTL.

72. In 1955 five Japanese citizens brought suit against the Japanese government claiming damages for injuries sustained from the use of the atomic bombs on Hiroshima and Nagasaki. On December 7, 1963, the District Court of Tokyo issued an opinion concluding that use of the atomic bombs violated international law but that the individual citizens did not have a private right of action under international law. For a detailed analysis of the Shimoda case, see Richard A. Falk, "The Shimoda Case: A Legal Appraisal of the Atomic Attacks Upon Hiroshima and Nagasaki," *American Journal of International Law*, Vol. 59 (1965), pp. 759–93. See also Francis A. Boyle, *The Future of International Law*

and American Foreign Policy (Dobbs Ferry, NY: Transnational Publishers Inc., 1989), pp. 321–26; Richard A. Falk, "The Claimants of Hiroshima," *Nation*, February 15, 1965, pp. 157–61; Jordan J. Paust, "The Nuclear Decision in World War II—Truman's Ending and Avoidance of War," *International Lawyer*, Vol. 8, No. 1 (1974), pp. 160–90, especially pp. 161–80; and Nagendra Singh and Edward McWhinney, *Nuclear Weapons and Contemporary International Law*, rev. ed. (Boston: Martinus Nijhoff Publishers, 1989), pp. 315–17.

73. Leahy, *I Was There*, p. 440.

74. Myron C. Cramer, "Memorandum for the Secretary of War," March 5, 1945, OPD 385 TS, OPD Decimal File 1945, Box 166, Entry 419, RG 165, NA. This finding is consistent with other instances in which the United States acknowledged during World War II that the use of poison would be a violation of customary international law. Jungk reports that "shortly before the decision to drop the atomic bomb" the Judge Advocate General of the Navy was asked to give a legal opinion concerning crop-destroying chemicals. The use of such weapons, he held, would be a violation of the laws of war. Robert Jungk, *Brighter Than a Thousand Suns: The Story of the Men Who Made the Bomb* (New York: Grove Press, 1956, 1958), p. 144. I have been unable to confirm Jungk's report.

75. Boyle, *The Future of International Law and American Foreign Policy*, pp. 341–43.

76. Morton William Royse, *Aerial Bombardment and the International Regulation of Warfare* (New York: H. Vinal, Ltd., 1928).

Chapter 43: Nagasaki and *"Year of Decisions"*

1. Summary of Target Committee Meetings on May 10 and 11, 1945, p. 4, File 5D (Selection of Targets), Roll 1, M1108, Top Secret Correspondence of the MED, NA.

2. Stimson Diary, June 1, July 22, and July 24, 1945; Stimson, "The Decision," p. 105; Stimson and Bundy, *On Active Service*, p. 625.

3. Truman, *Year of Decisions*, p. 420.

4. Stimson Diary, July 24, 1945.

5. Bundy, *Danger and Survival*, p. 94.

6. Victor Weisskopf, *The Joy of Insight: Passions of a Physicist* (New York, 1990), p. 156.

7. HST to HLS, December 31, 1946, Stimson Papers; a copy is also in the Vertical File, HSTL.

8. *Truman Speaks*, p. 73.

9. HST, cited from "Mr. Pres. Interviews by William Hillman," October 10, 1951, p. 1, Box 269, PSF, HSTL.

10. See, for instance, Stanley Goldberg, "General Groves and the Atomic West: The Making and the Meaning of Hanford," in Bruce Hevly and John Findlay, eds., *The Atomic West* (Seattle: University of Washington Press, forthcoming); see also Groves, *Now It Can Be Told*, p. 298.

11. Thomas T. Handy to Carl Spaatz, July 25, 1945, copy attached to James L. Cate to HST, December 6, 1952, Atomic Bomb, Box 112, PSF, HSTL. See also, Craven and Cate, eds., *The Army Air Forces In World War II*, Vol. 5, opposite p. 697; and Truman, *Year of Decisions*, p. 420.

12. Craven and Cate, *The Army Air Forces in World War II*, Vol. 5, p. 724.

13. Mission Planning Summary, Report Number 9, 509th Composite Group, Box 6, Entry 1, Groves Papers, RG 200, NA.

14. Ibid.

15. Ibid. Other evidence also strongly suggests the designated target was, in fact, the city center, making the field order even more of a puzzle. See F. L. Ashworth interview with A. D. Christman, April 1969, and LRG interview with A. D. Christman, May 1967

(reviewed by LRG, August 1967), Naval Weapons Center, CA, Collection on W. S. Parsons, NHC.

16. Wallace Diary, August 10, 1945; in Wallace, *The Price of Vision*, ed. Blum, p. 474.

17. Byrnes, *All in One Lifetime*, p. 306.

18. "President Truman to Dr. Compton," *Atlantic Monthly*, Vol. 179, No. 1 (February 1947), p. 27; Karl T. Compton, "If the Atomic Bomb Had Not Been Used," *Atlantic Monthly*, Vol. 178, No. 6 (December 1946), pp. 54–56.

19. Compton, "If the Atomic Bomb Had Not Been Used," p. 54. Like Henry Stimson's "The Decision," Compton's article had been written at the instigation of Harvard president James Conant. See Bernstein, "Seizing the Contested Terrain," pp. 35–72, especially pp. 43–45; and Hershberg, *James B. Conant*, p. 296.

20. "President Truman to Dr. Compton," *Atlantic Monthly*, Vol. 179, No. 1 (February 1947), p. 27.

21. Edward R. Winstead, "Harry S. Truman," unpublished draft paper in author's possession.

22. Truman, *Year of Decisions*, p. 416.

23. Leahy, *I Was There*, p. 245. In this passage, Leahy is referring to a July 10, 1944, Joint Chiefs meeting.

24. Forrestal, *The Forrestal Diaries*, ed. Millis, pp. xi, xiv.

25. Forrestal, *The Forrestal Diaries*, ed. Millis, especially pp. 74–76.

26. Concerning the May 28 meeting in which Grew urged him to provide assurances for the Emperor, Truman writes: "Acting Secretary of State Grew had spoken to me in late May about issuing a proclamation that would urge the Japanese to surrender but would assure them that we would permit the Emperor to remain as head of the state. Grew backed this with arguments taken from his ten years' experience as our Ambassador in Japan, and I told him that I had already given thought to this matter myself and that it seemed to me a sound idea." Truman, *Year of Decisions*, p. 416.

27. Truman, *Year of Decisions*, p. 428.

28. HST, "Discussion," February 11, 1954, Box 9, Post-Presidential File, HSTL.

29. Truman, *Year of Decisions*, pp. 416, 417.

30. Truman, *Year of Decisions*, p. 417.

31. See, for instance, Hillman, *Mr. President*, p. 248.

32. In discussing the August 10 surrender message, Truman makes an additional vague reference to this issue. He notes in passing that "Secretary Stimson had always expressed the opinion that it would be to our advantage to retain the Emperor." Truman, *Year of Decisions*, p. 428. Recall, however, Stimson's report that the president and Byrnes struck out the key passage—and that: "Japan accepted the Potsdam list of terms put out by the President 'with the understanding that the said declaration does not comprise any demand which prejudices the prerogatives of his majesty as a sovereign ruler'. It is curious that this was the very single point that I feared would make trouble." Stimson Diary, August 10, 1945.

33. Grew, *Turbulent Era*, Vol. II, p. 1434.

34. Truman, *Year of Decisions*, p. 417.

35. HST's August 6, 1945, statement; quoted in Truman, *Year of Decisions*, p. 422.

36. Butow, *Japan's Decision to Surrender*, pp. 145, 147. According to Truman, "Our proclamation had been referred to as 'unworthy of consideration,' 'absurd,' and 'presumptuous.' " Truman, *Year of Decisions*, p. 397.

37. HST's August 14, 1945, statement; quoted in Truman, *Year of Decisions*, p. 436.

38. "The War Ends," *Life*, Vol. 19, No. 8 (August 20, 1945), p. 25.

39. HST, handwritten journal, August 10, 1945, Box 333, PSF, HSTL; see also Truman, *Off the Record*, ed. Ferrell, p. 61.

40. Truman, *Year of Decisions*, especially pp. 79, 245, 264, 265, 314, 322–23, 387, and 411.

41. Instead, Truman writes that the Soviets were necessary to pin down Japanese troops in China: "Our military advisers had strongly urged that Russia should be brought into the war in order to neutralize the large Japanese forces on the China mainland and thus save thousands of American and Allied lives." Truman, *Year of Decisions*, p. 403. This, of course, had been a primary goal earlier in the year—and would still be important so long as the Emperor's position was threatened or if he were removed and could not order a surrender. See above, pp. 83–95.

42. HST, handwritten journal, July 17, 1945, "Ross, Mr. and Mrs. Charles G.," Box 322, PSF, HSTL; see also Truman, *Off the Record*, ed. Ferrell, p. 53; and HST to Bess [Truman], July 18, 1945, Box 9, Papers Pertaining to Family, Business and Personal Affairs, HSTL; see also Truman, *Dear Bess*, ed. Ferrell, p. 519.

43. Truman, *Year of Decisions*, p. 87. For Stimson's note, see *ibid.*, p. 85.

44. This despite Truman's claim in the Preface to his *Memoirs* that "What I have written here is based upon the circumstances and the facts and my thinking at the time I made the decisions, and not what they might have been as a result of later developments." Truman, *Year of Decisions*, p. x.

45. Truman, *Year of Decisions*, p. vii.

46. Truman, *Year of Decisions*, p. x.

47. Webster Schott, "How the Memoirs Were Written," *New Republic*, March 19, 1956, pp. 18–19, cited material from p. 19.

48. Francis H. Heller, "The Writing of the Truman Memoirs," *Presidential Studies Quarterly*, Vol. 13, No. 1 (Winter 1983), pp. 81–84, especially pp. 81–82.

49. Heller, "The Writing of the Truman Memoirs," p. 81.

50. "On one occasion the former President said to me that the Harris manuscript reminded him of a Saturday Evening Post story: 'My Life and Happy Times in the White House, by Harry S. Truman as told to Robert E. G. Harris.' " Heller, "The Writing of the Truman Memoirs," p. 81; repeated in Francis H. Heller, "Harry S. Truman and His Memoirs," unpublished paper prepared for the Conference on Political Memoirs, University of British Columbia, September 22–24, 1989 [p. 2].

51. Heller, "The Writing of the Truman Memoirs," p. 82.

52. "Discussion," February 11, 1954, p. 5, Box 9, Post-Presidential File, HSTL.

53. Herbert Lee Williams, "I Was Truman's Ghost," *Presidential Studies Quarterly*, Vol. 12, No. 2 (Spring 1982), pp. 256–59, cited material from p. 258.

54. Williams, "I Was Truman's Ghost," p. 259.

55. When Williams—who was still working on his doctorate—was offered the directorship of a university journalism program, Truman agreed that he should accept the position. Various papers on file suggest a less-than-amicable subsequent relationship.

56. Francis M. Heller, "Truman," in *History Makers: Leaders and Statesmen of the 20th Century*, ed. Frank P. Longford and John Wheeler-Bennett (London, 1973), p. 325.

57. Schott, "How the Memoirs Were Written," p. 19.

58. Heller, "The Writing of the Truman Memoirs," p. 83.

59. Ibid.

60. Heller, "The Writing of the Truman Memoirs," pp. 83–84.

61. Francis H. Heller, "The *Memoirs* of Harry S. Truman: Remarks Before the Jackson County Historical Society," May 18, 1958, unpublished paper, p. 10. Memoirs, Vertical File, HSTL. Heller notes that "Dean Acheson and Samuel Rosenman had read the entire manuscript. David Lloyd, Charles Sawyer and John Steelman had read some of the chapters." Heller, "The *Memoirs*," p. 11, n. 5.

Chapter 44: Certain Classes of Papers

1. As previously noted, although research on this subject was undertaken independently, see Barton Bernstein's similar account, Bernstein, "Writing, Righting, or Wronging," pp. 163–73.

2. *Public Papers of the Presidents: Harry S. Truman, 1945*, p. 199.

3. "President Truman to Dr. Compton," *Atlantic Monthly*, Vol. 179, No. 2 (February 1947), p. 27.

4. James L. Cate to HST, December 6, 1952, Atomic Bomb, Box 112, PSF, HSTL.

5. Ibid.

6. Thomas T. Handy to Carl Spaatz, July 25, 1945, copy attached to James L. Cate to HST, December 6, 1952, Atomic Bomb, Box 112, PSF, HSTL. See also Craven and Cate, *The Army Air Forces in World War II*, Vol. 5, opposite p. 697.

7. HST to James L. Cate, handwritten draft December 31, 1952, Atomic Bomb, Box 112, PSF, HSTL.

8. Kenneth W. Hechler to David L. Lloyd, January 2, 1953, Atomic Bomb, Box 112, PSF, HSTL.

9. David L. Lloyd to HST, January 6, 1953, Atomic Bomb, Box 112, PSF, HSTL.

10. HST to James L. Cate, January 12, 1953, Atomic Bomb, Box 112, PSF, HSTL; photostat in Craven and Cate, eds., *The Army Air Forces in World War II*, Vol. 5, between pp. 712 and 713.

11. Craven and Cate, eds., *The Army Air Forces in World War II*, Vol. 5, between pp. 712–13. For instance, Morton Grodzins, editor of the Press, wrote *Harper's*; and *Harper's*, in turn, gave additional publicity to the new version of events when it published Grodzins' letter (and quoted the relevant Truman letter paragraph). Morton Grodzins, "Japan's Surrender," *Harper's*, Vol. 206, No. 1237 (June 1953), p. 18.

12. Truman, *Year of Decisions*, pp. 420–21. Barton J. Bernstein observes that such an instruction would likely have been implicit, if not explicit, in Truman's discussions with Stimson at Potsdam: "Thus, what may have been an informal but clearly understood arrangement was transformed, in the aftermath, into *firm* instructions. That made the president seem both firm and authoritative, and allowed him again to emphasize that *he* had made the decision to use the atomic bombs." Bernstein, "Writing, Righting, or Wronging," p. 172.

13. *Public Papers of the Presidents, Harry S. Truman, 1945*, p. 199.

14. HST to James L. Cate, January 12, 1953, Atomic Bomb, Box 112, PSF, HSTL; reprinted in Craven and Cate, eds., *The Army Air Forces in World War II*, Vol. 5, between pp. 712–13.

15. Truman, *Year of Decisions*, p. 421.

16. HST, handwritten journal, July 25, 1945, "Ross, Mr. and Mrs. Charles G.," Box 322, PSF, HSTL; see also Truman, *Off the Record*, ed. Ferrell, p. 55.

17. HST, handwritten journal, July 18, 1945, "Ross, Mr. and Mrs. Charles G.," Box 322, PSF, HSTL; see also Truman, *Off the Record*, ed. Ferrell, p. 54.

18. HST, handwritten journal, July 25, 1945, "Ross, Mr. and Mrs. Charles G.," Box 322, PSF, HSTL; see also Truman, *Off the Record*, ed. Ferrell, p. 56.

19. Feis served under Henry Stimson and Cordell Hull at the State Department and under Henry Stimson, Robert Patterson (and briefly Kenneth Royall) at the War Department.

20. HST to Herbert Feis, [late April 1962]; as cited in Poen, *Strictly Personal and Confidential*, p. 34.

21. Herbert Feis to LRG, June 1, 1962, Box 3, Entry 2, Groves Papers, RG 200, NA.

22. LRG to Herbert Feis, August 9, 1962, Box 3, Entry 2, Groves Papers, RG 200, NA.

23. "The President's News Conference of October 26, 1950," in *Public Papers of the*

Presidents: Harry S. Truman, 1950 (Washington, D.C.: U.S. Government Printing Office, 1965), p. 273.

24. Eaker interview with Hugh N. Ahmann, February 10–11, 1975, pp. 552–53, United States Air Force Oral History Program, AFHRA; Spaatz Diary, August 1, 1945, "August 1945 Personal," Box 21, Spaatz Papers, LC.

25. Eben A. Ayers, memorandum beginning "*ATOM BOMB*, From Rigdon's book . . .," no date, "Atomic 1" File, Box 4, Eben A. Ayers Papers, HSTL. Ayers recorded on October 13, 1951: "I gave him [Truman] a rather lengthy document which I prepared about his participation in the development and use of the atomic bomb in 1945. I told him that I had put in much time on it but that I was not too satisfied with it as few documents bearing upon it are available. . . . I told the President I thought there probably were some in his personal files in his office and he told me to check over them with his secretary, Miss Conway. He said he had told her to make available anything he had there to George Elsey or me." Ayers Diary, October 13, 1951, Ayers Papers, HSTL.

26. Undated transcript beginning "Mr. Harris: I would like . . .," p. 5, Foreign Policy File, Box 4, Post-Presidential Memoirs, HSTL.

27. "Discussion," May 24, 1954, p. 14, Box 650, Post-Presidential Memoirs, HSTL.

28. Truman, *Off the Record*, ed. Ferrell, p. 348.

29. WAH to HST, May 26, 1964, "Truman, Harry S. and Bess," Box 515, Harriman Papers, LC.

30. HST to WAH, June 10, 1964, "Truman, Harry S. and Bess," Box 515, Harriman Papers, LC.

31. William M. Franklin to WAH, June 19, 1964, "Truman, Harry S. and Bess," Box 515, Harriman Papers, LC.

32. See Truman, *Off the Record*, ed. Ferrell, p. 6.

33. HST interview with Richard G. Hewlett, January 30, 1959, p. 1, Department of Energy Archives, Washington, D.C.; courtesy of Roger M. Anders.

34. HST interview with Richard G. Hewlett, January 30, 1959, p. 3, Department of Energy Archives, Washington, D.C.

35. HST interview with Richard G. Hewlett, January 30, 1959, p. 2, Department of Energy Archives, Washington, D.C.

36. HST interview with Richard G. Hewlett, January 30, 1959, pp. 2–3, Department of Energy Archives, Washington, D.C.

37. Phillips, *The Truman Presidency*, p. 436.

38. "Oral History Interview with Judge Samuel I. Rosenman," p. 103, Box 51, Oral History Interview Collection, HSTL.

39. Truman, *Off the Record*, ed. Ferrell, p. 6.

40. Messer, "New Evidence on Truman's Decision," p. 55.

41. Truman, *Dear Bess*, ed. Ferrell, p. vii.

42. Truman, *Dear Bess*, ed. Ferrell, p. viii.

43. Truman, *Off the Record*, ed. Ferrell, p. 50.

44. See HST to Mrs. Charles G. Ross, October 17, 1951, "Ross, Mr. and Mrs. Charles G.," Box 322, PSF, HSTL.

45. Eben A. Ayers to HST, October 15, 1951, "Ross, Mr. and Mrs. Charles G.," Box 322, PSF, HSTL.

46. Ibid.

47. Florence Ross to Bess [and Harry S.] Truman, October 16, 1951, "Ross, Mr. and Mrs., Charles G.," Box 322, PSF, HSTL. (Most of this letter is addressed to President Truman.)

48. HST to Mrs. Charles G. Ross, October 17, 1951, "Ross, Mr. and Mrs., Charles G.," Box 322, PSF, HSTL.

49. Florence Ross to Bess [and Harry S.] Truman, October 16, 1951, "Ross, Mr. and Mrs., Charles G.," Box 322, PSF, HSTL.

50. HST to Mrs. Charles G. Ross, October 17, 1951, "Ross, Mr. and Mrs., Charles G.," Box 322, PSF, HSTL.

51. HST to Eben A. Ayers, October 17, 1951, "Ross, Mr. and Mrs. Charles G.," Box 322, PSF, HSTL.

52. "Oral History Interview with Eben A. Ayers," Volume I, p. 59, Oral History Interview Collection, HSTL.

53. Myrtle Bergheim to HST, January 12, 1951, "Ross, Mr. and Mrs. Charles G.," Box 322, PSF, HSTL.

54. Hillman, *Mr. President*, cited from the title page.

55. Ayers Diary, March 6, 1952; Set 2, Part 3, Box 27, Eben A. Ayers Papers, HSTL. See also Ayers' March 1, 1952, diary entry: "He [Truman] commented that this would be good in this year's campaign and that seemed to have been one motive that actuated him in releasing this material."

56. Orville, Prescott, "Books of the Times," *The New York Times*, March 18, 1952.

57. Hillman, *Mr. President*, p. 1.

58. Hillman, *Mr. President*, p. 2.

59. Hillman, *Mr. President*, p. 3.

60. HST to William Hillman, cited in Hillman, *Mr. President*, pp. 251–52. This letter is also in Box 122, PSF, HSTL.

61. Hillman papers, courtesy of Mrs. William Hillman.

62. Hillman, *Mr. President*, pp. 122–25.

63. HST, handwritten journal, August 10, 1945, Box 333, PSF, HSTL; see also Truman, *Off the Record*, ed. Ferrell, p. 61.

64. Hillman, *Mr. President*, p. 125.

65. Hillman, *Mr. President*, p. 123.

66. Elsewhere Truman indicated that he was leaving various materials to Margaret. For instance, he wrote his cousin, Nellie Noland. "I've been offered a million dollars for my memoirs! They are not for sale at any price. But I intend to set 'em down and leave 'em to Margie." HST to Nellie Noland, August 8, 1951; printed in Truman, *Off the Record*, ed. Ferrell, p. 215. After his memoirs were published, Truman wrote Edward F. McFaddin, a justice of the Arkansas supreme court, "These memoirs of mine are not complete. I dictated over a million and a half words on the subject and we had to cut the number to about 520,000. I'm leaving the balance to Margaret, hoping it will be of some value to her and also an addition to the truth and the facts of the time." HST to Edward F. McFaddin, September 29, 1958; printed in Truman, *Off the Record*, ed. Ferrell, p. 369. See also, Truman, *Where the Buck Stops*, ed. Margaret Truman, pp. [v], vii.

67. My thanks to Leo C. Maley III for pointing out this connection.

68. Eben A. Ayers to HST, September 22, 1951, "Potsdam Conference," Box 11, Ayers Papers, HSTL.

69. HST, handwritten "Note for Mr. Ayers," "Personal—Truman, Harry S., Notes—Letters," Box 24, Ayers Papers, HSTL. Truman, however, did not provide Ayers with his recollections about Stalin and Churchill. Ayers noted: "The President said on October 13, that in response to my inquiry as to whether he had completed the attached memorandum about the Potsdam conference, that he decided when he was writing it that he would not make any comments about Churchill or Stalin at the time. He said he would rather wait until after the British election and that he would write some more for me some time thereafter." Eben A. Ayers, memorandum, October 15, 1951, "Potsdam Conference," Box 11, Ayers Papers, HSTL; see also Ayers Diary, October 13, 1951. Had Truman shown Ayers his Potsdam journal, Ayers would have discovered at least one comment. On July 17, 1945, Truman wrote, "I can deal with Stalin. He is honest—but smart as hell." HST, handwritten journal, July 17, 1945, "Ross, Mr. and Mrs. Charles G.," Box 322, PSF, HSTL; see also Truman, *Off the Record*, ed. Ferrell, p. 53.

70. HST, handwritten journal, July 17, 1945, "Ross, Mr. and Mrs. Charles G.," Box 322, PSF, HSTL; see also Truman, *Off the Record*, ed. Ferrell, p. 53.

71. HST, handwritten "Note for Mr. Ayers," "Personal—Truman, Harry S., Notes—Letters," Box 24, Ayers Papers, HSTL; Hillman, *Mr. President*, p. 123.

72. Messer, "New Evidence on Truman's Decision," p. 55.

73. Hillman, *Mr. President*, pp. 214, 217.

74. HST to Richard B. Russell, August 9, 1945, Misc. 45–46, Box 197, Official File, HSTL. My thanks to Leo C. Maley III for pointing this out. (Also, Truman's original phrase, "because they are beasts," was edited to read, "because they are cruel.")

75. HST, handwritten journal, July 16, 1945, "Ross, Mr. and Mrs. Charles G.," Box 322, PSF, HSTL; see also Truman, *Off the Record*, ed. Ferrell, p. 52.

76. Truman, *Year of Decisions*, p. 341.

77. For instance, the specific sequence "carrying," "pushing," and "pulling" is found in the journal but not in published accounts written by other members of Truman's party. See Byrnes, *Speaking Frankly*, p. 68; Leahy, *I Was There*, pp. 395–96; and Merriman Smith, *Thank You Mr. President* (New York: Harper & Brothers, 1946), p. 244.

78. Francis Heller interview with author, October 24, 1989.

79. Ibid.

Chapter 45: "The Most Terrible Bomb," "The Most Terrible Thing"

1. JJMc to Clark M. Clifford, September 17, 1984, Records of the Truman Centennial Commission, HSTL.

2. For a published collection of Truman's unsent letters, many of which display angry and emotional outbursts on a variety of topics, see Poen, ed., *Strictly Personal and Confidential*.

3. Samuel McCrea Cavert to HST, August 9, 1945, 692-A, Official File, HSTL.

4. HST to Samuel McCrea Cavert, August 11, 1945, 692-A, Official File, HSTL.

5. HST to Roman Bohnen, December 12, 1946, Atomic Energy, Box 2, PSF, HSTL.

6. HST to Irv Kupcinet, August 5, 1963, Box 58, PPF, HSTL; see also Poen, ed., *Strictly Personal and Confidential*, pp. 35–36.

7. HST, quoted in *The New York Times*, February 3, 1958, p. 16.

8. Hiroshima City Council "Resolution No. 11," February 13, 1958 attached to letter from Tsukasa Nitoguri to HST, March 1, 1958, Hiroshima File, Box 12, Post-Presidential Secretary's Office Files, HSTL. This protest was noted in *The New York Times*, February 14, 1958, p. 2.

9. Truman attached a handwritten note to an early draft of this statement which read, "Have it ready when I return. We'll have a press conference and release both letters. Have them mimeographed." Note attached to a draft of Truman's March 12, 1958, letter to Tsukasa Nitoguri; Hiroshima File, Box 12, Post-Presidential Secretary's Office Files, HSTL.

10. "For Immediate Release to the Press, Radio and Television," (HST to Tsukasa Nitoguri), Hiroshima File, Box 12, Post-Presidential Secretary's Office Files, HSTL. See also "Truman, in Letter to Hiroshima, Defends His Atom Bomb Order," *The New York Times*, March 15, 1958, pp. 1, 5.

11. HST, March 13, 1958, letter, reprinted in "Truman, in Letter to Hiroshima, Defends His Atom Bomb Order," *The New York Times*, March 15, 1958, pp. 1, 5.

12. Tsukasa Nitoguri, "A Protest against Mr. Truman's Reply to the Resolution passed by Hiroshima City Council," March 20, 1958, Hiroshima File, Box 39, Post-Presidential Files, HSTL.

13. Hiroshi Wakiyama to HST, March 29, 1958, Hiroshima File, Box 39, Post-Presidential Files, HSTL.

14. "R.I.P.," *National Review* (March 29, 1958), p. 296.

15. HST, handwritten journal, July 25, 1945, "Ross, Mr. and Mrs. Charles, G.," Box 322, PSF, HSTL; see also Truman, *Off the Record*, ed. Ferrell, pp. 55–56.

16. "Memorandum of Conference with the President, August 8, 1945, at 10:00 a.m.," Stimson Papers, Reel 128, YUL. Wallace Diary, August 10, 1945; in Wallace, *The Price of Vision*, ed. Blum, p. 474.

17. HST, handwritten speech delivered to the Gridiron Dinner, December 15, 1945, Speeches, Longhand Notes File, Box 46, PSF, HSTL. (A typed copy, signed by Truman, is in the same file.)

18. Lewis L. Strauss, "Memorandum for Files of Lewis L. Strauss," July 21, 1948, AEC-Memoranda to AEC Commissioners, Strauss Papers, HHPL.

19. David E. Lilienthal, *The Journals of David E. Lilienthal*, Vol. II: *The Atomic Energy Years, 1945–1950* (New York, 1964), p. 474.

20. HST, quoted in Lilienthal, *Journals, Atomic Energy Years*, p. 474.

21. UP teletype, "Washington, November 30, [1950]," copy in Atomic Energy File, Box 6, Elmer Davis Papers, LC; see also Eben Ayers' undated summary of this press conference (beginning "On November 30, 1950, . . .") in Atomic Bomb File, Box 4, Ayers Papers, HSTL.

22. HST to Thomas E. Murray, January 19, 1953, Atomic Bomb, Box 112, PSF, HSTL.

23. HST, handwritten memorandum, April 24, 1954; Trip File, Box 742, PPF, HSTL; see also Truman, *Off the Record*, ed. Ferrell, p. 304. Truman continues, "In the first place I could not bring myself to order the slaughter of 25,000,000 noncombatants. In 1945 I had ordered the A–Bomb dropped on Japan at two places devoted almost exclusively to war production. We were at war. We were trying to end it in order to save the lives of our soldiers and sailors. The new bomb was a powerful new weapon of war. In my opinion it had to be used to end the unnecessary slaughter on both sides. It was an entirely different situation from Korea. We stopped the war and saved thousands of casualties on both sides."

24. HST, "Discussion [with Hillman and Noyes]," February 18, 1954, p. 5, HST Quotes File, Box 9, Post-Presidential-Memoirs, HSTL.

25. Robert Arthur, quoted in Miller, *Plain Speaking*, p. 230. The film was never made; Truman never went to Hiroshima.

26. Margaret Truman, *Bess W. Truman* (New York, 1986), p. 270.

27. John A. Gronouski to Gar Alperovitz, October 4, 1989.

28. John A. Gronouski to Martha Hamilton, October 16, 1985; copy sent by John A. Gronouski to author, October 4, 1989.

29. "Oral History Interview with Tom C. Clark," October 17, 1972, pp. 88–89, Oral History Collection, HSTL.

Part III: James F. Byrnes

Chapter 46: Disappearing From—and Revising—History

1. Cousins and Finletter, "A Beginning for Sanity," pp. 5–9, 38–40, cited material from p. 7.

2. Stimson, "The Decision," pp. 98, 100. It also indirectly refers to him (though not by name) as the "public servant" who warned Roosevelt in a March 1945 memorandum of the costs of the Manhattan Project.

3. *The Beginning or the End*, MGM, February, 1947.

4. Ellis M. Zacharias, "How We Bungled the Japanese Surrender," *Look*, June 6, 1950, pp. 12–21, cited material from p. 21.

5. Blackett, *Fear, War, and the Bomb*, pp. 127–39.

6. Baldwin, *Great Mistakes of the War*, p. 91.

7. Walker, "The Decision to Use the Bomb," p. 102.

8. Williams, *The Tragedy of American Diplomacy*, pp. 243–58; Louis Morton, "The Decision to Use the Atomic Bomb," *Foreign Affairs*, Vol. 25 (January 1957), pp. 334–53.

9. Oppenheimer to author, November 4, 1964.

10. Brown, *James F. Byrnes* pp. 351–52; Robertson, Sly and Able, p. 493.

11. Brown, *James F. Byrnes*, p. 352.

12. Ibid.

13. For a discussion of Byrnes' gubernatorial career, see Robertson, *Sly and Able*, pp. 491–525.

14. Robertson, *Sly and Able*, p. 501.

15. Leo Szilard, "A Personal History of the Atomic Bomb," *The University of Chicago Round Table*, September 25, 1949, pp. 14–16, cited material from p. 15.

16. See Forrestal, *The Forrestal Diaries*, p. 78.

17. George M. Elsey, "Some White House Recollections," p. 361.

18. Feis, *The China Tangle*, p. 320.

19. Athan Theoharis, "James F. Byrnes: Unwitting Yalta Myth-Maker," *Political Science Quarterly*, Vol. 81, No. 4 (December 1966), pp. 581–92, cited material from p. 592.

20. Byrnes, *Speaking Frankly*, p. 205.

21. Byrnes, *Speaking Frankly*, pp. 204–05.

22. Byrnes, *Speaking Frankly*, p. 206.

23. Byrnes, *Speaking Frankly*, p. 209.

24. Byrnes, *Speaking Frankly*, p. 208.

25. Byrnes, *Speaking Frankly*, p. 261.

26. Notes of the Interim Committee Meeting, May 31, 1945, File 100, Roll 8, H-B Files, M1108, NA.

27. Byrnes, *Speaking Frankly*, p. 261.

28. Byrnes, *Speaking Frankly*, pp. 261–62.

29. Byrnes, *Speaking Frankly*, p. 262.

30. Ibid.

31. Ibid.

32. Byrnes, *All in One Lifetime*, p. 308.

33. Ibid.

34. Byrnes, *All in One Lifetime*, p. 297.

35. Stimson Diary, August 10, 1945.

36. Byrnes, *All in One Lifetime*, p. 296.

37. See Byrnes, *All in One Lifetime*, pp. 296, 305–06.

38. Byrnes, *All in One Lifetime*, p. 269.

39. Byrnes, *All in One Lifetime*, p. 291.

40. Byrnes, *All in One Lifetime*, p. 286.

41. Brown notes that in response to Byrnes' request (while he was preparing his 1947 *Speaking Frankly*), "I sent him a copy of my diary of the White House years . . ." (Brown, *James F. Byrnes of South Carolina*, pp. 351–52.) Similarly, Brown told Messer that ". . . when he got to writing his damn book, he was damn happy to refer to this thing . . . and I was glad to let him have it. Although I questioned his right to [publish] so soon after being in the State Department. . . ." (Brown interview with Robert Messer, December 20–21, 1972; provided to author courtesy of Dr. Messer.) A comparison of the text with certain passages in the diary is also instructive. For example, Byrnes notes Stalin's tribute to him at the end of the conference: "He has brought us together in reaching so many important decisions." (Byrnes, *Speaking Frankly*, p. 86.) Brown records Stalin as saying: "He [Byrnes] has brought us together in reaching so many important decisions. . . ." (WB's Book, August 1, 1945, Folder 602, Byrnes Papers, CUL.) The official minutes say only: "He has helped us to reach agreements." (FRUS, Pots. II, p. 601.) Neither of Byrnes' books notes Brown's July 18 entry: "JFB had hoped Russian declaration of war against Japan would come out of this conference" (WB's Book, July 18, 1945, Folder 602, Byrnes Papers, CUL); nor his August 3 observation: "President, Leahy, JFB

agrred [*sic*] Japas [*sic*] looking for peace. . . . President afraid [the Japanese] will sue for peace through Russia instead of some country like Sweden." (WB's Book, August 3, 1945, Folder 602, Byrnes Papers, CUL.) Byrnes does acknowledge in general that he used Brown's discussion in his 1958 *All in One Lifetime* (Byrnes, *All in One Lifetime*, acknowledgments.)

42. "Was A-Bomb on Japan a Mistake?," p. 66.

43. "Was A-Bomb . . . ?," p. 67.

44. "Was A-Bomb . . . ?," p. 65.

45. Ibid.

46. Byrnes interview with Fred Freed, 1964, pp. 13–14, Box 79, Feis Papers, LC.

47. Byrnes interview with Fred Freed, 1964, p. 21, Box 79, Feis Papers, LC.

48. Byrnes interview with Fred Freed, 1964, pp. 38–39, Box 79, Feis Papers, LC.

49. Byrnes interview with Fred Freed, 1964, p. 39, Box 79, Feis Papers, LC.

50. Ibid.

51. Ibid.

52. Byrnes interview with Fred Freed, 1964, pp. 7–8, Box 79, Feis Papers, LC.

53. Byrnes interview with Fred Freed, 1964, p. 9, Box 79, Feis Papers, LC.

54. Byrnes interview with Fred Freed, 1964, p. 11, Box 79, Feis Papers, LC.

55. Byrnes interview with Fred Freed, 1964, p. 9, Box 79, Feis Papers, LC.

56. Ibid.

57. Byrnes interview with Fred Freed, 1964, p. 16, Box 79, Feis Papers, LC.

58. Byrnes interview with Fred Freed, 1964, p. 18, Box 79, Feis Papers, LC.

59. Byrnes interview with Fred Freed, 1964, p. 15, Box 79, Feis Papers, LC.

60. Byrnes interview with Fred Freed, 1964, p. 14, Box 79, Feis Papers, LC.

61. WB's Book, Folder 602, Byrnes Papers, CUL; Brown Diary, Folder 54 (1), Byrnes Papers, CUL.

62. WB's Book, July 23, 1945, Folder 602, Byrnes Papers, CUL. See also entries for July 18, 24, 26.

63. Excerpts From Notes of Walter Brown, Folder 54 (1), Byrnes Papers, CUL.

64. Brown interview with Robert Messer, December 20–21, 1972. Provided to author courtesy of Dr. Messer.

65. In a 1990 interview with J.P. Rosensweig, Brown refused to grant direct access to any part of the diary. (Brown interview with J.P. Rosensweig, 1990.) Nor, of course, has he donated any further text to Clemson University for archival research. (Michael Kohl of Special Collections, Clemson University Libraries, to Williams, February 28, 1995, in author's possession.)

66. Omitted from the published version, for instance, are the details of Byrnes' swearing-in as Secretary of State. (WB's Book, July 3, 1945, Folder 602, Byrnes Papers, CUL.) Similarly omitted is Byrnes' comment that "somebody had made an awful mistake in bringing about a situation where Russia was permitted to come out of a war with the power she will have." (Brown Diary, July 24, 1945, Folder 54 (1), Byrnes Papers, CUL). See above, pp. 417–18, for other information which does not appear in the published version. Though editing is obvious in such instances, it is, of course, impossible to know of other omissions or changes without the actual texts in hand.

67. *The New York Times*, August 30, 1945, p. 1.

68. Ibid.

69. Ibid.

70. *The New York Times*, August 30, 1945, p. 4.

71. "Sec. Byrnes Verbatim Report of Press Conference at Dept. of State," Vol. XVI, August 29, 1945, pp. 17–19, RG 59, NA.

72. Ibid.

73. "The Bomb and the Peace," *The Commonweal*, Vol. XLII, No. 22 (September 14, 1945), p. 515.

74. Kennan to author, January 11, 1965.

Part IV: Managing History

Chapter 47: Leslie R. Groves

1. Peter Goodchild, *J. Robert Oppenheimer: Shatterer of Worlds.* (Boston, 1980), pp. 56–57. For a slightly different version of this comment, see Kenneth D. Nichols, *The Road to Trinity* (New York, 1987), pp. 107–108.

2. Leona Marshall Libby, *The Uranium People* (New York, 1979), p. 95. "His superiority complex was fed by the fact that he ruled by fiat over five Nobel Laureates. . . ."

3. Groves was not on the authorized list of MAGIC recipients; the leading expert on Groves, biographer Stanley Goldberg, confirms that nowhere in his papers is there evidence, so far as is known, of his knowledge of MAGIC. (Discussion of May 16, 1994 at National Press Club, Washington, D.C.)

4. Robert Jungk, *Brighter Than a Thousand Suns* (New York, 1958), p. 209 n.

5. Goldberg, Stanley. "General Groves and the Atomic West: The Making and Meaning of Hanford," in Bruce Hevly and John Findlay, eds., *The Atomic West* (Seattle, forthcoming).

6. See, for instance, Groves, *Now It Can Be Told*, p. 70; Goldberg, "General Groves and the Atomic West: The Making and Meaning of Hanford."

7. On this point, see Sigal, *Fighting to a Finish*; and Sigal, "Bureaucratic Politics and Tactical Use of Committees," pp. 326–364.

8. See Jones, *Manhattan: The Army and the Atomic Bomb*, pp. 74–75, for the story of how and why Groves was selected.

9. See Interim Committee Log, File 98, Roll 8, H-B Files, M1108, NA.

10. "Memorandum to the Chief of Staff" from LRG, March 26, 1945. File 5B, Sub-Series 1, Top Secret Files, MED, M1109, NA.

11. Meyer Berger, *The Story of The New York Times* (New York, 1951, 1970), pp. 511–12; see also Groves, *Now It Can Be Told*, pp. 325–26. There are conflicting accounts as to how Laurence was paid. According to the *Times* official history, Laurence worked under government contract for less than regular salary and the *Times* agreed to make up the difference. Groves states that he agreed "to have Laurence continue on the payroll of *The New York Times*, but with his expenses covered by the MED." (Groves, *Now It Can Be Told*, p. 326).

12. Notes of the Interim Committee Meeting, May 18, 1945, File 100, Roll 8, H-B Files, M1108, NA.

13. "Objectives," 000.71 (Releasing Information), MED, RG 77, NA, with handwritten note "Note: Called Page's Office 5/29 they will note we made 2 copies . . ." See also the nearly identical list of "Objectives," undated, File 74, Roll 6, H-B Files, M1108, NA.

14. For sources concerning the draft presidential statements, see below, note 24. On Nagasaki, see Craven and Cate, *The Army Air Forces in World War II*, Vol. 5, p. 724; Mission Planning Summary, Report Number 9, 509th Composite Group, Box 6, Entry 1, Groves Papers, RG 200, NA; United States Strategic Bombing Survey, *The Effects of Atomic Bombs on Hiroshima and Nagasaki*, (Washington, D.C.: Government Printing Office), June 30, 1946, p. 9. See also map of Nagasaki enclosed in the USSBS report.

15. "Draft" of presidential statement, June 7, 1945, File 74, Roll 6, H-B Files, M1108, NA.

16. FRUS, Pots. II, 1945, Conference Documents and Supplementary Papers, No. 1315, "White House Press Release," p. 1378.

17. Interim Committee Log, June 21, 1945, entry, File 98, Roll 8, H-B Files, M1108, NA.

18. Ibid. In final form, the statement gave a brief explanation of the atomic bomb and provided an account of how the United States had collaborated with Britain in building the weapon. It warned Japan that if its leaders "do not now accept our terms they may

expect a rain of ruin from the air, the like of which has never been seen on this earth" and cautioned that the Government would not "divulge the technical processes of production or all the military applications, pending further examination of possible methods of protecting us and the rest of the world from the danger of sudden destruction." The statement closed with an assurance that the president would recommend that Congress establish "an appropriate commission" to control atomic energy. (FRUS Pots. II, 1945, Conference Documents and Supplementary Papers, No. 1315, "White House Press Release", p. 1376.)

19. Interim Committee Log, File 98, Roll 8, H-B Files, M1108, pp. 16–17; see also Hewlett and Anderson, *The New World 1939/1946*, pp. 398–99.

20. Stimson Diary, July 30, 1945.

21. Compare final statement, FRUS Pots II Vol. II, 1945, Conference Documents and Supplementary Papers, No. 1315, "White House Press Release," p. 1377, to "Draft of 30 July 1945," Presidential statement, File 74, Roll 6, H-B Files, M1108, NA.

22. Stimson to Truman, July 31, 1945, File 74, Roll 6, H-B Files, M1108, NA.

23. President to the Secretary of War, July 31, 1945, File 74, Roll 6, H-B Files, M1108, NA.

24. See Groves, *Now It Can Be Told*, pp. 327–30; "The White House—Washington, DC—Immediate Release—Statement by the President of the United States," File 5D, Sub-Series 1, Roll 1, Top Secret Files, MED, M1109, NA, (and earlier drafts from File 74, H-B); and FRUS, Pots. II, 1945, No. 1315, "White House Press Release," p. 1376. For details of how the presidential statement was revised, see various drafts in File 74, Roll 6, H-B Files, M1108, NA; "Memorandum for Mr. Page" from Consodine, June 19, 1945, 000.71 (Releasing Information), Box 31, Entry 5, MED, RG 77, NA; Consodine to Page, June 20, 1945 and Consodine to Harrison, June 29, 1945, File 74, Roll 6, H-B Files, M1108, NA; and the Interim Committee Log, File 98, Roll 8, H-B Files, M1108, NA. Related files touching on the presidential release are also contained in Box 31, 000.71 (Releasing Information) and (Laurence Stories), Entry 5, MED, RG 77, NA.

25. "Interim Committee Log," May 19, 1945 entry, File 98, Roll 8, H-B Files, M1108, NA. p. 3.

26. "Memorandum for Mr. Page" from Consodine, June 19, 1945, 000.71 (Releasing Information), Box 31, Entry 5, MED, RG 77, NA.

27. Ibid. No reference was made to the U.S.-U.K. agreement, the Combined Development Trust, or the Belgian Agreement in the final statement. See "Statement of the Secretary of War," File 73, Roll 6, H-B Files, M1108, NA.

28. "Memorandum for Mr. Page" from Consodine, June 19, 1945, 000.71 (Releasing Information), Box 31, Entry 5, MED, RG 77, NA.

29. Interim Committee Log, June 21 to July 11 entries. File 98, Roll 8, H-B Files, M1108, NA, pp. 9–10. See also drafts of "Statement of the Secretary of War," File 73, Roll 6, H-B Files, M1108, NA.

30. Statement of the Secretary of War, File 73, Roll 6, H-B Files, M1108, NA.

31. Paul Boyer, "The Cloud over the Culture," p. 28.

32. "Suggestions regarding release of story," G. O. Robinson, June 6, 1945, 000.71 (Releasing Information), Box 31, Entry 5, MED, RG 77, NA.

33. "Memorandum for General Groves: Subject: MED Public Relations Program," from W.A. Consodine, June 27, 1945, 000.71 (Releasing Information), MED, RG 77, NA. Asterisks in text are used in place of letters and numbers in the original document.

34. "Memorandum for Mr. Harrison," from LRG, June 20, 1945, 000.71 (Releasing Information), Box 31, Entry 5, MED, RG 77, NA. On June 21, the Interim Committee agreed to put responsibility for the releases in the hands of Groves' organization with the cooperation of Mr. Page. (Interim Committee Log, June 21, 1945 entry, File 98, Roll 8, H-B Files, M1108, NA.)

35. "Manhattan Engineer District Public Relations Program," July 10, 1945. 000.71 (Releasing Information), Box 31, Entry 5, MED, RG 77, NA. The July 10 draft program

was revised on July 26. This approach to broadcast interviews overrode an earlier plan calling for a press conference with Stimson, Groves, and leading scientists one hour after Truman's announcement. See "Presidential Announcement," undated, 000.71 (Releasing Information), Box 31, Entry 5, MED, RG 77, NA.

36. "Subject: Manhattan Engineer District Public Relations Program," July 26, 1945, 000.71 (Releasing Information), Box 31, Entry 5, RG 77, MED, NA.

37. Copies of some of these draft stories are in 000.71 (Laurence), Box 31, Entry 5, MED, RG 77, NA. For the final press releases (authored by Laurence and others), see Manhattan District History, Book I, Volume 4, Chapter 8, NA.

38. For copies of alternative drafts of the Trinity test story, see File 4, Sub-Series 1, Roll 1, Top Secret Files, MED, M1109, NA.

39. Berger, *The Story of the New York Times*, p. 514.

40. Berger, *The Story of the New York Times*, p. 519 (Laurence not witnessing Hiroshima attack); p. 523 (Laurence witnessing attack on Nagasaki).

41. Henry D. Smyth, *Atomic Energy for Military Purposes* (Princeton, 1945). This edition includes minor changes from the version released in August (e.g., the addition of a few names and the inclusion of an index).

42. Groves to Smyth, April 17, 1944, and Smyth to Groves April 21, 1944, Administrative Files, General Correspondence, 319.1 (Smyth), MED, RG 77, NA; cited in Jones, *Manhattan*, pp. 556–57.

43. LRG to Smyth, May 21, 1945. Tab N, Folder 12, General Correspondence, Office of the Commanding General, MED, RG 77, NA. Cited in Jones, *Manhattan*, pp. 558–59. These rules were adopted after Smyth had prepared the original manuscript and were used as a guide to subsequent editing under the direction of Groves' scientific adviser, Richard Tolman.

44. At this same time Conant judged that "anyone could get the information contained in the report with very little money in less than three months." He was pleased that "if we gave out only these scientific data in addition to the Secretary's release . . . we could hold the fort." See "Notes of a Meeting on the Smyth Report in the Office of the Secretary of War, August 2, 1945," File 12, Sub-Series 1, Roll 2, Top Secret Files, MED, M1109, NA, pp. 3, 7.

45. LRG to Chief of Staff, August 6, 1945, File FB, Sub-Series 1, Roll 1, Top Secret File, MED, M1109, NA. Szilard disagreed: he believed that the Smyth Report revealed to other nations "knowledge of the methods that actually worked." (See Szilard dictation, May 22, 1956, Leo Szilard Papers, University of California, San Diego. Cited in Lanouette, *Genius in the Shadows*, p. 272.) In contrast, Conant had such confidence in the Report that in December 1945 he gave Molotov a copy for his daughter to use in school. (See Hershberg, *James B. Conant*, p. 256.)

46. Groves, *Now It Can Be Told*, p. 331.

47. Robert Karl Manoff, "Covering the Bomb: Press and State in the Shadow of Nuclear War," *War, Peace and the News Media: Proceedings* (New York, 1987), pp. 200–01. Paper delivered March 19, 1983, at the conference on "War, Peace, and the News Media," New York University, March 18–19, 1983.

48. Louis Liebovich, *The Press and the Origins of the Cold War, 1944–1947* (New York, 1988), pp. 85–86, p. 93, n. 12. Michael Yavenditti observes: ". . . [W]henever a government, for security or other reasons, enjoys a monopoly on information, the news is obviously controlled. In the initial period after Hiroshima, Americans were heavily dependent on government sources. . . . Restricted in its access to classified information, the media never seriously challenged government declarations about the bomb." Michael J. Yavenditti, "The American People and the Use of the Atomic Bomb On Japan: The 1940s," *The Historian*. Vol. 36, No. 2 (February 1974), pp. 224–47, quoted material from pp. 233–34.

49. "LRG Answers the queries for research study—Reference is made to Captain Wallace's letter of March 19, 1948," Box 1, Entry 4, Groves Papers, RG 200, NA.

50. LRG to Loew's (contractual agreement), December 31, 1945, Box 11, Entry 1, Groves Papers, RG 200, NA.

51. LRG to Carter Barron. April 15, 1946, Box 11, Entry 1, Groves Papers, RG 200, NA.

52. Brown, Harrison, "The Beginning or the End: A Review," *Bulletin of the Atomic Scientists*, III (March 1947), p. 99. For a discussion of the film's fictional portrayal of this leafletting and other inaccuracies, see Yavenditti, Michael J., "Atomic Scientists and Hollywood: *The Beginning or the End?*," *Film and History*, Vol. 8, No. 4 (December 1978), p. 84.

53. Yavenditti, "Atomic Scientists and Hollywood," p. 83. "Cochrane does not display all the symptoms of radiation poisoning. He merely faints. His subsequent death is probably meant to represent a token punishment for the inventors of the bomb." For a description of Harry Daghlian's death, see Weisgall, *Operation Crossroads*, pp. 138–39.

54. Walter Lippmann to Dr. Frank Aydelotte, October 28, 1946, Box 11, Entry 1, Groves Papers, RG 200, NA. On November 1, 1946, James McGuinness of MGM wrote to Lippmann to reassure him that a new scene would "sum up the many conferences the President had with his military, naval, diplomatic advisers—also with Churchill—and [show] the civilian and scientific advice he sought before he followed the urgings of his advisers and authorized the use of the bomb in combat." See McGuinness to Lippmann, November 1, 1946, Box 11, Entry 1, Groves Papers, RG 200, NA.

55. Lippman also wrote to McCloy, who passed his concerns on to Patterson. Patterson answered on November 5 that "I have instructed the Public Relations Division to hold up . . . final review until we get a chance to consider Walter Lippmann's criticism." In a memorandum to Patterson, Groves stated that "the White House had objected to [the Truman-Groves-Stimson] scene and it was already scheduled for deletion"—adding that had the White House not objected, "I would have insisted upon its removal." Groves to Carter Barron, April 15, 1946, Box 11, Entry 1, Groves Papers, RG 200, NA. In point of fact, this was the original Truman "decision" scene Groves had previously approved—indeed, the same scene in which Groves proposed that his character should state: "The minimum estimate of our losses is half a million men. . . ." See Secretary Patterson to John McCloy, Nov. 5, 1946, Atomic Energy Safe File #3, Box 1, Entry 75, Secretary of War, RG 107, NA; LRG Memorandum for the Secretary of War, November 15, 1946, Atomic Energy Safe File #3, Box 1, Entry 75, Secretary of War, RG 107, NA; and LRG to Carter Barron, April 15, 1946, Box 11, Entry 1, Groves Papers, RG 200, NA. See also script of *The Beginning or the End*, dated March 22, 1946, Public Relations Division—Motion Picture Scripts 1942–1946, Box 8, RG 165, NA, pp. 81–83.

56. Undated note, Box 1, Entry 3, Groves Papers, RG 200, NA.

57. Groves, *Now It Can Be Told*, pp. 185–86.

58. Groves, *Now It Can Be Told*, p. 201 n.

59. Groves, *Now It Can Be Told*, p. 202.

60. Wilson to LRG, November 3, 1959. Box 10, Entry 2, Groves Papers, RG 200, NA.

61. LRG, cover note to his diaries, August 23, 1960. Box 1, Entry 7, Groves Papers, RG 200, NA.

62. LRG to Alan Landsburg, August 30, 1963, Box 5, Entry 2, Groves Papers, RG 200, NA.

63. Jean O'Leary to Major Traynor, April 18, 1945, attached to "Some Notes for Guidance to Writers of Basic Data Books on DSM Project," March 30, 1945, 319.1 History, Box 51, Entry 5, MED, RG 77, NA.

64. Murray to Szilard, August 27, 1945, File 76, Roll 6, H-B Files, M1108, NA.

65. Miscellaneous Historical Document File, HSTL. Cited in Dan Kurzman, *Day of the Bomb* (New York, 1986), p. 502.

66. Szilard letter to the Editor of *Science*, dated "August 24, 1945," attached to a letter of August 18, 1945 explaining the document would not be available for publication until "on or about August 25.") Quotation from the August 24 letter. Documents contained in

the Leo Szilard Papers, University of California–San Diego, provided courtesy of William Lanouette.

67. Murray to Szilard, August 27, 1945, File 76, Roll 6, H-B Files, M1108, NA.

68. Murray to Szilard, August 28, 1945, File 76, Roll 6, H-B Files, M1108, NA.

69. Murray to Szilard, August 27, 1945, File 76, Roll 6, H-B Files, M1108, NA.

70. William Lanouette, *Genius in the Shadows*, p. 278.

71. Nichols to Adjutant General, October 27, 1953, Box 6, Entry 2, Groves Papers, RG 200, NA.

72. Groves retained 72 feet of files, comprising all of his "top secret" correspondence, as well as the Harrison-Bundy files (which had been turned over to Groves by Stimson in September 1945). See Elizabeth P. Epps and Robert Gruber, *Introduction to National Archives and Record Service Microfilm M1109*, "Correspondence (Top Secret) of the Manhattan Engineer District, 1942–1946," pp. 3–4; see also Clifford L. Muse and Robert Gruber, *Introduction to National Archives and Record Service Microfilm M1108*, "Harrison-Bundy Files Relating to the Development of the Atomic Bomb, 1942–1946," pp. 3–4.

73. LRG to Nichols, February 29, 1948, Box 6, Entry 2, Groves Papers, RG 200, NA.

74. LRG to Nichols, October 16, 1953, Box 6, Entry 2, Groves Papers, RG 200, NA.

75. Nichols to Adjutant General, October 27, 1953, Box 6, Entry 2, Groves Papers, RG 200, NA. See also Epps and Gruber, *Introduction to National Archives and Record Service Microfilm M1109*, pp. 3–4.

76. For evidence of how Groves held the petition, see Compton to Nichols, July 24, 1945; Nichols to LRG, July 25, 1945; and Memorandum for the Files by R. Gordon Arneson, May 24, 1946; all in File 76, Roll 6, H-B Files, M1108, NA. On the declassification issue, see C. L. Marshall to Szilard, July 23, 1957, and Hoylanne D. Young to Szilard, January 31, 1961, Leo Szilard Papers, University of California, San Diego. These documents were provided courtesy of William Lanouette.

77. Knebel and Bailey, *No High Ground*, pp. viii–ix.

78. Fletcher Knebel and Charles W. Bailey, "The Fight Over the A-bomb," *Look*, Vol. 27, No. 16 (August 13, 1963), p. 19.

79. LRG to HST, marked "Sent to Mr. Truman about August 20, 1963." Box 2, Entry 2, Groves Papers, RG 200, NA. The letter was actually sent August 16, 1963; see HST to LRG, September 4, 1963, Box 5, Entry 3, Groves Papers, RG 200, NA.

80. *The New York Times*, July 29, 1963, p. 2.

81. For instance, on July 30, 1945, Groves instructed Farrington Daniels to distribute a letter to scientists at the Met Lab in Chicago threatening prosecution under the provisions of the Espionage Act if they made unauthorized "disclosures of information." (See Groves to Daniels, July 30, 1945, and enclosure. Box 32, 000.73 (Censorship), Entry 5, MED, RG 77, NA.) Related to this: Donald A. Strickland reports that "Samuel Allison and Enrico Fermi were fired from the project shortly after V-J Day, when they wrote a congressman on Manhattan Project letterhead that there were no 'atomic secrets.'" They were reinstated the following day. (Donald A. Strickland, *Scientists in Politics: The Atomic Scientists Movement, 1945–46* [West Lafayette, Indiana: Purdue University, 1968], p. 84.)

Groves complained especially that Szilard "constantly stirred up differences and was a serious detriment to the program." The "situation finally got so bad that I talked to Harvey Bundy about it and told him I wished that there was some way that we could intern Szilard." ("Dictated Oct. 17, 1963—Re: Szilard," Box 9, Entry 2, Groves Papers, RG 200, NA.) A letter drafted by Groves for Stimson's signature requested that Szilard be locked up. (Stimson refused to send the letter.) (Box 88, "201 [Szilard, Leo]," Entry 5, RG 77, MED, NA.)

There is also evidence of attempts to intimidate the press. In September 1945, Groves threatened a *Newsweek* reporter, Harold Paynter, and demanded a list of sources for each point in an article analyzing the impact of atomic power on American policy. [See Harold

Paynter to LRG, October 6, 1945, and LRG to Paynter, October 22, 1945, Box 7, Entry 2, Groves Papers, RG 200, NA.] In another case Groves evidently used an FBI agent in an attempt to intimidate the editor of the *Newark Evening News*, Lloyd Felmly. (In July 1947, the *News* had published consecutive front-page stories criticizing Groves' security practices and implying that he was hypocritically manipulating reports of security lapses at Oak Ridge and Los Alamos to discredit the civilian Atomic Energy Commission.) (See *Newark Evening News*, July 16, 1947, p. 1; *Newark Evening News*, July 17, 1947, p. 1; Martin Agronsky ABC talk, July 26, 1947, Box 2, Entry 3, Groves Papers, RG 200, NA; Consodine to Felmly, July 21, 1947, Box 2, Entry 2, Groves Papers, RG 200, NA.)

For further discussion of Groves' activities, see Stanley Goldberg, *Fighting to Build the Bomb: The Private Wars of Leslie R. Groves* (Steerforth Press), forthcoming.

82. See Thad Williamson, "Memorandum on General Groves' Postwar Efforts to Shape Perceptions of the Bomb," unpublished memorandum in the author's collection. Hiroshima Project.)

83. To recall only one of numerous instances: In connection with the MGM film, he approved a speech by his character stating, "The minimum estimate of our losses is a half million men." LRG to Carter Barron, April 15, 1946, Box 11, Entry 1, Groves Papers, RG 200, NA.

84. LRG to Robert S. Stone, October 10, 1945. Box 9, Entry 2, Groves Papers, RG 200, NA.

Chapter 48: Censorship and Secrecy: Rules and Exceptions

1. Press Code for Japan, September 18, 1945; quoted in Monica Braw, *The Atomic Bomb Suppressed: American Censorship in Occupied Japan* (Armonk, NY, 1991), p. 41.

2. Press Code for Japan, September 18, 1945; quoted in Braw, *The Atomic Bomb Suppressed*, p. 41.

3. Braw, *The Atomic Bomb Suppressed*, p. 42.

4. Braw, *The Atomic Bomb Suppressed*, pp. 89–90; Glenn D. Hook, "Censorship and Reportage of Atomic Damage and Casualties in Hiroshima and Nagasaki," *Bulletin of Concerned Asian Scholars*, Vol. 23, No. 1 (January–March 1991), pp. 13–25, see especially pp. 17–18.

5. Quoted in Braw, *The Atomic Bomb Suppressed*, p. 89.

6. Quoted in Hook, "Censorship and Reportage," p. 18.

7. Wilfred Burchett, *Shadows of Hiroshima* (London, 1983), pp. 44–45; see also Boyer, *By the Bomb's Early Light*, p. 187.

8. Braw, *The Atomic Bomb Suppressed*, pp. 83–84.

9. Robert Karl Manoff, "The Silencer," *The Quill*, February 1984, pp. 7–11, cited material from p. 10.

10. Braw, *The Atomic Bomb Suppressed*, pp. 105–06.

11. See Erik Barnouw, "The Hiroshima-Nagasaki Footage: A Report," *Historical Journal of Film, Radio and Television*, Vol, 2, no. 1 (1982), pp. 91–100; see also " '45 Japanese Film of Hiroshima Suppressed by U.S. for 22 Years," *The New York Times*, May 18, 1967, p. 6.

12. Sueo Inoue interview with Monica Braw; quoted in Braw, *The Atomic Bomb Suppressed*, p. 5.

13. Akira Iwasaki, quoted in Barnouw, "The Hiroshima-Nagasaki Footage," pp. 91–92.

14. Michael J. Leahy, "N.E.T. to Show Japanese Film of Atom Bomb Damage," *The New York Times*, August 1, 1970, p. 47; "Hiroshima-Nagasaki, August '45—Not for Sensitive U.S. Eyes," *Boston Globe*, April 5, 1970, p. B6, reproduced in Barnouw, "The Hiroshima-Nagasaki Footage," p. 96.

15. The occasion of Mitchell's 1985 notice was Sussan's death. "Ironically," Mitchell notes, "the task of capturing the agony of atomic victims may have cost Sussan his own

life. He suffered, in his last years, from lymphoma, which he and his doctor believed may have been caused by his exposure to radiation in Hiroshima and Nagasaki." Sussan was sixty-four when he died. [Greg Mitchell], "Herbert Sussan," *Nuclear Times* (November–December 1985), p. 2.

16. John W. Dower, "The Bombed: Hiroshima and Nagasaki in Japanese Memory," unpublished manuscript forthcoming in *Diplomatic History*, ms. pp. 1–2.

17. Braw, *The Atomic Bomb Suppressed*, p. 133.

18. "U.S. War Prisoners Died at Hiroshima, A Japanese Asserts," *The New York Times*, July 12, 1970, p. 10; "Pentagon Disclaims Knowledge," *The New York Times*, July 12, 1970, p. 10.

19. September 23, 1945, document; quoted in Barton J. Bernstein, "Unraveling a Mystery: American POWs Killed at Hiroshima," *Foreign Service Journal* (October 1979), p. 18.

20. October 9, 1945, document; quoted in Bernstein, "Unraveling a Mystery," p. 18.

21. Bernstein, "Unraveling a Mystery," p. 19.

22. Walter R. Ross, quoted in Robert Karl Manoff, "American Victims of Hiroshima," *New York Times Magazine,* December 2, 1984, p. 123.

23. Bernstein, "Unraveling a Mystery," p. 19.

24. The other nine POWs were not in Hiroshima at all. Of these, eight may have been the subjects of human medical experiments—a fact the Japanese government wished to conceal during the occupation. Bernstein, "Unraveling the Mystery," pp. 19–20.

25. See, for instance, Iver Peterson, "G. I. Deaths in Hiroshima Are Documented," *The New York Times*, August 23, 1979, p. 16; Bernstein, "Unraveling a Mystery," p. 18; and Manoff, "American Victims."

26. Manoff, "American Victims," p. 110.

27. As Bernstein observes: "How the military determined the date, but not the cause, of death remained unanswered." Bernstein, "Unraveling a Mystery," p. 19.

28. Thomas G. Paterson, "Thought Control and the Writing of History," in *Freedom at Risk: Secrecy, Censorship, and Repression in the 1980s*, ed. Richard O. Curry (Philadelphia, 1988), p. 61.

29. On government information classification policies see: Steven Aftergood, "The Perils of Government Secrecy," *Issues in Science and Technology*, Vol. 8, No. 4 (Summer 1992), pp. 81–88; Sam Archibald, "The Early Years of the Freedom of Information Act—1955 to 1974," *PS: Political Science & Politics*, Vol. 26, No. 4 (December 1993), pp. 726–31; Lotte E. Feinberg, "Managing the Freedom of Information Act and Federal Information Policy," *Public Administration Review*, Vol. 46, No. 6 (November–December 1986), pp. 615–21; Harold C. Relyea, "Access to Government Information in the Information Age," *Public Administration Review*, Vol. 46, No. 6 (November–December 1986), pp. 635–39; and Harold C. Relyea, "The Evolution of Government Information Security Classification Policy: A Brief Overview (1775–1972)," and updated (1972–1992), published in various congressional reports (available through the Congressional Research Service, The Library of Congress, Washington, D.C.).

30. At times documents previously available were reclassified or otherwise withdrawn from public circulation. See, for instance, Anthony Leviero, "Army Tightens Secrecy On MacArthur Yalta Data," *New York Times*, April 2, 1955, pp. 1, 2; and Paterson, "Thought Control and the Writing of History," pp. 61–62.

31. The Atomic Energy Act of 1946: reprinted in Robert E. Summers, compiler *Federal Information Controls in Peacetime*. The Reference Shelf, Vol. 20, No. 6 (New York: H. W. Wilson, 1949), pp. 41–42. These provisions were amended in 1954 to facilitate the creation of a civilian nuclear power industry.

32. The Atomic Energy Act of 1946; reprinted in Summers, *Federal Information Controls in Peacetime*, p. 42.

33. "Secretary O'Leary Releases Classified Documents On Nuclear Testing, Radiation Releases, Fusion," *DOE This Month*, Vol. 16, No. 12 (December 1993), p. 3. The

32-million-page estimate was recently revised upward to 130 million pages. *Secrecy & Government Bulletin*, No. 46 (March–April 1995).

34. Memorandum: Declassification Section, G.O. Robinson, Public Relations Office, Clearance of Technical Documents, March 18, 1947, Department of Energy Archives.

35. O. G. Haywood, Jr., "Medical Experiments on Humans," ("Attention: Dr. Fidler"), April 17, 1947, Department of Energy Archives. This memorandum was itself stamped "SECRET" and "RESTRICTED DATA." It was not declassified until February 1994.

36. On some historians' privileged access to classified government information, see, for instance, Carol M. Barker and Matthew H. Fox, *Classified Files: The Yellowing Pages: A Report on Scholars' Access to Government Documents* (New York: Twentieth Century Fund, 1972); and Steve Weinberg, *For Their Eyes Only: How Presidential Appointees Treat Public Documents as Personal Property* (Washington, D.C.: Center for Public Integrity, 1992), especially pp. 22–28.

37. Herbert Feis, *The Road to Pearl Harbor: The Coming of the War Between the United States and Japan* (Princeton, NJ, 1950), p. vi.

38. Feis, *The Road to Pearl Harbor*, p. v.

39. Feis, *The China Tangle*, p. vi.

40. Feis, *Churchill-Roosevelt-Stalin*, p. v.

41. Feis, *Churchill-Roosevelt-Stalin*, p. vi.

42. Ibid.

43. Feis, *Churchill-Roosevelt-Stalin*, p. v.

44. Feis, *Between War and Peace*, p. v.

45. Ibid.

46. Feis, *Japan Subdued*, p. v.

47. Ibid.

48. Feis, *Churchill-Roosevelt-Stalin*, p. 640.

49. Stimson Diary, May 15, 1945.

50. Herbert Feis to McGeorge Bundy, March 3, 1958, "Correspondence about on Potsdam Book (Between War and Peace)" File, Box 23, Feis Papers, LC.

51. Undated, handwritten note, preceding Felix Frankfurter to McGeorge Bundy, March 7, 1956, Reel 19, Frankfurter Papers, LC.

52. Herbert Feis, Handwritten "Manuscript of Memoirs of H.F., 1971," p. 84, Box 101, Feis Papers, LC.

53. Stimson Diary, May 30, 1945.

54. McGeorge Bundy to Herbert Feis, February 9, 1949, "Harvard Club" File, Box 18, Feis Papers, LC.

55. McGeorge Bundy to Herbert Feis, November 27, 1949, "Harvard Club" File, Box 18, Feis Papers.

56. Herbert Feis, review of *On Active Service in Peace and War*, by Henry L. Stimson and McGeorge Bundy, *American Foreign Service Journal*, Vol. 25, No. 12 (December 1948), p. 30.

57. McGeorge Bundy to Herbert Feis, August 24, 1965, "H-B Files, Revisions—Japan Subdued" File, Box 20, Feis Papers, LC.

58. J. C. Lambert to Chief of Staff, United States Army, September 16, 1965; copy in "H-B Files, Revision—Japan Subdued" File, Box 20, Feis Papers, LC.

59. Herbert Feis to McGeorge Bundy, August 28, 1965, "H-B Files, Revision—Japan Subdued" File, Box 20, Feis Papers, LC.

60. Herbert Feis to McGeorge Bundy, September 13, 1965, "H-B Files, Revision—Japan Subdued" File, Box 20, Feis Papers, LC.

61. Alfred B. Fitt to Herbert Feis, September 16, 1965, "H-B Files, Revision—Japan Subdued" File, Box 20, Feis Papers, LC. In the end, Feis' notes were not cleared in time to be used in his revised edition of *Japan Subdued*. On September 29, 1965, Feis wrote McGeorge Bundy that he had "just sent off the following telegram to the Department of the Army: CIRCUMSTANCES COMPEL ME TO PROCEED AT ONCE TO DISPATCH FINAL PROOFS

OF MY BOOK. THEREFORE PLEASE INFORM EVERYONE CONCERNED NOT TO PROCEED WITH THE CLEARANCE OF MY NOTES AND TO DISPOSE OF THEM AS THEY SEE FIT." He continued with barely disguised bitterness: "It's a great victory for the committee structure of the government. . . . any well qualified person could dispose of the matter in two hours at most." Herbert Feis to McGeorge Bundy, September 29, 1965, "H-B Files, Revision—Japan Subdued" File, Box 20, Feis Papers, LC.

62. WAH to Herbert Feis, September 1, 1953, "Averell Harriman—Start of Churchill-Roosevelt-Stalin" File, Box 18, Feis Papers, LC; copy in "Memoirs—Feis Files—Subject File—Administrative and Financial Correspondence" File, Box 872, Harriman Papers, LC.

63. Herbert Feis to J. D. Powell, November 5 1954, "Harriman Project" File, Box 18, Feis Papers, LC; this letter is also quoted in Dennis K. Yergler, *Herbert Feis, Wilsonian Internationalism, and America's Technological-Democracy* (New York, 1993), pp. 136–37, n. 24.

64. G. Bernard Noble to Herbert Feis, March 2, 1956, "Noble, Dr. G. Bernard" File, Box 22, Feis Papers, LC.

65. Feis, *The Atomic Bomb and the End of World War II*, p. 200.

66. Herbert Feis, Handwritten "Manuscript of Memoirs of H.F., 1971," especially pp. 83R–86, Box 101, Feis Papers, LC; see also Yergler, *Herbert Feis*, pp. 102–03.

67. Dennis Yergler comments that ". . . Feis's own intellectual integrity was truly admirable, and he did his utmost to maintain his scholastic integrity. Yet human nature remains human nature; it becomes difficult to be objectively critical of friends when the friends become the supporting patrons." Yergler, *Herbert Feis*, p. 106.

68. Feis, *Japan Subdued*, p. 178.

69. "Discussion of the Question of Whether It Was Essential to Use the Atomic Bomb Against Japan," Box 66, Feis Papers, LC.

70. Feis, *Japan Subdued*, pp. 175–76. Curiously, Feis suggested: "But it is improbable that the Soviet government could have been prevailed on to reveal its intentions and so enable the Japanese better to prepare for the assault." Feis, *Japan Subdued*, p. 176. Earlier—before they had built up their troop levels in the Far East—the Russians had been made nervous by such matters. However, as we have seen, by July they clearly wished to get into the war and had little fear that the faltering Japanese would challenge the Red Army. Moreover, in May, when they fixed the time for the Soong mission, Stalin told Hopkins "that the first part of July would be the best time to raise the question since it would obviously be impossible to conceal from the Japanese very much longer the movement of Soviet troops." FRUS, Pots. I, p. 42. Again, in response to Byrnes' July 18 question as to whether the Emperor's approach to Moscow was inspired by "fear of what the Soviets intended to do," Molotov pointed out that "he was sure the Japanese could guess, and Stalin remarked that they had observed Soviet forces and tanks, etc., moving in the Far East." Memorandum of Conversation, July 17, 1945 (date apparently incorrect on memorandum), "July 16–19, 1945," Box 181, Harriman Papers, LC.

71. Feis, *The Atomic Bomb and the End of World War II*, p. 194.

Chapter 49: Final Perspectives

1. Writing privately in 1958 to Byrnes' close friend and adviser, Benjamin Cohen, Feis commented, "There are moments when I feel I am the only person who believes that the people have a right—short of some imperative contrary public interest—to know of the way in which the leaders of the nations at war dealt with those issues which are still troubling the world." Herbert Feis to Benjamin V. Cohen, March 24, 1958, "Permission to Examine" File, Box 23, Feis Papers, LC.

2. Herbert Feis, "The Shackled Historian," *Foreign Affairs*, Vol. 45, No. 2 (January 1967), pp. 332–43, cited material from p. 334.

3. Ibid.

4. LRG to Robert P. Patterson, June 19, 1946, Atomic Energy Safe File #2, Box 1, Entry 75, Patterson Safe Files, RG 107, NA.

5. Robert P. Patterson, "Memorandum for the Chief of Staff," June 24, 1946, Atomic Energy Safe File #2, Box 1, Entry 75, Patterson Safe Files, RG 107, NA.

6. Ibid.

7. Robert P. Patterson, "Memorandum for the Chief of Staff," June 25, 1946, Atomic Energy Safe File #2, Box 1, Entry 75, Patterson Safe Files, RG 107, NA.

8. Memorandum for Chief, Strategic Policy Section, S & P Group, OPD, Subject: Use of Atomic Bomb on Japan, from Ennis, April 30, 1946, p. 5, "ABC 471.6 Atom (17 Aug. 45), Sec. 7," Entry 421, RG 165, NA.

9. Memorandum for Chief, Strategic Policy Section, S & P Group, OPD, Subject: Use of Atomic Bomb on Japan, from Ennis, April 30, 1946, p. 5, "ABC 471.6 Atom (17 Aug 45), Sec. 7," Entry 421, RG 165, NA.

10. On December 12, 1945, Sen. McMahon, Chairman of the Senate Special Committee on Atomic Energy, informed a War Department liaison officer that he intended to call upon army and navy representatives to testify separately on the effect of atomic weapons on national defense. The next day Secretary of War Patterson informed Gen. Eisenhower "that it would be well to take early action in blocking out what our course of action will be." See "ABC 471.6 Atom (17 Aug 45), Sec. 2," Entry 421, RG 165, NA.

11. JCS 1477/3, JCS Central Decimal File 1948–50, "471.6 (8-15-45) Sec. 1," RG 218, NA.

12. We do know, however, that the study was commissioned in conjunction with this JCS statement. On January 29, 1946, Col. Bonesteel of OPD requested Gen. Weckerling of MID to conduct a study assuming the U.S. "had no capability to use atomic bombs" against Japan while taking into account the "effect on Operation 'OLYMPIC' of the October typhoon on Okinawa; and Japanese actions understood to have been underway in the summer of 1945 to counter a possible landing on Kyushu?" Memorandum for General Weckerling, January 29, 1946, "ABC 471.6 Atom (17 Aug 45), Sec. 2," Entry 421, RG 165, NA. For an early draft of the final report see "Probable Effect of October Typhoons on Operation 'OLYMPIC' and Japanese Reactions Thereto," February 4, 1946, Project 2918A, "P" File 1946–51, Box 1411, RG 319, NA.

13. JCS 1477/7, February 6, 1946, JCS Central Decimal File 1948–50, "471.6 (8-15-45), Sec. 2," RG 218, NA.

14. JCS 1477/8, February 23, 1946, JCS Central Decimal File 1948–50, "471.6 (8-15-45), Sec. 2," RG 218, NA.

15. "Memorandum for the Chief of Staff," February 23, 1946, "ABC 471.6 Atom (17 Aug 45), Sec. 2," Entry 421, RG 165, NA.

16. JCS 1477/9, March 13, 1946, JCS Central Decimal File 1948–50, "471.6 (8-15-45), Sec. 2," RG 218, NA.

17. "Statement of Effect of Atomic Weapons on National Security and Military Organization. JCS 1477/7; 1477/8; 1477/9." April 1, 1946, JCS Central Decimal File 1948–50, "471.6 (8-15-45), Sec. 2," RG 218, NA.

18. "Memorandum for the Acting Chief of Staff," February 27, 1946, "ABC 471.6 Atom (17 Aug 45), Sec. 2," Entry 421, RG 165, NA. Emphasis original.

19. "Memorandum for the Chief of Staff," April 2, 1946, "ABC 471.6 Atom (17 Aug 45), Sec. 2," Entry 421, RG 165, NA.

20. "Memorandum for the Chief of Staff," April 2, 1946, "ABC 471.6 Atom (17 Aug 45), Sec. 2," Entry 421, RG 165, NA.

Conclusion: The Complicity of Silence

1. Gallup Polls: July 31, 1990; November 1991; December 15, 1994.

2. "We Shouldn't Let the Japanese Rewrite Our History," *Dallas Morning News*, December 18, 1994, p. 7J; "War and the Smithsonian," *The Wall Street Journal*, August 29, 1994; "The Enola Gay's Place in History," *Chicago Tribune*, September 9, 1994, p. 12; "What Was Crueler Than 'Enola Gay'? Japan At War," *St. Petersburg Times*, September 5, 1994, p. 2.

3. Uday Mohan, "A Preliminary Survey of Press Coverage of the Smithsonian's Enola Gay Controversy," unpublished paper; see also Uday Mohan and Sanho Tree, "The Ending of World War II: Media Perspectives in the 1940s–1960s and Early 1990s," paper presented at the American Historical Association meeting, January 6, 1995, revised and forthcoming in the *Journal of American–East Asian Relations*.

4. Baldwin, *Great Mistakes of the War*, pp. 88–108.

5. Walker, "The Decision," p. 110.

6. Dower, "The Bombed," unpublished manuscript forthcoming in *Diplomatic History*.

7. Leahy, *I Was There*, p. 441.

8. Eisenhower, *Mandate for Change*, p. 313.

9. McCloy Diary, Memorandum of Conversation with General Marshall and the Secretary of War, May 29, 1945.

10. Ibid.

11. Eisenhower, *Crusade in Europe*, p. 444; Robert J. Donovan, *Conflict and Crisis: The Presidency of Harry S. Truman, 1945–1948* (New York: Norton, 1977), pp. 86–87, 338; see also McCullough, *Truman*, pp. 429–30, 584.

12. HLS to Joseph C. Grew, June 19, 1947, Stimson Papers, YUL.

13. Eisenhower, quoted in "Ike on Ike," *Newsweek*, November 11, 1963, p. 107.

14. Michael Walzer, *Just and Unjust Wars: A Moral Argument with Historical Illustrations* (New York, 1977), p. 268.

15. Barton J. Bernstein, "A Postwar Myth: 500,000 U.S. Lives Saved," *Bulletin of the Atomic Scientists*, Vol. 42, No. 6 (June–July 1986), pp. 38–40; Rufus E. Miles, Jr., "Hiroshima: The Strange Myth of Half a Million American Lives Saved," *International Security*, Vol. 10, No. 2 (Fall 1985), pp. 121–40; and Skates, *The Invasion of Japan*, pp. 76–83. See also Chapter 38, endnote 44, and Afterword, endnote 7.

16. Stimson and Bundy, *On Active Service*, p. 629; Martin J. Sherwin, "Hiroshima and Modern Memory," *Nation*, October 10, 1981, pp. 329, 349–53, especially p. 352.

17. Army battle-related deaths during the June–August period totaled 2,152; Navy and Marine battle-related deaths during the same period totaled 3,133—yielding a figure of 5,285 deaths for this time period. Battle Casualties of the Army, September 1, 1945, "Subject: Battle Casualties of the Army," OPD 704, Box 1684, Entry 418, RG 165, NA; The Division of Medical Statistics, Bureau of Medicine and Surgery, Navy Department, *The History of the Medical Department of the United States Navy in World War II: The Statistics of Disease and Injuries* (Washington, D.C., 1950), p. 179. A slightly different figure for Army battle-related deaths during the June–August period, 2,526, is given in Statistical and Accounting Branch office of the Adjutant General, *Army Battle Casualties and Nonbattle Deaths in World War II, Final Report, 7 December 1941–31 December 1946* (Washington, D.C., 1970), p. 110.

18. Herbert Hoover to John Callan O'Laughlin, August 8, 1945, O'Laughlin Correspondence File, Box 171, Post-Presidential Papers, HHPL.

19. "Oxnam, Dulles Ask Halt in Bomb Use," *The New York Times*, August 10, 1945, p. 6. See also, "Churchmen Speak on Atomic Bomb," p. 6.

20. Henry Luce, speech to the National Assembly of the United Council of Church Women at Milwaukee, November 16, 1948; reprinted in Jessup, ed., *The Ideas of Henry Luce*, p. 297.

21. Herbert Hoover to John Callan O'Laughlin, August 8, 1945, O'Laughlin Corre-

spondence File, Box 171, Post-Presidential Papers, HHPL; Leahy, *I Was There*, p. 441.

22. Henry A. Wallace Diary, August 10, 1945; printed in Wallace, *The Price of Vision*, ed. Blum, p. 474.

23. Judith Lewis Herman, *Trauma and Recovery* (New York, 1992), p. 2.

24. On the "mushroom cloud" image, see, for instance, Peter B. Hales, "The Atomic Sublime," *American Studies*, Vol. 32, No. 1 (Spring 1991), pp. 5–31; and Vincent Leo, "The Mushroom Cloud Photograph: From Fact to Symbol," *Afterimage*, Vol. 13, Nos. 1/2 (Summer 1985), pp. 6–12.

25. Raymond Hunthausen, "Bishop Urges Protest of Armaments," *Origins*, Vol. 11, No. 7 (July 2, 1981), p. 110.

26. See, in this regard, Boyer, "The Cloud Over Our Culture," pp. 26–31.

27. HLS to Joseph C. Grew, June 19, 1947, Stimson Papers, YUL.

28. Reinhold Niebuhr to JBC, March 12, 1946, Box 3, Niebuhr Papers, LC.

29. Kennan, "A Christian's View of the Arms Race"; reprinted in George F. Kennan, *The Nuclear Delusion: Soviet-American Relations in the Atomic Age* (New York, 1982), pp. 206–07.

30. Baldwin, *Great Mistakes of the War*, p. 105.

31. National Conference of Catholic Bishops, *The Challenge of Peace: God's Promise and Our Response: A Pastoral Letter on War and Peace, May 3, 1983* (Washington, D.C.: United States Catholic Conference, 1983), para. 302.

32. Constitution of the United States, Article 1, Section 8. See also Louis Fisher, *Presidential Power* (Lawrence, KS, 1995).

33. Clearly, not all those who believed the bombings were not dictated by military necessity also objected on ethical grounds. See, for instance, above discussion of LeMay and Halsey.

34. Leahy, *I Was There*, p. 441.

35. Richard Nixon, quoted in "A Nation Coming into Its Own," *Time*, July 29, 1985, pp. 48–53, cited material from p. 48; also in Roger Rosenblatt, *Witness: The World Since Hiroshima* (Boston, 1985), p. 63.

36. Leahy, *I Was There*, p. 441.

37. Eisenhower, quoted in "Ike on Ike," *Newsweek*, November 11, 1963, p. 107.

38. *The New York Times*, December 8, 1991, Sec. I, p. 26:1.

Afterword: Questions, Issues, and Major Theories Concerning the Use of the Atomic Bomb

1. See also Nitze, *From Hiroshima to Glasnost*, p. 37.

2. Feis, *Japan Subdued*, pp. 178–79.

3. Feis, *The Atomic Bomb and the End of World War II*, p. 191.

4. Stimson Diary, August 10, 1945.

5. Robert A. Pape, "Why Japan Surrendered," *International Security*, Vol. 18, No. 2 (Fall 1993), pp. 154–201, cited material from p. 156.

6. Pape, "Why Japan Surrendered," pp. 178–79.

7. See, for example, Edward J. Drea, *MacArthur's ULTRA: Codebreaking and the War Against Japan* (Lawrence, KS, 1992); and Drea, "Previews of Hell," *MHQ: The Quarterly Journal of Military History*, Vol. 7, No. 3 (Spring 1995), pp. 74–81; Richard Frank, "Downfall: The Invasion of Japan 'Not a Recipe for Victory,'" paper presented at the Admiral Nimitz Museum and Foundation, March 19, 1995; Bruce Lee, *Marching Orders*; Robert James Maddox, "Generals, Admirals, and Atomic Bombs: Ending the War with Japan," paper presented at the Conference of Army Historians, June 13–16, 1994, Center for Military History, Washington, D.C., provided courtesy of Judith Bellafaire. Noting this buildup, some writers imply that it is also evidence that a surrender was not likely—a step in logic which is unwarranted. While the unavailability of many high-level G-2 records

hampers all analysis in this area, available documents shed considerable light on the issue. For instance, the previously cited 1946 Military Intelligence Division (G-2) study—drawing upon contemporaneous intelligence materials—took into account "Japanese actions understood to have been underway in the summer of 1945 to counter a possible landing on Kyushu. . . ." This concluded that by "14 August 1945, the Japanese had already established on Kyushu the maximum troop strength planned for its defense. Even in the event of invasion, no further reinforcements were contemplated." Contrary to the implied arguments of recent after-the-fact accounts—this internal study, done at a point in time close to the events in question, judged that in any event the Japanese almost certainly would have surrendered upon Soviet entry into the war. As we have seen, as early as April 1945 War Department planning and intelligence documents contained similar judgments in connection with the "two-step" logic. (Surprisingly, few studies which emphasize the new ULTRA information cite or show any awareness of these contemporaneous documents.) Other assessments from the pre-Hiroshima period also demonstrate the vulnerability of the Japanese armed forces and the inadequacy of their arms and supplies. In general, Drea himself observes that the Japanese counterattack plans seem "wildly ambitious," and points to "the wretched state of communications, the devastated railway network, Allied mastery of the air and sea, and the lack of fast-moving motorized and mechanized combat formations." (Drea, *MacArthur's Ultra*, p. 218.) For skepticism about Japan's ability to counter a U.S. assault, also see Peter Maslowski, "Truman, the Bomb, and the Numbers Game," *MHQ: The Quarterly Journal of Military History,* Vol. 7, No. 3 (Spring 1995), pp. 103–07. Finally, we may note Truman's own judgments of July 17 and 18 and August 3. See above, pp. 242, 415. For the 1946 study, see Memorandum for General Weckerling, January 29, 1946, "ABC 471.6 Atom (17 Aug 45), Sec. 2," Entry 421, RG 165, NA; and Memorandum for Chief, Strategic Policy Section, S&P Group, OPD, from Ennis, Subject: Use of Atomic Bomb on Japan, April 30, 1946, "ABC 471.6 Atom (17 Aug 45), Sec. 7," Entry 421, RG 165, NA. For additional commentary on this study, see above, pp. 84–85. On the April 1945 judgments, see above, pp. 112–14. Also see G-2's "Estimate of the Enemy Situation," July 7, 1945, ID# 926728, ACSI, RG 319, NA. For a discussion of the related issue of casualty estimates, see above.

8. Interrogation of Prince Konoye, November 9, 1945, Roll 5, USSBS Interrogations of Japanese Leaders and Responses to Questionnaires, M1654, RG 243, NA.

9. Toland, *The Rising Sun*, p. 909, footnote.

10. Quoted in Sigal, *Fighting to a Finish*, p. 226.

11. JCS 924/15, "Pacific Strategy," April 25, 1945, p. 245, "ABC 384 Pacific (1-17-43) Sec. 9," Box 457, Entry 421, RG 165, NA; also DoD, *Entry*, p. 63.

12. McGeorge Bundy, "Pearl Harbor Brought Peace," *Newsweek*, December 16, 1991, p. 8.

13. Barton J. Bernstein's reply to Gar Alperovitz and Robert Messer, "Correspondence," *International Security*, Vol. 116, No. 3 (Winter 1991/2), pp. 214–21, cited material from p. 220. Also see Alperovitz's and Messer's extended comment in the same issue, pp. 204–14.

14. Skates, *The Invasion of Japan*, p. 239.

15. Stimson Diary, June 19, 1945.

16. Robert P. Newman, "Ending the War With Japan: Paul Nitze's 'Early Surrender Counterfactual," p. 11, Paper presented before the Modern History Faculty, Oxford, May 25, 1994.

17. Stimson Diary, July 23, 1945. Related to this: Given the continued threat to the Emperor—and the strong views of some army figures—spelling out terms in cables (rather than orally via an Imperial Envoy) was undoubtedly difficult.

18. Butow, *Japan's Decision to Surrender*, p. 131.

19. MAGIC, No. 1225 (August 2, 1945) and No. 1226 (August 3, 1945), RG 457, NA; WB's Book, August 3, 1945, Folder 602, Byrnes Papers, CUL.

20. Ehrman, *Grand Strategy*, p. 291.

21. Memorandum for the Assistant Chief of Staff, OPD, Subject: Estimate of the Enemy Situation, June 30, 1945, Appendix H, p. 2, "Estimate of the Enemy Situation," OPD 350.05 TS, Entry 419, RG 165, NA.

22. Pape, "Why Japan Surrendered," p. 187.

23. Bernstein, "The Perils and Politics of Surrender," p. 23.

24. Toland, *The Rising Sun*, p. 940.

25. Sigal, *Fighting to a Finish*, pp. 273–74. See also Thomas B. Allen and Norman Polmar, "The Voice of the Crane," *MHQ: The Quarterly Journal of Military History*, Vol. 7, No. 3 (Spring 1995), pp. 98–102.

26. Leahy, *I Was There*, p. 419.

27. Telephone Transcript, "General Hull and Colonel Seaman - 1325 -13 Aug 45," "Telephone Conversations 6 Aug. to 25 Aug. 45," Folder No. 2, Item 35A, Exec. 17, Box 101, OPD Executive Files, Entry 422, RG 165, NA. See Barton J. Bernstein, "Eclipsed by Hiroshima and Nagasaki: Early Thinking About Tactical Nuclear Weapons," *International Security*, Vol. 23, No. 4 (Spring 1991), pp. 149–73; and Marc Gallicchio, "After Nagasaki: General Marshall's Plan for Tactical Nuclear Weapons in Japan," *Prologue*, Vol. 23, No. 4 (Winter 1991), pp. 396–404. See also Gar Alperovitz's and Robert Messer's exchange with Bernstein, "Correspondence," *International Security*, Vol. 116, No. 3 (Winter 1991/92), pp. 204–21. In connection with Marshall's level of confidence, note that he agreed on August 11, 1945, that shipment of materials for a third bomb should be stopped. See Groves, *Now It Can Be Told*, p. 352; and Bernstein, "Eclipsed by Hiroshima and Nagasaki," p. 166. Further evidence in this connection comes from Gen. Maxwell Taylor, who recalls that in a discussion with Marshall after Potsdam, Marshall stated: "Gentlemen, on the first moonlight night in August, we will drop one of these bombs on the Japanese. I don't think we will need more than two." Maxwell D. Taylor, *The Uncertain Trumpet* (New York, 1960), p. 3. Also see Stimson's diary entry of July 23, where he writes that "Marshall felt as I felt sure he would that now with our new weapon we would not need the assistance of the Russians to conquer Japan."

28. Gallicchio, "After Nagasaki," p. 402.

29. Feis to Winnacker, September 7, 1965, Box 20, Feis Papers, LC. See also Winnacker to Feis, September 2, 1963, Box 20, Feis Papers, LC.

30. Harvey Bundy, "Remembered Words," *Atlantic*, March 1957, p. 57. Some historians imply incorrectly that Stimson's comment was in reaction to the use of the atomic bomb. In fact, Harvey Bundy recalled that this was Stimson's response to news of the successful atomic test at Alamogordo. Bundy writes that Stimson "had just received a cable telling him that the Alamogordo test had been successful. . . . [He] remarked to John J. McCloy and to me:—'Well, I have been responsible for spending two billions of dollars on this atomic venture. Now that it is successful I shall not be sent to prison in Fort Leavenworth.' "

31. Goldberg, "General Groves and the Atomic West," p. 66.

32. Robertson, *Sly and Able*, p. 405. On Szilard's report, see Szilard, "Reminiscences," p. 127.

33. See Szilard, "Reminiscences," p. 128. On the other hand, as previously noted, in March Byrnes had sent FDR a memorandum regarding his concerns about the mounting costs of the Manhattan project. See Stoff, Fanton, Williams, eds., *The Manhattan Project*, p. 84. However, I have not been able to find evidence that he subsequently returned to this argument.

34. "MEMO TO FILES," Subject: Report of Meeting with The President, April 25, 1945, Box 3, Entry 2, Groves Papers, RG 200, NA. For Truman's 1947 and 1954 comments see Truman, *Off the Record*, ed. Ferrell, p. 107, and HST, discussion with Noyes and Hillman, January 22, 1954, p. 9, HST Quotes File, Box 9, Post-Presidential-Memoirs, HSTL.

35. Kai Bird, "Roosevelt's Assistant President," *Washington Post Book World*, January 1, 1995, p. 10.

36. For details on the Berlin bombing, see Crane, *Bombs, Cities, & Civilians*, pp. 101–08.

37. CCS 643/3, "Estimate of the Enemy Situation (as of 6 July)," July 8, 1945, p. 10, "CCS 381 (6-4-43), Sec. 2, Part 5," RG 218, NA.

38. Fletcher Knebel and Charles W. Bailey, "The Fight Over the Atom Bomb," *Look*, Vol. 27, No. 16 (August 13, 1963), pp. 19–23, cited material from p. 20.

39. In a previously cited August 16, 1963, letter to Truman, Groves wrote that he "was annoyed by the recent article in *Look* Magazine entitled 'The Fight over the Atom Bomb.' " He added: "I would like to assure you personally that the reference to 'a little boy on a toboggan' bears little resemblance to anything I can recall saying. Particularly objectionable to me were the words, 'a little boy', which, with my respect for the office of the President and for you, I could never have used in any such way as is implied." LRG to HST, "Sent to Mr. Truman about Aug. 20, 1963," Box 2, Entry 2, Groves Papers, RG 200, NA.

40. See Crane, *Bombs, Cities, and Civilians*; and Michael Sherry, *The Rise of American Air Power: The Creation of Armageddon* (New Haven, 1987).

41. See, for example, Ambrose, *Rise to Globalism*; Bernstein, "The Perils and Politics of Surrender"; Wyden, *Day One*.

42. Sigal, *Fighting to a Finish*, p. 21. Variations on a "bureaucratic momentum" interpretation include Sherry, *The Rise of American Air Power*; Kenneth Glazier, "The Decision to Use Atomic Weapons Against Hiroshima and Nagasaki," *Public Policy*, Vol. 18 (1970), pp. 463–516; Brian L. Villa, "The U.S. Army, Unconditional Surrender, and the Potsdam Proclamation," pp. 66–92.

43. Sigal, *Fighting to a Finish*, p. 219.

44. Sigal, *Fighting to a Finish*, pp. 220–21.

45. Bob Woodward, *The Commanders*, (New York, 1991), p. 33.

46. See Thomas J. McCormick, *America's Half Century: United States Foreign Policy in the Cold War* (Baltimore, 1989), pp. 44–46.

47. William Appleman Williams, *The Tragedy of American Diplomacy* (New York, 1972), p. 253.

48. Stimson Diary, July 17, 1945.

49. Bernstein's reply to Alperovitz and Messer, "Correspondence," p. 220.

50. Hyde Park Aide-Memoire, September 18, 1944, President's Map Room Papers, Naval Aide's File, Box 172—General Folder, Franklin D. Roosevelt Library; reprinted in Stoff, Fanton, Williams, eds., *The Manhattan Project*, p. 70.

51. Bush to Conant, September 23, 1944, Document 186, OSRD, S-1 Historical File, AEC Files, NA; reprinted in Stoff, Fanton, Williams, eds., *The Manhattan Project*, pp. 74–75.

52. Bundy, *Danger and Survival*, p. 90.

53. See Nat S. Finney, "How FDR Planned to Use the A-Bomb," *Look*, Vol. 14, No. 6 (March 14, 1950), pp. 23–27; also Blum, ed., *The Price of Vision*, pp. 499–500.

54. Bernstein, "Roosevelt, Truman and the Atomic Bomb," p. 32.

55. Sherwin, "The Atomic Bomb and the Origins of the Cold War," p. 962.

56. Sherwin, *A World Destroyed*, p. xxii.

57. Sherwin, *A World Destroyed*, p. xxiv.

58. FRUS, Pots. I, p. 173.

59. For details on the terms of the Italian surrender, see Raymond G. O'Connor, *Diplomacy for Victory; FDR and Unconditional Surrender* (New York, 1971), pp. 59–60; also, United Nations, *Surrender of Italy, Germany and Japan, World War II* (Washington, D.C.: U.S. Government Printing Office, 1946), pp. 3–35.

60. *Sunday Express* (London), August 18, 1946, p. 4; this story was picked up by *The New York Times* and reported August 19, 1946, p. 1.

61. Feis, *The Atomic Bomb and the End of World War II*, p. 194.

62. Walker, "The Decision to Use the Bomb," pp. 111, 102.

63. Herken, *The Winning Weapon*, p. 4.

64. Roger M. Anders, "The President and the Atomic Bomb: Who Approved the Trinity Nuclear Test?," *Prologue*, Vol. 20, No. 4 (Winter 1988), pp. 268–82, cited material from p. 278.

65. Anders, "The President and the Atomic Bomb," p. 281.

66. Bernstein, "Roosevelt, Truman and the Atomic Bomb," pp. 24, 60; for a more recent statement of his position, see Bernstein's reply to Alperovitz and Messer, "Correspondence," p. 220.

67. Sherwin, "The Atomic Bomb and the Origins of the Cold War," pp. 966, 965.

68. Sherwin, "Hiroshima and Modern Memory," p. 352.

69. Stimson Diary, May 16 and June 6, 1945; HLS to HST, April 24, 1945, "White House Correspondence," Box 15, Stimson Safe File, Entry 74A, RG 107, NA; also, Truman, *Year of Decisions*, p. 85.

70. Szilard, "A Personal History of the Atomic Bomb," pp. 14–15.

71. Stimson diary, May 10 and May 14, 1945.

72. Stimson Diary, September 4, 1945.

73. See Messer, "The Making of a Cold Warrior, pp. 159–256; Messer, *The End of an Alliance*, pp. 53–92.

74. Given the strong recommendations of virtually all the other civilian and military advisers that the surrender formula be clarified—and the rather soft evidence concerning politics—an obvious question is whether there is any other way to explain Byrnes' position. The fact is, the goal of ending the war before the Russians got into Manchuria might well have been more easily achieved by an early clarification of the surrender terms—which, of course, is why Grew and others urged this in May. Moreover, not bombing Japan could have helped lay the groundwork for a better postwar relationship as the United States and Russia jockeyed for position. There were, in short, good military and diplomatic reasons—especially in Asia—why the war might better have been ended via diplomacy rather than the bomb. The question—as, to recall, William R. Castle put it—is whether U.S. leaders may perhaps have actually wished the war to carry on so they would have an opportunity to test the new weapon on various Japanese cities. (Castle Diary, February 9, 1947.) Robert Messer has also pointed out: "If [Truman] believed that the war could end with Soviet entry in mid-August, then he must have realized that if the bombs were not used before that date they might well not be used at all." (Messer, "New Evidence on Truman's Decision," p. 55.) Although ending the war without the bomb could have served American diplomatic aims in Asia, it clearly would not have added to the leverage available to American diplomacy in Europe. Byrnes may have been naïve to believe he could stall the Russians until August 15, but the disturbing fact is that only the actual use of the bomb could plausibly have achieved both objectives. Perhaps one day further documentary discoveries will allow deeper insight into the calculations of Truman's most important adviser.

Appendix: Byrnes' Activities: April to July 1945

1. Byrnes meets with Truman, 2:30 p.m. Brown, *James F. Byrnes of South Carolina*, p. 256.

2. Byrnes and Leahy meet with Truman, 2:30 p.m.; entrain for Hyde Park at 10:00 p.m. "Appointments for the First Thirty Days of the Administration of President Harry S. Truman," Daily Sheets, President's Appointment File, President's Secretary's Files, HSTL.

3. Byrnes meets with Truman en route from Hyde Park. *The New York Times*, April 16, 1945, p. 1.

4. Byrnes meets with Truman, 11:00 a.m., just before the latter's speech to Congress. "Appointments for the First Thirty Days of the Administration of President Harry S. Truman," Daily Sheets, President's Appointment File, President's Secretary's Files, HSTL; Brown, *James F. Byrnes of South Carolina*, p. 259. At a dinner in honor of Sir Anthony Eden at the British Embassy, Byrnes has informal discussions with Ambassador Halifax, Eden, Secretary of War Henry Stimson, and Chief of Staff William Leahy. Stimson Diary, April 16, 1945.

5. Byrnes meets "at length with Truman." Brown, *James F. Byrnes of South Carolina*, p. 259.

6. Byrnes in Washington from May 5 to May 9, according to Truman on May 4. Stimson Diary, May 4, 1945.

7. Byrnes in Washington from May 5 to May 9, according to Truman on May 4. Stimson Diary, May 4, 1945.

8. Byrnes meets with Truman, 3:15 p.m. *The New York Times*, May 8, 1945, p. 10.

9. Byrnes meets with Stimson, 3:30 p.m. The two are subsequently joined by Groves, Bundy, and Harrison, Stimson Diary, May 8, 1945.

10. Interim Committee meeting. Notes of an Informal Meeting of the Interim Committee, May 9, 1945, File 100, Roll 8, H-B Files, M1108, NA.

11. Interim Committee meeting. Notes of an Informal Meeting of the Interim Committee, May 14, 1945, File 100, Roll 8, H-B Files, M1108, NA.

12. Byrnes meets with Hopkins, 10:00 a.m. Hopkins appointments, diaries, Box 53, Hopkins Papers, Georgetown University Archives.

13. Interim Committee meeting. Notes of an Informal Meeting of the Interim Committee, May 18, 1945, File 100, Roll 8, H-B Files, M1108, NA; Byrnes meets with McCloy, 2:30 p.m. McCloy diary, May 18, 1945; Byrnes meets with Truman, 5:00 p.m. Truman. *Off the Record*, p. 30.

14. Byrnes meets with Leahy. Leahy Diary, May 20, 1945.

15. Interim Committee meeting. Notes of the Interim Committee Meeting, May 31, 1945, File 100, Roll 8, H-B Files, M1108, NA.

16. Interim Committee meeting. Notes of the Interim Committee Meeting, June 1, 1945, File 100, Roll 8, H-B Files, M1108, NA; subsequently, Byrnes meets with Truman. Byrnes interview with Fred Freed for NBC White Paper, 1964, pp. 11–12, Box 79, Feis Papers, LC.

17. Byrnes meets with Leahy, 5:30 p.m. Leahy diary, June 4, 1945.

18. Byrnes meets with Davies, noon. Byrnes meets with Truman, Leahy, and Davies, 3:10 p.m. Byrnes, *Speaking Frankly*, p. 64; Leahy, *I Was There*, pp. 378–80; Truman, *Year of Decisions*, p. 260; Diary, June 5, 1945 (1-25-54), Box 114, Davies Papers, LC. Another version of Davies' diary misdates this meeting as June 6. Journal, June 6, 1945, Box 17, Davies Papers, LC.

19. Byrnes meets with Davies during evening. Diary, June 6, 1945 (11-7-50), Box 17, Davies Papers, LC.

20. Byrnes meets with Hopkins, 9:30 a.m. Hopkins appointments diary, Box 53, Hopkins Papers, Georgetown University Archives.

21. Interim Committee meeting. Notes of the Interim Committee Meeting, June 21, 1945, File 100, Roll 8, H-B Files, M1108, NA.

22 Byrnes sworn in as Secretary of State. Brown, *James F. Byrnes of South Carolina*, p. 263.

23. Byrnes meets with State Department personnel and foreign diplomats, and prepares himself for the Potsdam Conference. Brown, *James F. Byrnes of South Carolina*, p. 267.

24. Byrnes meets with State Department personnel and foreign diplomats, and prepares himself for the Potsdam Conference. Brown, *James F. Byrnes of South Carolina*, p. 267.

25. Byrnes meets with State Department personnel and foreign diplomats, and prepares himself for the Potsdam Conference. Brown, *James F. Byrnes of South Carolina*, p. 267.

26. Stimson diary, May 3, 1945.

27. *The New York Times*, May 8, 1945, p. 10.

28. Truman, *Off the Record*, ed. Ferrell, p. 30.

29. Byrnes interview with Fred Freed for NBC White Paper, 1964, pp. 11–12, Box 79, Feis Papers, LC.

30. Byrnes, *Speaking Frankly*, p. 64; Leahy, *I Was There*, pp. 378–80; Harry s. Truman, *Year of Decisions*, p. 260; Diary, June 5, 1945 (1-25-54), Box 114, Davies Papers, LC. See endnote 18, above.

31. Brown, *James F. Byrnes of South Carolina*, p. 263.

32. Notes of an Informal Meeting of the Interim Committee, May 9, 1945, File 100, Roll 8, H-B Files, M1108, NA.

33. Notes of an Informal Meeting of the Interim Committee, May 14, 1945, File 100, Roll 8, H-B Files, M1108, NA.

34. Notes of an Informal Meeting of the Interim Committee, May 18, 1945, File 100, Roll 8, H-B Files, M1108, NA.

35. Notes of the Interim Committee Meeting, May 31, 1945, File 100, Roll. 8, H-B Files, M1108, NA.

36. Notes of the Interim Committee Meeting, June 1, 1945, File 100, Roll 8, H-B Files, M1108, NA.

37. Notes of the Interim Committee Meeting, June 21, 1945, File 100, Roll 8, H-B Files, M1108, NA.

38. Szilard, "Reminiscences," p. 126.

39. Stimson diary, April 16, 1945.

40. Stimson diary, May 8, 1945.

41. Hopkins appointments diary, Box 53, Hopkins Papers, Georgetown University Archives.

42. McCloy Diary, May 18, 1945.

43. Leahy Diary, May 20, 1945.

44. "Was A-Bomb on Japan a Mistake?," p. 69.

45. Leahy Diary, June 4, 1945.

46. Diary, June 6, 1945 (11-7-50), Box 17, Davies Papers, LC.

47. Interim Committee Log, June 13, 1945, File 98, Roll 8, H-B Files, M1108, NA.

48. Hopkins appointments diary, Box 53, Hopkins Papers, Georgetown University Archives.

49. Brown, *James F. Byrnes*, p. 263.

Selected Bibliography

Manuscript Collections

Air Force Historical Research Agency,
Maxwell Air Force Base, AL

U.S. Air Force Oral History Program
  Ira C. Eaker
  Roscoe C. Wilson
  Glen W. Martin
  Curtis E. LeMay
  Carl A. Spaatz
  George C. Kenney
  Laurence S. Kuter

Columbia University, New York, NY
Butler Library

Oral History Program
  Orvil A. Anderson
  Kenneth Tompkins Bainbridge
  Joseph Ballantine
  Hugh Borton
  William L. Clayton
  Eugene H. Dooman
  Donald B. Duncan
  Ira Eaker
  Leslie R. Groves
  Haywood Hansell
  W. Averell Harriman
  Arthur Krock
  Robert A. Lovett
  John J. McCloy
  Arthur W. Page
  Samuel I. Rosenman
  Carl Spaatz
  Lewis L. Strauss
  Harold Train

Dwight D. Eisenhower Presidential Library, Abilene, KS

Dwight D. Eisenhower
Milton Eisenhower
Harry Butcher
Lauris Norstad

Harry S. Truman Library, Independence, MO

Eben A. Ayers
Jonathan Daniels
George M. Elsey
Map Room Files
Oral History Collection
    Eben A. Ayers
    Tom C. Clark
    Matthew J. Connelly
    Robert G. Nixon
    Samuel I. Rosenman
    James W. Riddleberger
Records of the Truman Centennial Commission
Samuel I. Rosenman
Charles G. Ross
Papers of Harry S. Truman
    Confidential File, White House Central File
    Official Files
    Post-Presidential Memoirs
    Post-Presidential Papers
    Post-Presidential Secretary's Office Files
    President's Personal Files
    President's Secretary's Files
    Rose Conway File
    Vertical File

Harvard University, Cambridge, MA
Houghton Library

Joseph C. Grew
William R. Castle

Pusey Library

James B. Conant

Herbert Hoover Presidential Library, West Branch, IA

Herbert Hoover Post Presidential Files
William R. Castle
Westbrook Pegler
Lewis L. Strauss
Charles C. Tansill

Hoover Institution Archives, Stanford, CA

Elizabeth Churchill Brown
Charles M. Cooke
Eugene H. Dooman
Bonner Fellers
Stanley Hornbeck
Alfred Kohlberg
Paul M. A. Linebarger
T. V. Soong
Truman Smith
Albert C. Wedemeyer
Ivan D. Yeaton

George C. Marshall Library, Lexington, VA

George C. Marshall
Hanson W. Baldwin
Forrest C. Pogue
Frank McCarthy

Library of Congress, Washington, D.C.
Manuscripts Division

Clinton P. Anderson
Henry Harley "Hap" Arnold
Charles E. Bohlen
Vannevar Bush
Tom T. Connally
Joseph E. Davies
Elmer H. Davis
Ira C. Eaker
Herbert Feis
Foreign Copying Program, Great Britain
Felix Frankfurter
William F. Halsey
W. Averell Harriman
William D. Leahy
Curtis E. LeMay
Charles A. Lockwood
Claire Boothe Luce

Reinhold Niebuhr
William S. Parsons
Robert P. Patterson
Carl Spaatz
Raymond Swing
Nathan Twining

National Archives
Washington, D.C., Suitland, MD, and College Park, MD

RG 18 Army Air Forces
RG 38 Office of the Chief of Naval Operations
RG 59 Department of State
RG 77 Army Corps of Engineers (Manhattan Engineer District)
RG 107 Secretary of War
RG 153 Judge Advocate General
RG 165 War Department General and Special Staffs
RG 200 Gift Collection (Leslie R. Groves)
RG 208 Office of War Information
RG 218 Joint Chiefs of Staff
RG 226 Office of Strategic Services
RG 243 United States Strategic Bombing Survey
RG 263 Central Intelligence Agency
RG 319 Army Staff
RG 331 Allied Operational and Occupation Headquarters, WWII, International Prosecution Section
RG 341 Headquarters, United States Air Force
RG 353 Interdepartmental and Intradepartmental Committees
RG 457 National Security Agency

Naval Historical Center, Navy Yard, Washington, D.C.,
Operational Archives Branch

James V. Forrestal Diaries
Chester W. Nimitz
John Mason Interviews:
 Bernhard H. Bieri
 Robert L. Dennison
 Charles K. Duncan
 George C. Dyer
 Thomas H. Dyer
 Charles D. Griffin
 Edwin B. Hooper
 Felix Johnson
 Ruthven V. Libby
 Arthur H. McCollum
 Clarence E. Olsen
 Joseph J. Rochefort
 Malcolm F. Schoeffel
 William J. Sebald
 William R. Smedberg

Naval Weapons Center, China Lake, CA, Oral History Collection on W. S. Parsons:
F. L. Ashworth
Dr. Kenneth Bainbridge
Dr. A. F. Birch
Dr. N. E. Bradbury
Arthur Breslow
Mrs. Robert Burroughs
Dr. Vannevar Bush
Alfred M. Granum
Leslie R. Groves
M. R. Jeppson
Dr. G. B. Kistiakowski
Harry Parsons
Dr. Norman Ramsey
Malcolm Schoeffel
Levering Smith
Mrs. J. V. Stearns
Lewis L. Strauss

Naval Historical Collection
Naval War College, Newport, RI

Thomas Buell
Ernest J. King
Edwin T. Layton
Raymond A. Spruance
Walter Whitehill

Princeton University, Princeton, NJ
Mudd Manuscript Library

Bernard M. Baruch
Allen W. Dulles
James V. Forrestal
George F. Kennan
Arthur Krock
David Lawrence

Public Records Office, UK

Cabinet
Foreign Office
Premier
War Office

State Historical Society of Wisconsin, Madison, WI

Arthur W. Page
Byron Price
Richard H. Rovere

U.S. Army Military History Institute, Carlisle Barracks
Carlisle, PA

Charles H. Bonesteel III
Charles H. Donnelly
Thomas T. Handy
John E. Hull
Robert J. Wood
Ivan D. Yeaton

United States Naval Institute, Annapolis, MD

Oral History Program
 Hanson W. Baldwin
 Bernhard H. Bieri
 Robert E. Dornin
 E. B. Fluckey
 R. E. Libby
 Mrs. Chester W. Nimitz and Nancy Nimitz
 Robert Lee Dennison
 William J. Sebald
 William R. Smedberg, III

Yale University, New Haven, CT
Sterling Library

Hanson W. Baldwin
Walter Lippmann
Henry L. Stimson

Other Collections Consulted

James F. Byrnes papers, Robert Muldrow Cooper Library, Clemson University, Clemson, SC.
Anthony Eden papers, University of Birmingham, Edgbaston, Birmingham, UK.
Murray Green collection, U.S. Air Force Academy Library, CO.
Harry L. Hopkins papers, Georgetown University Archives, Washington, D.C.
George A. Lincoln papers, U.S. Military Academy Library, West Point, NY.
John J. McCloy papers, Amherst College Archives, Amherst, MA.
Louis Morton papers, Dartmouth College Library, Hanover, NH.
Records from General Headquarters, U.S. Army Forces, Pacific (USAFPAC), (RG 4), Douglas MacArthur Memorial Archives and Library, Norfolk, VA.
Leo Szilard papers, University of California, San Diego, San Diego, CA.

Government Publications

Division of Medical Statistics, Bureau of Medicine and Surgery, Navy Department. *The History of the Medical Department of the United States Navy in World War II*. Washington, D.C.: U.S. Government Printing Office, 1950.

National Archives Publications Pamphlets Describing M1108 (Harrison-Bundy Files) and M1109 (MED Top Secret Files). Washington, D.C.: National Archives Trust Fund Board, 1982.

Public Papers of the Presidents: Harry S. Truman, 1945. Washington, D.C.: U.S. Government Printing Office, 1961.

Public Papers of the Presidents: Harry S. Truman, 1948. Washington, D.C.: U.S. Government Printing Office, 1964.

Public Papers of the Presidents: Harry S. Truman, 1949. Washington, D.C.: U.S. Government Printing Office, 1964.

Public Papers of the Presidents: Harry S. Truman, 1950. Washington, D.C.: U.S. Government Printing Office, 1965.

Sextant Conference, November–December 1943, Papers and Minutes of Meetings, Sextant and Eureka Conferences. Washington, D.C.: Office U.S. Secretary, Office of the Combined Chiefs of Staff, 1943.

Supreme Commander Allied Powers. *Reports of General MacArthur*. Vol. II: *Japanese Operations in the Southwest Pacific Area*. Washington, D.C.: U.S. Government Printing Office, 1966.

United Nations. *Surrender of Italy, Germany and Japan, World War II*. Washington, D.C.: U.S. Government Printing Office, 1946.

United States Strategic Bombing Survey. *The Effects of Strategic Bombing on Japan's War Economy*. Washington, D.C.: U.S. Government Printing Office, 1946.

———. *The Effects of Atomic Bombs on Hiroshima and Nagasaki*. Washington, D.C.: United States Government Printing Office, 1946.

———. *Japan's Struggle to End the War*. Washington, D.C.: United States Strategic Bombing Survey, Chairman's Office, 1946.

U.S. Atomic Energy Commission. *In the Matter of J. Robert Oppenheimer; transcript of hearing before Personnel Security Board, Washington, D.C. April 12, 1954 through May 6, 1954*. Washington, D.C.: U.S. Government Printing Office, 1954.

U.S. Department of Defense. *The Entry of the Soviet Union into the War Against Japan: Military Plans, 1941–1945*. Washington, D.C.: U.S. Government Printing Office, 1955.

U.S. Department of State. *The Conferences at Malta and Yalta, 1945*. Washington, D.C.: U.S. Government Printing Office, 1955.

———. *Foreign Relations of the United States: Diplomatic Papers, 1944*. Vol. V. Washington, D.C.: Government Printing Office, 1965.

———. *Foreign Relations of the United States: Diplomatic Papers, 1945*. Vol. II. Washington, D.C.: U.S. Government Printing Office, 1967.

———. *Foreign Relations of the United States: Diplomatic Papers, 1945*. Vol. III. Washington, D.C.: U.S. Government Printing Office, 1968.

———. *Foreign Relations of the United States: Diplomatic Papers, 1945*. Vol. IV. Washington, D.C.: U.S. Government Printing Office, 1968.

———. *Foreign Relations of the United States: Diplomatic Papers, 1945*. Vol. V. Washington, D.C.: U.S. Government Printing Office, 1969.

———. *Foreign Relations of the United States: Diplomatic Papers, 1945*. Vol. VI. Washington, D.C.: U.S. Government Printing Office, 1969.

———. *Foreign Relations of the United States: Diplomatic Papers, 1945*. Vol. VII. Washington, D.C.: U.S. Government Printing Office, 1969.

———. *Foreign Relations of the United States: Conference of Berlin (Potsdam), 1945*. 2 vols. Washington, D.C.: U.S. Government Printing Office, 1960.

————. *United States Relations with China, 1944–1949.* Washington, D.C.: U.S. Government Printing Office, 1949.

U.S. Senate Committee on Armed Services and Committee on Foreign Relations. *Military Situation in the Far East.* Part 1. Washington D.C.: U.S. Government Printing Office, 1951.

Books Cited

Acheson, Dean. *Present at the Creation: My Years in the State Department.* New York: Norton, 1969.

————. *Among Friends: Personal Letters of Dean Acheson.* Edited by David S. McLellan and David C. Acheson. New York: Dodd, Mead, 1980.

Adams, Henry. *Witness to Power: The Life of Fleet Admiral William D. Leahy.* Annapolis, MD: Naval Institute Press, 1985.

Albion, Robert Greenhalgh, and Robert Howe Connery. *Forrestal and the Navy.* New York: Columbia University Press, 1962.

Alperovitz, Gar. *Atomic Diplomacy: Hiroshima and Potsdam: The Use of the Atomic Bomb and the American Confrontation with Soviet Power.* New York: Simon & Schuster, 1965. 1st rev. ed. New York: Penguin, 1985.

Ambrose, Stephen E. *Eisenhower.* New York: Simon & Schuster, 1983.

————. *Rise to Globalism: American Foreign Policy Since 1938.* 7th rev. ed. New York: Penguin, 1993.

Angelou, Maya. *On the Pulse of Morning.* New York: Random House, 1993.

Arai, Shinichi. *Genbaku Toka eno Michi* (The Road to the Atomic Bombing). Tokyo: University of Tokyo Press, 1985.

Arnold, H. H. *Global Mission.* New York: Harper & Brothers, 1949.

Ashley, Perry J. *Dictionary of Literary Biography.* Vol. 29: *American Newspaper Journalists, 1926–1950.* Detroit: Gale Research, 1984.

Attlee, Clement. *As It Happened.* New York: Viking Press, 1954.

Ayers, Eben A. *Truman in the White House: The Diary of Eben A. Ayers.* Edited by Robert H. Ferrell. Columbia: University of Missouri Press, 1991.

Backer, John H. *The Decision to Divide Germany: American Foreign Policy in Transition.* Durham, NC: Duke University Press, 1978.

Baldwin, Hanson. *Great Mistakes of the War.* New York: Harper & Brothers, 1950.

Barnet, Richard. *The Rocket's Red Glare: When America Goes to War—the Presidents and the People.* New York: Simon & Schuster, 1990.

Barnhart, Michael A. *Japan Prepares for Total War: The Search for Economic Security, 1919–1941.* Ithaca, NY: Cornell University Press, 1987.

Berger, Meyer. *The Story of the New York Times.* New York: Simon & Schuster, 1951, 1970.

Bernstein, Barton J., ed. *The Atomic Bomb: The Critical Issues.* Boston: Little, Brown, 1976.

Bird, Kai. *The Chairman: John J. McCloy, the Making of the American Establishment.* New York: Simon & Schuster, 1992.

Blackett, P.M.S. *Fear, War, and the Bomb: Military and Political Consequences of Atomic Energy.* New York: Whittlesey House, 1949.

Bohlen, Charles E. *Witness to History, 1929–1969.* New York: Norton, 1973.

Boll, Michael M. *Cold War in the Balkans: American Foreign Policy and the Emergence of Communist Bulgaria, 1943–1947.* Lexington, KY: University Press of Kentucky, 1984.

Borklund, Carl. *Men of the Pentagon: From Forrestal to McNamara.* New York: Praeger, 1966.

Boyer, Paul. *By the Bomb's Early Light: American Thought and Culture at the Dawn of the Atomic Age.* New York: Pantheon, 1985.

Bradley, Omar. *A Soldier's Story.* New York: Henry Holt, 1951.

Braw, Monica. *The Atomic Bomb Suppressed: American Censorship in Occupied Japan.* Armonk, NY: M. E. Sharpe, 1991.

Brown, Anthony Cave. *Bodyguard of Lies.* New York: Bantam Books, 1976.

Brown, Elizabeth Churchill. *The Enemy at His Back.* New York: Distributed by the Bookmailer, 1956.

Brown, Walter. *James F. Byrnes of South Carolina: A Remembrance.* Macon, GA: Mercer University Press, 1992.

Bryant, Arthur. *Triumph in the West: A History of the War Years Based on the Diaries of Field-Marshal Lord Alanbrooke, Chief of the Imperial General Staff.* Garden City, NY: Doubleday, 1959.

Bundy, McGeorge. *Danger and Survival: Choices about the Bomb in the First Fifty Years.* New York: Random House, 1988.

Burchett, Wilfred. *Shadows of Hiroshima.* London: Verso, 1983.

Butow, Robert J. C. *Japan's Decision to Surrender.* Stanford: Stanford University Press, 1954.

Byrnes, James F. *Speaking Frankly.* New York: Harper & Brothers, 1947.

————. *All in One Lifetime.* New York: Harper & Brothers, 1958.

Churchill, Winston S. *Triumph and Tragedy.* Boston: Houghton Mifflin, 1953.

————. *Winston S. Churchill: His Complete Speeches, 1897–1963.* Vol. VII: *1943–1949.* Edited by Robert Rhodes James. New York: Chelsea House, 1974.

Clayton James, D. *The Years of MacArthur.* Vol. II: *1941–1945.* Boston: Houghton Mifflin, 1975.

Clements, Kendrick, A., ed. *James F. Byrnes and the Origins of the Cold War.* Durham, NC: Carolina Academic Press, 1982.

Clifford, Clark, with Richard Holbrooke. *Counsel to the President: A Memoir.* New York: Random House, 1991.

Cline, Ray S. *Washington Command Post: The Operations Division.* Washington, D.C.: Department of the Army, Office of the Chief of Military History, 1951.

Coffin, Tristram. *Missouri Compromise.* Boston: Little, Brown, 1947.

Colville, John. *The Fringes of Power: Downing Street Diaries, 1939–1955.* London: Hodder and Stoughton, 1985.

The Committee for the Compilation of Materials on Damage Caused by the Atomic Bombs in Hiroshima and Nagasaki. *Hiroshima and Nagasaki: The Physical, Medical, and Social Effects of the Atomic Bombings.* Trans. Eisei Ishikawa and David L. Swain. New York: Basic Books, 1981.

Compton, Arthur. *Atomic Quest: A Personal Narrative.* New York: Oxford University Press, 1956.

Cottrell, Leonard S., and Sylvia Eberhart. *American Opinion on World Affairs in the Atomic Age.* Princeton: Princeton University Press, 1948.

Cousins, Norman. *The Pathology of Power.* New York: Norton, 1987.

Crane, Conrad C. *Bombs, Cities, and Civilians: American Airpower Strategy in World War II.* Lawrence, KS: University Press of Kansas, 1993.

Craven, Wesley Frank, and James Lea Cate, eds. *The Army Air Forces in World War II.* Vol V: *The Pacific: Matterhorn to Nagasaki, June 1944 to August 1945.* Chicago: University of Chicago Press, 1953.

Cray, Ed. *General of the Army: George C. Marshall, Soldier and Statesman.* New York: Norton, 1990.

Current, Richard N. *Secretary Stimson: A Study in Statecraft.* New Brunswick, NJ: Rutgers University Press, 1954.

Daniels, Jonathan. *The Man of Independence.* Port Washington, NY: Kennikat Press, 1971.

Davis, Nuel Pharr. *Lawrence and Oppenheimer.* New York: Simon & Schuster, 1968.

Deane, John R. *The Strange Alliance: The Story of Our Efforts at Wartime Cooperation with Russia.* New York: Viking Press, 1947.

Donovan, Robert J. *Conflict and Crisis: The Presidency of Harry S. Truman, 1945–1948.* New York: Norton, 1977.

———. *Tumultuous Years: The Presidency of Harry S. Truman, 1949–1953.* New York: Norton, 1982.

Dower, John W. *War Without Mercy: Race and Power in the Pacific War.* New York: Pantheon, 1986.

Drea, Edward J. *MacArthur's Ultra: Codebreaking and the War Against Japan, 1942–1945.* Lawrence, KS: University Press of Kansas, 1992.

Dulles, Allen. *The Secret Surrender.* New York: Harper & Row, 1966.

Dunar, Andrew J. *The Truman Scandals and the Politics of Morality.* Columbia: University of Missouri Press, 1984.

Dyer, George Carroll. *The Amphibians Came to Conquer: The Story of Admiral Richmond Kelly Turner.* Washington, D.C.: U.S. Government Printing Office, 1972.

Ehrman, John. *Grand Strategy.* Vol. VI: *October 1944–August 1945.* London: Her Majesty's Stationery Office, 1956.

Eisenhower, Dwight D. *Crusade in Europe.* Garden City, NY: Doubleday, 1948.

———. *Mandate for Change, 1953–1956: The White House Years.* Garden City, NY: Doubleday, 1963.

Eisenhower, John. *Strictly Personal.* Garden City, NY: Doubleday, 1974.

Eisenhower, Milton. *The President Is Calling.* Garden City, NY: Doubleday, 1974.

Ermenc, Joseph J. *Atomic Bomb Scientists: Memoirs, 1939–1945.* Westport, CT: Meckler, 1989.

Evans, Rowland, Jr., and Robert Novak. *Nixon in the White House: The Frustration of Power.* New York: Random House, 1971.

Farago, Ladislas. *Burn After Reading: The Espionage History of World War II.* New York: Walker, 1961.

Federal Council of the Churches of Christ in America, Commission on The Relation of the Church to the War in the Light of the Christian Faith. *Atomic Warfare and the Christian Faith.* New York: Federal Council of the Churches of Christ in America, March 1946.

Feis, Herbert. *The Road to Pearl Harbor: The Coming of the War Between the United States and Japan.* Princeton: Princeton University Press, 1950.

———. *The China Tangle: The American Effort in China from Pearl Harbor to the Marshall Mission.* Princeton: Princeton University Press, 1953.

———. *Churchill-Roosevelt-Stalin: The War They Waged and the Peace They Sought.* Princeton: Princeton University Press, 1957.

———. *Between War and Peace: The Potsdam Conference.* Princeton: Princeton University Press, 1960.

———. *Japan Subdued: The Atomic Bomb and the End of the War in the Pacific.* Princeton: Princeton University Press, 1961.

———. *The Atomic Bomb and the End of World War II.* Princeton: Princeton University Press, 1966.

Ferrell, Robert H. *Harry S. Truman: A Life.* Columbia: University of Missouri Press, 1994.

———. *Choosing Truman: The Democratic Convention of 1944.* Columbia: University of Missouri Press, 1994.

Ferrell, Robert H., and Samuel Flagg Bemis, eds. *The American Secretaries of State and Their Diplomacy.* Vol. 14. New York: Cooper Square, 1963.

Fleming, D.F. *The Cold War and Its Origins, 1917–1960.* 2 vols. Garden City, NY: Doubleday, 1961.

Fleming, Donald, and Bernard Bailyn, eds. *The Intellectual Migration: Europe and America, 1930–1960.* Cambridge, MA: Harvard University Press, 1969.

Forrestal, James V. *The Forrestal Diaries.* Edited by Walter Millis. New York: Viking Press, 1951.

Fox, Richard Wightman. *Reinhold Niebuhr: A Biography.* San Francisco: Harper & Row, 1985, 1987.

Fukai, Eigo. *Sumitsuin Jyuyogiji Oboegaki [The Memorandum of the Privy Council].* Tokyo: Iwanami Shoten, 1953.

Gaddis, John Lewis. *The United States and the Origins of the Cold War.* New York: Columbia University Press, 1972.

Gaimusho [Japan Foreign Ministry], ed. *Dainiji Sekaitaisen Shusenshi Roku (The Record of the Ending of World War II).* Tokyo: Yamate Shobo Shin Sha, 1990.

Gallicchio, Marc S. *The Cold War Begins in Asia: American East Asian Policy and the Fall of the Japanese Empire.* New York: Columbia University Press, 1988.

Gallu, Samuel. *"Give 'Em Hell Harry": Reminiscences.* New York: Avon, 1975.

Gaulle, Charles de. *War Memoirs.* Vol. 3: *Salvation, 1944–1946.* New York: Simon & Schuster, 1960.

Gallup, George H. *The Gallup Poll: Public Opinion, 1935–1971.* Vol. I: *1935–1948.* New York: Random House, 1972.

Gati, Charles. *Hungary and the Soviet Bloc.* Durham, NC: Duke University Press, 1986.

Gilbert, Martin. *'Never Despair': Winston S. Churchill, 1945–1965.* London: William Heinemann, 1988.

Giovannitti, Len, and Fred Freed. *The Decision to Drop the Bomb.* New York: Coward-McCann, 1965.

Gomikawa, Junpei. *Gozen Kaigi [The Imperial Council].* Tokyo: Bungeishunju, 1958.

Goodchild, Peter. *J. Robert Oppenheimer: Shatterer of Worlds.* Boston: Houghton Mifflin, 1980.

Goodman, Walter. *The Committee: The Extraordinary Career of the House Committee on Un-American Activities.* New York: Farrar, Straus and Giroux, 1968.

Gormly, James L. *From Potsdam to the Cold War: Big Three Diplomacy, 1945–1947.* Wilmington, DE: Scholarly Resources, 1990.

Gouldschmidt, Bertrand. *Atomic Adventure.* New York: Pergamon, 1964.

Gowing, Margaret. *Britain and Atomic Energy, 1939–1945.* New York: St. Martin's Press, 1964.

Greiner, Bernd. *Die Morgenthau-Legende. Zur Geschichte eines umstrittenen Plans.* Hamburg, Germany: Hamburger Edition HIS Verlages, 1995.

Grew, Joseph C. *Turbulent Era: A Diplomatic Record of Forty Years, 1904–1945.* Vol. II. Boston: Houghton Mifflin, 1952.

Grose, Peter. *Gentleman Spy: The Life of Allen Dulles.* Boston: Houghton Mifflin, 1994.

Groueff, Stephane. *The Manhattan Project: The Untold Story of Making the Atomic Bomb.* Little, Brown, 1967.

Groves, Leslie R. *Now It Can Be Told: The Story of the Manhattan Project.* New York: Harper & Brothers, 1962.

Hachiya, Michihiko, M.D. *Hiroshima Diary: The Journal of a Japanese Physician, August 6–September 30, 1945.* Chapel Hill: University of North Carolina Press, 1955.

Hacker, Barton. *The Dragon's Tail: Radiation Safety in the Manhattan Project, 1942–1946.* Berkeley: University of California Press, 1967.

Hansell, Haywood S. *Strategic Air War Against Japan.* Maxwell Air Force Base, AL: Air War College, 1980.

Harriman, W. Averell, and Elie Abel. *Special Envoy to Churchill and Stalin, 1941–1946.* New York: Random House, 1975.

Harris, Sheldon H. *Factories of Death: Japanese Secret Biological Warfare 1932–1945 and the American Cover-up.* New York: Routledge, 1994.

Hayashi, Saburo. *Taiheiyo Senso Rikusen Gaishi* (The Battle of the Army in the Pacific War). Tokyo: Iwanami Shinsho, 1951.

Hayashi, Shigeru, ed. *Nihon Shusen Shi* (The Road to Surrender). Tokyo: Yomiuri Shinbun Sha, 1962.

Hayes, Grace Pearson. *The History of the Joint Chiefs of Staff in World War II: The War Against Japan.* Annapolis, MD: Naval Institute Press, 1982.

Heller, Francis H., ed. *The Truman White House: The Administration of the Presidency, 1945–1953.* Lawrence: Regents Press of Kansas, 1980.

Herken, Gregg. *The Winning Weapon: The Atomic Bomb in the Cold War, 1945–1950.* New York: Alfred A. Knopf, 1980.

Herman, Judith Lewis. *Trauma and Recovery.* New York: Basic Books, 1992.

Hershberg, James G. *James B. Conant: Harvard to Hiroshima and the Making of the Nuclear Age.* New York: Alfred A. Knopf, 1993.

Hersey, John. *Hiroshima.* New York: Vintage Books, 1946, 1985.

Hewlett, Richard G., and Oscar E. Anderson. *The New World, 1939–1946.* University Park: Pennsylvania State University Press, 1962.

Hewlett, Richard G., and Francis Duncan. *Atomic Shield, 1947–1952.* University Park: Pennsylvania State University Press, 1969.

Hodgson, Godfrey. *The Colonel: The Life and Wars of Henry Stimson, 1867–1950.* New York: Alfred A. Knopf, 1990.

Holloway, David. *The Soviet Union and the Arms Race.* 2nd ed. New Haven: Yale University Press, 1984.

———. *Stalin and the Bomb: The Soviet Union and Atomic Energy, 1939–1956.* New Haven: Yale University Press, 1994.

Hoopes, Townsend, and Douglas Brinkley. *Driven Patriot: The Life and Times of James Forrestal.* New York: Alfred A. Knopf, 1992.

Hull, Cordell. *Memoirs of Cordell Hull.* Vol. II. New York: Macmillan, 1948.

Ienaga, Saburo. *The Pacific War: World War II and the Japanese, 1931–1945.* New York: Pantheon, 1968.

———. *Japan's Last War.* Canberra: Australian National University Press, 1979.

Inoki, Masamichi. *Nihon Seiji Gaiko Shiryosen* (The Diplomatic Document). Tokyo: Yushindo, 1967.

Inoue, Kiyoshi. *Gendai Nihon no Rekishi* (Japanese Modern History). Tokyo: Aoki Shoten, 1958.

———. *Showa no Gojunen* (Fifty Years of the Showa Period). Tokyo: Kodansha, 1976.

———. *Watashi no Gendaishi Ron* (The Modern History Theory). Osaka: Osaka Shoseki, 1982.

Ismay, Hastings Lionel. *Memoirs.* New York: Viking Press, 1960.

Isaacson, Walter, and Evan Thomas. *The Wise Men: Six Friends and the World They Made: Acheson, Bohlen, Harriman, Kennan, Lovett, McCloy.* New York: Simon & Schuster, 1986.

James, D. Clayton. *The Years of MacArthur, Vol. II: 1941–1945.* Boston: Houghton Mifflin, 1975.

Jones, Vincent C. *Manhattan: The Army and the Atomic Bomb.* Washington, D.C.: Center of Military History, U.S. Army, 1985.

Jucker-Fleetwood, Erin E. *The Per Jacobsson Mediation.* Basle Center for Economic and Financial Research, 1967.

Jungk, Robert. *Brighter Than a Thousand Suns: The Story of the Men Who Made the Bomb.* Trans. James Cleugh. New York: Grove Press, 1956, 1958.

———. *The Nuclear State.* London: John Calder, 1977.

Kase, Toshikazu. *Journey to the Missouri.* New Haven: Yale University Press, 1950.

Kennan, George F. *The Nuclear Delusion: Soviet-American Relations in the Atomic Age.* New York: Pantheon, 1982.

Kido, Koichi. *Kido Nikki* (Kido Diary). Tokyo: Tokyo Daigaku Shuppan Sha, 1966.

Kiernan, Ben, ed. *Burchett Reporting the Other Side of the World, 1939–1983*. London: Quartet Books, 1986.

King, Ernest J., and Walter Muir Whitehill. *Fleet Admiral King: A Naval Record*. New York: Norton, 1952.

Knebel, Fletcher, and Charles W. Bailey. *No High Ground*. New York: Harper & Brothers, 1960.

Kofsky, Frank. *Harry S. Truman and the War Scare of 1948: A Successful Campaign to Deceive the Nation*. New York: St. Martin's Press, 1993.

Kolko, Gabriel. *The Politics of War: The World and United States Foreign Policy, 1943–1945*. New York: Harper & Row, 1968.

Kubek, Anthony. *How the Far East Was Lost: American Policy and the Creation of Communist China, 1941–1949*. Chicago: Henry Regnery, 1963.

Kuklick, Bruce. *American Policy and the Division of Germany: The Clash with Russia over Reparations*. Ithaca, NY: Cornell University Press, 1972.

Lacey, Michael J., ed. *The Truman Presidency*. New York: Woodrow Wilson International Center for Scholars and Cambridge University Press, 1989.

Lafeber, Walter. *America, Russia & the Cold War, 1945–1984*. 6th ed. New York: McGraw-Hill, 1991.

Lane, Arthur Bliss. *I Saw Poland Betrayed: An American Ambassador Reports to the American People*. Indianapolis: Bobbs-Merrill, 1948.

Lang, Daniel. *Early Tales of the Atomic Age*. Garden City, NY: Doubleday, 1948.

Lanouette, William, with Bela Szilard. *Genius in the Shadows: A Biography of Leo Szilard, the Man Behind the Bomb*. New York: Scribner's, 1992.

Laurence, William L. *Dawn over Zero: The Story of the Atomic Bomb*. New York: Alfred A. Knopf, 1946.

————. *Men and Atoms: The Discovery, the Uses and the Future of Atomic Energy*. New York: Simon & Schuster, 1946, 1959.

Lawren, William. *The General and the Bomb: A Biography of General Leslie R. Groves, Director of the Manhattan Project*. New York: Dodd, Mead, 1988.

Leahy, William D. *I Was There: The Personal Story of the Chief of Staff to Presidents Roosevelt and Truman, Based on His Notes and Diaries Made at the Time*. New York: Whittlesey House, 1950.

Lee, Bruce. *Marching Orders: The Untold Story of World War II*. New York: Crown Publishers, 1995.

Leffler, Melvyn P. *A Preponderance of Power: National Security, the Truman Administration, and the Cold War*. Stanford: Stanford University Press, 1992.

Leighton, Alexander H. *Human Relations in a Changing World: Observations on the Use of Social Sciences*. New York: Dutton, 1949.

LeMay, Curtis E., with MacKinlay Kantor. *Mission with LeMay: My Story*. Garden City, NY: Doubleday, 1965.

LeMay, Curtis E., and Bill Yenne. *Superfortress: The Story of the B-29 and American Air Power*. New York: McGraw-Hill, 1988.

Libby, Leona Marshall. *The Uranium People*. New York: Scribner's, 1979.

Lieberman, Joseph. *The Scorpion and the Tarantula: The Struggle to Control Atomic Weapons, 1945–1949*. Boston: Houghton Mifflin, 1970.

Liebovich, Louis. *The Press and the Origins of the Cold War*. New York: Praeger, 1988.

Lilienthal, David E. *The Journals of David E. Lilienthal*. Vol. II: *The Atomic Energy Years, 1945–1950*. New York: Harper & Row, 1964.

Long, Edward LeRoy, Jr. *The Christian Response to the Atomic Crisis*. Philadelphia: Westminster Press, 1950.

Luce, Henry A. *The Ideas of Henry Luce*. Edited by John K. Jessup. New York: Atheneum, 1969.

Lunger, Harold L., ed. *Facing War/Waging Peace: Findings of the American Church Study Conferences, 1940–1960*. New York: Friendship Press, 1988.

Macdonald, Dwight. *Memoirs of a Revolutionist: Essays in Political Criticism.* New York: Farrar, Straus, and Cudahy, 1957.

MacIsaac, David. *Strategic Bombing in World War Two: The Story of the United States Strategic Bombing Survey.* New York: Garland, 1976.

MacLean, Elizabeth Kimball. *Joseph E. Davies: Envoy to the Soviets.* Westport, CT: Praeger, 1992.

Maddox, Robert James. *From War to Cold War: The Education of Harry S. Truman.* Boulder, CO: Westview Press, 1988.

Manchester, William. *American Caesar: Douglas MacArthur, 1880–1964.* Boston: Little, Brown, 1978.

Manne, Robert. *Agent of Influence: The Life and Times of Wilfred Burchett.* Toronto: The Mackenzie Institute for the Study of Terrorism, Revolution and Propaganda, 1989.

Masanori, Nakamura. *The Japanese Monarchy: Ambassador Joseph Grew and the Making of the "Symbol Emperor System," 1931–1991.* Armonk, NY: M.E. Sharpe, 1992.

Matloff, Maurice, and Edwin M. Snell. *Strategic Planning for Coalition Warfare, 1941–1942.* Washington, D.C.: Office of the Chief of Military History, Department of the Army, 1953.

Matsumoto Shunichi and Ando Yoshiro, eds. *Nihon Gaiko Shi* (Japanese Diplomatic History). Vol. 25: *Daitoa Senso, Shusen Gaiko* (Greater Asian War and Diplomacy). Tokyo: Kagoshima Kenkyu Sho Shuppan Kai, 1972.

McCloy, John J. *The Challenge to American Foreign Policy.* Cambridge, MA: Harvard University Press, 1953.

McCormick, Thomas J. *America's Half Century: United States Foreign Policy in the Cold War.* Baltimore: Johns Hopkins University Press, 1989.

McCullough, David. *Truman.* New York: Simon & Schuster, 1992.

McNeill, William Hardy. *America, Britain, & Russia: Their Co-operation and Conflict, 1941–1946.* New York: Oxford University Press, 1953.

Mee, Charles. *Meeting at Potsdam.* New York: M. Evans, 1975.

Messer, Robert L. *The End of an Alliance: James F. Byrnes, Roosevelt, Truman and the Origins of the Cold War.* Chapel Hill: University of North Carolina Press, 1982.

Miller, Merle. *Plain Speaking: An Oral Biography of Harry S. Truman.* New York: Distributed by Putnam, 1974.

Miller, Richard. *Truman: The Rise to Power.* New York: McGraw-Hill, 1986.

Morgenthau, Henry. *Morgenthau Diary (Germany).* Washington, D.C.: U.S. Government Printing Office, 1967.

Morison, Elting E. *Turmoil and Tradition: A Study of the Life and Times of Henry L. Stimson.* Boston: Houghton Mifflin, 1960.

Mumford, Lewis. *Programme for Survival.* London: Secker & Warburg, 1946.

———. *Values for Survival: Essays, Addresses, and Letters on Politics and Education.* New York: Harcourt, Brace, 1946.

Muresianu, John M. *War of Ideas: American Intellectuals and the World Crisis, 1938–1945.* New York: Garland, 1988.

Nakayama, Takashi. *Sorengun Shinko to Nihongun* (The Attack of Soviet Troops and the Japanese Military). Tokyo: Kokusho Kankokai, 1990.

National Conference of Catholic Bishops. *The Challenge of Peace: God's Promise and Our Response, A Pastoral Letter on War and Peace, May 3, 1983.* Washington, D.C.: United States Catholic Conference, 1983.

Nihon Gaiko Gakkai, ed. *Taiheiyo Senso Shuketsu Ron* (Some Discussions on the Ending of the Pacific War). Tokyo: University of Tokyo Press, 1958.

Nishijima, Ariatsu. *Genbaku ha Naze Toka Saretaka* (Why Were the Atomic Bombs Dropped?). Tokyo: Aoki Shoten, 1985.

Nitze, Paul H., with Ann M. Smith and Steven L. Rearden. *From Hiroshima to Glasnost: At the Center of Decision: A Memoir.* New York: Grove Weidenfeld, 1989.

Novick, Peter. *That Noble Dream: The "Objectivity Question" and the American Historical Profession.* New York: Cambridge University Press, 1988.

O'Connor, Raymond G. *Diplomacy for Victory: FDR and Unconditional Surrender.* New York: Norton, 1971.

Oppenheimer, Robert. *Robert Oppenheimer: Letters and Recollections.* Edited by Alice Kimball Smith and Charles Weiner. Cambridge, MA: Harvard University Press, 1980.

Pais, Abraham. *Niels Bohr's Times in Physics, Philosophy, and Polity.* New York: Oxford University Press, 1991.

Perry, Glen C. H. *"Dear Bart": Washington Views of World War II.* Westport, CT: Greenwood Press, 1982.

Phillips, Cabell. *The Truman Presidency: The History of A Triumphant Succession.* New York: Macmillan, 1966.

Podell, Janet, and Steven Anzovin, eds. *Speeches of the American Presidents.* New York: H.W. Wilson, 1988.

Pogue, Forrest C. *George C. Marshall: Organizer of Victory, 1943–1945.* New York: Viking Press, 1973.

————. *George C. Marshall: Statesman, 1945–1959.* New York: Penguin, 1987.

————. *George C. Marshall: Interviews and Reminiscences for Forrest C. Pogue.* Lexington, VA: George C. Marshall Research Foundation, 1986.

Potter, E. B. *Nimitz.* Annapolis, MD: Naval Institute Press, 1976.

Potter, E. B., and Chester W. Nimitz, eds. *Sea Power: A Naval History.* Engelwood Cliffs, NJ: Prentice-Hall, 1960.

Quigley, Martin S. *Peace Without Hiroshima: Secret Action at the Vatican in the Spring of 1945.* New York: Madison Books, 1991.

Reingold, Nathan. *Science, American Style.* New Brunswick, NJ: Rutgers University Press, 1991.

Reston, James. *Deadline: A Memoir.* New York: Random House, 1991.

Reuben, William. *Atom Spy Hoax.* New York: Action Books, 1955.

Rhodes, Richard. *The Making of the Atomic Bomb.* New York: Simon & Schuster, 1986.

Robertson, David. *Sly and Able: A Political Biography of James F. Byrnes.* New York: Norton, 1994.

Rose, Lisle A. *After Yalta.* New York: Scribner's, 1973.

Rosenblatt, Roger. *Witness: The World Since Hiroshima.* Boston: Little, Brown, 1985.

Royse, Morton William. *Aerial Bombardment and the International Regulation of Warfare.* New York: H. Vinal, 1928.

Rubin, David M., and Ann Marie Cunningham, eds. *War, Peace and the News Media.* New York: New York University Press, 1987.

Sadofsky, David. *Knowledge as Power: Political and Legal Control of Information.* New York: Praeger, 1990.

Sanbohonbu [The General Staff]. *Haisen no Kiroku* (The Record of Defeat). Tokyo: Hara Shobo, 1967.

Schaller, Michael. *Douglas MacArthur: The Far Eastern General.* New York: Oxford University Press, 1989.

Schell, Jonathon. *The Fate of the Earth.* New York: Alfred A. Knopf, 1982.

Schlesinger, Arthur, Jr. *A Thousand Days: John F. Kennedy in the White House.* Boston: Houghton Mifflin, 1965.

Schneir, Walter, and Miriam Schneir. *Invitation to an Inquest.* New York: Pantheon, 1983 ed.

Schoenberger, Walter Smith. *Decision of Destiny.* Athens: Ohio University Press, 1969.

Sha, Yomiuri Shimbun, [Yomiuri Newspaper] ed. *Showashi no Tenno* (History of the Showa Period and the Emperor). Vol. 2. Tokyo: Yomiuri Shimbun Sha, 1967.

Sherry, Michael. *The Rise of American Air Power: The Creation of Armageddon.* New Haven: Yale University Press, 1987.

Sherwin, Martin. *A World Destroyed: Hiroshima and the Origins of the Arms Race.* New York: Alfred A. Knopf, 1975; Vintage, 1987.

Sherwood, Robert E. *Roosevelt and Hopkins: An Intimate History.* New York: Grosset & Dunlap, 1948.

Shinobu, Seizaburo. *Sengo Nihon Seiji Shi I: Senryo to Minshu Shugi* (Political History of Japan After the War). Vol. I: (Occupation and Democracy). Tokyo: Keiso Shobo, 1966.

———. *Seidan no Rekishigaku* (Historical Meaning of the Emperor's Majestic Decision). Tokyo: Keiso Shobo, 1992.

Sigal, Leon V. *Fighting to a Finish: The Politics of War Termination in the United States and Japan, 1945.* Ithaca, NY: Cornell University Press, 1988.

Singh, Nagendra, and Edward McWhinney. *Nuclear Weapons and Contemporary International Law.* rev. ed. Boston: Martinus Nijhoff Publishers, 1989.

Skates, John Ray. *The Invasion of Japan: Alternative to the Bomb.* Columbia: University of South Carolina Press, 1994.

Smith, Alice Kimball. *A Peril and a Hope: The Scientists' Movement in America, 1945–1947.* Cambridge, MA: M.I.T. Press, 1971.

Smith, Jean. *Lucius D. Clay: An American Life.* New York: Henry Holt, 1990.

Smyth, Henry P. *Atomic Energy for Military Purposes.* Princeton: Princeton University Press, 1945.

Snell, John L. *Illusion and Necessity: The Diplomacy of Global War, 1939–1945.* Boston: Houghton Mifflin, 1963.

Snow, Edgar. *Journey to the Beginning.* New York: Random House, 1958.

Spector, Ronald H. *Eagle Against the Sun: The American War With Japan.* New York: Vintage, 1985.

Stalin, Joseph. *Stalin's Correspondence with Churchill, Attlee, Roosevelt and Truman, 1941–45.* Vol. 2. London: Lawrence & Wishart, 1958.

Steinberg, Alfred. *The Man from Missouri: The Life and Times of Harry S. Truman.* New York: Putnam's, 1962.

Stimson, Henry L., and McGeorge Bundy. *On Active Service in Peace and War.* New York: Harper & Brothers, 1948.

Stoff, Michael B., Jonathan F. Fanton, and R. Hal Williams, eds. *The Manhattan Project: A Documentary Introduction to the Atomic Age.* Philadelphia: Temple University Press, 1991.

Stowe, Leland. *While Time Remains.* New York: Alfred A. Knopf, 1946.

Strickland, Donald A. *Scientists in Politics: The Atomic Scientists Movement, 1945–46.* West Lafayette, IN: Purdue University Press, 1968.

Summers, Robert E. *Federal Information Controls in Peacetime.* New York: H.W. Wilson, 1949.

Swing, Raymond. *In the Name of Sanity.* New York: Harper & Brothers, 1945, 1946.

Szilard, Leo. *Leo Szilard: His Version of the Facts, Selected Recollections and Correspondence.* Edited by Spencer R. Weart and Gertrud Weiss Szilard. Cambridge, MA: M.I.T. Press, 1978.

Taylor, Telford. *The Anatomy of the Nuremberg Trials: A Personal Memoir.* New York: Alfred A. Knopf, 1992.

Teller, Edward, with Allen Brown. *The Legacy of Hiroshima.* Garden City, NY: Doubleday, 1962.

Theoharis, Athan. *The Yalta Myths: An Issue in U.S. Politics, 1945–1955.* Columbia: University of Missouri Press, 1970.

Thorne, Christopher. *Allies of a Kind: The United States, Britain, and the War Against Japan, 1941–1945.* New York: Oxford University Press, 1978.

Togo, Shigehiko. *Sofu Togo Shigenori no Shogai* (The Biography of Shigenori Togo). Tokyo: Bungei Shunshu, 1993.

Toland, John. *The Rising Sun: The Decline and Fall of the Japanese Empire, 1936–1945*. New York: Bantam Books, 1971.

Tolischus, Otto. *Tokyo Record*. New York: Reynal & Hitchcock, 1943.

Truman, Harry S. *Mr. President: The First Publication from the Personal Diaries, Private Letters, Papers, and Revealing Interviews of Harry S. Truman, Thirty-second President of the United States of America*. Edited by William Hillman. New York: Farrar, Straus and Young, 1952.

———. *Memoirs of Harry S. Truman*. Vol. I: *Year of Decisions*. Garden City, NY: Doubleday, 1955.

———. *Truman Speaks*. New York: Columbia University Press, 1960.

———. *The Autobiography of Harry S. Truman*. Edited by Robert H. Ferrell. Boulder: Colorado Associated University Press, 1980.

———. *Off the Record: The Private Papers of Harry S. Truman*. Edited by Robert H. Ferrell. New York: Harper & Row, 1980; Penguin, 1982.

———. *Strictly Personal and Confidential: Letters Harry Truman Never Mailed*. Edited by Monte M. Poen. Boston: Little, Brown, 1982.

———. *Dear Bess: The Letters from Harry to Bess Truman, 1910–1959*. Edited by Robert H. Ferrell. New York: Norton, 1983.

———. *Letters Home*. Edited by Monte M. Poen. New York: Putnam's, 1984.

———. *Where the Buck Stops: The Personal and Private Writings of Harry S. Truman*. Edited by Margaret Truman. New York: Warner Books, 1989.

Truman, Margaret. *Harry S. Truman*. New York: Morrow, 1973.

———. *Bess W. Truman*. New York: Macmillan, 1986.

Udall, Stewart L. *The Myths of August: A Personal Exploration of Our Tragic Cold War Affair with the Atom*. New York: Pantheon, 1994.

Ulam, Adam. *Stalin: The Man and His Era*. New York: Viking Press, 1973.

Vandenberg, Arthur H. *The Private Papers of Senator Vandenberg*. Edited by Arthur H. Vandenberg, Jr. Cambridge, MA: Riverside Press, 1952.

van der Vat, Dan. *The Pacific Campaign, World War II: The U.S.-Japanese Naval War, 1941–1945*. New York: Simon & Schuster, 1991.

Wallace, Henry A. *The Price of Vision: The Diary of Henry A. Wallace, 1942–1946*. Edited by John M. Blum. Boston: Houghton Mifflin, 1973.

Walzer, Michael. *Just and Unjust Wars: A Moral Argument with Historical Illustrations*. New York: Basic Books, 1977.

Weiner, Tim. *Blank Check: The Pentagon's Black Budget*. New York: Warner Books, 1991.

Weinstein, Allen, and Moshe Ma'oz, eds. *Truman and the American Commitment to Israel: A Thirtieth Anniversary Conference*. Jerusalem: Magnes Press, Hebrew University, 1981.

Weisgall, Jonathan M. *Operation Crossroads: The Atomic Tests at Bikini Atoll*. Annapolis, MD: Naval Institute Press, 1994.

Weisskopf, Victor. *The Joy of Insight: Passions of a Physicist*. New York: Basic Books, 1990.

Williams, William Appleman. *The Tragedy of American Diplomacy*. 2nd rev. ed. New York: Dell, 1972.

Williamson, Samuel R., and Steven L. Rearden. *The Origins of U.S. Nuclear Strategy, 1945–1953*. New York: St. Martin's Press, 1993.

Woodward, Bob. *The Commanders*. New York: Simon & Schuster, 1991.

———. *The Agenda: Inside the Clinton White House*. New York: Simon & Schuster, 1994.

Wyden, Peter. *Day One: Before Hiroshima and After*. New York: Simon & Schuster, 1984.

Yergin, Daniel. *Shattered Peace: The Origins of the Cold War and the National Security State.* Boston: Houghton Mifflin, 1977.

Yergler, Dennis K. *Herbert Feis, Wilsonian Internationalism, and America's Technological Democracy.* New York: Peter Lang, 1993.

Zacharias, Ellis M. *Secret Missions: The Story of an Intelligence Officer.* New York: Putnam's, 1946.

Articles

"A Petition to The President of The United States." *The Christian Century* (June 27, 1945): 762.

"A Report to the Secretary of War." *Bulletin of the Atomic Scientists* 1 (May 10, 1946): 2–4, 16.

"A Statement on Our Policy Toward Japan." *Christianity and Crisis* V (June 25, 1945): 1.

Aftergood, Steven. "The Perils of Government Secrecy." *Issues in Science and Technology* 8 (Summer 1992): 81–88.

Allen, Thomas B., and Norman Polmar. "The Voice of the Crane." *MHQ: The Quarterly Journal of Military History* 7 (Spring 1995): 98–102.

Alperovitz, Gar, and Robert L. Messer. "Correspondence." *International Security* 116 (Winter 1991/92):204–14.

Alperovitz, Gar, and Kai Bird. "The Centrality of the Bomb." *Foreign Policy* 94 (Spring 1994): 3–20.

Alsop, Joseph, and David Joravsky. "Was the Hiroshima Bomb Necessary? An Exchange." *New York Review of Books*, October 23, 1980, 33–35.

"America's Atomic Atrocity." *Christian Century* 62 (August 29, 1945): 974–76.

Anders, Roger M. "The President and the Atomic Bomb: Who Approved the Trinity Nuclear Test?" *Prologue* 20 (Winter 1988): 268–82.

Archibald, Sam. "The Early Years of the Freedom of Information Act—1955 to 1974." *Political Science & Politics* 26 (December 1993): 726–31.

"The Atomic Bomb and Our Cities." *Bulletin of the Atomic Scientists* 2 (August 1, 1946): 29–30.

"Atomic Warfare and the Christian Faith." *United States News*, March 22, 1946.

Baldwin, Hanson W. "Terms for Japanese: Allies' Declaration Omits Provision for Emperor as Foe Pleads for Soft Peace." *The New York Times* (July 27, 1945): 4.

———. "Big Questions in Asia Now Center on Russia." *The New York Times* (July 1, 1945): IV, 5.

———. "New Crisis in Pacific: Russian Move Plus Military Gains Said to Portend Quicker End of War." *The New York Times* (April 6, 1945): 5.

Barnes, Harry Elmer. "Hiroshima: Assault on a Beaten Foe." *National Review* (May 10, 1958): 441–443.

Barnouw, Erik. "The Hiroshima-Nagasaki Footage: A Report." *Historical Journal of Film, Radio and Television* 2 (1982): 91–100.

Bauer, K. Jack, and Alan C. Cox. "Olympic vs Ketsu-Go." *Marine Corps Gazette* 49 (August 1965): 32–44.

Bernstein, Barton J. "The Atomic Bomb and American Foreign Policy, 1941–1945: An Historiographical Controversy." *Peace and Change* 2 (Spring 1974): 1–16.

———. "Doomsday II." *New York Times Magazine* (July 27, 1975): 7.

———. "Roosevelt, Truman and the Atomic Bomb, 1941–1945: A Reinterpretation." *Political Science Quarterly* 90 (Spring 1975): 23–69.

———. "Triumph and Tragedy: Hiroshima and Nagasaki—30 Years Later." *Intellect* 104 (Summer 1975): 257–63.

————. "Shatterer of Worlds: Hiroshima and Nagasaki." *Bulletin of the Atomic Scientists* 31 (December 1975): 12–22.

————. "The Perils and Politics of Surrender: Ending the War with Japan and Avoiding the Third Atomic Bomb." *Pacific Historical Review* 46 (February 1977): 1–27.

————. "Unraveling a Mystery: American POWs Killed at Hiroshima." *Foreign Service Journal* (October 1979): 17–19, 40.

————. "Truman at Potsdam: His Secret Diary." *Foreign Service Journal* (July/August 1980): 29–34, 36.

————. "A Postwar Myth: 500,000 U.S. Lives Saved." *Bulletin of the Atomic Scientists* 42 (June/July 1986): 38–40.

————. "Ike and Hiroshima: Did He Oppose It?" *The Journal of Strategic Studies* 10 (Spring 1987): 377–89.

————. "An Analysis of 'Two Cultures': Writing About the Making and the Using of the Atomic Bombs." *The Public Historian* 12 (Spring 1990): 83–107.

————. "Eclipsed by Hiroshima and Nagasaki: Early Thinking About Tactical Nuclear Weapons." *International Security* 15 (Spring 1991): 149–73.

————. "Correspondence." *International Security* 116 (Winter 1991/92): 214–21.

————. "Writing, Righting or Wronging the Historical Record: President Truman's Letter on His Atomic-Bomb Decision." *Diplomatic History* 16 (Winter 1992): 163–73.

————. "Seizing the Contested Terrain of Early Nuclear History: Stimson, Conant, and Their Allies Explain the Decision to Use the Atomic Bomb." *Diplomatic History* 17 (Winter 1993): 35–72.

————. "The Atomic Bombings Reconsidered." *Foreign Affairs* 74 (January/February 1995): 135–52.

Besse, Janet, and Harold D. Lasswell. "Our Columnists on the A-Bomb." *World Politics* 3 (October 1950): 72–87.

"Big Three Asked to Tell Foe Price of Peace." *The New York Times* (July 13, 1945): 3.

Bird, Kai. "Roosevelt's Assistant President." *Washington Post Book World* (January 1, 1995): 1.

"Bishop Urges Protest of Armaments." *Origins* 11 (July 2, 1981): 110–12.

Blanton, Willard B. "Harry S Truman and Pendergast Politics." *Gateway Heritage* 11 (Winter 1990–91): 60–69.

Blumenthal, Sidney. "The Essential Clark Clifford." *Washington Post Magazine* (February 5, 1989): 12–18.

Boller, Paul F., Jr. "Hiroshima and the American Left: August 1945." *International Social Science Review* 57 (Winter 1982): 13–28.

Boyer, Paul. "The Cloud over Our Culture." *New Republic* 193 (August 12 and 19, 1985): 26–31.

Brown, Harrison. "The Beginning of the End: A Review." *Bulletin of the Atomic Scientists* 3 (March 1947): 99.

Budris, John. "Up-Close and 'Down to the Ground.'" *Christian Science Monitor* (June 12, 1992): 13.

Bundy, Harvey. "Remembered Words." *The Atlantic* 199 (March 1957): 56–57.

Bundy, McGeorge. "Pearl Harbor Brought Peace." *Newsweek* (December 16, 1991): 8.

Capaccio, Tony. "'Truman' Author Errs on Japan Invasion Casualty Memo." *Defense Week* 15 (October 11, 1994): 1, 8–9.

"Churchmen Speak on Atomic Bomb." *Federal Council Bulletin* 28 (September 1945): 6.

"Classified Universe Still Expanding." *Secrecy & Government Bulletin* 36 (June 1994): 1.

Clemens, Diane S. "Averell Harriman, John Deane, the Joint Chiefs of Staff, and the 'Reversal of Co-operation' with the Soviet Union in April 1945." *The International History Review* XIV (May 1992): 277–306.

Compton, Arthur H., and Farrington Daniels. "A Poll of Scientists at Chicago, July 1945." *Bulletin of the Atomic Scientists* 4 (February 1948): 44, 63.

Compton, Karl T. "If the Atomic Bomb Had Not Been Used." *Atlantic Monthly* 178 (December 1946): 54–56.

Cousins, Norman. "The Literacy of Survival." *The Saturday Review of Literature* (September 14, 1946): 14.

Cousins, Norman, and Thomas K. Finletter. "A Beginning for Sanity." *The Saturday Review of Literature* (June 15, 1946): 5–9, 38–40.

Curry, George. "James F. Byrnes." In *The American Secretaries of State and Their Diplomacy.* Edited by Robert H. Ferrell and Samuel Flagg Bemis. Vol. 14. New York, 1963.

Davis, Forrest. "Did Marshall Prolong the Pacific War?" *The Freeman* (November 5, 1951): 73–75; (November 19, 1951): 112–15.

"Deny Atomic Bomb Use Was Atrocity." *Christian Century* 64 (February 12, 1947): 196.

"Double Blow for Japan." *The New York Times* (April 6, 1945): 14.

Drea, Edward J. "Previews of Hell." *MHQ: The Quarterly Journal of Military History* 7 (Spring 1995): 74–81.

Eaker, Lt. Gen. Ira C. (USAF, Ret.). "Gen. Carl A. Spaatz, USAF." *Air Force Magazine* 57 (September 1974): 43–48.

Elsey, George M. "Some White House Recollections, 1942–1953." *Diplomatic History* 12 (Summer 1988): 357–64.

Evangelista, Matthew A. "Stalin's Postwar Army Reappraised." *International Security* 7 (Winter 1982/3): 110–38.

"Everyone's Wild About Harry." *Newsweek* (March 24, 1975): 28.

Falk, Richard A. "The Shimoda Case: A Legal Appraisal of the Atomic Attacks Upon Hiroshima and Nagasaki." *American Journal of International Law* 59 (1965): 759–93.

———. "The Claimants of Hiroshima." *Nation* (February 15, 1965): 157–61.

"Fatal Phrase." *The Washington Post* (June 11, 1945): 8.

Feinberg, Lotte E. "Managing the Freedom of Information Act and Federal Information Policy." *Public Administration Review* 46 (November–December 1986): 615–21.

Feis, Herbert. Review of *On Active Service in Peace and War,* by Henry L. Stimson and McGeorge Bundy. *American Foreign Service Journal* 25 (December 1948): 30.

———. "The Shackled Historian." *Foreign Affairs* 45 (January 1967): 332–43.

Ferrell, Robert H., and Francis H. Heller. "Plain Faking?," *American Heritage* 46 (May/June 1995): 14–16.

Finney, Nat S. "How FDR Planned to Use the A-Bomb." *Look* 14 (March 14, 1950): 23–27.

"The Fortune Survey." *Fortune* (December 1945): 303, 305–06, 309–10.

Fussell, Paul. "Hiroshima: A Soldier's View." *New Republic* (August 22 and 29, 1981): 26–30.

Gallicchio, Marc. "After Nagasaki: General Marshall's Plan for Tactical Nuclear Weapons in Japan." *Prologue* 23 (Winter 1991): 396–404.

———. "The Kuriles Controversy: U.S. Diplomacy in the Soviet-Japan Border Dispute, 1941–1956." *Pacific Historical Review* 60 (February 1991): 60–101.

Garthoff, Raymond L. "The Soviet Campaign, August 1945." *Military Affairs* XXXIII (October 1969): 312–36.

Gillis, James M. "The Atom Bomb." *Catholic World* (September 1945): 449–52.

Glantz, David M. "The Soviet Invasion of Japan." *MHQ: The Quarterly Journal of Military History* 7 (Spring 1995): 96–97.

Glazier, Kenneth. "The Decision to Use Atomic Weapons Against Hiroshima and Nagasaki." *Public Policy* 18 (1970): 463–516.

Goldberg, Stanley. "Grove Takes the Reins." *Bulletin of the Atomic Scientists* 48 (December 1992): 34–35.

Griffith, Robert. "Harry S. Truman and the Burden of Modernity." *Reviews in American History* 9 (September 1981): 295–306.

Grodzins, Morton. "Japan's Surrender." *Harper's* 206 (June 1953): 18.

Hales, Peter B. "The Atomic Sublime." *American Studies* 32 (Spring 1991): 5–31.

Hamby, Alonzo L. "The Mind and Character of Harry S. Truman." In *The Truman Presidency*. Edited by Michael J. Lacey. New York: Woodrow Wilson International Center for Scholars and Cambridge University Press, 1989.

———. "An American Democrat: A Reevaluation of the Personality of Harry S. Truman." *Political Science Quarterly* 106 (1991): 33–55.

Hayashi, Shigeru. "Tai So Kosaku no Tenkai [The Development of Maneuvering with the Soviets]." In *Taiheiyo Senso Shuketsu Ron* (Some Discussions on the Ending of the Pacific War), edited by Nihon Gaiko Gakkai. Tokyo: University Press, 1958.

"Heavy Allied Blows, Fear of Reds Make Jap Leaders Seek Way Out." *Newsweek* (July 30, 1945): 29–30.

Heller, Francis M. "Truman." In *History Makers: Leaders and Statesmen of the 20th Century*. Edited by Frank P. Longford and John Wheeler-Bennett. London: Sidgwick and Jackson, 1973.

———. "The Writing of the Truman Memoirs." *Presidential Studies Quarterly* 13 (Winter 1983): 81–84.

Herken, Gregg F. " 'Stubborn, Obstinate, and They Don't Scare': The Russians, The Bomb, and James F. Byrnes." In *James F. Byrnes and the Origins of the Cold War*. Edited by Kendrick A. Clements. Durham, NC: Carolina Academic Press, 1982.

Hook, Glenn D. "Censorship and Reportage of Atomic Damage and Casualties in Hiroshima and Nagasaki." *Bulletin of Concerned Asian Scholars* 23 (January–March 1991): 13–25.

Hutchinson, Russell S. "Hiroshima." *Christian Century* 63 (September 25, 1946): 1143–44.

"Ike on Ike." *Newsweek* (November 11, 1963): 107–10.

Iokibe, Makato. "American Policy Toward Japan's 'Unconditional Surrender.' " *The Japanese Journal of American Studies* 1 (1981): 19–53.

"Japan—An Opportunity for Statesmanship." *Life* (July 16, 1945): 22.

"Japan Will Seek Peace if Russia Joins War on Her, British Ex-Envoy to Tokyo Says." *The New York Times* (April 8, 1945): 5.

"Japanese Cabinet Weighs Ultimatum: Domei Says Empire Will Fight to the End—Rayburn Reports Tokyo Has Made Peace Bids." *The New York Times* (July 28, 1945): 1–2.

Johnson, Gerald W. "Truman Nostalgia." *New Republic* 172 (May 31, 1975): 17–19.

Kawai, Kazuo. " *'Mokusatsu,'* Japan's Response to the Potsdam Declaration." *Pacific Historical Review* 19 (November 1950): 409–14.

Kay, Lillian Wald. "Public Opinion and the Bomb." *Journal of Educational Sociology* 22 (January 1949): 357–60.

Kiernan, Ben. "Introduction." In *Burchett Reporting the Other Side of the World, 1939–1983*. Edited by Ben Keirnan. London: Quartet Books, 1987.

Kimball, Warren F. "The Cold War Warmed Over." *The American Historical Review* 79 (October 1974): 1119–36.

Kirkendall, Richard S. "Harry Truman as National Hero." *Reviews in American History* 21 (1993): 314–19.

Knebel, Fletcher, and Charles W. Bailey. "The Fight Over the Atom Bomb." *Look* 27 (August 13, 1963): 19–23.

Krock, Arthur. "Objects of Our Propaganda to Japan." *The New York Times* (July 24, 1945): 22.

———. " 'Soft' Peace for Japan?: Advocates of Terms Outlined in Capital Contend Country Will Support Demands." *The New York Times* (July 25, 1945): 4.

Kubek, Anthony. "How We Lost the Pacific War." *Human Events* 25 (December 1, 1958): 1–4.

Lanza, Conrad H. "The Surrender of Japan." *America* 73 (September 1, 1945): 428–30.

Lawrence, David. "What Hath Man Wrought!" *United States News* (August 17, 1945): 38–39.

———. "The Right to Kill." *United States News* (October 5, 1945): 34–35.

———. "Did Hitler Win the War?" *United States News* (November 2, 1945): 34–35.

———. "Where Is The Faith?" *United States News* (November 23, 1945): 34–35.

———. "Let's Rebuild Hiroshima!" *United States News* (March 1, 1946): 26–27.

Lee, R. Alton. "The Army 'Mutiny' of 1946." *The Journal of American History* 53 (December 1966): 555–71.

Lee, S. Y. "Hiroshima Not Remembered: The Story of the Korean Atomic Bomb Victims." *Korea Report* 1 (July–August 1987): 6–8.

Leffler, Melvyn P. "Adherence to Agreements: Yalta and the Experiences of the Early Cold War." *International Security* 11 (Summer 1986): 88–123.

Leo, Vincent. "The Mushroom Cloud Photograph: From Fact to Symbol." *Afterimage* 13 (Summer 1985): 6–12.

Libby, Justin H. "The Search for a Negotiated Peace." *World Affairs* 156 (Summer 1993): 35–45.

Lindley, Ernest K. "Byrnes, the Persuasive Reporter." *Newsweek* (March 12, 1945): 42.

———. "The Jap Does Have a Choice." *Newsweek* (July 16, 1945): 31.

———. "The Decisions We Face on Japan." *Newsweek* (July 30, 1945): 25.

Luft, Joseph, and W. M. Wheeler. "Reaction to John Hersey's 'Hiroshima.'" *Journal of Social Psychology* 28 (1948): 135–40.

Macdonald, Dwight. "The Bomb." *Politics* 2 (September 1945): 257–60.

Manoff, Robert Karl. "American Victims of Hiroshima." *New York Times Magazine* (December 2, 1984): 67, 110, 112, 114, 116, 118, 123, 125.

———. "The Silencer." *The Quill* (February 1984): 7–11.

———. "Covering the Bomb: Press and State in the Shadow of Nuclear War." In *War, Peace and the News Media*. Edited by David M. Rubin and Ann Marie Cunningham. New York: New York University, 1987.

Marmarelli, Ronald S. "David Lawrence." In *Dictionary of Literary Biography*. Vol. 29: *American Newspaper Journalists, 1926–1950*. Edited by Perry J. Ashley. Detroit: Gale Research, 1984.

Maslowski, Peter. "Truman, the Bomb, and the Numbers Game." *MHQ: The Quarterly Journal of Military History* 7 (Spring 1995): 103–07.

Mastny, Vojtech. "Kremlin Politics and the Austrian Settlement." *Problems of Communism* 31 (July–August 1982): 37–51.

May, Ernest R. "The United States, the Soviet Union, and the Far Eastern War, 1941–1945." *Pacific Historical Review* 24 (February 1955): 153–74.

McCloy, John J. "McCloy on the A-Bomb." Appendix in *Deadline: A Memoir*, by James Reston. New York: Random House, 1991.

McMahon, Brian. "Comment on Blackett's Book." *Bulletin of the Atomic Scientists* 5 (February 1949): 40–43.

Messer, Robert L. "New Evidence on Truman's Decision." *Bulletin of the Atomic Scientists* 41 (August 1985): 50–56.

Miles, Rufus E., Jr. "Hiroshima: The Strange Myth of Half a Million American Lives Saved." *International Security* 10 (Fall 1985): 121–40.

Moley, Raymond. "Attacking the Jap Mentality." *Newsweek* (July 2, 1945): 92.

Moll, Kenneth L. "The Birth of the A-bomb . . . And the Aftermath." *Air Force Magazine* (August 1965): 29–36.

Morley, Felix. "The Return to Nothingness." *Human Events* (August 29, 1945): 144–47.

Morton, Louis. "The Decision to Use the Atomic Bomb." *Foreign Affairs* 35 (January 1957): 334–53.

———. "The Atomic Bomb and the Japanese Surrender." *Marine Corp Gazette* 43 (February 1959): 20–29.

————. "Soviet Intervention in the War with Japan." *Foreign Affairs* 40 (July 1962): 653–62.

Motohashi, Tadashi. "Daresu Kikan wo Tsuzuru Wahei Kosaku [Peace Negotiation Through the Dulles Agency]." In *Taiheiyo Senso Shuketsu Ron* (Some Discussions on the Ending of the Pacific War), edited by Nihon Gaiko Gakkai. Tokyo: University of Tokyo Press, 1958.

"The Nation." *Time* (July 16, 1945): 15.

Nelson, Anna K., and Richard H. Kohn. "The U.S. Must Declassify Its Cold-War Documents." *Chronicle of Higher Education* (September 16, 1992): 56.

Niebuhr, Reinhold. "Our Relations to Japan." *Christianity and Crisis* 5 (September 17, 1945): 5–7.

Pakenham, Compton. "How the Jap Will Take Final Defeat." *Newsweek* (July 16, 1945): 40.

Pape, Robert A. "Why Japan Surrendered." *International Security* 18 (Fall 1993): 154–201.

Paterson, Thomas G. "The Abortive American Loan to Russia and the Origins of the Cold War, 1943–1946." *The Journal of American History* 56 (June 1969): 72–92.

————. "Potsdam, the Atomic Bomb, and the Cold War." *Pacific Historical Review* 41 (May 1972): 225–30.

————. "Thought Control and the Writing of History." In *Freedom at Risk: Secrecy, Censorship, and Repression in the 1980s*. Edited by Richard O. Curry. Philadelphia: Temple University Press, 1988.

Paust, Jordan J. "The Nuclear Decision in World War II—Truman's Ending and Avoidance of War." *International Lawyer* 8 (1974): 160–90.

Poore, Charles. "The Most Spectacular Explosion in the Time of Man." *The New York Times Book Review* (November 10, 1946): 7, 56.

Pope Paul VI. "Day of Peace Message: The Contrary and Positive Weapons of Peace." *Origins* 5 (January 1, 1976).

Rabi, I. I. "Playing Down the Bomb: Blackett versus the Atom." *Atlantic Monthly* 183 (April 1949): 21–24.

Reingold, Nathan. "MGM Meets the Atomic Bomb." *The Wilson Quarterly* 8 (Autumn 1984): 154–63.

Relyea, Harold C. "Access to Government Information in the Information Age." *Public Administration Review* 46 (November–December 1986): 635–39.

Rovere, Richard H. "Notes on the Establishment in America." *American Scholar* 30 (Autumn 1961): 489–95.

————. "The American Establishment." *Wilson Quarterly* 2 (Summer 1978): 170–81.

————. "Postscript: A 1978 Commentary." *Wilson Quarterly* 2 (Summer 1978): 182–83.

Schott, Webster. "How the Memoirs Were Written." *New Republic* (March 19, 1956): 18–19.

"Secretary O'Leary Releases Classified Documents on Nuclear Testing, Radiation Releases, Fusion." *DOE This Month* 16 (December 1993): 3, 14.

"Senator Urges Specific Terms Of Surrender Be Given Japan." *The Washington Post* (July 3, 1945): 1–2."

"Service News and Gossip." *Army and Navy Journal* (July 21, 1945): 1426.

"Service News and Gossip." *Army and Navy Journal* (August 4, 1945): 1482.

Sherwin, Martin J. "The Atomic Bomb and the Origins of the Cold War: U.S. Atomic Energy Policy and Diplomacy, 1941–1945." *American Historical Review* 78 (October 1973): 945–68.

————. "Hiroshima and Modern Memory." *The Nation* (October 10, 1981): 329, 349–53.

Shils, Edward A. "Blackett's Apologia for the Soviet Position." *Bulletin of the Atomic Scientists* 5 (February 1949): 34–37.

Sigal, Leon V. "Bureaucratic Politics & Tactical Use of Committees: The Interim Committee & the Decision to Drop the Atomic Bomb." *Polity* 10 (Spring 1978): 326–64.

Smith, Alice Kimball. "Behind the Decision to Use the Atomic Bomb: Chicago, 1944–45." *Bulletin of the Atomic Scientists* 14 (October 1958): 288–312.

Smith, Gaddis. "Was Moscow Our Real Target?" *The New York Times Book Review* (August 18, 1985): 16.

"Soviet-Japanese Contacts in 1945." *Vestnik* (August 1990): 64–73.

Steel, Ronald. "Harry of Sunnybrook Farm." Review of *Truman* by David McCullough. *New Republic* (August 10, 1992): 34–39.

Stimson, Henry L. "The Bomb and the Opportunity." *Harper's* 192 (March 1946): 204.

———. "The Decision to Use the Atomic Bomb." *Harper's* 194 (February 1947): 97–107.

Szilard, Leo. "A Personal History of the Atomic Bomb." *University of Chicago Roundtable* 601 (September 25, 1949): 14–16.

———. "Reminiscences." Edited by Gertrud Weiss Szilard and Kathleen R. Winsor. *Perspectives in American History* II (1968): 94–151.

Tanaka, Tadakichi. "Tai So Kosaku: Taiheiyo Senso Chu ni Okeru Nisso Kosho [Maneuvering with the Soviets: Negotiation Between Japan and the Soviets During the Pacific War]." In *Taiheiyo Senso Shuketsu Ron* (Some Discussions on the Ending of the Pacific War), edited by Nihon Gaiko Gakkai. Tokyo: University of Tokyo Press, 1958.

Tantur, Richard. "Voice and Silence in the First Nuclear War: Wilfred Burchett and Hiroshima." In *Burchett Reporting the Other Side of the World, 1939–1983*, edited by Ben Kiernan. London: Quartet Books, 1986.

"Terms for Japan." *The New York Times* (July 23, 1945): 18.

"Terms to End War Urged on Truman: Senator Wherry Links High U.S. Military Man to Letter—Plan Bars Occupation." *The New York Times* (July 24, 1945): 5.

Theoharis, Athan. "James F. Byrnes: Unwitting Yalta Myth-Maker." *Political Science Quarterly* 86 (December 1966): 381–92.

"Tokyo Radio Appeals to U.S. for a More Lenient Peace." *The New York Times* (July 26, 1945): 1.

Truman, Harry S. "President Truman to Dr. Compton." *Atlantic Monthly* 179 (February 1947): 27.

"Truman Approved Warning to Japan: Speech Viewed as Part of His Strategy for Securing Goals in the Far East." *The New York Times* (July 23, 1945): 5.

"Trumania in the '70s." *Time* (June 9, 1975): 45.

Villa, Brian L. "A Confusion of Signals: James Franck, the Chicago Scientists and Early Efforts to Stop the Bomb." *Bulletin of the Atomic Scientists* 31 (December 1975): 36–43.

———. "The U.S. Army, Unconditional Surrender, and the Potsdam Proclamation." *The Journal of American History* 63 (June 1976): 66–92.

Walker, J. Samuel. "The Decision to Use the Bomb: A Historiographical Update." *Diplomatic History* 14 (Winter 1990): 97–114.

Walz, Jay. "Japan Is Warned to Give Up Soon: U.S. Broadcast Says Speed Will Bring Peace Based on the Atlantic Charter." *The New York Times* (July 22, 1945): 1, 4.

"Was A-Bomb on Japan a Mistake?" *U.S. News and World Report* (August 15, 1960): 62–78.

Weinstein, Allen. "Presidential Reputations: Truman and the American Imagination." In *Truman and the American Commitment to Israel: A Thirtieth Anniversary Conference*. Edited by Allen Weinstein and Moshe Ma'oz. Jerusalem: Magnes Press, Hebrew University, 1981.

"White Urges Truman Give Terms to Tokyo." *The New York Times* (July 3, 1945): 3.

Williams, Herbert Lee. "I Was Truman's Ghost." *Presidential Studies Quarterly* 12 (Spring 1982): 256–59.

Wills, Garry. "I'm Not Wild About Harry." *Esquire* 85 (January 1976): 91–95.

Wilson, Don W. "The Declassification of Records: Remarks by the Archivist of the United States." *Society for Historians of American Foreign Relations Newsletter* 21 (December 1990): 32–34.

Winnacker, Rudolph A. "The Debate About Hiroshima." *Military Affairs* 11 (Spring 1947): 25–30.

Wolk, Herman S. "The B-29, the A-Bomb, and the Japanese Surrender." *Air Force Magazine* 58 (February 1975): 55–61.

"Writing on the Wall." *The Washington Post* (June 3, 1945): 4B.

"Yalta Legman." *Newsweek* (March 19, 1945): 52.

Yavenditti, Michael J. "The American People and the Use of Atomic Bombs on Japan: The 1940s." *Historian* 36 (February 1974): 224–47.

———. "John Hersey and the American Conscience: The Reception of 'Hiroshima.'" *Pacific Historical Review* 43 (1974): 24–49.

———. "Atomic Scientists and Hollywood: *The Beginning or the End?*" *Film and History* 8 (December 1978): 73–88.

Zacharias, Ellis M. "Eighteen Words That Bagged Japan." *Saturday Evening Post* 218 (November 17, 1945): 17, 117–20.

———. "We Did Not Need to Drop the A-Bomb," *Look* 14 (May 23, 1950): 29–35.

———. "How We Bungled the Japanese Surrender," *Look* 14 (June 6, 1950): 12–21.

Dissertations

Baggaley, Philip A. "Reparations, Security, and the Industrial Disarmament of Germany: Origins of the Potsdam Decisions." Ph.D. Diss., Yale University, 1980.

Brower, Charles F. "The Joint Chiefs of Staff and National Policy: American Strategy and the War with Japan, 1943–1945." Ph.D. Diss., University of Pennsylvania, 1987.

Crane, Conrad C. "The Evolution of American Strategic Bombing of Urban Areas." Ph.D. Diss., Stanford University, 1990.

Hershberg, James G. "James B. Conant, Nuclear Weapons, and the Cold War, 1945–1950." Ph.D. Diss., Tufts University, 1989.

Messer, Robert L. "The Making of a Cold Warrior: James F. Byrnes and American-Soviet Relations, 1945–1946." Ph.D. Diss., University of California, Berkeley, 1975.

Palumbo, John C. "Prince Konoe's Efforts for Peace, 1941–1945." Ph.D. Diss., St. John's University, 1972.

Preston, Edmund R. "Prelude to Cold War: American Reactions to the Growth of Soviet Power 1944–1945." Ph.D. Diss., University of Virginia, 1979.

Yavenditti, Michael J. "American Reactions to the Use of Atomic Bombs on Japan, 1945–1947." Ph.D. Diss., University of California, Berkeley, 1970.

Miscellaneous

ABC News, *Nightline*. "What If . . . We Hadn't Dropped the Bomb?" Transcript of Show No. 1096, August 5, 1985.

Kay, Alan. *Americans Talk Security*. Winchester, MA: October 1989.

MGM. *The Beginning or the End*. February 1947. Library of Congress.

Interviews and Unpublished Works

Alperovitz, Gar, and Kai Bird. "A Theory of the Cold War." Paper presented before the Organization of American Historians, Washington, D.C., March 31, 1995.

Alperovitz, Gar, Kai Bird, and Uday Mohan. "Fact and Fiction: The American Media, Pearl Harbor, and Hiroshima." Unpublished paper in possession of author.

Bidwell, Col. Bruce. "History of MID." Unpublished manuscript. Center for Military History, Washington, D.C.

Brown, Walter. Interview with Robert L. Messer, December 20–21, 1972. Tapes provided to author courtesy of Robert Messer.

———. Interview with J. P. Rosensweig, June 28, 1990.

Butow, Robert J. C. Interview with Kathryn C. Morris, August 23, 1994.

Bundy, McGeorge. Interview with Gar Alperovitz, April 6, 1995.

Carrington, Elsworth. Interview with Sanho Tree, October 13, 1993.

Current, Richard N. Interview with Gar Alperovitz, March 6, 1995.

Dower, John W. "The Bombed: Hiroshima and Nagasaki in Japanese Memory." Unpublished manuscript, forthcoming in *Diplomatic History*.

Eisenberg, Carolyn. *Drawing the Line: The American Decision to Divide Germany, 1944–49*. Cambridge: Cambridge University Press, forthcoming.

Elsey, George M. Interview with Gar Alperovitz, 1989.

Goldberg, Stanley. "Note on B. Bernstein's 'Seizing the Contested Terrain of Early Nuclear History.' " Unpublished paper provided to author courtesy of S. Goldberg.

———. "Groves and Oppenheimer: The Story of a Partnership." Unpublished paper provided to author courtesy of S. Goldberg.

———. "General Groves and the Atomic West: The Making and the Meaning of Hanford." In *The Atomic West*. Edited by Bruce Hevly and John Findlay. Seattle: University of Washington Press, forthcoming.

Goodpaster, Andrew J. Interview with Sanho Tree, January 29, 1992.

Gustafson, Milton O. "The Committee of 3: The Origins of the National Security Council, 1944–1947." Paper presented at the Conference on War and Diplomacy, The Citadel, March 10–12, 1977.

Heller, Francis H. "The *Memoirs* of Harry S. Truman: Remarks before the Jackson County Historical Society." Unpublished paper, May 18, 1958, Vertical File, Memoirs, HSTL.

———. "Harry S. Truman and His Memoirs." Unpublished paper prepared for the Conference on Political Memoirs, University of British Columbia, September 22–24, 1989.

———. Interview with Gar Alperovitz, October 24, 1989.

Hewlett, Richard. Interview with Kai Bird, March 9, 1993.

Joint Chiefs of Staff Historical Section. *United States Interest in Entry of the USSR in the War Against Japan*. April 25, 1955. Unpublished manuscript, formerly Top Secret. JCS Historical Section, Department of Defense.

Jordan, Gregory M. "But Was It Legal?: The Atomic Bomb and Hiroshima." March, 1, 1995. Draft essay in author's collection.

Leighton, Alexander. Interview with Sanho Tree, October 18, 1993.

Maddox, Robert James. "Generals, Admirals, and Atomic Bombs: Ending the War with Japan." Paper presented at the Conference of Army Historians, June 13–16, 1994, Center for Military History, Washington, D.C. Provided to author courtesy of Judith Bellafaire.

Maley, Leo, III. "Use of the Stimson Diary in *On Active Service*." March 1, 1995. In author's collection.

McCloy, John J. Interview with Walter Cronkite, undated. Transcript provided to author courtesy of Milton Leitenburg.

McKeever, Porter. Interview with J. P. Rosensweig, September 15, 1990.

Mohan, Uday. "A Preliminary Survey of Press Coverage of the Smithsonian's Enola Gay Controversy." Unpublished memorandum. Provided to author courtesy of Uday Mohan.

Mohan, Uday, and Sanho Tree, "The Ending of World War II: Media Perspectives in the

1940s–1960s and Early 1990s." Paper presented at the conference of the American Historical Association, Chicago, IL, January 6, 1995.

Morton, Louis. "The Soviet Union and the War Against Japan, September 1944–August 1945." Unpublished paper, MS 60-2:65, Dartmouth College Archives.

Newman, Robert P. "Ending the War With Japan: Paul Nitze's 'Early Surrender' Counterfactual." Paper presented before the Modern History Faculty, Oxford, May 25, 1994.

Nitze, Paul H. Interview with Gar Alperovitz, September 27, 1990.

Parten, J. R. Interviews with Gar Alperovitz, December 26, 1984, and January 5, 1985.

Sodei, Rinjiro. *Were We the Enemy? A Saga of Hiroshima Survivors in America.* Unpublished manuscript, 1982.

Tree, Sanho. Unpublished memorandum on "LOCKUP." September 11, 1994. In author's collection.

U.S. Army Medical Service. "Medical History of the Asiatic-Pacific Theater." Chapter XV. Draft, n.d. U.S. Army Military History Institute, Carlisle Barracks, Carlisle, PA.

Walker, J. Samuel. "History, Collective Memory, and the Decision to Use the Bomb." Forthcoming article. Provided to author courtesy of J. Samuel Walker.

Williams, David J. "Did the President Consult with the JCS at Potsdam Regarding the Atomic Bomb?" February 13, 1995. In author's collection.

Williamson, Thad. "Memorandum on General Groves' Postwar Efforts to Shape Perceptions of the Bomb." January 14, 1995. In author's collection.

Winstead, Edward R. "Harry S. Truman." June 11, 1993. In author's collection.

Wolk, Herman. Interview with Sanho Tree, April 13, 1995.

Acknowledgments

No book of this length and scope just happens; nor is it ever the product of one person working alone. First and foremost are the loved ones and friends who help through the hard places and hang in for the long haul. My wife, Sharon, leads the list: Her love and strength and support and personal sacrifices cannot be properly acknowledged, save to say that whatever she may feel of my love and gratitude is only a tiny fragment of the truth and depth of my feeling. My late parents, Emily and Julius Alperovitz, were there at the beginning—and ever present. My children, Kari and David, accepted my absorption in the enterprise with much-appreciated love and good cheer.

As I indicated at the outset, for better or worse Bernd Greiner and Ronald Goldfarb were responsible for nudging me from the passing thought of an article into what became a full-length study. Bernd also helped in many other ways, not the least of which was by providing a tough intellectual sounding board; Ron served as my agent—and, too, as a trusted adviser in connection with numerous matters that kept springing up along the way. My editor, Ash Green, went far beyond the call of professional duty to help transform a disjointed and repetitive manuscript into a book—and did so under the pressure of the relentless timetable set by the forthcoming Fiftieth Anniversary. He is the best editor with whom I have ever worked—and what used to be called a gentleman and a scholar as well.

A project which moves from an article to a full-scale study also requires money. Initial funding for the research that informs this work came from the Parten Foundation and the generosity of the late J. R. Parten (who knew all the players personally and had himself been at Potsdam as deputy to Edwin Pauley, the U.S. reparations negotiator). Thereafter support from the MacArthur Foundation made possible a two-year specialist symposium held at the Institute for Policy Studies. The ongoing dialogue among many of the nation's leading Cold War historians clarified numerous issues of context and interpretation. Once we reached the stage of serious research, the support of Jan Philipp Reemtsma, director of the Hamburg Institute for Social Research, was critical. Jan Philipp's generosity and intellectual integrity are extraordinary—as is his commitment to the depth of research which is needed to penetrate many difficult twentieth-century issues: This project would not have been possible without his concern and help. In like manner, Patricia Bauman and John Bryant have both been enormously supportive (even though projects assisted by the Bauman Family Foundation intersect with the subject of this book only in certain areas). Their generosity, patience, and many kindnesses were and are greatly treasured—as is their warm friendship. Other much-appreciated assistance was received from The Henry P. Kendall Foundation, The Nathan Cummings Foundation, Ms. Anne Bartley, The Samuel Rubin Foundation, W. H. and Carol Ferry, the late Philip Stern (and The Stern Family Fund), The Winston Foundation for World Peace, and The Jessie Smith Noyes Foundation, and from several individuals who traditionally have preferred to remain anonymous in their various philanthropic efforts.

The process by which this book was constructed was unusual. I have noted that my original work on the atomic bombing of Hiroshima and Nagasaki was done in the late 1950s and early 1960s as I was preparing a Cambridge University Ph.D. dissertation. Important as it is, however, this is not my central intellectual concern: The deepening crisis of twentieth-century political-economic systems—and alternatives for the future—continue to absorb the greatest share of my research energies. Indeed, after publishing *Atomic Diplomacy* in 1965 (and several related articles while at the Institute of Politics at Harvard), I did not continue with the usual follow-on studies which are the common practice of young scholars beginning a career devoted primarily to historical research. Instead, I largely put aside this field of study for almost a quarter century. What stimulated my renewed interest was a 1985 invitation to republish my early book at the time of the Fortieth Anniversary of the bombings—and the need to catch up, therefore, on the expert literature. Shortly thereafter the B.B.C. asked me to participate in the creation and production of a television documentary which centered on my work (and which in the end I helped narrate). Working with Robert Marshall on "Summer of the Bomb" reignited my passion for all the old questions. Then, reading an early draft of J. Samuel Walker's literature assessment for *Diplomatic History* prompted me to think of doing a short essay (as I have noted), and gradually, of getting serious about something larger.

It is possible to write an essay—or even the Introduction to a reissued version of an old book—on the basis of a review of the existing scholarly literature; it is not possible to undertake a full-length study. A great deal of time investigating the primary sources comes with the territory—especially when addressing a controversial subject: There is no other way to advance beyond the contours of the traditional (and somewhat shopworn) lines of debate. As Somerset Maugham once put it: "The writing of books is done by the application of the seat of the pants to the seat of the chair."

The first exploratory plunge was taken in a late 1989 series of preliminary inquiries—and in a round of interviewing, followed by high-intensity reading and photocopying at the Truman Library. I find tentative draft chapter sketches in my computer which date from the fall of 1989 and the winter of 1989–90. Beginning in 1989, too, a staff of sorts began to assemble—first mainly part-time assistants, then, slowly, a small group of dedicated young researchers working full-time (or, in most cases, far more than anything that can traditionally be termed "full-time"!). Slowly our initial inquiry began to force us into ever-wider and -deeper research. Ultimately we saw a rather expansive text begin to take shape.

There is no way to acknowledge fully the many people who helped build this book. Our team was (and is) extraordinary; time and again it produced critical information, documents, and insights under the pressure of an ever-tightening timetable. First on the list is Sanho Tree, who joined the project in 1989 and was our archival research director. Sanho had primary responsibility for research undertaken in virtually all the archival collections listed in the bibliography. (Not only was his intense and careful scholarship invaluable, but a back injury now limits my own ability to do such research on an extended basis.) Sanho was also responsible for managing various Freedom of Information Act matters, and, too, for supervising more than a dozen interns over the course of the project. One of his areas of special expertise and interest involved intelligence materials, and MAGIC and other signal communications traffic.

Ted Winstead came to the project in 1991 as a researcher. However, his position soon evolved into something quite different. Once we decided to go forward, a major task was to assemble and organize the information we found along the rough (and continually changing) outlines of the chapter-sketches I had begun in late 1989. At this time, too, we began systematically to plumb the depths of the archives for documents which I and other scholars had previously used. Soon the flow of information intensified, too, from an ever-widening circle of dispersed and little-studied sources. With great skill and dedication Ted bore the responsibility of editing and writing what I came to think of as our initial "scaffolding" materials—very long drafts which in the end were largely transcended but which provided the first backbone of what became the book. Additionally, Ted did a good deal of invaluable work on James F. Byrnes.

Katie Morris is listed first in the sequence of three names on the title page for two reasons: First, her area of special concern was the fundamental argument of Book I—and especially its formative structure in Parts I through IV. She is also listed first because of her extraordinary contribution, her many insights, and the depth of her commitment. Once an intern, Katie returned to the project as a professional in 1993 at the point when we were ready to begin to turn our crude scaffolding into a real building. It was also a moment when serious staff illnesses and other problems had slowed our work. Without her steady hand in every area—from basic research to the preparation of the Bibliography—this book could not have been written: Katie helped take the argument from rough blueprint to sophisticated and nuanced development. Related to this was her critical review of the complex interpretative literature which helped provide the research base for the argument of the Afterword.

Beginning in early 1994, Dave Williams' primary responsibilities included research on portions of the book next in sequence: several chapters in the "Potsdam" Part (especially, but not limited to, the Balkans, Germany, and the Dulles and Stockholm negotiations)—and, importantly, the views of the military reported in Part VI of Book I. In addition, Dave helped take Ted Winstead's initial work on Byrnes to the final stage of development in Book I, Book II, and the Appendix. A special contribution was the detailed tracking of timetables and chronology in connection with Byrnes' presence in Washington during the period April–July 1945—and (in other "Potsdam" chapters) in connection with the flow of information on the bomb as it intersected diplomatic developments at the Big Three meeting.

Leo Maley's initial research (beginning in 1993) concerned the scientists, and press and religious responses to the bombings (subjects which space limitations ultimately reduced to the modest reports of Chapters 14 and 36). Soon, however, Leo took over primary responsibility for helping prepare draft sections in connection with the overall argument of Book II—especially the "Truman" and "Stimson" parts, and the "Freedom of Information" chapter. Leo's extreme care and thoughtful insights are reflected throughout the complex analysis of the second half of the book. Time and again he was able to discern small contradictions in the evidence which (as in the case of Truman's suppression of his Potsdam journal) had eluded other researchers. His dissection of the record in connection with Stimson's postwar role helped add many new dimensions to the story.

The final two members of our team—Thad Williamson and Miranda Grieder—played somewhat different roles. Thad generously parachuted in from other research during the final year of the project to help with what was originally a much longer section on Groves (which space requirements, again, forced us to drastically reduce). Thad also helped with our periodic literature reviews, with "quality control" in general—and, too, with research on three special subjects: the work of the U.S. Strategic Bombing Survey; the role of James B. Conant; and a thicket of complex issues surrounding modern research on casualty estimates.

During the final two years of the project Miranda served as our in-house editor, managing with great skill, attention to detail, and dedication the extremely demanding process of producing a thirteen-hundred-page manuscript, and then taking it forward as it evolved in the editing process (and was prepared for simultaneous publication in five countries). She also typed a great deal of what became the final manuscript (and, too, supervised a small army of other typists). In the end many chapters went through more than a dozen drafts as, with the help of our team, I edited, wrote, edited, and rewrote sections again and again, striving for ever-greater clarity.

The production of this book taught us a good deal about the limitations and opportunities facing any research effort. As every researcher knows, it is impossible to cover all the conceivable sources in connection with a question as difficult and important as the decision to use the atomic bomb. Simply by way of illustration, there are innumerable secondary figures who were close to the principal decision-makers, and who knew a good deal about what went on. Many undoubtedly kept diaries or wrote letters which, if found, could yield important insights. To track the children, grandchildren, and other descendants of even a fraction of the long list of such people is extraordinarily time-consuming—and beyond the means of most individuals. Working as a team we were able to track a few more than is sometimes possible.

Another advantage of a team effort is the cross-stimulation of research. The project generated a subtle and highly charged group process—and, too, the interaction of several different minds. In the course of our work we had extremely intense discussions—often several times a day, and in various configurations, from one-on-one conversations to larger, project-wide meetings. Even the best graduate seminar can involve no more than one or two people who have spent significant amounts of time and energy on the same topic. A panel at an academic conference commonly lasts two to three hours. Our regular meetings involved a high-level debate over almost two years among a group of people who became extremely sophisticated in a wide range of specific but interrelated areas of research.

Several other professionals and consultants also helped in important ways. My thanks especially to Dawn Nakano, who graciously agreed to put aside other research in order to help manage the research and administrative staff and coordinate special projects during critical phases of the book's development. Special thanks also to J. P. Rosensweig, who began what became our extended exploration of Byrnes' role—and, too, undertook the first investigation of the papers of William Hillman; to Mary Coney and Mary Nell Harris for their assistance with research on Groves; to Kai Bird for generous help with documents on John J. McCloy (and, too, for his assistance early on in connection with the "Stimson" section); to Akiko Naono, for work with Japanese language publications and translations (and for reminding us by her presence and spirit of what was at stake); to Ted Howard for his assistance in numerous areas, from fund-raising to early, difficult integrative work on Groves; to Lee Ebersole for pitching in on several fronts with extraordinary goodwill at the last minute; to Laura Gilliam for her unfailing assistance with accounting and financial administration; to Nina Graybill for tough-minded and cheerful assistance with various legal matters; to Laura Garces for her early work on the Air Force; to Scott Pomfret for help above and beyond the call of duty in connection with typing, proofreading, and other administrative functions; to Ted Schenkelberg for library and archival support in the final stage of the project; to Ama Schulman for similar assistance in connection with this and related projects; to Uday Mohan for help with the early history of media reactions to the bombings; to Enrique Martinez Vidal for his supportive role in diverse areas from the very beginning; to Greg Jordan for his work on legal matters; to Laura Secor and Jennifer Washburn for administrative and research assistance; and to Jennifer Bernstein, Melvin Rosenthal, Peter Andersen, Jennifer Parkinson, and Bette Graber (and others unknown!) at Knopf for their patient assistance with an extremely complex and often behind-schedule manuscript.

I am indebted to Linda Michaels for the great skill with which she arranged foreign publications under pressure of a severe deadline, difficult embargo requirements, and complex translation scheduling. Special thanks also: to Paul Wolfson and Alan Morrison of the Public Citizen Litigation Group for assistance with Freedom of Information legal problems; to Robert Messer for providing tapes of his interview with Walter Brown; to William Lanouette for allowing us to use various documents in his possession concerning Leo Szilard; to Senator Joseph Tydings and Senator John Culver for help in arranging access to the restricted portions of the Joseph E. Davies papers; to Mrs. Margherita Bisconti Hillman and Alessandra Hillman Devine for graciously allowing access to the private papers of William Hillman; to Juan Garces for bringing certain critical documents to my attention; to Milton Leitenberg for generously allowing access to materials in his possession; to Francis Boyle, Stephen Badsey, David Kahn, and Duane Shank for thoughtful suggestions with regard to certain research questions; and to Alan Kay for help with the provision of various polling data.

The assistance of particularly helpful archivists at various institutions across the country is also gratefully acknowledged—including especially: Carey Conn, Glenn Cook, James Cross, Daria D'Arienzo, Marti Gansz, Bernice Holt, David Keogh, Michael Kohl, Dan Link, Will Mahoney, Dale Mayer, Duane Reed, Ed Reese, Essie Roberts, Sam Rushay, John Taylor, Mike Walker, and Nanci Young. Last but hardly least, David Langbart of the National Archives was a participant in our Cold War symposium and a helpful adviser on several matters requiring expert archival knowledge.

A number of people participated as volunteer researchers or graduate student interns at various points in time. I am grateful to the following interns for their hard work and dedication to the project: John Antush, John Coney, Andrew Craig, Matt Craver, Pat Dorsey, Jason Dougal, Ross Dunbar, Scott Goldstein, Alex James, Tom Marx, Akiko Naono, Carl Stevens, Michael Sutz, and Tom Yoritaka.

Many individuals have also assisted with typing and specific research tasks. The contributions of the following are similarly acknowledged: Karen Baker, David Brindley, Chris Chamberlin, Yogesh Chandrani, David Cochran, Jen Collet, Debra Durocher, Betsy Grout, Chris Herman, Millie Hopes, Hany Khalil, Edmund Lowson, Eyal Press, and Will Winter.

Several historians and other specialists were kind enough to review portions of the manuscript or advise on specific problems. The comments and suggestions of the following were especially helpful, and much appreciated: Steven Aftergood, Shinichi Arai, Kai Bird, Stanley Goldberg, James G. Hershberg, William Lanouette, Melvyn P. Leffler, Page Miller, Anna K. Nelson, and J. Samuel Walker. Additionally, informal discussions with Stanley Goldberg and William Lanouette helped sharpen many questions. I also wish to acknowledge the work of a very good historian with whom I disagree on some important matters of interpretation: In a world where hysteria, nitpicking, and charge and countercharge often substitute for true scholarly debate, Barton Bernstein's work is a model of integrity and seriousness. Repeatedly during our work we found ourselves asking whether Bart had covered an issue—and if we disagreed with his interpretation, what evidence, precisely, we had to back up our arguments. (Also, as noted, at several points in Book II we have drawn on work pioneered by Bernstein.) The debt I owe to the insight and example of an undergraduate professor in the mid-1950s—the late William Appleman Williams—also continues to be great. Finally, often writers who have pointed out errors of fact or interpretation in my earlier work were also helpful, as were several military historians who have probed certain areas in depth which diplomatic historians sometimes neglect.

It should be obvious that the writing of history is a deeply social—and continually evolving—project. No work stands on its own; every book rests on the shoulders of many, many others. As is evident throughout this text, the research efforts of many, many women and men, over several decades, are the foundation upon which this book has been built. I hope that whatever flaws remain in its structure—and in the work of the present builder—may be improved upon by those who take up the next phase of ongoing construction.

Index

Permissions Acknowledgments

Grateful acknowledgment is made to the following for permission to reprint previously published and unpublished material:

Amherst College Library: Material from the John J. McCloy Papers. Amherst College Archives, Amherst College Library, Amherst, Massachusetts. Reprinted by permission of Amherst College Library.

AP/Associated Press: Excerpts from "Truman Approved Warning to Japan" (Potsdam: *AP/Associated Press*, July 22, 1945). Reprinted by permission of *AP/Associated Press*.

James F. Byrnes Foundation: Excerpts from *Speaking Frankly* by James F. Byrnes (New York: Harper & Row, 1947), and excerpts from *All in One Lifetime* by James F. Byrnes (New York: Harper & Row, 1958). Reprinted by permission of the James F. Byrnes Foundation.

Clemson University Libraries: Material from the James F. Byrnes Papers. Special Collections, Clemson University Libraries, Clemson, South Carolina. Reprinted by permission of Clemson University Libraries.

Columbia University: Material from *The Reminiscences of Admiral Harold C. Train* (1965–1966), p. 218, Oral History Collection of Columbia University; material from *The Reminiscences of Isador Lubin* (1957), p. 86, Oral History Collection of Columbia University. Reprinted by permission of Columbia University.

The Controller of HMSO: Excerpts from *Grand Strategy*, Vol. VI by John Ehrman (London: HMSO, 1956). Crown copyright is reproduced by the permission of the Controller of HMSO.

Cornell University Press: Excerpts from *Fighting to a Finish* by Leon V. Sigal (1988). Reprinted by permission of Cornell University Press.

Doubleday: Excerpts from *Triumph in the West* by Arthur Bryant (Doubleday, 1959). Reprinted by permission of Doubleday, a division of Bantam Doubleday Dell Publishing Group, Inc.

H & C Communications, Inc.: Excerpts from "How We Bungled the Japanese Surrender" by Ellis M. Zacharias (*Look*, Vol. 14, No. 12, June 6, 1950). Reprinted by permission of H & C Communications, Inc.

HarperCollins Publishers, Inc.: Excerpts from *On Active Service in Peace and War* by Henry L. Stimson and McGeorge Bundy, copyright © 1948 by Henry L. Stimson and McGeorge Bundy, copyright renewed 1976 by McGeorge Bundy. Reprinted by permission of HarperCollins Publishers, Inc.

The Houghton Library: Excerpt from correspondence from Joseph C. Grew to Henry L. Stimson, February 12, 1947, Joseph Grew Papers, The Houghton Library, Harvard University. Reprinted by permission of The Houghton Library.

Houghton Mifflin Company: Excerpts from *The Price of Vision: The Diary of Henry A. Wallace*, edited by John Morton Blum, copyright © 1971 by the Estate of Henry A. Wal-

The Harry S. Truman Library: Material from The Papers of Harry S. Truman, The Records of the Truman Centennial Commission, the Papers of Eben A. Ayers, Jonathan Daniels, George M. Elsey, Samuel I. Rosenman, and Charles G. Ross, and the Oral History Collections of Eben A. Ayers, Tom C. Clark, Emilio Collado, Matthew J. Connelly, Robert G. Nixon, James W. Riddleberger, and Samuel I. Rosenman. The Harry S. Truman Library, Independence, Missouri. Reprinted by permission of The Harry S. Truman Library.

Margaret Truman, The Estate of Harry S. Truman: Excerpts from Harry S. Truman material as reprinted in *Mr. President*, edited by William Hillman (New York: Farrar, Straus and Young, 1952); excerpts from *Memoirs of Harry S. Truman,* Vol. I: *Year of Decisions* by Harry S. Truman (New York: Doubleday, 1955–1956). Reprinted by permission of Margaret Truman, The Estate of Harry S. Truman.

United States Naval Institute: Material from United States Naval Institute Oral History Program for Hanson W. Baldwin, Bernhard Bieri, Robert Dornin, H. Arthur Lamar, Mrs. Chester Nimitz, Mrs. Nancy Nimitz, Robert Dennison, and William Sebald; copyright © by the United States Naval Institute. Reprinted by permission of the United States Naval Institute.

U.S. News & World Report: Excerpts from "The Story Gen. Marshall Told Me" by John P. Sutherland (Nov. 2, 1959); excerpts from "Was A-Bomb on Japan a Mistake?" (Aug. 15, 1960). Reprinted by permission of *U.S. News & World Report.*

University of California Press Journals: Excerpts from " 'Mokusatsu,' Japan's Response to the Potsdam Declaration" by Kazuo Kawai (*Pacific Historical Review*, Vol. XIX, No. 4, Nov. 1950, pp. 409–414), copyright © 1950 by Pacific Coast Branch, American Historical Association. Reprinted by permission of University of California Press Journals.

University of Chicago: Excerpts from "A Personal History of the Atomic Bomb" by Leo Szilard (*The University of Chicago Roundtable*, Sept. 25, 1949, pp. 14–16). Reprinted by permission of the University of Chicago, Office of Public Affairs.

The University of Chicago Press: Excerpts from *The Army Air Forces in World War II*, Vol. V, edited by Wesley Frank Craven and James Lea Cate, copyright © 1953. Reprinted by permission of The University of Chicago Press.

Yale University Library: Correspondence from Walter Lippmann to James F. Byrnes, Walter Lippmann Papers, Manuscripts and Archives, Yale University Library; diary entries, correspondence, and memoranda from Henry L. Stimson Papers, Manuscripts and Archives, Yale University Library. Reprinted by permission of Yale University Library.